C000051533

WYATT AND DASHWOOD'S
EUROPEAN
COMMUNITY LAW

AUSTRALIA
The Law Book Company
Brisbane ● Sydney ● Melbourne ● Perth

CANADA
Carswell
Ottawa ● Toronto ● Calgary ● Montreal ● Vancouver

Agents:
Steimatzky's Agency Ltd., Tel Aviv;
N.M. Tripathi (Private) Ltd., Bombay;
Eastern Law House (Private) Ltd., Calcutta;
M.P.P. House, Bangalore;
Universal Book Traders, Delhi;
Aditya Books, Delhi;
MacMillan Shuppan KK, Tokyo;
Pakistan Law House, Karachi, Lahore

WYATT AND DASHWOOD'S
EUROPEAN COMMUNITY LAW

THIRD EDITION

By

DERRICK WYATT
M.A., LL.B. (Cantab.), J.D. (Chicago)
Of Lincoln's Inn, Barrister
Fellow of St. Edmund Hall, Oxford

and

ALAN DASHWOOD
B.A. (Rhodes), M.A. (Oxon)
Of the Inner Temple, Barrister
Director in the Legal Service of the Council
of the European Communities
Visiting Professor of Law in the University of Leicester

Assisted by

ANTHONY ARNULL
B.A. (Sussex), Ph.D. (Leicester)
Solicitor of the Supreme Court of England and Wales
Wragge Professor of European Law
University of Birmingham

AIDAN ROBERTSON
M.A., LL.M. (Cantab.)
Solicitor of the Supreme Court of England and Wales
Fellow of Wadham College, Oxford

MALCOLM ROSS
LL.B., M.Phil
Jean Monnet Lecturer in European Community Law
University of Leicester

PHILIPPA WATSON
M.A. (Dub.), LL.B. (Cantab.), Ph.D. (Cantab.)
Of King's Inn, Dublin and Middle Temple, Barrister

LONDON
SWEET & MAXWELL
1993

First Edition 1980
Second Impression 1981
Third Impression 1986
Second Edition 1987
Second Impression 1990
Third Impression 1991
Third Edition 1993

Published in 1993 by
Sweet & Maxwell Limited
of South Quay Plaza
183 Marsh Wall, London E14 9FT
Typeset by Mendip Communications Ltd., Frome, Somerset
Printed in England by Clays Ltd, St Ives plc

A CIP catalogue record for this book
is available from The British Library

ISBN 0421 468 904

*All rights reserved. No part of this publication may be
reproduced or transmitted in any form or by any means,
electronic, mechanical, photocopying, recording or otherwise,
or stored in any retrieval system of any nature, without the
written permission of the copyright holder and the publisher,
application for which shall be made to the publisher.*

©
D. Wyatt and A. Dashwood
1993

PREFACE

This book, in its third edition, has a change of title which reflects the broadening of its scope to cover institutional matters as well as substantive law. Our aim was to produce a work that could stand on its own as a textbook for general university courses on European Community law, while also providing analysis in depth of the main topics of European economic and social law which are explored in more specialised courses. We hope, too, that practitioners will find it useful to have the discussion of substantive legal issues placed in the context of the constitutional principles and institutional arrangements of the existing Communities and the future Union.

As always, to allow for treatment in depth of the subjects we are covering, we have had to be selective. One major sacrifice was the chapter on agriculture: space had to be made for new material, and with the details of C.A.P. reform still to be fully worked out, and the implications of a possible deal in the Uruguay Round not yet known, the omission seemed justified. On the other hand, we thought it appropriate, in a book to be published during 1993, that the specific legal techniques used, and the legal problems encountered, in implementing the programme on the completion of the internal market be analysed in a separate chapter. Nor was it possible to ignore the blueprint for the next phase of European integration, contained in the Treaty on European Union (or T.E.U.) which was signed in February 1992: innovations the T.E.U. will bring are discussed in the chapters on the institutions and on the legislative process; and our concluding chapter examines the structure envisaged for the European Union, the principal amendments to be made to the EEC Treaty and the intensified co-operation and common action to be established in the fields of foreign and security policy and of justice and home affairs. Other new chapters in this edition are those on the merger control regulation and on vocational training, reflecting important recent developments in legislation and in the case-law. In addition, the chapters on the Court of Justice have been substantially enlarged, and now include full analysis of the Courts' various heads of jurisdiction.

Uncertainty over the prospects for ratification of the T.E.U. complicated our work. Finishing touches were put to the manuscript after the European Council in Edinburgh when it seemed clear the Treaty would be ratified by all 12 of the Member States, although the process would certainly not be completed until after our publication date. Thus the future tense has been retained for describing the legal situation that will exist when the Treaty finally enters into force. Another problem was how we should refer to provisions included among the amendments and additions the T.E.U. will make to the EEC Treaty, the name of which is to be changed to "Treaty Establishing the European Community" (or EC Treaty): a solution adopted in some chapters was to refer to the "EC Treaty, as amended."

Owing to the various calls on our time, it was only possible to produce this edition as a team effort. However, we have done our best to preserve the structure and general approach adopted in the chapters carried over from previous editions, and to ensure the overall coherence of the work.

We are most grateful to our contributors, who have written or revised the following chapters: Anthony Arnull, Chapters 5 and 6; Aidan Robertson, Chapters 13, 14 and 16; Malcolm Ross, Chapters 15, 17, 18 and 19; Philippa Watson, Chapters 11, 21 and 22. Derrick Wyatt was directly responsible for revising Chapters 4, 7, 8, 9, 10 and 20 (the last with Aidan Robertson); and Alan Dashwood revised Chapter 1 and wrote Chapters 2, 3, 12 and 23.

Finally, our affectionate thanks go to Joan Wyatt and to Julie Dashwood for their encouragement with this edition, as with previous ones, and for very practical help in dealing with our proofs.

Derrick Wyatt
Alan Dashwood

December 1992

CONTENTS

PART I: HISTORICAL INTRODUCTION

Chapter

PART II: INSTITUTIONS AND LEGAL ORDER

PART III: THE FOUNDATIONS OF THE COMMUNITY

PART IV: POLICIES OF THE COMMUNITY

PART V: EUROPEAN UNION

TABLE OF CASES (ALPHABETICAL)

TABLE OF CASES

EUROPEAN COURT OF JUSTICE

EUROPEAN COURT OF FIRST INSTANCE

EC COMMISSION DECISIONS

NATIONAL CASES

FRANCE

GERMANY

UNITED KINGDOM

UNITED STATES

INTERNATIONAL TRIBUNAL CASES

EC TREATIES AND CONVENTIONS

REGULATIONS

DIRECTIVES

COUNCIL DECISIONS

RULES OF PROCEDURE (OF THE EUROPEAN COURT OF JUSTICE AND COURT OF FIRST INSTANCE)

UK LEGISLATION

INTERNATIONAL TREATIES AND CONVENTIONS

PART I: HISTORICAL INTRODUCTION

CHAPTER 1

FROM THE FOUNDING TREATIES TO THE TREATY ON EUROPEAN UNION

The Schuman Plan and the establishment of the ECSC

Although there was a certain ideological groundswell in favour of a "United Europe" shortly after the Second World War[1]—as evidenced by the call of the 1948 Hague Congress for Western European economic and political union—the first concrete steps towards integration were prompted by the spectre of Soviet expansion. Within days of the signature by France and the United Kingdom of the Dunkirk Treaty, providing for mutual assistance in the event of a renewal of hostilities with Germany, the breakdown of the Moscow Conference over the future of occupied Germany was to set the pattern for future strained relations between the U.S.S.R. on the one side, and the United States, Great Britain and France on the other. Despite the indispensable United States defence commitment affirmed in the North Atlantic Treaty, Western Europe stood divided and vulnerable in the face of a Soviet Union whose wartime military potential had been scarcely diminished by demobilisation, and whose political influence had been enhanced by successful Communist Party coups in Bulgaria, Rumania, Poland and Czechoslovakia.[2] It was in this context that Mr. Robert Schuman, the French Foreign Minister, made an historic proposal to a ministerial meeting in London on May 9, 1950.[3] His proposal was for no less than the fusion of the coal and steel industries of France and Germany, and any other countries wishing to participate, under a supranational High Authority. Not only would such a pooling of production make future conflict between France and Germany impossible, it would provide a sound basis for economic expansion. The implications of the scheme were clearly far-reaching, constituting, as Mr. Schuman explained, "the first concrete foundation for a European Federation which is indispensable for the preservation of peace."

The Schuman Plan was enthusiastically endorsed by the Benelux countries, France, Germany and Italy, but the United Kingdom declined to participate, refusing to accept the supranational role of the projected High Authority. The Treaty Establishing the European Coal and Steel Community (or ECSC) was signed in Paris on April 18, 1951, and came into

---

[1] See generally, Michael Palmer et al., *European Unity* (1968), Introduction; Gladwyn, *The European Idea* (1967), Chap. 4; A. H. Robertson, *European Institutions* (1973), pp. 5–17; Kapteyn and Verloren Van Themaat, *Introduction to the Law of the European Communities* (2nd ed., Gormley) (1989, Kluwer), Chap. 1.
[2] *NATO-Facts and Figures* (1971, Brussels), Chap. 1.
[3] For the French text, see *Documents on International Affairs* (1949–50), pp. 315–317. An English translation (from which the quotations in the text are extracted) appears in 22 Department of State Bulletin at pp. 936, 937.

force on July 20 of the following year. It was concluded for a period of 50 years from that date and is, therefore, due to expire in July 2002.[4]

The strategy of the Treaty, inspired by the Schuman Declaration, was to set limited and specific economic objectives as steps towards the long-term political objective of European unity. The preamble to the Treaty announced that Europe was to be built "through practical achievements which will first of all create real solidarity, and through the establishment of common bases for economic development." The economic community created pursuant to the Treaty was to constitute "the basis for a broader and deeper community among peoples long divided by bloody conflicts" and the foundations were to be laid "for institutions which will give direction to a destiny henceforward shared."

The central economic mechanism of the ECSC is a common market for coal and steel.[5] A definition of this mechanism, from a negative point of view, is given by Article 4 of the Treaty, which provides that the following are recognised as incompatible with the common market for coal and steel and shall accordingly be abolished and prohibited within the Community:

(a) import and export duties, or charges having equivalent effect, and quantitative restrictions on the movement of products;
(b) measures or practices which discriminate between producers, between purchasers or between consumers, especially in prices and delivery terms or transport rates and conditions; and measures or practices which interfere with the purchaser's free choice of supplier;
(c) subsidies or aids granted by States, or special charges imposed by States, in any form whatsoever;
(d) restrictive practices which tend towards the sharing or exploiting of markets.

Article 4 thus envisages a Community-wide market for coal and steel free from interference by the Member States or by economic operators tending to impede the flow of trade or to distort the play of competition. The Community is empowered to carry out its task under the Treaty "with a limited measure of intervention," *inter alia* by placing financial resources at the disposal of undertakings for investment and by bearing part of the cost of readaptation.[6] Only when circumstances so require is it authorised to exert direct influence upon production or upon the market, for instance by imposing production quotas.[7]

The EDC and EPC—a false dawn

Significant as the founding of the ECSC may have been, it contributed little of itself to the increasingly pressing problem of incorporating West

---

[4] Art. 97 ECSC. If no steps are taken to renew the ECSC Treaty (and there is currently no plan to do so) the coal and steel sectors will come within the purview of the EEC Treaty.
[5] Art. 1 ECSC proclaims that the Community is "founded upon a common market, common objectives and common institutions."
[6] Art. 5 ECSC.
[7] *Ibid.* second sub-para., third indent.

Germany into the defence network established by the Brussels and North Atlantic Treaties. While the United States was enthusiastic for German participation, France was naturally chary of seeing her recently vanquished enemy so soon rearmed. At the instigation of Sir Winston Churchill and Mr. Paul Reynaud[8] the Consultative Assembly of the Council of Europe[9] called for the "immediate creation of a unified European Army, under the authority of a European Minister of Defence, subject to proper European democratic control and acting in full co-operation with the United States and Canada."[10]

After a French initiative known as the "Pleven Plan," the Treaty Establishing the European Defence Community (EDC) was signed—subject to ratification—by the Benelux countries, France, Germany and Italy.[11] Once again the United Kingdom held aloof. If the ECSC had been calculated to bind Germany to France industrially, the European Defence Community was to provide the framework for German rearmament.

The projected Defence Community had two significant characteristics. First, it was to be endowed with a supranational institutional structure not unlike that of the Coal and Steel Community. Secondly, its statute assumed that it would be of a transitional nature, and would give way to some more comprehensive form of federal or confederal European Union.

The EDC Treaty provided for a European Army, composed of units placed at the disposal of the Council of Ministers by the Member States. A Common Budget would be drawn up, and an executive body, the "Commissariat," would lay down common programmes in the field of armaments, provisioning and military infrastructure. The objects of the Community were to be purely defensive, within the context of the North Atlantic Treaty.

The transitional nature of the proposed Community was evidenced by the terms of Article 8(2), which provided that the institutional structure laid down in the Treaty would remain in force until displaced by the establishment of the federal or confederal organisation envisaged by Article 38.

This latter Article required the Assembly of the EDC to make proposals to the Governments of the Member States on the establishment of a directly elected Assembly, and the powers it should exercise. Particular regard was to be had to the principle that such a modified Parliamentary body should be able to constitute one of the elements in a subsequent federal or confederal structure.

---

[8] Robertson, *op. cit.* note 1, *supra*, p. 18.
[9] The Council of Europe is an inter-governmental organisation established in 1949. Its aim is to achieve greater unity among its members, and to this end it seeks agreement on common action "in economic, social, cultural, scientific, legal and administrative matters and in the maintenance and further realisation of human rights and fundamental freedoms." See Bowett, *The Law of International Institutions* (1975), p. 149; Robertson, *op. cit.* p. 36.
[10] Resolution of the Consultative Assembly of the Council of Europe, August 11, 1950; *Documents on International Affairs* (1949–50), p. 331. As is clear from the quotation cited in the text, the Council at times interprets the terms of its statute with some liberality. Robertson, *op. cit.* note 1, *supra*, p. 19.
[11] May 27, 1952. See *Documents on International Affairs* (1952), pp. 116–162.

These proposals were to be presented to the Governments of the Six after the Assembly of the EDC assumed its functions, but within days of the signature of the Treaty the Consultative Assembly of the Council of Europe resolved that it would be "of great advantage if the basic principles of a European supranational political authority and the nature and limits of its powers were defined within the next few months, without waiting for the entry into force of the Treaty instituting the European Defence Community."[12] Despite the fact that the Assembly provided for in Article 38 of the EDC Treaty was not yet in existence, and that the Article only referred to the constitution of a future Parliamentary body, the Foreign Ministers of the Member States of the Coal and Steel Community requested the Members of the Coal and Steel Community Assembly to co-opt additional Members, reorganise the distribution of seats laid down in the Paris Treaty in accordance with that prescribed for the Assembly of the proposed EDC, and draw up a draft Treaty for a European Political Community (EPC). On March 10, 1953, the "Ad Hoc Assembly" presented the requested draft.[13]

The "European Community" proposed by the Ad Hoc Assembly provided for the extensive political and economic integration of its Members. Its aims were as follows:

— to contribute towards the protection of human rights and fundamental freedoms in Member States;
— to co-operate with the other free nations in ensuring the security of Member States against all aggression;
— to ensure the co-ordination of the foreign policy of Member States in questions likely to involve the existence, the security or the prosperity of the Community;
— to promote . . . the development of employment and the improvement of the standard of living in Member States, by means, in particular, of the progressive establishment of a common market. . . .

To ensure the protection of human rights in the proposed Community, provision was made for the application—as part of the Community Statute—of the provisions of section I of the European Convention on Human Rights, along with the first Protocol to that Convention, signed in Paris on March 20, 1952.

The Institutions of the EPC were to comprise a bicameral legislature, a European Executive Council, a Council of National Ministers, Court of Justice, and an Economic and Social Council. Financial resources would be derived from a combination of Community taxation and contributions from the Member States.

The hopes of those who saw the future of Western Europe in immediate

---

[12] Resolution of May 30, 1952, Texts Adopted (1952), and see *Report on the Constitutional Committee instituted to work out a Draft Treaty setting up a European Political Community* (Paris, December 20, 1952), p. 8.
[13] See *Information and Official Documents of the Constitutional Committee of the Ad Hoc Assembly* (Paris, 1953), pp. 53 *et seq.*

federation were dashed when the French Parliament voted against ratification of the EDC Treaty. A change of Government in France, and an easing of tension between East and West,[14] contributed to the rejection of the Treaty by the combined votes of Gaullists, Communists, Socialists and Radicals.[15]

In the event, Germany's participation in the defence of Western Europe was achieved by other means. The Paris Agreements of October 23, 1954 provided for the recognition of the Federal Republic of Germany as a sovereign state, and for its subsequent accession to the North Atlantic Treaty.[16]

The Spaak Report and the establishment of the EEC and Euratom

Despite the setback represented by the rejection of the EDC Treaty, the Six were still convinced of the need for closer integration. At a Conference held in the Sicilian city of Messina in 1955 the Foreign Ministers of the ECSC countries expressed the belief that the time had come to make "a fresh advance towards the building of Europe," but that this must be achieved "first of all, in the economic field."[17] The twin objectives were agreed of developing atomic energy for peaceful purposes, and establishing a European common market. An inter-governmental committee under the Chairmanship of the Belgian Foreign Minister, Mr. Paul-Henri Spaak, was entrusted with the task of making proposals to this end. The United Kingdom was invited to participate in the work of the committee, but although a Board of Trade official was initially dispatched, he was recalled after a few weeks.

The Spaak Report was published in April 1956.[18] In the light of its conclusions two new Treaties were negotiated, one providing for the establishment of a European Economic Community (EEC) and the other for the establishment of a European Atomic Energy Community (Euratom). The EEC and Euratom Treaties were signed in Rome on March 25, 1957 and came into force on January 1, 1958.

The preamble to the EEC Treaty expresses the determination of the High Contracting Parties "to lay the foundations of an ever closer union among the peoples of Europe." The Community's task is to promote "a harmonious development of economic activities, a continuous and balanced expansion, an increase in stability, an accelerated raising of the standard of living and closer relations between the States belonging to it." This is to be achieved by

---

[14] Robertson, *op. cit.* note 1, *supra*, p. 21.
[15] Palmer, *loc cit.* note 1, *supra*.
[16] *NATO-Facts and Figures* (Brussels, 1971), p. 35. For the Protocol to the North Atlantic Treaty on the Accession of the Federal Republic of Germany, and the texts known collectively as the "Paris Agreements," see Apps. 9 and 10.
[17] *Documents on International Affairs* (1955), p. 163; Cmnd. 9525.
[18] *Rapport des chefs de délégation aux ministres des affaires étrangères* (Brussels), April 21, 1956. A summarised translation of Part I of the Spaak Report—"The Common Market" was published by Political and Economic Planning as Broadsheet No. 405 of December 17, 1956.

two principal means—"establishing a common market and progressively approximating the economic policies of Member States."[19]

The common market provided for under the EEC Treaty covers all economic sectors other than those falling within the purview of the ECSC or Euratom Treaties.[20] As we shall see, the Treaty aims to create, on a Community scale, economic conditions similar to those on the market of a single state.[21] This involves the establishment of a customs union, through the elimination of all customs duties and quantitative restrictions (or quotas) in trade between the Member States and the erection of a common customs tariff (C.C.T.), as well as the removal of barriers to the free movement of "the factors on production"—labour, business and capital. In addition, the Treaty contains rules designed to prevent competition from being restricted by arrangements between private operators, or by government subsidies or the activities of state monopolies. There is also legal machinery for the harmonisation of national legislation that may have a bearing on the well-functioning of the common market. Last but not least, a common agricultural policy and a common transport policy are mentioned by the Treaty, along with the free movement of goods, persons, services and capital ("the Four Freedoms"), as constituting "Foundations of the Community."[22]

That is already enough to give an impression of the range and variety of matters falling within the competence of the EEC. The complex and far-reaching provisions of the Treaty defining that competence, and the acts of the Community institutions by which the Treaty rules have been developed and applied in key policy areas, are analysed more fully in subsequent chapters of this work.

A single set of institutions

The ECSC Treaty created four main institutions—a High Authority, a Special Council of Ministers, a Common Assembly and a Court of Justice. In accordance with the Schuman Plan, the leading role in the implementation of the Treaty was given to a supranational High Authority, whose members were under a duty to act with complete independence, in the Community interest.[23] The High Authority was empowered to take legally binding decisions[24] and was authorised, *inter alia*, to procure funds,[25] to fix maximum and minimum prices for certain products[26] and to fine undertakings in breach of the ECSC's rules on competition.[27] The Special Council of Ministers, a body composed of representatives of the Member States, was given the

---

[19] Art. 2 EEC.
[20] See Art. 232 EEC.
[21] See the description of the common market in Case 15/81, *Schul* v. *Inspecteur de Invoerrechten en Accijnzen* [1982] E.C.R. 1409 at pp. 1431–1432.
[22] See the list of activities in Art. 3 EEC. The drafting of the Art. ("... shall include ...") shows the list is not intended to be exhaustive.
[23] Art. 9 ECSC, replaced by Merger Treaty, Art. 10.
[24] Art. 14 ECSC.
[25] Art. 49 ECSC.
[26] Art. 61 ECSC.
[27] Arts. 65 and 66 ECSC.

function of harmonising "the action of the High Authority and that of Governments, which are responsible for the general economic policies of their countries."[28] With limited exceptions, the role of the Council in the institutional system of the ECSC is confined to consultation with the High Authority and the giving (or withholding) of its assent (*avis conforme*) to actions which the latter is proposing to take.

According to the EEC and Euratom Treaties, the two later Communities were each to have, in their turn, four main institutions—an Assembly, a Council, a Commission and a Court of Justice—but, to avoid unnecessary proliferation, a Convention was signed contemporaneously with the Treaties of Rome providing for there to be a single Assembly (now the European Parliament) and a single Court to carry out the functions assigned to those institutions under the three Community Treaties.[29] For some years after 1957, however, in addition to the High Authority and the Special Council of Ministers of the ECSC, there was a separate EEC Council and Commission and a separate Euratom Council and Commission. That situation was brought to an end by the Treaty establishing a Single Council and a Single Commission of the European Communities (known as the "Merger Treaty") which was signed in April 1965 and came into force in July 1967.[30] From that time, the ECSC, the EEC and Euratom have been served by the same set of institutions whose powers vary depending on the Treaty under which they act for a given purpose.

As will be seen in Chapters 2 and 3, below, in the institutional structure of the Rome Treaties, and particularly of the EEC Treaty, decision-making power is concentrated in the hands of the Council, and the role of the Commission is principally that of the initiator, and subsequently the executant, of Council decisions.[31] This difference, as compared with the institutional structure of the ECSC, is explained by the fact that, whereas the rules applicable to the coal and steel sectors are spelt out in considerable detail in the ECSC Treaty itself, in many areas of EEC competence the Treaty merely establishes a framework for common action, leaving fundamental political choices to be made by the Community institutions. It was inevitable that the final say in respect of such choices be left to the Council, the institution in which Member States are directly represented.

Enlargement—from six to twelve

Largely in response to the creation of the EEC, Austria, Denmark, Norway, Sweden, Switzerland, Portugal and the United Kingdom signed the Stockholm Convention on January 4, 1960, and the European Free

---

[28] Art. 26 ECSC.
[29] Convention on Certain Institutions Common to the European Communities, March 25, 1957; see Sweet & Maxwell's *Encyclopedia of European Community Law, European Community Treaties*, Vol. I, Pt. B8, B8–029.
[30] Treaty Establishing a Single Council and a Single Commission of the European Communities; see Sweet & Maxwell's *Encyclopedia*, B8–034.
[31] The Commission is also "guardian of the Treaties," with powers to ensure that the Member States and other Community institutions comply with their obligations: see, in particular, Art. 155 EEC, first indent and Arts. 169, 173 and 175 EEC.

Trade Association (or EFTA) came into being in May of that year. The primary object of the "Outer Seven" was to offset any detrimental effects to their trade resulting from the progressive elimination of tariffs inside the Community by a similar reduction within EFTA.

To a certain extent, EFTA was regarded as a stepping stone to possible future Community membership. As the White Paper that was published in July 1971 setting out the terms agreed, and the case for, United Kingdom membership of the Communities explained: "From the outset ... it was recognised that some members of the EFTA might eventually wish to join, and others to seek closer trading arrangements with, the European Communities."[32] Indeed, barely 14 months after the Stockholm Convention entered into force, the Macmillan Government applied for EEC membership. This was to be the first of two applications thwarted by the opposition of President de Gaulle of France. After lengthy negotiations had taken place with the Six, the French President made it clear, in January 1963, that he would not consent to British accession.

Applications in 1967 by the United Kingdom, Denmark, Ireland and Norway met with a similar rebuff. Nevertheless, these four countries left their applications "lying on the table," and at the Hague Summit Conference of the Six in December 1969, summoned on the initiative of the new President of France, Mr. Pompidou, it was agreed that "The entry of other countries of the continent to the Communities ... could undoubtedly help the Communities to grow to dimensions more in conformity with the present state of world economy and technology. ... In so far as the applicant States accept the Treaties and their political objective ... the Heads of State or Government have indicated their agreement to the opening of negotiations between the Community on the one hand and the applicant States on the other."[33]

Negotiations between the applicant States and the Six formally opened on June 30, 1970, and a Treaty of Accession was eventually signed on January 22, 1972. The provisions of the Treaty, and the detailed adaptations contained in the Act of Accession annexed to it, have served as a model, *mutatis mutandis*, for later enlargements. The only institutional changes required were those resulting from the need to accommodate the additional Member States. The elimination of customs duties and quotas between the prospective Member and the Six, and the adoption of the Common External Tariff, were to be phased in between April 1973 and July 1977. A transitional period was also to be allowed for the adoption of the Common Agricultural Policy, and for the build up of contributions to the Community budget. Although the United Kingdom would be compelled to forego Commonwealth preference as such, special arrangements were agreed for

---

[32] See *The United Kingdom and the European Communities*, Cmnd. 4715. After the accession of Denmark, Ireland and the United Kingdom of the European Communities, Austria, Finland, Norway, Portugal, Sweden and Switzerland entered into free trade agreements within the Nine. See *Seventh General Report on the Activities of the European Communities* (1973), p. 400.
[33] *Third General Report on the Activities of the Communities* (1969) Annex—Documents on the Summit Conference, pp. 487, 489.

the access of New Zealand dairy products and lamb, and the importation of sugar from Commonwealth suppliers. It was understood that association arrangements comparable with those already accorded to developing countries enjoying traditional relations with the original Six would be made with developing countries in the Commonwealth.

On January 1, 1973, the Treaty of Accession entered into force, and Denmark, Ireland and the United Kingdom became Members of the three Communities. Norway, which had signed the Treaty on January 22, 1972, did not proceed to ratification, following an adverse result in a national referendum held on the issue of membership.

British membership of the Communities was briefly put in doubt by the election in February 1974 of a Labour Government. Although the membership negotiations which were brought to a successful conclusion by the Conservative administration had been set in train by their predecessors, Labour in opposition declared themselves unable to accept the terms of entry finally agreed. When Labour returned to power, the Government of Mr. Harold Wilson set out to "renegotiate" the agreed terms in respect of agriculture, contributions to the Community Budget, economic and monetary union, state aids to industry, movement of capital, the Commonwealth and developing countries, and value added tax, and on January 23, 1975 it was announced that a national referendum would be held on the results of the renegotiation. The Government declared itself satisfied with those results and felt able to recommend to the British people that they cast their votes in favour of continued membership of the European Communities.[34] This view was endorsed by an overwhelming majority of the votes in the referendum which followed on June 5, 1975.[35]

The transitional period for the accession of the three new Member States was barely half spent when a further application for membership was received from Greece.[36] In its Opinion of January 28, 1976, the Commission recommended that the Communities give an affirmative answer to this request.[37] The Council acted upon this recommendation, and negotiations commenced on July 27, 1976. The instruments relating to Greece's accession were signed in Athens on May 28, 1979 and Greece became the tenth Member State on January 1, 1981.

Meanwhile, Spain and Portugal had also applied for membership. The Commission's Opinion in each case was, once again, favourable[38] and, after long and sometimes difficult negotiations, the instruments of accession were signed in Madrid and Lisbon on June 12, 1985 and Spain and Portugal joined the Communities on January 1, 1986.[39] Thus, in little more than a decade, the Six had become Twelve.

At the time of writing, applications for membership of the European

---

[34] See *Membership of the European Community*, Cmnd. 5999; *Report on Renegotiation*, Cmnd. 6003.
[35] See R. E. M. Irving, "The United Kingdom Referendum" (1975–76) 1 E.L.Rev. 1.
[36] On January 12, 1975, E.C. Bull. 1975, No. 6, points 1201 to 1212.
[37] E.C. Bull. 1976, No. 1, points 1101 to 1111 and Supplement 2/76.
[38] E.C. Bull. 1978, No. 5, points 111 *et seq.*; E.C. Bull. 1978, No. 11, points 111 *et seq.*
[39] E.C. Bull. 1985, No. 6, points 111 *et seq.*

Communities have been received from five EFTA countries, Austria, Finland, Sweden, Switzerland and Norway,[40] as well as from Cyprus, Malta and Turkey. In the light of the Presidency conclusions of the European Council held in Lisbon on June 26 and 27, 1992, formal enlargement negotiations with the EFTA applicants seem likely to begin in 1993.[41] For the three applicant countries in the Mediterranean area, no timetable has been laid down, but there is a clear commitment to intensifying co-operation under existing association agreements and to developing political dialogue.

As regards the countries of Central and Eastern Europe, partnership will be developed within the framework of agreements already negotiated (or in the course of negotiation) and political dialogue will be intensified and extended to include meetings at the highest level. Co-operation will be focused systematically on assisting those countries' efforts to prepare the accession which they seek.

Amendments and development of the founding treaties

Apart from the amendments contained in the Merger Treaty and in successive Accession Treaties, the texts of the three founding Treaties have been amended or developed over the years by a series of Treaties, Decisions or Acts, the most significant of which are identified below.

The Budgetary Treaties of 1970 and 1975

These two Treaties, which were signed, respectively, on April 22, 1970 and on July 22, 1975, replaced the original budgetary procedure of the Communities with a new one giving important powers to the European Parliament.[42] The different roles in that procedure of the Council, which has the last word in respect of so-called "compulsory expenditure," and the Parliament, which has the last word in respect of "non-compulsory expenditure," are analysed in the next chapter. The 1975 Treaty also created a new body, the Court of Auditors, to act as a financial watchdog for the Communities.

Own resources decisions

In the early years of the EEC and Euratom, the Communities' revenue came from direct financial contributions by the Member States, according to scales that were laid down by the Treaties.[43] However, Article 201 EEC and Article 173 Euratom looked forward to the replacement of financial contributions by a system giving the Communities their "own resources." A legislative procedure was provided for the establishment of such a system by

---

[40] The failure of Norway's first attempt at accession was noted above.

[41] See *Agence Europe*, Special Edition, June 28, 1992, pp. 5–6. The opening of negotiations is conditional on the ratification of the Treaty on European Union and the adoption of the packet of financial measures known as "Delors II" (see below).

[42] The text of the 1970 Treaty is published at O.J. 1971 L2/1 and that of the 1975 Treaty at O.J. 1977 L359/1.

[43] See Art. 200 EEC; Art. 172, Euratom. Different financial arrangements apply under the ECSC Treaty: see Arts. 49 ECSC *et seq.*

a unanimous decision of the Council, acting on the basis of proposals by the Commission and after consulting the European Parliament, with the additional step that the Council decision be recommended to the Member States for adoption in accordance with their respective national requirements. That especially solemn procedure gives the decisions to which it applies a legal status only slightly inferior to the Treaties themselves.

A first own resources Decision was adopted in 1970[44] and this was replaced by a Decision of 1985[45] which, in turn, was replaced by the currently applicable own resources Decision of 1988.[46] However, it should be noted that the package of financial proposals put forward by the Commission with a view to the implementation of the Treaty on European Union once it has been ratified by the Member States (known as the "Delors II" package, to distinguish it from "Delors I," whereby financial means were provided to give effect to the Single European Act) will entail the adoption of a new Decision on own resources.[46a]

According to the 1988 Decision, revenue from the following sources constitutes own resources entered in the budget of the Communities:

— levies and other charges imposed in respect of trade in agricultural products under the rules of the common agricultural policy;
— customs duties levied under the C.C.T. on imports from third countries;
— the application of a uniform rate (in principle 1.4 per cent.) to a uniform VAT assessment base determined in a uniform manner for Member States in accordance with Community rules;
— the application of a rate (variable from year to year, depending on the amount of additional revenue needed to balance the budget) to the sum of all the Member States' G.N.P.[47]

Of those four categories of own resources, only agricultural levies and customs duties (often referred to as "traditional own resources") have the true character of Community taxes. They are collected on behalf of the Communities by the Member States which have the right to retain, by way of collection costs, 10 per cent. of the amounts paid.[48] The VAT own resource does not give the Communities a fixed share of Member States' *actual* VAT receipts, since the prescribed rate is applied to an artificially constructed assessment basis. As for the G.N.P. own resource, its purpose is, in part, to redress the economically regressive effect of the VAT resource, which, because it is related to consumption, falls more heavily on the less prosperous Member States, by shifting the burden towards those that are more prosperous. The G.N.P. rate is fixed each year under the budgetary procedure, to cover the amount needed to balance the budget, after account has been taken of revenue from the other three resources.

---

[44] Council Dec. 70/243 of April 21, 1970, O.J. 1970 L94/19.
[45] Council Dec. 85/257 of May 7, 1985, O.J. 1985 L128/15.
[46] Council Dec. 88/376 of June 24, 1988, O.J. 1988 L185/24.
[46a] The Edinburgh European Council asked the Commission to prepare a new Decision for adoption before 1995.
[47] 1988 Dec., Art. 2(1).
[48] 1988 Dec., Art. 2(3).

It may be added that the Decisions both of 1985 and of 1988 included mechanisms for the correction, in favour of the United Kingdom of so-called "budgetary imbalances," *i.e.* the difference between payments to, and receipts from, the Community budget.[49] It was decided at the Edinburgh European Council in December 1992 that such a corrective mechanism will be included in the financial arrangements that are to apply during the period to 1999.

A directly elected European Parliament

Article 138(3) EEC and the corresponding provisions of the other Treaties[50] lay down a solemn procedure for the enactment of rules for direct elections to the European Parliament similar to the procedure applicable to own resources decisions, except that in this case the initiative belongs to the Parliament. Under that procedure, an Act concerning the election of the representatives of the European Parliament by direct universal suffrage was approved by the Council in September 1976 and recommended to the Member States for adoption in accordance with their respective constitutional requirements.[51] The first elections were held in June 1979 and these were followed by elections in 1984 and 1989. Further discussion of these developments is found in the section relating to the European Parliament in the next chapter.

The Single European Act

The Single European Act (S.E.A.) was signed on February 17, 1986 and entered into force on July 1, 1987.[52] Its odd-seeming title is explained by the fact that, within a single legal instrument, there were juxtaposed provisions amending the three European Community Treaties and provisions organising co-operation in the inter-governmental sphere of foreign policy.

The amendments to the Treaties contained in Title II of the S.E.A. were the most extensive adopted up to that time. They included the introduction of a new "co-operation procedure" giving the European Parliament a significantly enhanced role in the legislative process, which is discussed in detail in Chapter 3, below. One of the principal objectives of the S.E.A. was to ensure the completion of the EEC's internal market by the end of 1992 and the legal means provided in order to achieve this[53] are analysed in Chapter 11. Other provisions of the S.E.A. inserted into the EEC Treaty a number of specific new legal bases for Community action, for example on economic and social cohesion,[54] on research and technological development[55] and on the protection of the environment.[56]

Title III of the S.E.A. contains the Treaty provisions on European

---

[49] 1988 Dec., Arts. 4 and 5. See Chap. 2, *infra*, p. 21, note 7.
[50] Art. 21(3) ECSC; Art. 108(3) Euratom.
[51] Council Dec. 76/787 of September 20, 1976, O.J. 1976 L278/1.
[52] The S.E.A. is published at O.J. 1987 L169/1.
[53] Notably, Arts. 8a and 100a, which were added to the EEC Treaty.
[54] Arts. 130a to 130e EEC.
[55] Arts. 130f to 130q EEC.
[56] Arts. 130r to 130t EEC.

Co-operation in the sphere of foreign policy, known more shortly as "European Political Co-operation" (or EPC). The Title establishes a series of principles designed to bring about closer and more systematic co-operation in the formulation and implementation of foreign policy. For instance, the High Contracting Parties are required to inform and consult each other on any foreign policy matters of general interest,[57] and such consultations are to take place before a final position is decided on.[58] Due consideration must be given to the desirability of adopting and implementing common European positions,[59] and the determination of common positions constitutes "a point of reference for the policies of the High Contracting Parties."[60] There is provision for regular meetings between Political Directors within a Political Committee[61] and for the establishment in Brussels of a secretariat to assist the Presidency in preparing and implementing EPC activities and in administrative matters.[62] The philosophy of the S.E.A. was to keep EPC strictly separate from the institutional and decision-making system of the European Communities but practice is tending to erode that distinction, especially at meetings of Foreign Ministers where Community and EPC matters appear on the same Council agenda and are dealt with in the presence of both Community and EPC staff.

The Treaty on European Union

The latest step in the constitutional development of Europe was the signing in Maastricht of the Treaty on European Union (T.E.U.) on February 7, 1992.[63] At the time of writing, the process of ratifying the Treaty was still under way. Despite a set-back to the process owing to the negative outcome of a referendum in Denmark, it remained the hope that the ratification by all 12 Member States would be completed in time to enable the T.E.U. to enter into force, if not on January 1, 1993, at least within the first half of that year.[64]

An analysis of the new constitutional order that will be brought into being under the T.E.U., and of some of the Treaty's main substantive provisions, including those relating to the establishment and functioning of economic and monetary union, is found in Chapter 23 of this work. The amendments the Treaty will entail for the institutional system and for the legislative process of the Communities are examined in the context of the general discussion of these topics in Chapters 2 and 3.

---

[57] S.E.A., Art. 30(2)(a).
[58] S.E.A., Art. 30(2)(b).
[59] S.E.A., Art. 30(2)(c), first sub-para.
[60] S.E.A., Art. 30(2)(c), third sub-para.
[61] S.E.A., Art. 30(10)(c).
[62] S.E.A., Art. 30(10)(g).
[63] The T.E.U. has been published at O.J. 1992 C191/1. A consolidated text of the EC Treaty, as amended by the T.E.U., has been published at O.J. 1992 C224/6.
[64] See T.E.U., Art. R(1).

PART II: INSTITUTIONS AND LEGAL ORDER

CHAPTER 2

THE INSTITUTIONS OF THE COMMUNITIES AND OF THE UNION

Article 4 of the EC Treaty, as amended

According to Article 4 of the EC Treaty, as amended by the T.E.U., the tasks entrusted to the Community are to be carried out by five institutions—a European Parliament, a Council, a Commission, a Court of Justice and a Court of Auditors.[1] It is expressly provided that each of the institutions "shall act within the limits of the powers conferred on it by this Treaty." Thus the institutional system is founded on the idea of the "attribution of powers." The Community institutions have only the powers given to them expressly or impliedly by the Treaties.

The founding Treaties endowed each of the European Communities with separate institutions. However, as we have seen, a Convention on certain Institutions common to the European Communities, which came into force at the same time as the EEC and Euratom Treaties, provided for there to be a single Assembly and a single Court of Justice exercising the various powers attributed to those institutions by the three Treaties. This was followed by the establishment, from July 1967, of a single Council of the European Communities, replacing the Special Council of Ministers of the ECSC, and the EEC and Euratom Councils, and a Commission of the European Communities, replacing the High Authority of the ECSC, and the EEC and Euratom Commissions.[2] The unity of the institutions will be maintained by the provision in Article C, first paragraph of the T.E.U. that the Union shall be served by a single institutional framework.[3]

Besides the five Community institutions listed in its first paragraph, the new version of Article 4 mentions, in its second paragraph, the Economic and Social Committee and the Committee of the Regions. The role of these two bodies is to assist the Council and the Commission by giving advisory opinions. The Economic and Social Committee, which has been in existence since the establishment of the EEC and Euratom, consists of representatives of the different categories of economic and social life and of the general interest, while the Committee of the Regions, newly created by the Treaty

---

[1] For a short introduction to the Communities' institutional system, see E. Noël, *Working Together* (1991 ed.), Office for Official Publications of the European Communities. There is a full legal analysis of the provisions of the EEC Treaty relating to the political institutions in Mégret *et al.*, *Le droit de la CEE* (1979, Editions de l'Université de Bruxelles), Vol. 9, but this has been rather overtaken by events. On the impact of the S.E.A., see De Ruyt, *L'Acte unique européen* (1987, Editions de l'Université de Bruxelles), Chap. VI; D. A. W. Edward, (1987) C.M.L.Rev. 19. On the institutional aspects of the T.E.U., see J. Rideau, *Revue des Affaires européennes* 2/1992, p. 21.
[2] The Treaty Establishing a Single Council and a Single Commission of the European Communities was signed on April 8, 1965 and entered into force on July 13, 1967. For the text of the Convention on certain institutions common to the European Communities and that of the Merger Treaty, see, respectively, footnotes 29 and 30, *supra*.
[3] See the discussion of the structure of European Union in Chap. 23.

on European Union, will consist of representatives of regional and local bodies.[4] Power to appoint the members of these Committees is given to the Council acting unanimously on the basis of lists of names put forward by each of the Member States. The decision to establish a Committee of the Regions represents a response to political demands in certain Member States, particularly those with a federal structure, that regional and local interests be given a direct line of communication to the Community institutions. It remains to be seen whether the new Committee will become a significant political force.

The Court of Auditors was created by the Financial Treaty of 1975, replacing the former Audit Board. The T.E.U. "promotes" the Court of Auditors to paragraph (1) of Article 4, so that it will in future enjoy the full status of a Community institution: in the EEC Treaty, it is mentioned in a separate paragraph (3). Under powers which have been spelt out in greater detail in the T.E.U., the Court of Auditors is required to examine the accounts of all Community revenue and expenditure and ensure their reliability, and the legality and regularity of the underlying transactions.[5] Its annual report, and the replies of the institutions under audit to its observations, are essential elements in the exercise of giving a discharge to the Commission in respect of the implementation of the budget, and it may also, at any time, submit observations on specific questions and deliver opinions at the request of one of the Community institutions.

The remainder of the present chapter will be devoted to a closer examination of the Communities' three main *political* institutions—the Council, the Commission and the European Parliament. However, before turning to those institutions, it is necessary to consider a body which, although not an institution in the sense of Article 4(1), may be regarded as the supreme political authority of the Communities and of the future Union—the European Council.

The European Council

It was at the summit meeting of European Community leaders in Paris in December 1974 that the decision was taken to hold regular meetings at the highest political level, within a "European Council." The first European Council was held in Dublin in March 1975, and the series of meetings continued on an informal basis, until a legal basis was provided by Article 2 of the S.E.A.[6]

According to that Article, the European Council brings together the Heads of State or Government of the Member States and the President of the Commission, who are assisted by Ministers of Foreign Affairs and by a

---

[4] On the Economic and Social Committee, see EC Treaty, as amended, Arts. 193 to 198 (same numbering as in the EEC Treaty). On the Committee of the Regions, see EC Treaty, as amended, Arts. 198a to 198c.
[5] As to the composition and powers of the Court of Auditors, see EC Treaty, as amended, Arts. 188a to 188c (replacing, with amendments, Arts. 206 and 206a EEC).
[6] There is a recent monograph by J. Werts, *The European Council* (1992, North-Holland). See also A. H. Lauwaars, (1977) C.M.L.Rev. 25.

member of the Commission. The formula "Heads of State or Government" is designed to accommodate the constitutional position of the French President. Article D of the T.E.U. takes over the description of the European Council in the S.E.A., adding that meetings are to be chaired by the Head of State or Government of the Member State holding the Presidency of the Council. The rhythm of meetings was fixed by the S.E.A. as at least two per year, and this is maintained by the T.E.U.

The European Council does not deliberate formally and reach binding decisions under the discipline of rules of procedure. Its role, which over the years has become increasingly significant, is essentially a political one. This is emphasised by Article D of the T.E.U. which states in its first paragraph: "The European Council shall provide the Union with the necessary impetus for its development and shall define the general political guidelines thereof." To demonstrate the contribution European Councils have made to the strategic development of the Communities, it is enough to recall the meeting in Bremen in July 1978 when the foundations of the European monetary system were laid, the meeting in Fountainebleau in June 1984 when work was set in train which eventually bore fruit in the institutional reforms of the S.E.A. and the meeting in Hanover in June 1988 when the project of establishing an economic and monetary union was relaunched. The Fontainebleau meeting illustrates another function of the European Council—that of unravelling knotty political problems which have defeated the efforts of the institutions. It was at that meeting that a solution was found to the long-running dispute about the level of the United Kingdom's net contribution to the Community budget.[7] European Councils also provide an opportunity for reviewing foreign policy questions, both those falling within the Communities' external competence and those which have been the subject of European Political Co-operation (EPC) and which, under the T.E.U., will be covered by the common foreign and security policy (or C.F.S.P., more fully considered in Chapter 23, below). Thus the European Council in Maastricht in December 1991 found time, among its other preoccupations, to agree that concrete steps should be taken by the Community to ease the food supply situation in Moscow and St. Petersburg; and it also adopted, within the EPC framework, declarations on the peace process in the Middle East and on developments in the Soviet Union.

Does the existence of the European Council, unforeseen by the original Treaties, distort the institutional structure of the Communities? The question is a legitimate one, since the task of leading the Member States along the road towards the ever closer union referred to in the preamble to the EEC Treaty and in Article A of the T.E.U. might be thought to belong

---

[7] The solution consisted of providing for a "correction" of the amount payable by the United Kingdom under the rules for the calculation of the "own resources" which constitute the Communities' revenue. Provision was made for this correction in Dec. 85/257, O.J. 1985 L128/15, which revised the own resources system in the light of the decisions taken in Fontainebleau. That Decision was subsequently replaced by Dec. 88/376, O.J. 1988 L185/24, which formed part of the Delors I package of financial measures, and a new decision is due to be adopted before 1995. The advantage, from the United Kingdom's point of view, of incorporating the correction into successive own resources decisions is that these require unanimity for their adoption: see EC Treaty, as amended, Art. 201.

more particularly to the Commission. Recent experience, however, has shown that a strongly led Commission has nothing to fear and everything to gain from working in close partnership with the European Council to achieve its medium term objectives. Thus political support from successive European Councils was an important factor in the implementation of the White Paper of 1985 on completing the internal market and in the development of plans for economic and monetary union.

The Council

The Council consists of representatives of the Member States. According to the original drafting of the first paragraph of Article 146 EEC, "Each Government shall delegate to the Council one of its members." National representatives on the Council were thus required to be members of the central government. However, the T.E.U. changes the wording of the paragraph so that it reads, "The Council shall consist of a representative of each Member State *at ministerial level*, authorised to commit the government of that Member State."[8] The purpose of this amendment is to allow Member States with a federal structure to be represented, when the Council is dealing with matters falling within the exclusive competence of regional governments, by a member of one of those governments rather than by a minister in the federal government. In such a case, the regional minister concerned would have to be authorised to act on behalf of the Member State as a whole, so that his agreement to a matter on the Council agenda would bind that Member State both legally and politically. At all events, it is clear that a "member" of the Council within the meaning of Article 146 must be a person holding political office, *i.e.* a minister, and not a civil servant.

In law, the Council is a unitary institution: in other words, it is the same institution with the same powers under the Treaties, whatever the particular national responsibilities of the ministers attending a given meeting. However, the Council customarily meets in certain formations, determined in accordance with the matters on the agenda. The General Affairs Council, which brings together Foreign Ministers, deals with external relations and with broad institutional and policy issues, providing a measure of co-ordination of the Council's multifarious activities. It also has the task of preparing European Councils. Another Council with a wide remit is the Economic and Financial Affairs (or Ecofin) Council which, like the General Affairs Council, meets, in principle, monthly except in August. The Ecofin Council is responsible for, *inter alia*, the implementation of the legislative programme for the abolition of fiscal frontiers and, generally, for the co-ordination of the economic policies of Member States.[9] More specialised Council formations in which important legislative business is regularly transacted include the Agriculture, Internal Market, Environment and

---

[8] Emphasis added.
[9] In the context of E.M.U., the Ecofin Council will take the key decisions not reserved for the Heads of State and Government. See Decl. No. 3 to the Final Act of the T.E.U.

Transport Councils. There are also Councils which handle specific business at certain times of the year, such as the Budget Council, which normally meets in July to establish the draft general budget of the Communities and in November to give the draft budget a second reading. Other Councils meet more sporadically, depending on the priorities of different Presidencies.

The principle of the unicity of the Council is put under some strain by the provisions of Article 109j, paragraphs (2) to (4) of the EC Treaty, as amended by the T.E.U. Under the procedure laid down by those provisions, certain decisions connected with the transition to the third stage of E.M.U. and the establishment of a single currency are to be taken by the Council "meeting in the composition of the Heads of State or Government" on the basis of recommendations put to it by the Council meeting in one of its ordinary formations (in practice, the Ecofin Council). It is a constitutional innovation that powers should be expressly reserved for the Council in a particular formation and that the basis for the exercise of those powers should consist of recommendations from the same institution meeting in a different formation. A further point is that there is a clear distinction in law between the 12 Heads of State or Government taking decisions as a formation of the Council in the sense of Article 146 EEC—which will be the case here—and the same leaders meeting as the European Council, with the President of the Commission as a thirteenth member.

Article 4 of the Council's Rules of Procedure[10] allows a member of the Council (*i.e.* a minister) unable to be present at a meeting, or part of it, to arrange to be represented. His place will usually be taken by the Permanent Representative or the Deputy Permanent Representative of the Member State concerned. Since the latter are civil servants, they cannot, strictly speaking, cast their minister's vote, since Article 5(3) of the Rules of Procedure provides that delegation of the right to vote can only be made to another member of the Council: in practice, however, non-ministerial representatives vote in accordance with the instructions of their governments, theoretically under the "cover" of one of the ministers present. Article 5(3) of the Rules of Procedure must be read together with Article 150 EEC which provides that, where a vote is taken, a Council member may act on behalf of not more than one other member. The combined effect of the two rules is that, to enable a formal vote to be held, a "quorum" of at least six ministers must be present, each of them covering for an absent colleague.

The Presidency of the Council is held in turn by the Member States for periods of six months, following the order laid down in the second paragraph of Article 146 of the Treaty.[11] In the Community of 12 the order of rotation changes in the second of each cycle of six years to ensure that a Member State's Presidency will not always fall in the same half of the calendar year.

---

[10] The Rules were first published in 1979: see O.J. 1979 L268/1. They were revised in 1987: see O.J. 1987 L291/27. A further revision is being discussed in the context of the implementation of the T.E.U.

[11] The order, as from January 1993, will be: Denmark, Belgium, Greece, Germany, France, Spain, Italy, Ireland, Netherlands, Luxembourg, United Kingdom, Portugal.

The significance of this is that Presidencies in the second half of the year are considered more difficult to run successfully because working time is severely constricted, with the summer break at the beginning and Christmas at the end. As for the duties of the Presidency, these include, besides taking the chair at Council meetings, the convening of meetings[12] and the establishment of the provisional agenda, which must be circulated to other members of the Council at least a fortnight in advance and must contain an indication of the items on which a vote may be taken.[13] The Presidency has come to play an active role in managing the progress of Commission proposals through the Council. Negotiations between national delegations within the Council take place in relation to a series of compromise texts devised by the Presidency with a view to securing the necessary majority or unanimity for the adoption of the measure in question. A Presidency is expected to show objectivity in furthering proposals, without undue regard to its specific national interests. A certain rivalry has developed between Presidencies in seeking to achieve an impressive "score" of measures adopted, and this has undoubtedly been a factor in the acceleration of the legislative process in recent years.

The work of the Council is prepared by a Committee of Permanent Representatives (COREPER) who are senior national officials based in Brussels. The legal basis of COREPER's activities is Article 4 of the Merger Treaty, which is due to be replaced, under the T.E.U., by a new Article 151 EC. The Committee operates at two levels, that of COREPER II, composed of the Permanent Representatives, who are of ambassadorial rank, and that of COREPER I, composed of the Deputy Permanent Representatives. The distribution of files between the two parts of COREPER is intended to reflect the more political nature of those given to COREPER II (for example, external relations), and the more technical nature of those given to COREPER I (for example, internal market legislation), but in practice even technical-seeming matters, such as the organisation of veterinary checks, may have political implications for some Member States. COREPER does not concern itself with matters relating to agricultural market organisations: the task of preparing the work of the Agriculture Council on these matters has been effectively delegated to the Special Committee on Agriculture. A question debated during the negotiation of the T.E.U. was that of the relationship between COREPER and certain high level committees—the Monetary Committee, the Political Committee and the Co-ordinating Committee—which are given specific responsibilities under the Treaty. In the event, the relevant provisions of the T.E.U. state that the contribution made by those Committees in preparing Council business is to be "without prejudice to Article 151," thereby preserving the position of COREPER as the filter through which such

---

[12] Rules of Procedure, Art. 1(1).
[13] Rules of Procedure, Art. 2(1) and (2). The items on which a vote may be taken are indicated on the draft agenda by an asterisk. If no such indication is given, a matter cannot be put to the vote under Art. 5 of the Rules of Procedure, except by unanimous agreement of the Council.

business must pass.[14] The principle is important because, with so many different formations of the Council, there is a danger political coherence may be lost: COREPER is the only Council body able to take a horizontal view of the development of Community policies.

The business that comes to COREPER will have been prepared, in turn, by specialised working groups made up of national officials. In addition to the numerous standing groups, COREPER from time to time establishes *ad hoc* groups to deal with matters requiring specific expertise.

The Council, COREPER and working groups are assisted by an independent body of civil servants, the Secretariat General, under the direction of a Secretary General. The legal basis for the activities of the Council's Secretariat General has hitherto been Article 17 of the Rules of Procedure, but a legal basis in the new Article 151(2) of the EC Treaty, as amended, will be provided by the T.E.U.

Council agendas are divided into a Part A and a Part B.[15] Items listed in Part A (known as A-points) are those which COREPER has agreed may be adopted by the Council without discussion, which does not exclude the possibility for a delegation to have a statement or a negative vote recorded in the minutes. Any member of the Council or the Commission may ask for an item to be taken off the list of A-points, in which case the item will be held over for a later Council, unless a simple majority of Council members decides that it should remain on the agenda.[16] In the latter event, the item cannot be voted on unless the A-point list on which it appears was circulated within the 14-day time limit.[17] The A-point procedure is often used for the formal adoption of texts which have been agreed in principle at an earlier Council.

Turning from the composition and organisation of the Council to its powers, these are described in the first two indents of Article 145 in an oddly cursory way. The first indent says the Council is to "ensure co-ordination of the general economic policies of the Member States" and the second indent that it is to "have power to make decisions."[18]

With the advance towards Economic and Monetary Union (or E.M.U.), the co-ordination of general economic policy by the Council is taking on new importance.[19] Under a Decision of 1990, the Council undertakes, in stage one of E.M.U., multilateral surveillance of the economic policies and performance of the Member States.[20] The Decision calls for the examination by the Council, at least twice a year, of economic conditions, prospects and policies in the Community and its Member States, the compatibility of

---

[14] See, respectively, EC Treaty, as amended, Art. 109c(1) and T.E.U. Arts. J.8(5) and K.4(1). In the third stage of E.M.U., the Monetary Committee will be replaced by an Economic and Financial Committee: see Art. 109c(2).

[15] Rules of Procedure, Art. 2(6).

[16] Rules of Procedure, Art. 2(7).

[17] Rules of Procedure, Art. 2(2). In theory, the members of the Council might decide *unanimously* that the item be put to the vote.

[18] The third indent of Art. 145, which concerns implementing powers, is discussed *infra* in connection with the powers of the Commission.

[19] Chap. 23, *infra*, contains a fuller discussion of the three stages of E.M.U.

[20] Dec. 90/141, O.J. 1990 L78/23.

policies within Member States and in the Community at large, and the external economic environment and its interaction with the Community economy. These examinations are held in very restricted sessions of the Ecofin Council, which may, however, authorise the President to make public the results of its deliberations. In the second and third stages of E.M.U., as provided for under the T.E.U., the Council will be empowered to intervene more actively, in particular to prevent a Member State from running an excessive government deficit.

The reference in the second indent of Article 145 to the Council's "power to take decisions" highlights its essential role in the system of the EEC and Euratom Treaties—that of the institution that has to decide for or against measures developing or extending the body of primary rules contained in the Treaties. The system of the ECSC Treaty is different: powers of decision are given under that Treaty not so much for the creation of new primary rules as for the implementation of the rules laid down by the Treaty itself; the Commission is the natural recipient of such a power, its exercise being subject, however, to the assent of the Council in certain cases.[21] We return to the subject of decision-making by the Council, including the once vexed question of majority voting, in the next chapter.

Consistently with its central role in the creation of law in the internal Community sphere, the Council has to agree to the acceptance by the EEC of new obligations in international law resulting from the conclusion of agreements with third countries.[22] It is the Commission which negotiates with third countries on behalf of the Community, but Council authorisation is required for opening negotiations, and it is the Council that takes the decision to conclude agreements. In some important cases the assent (*avis conforme*) of the European Parliament also has to be obtained.

Another area in which the Council has important powers is that of the adoption of the Community budget. The Council and the European Parliament together constitute the budgetary authority of the Communities which has the annual task of elaborating and adopting the general budget, as well as any supplementary and amending budgets that may prove necessary in the course of the financial year.[23] The division of powers between the Council and the European Parliament in the budgetary procedure is further examined below.

The Commission

Unlike the Council, whose members directly represent the interests of their governments, the Commission has a vocation to further the interests of

---

[21] The Commission is given an independent power of decision on certain matters where, unusually, basic rules limiting the discretion of the legislator are found in the EEC Treaty itself: *e.g.* under the provisions for the completion of the customs union during the EEC's transitional period, for which a detailed timetable was provided by the Treaty. As noted in Chap. 23, *infra*, the European Central Bank, too, will have law-making powers on aspects of monetary policy: see EC Treaty, as amended, Art. 108a.

[22] The procedure for the negotiation and conclusion of agreements is found in EC Treaty, as amended, Art. 228.

[23] The budgetary procedure is laid down by Art. 203 EC.

the Community as a whole. The members of the Commission are required to be persons "whose independence is beyond doubt,"[24] and the Treaty provides that they "shall, in the general interest of the Community, be completely independent in the performance of their duties."[25] They may not seek or take instructions from any government or other body, and the Member States have undertaken to respect that principle and not to seek to influence Commissioners in the performance of their tasks.[26] The rule that the Commission acts by a majority of its members[27] provides a further guarantee that its decisions will not reflect, even inadvertently, particular national viewpoints.

At the time of the accession of Spain and Portugal to the Communities, the number of members of the Commission was fixed at 17 and this has not been changed by the T.E.U.[28] In practice, that has meant that a second Commissioner has been appointed from each of the five larger Member States. However, the Council has power to alter the size of the Commission,[29] and there is a Declaration to the Final Act of the T.E.U. recording the agreement of the negotiating Conference that the question of the number of members of the Commission (as well as of the European Parliament) be examined no later than the end of 1992.[30]

Article 11 of the Merger Treaty provided that the members of the Commission be appointed by common accord of the Governments of the Member States for a renewable term of four years. It may be noted in passing that "common accord" is a stricter voting rule than unanimity as defined by Article 148(3) EC, since it does not allow abstentions. The new Article 158 which will be inserted into the EC Treaty by the T.E.U. extends the term of office of Commissioners to five years and alters the procedure for their appointment. Under the new procedure, the Governments of the Member States will nominate by common accord, after consulting the European Parliament, the person they intend to appoint as President of the Commission and then, in consultation with the President designate, will nominate those they intend to appoint as members. The whole slate of Commissioners will then be presented to the European Parliament for approval and, if approved, will be formally appointed by common accord of the Governments. This change of procedure, effectively giving the European Parliament a right to veto the appointment of a Commission including members of which it disapproves, is symbolically important, since it emphasises the political link between the Commission and the Parliament, while also representating a real increase in the Parliament's powers. To align the Commission's term of office on that of the European Parliament, there is

---

[24] EC Treaty, as amended, Art. 157(1). This will replace Merger Treaty, Art. 10.
[25] EC Treaty, as amended, Art. 157(2).
[26] *Ibid.*
[27] EC Treaty, as amended, Art. 163. This will replace Merger Treaty, Art. 17.
[28] EC Treaty, as amended, Art. 157(1).
[29] *Ibid.*, second sub-para.
[30] Decl. No. 15.

to be an interim arrangement under which the Commission appointed with effect from January 7, 1993 will serve for only two years.[31]

The number and method of appointment of the Commission's Vice-Presidents will also be changed by the T.E.U. Instead of six Vice-Presidents, there will be one, or at most two, and they will no longer be appointed by common accord of the Member States but by the Commission itself.[32]

When a new Commission comes into office its members are assigned portfolios giving them responsibility for different policy areas. However, the Commission acts as a collegiate body, either by decisions taken at its weekly meetings (normally on Wednesdays) or by a written procedure. It is assisted by a staff of permanent officials under a Secretary General, who are organised into Directorates General and various other services, and, in addition, each Commissioner has a small personal staff (or *cabinet*) composed partly of political associates and seconded national officials and partly of seconded Community officials. Meetings of the heads of these personal staffs (the *Chefs de Cabinet*) prepare the weekly meetings of the Commission.

The various elements that define the complex role of the Commission are described in Article 155 EC in the following terms:

> "In order to ensure the proper functioning and development of the common market, the Commission shall:
> — ensure that the provisions of this Treaty and the measures taken by the institutions pursuant thereto are applied;
> — formulate recommendations or deliver opinions on matters dealt with in this Treaty, if it expressly so provides or if the Commission considers it necessary;
> — have its own power of decision and participate in the shaping of measures taken by the Council and by the European Parliament in the manner provided for in this Treaty;
> — exercise the powers conferred on it by the Council for the implementation of the rules laid down by the latter."

In the present section we consider two aspects of the Commission's role—as the initiator of decisions and as the institution that sees to their implementation once they have been adopted, whether by the Council or by the Commission itself. Another important role, that of "guardian of the Treaties," is associated with the Commission's right to invoke against the Council or against a Member State judicial remedies which are discussed in Chapter 5.

The Treaties contain no general rule reserving to the Commission the right to put forward proposals for Community acts. The Commission's right of initiative is, accordingly, nothing but an inference drawn from the numerous Treaty provisions that empower the Council to act "on a proposal of the Commission." That form of words, or a similar one, is used by the EC

---

[31] EC Treaty, as amended, Art. 158(3).
[32] EC Treaty, as amended, Art. 161.

Treaty in almost every case where the Council is given power to make new Community law. Thus the Council is usually able to exercise its legislative powers only in relation to a text which has been formulated by the institution with a duty to act independently of specific national interests. The way in which the Commission's right of initiative, and its right to amend its own proposals at any time before their adoption by the Council, interacts with the right of the Council to amend those proposals, is discussed in Chapter 3.

A feature of decision-making in the new areas of co-operation and common action created by Titles V and VI of the T.E.U., which contrasts with the system of the Community Treaties, is that the Commission will not enjoy an exclusive right of initiative. In the case of the common foreign and security policy, a right to refer to the Council any question relating to the policy, and to submit proposals to the Council, is shared by the Member States and the Commission. In the case of co-operation in the fields of judicial and home affairs, while the Council may act on the initiative of a Member State on all the matters listed in Article K, it may do so on the Commission's initiative only in respect of some of them.[33]

The Commission is sometimes described as the "executive" of the Communities but this is misleading. It implies that the Commission is like a government, with inherent or residual power to implement legislation, whereas Article 4(1), second sub-paragraph of the EC Treaty makes clear that it has only those powers of implementation that have been conferred on it either directly by the Treaties or by acts of the Council. In this respect, there is a clear contrast between the ECSC and EC Treaties: in ECSC matters the Commission, as successor to the High Authority, enjoys wide direct powers, whereas under the EEC Treaty, although directly empowered to act for certain purposes, for example the establishment of the customs union and the supervision of State aids to industry, the Commission derives the bulk of its powers from legislation enacted by the Council. A change introduced by the S.E.A. was the insertion into Article 145 EEC of a third indent establishing, as a general rule, that power to implement acts of the Council be conferred on the Commission: the Council is allowed to reserve implementing power for itself in specific cases but the Court of Justice has said, "it must state in detail the grounds for such a decision."[34] The Court has also stipulated that the essential elements of matters to be dealt with by the Commission under derived powers must be determined by the Council act directly based on the Treaty.[35] It would be a breach of the Treaty for the Commission to be given a discretion co-extensive with that which the Council is required under the Treaty to exercise in accordance with a prescribed procedure.

The grant of powers to the Commission may cover, besides the management of the policy in question, the development, by subordinate

---

[33] See Chap. 23, *infra*.
[34] Case 16/88, *Commission* v. *Council* [1989] E.C.R. 3457 at p. 3485.
[35] Case 25/70, *Köster* [1970] E.C.R. 1161 at p. 1170. The same principle applies where the Council reserves for itself power to adopt implementing acts by a simpler procedure than the one prescribed by the Treaty for the basic act.

legislation, of the rules contained in the basic Council act. This is most notably the case with the common agricultural policy where the Commission is responsible both for establishing the regulatory framework within which the competent national authorities are required to act and for the day-to-day management of agricultural markets, in close collaboration with those authorities. Competition policy provides another instructive example: this is an area where, unusually, the Commission has been given, pursuant to Regulation 17,[36] administrative and coercive powers which can be used against individual undertakings; in addition, it has been empowered, under a series of Council measures, to adopt regulations exempting certain categories of restrictive agreements and practices from the automatic prohibition to which they would otherwise be subject under the rules of Article 85 EEC.[37] Other areas in which the Commission has acquired, relatively recently, an enhanced administrative role are those of research, where it implements the specific programmes developed within the various activities envisaged by the multi-annual framework programme, and economic and social cohesion where, in partnership with beneficiary Member States, it manages the resources made available through the structural funds.

The exercise by the Commission of powers of implementation which it has been granted under acts of the Council is frequently subjected to procedural requirements. Article 145, third indent, expressly preserves the Council's right to impose such requirements, while providing that the latter "must be consonant with principles and rules to be laid down in advance." A closed catalogue of forms of procedure was, accordingly, established by Decision 87/373—known as the "Comitology" Decision because the different procedures all involve the submission of the Commission's draft implementing measures to a committee composed of national officials.[38] The degree of constraint placed on the Commission varies from one procedure to another: for instance, under the "advisory committee" procedure the Commission is required to take the utmost account of the opinion delivered by the Committee, but is not bound by it[39]; whereas, under the "management committee" procedure, in the event of a negative opinion by the committee, the matter is referred to the Council which may, within a prescribed time limit, substitute its own decision for that of the Commission.[40] It is for the Council, when it adopts an act conferring

---

[36] O.J. Eng.Sp.Ed. 1959–62, 87.
[37] See Chap. 17, *infra*.
[38] O.J. 1987 L197/33. The Decision provides for three main forms of procedure, two of them with variants, as well as a procedure applicable where the Council confers on the Commission the power to decide on safeguard measures.
[39] See Procedure I in Art. 2 of Dec. 87/373.
[40] See Procedure II, *ibid.*, which has a Variant (a) and a Variant (b). The main difference is that under Variant (b) the Commission is *required* to defer the application of implementing measures which have been rejected by the Committee, during the period allowed for the Council to take a different decision, whereas, under Variant (a), it has the option of doing so. For a recent example of a Council Decision adopted following a reference back under Procedure II, Variant (b), see Dec. 92/277, O.J. 1992 L144/18. The Commission is highly critical of the way in which the Council has applied the Comitology Decision: see the report it submitted to the Council pursuant to Art. 5 of the Decision, SEC(90) 2589 final.

implementing power on the Commission, to determine which, if any, procedure should be attached to the exercise of that power. The Court of Justice has rejected the argument that, where implementation does not involve adopting subordinate legislation but simply applying rules to individual cases, only the advisory committee procedure is legally acceptable.[41]

The European Parliament[42]

The European Parliament has undergone more fundamental changes in its history than any of the other Community institutions. First, as to its name: it was called the "Assembly" in the founding Treaties, and continued to be referred to as such in Council acts until its change of name was officially recognised by the S.E.A.[43] Secondly, as to its composition: originally a nominated body, its members drawn from the parliamentary institutions of the Member States, the European Parliament was transformed into a body of representatives directly elected by universal suffrage in June 1979 when the first elections were held under rules which had been laid down by an Act annexed to a Council decision of 1976.[44] Thirdly, as to its powers: described in the founding Treaties as exercising "advisory and supervisory powers," the European Parliament received significant new powers, in the budgetary sphere, under the Treaties of 1970 and 1975 and, in the legislative sphere, under the S.E.A.; and the T.E.U. will bring still more substantial changes, including a power to adopt legislation jointly with the Council.[45]

The Act of 1976 was approved by the Council under the procedure prescribed by Article 138(3) EEC. That procedure requires proposals to be drawn up by the European Parliament "for elections by direct universal suffrage in accordance with a uniform procedure in all Member States" and empowers the Council, acting unanimously, to lay down the appropriate provisions, which must then be recommended to the Member States for adoption in accordance with their respective constitutional requirements. It did not prove possible in 1976 to agree a uniform electoral procedure and Article 7(2) of the Act, accordingly, states that, pending the entry into force of such a procedure (and subject to specific provisions of the Act, such as those relating to the timing of elections and the counting of votes), "the electoral procedure shall be governed in each Member State by its national provisions." The three elections so far held (in 1979, 1984 and 1989) have therefore been organised under national electoral laws, all of them based on variants of proportional representation apart from that of the United Kingdom where the usual "first past the post" system applies, except in Northern Ireland. The T.E.U. includes an amendment to Article 138(3), inserting into the procedure a requirement that the decision of the Council

---

[41] Case 16/88, *loc. cit.* note 34, *supra.*
[42] See F. Jacobs and R. Corbett, *The European Parliament* (1990, Longman).
[43] S.E.A., Art. 3(1) speaks, rather coyly, of the institutions "henceforth designated as referred to hereafter," and goes on to refer to "the European Parliament" in subsequent provisions.
[44] Dec. 76/787, O.J. 1976 L278/1.
[45] See the discussion of legislative procedures in Chap. 3, *infra.*

be adopted "after obtaining the assent of the European Parliament." Thus the European Parliament will have to give its formal approval to any uniform electoral system that may be adopted in the future.

The number of members of the European Parliament (or M.E.P.s) is currently fixed at 518, divided up as follows: 81 each from Germany, France, Italy and the United Kingdom; 60 from Spain; 25 from the Netherlands; 24 each from Belgium, Greece and Portugal; 16 from Denmark; 15 from Ireland; 6 from Luxembourg.[46] Like the qualified majority as defined by Article 148(2), the number of seats given to the various Member States reflects, in a rough and ready way, differences in their populations. The issue of whether to increase the number of M.E.P.s from Germany, following reunification, was left unresolved by the T.E.U. However, as we have seen, it was mentioned in a Declaration, along with the number of Commissioners, as something to be examined before the end of 1992, with a view to establishing the necessary legal basis for fixing the number of M.E.P.s in good time for the 1994 elections.[47] The Declaration further notes that decisions will be taken in the light, *inter alia*, of the need to establish the overall size of the European Parliament in an enlarged Community.

The M.E.P.s are organised in cross-national political groups, broadly following the ideological divisions that are familiar in national politics. Thus the two largest groups are the Socialist Group, to which the British Labour Members belong, and the Group of the European People's Party, composed in the main of Christian Democrats from Continental Member States, who were joined in 1992 by the British Conservatives. Article 138a of the T.E.U. emphasises the importance of political parties at European level as a factor for integration within the Union.

Article 3(1) of the Act of 1976 provides for a fixed parliamentary term of five years. This can be varied by up to a month either way, if the Council, acting unanimously after consulting the European Parliament, decides that elections are to be held during a period not exactly corresponding to the period chosen for the first elections in 1979, *i.e.* June 7 to 10.[48]

The increase in the powers of the European Parliament under successive Treaties, which is taken a stage further by the T.E.U., was remarked on at the beginning of this section. The formal powers of the Parliament are broadly of three kinds: it participates in various ways, depending on the legal basis of the act in question, in the law-making process of the Communities; together with the Council, it constitutes the budgetary authority of the Communities; and it exercises political supervision over the performance by the Commission of its tasks. Besides these formal powers, the European Parliament evidently considers that it is entitled, as the collective voice of the Community electorate, to express reactions to political events both within the Communities and in the wider world. It does not have an independent right of initiative but brings its influence to bear on the Commission and, so far as it is able, on the Council, to provoke any action by

---

[46] Act, Art. 2, as replaced by Art. 10 of the Act of Accession of Spain and Portugal.
[47] Decl. No. 15.
[48] See Act, Art. 10(2).

those institutions that it considers necessary. For that purpose, the position of the European Parliament will be strengthened by the second paragraph of Article 138b of the EC Treaty, as amended by the T.E.U., which provides that it may "acting by a majority of its members, request the Commission to submit any appropriate proposal on matters on which it considers that a Community act is required for the purpose of implementing this Treaty."[49]

The participation of the European Parliament in the law-making process will be discussed in Chapter 3. In the present chapter we confine our attention to the budgetary powers of the Parliament and to its role as political watchdog of the Commission.

In the budgetary sphere, as a result of the Treaties of 1970 and 1975, the European Parliament has become an equal partner of the Council. Their respective powers are determined by the distinction between "compulsory expenditure" (usually referred to by its French acronym, DO) and "non-compulsory expenditure" (or DNO). DO has been defined as "such expenditure as the budgetary authority is obliged to enter in the budget to enable the Community to meet its obligations, both internally and externally, under the Treaties and acts adopted in accordance therewith."[50] The Council has the last word on DO, which consists largely of expenditure on the common agricultural policy, while the Parliament has the last word on DNO, which includes expenditure on the structural funds, on research and on aid to non-Community countries. At one time DNO accounted for only a small proportion of Community expenditure, but that proportion has risen very significantly with the doubling of expenditure on the structural funds between 1988 and 1993 and the high level of financial support for Central and Eastern European countries and the former Soviet Union. The increase not only in the amount but also in the political importance of DNO has reinforced the bargaining power of the European Parliament in financial matters.

The different roles assigned to the Council and the European Parliament in the budgetary procedure laid down by Article 203 reflect the division of competence between them. On the basis of a provisional draft budget proposed by the Commission, the Council establishes the draft budget, which it is required to submit to the European Parliament before October 5 in the year preceding the one in which the budget is to be implemented.[51] At its first reading of the draft budget, the Parliament has the right to propose modifications of items classified as DO and to amend items classified as DNO.[52] The draft budget then returns to the Council for a second reading. Proposed modifications to DO which are not explicitly accepted by the Council stand as rejected (except for those involving no increase in total expenditure whose rejection requires a positive decision by the Council) and

---

[49] *Cf.* the Council's rarely used right under Art. 152 EC to request the Commission to undertake studies and to submit to it any appropriate proposals.

[50] See Joint Declaration by the European Parliament, the Council and the Commission on various measures to improve the budgetary procedure, which was adopted on June 30, 1982: O.J. 1982 C194/1.

[51] Art. 203(4).

[52] *Ibid.*

the Council may also modify any of the amendments to DNO adopted by the Parliament.[53] All Council decisions connected with the budgetary procedure are taken by a qualified majority. At its second reading of the draft budget, the Parliament may, acting by a majority of its members and three-fifths of the votes cast, amend or reject any of the modifications made by the Council to its amendments to DNO, but it no longer has any right to touch DO.[54] The procedure concludes with the formal declaration by the President of the European Parliament that the budget has been finally adopted.[55] However, the Parliament may "for important reasons," decide, by a majority of its members and two-thirds of the votes cast, to reject the budget as a whole and ask for a new draft to be submitted to it.[56] Drastic as that power may seem, it has been used by the Parliament on three occasions, in respect of the general budgets for 1980 and 1985 and a supplementary and amending budget in 1982.

A complex mechanism to prevent DNO from increasing excessively from one year to another is provided by Article 203(9). The functioning of that mechanism was the subject of frequent disputes between the Council and the European Parliament, one of them, in respect of the 1986 budget, leading to proceedings before the Court of Justice and the annulment by the Court of the act of the President of the Parliament declaring the budget to have been finally adopted.[57] In 1988, however, the package of financial measures (now known as the "Delors I" package) was adopted, with the aim of ensuring adequate resources to achieve the objectives of the S.E.A., within a framework of budgetary discipline. The measures included an Inter-Institutional Agreement (or I.I.A.) between the European Parliament, the Council and the Commission containing "financial perspectives" by which annual ceilings were fixed for various categories of expenditure over the period 1988 to 1992.[58] The financial perspectives provided a basis for the orderly development of expenditure in accordance with agreed priorities. Thanks to the I.I.A., relative peace has reigned between the two branches of the budgetary authority since 1987, and this in spite of the fact that unforeseen events, notably in Central and Eastern Europe and the former Soviet Union, have made it necessary for some of the ceilings of the financial perspectives to be raised. The agreement of 1988 expires at the end of 1992 and it has been proposed, as part of the package of financial measures to give effect to the T.E.U. (the "Delors II" package), that a new I.I.A., with another set of multi-annual financial perspectives, be negotiated.

The I.I.A. of 1988 is interesting not only as a tool of budgetary policy but also from a legal point of view. It is not an agreement in international law, since the parties—Community institutions—do not have international legal

---

[53] Art. 203(5).
[54] Art. 203(6).
[55] Art. 203(7).
[56] Art. 203(8).
[57] Case 34/86, *Council* v. *European Parliament* [1986] E.C.R. 2155.
[58] The text of the I.I.A. was published, together with the other elements of the Delors I package, in O.J. 1988 L185.

personality. It should rather be regarded as a pact between equal partners in a constitutional order about the way in which they will exercise co-ordinate powers. In fact, this kind of arrangement between institutions seems to be characteristic of the Community order: other examples are the Joint Declaration of 1975 on the institution of a conciliation procedure[59] and the Joint Declaration of 1982 on various measures to improve the budgetary procedure.[60] Whether such arrangements create legal or purely political obligations is a matter which, ultimately, only the Court of Justice can decide. Perhaps they may be found to constitute a concrete expression of the obligation of loyal co-operation between the institutions. At all events, the parties to the I.I.A. have consistently behaved as if they expected its terms to be observed in good faith.

Detailed supervision by the European Parliament over the activities of the Commission is made possible by the regular attendance of members of the Commission at part-sessions of the Parliament, and of Commissioners or their officials at meetings of Parliamentary committees. There is an express Treaty obligation on members of the Commission to reply to written and oral questions[61] and, following the first enlargement of the Communities in 1973, a question time, clearly influenced by the British model, was introduced. The Treaty also requires the Commission to submit an annual general report to the Parliament,[62] and the practice has developed of publishing, in conjunction with that report, other reports of a more specialised character relating, for instance, to the agricultural situation in the Community or to competition policy, which are an important source of information.

Although not obliged by the Treaty to do so, the Council replies to written questions from the European Parliament and, through the President of the relevant Council formation, to oral questions.[63] Council Presidents are invited to appear before committees of the Parliament and they attend part-sessions to represent the views of the Council or to give an account of their management of Council business.

The supervisory powers of the European Parliament will be reinforced by the T.E.U. in three ways. First, the Parliament will have the right, under Article 138c, to set up temporary Committees of Inquiry to investigate "alleged contraventions or maladministration in the implementation of Community law," except where the matter is *sub judice*. It is interesting to note that the text does not explicitly limit the scope of such investigations to contraventions or maladministration for which Community institutions or bodies are allegedly responsible. Secondly, Article 138d confirms an established practice by giving any citizen of the Union or any resident of a Member State the right to petition the European Parliament on a matter within Community competence which affects him directly. Thirdly, under

---

[59] O.J. 1975 C89/1.
[60] See note 50, *supra*.
[61] Art. 140 EC, third para.
[62] Art. 143 EC.
[63] See Art. 140 EC, fourth para. and Rules of Procedure of the Council, Art. 19.

Article 138e, the European Parliament is to appoint an Ombudsman who will be empowered to receive complaints concerning instances of maladministration in the activities of Community institutions or bodies (other than the Court of Justice or the Court of First Instance acting judicially). If the Ombudsman establishes a case of maladministration, he will be required to give the institution concerned three months in which to inform him of its views and will then forward a report to the European Parliament and to the institution, while also informing the complainant of the outcome. The Ombudsman is to be appointed after each election for the duration of the newly elected Parliament's terms of office.

The effectiveness of the European Parliament's supervision of the Commission does not depend only on the moral authority of its democratic mandate: Article 144 EEC puts into the hands of the Parliament the supreme political weapon of a motion of censure by which it can force the resignation of the College of Commissioners. If a motion of censure is tabled, three days must elapse before a vote is taken; and, for the motion to be carried, there must be a two-thirds majority of the votes cast, representing a majority of the members of the Parliament. In the past it was sometimes said that the power to dismiss the Commission by a vote of censure was too powerful a weapon ever to be used; and, even if the Commission could be forced to resign in this way, it would immediately be reappointed by common accord of the Governments of the Member States. That argument was never very plausible and will lose all its force once the T.E.U. has brought in the requirement of a vote of approval by the European Parliament for an incoming Commission.

CHAPTER 3

THE LEGISLATIVE PROCESS

Legislative procedures

There is no single institution that constitutes the Community legislature: rather, the Community has a legislative process to which different institutions contribute in more or less important ways. The precise procedural steps to be taken for the enactment of a given measure are determined by the Treaty article that provides the legal basis. The S.E.A. introduced new procedures, giving an enhanced role to the European Parliament, and the T.E.U. contains further innovations. Once the T.E.U. has entered into force, the procedures for the adoption of law-making acts in the Community order will be of four main kinds.[1]

The consultation procedure

Before the amendment of the EEC Treaty by the S.E.A., this was the only procedure giving the European Parliament a guaranteed role in the enactment of legislation. Under the procedure, a piece of legislation is proposed by the Commission, the European Parliament is consulted on the proposal and the Council takes the final decision, acting by a qualified majority or unanimity, as laid down by the relevant provision of the Treaty (and depending on whether the Council exercises its power of amendment).[2]

Although it has been, to some extent, superseded by new procedures, the consultation procedure will continue to be used under the EC Treaty, as amended by the T.E.U. for legislation in several important policy areas, including the common agricultural policy,[3] harmonisation of indirect taxation[4] and certain aspects of the protection of the environment.[5] It is also prescribed by the T.E.U. for various matters on which a specific legal basis is to be created for the first time, for example visa policy[6] and matters connected with the establishment and functioning of E.M.U.[7]

Where the Treaty provides for the consultation of the European Parliament, that requirement must be strictly complied with. In practice, work on a Commission proposal begins immediately within Council bodies,

---

[1] The forms of procedure here examined all involve participation by the European Parliament. A simpler procedure, with no consultation of the Parliament, is provided by certain Treaty provisions, *e.g.* by Art. 113 EEC in respect of legislation on the common commercial policy.
[2] On the power of the Council to amend Commission proposals, see *infra*.
[3] Art. 43 EEC.
[4] Art. 99 EEC.
[5] See EC Treaty, as amended, Art. 130, s.(2). The matters in question comprise: provisions primarily of a fiscal nature; town and country planning, land use with the exception of waste management and measures of a general nature, and management of water resources; measures significantly affecting a Member State's choice between different energy sources and the general structure of its energy supply.
[6] EC Treaty, as amended, Art. 100c.
[7] *Eg.* EC Treaty, as amended, Art. 104c(14) (excessive deficit procedure); Art. 109f(7) (tasks of the E.M.I.). See Chap. 23, *infra*.

without waiting for the Parliament's Opinion, but the final decision cannot be taken until the Opinion has been received and considered by the Council. As the Court of Justice explained in the *Isoglucose* case:

> "The consultation provided for in the third sub-paragraph of Article 43(2), as in other similar provisions of the Treaty, is the means which allows the Parliament to play an actual part in the legislative process of the Community. Such power represents an essential factor in the institutional balance intended by the Treaty. Although limited, it reflects at Community level the fundamental democratic principle that the peoples should take part in the exercise of power through the intermediary of a representative assembly. Due consultation of the Parliament in the cases provided for by the Treaty therefore constitutes an essential formality disregard of which means that the measure concerned is void."[8]

In that case the Court annulled a Regulation[9] which the Council had adopted on the basis of Article 43(2) without having received the opinion of the Parliament which had been requested some months previously. The Court rejected the Council's argument that the Parliament, by its own conduct in failing to give an opinion on a measure it knew to be urgent, had made compliance with the consultation requirement impossible. Does it follow that the Parliament could indefinitely prevent the adoption of a measure of which it disapproved, simply by withholding its Opinion? The better view is that it could not, since the *Isoglucose* judgment lays emphasis on the fact that the Council had not formally invoked the emergency procedure for which the Parliament's own rules provide, nor had it taken advantage of its right, under Article 139 of the Treaty, to request an extraordinary session of the Parliament[10]: the implication is that, if the Council had exhausted all the procedural possibilities open to it, the adoption of the Regulation, without waiting any longer for the Opinion, might well have been justified.

The consultation of the European Parliament takes place in relation to the Commission's original proposal. If the Commission amends its proposal, or the Council intends to exercise its power of amendment, and this means that, considered as a whole, the substance of the text which was the subject of the first consultation will be altered, there is a duty to consult the Parliament a second time.[11] Reconsultation is not required if the change is one of method rather than of substance (for example, the substitution, in a draft regulation relating to officials' pay, of updated exchange rates); nor if the change goes in the direction of wishes expressed by the Parliament itself in its Opinion.[12] A new case for reconsultation, acknowledged in the practice

---

[8] Case 138/79, *Roquette Frères* v. *Council* [1980] E.C.R. 3333 at p. 3360.
[9] Council Reg. 1293/79, O.J. 1979 L162/10.
[19] Joint Decl., point 7.
[11] Case 41/69, *ACF Chemiefarma* v. *Commission* [1970] E.C.R. 661 at p. 702; Case 1253/79, *Battaglia* v. *Commission* [1982] E.C.R. 297; Case C–65/90, *European Parliament* v. *Council*, judgment of July 16, 1992 (not yet reported). See also Opinion of A.G. Mancini in Case 20/85, *Roviello* [1988] 2805 at pp. 2838 *et seq.*; Opinion of A.G. Darmon in Case 65/90, *European Parliament* v. *Council*, *supra*.
[12] Case 1253/79, *Battaglia*, *supra*.

of the Council since the introduction of the co-operation procedure by the S.E.A., is where the Council is minded to amend the legal basis proposed by the Commission from an article of the Treaty providing for co-operation to one requiring simple consultation of the Parliament. The same will, presumably, apply in the future if the Commission puts forward a proposal based on an article which, pursuant to the T.E.U., requires the new procedure under Article 189b of the EC Treaty, as amended, and the Council intends to substitute a legal basis with a less elaborate procedure.

Reconsultation, which is a legal requirement in certain circumstances, must not be confused with the conciliation procedure instituted by a Joint Declaration of the European Parliament, the Council and the Commission in 1975.[13] The procedure provides an opportunity, through a face-to-face meeting within a Conciliation Committee, for the European Parliament and the Council to find common ground in certain cases where the Council intends to depart from the Opinion adopted by the Parliament. The act in question must be one of "general application" (this would cover all acts of a normative character, including, by definition, all regulations) and it must have "appreciable financial implications."[14] Acts whose adoption is required pursuant to existing legislation are excluded,[15] because such legislation could itself have been the subject of conciliation. There are also procedural requirements: the Commission must indicate, in submitting its proposal, whether the act in question is a suitable subject for the procedure; and the European Parliament's request for conciliation must be made when it gives its Opinion.[16] Conciliation should normally be completed within three months, or within an appropriate time limit, to be fixed by the Council, if the matter is urgent.[17] It must be stressed that the aim is to *seek* an agreement between the Parliament and the Council[18]: if there is a sufficient *rapprochement*, the Parliament may give a fresh Opinion and the Council then proceeds to take definitive action[19]; however, even in the absence of agreement, the Council retains its legal right to adopt, according to the applicable voting procedure, the measure it considers appropriate. For the European Parliament, the advantage of the procedure is that it allows influence to be exerted in the final phase of decision-making, and this has been done with some effect in recent years, for example in respect of the amendments to the Financial Regulation that were adopted in 1988.[20]

It should finally be noted that there is nothing to prevent the Council from consulting the European Parliament, and it often does so, where this is not required by the Treaty. In such a case, if the Parliament fails, for some reason, to give an Opinion, the Council is free to withdraw the request, but,

---

[13] O.J. 1975 C89.
[14] Joint Decl., point 2.
[15] *Ibid.*
[16] Joint Decl., point 3.
[17] Joint Decl., point 6.
[18] *Ibid.*
[19] Joint Decl., point 7.
[20] Council Reg. 610/90, O.J. 1990 L70/1.

it is thought, reasonable notice should be given to the Parliament before such withdrawal.

The co-operation procedure

The S.E.A. introduced a new legislative procedure applicable wherever it was provided in the amended EEC Treaty that the Council act "in co-operation with the European Parliament."[21] The procedure, as set out in Article 149(2) EEC, will be retained in the EC Treaty, as amended by the T.E.U., where, however, it is to be found in Article 189c. As a matter of drafting technique, the mention of "co-operation" is to be dropped, and the EC Treaty, as amended, will speak of "the procedure referred to in Article 189c." However, for the sake of convenience, the term "co-operation procedure" is used in the discussion that follows.

In contrast to the consultation procedure, which in principle involves a single reading by the European Parliament and by the Council, the co-operation procedure involves two readings. The first reading corresponds to the consultation procedure except that it culminates not in the definitive enactment of the measure but in the adoption of a "common position" by the Council, acting by a qualified majority (unless it exercises its power to amend the Commission's proposal by unanimity).[22] The common position must be communicated to the European Parliament with a full account of the reasons that led to its adoption, as well as an explanation of the Commission's position.[23] The Parliament is given three months in which to react to the common position, and the action it decides on determines the further course of the second reading. There are three possibilities.

First, the European Parliament may approve the common position or allow the three-month period to elapse without taking a decision. In that event, the Council must proceed, without more ado, to the definitive adoption of the act in question, in accordance with the common position.[24]

Secondly, the Parliament may, by an absolute majority of its members, reject the common position. If that happens, it is still legally possible for the Council to adopt the act at second reading, but it may only do so by unanimity.[25] In practice, where the common position was adopted by a qualified majority, there is very little likelihood that the minority on the Council will be persuaded to join with the majority in overriding the Parliament's rejection, which will thus have the effect of a veto. Two such cases have occurred since the entry into force of the S.E.A.: in the first case the proposal lapsed at the end of the period of three months prescribed by Article 149(2)(f), while in the second one the Council, shortly after the

---

[21] See the discussion of the co-operation procedure in J. De Ruyt, *L'Acte unique européen* (1987, Editions de l'Université de Bruxelles), pp. 124 *et seq.* On the application of the procedure to internal market legislation, see J. Schwarze (ed.), *Legislation for Europe 1992* (1989, Nomos).

[22] Art. 149(2)(a) EEC (EC Treaty, as amended, Art. 189c(a)).

[23] Art. 149(2)(b), first sub-para. EEC (EC Treaty, as amended, Art. 189c(b), first sub-para.).

[24] Art. 149(2)(b), second sub-para. EEC (EC Treaty, as amended, Art. 189c(b), second sub-para.).

[25] Art. 149(2)(c), second sub-para. EEC (EC Treaty, as amended, Art. 189c(c), second sub-para.).

rejection, expressly declared itself unable to find the unanimity necessary to allow it to act at second reading.[26]

The European Parliament's third option, and the one it normally chooses, is to propose amendments to the common position, again by an absolute majority of its members.[27] The Commission is required, within a month, to re-examine the proposal on the basis of which the common position was adopted, taking as its starting point the amendments proposed by the Parliament. The intention (more evident from the language of the French version of the relevant provision than from its English version) seems to be that any change made to the proposal at that stage must go in the direction of the Parliament's amendments[28]: the Commission has a choice between taking those amendments into account or leaving its proposal intact, but it may not introduce complete new amendments. The re-examined proposal is finally sent back to the Council, which may adopt it by a qualified majority or amend it by unanimity (*inter alia*, by accepting any of the amendments put forward by the European Parliament which the Commission may not have incorporated into its proposal).[29]

In the scheme of the S.E.A., the co-operation procedure was closely associated with the objective of completing the internal market by the end of 1992. Nearly all of the legal bases providing for the use of the procedure[30] were either specifically created or adapted with that end in view, most notably Article 100a, the basis for the great bulk of approximation measures having as their object the establishment or functioning of the internal market. The T.E.U. will bring a significant change, substituting the Article 189b procedure for co-operation in most of the provisions for which the latter was required pursuant to the S.E.A.[31] On the other hand, the T.E.U. creates new uses for the co-operation procedure, *inter alia*, for measures in connection with the common transport policy,[32] and in the fields of vocational training[33] and development co-operation.[34] It will also become the normal procedure for taking action in furtherance of Community policy on the environment.[35]

The procedure referred to in Article 189b

This new legislative procedure, to be introduced by the T.E.U., is sometimes called "co-decision," reflecting the language of earlier versions of

---

[26] The first case, which occurred in 1988, concerned a draft directive on the protection of workers against risks related to exposure to benzene (see O.J. 1988 C290/64). The second case, which occurred in 1992, concerned a draft directive on sweetners.

[27] Art. 149(2)(c), first sub-para. EEC (EC Treaty, as amended, Art. 189c(c), first sub-para.).

[28] Art. 149(2)(d), first sub-para. EEC (EC Treaty, as amended, Art. 189c(d), first sub-para.). The French version says: "à partir des amendements proposés par le Parlement européen." *Cf.* the English version: "taking into account the amendments. . . ."

[29] Art. 149(2)(d), second sub-para., and (e) EEC (EC Treaty, as amended, Art. 189c(d), second sub-para., and (e)).

[30] See the list of provisions in S.E.A., Art. 6.

[31] In particular, the internal market provisions: see EC Treaty, as amended, Arts. 49, 54(2), 56(2), 57(1) and (2), 100a(1).

[32] EC Treaty, as amended, Art. 75(1).

[33] EC Treaty, as amended, Art. 127(4).

[34] EC Treaty, as amended, Art. 130w(1).

[35] EC Treaty, as amended, Art. 130s(1).

the Treaty. The decision to drop that terminology, for whatever political reasons, seems sound in principle: in our submission, it is misleading to apply the term "co-decision" to any procedure that does not give an equal power of final approval of the measure in question to the European Parliament and the Council. As we shall see, although the Article 189b procedure seeks to channel the two institutions towards approval of a joint text, the Council may still, in the absence of agreement, be able to act unilaterally.

The Article 189b procedure begins, like the co-operation procedure, with a first reading culminating in the adoption by the Council of a common position which must then be communicated with full explanations, to the European Parliament.[36] A difference, as compared with the co-operation procedure, is that the Commission's proposal is to be submitted directly to both the European Parliament and the Council. This is clearly of symbolic importance, but it may also have practical implications: if the Council does not formally consult the Parliament, but merely obtains its Opinion on a proposal which each of them has received independently, it is legitimate to wonder whether the case law[37] on the reconsultation of the Parliament will apply, should the Council wish to adopt a common position that would change the substance of the Commission's proposal.

At second reading, the European Parliament will, once again, be faced with a choice between expressly or tacitly approving the common position of the Council or rejecting it or proposing amendments to it. However, the consequences of taking either of the latter options differ markedly from those under the co-operation procedure.

Should the European Parliament indicate, by an absolute majority its members, that it intends to reject the common position, the Council must be informed immediately, and may convene a meeting of the Conciliation Committee provided for by Article 189b(4), in order further to explain its position. Following such a meeting (or if none is held), the European Parliament may either confirm its rejection of the common position or propose amendments to it. If the Parliament opts for rejection, the proposal will be deemed not to have been adopted.[38]

Where the European Parliament proposes amendments to the common position, the amended text must be forwarded to the Council and the Commission, the latter being required to deliver an opinion on the amendments.[39] If within three months the Council approves *all* the Parliament's amendments (by a qualified majority, or by unanimity in respect of amendments on which the Commission has delivered a negative opinion) and amends its common position accordingly, it may go on to adopt the act in question. If it does not, then the Conciliation Committee must be convened.[40]

---

[36] EC Treaty, as amended, Art. 189b(2), first and second sub-paras.
[37] See note 11, *supra*.
[38] As to all this, see EC Treaty, as amended, Art. 189b(2)(c).
[39] EC Treaty, as amended, Art. 189b(2)(d).
[40] EC Treaty, as amended, Art. 189b(3).

The Committee will be composed of the members of the Council or their representatives and an equal number of representatives of the European Parliament. Its task will be, within a six-week deadline, to reach agreement on a joint text by a qualified majority on the Council side and by a majority on the Parliament side. The Commission is to participate in the proceedings of the Committee and to act as broker between the two sides.[41] If the Committee succeeds in its task, the European Parliament, acting by an absolute majority of the votes cast, and the Council, acting by a qualified majority, will have six weeks in which to adopt the act in question in accordance with the joint text: should either of them fail to do so, the act will be deemed not to have been adopted.[42] If, on the other hand, no joint text is approved, the act will be deemed not to have been adopted, unless the Council, within six weeks of the end of the period granted to the Committee, confirms, by a qualified majority, the common position to which it agreed before the conciliation procedure was initiated, possibly incorporating some of the Parliament's proposed amendments. However, the final adoption of the act by unilateral decision of the Council can still be prevented by the Parliament if, within six months, it rejects the text by an absolute majority of its members.[43]

The Article 189b procedure will be available for the adoption of a much wider range of actions than seemed likely at one stage in the negotiations for the T.E.U. Those actions include (besides legislation relating to the internal market)[44]: incentive measures in the field of public health[45]; specific action supporting or supplementing national policies on consumer protection[46]; guidelines covering the objectives, priorities and broad lines of measures envisaged in the sphere of trans-European networks[47]; and general action programmes setting out priority objectives for policy on the environment.[48] In addition, the new procedure is prescribed for incentive measures in the field of culture[49] and for the adoption of the multinational framework programme for research[50]: a peculiar feature of the procedure in these last two cases, however, is that the Council will be required to act, at all stages, by unanimity.

The assent procedure (avis conforme)

Under the assent procedure, the Council acts on a proposal by the Commission after obtaining the assent of the European Parliament. The simplicity of the procedure belies its political significance: it is an example of

---

[41] EC Treaty, as amended, Art. 189b(4).
[42] EC Treaty, as amended, Art. 189b(5).
[43] EC Treaty, as amended, Art. 189b(6).
[44] The substitution of the Art. 189b procedure for the co-operation procedure in Treaty articles providing the legal basis for internal market legislation, including Art. 100a, was noted *supra*.
[45] EC Treaty, as amended, Art. 129(4).
[46] EC Treaty, as amended, Art. 129a(2).
[47] EC Treaty, as amended, Art. 129d.
[48] EC Treaty, as amended, Art. 130s(3).
[49] EC Treaty, as amended, Art. 128(5), first indent.
[50] EC Treaty, as amended, Art. 130i(1).

pure co-decision, where the act in question can only be adopted if it is formally approved by both the Parliament and the Council.

The S.E.A. introduced the assent procedure into the EEC Treaty for decisions under Article 237 on applications by States seeking membership of the Community and under Article 238 on the conclusion of association agreements. The category of international agreements to which the procedure applies is to be considerably enlarged by the T.E.U.,[51] which will also extend the procedure to the legislative sphere. Thus the enactment, pursuant to Article 8a(2) of the EC Treaty, as amended, of provisions with a view to facilitating the exercise of rights of free movement and residence for Union citizens will require the assent of the European Parliament. The same will be true of acts, adopted by the Council under Article 130d, defining the tasks, priority objectives and organisation of the structural funds, as well as of the decision that will have to be taken before the end of 1993 to set up the new Cohesion Fund. The assent procedure is also to be introduced for the amendment of certain provisions of the Statute of the ESCB[52] and for the adoption of acts regulating elections to the European Parliament.[53]

Under most of the Treaty articles providing for the use of the assent procedure, the Council is required to act by unanimity, but a qualified majority will be sufficient for the adoption of decisions on the conclusion of some, at least, of the international agreements to which the new Article 228(3), second sub-paragraph applies.[54] The European Parliament will give its assent by a majority of the votes cast in all cases, except for decisions on applications for membership, where an absolute majority of M.E.P.s is required.

Majority decisions by the Council

The general voting procedure, laid down by Article 148(1) EEC, is that, save as otherwise provided by the Treaty, the Council shall act by a majority of its members. However, there are few cases where the Treaty confers powers on the Council without specifically providing that acts shall be adopted either by a qualified majority or by unanimity. In the Community of 12, a qualified majority consists of 54 votes out of 76, the allocation of votes to the various Member States being weighted so as to correspond, very roughly, to differences in size of population.[55] In the rather rare cases where the Council may act without a proposal from the Commission, a qualified majority decision requires, in addition, the positive votes of at least eight Member States. Where the Treaty provides for the Council to act by

---

[51] See the new Art. 228(3), second sub-para.
[52] EC Treaty, as amended, Art. 106(5).
[53] EC Treaty, as amended, Art. 138(3).
[54] *E.g.* "agreements establishing a specific institutional framework by organising co-operation procedures" or "agreements having important budgetary implications for the Community" in a field where unanimity is not required for the adoption of internal rules: para. (3) of Art. 228, read together with para. (1), second sub-paragraph and para. (2), second sentence.
[55] Germany, France, Italy and the United Kingdom have 10 votes each; Spain has 8 votes; Belgium, Greece, the Netherlands and Portugal have 5 votes; Denmark and Ireland have 3 votes; Luxembourg has 2 votes.

unanimity, abstentions by the Member States do not prevent the act in question from being adopted[56]; in other words, "unanimity" connotes the absence of negative votes. By contrast, to obtain a qualified majority, 54 positive votes are needed, so any purported abstention will contribute to a blocking minority.

The T.E.U. provides for special qualified majorities in certain cases, more particularly in connection with decisions that have to be taken within the context of economic and monetary union. For example, when the Council decides under Article 104c(11) to impose sanctions on a Member State which has failed to comply with a decision requiring it to take the necessary measures to reduce an excessive government deficit, the Member State concerned will not be entitled to vote, and the qualified majority will consist of two thirds of the weighted votes of the other members of the Council. Similarly, in the third stage of economic and monetary union only the Member States qualifying for participation in the single currency will have a right to vote on matters connected with its establishment and management, and two thirds of the weighted votes of those Member States will constitute a qualified majority.[57]

Since the end of the second stage of the EEC's transitional period (December 31, 1965), the qualified majority has been the voting procedure prescribed in the core areas of Community competence—those of the common market and the common policies in agriculture and transport. The range of matters that could be decided by a qualified majority was extended by the S.E.A., most notably in the case of Article 100a, the legal basis for adopting measures for the approximation of national provisions where such measures have as their object the establishment and functioning of the internal market. With the further extension of qualified majority decisions by the T.E.U., the rule of unanimity will be confined to certain matters of special political sensitivity, such as the harmonisation of indirect taxation,[58] and to decisions of a fundamental character, such as the exercise of the residual power of action given by Article 235 EEC.[59]

Despite the opportunities for majority voting offered by the EEC Treaty, until the early 1980s the Council only regularly took decisions in this way on budgetary and staff matters, acting by consensus in other cases. The tedious process of negotiating a compromise acceptable to all delegations represented a serious impediment to progress in the development of the EEC in the decade following the end of the transitional period. That has now changed and it has become the normal practice for the Council to act by a qualified or simple majority where the Treaty allows.[60] The change in practice reflected a new political climate, influenced by the perception that rapid progress towards completing the internal market was necessary to

---

[56] Art. 148(3) EEC.
[57] EC Treaty, as amended, Art. 109k(5). On these matters, see Chap. 23, *infra*.
[58] Art. 99 EEC.
[59] Other typical examples are Art. 201 (own resources) and Art. 209 (financial legislation).
[60] See J.-L. Dewost in Capotorti *et al.* (eds.), *Du droit international au droit communautaire, Liber amicorum Pierre Pescatore* (1988, Nomos), pp. 167 *et seq.*; Dashwood in Schwarze (ed.), *Legislation for Europe 1992* (1989, Nomos), pp. 79 *et seq.*

enable the Community to deal on equal terms with its main international competitors. The trend towards majority voting predates the entry into force of the S.E.A.,[61] but it certainly received a fresh impetus from the introduction of new legal bases providing for majority decisions.

In connection with majority voting, something must be said about the so-called "Luxembourg Compromise." This was an "agreement to disagree," reached at a special meeting of the Council in January 1966, to resolve a political crisis precipitated in part because of the shift to decision-making by qualified majority which was foreseen under the EEC Treaty from the beginning of the final stage of the transitional period. The text of the Luxembourg Compromise[62] included a provision to the effect that when, in case of a decision that can be taken by a majority vote, very important interests of a Member State are at stake, the Council will attempt, within a reasonable time, to reach a solution acceptable to all its members. It was noted that, in the view of the French delegation, the discussion in such cases must continue until unanimous agreement is reached, a view not shared by the other delegations. This arrangement left the Council's legal powers fully intact, while influencing its practice. In assessing that influence, it is useful to draw a distinction between the encouragement that was undoubtedly given to the search for consensus within the Council, and formal invocation of the Compromise by a Member State to prevent a vote from being taken on a particular occasion.[63] In fact, Member States have formally invoked the Compromise only about a dozen times, and the political price for doing so is considered to be high. The outcome may also be uncertain: thus in 1982, when the United Kingdom sought to block the adoption of the agricultural price package in order to put pressure on the other Member States to agree a reduction of the British contribution to the Community budget, its purported "veto" was swept aside and a vote was taken[64]; whereas in 1985 Germany successfully invoked the Compromise to forestall a decision on the reduction of cereal prices. Whether in the era of the T.E.U. the Luxembourg Compromise can still be said to "exist" is not a question to which a legal answer can be given: it all depends on whether, in a concrete case, enough of the Member States to constitute a blocking minority can be persuaded, by the Member State claiming a vital interest, to refrain from voting. However, such cases, if they occur at all in future, will be very rare; more importantly, the Compromise has ceased to influence the Council towards acting by consensus, since, as we have seen, voting, if legally permissible, is now the normal practice.

---

[61] Evidence of the trend can be found in Council answers to Written Questions of the European Parliament: see, *e.g.* the answers to Written Questions No. 1121/86 (Elles), O.J. 1986 C306/42; Written Questions No. 2126/86 (Fontaine), O.J. 1987 C82/43.

[62] The full text of the Luxembourg compromise is published in Bulletin of the EEC, March 1966, pp. 8–10.

[63] Dashwood, *op. cit.* note 61, *supra*, pp. 82–83.

[64] A lesson from that episode is that the very important interest which is claimed must be directly linked to the particular measure under consideration. The United Kingdom had indicated that it was invoking the Luxembourg Compromise, not to protect important interests threatened by the price package, but as a purely tactical move.

The interaction between the institutions

The Commission's right to alter or withdraw its proposal

The Commission is expressly empowered, as long as the Council has not acted, to alter its proposal at any time during the procedures leading to the adoption of a Community act.[65] There are various reasons why it may choose to do so.

In the first place, the Commission may independently form the view that the proposal needs to be improved or completed; or perhaps to be updated, in order to keep abreast of scientific developments, especially if it has been lying on the Council's table for some time. Or account may have to be taken of changes in the legal situation: for instance, after the entry into force of the S.E.A., the Commission substituted Article 100a as the legal basis of a large number of proposals originally based on other provisions of the Treaty; and the new legal bases and procedures provided by the T.E.U. will require a similar exercise.

Secondly, the Commission may respond to an Opinion rendered by the European Parliament under the consultation procedure, or at first reading under the co-operation procedure or the Article 189b procedure, by incorporating into its proposal some or all of the amendments put forward by the Parliament. At second reading under the co-operation procedure, as we have seen, if the European Parliament proposes amendments, there is a legal duty on the Commission to re-examine its proposal, taking the Parliament's amendments as a starting point. The proposal to be re-examined is the one "on the basis of which the Council adopted its common position," which assumes that proposal has not previously been altered. This is an indication that the Commission's power of amendment, despite the general terms in which it is described by the Treaty, does not apply as long as the European Parliament, seised of the common position adopted by the Council, has not made up its mind how to react to it.[66]

Thirdly, the Commission may alter its proposal in order to facilitate decision-making within the Council. Decisions are reached by the Council through negotiations between national delegations in working groups, in COREPER and at ministerial level. These negotiations involve progressive adaptation of the Commission's proposal in order to take account of Member States' particular interests and difficulties. The process is managed by the Presidency, aided by the General Secretariat of the Council, with the aim of achieving a balanced compromise text, commanding the qualified majority or unanimity required for the adoption of the measure in question. The Commission is represented at meetings of Council bodies where its proposals are under discussion,[67] and it may play a vital part in the development of the Presidency compromise, both by providing technical

---

[65] Art. 149(3) EEC (EC Treaty, as amended, Art. 189a(2)).
[66] Art. 149(3) EEC, as the more general provision, must be read consistently with the specific requirements of the co-operation procedure.
[67] Art. 3(2) of the Council's Rules of Procedure provides: "The Commission shall be invited to take part in meetings of the Council. The Council may, however, decide to deliberate without the presence of the Commission."

assistance and by indicating amendments it is able to accept. In some cases, final amendments to the proposal are made orally by the Commissioner attending the Council meeting where a measure is adopted, who will have been mandated by the College of Commissioners to act within a certain margin of manoeuvre.

There is no explicit provision of the Treaty enabling the Commission to withdraw a proposal which it has submitted to the Council. However, it is generally agreed that, within certain limits, the Commission has such a power.[68] One view is that withdrawal may be regarded as the extreme case of amendment, but the better view is, perhaps, that both amendment and withdrawal are corollaries of the right of initiative: the latter would be incomplete, if the Commission, having put forward a proposal which it no longer considered appropriate, were unable to remedy the situation. At the same time, the power of withdrawal must not be used to prevent other institutions from performing the roles the Treaty has given them in the legislative procedure. Thus it would be an abuse of power for the Commission to withdraw a proposal which is on the point of being adopted by the Council, in order to prevent that institution from exercising its own power of amendment (as to which, see below). Similarly, it is submitted, under the co-operation procedure the Commission has no right to withdraw its proposal once the Council has adopted its common position. This seems to follow from the clear terms in which the Treaty specifies the options open to the European Parliament at second reading and the legal consequences that ineluctably follow from the course of action chosen.

The Council's power of amendment

The Council has a general power to amend proposals of the Commission but, in so doing, it must act unanimously.[69] The rule requiring unanimity for the amendment of Commission proposals was of limited practical significance during the period when the Council habitually acted by consensus; now, however, with the extension of the range of matters that can be decided by a qualified majority, and with majority decisions being taken as a matter of course where the Treaty permits, the rule has come into its own as a pivotal element of the Council/Commission relationship. This is because, if the Council is unwilling to adopt a proposal without making certain changes, the only way of avoiding the unanimity rule is for a compromise to be negotiated that the Commission can make its own; the compromise will then have the legal status of an amended Commission proposal and be capable of being enacted by a qualified majority. The Commission is thus able to maintain direct influence over the progress of its proposal, right up to the final outcome of the negotiations within the Council.

The right of the Council to amend the Commission's proposal by unanimity does not extend to the substitution of an entirely new proposal,

---

[68] See Mégret et al., Le droit de la CEE (1979, Editions de l'Université de Bruxelles), Vol. 9, pp. 135–136.
[69] Art. 149(1) EEC (EC Treaty, as amended, Art. 189a(1)).

since that would be to usurp the right of initiative.[70] It is submitted that Council amendments, however radical, will not be *ultra vires*, as long as the subject-matter of the measure in question remains the same. For instance, in a draft directive concerning animal welfare, the Council may decide to establish different criteria of welfare from those proposed by the Commission; but it would not be entitled to transform the directive into one fixing quality standards for fresh meat.

The requirement of unanimity for the amendment of Commission *proposals* does not extend to cases where the decision-making process is initiated by the submission to the Council of a *recommendation* by the Commission.[71] The main example of the EEC Treaty is found in Articles 113 and 114 which concern the negotiation and conclusion of commercial agreements with third countries. Where such agreements need to be negotiated, the Commission makes a recommendation to the Council which decides whether to authorise the opening of negotiations and, if so, whether any negotiating directives should be issued to the Commission; and, when negotiations have been completed, it is for the Council to decide on the conclusion of the agreement in question. On all of these matters the Council is free to act by a qualified majority, even if it departs from the Commission's recommendation.

That model has been followed in the case of various key decisions to be taken, pursuant to the T.E.U., in relation to the establishment and functioning of E.M.U. These include, notably, decisions in connection with the excessive deficit procedure (as to the existence of an excessive deficit in a Member State; recommendations for bringing such a deficit to an end; measures for deficit reduction; the imposition of sanctions)[72] and the transition to the third stage of E.M.U. (fulfilment of the conversion criteria[73]; grant of derogations).[74] Such an increase in the number of cases where the Council acts on a simple recommendation by the Commission might seem to represent a significant rebalancing of powers, to the Commission's disadvantage. However, it should be noted that the Council decisions in question are essentially executive in character: where *legislative* acts have to be adopted for the purposes of E.M.U. (for example for the further elaboration of the excessive deficit procedure[75] or for the irrevocable fixing of exchange rates),[76] the Council will act in the traditional way, on the basis of a Commission proposal.

The general rule requiring unanimity for the amendment of a Commission proposal is subject to an express exception in respect of Article 189b(4) and (5) of the EC Treaty as amended by the T.E.U. The exception relates to decisions adopted by the Council in accordance with a joint text agreed with

---

[70] Mégret, *op. cit.* note 68, *supra*, p. 133.
[71] This follows from the wording of Art. 149(1), which says: "Where, in pursuance of this Treaty, the Council acts *on a proposal from the Commission* . . ." (emphasis added). The same wording is found in EC Treaty, as amended, Art. 189a(1).
[72] EC Treaty, as amended, Art. 104c(6),(7),(9) and (11).
[73] EC Treaty, as amended, Art. 109j(2).
[74] EC Treaty, as amended, Art. 109k(1).
[75] EC Treaty, as amended, Art. 104c(14).
[76] EC Treaty, as amended, Art. 109l(4).

the European Parliament in the Conciliation Committee provided for by Article 189b(4). The Council will thus be able to adopt by a qualified majority a text representing the result of a successful conciliation, regardless of whether the Commission has altered its proposal accordingly.

More controversial is the question whether the Council would be able to act by a qualified majority where, conciliation having failed, it exercised its power under Article 189b(6) to confirm a common position differing in some degree from the latest version of the Commission's proposal. On the one hand, the fact that Article 189a(1) expressly mentions paragraphs (4) and (5) of Article 189b as falling outside the general rule, but is silent as to paragraph (6), might seem to indicate that unanimity would be required in such a case. On the other hand, paragraph (6) contrasts with paragraph (3) of the same Article, in referring to the possibility of incorporating into the common position amendments proposed by the European Parliament, while saying nothing about the need for unanimity if the Council acts on an amendment of which the Commission disapproves. The better view, it is submitted, is that, once the conciliation phase of the Article 189b procedure has been reached, the Commission's proposal simply ceases to be relevant: either the Council and the European Parliament will act jointly on the basis of a text agreed by the Conciliation Committee; or the Council will confirm its common position, subject to a possible Parliamentary veto. In neither case can the Council be said to be acting "on a proposal from the Commission."

The European Parliament's participation

We have seen that, where consultation of the European Parliament is required by the legal basis of a proposal, the Council must be formally seised of the Opinion rendered by the Parliament before proceeding to the adoption of the act in question (apart from urgent cases, where all procedural possibilities for obtaining the Opinion have been tried unsuccessfully).[77] However, the Council, having considered the Parliament's Opinion, is under no *legal* obligation to follow it. In practice, the most effective way for the European Parliament to influence the final shape of legislation is by putting political pressure on the Commission to incorporate elements of the Opinion into an amended proposal. If the Commission responds favourably, the Council will then be faced with a text which it will only be able to amend further by unanimity.

Under the co-operation procedure, the position of the European Parliament is similar at first reading, but at second reading there are significant differences. One difference is that the Parliament is able to influence the decision-making process directly (rather than by way of pressure brought to bear on other institutions): thus, by approving the common position, it places the Council under a legal duty to adopt the act in question in accordance with that position; while, by rejecting the common position, it prevents the Council from acting at second reading otherwise

---

[77] See the cases cited in notes 8 and 11, *supra*.

than by unanimity. Another difference is that the Commission is legally, and not merely politically, bound to re-examine the proposal on the basis of which the Council adopted the common position to see whether it should be changed to take account of amendments proposed by the European Parliament (no other changes being allowed at that stage). Over the period since the entry into force of the S.E.A., the Parliament has used its powers under the co-operation procedure to some effect, especially in respect of internal market legislation. Thus the Commission pointed out in a report published in June 1991 that the Council had adopted 32 per cent. of the amendments put forward by the European Parliament, adding that, "in many fields, such as public works contracts and public services, machine safety and insurance, Parliament has directly influenced the content of directives, in particular by taking account of their social dimension."[78]

The contribution of the European Parliament towards shaping Community legislation will be further enhanced by the introduction of the Article 189b procedure. The hallmark of that procedure is the combination of obligatory conciliation and a fully fledged Parliamentary veto. The Council and the Parliament will be required to make an effort at second reading to achieve agreement on a joint text which they can then go on to enact, each according to their own procedures. The creation of a new category of acts jointly adopted by the Council and the European Parliament emphasises their equality as partners in the legislative process. In case of a fundamental disagreement, where the Council's position remains firm, and this is unacceptable to a majority of the members of the European Parliament, the latter will have power to prevent the act in question from being adopted. Thus, where conciliation fails, the Council will not be able to impose a unilateral solution that is opposed by a majority of M.E.P.s.

---

[78] See COM(91) 237, point 22.

CHAPTER 4

THE COMMUNITY LEGAL ORDER

SOURCES OF COMMUNITY LAW

The sources of Community law are as follows:

— the Treaties establishing the three Communities, as supplemented and amended from time to time, and the secondary legislation made thereunder;
— related treaties concluded between Member States[1];
— treaties concluded between the Community and third countries[2];
— international treaties binding upon all the Member States, where the responsibilities of the latter have been assumed by the Community[3];
— decisions of the Member States having legal effect within the sphere of operation of the Treaties[4];
— decisions of the European Court of Justice[5];
— the general principles of law and the fundamental rights upon which the constitutional laws of the Member States are based[6];
— recommendations adopted on the basis of the EEC Treaty inasmuch as they may cast light on the interpretation of national law or Community law.[7]

For the purposes of simplicity, where consideration of the abovementioned sources requires reference to the Treaties and to the secondary legislation made thereunder, discussion will be limited to the legal effects of the Treaty establishing the European Economic Community, and the secondary legislation—regulations, directives and decisions—made thereunder.

Member States are bound to carry out the obligations imposed by the Treaty and secondary legislation. Breach of these obligations may give rise to an action before the Court of Justice at the suit of either the Commission, or another Member State.[8] The legal impact of Community law in the

---

[1] International agreements which are not based on the Treaties establishing the Communities do not fall within the scope of Article 177 of the EEC Treaty or Article 150 of the Euratom Treaty, see Case 44/84, *Hurd* v. *Jones* [1986] E.C.R. 29 at p. 76, para. 20.

[2] Appropriately worded provisions of such agreements may be invoked before the courts of Member States, see, *e.g.* Case 104/81, *Kupferberg* [1982] E.C.R. 3641, *infra*, p. 76.

[3] Cases 21–24/72, *International Fruit* [1972] E.C.R. 1219.

[4] *E.g.* the "acceleration" decisions of May 12, 1960, J.O. 1960 1217, and May 15, 1962, J.O. 1962 1284. See Case 22/70, *E.R.T.A.* [1971] E.C.R. 263.

[5] Decisions of the Court under Article 177 EEC are binding on the referring Court; see Case 29/68, *Milchkontor* [1969] E.C.R. 165; Case 52/76, *Benedetti* [1977] E.C.R. 163. *Stare decisis* applies in the United Kingdom by virtue of s.3(1) of the European Communities Act 1972. A ruling of the Court under Art. 177 on the invalidity of a Community act is binding *erga omnes*; see Case 66/80, *International Chemical Corporation* [1981] E.C.R. 1191. Prior decisions of the Court of Justice may extinguish the duty to refer under Art. 177(3), see Case 283/81, *CILFIT* [1982] E.C.R. 3415.

[6] See *infra* at p. 88.

[7] Case 113/75, *Frecassetti* [1976] E.C.R. 983; Case 90/76, *Van Ameyde* [1977] E.C.R. 1091; Case C–322/88, *Grimaldi* [1989] E.C.R. 4407.

[8] Arts. 169, 170, *infra* at p. 109.

Member States, however, springs from its capacity, even its tendency to give rise to rights in individuals which national courts are bound to safeguard. The position is complicated by a rather confusing terminology, which describes provisions of Community law as being either "directly applicable," or "directly effective." The latter expression describes a provision endowed with sufficient clarity and precision to bestow a legal right on a natural or legal person, as against another natural or legal person, or a Member State. Establishing direct effect is a matter of interpretation, and it is clear that specific provisions of the Treaty, as well as specific provisions of regulations, directives or decisions, may be endowed with this quality. It has been argued that direct effect, in the sense of practical operation for all concerned, is to be presumed unless established to the contrary.[9] Direct applicability, on the other hand, is that attribute of a regulation which ensures its access, in its entirety, to the national legal order, without the need for specific incorporation. National reproduction of the text of a regulation is not only otiose, but impermissible, and its status as direct Community legislation allows it to pre-empt national legislative competence. It should be noted that Member States are obliged to implement Treaty provisions and directives by legislative measures, notwithstanding the fact that in the absence of such implementation, the provisions concerned would be directly effective. Direct effect of Treaty provisions and directives is a consequence of a Member State's failure properly to implement Community law and national law and national judicial recognition of direct effect does not remedy the Member State's failure to adopt appropriate legislative measures.[10] By way of contrast, the direct effect of a regulation is not a consequence of the default of the Member State, but the corollary of the direct applicability of regulations, and of the specific text and context of particular provisions of the regulation.

Confusion arises because the expressions "directly applicable" and "directly effective" are sometimes used interchangeably, even by the Court.[11] While specific provisions of the Treaty, and of directives and decisions, may be directly effective, these instruments as a whole lack the unique pre-emptive quality of regulations.

NATURE OF THE COMMUNITY LEGAL ORDER

The European Community is a developed form of international organisation which displays characteristics of an embryonic federation. Analysis of the nature of the Community legal system is of intrinsic interest, and may facilitate the solution of practical problems. The debt owed by

---

[9] Pescatore, "The Doctrine of 'Direct Effect': An Infant Disease of Community Law" (1983) 8 E.L.Rev. 155.

[10] Case 104/86, *Commission* v. *Italy* [1988] E.C.R. 1799 (duty of Member States to repeal inconsistent legislation); Case C–120/88, *Commission* v. *Italy* [1991] E.C.R. I–621 (duty of Member State to implement Article 95); Case C–208/90, *Emmott* [1991] E.C.R. I–4869 at paras. 20–22.

[11] See the ruling in Case 2/74, *Reyners* [1974] E.C.R. 631, to the effect that Article 52 of the Treaty is directly applicable. In similar vein, see Case 17/81, *Pabst* [1982] E.C.R. 1331; Case 104/81, *Kupferberg* [1982] E.C.R. 3641.

Community law to public international law is considerable, and usually understated.[12] The twin pillars of the Community legal system are the doctrines of direct applicability/direct effect, and the supremacy of Community law. Both doctrines are derived from international law.[13] Equally, however, the relationship between Community law and national law clearly lends itself to comparison with the relationship between state and federal law in a federal system. In *Simmenthal* the Court of Justice held that Community law was competent to "preclude the valid adoption"[14] of inconsistent national legislation. This is a controversial formulation, and seems to equate the relationship between Community law and national law to a constitutional relationship, thereby distancing Community law from international law. As one learned writer on international law has put it: "International tribunals cannot declare the internal invalidity of rules of national law since the international legal order must respect the reserved domain of domestic jurisdiction."[15] Nevertheless, the International Court of Justice has pronounced certain official acts of South Africa in Namibia to be "illegal and invalid,"[16] and there appears to be no difference in principle between the demands of public international law and Community law in this regard.

For its own part, the European Court of Justice has contrasted the EEC Treaty with "ordinary international treaties,"[17] and even before the establishment of the EEC Advocate General Lagrange, in the *Fedechar* case,[17a] had floated the argument that the Court of Justice was not "an international court but the court of a Community created by six States as a model which is more closely related to a federal than to an international organisation," though he then dismissed the international court versus federal court argument as an "academic discussion." The Court of Justice referred in the event to a "rule of interpretation generally accepted in both international and national law."[18] More significantly, in *Commission* v. *Luxembourg and Belgium*,[19] the Court rejected an argument based on international law, that a default by the Commission in its obligations to a Member State had the effect of suspending the reciprocal obligations of the

---

[12] Wyatt, "New Legal Order or Old?" (1982) 7 E.L.Rev. 147; De Witte, "Retour a 'Costa': La primauté du droit communautaire à la lumière du droit international" (1984) 20 R.T.D.E. 425.

[13] For direct applicability, see "Jurisdiction of the Courts of Danziq" (1928) P.C.I.J.Ser. B., No. 15. For the principle that treaty obligations take priority over national law, see Vienna Convention on the Law of Treaties, Art. 27: "Treatment of Polish Nationals in Danziq" (1932) P.C.I.J. Rep.Ser. A/B, No. 44, p. 24.

[14] Case 106/77 [1978] E.C.R. 629 at 643, para. 17.

[15] Brownlie, *Principles of Public International Law* (3rd ed.), p. 43, citing "Interpretation of the Statute of the Memel Territory" P.C.I.J.Ser. A/B, No. 49, p. 236. Yet the Permanent Court's judgment makes it clear that it confined itself to interpreting the statute because that was the intention of the Four Powers when they submitted the point in question to the Court.

[16] *Namibia Case* [1971] I.C.J.Rep., p. 16 at p. 56, para. 125.

[17] *Costa* v. *ENEL*, see *infra*, note 33.

[17a] Case 8/55 [1954–56] E.C.R. 245.

[18] [1954–56] E.C.R. 292 at p. 299. For consideration of internationalist, federalist, and functionalist theories of the Community legal order, see Dagtoglou, "The legal nature of the European Community" in *Thirty Years of Community Law* (EC Publication, 1983), Chap. II.

[19] Cases 90 and 91/63 [1964] E.C.R. 625.

latter.[20] The Court has subsequently rejected the proposition that a default by one Member State suspends the reciprocal obligations of other Member States.[21] Yet this conclusion is perfectly consistent with the public international law basis of the Community legal system; the International Court of Justice has similarly denied that the "self-contained regime" established by the Vienna Convention on Diplomatic Relations leaves any room for self-help.[22] The principle affirmed by the International Court of Justice is that the provision of procedures capable of providing a remedy for the breach of an international obligation may be held to oust the customary law right of self-help.

The truth is that there are certain legal characteristics which may be encountered both in international organisations and in federal systems. Thus the principles of direct applicability/direct effect, the supremacy of Community law, and the predominance of judicial remedies over self-help, allow analogies to be drawn with both federal constitutional and international law. A federal state is characterised *inter alia* by the central government's legal monopoly over foreign relations. In the Community, the Commission and Council as yet enjoy no such monopoly, though the potential exists for an increase in Community competence in this field.[23] Secondly, the Community is based upon international treaties concluded between states, and the efficacy of Community law is in some Member States still dependent upon its status as international law.[24] In a federal system, state courts resolve conflicts exclusively upon the basis of federal "conflict," or supremacy rules. In the Community, national courts resolve conflicts between national law and Community law upon the basis both of national law and of Community law. Community law is thus applied to the extent that it has been incorporated into national law in accordance with national constitutional requirements. Nevertheless, it has been said that the European Court "has sought to 'constitutionalise' the Treaty, that is to fashion a constitutional framework for a federal type structure in Europe."[25] Consistently with this approach the Court itself has said that: "The EEC Treaty, albeit concluded in the form of an international agreement, none the less constitutes the constitutional charter of a Community based on the rule of law."[26] It is this latter conception of the Community legal system,

---

[20] For the doctrine in international law, see *Tacna-Arica Arbitration* (1925) 2 R.I.A.A. 921; *U.S.-France Air Services Arbitration* 54 I.L.R. 303; *Vienna Convention on the Law of Treaties*, Art. 60.

[21] Case 43/75, *Defrenne* [1976] E.C.R. 455; Case 232/78, *Commission* v. *France* [1979] E.C.R. 2729.

[22] *Hostages* (1980) I.C.J.Rep., p. 3, p. 28, para. 83.

[23] Case 22/70, *E.R.T.A.* [1971] E.C.R. 263; Cases 3, 4 and 6/76, *Kramer* [1976] E.C.R. 1279.

[24] For example, in France the supremacy of Community law appears to be based upon the status accorded to treaties by Article 55 of the French Constitution, see P. Manin, "The Nicolo case of the Conseil D'Etat: French constitutional law and the Supreme Administrative Court's acceptance of the Primacy of Community law over subsequent national statute law" (1991) 28 C.M.L. Rev. 499.

[25] G. F. Mancini, "The Making of a Constitution for Europe" (1989) 26 C.M.L. Rev. 595 at p. 596; and see K. Lenaerts, "Fundamental Rights to be included in a Community Catalogue" (1991) 16 E.L. Rev. 367 at p. 367.

[26] Opinion 1/91 on *Draft Agreement between EEC and EFTA*, of December 13, 1991 at para. 21.

quasi-federal yet undeniably *sui generis*, which seems likely to influence the future development of Community law.

THE SUPREMACY OF COMMUNITY LAW

International law by its nature binds the State in its executive, legislative and judicial activities, and no international tribunal would permit a respondent State to plead provisions of its own law or constitution as a defence to an alleged infringement of an international obligation.[27] The same is true of European Community law, "over which no appeal to provisions of internal law of any kind whatever can prevail,"[28] and the Court has always declined to accept a plea of force majeure where a Member State has attempted to comply with Community obligations, but failed as a result of delays in the constitutional process. The Court's decision in *Commission v. Belgium*[29] is illustrative. Belgian indirect taxation of home grown and imported timber discriminated against the latter, contrary to Article 95 of the Treaty. In its defence to an action by the Commission under Article 169 of the Treaty, the Belgian Government argued that it had introduced draft legislation to the Chamber of Representatives two years previously, to remedy the situation, but that it had yet to be passed. Under the principle of the separation of powers prevailing in Belgium, pointed out the Government, it could do no more. The Court was unmoved. "The obligations arising from Article 95 of the Treaty," it observed, "devolve upon States as such and the liability of a Member State under Article 169 arises whatever the agency of the State whose action or inaction is the cause of the failure to fulfil its obligations, even in the case of a constitutionally independent institution."[30]

The duty of Member States to take all appropriate measures to ensure the fulfilment of obligations arising under the Treaty or secondary legislation is laid down explicitly in Article 5, and this duty devolves directly upon national courts where directly effective provisions of Community law are involved.[31] This factor was emphasised in *Costa v. ENEL*,[32] in which it was argued that the Court's ruling would be irrelevant to the solution of the main suit, since the national tribunal which had made the reference would be bound to apply national law in any event. The Court responded with an analysis of the Community legal system, and an affirmation of its supremacy over national law:

"By contrast with ordinary international treaties, the EEC Treaty has created its own legal system which on the entry into force of the Treaty,

---

[27] "Treatment of Polish Nationals in Danziq" (1932) P.C.I.J.Rep. Ser. A/B, No. 44, at p. 24. *Vienna Convention on the Law of Treaties*, 1969, Art. 27.
[28] Case 48/71 *Commission* v. *Italy* [1972] E.C.R. 527 at 535.
[29] Case 77/69 [1970] E.C.R. 237. The Court has taken the same position in a consistent line of cases, see, *e.g.* Case 254/83, *Commission* v. *Italy* [1984] E.C.R. 3395.
[30] [1970] E.C.R. 237 at 243, para. 15.
[31] See, *e.g.* Case 45/76, *Comet* [1976] E.C.R. 2043 at 2053, para. 12.
[32] Case 6/64 [1964] E.C.R. 585. And see Case 17/67, *Neumann* [1967] E.C.R. 441 at 453.

became an integral part of the legal systems of the Member States and which their courts are bound to apply.

By creating a Community of unlimited duration, having ... powers stemming from a limitation of sovereignty, or a transfer of powers from the States to the Community, the Member States have limited their sovereign rights, albeit within limited fields, and have thus created a body of law which binds both their nationals and themselves."[33]

As the Court acknowledged in *Costa*, the supremacy of Community regulations is implicit in the legal characteristics ascribed to them in Article 189 of the Treaty.[34] Not only does direct applicability require their access to the national legal order without the favour of specific incorporation, but they have the capacity to pre-empt national legislative competence.[35] Their very nature precludes their modification by inconsistent measures of national law.

That the duty of national courts to give precedence to Community law over national law extends to national legislation adopted after the incorporation of the relevant Community rules into the national legal order was made clear in *Simmenthal*[36]:

"Furthermore, in accordance with the principle of the precedence of Community law, the relationship between provisions of the Treaty and directly applicable measures of the institutions on the one hand and the national law of the Member States on the other is such that those provisions and measures not only by their entry into force render automatically inapplicable any conflicting provision of current national law but—insofar as they are an integral part of, and take precedence in, the legal order applicable in the territory of each of the Member States—also preclude the valid adoption of new national legislative measures to the extent to which they would be incompatible with Community provisions. ... It follows from the foregoing that every national court must, in a case within its jurisdiction, apply Community law in its entirety and protect rights which the latter confers on individuals and must accordingly set aside any provision of national law which may conflict with it, whether prior or subsequent to the Community rule."

The principle of the supremacy of Community law, well-established as it is in the jurisprudence of the Court, may be denied its full effect by national tribunals. Although as a matter of Community law it is impermissible to condition the effects of its provisions on the requirements of national law, however fundamental,[37] national courts may nevertheless feel constrained to temper the rigour of the Treaty's requirements, for national courts are

---

[33] [1964] E.C.R. 585 at 593.
[34] "The precedence of Community law is confirmed by Article 189, Whereby a regulation 'shall be binding' and 'directly applicable in all Member States.' " [1964] E.C.R. 585 at 594.
[35] *Infra*, p. 69.
[36] Case 106/77 [1978] E.C.R. 629 at pp. 643, 644.
[37] Case 11/70, *Internationale Handelsgesellschaft* [1970] E.C.R. 1125.

instituted under national law, and are entrusted first and foremost with maintaining the integrity of the national legal order. In the United Kingdom, section 2(1) of the European Communities Act 1972 provides for the recognition of all directly enforceable Community law. In *Factortame* v. *Secretary of State for Transport*,[38] the House of Lords expressed the view that section 2(1) of the 1972 Act has precisely the same effect as if a section were incorporated in an Act of 1988 which in terms enacted that that latter Act was to be without prejudice to the directly enforceable rights of nationals of any Member State of the EEC.[39] The *Factortame* litigation[40] makes it clear that an Act of Parliament subsequent to the 1972 European Communities Act may be subject to judicial review if it contravenes the directly enforceable Community rights of the Applicant, and that the doctrine of implied repeal has no application to the 1972 Act, nor to directly enforceable Community rights taking effect thereunder. This is surely a landmark in the evolution of our constitutional system. Express repeal of, or derogation from, section 2(1) of the European Communities Act, would, however, be likely to be given effect by courts in the United Kingdom, since such a step would remove or amend *pro tanto* the constitutional basis for the application of Community law in the United Kingdom.

THE LEGAL EFFECT OF TREATY PROVISIONS IN NATIONAL COURTS

1. Rights of the individual against the state

The judicial *fons et origo* of the principle that certain provisions of the Treaty may be invoked by individuals in national courts is the decision in *Van Gend en Loos* v. *Nederlandse Administratie der Belastingen*.[41] Dutch importers challenged the rate of import duty charged on a chemical product imported from the Federal Republic of Germany, alleging that reclassifying it under a different heading of the Dutch customs tariff had resulted in an increase in duty prohibited under Article 12 of the Treaty, which provides that: "Member States shall refrain from introducing between themselves any new customs duties on imports . . . or any charges having equivalent effect, and from increasing those which they already apply in their trade with each other." The Tarief-commissie, an administrative tribunal having final jurisdiction in revenue cases, asked the Court whether the Article in question had "direct application within the territory of a Member State, in other words, whether nationals of such a State can, on the basis of the Article in question, lay claim to individual rights which the courts must protect." The Dutch Government, in its submissions to the Court, argued that an infringement of the Treaty by a Member State could be submitted to

---

[38] [1990] 2 A.C. 85.
[39] [1990] 2 A.C. 85 at p. 140, *per* Lord Bridge.
[40] *Factortame*, notes 38 and 39 above, and *Factortame* (No. 2) [1991] 1 A.C. 603. For the constitutional implications of these cases, see Craig, "Supremacy of the United Kingdom Parliament after Factortame" (1991) 11 Y.E.L. 221.
[41] Case 26/62 [1963] E.C.R. 1.

the Court only under the procedure laid down by Articles 169 and 170, *i.e.* at the suit of the Commission or another Member State.[42] This view, to the effect that the provisions of the Treaty simply give rise to rights and obligations between Member States in international law, was rejected by Advocate General Roemer, who argued that anyone "familiar with Community law" knew that "in fact it does not just consist of contractual relations between a number of States considered as subjects of the law of nations."[43] This followed from the fact that the Community was authorised to make rules of law capable of bestowing rights and imposing obligations on private individuals as well as on Member States.[44] The Court, in a landmark judgment, upheld the Advocate General's reasoning:

> "The objective of the EEC Treaty, which is to establish a Common Market, the functioning of which is of direct concern to interested parties in the Community, implies that this Treaty is more than an agreement which merely creates mutual obligations between the contracting States. The task assigned to the Court of Justice under Article 177, the object of which is to ensure uniform interpretation of the Treaty by national courts and tribunals, confirms that the States have acknowledged that Community law has an authority which can be invoked by their nationals before those courts and tribunals.
>
> The conclusion to be drawn from this is that the Community constitutes a new legal order of international law for the benefit of which the States have limited their sovereign rights, albeit within limited fields, and the subjects of which comprise not only Member States but also their nationals. Independently of the legislation of Member States, Community law therefore not only imposes obligations on individuals but is also intended to confer upon them rights which become part of their legal heritage. These rights arise not only where they are expressly granted by the Treaty, but also by reason of obligations which the Treaty imposes in a clearly defined way upon individuals as well as upon the Member States and the institutions of the Community."[45]

Although the Advocate General had taken the view that certain Treaty provisions were "clearly intended to be incorporated into national law and to modify or supplement it,"[46] he had not numbered among them Article 12, since its application required the resolution of complex issues of interpretation. To hold such a provision directly applicable, he pointed out, would create uncertainty in the law: enterprises would be far more likely to rely upon national customs legislation than upon the text of the Treaty. The Court's approach was less cautious. "The wording of Article 12," it argued, "contains a clear and unconditional prohibition which is not a positive but a

---

[42] [1963] E.C.R. 1 at p. 6.
[43] [1963] E.C.R. 1 at p. 20.
[44] The Adv. Gen. cited in support of this proposition Arts. 187, 189, 191 and 192 of the Treaty.
[45] [1963] E.C.R. 1 at p. 12.
[46] He cited Arts. 85, 86, 88, 177 and 192.

negative obligation. This obligation, moreover, is not qualified by any reservation on the part of states which would make its implementation conditional upon a positive legislative measure enacted under national law. The very nature of this prohibition makes it ideally adapted to produce direct effects in the legal relationship between Member States and their subjects."[47]

The *Van Gend en Loos* judgment affirms the existence of the "new legal order" in which individuals, as well as Member States, may have rights and obligations, and it lays down the criteria to be applied in deciding whether or not a particular provision may be invoked by individuals in national courts. These criteria were to be applied subsequently in numerous cases,[48] and were summed up as follows by Advocate General Mayras in *Reyners* v. *Belgian State*:

— the provision in question must be sufficiently clear and precise for judicial application[49];
— it must establish an unconditional obligation[50];
— the obligation must be complete and legally perfect, and its implementation must not depend on measures being subsequently taken by Community institutions or Member States with discretionary power in the matter.[51]

The second requirement, that the obligation be unconditional, was of considerable importance in the transitional period, during which national restrictions on the free movement of goods, persons and services were to be progressively abolished.[52] These conditional prohibitions in the Treaty become unconditional on the expiration of the transitional period, and national measures in force when the Treaty came into effect could be challenged in national courts.[53]

The first and third requirements, that a legal provision be clear and precise, and be independent of measures to be taken subsequently by the Community institutions or the Member States, may be illustrated by reference to *Salgoil* v. *Italian Ministry for Foreign Trade*,[54] in which the

---

[47] [1963] E.C.R. 1 at p. 13.
[48] *E.g.* provisions of the Treaty were held directly effective in the following cases: Case 6/64, *Costa* [1964] E.C.R. 585 (Arts. 53 and 37(2)); Case 57/65, *Lutticke* [1966] E.C.R. 205 (Arts. 95(1) and 95(3)); Case 28/67, *Molkerie-Zentrale* [1968] E.C.R. 143 (Art. 95(1)); Case 27/67, *Fink-Frucht* [1968] E.C.R. 223 (Art. 95(2)); Case 13/68, *Salgoil* [1968] E.C.R. 453 (Arts. 31 and 32(1)); Case 33/70, *SACE* [1970] E.C.R. 1213 (Art. 13(2)); Case 18/71, *Eunomia* [1971] E.C.R. 811 (Art. 16); Case 127/73, *SABAM* [1974] E.C.R. 51 (Arts. 85 and 86).
[49] See, *e.g.* Case 26/62, *Van Gend en Loos*, see note 41: Case 6/64, *Costa*; Case 33/70, *SACE*; Case 18/71, *Eunomia*; for references, see note 48; Case 41/74, *Van Duyn* [1974] E.C.R. 1337 (Art. 48).
[50] See, *e.g.* Case 26/62, *Van Gend en Loos*; Case 6/64, *Costa*; Case 57/65, *Lutticke*; for references, see note 48.
[51] See, *e.g.* Case 26/62, *Van Gend en Loos*; Case 57/65, *Lutticke*; Case 33/70, *SACE*; Case 18/71, *Eunomia*; for references, see note 48; Case 41/74, *Van Duyn*, note 49.
[52] See, *e.g.* Arts. 13(1), (2); Arts. 30, 32(1); Art. 48(1), Art. 52; Art. 59.
[53] Ranbow, "The End of the Transitional Period" (1969) 6 C.M.L.Rev. 434. For obligations directly effective as of the end of the transitional period, see, *e.g.* Case 77/72, *Capolongo* [1973] E.C.R. 611 (Art. 13(2)); Case 74/76, *Ianelli & Volpi* [1977] E.C.R. 557 (Art. 30); Case 59/75, *Manghera* [1976] E.C.R. 91 (Art. 37(1)); Case 41/74, *Van Duyn* [1974] E.C.R. 1337 (Art. 48); Case 2/74, *Reyners* [1974] E.C.R. 631 (Art. 52); Case 33/74, *Van Binsbergen* [1974] E.C.R. 1299 (Art. 59).
[54] Case 33/68 [1968] E.C.R. 453.

Court denied direct effect to Article 32(1), last sentence, and Article 33, of the Treaty. These provisions required Member States to phase out quantitative restrictions on imports, by converting bilateral quotas into global quotas, and by progressively increasing their total value. The rate of liberalisation was prescribed for products where "the global quotas amounted to less than 3 per cent. of the national production of the State concerned." The court conceded that these provisions laid down obligations which were not subject to the adoption of measures by the institutions of the Community, but pointed out that: "Some discretion does fall to be exercised by the Member States from the obligation to 'convert any bilateral quotas . . . into global quotas' and from the concepts of 'total value' and 'national production.' In fact, since the Treaty gives no indication as to the data . . . or as to the methods applicable, several solutions may be envisaged."[55] It followed, in the court's view, that the provisions in question were insufficiently precise to be considered directly effective.

It must be emphasised that the fact that provisions of Community law may require the appreciation of complex economic issues does not preclude their being directly effective, providing the requisite conditions are satisfied. Thus Article 95(1) of the Treaty prohibits the imposition "on the products of other Member States" of "any internal taxation of any kind in excess of that imposed directly or indirectly on similar domestic products." The second paragraph of that Article adds that: "no Member State shall impose on the products of other Member States any internal taxation of such a nature as to afford indirect protection to other products." In *Fink-Frucht* v. *Hauptzollamt Munchen*,[56] the Court considered whether or not this latter provision was directly effective. It decided that it was, in face of the arguments of the Federal Republic that the paragraph was "vague and incomplete" and that the "value-judgments" it required should not be forced on national courts.[57] In the Court's view, the provision contained a straightforward prohibition against protection; "it established an unconditional obligation, and no action was required on the part of the institutions of the Community or the Member States for its implementation." "Although this provision involves the evaluation of economic factors," observed the Court, "this does not exclude the right and duty of national courts to ensure that the rules of the Treaty are observed whenever they can ascertain . . . that the conditions necessary for the application of the article are fulfilled."[58]

2. The rights and obligations of individuals *inter se*

In the cases discussed above, the Court of Justice was called upon to consider whether or not a provision of the Treaty had modified the legal position of individuals *vis-à-vis* the State. Beginning with the decision in

---

[55] [1968] E.C.R. 453 at p. 461.
[56] Case 27/767 [1968] E.C.R. 223.
[57] [1968] E.C.R. 223 at p. 229.
[58] [1968] E.C.R. 223 at p. 232.

Belgische Radio en Televisie v. *SABAM*,[59] we see a new development; the acknowledgment that provisions of the Treaty are capable of modifying the rights of individuals *inter se*. Thus in *SABAM* the Court observed that the prohibitions of Articles 85(1) and 86 "tend by their very nature to produce direct effects in relations between individuals," and "create direct rights in respect of the individuals concerned which the national courts must safeguard."[60] It might have been arguable that Articles 85 and 86, being explicitly concerned with private action, could be treated as special cases, but the Court's later decision in *Walrave and Koch* v. *Association Union Cycliste Internationale*[61] suggested a more general principle. Motorcyclists who earned their living "pacing" pedal cyclists in international events asked the Arrondissementsrechtsbank, Utrecht, for a declaration that certain rules of the defendant association infringed the Treaty's prohibition of discrimination on grounds of nationality. Doubts were expressed by the Commission[62] as to whether the prohibition in question applied to private action, and the Court, although the issue was not explicitly before it, addressed itself to the question as follows:

> "It has been alleged that the prohibitions in these Articles refer only to restrictions which have their origin in acts of an authority and not to those resulting from legal acts of persons or associations who do not come under public law.
>
> Articles 7, 48, 59 have in common the prohibition, in their respective spheres of application, of any discrimination on grounds of nationality.
>
> Prohibition of such discrimination does not only apply to the acts of public authorities, but extends likewise to rules of any other nature aimed at regulating in a collective manner gainful employment and the provision of services."[63]

It followed, in the Court's view that the provisions of Articles 7, 48 and 59 of the Treaty could be taken into account in judging the validity and the effects of the rules of a sporting association.

The extent to which the Treaty may impose obligations on individuals was once again raised in *Defrenne* v. *Sabena*,[64] a reference from the Belgian Tribunal du Travail. The national suit arose from proceedings brought by a former air-hostess against her former employer, Sabena, in which she alleged infringement of Article 119 of the Treaty. The latter Article provides that during the first stage "Each Member State shall ... ensure and subsequently maintain the application of the principle that men and women should receive equal pay for equal work." The original Six had not complied with this obligation by January 1, 1973, nor had the new Member States been

---

[59] Case 127/73 [1974] E.C.R. 51.
[60] [1974] E.C.R. 51 at p. 62.
[61] Case 36/74 [1974] E.C.R. 1405.
[62] [1974] E.C.R. 1405 at p. 1410.
[63] [1974] E.C.R. 1405 at p. 1418, paras. 15, 16, 17.
[64] Case 43/75 [1976] E.C.R. 455. The decision provoked a great deal of discussion, see Wyatt, (1975–76) 1 E.L.Rev. 399–402, 418, 419; Crisham, (1977) 14 C.M.L.Rev. 102, and references cited at pp. 108, 109, note 1. Allott, [1977] C.L.J. 7.

in a position to do so on accession. The Tribunal du Travail asked the Court of Justice whether the Article in question entitled workers to undertake proceedings before national courts in order to ensure its observance. The Court replied in the affirmative; even though the complete implementation of the equal pay principles could not be achieved without legislative elaboration at the Community or national level, the requirement was nevertheless apt for national judicial application in cases of "direct and overt discrimination which may be identified solely with the aid of the criteria based on equal work and equal pay referred to by the article in question."[65] The Court went on to reject the argument that the Article could not be applied to the activities of private parties. The fact that the obligation in Article 119 was addressed to Member States did not preclude application by judicial authorities as well as implementation by legislative authorities.[66] "In fact," declared the Court, "since Article 119 is mandatory in nature, the prohibition on discrimination between men and women applies not only to an action of public authorities, but also extends to all agreements which are intended to regulate paid labour collectively, as well as to contracts between individuals."[67] The Treaty's prohibition on discrimination, whether it be on the grounds of nationality or sex (at any rate as far as pay is concerned) may, it seems, be invoked against natural and legal persons, as well as against Member States.

3. The exceptional case—the prospective effect of a holding of direct applicability

Although the Court in *Defrenne* held that Article 119 of the Treaty was directly applicable—at least in part—it also held that the Article could not be relied upon to support claims in respect of pay periods prior to the date of its judgment, except as regards workers who had already brought legal proceedings or made equivalent claims. The Court seems to have been moved by the pleas of Ireland and the United Kingdom that claims to back pay based on Article 119 could have disastrous economic effects in these countries. It responded as follows:

> "Although the practical consequences of any judicial decision must be carefully taken into account, it would be impossible to go so far as to diminish the objectivity of the law and compromise its future application on the ground of the possible repercussions which might result, as regards the past, from such a judicial decision.
>
> However, in the light of the conduct of several of the Member States and the views adopted by the Commission and repeatedly brought to the notice of the circles concerned, it is appropriate to take exceptionally into account the fact that, over a prolonged period, the

---

[65] [1976] E.C.R. 455 at p. 473, para. 18, *e.g.* discrimination in national legislation or in collective labour agreements, which could be detected on the basis of a purely legal analysis of the situation, [1976] E.C.R. 455 at p. 473, para. 21.
[66] [1976] E.C.R. 455 at p. 475, para. 37.
[67] [1976] E.C.R. 455 at p. 476, para. 39.

parties concerned have been led to continue with practices which were contrary to Article 119, although not yet prohibited under their national law.

The fact that, in spite of the warnings given, the Commission did not initiate proceedings under Article 169 against the Member States concerned on grounds of failure to fulfil an obligation was likely to consolidate the incorrect impression as to the effects of Article 119.

In these circumstances, it is appropriate to determine that, as the general level at which pay would have been fixed cannot be known, important considerations of legal certainty affecting all the interests involved, both public and private, make it impossible to re-open the question as regards the past."[68]

In other words, the unexpectedness of the Court's ruling militated against its retrospective application. The legal basis of the decision is the principle of "legal certainty," which embraces the notion that parties acting reasonably on the basis of the law as it stands ought not to have their expectations frustrated by subsequent legislative action.[69] Analogous principles underlie the practice of the Supreme Court of the United States, which has declared in certain cases that constitutional rulings shall have only prospective effect.[70] In so doing, it has emphasised three criteria: (i) the purpose to be served by the new rule; (ii) the extent of reliance by law enforcement authorities on the old rule; and (iii) the effect on the administration of justice of a retrospective application of the new rule.[71] Application of these criteria to the equal pay situation before the Court in *Defrenne* is instructive. Commission, State authorities and private individuals had certainly relied in good faith on the fact that Article 119 did not have direct effect as of the end of the first stage. Again, there can be little doubt that a retroactive ruling in *Defrenne* could have created insuperable problems for the "administration of justice," for, as the Court pointed out, it would have been impossible to have ascertained the wage patterns that would have emerged had the requirement of the Treaty been observed at the proper time.[72] Nor would a retroactive ruling have accorded with the "purpose of the rule"—its social aims might well have been frustrated by national courts giving judgments against employers resulting in unemployment or even bankruptcy.[73]

The Court's ruling that Article 119 should have direct effect only prospectively is novel, and clearly exceptional,[74] but that is not to deny that it

---

[68] [1976] E.C.R. 455 at pp. 480, 481, paras. 71–74.

[69] For the relationship between "legal certainty" and "legitimate expectation," see Usher, "The Influence of National Concepts on Decisions of the European Court" (1975–76) 1 E.L.Rev. 359 at 363. For these concepts as general principles of Community Law, see *infra* at p. 91.

[70] See Wilson, 42 Fordham L.Rev. 653.

[71] *Stovall* v. *Denno* 388 U.S. 293 at p. 297; L.Ed. 2d 1199; 87 S.Ct. 1967.

[72] It is fanciful to suppose that the increased cost of equal pay would have had no impact on the level of earnings.

[73] "Levelling down" is not a permissible method of complying with Art. 119, see [1976] E.C.R. 455 at p. 472, para. 15.

[74] Case 61/79, *Denkavit* [1980] E.C.R. 1200 (prospective effect ruling for Court of Justice alone); Case 69/80, *Worringham & Humphreys* [1981] E.C.R. 767; Cases 142 and 143/80, *Essevi* and *Salengo* [1981] E.C.R. 1413; (Case 811/79, *Ariete* [1980] E.C.R. 2545; 826/79, *Mireco* [1980] 2559). Rulings on the invalidity of Community legislation are more readily

is firmly founded in principles affirmed consistently by the Court in its previous jurisprudence, unexceptionable in themselves, and essential to a court exercising a quasi-constitutional function in the legal order established by the founding Treaties. In *Barber* v. *Guardian Royal Exchange*,[75] the Court held that Article 119 applied with direct effect to pensions paid under "contracted-out" pension schemes, *i.e.* schemes recognised in the United Kingdom in substitution for the earnings-related part of the State pension. Nevertheless, the Court acknowledged that the Member States and the parties concerned were reasonably entitled to consider that Article 119 did not apply to pensions paid out under contracted-out schemes. The Court ruled accordingly that the direct effect of Article 119 in such circumstances had only prospective effect.[76]

4. Direct application of rules of the Treaty which do not give rise to rights in individuals

The law is not exclusively concerned with bestowing rights, or imposing obligations, on individuals; it may, for instance, authorise public authorities to take action which they would not otherwise be authorised to take. Treaty provisions which fall into this category are not "directly effective," as that expression has been defined by the Court in the cases discussed above, but they may nevertheless be susceptible to direct application in national courts. It will be recalled that the Advocate General in *Van Gend en Loos* referred to Treaty provisions being "clearly intended to be incorporated into national law and to modify or supplement it,"[77] and this approach is echoed in the words of the Court of Justice in *Costa* v. *ENEL* to the effect that the "EEC Treaty has created its own legal system which, on the entry into force of the Treaty, became an integral part of the legal systems of the Member States and which their courts are bound to apply."[78]

Whether or not a Treaty provision is to be applied by a national court, independently of national implementation, depends on the interpretation of the provision in question. If, on its proper construction, it is intended to have legal effect, then English courts are bound to give it such, under the appropriately worded text of section 2(1) of the European Communities Act 1972.[79] Thus Article 177 of the Treaty directly bestows on national courts the competence to refer questions to the Court of Justice for a preliminary ruling. National provisions may establish the relevant details of procedure,[80] but they neither create, nor may they condition, the capacity to make the reference. The provision is not directly effective, in that it does not give rise

---

given prospective effect; see, *e.g.* Case 4/79, *Providence Agricole* [1980] E.C.R. 2823, p. 2853; Case 109/79, *Maiseries de Beauce* [1985] E.C.R. 2883 at 2913; Case 145/79, *Roquette* [1985] E.C.R. 2917 at p. 2946; Case 41/84, *Pinna* [1986] E.C.R. 1 at p. 26.
[75] Case C–262/88 [1990] 1 E.C.R. 1989.
[76] The effect of the ruling on prospective effect gave rise to further references to the Court of Justice and to a protocol to the T.E.U.
[77] [1963] E.C.R. 1 at p. 20.
[78] [1964] E.C.R. 585 at p. 593. And see Case 17/67, *Neumann* [1967] E.C.R. 441 at p. 453.
[79] See Mitchell et al., (1972) 9 C.M.L.Rev. 134, 137.
[80] See, *e.g.* R.S.C., Ord. 114.

to rights in individuals which national courts are bound to safeguard (apart, perhaps, from the third paragraph of Article 177), but is nevertheless directly applicable, in the sense that it has direct application, in the national legal order.

THE LEGAL EFFECTS OF COMMUNITY ACTS

One of the most striking characteristics of the legal order established by the Treaty is the competence vested in the Council, and to a lesser extent in the Commission, to enact legislation for the purpose of attaining the objectives of the Treaty. Thus Article 189 provides that: "In order to carry out their task the Council and the Commission shall, in accordance with the provisions of this Treaty, make regulations, issue directives, take decisions, make recommendations, or deliver opinions." Since "recommendations and opinions have no binding force,"[81] emphasis will be placed on regulations, directives and decisions.

Regulations

Article 189 of the Treaty provides that: "A regulation shall have general application. It shall be binding in its entirety and directly applicable in all Member States." At first sight, this description of regulations appears to attribute to them the characteristics of those Treaty provisions capable of giving rise to rights in individuals which national courts are bound to safeguard. Even a cursory scrutiny of the Official Journal, however, reveals that each and every provision of each and every regulation does not give rise to rights in individuals as against other individuals or as against Member States. Various explanations have been offered for this unsurprising phenomenon. On the one hand, it has been suggested[82] that since characterisation as a regulation *vel non* is a matter of substance, not form,[83] the provisions of a regulation which do not satisfy the conditions for direct applicability are not regulations in the true sense at all. "In such an instance," the argument runs, "the merely formal regulations could be denied direct application."[84] This view is not without difficulty. It seems to discount the possibility that Community law may empower national courts to apply rules which do not actually bestow rights on individuals. Again, it leads to the conclusion that if the Treaty authorised the Council to legislate on certain matters by regulation and regulation only, each and every provision of such a regulation must give to rights in individuals which national courts are bound to safeguard; any such provision which does not have this quality is not part of the regulation, in law, is unauthorised by the Treaty Article in question and therefore invalid.[85]

---

[81] But recommendations are to be taken into account for interpretative purposes, see *supra*, p. 52, and note 7.
[82] Bebr, [1970] I.C.L.Q. 257 at pp. 290 *et seq.*
[83] Cases 16, 17, 19–22/62, *Confederation Nationale* [1962] E.C.R. 471; Case 30/67, *Industria Molitoria* [1968] E.C.R. 115; Case 6/68, *Zuckerfabrik* [1968] E.C.R. 409.
[84] [1970] I.C.L.Q. 257 at p. 290.
[85] Art. 94 of the Treaty authorises only regulations.

Another view[86] is that the reference to direct applicability in Article 189 concerns the process of incorporation of regulations into the national legal order. This description emphasises that national courts must take cognisance of regulations as legal instruments whose validity and recognition by national courts must not be conditioned on national procedures of incorporation into the national legal order. Whether or not particular provisions of such an instrument in fact give rise to rights in individuals which national courts must safeguard is a matter of interpretation of the provisions concerned, in light of the criteria established by the Court of Justice with respect to the direct application of provisions of the Treaty. This is the better view, and is quite consistent with the decided cases, though the Court has not gone out of its way to clarify the matter. Thus in *Politi* v. *Italian Ministry of Finance*,[87] the Turin Tribunale asked the Court whether certain provisions of an agricultural regulation were (i) directly applicable, and (ii) if so, whether they created rights for individuals which national courts were bound to safeguard. The question presented to the Court reflects neatly the distinction indicated above; the Court's response does not. "Under the terms of the second paragraph of Article 189," it declared, "regulations 'shall have general application' and 'shall be . . . directly applicable in all Member States.' " Therefore, by reason of their nature and their function in the system of the sources of Community law, regulations have direct effect and are as such capable of creating individual rights which national courts must protect."[88] Similar reasoning appears in *Leonesio* v. *Italian Ministry of Agriculture and Forestry*,[89] in which the Pretore of Lonato posed questions which again separated the issues of direct applicability and direct effect. The Court ruled that: "A Community regulation has direct effect and is, as such capable of creating individual rights which national courts must protect." Advocate General Roemer, on the other hand, pointed out that simply to acknowledge the status of the instrument in question did not solve the problem before the Court, *i.e.* whether certain of its provisions bestowed enforceable rights on individual farmers as against the Italian State "wherefore an answer to the question of the legal effects," he argued, "depends on the questions whether an area of discretion was left to the national authorities in the matter of implementation and in what manner the national provisions were to supplement the measures adopted."[90]

Although the Court of Justice had not explicitly acknowledged that the direct applicability of regulations does not require the automatic effect of their provisions at the suit of individuals, such is clearly the case, and it is always possible that the Court's reticence results from the conviction that the distinction is either obvious, or of little practical importance. If the question were raised before the Court that on its true construction a

---

[86] J. A. Winter, (1972) 9 C.M.L. Rev. 425.
[87] Case 43/71 [1971] E.C.R. 1039.
[88] [1971] E.C.R. 1039 at p. 1048, para. 9.
[89] Case 93/71 [1972] E.C.R. 287.
[90] [1972] E.C.R. 287 at p. 300.

particular provision of a regulation was incapable of giving rise to rights in individuals because it was conditioned on national implementation, the Court would no doubt construe the provision in question, to see if it were apt for judicial enforcement. Thus in *Caisse commune D'assurances "la prevoyance sociale"* v. *Bertholet*,[91] the Court was asked whether Article 52 of Regulation 3 was applicable in national courts before the bilateral agreements referred to therein had been concluded between the Member States concerned. The Court answered in the affirmative, on the grounds that the first paragraph of that Article was couched in unequivocal terms, while its provisions were clear and could be applied without difficulty. Obviously the mere status of the instrument in which the provision was found could not determine a question dependent on the true construction of the provision itself.

A corollary of the proposition that regulations must be recognised as legal instruments without the need for national implementation is that such implementation, unless authorised in a particular case,[92] is impermissible, inasmuch as it tends to disguise from those subject to the law the Community source of their rights and obligations. That the legislative duplication of regulations might in itself be inconsistent with community law was made clear in *Commission* v. *Italy*,[93] in which the Italian Government had failed to implement certain regulations concerning slaughter premia and the withholding of milk supplied from the market, resulting in an action by the Commission under Article 169 of the Treaty. Not only did the Commission complain of the delay of the Italian Government in instituting the scheme, but also of the technique of reproducing the texts of regulations in Italian legislation. This, said the Court, itself constituted a default, since by adopting this procedure, the Italian Government had brought into doubt both the legal nature of the applicable provisions and the date of their coming into force. The Court reiterated its position in *Fratelli Variola* v. *Amministrazione italiana delle Finanze*. "No procedure is permissible," it emphasised, "whereby the Community nature of a legal rule is concealed from those subject to it."[94] Member States are *a fortiori* prohibited from adopting national measures designed to alter the scope of regulations, or amend their provisions.[95] Nevertheless, the Court has acknowledged that where Community regulations require implementation by national measures, the incorporation of the texts of such regulations may be justified for the sake of coherence and in order to make them comprehensible to the persons to whom they apply.[96]

Since regulations constitute direct legislation by the Community, not only may individuals rely on specific provisions as against other individuals and Member States, they may invoke the general objective and purpose of

---

[91] Case 31/64 [1965] E.C.R. 81.
[92] Case 31/78, *Bussone* [1978] E.C.R. 2429; Case 230/78, *Zuccheri* [1979] E.C.R. 2749.
[93] Case 39/72 [1973] E.C.R. 101.
[94] Case 34/73 [1973] E.C.R. 981 at p. 991, para. 11.
[95] Case 74/69, *Krohn* [1970] E.C.R. 451; Case 40/69, *Bollmann* [1970] E.C.R. 69 at p. 79; Case 18/72, *Granaria* [1972] E.C.R. 1163.
[96] Case 272/83, *Commission* v. *Italy* [1985] E.C.R. at p. 1074, para. 27.

regulations as against national legal provisions. This pre-emptive quality of regulations has become most obviously apparent in the context of the common agricultural policy, where the Court has ruled on several occasions that national measures have been incompatible with the legal regime established by a Community regulation (as opposed to specific provisions vesting rights in individuals).[97] Thus national measures which hinder agricultural producers from selling on the market at a price equal to the target price may be challenged by individuals concerned in national courts, although producers have no "right" to sell at that price. In effect, they are allowed to invoke the encroachment by national legislation on an area of Community competence.[97a] As the Court explained in *Amsterdam Bulb BV* v. *Produktschap voor Siergewassen*:

> "From the moment that the Community adopts regulations under Article 40 of the Treaty establishing a common organisation of the market in a specific sector the Member States are under a duty not to take any measure which might create exemptions from them or affect them adversely.
>
> The compatibility with the Community regulations of the provisions referred to by the national court must be considered in the light not only of the express provisions of the regulations *but also of their aims and objectives.*"[98] (emphasis added)

In certain cases, it seems that the subject-matter of a regulation may preclude the enactment of national legislation entirely in the field in question. Thus in *Hauptzollamt Bremen* v. *Krohn*, the Court declared: "In so far as the Member States have conferred on the Community legislative powers in tariff matters, in order to ensure the proper functioning of the common market in agriculture, they no longer have the power to issue independent provisions in this field."[99]

Regulations, in short, are to be treated as "law" in every sense of the word. National courts must take judicial notice of them in their entirety; specific provisions contained therein may bestow on individuals rights as against other individuals or Member States; and their effect in a particular area may be to pre-empt national legislative competence.

Directives and decisions

(a) *General*

Article 189 says of directives and decisions:

> "A directive shall be binding, as to the result to be achieved, upon each

---

[97] See, *e.g.* Case 60/75, *Russo* [1976] E.C.R. 45; Case 77/76, *Fratelli Cucchi* [1977] E.C.R. 987; see Wyatt, [1977] C.L.J. 216 at p. 217.
[97a] Case 77/76, *Cucchi*, see *supra*, note 97.
[98] Case 50/76 [1977] E.C.R. 137 at p. 147, para. 8.
[99] Case 74/69 [1970] E.C.R. 451 at p. 458. And see Case 40/69, *Bollmann* [1970] E.C.R. 69 at p. 79.

Member State to which it is addressed, but shall leave to the national authorities the choice of form and methods.

A decision shall be binding in its entirety upon those to whom it is addressed."

Whereas a directive may be addressed only to a state, a decision may also be addressed to a natural or legal person. An example of an individual decision would be a Commission ruling that a firm or firms had acted in breach of Articles 85 and 86 of the Treaty. Such a decision might include the imposition of a fine.[1] An example of a decision addressed to a Member State, by contrast, would be an act of the Commission requiring a Member State to abolish or amend measures of aid to national undertakings.[2] The choice of form and methods for the implementation of directives left to Member States allows a Member State to choose the legislative format which it considers appropriate.[3] Thus the legislation adopted to implement a directive need not use the same words as the directive itself.[4] National implementing rules should however give persons concerned a clear and precise understanding of their rights and obligations and enable national courts to ensure that those rights and obligations are observed.[5] This may be a counsel of perfection, in view of the vagueness to be found on occasion in the text of directives.

Mere administrative practices, which by their nature may be altered at the whim of the authorities and lack the appropriate publicity cannot be regarded as a valid fulfilment of the obligation imposed by Article 189 on Member States to which directives are addressed.[6] However, the Court has held that directives do not require legislative implementation where there exist general principles of constitutional or administrative law which render specific legislation superfluous, provided that these principles guarantee the application of the directive, are clear and precise, are made known to those subject to the law, and are capable of being invoked in the courts.[7] It follows that legislation is also superfluous where national legislative provisions in force afford similar guarantees that a directive will be effectively implemented.

(b) *Rights of individuals against the state*

It was initially believed that directives and decisions gave rise exclusively to rights and obligations as between their addressees on the one hand, and the Community institutions and Member States on the other.[8]

---

[1] See Arts. 85–87; Reg. 17, O.J. Sp.Ed. 1959–62, p. 87, Arts. 15, 16. See *infra*, p. 486.
[2] Art. 93(2) EEC; see *infra*, p. 538.
[3] Case 163/82, *Commission* v. *Italy* [1983] E.C.R. 3723 at pp. 3286, 3287.
[4] Case 247/85, *Commission* v. *Belgium* [1987] E.C.R. 3029 at p. 3060, para. 9; Case 262/85, *Commission* v. *Italy* [1987] E.C.R. 3073 at p. 3097, para. 9; Case 252/85, *Commission* v. *France* [1988] E.C.R. 2243 at p. 2263, para. 5.
[5] Case 257/86, *Commission* v. *Italy* [1988] E.C.R. 3249 at p. 3267.
[6] Case 102/79, *Commission* v. *Belgium* [1980] E.C.R. 1473; Case 96/81, *Commission* v. *Netherlands* [1982] E.C.R. 1791; Case 145/82, *Commission* v. *Italy* [1982] E.C.R. 1791; Case 145/82, *Commission* v. *Italy* [1983] E.C.R. 711.
[7] Case 29/84, *Commission* v. *Germany* [1985] E.C.R. 1661.
[8] See, *e.g. Joseph Aim* [1972] C.M.L.R. 901 (*Cour d'Appel de Paris*); *Firma Baer Getreide GmbH* [1972] C.M.L.R. 539 (Hessischer Verwaltungsgerichtschof); and more recently,

A series of decisions of the Court of Justice, beginning with that in *Franz Grad* v. *Finanzamt Traunstein*,[9] necessitated a radical reappraisal of the traditional view. In the *Grad* case, the Finanzgericht, Munich, asked the Court of Justice whether the obligation imposed upon Member States by Article 4 of Council Decision 65/271,[10] coupled with the deadline for its fulfilment contained in Article 1 of Directive 67/227[11] were capable of vesting rights in individuals which national courts were bound to safeguard.

The Court of Justice held that directives and decisions might contain directly effective provisions. "Although it is true," declared the Court, "that by virtue of Article 189, regulations are directly applicable and therefore by virtue of their nature capable of producing direct effects, it does not follow from this that other categories of legal measures mentioned in that Article can never produce similar effects. In particular, the provision according to which decisions are binding in their entirety on those to whom they are addressed enables the question to be put whether the obligation created by the decisions can only be invoked by the Community institutions against the addressee or whether such a right may possibly be exercised by all those who have an interest in the fulfilment of this obligation."[12] In the Court's view to adopt the alternative solution would call in question the binding nature of decisions, and diminish their useful effect. While the effects of a decision might not be identical with those of a provision contained in a regulation, this difference did not preclude the possibility that the end result, namely the right of the individual to invoke the measure before the courts, might be the same as that of a directly applicable provision of a regulation. This conclusion was reinforced by the wording of Article 177 of the Treaty:

> "Article 177, whereby the national courts are empowered to refer to the Court all questions regarding the validity and interpretation of all acts of the institutions without distinction, also implies that individuals may invoke such acts before the national courts. Therefore, in each particular case, it must be ascertained whether the *nature, background and wording of the provision in question* are capable of producing direct effects in the legal relationships between the addressee of the act and third parties."[13] (emphasis added)

The reasoning of the Court has been reiterated in subsequent cases,[14] and the Court has upheld the direct effect of appropriately worded provisions of directives in a consistent case-law.[15]

Cohn-Bendit [1979] Dalloz Jur. 155 (Conseil d'Etat); and *Kloppenburg*, Judgment of April 25, 1985 (Bundesfinanzhof), see (1985) 10 E.L.Rev. 303.

[9] Case 9/70 [1970] E.C.R. 825; see also Case 20/70, *Transports Lesage* [1970] E.C.R. 861; and Case 23/70, *Haselhorst* [1970] E.C.R. 881.

[10] O.J.Sp.Ed. 1965–66, p. 67, providing for the application of the common value added tax system to transport of goods by road, rail and inland waterway.

[11] O.J.Sp.Ed. 1967, p. 14 on the harmonisation of legislation of Member States concerning turnover taxes.

[12] [1970] E.C.R. 825 at p. 837, para. 5.

[13] [1970] E.C.R. 825 at p. 837, para. 6.

[14] See, *e.g.* Case 41/74, *Van Duyn* [1974] E.C.R. 1337; Case 36/75, *Rutili* [1975] E.C.R. 1219; Case 51/76, *Verbond* [1977] E.C.R. 113.

[15] See, *e.g.* Case 38/77, *Enka* [1977] E.C.R. 2203; Case 148/78, *Ratti* [1979] E.C.R. 1629; Case 8/81, *Becker* [1982] E.C.R. 53; Case 255/81, *Grendel* [1982] E.C.R. 2301; Case 70/83,

The provisions of a directive may only have direct effect where they have not been correctly implemented by the Member State in question before the end of the period prescribed for that purpose.[16] Where a directive has been properly implemented by national measures, its effects extend to individuals through the medium of those implementing measures,[17] though the directive may be invoked before national courts as an aid to the construction of national statutes,[18] and national courts are obliged to construe national law, whether specifically introduced to implement the directive or not, and whether introduced prior of subsequent to the directive,[19] in the light of the wording and purpose of the directive in order to achieve the result referred to in the third paragraph of Article 189.[20] In *Marleasing* v. *La Comercial* the Court of Justice seems to suggest that it is impossible for a national court to interpret the provisions of national law in such a way as to deviate from the requirements of a relevant directive,[21] but this would seem to undermine the distinction between consistent interpretation and direct effect. Where a directive has been properly implemented by national measures, it is not open to a litigant to side-step the appropriate provisions of national law and rely upon the direct effect of the provisions of the directive.[22] This follows from the terms of Article 189 EEC, which provides that directives, while binding as to the result to be achieved, "shall leave to the national authorities the choice of form and methods." National legislative implementation of a directive constitutes both the due performance of a Community obligation, and the exercise of a sovereign choice to exclude the direct application of the directive itself by the national courts.

While the appropriate test for the direct effect of a directive is said to be the clarity and precision of its terms,[23] it must be added that even the precise and unconditional terms of a directive will not be directly effective (as far as judicial application is concerned) unless intended to be given effect by the national judicial authorities, rather than national administrative authorities.[24] Nevertheless, a provision of a directive which satisfies the conditions for direct effect, and has not been implemented by national law, is binding on all the organs of the administration, including decentralised authorities and municipalities.[25]

Irrespective of the direct effect of the substantive provisions of a directive, its terms may lack an unconditional and precise obligation as to the specific

---

Kloppenburg [1984] E.C.R. 1075; Case 5/84, *Direct Cosmetics* [1985] E.C.R. 617; Case 152/84, *Marshall* [1986] E.C.R. 723.

[16] Case 148/78, *Ratti* [1979] E.C.R. 1629; Case 8/81, *Becker* [1982] E.C.R. 53; Case 126/82, *D. J. Smit* [1983] E.C.R. 73.

[17] Case 102/79, *Commission* v. *Belgium* [1980] E.C.R. 1473; Case 8/81, *Becker* [1982] E.C.R. 53.

[18] Case 32/74, *Haaga* [1974] E.C.R. 1201; Case 11/75, *Mazzalai* [1976] E.C.R. 657; Case 270/81, *Felicitas* [1982] E.C.R. 2771.

[19] Case C–106/89, *Marleasing* v. *La Comercial* [1990] E.C.R. 4135.

[20] Case 14/83, *Von Colson* [1984] E.C.R. 1891 at p. 1909, para. 26; Case 79/83, *Harz* [1984] E.C.R. 1921 at p. 1942, para. 26.

[21] Case C–106/89, *supra*, note 19.

[22] Case 270/81, *Felicitas* [1982] E.C.R. 2771.

[23] Case 126/82, *D. J. Smit* [1983] E.C.R. 73.

[24] Case 815/79, *Cremonini & Vrankovich* [1980] E.C.R. 3583.

[25] Case 103/88, *Constanzo* [1989] E.C.R. 1839 at pp. 1870 and 1871, paras. 31 and 32.

remedies to be made available in national courts.[26] If however a Member State chooses to remedy the breach of an obligation required to be imposed under a directive by the award of compensation, that compensation must be adequate in relation to the damage sustained,[27] and it is incumbent upon national courts to construe national legislation accordingly.[28]

(c) *Rights of individuals* inter se

The Court has held that while directives may be invoked against the State, both in its private law and public law capacities, they can never be invoked against private individuals.[29] The legal effects of directives (and presumably decisions addressed to Member States) thus differ from those of both treaty provisions and regulations, and the reasons for this merit consideration.

Before the judgment in the *Ratti* case,[30] there was nothing in the Court's case-law to suggest that the legal effects of a directly effective provision in a directive would be any different from those of a directly effective treaty provision. Since the court had held that treaty provisions were capable of binding individuals, as well as States,[31] it would have followed that directives could have similar effects. There were several arguments, however, which could be marshalled against this conclusion.[32] First, since there was no legal requirement to publish directives, it might seem to be implied that directives could only bind those to whom they were addressed. Secondly, it was arguable that to allow directives to be pleaded against individuals would assimilate directives to regulations, which would run counter to Article 189 of the Treaty. Thirdly, there was the argument that to allow directives to be pleaded against individuals would be contrary to the principle of legal certainty, since those subject to obligations contained in directives might be unsure whether to rely upon national implementing legislation, or upon the underlying directives. While none of these arguments were conclusive, there was a further argument, of a political, rather than legal nature: the courts in some Member States were having difficulty in accepting that directives could have direct effect at all[33]; to go further and to allow "horizontal" effect to directives might further diminish the credibility of the Court of Justice in such Member States, and lead to the uneven enforceability of directives in the Community.

The Court laid the conceptual foundations for its later compromise solution in a judgment of April 5, 1979. In the *Ratti* case[34] the Court of Justice declared that:

"a Member State which has not adopted the implementing measures required by the directive in the prescribed period *may not rely, as*

---

[26] Case 14/83, *Von Colson* [1984] E.C.R. 1891; Case 79/83, *Harz* [1984] 1921.
[27] See, *supra*, note 26.
[28] Case 14/83, *Von Colson* [1984] E.C.R. 1891 at p. 1909, para. 28.
[29] Case 152/84, *Marshall* [1986] E.C.R. 723.
[30] Case 148/78, *Ratti* [1979] E.C.R. 1629.
[31] See, *supra*, p. 62.
[32] See, in general, Easson, (1979) 4 E.L.Rev. 67 at pp. 70–73.
[33] Pescatore, (1983) 8 E.L.Rev. 155 at pp. 169–170.
[34] Case 148/78 [1979] E.C.R. 1629.

against individuals, on its own failure to perform the obligations which the directive entails."[35]

The italicised words indicated that the legal basis for the direct effect of directives was that a State could not rely upon its own wrong as a defence to an action based upon a directive before its own courts. This doctrine seemed to restrict the application of directives by national courts to actions against defaulting Member States, and to rule out actions against individuals. The Court's case-law following *Ratti* incorporated the above-mentioned formulation.[36]

The Court's decision in *Marshall*[37] finally laid speculation to rest. The appellant in the national proceedings. Miss M. H. Marshall, was an employee of an Area Health Authority in the United Kingdom. She had been dismissed at the age of 62, since she had passed "the normal retirement age" (of 60) applied by the Authority to women employees.

An exception had in fact been made for Miss Marshall to work until the age of 62. The normal retiring age for men was 65. Miss Marshall instituted proceedings against the Authority alleging sex discrimination contrary to the principle of equality of treatment laid down in Directive 76/207.[38] The Area Health Authority argued before the Court of Justice: (1) that the directive could not be relied upon against individuals; (2) that the Authority, although a public authority emanating from the central government, had acted *qua* employer in dismissing Miss Marshall, rather than *qua* State. The Court held that since a directive was binding under Article 189 EEC only upon "each Member State to which it was addressed," it could not of itself impose obligations upon an individual. However, this did not preclude an individual relying upon a directive against the State, regardless of the capacity in which the latter was acting, whether as an employer or as a public authority. The United Kingdom had argued that the possibility of relying on provisions of the directive against the Authority would give rise to arbitrary and unfair distinctions between the rights of state employees and those of private employees. The Court of Justice did not find this argument convincing. On the contrary, such a distinction might easily be avoided if the Member State concerned correctly implemented the directive in national law.

The *Marshall* decision allows the invocation of the "private law" directives against the State, but rules out such actions against private parties. While the compromise may be justifiable on policy grounds, the Court's reasoning seems less than compelling. The Court avers that directives bind the State, and therefore cannot be invoked against individuals. Yet this very argument failed in *Defrenne*[39] to prevent Article 119 of the Treaty being held to bind private parties as well as the State. What is true of the Treaty should also, it might be thought, be true of directives, for the obligation to comply

---

[35] [1979] E.C.R. 1629 at para. 22. Emphasis added.
[36] See, *e.g.* Case 8/81, *Becker* [1982] E.C.R. 53.
[37] Case 152/84, *Marshall* [1986] E.C.R. 723.
[38] O.J. 1976 L39/40.
[39] Case 43/75 [1976] E.C.R. 455.

with a directive is itself a treaty obligation, and the Court has held that directives have an effect no less binding than that of any other rule of Community law.[40]

That is not to say that the Court's ruling in *Marshall* cannot be justified on legal grounds; on the contrary, there has always been a strong case against the horizontal effect of directives based on the principal of legal certainty.[41] Private individuals should clearly not be placed in unreasonable doubt as to their obligations by requiring the scrutiny of overlapping texts at both the national and community level as a prerequisite to a complete appreciation of the law. The fact that individuals may be bound by treaty provisions and regulations does not give rise to the same risk of uncertainty. The Treaty is a finite document; the threat to legal certainty posed by the fact that its provisions may create obligations for individuals as well as rights is insignificant. Regulations, again, constitute direct Community legislation; they are as capable of binding individuals as any provision of national law, and are only subject to national implementation where they so provide. In this respect they must be distinguished from directives, and decisions addressed to Member States, which must be implemented by national legislation, resulting in the duplication of the substance of Community texts, and possible legal insecurity for individuals. For obvious reasons, the principle of legal certainty can hardly be invoked by a national authority as a ground for denying the legal efficacy of a directive, irrespective of the capacity in which the authority is alleged to be bound.

The disadvantage of the Court's approach in *Marshall* however, is that it rules out horizontal direct effect for directives even in cases where such effect could not prejudice the legal security of individuals, for example in cases where the direct effect of provisions of a "private law" directive have already been established in proceedings against the authorities of a Member State. The advantages of a case by case approach, allowing the principle of legal certainty to be pleaded as a complete defence to private individuals in some cases, and as justifying prospective effect for the Court's rulings in others, has apparently been foregone.

Two developments since *Marshall* may serve to remedy the uneven application of directives resulting from the above decision. The first is a broad approach to the concept of "Member State" for the purpose of the principle in *Marshall* that directives may be invoked against Member States but not against individuals. In *Foster* v. *British Gas* the Court of Justice held that:

> "a body, whatever its legal form, which has been made responsible, pursuant to a measure adopted by the state, for providing a public service under the control of the state and which has for that purpose special powers beyond those which result from the normal rules applicable in relations between individuals is included in any event

---

[40] Case 79/72, *Commission* v. *Italy* [1972] E.C.R. 667; Case 52/75, *Commission* v. *Italy* [1976] E.C.R. 277.
[41] See the first edition of this book, pp. 40, 41.

among the bodies against which the provisions of a directive capable of having direct effect may be relied upon."[42]

The second development concerns the obligation to interpret national law consistently with relevant directives. In *Marleasing* v. *La Comercial* the Sixth Chamber made it clear that the duty of consistent interpretation applies to national legislation which predates a directive, as well as to legislation which postdates it.[43] The court even uses language which suggests that a national court is prohibited from interpreting national legislation inconsistently with a directive,[44] but this would seem to confuse the principle of consistent interpretation with that of direct effect.

The legal effect of ancillary treaties[45]

It is established that international agreements between the Community and third countries constitute part of the Community legal order, and that appropriately worded provisions of such agreements may be invoked before national courts in the Member States. The exact position was for some time unclear.[46]

In *Kupferberg*[47] the Court was asked whether Article 21 of the EEC-Portuguese Association Agreement was directly applicable. The Court held the provisions in issue to be directly applicable, justifying its conclusion at some length, and in terms applicable generally to international agreements between the Community and third countries. In ensuring respect for commitments arising from an agreement concluded by the Community institutions, declared the Court, the Member States fulfilled an obligation not only in relation to the Community which had assumed responsibility for the due performance of the agreement. It followed from the Community nature of such provisions that their effect in the Community could not be allowed to vary according to whether their application was in practice the responsibility of the Community institutions or the Member States, and, in the latter case, according to the effects in the internal legal order of each Member State which the law of that State assigns to international agreements concluded by it. Furthermore, the possibility that the courts of third countries might not accord direct effect to Association Agreements was not incompatible with the direct applicability of appropriately worded provisions of such agreements. The international legal obligations of states to fulfil their treaty commitments left them freedom to determine the legal

---

[42] See Case C–188/89 [1990] E.C.R. I–3313 at p. 3348, para. 20. The Court pointed out that its previous case law indicated that directives could be relied upon against tax authorities, (*e.g.* Case 8/81, *Becker* [1982] E.C.R. 53), local or regional authorities (Case 103/88, *Constanzo* [1989] E.C.R. 1839), and constitutionally independent authorities responsible for the maintenance of public order and safety (Case 222/84, *Johnston* v. *RUC* [1986] E.C.R. 1651), see [1990] E.C.R. I–3313 at p. 3348, para. 19.
[43] Case C–106/89 [1990] E.C.R. I–4135 at p. 4159, para. 8.
[44] *Ibid.* at para. 9.
[45] See Pescatore, (1983) 8 E.L.Rev. 155, at p. 171.
[46] See Case 181/73, *Haegeman* [1974] E.C.R. 449; Case 87/75, *Bresciani* [1976] E.C.R. 129; Case 270/80, *Polydor* [1982] E.C.R. 329; Case 17/81, *Pabst* [1982] E.C.R. 1331.
[47] Case 104/81 [1982] E.C.R. 3641.

means for attaining that end in their own legal system, unless the agreement itself specified such means. Thus the fact that the courts of one country might accord a provision direct effect while the courts of another might not would not of itself constitute a lack of reciprocity in the implementation of the agreement. Again, the existence of joint committees designed to secure the proper implementation of the agreements did not exclude their judicial implementation. Application by a national court of an unconditional treaty obligation could not adversely affect the powers that the agreement conferred upon a joint committee.

The decision of the Court in *Kupferberg* is of considerable significance, providing as it does for the justiciability before the national courts of Member States of the world-wide trading relations of European countries, their residents, and their overseas trading partners.[48]

The Court of Justice has held that if an international agreement to which the Community was party provided for an international court to settle disputes between the Community and third countries, the decisions of that court would bind the Court of Justice when it was called upon to rule, by way of preliminary ruling or in a direct action, on the interpretation of the international agreement as part of the Community legal order.[49] The Court of Justice has also held that it is competent to review the validity of Community acts for consistency with rules of international law which are both binding on the Community and directly effective.[50] The General Agreement on Tariffs and Trade is binding on the Community, since under the EEC Treaty the Community has assumed the powers previously exercised by Member States with respect to the GATT.[51] However, the Court has rejected arguments that direct effect can be attributed to the GATT as regards Article II, Article XI, the Protocols concluded within the framework of the GATT, and those provisions of the GATT which determine the effect of such Protocols.[52] These conclusions are based on the general scheme of the GATT, and the flexibility of its provisions, in particular those concerning the possibility for derogation by Contracting States. Nevertheless, undertakings which complain to the Commission of illicit commercial practices attributable to third countries under the Community commercial policy instrument may rely upon the GATT as forming part of the rules of international law to which the instrument applies.[53]

---

[48] See Case C–18/90, *ONEM* v. *Bahia Kziber* [1991] E.C.R. I–119 for the direct effect of Art. 41(1) of the EEC-Morocco Co-operation Agreement of 1976.

[49] Opinion 1/91 on EC-EFTA Agreement, Opinion of December 14, 1991 at paras. 39 and 40.

[50] Cases 21–24/72, *International Fruit* [1972] E.C.R. 1219; Case 9/73, *Schluter* [1973] E.C.R. 1135; Cases 267–269/81, *Societa Petrolifera Italiana* [1983] E.C.R. 801; Cases 290–291/81, *Compagnia Singer* [1983] E.C.R. 847.

[51] See note 50, *supra*.

[52] See note 50, *supra*.

[53] Case 70/87, *Fediol* [1989] E.C.R. 1781 at pp. 1830, 1831, paras. 19, 20, dealing with the scope of Regulation 2641/84 on protection against illicit commercial practices.

RIGHTS AND REMEDIES

1. Introduction

In the main, the Community system is administered by national authorities,[54] with the result that national agencies, courts, and tribunals are entrusted with the application of sometimes subtle combinations of Community law and national law, based on variations of the following:

— rules of Community law incapable of direct application incorporated into national law in discharge of Community obligations;
— directly applicable rules of Community law, supplemented by directly applicable Community procedural rules [supplemented by national procedural rules and national remedies];
— directly applicable rules of Community law, supplemented by national procedural rules and national remedies.

2. Rules of Community law incapable of direct application

Where non-directly applicable rules of Community law are incorporated into national law, the Community source of the national rules in question will only be relevant for purposes of interpretation.[55]

The validity *vel non* of a national measure implementing an invalid Community act raises questions, not of Community law, but of national law.[56] In the United Kingdom, an order made under section 2(2) of the European Communities Act 1972, implementing such an act, would almost certainly be *ultra vires*.[57]

3. Directly applicable provisions of Community law supplemented by directly applicable Community procedural rules

Community regulations may not only vest rights in individuals as against national authorities; they may also provide detailed procedural rules for the enjoyment of these rights, including the standard and burden of proof necessary to sustain a claim to the payment of money. Such provisions are a commonplace.[58]

It is important to establish whether or not a regulation lays down comprehensive procedural rules in a specific area, since if it does not, the national authorities are free to supplement Community law with the rules of

---

[54] Though not entirely, for the Commission and the Court of Justice play a significant role.
[55] References from national courts under Art. 177 for the purpose of simply ensuring the consistent interpretation of national law with Community law are not infrequent, see p. 72, note 18, *supra*.
[56] Case 23/75, *Rey Soda* [1975] E.C.R. 1279.
[57] *Hayward* v. *Cammell Laird* [1988] A.C. 894 at p. 903; *R.* v. *MAFF, ex p. FEDESA* [1988] 3 C.M.L.R. 661 at p. 665.
[58] For example, see second edition of this book, Chap. 8, in particular the section on buying-in, and import and export licences at pp. 313 *et seq.*

the forum.[59] For the sake of the uniform application of Community law, however, resort to provisions of internal law is permissible only to the extent necessary to give effect to the regulation in question.[60]

4. Directly applicable provisions of Community law supplemented by national procedural rules and remedies

While regulations may, and sometimes do, provide detailed procedural rules for the vindication of Community rights, Community law more often than not vest rights in individuals (either against the State, or against other individuals), without prescribing explicitly the procedural rules applicable in national tribunals, or providing the remedies for infringement of these rights. In these cases, it is for national law to specify the appropriate court or tribunal in which an individual alleging violation of his rights is to present his claim,[61] and for such court or tribunal to choose an appropriate remedy from those available under national law.[62] As the Court observed in *Comet* v. *Produktschap*,[63] a decision in which it upheld the rights of Member States to apply national statutes of limitation to proceedings in national courts based on directly applicable provisions of Community law:

> "... in the absence of any relevant Community rules, it is for the national legal order of each Member State to designate the competent courts and to lay down the procedural rules for proceedings designed to ensure the protection of the rights which individuals acquire through the direct effect of Community law, provided that such rules are not less favourable than those governing the same right of action on an internal matter. ... The position would be differently only if those rules and time-limits made it impossible in practice to exercise rights which the national courts have a duty to protect."[64]

While it is incumbent upon national courts to deploy all available national remedies to secure the implementation of Community law, the Court of Justice has said that national courts cannot be expected to create new remedies for this purpose. As the Court of Justice explained in *Rewe* v. *Hauptzollamt Kiel*:

> "... although the Treaty has made it possible in a number of instances for private persons to bring a direct action, where appropriate, before the Court of Justice, it was not intended to create new remedies in national courts to ensure the observance of Community law other than those already laid down by national law. On the other hand the system of legal protection established by the Treaty, as set out in Article 177 in

---

[59] Case 31/69, *Commission* v. *Italy* [1970] E.C.R. 25.
[60] Case 39/70, *Norddeutsches Vieh-und Fleischkontor* [1971] E.C.R. 49.
[61] Case 13/68, *Salgoil* [1968] E.C.R. 453.
[62] See, *e.g.* Case 28/67, *Mokerei-Zentrale* [1968] E.C.R. 143; Case 34/67, *Luck* [1968] 245.
[63] Case 45/76 [1976] E.C.R. 2043; and see Case 33/76, *Rewe-Zentralfinanz* [1976] E.C.R. 1989.
[64] [1976] E.C.R. 2043 at p. 2053, paras. 13, 16. On the consistency of national time limits with these principles, see Case 386/87, *Bessin and Salson* [1989] E.C.R. 3551; Case C–208/90, *Emmott*, Judgment of July 25, 1991.

particular, implies that it must be possible for every type of action provided for by national law to be available for the purpose of ensuring observance of Community provisions having direct effect, on the same conditions concerning the admissibility and procedure as would apply were it a question of ensuring observance of national law."[65]

While it may be a general principle that national courts need not create new remedies in order to secure the enforcement of Community rights, it will be seen that the exceptions are almost as wide as the rule.[66]

There can be no doubt that it is for national law to specify the appropriate court, and the appropriate remedy, to enable an individual to pursue his rights under Community law, but this principle cannot preclude a national court from applying directly effective rules of Community law in all cases falling within its jurisdiction. This problem arose in stark form in *Simmenthal*.[67] Should an Italian court refuse to apply national legislation already held by the Court of Justice to be incompatible with Community law, or should the Italian court only do so after first referring the question to the Italian Constitutional Court? The Court of Justice ruled that:

"A national court which is called upon, within the limits of its jurisdiction, to apply provisions of Community law is under a duty to give full effect to those provisions, if necessary refusing of its own motion to apply any conflicting provisions of national legislation, even if adopted subsequently, and it is not necessary for the court to request or await the prior setting aside of such provisions by legislative or other constitutional mean."[68]

It would seem to follow that if a national tribunal is acting within its subject-matter jurisdiction (for example, sex discrimination), it must give effect to Community rights in this regard even if its jurisdiction under national law is limited to rights specified under certain national enactments.[69]

5. Recovery of money levied contrary to Community law

That the distinction between Community rights and national remedies may be less than clear cut is well illustrated by the cases on the recovery of money levied by Member States contrary to Community law. In *Pigs and Bacon Commission* v. *McCarren*[70] the Court considered the case of a trader

---

[65] [1981] E.C.R. 1805 at p. 1838.
[66] See in particular Case 199/82, *San Giorgio* [1983] E.C.R. 3595, and Case C–213/89, *Factortame* [1990] E.C.R. I–2433.
[67] Case 196/77 [1978] E.C.R. 629.
[68] [1978] E.C.R. 629 at p. 644. For the acceptance in Italian constitutional law of the European Court's position, see Petriccione, (1986) 11 E.L.Rev. 320.
[69] For the effect of direct claims under Art. 119 EEC before industrial tribunals in the United Kingdom, see *Pickstone* v. *Freemans* [1987] 3 All E.R. 756 at 777; Wyatt, "Enforcing EEC Social Rights in the United Kingdom" (1989) 18 I.L.J. 197 at pp. 207 *et seq.*; *Greater Glasgow Health Board* v. *Wright and Hannah* [1991] I.R.L.R. 187; *McKechnie* v. *UBM Building Supplies Ltd.* [1991] I.R.L.R. 283; *Livingston* v. *Hepworth Refractories Plc.* [1992] I.R.L.R. 63.
[70] Case 177/78 [1979] E.C.R. 2161.

who had paid a levy demanded, contrary to Community rules, within the framework of a national marketing system for pork. The Court declared that:

> "In principle any trader who is required to pay the levy has therefore the right to claim the reimbursement of that part of the levy which is then devoted to purposes incompatible with Community law. However, it is for the national court to assess, according to its national law, in each individual case, whether and to what extent the levy paid may be recovered and whether there may be set off against such a debt the sums paid to a trader by way of export bonus."[71]

This formulation is not without difficulty. In particular, the words "*whether and to what extent* ..." (emphasis added) imply that there may be circumstances in which a trader's right in principle to reimbursement may fail to be upheld for want of an appropriate national remedy. What, for instance, would be the position where national rules provided no general right to restitution for monies paid under a mistake of law?

In *San Giorgio*,[72] the Court of Justice considered a national rule which precluded the repayment of duties or taxes unduly paid where such duties or taxes had been passed on to third parties. However, under the national rule in question, duties or taxes were presumed to have been passed on whenever the goods in respect of which a charge had been levied had been transferred to third parties, in the absence of documentary proof to the contrary. The Court of Justice confirmed that national courts might legitimately take into account the fact that unduly levied charges had been incorporated in the price of goods and thus passed on to purchasers. However, any requirement of proof which had the effect of making it "virtually impossible or excessively difficult" to secure the repayment of charges levied contrary to Community law would be incompatible with Community law. That was particularly so in the case of presumptions or rules of evidence placing upon the taxpayer the burden of establishing that the charges had not been passed on to other persons, or in the case of special limitations concerning the form of evidence to be adduced, such as the exclusion of any kind of evidence other than documentary evidence. Once it was established that the levying of the charge was incompatible with Community law, the national court must be free to decide whether or not the burden of the charge had been passed on, wholly or in part, to other persons. Furthermore, the Court emphasised that national rules rendering recovery virtually impossible could not be justified on the basis that they were not discriminatory, inasmuch as recovery of taxes paid unduly under national law was also virtually impossible.

> "It must be pointed out in that regard that the requirement of non-discrimination laid down by the Court cannot be construed as

---

[71] [1979] E.C.R. 2161 at p. 2192.
[72] Case 199/82 [1983] E.C.R. 3595. See also Case 68/79 [1980] E.C.R. 501; see also Case 61/79, *Denkavit Italiana* [1980] E.C.R. 1205; Case 826/79, *Ariete* [1980] E.C.R. 2545; Case 826/79, *Mireco* [1980] E.C.R. 2559.

justifying legislative measures intended to render any repayment of charges levied contrary to Community law virtually impossible, even if the same treatment is extended to taxpayers who have similar claims arising from an infringement of national tax law. The fact that rules of evidence which have been found to be incompatible with the rules of Community law are extended, by law, to a substantial number of national taxes, charges and duties or even to all of them is not therefore a reason for withholding the repayment of charges levied contrary to Community law."[73]

National procedural conditions which may lawfully be taken into account in relation to the repayment of taxes levied contrary to Community law include time limitations[74]; unjust enrichment resulting from the taxes having been passed on to third parties[75]; damage to the trade of taxpayers resulting from the imposition of the unlawful tax[76]; and any benefits accruing to a person paying unlawful taxes by virtue of the payment.[77] Again, if national authorities exact money payments in contravention of Community law, the question whether interest is payable on repayment is one for national, not Community law.[78]

6. The extent to which national courts must adapt national remedies in aid of Community law

The Court of Justice held in *Rewe* v. *Hauptzollamt Kiel*[79] that national courts are under a duty to make available all national remedies in aid of Community law, but that they are not bound to create new remedies. This is logical, since the creation of a new remedy is a legislative, rather than a judicial act.

On the other hand, however, the Court in *San Giorgio*[80] held that a Member State cannot subject the repayment of national charges levied contrary to Community law to procedural requirements which make recovery virtually impossible.

Subsequent case law of the Court of Justice indicates that national courts are obliged to do everything necessary by way of provision of remedies to ensure the full force and effect of Community law.

In *UNECTEF* v. *Heylens*[81] the Court of Justice held that where an employed person relying upon Article 48 of the EEC Treaty claims that a

---

[73] [1983] E.C.R. at p. 3614. Confirmed in Case 331/84, *Bianco* [1988] E.C.R. 1099, and Case 240/87, *Deville* [1988] E.C.R. 3513.
[74] Case 33/76, *Rewe* [1976] E.C.R. 1989; Case 45/76, *Comet* [1976] E.C.R. 2043; Case 386/87, *Bessin & Salson* [1989] E.C.R. 3551; Case C–208/90, *Emmott* [1991] E.C.R. I–4869.
[75] Case 68/79, *Just* [1980] E.C.R. 501; Case 61/79, *Denakvit Italiana* [1980] E.C.R. 1205; Cases 142 and 143/80, *Essevi and Salengo* [1981] E.C.R. 1413; Case 199/82, *San Giorgio* [1983] E.C.R. 3595.
[76] Case 68/69, *Just* [1980] E.C.R. 501.
[77] Case 177/78, *Pigs and Bacon Commission* [1979] E.C.R. 2161.
[78] Case 6/60, *Humblet* [1960] E.C.R. 559; Case 26/74, *Roquette* [1976] E.C.R. 677.
[79] Case 158/80 [1981] E.C.R. 1805 at p. 1838.
[80] Case 199/82 [1983] E.C.R. 3595.
[81] Case 222/86 [1987] E.C.R. 4097.

foreign diploma merits recognition as a job qualification in the host State, the competent authority which adjudicates on this question is bound to give its reasons if it refuses to recognise the diploma in question. Furthermore, it must be possible for such a decision to be made the subject of judicial proceedings in which its legality under Community law can be reviewed. The Court has emphasised that the existence of effective judicial protection is a general principle of Community law.[82]

A major step in the development of the duty of national courts to adapt national remedies in aid of Community law was taken in the *Factortame* case.[83] The House of Lords asked whether Community law either obliged or authorised a national court to grant interim relief against a national measure pending a decision of the Court of Justice under Article 177 of the EEC Treaty on the compatibility of such a measure with Community law. The House of Lords specified circumstances in which *inter alia* the national court had no power to give interim protection to the rights claimed by suspending the application of a national measure. The question thus asked directly whether Community law could authorise or require the provision of a remedy which could not be granted under national law. The Court of Justice subtly reformulated the issue as follows:

> ". . . the House of Lords seek essentially to ascertain whether a national court which, in a case before it concerning Community law, considers that the sole obstacle which precludes it from granting interim relief is a rule of national law, must disapply that rule."[84]

Thus the Court of Justice presented the issue as not so much involving the capacity of Community law to create judicial remedies, as the limits on the capacity of national law to impede the application of Community law. The Court of Justice, referring to the principle of the supremacy of Community law, and to the duty of national courts to ensure the legal protection which individuals derive from the direct effect of provisions of Community law, continued:

> "The Court has also held that any provision of a national legal system and any legislative, administrative or judicial practice which might impair the effectiveness of Community law by withholding from the ..ational court having jurisdiction to apply such law the power to do everything necessary at the moment of its application to set aside national legislative provisions which might prevent, even temporarily, Community rules from having full force and effect are incompatible with those requirements, which are the very essence of Community law . . ."[85]

---

[82] Case 222/86 [1987] E.C.R. 4097 at p. 4117, para. 14, and see Case 222/84, *Johnston* v. *RUC* [1986] E.C.R. 1651 at p. 1663.

[83] Case C–213/89 [1990] E.C.R. I—2433. For the position where a litigant seeks interim relief against a national measure implementing a Community act pending a preliminary ruling on the validity of the Community act, see Case C–92/89, *Zuckerfabrik* [1991] E.C.R. I–415.

[84] [1990] E.C.R. I 2433 at p. 2473, para. 17.

[85] [1990] E.C.R. I 2433 at p. 2473, para. 20.

At the least this judgment holds that national remedies must be made available in aid of Community rights, but that any qualifying rules of national law which render those remedies inadequate in the judgement of the national court seised of the case must be set aside. It might even support the wider proposition that a remedy unknown to national law must be made available by a national court if in the view of the court that is the only way of securing full force and effect for Community law. After cases such as *San Giorgio* and *Factortame*, drawing a hard and fast distinction between Community rights on the one hand and national remedies on the other, is somewhat misleading. Community law, as well as defining rights, may in certain cases also determine the nature of the remedies provided by national courts. Such remedies are in truth hybrids, based on national law, but taking on Community characteristics in certain categories of case.

7. Damages as a remedy for breach of Community law

It has been demonstrated[86] that Community law requires restitution in certain cases as an adjunct to the directly effective Community right to resist the application of customs duties, discriminatory internal taxation, etc. Are there any directly effective provisions of Community law which have as their adjunct the right to damages for breach? There were early suggestions in the Court's case-law that this might indeed be the case. In *Humblet*[87] the Court declared:

> "In fact if the Court rules in a judgment that a legislative or administrative measure adopted by the authorities of a Member State is contrary to Community law, that Member State is obliged, by virtue of Article 86 of the ECSC Treaty[88] to rescind the measure in question and to make reparation for any unlawful consequences which may have ensued ..."[89]

The Court indicated that damages might be available for a breach of Community law in *Russo*[90]:

> "If an individual producer has suffered damage as a result of the intervention of a Member State in violation of Community law it will be for the State, as regards the injured party, to take the consequences upon itself in the context of the provisions of national law relating to the liability of the State."[91]

That the principle of liability of the state for damage caused to individuals by infringements of Community law is inherent in the scheme of the EEC

---

[86] *Supra* at p. 80.
[87] Case 6/60 [1960] E.C.R. 559.
[88] Art. 86 provides, that "Member States undertake to take all appropriate measures, whether general or particular, to ensure fulfilment of the obligations resulting from decisions and recommendations of the institutions of the Community and to facilitate the performance of the Community's tasks." *Cf.* Art. 5 EEC.
[89] [1960] E.C.R. 559 at p. 569.
[90] Case 60/75 [1976] E.C.R. 45 at p. 57.
[91] [1976] E.C.R. 45 at p. 57.

Treaty was confirmed by the Court of Justice in *Francovich* v. *Italian Republic*.[92] Directive 80/987[93] sought to ensure for employees throughout the Community a minimum level of protection in the event of the insolvency of their employer. To this end it provided, in particular, specific guarantees for the payment of unpaid remuneration. Italy failed to enact national legislation implementing the Directive, and failed in particular to establish the funds necessary to secure payments to employees. This failure was established in infringement proceedings brought by the Commission.[94] Certain employees, owed arrears of salary by their employer undertakings, which had become insolvent, sued the Italian state in a national court for damages for failing to implement the Directive. The Court of Justice, despite holding that the Directive in question was not directly effective since guarantor institutions were not identified,[95] held that a Member State was bound to make good any damage to individuals arising from the non-implementation of the Directive in question. The Court of Justice, referring to the *Factortame* case,[96] observed that the full effectiveness of Community rules might be called in question and the protection of the rights which they conferred would be weakened if individuals could not obtain compensation where their rights were infringed by a breach of Community law for which a Member State was responsible. The Court concluded that the principle of state liability for damages caused to individuals by infringements of Community law for which they were responsible was inherent in the scheme of the Treaty. In a case such as that in issue, where a Member State had failed to fulfil its obligations under Article 189 of the EEC Treaty to take all measures necessary in order to achieve the result laid down by a Directive, the full effectiveness of that rule of Community law required that there should be a right to compensation where three conditions were fulfilled. The first was that the result laid down by the Directive involved rights conferred on individuals. The second was that the content of the rights might be identified on the basis of the provisions of the Directive. And the third was the existence of a causal link between the failure by the Member State to fulfil its obligations and the damage suffered by the persons affected.

The potential scope of *Francovich* is wide. In that case Italy had completely failed to transpose the Directive in question. But would the three conditions be regarded as being fulfilled where a Member State adopted legislation to implement a Directive, but later interpretation of the Directive by the Court of Justice revealed that the national implementing rules had not given full effect to its terms? There are several possible approaches. One is to argue that a Member State is free to adopt the specific words of a Directive in its national implementing rules if it so chooses, but that if it adopts the

---

[92] Cases C–6/90 and C–9/90 Judgment of November 19, 1991. See Barav, (1991) 141 N.L.J. 1584.
[93] O.J. 1980 L283/23.
[94] Case 22/87, *Commission* v. *Italy* [1989] E.C.R. 143.
[95] Case 380/87, *Enichem* [1989] E.C.R. 2491 appears to assume that a right to compensation would not arise in the absence of the direct effect of the directive in question, [1989] E.C.R. at p. 2518, para. 25.
[96] See note 83, *supra.*

option of transposing the words of the Directive into its own national legal language, it must assume the risk of liability if in so doing it prevents full effect being given to Community law. Another approach is to argue that since Member States are given a discretion under Article 189 of the Treaty as to the choice of means to implement a Directive, they should not be held liable in damages for mis-implementation unless the terms of the Directive are sufficiently clear and precise to have put the Member State on warning and render the State culpable as to any loss incurred by individuals as a consequence of national implementing rules failing to ensure the full effect of the Directive. Automatic State liability for exceeding the scope of discretionary powers should perhaps not be assumed to follow from *Francovich* in the absence of a clearer indication from the Court of Justice. Indeed, it might be thought that some element of culpability on the part of the State ought to be regarded as a precondition for liability in cases where a claim is based on legislative mis-implementation by a Member State. The Court in *Francovich* does acknowledge that while the liability of the Member State was laid down in Community law, the conditions in which such liability gave rise to a right to compensation depended upon the nature of the infringement of Community law which gave rise to the damage.[97] As far as the transposition of directives is concerned, the possibility of individuals suing the State for failing to provide rights and effective remedies against third parties in accordance with the terms of a relevant Directive surely arises after *Francovich*. The safest advice for Member States is to adopt a cautious approach pending clarification of *Francovich*. First, Directives should be implemented on time! Secondly, if a State is in doubt as to the meaning of the text of a directive, it might transpose the specific words of the Directive, rather than seeking to "translate" the Directive into national legal language, which introduces the possibility of error. Thirdly, states might ensure that the most favourable remedies under national law are made available to give effect to rights intended to be bestowed upon individuals by directives.

It seems likely that *Francovich* liability might arise in contexts other than that of the implementation of directives. Where national authorities take administrative decisions on the basis of regulations, liability might arise if a national authority mistakenly denies a valuable right to a beneficiary of Community rules, for example, if a national authority denies a milk quota to a dairy farmer entitled to a quota under the applicable Community regulations. Where, however, a national authority exercises pursuant to Community law a discretion in the public interest, liability in damages should not be automatic in the event of a mistake of law tainting the national action with illegality. Those authorities which exercise policy choices in the public interest should not be made insurers for the consequences of illegality in measures they adopt as a result of good faith errors of law.[98] Liability in

---

[97] Judgment of November 19, 1991, para. 38.
[98] Support for this approach is found in the case-law of the Court of Justice on the liability of Community institutions under Art. 215 EEC, see in particular Cases 83 and 94/76, 4, 15 and 40/77, *HNL* v. *Council and Commission* [1978] E.C.R. 1209 at p. 1224, para. 5.

damages in such cases should be exceptional, and confined to cases where a national authority has manifestly and gravely disregarded the limits on the exercise of its powers.[99]

8. National procedures subject to Community standards

Member States are under an obligation to take all "appropriate" measures to ensure the fulfilment of the obligations arising out of the Treaty or resulting from action taken by the institutions of the Community.[1] Although the Court has suggested on occasion that what is "appropriate" is for the Member State in question to decide,[2] this would render the obligation nugatory, and an objective interpretation is more in accordance with principle.[3] It follows that national procedural rules and remedies are subject in principle to Community minimum standards, and support for this proposition may be found in *Rheinmuhlen-Dusseldorf* v. *EVSt*,[4] in which the Court acknowledged the competence of national authorities to adopt the standard of proof they thought fit for the purpose of assessing claims of export refunds, but added that complete reliance on shipment without a Community transit document as proof of exportation might nevertheless constitute an abuse of their discretion.

Whether or not Community law provides implicit procedural rules may often be difficult to establish without the benefit of a reference to the Court of Justice. In certain cases the Court of Justice has interpreted Community law as implicitly placing the burden of proof on one party or the other in national proceedings. Thus, the Court has held that it is for the national authorities of a Member State to prove that national trading rules inhibiting imports may be justified under Article 36 of the EEC Treaty.[5] Again, in the context of equal pay, the Court has held that if an employer applies a system of pay which is totally lacking in transparency, it is for the employer to prove that this practice in the matter of wages is not discriminatory, if a female worker establishes, in relation to a relatively large number of employees, that the average pay for women is less than that for men.[6]

The intrusion of Community law into the question of the burden, and the standard of proof, will only be necessary in cases where the application of diverse rules is likely to prejudice unduly the uniform application of Community law. The Court of Justice will no doubt be slow to reach such a conclusion; it certainly does not consider that the application of different

---

[99] See note 98, [1978] E.C.R. at p. 1224, para. 6.
[1] Art. 5 EEC.
[2] Case 50/76, *Amsterdam Bulb* [1977] E.C.R. 137 at p. 150, para. 32.
[3] The Court has held that although the "choice of form and methods" in implementing directives is left to the Member States, they are nevertheless obliged to choose the most appropriate form and method to ensure the effective functioning of directives, account being taken of their aims; Case 48/75, *Royer* [1976] E.C.R. 497 at p. 518, para. 73.
[4] Case 6/71 [1971] E.C.R. 823.
[5] See *infra*, p. 229.
[6] Case 109/88, *Handels-og Kontorfunktionaerernes Forbund* [1989] E.C.R. 3199. See also Case 170/84, *Bilka* v. *Weber* [1986] E.C.R. 1607.

periods of limitation in the various Member States is itself likely to lead to such a result.[7]

9. Penal sanctions

The possibility of having to compensate the legally wronged may not always provide sufficient encouragement to those subject to the law to comply with its terms. Again, the infringement of certain rules may damage the public interest rather than infringe individual rights. Exceptionally, Community law resorts to coercion to secure compliance with its norms. One example is the authority of the Commission to fine undertakings for conduct prohibited under Articles 85 and 86 of the Treaty.[8] Milder forms of encouragement are encountered in the field of agriculture, deposits subject to forfeiture being especially favoured.[9] For the rest, Community law relies upon the enforcement procedures of the Member States. "Article 5 of the Treaty ..." commented the Court in one case, "... allows the various Member States to choose the measures which they consider appropriate, including sanctions which may be criminal in nature."[10] While the choice of penalties remains within the discretion of Member States, they must ensure in particular that infringements of Community law are penalised under conditions, both procedural and substantive, which are analogous to those applicable to infringements of national law of a similar nature and importance and which, in any event, make the penalty effective, proportionate, and dissuasive.[11]

THE GENERAL PRINCIPLES OF COMMUNITY LAW

1. A judicial development

In addition to the explicit rules laid down in the Treaty and secondary legislation, the Court of Justice has developed certain general principles of law, inspired by the national laws of the Member States, in accordance with which it interprets the express provisions of Community law, and evaluates the legality of acts of the institutions, and of the Member States when they take administrative or legislative measures to implement Community law.[12] Although a distinction may be drawn between "general principles" on the one hand, and "fundamental rights" on the other, the latter rights have been declared by the Court of Justice to constitute an integral part of the general principles of law which it is bound to uphold.[13]

---

[7] Case 33/76, *Rewe* [1976] E.C.R. 1989; Case 45/76, *Comet* [1976] E.C.R. 2043.
[8] See *infra*, p. 486. Provision is made for penalties against defaulting Member States in Art. 171(2) of the EC Treaty as amended by the T.E.U.
[9] For example, Case 11/70, *Internationale Handelsgesellschaft* [1970] E.C.R. 1125.
[10] Case 50/76, *Amsterdam Bulb* [1977] E.C.R. 137 at p. 150, para. 32.
[11] Case 68/88, *Commission* v. *Greece* [1989] E.C.R. 2965; Case C–326/88, *Hansen* [1990] E.C.R. 2911.
[12] Case 316/86, *HZ Hamburg-Jonas* v. *Krucken* [1988] E.C.R. 2213 at p. 2239, para. 22; Cases 201 & 202/85, *Klensch* [1986] E.C.R. 3477 at p. 3508, para. 10.
[13] Case 4/73, *Nold* v. *Commission* [1974] E.C.R. 491.

2. Juridical basis

The Court can hardly be said to have exceeded its jurisdiction by its recourse to the general principles of law. No treaty regime, let alone the "new legal order" of the Community, could be interpreted in a legal vacuum. International tribunals have long been regarded as competent to draw upon the general principles of municipal law as a source of international law,[14] and the competence of the Court of Justice in the interpretation and application of Community law could surely be no less. The Treaty itself implies as much. Article 164 states: "The Court of Justice shall ensure that in the interpretation and application of this Treaty the law is observed."

This exhortation is not merely tautologous. The words "the law" render the French phrase "*respect du droit*," which suggests a corpus juris transcending the treaty texts.[15] Other provisions of the Treaty are consistent with the proposition that the general principles of law constitute a source of Community law.

Article 173 includes among the grounds of invalidity of Community acts infringement of "any rule of law" relating to the Treaty's application, an expression wide enough to encompass the principles under consideration. Furthermore, Article 215 of the Treaty provides that the non-contractual liability of the Community shall be determined "in accordance with the general principles common to the laws of the Member States," which amounts to express recognition of the role of the general principles of national law as a source of Community law.

3. Particular principles

(a) *Proportionality*

One of the most oft-invoked of the general principles of law developed by the Court of Justice[16] is that of proportionality. This principle holds that "the individual should not have his freedom of action limited beyond the degree necessary for the public interest,"[17] and the Court of Justice has described the principle as follows:

> "In order to establish whether a provision of Community law is consonant with the principle of proportionality it is necessary to establish, in the first place, whether the means it employs to achieve the

---

[14] See Wyatt, "New Legal Order, or Old?" (1982) 7 E.L.Rev. 147 at p. 157. *Cf.* Art. 38 of the Statute of the International Court of Justice, which lists as a source of international law, "the general principles of law recognised by civilised nations."
[15] See Pescatore, "Fundamental Rights and Freedoms in the System of the European Communities" [1970] A.J.I.L. 343, at p. 348.
[16] See in general Usher, "The Influence of National Concepts in Decisions of the European Court" (1975–76) 1 E.L.Rev. 359.
[17] Case 11/70, *Internationale Handelsgesselschaft* [1970] E.C.R. 1125 at p. 1127, *per* Adv. Gen. Dutheillet de Lamothe.

aim correspond to the importance of the aim and, in the second place, whether they are necessary for its achievement."[18]

This principle finds explicit expression in the Treaty as a constraint on Community action. Thus Article 40(3), which authorises the establishment of a common organisation of the market, declares that such organisation "may include all measures *required* to attain the objectives set out in Article 39."[19] (emphasis added). On the other hand, the wording of the Treaty does not seem to be a decisive factor. The Court examined the proportionality of Regulation 974/71 in *Balkan-Import-Export* v. *Hauptzollamt Berlin-Packhof*,[20] a regulation which was at that time based on Article 103(2) of the Treaty which provides that the Council may take "appropriate" measures. The Court observed that: "In exercising their powers, the Institutions must ensure that the amounts which commercial operators are charged are no greater than is *required* to achieve the aim which the authorities are to accomplish" (emphasis added).[21] There can be little doubt that the principle is applicable in its own right as a criterion of the validity of Community action.

The principle has operated to invalidate a provision of a regulation providing for the forfeiture of a security for any failure to perform a contractual undertaking, irrespective of the gravity of the breach.[22] The Court held that the:

> "absolute nature . . . of the above-mentioned regulation is contrary to the principle of proportionality in that it does not permit the penalty for which it provides to be made commensurate with the degree of failure to implement the contractual obligations or with the seriousness of the breach of those obligations."[23] In the context of the common agricultural policy, the Council has a wide discretionary power, and the Court of Justice will only interfere if a measure is manifestly inappropriate having regard to the objective which the competent institution is seeking to pursue.[24]

As well as constituting a constraint upon Community legislative activities, the principle of proportionality may be resorted to in assessing the legitimacy of State action otherwise authorised under the Treaty. Thus in *Rivoira*[25] the Court held that it was disproportionate for a Member State to apply a criminal penalty provided under national law for false declarations in

---

[18] Case 66/82, *Fromancais* [1983] E.C.R. 395 at p. 404, para. 8.
[19] For the application of the principle of proportionality in the agricultural context, see, *e.g.* Case 114/76, *Bergmann* [1977] E.C.R. 1211.
[20] Case 5/73 [1973] E.C.R. 1091.
[21] [1973] E.C.R. 1091 at pp. 1111–1112, para. 22. Though as the Court acknowledges, it does not necessarily follow that the obligation to respect the principle of proportionality must be measured in relation to the individual situation of any one particular group of operators. See also Cases 26 and 86/79, *Furges* [1980] E.C.R. 1083 at p. 1093.
[22] Case 240/78, *Atalanta* [1979] E.C.R. 2137.
[23] [1979] E.C.R. 2137 at p. 2151. And see Case 122/78, *Buitoni* [1975] E.C.R. 677, and Case 181/84, *E. D. & F. Man* [1985] E.C.R. 2889.
[24] Case 265/87, *Schrader* [1989] E.C.R. 2237 at pp. 2269, 2270, paras. 21, 22; Case 331/88, *Ex p. Fedesa* [1990] E.C.R. I–4023 at p. 4063, para. 14.
[25] Case 179/78 [1979] E.C.R. 1147.

connection with prohibited imports to an import which could not be subjected to prohibition or restriction. The principle applies in particular to State action in the context of those Treaty provisions allowing limited derogation from basic Treaty rules, such as Articles 36, 48(3) and (4), 55 and 56. Thus, while Article 48 provides for the free movement of workers between Member States, Article 48(3) allows for exceptions justified on grounds, *inter alia*, of public policy. The court has made it clear that this provision only allows derogations from the fundamental rule of Article 48 in case of a genuine and sufficiently serious threat to the requirements of public policy.[26] Again, where national authorities enact penalties to secure compliance with Community regulations, such penalties must be effective, proportionate, and dissuasive.[27] One may discern in the notion of the dissuasive penalty, a sort of reverse proportionality—the national penalty must be adequate to secure compliance.[28]

(b) *Legal certainty and legitimate expectation*

The principle of legal certainty requires that those subject to the law should not be placed in a situation of uncertainty as to their rights and obligations. The related concept of legitimate expectation constitutes an important corollary to this principle: those who act in good faith on the basis of the law as it is or seems to be should not be frustrated in their expectations.

The Court of Justice held in *Gondrand Freres*[29] that the principle of legal certainty requires that ambiguity or lack of clarity in measures imposing charges should be resolved in favour of the taxpayer. The Court declared:

> "The principle of legal certainty requires that rules imposing charges on the taxpayer must be clear and precise so that he may know without ambiguity what are his rights and obligations and may take steps accordingly.
>
> The rules in question are obviously unclear as is apparent *inter alia* from the fact that even the competent customs authorities originally interpreted them in the same way as the respondent in the main action and it was not until three years after the date of the first imports that they sought to recover the monetary compensatory amounts which would have been due in respect of the exports in question."[30]

The principle is capable of operating in favour of Member States. In *Germany* v. *Commission*[31] the court held that the principle of legal certainty:

---

[26] Case 36/75, *Rutili* [1975] E.C.R. 1219; Case 30/77, *Bouchereau* [1977] E.C.R. 1999.
[27] Case C–326/88, *Hansen* [1990] E.C.R. I–2911 at p. 2935, para. 17.
[28] And see Case 14/83, *Von Colson*: where a Member State chooses to penalise the breach of the prohibition of discrimination by the award of compensation, that compensation must be adequate in relation to the damage sustained, [1984] E.C.R. 1891 at p. 1908, para. 23.
[29] Case 169/80 [1981] E.C.R. 1931.
[30] [1981] E.C.R. 1931 at p. 1942. But where a regulation authorises the total or partial suspension of imports, a power to impose charges, as a less drastic measure, may be implied, Case 77/86, *Ex p. National Dried Fruit Association* [1988] E.C.R. 757.
[31] Case 44/81 [1982] E.C.R. 1855.

"... requires that a provision laying down a preclusive period, particularly one which may have the effect of depriving a Member State of the payment of financial aid its application for which has been approved and on the basis of which it has already incurred considerable expenditure, should be clearly and precisely drafted so that the Member States may be made fully aware of the importance of their complying with the time limit."[32]

An important judgment in the development of the principle of legitimate expectation was that in the *Mulder* case.[33] In order to stabilise milk production, Community rules provided for dairy farmers to enter into non-marketing agreements for a period of five years, in return for which they received a premium. In 1984 milk quotas were introduced, whereby milk producers would pay super levy on milk produced in excess of a quota determined by reference to their production during the 1983 marketing year. No provision was made for the grant of quota to those who did not produce during 1983 because of the existence of a non-marketing agreement! Having been urged to suspend milk production under Community rules, farmers were then excluded from milk production when their non-marketing period came to an end. One such farmer challenged the regulations in this regard. The Court of Justice held that the relevant regulation was invalid to the extent that no provision for allocation of quota was made in such cases. The basis of the ruling was the principle of legitimate expectation. As the Court explained:

"where such a producer, as in the present case, has been encouraged by a Community measure to suspend marketing for a limited period in the general interest and against payment of a premium he may legitimately expect not to be subject, upon the expiry of his undertaking, to restrictions which specifically affect him because he availed himself of the possibilities offered by the Community provisions."[34]

The Court has held that Member States are bound to implement directives in a way which meets the requirements of clarity and certainty, and that mere administrative practices will be inadequate for this purpose.[35] However, the drafting of some directives is lacking in precision. It remains to be seen whether the Court of Justice would be willing to hold a sufficiently vague and imprecise provision to be void for violation of the principle of legal certainty.

The principle of legal certainty militates against administrative and legislative measures taking effect without adequate notice to persons concerned. As the Court declared in *Racke*[36]:

---

[32] [1982] E.C.R. 1855 at p. 1877. But the principle of legal certainty does not necessarily play the same role between the authorities of Member States and the Community as it does in relations between authorities and individuals, see Case 262/87, *Netherlands* v. *Commission* [1989] E.C.R. 225 at p. 227, *per* Adv.-Gen. Van Gerven.

[33] Case 120/86 [1988] E.C.R. 2321. For an impressive survey of the extensive case-law of the Court, see Sharpston, "Legitimate Expectations and Economic Reality" (1990) 15 E.L. Rev. 103.

[34] [1988] E.C.R. 2321 at p. 2352, para. 24.

[35] Case 102/79, *Commission* v. *Belgium* [1980] E.C.R. 1473 at p. 1486. And see *supra*, p. 70.

[36] Case 98/78 [1979] E.C.R. 69.

"A fundamental principle in the Community legal order requires that a measure adopted by the public authorities shall not be applicable to those concerned before they have the opportunity to make themselves acquainted with it."[37]

The Court explained the implications of the principle for the retroactive effect of Community measures in *Decker*[38]:

"Although in general the principle of legal certainty precludes a Community measure from taking effect from a point in time before its publication, it may exceptionally be otherwise where the purpose to be achieved so demands and where the legitimate expectations of those concerned are duly respected."[39]

The above principles have implications for both the vires of Community measures, and their interpretation. In *Salumi*[40] the court stated:

"Although procedural rules are generally held to apply to all proceedings pending at the time when they enter into force, this is not the case with substantive rules. On the contrary, the latter are usually interpreted as applying to situations existing before their entry into force only insofar as it clearly follows from the terms, objectives or general scheme that such an effect must be given to them.

This interpretation ensures respect for the principles of legal certainty and the protection of legitimate expectation, by virtue of which the effect of Community legislation must be clear and predictable for those who are subject to it."[41]

Measures taken by the Commission under powers delegated by the Council may be precluded from having retroactive effect at all.[42]

If retroactive effect for administrative and legislative measures is the exception, it is for judicial decisions the rule. Yet, exceptionally, in *Defrenne* v. *Sabena*[43] the Court held that legal certainty precluded the retroactive effect of its ruling that Article 119 of the Treaty was directly effective. In *Defrenne*, the Court took into account "the conduct of several of the Member States and the views adopted by the Commission and repeatedly brought to the notice of the circles concerned" and noted that "the fact that, in spite of the warnings given, the Commission did not initiate

---

[37] [1979] E.C.R. 69 at p. 84. And see Case 84/81, *Staple Dairy Products* [1982] E.C.R. 1763 at p. 1777; Case 108/81, *Amylum* [1982] E.C.R. 3107 at p. 3130. A regulation is deemed to be published throughout the Community on the date appearing on the issue of the *Official Journal* containing the text of the regulation, unless the date of actual issue was later, Case C–337/88, *SAFA* [1990] E.C.R. I–1.

[38] Case 99/78 [1979] E.C.R. 101.

[39] [1979] E.C.R. 101 at p. 111. See also Case 276/80, *Pedana* [1982] E.C.R. 517 at p. 541; Case 258/80, *Rumi* [1982] E.C.R. 487 at p. 503. Thus a public statement of intention to alter monetary compensatory amounts justifies a later regulation altering the rates retrospectively to the earlier date, see Case 338/85, *Pardini* [1988] E.C.R. 2041 at p. 2078, paras. 24–26.

[40] Cases 212–217/80 [1981] E.C.R. 2735.

[41] [1981] E.C.R. 2735 at p. 2751.

[42] Case 77/71, *Gervais-Danone* [1971] E.C.R. 1127; Case 158/78, *Biegi* [1979] E.C.R. 1103; Case 196/80, *Anglo-Irish Meat* [1981] E.C.R. 2263. These cases probably turn on the nature of the rules in question rather than on the fact of delegation.

[43] Case 43/75, *Defrenne* [1976] E.C.R. 455. See *supra*, p. 63.

proceedings under Article 169 against the Member States concerned. . . was likely to consolidate the incorrect impression as to the effects of Article 119."[44] The Court has subsequently stressed the exceptional nature of a ruling on the interpretation of Community law having only prospective effect, and has rarely ruled to this effect.[45] In *Maizena*[46] the Court rejected the argument that inaction by the Commission in the face of conduct of the Federal Republic of Germany contrary to Community law could give rise to legitimate expectation in a trader as follows:

> "A practice of a Member State which does not conform to Community rules may never give rise to legal situations protected by Community law and this is so even where the Commission has failed to take the necessary action to ensure that the State in question correctly applies the Community rules."[47]

Nevertheless, delay in requiring a Member State to order the refund of an unlawful state aid may establish a legitimate expectation in a trader that no refund will be ordered.[48]

The Court has been ready to modify the temporal effect of judgments determining the invalidity of regulations, where legal certainty so required. It is the principle of legal certainty which underlies Article 174 of the Treaty, which allows the Court of Justice to determine which of the legal effects of a regulation declared to be void by the Court shall be considered as definitive. On the basis of this same principle, the Court of Justice has in a number of cases applied Article 174 by analogy in preliminary rulings on invalidity under Article 177 of the Treaty, denying retroactivity to its decisions.[49] The application of the principle in a direct action for annulment is strikingly illustrated in *Simmenthal*,[50] in which the Court annulled a Commission decision fixing the minimum selling prices for frozen beef put up for sale by intervention agencies. However, "for reasons of legal certainty and taking special account of the established rights of the participants in the invitation to tender whose tenders have been accepted"[51] the Court ruled that the annulment must be restricted to the specific decision to reject the applicant's tender which stemmed from the decision in question.

Respect for vested rights is itself an aspect of the principles of legal certainty and legitimate expectation. In *Rossi*[52] the Court stressed that:

> "The Community rules could not, in the absence of an express

[44] [1976] E.C.R. 455 at p. 473.
[45] See, *e.g.* Case 61/79, *Denkavit Italiana* [1980] E.C.R. 1205 at p. 1223; Case 826/79, *Mireco* [1980] E.C.R. 2559 at p. 2573.
[46] Case 5/82 [1982] E.C.R. 4601. And see Case 316/86, *Krucken* [1988] E.C.R. 2213 at p. 2239, para. 23.
[47] [1982] E.C.R. 4601 at p. 4615.
[48] Case 223/85, *RSV v. Commission* [1987] E.C.R. 4617.
[49] Case 4/79, *Providence Agricole* [1980] E.C.R. 2883 at p. 2853; Case 109/79, *Maizeries de Beauce* [1980] E.C.R. 2883 at p. 2913; Case 145/79, *Roquette* [1980] E.C.R. 2917 at p. 2946; Case 41/184, *Pinna* [1986] E.C.R. 1.
[50] Case 92/78 [1979] E.C.R. 777.
[51] [1979] E.C.R. 777 at p. 811.
[52] Case 100/78 [1979] E.C.R. 831.

exception consistent with the aims of the Treaty, be applied in such a way as to deprive a migrant worker or his dependents of the benefit of a part of the legislation of a Member State."[53]

Yet the principle cannot be stretched too far. Vested interests are not to be equated with vested rights, and cannot insulate traders from changes in the law. As the Court explained in *Eridania*[54]:

"... an undertaking cannot claim a vested right to the maintenance of an advantage which it obtained from the establishment of a common organisation of the market and which it enjoyed at a given time."[55]

The principle of legitimate expectation operates to protect individuals where they have acted in reliance upon measures taken by the Community institutions. Thus if an undertaking purchases grain for denaturing with a view to qualifying for a Community subsidy, it is not permissible to discontinue or reduce the subsidy without giving the interested party a reasonable opportunity of denaturing the grain in question at the old rate.[56] Again, if the Community induces prudent traders to omit to cover their transactions against exchange risks, by establishing a system of compensatory amounts which in practice eliminate such risks, it must not withdraw such payments with immediate effect, without providing appropriate transitional measures.[57] Similar reasoning protected certain former Community officials in receipt of pensions which had increased in value over a number of years as a result of the Council's failure to adjust the exchange rates used to calculate the amounts due. The Council sought to rectify the situation and phase out the advantages which had accrued over a ten-month period. The Court held that respect for the legitimate expectations of those concerned required a transitional period twice as long as that laid down by the Council.[58] Where Community or national subsidies are paid to undertakings in contravention of Community law, the question arises whether the protection of legitimate expectation precludes recovery. This may well be the case, unless the beneficiary was in a position to appreciate that the aid in question was granted in contravention of mandatory provisions of Community law.[59]

(c) *Equality*

A further principle binding upon the Community in its administrative and legislative activities is the principle of equality, whereby comparable

---

[53] [1979] E.C.R. 831 at p. 844.
[54] Case 230/78 [1979] E.C.R. 2749.
[55] [1979] E.C.R. 2749 at p. 2768.
[56] Case 48/74, *Deuka* [1975] E.C.R. 421; Case 5/75, *Deuka* [1975] E.C.R. 759.
[57] Case 74/74, *C.N.T.A.* [1975] E.C.R. 533. And prudent traders are deemed to know the content of the *Official Journal*, see Case C–174/89, *Hoche* [1990] E.C.R. I–2681 at p. 2713, para. 35.
[58] Case 127/80, *Grogan* [1982] E.C.R. 869; Case 164/80, *De Pascale* [1982] E.C.R. 909; Case 167/80, *Curtis* [1982] E.C.R. 931.
[59] Cases 205–215/82, *Deutsche Milchkontor* [1983] E.C.R. 2633 at p. 2669, para. 30; Case C–5/89, *Commission* v. *Germany* [1990] E.C.R. I–3437 at p. 3457, para. 14.

situations must not be treated differently and different situations must not be treated in the same way unless such treatment is objectively justified.[60]

The principle applies in the relationship between the Community institutions and its officials. As the Court has stated:

"According to the Court's consistent case law the general principle of equality is one of the fundamental principles of the law of the Community civil service."[61]

On this basis the Court has invalidated differentiation between Community officials on grounds of sex in the payment of expatriation allowances.[62] However, the Community cannot be called to account for inequality in the treatment of its officials for which it is not itself responsible. In *Souasio*[63] it was alleged that a Community dependent child tax allowance paid only once in respect of each child, even where both parents were employed by the Community, was contrary to the principle of equality, since it did not take into account tax allowances which might be claimed by a spouse who did not work for the Community, under national law. The Court rejected this argument:

"The principle of equality does not require account to be taken of possible inequalities which may become apparent because the Community and national systems overlap."[64]

The principle of equality provides a basis for the judicial review of measures adopted by the Community in all its various activities. Thus the Court has invalidated a Regulation which provided substantially more severe criteria for the determination of the origin of cotton yarn than for the determination of the origin of cloth and fabrics.[65] The Court has also required consistency in the Commission's policy of imposing fines upon undertakings for the infringement of production quotas for steel.[66]

The principle of equality has been held to add a gloss to Article 40(3) of the Treaty, which provides that the common organisations of the agricultural markets "shall exclude any discrimination between producers or consumers within the Community." In *Ruckdeschel*[67] and *Moulins*[68] proceedings arose from challenges in national courts to the validity of the Council's action in abolishing production refunds on maize used to make quellmehl and gritz, while continuing to pay refunds on maize used to make starch, a product in competition with both quellmehl and gritz. Producers of the latter product argued that they had been placed at a competitive

[60] Case 106/83, *Sermide* [1984] E.C.R. 4209 at p. 4231, para. 28. See also Case 139/77, *Denkavit* [1978] E.C.R. 1317; Case 106/81, *Kind* [1982] E.C.R. 2885.
[61] Cases 152, etc./81, *Ferrario* [1983] E.C.R. 2357 at p. 2367.
[62] Case 20/71, *Sabbatini* [1972] E.C.R. 345; Case 21/74, *Airola* [1972] E.C.R. 221; see also *Razzouk and Beydoun* [1984] E.C.R. 1509.
[63] Cases 81, 81 and 146/79 [1980] E.C.R. 3557.
[64] [1980] E.C.R. 3557 at p. 3572.
[65] Case 162/82, *Cousin* [1983] E.C.R. 1101.
[66] Case 234/82, *Ferriere di roe Volciano* [1983] E.C.R. 3921.
[67] Cases 117/76 and 16/77 [1977] E.C.R. 1753.
[68] Cases 124/76 and 20/77 [1977] E.C.R. 1795.

disadvantage by the Council's discriminatory, and hence unlawful action. Their pleas were upheld. Referring to Article 40(3) of the Treaty, the Court observed:

> "Whilst this wording undoubtedly prohibits any discrimination between producers of the same product it does not refer in such clear terms to the relationship between different industrial or trade sectors in the sphere of processed agricultural products. This does not alter the fact that the prohibition of discrimination laid down in the aforesaid provision is merely a specific enunciation of the general principle of equality which is one of the fundamental principles of Community law. This principle requires that similar situations shall not be treated differently unless differentiation is objectively justified."[69]

The *Wagner* case[70] affords a helpful illustration of objective criteria justifying differentiation between apparently similar situations. Community rules provided for reimbursement of storage costs in respect of sugar in transit between two approved warehouses situated in the same Member State, but not in respect of sugar in transit between two approved warehouses in different Member States. The Court rejected the argument that this was discriminatory, since the difference in treatment was based on requirements of supervision which could be objectively justified. The Court's ruling is a reminder that the principle of non-discrimination is only infringed by differences in treatment where the Community legislator treats *comparable* situations in different ways.[71] It follows that an allegation of discrimination cannot be based on differences in treatment of products subject to different market organisations which are not in competition with each other.[72]

The principle of equality has also been invoked in the budgetary context,[73] and the "equality of states" has been resorted to as a general principle for the interpretation of the Treaties.[74] It seems that in the Community legal order, the notion of "equality before the law," far from constituting merely an appeal to the better judgment of the legislator, provides a ground for invalidating administrative or legislative action adjudged by the Court either to differentiate arbitrarily between persons in comparable circumstances, or to fail to differentiate between situations which are not truly comparable.

---

[69] [1977] E.C.R. 1753 at p. 1769; [1971] E.C.R. 1795 at p. 1811. And see Case 300/86, *Landschoot* v. *Mera* [1988] E.C.R. 3443; Case C–37/89, *Weiser* [1990] E.C.R. I–2395. The principle applies as between identical or comparable situations, Case T–48/89, *Beltrante* [1990] E.C.R. II–493 at p. 506, para. 34.

[70] Case 8/82 [1983] E.C.R. 271.

[71] See, *e.g.* Case 6/71, *Rheinmuhlen Dusseldorf* [1971] E.C.R. 719; Case 283/83, *Racke* [1984] E.C.R. 3791.

[72] Cases 292 and 293/81, *Jean Lion* [1982] E.C.R. 3887.

[73] Case 265/78, *Ferwerda* [1980] E.C.R. 617.

[74] Case 128/78, *Commission* v. *United Kingdom* [1979] E.C.R. 419 at p. 419; Case 231/78, *Commission* v. *United Kingdom* [1979] E.C.R. 1447 at p. 1462.

(d) *Fundamental rights*

Unlike the abortive Treaty for the establishment of a European Political Community, which provided explicitly for the application of Section I of the European Convention on Human Rights,[75] the Treaty establishing the European Economic Community makes no provision in this regard. Although the circumstances in which Community activities are likely to encroach upon rights generally regarded as fundamental will be rare,[76] the Court has made it clear that there are such rights enshrined in Community law, and that they are capable of limiting the legislative competence of the Community. Thus in *Stauder* v. *City of Ulm*,[77] the Court was asked by the Verwaltungsgericht, Stuttgart, whether a Commission Decision which conditioned the distribution of butter at reduced prices on the disclosure of the name of the recipient was compatable "with the general principles of Community law in force." The Court replied that on its true construction the Decision in question did not require the disclosure of the names of beneficiaries to retailers, and added that: "Interpreted in this way the provision at issue contains nothing capable of prejudicing the fundamental human rights ... protected by the Court."[78] The existence of fundamental Community principles (albeit in the main unspecified) was confirmed in *Internationale Handelsgesellschaft* v. *EVSt*,[79] a request for a ruling on the validity of the import and export licensing system established under the common organisation of the grain market. The grant of licences was conditioned on the lodging of a deposit, which was forfeited in the event of the licence being unused in whole or in part during its period of validity. The Verwaltungsgericht, Frankfurt-am-Main sought the ruling in question because of doubts as to the compatibility of such arrangements with the principles of German constitutional law. The Court denied that the validity of a Community act could be impugned for inconsistency with principles of national constitutional law, however fundamental, but added:

> "However, an examination should be made as to whether or not any analogous guarantee inherent in Community law has been disregarded. In fact, respect for fundamental rights forms an integral part of the general principles of law protected by the Court of Justice. The protection of such rights, whilst inspired by the constitutional traditions common to the Member States, must be ensured within the framework of the structure and objectives of the Community. It must therefore be ascertained ... whether the system of deposits has infringed rights of a fundamental nature, respect for which must be ensured in the Community legal system."[80]

If *Stauder* confirmed the existence of fundamental rights in Community law, and *Internationale Handelsgesellschaft* identified their primary source as

---

[75] See *supra*, p. 6.
[76] Pescatore, (1970) A.J.I.L. 343 at p. 348.
[77] Case 29/69 [1969] E.C.R. 419.
[78] [1969] E.C.R. 419 at p. 425, para. 7.
[79] Case 11/70 [1970] E.C.R. 1125.
[80] [1970] E.C.R. 1125 at p. 1134, para. 4.

the national constitutions of the Member States, *Nold* v. *Commission* introduced a secondary source: "international treaties for the protection of human rights on which the Member States have collaborated or of which they are signatories."[81]

The Court's case-law was endorsed by the Parliament, the Council and the Commission in their Joint Declaration of April 5, 1977.[82] The Declaration notes that the Treaties are based on the principle of respect for the law, and acknowledges that "law" comprises, over and above the rules embodied in the treaties and secondary Community legislation, the general principles of law and in particular the fundamental rights, on which the constitutional law of the Member States is based. The Institutions stress in the Declaration that they attach prime importance to the protection of fundamental rights, as derived in particular from the constitutions of the Member States and the European Convention on Human Rights, and commit themselves to respect for those rights. Furthermore, the preamble to the Single European Act refers to both the European Convention on Human Rights and the European Social Charter. The Treaty on European Union makes reference in Article F simply to the European Convention on Human Rights.

In *Hauer*[83] the Court held that the right to property is guaranteed in the Community legal order in accordance with the ideas common to the constitutions of the Member States, which are reflected in the First Protocol to the European Convention on Human Rights. However, the Court upheld a Community imposed restriction on the planting of vines to constitute as a legitimate exception to the principle of a type recognised in the constitutional systems of the Member States.[84] The Court has denied that the guarantee afforded to the ownership of property can be extended to protect commercial interests, the uncertainties of which are part of the very essence of economic activity.[85]

The Court has referred to specific provisions of the European Convention on Human Rights in a number of judgments. In *National Panasonic*[86] the Court relied upon an exception to the guarantee of respect for private and family life to be found in Article 8 of the European Convention on Human Rights, in considering the scope of the investigative powers of the Commission under Regulation 17.[87] In *Dow Benelux*[88] the Court held that Article 8 applied in Community law to protect the private dwellings of natural persons rather than the premises of undertakings. Nevertheless, the investigative powers of the Commission were subject to the principle of proportionality.[89] In *Kirk*[90] the Court held that the retroactivity of a

---

[81] Case 4/73 [1974] E.C.R. 491 at p. 507, para. 13.
[82] O.J. 1977 C103/1.
[83] Case 44/79 [1979] E.C.R. 3727.
[84] [1979] E.C.R. 3727 at p. 3747.
[85] Case 4/73, *Nold* [1974] E.C.R. 491; Cases 154, etc./78, and 39, etc./79, *Valsabbia* [1980] E.C.R. 907.
[86] Case 136/79 [1980] E.C.R. 2033 at p. 2057.
[87] As to which see *infra* at p. 476.
[88] Case 85/87 [1989] E.C.R. 3137.
[89] [1989] E.C.R. 3137 at p. 3157 at paras. 28–30.
[90] Case 63/83 [1984] E.C.R. 2689.

Community regulation could not have the effect of validating *ex post facto* national measures of a penal nature which imposed penalties for an act which was not punishable at the time it was committed. The Court declared:

> "The principle that penal provisions may not have retroactive effect is one which is common to all the legal orders of the Member States and is enshrined in Article 7 of the European Convention ... as a fundamental right; it takes its place among the general principles of law whose observance is ensured by the Court of Justice."[91]

The above cases support the following propositions. First, for the purpose of applying Article 173 of the Treaty,[92] which provides for the judicial review of Community legislation, and Article 215, which provides for the tortious liability of the Community, certain fundamental rights will be taken into account as part of Community law. Secondly, these rights are to be deduced from the common constitutional principles of the Member States, and from international treaties on which the Member States have collaborated or of which they are signatories. It will be noted that these propositions are exclusively concerned with constraints on Community legislative or executive action, not with restrictions on the activities of Member States.

In *Rutili* v. *French Minister of the Interior*[93] the Court observed that the criterion of proportionality amounted to a specific manifestation of a general principle referred to in various provisions of the European Convention on Human Rights. Apart from highlighting the European Convention as a potential source of the general principles to which the Court will resort, the observation is significant in that the *Rutili* case concerned the legitimacy of State action under Article 48(3) of the Treaty, and it inevitably implied that provisions such as Article 48(3) of the Treaty must be interpreted in the light of the substantive guarantees provided in the European Convention on Human Rights. That this is indeed the case is demonstrated by *Elliniki Radiophonia Tileorassi*,[94] in which the Court held that the limitations imposed on the power of the Member States to apply the public policy proviso in Articles 66 and 56 of the EEC Treaty were to be appraised in light of the general principle of freedom of expression embodied in Article 10 of the European Convention on Human Rights.

Article 5 of the Treaty requires Member States to take all "appropriate" measures to fulfil the obligations arising out of the Treaty or the acts of the institutions. It would seem to follow that whenever a Member State takes action in fulfilment of a Community obligation, its action must be proportional, it must respect the principle of legal certainty, and it must conform with those fundamental rights which find expression in the general principles of Community law. The Court has held that in implementing directives, the Member States are obliged to use the most appropriate means.[95] And the Court has indicated that this obligation entails respect for

---

[91] [1984] E.C.R. 2689 at p. 2718.
[92] And of course Arts. 177 and 184.
[93] Case 36/75 [1975] E.C.R. 1219.
[94] Case C-260/89, *Elliniki Radiophonia Tileorassi*, [1991] E.C.R. I-2925.
[95] Case 48/75, *Royer* [1976] E.C.R. 497.

the general principles of law.[96] It follows that a similar obligation exists in respect of regulations, decisions, and provisions of the Treaty. In *Eridania*[97] the Court held that the general principles of Community law are binding on all authorities entrusted with the implementation of Community provisions. And in *Zuckerfabrik*, the Court examined whether national rules implementing a regulation laying down common rules for the denaturing of sugar for animal feed were consistent with "superior rules of Community law, in particular with the principles of legal certainty and proportionality. . . ."[98] In *Klensch*,[99] the Court held that where Community rules leave Member States to choose between various methods of implementation of Community law, the Member States must comply with the principle of non-discrimination.

An important decision on the applicability of general principles of Community law to national authorities when they implement Community rules is that in the *Wachauf* case.[1] Under Community regulations concerned with milk quotas it was provided that the milk quota should be transferred when the holding to which the quota related was transferred. A producer acquired a quota in the first place by virtue of his having produced milk during the applicable reference year. The issue in *Wachauf* was whether a transfer of quota from lessee to lessor on the expiry of a lease in accordance with the applicable regulation would be consistent with the general principles of Community law where it had been the lessee's milk production which had secured entitlement to the milk quota. The Court of Justice referred to the *Hauer* case for the applicability of fundamental rights in the Community system, subject to such proportional restrictions as might be imposed in the general interest. The Court stated:

> "Having regard to those criteria, it must be observed that Community rules which, upon the expiry of the lease, had the effect of depriving the lessee, without compensation, of the fruits of his labour and of his investments in the tenanted holding would be incompatible with the requirements of the protection of fundamental rights in the Community legal order. Since those requirements are also binding on the Member States when they implement Community rules, the Member States must, as far as possible, apply those rules in accordance with those requirements."[2]

It is interesting to note that the Court, rather than invalidating the Community transfer rules by reference to the general principles of law, upheld the Community rules but held that the national authorities must secure respect for the fundamental rights in question. In the view of the Court of Justice, the regulations in question left the competent national authorities a sufficiently wide margin of appreciation to enable them to

---

[96] Case 5/83, *Rienks* [1983] E.C.R. 4233 at p. 4245.
[97] Case 230/78 [1979] E.C.R. 2749 at p. 2771, para. 31.
[98] Case 77/81 [1982] E.C.R. 681 at pp. 694, 695.
[99] Case 202/85 [1986] E.C.R. 3477 at p. 3508, paras. 10, 11.
[1] Case 5/88 [1989] E.C.R. 2609.
[2] [1989] E.C.R. at p. 2639, para. 19.

apply those rules in a manner consistent with the protection of fundamental rights, either by giving the lessee the opportunity of keeping all or part of the milk quota if he intended to continue milk production, or by compensating him if he undertook to abandon milk production.[3]

Other principles

The categories of general principles which the Court will uphold do not appear to be closed. In *Transocean Marine Paint*[4] the Court resorted to the general principle that a person whose interests are affected by a decision taken by a public authority must be given an opportunity to make his point of view known. In a subsequent staff case,[5] the Court referred to:

"... a general principle of good administration to the effect that an administration which has to take decisions, even legally, which cause serious detriment to the person concerned, must allow the latter to make known their point of view, unless there is a serious reason for not doing so."[6]

With respect to the relations between the Community and its officials, the Court may take it upon itself to urge consultation, even where this is not legally required. In one case,[7] the Court acknowledged that there was no duty to consult, but added:

"Nevertheless, it is in accordance with the requirements of good faith and mutual confidence, which should characterise the relationship between officials and the administration, that the latter should, as far as possible, put the official in a position to make his point of view on the projected decision known. Such a practice is also likely to prevent legal disputes."[8]

Not all determinations are subject to the requirements of natural justice however. Thus the right to a fair hearing does not extend to the work of a Medical Committee engaged in the medical appraisal of an individual.[9]

The right to be assisted by counsel has been recognised by the Court as a general principle of law. In a staff case[10] the Court held that the refusal of the Commission to allow the applicant's counsel, as well as the applicant, access to the disciplinary file in the course of proceedings which resulted in a disciplinary measure being taken, amounted to a breach of a fundamental legal principle which the Court would uphold. The Court emphasised that

---

[3] [1989] E.C.R. at p. 2640, para. 22.
[4] Case 17/74 [1974] E.C.R. 1063. See also Case 264/82, *Timex* [1985] E.C.R. 849; Case 85/87, *Dow Benelux* [1989] E.C.R. 3137; Case C–49/88, *Al-Jubail Fertiliser*, [1991] E.C.R. I–3187. The principle may be invoked by a Member State as well as by an individual, see Case 259/85, *France* v. *Commission* [1987] E.C.R. 4393.
[5] Cases 33 and 75/79, *Kuhner* [1980] E.C.R. 1677.
[6] [1980] E.C.R. 1671 at p. 1698.
[7] Case 125/80, *Arning* [1981] E.C.R. 2539.
[8] [1981] E.C.R. 2439 at p. 2554.
[9] Case T–154/89, *Vidranyi* [1990] E.C.R. II–455.
[10] Case 115/80, *Demont* [1981] E.C.R. 3147.

respect for the rights of the defence was all the more important when the disciplinary proceedings were likely to result in particularly severe disciplinary measures.[11]

In an important decision,[12] the Court held that Article 14 of Regulation 17,[13] empowering the Commission to require the production of the business records of an undertaking, was subject to the principle that the confidentiality of certain communications between a lawyer and his client was to be protected.[14]

The Court has however refused to accept that the right normally recognised in a natural person not to incriminate himself extends to a legal person in relation to infringements of competition law.[15]

The Court has recognised the existence of a right to exercise a professional activity, subject to those limitations on the exercise of that right which may be justified in the general interest.[16]

The general principles of "good administration" clearly provide fertile ground for judicial development. For example, the Court has stigmatised the failure to respond to a communication as a "neglect of the rules of good administration," and reduced a fine accordingly.[17]

A further principle which has been invoked by the Court as a guide to the construction of secondary legislation is that of Community preference.[18]

---

[11] [1981] E.C.R. 3147 at p. 3158.
[12] Case 155/79, *A. M. & S.* [1982] E.C.R. 1575.
[13] Reg. 17 deals with the power of the Commission to establish violations of Arts. 85 and 86 EEC. See *infra* at p. 472.
[14] Communications between a lawyer and his client are protected providing they are made for the purposes of and in the interests of the client's rights of defence, and that they emanate from independent lawyers, that is, lawyers who are not bound to the client by a relationship of employment.
[15] Case 374/87, *Orkem* [1989] E.C.R. 3283 at p. 3350, paras. 28, 29.
[16] Case 234/85, *Keller* [1986] E.C.R. 2897; Case C–370/88, *Marshall* [1990] E.C.R. I–4071.
[17] Case 179/82, *Lucchini* [1983] E.C.R. 3083 at p. 3095.
[18] Case 6/78, *Union Francaise* [1978] E.C.R. 1695.

CHAPTER 5

THE COURT OF JUSTICE OF THE EUROPEAN COMMUNITIES

The Court of Justice of the European Communities plays a central rôle in the system created by the Treaties. Some of the concepts which are fundamental to the way in which the Community functions are to be found, not in the Treaties themselves, but in the case-law of the Court. Although its decisions have sometimes been controversial, few would deny that the Court has made a vital contribution to the Community's development.

A single Court of Justice was established under the 1957 Convention on Certain Institutions Common to the European Communities.[1] The Court of Justice exercises the jurisdiction enjoyed by the courts for which separate provision was made in the ECSC, EEC and Euratom Treaties.[2] It sits in Luxembourg.[3]

The primary sources of law on the Court of Justice are the Treaties themselves and the Statutes of the Court, which are annexed as Protocols to each of them.[4] Detailed effect is given to the Statutes by the Rules of Procedure of the Court (hereafter "the Rules"). The Rules are adopted by the Court itself but they require the unanimous approval of the Council.[5] The existence of Supplementary Rules and Instructions to the Registrar may also be noted.[6]

The organisation of the Court

(a) *The Members*

The Court of Justice consists of 13 Judges[7] and is assisted by six Advocates General.[8] The Judges and Advocates General are sometimes referred to collectively as the Members of the Court. The general function of a Judge needs no explanation. The distinctive rôle played by the Advocate General in the judicial process of the Court is considered below.

Judges and Advocates General "rank equally in precedence according to

---

[1] The other institutions concerned were the European Parliament and the Economic and Social Committee.
[2] See Art. 3 of the Convention.
[3] Although sometimes referred to as "the European Court" (see, *e.g.* the European Communities Act 1972), the Court of Justice should not be confused with the European Court of Human Rights, which sits in Strasbourg, France, and which is not an institution of the European Community.
[4] The Statutes are practically identical. Unless the context indicates otherwise, references hereafter are to the EEC Statute.
[5] See Art. 188 EEC and Art. 44 of the Statute.
[6] These instruments are published by the Office for Official Publications of the European Communities, together with certain other materials, in a volume entitled *Selected Instruments relating to the Organization, Jurisdiction and Procedure of the Court*, which is updated periodically. The Rules are also published at O.J. 1991 L176/7 and [1991] 3 C.M.L.R. 745.
[7] Art. 165 EEC.
[8] Art. 166 EEC.

their seniority in office."[9] The rules relating to their appointment are the same. Thus, according to Article 167 EEC, they must be "persons whose independence is beyond doubt and who possess the qualifications required for appointment to the highest judicial offices in their respective countries or who are jurisconsults of recognized competence." The term "jurisconsult," at least in the English version of the Treaty,[10] is wide enough to cover lawyers in private practice and academic lawyers, even where they are not eligible for appointment to the Bench at home. In practice, the Members of the Court have come from a variety of backgrounds, including the national judiciary, the civil service, the Bar and the academic world.[11] A President of the Court[12] has suggested[13] that a Member's professional background can have at least as significant an influence on his approach to a case as his national origin.

According to Article 167 EEC, the Members of the Court are appointed "by common accord of the Governments of the Member States for a term of six years," which is renewable. It is worth emphasising that the Members are not appointed by the Council of Ministers or by any single Member State.[14] This means that a Member's appointment can in theory be blocked by any of the Member States.

There is nothing in the Treaties about the national composition of the Court. In practice, however, one Judge is appointed from each Member State, the 13th post[15] being held by nationals of the five larger States[16] in turn. There is one Advocate General from the four largest Member States,[17] while the fifth and sixth posts rotate among the eight smaller Member States.[18]

The judicial business and the administration of the Court are directed by the President, who is elected by the Judges from among their own number for a term of three years. He may be re-elected.[19] The President presides at hearings and deliberations of the full Court,[20] fixes or extends the time limits for the lodging of pleadings and deals with most applications for

---

[9] Rules, Art. 6. Where there is equal seniority in office, precedence is determined by age. On two occasions, Judges have subsequently become Advocates General (Trabucchi in 1973 and Capotorti in 1976). Advocates General have twice become Judges (Mancini and Slynn in 1988).

[10] K. P. E. Lasok points out that, in some language versions, it is possible to argue that the term "jurisconsult" means a professional legal adviser and not simply a person learned in the law: *The European Court of Justice: Practice and Procedure* (1984), p. 5.

[11] For more information on the backgrounds of the Members of the Court, see Brown and Jacobs, *The Court of Justice of the European Communities* (3rd. ed., 1989), pp. 47–52 and 61–63; Lecourt, "La Cour de Justice des Communautés européennes vue de l'intérieur" in Grewe, Rupp and Schneider (eds.), *Europäische Gerichtsbarkeit und Nationale Verfassungsgerichtsbarkeit: Festschrift zum 70. Geburtstag von Hans Kutscher*, 261 at p. 263.

[12] Judge Ole Due of Denmark, who, before his appointment to the Court, held a number of posts in the Danish Ministry of Justice.

[13] In an interview broadcast on BBC radio on May 18, 1990.

[14] A point made by Slynn, Lasok and Millett in Vaughan (ed.), *Law of the European Communities*, para. 2.05.

[15] Which prevents the full Court from being evenly divided. The Court's decision-making process is discussed below.

[16] France, Germany, Italy, Spain and the United Kingdom.

[17] The States mentioned above with the exception of Spain.

[18] *i.e.* including Spain.

[19] See Art. 167 EEC and Art. 7 of the Rules.

[20] Rules, Art. 8.

interlocutory relief. He also appoints a Judge Rapporteur in each case[21] with responsibility for managing the case as it progresses through the various stages of the Court's procedure. The Judge Rapporteur's principal task is the drafting of the judgment.

As soon as the Judge Rapporteur has been designated by the President, an Advocate General is assigned to each case by the First Advocate General.[22] The office of First Advocate General rotates annually among the Advocates General.

(b) *The rôle of the Advocate General*[23]

The model before the minds of those who decided to endow the Court of Justice with Advocates General is believed to have been the *commissaire du gouvernement* in the procedure of the French Conseil d'Etat.[24] However, commentators are agreed that the office, as it has developed in the unique context provided by the Community Treaties, must be regarded as *sui generis*.[25]

An Advocate General is not a Judge but his rôle is, in a broad sense, judicial. After the parties have concluded their submissions, and before the Judges begin their deliberation, the Advocate General presents an independent and impartial Opinion on the case. The Opinion is fully reasoned, in the manner of a reserved judgment in the higher English courts. It sets out any relevant facts and legislation, discusses the issues that have been raised, situating them in the envolving pattern of the Court's case-law, and recommends a decision to the Judges. There is good reason to believe that a persuasive Opinion will strongly influence the subsequent deliberation.[26] Certainly, in the majority of cases the judgment and its rationale follow the Advocate General fairly closely, but it is an important safeguard that, even where the Court of Justice sits as a court of first and last resort, its decisions are in effect judicially considered twice over. Nor is the impact of an Opinion limited to the case in which it is given. It will be published alongside the judgment in the European Court Reports and may

---

[21] Rules, Art. 9(2).
[22] Rules, Art. 10(2).
[23] See Dashwood, (1982) 2 Legal Studies 202.
[24] See further Barav, (1974) Revue Internationale de Droit Comparé 809; Gori, (1976) C.D.E. 375; Borgsmidt, (1988) 13 E.L.Rev. 106; Condorelli-Braun in Rideau *et al.* (eds.), *La France et les Communautés Européennes* (1975), p. 455.
[25] This was the view taken by A. G. Warner in an unpublished lecture on "The rôle of the Advocate General at the European Court of Justice," delivered in Luxembourg on November 19, 1976. The same conclusion is reached by Gori, *loc. cit.* at p. 393. See also Vandersanden and Barav, *Contentieux Communautaire* (1977) at p. 16.
[26] An important witness is Mr. Robert Lecourt, a former President of the Court, whose speech of farewell on the occasion of the retirement of A. G. Roemer included this passage:
"Pour avoir une idée vraie du rôle des conclusions, c'est au délibéré qu'il faut avoir accès. On y decouvrirait l'intérêt de cet ultime répit entre le débat de l'audience et la médiation du juge et l'utile décantation de conflit judiciare qui en résulte. On y apprécierait qu'une voix autorisée et libre, s'élevant au-dessus des parties, ait pu analyser avec le recul nécessaire l'argumentation de chacune et pris le risque de porter sur le litige un premier jugement. On relèverait, enfin, l'importance de cette tension de l'esprit que provoque, en chaque juge, des orientations qui alimenteront les éventuelles confrontations du délibéré, en l'absence de votre personne, mais non dans le silence de votre voix."
The speech was delivered at the ceremonial sitting of the Court held on October 9, 1973.

be cited as authority by counsel or Advocates General in future cases, or in legal literature.

According to Article 166 EEC, the Advocate General must "... make, in open court, reasoned submissions on cases brought before the Court of Justice. ..." Under Article 18 of the Statute, the delivery of the Opinion marks the last stage of the *oral* procedure. For many years, either the complete text or extracts of Opinions were read out in public before the appropriate formation of the Court. This was a time-consuming process of little apparent value. The Court accordingly decided at its administrative meeting of July 11, 1990 that, unless an Advocate General wished to read out his entire Opinion in public, the normal practice would be for the recommendation at the end of the Opinion only to be read out. This is usually done prior to the hearing in another case by the Advocate General to whom that case has been assigned rather than by the author of the Opinion. Whether the new practice is compatible with Article 166 of the Treaty may be a moot point, but there is no doubt that it has enabled the Court to streamline its procedures without any apparent reduction in the influence of the Advocates General.[27]

(c) *Chambers*

The Court of Justice may decide cases either in plenary session (where the quorum is seven Judges)[28] or in Chambers of three or five Judges.[29] The Chambers are reconstituted, and their Presidents elected, on a yearly basis.[30]

The Treaties currently provide that cases brought by a Member State or by a Community institution must be heard by the full Court.[31] The types of case that may be assigned to Chambers are identified in Article 95 of the Rules. The include appeals against decisions of the Court of First Instance[32] and references for preliminary rulings, as well as actions for annulment, for failure to act or for damages[33] where the applicant is a private party. A case falling within one of these categories will be assigned to a Chamber "in so far as the difficulty or the importance of the case or particular circumstances are not such as to require that the Court decide it in plenary session."[34] However, a Member State or a Community institution which is a party to such a case has the right to insist upon trial by the full Court.[35] It should be noted that a party may not apply for a change in the composition of the Court

---

[27] The fears of some that the Opinion would become just another document among the mountain of paper received by the Judges seem to have proved unfounded.
[28] Statute, Art. 15.
[29] Art. 165 EEC.
[30] Rules, Art. 10.
[31] Art. 165 EEC.
[32] See the next chapter.
[33] These types of proceedings are discussed below.
[34] Rules, Art. 95(1)
[35] Rules, Art. 95(2). A Member State or Community institution counts as a "party" for this purpose where it intervenes in a direct action or submits written observations in a reference for a preliminary ruling.

or of one of its Chambers on the grounds of the nationality of a Judge or the absence of a Judge of the nationality of that party.[36]

The establishment of the Court of First Instance has resulted in the transfer to that body of many cases which would previously have been assigned to a Chamber of the Court of Justice.[37] The result under the current rules is that, while the workload of the Court of Justice continues to expand, the Chambers are relatively under-used. The Treaty on European Union would therefore replace Article 165 with a new text, the third paragraph of which would read: "The Court of Justice shall sit in plenary session when a Member State or a Community institution that is a party to the proceedings so requests." In the absence of such a request, the Court would no longer be required to sit in plenary session.

(d) *Language*

The language in which a case is conducted may be any one of the Communities' nine official languages as well as Irish.[38] The general rule is that the choice of language lies with the applicant.[39] However, where the defendant is a Member State or a natural or legal person having the nationality of a Member State, the language of the case is the official language of that State.[40] In references for preliminary rulings, it is the language of the referring court.[41] In direct actions, that is, actions which start and finish in the Court of Justice, the Court has the power, at the request of one of the parties, to authorise another procedural language to be used for all or part of the proceedings. Such a request may not be made by the Community institutions, as they are expected to be able to operate in all the procedural languages.[42] There is no express provision for the Court to authorise the use of a language other than that of the referring court in proceedings for a preliminary ruling. In practice, however, the Court may allow another language to be used at the hearing if none of the parties to the main action objects.[43]

The submissions of the parties, both written and oral, must be made in the language of the case and supporting documents must be either in that language or accompanied by a translation.[44] The Member States may use their own official languages when intervening in a case or taking part in a reference for a preliminary ruling.[45] The Registrar of the Court arranges for translation into the language of the case.

Inside the Court itself French is the working language, although English is now used a good deal. At hearings, Members of the Court are entitled to put

---

[36] Statute, Art. 16.
[37] For example, disputes between the Community institutions and their employees, which were previously assigned automatically to Chambers of three Judges.
[38] Rules, Art. 29(1).
[39] Rules, Art. 29(2).
[40] Rules, Art. 29(2)(a).
[41] Rules, Art. 29(2).
[42] Rules, Art. 29(2)(c).
[43] See Lasok, *op. cit.* p. 27.
[44] Rules, Art. 29(3).
[45] Rules, Art. 29(3). For the right to intervene, see Art. 37 of the Statute; Lasok, *op. cit.* Chap. 5; Usher, *European Court Practice* (1983), Chap. 11.

questions to the parties in any of the Court's procedural languages.[46] The Advocates General draft their Opinions in their own languages.[47]

(e) *Deliberation and judgment*

Once the Advocate General has delivered his Opinion, the Court begins its deliberations.[48] The process of reaching a decision is usually conducted in French. The authentic version of the judgment in the language of the case, if it is one other than French, will therefore be a translation.

An attempt is usually made to reach a consensus on the outcome. Every Judge taking part in the deliberations is obliged to give his view and the reasons for it and to cast a vote.[49] The final decision on a case is, if necessary, taken by majority vote,[50] but all the Judges who took part in the deliberations are required to sign the judgment.[51] There are no dissenting judgments. Moreover, under Article 32 of the Statute, the deliberations of the Court take place in secret. Only the Judges taking part attend.

Two reasons are usually put forward to justify the collegiate nature of the Court's judgments. The first is that, as a young judicial institution, the Court needed to build up its authority by presenting a united front to the world. The second is that anonymity protects the Judges from the various forms of political pressure to which they might otherwise be subject. Those seem on balance to be good and sufficient reasons, although the resulting judgment may perhaps have the look of a "committee" document, lacking in elegance and occasionally even in coherence.

Article 64(1) of the Rules requires that judgments be delivered in open court. However, to save time it is only the short operative part of the judgment that is read out. This is done in the language of the case.

The jurisdiction of the Court

The Court's general task is laid down in Article 164 EEC, which provides that "The Court of Justice shall ensure that in the interpretation and application of this Treaty the law is observed." The Treaty then sets out a number of more detailed provisions which confer on the Court specific heads of jurisdiction. The most important of those provisions will now be examined.

(a) *Enforcement actions against Member States*

One of the novel features of the Community legal order is the power given to the Commission to supervise compliance by the Member States with their

---

[46] Rules, Art. 29(5).
[47] See Rules, Art. 29(5).
[48] See further Lecourt, *loc. cit.* pp. 264–265.
[49] Rules, Art. 27.
[50] Rules, Art. 27(5).
[51] Rules, Art. 64(2). See also Art. 63 of the Rules and Art. 33 of the Statute.

obligations under the Treaties.[52] As far as the EEC Treaty is concerned, that power derives principally from Article 169,[53] which provides as follows:

> "If the Commission considers that a Member State has failed to fulfil an obligation under this Treaty, it shall deliver a reasoned opinion on the matter after giving the State concerned the opportunity to submit its observations.
>
> If the State concerned does not comply with the opinion within the period laid down by the Commission, the latter may bring the matter before the Court of Justice."

Article 169 is complemented by Article 170 EEC, the first paragraph of which provides that "A Member State which considers that another Member State has failed to fulfil an obligation under this Treaty may bring the matter before the Court of Justice." A Member State wishing to institute proceedings under this provision must first bring the matter before the Commission, which is required to deliver a reasoned opinion on the matter "after each of the States concerned has been given the opportunity to submit its own case and its observations on the other party's case both orally and in writing." The applicant State may then refer the matter to the Court, regardless of whether the respondent State complies with the reasoned opinion.[54] The first State may also bring the matter before the Court if the Commission does not deliver an opinion within three months of the date on which the matter was brought before it.

In practice, the Member States have shown a marked reluctance to commence proceedings under Article 170, only one case having proceeded to judgment under that provision at the time of writing.[55] The Member States evidently prefer to rely on the Commission to act under Article 169, sometimes intervening in its support when the matter is brought before the Court.

Articles 169 and 170 both speak of failure to fulfil "an obligation under this Treaty." This expression covers, in addition to the Treaty itself, provisions contained in the Treaties of Accession and legislative acts adopted by the Community institutions. It seems that it also covers agreements concluded by the Community with non-member States or international organisations, for according to Article 228(2) EEC, such agreements "shall be binding . . . on Member States."[56] It should be noted, however, that the right to bring proceedings under Articles 169 and 170 in respect of the obligations of the

---

[52] The most detailed examination is to be found in Audretsch, *Supervision in European Community Law* (2nd ed., 1986). For shorter accounts, see Brown and Jacobs, *op. cit.* Chap. 6; Dashwood and White, "Enforcement Actions under Articles 169 and 170 EEC" (1989) 14 E.L.Rev. 388; Hartley, *The Foundations of European Community Law* (2nd ed., 1988), Chap. 10.

[53] An expedited procedure is applicable in the context of State aid under the second para. of Art. 93(2) EEC.

[54] See further Hartley, *op. cit.* p. 305.

[55] Case 141/78, *France* v. *United Kingdom* [1979] E.C.R. 2923.

[56] *Cf.* Case 104/81, *Hauptzollamt Mainz* v. *Kupferberg* [1982] E.C.R 3641; Case 181/73, *Haegeman* v. *Belgium* [1974] E.C.R. 449. It is less clear whether conventions concluded by the Member States under Art. 220 EEC are covered: see Hartley, *op. cit.* pp. 286–287; Dashwood and White, *loc. cit.* p. 390.

Member States under the Treaty on European Union with regard to government deficits would be restricted by Article 104c(10).

Article 169 may be contrasted with Article 88 ECSC, which gives the Commission power to record in a binding decision the failure of the State concerned to fulfil its obligations. That State may then challenge the Commission's decision before the Court.

The procedure laid down in Article 169 falls into two distinct phases, the administrative phase (or pre-litigation procedure, as it is sometimes called in the Court's decisions) and the judicial phase.

The administrative phase

The administrative phase corresponds to the first paragraph of Article 169, which requires the Commission to take two steps: it must give the State concerned "the opportunity to submit its observations" and then, if it is still not satisfied, it must consider whether to "deliver a reasoned opinion on the matter." The purpose of this phase of the procedure, "which comes within the general scope of the supervisory task entrusted to the Commission under the first indent of Article 155 is, in the first place, to give the Member State an opportunity to justify its position and, as the case may be, to enable the Commission to persuade the Member State to comply of its own accord with the requirements of the Treaty. If this attempt to reach a settlement is unsuccessful, the function of the reasoned opinion is to define the subject-matter of the dispute."[57]

In practice, when the Commission becomes aware of a possible breach of Community law by a Member State, it will raise the matter on an informal basis through the Permanent Representative of the State concerned in Brussels. Discussions may then take place between officials of the Commission and the national authorities. If the Commission is not satisfied that Community law is being respected, it may decide to send to the Member State a letter of formal notice. That letter represents the first formal step in the procedure laid down in Article 169 and gives the Member State the opportunity to submit its observations on the matter, although the Member State is not obliged to avail itself of the opportunity.[58] The purpose of the letter of formal notice is "to delimit the subject-matter of the dispute and to indicate to the Member State which is invited to submit its observations the factors enabling it to prepare its defence." It constitutes "an essential formal requirement of the procedure under Article 169."[59] The Commission is required to allow the Member State a reasonable period in which to reply to the letter of formal notice. What is reasonable depends on the circumstances of the case, but very short periods may sometimes be justified, particularly where there is an urgent need to remedy a breach or where the Member

---

[57] Joined Cases 142 and 143/80, *Amministrazione delle Finanze dello Stato* v. *Essevi and Salengo* [1981] E.C.R. 1413, para. 15.
[58] See Case 211/81, *Commission* v. *Denmark* [1982] E.C.R. 4547, para. 9.
[59] *Ibid.* paras. 8 and 9.

State concerned was aware of the Commission's view before the procedure started.[60]

The letter of formal notice may lead to a further round of discussion between the Commission and the Member State concerned in an attempt to reach a settlement. If this does not prove possible, the Commission may decide to deliver a reasoned opinion on the matter. Although the Treaty uses the word "shall" in this context, it seems that the Commission is not obliged to take this step. In the first place, the Commission may only deliver a reasoned opinion where it "considers" that a Member State is in breach of Community law, which involves an essentially discretionary assessment. Secondly, the second paragraph of Article 169 makes it clear that, even if the Member State concerned fails to comply with the reasoned opinion, the Commission is not obliged, but merely empowered, to bring the matter before the Court.[61] There would therefore have been little point in imposing on the Commission an obligation to deliver a reasoned opinion whenever it took the view that a Member State was in breach of its obligations under the Treaty.[62]

The reasoned opinion should contain "a coherent statement of the reasons which led the Commission to believe that the State in question has failed to fulfil an obligation under the Treaty."[63] Since the reasoned opinion defines the scope of the proceedings, any subsequent application by the Commission to the Court must be founded on the same grounds and submissions. The Court will not consider a complaint that was not formulated in the reasoned opinion.[64] Although the reasoned opinion must be preceded by a letter inviting the Member State concerned to submit its observations, it need not simply repeat the contents of that letter. The Court has said that "there is nothing to prevent the Commission from setting out in detail in the reasoned opinion the complaints which it has already made more generally in its initial letter. Indeed, the reply to that letter may give rise to a fresh consideration of those complaints."[65]

In an early case, Advocate General Lagrange said that the reasoned opinion "must inform the government of the State of the measures which the Commission considers necessary to bring the failure to an end."[66] It must also lay down a deadline for compliance by the Member State.[67] That deadline determines the relevant date for the purposes of any subsequent proceedings before the Court,[68] for compliance with its obligations by the Member State concerned after the deadline has passed does not prevent the Commission from bringing the matter before the Court. The Court has said that the Commission retains an interest in continuing with a case in these

---

[60] Case 293/85, *Commission* v. *Belgium* [1988] E.C.R. 305, para. 14.
[61] See Case 247/87, *Star Fruit* v. *Commission* [1989] E.C.R. 291, paras. 11 and 12.
[62] See further Evans, "The Enforcement Procedure of Article 169 EEC: Commission Discretion" (1979) 4 E.L.Rev. 442; Dashwood and White, *loc. cit.* pp. 398–399.
[63] Case 325/82, *Commission* v. *Germany* [1984] E.C.R. 777, para. 8.
[64] See, *e.g.* Case 186/85, *Commission* v. *Belgium* [1987] E.C.R. 2029, para. 13.
[65] Case 74/82, *Commission* v. *Ireland* [1984] E.C.R. 317, para. 20.
[66] Case 7/61, *Commission* v. *Italy* [1961] E.C.R. 317, 334.
[67] See the second para. of Art. 169.
[68] See, *e.g.* Case C–362/90, *Commission* v. *Italy*, judgment of March 31, 1992.

circumstances, since a judgment of the Court "may be of substantive interest as establishing the basis of a responsibility that a Member State can incur as a result of its default, as regards other Member States, the Community or private parties."[69]

As in the case of the letter of formal notice, the Commission must allow the Member State concerned a reasonable period in which to comply with the reasoned opinion. The Court does not have the power to substitute a different period for that laid down by the Commission,[70] but if it considers the period allowed too short, it may dismiss any subsequent application to the Court as inadmissible.[71] Member States are usually allowed a month or two to take the necessary steps. It has been suggested that, "where short notice is given, the Commission will have to show both that the need for action was urgent, and that it had itself acted as soon as it was practically possible to do so."[72]

None of the measures taken by the Commission during the administrative phase of the procedure under Article 169 has binding force. Such measures may not therefore be the subject of annulment proceedings under Article 173 EEC.[73] The legality of those measures may be reviewed only in the context of a subsequent application by the Commission to the Court under Article 169.[74] Moreover, since the Commission enjoys a discretion whether to institute proceedings under Article 169, no action for failure to act under Article 175 EEC lies against it should it decline to do so.[75]

The judicial phase

If the Member State fails to comply with the reasoned opinion within the deadline laid down in it, the Commission has the power to bring the matter before the Court of Justice. The Court has stated in relation to Article 141 Euratom, the terms of which are identical to those of Article 169 EEC, that proceedings before the Court do not have to be instituted within any particular period, "since, by reason of its nature and its purpose, this procedure involves a power on the part of the Commission to consider the most appropriate means and time-limits for the purposes of putting an end to any contraventions of the Treaty."[76] However, the Commission's attitude

---

[69] See Case 39/72, *Commission* v. *Italy* [1973] E.C.R. 101, para. 11; Case C–29/90, *Commission* v. *Greece*, judgment of March 18, 1992, para. 12. On the liability of Member States to private parties for breaches of Community law, see Joined Cases C–6/90 and C–9/90, *Francovich and Bonifaci* v. *Italy*, judgment of November 19, 1991.

[70] Case 28/81, *Commission* v. *Italy* [1981] E.C.R. 2577, para. 6; Case 29/81, *Commission* v. *Italy* [1981] E.C.R. 2585, para. 6.

[71] See, *e.g.* Case 293/85, *Commission* v. *Belgium, supra*, where Belgium was given eight days to reply to the letter of formal notice and 15 days to comply with the reasoned opinion. *Cf.* Case 74/82, *Commission* v. *Ireland* [1984] E.C.R. 317, where Ireland was given five days to amend legislation which had been on the statute book for over 40 years. The Court made it clear that it disapproved of so short a deadline, but declined to rule the application inadmissible.

[72] Dashwood and White, *loc. cit.* p. 398.

[73] Case 48/65, *Lütticke* v. *Commission* [1966] E.C.R. 19. The action for annulment is discussed below.

[74] *Cf.* Joined Cases 76 and 11/69, *Commission* v. *France* [1969] E.C.R. 523, para. 36.

[75] Case 247/87, *Star Fruit* v. *Commission* [1989] E.C.R. 291. The action for failure to act is discussed below.

[76] Case 7/71, *Commission* v. *France* [1971] E.C.R. 1003, para. 5. See also Case 7/68, *Commission* v. *Italy* [1968] E.C.R. 423, 428.

does not affect the Member State's obligations under the Treaty or the rights which individuals may derive from it. These are matters which can only be determined by a judgment of the Court.[77]

If the Commission decides to make an application to the Court, it will be required to prove its allegation that the obligation in question has not been fulfilled. Where a Member State is required by a directive to inform the Commission of the steps taken to comply with it, failure to satisfy that requirement may itself amount to a breach of Community law, but it will not entitle the Commission to assume that no implementing measures have in fact been adopted.[78]

The application must state precisely the grounds on which it is founded and give some indication of their legal and factual basis. It is not enough simply to refer to the letter of formal notice and the reasoned opinion. If the application fails to satisfy these conditions, it will be dismissed by the Court as inadmissible.[79]

If the Commission's application to the Court is successful, the Court will declare that the Member State in question has failed to fulfil its obligations under the Treaty. The Court will specify the act or omission giving rise to the failure, but it has no power to tell the Member State what it must do to remedy the breach or to quash any national measure which it may have found unlawful. The Member State is required by Article 171 of the Treaty "to take the necessary measures to comply with the judgment of the Court of Justice." If it fails to do so, it commits a further breach of its obligations and exposes itself to a second action under Article 169, this time for breach of Article 171. At present, the Court has no power to impose sanctions on the Member State concerned, but, as we shall see, this will change if the Treaty on European Union enters into force.

The effect of the Court's ruling

The Court has said that a ruling against a Member State under Article 169 amounts to "a prohibition having the full force of law on the competent national authorities against applying a national rule recognized as incompatible with the Treaty and, if the circumstances so require, an obligation on them to take all appropriate measures to enable Community law to be fully applied."[80] The Court added in a later case that "by reason solely of the judgment declaring the Member State to be in default, the State concerned is required to take the necessary measures to remedy its default and may not create any impediment whatsoever."[81] Action to comply with the Court's judgment must be commenced as soon as it is delivered and completed as soon as possible.[82]

---

[77] See Joined Cases 142 and 143/80, *Amministrazione delle Finanze dello Stato* v. *Essevi and Salengo* [1981] E.C.R. 1413, paras. 16–18.
[78] See Case 96/81, *Commission* v. *Netherlands* [1982] E.C.R. 1791, paras. 4–6.
[79] See Case C–347/88, *Commission* v. *Greece* [1990] E.C.R. I–4747; Case C–43/90, *Commission* v. *Germany*, judgment of March 13, 1992; Case C–52/90, *Commission* v. *Denmark*, judgment of March 31, 1992.
[80] Case 48/71, *Commission* v. *Italy* [1972] E.C.R. 527, para. 7.
[81] Joined Cases 24 and 97/80 R, *Commission* v. *France* [1980] E.C.R. 1319, para. 16.
[82] See, *e.g.* Joined Cases 227 to 230/85, *Commission* v. *Belgium* [1988] E.C.R. 1, para. 11.

The effect produced by a ruling of the Court of Justice under Article 169 in the legal order of the Member State concerned was considered in *Procureur de la République* v. *Waterkeyn*,[83] where it was held that:

"if the Court finds in proceedings under Articles 169 to 171 of the EEC Treaty that a Member State's legislation is incompatible with the obligations which it has under the Treaty the courts of that State are bound by virtue of Article 171 to draw the necessary inferences from the judgment of the Court. However, it should be understood that the rights accruing to individuals derive, not from that judgment, but from the actual provisions of Community law having direct effect in the internal legal order."

This means that a judgment of the Court under Article 169 does not in itself confer rights on individuals. Such a judgment merely establishes whether or not a given course of conduct by a Member State is compatible with Community law. However, where the Court decides that the Member State is in breach of its obligations under a provision of Community law which produces direct effect, the national courts must draw the appropriate consequences and protect rights claimed by individuals under that provision. The ruling of the Court of Justice under Article 169 establishes conclusively that the provision in question has been breached. Moreover, the Court's ruling in *Francovich and Bonifaci* v. *Italy*[84] makes it clear that a ruling of the Court under Article 169 establishing that a Member State has failed to comply with a provision of Community law, even one that does not have direct effect, may render the State concerned liable to pay compensation to anyone who has thereby suffered loss.

Interim measures

Although the Court has no power under Article 169 to order the State concerned to pursue or refrain from pursuing a particular course of conduct, somewhat anomalously such an order may be made in the context of an application for interim measures[85] under Article 186 EEC.[86] Interim measures are not, however, available in proceedings against a Member State for failure to take the steps necessary to comply with a previous ruling of the Court under Article 169 where the measures sought would merely repeat the substance of the Court's earlier ruling.[87] Moreover, according to the second paragraph of Article 83(1) of the Rules, an application for interim measures under Article 186 EEC "shall be admissible only if it is made by a party to a case before the Court and relates to that case." In proceedings under Article 169, no such application may therefore be made before the Commission has

---

[83] Joined Cases 314 to 316/81 and 83/82 [1982] E.C.R. 4337.
[84] Joined Cases C–6/90 and C–9/90, judgment of November 19, 1991.
[85] Effectively an interlocutory injunction. Interim measures are discussed below.
[86] See Case 61/77 R, *Commission* v. *Ireland* [1977] E.C.R. 937 and 1411 (note in particular the remarks of A. G. Reischl at pp. 953–954); Case 246/89 R, *Commission* v. *United Kingdom* [1989] E.C.R. 3125.
[87] Joined Cases 24 and 97/80 R, *Commission* v. *France* [1980] E.C.R. 1319.

brought the matter before the Court, although both steps may be taken simultaneously.[88]

Defences

In the absence of procedural irregularities, it seems that the only defence to an action under Article 169 is that the Commission's view of what Community law requires, or of what the Member State concerned has done, is incorrect. The Court has been steadfast in refusing to allow Member States to rely on more subjective factors. The importance attached by the Court to compliance by the Member States with their obligations under the Treaty was emphasised in *Commission* v. *Italy*,[89] where it was pointed out that:

> "In permitting Member States to profit from the advantages of the Community, the Treaty imposes on them also the obligation to respect its rules.
>
> For a state unilaterally to break, according to its own conception of national interest, the equilibrium between advantages and obligations flowing from its adherence to the Community brings into question the equality of Member States before Community law and creates discriminations at the expense of their nationals, and above all of the nationals of the State itself which places itself outside the Community rules."

Thus, it is no defence that national legislation, although technically incompatible with Community law, is in practice applied in accordance with the requirements of the Treaty. The Court has said that the mere maintenance in force of such legislation "gives rise to an ambiguous state of affairs by maintaining, as regards those subject to the law who are concerned, a state of uncertainty as to the possibilities available to them of relying on Community law."[90]

The need to avoid this type of uncertainty has also led the Court to refuse to allow Member States to rely on the fact that the provisions of Community law which have been breached are directly effective and may therefore be relied on in the national courts, which, in accordance with the doctrine of the primacy of Community law, are required to accord them precedence over inconsistent provisions of national law. The Court has stated that "the primacy and direct effect of the provisions of Community law do not release Member States from their obligation to remove from their domestic legal order any provisions incompatible with Community law. . . ."[91]

Nor can Member States rely on a failure by the Community institutions to comply with their own obligations under the Treaty. In *Commission* v. *Luxembourg and Belgium*,[92] the Court said that "the Treaty is not limited to

---

[88] See, *e.g.* Case 246/89 R, *Commission* v. *United Kingdom, supra.*
[89] Case 39/72 [1973] E.C.R. 101, para. 24.
[90] Case 167/73, *Commission* v. *French Republic* [1974] E.C.R. 359, para. 41. See also Case C–58/90, *Commission* v. *Italy*, judgment of July 25, 1991, para. 12.
[91] Case 104/86, *Commission* v. *Italy* [1988] E.C.R. 1799, para. 12.
[92] Joined Cases 90 and 91/63 [1964] E.C.R. 625, 631.

creating reciprocal obligations between the different natural and legal persons to whom it is applicable . . . [E]xcept where otherwise expressly provided, the basic concept of the Treaty requires that the Member States shall not take the law into their own hands. Therefore the fact that the Council failed to carry out its obligations cannot relieve the defendants from carrying out theirs." The appropriate remedy for a Member State in such circumstances would be a direct action against the institution in question.

Similarly, a Member State may not justify a breach of Community law on the ground that its object was to correct the effects of such a breach by another Member State. The Court made it clear in *Commission* v. *France*[93] that "A Member State cannot under any circumstances unilaterally adopt, on its own authority, corrective measures or measures to protect trade designed to prevent[94] any failure on the part of another Member State to comply with the rules laid down by the Treaty." The Court pointed out that a Member State which considers the action of another Member State incompatible with Community law can take action at the political level, invite the Commission to bring proceedings against that State under Article 169 or take action itself under Article 170.

Moreover, reservations or statements made by the Member State concerned in the course of the procedure leading to the adoption of an act which is alleged to have been breached will not be taken into account by the Court, since "the objective scope of rules laid down by the common institutions cannot be modified by reservations or objections which Member States have made at the time the rules were being formulated.[95]

As the Court pointed out in *Commission* v. *Ireland*,[96] "It is well established in the case-law of the Court . . . that a Member State may not plead internal circumstances in order to justify a failure to comply with obligations and time-limits resulting from Community law. Moreover, it has been held on several occasions . . . that practical difficulties which appear at the stage when a Community measure is put into effect cannot permit a Member State unilaterally to opt out of fulfilling its obligations." In particular, the Court has made it clear that the obligations arising from the Treaty "devolve upon States as such and the liability of a Member State under Article 169 arises whatever the agency of the State whose action or inaction is the cause of the failure to fulfil its obligations, even in the case of a constitutionally independent institution."[97]

Thus, it is no defence that draft legislation intended to give effect to the requirements of Community law lapsed due to the dissolution of the national parliament.[98] It appears to follow that proceedings under Article 169 could be brought against a Member State if its courts failed to comply with their

---

[93] Case 232/78 [1979] E.C.R. 2729, para. 9.
[94] [*Sic.*] The French text reads ". . . destinées à obvier à une méconnaissance éventuelle, par un Etat membre, des règles du traité."
[95] Case 39/72, *Commission* v. *Italy* [1973] E.C.R. 101, para. 22. See also Case 38/69, *Commission* v. *Italy* [1970] E.C.R. 47, para. 12.
[96] Case C–39/88 [1990] E.C.R. I–4271, para. 11.
[97] Case 77/69, *Commission* v. *Belgium* [1970] E.C.R. 237, para. 15.
[98] *Ibid.* See also, *e.g.* Case 91/79, *Commission* v. *Italy* [1980] E.C.R. 1099.

obligations under the Treaty.[99] It seems clear, however, that an isolated failure by a national court to apply Community law correctly would not give rise to a right of action. Only a deliberate refusal by a national court to comply with its obligations under the Treaty[1] could have this result. Even then, proceedings under Article 169 might not be desirable.[2]

The question whether Member States may challenge the validity of Community acts in proceedings under Article 169 is considered below.[3]

The effectiveness of proceedings under Article 169

In considering the effectiveness of proceedings under Article 169 in securing compliance by the Member States with their obligations under the Treaty, there is an important preliminary point to be borne in mind. This is that many provisions of Community law produce direct effect and may therefore be relied on in the national courts of the Member States, which are bound to accord them precedence over inconsistent provisions of national law. Thus, even where a Member State has failed to implement a rule of Community law, it may be possible for effect to be given to that rule by the national courts. The Court of Justice is able to exercise a significant measure of control over the way in which Community law is applied by the national courts through the preliminary rulings procedure established by Article 177 EEC. As the Court pointed out in *Van Gend en Loos*,[4] "The vigilance of individuals concerned to protect their rights amounts to an effective supervision in addition to the supervision entrusted by Articles 169 and 170 to the diligence of the Commission and of the Member States."

Of the cases in which the Commission sends a letter of formal notice under Article 169, the vast majority are settled following receipt of that letter by the State concerned or following dispatch by the Commission of the reasoned opinion. In practice, the Commission is even willing to settle some cases after the expiry of the deadline laid down in the reasoned opinion, so that only a small proportion of the cases in which proceedings are instituted proceed to judgment.[5] This suggests that, in many cases, the threat of proceedings under Article 169 is enough to bring recalcitrant Member States to heel.

Of the cases which result in a ruling of the Court adverse to the Member State concerned, most are in due course complied with, although sometimes only after considerable delay. However, since 1985 there has been a marked increase in the number of rulings given by the Court against Member States for breach of Article 171. Until that date, the Court only appears to have

---

[99] This was the view taken by A. G. Warner in Case 9/75, *Meyer-Burckhardt* v. *Commission* [1975] E.C.R. 1171, 1187.
[1] *E.g.* a refusal by a national court against whose decisions there is no judicial remedy under national law to comply with the obligation imposed on it by the third paragraph of Art. 177 EEC.
[2] See Dashwood and White, *loc. cit.* p. 391 and the materials cited there.
[3] See "The plea of illegality and non-existent acts."
[4] Case 26/62 [1963] E.C.R. 1, 13.
[5] See Dashwood and White, *loc. cit.* pp. 411–413 and the materials cited there.

given one such ruling,[6] but between 1985 and 1990 nine applications by the Commission in respect of breaches of Article 171 were upheld by the Court.[7]

The explanation for this development may lie partly in the increased vigour with which the Commission has, since the late 1970s, pursued Member States which fail to comply with their Treaty obligations.[8] This has led to an increase in the number of rulings given by the Court under Article 169[9] and a concomitant rise in the possibility that some of those judgments will not be complied with in the absence of further action by the Commission. The Commission's change of policy may also have deprived decisions of the Court under Article 169 of some of their impact, since such decisions, often for relatively minor breaches of Community law, are now commonplace.

In an attempt to reinforce the effectiveness of proceedings under Article 169, the Member States agreed at Maastricht to add a second paragraph to Article 171 giving the Court power to impose sanctions on Member States which fail to comply with rulings under Article 169.[10] The new Article 171(2) provides that the Commission, if it considers that a Member State has not taken the measures necessary to comply with the Court's judgment,

"... shall, after giving that State the opportunity to submit its observations, issue a reasoned opinion specifying the points on which the Member State concerned has not complied with the judgment of the Court of Justice. If the Member State concerned fails to take the necessary measures to comply with the Court's judgment within the time-limit laid down by the Commission, the latter may bring the case before the Court of Justice. In so doing it shall specify the amount of the lump sum or penalty payment to be paid by the Member State concerned which it considers appropriate in the circumstances. If the Court of Justice finds that the Member State concerned has not complied with its judgment it may impose a lump sum or penalty payment on it. This procedure shall be without prejudice to Article 170."

The distinction between a lump sum and a penalty payment seems to be that the former resembles a fine of a fixed amount, while the latter is a sum which the Member State concerned is required to pay at regular intervals until the

---

[6] Case 48/71, *Commission* v. *Italy* [1972] E.C.R. 529. See also Joined Cases 24 and 97/80 R, *Commission* v. *France* [1980] E.C.R. 1319, which were eventually resolved through political channels.

[7] Case 281/83, *Commission* v. *Italy* [1985] E.C.R. 3397; Case 131/84, *Commission* v. *Italy* [1985] E.C.R. 3531; Case 160/85, *Commission* v. *Italy* [1986] E.C.R. 3245; Case 69/86, *Commission* v. *Italy* [1987] E.C.R. 773; Joined Cases 227, 228, 229 and 230/85, *Commission* v. *Belgium* [1988] E.C.R. 1; Case 391/85, *Commission* v. *Belgium* [1988] E.C.R. 579; Case 225/86, *Commission* v. *Italy* [1988] E.C.R. 2271; Case 169/87, *Commission* v. *France* [1988] E.C.R. 4093; Case 383/85, *Commission* v. *Belgium* [1989] E.C.R. 3069.

[8] See Dashwood and White, *loc. cit.* pp. 399–400.

[9] See Everling, "The Member States of the European Community before their Court of Justice" (1984) 9 E.L.Rev. 215, 218–222.

[10] The Member States also attached to the Treaty on European Union a Declaration stressing that "each Member State should fully and accurately transpose into national law the Community Directives addressed to it within the deadlines laid down therein. . . ." Actions under Art. 169 for failure to implement directives in good time are at present fairly common.

breach is terminated.[11] Somewhat surprisingly, there is apparently to be no limit to the amount which Member States can be required to pay. Even more surprisingly, the consequences should the Member State concerned refuse to pay are not specified. If it is to avoid exacerbating the situation, the Court would have to exercise this new power with considerable tact and it may be doubted whether much use would be made of it, although a threat by the Commission to propose the imposition of sanctions might have some effect.[12] It is submitted that the ruling in the *Francovich* case,[13] referred to above, is likely to prove more effective in securing compliance by the Member States with their obligations under the Treaty.

(b) *The action for annulment*[14]

The extensive legislative authority conferred on the Community institutions by the Treaties made it essential that a system be created for reviewing the legality of the way in which that authority was exercised. The principal device for achieving that objective is Article 173 EEC, under which direct actions for the annulment of Community acts may be brought before the Court of Justice. It may also be possible to challenge the validity of Community acts in proceedings before the courts of the Member States, which must, where there is a serious doubt about the validity of the act in question, ask the Court of Justice for a preliminary ruling on the matter under Article 177 EEC.[15] The preliminary rulings procedure is discussed below.

Article 173 EEC provides as follows:

> "The Court of Justice shall review the legality of acts of the Council and the Commission other than recommendations or opinions. It shall for this purpose have jurisdiction in actions brought by a Member State, the Council or the Commission on grounds of lack of competence, infringement of an essential procedural requirement, infringement of this Treaty or of any rule of law relating to its application, or misuse of powers.
>
> Any natural or legal person may, under the same conditions, institute proceedings against a decision addressed to that person or against a decision which, although in the form of a regulation or a decision addressed to another person, is of direct and individual concern to the former.
>
> The proceedings provided for in this Article shall be instituted within two months of the publication of the measure, or of its notification to

---

[11] *Cf.* Arts. 15 and 16 of Regulation No. 17, which implements Arts. 85 and 86 EEC (O.J. English Sp.Ed. 1959–62, p. 87).

[12] *Cf.* the third paragraph of Art. 88 ECSC, which provides for the imposition of sanctions on Member States which fail to fulfil their obligations under the ECSC Treaty, but which has never been invoked.

[13] Joined Cases C–6/90 and C–9/90, judgment of November 19, 1991.

[14] See generally Brown and Jacobs, *op. cit.* pp. 95–123; Hartley, *op. cit.* Chaps. 11, 12, 15 and 16; Toth, *The Oxford Encyclopaedia of European Community Law* (1990), Vol. I, under the relevant entries. The last-mentioned work makes extensive reference to the considerable body of literature on the subject.

[15] See Case 314/85, *Foto-Frost* v. *Hauptzollamt Lübeck-Ost* [1987] E.C.R. 4199.

the plaintiff, or, in the absence thereof, of the day on which it came to the knowledge of the latter, as the case may be."

Reviewable acts

Under the first paragraph of Article 173, proceedings may be brought against "acts of the Council and the Commission other than recommendations or opinions." According to Article 189 EEC, the last two categories of act "have no binding force."[16] The other categories of act mentioned in Article 189 (regulations, directives and decisions) do have binding force and are in principle susceptible to review under Article 173.

The question whether measures adopted by the Council or the Commission which produce legal effects, but which do not take the form of any of the binding acts referred to in Article 189, are susceptible to review under Article 173 was considered in the "ERTA" case,[17] where the Commission sought the annulment of certain "conclusions" reached by the Council concerning the negotiating position to be adopted by the Member States in discussions on a European road transport agreement. The Court stated that "Article 173 treats as acts open to review by the Court all measures adopted by the institutions which are intended to have legal force." The Court said that it would be inconsistent with the purpose of Article 173, which was to ensure that the law was observed in accordance with Article 164 EEC, "to limit the availability of this procedure merely to the categories of measures referred to by Article 189." It concluded that "An action for annulment must therefore be available in the case of all measures adopted by the institutions, whatever their nature or form, which are intended to have legal effects."

The Court's decision in the "ERTA" case was followed in *Les Verts* v. *Parliament*,[18] where a French political grouping sought the annulment of two measures adopted by the European Parliament. At present, the Parliament is not mentioned in the first paragraph of Article 173 and has no power under the Treaty to adopt regulations, directives or decisions.[19] Nonetheless, the Court held that it would be inconsistent with the spirit of the Treaty for measures adopted by the Parliament which produced legal effects *vis-à-vis* third parties to be excluded from the scope of the action under Article 173. Similarly, in *Maurissen and others* v. *Court of Auditors*,[20] the Court accepted as admissible an action brought under Article 173 against a measure adopted

---

[16] Recommendations are not, however, entirely devoid of legal significance: see Case C–322/88, *Grimaldi* v. *Fonds des Maladies Professionnelles* [1989] E.C.R. 4407; Arnull, (1990) 15 E.L.Rev. 318.

[17] Case 22/70, *Commission* v. *Council* [1971] E.C.R. 263. See also Case C–366/88, *France* v. *Commission* [1990] E.C.R. I–3571.

[18] Case 294/83 [1986] E.C.R. 1339. See also Case 34/86, *Council* v. *Parliament* [1986] E.C.R. 2155.

[19] The position will change if the Treaty on European Union enters into force.

[20] Joined Cases 193 and 194/87 [1989] E.C.R. 1045. See in particular the Opinion of A. G. Darmon at pp. 1063–1065. *Cf.* Case 110/75, *Mills* v. *European Investment Bank* [1976] E.C.R. 955, where the Court held that it had jurisdiction under Art. 179 EEC in disputes between the Bank and its servants.

by the Court of Auditors[21] which produced legal effects, notwithstanding the absence of any reference to the Court of Auditors in Article 173.

Thus, "any measure the legal effects of which are binding on, and capable of affecting the interests of, the applicant by bringing about a distinct change in his legal position"[22] is in principle open to review under the first paragraph of Article 173. Despite the terms of that provision, the action is not confined to acts of the Council and the Commission, nor even to the institutions mentioned in Article 4(1) of the Treaty. However, an act adopted in the context of a procedure involving several stages is susceptible to challenge only if it definitively lays down the adopting body's position at the culmination of that procedure and is not merely a provisional measure intended to pave the way for the final decision. Legal defects in measures of a purely preparatory nature may be relied on in proceedings for the annulment of the definitive act for which they represent a preparatory step.[23]

Capacity to bring proceedings

In order to bring proceedings under Article 173, an applicant must show that he satisfies the conditions regarding standing, or *locus standi*, laid down in the Treaty. Article 173 draws a distinction in this respect between the Member States, the Council and the Commission on the one hand and natural and legal persons, such as individuals and companies, on the other. Applicants falling within the former category automatically have standing to bring proceedings and do not have to establish any particular interest.[24] To put the point another way, such applicants are presumed to have an interest in the legality of all Community acts. For this reason, they are sometimes referred to as "privileged applicants." Where a Member State seeks the annulment of a measure adopted by the Council, its right to bring proceedings is not affected by whether or not it voted for the measure when it was adopted.[25]

It will be observed that, as presently drafted,[26] Article 173 confers no right of action on the European Parliament, but the Court held in the *Chernobyl* case[27] that the Parliament had the right to seek the annulment of acts adopted by the Council or by the Commission where the purpose of the proceedings was to protect the Parliament's prerogatives, such as the right to participate to the extent envisaged by the Treaty in the legislative process leading to the adoption of a Community act. The Court made it clear

---

[21] The Court of Auditors, which is at present mentioned in Art. 4(3) EEC, was established by the Treaty Amending Certain Financial Provisions signed in Brussels on July 22, 1975. It is not a court in the legal sense, but has the task of examining the revenue and expenditure of the Community and its financial management. The Treaty on European Union would add it to the list of institutions mentioned in Art. 4(1) of the EC Treaty. See further Arts. 188a-c of the EC Treaty, to be added by the Treaty on European Union; Kok, "The Court of Auditors of the European Communities: 'The other European Court in Luxembourg' " (1989) 26 C.M.L.Rev. 345.
[22] Case 60/81, *IBM* v. *Commission* [1981] E.C.R. 2639, para. 9.
[23] *IBM* v. *Commission, supra.*
[24] See Case 45/86, *Commission* v. *Council* [1987] E.C.R. 1493, para. 3.
[25] Case 166/78, *Italy* v. *Council* [1979] E.C.R. 2575, para. 6.
[26] The position will change if the Treaty on European Union enters into force: see below.
[27] Case C–70/88, *Parliament* v. *Council* [1990] E.C.R. I–2041.

that such proceedings were not brought under Article 173,[28] but under a right of action created by the Court to ensure respect for the institutional balance established by the Treaties. However, where the Parliament's prerogatives are in issue, such proceedings are subject to the same conditions as annulment proceedings instituted by the Council or by the Commission under the first paragraph of Article 173. Thus, notwithstanding the absence in Article 173 in its present form of any reference to the European Parliament, that institution may both institute annulment proceedings and be the defendant in such proceedings.

The standing of natural and legal persons to institute annulment proceedings is limited and for this reason they are sometimes referred to as "non-privileged applicants." According to the second paragraph of Article 173, an applicant falling within this category[29] may only bring proceedings against three types of act, namely:

(i) a decision addressed to him;
(ii) a decision in the form of a regulation which is of direct and individual concern to him;
(iii) a decision addressed to another person[30] which is of direct and individual concern to the applicant.

Article 173 makes no express provision for natural and legal persons to seek the annulment of directives, although it could perhaps be argued that directives are in essence decisions addressed to the Member States which may be challenged by anyone who is directly and individually concerned by them.[31]

In order to explain the standing of natural and legal persons under Article 173, it is therefore necessary to examine the following three questions: the distinction between regulations and decisions, the meaning of direct concern and the meaning of individual concern.

(a) **The distinction between regulations and decisions.** The reference in Article 173 to a decision *in the form of* a regulation implies that the nature of a measure depends on its substance rather than on the name the adopting institution has chosen to give it. This is the approach which underlies the case law of the Court, which has said that, in examining the question whether a measure constitutes a regulation or a decision, it "cannot restrict itself to considering the official title of the measure, but must first take into account its object and content."[32]

According to Article 189 EEC, "A regulation shall have general

---

[28] Indeed, the Court had held less than two years previously that the Parliament had no right of action under Art. 173: see Case 302/87, *Parliament* v. *Council* ("Comitology") [1988] E.C.R. 5615. The Court followed that ruling on this point in the *Chernobyl* case.
[29] Which extends to all natural and legal persons, regardless of their nationality or place of residence.
[30] For the purposes of the second paragraph of Art. 173, this expression includes the Member States: Case 25/62, *Plaumann* v. *Commission* [1963] E.C.R. 95.
[31] See further Toth, *op. cit.* p. 37. *Cf.* Case C–298/89, *Government of Gibraltar* v. *Council*, which is pending at the time of writing.
[32] Joined Cases 16 and 17/62, *Producteurs de Fruits* v. *Council* [1962] E.C.R. 471, 478.

application. It shall be binding in its entirety and directly applicable in all Member States." The same Article provides that "A decision shall be binding in its entirety upon those to whom it is addressed." In *Producteurs de Fruits* v. *Council*, the Court rejected a suggestion that these terms were used in a different sense in Article 173. The Court deduced from the terms of Article 189 that "The criterion for the distinction [between regulations and decisions] must be sought in the general 'application' or otherwise of the measure in question."[33]

Thus, regulations are essentially legislative in nature and apply to "categories of persons viewed abstractly and in their entirety."[34] In *Zuckerfabrik Watenstedt* v. *Council*,[35] the Court held that the measure at issue there was a true regulation because it was "applicable to objectively determined situations" and involved "legal consequences for categories of persons viewed in a general and abstract manner." The Court made it clear that a measure did not lose its character as a regulation simply because it was possible to ascertain the number or even the identity of those to whom it applied, provided it was clear that the measure was "applicable as the result of an objective situation of law or of fact."

Decisions are more specific in their application than regulations. In *Plaumann* v. *Commission*,[36] the Court said that "decisions are characterized by the limited number of persons to whom they are addressed. In order to determine whether or not a measure constitutes a decision one must enquire whether that measure concerns specific persons." Nonetheless, it has been observed that the distinction between regulations and decisions "is hard to draw where the number of persons making up the class is small and where the persons affected are designated as a general class but their identity is fixed and ascertainable at the time when the measure is adopted."[37]

It should be emphasised that, where the annulment of only some of the provisions of an act is being sought, it is the proper classification of those provisions and not that of the act as a whole that is important. The Court has acknowledged that a true regulation may contain provisions which amount in substance to decisions and which can therefore be challenged by non-privileged applicants under Article 173.[38] The Court has stated, however, that "A single provision cannot at one and the same time have the character of a measure of general application and of an individual measure."[39]

(b) **The meaning of direct concern.** If it is inevitable that a measure will affect someone's legal position in a particular way, that measure will be of direct concern to him. As Advocate General Warner put it in *C.A.M.* v.

---

[33] *Ibid.*
[34] *Ibid.*
[35] Case 6/68 [1968] E.C.R. 409, 415.
[36] Case 25/62 [1963] E.C.R. 95, 107.
[37] Slynn, Lasok and Millett in Vaughan (ed.) *op. cit.* para. 2.47.
[38] See the *Producteurs de Fruits* case, *supra* at p. 479.
[39] Case 45/81, *Moksel* v. *Commission* [1982] E.C.R. 1129, para. 18. See further the Opinion of A. G. Jacobs in Case C–358/89, *Extramet Industrie* v. *Council* [1991] E.C.R. I–2501.

Commission,[40] a measure is of direct concern to an applicant if it is "the direct cause of an effect" on him. The Court stated in *Les Verts* v. *Parliament*[41] that a measure which constitutes "a complete set of rules which are sufficient in themselves and which require no implementing provisions" is of direct concern to an applicant since in such circumstances the application of the measure "is automatic and leaves no room for any discretion."

The fact that a measure requires implementation by a third party does not prevent it from being of direct concern to an applicant, provided the third party has no discretion in the matter. For example, in *N.T.N. Toyo Bearing Company* v. *Council*,[42] the Court held that the applicant was directly concerned by a measure which required implementation by the Member States because implementation was required by Community law and was "purely automatic."

If, however, the measure only affects the applicant because a third party has exercised a discretion in a particular way, it will not be possible to establish direct concern. Thus, a decision addressed to two Member States refusing to grant them import quotas was held not to be of direct concern to an applicant where the allocation of any quota would have been a matter for the discretion of the Member States concerned.[43] In order to defeat a claim of direct concern, however, the manner in which any discretion left to third parties would be exercised must have been genuinely unpredictable at the time the contested measure was adopted. In *Piraiki-Patraiki* v. *Commission*,[44] for example, the applicants sought the annulment of a Commission decision authorising France to impose a quota system restricting imports of cotton yarn from Greece during a specific period. The Commission argued that the applicants were not directly concerned by the contested decision, since it required implementation by the French authorities, which were free not to make use of the authorisation. That argument was rejected by the Court, since before the decision was adopted France had already been restricting imports of Greek cotton yarn and the contested decision had been adopted in response to a request from the French authorities for permission to impose an even stricter quota system. In these circumstances, the Court concluded that "the possibility that the French Republic might decide not to make use of the authorization granted to it by the Commission decision was entirely theoretical, since there could be no doubt as to the intention of the French authorities to apply the decision."[45]

(c) **The meaning of individual concern.** This is the most difficult of the three requirements, both to describe and to establish. The Court has stated that "In order for a measure to be of individual concern to the persons to

---

[40] Case 100/74 [1975] E.C.R. 1393, 1410.
[41] Case 294/83 [1986] E.C.R. 1339, para. 31.
[42] Case 113/77 [1979] E.C.R. 1185 (one of the "First Ball Bearings" cases).
[43] Case 69/69, *Alcan* v. *Commission* [1970] E.C.R. 385.
[44] Case 11/82 [1985] E.C.R. 207.
[45] Para. 9 of the judgment.

whom it applies, it must affect their legal position because of a factual situation which differentiates them from all other persons and distinguishes them individually in the same way as a person to whom it is addressed."[46] The test is expressed by the Court in basically the same terms whether the contested measure is in the form of a regulation or in that of a decision,[47] although a measure in the form of a regulation will not be specifically addressed to anyone.

It is perhaps easiest for an applicant to establish individual concern where he can show that he was affected by the contested measure because he is a member of a class the membership of which was closed, both in theory and in practice, at the time the measure was adopted. In *Toepfer* v. *Commission*,[48] for example, the applicants sought the annulment of a Commission decision authorising Germany to maintain protective measures concerning imports of certain products. The only persons affected by the decision were importers who had applied for an import licence during the course of a particular day, since on the following day the danger against which the protective measures were intended to guard disappeared. The Court held that the number and identity of the importers affected had become fixed and ascertainable by the time the contested decision was adopted and that the Commission was therefore in a position to know that its decision would only affect their interests. Those importers were therefore held to be individually concerned by the contested decision.

Similarly, in *International Fruit Company* v. *Commission*,[49] the question arose whether a provision contained in a regulation concerning requests for import licences made in a particular week prior to its adoption was of individual concern to the applicants. The Court pointed out that, when the contested regulation was adopted, the number of applications which could be affected by it was fixed and that no new applications could be added. The Court concluded that the contested provision "must be regarded as a conglomeration of individual decisions taken by the Commission under the guise of a regulation ... each of which affects the legal position of each author of an application for a licence." It was therefore of individual concern to the applicants. Again, in *C.A.M.* v. *Commission*,[50] the Court held that a measure which affected "a fixed number of traders identified by reason of the individual course of action which they pursued or are regarded as having pursued during a particular period" was of individual concern to those to whom it applied.

It is not only dealings with the Community or with national authorities which may be relied on to establish individual concern. Arrangements of a

---

[46] Case 26/86, *Deutz and Geldemann* v. *Council* [1987] E.C.R. 941, para. 9. See also, *e.g.* Case 25/62, *Plaumann* v. *Commission* [1963] E.C.R. 95, 107; Case 100/74, *C.A.M.* v. *Commission* [1975] E.C.R. 1393, para. 19.
[47] Of the cases referred to in the preceding note, the first and third were for the annulment of regulations, the second for the annulment of a decision.
[48] Joined Cases 106 and 107/63 [1965] E.C.R. 405. *Cf.* Case 38/64, *Getreide-Import* v. *Commission* [1965] E.C.R. 203.
[49] Joined Cases 41 to 44/70 [1971] E.C.R. 411.
[50] Case 100/74, *supra*. See further Case 62/70, *Bock* v. *Commission* [1971] E.C.R. 897; Case 88/76, *Exportation des Sucres* v. *Commission* [1977] E.C.R. 709.

private law nature may also be invoked. In *Piraiki-Patraiki* v. *Commission*,[51] the Court held that the contested decision was of individual concern to those of the applicants which, prior to its adoption, had entered into contracts to be performed while it was in force, insofar as the execution of those contracts was wholly or partly prevented by its adoption. The Court ruled that the Commission had been in a position to discover the existence of contracts to be performed during the period of application of the contested decision. Undertakings which were parties to such contracts were therefore individually concerned "as members of a limited class of traders identified or identifiable by the Commission and by reason of those contracts particularly affected by the decision at issue."

This line of authority may present applicants with considerable difficulty, for it effectively requires them to establish that the contested measure produced some kind of retrospective effect.[52] The Court has stated that "The possibility of determining more or less precisely the number or even the identity of the persons to whom a measure applies by no means implies that it must be regarded as being of individual concern to them."[53] In particular, the Court has consistently held that the fact that an applicant is affected by a measure solely because he carries on a given commercial activity is not enough to establish individual concern. This is because the Court treats such activities as capable of being practised by anyone at any time and therefore not such as to distinguish the applicant individually, the class of which he is a member being, theoretically at least, an open one.[54] The Court has applied this criterion fairly strictly. In *Glucoseries Réunies* v. *Commission*,[55] the applicant sought the annulment of a Commission decision authorising France to levy countervailing charges on the importation of glucose from a number of other Member States, including Belgium. The applicant claimed that it was the only Belgian undertaking with an economic interest in the matter which was willing and able to export glucose from Belgium to France in significant quantities while the contested decision was in force. The Court noted, however, that the effects of the decision were not limited to exports from Belgium to France and stated that consideration of its effects could not therefore be confined to one exporter in one Member State, however important its position. The Court concluded that, in the light of the general economic scope of the decision, it was not of individual concern to the applicant.

Moreover, it has been held that an association, in its capacity as representative of its members, is not individually concerned by a measure

---

[51] Case 11/82 [1985] E.C.R. 207, *supra*.
[52] See Barav, "Direct and Individual Concern: An Almost Insurmountable Barrier to the Admissibility of Individual Appeal to the EEC Court" (1974) 11 C.M.L.Rev. 191; Rasmussen, "Why is Article 173 Interpreted against Private Plaintiffs?" (1980) 5 E.L.Rev. 122.
[53] Case 123/77, *UNICME* v. *Council* [1978] E.C.R. 845, para. 16.
[54] See, *e.g.* Case 25/62, *Plaumann* v. *Commission, supra*; Joined Cases 10 and 18/68, *Eridania* v. *Commission* [1969] E.C.R. 459. It appears that this rule is relaxed in anti-dumping cases: see Case C–358/89, *Extramet Industrie* v. *Council* [1991] E.C.R. I–2501.
[55] Case 1/64 [1964] E.C.R. 413.

which affects the general interests of those members.[56] It appears that such a measure must be challenged by the members themselves.

A decision which, it is submitted, is impossible to reconcile with the rest of the Court's case-law on individual concern but which seems to have been based on considerations of pure policy is *Les Verts* v. *Parliament.*[57] The applicant in that case sought the annulment of two measures adopted by the European Parliament, in 1982 and 1983 respectively, concerning the reimbursement of expenditure incurred by political groupings taking part in the 1984 European elections. The contested measures affected all groupings participating in those elections, whether or not they were already represented in the Parliament. However, groupings which were already represented took part in the procedure leading to the adoption of the contested measures. The applicant, which was not represented in the Parliament at the time the contested measures were adopted but which intended to contest the 1984 elections, alleged that the measures discriminated in favour of groupings which were already represented and sought the annulment of those measures under the second paragraph of Article 173.

The applicant faced two serious obstacles. First, it had to establish that measures adopted by the European Parliament could be challenged under that Article. As we have seen, the Court acknowledged that such a challenge was possible. Secondly, it had to establish that it was individually concerned by the contested measures. On the basis of the Court's existing case law, this might have seemed an impossible task, since at the time the contested measures were adopted, political groupings which were not represented in the Parliament but which might wish to contest the 1984 elections, and which would therefore be affected by the measures, could not be identified. In other words, the class to which the applicant belonged was an open one. The only class the members of which could be identified at the time the measures were adopted were groupings which were already represented, but they had no interest in mounting a challenge.

The Court noted the unprecedented circumstances of the action and said that, because the main measure being challenged concerned "the allocation of public funds for the purpose of preparing for elections and it is alleged that those funds were allocated unequally, it cannot be considered that only groupings which were represented and which were therefore identifiable at the date of the adoption of the contested measure were individually concerned by it." The Court concluded that "the applicant association, which was in existence at the time when the 1982 Decision was adopted and which was able to present candidates at the 1984 elections, is individually concerned by the contested measures."[58] The Court's emphasis on the unusual circumstances of the case suggests that it should be regarded as

---

[56] See, *e.g.* Joined Cases 16 and 17/62, *Producteurs de Fruits* v. *Council* [1962] E.C.R. 471, 479–480; Case 117/86, *UFADE* v. *Council and Commission* [1986] E.C.R. 3255, para. 12.
[57] Case 294/83 [1986] E.C.R. 1357.
[58] Paras. 35 and 37 of the judgment. The Court went on to annul the contested measures.

confined to its own special facts and should not in itself be taken as heralding any general relaxation of the criteria for establishing individual concern.

Despite the strictness of the main body of the case law on individual concern, however, there are certain particular situations in which the Court is more willing to allow proceedings to be brought by natural and legal persons. These situations all involve quasi-judicial measures taken at the end of a procedure in which the views of interested parties are heard.[59] Such procedures are particularly prominent in three fields: competition,[60] dumping[61] and State aid.[62] It seems, however, that the Court's case law on admissibility in these fields can only be applied with caution in other contexts.

Are there really three tests?

The terms of the second paragraph of Article 173 suggest that, where a non-privileged applicant wishes to seek the annulment of a regulation, he must establish that he satisfies each of the three conditions relating to admissibility identified above. The Court stated in *Alusuisse* v. *Council and Commission*[63] that all three requirements had to be met in order to establish *locus standi*. If this is correct, it must be theoretically possible to contemplate cases in which one of the requirements might not be satisfied. Direct concern raises no problems in this context: a measure may be a true regulation even though it is of direct concern to certain applicants. Equally clearly, a regulation which is in substance a decision may nonetheless not be of direct concern to an applicant. However, it would also have to be possible to conceive of a measure which, although of individual concern to certain applicants, remained a true regulation, or conversely of a regulation which, although in substance a decision, was not of individual concern to an applicant. This in turn would imply that the criteria for distinguishing regulations from decisions on the one hand, and the criteria for establishing individual concern on the other, were different.

It will be apparent from the cases discussed above, however, that this is not the case. Decisions, which the Court has said are characterised by the limited number of persons affected by them,[64] will necessarily affect those persons "by reason of certain attributes which are peculiar to them or by reason of circumstances in which they are differentiated from all other persons. . . ."[65] This blurring of the distinction evidently intended by the authors of the Treaty between the way in which regulations are distinguished from decisions and the way in which individual concern is established has

---

[59] See generally Hartley, *op. cit.* pp. 354–359.
[60] See Case 26/76, *Metro* v. *Commission* (No. 1) [1977] E.C.R. 1875; Case 210/81, *Demo-Studio Schmidt* v. *Commission* [1983] E.C.R. 3045; Case 75/84, *Metro* v. *Commission* (No. 2) [1986] E.C.R. 3021.
[61] See Arnull, "Challenging EC Anti-dumping Regulations: the Problem of Admissibility" [1992] E.C.L.R. 73.
[62] See Case 169/84, *Cofaz* v. *Commission* [1986] E.C.R. 391; Joined Cases 67, 68 and 70/85, *Van der Kooy and others* v. *Commission* [1988] E.C.R. 219.
[63] Case 307/81 [1982] E.C.R. 3463, para. 7.
[64] See the *Plaumann* case, *supra*.
[65] *Ibid.*

effectively resulted in a reduction of the conditions which must be satisfied by non-privileged applicants wishing to challenge regulations from three to two: direct concern and individual concern. The Court's case-law seems to show that, once these tests are satisfied, the applicant has nothing more to do to establish admissibility.[66]

In *Extramet Industrie* v. *Council*,[67] that case-law was the subject of a detailed analysis by Advocate General Jacobs, who said "the Court should in my view make clear what is already implicit in the prevailing trend of its case-law, namely that the requirement of a decision does not exist independently of the requirement of individual concern." Disappointingly, but perhaps unsurprisingly, the judgment of the Court does not contain a clear statement to that effect, but it may be taken impliedly to have endorsed the view of Advocate General Jacobs. The Court acknowledged that a measure might, without losing its character as a regulation, be of individual concern to certain undertakings, which would as a result have standing to seek its annulment. The Court accepted that undertakings which were individually concerned by such measures by reason of certain characteristics which were peculiar to them were entitled to challenge them before the Court.[68]

Although *Extramet* was a dumping case and the extent to which it is of general application may therefore be doubtful, it does provide support for the view that non-privileged applicants wishing to challenge regulations under the second paragraph of Article 173 no longer need to establish that the contested measure is in substance a decision. If this is so, it can hardly be denied that the approach of the Court is incompatible with the terms of Article 173. Much of the Court's case-law is, however, probably now too well established to be unravelled. Against that background, the outcome may be justified by the need to ensure effective judicial review.

Grounds of review

In order to succeed in an action for the annulment of a Community act, the applicant must establish that the contested act was unlawful. The first paragraph of Article 173 mentions four grounds, derived from French administrative law,[69] on which this may be done. They are lack of competence, infringement of an essential procedural requirement, infringement of the Treaty or of any rule of law relating to its application,

---

[66] See, *e.g. Producteurs de Fruits, supra; C.A.M.* v. *Commission, supra*; Joined Cases 239 and 275/82, *Allied Corporation* v. *Commission* [1984] E.C.R. 1005; Joined Cases C–133/87 and C–150/87, *Nashua Corporation* v. *Commission* [1990] E.C.R. I–719; Case C–156/87, *Gestetner Holdings* v. *Council* [1990] E.C.R. I–781; Case C–152/88, *Sofrimport* v. *Commission* [1990] E.C.R. I–2477; Joined Cases C–304/86 and C–185/87, Joined Cases C–305/86 and C–160/87, Joined Cases C–320/86 and C–188/87, and Case C–157/87 "Electric Motors" [1990] E.C.R. I–2939, I–2945, I–3013 and I–3021 respectively. *Cf.* Case 264/82, *Timex* v. *Council* [1985] E.C.R. 849, where the Court implied that a measure which was of individual concern to the applicant was automatically to be considered in substance a decision.

[67] Case C–358/89 [1991] E.C.R. I–2501.

[68] See also Case C–49/88, *Al-Jubail Fertilizer Company* v. *Council* [1991] 3 C.M.L.R. 377, para. 15.

[69] See the Opinion of A. G. Lagrange in Case 3/54, *ASSIDER* v. *High Authority* [1954 to 1956] E.C.R. 63, a case decided under the ECSC Treaty.

and misuse of powers. In practice, these grounds overlap to a considerable extent and the Court does not distinguish rigidly between them. As one commentator has remarked, "almost any well-substantiated infringement of Community law, other than a really minor one, may be invoked to establish the illegality of a measure and may in principle lead to its annulment. This is a consequence of the fact that the various grounds are drawn up in such wide terms that they encompass amongst themselves almost all conceivable cases of illegality."[70]

A measure may be annulled by the Court for lack of competence if the adopting institution lacked the authority to adopt it. This typically arises where the enabling provision under which the adopting institution purported to act is found by the Court not to be wide enough to cover the contested measure.[71] Examples of breaches of essential procedural requirements are failure to consult the Parliament prior to the adoption of an act where consultation is required by the Treaty[72] and failure to hear the views of interested parties before a measure is adopted.[73] Irregularities such as these are regarded by the Court as "essential" in the sense that, if they had not been committed, the content of the measure in question might have been different.[74] However, procedural irregularities may be treated as "essential" for the purposes of Article 173 even where it cannot be said that they might have affected on the content of the measure. An example is failure to give an adequate statement of the reasons on which an act is based.[75] The third ground, infringement of the Treaty or of any rule of law relating to its application, is the widest one and is capable of subsuming the other three. A measure may be declared void on this ground if it contravenes a general principle of law recognised by the Court, such as the principles of legal certainty, proportionality, equality and respect for fundamental rights.[76] Finally, a measure may be annulled by the Court for misuse of powers where the applicant establishes that the purpose pursued by the adopting institution was not that for which the power under which it purported to act was granted.[77] This ground is difficult to establish because it requires the applicant to identify the intentions of the defendant institution.

Time limits

Under the third paragraph of Article 173, proceedings must be instituted "within two months of the publication of the measure, or of its notification to

---

[70] Toth, *op. cit.* p. 282.
[71] See, *e.g.* Joined Cases 281, 283 to 285 and 287/85, *Germany, France, Netherlands, Denmark and United Kingdom* v. *Commission* [1987] E.C.R. 3203; Case 264/86, *France* v. *Commission* [1988] E.C.R. 973. *Cf.* Case 45/86, *Commission* v. *Council* [1987] E.C.R. 1493.
[72] Case 138/79, *Roquette Frères* v. *Council* [1980] E.C.R. 3333.
[73] See, *e.g.* Case 17/74, *Transocean Marine Paint Association* v. *Commission* [1974] E.C.R. 1063; Case C–49/88, *Al-Jubail Fertilizer Company* v. *Council* [1991] 3 C.M.L.R. 377.
[74] See, *e.g.* Case 30/78, *Distillers Company* v. *Commission* [1980] E.C.R. 2229, para. 26.
[75] Such a statement is required by Art. 190 EEC. For a failure to comply with that Article, see Case 45/86, *Commission* v. *Council, supra.* The amount of detail required by the Court to satisfy Art. 190 depends on the nature of the act and the context in which it is intended to operate. See further Toth, *op. cit.* pp. 497–499.
[76] The general principles of Community law are discussed in Chap. 4.
[77] See, *e.g.* Joined Cases 18 and 35/65, *Gutmann* v. *Commission* [1966] E.C.R. 103; Case 105/75, *Giuffrida* v. *Council* [1976] E.C.R. 1395.

the plaintiff, or, in the absence thereof, of the day on which it came to the notice of the latter." Article 191 of the Treaty, as presently drafted, requires regulations to be published in the Official Journal of the Communities, but only requires directives and decisions to be notified to those to whom they are addressed. In practice, they are frequently published in the Official Journal too, but it is thought that this has no effect on the date from which time begins to run.[78] Similarly, it seems that knowledge of a regulation prior to its publication does not alter the date on which time starts running.[79]

Detailed provisions for the calculation of time limits such as that laid down in Article 173 are contained in Article 80 of the Rules. Under Article 81(1) of the Rules, the period of time allowed for bringing annulment proceedings runs "from the day following the receipt by the person concerned of notification of the measure or, where the measure is published, from the 15th day after publication thereof in the *Official Journal of the European Communities*."[80] Moreover, in accordance with Article 81(2) of the Rules, extensions of the prescribed time limit are laid down on account of the distance between the Court and the place where the applicant is habitually resident.[81]

The expiry of the period of time allowed for bringing proceedings will not be fatal if the applicant can rely on the second paragraph of Article 42 of the Statute, which provides that "No right shall be prejudiced in consequence of the expiry of a time-limit if the party concerned proves the existence of unforeseeable circumstances or of *force majeure*." This provision is interpreted fairly strictly by the Court.[82]

Once the time limit laid down in the third paragraph of Article 173 has expired, it may still be possible to challenge the validity of a Community act in other proceedings before the Court of Justice by means of a so-called plea of illegality. This is discussed below.

The effects of annulment[83]

According to the first paragraph of Article 174 EEC, where the Court of Justice finds an action under Article 173 well founded, it "shall declare the act concerned to be void." The Court has no power to substitute its own views for those of the defendant institution, which is required by the first paragraph of Article 176 EEC to take the measures necessary to comply with the Court's judgment. This may mean that a new measure to replace the one declared void by the Court has to be adopted. The principle of legal certainty

---

[78] If the Treaty on European Union enters into force, directives and decisions adopted jointly by the Parliament and the Council and directives adopted by the Council and the Commission which are addressed to all the Member States will have to be published in the Official Journal. They will enter into force on the date specified in them or, in the absence thereof, on the 20th day following that of their publication: see the new version of Art. 191.

[79] See the Opinion of A. G. Reischl in Case 88/76, *Exportation des Sucres* v. *Commission* [1977] E.C.R. 709, 730–731.

[80] This rule seems difficult to reconcile with the terms of Art. 173, but was described by A. G. Reischl in *Exportation des Sucres, supra* at p. 731, as "certainly not contrary to the Treaty."

[81] The period laid down for the United Kingdom is 10 days.

[82] See, *e.g.* Case C–59/91, *France* v. *Commission*, Order of February 5, 1992.

[83] See Toth, "The Authority of Judgments of the European Court of Justice: Binding Force and Legal Effects" (1984) 4 Y.E.L. 1.

will generally mean that such a measure cannot be made retrospective, but in exceptional cases this is permitted "where the purpose to be achieved so demands and where the legitimate expectations of those concerned are duly respected."[84] The Court's ruling may also lead to a claim for compensation against the defendant institution in accordance with Article 178 and the second paragraph of Article 215 of the Treaty.[85]

In principle, a declaration by the Court under Article 173 that an act is void takes effect *erga omnes* and *ex tunc*, that is with regard to the whole world and with retrospective effect. The second paragraph of Article 174 states that "In the case of a regulation, however, the Court of Justice shall, if it considers this necessary, state which of the effects of the regulation which it has declared void shall be considered as definitive." This enables the Court to minimise any disruption which might be caused by the gap left by the disappearance of the measure which has been quashed. For example, in a case in which the Court declared void certain provisions of a regulation relating to the remuneration of Community officials, it declared that those provisions should continue to have effect until they were replaced "to avoid discontinuity in the system of remuneration."[86] In *Timex* v. *Council*, the Court declared void a provision in a regulation imposing an anti-dumping duty. The aim of the action had been to have the rate of the duty increased and to secure the imposition of a duty on a wider range of products. The Court therefore ruled that the provision in question should remain in force until it had been replaced.[87]

The Treaty on European Union

The Treaty on European Union would replace the existing text of Article 173 with a new text extending the class of acts susceptible to review to include "acts adopted jointly by the European Parliament and by the Council,"[88] acts of the ECB[89] and "acts of the European Parliament intended to produce legal effects *vis-à-vis* third parties." The Court would also be given express jurisdiction under Article 173 "in actions brought by the European Parliament and by the ECB for the purpose of protecting their prerogatives." In addition, Article 176 of the Treaty would be extended to the ECB.

As far as the Parliament is concerned, these proposed changes to Article 173 seem designed to embody the effects of the Court's decisions in *Les Verts* and *Chernobyl*, discussed above. Those decisions will, however, remain of

---

[84] See, *e.g.* Case 108/81, *Amylum* v. *Council* [1982] E.C.R. 3107.
[85] See the second paragraph of Art. 176 EEC. Claims under the second paragraph of Art. 215 are discussed below.
[86] Case 81/72, *Commission* v. *Council* [1973] E.C.R. 575, para. 15.
[87] Case 264/82 [1985] E.C.R. 849, para. 32.
[88] See the procedure laid down in the new Art. 189b of the EC Treaty.
[89] European Central Bank, the full exercise of the powers of which are intended to start at the beginning of the third stage for achieving economic and monetary union, *i.e.* January 1, 1999 at the latest: see Arts. 109j(4) and 109l(1) EC. During the second stage, which is to begin on January 1, 1994 (Art. 109e(1) EC), the term "ECB" used in Arts. 173, 175, 176, 177, 180 and 215 is to be read as referring to the European Monetary Institute to be set up under Art. 109f EC: see Art. 109f(9).

the utmost importance as examples of the extent to which the Court is prepared to stretch the Treaty.

The express limitation of the right to bring proceedings against the Parliament to cases involving acts of the Parliament "intended to produce legal effects *vis-à-vis* third parties" is, however, curious. As we have seen, proceedings under Article 173 are in any event confined to acts intended to produce such effects. The reference to this condition in the particular context of proceedings brought against acts of the Parliament could therefore be taken to imply that it no longer applied to actions brought against other types of act. This does not seem to have been the intention of the authors of the new provision, however, since recommendations and opinions, which have no binding force, will remain excluded from the class of acts susceptible to review under Article 173.

Finally, it should be noted that, if the Treaty on European Union enters into force, the requirements of Articles 190 and 191 EEC will be extended to acts of the European Central Bank and of the European Monetary Institute.[90]

(c) *The action for failure to act*[91]

The action for annulment under Article 173 EEC is complemented by the action for failure to act, for which Article 175 EEC provides in the following terms:

> "Should the Council or the Commission, in infringement of this Treaty, fail to act, the Member States and the other institutions of the Community may bring an action before the Court of Justice to have the infringement established.
>
> The action shall be admissible only if the institution concerned has first been called upon to act. If, within two months of being so called upon, the institution concerned has not defined its position, the action may be brought within a further period of two months.
>
> Any natural or legal person may, under the conditions laid down in the preceding paragraphs, complain to the Court of Justice that an institution of the Community has failed to address to that person any act other than a recommendation or an opinion."

As we shall see, Article 175 has been interpreted so strictly by the Court that proceedings for failure to act are rarely successful. They may be regarded mainly as a last resort.[92]

---

[90] See, in relation to the former, Art. 108a(2) EC and Art. 34.2 of the Statute of the European System of Central Banks and of the European Central Bank, and, in relation to the latter, Art. 15.4 of the Statute of the European Monetary Institute.

[91] See Hartley, *op. cit.* Chap. 13.

[92] See Due, "Legal Remedies for the Failure of European Community Institutions to Act in Conformity with EEC Treaty Provisions" (1990–91) 14 Fordham International Law Journal 341.

Privileged applicants

The distinction drawn by Article 173 between privileged and non-privileged applicants is reproduced in Article 175, the Member States and the Community institutions enjoying broader rights than natural and legal persons to institute proceedings for failure to act.

Like Article 173, Article 175 as presently drafted makes no express mention of the European Parliament. The Court held in the *Transport* case,[93] however, that the first paragraph of Article 175, in referring to "the other institutions of the Community," gave the same right of action to all the Community institutions, including the Parliament. The Court stated that "It is not possible to restrict the exercise of that right by one of them without adversely affecting its status as an institution under the Treaty, in particular Article 4(1)."

It seems to follow that the expression "an institution of the Community" in the third paragraph of Article 175 also embraces the Parliament, so that a natural or legal person may in principle bring proceedings for failure to act against that institution. This might give rise to an anomaly, for the first paragraph of Article 175 only expressly enables the Member States and the institutions to bring such proceedings against the Council or the Commission. However, by analogy with the Court's reasoning in *Les Verts*, where it was held that Acts of the Parliament were subject to review under Article 173 notwithstanding the absence of any reference to the Parliament in that Article, it is submitted that proceedings under the first paragraph of Article 175 may also be brought by the Member States and the other institutions against the Parliament. This is consistent with the Treaty on European Union, which would amend the first paragraph of Article 175 to make it clear that proceedings for failure to act may be brought against the Parliament as well as the Council and the Commission.

The Court said in *Chevalley* v. *Commission*[94] that "The concept of a measure capable of giving rise to an action is identical in Articles 173 and 175, as both provisions merely prescribe one and the same method of recourse." Similarly, in the *Transport* case[95] the Court emphasised that "in the system, of legal remedies provided for by the Treaty there is a close relationship between the right of action given in Article 173 ... and that based on Article 175. ..." It appears, however, that these statements no longer fully reflect the approach of the Court and that the analogy with Article 173 should not be pushed too far. More recently, the Court said in the *Comitology* case[96] that "There is no necessary link between the action for annulment and the action for failure to act." The Court stated that this was demonstrated by the fact that the Parliament could bring proceedings under Article 175 for failure to adopt measures which might not be susceptible to review under Article 173. By way of example, the Court referred to its

---

[93] Case 13/83, *Parliament* v. *Council* [1985] E.C.R. 1513, para. 17.
[94] Case 15/70 [1970] E.C.R. 975, para. 6.
[95] *Supra*, para. 36.
[96] Case 302/87, *Parliament* v. *Council* [1988] E.C.R. 5615, para. 16.

judgment in *Parliament* v. *Council*,[97] where it was held that the Parliament could bring proceedings against the Council under Article 175 if it failed to present a draft budget within the deadline laid down in Article 203(4) EEC. The Court pointed out that, as a preparatory measure, the draft budget could not, once established, be challenged under Article 173.[98]

It is clear that the Member States and the institutions may bring proceedings under Article 175 against a failure to adopt a legally binding act, such as a regulation, directive or decision. Moreover, unlike the third paragraph of Article 175, which excludes proceedings in respect of a failure to adopt a recommendation or an opinion, the first paragraph of Article 175 speaks of a failure to act in general terms. It therefore seems that proceedings may be instituted under that paragraph against a failure to adopt measures which do not have binding force, such as recommendations, opinions or proposals for legislation.

Nevertheless, the Court stated in the *Transport* case[99] that an action under Article 175 would only lie in respect of "failure to take measures the scope of which can be sufficiently defined for them to be identified individually and adopted in compliance with the Court's judgment. . . ." That case arose out of the Council's failure to adopt a common transport policy. The field of transport is in principle capable of falling within the scope of the Treaty rules on freedom to provide services,[1] but Article 61(1) EEC states that "Freedom to provide services in the field of transport shall be governed by the provisions of the Title relating to transport." The Title relating to transport consists of Articles 74 to 84 EEC. According to Article 74, the objectives of the Treaty are, as far as transport is concerned, to be pursued by the Member States within the framework of a common transport policy. For the purpose of giving effect to Article 74, Article 75(1) requires the Council to lay down:

"(a) common rules applicable to international transport to or from the territory of a Member State or passing across the territory of one or more Member States;

(b) the conditions under which non-resident carriers may operate transport services within a Member State;

(c) any other appropriate provisions."

The provisions referred to in (a) and (b) above were required by Article 75(2) to be laid down during the transitional period, which ended on December 31, 1969.

In the *Transport* case, the Parliament brought proceedings under Article 175 for a declaration that the Council had infringed the Treaty *inter alia* by failing to introduce a common policy for transport. The application was successful in part only. The Court made it clear that it was irrelevant how difficult it might be for the institution concerned to comply with its

---

[97] Case 377/87 [1988] E.C.R. 4017.
[98] See Case 60/81, *IBM* v. *Commission* [1981] E.C.R. 2639, *supra.*
[99] *Supra*, para. 37.
[1] Arts. 59–66 EEC.

obligations, but found that under the Treaty the Council enjoyed a discretion with regard to the implementation of the common transport policy. Although that discretion was subject to certain limits, the Court said that it was for the Council to determine "the aims of and means for implementing a common transport policy."[2] The Court concluded that the absence of such a policy "does not in itself necessarily constitute a failure to act sufficiently specific in nature to form the subject of an action under Article 175."[3]

The Commission, which intervened in support of the Parliament, argued, however, that the common transport policy envisaged by the Treaty contained one element which was sufficiently well-defined to be regarded as imposing on the Council a specific obligation, namely a requirement to ensure freedom to provide services. The scope of that requirement could be determined by reference to the Treaty rules on services and to the relevant directives and case-law. That argument found favour with the Court, which stated that "Insofar as the obligations laid down in Article 75(1)(a) and (b) relate to freedom to provide services . . . they are sufficiently well-defined for disregard of them to be the subject of a finding of failure to act pursuant to Article 175."[4] The Court concluded "that the Council has failed to act since it has failed to adopt measures which ought to have been adopted before the expiry of the transitional period and whose subject-matter and nature may be determined with a sufficient degree of precision."[5]

Non-privileged applicants

Under the third paragraph of Article 175, any natural or legal person may complain to the Court "that an institution of the Community has failed to address to that person any act other than a recommendation or an opinion." There are two respects in which the right of action conferred by that paragraph is more limited than that conferred on privileged applicants by the first paragraph of Article 175. First, the category of acts failure to adopt which gives rise to a right of action is restricted. Secondly, a non-privileged applicant must show that the act he alleges should have been adopted would have been addressed to him had the defendant institution complied with its obligations under the Treaty. It is not enough that the act would have been of direct and individual concern to him. These two aspects of the action under the third paragraph of Article 175 will now be considered in a little more detail.

The explicit exclusion of recommendations and opinions from the class of acts a failure to adopt which gives rise to a right of action under the third paragraph of Article 175 suggests that it is only a failure to adopt a legally binding act which may be the subject of proceedings under that provision. That suggestion is confirmed by *Chevalley* v. *Commission*,[6] where the Court

---

[2] Para. 49 of the judgment.
[3] Para. 53.
[4] Para. 66.
[5] Para. 68.
[6] Case 15/70 [1970] E.C.R. 975.

held that a definition of the Commission's position on a question, which would have amounted in substance to an opinion within the meaning of Article 189 EEC, was not capable of forming the subject-matter of an action under the third paragraph of Article 175.

The second point made above led to the failure of the application in *Lord Bethell* v. *Commission*,[7] where the applicant was seeking the adoption of binding measures in respect of third parties rather than in respect of himself. In that case, Lord Bethell brought proceedings against the Commission under the third paragraph of Article 175 for a declaration that the Commission had failed, in breach of the Treaty, to act against anti-competitive practices allegedly being pursued by a number of European airlines. The Court acknowledged that the applicant had an indirect interest in the outcome of any action the Commission might decide to take because he was a user of the airlines and a leading member of an organisation of users of air passenger services. Nevertheless, the Court pointed out that he was "not in the precise legal position ... of the potential addressee of a legal measure which the Commission has a duty to adopt with regard to him."[8] The application was therefore held inadmissible.

It should be noted that since, according to Article 189 EEC, a regulation is not addressed to anyone, it follows that a natural or legal person may not challenge a failure to adopt such a measure.[9]

Procedural aspects

Article 175 does not specify how soon proceedings must be instituted after the alleged failure to act has come to light. In a case decided under Article 35 of the ECSC Treaty, which corresponds to Article 175 EEC, the Court held that proceedings for failure to act must be instituted within a reasonable period once it has become clear that the Commission has decided to take no action.[10] In the *Transport* case, however, the Court partially upheld an application made under Article 175 in January 1983 in respect of a failure to discharge an obligation which should have been fulfilled by the end of 1969, by which time the applicant was fully aware of the failure concerned. These cases may perhaps be distinguished on the ground that in the former the defendant had made it clear that it had decided not to take any action, whereas in the latter the defendant accepted the need for it to take further steps. It seems that it is only in the former type of case that proceedings must be brought within a reasonable period of the alleged failure to act having come to light.

According to the second paragraph of Article 175, the institution concerned must first be "called upon to act." In the *Transport* case, the Council argued that that requirement had not been met. The Court

---

[7] Case 246/81 [1982] E.C.R. 2277.
[8] Para. 16 of the judgment.
[9] See, *e.g.* Case 134/73, *Holtz* v. *Council* [1974] E.C.R. 1, para. 5; Case 60/79, *Producteurs de Vins de Table et Vins de Pays* v. *Commission* [1979] E.C.R. 2429; Case 90/78, *Granaria* v. *Council and Commission* [1979] E.C.R. 1081, para. 14 (from the final sentence of which the word "not" has inadvertently been omitted in the English version).
[10] Case 59/70, *Netherlands* v. *Commission* [1971] E.C.R. 639.

disagreed, however, since the President of the Parliament had sent a letter to the Council which referred to Article 175 and which stated that the Parliament was calling on the Council to act pursuant to that provision. Moreover, annexed to the letter was a list of the steps which the Parliament considered the Council should take to remedy the failure.

If the institution concerned has not "defined its position" within two months of having been called upon to act, an application may be made to the Court within a further period of two months. Thus, where the institution does define its position, it is not possible to bring the matter before the Court under Article 175. An institution may define its position by means of a measure which is not itself susceptible to review under Article 173. For example, in Lütticke v. Commission,[11] the applicants commenced proceedings under Articles 173 and 175 in an attempt to force the Commission to bring an action against the Federal Republic of Germany under Article 169. The Commission had informed the applicants by letter that it did not consider the Federal Republic to be in breach of its obligations under the Treaty in the manner alleged. The applicants sought the annulment of that letter under Article 173 and, in the alternative, a declaration under Article 175 that the Commission's failure to bring an action against the Federal Republic was unlawful. The action under Article 173 was held inadmissible because the Commission's letter did not have any binding force. The action under Article 175 was also held inadmissible, since "the Commission has defined its position and has notified this position to the applicants within the prescribed period."[12]

In the Transport case, on the other hand, the Court declined to treat as a definition of its position within the meaning of the second paragraph of Article 175 the Council's reply to the letter from the Parliament calling upon it to act. The Court observed[13] that the Council's reply "was confined to setting out what action it had already taken in relation to transport without commenting 'on the legal aspects' of the correspondence initiated by the Parliament. The reply neither denied nor confirmed the alleged failure to act nor gave any indication of the Council's views as to the measures which, according to the Parliament, remained to be taken."

The act by which the institution defines its position will only be susceptible to review under Article 173 where the measure requested could itself have been challenged by the applicant under that Article had it been adopted. In Nordgetreide v. Commission,[14] for example, the applicant, a private undertaking, sought the annulment of a refusal by the Commission to adopt an act which would have taken the form of a regulation. Since the measure requested "would have affected the applicant only insofar as it belongs to a category viewed in the abstract and in its entirety," it could not have been

---

[11] Case 48/65 [1966] E.C.R 19.
[12] An alternative ground for dismissing the action under Art. 175 would have been that the Commission enjoys a discretion in deciding whether to commence proceedings under Art. 169: see Case 247/87, Star Fruit v. Commission [1989] E.C.R. 291.
[13] Para. 25 of the judgment.
[14] Case 42/71 [1972] E.C.R. 105.

challenged by the applicant under the second paragraph of Article 173. The application was therefore declared inadmissible.

The Court's decision in *Nordgetreide* suggested that a refusal to adopt the act requested constituted a definition of the institution's position and therefore excluded proceedings for failure to act. That position appears to have been relaxed in the *Comitology* case,[15] which concerned the question whether the Parliament had the right to institute annulment proceedings under Article 173. One of the arguments put forward by the Parliament was that, in the absence of any power to institute annulment proceedings, it would be unable to challenge an express refusal to act issued by the Council or the Commission after the Parliament had called upon them to act under Article 175. The Court replied: "that argument is based on a false premise. A refusal to act, however explicit it may be, can be brought before the Court under Article 175 since it does not put an end to the failure to act."[16]

It is possible that the Court's statement in *Comitology* is limited to cases where the applicant would not have standing to challenge an express refusal to act under Article 173.[17] It is submitted, however, that the statement should be regarded as having general application. As the Court acknowledged, a refusal, however clear, by an institution to take the action requested can have no bearing on the question whether the alleged failure to act is lawful.

It should be noted that Article 175 cannot be used to challenge a refusal by an institution to revoke a Community act which has not been challenged within the deadline laid down in Article 173, since this would provide applicants "with a method of recourse parallel to that of Article 173, which would not be subject to the conditions laid down by the Treaty."[18]

Where the failure to act is remedied within two months of the institution concerned having been called upon to act, no action may be brought before the Court. The steps taken need not be the same as those requested by the applicant, for the Court has said that "Article 175 refers to failure to act in the sense of failure to take a decision or to define a position, and not the adoption of a measure different from that desired or considered necessary by the persons concerned."[19] Thus, an institution which proposes a particular legal basis for a measure cannot use Article 175 to challenge the choice of a different legal basis by the adopting institution.[20]

Where the defendant institution takes the steps requested over two months after being called upon to do so but before judgment is given, the Court will decline to give a ruling on the basis that "the subject-matter of the action has ceased to exist."[21] This is surprising, since according to the second paragraph of Article 176 EEC a ruling by the Court under Article 175 is

---

[15] Case 302/87 [1988] E.C.R. 5615.
[16] Para. 17 of the judgment. *Cf.* the Opinion of A. G. Darmon at pp. 5630–5631.
[17] *Cf.* Due, *loc. cit.* p. 356; the Opinion of A. G. Gulmann in Joined Cases C–15/91 and C–108/91, *Josef Buckl & Söhne and others*, delivered on July 8, 1992.
[18] Joined Cases 10 and 18/68, *Eridania* v. *Commission* [1969] E.C.R. 459, para. 17.
[19] Joined Cases 166 and 220/86, *Irish Cement Ltd.* v. *Commission* [1988] E.C.R. 6473, para. 17.
[20] See Case C–70/88, *Parliament* v. *Council* ("Chernobyl") [1990] E.C.R. I–2041.
[21] See Case 377/87, *Parliament* v. *Council* [1988] E.C.R. 4017.

without prejudice to the liability of the institution concerned under the second paragraph of Article 215 EEC[22] to pay compensation for any damage resulting from its failure to act. By analogy with its case law under Article 169 EEC,[23] the Court might have been expected to regard a judgment on the substance as desirable in these circumstances in order to establish the legality of the alleged failure for the purposes of any subsequent proceedings under Article 215.

The effects of the Court's ruling

Where an application under Article 175 is upheld, the Court declares that the failure of the institution concerned to act is contrary to the Treaty. The Court cannot remedy the failure itself, but the institution concerned is required by the first paragraph of Article 176 EEC "to take the necessary measures to comply with the judgment of the Court of Justice." The Court has said that those measures must be taken within a reasonable period of the judgment.[24]

The Treaty on European Union

As well as adding the Parliament to the institutions against which proceedings for failure to act may be brought under the first paragraph of Article 175, the Treaty on European Union would insert a fourth paragraph in the following terms:

> "The Court of Justice shall have jurisdiction, under the same conditions, in actions or proceedings brought by the ECB[25] in the areas falling within the latter's field of competence and in actions or proceedings brought against the latter."

The meaning of the expression "under the same conditions" is not entirely clear. The preceding paragraph would be that dealing with the conditions under which natural and legal persons may bring proceedings for failure to act and it is possible that these are the conditions referred to in the new fourth paragraph. However, proceedings for failure to act evidently cannot be brought against natural and legal persons, yet it would be possible to bring such proceedings against the ECB. It is therefore submitted that the "conditions" referred to are those governing proceedings under the first, rather than the third, paragraph of Article 175.

As already noted, the Treaty on European Union would also extend Article 176 of the Treaty to the ECB.[26]

---

[22] This provision is discussed below.
[23] See, *e.g.* Case 39/72, *Commission* v. *Italy* [1973] E.C.R. 101, *supra.*
[24] See the *Transport* case, *supra* at para. 69.
[25] European Central Bank. During the second stage for achieving economic and monetary union, the term "ECB" in Art. 175 is to be read as referring to the European Monetary Institute: see Art. 109f(9) EC.
[26] And, during the second stage for achieving economic and monetary union, the European Monetary Institute.

(d) *The preliminary rulings procedure*

Introduction

The responsibility for giving effect to Community law cast by the Treaties on the national courts gave rise to a danger that equivalent provisions would not be interpreted and applied in the same way in different Member States. Such a situation would be inimical to the proper functioning of the common market. In an attempt to safeguard the uniform application of Community law,[27] the authors of the Treaty established a procedure which enables national courts to seek the guidance of the Court of Justice on points of Community law they are called on to decide. That procedure is laid down in Article 177 EEC, which provides as follows:

"The Court of Justice shall have jurisdiction to give preliminary rulings concerning:
(a) the interpretation of this Treaty;
(b) the validity and interpretation of acts of the institutions of the Community;
(c) the interpretation of the statutes of bodies established by an act of the Council, where those statutes so provide.

Where such a question is raised before any court or tribunal of a Member State, that court or tribunal may, if it considers that a decision on the question is necessary to enable it to give judgment, request the Court of Justice to give a ruling thereon.

Where any such question is raised in a case pending before a court or tribunal of a Member State, against whose decisions there is no judicial remedy under national law, that court or tribunal shall bring the matter before the Court of Justice."

The Treaty on European Union would amend Article 177 to enable the Court to give preliminary rulings on the validity and interpretation of acts of the ECB.[28]

The Court of Justice enjoys similar jurisdiction under the ECSC Treaty[29] and under the Euratom Treaty.[30] Provision for the Court of Justice to give preliminary rulings has also been made in relation to the Brussels Convention,[31] although the range of courts which may ask it to do so is more limited.

As we shall see, a reference to the Court of Justice may in principle be made at any stage in the proceedings pending before the national court. The ruling of the Court of Justice is interlocutory in that it constitutes a step in the proceedings before the national court, which must apply the ruling to the

---

[27] See Case 166/73, *Rheinmühlen* v. *Einfuhr- und Vorratsstelle Getreide* [1974] E.C.R. 33.
[28] European Central Bank. During the second stage for achieving economic and monetary union, this term is to be read as referring to the European Monetary Institute: see Art. 109f(9) EC.
[29] See Art. 41 ECSC, as interpreted by the Court of Justice in Case C–221/88, *ECSC* v. *Busseni* [1990] E.C.R. I–495.
[30] See Art. 150.
[31] The Convention of September 27, 1968 on Jurisdiction and the Enforcement of Judgments in Civil and Commercial Matters, O.J. 1978 L304/1.

facts of the case. It is in this sense that the ruling of the Court of Justice is preliminary. Thus, the national court must be in a position to take account of the ruling of the Court of Justice when giving judgment. The Court of Justice has no jurisdiction to give a preliminary ruling if the proceedings before the referring court have already been terminated.[32]

Questions which may be referred

Article 177 enables any question of EEC law to be referred to the Court of Justice for a preliminary ruling by any national court or tribunal which considers a decision on the question "necessary to enable it to give judgment." The question may be raised either by one of the parties or by the judge of his own motion.[33] A decision is "necessary" for these purposes if the national court sees it as a step, which need not be the final one, in its strategy for disposing of the case. The Community point need not be conclusive.[34]

Questions which may be the subject of a reference include, as well as questions on the interpretation of the EEC Treaty itself, questions on one of the amending Treaties or on one of the Treaties of Accession, and questions on the validity and interpretation of acts of the Community institutions, such as regulations, directives and decisions of the Council or Commission and non-binding measures such as recommendations.[35] Acts of the European Parliament may also be the subject of references to the Court of Justice.[36] Cases may be referred on the interpretation of an agreement concluded by the Community with a third State, since such an agreement constitutes, as far as the Community is concerned, an act of one of the institutions[37]; or even, in certain circumstances, on the interpretation of agreements to which the Community is not a party, notably the General Agreement on Tariffs and Trade (GATT).[38] References may also be made on whether a provision of Community law produces direct effect, that, is, whether it confers rights on individuals which national courts are bound to protect.

In *Dzodzi* v. *Belgium*,[39] the Court of Justice held that it has jurisdiction under Article 177 to give preliminary rulings on the effect of provisions of Community law which are applicable in the action pending before the national court only because their scope has been extended by national law. Advocate General Darmon had taken the view that the Court had no jurisdiction to give a ruling in circumstances such as these, where

---

[32] Case 338/85, *Pardini* v. *Ministero del Commercio con l'Estero* [1988] E.C.R. 2041, para. 11. *Cf.* Case C–3/90, *Bernini*, judgment of February 26, 1992; the decision of the Divisional Court in *S.A. Magnavision N.V.* v. *General Optical Council* [1987] 2 C.M.L.R. 262.

[33] Case 166/73, *Rheinmühlen* v. *Einfuhr- und Vorratsstelle Getreide* [1974] E.C.R. 33. See also Joined Cases C–87/90, C–88/90 and C–89/90, *Verholen and others*, judgment of July 11, 1991.

[34] See Joined Cases 36 and 71/80, *Irish Creamery Milk Suppliers Association* v. *Ireland* [1981] E.C.R. 735; *Polydor Ltd.* v. *Harlequin Record Shops Ltd.* [1980] 2 C.M.L.R. 413 (Court of Appeal).

[35] See, *e.g.* Case C–322/88, *Grimaldi* v. *Fonds des Maladies Professionelles* [1989] E.C.R. 4407.

[36] See, *e.g.* Case 208/80, *Lord Bruce of Donington* [1981] E.C.R. 2205.

[37] See Case 181/73, *Haegeman* v. *Belgium* [1974] E.C.R. 449; Opinion 1/76 [1977] E.C.R. 741.

[38] See Joined Cases 267 to 269/81, *Amministrazione delle Finanze dello Stato* v. *S.P.I. and S.A.M.I.* [1983] E.C.R. 801.

[39] Joined Cases C–297/88 and C–197/89 [1990] E.C.R. I–3763, followed in Case C–231/89, *Gmurzynska-Bscher* v. *Oberfinanzdirektion Köln* [1990] E.C.R. I–4003. See Bravo-Ferrer Delgado and La Casta Muñoa, (1991) 29 C.M.L.Rev. 152.

Community law was not applicable in its own right and where the guidance of the Court was being sought essentially to enable the national court to apply provisions of national law. The Court stated, however, that the proper functioning of the Community legal order made it imperative that provisions of Community law be given a uniform interpretation regardless of the circumstances in which they fell to be applied. It proceeded to deal with the substance of the questions which had been put to it.[40]

Courts and tribunals of the Member States

The power to make a reference under Article 177 belongs to "any court or tribunal of a Member State." This notion has been interpreted broadly by the Court of Justice as encompassing all organs of the Member States exercising a judicial function. Thus, in *Vaassen* v. *Beamtenfonds Mijnbedrijf*[41] a Dutch social security tribunal which gave "non-binding opinions" and which did not consider itself a court or tribunal under Dutch law was held to be a court or tribunal of a Member State for the purposes of Article 177. This was due to the fact that the members of the tribunal were appointed, its chairman designated and its rules of procedure laid down by the responsible minister, and that it was a permanent body which heard disputes according to an adversarial procedure and was bound to apply rules of law.

The fact that a body which exercises a judicial function also performs other tasks which are not judicial in character does not prevent it from being a court or tribunal for the purposes of Article 177. Thus, in *Pretore di Salò* v. *Persons Unknown*,[42] the Court of Justice accepted a reference from an Italian pretore, a magistrate combining the tasks of public prosecutor and investigating judge. On the other hand, in *Borker*,[43] the Court of Justice declined to give a ruling on a reference from the Paris Bar Council on the ground that the Council was not exercising a judicial function. Moreover, in *Nordsee* v. *Reederei Mond*,[44] an arbitrator appointed under a private contract was held not to be a court or tribunal of a Member State, notwithstanding (or perhaps because of) the commercial importance of arbitration and the finality of arbitrators' decisions.

It seems that Article 177 may be invoked by judicial bodies situated in any territory to which the Treaty applies, even if only in part. In *Department of Health and Social Security (Isle of Man)* v. *Barr and Montrose Holdings Ltd.*,[45] the Deputy High Bailiff's Court, Douglas, Isle of Man, purported to make a reference to the Court of Justice under Article 177. There was no doubt that the Deputy High Bailiff's Court was a "court" for the purposes of that Article, but since the Isle of Man is not part of the United Kingdom in constitutional terms,[46] the question arose whether it could be regarded as a

---

[40] Which concerned the rules on the free movement of persons.
[41] Case 61/65 [1966] E.C.R. 261.
[42] Case 14/86 [1987] E.C.R. 2545.
[43] Case 138/80 [1980] E.C.R. 1975.
[44] Case 102/81 [1982] E.C.R. 1095.
[45] Case C–355/89 [1991] E.C.R. I–3479. *Cf.* Joined Cases C–100/89 and C–101/89, *Kaefer and Procacci* v. *France* [1990] E.C.R. I–4647.
[46] See the Opinion of A. G. Jacobs.

court "of a Member State." Under Article 227(5)(c) of the Treaty and Protocol No. 3 to the United Kingdom Act of Accession, certain provisions of Community law are applicable in the island. Accordingly, the Court of Justice ruled that Article 177 could be invoked by the Deputy High Bailiff's Court, pointing out that otherwise it would be impossible to ensure the uniform application in the island of the provisions of Community law applicable there.

The dialogue between the Court of Justice and the national court

The relationship between the national court and the Court of Justice in proceedings under Article 177 is co-operative rather than hierarchical in nature. A reference to the Court of Justice is not in any sense an appeal against the decision of the national court. There are technically no parties to the proceedings before the Court of Justice, which may be regarded as a form of dialogue between that court and the referring court. The parties to the action before the referring court have the right, however, along with the Member States, the Commission,[47] and the Council, where the validity or interpretation of one of its acts is in issue, to submit written and oral observations to the Court of Justice in accordance with Article 20 of the Statute of the Court. In order to enable them to exercise that right, Article 20 requires the Court to notify them of the reference.

The Court of Justice will not, in the context of a reference for a preliminary ruling, rule on the application of the law to the specific facts of the case before the national court or on the compatibility of a provision of national law with the requirements of Community law.[48] These are matters within the exclusive jurisdiction of the national court in proceedings under Article 177. The questions referred should therefore be couched in terms which pose a general question of law rather than the concrete issue as it falls to be decided in the instant case. If they are not, the Court of Justice may reformulate them. Questions may also be reformulated if the Court of Justice considers this necessary to furnish the national court with all the elements of Community law which it requires to give judgment in the case before it.[49] The Court of Justice will in any event endeavour to extract from all the information provided by the national court and from the documents concerning the main proceedings the elements of Community law that need to be interpreted having regard to the subject-matter of the dispute.[50]

Where the questions are designed to permit the national court to rule on the compatibility of national provisions with Community law, the Court of Justice will endeavour to provide the necessary guidance on the correct interpretation of Community law. This is so even where the questions relate

---

[47] It is the practice of the Commission to submit observations in all references for preliminary rulings and these are often of great assistance to the Court.
[48] See, *e.g.* Joined Cases 91 and 127/83, *Heineken Brouwerijen* [1984] E.C.R. 3435.
[49] See, *e.g.* Case 28/85, *Deghillage* v. *Caisse Primaire d'Assurance Maladie* [1986] E.C.R. 991, para. 13; Case C–221/89, *R.* v. *Secretary of State for Transport, ex p. Factortame*, judgment of July 25, 1991.
[50] See, *e.g.* Case 251/83, *Haug-Adrion* v. *Frankfurter Versicherungs-AG* [1984] E.C.R. 4277.

to the national law of a Member State which is not that of the referring court.[51]

Although the reference itself is not required to take any particular form, the Court of Justice has provided guidance on what references should contain. In *Foglia* v. *Novello*,[52] the Court stated that national courts must explain the grounds on which they consider an answer to their questions necessary for judgment to be given in the main proceedings, if those grounds are not unequivocally evident from the file on the case. The Court pointed out in *Holdijk*[53] that the information furnished in the decision making the reference served not only to enable the Court to give helpful answers but also to enable the governments of the Member States and other interested parties to submit observations in accordance with Article 20 of the Statute of the Court. It was the Court's duty to ensure that the opportunity to submit observations was safeguarded. The reference should therefore be self-contained and self-explanatory, since only the reference itself, and not any accompanying documents, will be notified to those who are entitled to submit observations.

The discretion conferred by the second paragraph of Article 177

Under the second paragraph of Article 177, courts and tribunals in the Member States whose decisions are subject to a judicial remedy under national law enjoy a discretion in deciding whether or not to ask for a preliminary ruling on points of Community law they are called on to decide. The proper functioning of the preliminary rulings procedure depends to a large extent on the way in which that discretion is exercised. Some national courts have purported to lay down guidelines on the matter,[54] but since the extent of the discretion depends on the correct interpretation of Article 177, only the Court of Justice is competent to make authoritative pronouncements on the matter.

It is well established that the national court is in principle the sole judge of whether a preliminary ruling is necessary and of the relevance of the questions referred to the Court of Justice.[55] The latter court made it clear in *Rheinmühlen*[56] that the power to make a reference arises "as soon as the judge perceives either of his own motion or at the request of the parties that the litigation depends on a point referred to in the first paragraph of Article 177." It followed, the Court said, that national courts enjoyed "the widest discretion" in seeking preliminary rulings on points of Community law raised before them. This meant that "the existence of a rule of domestic law whereby a court is bound on points of law by the rulings of the court superior to it cannot of itself take away the power provided for by Article 177 of referring cases to the Court of Justice."

---

[51] See Case C–150/88, *Parfümerie-Fabrik 4711* v. *Provide* [1989] E.C.R. 3891.
[52] Case 244/80 [1981] E.C.R. 3045.
[53] Joined Cases 141 to 143/81 [1982] E.C.R. 1299.
[54] See, *e.g.* Lord Denning's now largely discredited guidelines in *H. P. Bulmer Ltd.* v. *J. Bollinger S.A.* [1974] Ch. 401.
[55] See, *e.g. Dzodzi* v. *Belgium, supra.*
[56] Case 166/73 [1974] E.C.R. 33, paras. 3 and 4.

In *Irish Creamery Milk Suppliers Association* v. *Ireland*, the Court of Justice made it clear that it was for the national court to decide at what stage in the proceedings it was appropriate for a preliminary ruling to be requested. In order for the Court of Justice to be in a position to give a useful answer, it was essential for the national court "to define the legal context" in which the reference was made. Thus, "it might be convenient, in certain circumstances, for the facts in the case to be established and for questions of purely national law to be settled at the time the reference is made to the Court of Justice so as to enable the latter to take cognizance of all the features of fact and of law which may be relevant. . . ." The Court of Justice emphasised, however, that:

> "Those considerations do not in any way restrict the discretion of the national court, which alone has a direct knowledge of the facts of the case and of the arguments of the parties, which will have to take responsibility for giving judgment in the case and which is therefore in the best position to appreciate at what stage in the proceedings it requires a preliminary ruling from the Court of Justice."[57]

Although the Court of Justice will not normally review the exercise by the national court of its discretion,[58] a reference will be rejected "if it is quite obvious that the interpretation of Community law or the examination of the validity of a rule of Community law sought by that court bears no relation to the actual nature of the case or to the subject-matter of the main action."[59] Moreover, in *Foglia* v. *Novello*[60] the Court of Justice refused to entertain a reference made in the context of a collusive action brought in one Member State by parties who are not really in dispute with each other with the intention of challenging the law of another Member State as contrary to Community law. The Court's ruling in that case was heavily criticised,[61] but has in practice been applied with considerable restraint.[62]

Despite the emphasis placed by the Court of Justice on the extent of the discretion enjoyed by national courts which are covered by the second paragraph of Article 177, it has nevertheless accepted that the Treaty does not preclude a decision to refer from remaining subject to the remedies normally available under national law. However, the Court will act on the decision to refer until it has been revoked.[63]

---

[57] Joined Cases 36 and 71/80 [1981] E.C.R. 735, paras. 6 and 7. The Court's ruling in the *Irish Creamery* case was reiterated in Case 72/83, *Campus Oil* v. *Minister for Industry and Energy* [1984] E.C.R. 2727 and Case 14/86, *Pretore di Salò* v. *Persons Unknown* [1987] E.C.R. 2545.

[58] See Case 6/64, *Costa* v. *ENEL* [1964] E.C.R. 585.

[59] Case 126/80, *Salonia* v. *Poidomani* [1981] E.C.R. 1563, 1576–1577. See also Case C–286/88, *Falciola* [1990] E.C.R. I–191.

[60] Case 104/79 [1980] E.C.R. 745.

[61] See, *e.g.* Barav (1980) 5 E.L.Rev. 443; Bebr (1980) 17 C.M.L.Rev. 525 and (1982) 19 C.M.L.Rev. 428.

[62] *Cf.*, however, Case C–83/91, *Meilicke* v. *ADV/ORGA*, judgment of July 16, 1992.

[63] See Case 146/73, *Rheinmühlen-Düsseldorf* v. *Einfuhr- und Vorratsstelle Getreide* [1974] E.C.R. 139, para. 3.

Preliminary rulings on validity

It will be observed that the Court of Justice may, under the first paragraph of Article 177, be asked for a preliminary ruling on the validity as well as on the interpretation of acts of the Community institutions. The Treaty appears to confer on national courts (other than those of last resort) the same discretion whether the question of Community law raised is one of interpretation or one of validity. However, in *Foto-Frost* v. *Hauptzollamt Lübeck-Ost*[64] the Court of Justice held that, while national courts were entitled to find that acts adopted by the institutions of the Community were valid, they had no power to declare such acts invalid. This was because "Divergences between courts in the Member States as to the validity of Community acts would be liable to place in jeopardy the very unity of the Community legal order and detract from the fundamental requirement of legal certainty." Accordingly, where a real and substantial doubt is raised in a national court on the validity of a Community measure, and where it is clear that a decision on the validity of the measure is necessary for the resolution of the case, then the issue must be referred. This is so even where similar provisions have been declared void by the Court of Justice in other cases.[65]

The jurisdiction of the Court of Justice to rule on the validity of Community provisions under Article 177 of the Treaty complements its jurisdiction to review the legality of acts of the institutions under Article 173 of the Treaty.[66] The former jurisdiction typically arises where a national measure, purportedly based on a Community act, is challenged in a national court on the ground that the Community act is itself invalid. A person affected by a Community act may thus challenge the validity of the act independently of the direct action which may be available before the Court of Justice under Article 173. The Court's jurisdiction to rule on validity under Article 177 is not subject to the restrictive conditions on standing or the two-month time limit laid down in Article 173. Moreover, unlike Article 173, Article 177 does not specify the grounds on which the validity of a Community act may be challenged. However, in practice the grounds appear to be substantially similar under both Articles.

The Court's judgment in *Foto-Frost* suggested[67] that national courts might have jurisdiction to declare Community acts invalid in interlocutory proceedings, where it might for reasons of urgency be impractical to wait for a ruling on the matter from the Court of Justice. The powers of national courts in such proceedings were considered in more detail in *Zuckerfabrik Süderditmarschen* v. *Hauptzollamt Itzehoe*.[68] In that case, the Court ruled

---

[64] Case 314/85 [1987] E.C.R. 4199. See Bebr, "The reinforcement of the constitutional review of Community acts under Article 177 EEC Treaty" (1988) 25 C.M.L.Rev. 667.

[65] *Cf. R.* v. *Intervention Board for Agricultural Produce, ex p. E.D. and F. Man (Sugar) Ltd.* [1986] 2 All E.R. 126 (Q.B.); *R.* v. *Minister of Agriculture, ex p. Fédération Européenne de la Santé Animale* [1988] 3 C.M.L.R. 207 and 661 (D.C.).

[66] Discussed above.

[67] See para. 19 of the judgment.

[68] Joined Cases C–143/88 and C–92/89 [1991] E.C.R. I–415. See Schermers, (1992) 29 C.M.L.Rev. 133.

that a national court may, on an interim basis, suspend a domestic measure based on a Community regulation[69] which is alleged to be invalid, provided:

(a) it has serious doubts about the validity of the Community act;
(b) it asks the Court of Justice for a preliminary ruling on the validity of the act (unless such a ruling has already been requested);
(c) the matter is urgent and the applicant is liable to suffer serious and irreparable damage if relief is refused; and
(d) due account is taken of the interest of the Community and the need to ensure the effectiveness of Community law.

Mandatory references

Where a question of Community law, within the meaning of the first paragraph of Article 177, is raised in a case pending before a court or tribunal of a Member State against whose decisions there is no judicial remedy under national law, that court or tribunal is obliged, under the third paragraph of the Article, to refer the question to the Court of Justice. The expression "court or tribunal . . . against whose decisions there is no judicial remedy under national law" is not confined to courts whose decisions are always final, such as the House of Lords. It means any court, even if not the highest court, against whose decision there is no judicial remedy in the instant case.[70] Accordingly, the Court of Appeal is obliged to refer if leave to appeal to the House of Lords is refused.[71] It would appear to follow that, if the Court of Appeal refuses either to refer or to grant leave to appeal against its substantive decision, then the House of Lords must itself grant leave to appeal. Similar considerations apply where the High Court is considering whether to grant leave to apply for judicial review of a decision from which there is no appeal.[72]

Although Article 177(3) states that a reference is obligatory "where any such question is raised," this does not mean that the obligation arises wherever a party contends that a question of Community law needs to be decided. In *CILFIT* v. *Ministry of Health*,[73] the Court of Justice held that final courts are in the same position as other national courts in deciding whether they need to resolve a question of Community law before giving judgment. A final court is not therefore obliged to ask for a preliminary ruling where the answer to the question raised cannot affect the outcome of the case.

Even where a question of Community law is relevant, the Court of Justice went on to hold that a final court is under no obligation to refer if:

(a) the point has already been decided by a previous decision of the Court

---

[69] Although the case concerned a regulation, it is submitted that similar considerations would apply in relation to other types of Community act.
[70] Case 6/64, *Costa* v. *ENEL* [1964] E.C.R. 585. See also Case 107/76, *Hoffmann-La Roche* v. *Centrafarm* [1977] E.C.R. 957 and Joined Cases 35 and 36/82, *Morson and Jhanjan* v. *Netherlands* [1982] E.C.R. 3723.
[71] See the decision of the Court of Appeal in *Hagen* v. *Fratelli D. & G. Moretti S.N.C.* [1980] 3 C.M.L.R. 253.
[72] For a more detailed discussed, see Hartley, *op. cit.* pp. 261–266.
[73] Case 283/81 [1982] E.C.R. 3415.

of Justice (although in that event the national court remains free to refer if it wishes the Court of Justice to reconsider its earlier ruling); or

(b) the correct application of Community law is so obvious as to leave no scope for any reasonable doubt as to the manner in which the question raised is to be resolved.[74] However, before the national court reaches this conclusion, it must be convinced that the matter would be equally obvious to the courts of the other Member States and to the Court of Justice. In that regard, it must take account of the characteristic features of Community law and the particular difficulties to which its interpretation gives rise.

If follows from the decision of the Court of Justice in the *Foto-Frost* case, where it was held that no national court is competent to declare an act adopted by one of the Community's political institutions invalid, that the considerations laid down in *CILFIT* apply only where the question of Community law raised before the national court is one of interpretation. Accordingly, where there is a real possibility in proceedings before a national court of last resort that a Community measure is invalid, the matter must be referred to the Court of Justice.

The criteria set out by the Court of Justice in the *CILFIT* case are also relevant where courts which are not covered by the third paragraph of Article 177 have to interpret Community law. This is because, where those criteria are satisfied, such courts may properly decline, in the exercise of their discretion, to make a reference.

In England, there is some evidence that the *CILFIT* decision is occasionally used by the courts to justify declining to make a reference where such a step ought probably to be taken.[75] On the whole, however, English courts seem to regard the criteria laid down in *CILFIT* as difficult to satisfy.[76]

A national court is not required to refer a question of interpretation or validity when the question is raised in interlocutory proceedings for an interim order, provided that each of the parties is entitled to institute proceedings or to require proceedings to be instituted on the substance of the case, and that during such proceedings the question provisionally decided at the interlocutory stage may be re-examined and referred to the Court of Justice.[77] This is so even where the criteria laid down in the *CILFIT* case are not satisfied and no judicial remedy is available against the interlocutory decision itself.

---

[74] This situation is sometimes called "*acte clair.*"
[75] See further Arnull, "The Use and Abuse of Article 177 EEC" (1989) 52 M.L.R. 622.
[76] Some of those criteria were described by Hodgson J. in *R.* v. *Secretary of State for Transport, ex p. Factortame* [1989] 2 C.M.L.R. 353, 379 as "intimidating to an English judge."
[77] Case 107/76, *Hoffman-La Roche* v. *Centrafarm* [1977] E.C.R. 957; Joined Cases 35 and 36/82, *Morson and Jhanjan* v. *Netherlands* [1982] E.C.R. 3723.

Deciding the point without a reference

The mere existence of the right to ask the Court of Justice for a preliminary ruling does not deprive national courts and tribunals (other than those against whose decisions there is no judicial remedy) of the right to reach their own conclusions on questions of Community law it may be necessary for them to decide.[78] Indeed, where the point raised is reasonably clear or it is possible to deduce from the case-law of the Court of Justice a clear general approach to a particular question, it may be preferable for such a national court to decide the point itself.[79]

However, where it seems likely that a reference will be made at some stage in the proceedings, it is sensible for that step to be taken sooner rather than later, for an early reference saves time and costs.[80] Moreover, as Bingham J. acknowledged in *Commissioners of Customs and Excise* v. *Samex ApS*,[81] the Court of Justice is far better equipped than national courts to resolve issues of Community law:

> "Sitting as a judge in a national court, asked to decide questions of Community law, I am very conscious of the advantages enjoyed by the Court of Justice. It has a panoramic view of the Community and its institutions, a detailed knowledge of the Treaties and of much subordinate legislation made under them, and an intimate familiarity with the functioning of the Community market which no national judge denied the collective experience of the Court of Justice could hope to achieve. Where questions of administrative intention and practice arise the Court of Justice can receive submissions from the Community institutions, as also where relations between the Community and non-Member States are in issue. Where the interests of Member States are affected they can intervene to make their views known. . . . Where comparison falls to be made between Community texts in different languages, all texts being equally authentic, the multi-national Court of Justice is equipped to carry out the task in a way which no national judge, whatever his linguistic skills, could rival. The interpretation of Community instruments involves very often not the process familiar to common lawyers of laboriously extracting the meaning from words used but the more creative process of applying flesh to a spare and loosely constructed skeleton. The choice between alternative submissions may turn not on purely legal considerations, but on a broader view of what the orderly development of the Community requires. These are matters which the Court of Justice is very much better placed to assess and determine than a national court."

---

[78] See Slade L.J. in *J. Rothschild Holdings plc* v. *Commissioners of Inland Revenue* [1989] 2 C.M.L.R. 621, 645 (C.A.).
[79] See *Pickstone* v. *Freemans Plc* [1987] 2 C.M.L.R. 572, 591 (C.A.), *per* Purchas L.J.
[80] This was acknowledged by Kerr L.J. in *R.* v. *Pharmaceutical Society of Great Britain, ex p. The Association of Pharmaceutical Importers* [1987] 3 C.M.L.R. 951, 972.
[81] [1983] 3 C.M.L.R. 194, 210–211 (H.C.).

The effects of the ruling of the Court of Justice

A ruling on interpretation given by the Court of Justice under Article 177 "is binding on the national courts as to the interpretation of the Community provisions and acts in question."[82] The referring court is under a duty to give full effect to the provisions of Community law as interpreted by the Court of Justice. This may require it to refuse to apply conflicting provisions of national law, even if adopted subsequently.[83] Moreover, other courts are entitled to treat the ruling of the Court of Justice as authoritative and as thereby obviating the need for the same points to be referred to the Court of Justice again.[84]

A ruling by the Court under Article 177 declaring an act of one of the institutions void is also binding on the referring court.[85] The effect of the ruling is not formally to annul the measure, but the practical result is the same: the measure will be treated as void for all purposes unless exceptionally, as indicated below, the Court limits the effects of its ruling on past transactions. Moreover, such a ruling "is sufficient reason for any other national court to regard that act as void for the purposes of a judgment which it has to give."[86] If, on the other hand, the Court rejects the challenge to the validity of the measure, it will rule that consideration of the questions raised has disclosed no factor of such a kind as to affect the validity of the contested act,[87] thus leaving open the possibility of a subsequent challenge on other grounds.

It is important to emphasise, however, that national courts remain free to bring matters of Community law before the Court of Justice under Article 177 whenever they feel it necessary to do so: they are not precluded from doing so by the fact that the point in question seems already to have been settled by the Court.[88] Indeed, a national court may if it wishes make more than one reference in the same proceedings, although in practice this happens only exceptionally.[89] However, the Court of Justice acknowledged in *Pretore di Salò* v. *Persons Unknown*[90] that a second reference "may be justified when the national court encounters difficulties in understanding or applying the judgment, when it refers a fresh question of law to the Court, or again when it submits new considerations which might lead the Court to give

---

[82] Case 52/76, *Benedetti* v. *Munari* [1977] E.C.R. 163, para. 26. This obligation is reinforced for courts in the United Kingdom by section 3(1) of the European Communities Act 1972. For a detailed discussion of the effects of rulings given by the Court of Justice under Article 177, see Toth, "The Authority of Judgments of the European Court of Justice: Binding Force and Legal Effects" (1984) 4 Y.E.L. 1.

[83] See, *e.g.* Case 106/77, *Amministrazione delle Finanze dello Stato* v. *Simmenthal* [1978] E.C.R. 629; Case 170/88, *Ford España* v. *Estado Español* [1989] E.C.R. 2305.

[84] See Joined Cases 28–30/62, *da Costa en Schaake* [1963] E.C.R. 31; Case 283/81, *CILFIT* v. *Ministry of Health* [1982] E.C.R. 3415.

[85] Case 66/80, *International Chemical Corporation* v. *Amministrazione delle Finanze dello Stato* [1981] E.C.R. 1191.

[86] *Ibid.* para. 13.

[87] See, *e.g.* Case C–323/88, *Sermes* [1990] E.C.R. I–3027.

[88] See *International Chemical Corporation*, para. 14; *CILFIT*, para. 15.

[89] For examples, see Case 117/77, *Pierik* [1978] E.C.R. 825 and Case 182/78 [1979] E.C.R. 1977; Case 104/79, *Foglia* v. *Novello* [1980] E.C.R. 745 and Case 244/80 [1981] E.C.R. 3045; Case 283/81, *CILFIT* [1982] E.C.R. 3415 and Case 77/83 [1984] E.C.R. 1257; Case C–213/89, *Factortame* [1990] E.C.R. I–2433 and Case C–221/89, judgment of July 25, 1991.

[90] Case 14/86 [1987] E.C.R. 2545.

a different answer to a question submitted earlier." Nonetheless, national courts should not use the right to refer further questions "as a means of contesting the validity of the judgment delivered previously."[91]

The right of the national courts to refer to the Court of Justice questions which it has already addressed is the corollary of the fact that the Court of Justice is not bound by its own previous decisions. It is therefore always at liberty to reconsider points which have been dealt with previously. In the absence of any suggestion that the previous case was wrongly decided, however, the Court will simply repeat its earlier ruling.[92] Indeed, where a question referred to the Court for a preliminary ruling is "manifestly identical to a question on which the Court has already ruled," the Court is empowered by Article 104(3) of the Rules to give its decision by reasoned order in which reference is made to its previous judgment.

A ruling on interpretation, or a declaration that a measure is invalid, will normally relate back to the facts of the case. A preliminary ruling on the interpretation of a rule of Community law "clarifies and defines where necessary the meaning and scope of that rule as it must be or ought to have been understood and applied from the time of its coming into force. It follows that the rule as thus interpreted may, and must, be applied by the [national] courts even to legal relationships arising and established before the judgment ruling on the request for interpretation. ..."[93] Very exceptionally the Court of Justice may, in the interests of legal certainty, be led to limit the effects on past transactions of preliminary rulings on questions of both interpretation and validity.[94] Any such limitation will always be laid down in the ruling itself.[95]

(e) *The plea of illegality and non-existent acts*

The strict time limits and rules as to standing laid down in Article 173 EEC are to some extent mitigated by the so-called plea of illegality,[96] for which provision is made in Article 184 EEC in the following terms:

"Notwithstanding the expiry of the period laid down in the third paragraph of Article 173, any party may, in proceedings in which a regulation of the Council or the Commission is in issue, plead the grounds specified in the first paragraph of Article 173, in order to

---

[91] See Case 69/85, *Wünsche* v. *Germany* [1986] E.C.R. 947.

[92] See, *e.g.* Case C–350/89, *Sheptonhurst Ltd.* v. *Newham Borough Council*, judgment of May 7, 1991, where the Courts simply repeated its ruling in Case C–23/89, *Quietlynn Ltd.* v. *Southend Borough Council* [1990] E.C.R. I–3059, and Case C–295/89, *Donà*, judgment of June 18, 1991, where the Court repeated aspects of its ruling in Case 103/88, *Fratelli Costanzo* [1989] E.C.R. 1839. In practice, the Court will sometimes instruct its Registrar to write a letter to the referring court drawing its attention to the earlier judgment and asking the referring court whether it wishes to maintain the reference. References are often withdrawn following the dispatch of such letters.

[93] Case 61/79, *Amministrazione delle Finanze dello Stato* v. *Denkavit Italiana* [1980] E.C.R. 1205, para. 16.

[94] See, *e.g.* Case 43/75, *Defrenne* v. *SABENA* [1976] E.C.R. 455; Case 41/84, *Pinna* v. *Caisse d'Allocations Familiales de la Savoie* [1986] E.C.R. 1; Case 24/86, *Blaizot* v. *University of Liège* [1988] E.C.R. 379; Case 262/88, *Barber* v. *Guardian Royal Exchange* [1990] E.C.R. I–1889.

[95] See *Denkavit Italiana, supra.*

[96] See Hartley, *op. cit.* Chap. 14.

invoke before the Court of Justice the inapplicability of that regulation."

The Treaty on European Union would extend Article 184 to regulations adopted jointly by the Parliament and the Council and to regulations adopted by the European Central Bank.

Article 184 does not give rise to a separate cause of action. It merely allows the illegality of certain types of act to be pleaded indirectly in proceedings which are pending before the Court of Justice under some other provision.[97] Where, for example, a natural or legal person seeks the annulment of a decision addressed to him which is based on a regulation, he may contest the validity of that regulation notwithstanding the fact that he would not have been able to challenge it directly under Article 173. The plea of illegality therefore represents a compromise between the principle of legal certainty, which would rule out a challenge to a Community act once the deadline laid down in Article 173 had expired, and the principle of legality, which would preclude reliance on acts which were invalid.

Although Article 184 only refers to regulations, the Court said in *Simmenthal* v. *Commission*[98] that:

> "Article 184 of the EEC Treaty gives expression to a general principle conferring upon any party to proceedings the right to challenge, for the purpose of obtaining the annulment of a decision of direct and individual concern to that party, the validity of previous acts of the institutions which form the legal basis of the decision which is being attacked, if that party was not entitled under Article 173 of the Treaty to bring a direct action challenging those acts [and] by which it was thus affected without having been in a position to ask that they be declared void."

The Court concluded that Article 184 extended to "acts of the institutions which, although they are not in the form of a regulation, nevertheless produce similar effects and on those grounds may not be challenged under Article 173 by natural or legal persons other than Community institutions and Member States."[99]

While the logic and equity of the Court's decision in the *Simmenthal* case are self-evident, it may be doubted whether Article 184 really embodies the general principle to which the Court claimed it gave expression. The position adopted by the Court would suggest that Article 184 could never be invoked by the institutions or by the Member States, since they have unlimited standing to bring proceedings under Article 173. According to the terms of Article 184, however, the plea of illegality may be invoked by "any party," an expression which is clearly broad enough to cover privileged applicants for the purpose of Article 173. The case law suggests that a

---

[97] See Joined Cases 31 and 33/62, *Wöhrmann* v. *Commission* [1962] E.C.R. 501.
[98] Case 92/78 [1979] E.C.R. 777, para. 39.
[99] *Ibid.* para. 40 of the judgment. Thus, the Court held that Art. 184 could be invoked in relation to notices of invitation to tender.

Member State may challenge the validity of a regulation indirectly in proceedings under both Articles 173[1] and 169.[2] It is submitted that the institutions are in principle also entitled to invoke Article 184.

Moreover, the mischief against which the Court was seeking to guard in *Simmenthal* is, at least in theory, capable of arising in relation to any act producing legal effects which natural and legal persons are unable to challenge directly under Article 173. Article 184 is apparently confined, however, to measures which are in substance (if not in form) regulations. Thus, in *Commission* v. *Greece*,[3] the Court held that a Member State may not "plead the unlawfulness of a decision addressed to it as a defence in an action for a declaration that it has failed to fulfil its obligations arising out of its failure to implement that decision." It would seem to follow that the validity of a directive may not be challenged by the Member States to which it is addressed once the deadline laid down in Article 173 has expired.

In *Commission* v. *Greece*, the Court said that the position would be different "only if the measure at issue contained such particularly serious and manifest defects that it could be deemed non-existent."[4] Thus, notwithstanding the expiry of the deadline laid down in Article 173 and independently of Article 184, any party may argue that an act, regardless of its nature, is vitiated by such fundamental defects that it should be regarded as non-existent. This test is extremely difficult to satisfy, but where such an argument succeeds the measure in question will be treated as incapable of producing any legal effects.[5]

Where a plea of illegality is successful, the Court does not formally annul the measure in question, but simply declares it inapplicable. This has the effect of depriving any act adopted under it of its legal basis. Nevertheless, although the Court's ruling in relation to the first measure is technically limited to the case in which it is made, it is tantamount in practical terms to a declaration of invalidity, for the institutions will immediately cease to apply the measure and the Court will henceforth treat it as invalid.

It may be observed that, since Article 184 applies only in proceedings before the Court of Justice, it does not affect the circumstances in which the validity of Community acts may be contested in the national courts. It seems, however, that a declaration of inapplicability made by the Court of Justice under Article 184 in a previous case would enable a national court to

---

[1] See Case 32/65, *Italy* v. *Council and Commission* [1966] E.C.R. 389, in particular the Opinion of A. G. Roemer at p. 414.
[2] See Case 116/82, *Commission* v. *Germany* [1986] E.C.R. 2519; the Opinion of A. G. Darmon in Case C–258/89, *Commission* v. *Spain*, judgment of July 25, 1991. In the latter case, the Court did not discuss the issue of validity, treating the dispute instead as relating to interpretation.
[3] Case 226/87 [1988] E.C.R. 3611, para. 14. See also Case 156/77, *Commission* v. *Belgium* [1978] E.C.R. 1881, para. 22.
[4] *Ibid.* para. 16 of the judgment.
[5] See Case 15/85, *Consorzio Cooperative d'Abruzzo* v. *Commission* [1987] E.C.R. 1005, para. 10; Joined Cases T–79/89 etc., *BASF and others* v. *Commission*, judgment of February 27, 1992 (at the time of writing, this judgment was the subject of an appeal to the Court: see Case C–137/92 P). See further Hartley, *op. cit.* pp. 331–334.

treat the act in question as invalid without referring the matter to the Court of Justice under Article 177.[6]

(f) *Non-contractual liability*[7]

Article 178 EEC gives the Court of Justice jurisdiction in actions for damages brought under the second paragraph of Article 215 EEC, which provides:

> "In the case of non-contractual liability, the Community shall, in accordance with the general principles common to the laws of the Member States, make good any damage caused by its institutions or by its servants in the performance of their duties."

The Treaty on European Union would insert a new third paragraph in Article 215[8] stating:

> "The preceding paragraph shall apply under the same conditions to damage caused by the ECB[9] or by its servants in the performance of their duties."

Unlike its powers under Articles 173 and 175, the jurisdiction of the Court of Justice under the second paragraph of Article 215 is sometimes described as "unlimited." This means that the Court is not confined to reviewing the legality of the conduct of the defendant but may substitute its own views as to the appropriateness of that conduct in the light of all the prevailing circumstances.

The Court has said that the action for damages constitutes an independent or autonomous form of action. Its purpose is different from that of proceedings under Article 173 or 175 and it is not therefore necessary to have recourse to one of those Articles before commencing an action under the second paragraph of Article 215.[10] The latter provision may therefore be used as a means of challenging indirectly the legality of an act or failure to act which has not been contested directly under Article 173 or 175.

Although the second paragraph of Article 215 refers to "the general principles common to the laws of the Member States," it has been observed that "There does not exist within the 12 countries of the Communities a common *corpus* of legal principles governing State liability in tort."[11] The

---

[6] See Case 314/85, *Foto-Frost* v. *Hauptzollamt Lübeck-Ost* [1987] E.C.R. 4199, para. 16, where the Court refers to Art. 184; Toth, *op. cit.* p. 415.

[7] See generally Brown and Jacobs, *op. cit.* pp. 134–157; Hartley, *op. cit.* pp. 453–492. For extremely thorough and up-to-date accounts, see Slynn, Lasok and Millett in Vaughan (ed.), *op. cit.* paras. 2.76–2.100; Toth, *op. cit.* under the relevant entries. The last-mentioned work makes extensive reference to the literature on the subject.

[8] There is to be no corresponding amendment to Article 178 of the Treaty, but see Art. 35.1 of the Statute of the European System of Central Banks and of the European Central Bank and Art. 19.1 of the Statute of the European Monetary Institute.

[9] European Central Bank. During the second stage for achieving economic and monetary union, the term "ECB" is here to be read as referring to the European Monetary Institute: see Art. 109f(9) EC.

[10] See, *e.g.* Case 4/69, *Lütticke* v. *Commission* [1971] E.C.R. 325; Case 5/71, *Zuckerfabrik Schöppenstedt* v. *Council* [1971] E.C.R. 975. The Court's decision to the contrary in Case 25/62, *Plaumann* v. *Commission* [1963] E.C.R. 95 seems to be confined to its facts: *cf.* Case 175/84, *Krohn* v. *Commission* [1986] E.C.R. 753.

[11] Brown and Jacobs, *op. cit.* p. 137.

wording of the Treaty therefore gives the Court a good deal of freedom in developing a body of principles appropriate to the Community system. Those principles have yet to be fully elaborated.

According to the Treaty, it is the Community as a whole whose liability is in issue in proceedings under the second paragraph of Article 215. However, the Court has said that "where Community liability is involved by reason of the act of one of its institutions, it should be represented before the Court by the institution or institutions against which the matter giving rise to liability is alleged."[12] Where the action relates to a legislative measure adopted by the Council on a proposal from the Commission, proceedings may be brought against both institutions jointly.[13]

Damage caused by servants of the Community in the performance of their duties

Where the applicant relies on an act performed by a Community official in the performance of his duties, the Court applies a very strict test. In *Sayag* v. *Leduc*,[14] a case concerning the identical provision of the Euratom Treaty,[15] the Court held that the Community was not liable for an accident caused by one of its servants while using his private car during the performance of his duties. The Court said that "Only in the case of *force majeure* or in exceptional circumstances of such overriding importance that without the servant's using private means of transport the Community would have been unable to carry out the tasks entrusted to it, could such use be considered to form part of the servant's performance of his duties. . . . ."

Damage caused by an institution of the Community

Acts adopted by the institutions which do not have general application may give rise to non-contractual liability on the part of the Community where certain conditions are satisfied. In *Compagnia Italiana Alcool* v. *Commission*,[16] the Court stated that "those conditions are the incurrence [*sic*] of damage, the existence of a causal link between the damage relied on and the conduct alleged against the institutions, and the unlawful nature of that conduct."

Measures having general application[17] may also give rise to non-contractual liability on the part of the Community, but only where certain additional criteria are satisfied. In *Zuckerfabrik Schöppenstedt* v. *Council*,[18] the Court stated: "Where legislative action involving measures of economic policy is concerned, the Community does not incur non-contractual liability for damage suffered by individuals as a consequence of that action . . . unless a sufficiently flagrant violation of a superior rule of law for the protection of

---

[12] Joined Cases 63 to 69/72, *Werhahn* v. *Council* [1973] E.C.R. 1229, para. 7.
[13] *Ibid.* para. 8.
[14] Case 9/69 [1969] E.C.R. 329.
[15] The second para. of Art. 188.
[16] Case C–358/90, judgment of April 7, 1992, para. 46. See also Case C–55/90, *Cato* v. *Commission*, judgment of April 8, 1992, para. 18.
[17] But not the provisions of an Act of Accession, since they are the result of an agreement between the Member States and the applicant State: see Joined Cases 31 and 35/86, *Laisa* v. *Council* [1988] E.C.R. 2285.
[18] Case 5/71 [1971] E.C.R. 975, para. 11.

the individual has occurred." Since nearly all Community legislation of a type liable to give rise to a claim in damages is concerned in some way with economic policy, the test laid down in the *Schöppenstedt* case may be regarded as of general application. It is not enough to establish liability that the measure in question has previously been declared void by the Court.[19]

A superior rule of law for these purposes may include a provision of the Treaty, such as the rule in Article 40(3) EEC prohibiting discrimination between producers and consumers in the Community in the context of the common organisation of agricultural markets.[20] It may also include a general principle of law, such as the protection of legitimate expectations.[21] It seems that an applicant need only show that the rule in question was for the protection of individuals generally, not that it was for the protection of a particular class of which he was a member.[22] It should be noted, however, that an inadequacy in the statement of the reasons on which a measure is based is apparently not sufficient to make the Community liable under the second paragraph of Article 215,[23] nor does the Community incur such liability as a result of a failure to respect the institutional balance laid down in the Treaties. The Court does not regard the division of powers among the institutions as intended to protect individuals.[24]

The main problem for applicants in such cases is to establish that a sufficiently serious breach of the rule in question has occurred. In *HNL* v. *Council and Commission*,[25] the Court said that, in a legislative field which involved the exercise of a wide discretion, such as that of the Common Agricultural Policy, the Community did not incur non-contractual liability "unless the institution concerned has manifestly and gravely disregarded the limits on the exercise of its powers." The Court went even further in *Amylum* v. *Council and Commission*,[26] where it stated that a legal situation resulting from legislative measures would only be sufficient to fix the Community with liability if the conduct of the institutions concerned "was verging on the arbitrary."

The result is that actions in respect of legislative measures are rarely successful.[27] The Court seems to regard the strictness of its approach as justified by two factors. The first is that, if liability were too easy to establish, the institutions would be unduly hampered in the performance of the tasks

---

[19] See, *e.g.* Joined Cases 83 and 94/76, 4, 15 and 40/77, *HNL* v. *Council and Commission* [1978] E.C.R. 1209, para. 4.
[20] See, *e.g.* Joined Cases 83 and 94/76, 4, 15 and 40/77, *HNL* v. *Council and Commission* [1978] E.C.R. 1209, para. 5; Case 238/78, *Ireks-Arkady* v. *Council and Commission* [1979] E.C.R. 2955, para. 11.
[21] See, *e.g.* Case 74/74, *CNTA* v. *Commission* [1975] E.C.R. 533, para. 44; Joined Cases C–104/89 and C–37/90, *Mulder and others* v. *Council and Commission*, judgment of May 19, 1992, para. 15.
[22] See Joined Cases 5, 7 and 13 to 24/66, *Kampffmeyer* v. *Commission* [1967] E.C.R. 245, 262–263.
[23] Case 106/81, *Kind* v. *EEC* [1982] E.C.R. 2885, para. 14. Cf. Case C–358/90, *Compagnia Italiana Alcool* v. *Commission*, judgment of April 7, 1992, para. 47.
[24] Case C–282/90, *Vreugdenhil* v. *Commission*, judgment of March 13, 1992, paras. 20–21.
[25] *Supra* at para. 6.
[26] Joined Cases 116 and 124/77 [1979] E.C.R. 3497, para. 19.
[27] For an example of such an action which was successful in part, see Joined Cases C–104/89 and C–37/90, *Mulder and others* v. *Council and Commission*, judgment of May 19, 1992.

conferred on them by the Treaty.[28] The second is that an individual who considers himself injured by a Community act which has been implemented by the national authorities may challenge the act's validity before the national courts. The matter can then be referred to the Court of Justice under Article 177. According to the Court, "The existence of such an action is by itself of such a nature as to ensure the efficient protection of the individuals concerned."[29]

The Community also incur liability under the second paragraph of Article 215 for administrative acts and omissions, as the Stanley Adams saga illustrates.[30] Stanley Adams was an employee of the Swiss pharmaceutical company, Hoffmann-La Roche. He formed the view that some of the company's practices were incompatible with the competition rules laid down in the EEC Treaty. He therefore alerted the Commission and supplied it with copies of a number of internal company documents. The Commission subsequently commenced an investigation into the company's activities, in the course of which it handed over to the company edited copies of some of the documents supplied by Adams. The Commission ultimately adopted a decision imposing a substantial fine on the company for breach of Article 86 EEC.[31]

In the meantime, the company, realising the Commission must have had an informant, attempted to discover his identity. The company's lawyer told the Commission that it was considering taking criminal proceedings against the informant for economic espionage under the Swiss Penal Code. The company eventually succeeded in identifying Adams from the copies of its own documents which had been handed to it by the Commission.

Adams had by now left his employment with the company and moved to Italy, but he was arrested by the Swiss authorities as he attempted to enter Switzerland on a visit. While he was being held in custody, his wife committed suicide. He was subsequently released on bail, but was in due course found guilty of economic espionage and sentenced *in absentia* to a suspended term of one year's imprisonment. His conviction damaged his creditworthiness and led to the failure of a business he had established after leaving the company.

In proceedings against the Commission under the second paragraph of Article 215, the Court found that two aspects of the Commission's conduct gave rise to liability[31a]: first, the disclosure to the company of the documents which enabled Adams to be identified; and secondly, the failure to warn Adams of the risk that he would be prosecuted if he returned to Switzerland, a risk of which the Commission should have been aware following its discussions with the company's lawyer. However, the Court took the view that Adams was partly to blame for his misfortunes: he had not, for example, warned the Commission that he could be identified from the documents he

---

[28] See, *e.g.* the *HNL* case, *supra* at para. 5.
[29] See the *Amylum* case, *supra* at para. 14.
[30] The story is recounted by Stanley Adams in *Roche versus Adams* (1984). See also Hunnings, "The Stanley Adams Affair or the Biter Bit" (1987) 24 C.M.L.Rev. 65.
[31] The essence of the Commission's decision was upheld by the Court in Case 85/76, *Hoffmann-La Roche* v. *Commission* [1979] E.C.R. 461.
[31a] Case 145/83, *Adams* v. *Commission* [1985] E.C.R. 3539.

had supplied and he had returned to Switzerland without inquiring as to the risks involved in doing so. The Court therefore decided that responsibility for the damage he had suffered should be apportioned equally between himself and the Commission.

Concurrent liability of the Community and the Member States[32]

Under the system established by the Treaties, it is common for Community legislation to require implementation by the national authorities of the Member States. If a person suffers damage as a result of such implementation, the question may arise whether he should commence proceedings against the competent national authorities in the national courts, which might have to ask the Court of Justice for a preliminary ruling under Article 177, or against the Community under the second paragraph of Article 215.

The Court has acknowledged that, in some cases, proceedings under the second paragraph of Article 215 will only be admissible if the applicant has exhausted any cause of action he might have against the national authorities in the domestic forum.[33] It seems that such a cause of action must be pursued first where the actions of the national authorities, although based on Community legislation, are the most direct cause of the damage suffered by the applicant.[34] Where the conduct in question is in fact the responsibility of a Community institution and cannot be attributed to a national body, however, the Court of Justice has jurisdiction.[35] In any event, it is not necessary to exhaust any national rights of action that may be available where they are not capable of providing an effective means of protection for the applicant and compensating him for the damage he claims to have suffered.[36]

Damage

The Court has not so far laid down any general principles in respect of the types of damage which may be the subject of a claim or as to how the damage is to be assessed. It seems clear that actual financial loss may be recovered,[37] as in principle may loss of profits.[38] In staff cases, small amounts have been recovered for shock, disturbance and uneasiness.[39] Moreover, the Court has acknowledged that it may be asked "to declare the Community liable for

---

[32] For further discussion of the Court's complex and inconclusive case-law on this topic, see Brown and Jacobs, *op. cit.* pp. 152–157; Hartley, *op. cit.* pp. 483–492.

[33] See, *e.g.* Case 175/84, *Krohn* v. *Commission* [1986] E.C.R. 753, para. 27.

[34] See, *e.g.* Case 133/79, *Sucrimex* v. *Commission* [1980] E.C.R. 1299; Case C–282/90, *Vreugdenhil* v. *Commission*, judgment of March 13, 1992.

[35] See, *e.g.* Case 175/84, *Krohn* v. *Commission* [1986] E.C.R. 753. *Cf.* Slynn, Lasok and Millett in Vaughan (ed.), *op. cit.* paras. 2.93–2.95.

[36] *Krohn* v. *Commission*, *supra*, para. 27; Case 20/88, *Roquette Frères* v. *Commission* [1989] E.C.R. 1553, para. 15.

[37] See Joined Cases 5, 7 and 13 to 24/66, *Kampffmeyer* v. *Commission* [1967] E.C.R. 245; Case 74/74, *CNTA* v. *Commission* [1975] E.C.R. 533.

[38] See, *e.g.* the *Kampffmeyer* case, *supra*; Joined Cases C–104/89 and C–37/90, *Mulder and others* v. *Council and Commission*, judgment of May 19, 1992. *Cf.* Joined Cases 54 to 60/76, *Compagnie Industrielle du Comité de Loheac* v. *Council and Commission* [1977] E.C.R. 645.

[39] See, *e.g.* Joined Cases 7/56 and 3 to 7/57, *Algera* v. *Common Assembly* [1957 and 1958] E.C.R. 39, 66–67.

imminent damage foreseeable with sufficient certainty even if the damage cannot yet be precisely assessed."[40] However, the applicant must take steps to mitigate any damage[41] and will not be able to recover compensation where he could have passed the loss on to his customers.[42] The applicant must also show that the damage he has suffered "exceeds the limits of the economic risks inherent in operating in the sector concerned."[43]

Where a claim under the second paragraph of Article 215 is successful, the Court does not normally make a specific award of damages. Instead, the judgment will usually establish the acts or omissions giving rise to liability and, if appropriate, make an award of interest. It will then order the parties to attempt to reach an agreement, within a specified period, on the amount of compensation payable. The judgment will require the parties to transmit to the Court a statement of their views, with supporting figures, if they are unable to reach agreement.[44]

Causation

The applicant must be able to establish a causal link between the defendant's conduct and the damage he claims to have suffered. The Court has said that the second paragraph of Article 215 does not require the Community "to make good every harmful consequence, even a remote one, of unlawful legislation."[45] The applicant must therefore establish that the damage is a "sufficiently direct consequence of the unlawful conduct."[46] In *Compagnia Italiana Alcool* v. *Commission*,[47] the Court said that there was no causal link between the damage allegedly suffered by the applicant and a deficiency in the statement of reasons contained in a Commission decision. As the Court explained, "If that deficiency had not existed, the damage allegedly suffered by [the applicant] would have been the same."

The chain of causation may be broken by, for example, the actions of national authorities or by the behaviour of the applicant himself. In this respect, traders are expected to behave in a prudent manner and to apprise themselves of the conditions on the markets in which they operate. If they fall short of this standard, the Community will not be held responsible for any loss that ensues.[48]

---

[40] Joined Cases 56 to 60/74, *Kampffmeyer* v. *Commission and Council* [1976] E.C.R. 711, para. 6.
[41] Case 120/83 R, *Raznoimport* v. *Commission* [1983] E.C.R. 2573, para. 14; *Mulder and others, supra*, para. 33.
[42] See Joined Cases 64 and 113/76, 167 and 239/78, 27, 28 and 45/79, *Dumortier Frères* v. *Council* [1979] E.C.R. 3091, para. 15; Case 238/78, *Ireks-Arkady* v. *Council and Commission* [1979] E.C.R. 2955, para. 14; Joined Cases 241, 242 and 245 to 250/78, *DGV* v. *Council and Commission* [1979] E.C.R. 3017, para. 15; Joined Cases 261 and 262/78, *Interquell Stärke* v. *Council and Commission* [1979] E.C.R. 3045, para. 17 (the so-called *Gritz and Quellmehl* cases, after the products with which they were concerned). See Rudden and Bishop, "Gritz and Quellmehl: Pass It On" (1981) 6 E.L.Rev. 243.
[43] Case 59/83, *Biovilac* v. *EEC* [1984] E.C.R. 4057, para. 28.
[44] See, *e.g.* the *Gritz and Quellmehl* cases, *supra*; Case 145/83, *Adams* v. *Commission* [1985] E.C.R. 3539; *Mulder and others, supra*.
[45] *Dumortier-Frères* v. *Council, supra*, para. 21.
[46] *Ibid.*
[47] Case C–358/90, judgment of April 7, 1992, para. 47.
[48] See Case 169/73, *Compagnie Continentale* v. *Council* [1975] E.C.R. 117, paras. 22–32; Case 26/81, *Oleifici Mediterranei* v. *EEC* [1982] E.C.R. 3057, paras. 22–24.

Limitation

A limitation period of five years is laid down by Article 43 of the Statute of the Court, which provides as follows:

> "Proceedings against the Community in matters arising from non-contractual liability shall be barred after a period of five years from the occurrence of the event giving rise thereto. The period of limitation shall be interrupted if proceedings are instituted before the Court or if prior to such proceedings an application is made by the aggrieved party to the relevant institution of the Community. In the latter event the proceedings must be instituted within the period of two months provided for in Article 173 [of the Treaty]; the provisions of the second paragraph of Article 175 [of the Treaty] shall apply where appropriate."

It should be noted that the last sentence of Article 43 does not have the effect of reducing the five-year period. It merely prevents certain periods from being taken into account in the calculation of that period.[49]

The limitation period does not start to run "before all the requirements governing an obligation to provide compensation for damage are satisfied and in particular before the damage to be made good has materialized." Thus, where the liability of the Community derives from a legislative measure, the limitation period does not begin "before the injurious effects of that measure have been produced."[50] Where the cause of the damage suffered by the applicant is an administrative act or omission, the limitation period does not start to run until he becomes aware of it.[51]

(g) *Other heads of jurisdiction*

Among the Court of Justice's other heads of jurisdiction, brief mention may be made of the following:

(i) *Penalties provided for in Council regulations.* Under Article 172 EEC, a regulation of the Council that creates a power to impose a penalty may give the Court unlimited jurisdiction in cases arising out of the exercise of the power. Thus, Regulation No. 17, the chief implementing measure concerning the Treaty competition rules, provides in Article 17 that the Court may cancel, reduce or increase fines or periodic penalty payments imposed by the Commission for infringement of those rules. If the Treaty on European Union enters into force, Article 172 will be extended to cover regulations adopted jointly by the Parliament and the Council.

(ii) *Staff cases.* Under Article 179 EEC, the Court of Justice has jurisdiction in disputes between institutions of the Community and

---

[49] See Joined Cases 5, 7 and 13 to 24/66, *Kampffmeyer* v. *Commission* [1967] E.C.R. 245, 260.
[50] Joined Cases 256, 257 and 267/80 and 5/81, *Birra Wührer* v. *Council and Commission* [1982] E.C.R. 85, para. 10; Case 51/81, *De Franceschi* v. *Council and Commission* [1982] E.C.R. 117, para. 10.
[51] See Case 145/83, *Adams* v. *Commission* [1985] E.C.R. 3539, paras. 50–51.

their employees. Such disputes are now dealt with initially by the Court of First Instance, which is discussed in the following chapter. The number of staff cases pending before the Court of First Instance at any one time is considerable, but they do not often involve issues of general concern. If the Treaty on European Union enters into force, the Court of Justice will be given jurisdiction in disputes between the European Central Bank and its servants[52] and between the European Monetary Institute and its servants.[53] It is envisaged that these classes of action will be heard by the Court of First Instance and the relevant rules are to be adapted accordingly.[54]

(iii) *Actions against national central banks.* The Court of Justice has jurisdiction under Article 180 EEC in various classes of dispute concerning the European Investment Bank. If the Treaty on European Union enters into force, Article 180 will be extended to give the Court jurisdiction in disputes concerning the fulfilment by national central banks of their obligations under the Treaty and under the Statute of the European System of Central Banks. The Council of the European Central Bank[55] is to enjoy powers in respect of national central banks which are the same as those enjoyed by the Commission *vis-à-vis* the Member States under Article 169.[56] A national central bank which is found by the Court to have failed to fulfil its obligations under the Treaty will be required to take the measures necessary to comply with the Court's judgment. If it fails to do so, however, the European Central Bank will not have the power conferred on the Commission by the new second paragraph of Article 171 to ask the Court to impose on the bank concerned a lump sum or penalty payment.

(iv) *Interlocutory relief.* The Court of Justice has jurisdiction under Article 185 EEC to order that the application of a contested measure be suspended if it considers that circumstances so require. In addition, Article 186 EEC provides that the Court may in any case before it prescribe any necessary interim measures.[57] Interim measures can only be granted in respect of a case pending before the Court.[58] The applicant must establish that the order requested is

---

[52] See Art. 36.2 of the Statute of the European System of Central Banks and of the European Central Bank.

[53] See Art. 18.2 of the Statute of the European Monetary Institute.

[54] See the Declaration on Disputes between the ECB and the EMI and their Servants annexed to the Treaty on European Union.

[55] During the second stage for achieving economic and monetary union, the powers of the European Central Bank under Art. 180 are to be exercised by the European Monetary Institute: see Art. 109f(9) EC.

[56] See further Art. 35.6 of the Statute of the European System of Central Banks and of the European Central Bank. Curiously, there appears to be no equivalent of that provision in the Statute of the European Monetary Institute.

[57] See further Usher, *op. cit.* pp. 269–286; Lasok, *op. cit.* pp. 145–176; Oliver, "Interim Measures: Some Recent Developments" (1992) 29 C.M.L.Rev. 7.

[58] Rules, Art. 83(1).

urgently necessary because, without it, he would be liable to suffer serious and irreparable harm.[59] He must also show that the claim in the main proceedings is not manifestly unfounded.[60] For his part, the defendant may argue that he would be seriously and irreparably harmed by the granting of the order.[61] Because of the urgent nature of such applications, the President of the Court has been given power to decide on them himself,[62] and generally does so. Where a case is difficult or important, however, the President may refer the application instead to the Court.

(v) *Contractual liability of the Community.* According to the first paragraph of Article 215 EEC, the contractual liability of the Community is governed by the national law applicable to the contract in question. Disputes arising out of such contracts are heard by the appropriate national courts,[63] except where jurisdiction is conferred on the Court of Justice under an arbitration clause inserted pursuant to Article 181 EEC. In such cases, the Court of Justice applies the relevant national law.[64] If the Treaty on European Union enters into force, Article 35.4 of the Statute of the European System of Central Banks and of the European Central Bank will confer on the Court of Justice jurisdiction to give judgment pursuant to an arbitration clause contained in a contract concluded by or on behalf of the European Central Bank. Article 19.4 of the Statute of the European Monetary Institute will give the Court the same jurisdiction in respect of arbitration clauses contained in contracts concluded by or on behalf of the European Monetary Institute. Save where jurisdiction has been specifically conferred on the Court of Justice, disputes involving the European Central Bank or the European Monetary Institute will otherwise be dealt with by the competent national courts.[65]

(vi) *Opinions pursuant to Article 228(1) EEC.* Where it is envisaged that an agreement be concluded between the Community and a third State or an international organisation, the opinion of the Court of Justice may be sought by the Council, the Commission or a Member State under the second sub-paragraph of Article 228(1) EEC on the compatibility of the agreement with the EEC Treaty. If the Court's

---

[59] See, *e.g.* Case 31/59, *Acciaieria de Brescia* v. *High Authority* [1960] E.C.R. 98; Case 61/76 R II, *Geist* v. *Commission* [1976] E.C.R. 2075; Case 113/77 R and 113/77 R-Int., *NTN Toyo* v. *Council* [1977] E.C.R. 1721; Case 121/77 R, *Nachi Fujikoshi* v. *Council* [1977] E.C.R. 2107; Joined Cases 225 and 229/82 R, *Ford AG and Ford of Europe* v. *Commission* [1982] E.C.R. 3091. (The suffix "R" stands for the French word *référé* and denotes a decision taken on an application for interim measures.)

[60] Case 3/75 R, *Johnson and Firth Brown* v. *Commission* [1975] E.C.R. 1.

[61] *Ibid.* See also Case 26/76 R, *Metro* v. *Commission* [1977] E.C.R. 1875.

[62] Rules, Art. 85.

[63] See further Brown and Jacobs, *op. cit.* at pp. 132–134; Hartley, *op. cit.* at pp. 445–449.

[64] See, *e.g.* Case 23/76, *Pellegrini* v. *Commission* [1976] E.C.R. 1807.

[65] See Art. 35.2 of the Statute of the European System of Central Banks and of the European Central Bank and Art. 19.2 of the Statute of the European Monetary Institute.

opinion is adverse, the agreement in question may only enter into force if the Treaty is amended in accordance with Article 236 EEC. The notion of compatibility is interpreted extremely broadly by the Court as embracing not only textual compatibility but also compatibility with the proper functioning of the Community legal order.[66] Article 228(1) may therefore be used for, *inter alia*, the resolution of a difference of opinion between the Commission and the Member States as to the extent to which a particular agreement falls within the exclusive jurisdiction of the Community.[67] If the Treaty on European Union enters into force, the second sub-paragraph of Article 228(1) EEC will be replaced by Article 228(6) EC, which is in substantially the same terms.

(vii) *The Agreement on the European Economic Area.* If this Agreement enters into force, it will confer a number of new powers on the Court. It is not possible to summarise them all in the space available here, but particular mention may be made of the power the Court will have to decide on the interpretation of an E.E.A. rule at the request of a court or tribunal of any member country of the European Free Trade Association which has authorised its courts and tribunals to make such requests.[68]

(h) *The nature of the Court's jurisdiction*[69]

It used to be widely believed that the jurisdiction of the Court was what the French call a *compétence d'attribution*, in other words that it had jurisdiction only in the specific cases in which this was given to it by the Treaties. That view was supported by the Court's decision in *CFDT* v. *Council*,[70] a case brought under the ECSC Treaty, where the applicant sought to establish the admissibility of the action by invoking the principle laid down in Article 31 ECSC (the equivalent of Article 164 EEC) and the duty of any court to avoid a denial of justice. In dismissing the action as inadmissible, the Court remarked that the principles invoked by the applicant "do not permit the Court on its own authority to amend the actual terms of its jurisdiction."[71]

It seems, however, that in exceptional cases the Court no longer regards itself as confined by the provisions of the Treaty expressly giving it certain types of jurisdiction. As we have seen, in the *Chernobyl* case the Parliament was allowed to bring annulment proceedings, not under Article 173, which does not mention the Parliament, but under a right of action created by the

---

[66] See, *e.g.* Opinion 1/76 [1977] E.C.R. 741; Opinion 1/91, O.J. 1992 C110/1.
[67] See Opinion 1/75 [1975] E.C.R. 1355; Opinion 1/78 [1979] E.C.R. 2871. *Cf.* Rules, Art. 107(2).
[68] For a detailed examination of the powers which the Court will enjoy under the Agreement, see Opinion 1/91, O.J. 1992 C110/1, and Opinion 1/92, O.J. 1992 C136/1, both delivered by the Court under Art. 228(1) EEC.
[69] See Arnull, "Does the Court of Justice Have Inherent Jurisdiction?" (1990) 27 C.M.L.Rev. 683.
[70] Case 66/76 [1977] E.C.R. 305.
[71] Para. 8 of the judgment.

Court to enable the Parliament to protect its prerogatives. The approach taken in that case was followed in *Zwartveld*,[72] where a Dutch judge asked the Court to order the Commission to release certain reports prepared by the Commission's officials and to authorise those officials to give evidence before him in connection with an investigation he was carrying out into an alleged fraud relating to the Community legislation on fisheries.

Before the Court, the Commission put forward the traditional view that the circumstances in which proceedings could be instituted before the Court were set out exhaustively in the Treaty. According to the Commission, the only way in which a national judge could bring a matter relating to the EEC Treaty before the Court was by way of a reference for a preliminary ruling under Article 177. That provision was not relevant here, since the Dutch judge had not asked for a preliminary ruling on a question of Community law within the meaning of that Article. The Commission concluded that the judge's request was inadmissible.

The Court disagreed and held the judge's request admissible. Reiterating a statement it had made in the *Chernobyl* case,[73] the Court said that, by virtue of the duty cast on it by Article 164 of the Treaty, it had to be in a position to ensure, by a suitable legal remedy, that the Commission complied with the duty imposed on it by Article 5 EEC to co-operate with the national judicial authorities. It therefore ordered the Commission to release certain reports to the Dutch judge and to authorise its officials to testify before him unless it could convince the Court that to do so would be contrary to the interests of the Community.

It therefore seems that the Court is willing, in exceptional cases, to create new heads of jurisdiction where it considers this necessary to ensure that the law is observed in the interpretation and application of the Treaties. The circumstances in which the Court will be prepared to exercise this new-found freedom remain unclear. It should, however, be noted that Article L of the Treaty on European Union would expressly exclude from the jurisdiction of the Court *inter alia* the new provisions on a common foreign and security policy and practically all the new provisions on co-operation in the fields of justice and home affairs.

---

[72] Case C–2/88 Imm. [1990] E.C.R. I–3365. See Watson (1991) 28 C.M.L.Rev. 428.
[73] Compare para. 23 of the judgment in *Chernobyl* with para. 23 of the Order in *Zwartveld*.

CHAPTER 6

THE COURT OF FIRST INSTANCE

The establishment of the Court of First Instance[1]

By virtue of Article 11 of the Single European Act, a new Article 168a was added to the provisions of the EEC Treaty dealing with the Court of Justice.[2] Article 168a provides as follows:

"1. At the request of the Court of Justice and after consulting the Commission and the European Parliament, the Council may, acting unanimously, attach to the Court of Justice a court with jurisdiction to hear and determine at first instance, subject to a right of appeal to the Court of Justice on points of law only and in accordance with the conditions laid down by the Statute, certain classes of action or proceeding brought by natural or legal persons. That court shall not be competent to hear and determine actions brought by Member States or by Community institutions or questions referred for a preliminary ruling under Article 177.

2. The Council, following the procedure laid down in paragraph 1, shall determine the composition of that court and adopt the necessary adjustments and additional provisions to the Statute of the Court of Justice. Unless the Council decides otherwise, the provisions of this Treaty relating to the Court of Justice, in particular the provisions of the Protocol on the Statute of the Court of Justice, shall apply to that court.

3. The members of that court shall be chosen from persons whose independence is beyond doubt and who possess the ability required for appointment to judicial office; they shall be appointed by common accord of the Governments of the Member States for a term of six years. The membership shall be partially renewed every three years. Retiring members shall be eligible for reappointment.

4. That court shall establish its rules of procedure in agreement with the Court of Justice. Those rules shall require the unanimous approval of the Council."

A Council Decision establishing a Court of First Instance of the European Communities was adopted on October 24, 1988[3] and the Court of First

---

[1] See generally the Report of the House of Lords Select Committee on the European Communities entitled "A European Court of First Instance" (Session 1987–88, 5th Report); Millett, *The Court of First Instance of the European Communities* (1990); Kennedy, "The Essential Minimum: the Establishment of the Court of First Instance" (1989) 14 E.L.Rev. 7 and (1990) 15 E.L.Rev. 54; Toth, "The Court of First Instance of the European Communities" in White and Smythe (eds.), *Current Issues in European and International Law* (1990), p. 19.

[2] Similar adjustments were made to the ECSC and Euratom Treaties: see Articles 32d and 140a respectively.

[3] Dec. 88/591, referred to in the rest of this section as "the Decision." The version originally published contained a number of errors and a corrected version was published in O.J. 1989 C215/1 and [1989] 3 C.M.L.R. 458.

Instance commenced operations on October 31, 1989.[4] On that date, 151 cases falling within the jurisdiction of the Court of First Instance which were pending before the Court of Justice were transferred to the Court of First Instance pursuant to Article 14 of the Decision. The Rules of Procedure of the Court of First Instance entered into force on July 1, 1991.[5] Until that date, the Rules of Procedure of the Court of Justice were applied *mutatis mutandis*.[6]

The Court of First Instance is housed in a well-appointed annex to the main court building in Luxembourg.[7] It has its own Registry, but otherwise shares the services of the Court of Justice.

The purpose of the Court of First Instance is essentially twofold. First, it is intended to reduce the case-load of the Court of Justice and thereby to reduce the amount of time taken by that Court to dispose of cases. The burgeoning case-load of the Court of Justice has been giving rise to concern for a number of years. The figures speak for themselves.[8] The number of cases brought rose from 279 in 1980 to 373 in 1988. Although the Court's productivity also increased over that period, 206 cases being disposed of in 1980 and 386 in 1988, the increase was not enough to keep pace with the growing number of new cases being brought. Thus, in 1980 there were 328 cases pending at the end of the year, but that figure had risen to 605 by the end of 1988. The Court's case-load was having a serious effect on the average duration of proceedings: in 1980, it took the Court nine months on average to deal with a reference for a preliminary ruling and 18 months to dispose of a direct action. The corresponding figures for 1988 were 18 months and 24 months respectively.

Secondly, the Court of First Instance is intended to improve the administration of justice in the Community by engaging in more detailed investigation of factual matters.[9] The fact-finding procedures of the Court of Justice have been widely criticised[10] and it was hoped that the Court of First Instance would develop into a specialised fact-finding tribunal with particular expertise in cases concerning the economic effects of complex factual issues.

The jurisdiction of the Court of First Instance

Article 3(1) of the Decision provides that, in certain specified types of case, the Court of First Instance exercises "at first instance the jurisdiction conferred on the Court of Justice by the Treaties establishing the

---

[4] Following the publication in the Official Journal, in accordance with Article 13 of the Decision, of the ruling by the President of the Court of Justice that the Court of First Instance had been constituted in accordance with law: see O.J. 1989 L317/48. (Since then, judgments delivered by the Court of Justice have borne the prefix "C." Judgments delivered by the Court of First Instance bear the prefix "T," for the French word *tribunal*.)

[5] See O.J. 1991 L136/1; [1991] 3 C.M.L.R. 795.

[6] See Art. 11 of the Decision.

[7] *Cf.* Art. 1 of the Decision.

[8] Those which follow are taken from Millett, *op. cit.* p. 2.

[9] See the fourth recital to the Decision.

[10] See, *e.g.* the Report of the House of Lords Select Committee, paras. 35–36 and 63–65.

Communities and by the acts adopted in implementation thereof." As this provision makes clear, the establishment of the Court of First Instance did not therefore result in the creation of new heads of jurisdiction, but simply in a redistribution of responsibility for dealing at first instance with certain cases brought under the existing heads.

It will be observed that the first paragraph of Article 168a of the Treaty excludes certain matters from the jurisdiction of the Court of First Instance. Within the limits set by the Treaty, the precise jurisdiction of the Court of First Instance is laid down in Article 3 of the Decision. Broadly speaking, the Court of First Instance has jurisdiction in three categories of case:

(a) staff cases, that is disputes between the Communities and their servants;

(b) certain actions brought against the Commission by undertakings or associations of undertakings under the second paragraph of Article 33 and Article 35 of the ECSC Treaty; and

(c) "actions brought against an institution of the Communities by natural or legal persons pursuant to the second paragraph of Article 173 and the third paragraph of Article 175 of the EEC Treaty relating to the implementation of the competition rules applicable to undertakings."

The Court of First Instance also had jurisdiction in claims for compensation brought against a Community institution where the applicant claims that the damage it has suffered results from an act or failure to act which it is challenging under (a), (b) or (c) above.

The Court of Justice had originally proposed that the Court of First Instance also be given jurisdiction in actions for annulment or failure to act in the field of anti-dumping and subsidies.[11] The Commission, supported by France, opposed this proposal, ostensibly on the ground that it would make the procedure for imposing duties, which already required the intervention of both the Commission and the Council, too cumbersome. It was also suggested that the case-law of the Court of Justice was not sufficiently developed to enable the principles applicable in such cases to be clearly identified by the Court of First Instance. Although the Council did not therefore transfer jurisdiction in such cases to the Court of First Instance immediately, it committed itself in Article 3(3) of the Decision to re-examining the matter "in the light of experience, including the development of jurisprudence,[12] and after two years of operation of the Court of First Instance."

---

[11] The formal proposal of the Court of Justice has not been published, but a draft is reproduced at [1988] 1 C.M.L.R. 185. The contents of the Court's formal proposal are discussed by Kennedy, *loc. cit.* and by Toth, *loc. cit.*

[12] As Millett, *op. cit.* p. 32 note 11, points out, "jurisprudence" here means "case-law."

The Members of the Court of First Instance

The Court of First Instance consists of 12 Members,[13] and sits in Chambers of three or five Judges or in plenary session. Although the Treaty and the Council's Decision are silent on the question of the nationality of the Members, there is currently one Judge from each Member State. The judicial business and administration of the Court of First Instance is directed by its President, who presides at plenary sittings and deliberations.[14] The first President of the Court of First Instance was appointed by common accord of the Governments of the Member States,[15] but subsequent Presidents will be elected by the members from among their number. The President holds office for a term of three years and may be re-elected.[16]

The Court of Justice proposed that the Court of First Instance should have only seven Members, but, perhaps inevitably, the Member States preferred a solution which would enable them to appoint one Member each. Similarly, the proposal of the Court of Justice made no provision for the Court of First Instance to sit in plenary session, but the Council took the view, probably rightly, that the Court of First Instance should not be precluded from doing so when it considered this appropriate. Under Article 14 of its Rules of Procedure, a case may be referred to the Court of First Instance sitting in plenary session, or to a chamber consisting of a different number of Judges, "[w]henever the legal difficulty or the importance of the case or special circumstances so justify." Otherwise, staff cases are generally assigned to Chambers of three Judges and other cases to Chambers of five Judges.[17]

As a rule, each Member of the Court of First Instance performs the function of Judge.[18] There are no full-time Advocates General in the Court of First Instance, but any of the Members (with the exception of the President) may be called upon to perform the function of Advocate General.[19] A Member who is called upon to act as Advocate General in a case may not then take part in deciding that case,[20] although he can of course perform the function of Judge in other cases where the same issues arise.

According to Article 17 of its Rules of Procedure, when the Court of First Instance sits in plenary session, it must be assisted by an Advocate General, who is designated by the President. A Chamber of the Court of First Instance "may be assisted by an Advocate General if it is considered that the legal difficulty or the factual complexity of the case so requires."[21] The decision to designate an Advocate General in a particular case is taken by the Court of First Instance sitting in plenary session at the request of the Chamber to which the case has been assigned. The Judge who is to perform the function of Advocate General in such a case is designated by the President.[22] Where

---

[13] Decision, Art. 2.
[14] See Art. 8 of the Rules of Procedure of the Court of First Instance.
[15] See Art. 11 of the Decision.
[16] *Ibid.* Art. 2(2).
[17] Art. 12 of the Rules of Procedure of the Court of First Instance.
[18] See Art. 2 of the Rules of Procedure of the Court of First Instance.
[19] For an example, see Case T–51/89, *Tetra Pak Rausing* v. *Commission* [1990] E.C.R. II–309.
[20] Art. 2(3) of the Decision.
[21] Art. 18 of the Rules of Procedure of the Court of First Instance.
[22] *Ibid.* Art. 19.

an Advocates General is designated, he may deliver his Opinion orally or in writing.[23]

It is worth noting that the proposal of the Court of Justice made no provision for the Court of First Instance to be assisted by Advocates General, as it did not consider them necessary in a tribunal whose main function was to apply the decisions of the Court of Justice to new factual situations. Many interested parties, however, favoured the inclusion of Advocate General in the Court of First Instance [24] and the solution arrived at by the Council is a happy compromise between these opposing points of view, recognising that the assistance of an Advocate General would be an unnecessary luxury in many of the cases which fall within the jurisdiction of the Court of First Instance but that in certain cases the Opinion of an Advocate General might be helpful.

With regard to the qualifications for appointment to the Court of First Instance, the House of Lords Select Committee on the European Communities highlighted the disparity between Article 168a of the Treaty, which refers to "persons whose independence is beyond doubt and who possess the ability required for appointment to judicial office," and Article 167 of the Treaty, according to which the Members of the Court of Justice must be "persons whose independence is beyond doubt and who possess the qualifications required for appointment to the highest judicial offices in their respective countries or who are jurisconsults of recognized competence." The Committee stated: "The possibility of appointment of persons who have only the minimum qualifications for judicial posts in their own countries was rightly deplored by many of the witnesses ... The Committee share their view that judges should be of a calibre suitable for appointment to senior judicial posts in the courts of Member States; they trust that only persons of calibre well above the minimum requirement will be appointed to the CFI."[25] Another commentator has observed, more bluntly, that "As regards the quality of judicial review, it is difficult to envisage that this would be enhanced by the addition of the CFI consisting of judges with lower qualifications, particularly since the ultimate decision lies with the European Court."[26]

It is submitted that too much should not be made of the difference between the wording of Article 168a and Article 167 in this respect. Given the hierarchical relationship between the Court of Justice and the Court of First Instance, it would have been illogical to have laid down equivalent qualifications for appointment. In practice, the criteria laid down in both Articles are essentially subjective and the quality of the appointees to both courts depends ultimately on the willingness of the Member States to appoint Members who are up to the task.

---

[23] See Art. 61 of the Rules of Procedure of the Court of First Instance.
[24] See Millett, *op. cit.* pp. 15–16.
[25] *Loc. cit.* para. 72.
[26] Toth, *loc. cit.* p. 35.

The judgment

Like the Court of Justice, the Court of First Instance gives one collegiate judgment which is agreed, if necessary, by majority vote. No dissenting judgments are delivered.

The question whether it would be desirable for dissenting judgments to be published by the Court of First Instance was considered by the House of Lords Select Committee on the European Communities.[27] The argument in favour is that such judgments may help to clarify the judgment of the majority, particularly where no Advocate General has been designated, and that they may assist the Court of Justice in dealing with appeals. The main argument against is that, as with the Court of Justice, the collegiate nature of the judgments of the Court of First Instance shields its members from political pressure. Moreover, in many cases participation in the proceedings by other institutions and by the Member States will be enough to ensure that the Court of Justice is left in no doubt about the points at issue.

The need to protect the Members of the Court of First Instance from external pressure seems decisive. Dissenting judgments would, it is submitted, only be feasible if the Members of the Court of First Instance were appointed for much longer terms, say 12 years, which could not be renewed.[28]

Measures of organisation of procedure

In view of the Court of First Instance's intended role as a specialised fact-finding tribunal, provision is made in Article 64 of its Rules of Procedure for the adoption of so-called "measures of organization of procedure," which have no direct equivalent in the Rules of Procedure of the Court of Justice. The broad aim of such measures is "to ensure that cases are prepared for hearing, procedures carried out and disputes resolved under the best possible conditions." More specifically, their purpose is:

"(a) to ensure efficient conduct of the written and oral procedure and to facilitate the taking of evidence;
(b) to determine the points on which the parties must present further argument or which call for measures of enquiry;
(c) to clarify the forms of order sought by the parties, their pleas in law and arguments and the points at issue between them;
(d) to facilitate the amicable settlement of proceedings."

Measures of organisation of procedure are prescribed by the Court of First Instance after hearing the Advocate General, if one has been appointed. The adoption or modification of such measures may also be proposed by any of the parties. They are undertaken either by the Court of First Instance sitting in plenary session, by the Chamber to which the case has been

---

[27] See the Addendum to its Report, para. 12.
[28] *Cf.* the evidence given to the House of Lords Select Committee by Professor J. A. Usher at q. 247 of the Report.

assigned or by the Judge Rapporteur. If an Advocate General has been designated, he also takes part in the measures.

According to Article 64(3) of the Rules of Procedure of the Court of First Instance,

> "Measures of organisation of procedure may, in particular, consist of:
> (a) putting questions to the parties;
> (b) inviting the parties to make written or oral submissions on certain aspects of the proceedings;
> (c) asking the parties or third parties for information or particulars;
> (d) asking for documents or any papers relating to the case to be produced;
> (e) summoning the parties' agents or the parties in person to meetings."

It is clear from the use of the words "in particular" at the beginning of that provision that this list is illustrative only, although it should doubtless be construed *ejusdem generis*. Thus, the Court of First Instance may prescribe other such measures if it considers them necessary to ensure that "cases are prepared for hearing, procedures carried out and disputes resolved under the best possible conditions."

It may be observed, however, that the success of the Court of First Instance as a fact-finding tribunal depends as much on the use it makes of its powers as on their formal existence. It is interesting to note that the measures of organisation of procedure enumerated in the Rules of Procedure of the Court of First Instance could all be adopted by the Court of Justice under Articles 21 and 22 of the Statute or as measures of inquiry under Article 45 of its own Rules of Procedure. Moreover, Articles 21 and 22 of the Statute are applicable in proceedings before the Court of First Instance[29] and the Rules of Procedure of the Court of First Instance contain provisions relating to measures of inquiry which are substantially the same as those contained in the Rules of Procedure of the Court of Justice. It therefore appears that the provisions relating to measures of organisation of procedure amount to little more than an elaborate way of encouraging the Court of First Instance to take a more active role in establishing the facts.

Appeals to the Court of Justice

It will be recalled that, under Article 168a of the EEC Treaty, decisions of the Court of First Instance are "subject to a right of appeal to the Court of Justice on points of law only and in accordance with the conditions laid down by the Statute." According to Article 51 of the Statute, an appeal "shall lie on the grounds of lack of competence of the Court of First Instance, a breach of procedure before it which adversely affects the interests of the appellant as well as the infringement of Community law by the Court of First

---

[29] See Art. 46 of the Statute.

Instance." The third of these grounds is capable of subsuming the other two and is very wide. The only substantial restriction on the right of appeal is the requirement that appeals be limited to points of law. It is trite, but nonetheless valid, to observe that the distinction between questions of law and questions of fact is often difficult to draw.[30] The Court of Justice will have to be alert to attempts to expand the former category at the expense of the latter, for otherwise the right to appeal against decisions of the Court of First Instance will become virtually unlimited.[31]

According to Article 49 of the Statute, appeals to the Court of Justice may be brought "against final decisions of the Court of First Instance and decisions of that Court disposing of the substantive issues in part only or disposing of a procedural issue concerning a plea of lack of competence or inadmissibility." No appeal lies against certain procedural matters, such as decisions on the amount of costs or the party ordered to pay them[32] or on whether to grant legal aid.[33] Appeals must be brought within two months of the notification of the contested decision and may be lodged by any party which has been unsuccessful, in whole or in part, in its submissions. Interveners, other than the Member States and the Community institutions, may bring an appeal only where the decision of the Court of First Instance directly affects them. It is submitted that this means that they must establish an interest in the outcome of the case, not just in the success of certain arguments.[34] Except in staff cases, an appeal may also be brought by Member States and institutions which did not take part in the proceedings at first instance.[35]

In principle, an appeal to the Court of Justice does not have suspensory effect. Where a regulation is declared void by the Court of First Instance, however, its decision does not take effect until the period for bringing an appeal has expired and, if an appeal is brought, until it is dismissed. The powers of the Court of Justice to prescribe interim measures under Articles 185 and 186 of the Treaty are not affected.[36]

The right to bring an appeal against a decision of the Court of First Instance is not subject to any requirement that leave be obtained beforehand. It is arguable that any such requirement would be inconsistent with Article 168a of the Treaty, which speaks of "a *right* to appeal to the

---

[30] See further Jacobs, "Proposals for Reform in the Organisation and Procedure of the Court of Justice of the European Communities: with Special Reference to the Proposed Court of First Instance" in Capotorti *et al.* (eds.), *Du droit international au droit de l'intégration* (1987), 287 at pp. 294–296.

[31] For early decisions on the distinction between questions of law and questions of fact, see Case C–283/90 P, *Vidrányi* v. *Commission*, judgment of October 1, 1991; Case C–132/90 P, *Schwedler* v. *Parliament*, judgment of November 28, 1991; Case C–346/90 P, *F.* v. *Commission*, judgment of April 8, 1992; Case C–378/90 P, *Pitrone* v. *Commission*, judgment of April 2, 1992. (The suffix "P" after the number of the case stands for the French word *pourvoi* and denotes a decision given by the Court of Justice on appeal from the Court of First Instance.)

[32] Art. 51 of the Statute.

[34] *Cf.* the right of private parties to intervene in proceedings before the Court of Justice. See Lasok, *The European Court of Justice: Practice and Procedure* (1984), pp. 100–106.

[35] Art. 49 of the Statute.

[35] Art. 49 of the Statute.

[36] Art. 53 of the Statute.

Court of Justice" (emphasis added). The House of Lords Select Committee on the European Communities pointed out that, while a requirement that leave be obtained would have been familiar to lawyers trained in the common law tradition, it would not have been acceptable to some Member States from the civil law tradition, where the right to appeal is not subject to the exercise of discretion by the courts. Nonetheless, the Committee took the view that a requirement of leave to appeal would eventually have to be introduced in order to prevent the Court of Justice from becoming overloaded with appeals.[37] That prediction may well prove correct, although Article 119 of the Court's Rules of Procedure provides some scope for discouraging hopeless appeals. That provision states that "Where the appeal is, in whole or in part, clearly inadmissible or clearly unfounded, the Court may at any time, upon report of the Judge-Rapporteur and after hearing the Advocate-General, by reasoned order dismiss the appeal in whole or in part." Article 119 does not necessarily go as far as a system of leave to appeal, under which it might be envisaged that leave could be refused even where the appellant had an arguable case. It should prove adequate, however, to exclude frivolous appeals.

Where an appeal to the Court of Justice is successful, the decision of the Court of First Instance has to be quashed. The Court of Justice may then proceed to give final judgment in the matter, where the state of the proceedings so permits, or it may refer the case back to the Court of First Instance for judgment, in which case the Court of First Instance is bound by the decision of the Court of Justice on points of law. Where a successful appeal is brought by a Member State or Community institution which did not take part in the proceedings at first instance, the Court of Justice may state which, if any, of the effects of the decision of the Court of First Instance which has been quashed are to be considered definitive as between the parties.[38]

Since the jurisdiction of the Court of Justice is limited, on appeals from the Court of First Instance, to points of law, these arrangements may prove cumbersome where an applicant raises a number of grounds before the Court of First Instance and is successful on one of them. If the Court of Justice then upholds an appeal against the decision of the Court of First Instance, it may not be in a position to give final judgment if the Court of First Instance has not made the necessary findings of fact in relation to the other grounds raised by the applicant. In these circumstances, the case would have to be referred back to the Court of First Instance, giving rise to the possibility of a further appeal and the possibility that the entire process might have to be repeated.

The Court of Justice was confronted with a situation of this sort in *Commission v. Gill*.[39] In the interests of procedural economy, Advocate General Jacobs suggested that:

---

[37] See paras. 58–61 and 89 of the Committee's Report.
[38] See Art. 54 of the Statute.
[39] Case C–185/90 P, judgment of October 4, 1991. See also the Court's Order of February 25, 1992 in the same case.

"in general it would be helpful if the Court of First Instance, when giving judgment on one ground in favour of an applicant, were to make the necessary findings of fact relevant to any other grounds on which the applicant has relied and on which, in the event of an appeal, he might seek to rely as respondent."

This would enable the Court of Justice to give final judgment on appeal and avoid the need for the case to be referred back to the Court of First Instance for further findings of fact to be made. Despite the merits of the Advocate General's proposal, the point was not discussed by the Court,[40] which simply quashed the decision of the Court of First Instance and referred the case back for judgment.[41]

Overlapping jurisdiction

It will be apparent that situations may arise in which essentially the same question is raised in cases which are pending before both the Court of Justice and the Court of First Instance. This possibility is dealt with in the third paragraph of Article 47 of the Statute, which states in essence that either court may stay the proceedings pending before it until the other has given judgment. Where the Court of Justice decides to stay the proceedings before it, however, the proceedings before the Court of First Instance must continue. The third paragraph of Article 47 seems wide enough to cover cases which have come before the Court of Justice under Article 177 of the Treaty. However, because of the special need to deal with such cases promptly, it is submitted that the Court of Justice should as a rule allow proceedings under Article 177 to continue, leaving it to the Court of First Instance to consider whether to stay its own proceedings.

Cases may also arise in which it is not immediately apparent which court has jurisdiction. The rule applicable here is simple and sensible.[42] Where the Court of First Instance finds that is does not have jurisdiction to deal with a case falling within the jurisdiction of the Court of Justice, it is required to refer the action to the Court of Justice.[43] Likewise, where the Court of Justice finds that an action brought before it falls within the jurisdiction of the Court of First Instance, it is required to refer the action to the Court of First Instance, in which event the latter may not decline jurisdiction.

---

[40] But *cf.* Case T–15/91, *Bollendorff* v. *European Parliament*, judgment of April 10, 1992, where the Court of First Instance dealt with the substance of an application it considered inadmissible.

[41] For a case where the Court of Justice, having upheld an appeal from the Court of First Instance, decided to give final judgment in the matter, see Case C–345/90 P, *European Parliament* v. *Hanning*, judgment of February 20, 1992.

[42] See the second paragraph of Art. 47 of the Statute.

[43] For an example, see Case T–78/91, *Moat and TAO/AFI* v. *Commission*, Order of December 4, 1991, registered at the Court of Justice as Case C–322/91.

The effect of the Court of First Instance on the case-load of the Court of Justice

It is widely acknowledged that the establishment of the Court of First Instance will only provide the Court of Justice with temporary respite from its heavy case-load.[44] That case-load is likely to increase in the foreseeable future, as the validity and interpretation of the vast body of legislation adopted to give effect to the single market programme is questioned and courts in the newer Member States become more accustomed to using the preliminary rulings procedure. Moreover, a number of other instruments conferring on the Court jurisdiction to give preliminary rulings or a similar power, such as the Community Patent Convention,[45] the Rome Convention on the Law Applicable to Contractual Obligations[46] and the Agreement on the European Economic Area can be expected to enter into force fairly soon. In addition, early experience of the operation of the Court of First Instance suggests that the fears expressed by the House of Lords Select Committee[47] that a high proportion of its decisions would be taken on appeal to the Court of Justice are likely to prove justified.[48] At the same time, it is probably fair to say that the Court of First Instance is not yet working to its full capacity. It would seem to follow that further steps will need to be taken to reduce the case-load of the Court of Justice and to expand the jurisdiction of the Court of First Instance.[49]

Accordingly, in October 1991 the Court of Justice sent to the Council a draft decision extending the jurisdiction of the Court of First Instance to virtually all actions brought by natural and legal persons. Given that the Council was in any event required by Article 3(3) of the Decision to consider, in the autumn of 1991, whether the Court of First Instance should be given jurisdiction in dumping and subsidy cases, the Court's draft was intended to prompt a general review of the jurisdiction of the Court of First Instance. If adopted, it would virtually exhaust the possibilities for extending the jurisdiction of the Court of First Instance made available to the Council by Article 168a in its present form.

The Treaty on European Union would, however, replace Article 168a with a new text reflecting the fact that the Court of First Instance is now in existence. The only class of proceedings expressly excluded from the jurisdiction of the Court of First Instance would be references for preliminary rulings. Actions brought by Member States or by Community institutions would no longer be excluded in principle from its jurisdiction.

---

[44] See, *e.g.* the Report of the House of Lords Select Committee, paras. 76–79.

[45] O.J. 1976 L17/1.

[46] O.J. 1980 L266/1.

[47] See para. 83 of its Report.

[48] Although the Committee acknowledged the possibility that disposing of an appeal would be less time-consuming than dealing with a case from the beginning, as the facts would have been established and the legal issues clarified by the Court of First Instance: see para. 85 of its Report.

[49] See further the paper prepared by the Court of First Instance entitled "Reflections on the Future Development of the Community Judicial System" (1991) 16 E.L.Rev. 175; Jacqué and Weiler, "On the Road to European Union—A New Judicial Architecture: An Agenda for the Intergovermental Conference" (1990) 27 C.M.L.Rev. 185.

The Council, acting unanimously at the request of the Court of Justice and after consulting the Parliament and the Commission, would have the power to determine the particular classes of action or proceeding which are to be dealt with by the Court of First Instance. In the light of these proposed amendments to Article 168a and of the Court's proposal, it seems likely that there will soon be a significant extension in the jurisdiction of the Court of First Instance.

PART III: THE FOUNDATIONS OF THE COMMUNITY

CHAPTER 7

CUSTOMS DUTIES AND DISCRIMINATORY INTERNAL TAXATION

ESTABLISHMENT OF A CUSTOMS UNION

Whereas a free trade area comprises a group of customs territories in which duties are eliminated on trade in goods originating in such territories, a customs union represents a further step in economic integration, since a common tariff is adopted in trade relations with the outside world.

Article 9 of the Treaty[1] provides that the Community "shall be based on a customs union which shall cover all trade in goods and which shall involve the prohibition between Member States of custom duties on imports and exports and all charges having equivalent effect, and the adoption of a common customs tariff in their relations with third countries." The "goods" referred to are all products which have a monetary value and may be the object of commercial transactions. The Court rejected an argument adduced by the Italian Government that the free movement provisions of the Treaty could have no application to a charge levied on the export of goods of historic or artistic interest. The products covered by the Italian law in issue, said the Court, regardless of any other qualities which might distinguish them from other commercial goods, resembled such goods in that they had a monetary value and could constitute the object of commercial transactions—indeed, the Italian law recognised as much by fixing the charge in relation to the value of the object in question.[2]

The reason why the abolition of duties between the constituent territories of a free trade area is normally restricted to goods originating in such territories, is that otherwise members of the area maintaining high tariffs against non-Member countries would find their markets open to imports from such countries via the territory of low tariff neighbours. The problem is obviated if all members adopt the same tariffs in their trade with third countries. Thus the Treaty provides[3] that its free movement provisions[4] apply not only to goods originating in Member States, but also to products coming from third countries which are in free circulation in the Member States.

---

[1] Directly applicable in conjunction with other Treaty Articles; Cases 2 & 3/69, *Sociaal Fonds, etc.* v. *Brachfeld and Chougol Diamond Co.* [1969] E.C.R 211, (Arts. 9 and 12); Case 33/70, *SACE* v. *Italian Ministry of Finance* [1970] E.C.R. 1213, (Arts. 9 and 13(2)); Case 18/71, *Eunomia* v. *Italian Ministry of Education* [1971] E.C.R. 811, (Arts. 9 and 16).

[2] Case 7/68, *Commission* v. *Italy* [1968] E.C.R. 423. It is open to Member States to prohibit the export of national treasures under Art. 36. Coins may constitute "goods" if they do not constitute a means of payment in the Member States, see Case 7/78, *R.* v. *Johnson* [1978] E.C.R. 2247. For goods as waste under Art. 30, see Case C-2/90, *Commission* v. *Belgium*, judgment of July 9, 1992.

[3] Art. 9(2).

[4] Arts. 12–17, 31–37.

GOODS ORIGINATING IN MEMBER STATES

Although products from third countries in free circulation benefit in equal measure from the provisions guaranteeing the free movement of goods, it is nevertheless necessary to differentiate between products according to origin in several circumstances:

— for the purposes of the application of the Common Customs Tariff, in the case of imports from third countries;
— where Member States have to certify the origin of goods exported to third countries, because required to do so by the authorities in such countries;
— where the Commission, acting under Article 115 of the Treaty, authorises Member State A to take protective measures against the import of a certain product, originating in a third country, which has been imported into Member State B, and is in free circulation therein.

Rules for determining the origin of goods in such circumstances are contained in Regulation 802/68.[5] Under the latter Regulation, a product is considered to have originated in a particular country if it has been wholly obtained or produced in that country.[6] Goods in the production of which two or more countries have been concerned are considered to have originated in the country in which the last economically justifiable process was performed, provided that such operation was carried out in an undertaking equipped for the purpose, and resulted in the manufacture of a new product or represented an important stage of manufacture.[7] The Court has held[8] that the stage of manufacture referred to must bring about a "significant qualitative change" in the properties of the original product. An assembly operation may confer origin where it represents the decisive production stage.[9] But in some cases involving assembly operations it is necessary to take account of the value added by the assembly as an ancillary criterion.[10] Special rules for determining the origin of particular products have been made under the parent Regulation (for example regarding the origin of photocopiers, and integrated circuits).[11] Provision is made for the issue of certificates of origin by authorised national agencies.[12]

---

[5] O.J. English Sp.Ed. 1968 (I), p. 165. See in general, Forrester, (1980) 5 E.L.Rev. 167.
[6] Art. 4. On origin of fish under Art. 4(2)(f), see Case 100/84, *Commission* v. *United Kingdom* [1985] E.C.R. 1169.
[7] Art. 5.
[8] Case 49/76, *Uberseehandel* [1977] E.C.R. 41. See also Case 93/83, *ZENTRAG* [1984] E.C.R. 1095.
[9] Case 114/78, *Yoshida* [1979] E.C.R. 151; Case C–26/88, *Brother* [1989] E.C.R. 4253 at p. 4280, para. 19.
[10] Case 26/88, *Brother* [1989] E.C.R. 4253 at p. 4280, para. 20.
[11] See, *e.g.* Reg. 288/89, O.J. 1989 L33/23 on the origin of integrated circuits, and Reg. 2071/89, O.J. 1989 L196/24 on the origin of photocopier apparatus. The Court has held two such Regulations invalid. Reg. 2067/77 (zip-fasteners) in Case 34/78, *Yoshida* [1979] E.C.R. 115, and Case 114/78, *Yoshida* [1979] E.C.R. 151; and Reg. 749/78 (textile products), in Case 162/82, *Cousin* (1983) E.C.R. 1101.
[12] Reg. 802/68, Art. 10.

GOODS IN FREE CIRCULATION IN THE MEMBER STATES

Article 10 of the Treaty provides that products coming from a third country shall be considered to be in free circulation in a Member State:

— if import formalities have been complied with;
— if customs duties or charges having equivalent effect have been levied; and
— if there has been no reimbursement of such duties or charges.

The reimbursement referred to is possible in the case of inward processing, when goods are imported simply for the purposes of processing followed by re-export.[13]

EVIDENCE OF ENTITLEMENT TO FREEDOM OF MOVEMENT—COMMUNITY TRANSIT

Article 10(2) provides for administrative co-operation to facilitate the application of the free movement of goods provisions to all products qualifying under Article 9(2). An early Commission Decision laid down that such products should be admitted to the benefit of the relevant Treaty provisions on the presentation of documentary evidence, which would be issued by the customs authorities of the Member State of export, at the request of the exporter.[14] Two certificates were specified in the Decision; Form DD1, issued in respect of goods transported directly from the Member State of export to that of import, and Form DD3, issued in other cases. This requirement simplified customs clearance, but it did not obviate the necessity of a succession of customs formalities in the case of goods traversing several Member States. It was to minimise such formalities that the Community transit system was instituted. Regulation 222/77[15] establishes two procedures: one for external Community transit, and one for internal Community transit. The first procedure applies, essentially, to goods which neither originate in a Member State nor are in free circulation (*i.e.* goods from third countries on which duty has not been paid), while the second applies to goods which either do originate in a Member State, or, if not, are in free circulation.

An example of the external transit procedure would be as follows. Suppose that eligible goods are to be transported between Member States A and D, via Member States B and C. The exporter must make a "T1" declaration in the customs office in State A.[16] The office will register the T1 declaration, prescribe the period within which the goods must be produced at the requisite customs office in State D, retain a copy of the T1 declaration,

---

[13] See Reg. 1999/85, J.O. 1985 L188/1.
[14] Dec. December 5, 1960, J.O. 1961, 29.
[15] O.J. 1977 L38/1, superseding Reg. 542/69, O.J. 1969 L77/1, and consolidating its amending texts. Reg. 222/77 has been the subject of numerous amendments. For a consolidated text, see *Encyclopedia of European Community Law*, (Sweet and Maxwell), C10–193.
[16] Art. 12.

and return copies to the exporter.[17] Identification of the goods will in general be secured by sealing.[18] Transit through Member States B and C will be accomplished simply by presentation of the T1 declaration, and customs inspection to ensure that the seals are not broken.[19]

The procedure is similar for internal Community transit, except that the relevant document is a "T2" declaration.

Simplified procedures are available for persons who frequently consign goods and who satisfy certain other conditions.[20]

The Community transit procedure is mandatory for all movement of goods between two points situated in the Community,[21] with certain limited exceptions.[22] Even when the exceptions apply, the Community nature of goods is certified, for the purposes of the free movement provisions of the Treaty, by Community transit documents. In these cases a slight modification of the form T2 is specified, and termed T2L.[23] The requirement that the Community status of goods be proven *vis-à-vis* the customs authorities of the Member State of destination exclusively by means of transit documents T2 or T2L has been held to be consistent with Articles 9 and 10 of the EEC Treaty.[24]

The EEC Treaty does not expressly prohibit transit charges. In *SIOT*[25] an Italian undertaking challenged before an Italian court charges imposed upon oil landed at Trieste for consignment via the transalpine oil pipeline to Germany. The court asked the Court of Justice whether such transit charges were compatible with Community law. The Court held that it was a necessary consequence of the Customs Union and the mutual interest of the Member States that there be recognised a general principle of freedom of transit of goods within the Community. The imposition of transit charges was incompatible with this principle, unless the charges in question represented the costs of transportation or of other services connected with transit, including general benefit derived form the use of harbour works or installations, for the navigability and maintenance of which public authorities were responsible. It is to be noted that the oil in question did not originate in a Member State, and it is not clear that it was in free circulation in a Member State.[26] While the Treaty states that the elimination of customs duties and quantitative restrictions applies to products originating in Member States and to products coming into third countries which are in free circulation in Member States,[27] the *SIOT* case implies that the

---

[17] Art. 17.

[18] Art. 18.

[19] Art. 20.

[20] Reg. 1062/87 O.J. 1987 L107/1, Arts. 62–77.

[21] Art. 1.

[22] Arts. 2–8, 42–49.

[23] Reg. 1062/87, O.J. 1987 L107/1, Arts. 82–88. Reg. 1062/87 has been amended on numerous occasions. For a consolidated text, see *Encyclopedia of European Community Law*, (Sweet and Maxwell), C10–413.

[24] Case C–117/88, *Trend-Moden* [1990] E.C.R. I–631. The Court notes that T2 or T2L documents may be issued retroactively, [1990] E.C.R. I—at p. 645, para. 15.

[25] Case 266/81 [1983] E.C.R. 731.

[26] The reference by the Trieste Port Authority to external Community transit suggests that the goods were not in free circulation, [1988] E.C.R. at p. 752.

[27] Art. 9(2) EEC Treaty.

abovementioned provisions apply by analogy to third country goods which are not in free circulation where such goods are in lawful transit in one Member State and destined for another. In the *Richardt*[28] case goods of third country origin in free circulation in France were mistakenly consigned via the external community transit procedure (rather than via internal community transit) to Luxembourg for export to the Soviet Union. The Court of Justice confirmed the principle of freedom of transit without stating in so many words that the principle applied to goods in external community transit as well as to goods in free circulation. The implication is that goods in external community transit or which would be so conveyed unless exempted from that procedure are subject to the application of analogy of the provisions of the Treaty prohibiting customs duties and charges having equivalent effect, and quantitative restrictions and measures having equivalent effect.

Elimination of customs duties and measures having equivalent effect on imports and exports—the framework of Articles 12 to 17 of the Treaty.

Articles 12 to 17 EEC provide for the abolition of customs duties and similar charges, calling for:

— a standstill on customs duties and measures having equivalent effect on imports and exports (Article 12);
— the progressive elimination of customs duties on imports during the transitional period (Articles 13(1), 14 and 15);
— the progressive elimination of charges having an effect equivalent to customs duties on imports during the transitional period (Article 13(2));
— the abolition of customs duties and charges having equivalent effect on exports by the end of the first stage (Article 16).

THE STANDSTILL

Article 12 provides that Member States shall refrain from introducing between themselves any new customs duties on imports and exports or any charges having equivalent effect, and from increasing those which they already apply in their trade with each other. The Article, which applies equally to agricultural goods,[29] is directly applicable.[30]

The Court emphasised the central role of the prohibition of customs duties and similar charges, contained in Articles 9 and 12, in *Commission* v. *Luxembourg and Belgium*,[31] basing its view on the respective provisions of these Articles in the scheme of the Treaty, Article 9 being placed at the beginning of the Title relating to "Free Movement of Goods" and Article 12 at the beginning of the section dealing with the "Elimination of Customs

---

[28] Case C–367/89 [1991] E.C.R. I–4621.
[29] Cases 90 and 91/63, *Commission* v. *Luxembourg and Belgium* [1964] E.C.R. 65.
[30] Case 26/62, *Van Gend en Loos* v. *Nederlandse Administratie der Belastingen* [1963] E.C.R. 1; Cases 2 & 3/69 *Sociaal Fonds etc.* v. *Brachfeld and Chougol Diamond Co.* [1969] E.C.R. 211.
[31] Cases 2 and 3/62 [1962] E.C.R. 425.

Duties."[32] Any exception to such an essential rule would require to be clearly stated, and would receive a narrow construction.[33] Thus, to the extent that a Council Regulation concerning the common organisation of the market in wine authorised Member States to impose charges on intra-Community trade, it was held to be invalid by the Court of Justice.[34] The Court's rigorous approach is reflected in its subsequent case-law. In *Social Fonds voor de Diamantarbeiders* v. *Brachfeld and Chougol Diamond Co.*,[35] the Court was faced with a reference from an Antwerp magistrate, concerning a levy imposed under Belgian law on imported diamonds. The Belgian Government submitted that the levy could not be regarded as infringing Articles 9 and 12, since it was devoid of protectionist purpose in the first place, Belgium did not even produce diamonds, and in the second place, the purpose of the levy was to provide social security benefits for workers in the diamond industry. The following statement of the Court emphasises that the achievement of a single market between Member States requires more than the elimination of protection:

"In prohibiting the imposition of customs duties, the Treaty does not distinguish between goods according to whether or not they enter into competition with the products of the importing country. Thus, the purpose of the abolition of customs barriers is not merely to eliminate their protective nature, as the Treaty sought on the contrary to give general scope and effect to the rule on elimination of customs duties and charges having equivalent effect in order to ensure the free movement of goods. It follows from the system as a whole and from the general and absolute nature of the prohibition of any customs duty applicable to goods moving between Member States that customs duties are prohibited independently of any consideration of the purpose for which they were introduced and the destination of the revenue obtained therefrom. The justification for this prohibition is based on the fact that any pecuniary charge—however small—imposed on goods by reason of the fact that they cross a frontier constitutes an obstacle to the movement of such goods."[36]

Whether or not a customs duty is a "new" customs duty, or whether or not it represents an increase in one already applied, must be determined in relation to the duties actually applied at the date the Treaty entered into force, rather than those which in strict law ought to have been applicable. The significance of the point is illustrated in *Commission* v. *Italy*,[37] arising out of proceedings instituted under Article 169 of the Treaty. As the result of legislative oversight, two different duties became applicable in Italy to

---

[32] [1962] E.C.R. 425 at p. 431.
[33] Art. 115 permitted unilateral derogation from the free movement provisions of the Treaty, in cases of urgency, during the transitional period. Now a Commission authorisation is necessary.
[34] Cases 80 & 8/77, *Société Les Commissionaires Reunis Sarl* v. *Receveurs des Douanes* [1978] E.C.R. 927.
[35] Note 30.
[36] [1969] E.C.R. 211 at pp. 221, 222.
[37] Case 10/61 [1962] E.C.R. 1.

imported radio parts as of July 14, 1956: one of 35 per cent. and one of 30 per cent. coupled with a specific minimum of 150 lira. In these circumstances the Italian customs authorities were instructed to apply to each particular case the duty more favourable to the importer. In its application of Articles 12 and 14 of the Treaty, the Italian Government treated the 35 per cent. duty as being without lawful effect, and applied the Treaty on the basis of the alternative charge. The Court held that the provisions of the Treaty in question must be given effect on the basis of the duties actually applied in each case. Any other solution would leave the Commission the task of inquiring into the validity of domestic administrative measures with respect to the law of the Member States. This view was reiterated in *Van Gend en Loos* v. *Netherlands Inland Revenue Administration*,[38] the Court adding that a reclassification of a particular product under a tariff heading attracting a higher duty was no more consistent with Article 12 than a straightforward increase in the original rate.

DEFINITION OF "CHARGES HAVING EQUIVALENT EFFECT"

Article 13(2) EEC provides for the progressive abolition of charges having an effect equivalent to customs duties on imports. This requirement has been described by the Court as the "logical and necessary complement"[39] to the first paragraph of the Article in question, which calls for the elimination of customs duties proper. The prohibition of charges having equivalent effect, like the prohibition on customs duties, constitutes a basic Treaty norm, and any exceptions must be clearly and unambiguously provided for.[40]

The concept of charges having equivalent effect must be interpreted in the light of the objects and purposes of the Treaty, in particular the provisions dealing with the free movement of goods.[41] "Consequently," the Court has declared, "any pecuniary charge, however small and whatever its designation and mode of application, which is imposed unilaterally on domestic or foreign goods by reason of the fact that they cross a frontier, and which is not a customs duty in the strict sense, constitutes a charge having equivalent effect within the meaning of Articles 9, 12, 13 and 16 of the Treaty, even if it is not imposed for the benefit of the State, is not

---

[38] Note 30.
[39] Cases 52 & 55/65, *Germany* v. *Commission* [1966] E.C.R. 159; and see, *e.g.* Cases 2 & 3/69, *Chougol Diamond* [1969] E.C.R. 211; Case 24/68, *Commission* v. *Italy* [1969] E.C.R. 193.
[40] Cases 52 & 55/65 note 39.
[41] See, *e.g.* Cases 2 & 3/69, Case 24/68 note 39. A prohibition on charges having equivalent effect often appears in secondary legislation. Such a provision is invariably given the same meaning as the similar provision in the Treaty: Case 25/67, *Milch-, Fett- und Eirkontor* v. *Hauptzollamt Saarbrucken* [1968] E.C.R. 207; Case 34/73, *Variola* v. *Italian Ministry of Finance* [1973] E.C.R. 981; Case 21/75, *Schroeder* v. *Oberstadtdirektor* Cologne [1975] E.C.R. 905. This may not be the case, however, in the case of imports from a third country: Case 70/77, *Simmenthal* v. *Italian Ministry of Finance* [1978] E.C.R. 1453; see *infra* at p. 206.

discriminatory or protective in effect and if the product on which the charge is imposed is not in competition with any domestic product."[42]

On several occasions the Court has been confronted with the argument that a charge levied on the crossing of a frontier was not a charge having equivalent effect to a customs duty, but a "fee" for a service rendered. This argument has been adduced in the case of a "fee" charged by a national agricultural intervention agency for the issue of import licences,[43] a fee levied on all imports and exports to defray the costs of compiling statistical data, the availability of which allegedly benefited traders,[44] and "fees" to offset the costs of compulsory health and sanitary inspections.[45] The Court has taken the view that "a charge may escape prohibition as a charge having equivalent effect if the charge in question is the consideration for a service actually rendered to the importer and is of an amount commensurate with that service."[46] The Court has rejected the "consideration for services" argument in the case of unilateral measures, either because the services in question were rendered in the general interest (for example, health inspections), rather than in the interests of traders themselves, or, if the services did benefit traders, because they benefited them as a class in a way which was impossible to quantify in a particular case (for example, compilation of statistical data). Charges imposed by a Member State to cover the cost of complying with Community measures will not however amount to measures having equivalent effect, at any rate where the Community measures reduce obstacles to intra-Community trade which would otherwise result from divergent national measures.[47] It is not necessary in such a case to establish whether or not the service is of direct benefit to importers or exporters.[48] Measures taken by a Member State under an international Treaty to which all Member States are parties, and which encourage the free movement of goods, may be assimilated to Community measures, and fees covering costs may be charged accordingly.[49]

A case neatly illustrating the difficulties of establishing whether or not

---

[42] Case 24/68, *Commission* v. *Italy* [1969] E.C.R. 193, at p. 201. And see Case C–137/89, *Commission* v. *Italy* [1990] E.C.R. I–847; Case 340/87, *Commission* v. *Italy* [1989] E.C.R. 1483.

[43] Cases 52 & 55/65 note 36. Note that even if Art. 36 permitted a quantitative restriction or measure having equivalent effect, it would not justify a fee charged in connection with such a measure, Case 29/72, *Marimex* v. *Italian Finance Administration* [1972] E.C.R. 1309. But *cf.* Case 46/76, *Bauhuis* v. *Netherlands State* [1977] E.C.R. 5, where Community rules justified the restriction in question.

[44] Case 24/68 note 39.

[45] Case 39/73, *Rewe-Zentralfinanz* v. *Landwirtschaftskammer* [1973] E.C.R. 1039; Case 87/75, *Bresciani* v. *Italian Finance Administration* [1976] E.C.R. 129; Case 35/76, *Simmenthal* v. *Italian Minister of Finance* [1976] E.C.R. 1871; Case 251/78, *Firma Denkavit Futtermittel GmbH* v. *Minister for Food* [1979] E.C.R. 3369.

[46] Case 132/82, *Commission* v. *Belgium* [1983] E.C.R. 1649. An *ad valorem* charge will not meet the requirement that the charge be commensurate to the service, Case 170/88, *Ford Espana* [1989] E.C.R. 2305.

[47] Case 46/76, *Bauhuis* v. *Netherlands State* [1977] E.C.R. 5. Case 18/87, *Commission* v. *Germany* [1988] E.C.R. 5427, at p. 5441.

[48] *Ibid.*

[49] Case 89/76, *Commission* v. *Netherlands* [1977] E.C.R. 1355; Case C–111/89, *Hillegom* [1990] E.C.R. I–1735. May 2, 1990. A charge based on the invoice value of the goods will not be sufficiently linked to the cost of the operation for these purposes.

national charges may be regarded as charges having equivalent effect was *Commission* v. *Belgium*.[50] The development of Community transit[51] enabled importers to convey their goods from the frontier to public warehouses situated in the interior of the country without paying duties and taxes. In these warehouses, importers could have customs clearance operations carried out, and they also had the opportunity of placing their goods in temporary storage, pending their consignment to a particular customs procedure. The Belgian Government levied storage charges on goods deposited in such public warehouses in the interior of the Community. The Court held that these charges were charges having equivalent effect when they were imposed solely in connection with the completion of customs formalities, but that they were justified in cases where the trader elected to place his goods in storage. In the latter case, the Court accepted that the storage represented a service rendered to traders. A decision to deposit the goods could only be taken at the request of the trader concerned, and ensured storage of the goods without payment of duties. The Belgian Government argued that also in the former case—where the goods were cleared through customs without storage—a service was rendered to the importer. It was always open to the latter to avoid payment by choosing to have his goods cleared through customs at the frontier, where such a procedure was free of charge. By using a public warehouse, the importer could have the goods declared through customs near the places for which his products were bound. The Court acknowledged that the use of a public warehouse in the interior of the country offered certain advantages, but noted that such advantages were linked solely with the completion of customs formalities which, whatever the place, was always compulsory. Furthermore, the advantages in question resulted from the scheme of Community transit, which had been established not in the interest of individual traders, but in order to encourage the free movement of goods and facilitate transport in the Community. "There can therefore," concluded the Court, "be no question of levying charges for customs clearance facilities accorded in the interests of the Common Market."[52]

Article 13(2) EEC was held to be directly applicable as of the end of the transitional period in *SACE* v. *Italian Ministry of Finance*, and *Capolongo* v. *Azienda Agricola Maya*.[53]

---

[50] Case 132/82 [1983] E.C.R. 1649.
[51] See *supra* at p. 183.
[52] It is not clear whether or not this represents a retreat from Case 46/76, *Bauhuis* [1977] E.C.R. 5, and Case 89/76, *Commission* v. *Netherlands* [1977] E.C.R. 1355, which allow national charges for the completion of procedures established in the general interests of the Community. These latter cases were referred to by the Court with approval in Case 1/83, *IFG* [1984] E.C.R. 349. It may be that a charge could be made for completion of customs formalities outside normal working hours, *cf.* Case 340/87, *Commission* v. *Italy* [1989] E.C.R. 1483.
[53] Case 33/70 [1970] E.C.R. 1213 and Case 77/72 [1973] E.C.R. 611. But not before the end of the transitional period; the Council's "acceleration" Decision of July 26, 1966, J.O. 1966 2971, applied only to customs duties, not to charges having equivalent effect.

In the appropriate context, a prohibition of customs duties *simpliciter* will be construed as including by implication charges having equivalent effect.[54]

CUSTOMS DUTIES AND CHARGES HAVING EQUIVALENT EFFECT ON EXPORTS—ARTICLE 16 EEC

The fact that the achievement of a single market between Member States is dependent on more than the suppression of measures calculated to protect domestic industry is well illustrated by the prohibition of customs duties and charges having equivalent effect on exports as well as imports. As Advocate General Gand pointed out in *Commission* v. *Italy*, "What distinguishes customs duties on exports is not that they protect the national industry but that they increase the price of goods and thus tend to hinder their exportation and, without prohibiting trade in goods, to make it more difficult."[55] The concept of charges having equivalent effect in the context of exports is the same as in the context of imports, as is indicated by the repeated formulations of the Court of Justice, which make reference to Article 16 of the Treaty, as well as to Articles 12 and 13.[56]

Article 16 required the abolition of all duties and charges having equivalent effect by the end of the first stage at the latest (December 31, 1961), and the Court held in *Eunomia di Porro & Co.* v. *Italian Ministry of Education*[57] that this Article, in conjunction with Article 9, produced direct effects in the Member States. The Court has held that an internal duty which falls more heavily on exports than on domestic sales amounts to a charge having equivalent effect to a customs duty.[58] Fees for inspections of plants charged only in respect of exported products, and not in respect of those intended for the home market, constitute charges having equivalent effect on exports, even if those inspections are carried out to meet the requirements of international conventions affecting only exported products. The contrary would be true only if it were established that the products intended for the home market derived no benefit from the inspections.[58a]

THE PROHIBITION OF DISCRIMINATORY FISCAL CHARGES ON IMPORTS

Article 95

The first paragraph of Article 95 of the Treaty provides that no Member State shall impose, directly or indirectly, on the product of any other Member State any internal taxation of any kind in excess of that imposed

---

[54] Cases 37 and 38/83, *Indiamex* [1973] E.C.R. 1609; Case C–260/90 *Leplat*, Judgment of February 12, 1992.
[55] Case 7/68 [1968] E.C.R. 423 at p. 434. And see the *Chougol Diamond* case, *supra*, p. 186.
[56] See, *e.g.* Case 24/68, *Commission* v. *Italy* [1969] E.C.R. 193, at p. 201, *supra*, p. 187.
[57] Case 18/71 [1971] E.C.R. 811.
[58] Cases 36 & 71/80, *Irish Creamery Milk Suppliers Assn.* v. *Govt. of Ireland* [1981] E.C.R. 735.
[58a] Case C–111/89, *Hillegom* [1990] E.C.R. I–1735.

directly or indirectly on similar domestic products. Paragraph 2 adds that Member States shall furthermore impose no taxation of such a kind as to afford indirect protection to other products. The first paragraph is concerned with imports having such a close competitive relationship with similar domestic products as to merit the same tax treatment as that applicable to those products. The second paragraph contemplates imports which are not in such a close competitive relationship with relevant domestic products as to merit the same tax treatment, but which are nevertheless sufficiently interchangeable from the point of view of consumers to merit tax treatment which is even handed and free of any protective effect in favour of such domestic products. Although Article 95 refers to products "of other Member States," this has been held to include products from third countries which are in free circulation in Member States.[59] Furthermore, once a product has been imported from another Member State and placed on the market, it becomes a domestic product for the purposes of comparison of its tax position with an import from another Member State under Article 95.[60]

Purpose of Article 95

The Court has stated that the Article is calculated to close any loopholes which internal taxation might open in the prohibition on customs duties and charges having equivalent effect.[61] The purpose of the Article has been explained as follows in a consistent line of cases:

"... Article 95 supplements the provisions on the abolition of customs duties and charges having equivalent effect. Its aim is to ensure free movement of goods between the Member States in normal conditions of competition by the elimination of all forms of protection which may result from the application of internal taxation that discriminates against products from other Member States. Thus Article 95 must guarantee the complete neutrality of internal taxation as regards competition between domestic products and imported products."[62]

The rule prohibiting discriminatory internal taxation on imported goods constitutes an essential basic principle of the common market,[63] and has produced direct effects in the Member States from January 1, 1962.[64]

---

[59] Case 193/85, *Co-Frutta* [1987] E.C.R. 2085 at p. 2110, para. 25.
[60] Case C–47/88, *Commission* v. *Denmark* [1990] E.C.R. I–4509, para. 17.
[61] Cases 2 & 3/62, *Commission* v. *Belgium and Luxembourg* [1962] E.C.R. 425 at p. 431.
[62] Case 252/86, *Bergandi* [1988] E.C.R. 1343 at p. 1374, para. 24, citing earlier case law.
[63] Case 57/65, *Lutticke* [1966] E.C.R. 205 at p. 214.
[64] Case 57/65 note 63; Case 28/67, *Mokerei-Zentrale* v. *Hauptzollampt Paderborn* [1968] E.C.R. 143; Case 45/75, *Rewe-Zentrale, etc.* v. *Hauptzollampt Landau/Pfalz* [1976] E.C.R. 181; Case 74/76, *Iannelli & Voloi* v. *Paolo Meroni* [1977] E.C.R. 557.

Member States free to choose system of internal taxation, providing its advantages are extended to imported products

Article 95, first paragraph, prohibits discrimination against similar imported products, with respect to the rate of taxation, basis of assessment,[65] or detailed rules.[66]

Article 95 leaves each Member State free to establish the system of taxation which it considers the most suitable in relation to each product, provided that the system is treated as a point of reference for determining whether the tax applied to a similar product of another Member State complies with the requirements of the first paragraph of that Article.[67] It matters not that tax concessions for domestic products rest, not directly upon national law, but on administrative instructions to the authorities.[68]

In the *Hansen* case[69] the question arose whether an importer of spirits into Germany was entitled to take advantage of tax relief available, *inter alia*, in respect of spirits made from fruit by small businesses and collective farms. The Court acknowledged that advantages of this kind could serve legitimate economic or social purposes, such as the use of certain raw materials, the continued production of particular spirits of high quality, or the continuance of certain classes of undertakings such as agricultural distilleries. However, Article 95 required that such preferential systems must be extended without discrimination to spirits coming from other Member States.[70]

The above principle was applied to the Republic of Italy when that country charged lower taxes on regenerated oil than on ordinary oil, on ecological grounds, while refusing to extend this advantage to imported regenerated oil. Italy argued that it was impossible to distinguish whether oil was of primary distillation, or regenerated. The Court of Justice[71] refused to accept this argument as a justification. It was for importers to establish that their oil qualified for the relief in question, while the Italian authorities were to set standards of proof no higher than was necessary to prevent tax evasion. The Court of Justice observed that certificates from the authorities of exporting Member States could provide one means of identifying oil which had been regenerated.

---

[65] Case 54/72, *F.O.R.* v. *V.K.S.* [1973] E.C.R. 193; Case 20/76, *Schottle & Sohne* v. *Finanzamt Freudenstadt* [1977] E.C.R. 247; Case 74/76, *Iannelli & Volpi* v. *Paolo Meroni* [1977] E.C.R. 557.

[66] Case 169/78, *Commission* v. *Italy* [1980] E.C.R. 385; Case 55/79, *Commission* v. *Ireland* [1980] E.C.R. 385.

[67] Case 127/75, *Bobie-Getrankevertrieb* v. *Hauptzollampt Aachen-Nord* [1976] E.C.R. 1079.

[68] Case 17/81, *Pabst & Richarz* [1982] E.C.R. 1331.

[69] Case 148/77, *H. Hansen* v. *Hauptzollampt Flensburg* [1978] E.C.R. 1787. See also Case 26/80, *Schneider-Import* [1980] E.C.R. 3469; Case 277/83, *Commission* v. *Italy* [1985] E.C.R. 2049 at p. 2058, para. 17; Case 196/85, *Commission* v. *France* [1987] E.C.R. 1597.

[70] *Ibid.*

[71] Case 21/79, *Commission* v. *Italy* [1980] E.C.R. 1. See also Case 140/79, *Chemial* v. *DAF* [1981] E.C.R. 1; Case 46/80, *Vinal* v. *Orbat* [1981] E.C.R. 77.

Criteria for differentiating between products for tax purposes must not discriminate against similar imported products

The Court has on a number of occasions considered progressive national taxes which at their higher level apply in practice exclusively to imports.

Humblot[72] arose from a challenge to a French special car tax payable by reference to "fiscal horsepower" or CV. Cars were subject in the first place to a tax which rose uniformly in proportion to increases in CV, and in the second place to a special tax levied at a single and considerably higher rate on cars rated at more than 16CV. No cars of more than 16CV were manufactured in France, all were imported. The Court emphasised that Member States were free to subject products such as cars to a system of tax which increases progressively in amount depending on an objective criterion, such as the power rating for tax purposes, which might be determined in various ways. Such a system of domestic taxation would only be compatible with Article 95 however if it were free of any discriminatory or protective effect. France denied any protective effect, arguing that there was no evidence that a consumer who might have been dissuaded from buying a vehicle of more than 16CV would purchase a car of French manufacture of 16CV or less. The Court of Justice rejected this argument, noting that cars on each side of the 16CV line were in competition with each other. The substantial additional increase in tax on cars of more than 16CV was liable to cancel out advantages which certain cars imported from other Member States might have in consumers' eyes over comparable cars of domestic manufacture. "In that respect," said the Court, "the special tax reduces the amount of competition to which cars of domestic manufacture are subject and hence is contrary to the principle of neutrality with which domestic taxation must comply."[73]

It fell to the Court to consider the successor tax to the above in the *Feldain* case.[74] The successor tax was progressive, but not uniformly progressive in two respects. Firstly, it progressed less sharply at the level which applied to top of the range French cars. According to the court, "It thus exhibits a discriminatory or protective effect ... in favour of cars manufactured in France."[75] Secondly, it incorporated a factor in calculating the power rating which had the effect of placing in the higher tax bands only imported vehicles. The Court noted that the factor in question was not justified by considerations relating to fuel consumption which France had argued as the basis for the system. "It must therefore be held that that method of determining the power rating for tax purposes is not objective in character and favours cars manufactured in France."[76]

In *Commission* v. *Greece*[77] the Court confronted another system of progressive taxation of cars, relating the tax payable to the cylinder capacity

---

[72] Case 112/84 [1985] E.C.R. 1367.
[73] [1985] E.C.R. 1367 at p. 1379, para. 15.
[74] Case 433/85 [1987] E.C.R. 3521.
[75] [1987] E.C.R. 3521 at p. 3540, para. 14.
[76] [1987] E.C.R. 3521 at p. 3541, para. 16.
[77] Case C–132/88 [1990] E.C.R. I–1567.

of the car. Greece argued that progression was justified by the fact that larger capacity cars were luxury products, and generated pollution. The progression was not uniform, increasingly sharply at 1201 cc, and then at 1801 cc. Most cars produced in Greece were of 1300 cc; none were produced of more than 1600 cc capacity, and the tax rates which applied above that level applied exclusively to imports. The Court of Justice held that the system was compatible with Article 95 since a consumer deterred from buying a car of over 1800 cc would either buy one of 1600 to 1800 cc (all of which were of foreign manufacture), or one of below 1600 cc (which range included imports and cars of Greek manufacture). "Consequently," held the Court, "the Commission has not shown how the system of taxation at issue might have the effect of favouring the sale of cars of Greek manufacturers."[78] Yet surely, in the words of the Court in *Humblot*, the tax in question "reduces the amount of competition to which cars of domestic manufacture are subject and hence is contrary to the principle of neutrality with which domestic taxation must comply."[79] The reasoning in this case seems defective, and the result could only be supported on the ground that the steep progression in the tax for cars of more than 1800 cc was justified on the objective grounds cited by the Greek authorities.

While it is open to Member States to differentiate between like products on objective grounds consistent with the Treaty, they are not permitted to discriminate by conditioning tax concessions on requirements which can only be, or in fact only are, satisfied by national products. Examples of such discrimination would be charging lower tax rates on those products which could be inspected on national territory at the manufacturing stage,[80] and charging lower rates on products without a designation of origin or provenance where no such protection was available for domestic products and the higher rate applied in practice only to imports.[81]

Article 95(1)—taxation in excess of that imposed "indirectly" on domestic products

It will be recalled that Article 95 first paragraph, prohibits internal taxation of any kind in excess of that imposed directly or indirectly on similar domestic products. In *Molkerei-Zentrale* v. *Hauptzollamt Paderborn*[82] the Court was asked for a definition of the "indirect" taxation in question. Advocate General Gand suggested that the charges in question must include all those imposed on raw materials and component goods and services. The Court agreed that the words "directly or indirectly" were to be construed broadly, and defined them as embracing all taxation which was actually and specifically imposed on the domestic product at earlier stages of the manufacturing and marketing process. This formulation might suggest that

---

[78] [1990] E.C.R. I–1567 at p. 1593, para. 20.
[79] See note 73.
[80] Case 142 & 143/80, *Italian Finance Administration* v. *Essevi S.p.A.* [1981] E.C.R. 1413. See also Case 277/83, *Commission* v. *Italy* [1985] E.C.R. 2049.
[81] Case 319/81, *Commission* v. *Italy* [1983] E.C.R. 601; see also Case 106/84, *Commission* v. *Denmark* [1986] E.C.R. 833.
[82] Case 28/67 note 64.

taxes on components, not being actually and specifically imposed on the product, might be excluded. This is not the case. As the Court's interpretation of the words "directly or indirectly" in Article 96 indicates,[83] "indirect" taxation indeed includes charges levied on raw materials and semi-finished products incorporated in the goods in question. Nevertheless, the Court entered a caveat in *Molkerei-Zentrale*: the effect of these charges diminished with the incidence of stages of production and distribution and tended rapidly to become negligible, and that fact ought to be taken into account by Member States when calculating the indirect charges applied to domestic products.

Although the taxation of undertakings manufacturing products will not in general be regarded as constituting taxation of the products themselves, the taxation of specific activities of an undertaking which has an "immediate effect" on the cost of the national imported product must by virtue of Article 95 be applied in a manner which is not discriminatory to imported products. Thus taxation imposed indirectly upon products within the meaning of Article 95 must be interpreted as including charges imposed on the international transport of goods by road according to the distance covered on the national territory and the weight of the goods in question.[84] Again, Article 95 applies to internal taxation which is imposed on the use of imported products where these products are intended for such use and have been imported solely for that purpose.[85]

The object of Article 95 is to abolish direct or indirect discrimination against imported products, but not to place them in a privileged tax position.[86] Internal taxation may therefore be imposed on imported products, even in the absence of a domestically produced counterpart.[87] In *Stier*,[88] the Court of Justice held that although Article 95 does not prohibit Member States from imposing taxation on imported products which lack a domestic counterpart, it would not be permissible to impose on such imports charges of such an amount that the free movement of goods would be impeded. In *Commission* v. *Denmark*[89] the Court held that such impediment to the free movement of goods would fall to be governed by Articles 30–36 of the EEC Treaty, rather than within the framework of Article 95 of the EEC Treaty.

Domestic products may not claim equality with imports

However, Article 95 does not prohibit the imposition on national products of internal taxation in excess of that on imported products.[90] It has been noted that Member States may differentiate for tax purposes between

---

[83] Case 45/64, *Commission* v. *Italy* [1965] E.C.R. 857.
[84] Case 20/76, *Schottle & Sohne* v. *Finanzamt Freudenstadt* [1977] E.C.R. 247.
[85] Case 252/86, *Bergandi* [1988] E.C.R. 1343.
[86] Case 153/80, *Rumhaus Hansen* [1981] E.C.R. 1165; Case 253/83, *Kupferberg* [1985] E.C.R. 157.
[87] Case 31/67, *Stier* [1968] E.C.R. 235; Case 27/67, *Fink-Frucht* v. *Hauptzollamt Munchen-Landsbergstrasse* [1968] E.C.R. 223 at p. 231.
[88] Case 31/67 [1968] E.C.R. 235.
[89] Case C–47/88 [1990] E.C.R. I–4509.
[90] Case 86/78, *Grandes Distilleries Peureux* v. *Directeur des Services Fisceaux* [1979] E.C.R. 89.

products, provided that discrimination against importers does not result. What if national law imposes a higher rate of tax on product X than on competing product Y, where product X is largely, but not entirely, imported and where the higher rate of tax contravenes Article 95 of the EEC Treaty? While importers of product X may claim the protection of Article 95, domestic producers may legitimately be taxed at the higher rate. Thus Danish revenue laws imposed a lower rate of tax on aquavit than on other spirits, which other spirits were mainly, but not entirely, imported. In proceedings instituted by the Commission under Article 169 EEC the Court held that these rules were contrary to Article 95,[91] and in later proceedings the Court emphasised that only importers could rely on Article 95, and not domestic producers of those spirits subject to the "discriminatory" tax.[92]

Respective scope of Article 95(1) and 95(2)

Whereas Article 95, first paragraph, prohibits internal taxation in excess of that imposed on similar domestic products, paragraph 2 adds that Member States shall furthermore impose no taxation of such a kind as to afford indirect protection to other products.

The respective scope of these two paragraphs is as follows. Under Article 95(1) it is necessary to consider as similar products those which have similar characteristics and which meet the same needs from the point of view of consumers. The appropriate criterion is not the strictly identical nature of the products but their similar and comparable use.[93] The Court at one stage held that "similarity" within Article 95(1) existed when the products were normally, for tax, tariff or statistical purposes, placed in the same classification.[94] In a later case the Court confirmed that classification under the same heading in the Common Customs Tariff was an important consideration in assessing similarity under Article 95.[95] But the Court has stressed that the fact that rum and whisky are given separate subdivisions under the C.C.T. is not conclusive on the question of "similarity" under Article 95(1),[96] and when asked by an Italian court whether it should apply the "tariff classification" test, or the broader economic approach referred to above, the Court reiterated the latter criterion, without adverting to the former.[97] Nevertheless, it would seem that C.C.T. classification constitutes at least evidence one way or the other of "similarity" within the meaning of Article 95(1).

In *John Walker*,[98] the Court held that in order to determine whether the

---

[91] Case 171/78, *Commission* v. *Denmark* [1980] E.C.R. 447. And see Case 168/78, *Commission* v. *France* [1980] E.C.R. 347.
[92] Case 68/79 [1980] E.C.R. 501.
[93] Case 169/78, *Commission* v. *Italy* [1980] E.C.R. 385.
[94] Case 27/67, *Fink-Frucht* v. *Hauptzollamt Munchen-Landsbergerstrasse* [1968] E.C.R. 223. Case 28/69, *Commission* v. *Italy* [1979] E.C.R. 187.
[95] Case 45/75, *Rewe-Zentrale, etc.* v. *Hauptzollamt Landau/Pfalz* [1976] E.C.R. 181.
[96] Case 169/78, *Commission* v. *Italy* [1980] E.C.R. 385; Case 168/78, *Commission* v. *France* [1980] E.C.R. 347; Case 106/84, *Commission* v. *Denmark* [1986] E.C.R. 833.
[97] Case 216/81, *Cogis SpA* v. *Italian Finance Ministry* [1982] E.C.R. 2701.
[98] Case 243/84, *John Walker* [1986] E.C.R. 875.

products in question (fruit liqueur wines and whisky) were "similar" within the meaning of Article 95(1), it was first necessary to consider objective characteristics of the respective products, such as their origin, method of manufacture, and their organoleptic qualities, in particular taste and alcohol content, and secondly necessary to consider whether both categories of beverages were capable of meeting the same needs from the point of view of consumers. Applying the first test, it was not sufficient that the same raw material, alcohol, was to be found in both products. For the products to be regarded as similar that raw material would have to be present in more or less equal proportions in both products. Since whisky contained twice the alcoholic content of fruit liqueur wines, the products could not be regarded as "similar" within the meaning of Article 95(1).

Once similarity is established and Article 95(1) applies, the tax rates on the domestic product and the similar imported product must be the same. Article 95(2), by way of contrast, covers all forms of indirect tax protection in the case of products which, without being similar within the meaning of Article 95(1), are nevertheless in competition, even partial, indirect or potential, with products of the importing country. It is sufficient for the imported product to be in competition with the protected domestic product by reason of one or several economic uses to which it may be put, even though the conditions of similarity for the purposes of Article 95(1) are not fulfilled.[99]

To illustrate the inter-relation between Article 95(1) and (2), reference may be made to the great range of spirit drinks aquavit, geneva, grappa, whisky, etc. While these drinks; have common generic factors (distillation, high alcohol level), there are different types of spirits, characterised by the raw material used, their flavour, and processes of manufacture.[1] Furthermore, spirits may be consumed in different forms: neat, diluted, or in mixtures.[2] They may also be consumed on different occasions, as aperitifs or digestifs, at meal times, or on other occasions.[3] The Court of Justice has held that among spirit drinks there exists an indeterminate number which can be regarded as similar products within the meaning of Article 95(1), and that where it is impossible to identify a sufficient degree of similarity between the products concerned for the purposes of Article 95(1), there exist nevertheless characteristics common to all spirits which are sufficiently marked for it to be said that they are all at least partly, indirectly or potentially in competition for the purposes of Article 95(2).[4] The result is that in a case involving alleged discrimination between domestic spirits and imported spirits, it may not be necessary to distinguish between the application of Article 95(1) and that of Article 95(2), since it cannot reasonably be denied that the products are in at least partial, indirect or

---

[99] Case 169/78 note 96.
[1] See Case 168/78 note 96; Case 169/78 note 96; and Case 171/78, *Commission* v. *Denmark* [1980] E.C.R. 447.
[2] Case 169/78 note 96.
[3] Case 168/78 note 96.
[4] Case 319/81, *Commission* v. *Italy* [1983] E.C.R. 601; referring to Case 168/78 note 96; Case 169/78 note 96; Case 171/78 note 1.

potential competition.[5] It will however be necessary to distinguish between the application of Article 95(1) and (2) if the tax on the import in question is greater than that on the domestic product without being sufficient to be shown to afford indirect protection to domestic products. In such a case, Article 95(1) would be infringed if the products were similar, but Article 95(2) would not be infringed if they were not.

The fact that Article 95(2) embraces potential as well as actual competition significantly widens its ambit. In *Commission* v. *United Kingdom*,[6] the United Kingdom argued that wine and beer could not be considered to be competing beverages, since beer was a popular drink consumed generally in public houses, while wine was generally consumed on special occasions. The Court of Justice stressed that it was necessary to examine not only the present state of the market in the United Kingdom but also possible developments in the free movement of goods within the Community and the further potential for the substitution of products for one another which might result from an intensification of trade. Consumer habits varied in time and space, and the tax policy of a Member State must not crystallise given consumer habits so as to consolidate an advantage required by the national industries concerned to respond to them. The Court held that to a certain extent at least wine and beer were capable of meeting identical needs and that there was a degree of substitution one for another.

While Article 95(1) prohibits a higher tax on imported products than similar domestic products, Article 95(2), because of the difficulty of making a sufficiently precise comparison between the products in question, employs a more general criterion, *i.e.* the indirect protection afforded by a domestic tax system. It follows that a tax on an imported product need not be identical with the tax imposed on a domestic product with which it is in partial or indirect competition, as it would have to be if the products were in a sufficiently close competitive relationship to be regarded as similar within the meaning of Article 95(1). In *Commission* v. *Belgium*[7] it was alleged that VAT on wine (imported) at 25 per cent. afforded indirect protection to beer (a domestic product) which was subject to VAT at 19 per cent. The Court rejected this argument, in view of the insignificant impact of the difference in tax on the difference in price between the two products. The Commission had not shown that the difference in question gave rise to any protective effect favouring beer intended for domestic consumption. It seems that what the Court was looking for was not complex market analysis, but a price difference which on a common sense basis would suggest an advantage for beer over wine. Protective effect need not, however, be shown statistically. It is sufficient for the purposes of Article 95(2) for it to be shown that a given system of taxation is likely, in view of its inherent characteristics, to bring about the protective effect referred to by the Treaty.[8] Furthermore,

---

[5] Case 168/78 note 96.
[6] Case 170/78 [1980] E.C.R. 417; [1983] E.C.R. 2265.
[7] Case 356/85 [1987] E.C.R. 3299. And for "*de minimis*" effect see Case 27/67, *Fink-Frucht* [1968] E.C.R. 223 at p. 233.
[8] Case 170/78, *Commission* v. *United Kingdom* [1980] E.C.R. 417.

statistics showing import penetration by products allegedly discriminated against cannot rebut the inference of protective effect to be drawn from the inherent characteristics of a national tax system.[9] However, statistics are admissible to show that a tax system which is apparently neutral in fact burdens imports to a greater extent than domestic products.[10]

And it must be admitted that in the case of some products found to have a competitive relationship it may be extremely difficult to establish the appropriate basis for comparison of the tax applied to the respective products, and the appropriate rate to be applied to ensure fiscal neutrality. A striking illustration is afforded by the Court's decision in *Commission* v. *United Kingdom*,[11] in which the Court attempted to establish the degree of indirect protection afforded beer by the excessive taxation of wine. On the basis of tax per unit of volume, wine bore an overall tax burden of 400 per cent. of that on beer; while on the basis of alcoholic strength per unit of volume, wine was subject to a tax burden 100 per cent. in excess of that on beer. On the basis of tax as a proportion of the net price of the beverage free of tax, the Court admitted that the evidence was difficult to assess, suggesting additional tax burdens of between 58 per cent. and 286 per cent.! The Court concluded that whichever criterion for comparison was used, the tax system offered indirect protection to national production, and that there was no need to express a preference for one or other of the criteria discussed! Though Article 95(2) was long ago held to be directly effective,[12] in such a case one might well sympathise with an importer challenging a national tax claim who seeks to quantify the amount by which his national tax demand offends Article 95(2) EEC!

Article 95(2) only applicable to comparison between imports and domestic products if no similar domestic product exists for purposes of Article 95(1) comparison

A Member State may impose the same tax on an import as on a similar domestic product, even if the tax in question affords indirect protection to other domestic products. In *Commission* v. *United Kingdom*,[13] the Commission, arguing (successfully in the event) that the United Kingdom was imposing a discriminatory tax on wine as compared with beer, nevertheless conceded that if a Member State produced both wine and beer, and taxed the former more heavily, the tax on imported wine would be judged, not by reference to domestic beer, but domestic wine. In that case the Court regarded British wine production as being commercially insignificant and left it out of account. Similarly, in *Commission* v. *Italy*,[14] the Court regarded Italian production of bananas as negligible and left it out of account, applying Article 95(2) to the competitive relationship between

---

[9] Case 168/78 note 96; Case 319/81 note 4.
[10] Case 319/81 note 4.
[11] Case 170/78 note 6.
[12] Case 27/67, *Fink-Frucht* [1968] E.C.R. 223.
[13] Case 170/78 [1980] E.C.R. 417, [1983] E.C.R. 2265.
[14] Case 184/85 [1987] E.C.R. 2013.

imported bananas and domestically produced table fruit. It may prove difficult to decide when domestic production of highly taxed product X which is largely but not entirely imported and in partial competition with a less highly taxed domestic product Y, becomes sufficiently substantial to establish the tax rate on product X (rather than product Y) as the appropriate comparator for imports of X for the purposes of Article 95. The Court has acknowledged that an internal tax system cannot be said to favour domestic fruit liqueur wine over imported whisky, bearing a higher rate of tax, where all spirits, and the majority of those domestically produced, bear the higher rate of tax. Such a system will be consistent with Article 95 where a significant proportion of domestic production of alcoholic beverages falls within each of the relevant tax categories.[15]

Only true fiscal charges subject to Article 95

It must be emphasised that while Article 95 permits the imposition of internal taxation on imports to the extent that domestic goods bear similar charges, it cannot justify any charges imposed with a view to assimilating the prices of imports to those of domestic goods. The point arose in *Commission v. Luxembourg and Belgium*,[16] a proceeding under Article 169 in which the Commission alleged infringement of Articles 9 and 12 in respect of charges levied on the issue of import licences for gingerbread. The defendants argued that the charges compensated for the effect of measures of price support for domestically produced rye, and were accordingly justified under Article 95. The purpose of the disputed charge, said the Court, was not to equalise charges which would otherwise unevenly burden domestic and imported products, but to equalise the very prices of such products.[17] A similar point arose in *Hauptzollamt Flensburg* v. *Hermann C. Andresen & Co. KG*.[18] A charge was imposed on spirits imported into Germany, being a charge also applicable to domestic spirits, and calculated to defray (in the case of domestic spirits) the administrative and operating costs of the Federal Spirits Monopoly. The Court held that a charge such as this was not a true fiscal charge, and that Article 95 only permitted the imposition on imports of such elements of the price of domestic spirits which the monopoly was required by law to remit to the State Treasury.

PROHIBITION OF CUSTOMS DUTIES AND CHARGES HAVING EQUIVALENT EFFECT AND PROHIBITION OF DISCRIMINATORY INTERNAL TAXATION MUTUALLY EXCLUSIVE

The prohibitions of Articles 12 and 13 on the one hand, and Article 95 on the other, have often been contrasted by the Court. The former applies to all

---

[15] Case 243/84, *John Walker* [1986] E.C.R. 833.
[16] Cases 2 & 3/62 [1965] E.C.R. 425.
[17] See also Case 45/75, *Rewe-Zentrale* [1976] E.C.R. 181.
[18] Case 4/81 [1981] E.C.R. 2835.

charges exacted at the time of or by reason of importation which are imposed specifically on an imported product to the exclusion of the similar domestic product; the latter embraces financial charges levied within a general system of internal taxation applying systematically to domestic and imported goods.[19] The application of these respective prohibitions has been held to be mutually exclusive, not only because one and the same charge could not have been both removed during the transitional period (Articles 13 and 14), and by no later than the beginning of the second stage (Article 95),[20] but also because customs duties and charges having equivalent effect are required to be simply abolished, while Article 95 provides solely for the elimination of any form of discrimination between domestic products and products originating in other Member States.[21] The Court has explicitly rejected the argument that an equalisation tax on an imported product which exceeds the charges applied to similar domestic products takes on the character of a "charge having equivalent effect" as to the difference.[22] Again, since the respective fields of application of the Treaty's prohibition on obstacles to the free movement of goods are to be distinguished, obstacles which are of a fiscal nature or have equivalent effect and are covered by Articles 9 to 16 or 95 of the Treaty cannot fall within the prohibition of Article 30, on quantitative restrictions and measures having equivalent effect.[23] Though an excessive tax impeding the free movement of goods which falls outside the scope of Article 95 because it lacks a domestically produced counterpart will fall to be governed by Articles 30–36 EEC.[24]

Charges on imports falling within Article 95, rather than Articles 12 and 13, are all those which are imposed in the same way within the State on similar or comparable products, or, where there are no comparable products, where the charge in question applies to whole classes of domestic or foreign products which are all in the same position no matter what their origin.[25]

However, the Court has held that such a limited number of products as "groundnuts, groundnut products and Brazil nuts" cannot fall within the concept of such whole classes of products, a concept which implies a much larger number of products determined by general and objective criteria.[26]

But charges must be levied at the same marketing stage on both domestic goods and imports to fall within the ambit of Article 95,[27] and if there is an insufficiently close connexion between the charges levied on domestic

---

[19] Case 77/82, *Capolongo* v. *Azienda Agricola Maya* [1973] E.C.R. 611.
[20] Case 10/65, *Deutschmann* v. *Federal Republic of Germany* [1965] E.C.R. 469. And see Case 57/65, *Lutticke* v. *Hauptzollamt Saarlouis* [1966] E.C.R. 205; Case 27/74, *Demag* v. *Finanzamt Duisburg-Sud* [1974] E.C.R. 1037.
[21] Case 94/74, *IGAV* v. *ENCC* [1975] E.C.R. 699.
[22] Case 25/67, *Milch- Fett- und Eierkontor* v. *Hauptzollamt Saarbrucken* [1968] E.C.R. 207; Case 32/80, *Officier van Justitie* v. *Kortmann* [1981] E.C.R. 251.
[23] Case 74/76, *Iannelli & Volpi* v. *Paolo Meroni* [1977] E.C.R. 557 at para. 9.
[24] Case C–47/88, *Commission* v. *Denmark* [1990] E.C.R. I–4509.
[25] Cases 2 & 3/69, *Chougol Diamond Co.* [1969] E.C.R. 211.
[26] Case 27/67, *Fink-Frucht* [1968] E.C.R. 223. Case 158/82, *Commission* v. *Denmark* [1983] E.C.R. 3573.
[27] Case 132/78, *Denkavit Loire Sarl* v. *France* [1979] E.C.R. 1923. But VAT levied on imports does not amount to a charge having equivalent effect. Case 249/84, *Profant* [1986] E.C.R. 3237.

goods, and those levied on imports, in that they are determined on the basis of different criteria, they will fall to be classified under Article 12 EEC, rather than Article 95.[28]

The Court added a qualification in *Wohrmann* v. *Hauptzollamt Bad Reichenhall*,[29] that, *in the absence of any protective purpose*, an internal tax could not be regarded as a charge having equivalent effect to a customs duty. This seems at first sight surprising, since the Court has often emphasised that a charge may have an effect equivalent to a customs duty under Articles 12 and 13 independently of either its purpose or the destination of its revenue.[30] The significance of protective purpose in this context is that a charge applicable equally to domestic and imported products—and therefore ostensibly "internal taxation" under Article 95—may nevertheless fall to be classified as a charge having equivalent effect, if the revenue from the charge is devoted exclusively to benefit domestic producers. In *Interzuccheri* v. *Ditta Rezzano e Cassava*,[31] the Court considered a charge imposed on sales of sugar, whether home produced or imported, the proceeds of which were used for the exclusive benefit of national sugar refineries and sugar beet producers. The Court held that such a charge, on the face of it internal taxation, could only be considered a charge having equivalent effect if:

— it had the sole purpose of financing activities for the specific advantage of the taxed domestic product;
— the taxed product and the domestic product benefiting from it were the same;
— the charges imposed on the domestic product were made good in full.

Since the charge in issue in the national proceedings financed sugar beet producers, as well as sugar refiners, it would not seem to constitute a charge having equivalent effect, according to the Court's stringent criterion.

In the later case of *Commission* v. *Italy*,[32] the Commission challenged the same Italian charge in contentious proceedings, arguing that if the charge were entirely offset by reimbursements in the form of aid, it amounted to a charge having an equivalent effect to a customs duty, while if it were only partly offset, it infringed Article 95. Somewhat puzzlingly, the Court held that Italy had violated Article 95, and that internal taxation would be regarded as indirectly discriminatory within the meaning of that Article if its proceeds were used *exclusively* or principally to finance aids for the sole benefit of domestic products. Yet in the later case of *Officier van Justitie* v. *Kortmann*,[33] the Court confirmed the *Interzuccheri* proposition that an internal tax amounted to a charge having equivalent effect to a customs duty when in fact it was imposed solely on imported products to the exclusion of

---

[28] Case 132/80, *United Foods* [1981] E.C.R. 995.
[29] Case 7/67 [1968] E.C.R. 177.
[30] *E.g.* Case 63/74, *Cadskey* [1975] E.C.R. 281; Cases 2 & 3/69, *Chougol Diamond Co.* [1969] E.C.R. 211.
[31] Case 195/76 [1977] E.C.R. 1029; Case 77/72, *Capolongo* [1973] E.C.R. 611; Case 94/74, *IGAV* [1975] E.C.R. 699; Case 77/76, *Fratelli Cucchi* [1977] E.C.R. 987; Case 222/78, *ICAP* v. *Walter Beneventi* [1979] E.C.R. 1163.
[32] Case 73/79 [1980] E.C.R. 1533.
[33] Case 32/80 [1981] E.C.R. 251.

domestic products. The explanation for the apparent inconsistency seems to be that *Commission* v. *Italy*[34] concerned a charge on one product (imported sugar) which was used to benefit sugar beet as well as sugar. Indeed, this was why it is clear from the Court's ruling in *Interzuccheri*[35] that the charge in question could not be regarded as a charge having equivalent effect. Thus the ruling in *Commission* v. *Italy* that an equal charge imposed on both imported and domestic products may amount to discriminatory internal taxation if used *exclusively* or principally to finance aids for the sole benefit of domestic products (which appears to be categorising as discriminatory internal taxation that which is a charge having equivalent effect to a customs duty) would seem to be confined to cases where the domestic products benefited are not identical to the imported products subject to the charge. The proposition is of course unexceptionable insofar as it refers to the proceeds of a charge used principally (or indeed at all) to benefit domestic products alone. Where the products are identical, and the *Interzuccheri*[36] criteria are satisfied, the ostensible internal tax is to be categorised as a charge having equivalent effect to a customs duty. It will be noted that these problems only arise if a Member State has resort to ear-marked taxes, as Italy pointed out to the Court during the proceedings in *Commission* v. *Italy*.[37]

DISCRIMINATORY TAX TREATMENT OF EXPORTS

The system adopted for taxing products in intra-Community trade is based on the "destination principle," *i.e.* goods exported from a Member State receive a rebate of internal taxation paid, and are in turn subjected to internal taxation in the country of destination. The purpose of Article 95 is to prevent this process being used to place a heavier burden on imports than on domestic goods, but the system is vulnerable to another, equally damaging abuse: the repayment to exporters of an amount exceeding the internal taxation in fact paid, which would amount to an export subsidy for domestic production. It is to counteract this possibility that Article 96 provides that where products are exported to the territory of any Member State, any repayment of internal taxation shall not exceed the internal taxation imposed on them, whether directly or indirectly.

The Court laid down decisive guidelines as to the extent of repayments permissible under this Article in *Commission* v. *Italy*,[38] a case arising from proceedings under Article 169 alleging excessive repayment of taxes levied on certain engineering products. The Commission claimed that the repayment of duties paid on licenses, concessions, motor vehicles and advertising, in connection with the production and marketing of the

---

[34] Case 73/79 note 32.
[35] Case 105/76 [1977] E.C.R. 1029.
[36] Note 31.
[37] Note 32.
[38] Case 45/64 [1965] E.C.R. 857. For infringements of Art. 96, see Case C–152/89, *Commission* v. *Luxembourg* [1991] E.C.R. I–3141; and Case C–153/89, *Commission* v. *Belgium* [1991] E.C.R. I–3171.

products in question, were ineligible for repayment under Article 96. The Court ruled that the words "directly or indirectly" referred to the distinction between taxes which had been levied on the products themselves (directly), and taxes levied on the raw materials and semi-finished goods used in their manufacture (indirectly).[39] It followed that the charges referred to by the Commission could not be repaid consistently with Article 96, for the simple reason that they were not taxes imposed on the products at all, but "upon the producer undertaking in the very varied aspects of its general commercial and financial activity."[40]

But whereas Article 12 applies to customs duties and charges having equivalent effect on both imports and exports, Article 95, on its face, applies only to tax discrimination against imports. Nevertheless, in *Staten Kontrol* v. *Larsen*,[41] the Court held that the rule against discrimination underlying Article 95 also applied when the export, rather than import, of a product constituted, within the context of a system of internal taxation, the chargeable event giving rise to a fiscal charge. It would be incompatible with the system of tax provisions laid down in the Treaty to acknowledge that a Member State, in the absence of an express prohibition laid down in the Treaty, were free to apply in a discriminatory manner a system of internal taxation to products intended for export to another Member State. Article 95, it seems, prohibits internal taxation which either discriminates against imports or exports, as compared to domestic products.[42]

Furthermore, in *Hulst* v. *Produktschap voor Siergewassen*,[43] the Court held that an internal levy applying to domestic sales and exports could have an effect equivalent to a customs duty when either its application fell more heavily on export sales than on sales within the country, or when the levy was intended to finance activities likely to give preferential treatment to the product intended for marketing within the country, to the detriment of that intended for export.

THE RELATIONSHIP BETWEEN ARTICLES 12 AND 95, AND OTHER PROVISIONS OF THE TREATY

Where national measures are financed by a discriminatory internal tax, Article 95 is applicable to the latter, despite the fact that it forms part of a national aid, subject to scrunity under Articles 92 and 93 EEC.[44] Equally, Article 12 and Articles 92 and 93, would seem to be cumulatively applicable in such circumstances.

---

[39] On a similar wording in Art. 95(1), see *supra*, p. 194, and Case 28/67, *Molkerei-Zentrale* [1968] E.C.R. 143 at p. 155.
[40] [1965] E.C.R. 857 at p. 866.
[41] [1978] E.C.R. 1787.
[42] *Cf.* Case 27/74, *Demag* (1974) E.C.R. 1037.
[43] Case 51/74 [1975] E.C.R. 79.
[44] Case 47/69, *France* v. *Commission* [1970] E.C.R. 487; Case 73/79, *Commission* v. *Italy* [1980] E.C.R. 1547; Case 17/81, *Pabst and Richarz* v. *Hauptzollamt Oldenburg* [1982] E.C.R. 1331; Case 277/83, *Commission* v. *Italy* [1985] E.C.R. 2049.

Articles 9–16 and Article 95 do not however overlap with Article 30. The Court held in *Ianelli & Volpi* v. *Paolo Meroni*[45] that:

"However wide the field of application of Article 30 may be, it nevertheless does not include obstacles to trade covered by other provisions of the Treaty. Thus obstacles which are of a fiscal nature or have equivalent effect and are covered by Articles 9 to 16 and 95 of the Treaty do not fall within the prohibition of Article 30."

The relationship between Article 37 on state monopolies, and Article 95, was considered by the Court in *Grandes Distilleries Peureux*.[46] Whereas Article 37 was acknowledged to have provided an exception to certain rules of the Treaty—*in casu* Article 95—during the transitional period, this was declared to be no longer the case. Where internal taxation is concerned, Article 95 apparently constitutes a *lex specialis*, even it seems in the case of activities which would otherwise qualify for scrutiny under Article 37.

It will be recalled that in *Staten Kontrol* v. *Larsen*,[47] the Court held that, while a Member State was precluded under Article 95 from taxing exports more heavily than domestically traded goods, it was open to a Member State to tax exports in the same way as domestic goods, even if this led to taxes overlapping with those imposed in the country of destination: this latter problem would fall to be solved by harmonisation of national legislation under Articles 99 or 100 of the Treaty. However, in *Gaston Schul*,[48] the Court held that a Member State was required by Article 95, when imposing value added tax on imports, to take into account value added tax paid but not refunded (and not refundable under the applicable VAT Directive) in the country of export. So far from the harmonisation of national tax provisions ousting Article 95, the Court held that the applicable VAT Directive must be construed in accordance with the terms of Article 95, which were mandatory and binding upon the Community institutions in the enactment of such legislation.

COMMON CUSTOMS TARIFF AND EXTERNAL RELATIONS

The preceding exposition has been concerned with the elimination of customs duties and other financial charges on trade between the Member States, but brief mention must be made of imports and exports between the Community and third countries.

Neither the relevant Articles of the Treaty, nor Regulation 950/68 on the

---

[45] Case 74/76 [1977] E.C.R. 557. But if Art. 95 is inapplicable because an import lacks a domestic counterpart, Art. 30 may apply to the tax in question, see Case C–47/88, *Commission* v. *Denmark* [1990] E.C.R. I–4509.
[46] Case 86/78 [1979] E.C.R. 897.
[47] Case 142/77 [1978] E.C.R. 1787 *supra*, p. 204.
[48] Case 15/81, *Gaston Schul* [1982] E.C.R. 1409, and see Case 39/85, *Bergeres-Becque* [1986] E.C.R. 259; Case C–120/88, *Commission* v. *Italy* [1991] E.C.R. I–621; Case C–119/89, *Commission* v. *Spain* [1991] E.C.R. I–641; Case 159/89, *Commission* v. *Greece* [1991] E.C.R. I–691.

Common Customs Tariff,[49] explicitly provided for the regulation of charges having an equivalent effect in trade relations between the Member States and third countries. Nevertheless, the Court held in *Sociaal Fonds voor de Dimantarbeiders* v. *Indiamex*[50] that the unilateral imposition of such charges after the adoption of the Common Customs Tariff was inconsistent with the aim of the Treaty that Member States adopt a common policy in their trade relations with the outside world.

But the Treaty itself has no provision analogous to Article 95 applying to imports from non-member countries.[51] Agreements between the EEC and third countries, and the provisions of agricultural regulations, may prohibit customs duties, charges having equivalent effect, and discriminatory internal taxation, on trade between the EEC and third countries. It cannot be assumed without more than such provisions as these are to be construed as strictly as analogous provisions governing intra-Community trade. Even where a provision of a regulation prohibits charges having equivalent effect on trade with third countries, and the Court takes the view that the concept is the same as that embodied in Article 9 *et seq.* of the EEC Treaty, the requirement may be subject to derogation authorised by the Community institutions in a way that would not be possible where intra-Community trade involved.[52] And where health inspections are permitted by Community regulations on imports from third countries, the inspections may be more strict, and the fees charged higher, than in intra-Community trade, since Community law does not require Member States to show the same degree of confidence towards non-member countries as they are required to show other Member States.[53]

Where a treaty prohibits discriminatory internal taxation on imports from third countries, it will be a matter of interpretation whether or not the provision in question is intended to fulfil the same purpose in relations between the EEC and third countries as Article 95 fulfils in respect of intra-Community trade. Thus a three-Judge Chamber held in *Pabst & Richarz* v. *HZ Oldenburg*[54] that Article 53 of the Association Agreement between the EEC and Greece fulfilled, within the framework of the Association between the Community and Greece, the same function as that of Article 95. A full Court in *HZ Mainz* v. *Kupferberg*[55] however, considering Article 21 of the EEC–Portugal free trade agreement, also prohibiting discriminatory internal taxation, observed that although Article 21 of the Agreement and Article 95 of the EEC Treaty had the same object, they were nevertheless worded differently, and must be considered and interpreted in their own context. The Court concluded that interpretation given to Article 95 of the Treaty could not be applied by way of simple

---

[49] O.J.Sp.Ed. 1968 (1), p. 275. Repealed with effect from December 31, 1987 by Reg. 2658/87, O.J. 1987 L256/1.
[50] Cases 37 & 38/73 [1973] E.C.R. 1609.
[51] Case 148/77, *Hansen* [1978] E.C.R. 1787.
[52] Case 70/77, *Simmenthal* [1978] E.C.R. 1543.
[53] Case 30/79, *Land Berlin* v. *Wigei* [1980] E.C.R. 151.
[54] Case 17/71 [1982] E.C.R. 1331.
[55] Case 104/81 [1982] E.C.R. 3641.

analogy to the agreement on free trade. It is to be noted that Article 14 of the Agreement on the European Economic Area between the EEC and the Member States on the one hand, and Austria, Finland, Iceland, Liechtenstein, Norway, Sweden and Switzerland, on the other, provides for the abolition of discrimination taxation on trade between Contracting States in terms identical to those of Article 95. Furthermore, Article 6 of the Agreement provides that such provisions are to be interpreted in accordance with the prior case law of the Court of Justice on the corresponding provisions of the EEC Treaty.

Since the Court has held that Conventions concluded by the Council pursuant to Article 228 and 238 (conclusion of agreements with third countries) constitute an integral part of Community law,[56] and that appropriately worded provisions of such agreements are capable of giving rise to rights in individuals which national courts are bound to safeguard,[57] it is clear that the principles discussed above have a significance extending far beyond the confines of intra-Community trade.

Customs duties on trade with third countries are established by the Common Customs Tariff,[58] which the Court has held must be interpreted in such a way as to give effect to a single trading system with third countries, and not in such a way that products are treated differently according to the country by which they enter the Community.[59] But the customs duties are only chargeable under the C.C.T. upon goods capable of being lawfully traded within the Community, and not, for example, upon smuggled narcotic drugs,[60] or counterfeit currency.[61]

---

[56] Case 181/73, *Haegeman* v. *Belgian State* [1974] E.C.R. 449.
[57] Case 87/75, *Bresciani* [1976] E.C.R. 129; Case 17/81, *Pabst & Richarz* [1982] E.C.R. 1331; Case 104/78, *Kupferberg* [1982] E.C.R. 3641.
[58] Note 50.
[59] Case 135/79, *Gedelfi* [1980] E.C.R. 1713.
[60] Case 50/80, *Horvath* [1981] E.C.R. 385; Case 221/81, *Wolf* [1982] E.C.R. 3681; Case 240/81, *Einberger* [1982] E.C.R. 3699.
[61] Case C–343/89, *Witzemann* [1990] E.C.R. I–4477.

CHAPTER 8

QUANTITATIVE RESTRICTIONS AND MEASURES HAVING EQUIVALENT EFFECT

INTRODUCTION

A quantitative restriction, or a quota, is a measure restricting the import of a given product by amount or by value. In order to obviate the risk of importers ordering goods only to have them excluded at the frontier because the quota has been filled, a licensing system may be adopted, whereby a government agency formally authorises particular importers to import stated quantities, or money's worth, of goods.[1] Since quotas are capable of disturbing the flow of international trade to a greater extent than tariffs,[2] and indeed found favour during the 1930s as a means of restricting imports without infringing international agreements prohibiting the introduction of customs duties,[3] it is hardly surprising that the authors of the Spaak Report considered their elimination as a "fundamental element" in the creation of a common market.[4] Accordingly, the Treaty provided for the abolition of quantitative restrictions and measures having equivalent effect on imports and exports,[5] in the former case by the end of the transitional period,[6] and in the case of exports by the end of the first stage.[7] "Standstill"[8] provisions prevented Member States from introducing new quantitative restrictions or measures having equivalent effect,[9] or making more restrictive those measures already in existence when the Treaty entered into force.[10]

The prohibition on quantitative restrictions and measures having equivalent effect is applicable without distinction to products originating in Member States and to those coming from non-member countries which are in free circulation.[11]

---

[1] Jackson, *World Trade and the Law of GATT* (1969), p. 305.
[2] The volume of imports cannot expand to meet increased demand, nor can the improvement of efficiency of manufacturers in exporting countries secure their access to the protected markets, Wilcox, *A Charter for World Trade* (1949), pp. 81 *et seq.*; K. Dam, *The GATT* (1970), p. 148; Jackson, *op. cit.* pp. 309–310.
[3] Jackson, *op. cit.* p. 306.
[4] *Rapport des Chefs de Delegation aux Ministres des Affaires Ètrangeres* (1956), p. 35.
[5] The Spaak Report points out that one result of the removal of restrictions on imports would be increased interdependence of the Member States. This would require, as necessary corollary, that importing countries be able to rely on continuity of supplies from exporting countries. *Rapport*, p. 38.
[6] Arts. 30, 32, 33.
[7] Art. 34. For detailed treatment of Arts. 30–36, see Oliver, *Free Movement of Goods in the EEC* (1988); Gormley, *Prohibiting Restrictions on Trade within the EEC* (1985).
[8] *Cf. supra*, p. 185.
[9] Art. 31.
[10] Art. 32. There is no explicit standstill for quantitative restrictions and measures having equivalent effect on exports, but Art. 34(1) prohibits such measures outright.
[11] Case 41/76, *Donckerwolcke*; [1976] E.C.R. 1921; Case 288/83, *Commission* v. *Ireland* [1985] E.C.R. 1761; Case 212/88, *Levy* [1989] E.C.R. 3511.

QUANTITATIVE RESTRICTIONS

The notion of a quantitative restriction is well understood, and definition poses little difficulty. As the Court explained in *Geddo* v. *Ente Nazionale Risi*, "The prohibition on quantitative restrictions covers measures which amount to a total or partial restraint of, according to the circumstances, imports, exports, or goods in transit."[12] Thus, when the Italian authorities suspended imports of pork into Italy from other Member States in June 1960, the Court ruled that such a measure amounted to an infringement of the "standstill" provision of Article 31, first paragraph, of the Treaty.[13] Again, a prohibition on the import of pornographic material amounts to a quantitative restriction contrary to Article 30, subject to possible justification under Article 36.[14]

MEASURES HAVING EQUIVALENT EFFECT TO QUANTITATIVE RESTRICTIONS ON IMPORTS— DIRECTIVE 70/50

The concept of measures having equivalent effect to quantitative restrictions is rather more complex. Article 2(1) of Directive 70/50[15] prohibits measures, other than those applicable equally to domestic or imported products, which hinder imports which could otherwise take place, including those "which make importation more difficult or costly than the disposal of domestic production." This provision was relied upon by the Court in terms in *Ianelli & Volpi*.[16] In other cases the Court has relied upon the principle involved without reference to the Directive. Thus in *Commission* v. *Italy*[17] the Court held that an import deposit scheme was contrary to Article 30 because its effect was to render imports "more difficult or burdensome" than internal transactions, and thereby produced restrictive effects on the free movement of goods. With respect to imports, Article 2(2) of Directive 70/50 provides that measures having equivalent effect include those which "make imports or the disposal, at any marketing stage, of imported products subject to a condition—other than a formality—which is required in respect of imported products only, or a condition differing from that required from domestic products and more difficult to satisfy." This provision was cited with approval in *Rewe-Zentralfinanz* v. *Landwirtschaftskammer*,[18] in which the Court declared that health inspections of plant products at national frontiers constituted a measure

---

[12] Case 2/73 [1973] E.C.R. 865 at p. 879.
[13] Case 7/61, *Commission* v. *Italy* [1961] E.C.R. 317.
[14] Case 34/79, *Henn and Darby* [1979] E.C.R. 3795. For exceptions under Article 36, see *infra* at p. 225. United Kingdom restrictions on imports of main crop potatoes amounted to quantitative restrictions, see Case 118/78, *Meijer* [1979] E.C.R. 1387; Case 231/178, *Commission* v. *United Kingdom* [1979] E.C.R. 1447.
[15] O.J.Sp.Ed. 1970(I), p. 17. Technically applicable only to measures in force at the end of the transitional period, it provides valuable guidance on the meaning of measures having equivalent effect.
[16] Case 74/76 [1977] E.C.R. 557.
[17] Case 95/81 [1982] E.C.R. 2187.
[18] Case 4/75 [1975] E.C.R. 843.

having equivalent effect, where similar domestic products were not subject to a similar examination. Although the Article refers to measures other than formalities, the Court has held that national measures requiring import and export licences in intra-Community trade—even though such licences are granted automatically—infringe the prohibition of Articles 30 and 34(1).[19]

Article 2(3) lists examples of the national measures covered by the definitions contained in Articles 2(1) and 2(2). Thus Article 2(3)(g) refers to measures which make the access of imported products to the domestic market conditional upon having an agent or representative in the territory of the importing Member State. This provision was relied upon by the Commission in an action against the Federal Republic of Germany.[20] German legislation provided that pharmaceutical products could be placed on the market only by a pharmaceutical undertaking having its headquarters in the area in which that legislation was applicable. The Court held—without reference to the Directive—that the legislation in question was likely to involve additional costs for undertakings which found no good reason for having a representative of their own established in Germany, and which sold directly to customers. The legislation was therefore likely to hinder trade within the Community and amounted to a measure having equivalent effect. Again, Article 2(3)(s) refers to national measures which "confine names which are not indicative of origin or source to domestic products only."[21] However, even names which are indicative of origin or source may only be confined to domestic products if the geographical area of origin of a product confers upon it a specific quality and characteristic of such a nature as to distinguish it from all other products.[22] It follows that making the application of a designation of quality which is neither an indication of origin or source conditional upon one or more stages of the production process taking place on national territory, amounts to a measure having equivalent effect.[23]

Article 3 of Directive 70/50 covers measures governing the marketing of products which deal in particular with the presentation or identification of products and which apply equally to domestic and imported products, where the restrictive effect of such measures on the free movement of goods exceeds the effects intrinsic to trade rules. This is stated to be the case, in particular, where the restrictive effects on the free movement of goods are out of proportion to their purpose, or where the same objective can be attained by other means which are less of a hindrance to trade. This provision has been cited by the Court of Justice.[24] Although the tenth recital to the preamble of Directive 70/50 might suggest that Article 3, despite

---

[19] Cases 51–54/71, *International Fruit* [1971] E.C.R. 1107; Case 53/76, *Bouhelier* [1977] E.C.R. 197; Case 68/76, *Commission* v. *French Republic* [1977] E.C.R. 515; Case 124/82, *Commission* v. *United Kingdom* [1983] E.C.R. 203.

[20] Case 247/81, *Commission* v. *Germany* [1984] E.C.R. 1111. See also Case 87/85, *Laboratoires de Pharmacie Legia* [1986] E.C.R. 1707. Art. 2(3) contains a list of examples and connot be pleaded to defeat the purpose of Art. 30; Case 103/84, *Commission* v. *Italy* [1986] E.C.R. 1759.

[21] Case 12/74, *Commission* v. *Germany* [1975] E.C.R. 181; Case 13/78, *Eggers* [1978] E.C.R. 1935.

[22] Case 12/74 note 21; Case 13/78 note 21.

[23] Case 13/78 note 21.

[24] Case 75/81, *Blesgen* [1982] E.C.R. 1211.

referring to measures which "are equally applicable" to domestic and imported products, only covers national measures which are indirectly discriminatory, since the recital refers to imports which are "either precluded or made more difficult or costly than the disposal of domestic production," the better view is probably that Article 3 also applies to national measures which are simply capable of restricting the volume of imports, by, for example, affecting marketing opportunities for both domestic products and imports.[25]

MEASURES HAVING EQUIVALENT EFFECT TO QUANTITATIVE RESTRICTIONS—JURISPRUDENCE OF THE COURT

General scope of the prohibition on measures having equivalent effect

The Court has adopted a broad definition of measures having equivalent effect to quantitative restrictions on imports, defining them as "all trading rules enacted by Member States which are capable of hindering, directly or indirectly, actually or potentially, intra-Community trade."[26] The prohibition in question has direct effect and creates individual rights which national courts must protect.[27]

It is not necessary for a national measure to have an appreciable effect on trade for it to fall within the prohibition of Article 30.[28] Indeed, in *Jan Van der Haar* the Court stressed that Article 30:

"... does not distinguish between measures ... according to the degree to which trade between Member States is affected. If a national measure is capable of hindering imports it must be regarded as a measure having an effect equivalent to a quantitative restriction, even though the hindrance is slight and even though it is possible for imported products to be marketed in other ways."[29]

In one case the Court referred to a "national measure which has, or *may* have, a restrictive effect on trade."[30] The position appears to be that even the possibility of a slight effect on intra-Community trade is sufficient to bring a national measure within the ambit of Article 30. Nevertheless, the Court has held that the possibility that nationals of one Member State might hesitate to sell goods on instalment terms to purchasers in another Member State

---

[25] This view is supported by the reasoning in Case 286/81, *Oosthoek's* [1982] E.C.R. 4575 at para. 15; Cases 60 and 61/83, *Cinéthèque* [1985] E.C.R. 2605; and Case 145/88, *Torfaen B.C. v. B&Q Plc* [1989] E.C.R. 3851.

[26] Case 8/74, *Dassonville* [1974] E.C.R. 837 at 852, para. 5; Case 4/75, *Rewe-Zentralfinanz* [1975] E.C.R. 843; Case 65/75, *Tasca* [1976] E.C.R. 291; Cases 88–90/75, *SADAM* [1976] E.C.R. 323. The formulation has been confirmed on numerous occasions, either in identical, or similar terms. See, *e.g.* more recently, Case C–69/88, *Krantz* [1990] E.C.R. I–583.

[27] Case 74/76, *Ianelli & Volpi* [1977] E.C.R. 557 at para. 13.

[28] Case 16/83, *Prantl* [1984] E.C.R. 1299.

[29] Cases 177 & 178/82, *Jan van de Haar* [1984] E.C.R. 1797 at para. 13.

[30] Case 97/83, *Melkunie* [1984] E.C.R. 2367 at para. 12. Emphasis added.

because such goods would be liable to seizure in the latter Member State by the collector of taxes if the purchasers failed to discharge their tax debts is "too uncertain and indirect" to warrant the conclusion that a national provision authorising such seizure is liable to hinder trade between Member States.[31]

The fact that Article 30 extends to indirect as well as direct restrictions on imports is of considerable significance. It extends the reach of Community law beyond frontier restrictions and the formalities of import transactions to the whole range of commercial and marketing rules applied in the Member States. Thus, for example national rules on advertising and promotion are capable of amounting to measures having equivalent effect if there is a possibility that they may affect the prospects of importing products from other Member States.[32] As the Court explained in *Oosthoek's Uitqeversmaatschappij B.V.*[33]:

> "Legislation which restricts or prohibits certain forms of advertising and certain means of sales promotions may, although it does not directly affect imports, be such as to restrict their value because it affects marketing opportunities for the imported products."

Yet it must be said that the Court's case law on the application of the abovementioned principles is not entirely consistent. In *Blesgen*[34] the Court considered that a legislative provision that concerned only the sale of strong spirits for consumption on the premises in all places open to the public and did not concern other forms of marketing the same drinks had in fact no connection with the import of the products and for that reason was not of such a nature as to impede trade between Member States. In *Quietlynn*[35] the Court referred to *Blesgen* in holding that national provisions prohibiting the sale of lawful sex articles from unlicensed sex establishments did not constitute a measure having equivalent effect. Yet it is difficult to reconcile the approach in these decisions with the statement from *Jan van der Haar* referred to above and with the reasoning of the Court in the decisions on Sunday trading. In *Torfaen B.C.* v. *B&Q Plc*,[36] the Court held that Sunday trading restrictions are not prohibited by Article 30 where the restrictive effects on Community trade which may result therefrom do not exceed the effects intrinsic to rules of that kind. In other words, such rules might fall within Article 30 unless justified.[37] Furthermore, the Court stated in *André Marchandise*[38] that a prohibition on the employment of workers in retail shops on Sundays after 12 noon might have negative repercussions on the volume of sales and hence on the volume of imports (though the Court regarded any such restrictions as being justified).[39] On the one hand, it is

---

[31] Case C–69/88, *Krantz* [1990] E.C.R. I–583.
[32] Case 152/78, *Commission* v. *France* [1980] E.C.R. 2299.
[33] Case 286/81 [1982] E.C.R. 4575 at p. 4587, para. 15.
[34] Case 75/81 [1982] E.C.R. 1211.
[35] Case C–23/89 [1990] E.C.R. I–3059.
[36] Case 145/88 [1989] E.C.R. 3851.
[37] On justification for restrictive measures see *infra* at p. 225.
[38] Case C–332/89 [1991] E.C.R. I–1027.
[39] On justification for such measures see *infra* at p. 225.

difficult to see the difference in principle, as regards potential effect on imports, between restrictions such as those in issue in *Blesgen* and *Quietlynn* on the one hand, and those in *Torfaen* and *Marchandise* on the other, though differences in degree there may be. On the other hand, it seems clear that all such "restrictions" should be regarded as compatible with Article 30 without the need to treat some of them as potentially contrary to Article 30 unless justified on grounds recognised under Community law. It is submitted that Article 30 should never apply on the sole ground that the restrictive effect on imports of a national measure is a consequence of its effect on the overall volume of sales of domestic goods and imports alike. The purpose of Article 30 is to exclude the application of national measures which partition national markets one from the other.[40] If construed and applied accordingly there would be no need to devise further and better justifications for national measures which only restrict imports by virtue of their restrictive effect on the total volume of sales of all relevant goods irrespective of origin in the Member State in question.

The Court in the *Kramer*[41] case contrasted the production stage of the economic process with the marketing stage, and indicated that Articles 30 *et seq.* applied to the latter but not to the former. Furthermore, Article 30 would not seem capable, in principle, of extending to the general powers of economic management vested in the Member States. For example, restrictions on the availability of credit are capable of reducing the volume of imports, but would not, it is submitted, fall foul of Article 30 in the absence of some element of discrimination.[42]

A common defence advanced by national authorities has been that although a particular measure is apparently contrary to Articles 30 *et seq.* it is in fact administered with flexibility, and exceptions may be made. The Court has consistently rejected this argument.[43] As the Court explained in *Kelderman*[44]:

> ". . . a measure caught by the prohibition provided for in Article 30 . . . does not escape that prohibition simply because the competent authority is empowered to grant exemptions, even if that power is freely applied to imported products. Freedom of movement is a right whose enjoyment may not be dependent upon a discretionary power or on a concession granted by the national administration."

The measures defined by the Court as infringing Articles 30 *et seq.* are invariably described as "national" measures, or trading rules "of the Member States" or "enacted by Member States." This would seem to exclude the conduct of private individuals and undertakings unsupported by

---

[40] See Adv. Gen. Van Gerven in Case 145/88 [1989] E.C.R. 3877 to 3879.
[41] Cases 3, 4 & 6/76 [1976] E.C.R. 1279 at para. 27.
[42] This may be an explanation of the Court's reasoning in Case 238/82, *Duphar* [1984] E.C.R. 523. See *infra* at p. 233.
[43] Case 82/77, *Van Tiggele* [1978] E.C.R. 25; Case 251/78, *Denkavit* [1979] E.C.R. 3369; Case 27/80, *Fietje* [1980] E.C.R. 3839. It is of course otherwise if the restrictions are capable of being justified in accordance with the Treaty, as to which, see *infra* at p. 225.
[44] Case 130/80 [1981] E.C.R. 517 at para. 14. See also Case 124/81, *Commission* v. *United Kingdom* [1983] E.C.R. 203 at para. 10.

state action of a legislative, executive or judicial character. The Court has condemned as a measure having equivalent effect a campaign funded by a Member State to promote the sale of domestic goods with a view to limiting imports, despite the fact that the campaign was conducted by a private company limited by guarantee. The management committee of the company was appointed by the national authorities, and the aims and outlines of the campaign were decided upon by those authorities. The Court held that the Member State in question could neither rely upon the fact that the campaign was conducted by a private company, nor upon the fact that the campaign was based upon decisions which were not binding upon undertakings, to avoid liability under Article 30.[45] The Court observed in another case that a body established and funded by Government with a view, *inter alia*, to promoting the sale of domestic products could not under Community law enjoy the same freedom as regards methods of advertising as that enjoyed by producers themselves or producers' associations of a voluntary character.[46]

It is clear that many barriers to intra-Community trade are capable of elimination through the technique of harmonisation of national laws under Article 100 or 100a of the EEC Treaty. The possibility of harmonisation, however, cannot justify derogation from the requirements of Article 30. In *Commission* v. *Republic of Italy*[47] the defendant Member State argued that the Commission should have sought harmonisation before resorting to Articles 30 to 36 of the Treaty. The Court rejected the argument as follows:

> "The fundamental principle of a unified market and its corollary, the free movement of goods, must not under any circumstances be made subject to the condition that there should first be an approximation of national laws for if that condition had to be fulfilled the principle would be reduced to a mere cipher."[48]

Articles 30 to 36 apply to trade in all goods, subject only to the exceptions provided in the Treaty itself.[49] In *Campus Oil*[50] the Irish Government argued unsuccessfully that oil, being of vital national importance, should be regarded as impliedly exempt from Article 30. The Court held that goods could not be considered to be exempt merely because they were of particular importance for the life or economy of the Member State.[51] Coins which constitute legal tender do not fall within Articles 30 to 36; coins which no longer constitute legal tender do.[52]

Where national procedures are contrary to Articles 30 to 36, any charge

---

[45] Case 249/81, *Commission* v. *Ireland* [1982] E.C.R. 4005. In Cases 266 and 267/87, *ex p. API* [1989] E.C.R. 1295 the Court held that measures adopted by a professional body vested with statutory disciplinary powers might constitute "measures" within the scope of Art. 30.

[46] Case 222/82, *Apple and Pear Development Council* [1983] E.C.R. 4083.

[47] Case 193/80 [1981] E.C.R. 3019.

[48] *Ibid.*, at para. 17.

[49] See Art. 36, *infra* at p. 138; and Art. 223, dealing with trade in arms, munitions and war materials. Case 72/83, *Campus Oil* [1984] E.C.R. 2727. Case C–2/90, *Commission* v. *Belgium*, judgment of July 9, 1992.

[50] Case 72/83 note 49.

[51] Case 72/83 note 49, para. 17.

[52] Case 7/78, *Thompson* [1978] E.C.R. 2247.

made by the national authorities for completion of such procedures is likewise unlawful.[53]

It should be noted that the inconsistency of national rules with Articles 30 to 36 is a point which can only be taken in respect of goods imported or to be imported from another Member State.[54] Where Article 30 precludes the application of national law to imports, the result may be that imported products are placed at a disadvantage in comparison with imports. But this is consistent with Community law.[55] It is a consequence of, on the one hand, the choice of the national legislator, and, on the other hand, the fact that Article 30 applies exclusively to imported products. The position is different where Community rules lay down the same conditions for the marketing of domestic products and imports alike.[56]

Measures having equivalent effect to quantitative restrictions on exports

Article 34(1) of the EEC Treaty provides that quantitative restrictions on exports, and all measures having equivalent effect, shall be prohibited between Member States. The notion of measures having equivalent effect clearly embraces measures which formally differentiate between domestic trade on the one hand, and the export trade on the other, as the *Bouhelier* case illustrates.[57] In order to ensure quality control, French legislation authorised a public authority to inspect pressed lever watches and watch movements made in France and destined for export to other Member States. If the watches or movements complied with the relevant quality standards, a certificate was issued to that effect. The export of such watches and movements was subject to the grant of a licence, except in the case of consignments in respect of which a standards certificate had been issued. The Court held that Article 34 of the Treaty precluded both export licensing and the imposition of quality controls on exports. Since the latter controls were not required in the case of products for the domestic market, their imposition amounted to arbitrary discrimination and constituted an obstacle to intra-Community trade.

In the case of quantitative restrictions on imports the Court's case-law has developed to the stage where it is not necessary to establish discrimination in order to invoke the terms of Article 30. The Court takes judicial notice of the "protective effect" of national trading rules which, while applying to domestic products and imports alike, exclude or discourage imports from other Member States.[58]

It seems that the concept of measures having equivalent effect to

---

[53] Case 50/85, *Schloh* [1986] E.C.R. 1855.
[54] Cases 314–316/82, *Waterkeyn* [1982] E.C.R. 4337.
[55] Case 355/85, *Driancourt* v. *Cognet* [1986] E.C.R. 3231; Cases 80 & 159/85, *EDAH BV* [1986] E.C.R. 3359.
[56] Case 98/86, *Mathot* [1987] E.C.R. 809.
[57] Case 53/76 [1977] E.C.R. 197.
[58] For the *Cassis* decision, Case 120/78, *Rewe* [1979] E.C.R. 649, and its progeny, see *infra* at p. 221.

quantitative restrictions on exports is not as broad as the same concept applicable to imports. Discrimination, either formal or material, still seems to be an essential element in the former case. As the Court explained in *Groenveld*[59]:

> "That provision [*i.e.* Art. 34(1)] concerns the national measures which have as their specific object or effect the restrictions of patterns of exports and thereby the establishment of a difference in treatment between the domestic trade of a Member State and its export trade in such a way as to provide a particular advantage for national production or for the domestic market of the State in question at the expense of the production or of the trade of other Member States. This is not so in the case of a prohibition like that in question which is applied objectively to the production of goods of a certain kind without drawing a distinction depending on whether such goods are intended for the national market or for export."

The Court has repeated this formulation on numerous occasions.[60] An obligation on producers to deliver poultry offal to their local authority has been held to involve by implication a prohibition of exports and to fall accordingly within the scope of application of Article 34.[61]

The prohibition in question binds the Community institutions as well as the Member States, and the requirements of Article 34 have been held to be satisfied where Community rules made equivalent but not identical provision for administrative supervision both for exports in bulk of compound feedingstuffs and for the marketing thereof within the country of origin.[62]

Import licences, declarations, etc.

Apart from the exceptions for which provision is made by Community law itself,[63] Articles 30 and 34 of the EEC Treaty preclude the application to intra-Community trade of a national provision which requires, even purely as a formality, import or export licences or any other similar procedure.[64]

An obligation imposed by an importing Member State to produce a certificate of fitness issued by an exporting Member State in connection with the import of a product amounts to a measure having equivalent effect.[65]

However, requiring declarations from importers concerning the origin of

---

[59] Case 15/79 [1979] E.C.R. 3409 at para. 7.
[60] See, *e.g.* Case 155/80, *Oebel* [1981] E.C.R. 1993 at para. 15; Case 286/81, *Oosthoek's* [1982] E.C.R. 4575 at para. 13; Case 172/82, *Inter-Huiles* [1983] E.C.R. 555 at para. 12.
[61] Case 118/86, *Nertsvoederfabriek Nederlandse* [1987] E.C.R. 3883.
[62] Case 15/83, *Denkavit* [1984] E.C.R. 2171.
[63] Note that import licences may in principle be excused in appropriate cases under Article 36 (as to which see *infra* at p. 225), Case 124/81, *Commission* v. *United Kingdom* [1983] E.C.R. 203; Case 74/82, *Commission* v. *Ireland* [1984] E.C.R. 317; Case 40/82, *Commission* v. *United Kingdom* [1984] E.C.R. 283.
[64] Cases 51–54/71, *International Fruit* [1971] E.C.R. 1107; Case 68/76, *Commission* v. *French Republic* [1977] E.C.R. 515; Case 41/76, *Donckerwolcke* [1976] E.C.R. 1921; Case 124/81, *Commission* v. *United Kingdom* [1983] E.C.R. 203.
[65] Case 251/78, *Denkavit* [1979] E.C.R. 3369 at para. 11.

goods for the purpose of monitoring the movement of goods does not amount to a measure having equivalent effect provided that the importer is not required to declare more than he knows or can reasonably be expected to know, and provided that penalties for failure are not disproportionate.[66]

Specific preference for domestic products

National measures which express a preference for domestic products or confer some advantage on domestic products alone will amount to measures having equivalent effect to quantitative restrictions. The Court of Justice has so ruled in the case of a quality designation reserved for alcoholic drinks containing 85 per cent. spirits distilled on national territory.[67] Similarly, in *Campus Oil* the Court held that Irish rules requiring importers of petroleum products to purchase a certain proportion of their requirements at prices fixed by the competent Minister from a state-owned company operating a refinery in Ireland amounted to a measure having equivalent effect.[68] In *Commission* v. *Hellenic Republic*[69] it was conceded by the defendant Member State that requiring the Agricultural Bank of Greece not to finance purchases of imported agricultural machinery except upon proof that machinery of that kind was not manufactured in Greece amounted to a measure having equivalent effect. The Court held that the concession was rightly made. In *Du Pont de Nemours Italiana* the Court held that Article 30 precluded national rules which reserved to undertakings established in particular regions of the national territory a proportion of public supply contracts.[70] It has even been held that state-financed publicity campaigns promoting the purchase of national products on the grounds of national origin and disparaging products from other Member States infringe Article 30.[71]

Conditions imposed in respect of imported products only

One of the most easily detected infringements of the Treaty's prohibition on measures having equivalent effect to quantitative restrictions is a national rule imposing conditions on imported products which are not imposed on their domestic counterparts. Thus phyto-sanitary inspections on imports of plant products where no compulsory examination is made of domestic products amounts to a measure having equivalent effect.[72] Again, a national requirement that imported drinks be at least of the alcohol content specified as the minimum in the country of origin, where no minimum alcoholic

---

[66] Case 41/76, *Donckerwolcke* [1976] E.C.R. 1921; Case 179/78, *Rivoira* [1979] E.C.R. 1147.
[67] Case 13/78, *Eggers* [1978] E.C.R. 1935.
[68] Case 72/83 [1984] E.C.R. 2727. But the Court held that such a measure might in principle be excused under Art. 36 on grounds of national security.
[69] Case 192/84 [1985] E.C.R. 3967; Case 103/84, *Commission* v. *Italy* [1986] E.C.R. 1759 (subsidies for vehicles of national manufacture).
[70] Case C-21/88 [1990] E.C.R. I-889.
[71] Case 249/81, *Commission* v. *Ireland* [1982] E.C.R. 4005; Case 222/82, *Apple and Pear Development Council* [1983] E.C.R. 4083.
[72] Case 4/75, *Rewe* [1975] E.C.R. 843. In this case the measures were justified under Art. 36.

content was specified for similar domestic products, has been held to be contrary to Article 30.[73] In *Commission* v. *Italy* the Court condemned an Italian measure prohibiting the testing, for the purposes of registration, of buses which were more than seven years old and came from other Member States, where no such prohibition applied to Italian buses.[74]

Measures making imports more difficult or more costly

A ground advanced by the Court for holding frontier checks of imported products to amount to measures having equivalent effect is that such checks make imports more difficult or costly.[75] Examples of national measures which have been held to be contrary to Article 30 (subject to appropriate justification in accordance with the Treaty)[76] on this ground are an import deposit scheme for imports for which payment was made in advance[77]; the extension to imported products of national rules which prohibited the sales of silver goods without hallmarking[78]; the extension to imported products of a national rule which required that margarine be sold in cube-shaped packs[79]; the extension to imported products of a requirement that certain information be not provided on the packaging of certain products[80]; the extension to imported products of a national rule which prohibited the sale of goods by retail unless they bore an indication of their country of origin[81]; and the roadworthiness testing of imported vehicles.[82]

Impeding access to certain channels of distribution

The definition of measures having equivalent effect which the Court has adopted has led it to conclude that measures are forbidden which "favour, within the Community, particular trade channels or particular commercial operators in relation to others."[83] An example of such a measure is provided by the proceedings in *Procureur du Roi* v. *Dassonville*.[84] The defendants in the national suit imported into Belgium Scotch whisky which they had purchased from French distributors. Belgian legislation required such goods to be accompanied by a British certificate of origin made out in the name of the Belgian importers, and the goods in question were without such certificates, which could have been obtained only with the greatest difficulty once the goods had been imported previously into France. The Court of Justice held that a requirement such as that laid down by the Belgian

---

[73] Case 59/82, *Schutzverband* [1983] E.C.R. 1217.
[74] Case 50/83 [1984] E.C.R. 1633.
[75] Case 4/75, *Rewe* [1975] E.C.R. 843 at para. 11; Case 42/82, *Commission* v. *French Republic* [1983] E.C.R. 1013 at para. 50.
[76] As to which, see *infra* at p. 225.
[77] Case 95/81, *Commission* v. *Italy* [1982] E.C.R. 2187.
[78] Case 220/81, *Robertson* [1982] E.C.R. 2349.
[79] Case 261/81, *Rau* [1982] E.C.R. 3961.
[80] Case 94/82, *De Kikvorsch* [1983] E.C.R. 947.
[81] Case 207/83, *Commission* v. *United Kingdom* [1985] E.C.R. 1201.
[82] Case 50/85, *Schloh* [1986] E.C.R. 1855.
[83] Case 155/73, *Sacchi* [1974] E.C.R. 409 at p. 427, para. 8.
[84] Case 8/74 [1974] E.C.R. 837.

legislation in issue constituted a measure having equivalent effect, inasmuch as it favoured direct imports from the country of origin over imports from a Member State where the goods were in free circulation.

The Court reiterated its view that there must be no discrimination between channels of trade in *de Peijper*.[85] Dutch legislation laid down certain safety requirements in the case of imports of medicinal preparations. The importer was bound to present certain documentation, verified by the manufacturer, to the Dutch public health authorities. Centrafarm purchased quantities of Valium, manufactured by Hoffmann-La Roche in England, from a British wholesaler, packed the tablets in packages bearing the name Centrafarm and marked with the generic name of the product in question, and distributed them to pharmacies in the Netherlands. Centrafarm could not rely on Hoffmann-La Roche's co-operation with regard to the relevant documentation, and was charged under Dutch law. On a reference from the Kantongerecht, Rotterdam, the Court ruled that national practices which resulted in imports being channelled in such a way that certain traders could effect these imports, while others could not, constituted measures having equivalent effect.

Price restrictions

The Court has considered on a number of occasions the compatibility with Article 30 of national measures fixing the selling prices of products.

Selective price measures taken by national authorities to restrict importation of products from other Member States will clearly be incompatible with Article 30.[86]

Where a maximum selling price applies without distinction to domestic and imported products it does not of itself amount to a measure having equivalent effect. It will only do so when it is fixed at such a low level that the sale of imported products becomes, if not impossible, at any rate more difficult than that of domestic products.[87] This would be the case where imports could only be effected at a loss,[88] or where traders were impelled by the disparity between the lower cost of domestic goods and imports to give preference to the latter.[89] Imports would equally be impeded if the minimum prices which could be charged by traders were fixed at such a high level that the price advantage enjoyed by imports over domestic goods were cancelled out.[90]

Even if national rules establish different criteria for fixing the selling prices of imports than are established for fixing the selling prices of domestic goods, there will only be a violation of Article 30 if imports are actually put

---

[85] Case 104/75 [1976] E.C.R. 613. See also Case 261/81, *Rau* [1982] E.C.R. 3961 at para. 13.
[86] Case 90/82, *Commission* v. *France* [1983] E.C.R. 2011 at para. 27.
[87] See, *e.g.* Case 65/75, *Tasca* [1976] E.C.R. 291, at para. 13; Cases 88–90/75, *SADAM* [1976] E.C.R. 323 at para. 15; Case 5/79, *Hans Buijs* [1979] E.C.R. 3203 at para. 26; Cases 16–20/79, *Danis* [1979] E.C.R. 3327.
[88] Case 65/75 and Cases 88–90/75, note 87.
[89] Case 5/79, *Hans Buijs* [1979] E.C.R. 3203 at para. 26; Cases 16–20/79, *Danis* [1979] E.C.R. 3327.
[90] Case 82/77, *Van Tiggele* [1978] E.C.R. 25.

at some disadvantage. This follows from the *Roussel* case,[91] in which the Court held that:

> "Legislation ... which differentiates between the two groups of products, must be regarded as a measure having an effect equivalent to a quantitative restriction where it is capable of making more difficult, in any manner whatever, the sale of imported products."[92]

That separate rules for the price fixing of imports do not of themselves infringe Article 30 is confirmed in *Leclerc*, in which the Court condemned separate price-fixing rules for imported books which were liable to impede trade between Member States.[93] Nevertheless, if price-fixing rules applied exclusively to imported products, this would violate Article 30 without more since it would of itself place imported products at some disadvantage.

Discrimination may be either formal or material

Where it is alleged that a national measure amounts to a measure having equivalent effect to a quantitative restriction on imports it will invariably be sufficient—whether or not it is also necessary[94]—to show that it discriminates against imports. Discrimination exists not only when a national measure treats similar situations in different ways—so-called "formal" discrimination—(for example prohibiting the testing of imported buses more than seven years old while allowing it in the case of similar buses of domestic manufacture),[95] but also when a national measure treats different situations in the same way[96]—so-called "material" discrimination—(for example applying the same maximum selling price to imported goods as to domestic goods where the former cost more than the latter).[97] The adoption of apparently neutral criteria will amount to material discrimination where the criteria in practice are satisfied entirely or mainly by domestic products rather than imports. In *Commission* v. *Ireland*[98] the Court considered the terms of a contract specification publicised for tender in connection with the augmentation of the Dundalk water supply. The specification referred to asbestos cement pressure pipes "certified as complying with Irish Standard Specification 188:1975 in accordance with the Irish Standards Mark Licensing Scheme of the Institute for Industrial Research and Standards." It appeared that only one undertaking—located in Ireland—had been certified to apply the Irish Standard Mark to pipes of the type required. Since the contract specification did not allow for pipes of

---

[91] Case 181/82 [1983] E.C.R. 3849.
[92] Case 181/82 at para. 19.
[93] Case 229/83 [1985] E.C.R. 2.
[94] For discrimination as an element in establishing infringement of Article 30, see *infra* at p. 232.
[95] Case 50/83 [1984] E.C.R. 1633.
[96] Case 13/63, *Republic of Italy* v. *Commission* [1963] E.C.R. 165.
[97] Case 65/75, *Tasca* [1976] E.C.R. 291; Cases 88–90/75, *SADAM* [1976] E.C.R. 323. See *supra* at p. 219.
[98] Case 45/87 [1988] E.C.R. 4929.

equivalent standard, the Court held that the inclusion of the specifications in question impeded imports contrary to Article 30 of the EEC Treaty.

Disparities between national laws as measures having equivalent effect

Prior to the landmark decision of the Court of Justice in the *Cassis* case[99] it was generally assumed—and the Court's case-law was consistent with this assumption—that Article 30 had no application to a national measure unless it could be proved that the measure in question discriminated in some way, formally or materially, between either imports and domestic products, or between channels of intra-Community trade.

The *Cassis* case involved the intended importation into Germany of a consignment of the alcoholic beverage "Cassis de Dijon." Under German legislation fruit liqueurs such as "Cassis" could only be marketed if they contained a minimum alcohol content of 25 per cent., whereas the alcohol content of the product in question was between 15 per cent. and 20 per cent. A German court asked the Court of Justice whether legislation such as that in issue was consistent with Article 30 of the Treaty. Before the Court of Justice the Federal Republic of Germany argued that the legislation in question was discriminatory in neither a formal nor a material sense; any obstacles to trade resulted simply from the fact that France and Germany contained different rules for the minimum alcohol contents of certain drinks. The Court's judgment makes no reference at all to the issue of discrimination. Rather it regards incompatibility with Article 30 as flowing from the very fact that the "Cassis" could not be placed lawfully on the German market, and addresses itself at once to the question whether there existed any justification for the restriction.

> "In the absence of common rules relating to the production and marketing of alcohol ... it is for the Member States to regulate all matters relating to the production and marketing of alcohol and alcoholic beverages on their own territory.
>
> Obstacles to movement within the Community resulting from disparities between the national laws relating to the marketing of the products in question must be accepted in so far as those provisions may be recognized as being necessary in order to satisfy mandatory requirements relating in particular to the effectiveness of fiscal supervision, the protection of public health, the fairness of commercial transactions and the defence of the consumer."[1]

The Court rejected the arguments of the Federal Republic of Germany relating to the protection of public health and to the protection of the consumer against unfair commercial practices, and continued:

> "It is clear from the foregoing that the requirements relating to the

---

[99] Case 120/78, *Rewe* [1979] E.C.R. 649.
[1] Case 120/78 note 99 at paras. 8, 9.

minimum alcohol content of alcoholic beverages do not serve a purpose which is in the general interest and such as to take precedence over the requirements of the free movement of goods, which constitute one of the fundamental rules of the Community."[2]

In the paragraphs which follow the Court describes the restrictive effect of national rules such as those in issue in terms which either make the existence of an element of discrimination irrelevant in establishing violation of Article 30, or presume it to exist from the very fact of exclusion of products lawfully produced and marketed in one of the Member States.

"In practice, the principal effect of requirements of this nature is to promote alcoholic beverages having a high alcohol content by excluding from the national market products of other Member States which do not answer that description.

It therefore appears that the unilateral requirement imposed by the rules of a Member State of a minimum alcohol content for the purposes of the sale of alcoholic beverages constitutes an obstacle to trade which is incompatible with the provisions of Article 30 of the Treaty.

There is therefore no valid reason why, provided that they have been lawfully produced and marketed in one of the Member States, alcoholic beverages should not be introduced into any other Member State; the sale of such products may not be subject to a legal prohibition on the marketing of beverages with an alcohol content lower than the limit set by the national rules."[3]

The Court was soon to confirm the approach it had adopted in *Cassis* in *Gilli & Andres*,[4] a case concerning national legislation prohibiting the marketing of vinegar containing acetic acid derived otherwise than from the acetic fermentation of wine. In this case the Court slightly modified one of its observations in *Cassis*:

"In practice, the principal effect of provisions of this nature is to protect domestic production by prohibiting the putting on to the market of products from other Member States which do not answer the descriptions laid down by the national rules."[5]

If discrimination was the distinguishing feature of national measures prima facie contrary to Article 30 before the *Cassis* decision, emphasis after that case was placed upon the protective effect of national rules which excluded from the market of one Member State goods lawfully produced and marketed in the territory of another. As the Commission stated in its Communication of October 3, 1980 concerning the consequences of the *Cassis* case:

"Any product imported from another Member State must in principle

---

[2] *Ibid.* at para. 14.
[3] *Ibid.* at para. 14.
[4] Case 788/79 [1980] E.C.R. 2071.
[5] Case 788/79 note 96 at para. 10.

be admitted to the territory of the importing Member State if it has been lawfully produced, that is, conforms to rules and processes of manufacture that are customarily and traditionally accepted in the exporting country, and is marketed in the territory of another."[6]

Examples of measures held by the Court to fall foul of the *Cassis* formulation (subject to justification in accordance with the Treaty)[7] are national rules imposing a labelling requirement[8]: national rules prohibiting use of the additive nisin in cheese[9]; national rules regulating the dry matter content of bread[10]; national rules requiring silver products to be hallmarked[11]; national rules requiring margarine to be sold in cube-shaped packets[12]; national rules restricting or prohibiting certain forms of advertising[13]; national rules prohibiting the retail sale of certain products unless marked with their country of origin[14]; national rules prohibiting the marketing under the designation "beer" of beers manufactured in other Member States in accordance with rules different to those applicable in the Member State of import, and prohibiting the import of beers containing additives whose use is authorised in the Member State of origin but forbidden in the Member State of import[15]; national rules prohibiting the use of common wheat flour in the production of pasta products[16]; national rules restricting the term "yoghurt" to fresh yoghurt and prohibiting its application to deep frozen yoghurt[17]; national rules restricting the name "Edam" to cheese having a minimum fat content of 40 per cent.[18]; and national rules providing that sales offers involving a temporary price reduction may not state the duration of the offer or refer to previous prices.[19]

There can be no doubt that the *Cassis* formulation may cover national measures which are discriminatory and which are capable of infringing Article 30 on that ground. At times the new notion of protective effect and the old notion of discrimination appear to coalesce. Thus in *Prantl* the Court declared:

> "... even national legislation on the marketing of a product which applies to national and imported products alike falls under the prohibition laid down in Article 30 ... if in practice it produces protective effects by favouring typical national products and, by the same token, operating to the detriment of certain types of products from other Member States."[20]

---

[6] O.J. 1980 C–256/2.
[7] As to which, see *infra* at p. 225.
[8] Case 27/80, *Fietje* [1980] E.C.R. 3839; Case 94/82, *De Kikvorsch* [1983] E.C.R. 947.
[9] Case 53/80, *Eyssen* [1981] E.C.R. 409.
[10] Case 30/80, *Kelderman* [1981] E.C.R. 517.
[11] Case 220/81, *Robertson* [1982] E.C.R. 2349.
[12] Case 261/81, *Rau* [1982] E.C.R. 3961.
[13] Case 286/81, *Oosthoek's*, etc. [1982] E.C.R. 4575.
[14] Case 207/83, *Commission* v. *United Kingdom* [1985] E.C.R. 1201.
[15] Case 178/84, *Commission* v. *Germany* [1987] E.C.R. 1227.
[16] Case 407/85, *Drei Glocken GmbH* [1988] E.C.R. 4233.
[17] Case 298/87, *SMANOR SA* [1988] E.C.R. 4489.
[18] Case 286/86, *Deserbais* [1988] E.C.R. 4907.
[19] Case C–362/88, *GB-INNO-BM* [1990] E.C.R. I–667.
[20] Case 16/83 [1984] E.C.R. 1299 at para. 21.

Nevertheless, the Court made it clear in the *Cinéthèque* case[21] that the *Cassis* formulation is not limited in its application to national measures which are proved to have or assumed to have some discriminatory purpose or effect. The case concerned French rules which provided that video-cassettes of films could not be distributed within one year of the release of the films in question at the cinema. The Court made the following observations:

"... such a system, if it applies without distinction to both video-cassettes manufactured in the national territory and to imported video-cassettes, does not have the purpose of regulating trade patterns; its effect is not to favour national production as against the production of other Member States, but to encourage cinematograph production as such.

Nevertheless, the application of such a system may create barriers to intra-Community trade in video-cassettes because of the disparities between the systems operated in the different Member States and between the conditions for the release of cinematographic works in the cinemas of those States. In those circumstances a prohibition of exploitation laid down by such a system is not compatible with the principle of the free movement of goods provided for in the Treaty unless any obstacle to intra-Community trade thereby created does not exceed what is necessary in order to ensure that attainment of the objective in view and unless that objective is justified with regard to Community law."[22]

While the existence of the non-discriminatory trade restriction has been unequivocally confirmed by the Court, it does not follow that establishing discrimination is no longer appropriate where infringement of Article 30 is alleged. First, even if not a necessary ingredient in all Article 30 cases, the existence of discrimination against imported products will invariably give rise to the inference that a national rule amounts to a measure having equivalent effect. Secondly, there are clearly certain cases where discrimination remains a necessary element in establishing violation of Article 30.[23] Thirdly, the existence of discrimination may be crucial in determining whether a measure having equivalent effect may be justified on the grounds recognised under Community law.[24]

---

[21] Cases 60 & 61/84 [1985] E.C.R. 2605.

[22] Cases 60 & 61/84 note 21, paras. 21, 22. *Cinéthèque* was relied upon by the Court in Case 145/88, *Torfaen B.C.* v. *B&Q Plc* [1989] E.C.R. 3851 in support of the proposition that Sunday trading legislation might infringe Art. 30, (though any impediment to intra-Community trade resulting from such rules is unconnected with disparities between the rules in different Member States).

[23] For example, the price control cases, and cases where a Member State takes steps to promote the financial stability of a national social security scheme, see *infra* at p. 232.

[24] See *infra* at p. 226 and 232.

DEROGATION FROM ARTICLES 30 TO 34

Article 36 of the EEC Treaty

Article 36 of the Treaty provides:

"The provisions of Articles 30 to 34 shall not preclude prohibitions or restrictions on imports, exports or goods in transit justified on grounds of public morality, public policy or public security; the protection of health and life of humans, animals or plants; the protection of national treasures possessing artistic, historic or archaeological value; or the protection of industrial and commercial property. Such prohibitions or restrictions shall not, however, constitute a means of arbitrary discrimination or a disguised restriction on trade between Member States."

The grounds of derogation

Article 36 constitutes an exception to the fundamental rules that all obstacles to the free movement of goods between Member States shall be abolished and the Article must be interpreted strictly.[25] It follows that the list of exceptions is exhaustive.[26] Thus the Court has held that Article 36 does not justify derogation from Article 30 on the grounds of the protection of consumers or the fairness of commercial transactions,[27] economic policy,[28] or the protection of creativity and cultural diversity,[29] since none of the foregoing are referred to in the Article.

While the Court has accepted that the expression "public policy" is capable of embracing a national ban on the export of coins no longer constituting legal tender,[30] it has refused to accept that the expression includes the protection of consumers.[31]

In the absence of harmonised rules at the Community level, recourse to Article 36 may entail the application of different standards in different Member States, as a result of different national value-judgments, and different factual circumstances. Thus the Court has emphasised that:

"In principle, it is for each Member State to determine in accordance

---

[25] Case 46/76 [1977] E.C.R. 5; Case 113/80, *Commission* v. *Ireland* [1981] E.C.R. 1625; Case 95/81, *Commission* v. *Italy* [1982] E.C.R. 2187.
[26] Case 95/81, *Commission* v. *Italy* [1982] E.C.R. 2187.
[27] Case 95/81, *Commission* v. *Italy* [1982] E.C.R. 2187; Case 220/81, *Robertson* [1982] E.C.R. 2349; Case 229/83, *Leclerc* [1985] E.C.R. 2. Such considerations may however, in the case of non-discriminatory restrictions, amount to mandatory requirements justifying reasonable restrictions on the free movement of goods in the general interest, see *infra* at p. 229.
[28] Case 7/61, *Commission* v. *Italy* [1961] E.C.R. 317; Case 95/81 note 13; Case 238/82, *Duphar* [1984] E.C.R. 523; Case 72/83, *Campus Oil* [1984] E.C.R. 2727; Case 288/82, *Commission* v. *Ireland* [1985] E.C.R. 1761. Such considerations may however, in the case of non-discriminatory restrictions, amount to mandatory requirements justifying reasonable restrictions on the free movement of goods in the general interest, see Case 238/82, *Duphar* E.C.R. 523 *infra* at p. 233.
[29] Case 229/83, *Leclerc* [1985] E.C.R. 2.
[30] Case 7/78, *Thompson* [1978] E.C.R. 2247.
[31] Case 177/83, *Kohl* [1984] E.C.R. 3651.

with its own scale of values and in the form selected by it the requirements of public morality in its territory."[32]

Again, in connection with the protection of public health, it has stated:

"In so far as the relevant Community rules do not cover certain pesticides, Member States may regulate the presence of residues of those pesticides in a way which may vary from one country to another according to the climatic conditions, the normal diet of the population and their state of health."[33]

While Article 36 leaves a margin of discretion in the national authorities as to the extent to which they wish to protect the interests listed therein, the discretion is limited by two important principles. First, that any discrimination between imports and domestic products must not be arbitrary. Secondly, that national measures must not restrict trade any more than is necessary to protect the interest in question.

Arbitrary discrimination or a disguised restriction on trade

Article 36 provides that prohibitions or restrictions permitted under that Article shall not, however, constitute a means of arbitrary discrimination or a disguised restriction on trade between Member States. The purpose of this formulation has been said by the Court to be to:

". . . prevent restrictions on trade based on the grounds mentioned in the first sentence of Article 36 from being diverted from their proper purpose and used in such a way as either to create discrimination in respect of goods originating in other Member States or indirectly to protect certain national products."[34]

In determining whether or not discrimination against imported goods is arbitrary, the crucial test will be a comparison with measures taken *vis-à-vis* domestic goods: *Rewe-Zentralfinanz* v. *Landwirtschaftskammer.*[35] As a precaution against transmission of the destructive San José scale insect, German legislation provided for the phytosanitary examination of certain imported fruit and vegetables at point of entry. On a reference from the Verwaltungsgericht Cologne, the Court held that such measures must be considered to be justified in principle under Article 36, provided that they did not constitute a means of arbitrary discrimination. This would not be the case where effective measures were taken to prevent the distribution of contaminated domestic products, and where there was reason to believe that there would be a risk of the harmful organism spreading if no inspections were held on importation.

---

[32] Case 34/79, *Henn & Darby* [1979] E.C.R. 3795.
[33] Case 94/83, *Heijn* [1984] E.C.R. 3263.
[34] Case 34/79, *Henn & Darby* [1979] E.C.R. 3795 at para. 21; Case 40/82, *Commission* v. *United Kingdom* [1984] E.C.R. 283 at para. 36.
[35] Case 4/75 [1975] E.C.R. 843.

National measures are only justified if they are no more restrictive than is strictly necessary

The Court has emphasised that Article 36 is not designed to reserve certain matters to the exclusive jurisdiction of Member States, but only permits national laws to derogate from the principle of the free movement of goods to the extent to which such derogation is and continues to be justified for the attainment of the objectives referred to in that Article.[36] The word "justified" is to be construed as meaning "necessary."[37] Application of the Article is thus to be conditioned upon compliance with the principle of proportionality.[38] As the Court explained in *Commission* v. *Belgium*:

> "However [public health] measures are justified only if it is established that they are necessary in order to attain the objective of protection referred to in Article 36 and that such protection cannot be achieved by means which place less of a restriction on the free movement of goods within the Community."[39]

Thus, in *de Peijper*,[40] the Court considered the argument that restrictive provisions of Netherlands legislation which favoured imports by dealers securing the co-operation of the manufacturer were justified on the basis that they were necessary for the protection of the health and life of humans. While the Court acknowledged that this interest ranked first among the interests protected by Article 36 of the Treaty, it emphasised that national measures did not fall within the exception if the health or life of humans could be as effectively protected by means less restrictive of intra-Community trade. In particular, Article 36 did not justify restrictions motivated primarily by a concern to facilitate the task of the authorities, or reduce public expenditure, unless alternative arrangements would impose unreasonable burdens on the administration.

As long as the rules relating to health protection in a particular sector have not been harmonised, it is open to the Member States to carry out any necessary inspections at national frontiers.[41] However, the free movement of goods is facilitated by the carrying out of health inspections in the country of production and the health authorities of the importing Member State should co-operate in order to avoid the repetition, in the importing country, of checks which have already been carried out in the country of production.[42] Similar considerations apply to approval by national authorities of products which have been approved on health grounds in other Member States. Whilst a Member State is free to require such products to undergo a fresh procedure of examination and approval, the authorities of that Member State are bound to assist in bringing about a relaxation of the controls

---

[36] Case 5/77, *Tedeschi* [1977] E.C.R. 1556; Case 251/78, *Denkavit* [1979] E.C.R. 3327.
[37] Case 153/78, *Commission* v. *Germany* 2555 at para. 8; Case 251/78, *Denkavit* [1979] E.C.R. 3327 at para. 21.
[38] As to which, see *supra* at p. 89.
[39] Case 155/82 [1983] E.C.R. 531. See also Case 97/83, *Melkunie* [1984] E.C.R. 2367 at para. 12.
[40] Case 104/75 [1976] E.C.R. 613.
[41] Case 73/84, *Denkavit* [1985] E.C.R. 1013.
[42] Case 251/78, *Denkavit* [1979] E.C.R. 3327. Case 73/84, *Denkavit* [1985] E.C.R. 1013.

applied in intra-Community trade,[43] and are not entitled unnecessarily to require technical or chemical analyses or tests where those analyses or tests have already been carried out in another Member State and their results are available to those authorities, or may at their request be placed at their disposal.[44]

Disguised restrictions, arbitrary discrimination, and proportionality

The requirements that measures taken by Member States under Article 36 must not constitute a means of arbitrary discrimination, nor a disguised restriction on trade, and must comply with the principle of proportionality, overlap, and should not be considered in isolation. Thus, infringement of the principle of proportionality may lead to a measure being categorised as a disguised restriction on trade.[45] Again, in deciding in *Commission* v. *France*[46] whether or not the frequency of French frontier tests of Italian wine complied with the principle of proportionality, the Court took into account not only the fact that similar checks on Italian wine were carried out by the Italian authorities, but also the fact that the frequency of the French frontier inspections was distinctly higher than the occasional checks carried out on the transportation of French wine within France.

The effect of harmonisation directives and other Community measures on recourse to Article 36

Recourse to Article 36 is no longer justified if Community rules provide for the necessary measures to ensure protection of the interests set out in that article.[47] This may be the case, for example, when directives enacted under Article 100 or 100a of the EEC Treaty provide for the full harmonisation of the measures necessary for the protection of animal and human health, and establish the procedures to check that they are observed.[48] Thus, if such a directive places the responsibility for public health inspections of a product upon the Member State of export, the national authorities of the importing Member State will no longer be entitled to subject the product to systematic inspection upon importation; only occasional inspections to check compliance with the Community standards will be permissible.[49] But procedures for checking imports authorised under Community law must not entail unreasonable cost or delay.[50]

---

[43] Case 104/75, *de Peijper* [1976] E.C.R. 613; Case 272/80, *Frans-Nederlandse* [1981] E.C.R. 3277.
[44] Case 272/80, *Frans-Nederlandse* [1981] E.C.R. 3277.
[45] Case 272/80, *Frans-Nederlandse* [1981] E.C.R. 3277, paras. 13, 14; Cases 2–4/82, *Le Lion* [1983] E.C.R. 2973 at para. 12.
[46] Case 42/82 [1983] E.C.R. 1013 at paras. 51 to 57.
[47] Case 72/83, *Campus Oil* [1984] E.C.R. 2727 at para. 27.
[48] Case 251/78, *Denkavit* [1979] E.C.R. 3369 at para. 14; Case 227/82, *Leendert* [1983] E.C.R. 3883 at para. 35; Case 29/87, *Denkavit* [1988] E.C.R. 2965; Case 190/87, *Moormann BV* [1988] E.C.R. 4689; Case C–304/88, *Commission* v. *Belgium* [1990] E.C.R. I–2801.
[49] Case 35/76, *Simmenthal* [1976] E.C.R. 1871; Cases 2–4/82, *Le Lion* [1983] E.C.R. 2973.
[50] Case 406/85, *Goffette* [1987] E.C.R. 2525.

Burden of proof lies on the national authorities

It is for the national authorities of the Member States to prove that their restrictive trading rules may be justified under Article 36. As the Court stated in *Leendert van Bennekom*[51]:

> "it is for the national authorities to demonstrate in each case that their rules are necessary to give effective protection to the interests referred to in Article 36 of the Treaty."

Thus in *Cullet* the French Government defended national rules fixing retail selling prices for fuel on grounds of public order and security represented by the violent reactions which would have to be anticipated on the part of retailers affected by unrestricted competition. The Court rejected this argument summarily:

> "In that regard, it is sufficient to state that the French Government has not shown that it would be unable, using the means at its disposal, to deal with the consequences which an amendment of the rules in question . . . would have upon public order and security."[52]

The burden of proving that Article 36 applies accordingly entails: (i) showing that the national measures in question fall within one of the categories (for example public health, public policy or public morality) referred to in Article 36[53]; (ii) establishing that the measure does not constitute a means of arbitrary discrimination, that is to say, that if it differentiates between domestic products and imports, it does so on objective and justifiable grounds[54]; (iii) establishing that the measure does not constitute a disguised restriction on trade, that is to say, that any restrictive effect on the free movement of goods is limited to what is necessary to protect the interest in question.[55]

Mandatory requirements in the general interest

Although the Court has stated repeatedly that the exceptions listed in Article 36 are exhaustive,[56] it in effect established further grounds upon which Member States may derogate from Article 30 in the *Cassis* case, in which it held that obstacles to the free movement of goods in the Community resulting from disparities between national marketing rules must be accepted insofar as they were necessary to satisfy mandatory requirements relating in particular to the effectiveness of fiscal supervision, the protection of public health, the fairness of commercial transactions, and the defence of the consumer.[57] The theoretical explanation for this apparent inconsistency

---

[51] Case 227/82 [1983] E.C.R. 3883 at para. 40; see also Case 104/75, *de Peijper* [1976] E.C.R. 613; Case 251/78, *Denkavit* [1979] E.C.R. 3369 at para. 24; Case 174/82, *Sandoz* [1983] E.C.R. 2445 at para. 22.
[52] Case 231/83 [1985] E.C.R. 306 at paras. 32, 33.
[53] *Supra* at p. 225.
[54] *Supra* at p. 226.
[55] *Supra* at p. 226.
[56] See *supra* at p. 227.
[57] Case 120/78, *Rewe* [1979] E.C.R. 649. See *supra* at p. 221.

is that the *Cassis* list does not so much provide grounds for derogating from Article 30 as define the circumstances in which national measures fall within Article 30 in the first place.

The categories of justification under the *Cassis* formulation are not closed, as appears from the formulation itself, which refers to four categories "in particular." The Court has added to the list environmental protection,[58] and the encouragement of film-making, upholding on this latter ground national rules providing that video-cassettes of films could not be distributed until one year after the release of the films at the cinema.[59] In *Oebel* the Court stated that legitimate interests of economic and social policy, consistent with the Treaty, might similarly justify impediments to the free movement of goods.[60] And the Court has held that restrictions on imports which result from national rules governing the opening hours of retail premises, in particular as regards Sunday trading, may be justified by reference to national or regional socio-cultural characteristics.[61]

A useful example of mandatory requirements justifying national measures is provided in *Oosthoek's Uitgeversmaatschaapij B.V.*[62] The national measures in question restricted the giving of free gifts as a means of sales promotion. The Court took the view that to compel a producer either to adopt advertising or sales promotion schemes which differed from one Member State to another or discontinue a scheme which he considered to be particularly effective might constitute an obstacle to imports even if the legislation in question applied to domestic goods and to imports without distinction. Nevertheless, the Court upheld such rules on the grounds of the fairness of commercial transactions and the defence of the consumer:

> "It is undeniable that the offering of free gifts as a means of sales promotion may mislead consumers as to the real prices of certain products and distort the conditions on which genuine competition is based. Legislation which restricts or even prohibits such commercial practices for that reason is therefore capable of contributing to consumer protection and fair trading."[63]

In *GB-INNO-BM*,[64] however, the Court took a different view of the need for state intervention in the interests of consumer protection. A Belgian company had distributed advertising leaflets in Luxembourg territory as well as on Belgian territory allegedly contrary to Luxembourg rules according to which sales offers involving a temporary price reduction may not state the duration of the offer or refer to previous prices. The Court held that under

---

[58] Case 240/83, *Bruleurs d'Huiles Usagees* [1985] E.C.R. 532.
[59] Cases 60 & 61/84, *Cinéthèque* [1985] E.C.R. 2605.
[60] Case 155/80, *Oebel* [1981] E.C.R. 1993 at para. 12.
[61] Case 145/88, *Torfaen B.C.* v. *B&Q Plc* [1989] E.C.R. 3851; Case C–332/89, *Andre Marchandise* [1991] E.C.R. I–1027.
[62] Case 286/81 [1982] E.C.R. 4575.
[63] Case 286/81 note 62 at para. 18. And in Cases C–1/90 and C–176/90, *Aragonesa de Publicidad Exterior S.A.* [1991] E.C.R. I–4151 the Court upheld on public health grounds restrictions on advertising of certain alcoholic beverages. See also Case 382/87, *Buet* [1989] E.C.R. 1235 (prohibition of door to door canvassing of educational material justified).
[64] Case C–362/88 [1990] E.C.R. I–667.

Community law concerning consumer protection the provision of information to the consumer is considered one of the principal requirements. It followed that Article 30 could not be interpreted as meaning that national legislation which denies the consumer access to certain kinds of information might be justified by mandatory requirements concerning consumer protection.[65]

Consumer protection and fair trading, however, raise issues which extend beyond the market of the importing Member State. In *Prantl*[66] the Court considered trading rules reserving to national wine producers the use of the characteristically-shaped "Bocksbeutel" bottle. Consumer protection and fair trading were pleaded in support of the national rules. The Court noted, however, that in the common market consumer protection and fair trading as regards the presentation of wines must be guaranteed "with regard on all sides for the fair and traditional practices observed in the various Member States."[67] It followed that an exclusive right to use a certain type of bottle granted by national legislation in a Member State could not be used to bar imports of wines originating in another Member State put up in bottles of the same or similar shape in accordance with a fair and traditional practice in that Member State.

Recourse to mandatory requirements is subject to the principle of proportionality, as the Court made clear in the *Rau* case:

> "It is also necessary for such rules to be proportionate to the aim in view. If a Member State has a choice between various measures to attain the same objective it should choose the means which least restrict the free movement of goods."[68]

A further limitation on recourse to mandatory requirements is that they may only be invoked in the case of national rules which apply without discrimination to both domestic and imported products.[69] Thus in the case of national rules requiring certain imported products but not their domestically produced counterparts to bear an indication of country of origin, the Court held that considerations of consumer protection and the fairness of commercial transactions could have no application.[70] In the case of national rules requiring both domestic goods and imports to bear an indication of country of origin, the Court again refused to consider arguments based on considerations of consumer protection on the grounds that the national rules were in fact discriminatory:

> "The requirements relating to the indication of origin of goods are applicable without distinction to domestic and imported products only in form because, by their very nature, they are intended to enable the consumer to distinguish between those two categories of products,

---

[65] But *cf.* Cases C–1/90 and C–176/90 above note 63.
[66] Case 16/83 [1984] E.C.R. 1299.
[67] Case 16/83 [1984] E.C.R. 1299 at para. 27.
[68] Case 261/81 [1982] E.C.R. 3961 at para. 12.
[69] Case 113/80, *Commission* v. *Ireland* [1981] E.C.R. 1625.
[70] Case 113/80, *Commission* v. *Ireland* [1981] E.C.R. 1625.

which may thus prompt him to give his preference to national products."[71]

It seems that recourse to mandatory requirements is impermissible if national rules are discriminatory, either in a formal[72] or material sense,[73] from the point of view of their effect on trade,[74] or if national rules are applied in a similarly discriminatory manner.[75] However, care must be taken to differentiate discrimination, which ousts the application of mandatory requirements, from the "protective effect" characteristic of *Cassis* restrictions.[76]

COLOURABLE TRANSACTIONS

In *Leclerc* the Court held that a national price-fixing measure amounting to a measure having equivalent effect was not to be so regarded *vis-à-vis* products exported for the sole purpose of reimportation in order to circumvent the national legislation in question.[77] This conclusion is to be supported, not on the basis of the theory of "abuse of rights," but on the basis that the so-called "imports" were in commercial reality purely internal transactions.

CASES IN WHICH DISCRIMINATION IS A NECESSARY ELEMENT IN ESTABLISHING A MEASURE HAVING EQUIVALENT EFFECT

It has been noted that prior to the *Cassis*[78] decision it was generally assumed that discrimination was a necessary element in establishing a measure having equivalent effect.[79] Since that decision two things have become clear. First, that national rules may amount to measures having equivalent effect despite applying equally and without any discrimination to domestic products and to imports.[80] Secondly, that there nevertheless remain cases where discrimination is an indispensable element in establishing the existence of a measure having equivalent effect. The principle example is that of the price-control cases.[81] There are several

---

[71] Case 207/83, *Commission* v. *United Kingdom* [1985] E.C.R. 1201.

[72] For the distinction between formal and material discrimination, see *supra* at p. 220. Cases of formal discrimination ousting mandatory requirements are Case 113/80, *Commission* v. *Ireland* [1981] E.C.R. 1625; Case 59/82, *Shutzverband* [1983] E.C.R. 1217.

[73] Case 177/83, *Kohl* [1984] E.C.R. 3651; Case 207/83, *Commission* v. *United Kingdom* [1985] E.C.R. 1201.

[74] Case 177/83, *Kohl* [1984] E.C.R. 3651 at para. 14.

[75] Case 177/83, *Kohl* [1984] E.C.R. 3651 at para. 14.

[76] See *supra* at p. 222, in particular the definition of protective effect in Case 16/83, *Prantl* [1984] E.C.R. 1299 at para. 21.

[77] Case 229/83 [1985] E.C.R. 1. For reference to the view that this is an example of "abuse of rights," see reference in Oliver, (1986) 23 C.M.L.Rev. 325 at 327.

[78] As to which, see *supra* at p. 221.

[79] As to which, see *supra* at p. 134. See Wyatt, "Article 30 and non-discriminatory trade restrictions" (1981) 6 E.L.Rev. 185.

[80] Case 286/81, *Oosthoek's* [1982] E.C.R. 4575; Cases 60 & 61/84, *Cinéthèque* [1985] E.C.R. 2605; see *supra* at p. 224.

[81] As to which, see *supra* at p. 219.

possible explanations for the continuing requirement of discrimination in these cases. One is simply that the first cases were decided before *Cassis*, they were followed thereafter, and the resulting case law is *sui generis* and anomalous. However, in a more recent case, *Duphar*,[82] the Court made it clear that a national measure excluding certain types of drugs from reimbursement under a state social security scheme would only fall foul of Article 30 if it were discriminatory. The decision is to be welcomed. To have eschewed the requirement of discrimination and to have applied the principle of proportionality would have been tantamount to subjecting the public expenditure policy of the Member State concerned to judicial review. There can be no doubt that many of the public expenditure decisions of public authorities have an indirect effect upon imports, as indeed do many of the fiscal and monetary measures adopted with a view to the general management of the economy. It may be that measures of this type either do not in their nature amount to measures having equivalent effect, or do not constitute such measures unless they discriminate against imports. This view could explain the price control cases as well as *Duphar*, because price-fixing legislation is an instrument of general economic management; indeed it constitutes an alternative or supplementary policy instrument to fiscal and monetary measures in times of inflation. Furthermore, in the absence of discrimination against imports, such measures do not have the effect of partitioning national markets.

THE RELATIONSHIP BETWEEN ARTICLES 30 TO 36 AND OTHER PROVISIONS OF THE TREATY

However wide the field of application of Articles 30 and 34 may be, it does not include obstacles to trade covered by other provisions of the Treaty, such as Articles 9 to 16 (customs duties and charges having equivalent effect), 95 (discriminatory internal taxation), and 92 and 93 (state aids).[83] Where national taxes are imposed on an import which lacks a domestic counterpart, the rate of tax must not be so high as to impede the free movement of goods. Such an impediment to free movement would fall to be governed by Articles 30–36 of the EEC Treaty, rather than within the framework of Article 95 of the Treaty.[84]

National measures which fall to be scrutinised by the Commission under Articles 92 and 93 cannot be categorised as measures having equivalent effect simply by virtue of their effects upon trade, unless the aid in question produces "restrictive effects which exceed what is necessary to enable it to attain the objectives permitted by the Treaty."[85] This may be the case where aid is granted to traders who obtain supplies of imported products through a state agency but is withheld when the products are imported direct, if this

---

[82] Case 238/82 [1984] E.C.R. 523.
[83] Case 74/76, *Iannelli & Volpi* [1977] E.C.R. 557; Case 222/82, *Apple and Pear Development Council* [1983] E.C.R. 4083 at para. 30.
[84] Case C–47/88, *Commission* v. *Denmark* [1990] E.C.R. I–4509.
[85] Case 74/76, *Iannelli & Volpi* [1977] E.C.R. 557.

distinction is not clearly necessary for the attainment of the objectives of the said aid or for its proper functioning.[86] Furthermore, the Court has held that the possibility that state subsidies to a campaign designed to favour domestic products might fall within Articles 92 and 93 does not mean that the campaign itself thereby escapes the prohibitions laid down in Article 30.[87] The fact that a public works contract relates to the provision of services cannot remove a clause in an invitation to tender restricting the material that may be used from the scope of the prohibitions set out in Article 30.[88]

Other provisions of the Treaty may at times affect the application of Articles 30 to 36, in particular Articles 39 to 46 (common agricultural policy), Article 103 (conjunctural policy), Articles 108–109 (measures to combat balance of payments problems), Article 115, and Articles 223 to 225 (safeguard measures). Particular reference should also be made to Article 37 of the Treaty, on state monopolies of a commercial character.

Article 37—state monopolies of a commercial character

Article 37 of the Treaty provides, in part:

"1. Member States shall progressively adjust any State monopolies of a commercial character so as to ensure that when the transitional period has ended no discrimination regarding the conditions under which goods are procured and marketed exists between nationals of Member States.

The provisions of this Article shall apply to any body through which a Member State, in law or in fact, either directly or indirectly supervises, determines or appreciably influences imports or exports between Member States. These provisions shall likewise apply to monopolies delegated by the State to others.

2. Member States shall refrain from introducing any new measure which is contrary to the principles laid down in paragraph 1 or which restricts the scope of the Articles dealing with the abolition of customs duties and quantitative restrictions between Member States."

The provisions of paragraph 2 were held to be directly applicable from the date of entry into force of the Treaty in *Costa* v. *ENEL*.[89] Paragraph 1 was held to have similar effect from the end of the transitional period in *Pubblico Ministero* v. *Flavia Manghera*[90] and *Rewe-Zentrale des Lebensmittel-Grosshandels* v. *Hauptzollamt Landau/Pfalz*.[91] The state monopolies in question are those enjoying exclusive rights in the procurement and distribution of goods, not services.[92] But the existence of national rules

---

[86] Case 74/76, *Iannelli & Volpi* [1977] E.C.R. 557.
[87] Case 249/81, *Commission* v. *Ireland* [1982] E.C.R. 4005 at para. 18.
[88] Case 45/87, *Commission* v. *Ireland* [1988] E.C.R. 4929.
[89] Case 6/64 [1964] E.C.R. 585.
[90] Case 59/75 [1976] E.C.R. 91.
[91] Case 45/75 [1976] E.C.R. 181.
[92] Case 155/73, *Sacchi* [1974] E.C.R. 409; Case 271/81, *Société d'Insemination Artificielle* [1983] E.C.R. 2057. In the latter case the Court recognised the possibility that a monopoly over the provision of services might have an indirect influence on trade in goods.

requiring the licensing of particular activities is not sufficient to amount to a state monopoly of a commercial character.[93]

As from the end of the transitional period every national monopoly of a commercial character must have been adjusted so as to eliminate the exclusive right to import from other Member States.[94] Article 37 only applies to activities intrinsically connected with the specific business of the monopoly and is irrelevant to national provisions which have no connection with such specific business.[95] While, during the transitional period, Article 37 suspended the operation of Article 95, prohibiting discriminatory internal taxation,[96] as of the end of the transitional period, the position of internal taxes has been subject exclusively to Article 95.[97] Furthermore, while Article 37 permits the continuation of the obligation to deliver goods to the monopoly, and a corresponding obligation upon the monopoly to purchase such goods, Article 30 applies so as to ensure equal treatment of domestic goods and imports.[98] It thus seems that Article 37 is cumulatively applicable with the earlier provisions of the chapter on the elimination of quantitative restrictions, and perhaps the provision on customs duties and charges having equivalent effect.

In the second *Hansen* case,[99] arising from the operation of the German alcohol monopoly, the Court held: (i) that after the end of the transitional period, Article 37 remained applicable wherever the exercise by a state monopoly of its exclusive rights entailed a discrimination or restriction prohibited by that Article; (ii) that Article 37 prohibited a monopoly's right to purchase and resell national alcohol from being exercised so as to undercut imported products with publicly subsidised domestic products; and (iii) that Articles 37 and 92/93 were capable of cumulative application to one and the same fact situation.

In *Pigs and Bacon Commission* v. *McCarren*[1] the Court held that Article 38(2) of the Treaty[2] gave priority to the rules for the organisation of the agricultural markets over the application of Article 37. The better view is that this means merely that Article 37 cannot be pleaded by way of derogation from rules imposed by a common organisation: the positive obligations of the Article are surely to be implied into the framework of a common organisation and it is trite law that common organisations can derogate only in exceptional circumstances from the free movement provisions of the Treaty.[3]

Article 37(4) of the Treaty provides:

---

[93] Case 118/86, *Nertsvoederfabriek Nederland BV* [1987] E.C.R. 3883.
[94] Case 59/75, *Manghera* [1986] E.C.R. 91.
[95] Case 86/78, *Grandes Distilleries* [1979] E.C.R. 897.
[96] As to which, see *supra* at p. 205.
[97] Case 86/78 note 95.
[98] Case 119/78, *Grandes Distilleries* [1979] E.C.R. 975.
[99] Case 91/78 [1979] E.C.R. 935.
[1] Case 177/78 [1979] E.C.R. 2161.
[2] Art. 38(2) provides that "save as otherwise provided in Articles 39 to 46, the rules laid down for the establishment of the common market shall apply to agricultural products."
[3] Cases 80 & 81/77, *Commissionaires Reunis* [1978] E.C.R. 927; Case 83/78, *Redmond* [1978] E.C.R. 2347.

"If a State monopoly of a commercial character has rules which are designed to make it easier to dispose of agricultural products or obtain for them the best return, steps should be taken in applying the rules contained in this Article to ensure equivalent safeguards for the employment and standard of living of the producers concerned, account being taken of the adjustments that will be possible and the specialisation that will be needed with the passage of time."

In *Charmasson*[4] the Court emphasised that Article 37(4) had never allowed any derogation from Article 37. The "equivalent safeguards" referred to in Article 37(4) must themselves be compatible with the provisions of Article 37(1) and (2).

---

[4] Case 48/74 [1974] E.C.R. 1383.

CHAPTER 9

FREE MOVEMENT OF WORKERS

GENERAL

The Treaties establishing the European Communities each contain provisions designed to facilitate the movement of workers between the Member States. The signatories to the Treaty establishing the European Coal and Steel Community undertook in Article 69 to remove any restrictions based on nationality upon the employment in the coal and steel industries of workers holding the nationality of one of the Member States and having recognised qualifications in coal-mining or steel-making, and a similar provision appears in Article 96 of the Treaty establishing the European Atomic Energy Community, declaring the right of nationals of the Member States to take skilled employment in the field of nuclear energy. Acting under this latter Article the Council issued a Directive in 1962[1] defining the scope of skilled employment and requiring that Member States adopt all necessary measures to ensure that any authorisation required for taking up employment in the field specified should be automatically granted.

As Treaties concerned only with limited economic integration, the ECSC and Euratom Treaties naturally only dealt with workers in their respective sectors. The EEC Treaty, on the other hand, seeks to promote comprehensive economic integration, and its provisions requiring that "freedom of movement for workers shall be secured within the Community by the end of the transitional period at the latest" are applicable to all "workers of the Member States" regardless of occupation.[2] It is with the provisions of the EEC Treaty, and the implementing legislation made thereunder, that we shall be hereafter concerned.

Since a common market requires the removal of all obstacles to the free movement of the factors of production, as well as of goods and services, the free movement of workers in the Community may be seen simply as a prerequisite to the achievement of an economic objective. Support for this view may be found in the Spaak Report,[3] and in the texts of Articles 48, 49 and 51 of the Treaty. Under Article 48, workers of the Member States are to be free to accept offers of employment actually made, and to remain in a Member State for the purposes of carrying on employment. Article 49 authorises legislation by the Council to eliminate administrative procedures likely to impede the movement of workers, and to set up machinery for matching offers of employment in one Member State with available candidates in another. The provisions of Article 51 of the Treaty

---

[1] J.O. 1962 1650.
[2] Art. 48. But the EEC Treaty does not "affect" the provisions of the ECSC Treaty, nor "derogate" from those of the Euratom Treaty; see Art. 232 EEC.
[3] *Rapport des chefs de delegation aux ministres des affaires etrangères* (Brussels, April 21, 1856), pp. 18, 88.

empowering the Council to take legislative action in the field of social security appear to extend this authorisation only to measures necessary for safeguarding the rights of the migrant worker *stricto sensu*.

Yet such a functional economic approach to the interpretation of the free movement provisions is likely to be inadequate for two reasons. First, in the graphic words of Article 6 of the Clayton Anti-Trust Act, because of the notion that "the labour of a human being is not a commodity or article of commerce," or as Advocate General Trabucchi has put it: "The migrant worker is not regarded by Community law—nor is he by the internal legal system—as a mere source of labour but is viewed as a human being."[4] A similar sentiment may be discerned in the fifth recital to the preamble to Regulation 1612/68 of the Council,[5] which speaks of the exercise of workers' rights in "freedom and dignity," and describes freedom of movement for workers as a "fundamental right" and "one of the means by which the worker is guaranteed the possibility of improving his living and working conditions and promoting his social advancement, while helping to satisfy the requirements of the economies of the Member States." As Advocate General Jacobs has observed, "The recital makes it clear that labour is not, in Community law, to be regarded as a commodity and notably gives precedence to the fundamental rights of workers over satisfying the requirements of the economies of the Member States."[6]

But for another reason a purely economic approach is likely to be deficient. The EEC was established after the failure of rather more grandiose attempts to institute a Western European military and political union, and it represented an attempt to achieve a similar political aim by means of economic integration. Thus the first recital to the preamble to the Treaty of Rome records the determination of the signatories to lay the foundation of an ever closer union among the peoples of Europe, and the eighth records their resolve to strengthen peace and liberty by a pooling of their respective resources. The last sentence of Article 2 of the Treaty lays down as one of the Community's allotted tasks that of promoting closer relations between the Member States. To this extent, there may be said to be a political objective enshrined in the provisions relating to the free movement of persons. The halting steps of the Member States towards "European Union" are apparently taken in the belief that they are taking the Community concept to its logical conclusion. It is significant that the Declaration issued after the Summit Conference of October 1972 included the words: "The Member States reaffirm their resolve to base their Community's development on democracy, freedom of opinion, free

---

[4] Case 7/75, *Mr. and Mrs. F.* v. *Belgian State* [1975] E.C.R. 679 at p. 696; [1975] 2 C.M.L.R. 442 at p. 450.
[5] J.O. 1968 L257/2. The Court has referred to the fifth recital both as a guide to the interpretation of the Regulation, and as an indication of the scope of the application of the Treaty: Case 76/72, *Michel S.* [1973] E.C.R. 457; Case 9/74, *Casagrande* [1974] E.C.R. 773 (interpretation of Reg. 1612/68); Case 152/81, *Forcheri* [1983] E.C.R. 2323 (scope of application of the Treaty).
[6] Case 344/87, *Bettray* [1989] E.C.R. 1621 at p. 1637.

movement of men and ideas and participation by the people through their elected representatives."[7]

The Court of Justice has sometimes interpreted the provisions of Articles 48 to 51 of the Treaty, and the implementing legislation made thereunder, in a rather more liberal manner than would be dictated by a purely functional view of the Treaty based on its economic objectives. In *Hessische Knappschaft* v. *Maison Singer*[8] a German national on holiday in France had been killed in a road accident. His dependants were paid benefit by a German social security institution, which then brought an action in France against the employer of the driver of the other vehicle, claiming that the French court was bound to recognise the subrogation that German law allowed, by virtue of Article 52 of Regulation 3.[9] In the course of the proceedings before the Court of Justice, it was argued that to apply Article 52 of the Regulation in circumstances such as those before the national court would be incompatible with Article 51 of the Treaty, inasmuch as that provision only allowed the Council to adopt such measures as were necessary to provide freedom of movement for workers *qua* workers, not *qua* holidaymakers. The Court responded:

> "Since the establishment of as complete as possible a freedom of movement of labour is among the 'foundations' of the Community, it is the ultimate goal of Article 51 and, therefore, governs the exercise of the power it confers upon the Council. It would not be in keeping with such a concept to limit the idea of 'worker' to migrant workers strictly speaking or to travel connected with their employment. Nothing in Article 51 requires such a distinction; moreover, such a distinction would make the application of the contemplated rules unfeasible. On the other hand, the system adopted for Regulation No. 3, which consists in removing, as much as possible, the territorial limitations for applying the various social security systems, is quite in keeping with the objectives of Article 51 of the Treaty."[10]

It was in a similar spirit that the Court of Justice considered the purpose and effect of Regulation 1612/68[11] in *Commission* v. *Germany*[12] in the following terms:

> "It is apparent from the provisions of the regulation, taken as a whole, that in order to facilitate the movement of members of workers' families the Council took into account, first, the importance for the worker, from a human point of view, of having his entire family with him, and secondly, the importance, from all points of view, of the integration of

---

[7] Emphasis added. Bull. E.C. 10/72 at p. 15.
[8] Case 44/65 [1965] E.C.R. 965; [1966] C.M.L.R. 82.
[9] J.O. 1958, 561.
[10] [1965] E.C.R. 965 at p. 971; [1966] C.M.L.R. 82 at p. 94.
[11] Note 5, *supra*.
[12] Case 249/86 [1989] E.C.R. 1263.

the worker and his family into the host Member State without any difference in treatment in relation to nationals of that State."[13]

In Articles 8 and 8a of the Treaty on European Union provision is made for citizenship of the Union, under which any citizen of the Union shall have the right to move and reside freely within the territory of the Member States, subject to the limitations and conditions laid down in the Treaty and by measures adopted thereunder.[14] Under Article 8b every citizen of the Union residing in a Member State of which he is not a national shall have the right to vote and to stand as a candidate at municipal elections in the Member State in which he resides, under the same conditions as nationals of that State. In the concept of citizenship of the Union there appears to be manifested a purpose which transcends the economic requirements of the single market.

THE AMBIT OF ARTICLE 48 OF THE TREATY

Article 48 aims to secure freedom of movement for workers. While this provision may require Member States to amend their legislation, even with respect to their own nationals (for example to allow them to leave their own Member State to seek work in another),[15] it does not extend to situations wholly internal to a Member State,[16] for example the binding over of a person charged with theft on condition that she proceed to Northern Ireland and not return to England or Wales for three years.[17] A worker cannot rely upon Article 48 unless he or she has exercised the right to freedom of movement within the Community,[18] or is seeking to exercise that right, and the purely hypothetical possibility that an individual may at some time in the future seek work in another Member State is not sufficient.[19]

The application of Article 48 is not conditional upon all conduct pertaining to an economic relationship or activity occurring within the territory of the Member States: it applies in judging all legal relationships which can be localised with the Community, by reason either of the place where they were entered into, or the place where they take effect.[20]

THE CONCEPT OF "WORKER"

Article 48 refers to freedom of movement for "workers." Article 1 of Regulation 1612/68 (freedom of movement for workers within the Community) refers to the right to "take up an activity as an employed person." Neither formulation is defined,[21] but the concepts must be

---

[13] [1989] E.C.R. 1263 at p. 1290, para. 11.
[14] See *infra* at p. 277.
[15] See, *e.g.* Art. 2(1) of Dir. 68/360; see *infra* at p. 243.
[16] Case 175/78, *Saunders* [1979] E.C.R. 1129; Case 298/84, *Iorio* [1986] E.C.R. 247.
[17] *Ibid.*
[18] Cases 35, 36/82, *Morson* [1982] E.C.R. 3723.
[19] Case 180/83, *Moser* [1984] E.C.R. 2539.
[20] Case 36/74, *Walgrave* [1974] E.C.R. 1405; Case 237/83, *Prodest* [1984] E.C.R. 3153; Case 9/88, *Lopes da Veiga* [1989] E.C.R. 2989.
[21] Except for the purposes of Reg. 1408/71, on social security; see Art. 1(a).

interpreted according to their ordinary meaning, and in the light of the objectives of the Treaty.[22] The terms cannot be defined according to the national laws of the Member States,[23] but have a Community meaning.[24] Since these concepts define the field of application of one of the fundamental freedoms guaranteed by the Treaty, they must not be interpreted restrictively.[25] A person may be a "worker," or person pursuing an "activity as an employed person" even if engaged in only part-time work, and in receipt of pay below the minimum guaranteed wage in the sector in question.[26] However, the concepts cover only the pursuit of effective and genuine activities, and not activities on such a small scale as to be regarded as "marginal and ancillary."[27] Work cannot be regarded as an effective and genuine economic activity if it constitutes merely a means of rehabilitation or reintegration for the persons concerned and the purpose of the paid employment, which is adapted to the physical and mental capabilities of each person, is to enable those persons sooner or later to recover their capacity to take ordinary employment or to lead as normal as possible a life.[28] Furthermore, the motives which may have prompted a "worker" to seek employment in another Member State are of no account as regards his right to enter and reside in the territory of that State, provided that he pursues or wishes to pursue an effective and genuine activity.[29]

A person who has never been employed, and who goes to another Member State to study, is not to be regarded as a "worker," at any rate where he is not during his sojourn in the latter Member State subject to a social security scheme designed to benefit employed persons.[30]

The definition of "worker" in the Community sense rarely causes difficulty because if an economically active claimant under Article 48 is not a worker, he is as like as not self-employed, in which case Articles 52 or 59 EEC come into play. The Court has held that Articles 48, 52 and 59 are based on the same principles both as far as entry and residence and non-discrimination on grounds of nationality are concerned,[31] and so categorisation under Article 48, as opposed to Articles 52 or 59, will rarely be crucial.[32] Thus, for example, Member States are obliged to issue a residence permit to a national of another Member State if it is not disputed that that person is engaged in economic activity, without it being necessary in that regard to classify the activity as that of an employed or self-employed person.[33] Nevertheless, the distinction may be significant in certain cases,

---

[22] Case 53/81, *Levin* [1982] E.C.R. 1035.
[23] Though to some extent they are: in the context of the social security rules: see Reg. 1408/71, Art. 1(a); *infra* at p. 318.
[24] Case 75/63, *Hoekstra (née Unger)* [1964] E.C.R. 177; Case 53/81, *Levin* [1982] E.C.R. 1035.
[25] Case 53/81, *Levin* [1982] E.C.R. 1035; Case 139/85, *Kempf* [1986] E.C.R. 1741; Cases 389 and 390/81, *Echternach* [1989] E.C.R. 723.
[26] *Ibid.*
[27] *Ibid.*
[28] Case 344/87, *Bettray* [1989] E.C.R. 1621.
[29] Note 25, *supra*.
[30] Case 66/77, *Kuyken* [1977] E.C.R. 2311; Case 238/83, *Meade* [1984] E.C.R. 2631.
[31] Case 48/75, *Royer* [1976] E.C.R. 497; see *infra* at p. 288.
[32] See *infra* at p. 288.
[33] Case C–363/89, *Roux* [1991] E.C.R. I–273.

and a person who has worked only in a self-employed capacity in the relevant Member State cannot be regarded as a "worker" within the meaning of Article 48 of the Treaty and therefore cannot rely upon that provision.[34]

REMOVAL OF RESTRICTIONS ON MOVEMENT AND RESIDENCE IN THE MEMBER STATES

The Treaty provides that freedom of movement for workers shall entail the right to move freely within the Member States for the purpose of accepting offers of employment actually made and empowers the Council to implement this object by legislation. Acting under this authority the Council issued Directive 68/360 of October 15, 1968, on the abolition of restrictions on movement and residence for workers of the Member States and their families.[35] The provisions of Article 48 of the Treaty have been held to be directly applicable,[36] as have those of Directive 68/360.[37] As the Court explained in *Procureur du Roi* v. *Royer*,[38] "the directives concerned [including 68/360] determined the scope and detailed rules for the exercise of rights conferred directly by the Treaty."

Persons to whom Directive 68/360 is applicable

The Directive applies to nationals of the Member State and those members of their families to whom Regulation 1612/68 is applicable.[39] In Article 10(1) of the latter Regulation we find members of the worker's family defined as:

(a) his spouse and their descendants who are under the age of 21 years or are dependants[40];

(b) dependant[41] relatives in the ascending line of the worker and his spouse.

The Article declares that these members of the family, irrespective of nationality, have the right to "install" themselves with a worker who is a national of one Member State employed in the territory of another. In the *Morson* case[42] the Court held that Article 10(1) does not cover the relatives of a worker who is a national of the host State, and has never exercised the right of free movement. But it follows from the decision in *Surinder Singh*[43]

---

[34] Case C–15/90, *Middleburgh* [1991] E.C.R. I–4655.
[35] J.O. 1968 L257/13.
[36] Case 167/73, *Commission* v. *French Republic* [1974] E.C.R. 359; [1974] 2 C.M.L.R. 216; Case 41/74, *Van Duyn* v. *Home Office* [1974] E.C.R. 1337; [1975] 1 C.M.L.R. 1.
[37] Case 36/75, *Rutili* v. *French Minister of the Interior* [1975] E.C.R. 1219; [1976] 1 C.M.L.R. 140.
[38] Case 48/75, *Procureur du Roi* v. *Royer* [1976] E.C.R. 497; [1976] 2 C.M.L.R. 619.
[39] Art. 1.
[40] Dependency is a matter of fact and the reasons are immaterial: Case 316/85, *Lebon* [1987] E.C.R. 2811.
[41] *Ibid.*
[42] Cases 35 and 36/82, *Morson* [1982] E.C.R. 3723.
[43] Case C–370/90, judgment of July 7, 1992.

that Article 10(1) applies to members of the family where a worker of one Member State who has been employed in another returns to his Member State of origin. The members of the family referred to need not actually reside under the same roof as the worker, in order to claim the benefit of Article 10(1), and a spouse retains that status until the formal dissolution of the marriage.[44]

Article 10(2) of the Regulation provides that Member States shall "facilitate the admission" of dependent members of a worker's family other than children or those in the ascending line, and any members of the family living under the worker's roof in the country whence he came.

The right of the worker and members of his family to leave their home country in order to pursue employment in another Member State

The Directive deals not only with the right to enter other Member States, it also grants the right to leave one's own.[45] Member States are obliged to grant workers the right to leave their territory for the purpose of taking up activities as employed persons and pursuing such activities in the territory of another Member State. Members of their family enjoy the same right as the national on whom they are dependant. The exercise of this right is conditioned simply on the production of a valid identity card or passport, which Member States are under a duty both to issue and to renew. Passports must be valid for all Member States and for countries through which the holder must pass when travelling between Member States. Where a passport is the only document on which the holder may lawfully leave the country, its period of validity shall be at least five years. Member States may not demand exit visas or equivalent documents from workers or members of their families.

The right of a worker and members of his family to enter another Member State

Member States are required to allow the persons to whom Directive 68/360 applies to enter their territory simply on production of a valid identity card or passport.[46] No entry visas or equivalent documents may be demanded save from members of the family who are not EEC nationals. Member States must accord to such persons every facility for obtaining the necessary visas.[47] The Court has construed "entry visa or equivalent document" as covering any formality for the purpose of granting leave to enter the territory of a Member State which is coupled with a passport check

---

[44] Case 267/83, *Diatta* [1985] E.C.R. 567. In referring to "spouse," Art. 10(1) refers to a relationship based on marriage: see Case 59/85, *Reed* [1986] E.C.R. 1283.
[45] Art. 2.
[46] Art. 3(1).
[47] Art. 3(2).

at the frontier, whatever the place or time at which leave is granted, and in whatever form it may be granted.[48]

Article 48(3)(b) of the Treaty envisages free movement of workers for the purpose of accepting offers of employment actually made, but makes no mention of a right to move freely in search of employment. It would seem to follow that Member States are only bound to apply Article 3 of the Directive in the case of workers who have already been offered a job, but the Court of Justice in *Procureur de Roi* v. *Royer*[49] referred to the right of workers to enter the territory of a Member State and reside there for the purposes intended by the Treaty, in particular to look for or pursue an activity as an employed person. Such a construction of Article 48 is clearly consistent with its purpose and wording. Freedom of movement entails the abolition of any discrimination based on nationality between workers of the Member States as regards, *inter alia*, employment. In Article 7 of Regulation 1612/68 the notion of equality in matters of employment is construed by the Council as involving reinstatement and re-employment. Preventing a national of a Member State who has lost his job from entering another Member State to seek employment could be said to amount to discrimination based on nationality, since he would be restricted to seeking employment in that Member State via the postal services and his own local labour exchange. Article 69 of Regulation 1408/71[50] on the social security rights of migrant workers, in providing unemployment benefit to a national of one Member State seeking employment in another, certainly assumes that he will be admitted for such a purpose.

When the Council of Ministers was drafting Directive 68/360, it was understood that a worker entering a Member State for employment could stay for three months to find a job and thus qualify for residence, but no specific provision was made.[51] Consistently with this view, Regulation 1408/71, Article 69(1)(c) provides that entitlement to unemployment benefit under that Article should continue for no more than three months. In *Antonissen*[52] the Court considered whether national rules specifying a six-month period in which to find work were compatible with the right to enter and remain in a Member State in order to look for work. The Court held that in the absence of a Community provision prescribing the period during which Community nationals seeking employment in a Member State may stay there, a period of six months did not appear in principle to be insufficient to enable the persons concerned to apprise themselves, in the host Member State, of offers of employment corresponding to their occupational qualifications and to take, where appropriate, the necessary steps in order to be engaged, and therefore did not jeopardise the

---

[48] Case 157/79, *Pieck* [1980] E.C.R. 2171. But, for non-discriminatory checks of identity cards, see Case 321/87, *Commission* v. *Belgium* [1989] E.C.R. 997.
[49] Case 48/75 [1976] E.C.R. 497. This approach was confirmed in Case C–292/88, *Antonissen* [1991] E.C.R. I–745.
[50] J.O. 1971 L149/2; consolidated in Reg. 2001/83, O.J. 1983 L230/6.
[51] H. Ter Heide, 6 C.M.L.Rev. 466, 476. The U.K. allows a stay of six months: see Statement of Changes in Immigration Rules H.C. Papers (1982–83) 169, paras. 67, 70.
[52] Note 49, *supra*.

effectiveness of the principle of free movement. The Court added that if, after the expiry of the six-month period, the person concerned provided evidence that he was continuing to seek work, and that he had genuine chances of being engaged, he could not be required to leave the territory of the host Member State.

The right of residence

The worker, the worker's spouse, and children under age 21 years[53]

In accordance with Article 48(3)(c) of the Treaty, Directive 68/360 provides that Member States shall grant the right of residence to workers able to produce:

  (a) the document with which they entered the Member State's territory, and
  (b) a confirmation of engagement from an employer, or a certificate of employment.

In the case of a worker's spouse and children under the age of 21 years, the right of residence is acquired upon production of:

  (a) the document with which they entered the territory, and
  (b) a document proving their relationship, issued either by their State of origin, or the State whence they came.

Dependent children over the age of 21 years, and other dependent relatives in the ascending line of the worker and the worker's spouse[54]

In the case of the aforementioned, there is required in addition to the document with which they entered the territory a document testifying to their dependence, issued either by the State of origin or the State whence they came.

Dependent relatives other than children or those in the ascending line, and relatives living under the worker's roof in the country whence they came

According to Article 10(2) of Regulation 1612/68, such members of the family do not have a right of entry, much less a residence, merely on account of their relationship to the worker, and Member States are simply under an obligation to "facilitate" their admission. Directive 68/360, however, provides in Article 4(1) that Member States shall grant the right of residence to those persons: (a) referred to in Article 1 of the Directive; (b) who are able to produce the documents specified in Article 4(3). As to (a), Article 1 of the Directive refers to members of the worker's family to whom Regulation 1612/68 is applicable. Article 10(2) of that Regulation, as has been pointed out, indeed makes provision for the relatives in question,

---

[53] Dir. 68/360, Art. 4(3)(c), (d). A Member State is required to recognise the right of residence of workers if they are in possession of a valid identity card, even if that card does not allow the holder to leave the territory of the Member State in which it was issued: Case C–376/89, *Panagiotis Giagounidis* [1991] E.C.R. I–1069.
[54] Dir. 68/360, Art. 4(3)(e).

albeit to a limited extent. As to (b), Article 4(3)(e), in specifying those documents production of which gives rise to a right of residence, provides in pertinent part: "in the cases referred to in Article 10(1) and (2) of Regulation (EEC) No. 1612/68, a document issued by the competent authority . . . testifying that they are dependent on the worker or that they live under his roof in such country." Just as Article 4 assumes that the members of the family in question may claim a right of residence, so Article 3 suggests that they are entitled to enter a Member State simply on production of a valid identity card or passport, as "persons referred to in Article 1. . . ."

The contrary argument is that Article 4(1) of the Directive, in requiring Member States to grant a right of residence to a members of worker's family to whom Regulation 1612/68 is applicable, contemplates that this right of residence will be co-extensive with the right of "installation" granted by Article 10(1) of Regulation 1612/68 to spouse, children under 21 years or over that age and dependent, and dependent relatives in the ascending line, but not to the other relatives in question. A legislative intent to ensure the conformity of the Directive with the Regulation may be discerned in the first recital to the preamble to the former, which states: ". . . whereas, measures should be adopted . . . which conform to the rights and privileges accorded by the said Regulation to nationals of any Member States . . . and to members of their families."

It is doubtful whether a restrictive interpretation of Article 10 of Regulation 1612/68 would be consistent in all cases with the purposes of the Regulation. It would seem that dependent relatives in an analogous position to those specified in Article 10(1) of the Regulation could enter and reside as of right, for example a dependent guardian, or dependent brother or sister. One cannot imagine a more potent disincentive to immigration than the inability to provide a home for and personal support to a dependent relative for whom one has assumed responsibility. It is uncertain whether the Court of Justice would uphold the somewhat arbitrary distinctions necessitated by a restrictive interpretation.

The residence permit

Article 4 of Directive 68/360 provides that a residence permit shall be issued to the worker and members of his family who are nationals of Member States of the EEC, as proof of the right of residence. This document must include a statement that it has been issued pursuant to Regulation 1612/68 and to the measures taken by the Member States for the implementation of the Directive. The text of the statement is given in the Annex to the Directive. A member of a worker's family who is not a national of a Member State must be issued with a residence document having the same validity as that issued to the worker on whom he or she is dependent.[55]

The drafting of the provisions of the Directive relating to the issue,

---

[55] Art. 4(4).

validity, expiry and renewal of residence permits is not entirely satisfactory. Whereas Article 4(2) provides that a residence permit is issued as proof of the right of residence, subsequent provisions define the extent of the migrant's rights in terms of the validity of his or her permit. The conceptual confusion led the Tribunal de Première Instance of Liège in *Procureur du Roi* v. *Royer*[56] to seek a preliminary ruling from the Court of Justice on the question, *inter alia*, whether a worker's right of residence was conferred directly by the Treaty and the terms of Directive 68/360, or was conditional on the issue of a document drawn up by national authorities. The Court held that Article 48 vested rights directly in all persons falling within its ambit. Implementing legislation gave rise to no new rights in favour of persons protected by Community law, but simply determined the scope and detailed rules for the exercise of rights conferred directly by the Treaty. The grant of a permit was to be regarded "not as a measure giving rise to rights but as a measure by a Member State serving to prove the individual position of a national of another Member State with regard to provisions of Community law."[57] It followed that Member States were under a duty to grant the right of residence to any person who was able to prove, by producing the documents specified in Article 4(3) of the Directive, that he or she fell within one of the categories referred to in Article 1.

The Directive provides that completion of the formalities for obtaining a residence permit shall not hinder the immediate commencement of employment under a concluded contract.[58]

The residence documents granted to nationals of the Member States must be issued and renewed free of charge or on payment of an amount not exceeding the dues and taxes charged for the issue of identity cards to nationals. The visa which may be demanded of members of a worker's family who are not nationals of a Member State of the EEC shall be free of charge.[59]

Expiry and renewal of the residence permit

Although *Royer* and subsequent case-law[60] make it clear that a right of residence arises independently of the issue of a residence permit, the Directive defines the substantive rights of migrants in terms of the validity of their permits. The transference of thought is confusing, but it is proposed to adopt it for the sake of consistency with the terms of the Directive.

A residence permit, issued when the worker or member of his family satisfies the conditions stated in Article 4 of the Directive, must be valid throughout the territory of the Member State which issued it for a period of

---

[56] Case 48/75 [1976] E.C.R. 497.
[57] [1976] E.C.R. 497 at 513. No other permit may be required of workers of the Member States: Case 8/77, *Sagulo* [1977] E.C.R. 1495; Case 157/79, *Pieck* [1980] E.C.R. 2171. And see Cases 389 & 390/87, *Echternach* [1989] E.C.R. 723 at p. 762, para. 25, "The issue of such a permit does not create the rights guaranteed by Community law, and the loss of a permit cannot affect the exercise of those rights."
[58] Art. 5.
[59] Art. 9.
[60] Cases 389 & 390/87, *Echternach*, note 57.

at least five years from the date of issue, and be automatically renewable.[61] Although original acquisition of the residence permit requires a certification of employment, it must be noted that a valid residence permit may not be withdrawn from a worker solely on the grounds that he is involuntarily unemployed, this being duly confirmed by the competent unemployment office.[62] It would seem to follow that a worker who is voluntarily unemployed may have his permit withdrawn, *i.e.* lose his right of residence in the territory. This is certainly in accord with the scheme of Article 48 of the Treaty which guarantees residence for the purpose of seeking or engaging in activities as an employed person. An individual who is voluntarily unemployed can no longer be considered a "worker" within the meaning of Article 48.[63]

If a Member State wishes to terminate a residence permit valid for five years for any other reason apart from voluntary unemployment or prolonged absence, it must have resort to the proviso contained in Article 48(3) of the Treaty, to the effect that the rights defined therein are subject to limitations justified on grounds of public policy, public security or public health.[64]

At the end of a five-year period, a Member State is obliged to renew the document automatically for a further five years. The only exception to this, apart from cases of voluntary unemployment, prolonged absence, or the public policy proviso, is on the occasion of renewal of a residence permit for the first time. In this case, the period of residence may be restricted to a period of not less than 12 months, if the worker has been involuntarily unemployed for more than 12 consecutive months.[65] When this second, curtailed period of residence expires, it would seem that the worker has no right to an automatic renewal of his permit, and must acquire his right of residence afresh, by producing the documents referred to in Article 4 of the Directive, *i.e.* an entry document and a declaration of employment.

The validity of a residence permit is stated to be unaffected by either breaks in residence not exceeding six consecutive months, or absence on military service.[66] It would seem to follow that breaks in residence lasting longer than six consecutive months may provide grounds for withdrawal of a residence permit, and loss of the right of residence, pending compliance once again with the provisions of Article 4 of the Directive.

Temporary residence permit

Workers employed for periods exceeding three months but not exceeding a year must be issued with a temporary residence permit, the validity of which may be limited to the expected period of their employment.[67] Such a

---

[61] Art. 6.
[62] Art. 7(1).
[63] This follows from the reasoning in Case 53/81, *Levin* [1982] E.C.R. 1035.
[64] See *infra* at pp. 266 *et seq.*
[65] Art. 7(2).
[66] Art. 6(2).
[67] Art. 6(3).

permit is not stated to be automatically renewable, and on expiry the worker would be obliged to present anew the documents referred to in Article 4 of the Directive. Temporary residence permits are similarly issued to seasonal workers employed for more than three months. The period of employment must be indicated in the certificate of employment required, along with their entry document, for the acquisition of the residence permit.[68]

Recognition of the right of residence without the issue of permits

In three cases the Directive requires Member States to recognise the right of workers to reside in their territory without the issue of residence permits.[69] The first category comprises workers pursuing activities expected to last not more than three months. Presentation of the worker's entry document coupled with a certification from his employer stating the expected duration of his employment is sufficient to cover his stay.

The Directive makes similar provision for frontier workers, *i.e.* workers who, having their residence in one Member State to which they return in principle once a day or at least once a week, work in another Member State.[70] Although such a worker would prima facie be entitled to a full residence permit under Article 4 of the Directive (although, of course, he is not really "resident" at all), Article 8(1)(b) relieves the State where he is employed of any duty to provide such a permit, and provides that it may issue such a worker with a special permit valid for five years and automatically renewable.

The final category of workers, seasonal workers, has already been considered in the context of workers who must be issued with temporary residence permits. Such workers holding contracts of employment stamped by the competent authority of the Member State on whose territory they have come to work need not be issued with residence permits where they are employed for less than three months.[71]

In all three cases cited *supra*, the Member Sate may require the worker to report his presence in its territory.

The three "degrees" of residence

It will be appreciated that several groups of workers falling within Article 4 of the Directive enjoy varying degrees of "security of tenure" in the State of employment.

The first group, those who find a job of an expected duration of more than 12 months, receive a permit entitling them to at least six years' residence in the host State, providing, of course, that they do not become voluntarily

---

[68] *Ibid.*
[69] Art. 8.
[70] Dir. 68/360 does not use the term "frontier worker," but see Art. 1(b) of Reg. 1408/71. Does Art. 8(1)(b) intend to confer a right of "residence" in both the State of employment and the State of residence? The final sentence of the provision suggests only the former.
[71] Art. 6(3), second paragraph, and Art. 8(1)(c).

unemployed or conduct themselves in such a way as to fall within the scope of the "public policy proviso" of Article 48(3) of the Treaty.

The second group of workers comprises those who take up employment for a period of between three and 12 months, and seasonal workers who are employed for more than three months. Here security of residence is restricted by means of a temporary residence permit to the expected duration of the employment in question. Should such a worker become involuntarily unemployed, he would seem to retain his right of residence—by virtue of Article 7(1) of the Directive—until expiry of the temporary residence permit.

The final group of workers contemplated by Directive 68/360 have the most precarious right of all—the right to reside in a Member State only for the actual duration of their employment. This group comprises workers who expect to pursue employment for less than three months, seasonal workers employed for less than three months holding stamped employment contracts, and frontier workers. In the case of the latter, a "special residence permit" may be issued at the option of the host State. Such a permit must be valid for five years and be renewable automatically. On this occasion the context suggests that the Directive's reference to renewal of the permit is a reference to its formal validity rather than to the rights of its holder.

A right bestowed by the Treaty

The rights of workers may be rather less clear than the above scheme suggests, since their rights stem directly from the Treaty, and it is the function of secondary legislation merely to define their scope and provide the detailed rules for their employment. For instance, suppose a worker enters a Member State in search of a job. After three months he finds a job of an expected duration of six months. He is issued with a temporary residence permit for that period. After six months permit and employment expire. Is the worker entitled to remain in the Member State concerned for a reasonable time in order to seek further employment? The spirit of Article 48 suggests an affirmative answer: the text of the Directive the contrary. Other problems arise; how often is a worker entitled to enter the same Member State in search of employment? The answer to such questions may turn less on the interpretation of the detailed provisions of Community secondary legislation, than on the Court's view of the ambit of Article 48 itself. It is arguable that the latter Article requires absolute freedom of movement and residence for all nationals of the Member States engaged in employment or genuinely in search of it. On the other hand, Article 48 does not preclude a Member State from drawing distinctions between workers on the basis of the length and continuity of their relationship with that State.[72] A worker is entitled to remain in a Member State for a reasonable time seeking employment, but if it becomes apparent that he is unlikely to find a job, he may be required to return to his country of origin, or to the Member State

---

[72] *Cf.* Case 20/75, *D'Amico* v. *Landesversicherungsanstalt* [1975] E.C.R. 891.

where he was last employed.[73] An extended period of employment in a Member State, however, entitles an unemployed worker to the same opportunities as a member of the indigenous workforce, *i.e.* indefinite equal access to the host State's employment exchanges and unemployment benefits. On this view, the provisions of secondary legislation such as Directive 68/360 will be applicable to the extent that they regulate the modalities to the exercise of rights enjoyed directly under the Treaty, but ineffective to restrict their scope.

EQUALITY OF TREATMENT

Article 48(2) of the Treaty provides that freedom of movement for workers shall entail the abolition of any discrimination based on nationality between workers of the Member States as regards employment, remuneration and other conditions of work and employment. Although, as we shall see later, this prohibition is not restricted to national measures which directly relate to the employment context, it is restricted to discrimination which may, at least in principle, impede the free movement of persons. This may be why Article 48 does not exclude the right of Member States to adopt reasonable measures to keep track of the movement of aliens within their territory.[74] On the other hand, while Member States may impose penalties to compel compliance with the requirements of Community law relating to migrants, such penalties must be comparable to those attaching to the infringement of provisions of equal importance by nationals,[75] and such punishment must be proportional[76] to the gravity of the offences involved. However, where Community law permits differentiation between migrants and national workers, for instance in allowing Member States to require the possession of residence permits by aliens,[77] Member States may impose more serious penalties for infractions of such requirements than would be imposed in the case of the commission by nationals of comparable offences, for instance the failure to comply with the requirement that nationals possess identity cards.[78]

Whereas Directive 68/360 ensures entry and residence for Community workers, the right to equal treatment in respect of job opportunity and conditions of employment is governed by Regulation 1612/68 of October 15, 1968 on freedom of movement for workers within the Community.[79] Part I of the Regulation is divided into three Titles:

---

[73] Case C–292/88, *Antonissen* [1991] E.C.R. I–745 supports this approach.

[74] Case 118/75, *The State* v. *Watson and Belmann* [1976] E.C.R. 1185, discussed (1975–76) 1 E.L.Rev. 556. But a requirement that nationals of other Member States make a declaration of residence within three days of arrival is unreasonable and contrary to Community law: Case 265/88, *Messner* [1989] E.C.R. 4209.

[75] Case 118/75, note 74.

[76] For the concept of "proportionality," see *supra* at p. 89.

[77] As to which, see *supra* at p. 246.

[78] Case 8/77, *The State* v. *Sagulo* [1977] E.C.R. 1495, discussed (1977) 2 E.L.Rev. 445. It may be that Case 118/75, *Watson & Belmann*, note 74, may be explained on the basis that keeping track of aliens constitutes objective differentiation between nationals and non-nationals.

[79] J.O. 1968 L257/2.

— Eligibility for employment;
— Employment and equality of treatment; and
— Workers' families.

It is convenient to adopt the scheme of the Regulation for the purposes of exposition of its terms and discussion of the case law of the Court.

Eligibility for employment

The Regulation guarantees to workers the right to take up employment in the territory of a Member State with the same priority as the nationals of the State in question.[80] Employees and employers are entitled to exchange their applications for and offers of employment, and to conclude and perform contracts in accordance with "the provisions in force laid down by law, regulation or administrative action, without any discrimination resulting therefrom."[81]

National provisions, whether the result of legal regulation or administrative action, are stated to be inapplicable if they limit explicitly or implicitly the right of workers to take up and pursue employment.[82] An exception is made in the case of linguistic requirements necessitated by the nature of the post to be filled.[83] In the *Groener* case[84] the Court considered the compatibility with Regulation 1612/68 of national rules making appointment to a permanent full-time post as a lecturer in public vocational educational institutions conditional upon proof of an adequate knowledge of the Irish language. Knowledge of the Irish language was not required for the performance of the duties which teaching of the kind at issue specifically entailed. The Court held, however, that the post justified the requirement of linguistic knowledge, provided that the requirement in question was imposed as part of a policy for the promotion of the national language which was the first official language, and provided that the request was applied in a proportionate and non-discriminatory manner.

Article 3 of the Regulation itemises, as particular instances of the provisions declared inapplicable by the foregoing, those which:

"(a) prescribe a special recruitment procedure for foreign nationals;
(b) limit or restrict the advertising of vacancies in the press or through any other medium or subject it to conditions other than those applicable in respect of employers pursuing their activities in the territory of that Member State;
(c) subject eligibility for employment to conditions of registration with employment offices or impede recruitment of individual workers where persons who do not reside in the territory of that State are concerned."

---

[80] Art. 1(2).
[81] Art. 2.
[82] Art. 3(1).
[83] Art. 3(1), last sub-para.
[84] Case 378/87 [1989] E.C.R. 3967.

Article 4 of the Regulation provides that national rules restricting by number or percentage the employment of foreign nationals are to be inapplicable to nationals of the Member States. Alleged infringement of this requirement by the Republic of France gave rise to proceedings before the Court of Justice at the suit of the Commission.[85] Article 3(2) of the Code du Travail Maritime of 1926 provided that such proportion of the crew of a ship as was laid down by order of the Minister for the Merchant Fleet must be French nationals. Ministerial Orders of November 1960 and June 1969 provided that certain employments on board ship were restricted exclusively to French nationals, and an overall ratio was imposed of three French to one non-French. The Commission took the view that such legislation contravened Article 48 of the Treaty and Article 4 of Regulation 1612/68. The French Government argued that Article 48 of the Treaty had no application to sea transport, but nevertheless proceeded to lay a draft amendment before the French Parliament. No legislation was in the event forthcoming, and the Commission referred the matter to the Court of Justice under Article 169 of the Treaty, claiming a declaration that the failure of the French Republic to amend Article 3(2) of the Code in so far as it applied to nationals of the Member States amounted to a breach of Community law.

In order to appreciate the significance of the Court's ruling, it must be noted that the French Government insisted that no discrimination had in fact taken place, since oral instructions had been given not to apply Article 3(2) of the Code to Community nationals, and that no finding was made on this issue. The Court (holding that Article 48 indeed applied to sea transport) acknowledged that the objective legal situation was clear— namely, that Article 48 of the Treaty and Regulation 1612/68 were directly applicable in France—yet found that by failing to amend Article 3(2) of the Code du Travail Maritime in so far as it appeared to nationals of the Member States, France was in breach of her legal obligations. In view of the position adopted by the French Government to the effect that the non-discriminatory application of the offending Article was a matter of grace, not of law, she had thereby brought about an ambiguous situation creating uncertainty for those subject to the law. Such an admittedly "secondary" obstacle to equal access to employment was nevertheless caught by the general prohibition of Article 48, and the specific provisions of Article 4 of Regulation 1612/68.

Since covert discrimination can be as effective in excluding foreign workers as express legal provisions or administrative measures, the Regulation further provides that the engagement or recruitment of a national of one Member State for a post in another shall not depend on medical, vocational or other criteria which are discriminatory by comparison with those applied in the case of national workers.[86] Nevertheless, when an employer actually offers a job to a national of another Member State he may expressly condition this offer on the candidate undergoing a vocational test.[87]

---

[85] Case 167/73, *Commission* v. *French Republic* [1974] E.C.R. 359; [1974] 2 C.M.L.R. 216.
[86] Art. 6(1).
[87] Art. 6(2).

A worker seeking employment in a Member State other than his own is entitled to receive from its employment services the same assistance as that afforded to national workers.[88]

Equality in employment

Article 48(2) of the Treaty provides for the abolition of discrimination based on nationality in the terms and conditions of employment and this prohibition is reiterated and expanded in Article 7(1) of the Regulation, as follows:

> "A worker who is a national of a Member State may not, in the territory of another Member State, be treated differently from national workers by reason of his nationality in respect of any conditions of employment and work, in particular as regards remuneration, dismissal, and should he become unemployed, re-instatement or re-employment."

Infringement of the principle of equality will occur where national legislation expressly attaches different terms to the conditions of employment of national workers and workers from other Community countries. In *Marsman* v. *Rosskamp*,[89] a Dutch national resident in the Netherlands was employed in Gronau, in the Federal Republic. After becoming incapacitated as a result of an accident at work, he was dismissed by his employer. German legislation provided that seriously disabled workers could not be dismissed without the approval of the main public assistance office. While this protection extended to nationals resident outside Germany, it applied only to non-nationals within the jurisdiction. Mr. Marsman challenged the legality of his dismissal before the Arbeitsgericht, which sought a ruling from the Court of Justice as to whether a Community national in the position of Mr. Marsman was entitled to the same protection against dismissal as that afforded to German nationals. The Court replied in the affirmative, emphasising that the social law of the Community was based on the principle that the laws of every Member State were obliged to grant nationals of the other Member States employed in its territory all the legal advantages that it provided for its own citizens. A slightly more complex situation arises when legislation conditions certain advantages on criteria which, although theoretically applicable to nationals and non-nationals alike, will in practice be fulfilled only by nationals. The point is illustrated in *Württembergische Milchverwertung-Sudmilch* v. *Ugliola*.[90] The respondent in the main suit was an Italian national employed by the appellant concern in the Federal Republic. He performed his military service in Italy between May 1965 and August 1966, and claimed the right to have this period taken into account in calculating his seniority with his employer. German legislation provided that military service in the Bundeswehr was to be taken into account for such purposes, but made no

---

[88] Art. 5.
[89] Case 44/72 [1972] E.C.R. 1243.
[90] Case 15/69 [1969] E.C.R. 363.

similar provision for services in the forces of other States. The Bundesarbeitsgericht sought a preliminary ruling from the Court of Justice on the question whether Article 7 of Regulation 1612/68 entitled a Community national in the position of Mr. Ugliola to have military service in his home country taken into account for the purposes of the German legislation in question. In its observations to the Court, the German Government argued that the job-protection law was not discriminatory, since (a) it did not apply to nationals who served in the forces of other States and (b) it did not apply to non-nationals who served in the Bundeswehr.

Advocate General Gand regarded such an argument as tempting, but was not convinced, since performance of military service in the army of a Member State other than the one whose nationality was possessed was a hypothesis which the German Government agreed was quite theoretical. The Court agreed. The provisions of Community law in question prohibited Member States from indirectly establishing discrimination in favour of their own nationals. The Court's decision may be explained as follows. First, by recourse to the notion of discrimination itself, which comprises not only differentiation between the like, but also the failure to differentiate between the unlike.[91] Thus to treat non-nationals in the same way as nationals, where this results in disadvantage in view of an objective difference between their respective situations, is discriminatory. The principle is identical to that discussed in the context of measures having an equivalent effect to quantitative restrictions: fixing the same prices for domestic and imported goods can amount to discrimination against the latter where differing costs hinder their competitive disposal on the market.[92] Secondly, the prohibition on discrimination contained in Article 48 must be considered in the light of the preamble to the Treaty, which calls for the elimination of the barriers which divide Europe, and the words of Article 3(c), which prescribe the "abolition, as between Member States, of obstacles to freedom of movement for persons, services and capital." Realisation of these aims calls for no less than the assimilation of the several legal orders of the Member States to a single legal order within the sphere of operation of the Treaty. It follows that if the performance of military duties is to be taken into account in the employment context, it can amount to discrimination to differentiate between the flags of the Member States.

The Court was faced with the problem of allegedly indirect discrimination once more in *Sotgiu* v. *Deutsche Bundespost*.[93] The plaintiff, an Italian whose family lived in Italy, was employed by the German postal service. He received a separation allowance at 7.50 DM per day, on the same basis as workers of German nationality. In accordance with a Government circular the allowance paid to workers residing within Germany at the time of their recruitment was increased to 10 DM per day, while those workers residing abroad at the time of their recruitment—German and foreign alike— continued to receive the allowance at the old rate. *Sotgiu* invoked

---

[91] Case 13/63, *Italy* v. *Commission* [1963] E.C.R. 165.
[92] See *supra* at p. 219.
[93] Case 152/73, *Sotgiu* v. *Deutsche Bundespost* [1974] E.C.R. 153.

Regulation 1612/68 in the German courts, and the Bundesarbeitsgericht sought a ruling, *inter alia*, on whether Article 7(1) of the Regulation could be interpreted as prohibited discrimination on the basis of residence as well as on the basis of nationality. In the course of the arguments before the Court it became apparent that, although workers residing within Germany at the time of the recruitment indeed received a larger allowance, it was conditional on their willingness to move to their place of work, and in any event was no longer paid after two years. No such conditions were attached to payment of the allowance to workers residing abroad at the time of the recruitment.

The Court affirmed that Article 7 prohibited all covert forms of discrimination which, by the application of criteria other than nationality, nevertheless led to the same result. Such an interpretation was consonant with the fifth recital to the Regulation, which required that equality of treatment for workers be established in fact as well as in law. Application of criteria such as place of origin or residence, argued the Court, could, in appropriate circumstances, have a discriminatory effect in practice that would be prohibited by the Treaty and the Regulation. This would not, however, be the case where the payment of a separation allowance was made on conditions which took account of objective differences in the situation of workers, which differences could involve the place of residence of a worker when recruited. Similarly, the fact that in the case of one group of workers allowances were only temporary while in the case of another they were of unlimited duration, could be a valid reason for differentiating between the amounts paid. A factual assessment of the situation would of course be a matter for the national court.

In *Biehl*[94] the Court considered a national rule whereby overpaid tax deducted from salaries and wages was not repayable to taxpayers resident during only part of the year in the relevant Member State. The national tax administration argued that a difference in treatment between two distinct categories of taxpayers did not constitute discrimination if it was objectively justified, and that the rule prevented taxpayers from avoiding the effects of progressive taxation by spreading their tax liability between different States. The Court noted that there was a risk that the criterion of permanent residence in national territory would work in particular against taxpayers who were nationals of other Member States. The Court rejected the justification offered by the national tax authorities since a national rule such as that in issue was liable to infringe the principle of equal treatment in various situations; in particular where no income arose during the year of assessment to the temporarily resident taxpayer in the country which he had left or in which he had taken up residence. In such a situation, the taxpayer would be treated less favourably than a resident taxpayer because he would lose the right to repayment of the over-deduction of tax which a resident taxpayer would always enjoy. It followed in the Court's view that such a measure was contrary to Article 48(2). The *Biehl* case is not entirely

---

[94] Case C–175/88 [1990] E.C.R. I–1779.

satisfactory. Its ruling is based merely on the risk that non-nationals would be treated less favourably than nationals,[95] and the consequence of the ruling seems to be that such a national rule cannot be applied by the national court, even in a case in which the rule would produce neutrality as between residents and non-residents. Nevertheless, the Court has acknowledged that the coherence of the tax system may sometimes justify measures otherwise contrary to Article 48. Thus in *Backmann*[96] the Court held that, while a national rule making pension contributions tax-deductible but confining this advantage to contributions made in national territory was in principle contrary to Article 48, it could be justified where the counterpart of making such contributions tax-deductible was subjecting the resulting pensions to tax liability.

In order to ensure equality for Community workers in the employment context, Regulation 1612/68 provides that they shall have "by virtue of the same right and under the same conditions as national workers . . . access to training in vocational schools and retraining centres."[97] Similarly, they are entitled to equality of treatment as regards membership of trade unions and the exercise of rights attaching thereto, including the right to vote.[98]

Freedom from discrimination for Community workers, although limited explicitly to the employment context in the Treaty, could not be achieved without requiring appropriate adjustments to all fields of national law and practice which might be likely to have an effect on the conditions under which migrants take up and pursue employment. Thus Article 7(2) of the Regulation provides that a national of one Member State employed in another "shall enjoy the same social and tax advantages as national workers." The wording and context of the Article suggest that it might be restricted to social and tax advantages conferred by national law *qua* worker, but the Court of Justice has taken a more liberal view, as its judgment in *Fiorini* v. *SNCF*[99] illustrates. French legislation provided that in families of three or more children under the age of 18 years, the father, mother, and each child under 18 years should receive a personal identity card entitling them to a reduction of between 30 and 75 per cent. in the scheduled fare charged by the Société Nationale des Chemins de Fer Français (SNCF). The Cour d'Appel of Paris sought a preliminary ruling from the Court of Justice on the question whether the reduction card issued by the SNCF to large families constituted for the workers of the Member States a "social advantage" within the meaning of Article 7(2) of the Regulation. The SNCF, in its observations to the Court, argued that Article 7(2) referred exclusively to advantages attaching to the nationals of Member States by virtue of their status as workers, and accordingly had no

---

[95] In Case 33/88, *Allue and Coonan* [1989] E.C.R. 1591 the Court found indirect discrimination where "only" 25 per cent. of persons affected were nationals of the host State. *Ibid.* at para. 12 of judgment.

[96] Case C–204/90, judgment of January 28, 1992.

[97] Art. 7(3).

[98] Art. 8, as amended by Reg. 312/76, O.J. 1976 L39/2.

[99] Case 32/75 [1975] E.C.R. 1985; [1976] 1 C.M.L.R. 573.

application to a benefit such as the reduction card issued by the SNCF. The Court rejected this view, reasoning as follows:

> "Although it is true that certain provisions in this article refer to relationships deriving from the contract of employment, there are others, such as those concerning reinstatement and re-employment should a worker become unemployed, which have nothing to do with such relationships and even imply the termination of a previous employment.
>
> It therefore follows that, in view of the equality of treatment which the provision seeks to achieve, the substantive area of application must be delineated so as to include all social and tax advantages, whether or not attached to the contract of employment, such as reductions in fares for large families."[1]

The Court has subsequently held that Article 7(2) applies to any benefit payable by virtue of an individual's status as a worker, or residence on national territory, where the extension of the benefit to nationals of other Member States seems suitable to facilitate free movement of workers.[2] Applying this test, the Court has excluded from the ambit of Article 7(2) early retirement on full pension for those in receipt of an invalidity pension granted by an Allied Power in respect of war service.[3] The abovementioned formulation has on the other hand been held to cover seven-year interest-free means-tested loans to families in respect of newly born children, even though the loans were of a discretionary nature.[4] Benefits held to fall within the ambit of the Article include an allowance to handicapped adults covered by Regulation 1408/71 on social security[5]; a guaranteed minimum subsistence allowance[6]; the possibility of using one's own language in court proceedings[7]; a special unemployment benefit for young persons falling outside the ambit of Regulation 1408/71[8]; an old-age benefit for those lacking entitlement to a pension under the national social security system[9]; and a guaranteed minimum income for old persons.[10]

Article 8 of the Regulation provides that a worker who is a national of a Member State and who is employed in the territory of another Member State shall enjoy equality of treatment as regards membership of trade unions and the exercise of rights attaching thereto, including the right to vote and to be eligible for the administration and management posts of a trade union. He may, however, be excluded from taking part in the management of bodies governed by public law and from holding an office governed by public law.[11]

---

[1] [1975] E.C.R. 1985 at p. 1094, 1095; [1976] 1 C.M.L.R. 582.
[2] Case 107/78, *Even* [1979] E.C.R. 2019.
[3] *Ibid.*
[4] Case 65/81, *Reina* [1982] E.C.R. 33.
[5] Case 63/76, *Inzirillo* [1976] E.C.R. 2057.
[6] Case 249/83, *Hoecks* [1985] E.C.R. 973; Case 122/84, *Scrivner* [1985] E.C.R. 1027.
[7] Case 137/84, *Mutsch* [1985] E.C.R. 2681.
[8] Case 94/84, *Deak* [1985] E.C.R. 1873.
[9] Case 157/84, *Frascogna* [1985] E.C.R. 1739.
[10] Case 261/83, *Castelli* [1984] E.C.R. 3199.
[11] See Case C–213/90, *Association de Soutien aux Travailleurs Immigrés* [1991] E.C.R. I–3507.

The Regulation recognises the importance of freely available housing to the migrant worker when it provides that he shall "enjoy all the rights and benefits accorded to national workers in matters of housing, including ownership of the housing he needs."[12] He may also, "with the same right as nationals, put his name down on the housing lists in the region in which he is employed, where such lists exist; he shall enjoy the resultant benefits and priorities." If the workers' family have remained in the country whence he came, they must be considered, for the purposes of priority on housing lists, as residing in the area where the worker is employed, where national workers benefit from a similar presumption.[13]

WORKERS' FAMILIES

Under Article 10 of Regulation 1612/68, the following members of a worker's family are entitled to install themselves with the worker in the host State:

"(a) his spouse and their descendants who are under the age of 21 years or are dependants[14];
(b) dependent[15] relatives in the ascending line of the worker and his spouse."

In the case of other members of the family who are dependent on the worker, or who were living under his roof in the country whence he came, Article 10(2) requires merely that Member States shall "facilitate" their admission.

The migrant is obliged to provide housing for his family that is considered normal for national workers in the region where he is employed. This requirement must not, however, give rise to discrimination between national workers and workers from other Member States.[16] Since discrimination must not occur in fact or in law, housing must be "considered normal" when it attains a standard equivalent to that actually enjoyed by workers in the region, even though such a standard may not accord with officially recommended levels of occupancy, or even legal requirements. The discriminatory application of national rules in themselves non-discriminatory could clearly amount to a breach of the Treaty. The Court has held that once normal housing has been made available, and the family brought together, the fact that housing ceases to be normal, because, for example, of the birth of a child, cannot justify non-renewal of the residence permit.[17]

Although the protection of the Regulation is limited to workers who are nationals of the Member State, their spouses and children under 21 years or

---

[12] Art. 9(1).
[13] Art. 9(2).
[14] The status of dependency is a result of a factual situation, namely the provision of support by the worker, without there being any need to determine the reasons for recourse to such support: see Case 316/85, *Lebon* [1987] E.C.R. 2811.
[15] *Ibid.*
[16] Art. 10(3).
[17] Case 249/86, *Commission* v. *Germany* [1989] E.C.R. 1263.

dependent, regardless of nationality, are entitled to take up employment throughout the territory in which the worker is employed.[18]

The third recital of the preamble to Regulation 1612/68 describes freedom of movement as a fundamental right of workers and their families, and indeed, genuine equality for the worker would be a chimera if the members of his family could be deprived of social advantages in the host State on account of their nationality. Thus Article 12 provides that the children of a worker residing in the territory of a Member State shall be admitted to that State's general educational, apprenticeship and vocational training courses under the same conditions as nationals of that State. This provision clearly bestows rights directly upon such children, although the second paragraph of Article 12, to the effect that "Member States shall encourage all efforts to enable such children to attend courses under the best possible conditions," is not directly effective, and provides merely an admonition to Member States as to the spirit in which they should apply the first paragraph of that Article, and a guide to courts in its interpretation.

The Court of Justice has had cause to interpret Article 12 on several occasions. In *Michel S.* v. *Fonds national de reclassement social des handicapés*,[19] the plaintiff in the main suit was the mentally handicapped son of a deceased Italian national who had worked as a wage-earner in Belgium. He was refused benefit from a national fund established to assist persons of Belgian nationality whose chances of employment had been seriously diminished by physical or mental handicap. The Court, having declared that Article 7 of the Regulation protected workers, but not their families, went on to consider Article 12, drawing on the wording of the fifth recital of the preamble as an aid to its interpretation. According to the Court, the "integration" contemplated by the preamble presupposed that the handicapped child of a foreign worker would be entitled to take advantage of benefits provided by the law of the host country for rehabilitation of the handicapped on the same basis as nationals in a similar position. No conclusion to the contrary could be drawn from the failure of the Council explicitly to mention such benefits in the text of the Article; rather, this omission could be explained by the difficulty of including all possible hypotheses.

The Court's liberal approach to the text of Article 12 in *Michel S.* was followed in *Casagrande* v. *Landeshaupstadt München*,[20] in which the son of a deceased Italian national who had worked as a wage-earner in the Federal Republic was refused, on grounds of nationality, a means-tested educational grant under a Bavarian statute. The Bayerisches Verwaltungsgericht sought a ruling from the Court of Justice on the consistency of such discriminatory provisions with Article 12. The Court resorted once again to the fifth recital of the Regulation's preamble. Read with the words of the second paragraph of Article 12, it became apparent that the Article guaranteed not simply

---

[18] Art. 112. See Case 131/85, *Gul* [1986] E.C.R. 1263.
[19] Case 76/72 [1973] E.C.R. 457.
[20] Case 9/74 [1974] E.C.R. 773, and see Case 68/74, *Alaimo* v. *Prefect of the Rhone* [1975] E.C.R. 109.

access to educational courses, but all benefits intended to facilitate educational attendance. In *Echternach*[21] the Court held that Article 12 of Regulation 1612/68 refers to any form of education, including university courses in economics and advanced vocational studies at a technical college. The Court also accepted that a child of a worker of a Member State, which latter has been in employment in another Member State, retains the status of member of a worker's family within the meaning of the Regulation when that child's family returns to the Member State of origin and the child remains in order to continue his studies, which he could not pursue in the Member State of origin.

The Court has retreated from its position in *Michel S.* that Article 7 of the Regulation protects workers but not their families. This will not be the case where the survivors of a worker living in the State where he was last employed claim a social advantage granted to the dependants of survivors of national workers in similar circumstances. In *Fiorini*, it will be recalled that the widow of a deceased Italian national applied for a reduced fare card on French national railways. The Court of Justice held that Article 7(2) must be interpreted as meaning "that the social advantages referred to by that provision include fares reduction cards issued by a national railway authority to large families and that this applies, even if the said advantage is only sought after the worker's death, to the benefit of his family remaining in the same Member State."[22] In *Inzirillo*,[23] the Court, dealing with a reference on the scope of Regulation 1408/71, observed that the protection of Article 7(2) of Regulation 1612/68 extended to handicapped dependant adult children of a worker who have installed themselves with the worker in accordance with Article 10 of Regulation 1612/68. More recently, in *Castelli*,[24] and *Frascogna*,[25] the Court has held that Article 7(2) is intended to protect, as well as workers themselves, their dependant relatives in the ascending line who have installed themselves with the worker. It follows from the above cases that any member of a worker's family who is entitled to, and does, install himself with the worker, is also entitled to equal treatment with nationals of the host State in the grant of all social and tax advantages. The rationale of this proposition would seem to be the deterrent effect upon free movement for workers which would result from the possibility of discriminating against dependent members of his family.[26] The Treaty basis of this right to equality in the relatives (as opposed to rights vested in the workers) is to be found in Article 7 EEC. Indeed, the Commission argued as much in *Fiorini*. Support for this view is to be found in the *Forcheri*[27] case, which held that discrimination against a national of one Member State lawfully established in another in the provision of vocational training

---

[21] Case 389/87 [1989] E.C.R. 723.
[22] [1975] E.C.R. 1085 at 1095.
[23] Case 63/76 [1976] E.C.R. 2057.
[24] Case 261/83 [1984] E.C.R. 3199.
[25] Case 157/84 [1985] E.C.R. 1739.
[26] Case 63/76, *Inzirillo* [1976] E.C.R. 2057, para. 17 of the judgment. And see Case 316/85, *Lebon* [1987] E.C.R. 2811 at para. 11 of judgment.
[27] Case 152/82 [1983] E.C.R. 2323. See also Case 293/83, *Gravier* [1985] E.C.R. 593. For vocational training see Chap. 22.

infringed Article 7 EEC. The plaintiffs in the national proceedings were a Commission official and his wife (the latter being the victim of the alleged discrimination). The Court's reasoning appears to be based on Article 7 EEC, the Court being of the opinion that vocational training fell squarely within the "scope of application of the Treaty."

RESIDENCE AFTER RETIREMENT OR INCAPACITY

The preamble to Regulation 1251/70 of June 29, 1970,[28] describes the right of workers to remain in the territory of a Member State after having been employed there as a corollary to the freedom of movement secured by Regulation 1612/68 and Directive 68/360. The Regulation applies to nationals of one Member State who have worked in the territory of another, and to the members of their family referred to in Article 10 of Regulation 1612/68.

The right of workers to remain in a Member State after having been employed there

The Regulation grants a right of residence after termination of employment to two classes of workers—the retired and the incapacitated. A worker acquires a right of residence on retirement provided; (i) that he has reached the age laid down by the law of the host State for entitlement to an old-age pension; (ii) that he has been employed in the host State for at least 12 months; and (iii) that he has resided continuously in the host State for more than three years.[29]

A worker who ceases employment as a result of permanent incapacity acquires a right to remain if he has resided in the host State for at least two years. If the permanent incapacity is the result of an accident at work, or an occupational disease entitling him to a pension for which an institution of the host State is entirely or partially responsible, he is entitled to remain regardless of the length of his previous residence.[30]

The above rules assume that a worker is employed and resident in the same Member State, but Regulation 1251/70 also makes limited provision for workers who live in one State while working in another. In the case of a worker who has completed three years' continuous employment and residence in the territory of one Member State, and then takes up employment in the territory of another, periods of employment completed in the latter are taken into account for the purposes of establishing a right to remain in the former State on retirement or in the event of incapacity, providing that the worker retains his residence in the former State, to which he returns, as a rule, each day, or at least once a week.[31] The preamble to the Regulation, after rehearsing the importance of guaranteeing to workers who

---

[28] J.O. 1970 L142/24. And see Dir. 90/365, J.O. 1990 L180/28, *infra* at p. 277.
[29] Art. 2(1)(a).
[30] Art. 2(1)(b).
[31] Art. 2(1)(c).

have been resident and employed in a Member State the right to remain after ceasing work through retirement or incapacity, continues: "it is equally important to ensure that right for a worker who, after a period of employment or residence in the territory of a Member State, works as an employed person in the territory of another Member State while still retaining his residence in the territory of the first State." It is difficult to see why this general consideration should be limited in its application to "frontier workers." Suppose a national of Member State X works and resides in Member State Y, and then takes a job in Member State Z, returning to his home and family in Member State Y every two weeks. On retirement, Regulation 1251/70 apparently gives him no right of residence in Member State Y, where his home and family are located. Such differentiation between workers residing in a State other than that of employment would seem to be arbitrary, and unjustified by the object and purpose of Article 48 of the Treaty.

In order to establish the requisite periods of residence, retiring or incapacitated workers are entitled to adduce any evidence normally accepted in the country of residence. Continuity is not affected by temporary absences totalling up to three months per year, nor by longer absences due to military service.[32] Periods of involuntary unemployment, duly recorded by the competent employment office, and absences due to illness or accident, are treated as equivalent to periods of employment.[33]

A retiring or incapacitated worker is not bound to fulfil the requisite periods of employment or residence if his spouse is a national of the Member State in question, or lost that nationality as a result of marriage to the worker.[34]

Once a worker has acquired a right to remain in a Member State under the terms of Regulation 1251/70, he has two years in which to decide whether or not to exercise it. During this period he is free to leave the territory of the State in question without prejudice to his right of permanent residence, which may be exercised without formality.[35]

Rights of workers' families

If a retiring or incapacitated worker has acquired a right of residence in a Member State, the members of his family to whom the Regulation applies are entitled to remain in the host State after his death.[36]

If, however, a worker dies during his working life and before having acquired a right of residence, members of his family are nevertheless entitled to remain, provided that: (a) the worker, at the date of his death, has resided continuously in the territory of that Member State for at least two years; or (b) his death resulted from an accident at work or an

---

[32] Art. 4(1).
[33] Art. 4(2).
[34] Art. 2(2).
[35] Art. 5.
[36] Art. 3(1).

occupational disease; or (c) the surviving spouse is a national of the State of residence or lost the nationality of that State by marriage to the worker.[37]

Equality of treatment

The right to equality of treatment provided by Regulation 1612/68 is also enjoyed by the beneficiaries of Regulation 1251/70.[38] As far as the survivors of workers are concerned, this seems at first sight to provide but a slender guarantee, since the provisions apparently applicable are those contained in Title III of that Regulation, headed Workers' Families, and covering: (a) the right to take up employment in a Member State (Art. 11); and (b) the right to equal access to educational and vocational facilities (Art. 12). Social security rights would be safeguarded by Regulation 1408/71, but what of rights classified as "social assistance," excluded from the ambit of Regulation 1408/71 by Article 4(4) of that Regulation? Article 7(2) of Regulation 1612/68 would seem to provide a right to such benefits *qua* "social . . . advantages," but in *Michel S.*[39] the Court held that Article 7(3) of the Regulation had no application to the families of workers, only to workers themselves. However, it will be recalled that in *Fiorini*,[40] the Court countenanced a claim founded on Article 7(2) being brought by the survivors of a worker. Thus the survivors of a deceased worker who enjoy the right to remain in a Member State are entitled to the same "social and tax advantages" as the survivors of national workers.

Residence permits

Persons who have acquired a right to remain in the territory of a Member State are entitled to receive a residence permit which must be valid throughout the territory of the issuing State for a period of at least five years, and be automatically renewable. Any charge made must not exceed the amount charged to nationals for the issue or renewal of identity documents.[41]

Periods of non-residence not exceeding six consecutive months may not affect the validity of a residence permit, but it would seem to follow that periods exceeding six months may affect such validity.[42] Whether absence exceeding six months is capable of prejudicing a person's substantive right to remain is unclear, since the function of the permit is not made explicit. It will be recalled that Article 4(2) of Directive 68/360 provides that the residence permit therein described be issued as proof of the right of residence,[43] but subsequent provisions, in particular Article 7, suggest that withdrawal of the

---

[37] Art. 3(2).
[38] Art. 7.
[39] Case 9/74 [1974] E.C.R. 773.
[40] Case 32/75 [1975] E.C.R. 1085. See also Case 261/83, *Castelli* [1984] E.C.R. 3199, and Case 157/84, *Frascogna* [1985] E.C.R. 1739.
[41] Art. 6(1).
[42] Art. 6(2).
[43] *Supra* at p. 246.

residence permit has substantive implications. The better view would seem to be that Article 6 of Regulation 1251/70 provides for the possible forfeiture of the right to remain in a Member State in the event of non-residence exceeding six months. It is difficult to discern any other purpose in the provision.

Derogation from national rules

The provisions of the Regulation in no way derogate from national rules more favourable to Community workers.[44] An express provision to this effect is probably unnecessary, since the Court has often expressed the view that the free movement provisions of the Treaty authorise legislative action only to improve the legal situation in which the worker would have found himself but for the Community rules.[45]

Admittance of workers without a strict right to residence

The Regulation places a duty on Member States to "facilitate readmission" to their territories of workers who have left after a long period of residence and employment and wish to return when they have reached retirement, or become incapacitated.[46] The legal effect of such a generalised provision is unclear. It can hardly be said to provide a right of re-entry; its terms are far too vague for that, nor can it be said to provide a principle in light of which related provisions must be interpreted.[47] At best it would seem to provide a principle account of which must be taken by national authorities when considering whether or not a person falling within the relevant category ought to be readmitted to national territory.

LIMITATIONS JUSTIFIED ON GROUNDS OF PUBLIC POLICY, PUBLIC SECURITY OR PUBLIC HEALTH

General

Article 48(3) of the Treaty subjects the free movement of workers to limitations justified on grounds of public policy, public security or public health. The text makes it clear that the exception limits the right itemised in the third paragraph of the Article, but not the right to equality in terms and conditions of employment guaranteed in Article 48(2). As Advocate General Gand explained in *Ugliola*, "on grounds of public policy or public security a foreigner may not be permitted to enter a country and take up

---

[44] Art. 8(1).
[45] See, *e.g.* Case 191/73, *Niemann* v. *Bundesversicherungsanstalt für Angestellte* [1974] E.C.R. 571; Case 27/75, *Bonaffini* v. *INPS* [1975] E.C.R. 971.
[46] Art. 8(2).
[47] *Cf. Casagrande*, in which the second paragraph of Art. 12 of Reg. 1612/68 was resorted to as an aid to interpretation of the first, *supra* at p. 260.

employment there, but those considerations have no bearing on conditions of work once employment has been taken up in an authorised manner."[48]

The Court agreed; the proviso applied only to "the cases expressly referred to in paragraph 3."[49]

Since Article 48(3) can be invoked to exclude a worker from the territory of a Member State, it would seem to follow that the exception could justify a partial restriction on residence, but this is not the case. In *Rutili* v. *French Minister of the Interior*,[50] an Italian national resident in France was issued with a residence permit subject to a prohibition on residence in certain French departments. The Court of Justice held that the reservation contained in Article 48(3) had the same scope as the right subject to limitation. It followed that any prohibition on residence could be imposed only in respect of the whole of the national territory. In the case of partial prohibitions on residence Article 7 of the Treaty required that persons covered by Community law must be treated on a footing of equality with nationals of the host State.

The Court held in the *Pieck* case[51] that the public policy proviso in Article 48(3) did not amount to a condition precedent to the acquisition of a right of entry and residence, but provided a possibility, in individual cases where there was sufficient justification, of imposing restrictions on the exercise of a right derived directly from the Treaty. It did not therefore justify general formalities at the frontier other than the simple production of a valid identity card or passport.

Directive 64/221

The scope of Article 48(3) may be clarified by reference to Directive 64/221 of February 25, 1964, on the co-ordination of special measures concerning the movement and residence of foreign nationals which are justified on grounds of public policy, public security or public health.[52] The Directive *in toto* gives rise to rights in individuals which national courts are bound to safeguard.[53]

The Directive applies to workers of one Member State travelling to or residing in another for the purpose of employment, and to members of their families.[54] It declares that the proviso may not be invoked to serve economic ends.[55] All measures relating to entry, the issue and renewal of residence permits, and expulsion, which are taken by Member States on grounds of public policy, public security or public health, are subject to its terms,[56] and

---

[48] Case 15/69 [1969] E.C.R. 363 at p. 365; [1970] C.M.L.R. 194 at p. 200.
[49] [1969] E.C.R. 363 at p. 369; [1970] C.M.L.R. 194 at p. 202. This suggests that the right to enter a Member State in search of work must be founded on Art. 48(3), rather than upon 48(2): see Case C–292/89, *Antonissen* [1991] E.C.R. I–745 at para. 13 of judgment.
[50] Case 36/75 [1975] E.C.R. 1219; [1976] 1 C.M.L.R. 140.
[51] Case 157/79, [1980] E.C.R. 2171.
[52] J.O. 1964, 850.
[53] Case 36/75, *Rutili* [1975] E.C.R. 1219.
[54] Art. 1.
[55] Art. 2(2).
[56] Art. 2(1).

must be based on the personal conduct of the individual concerned.[57] Previous criminal convictions, while no doubt relevant to the assessment of an individual's conduct, do not in themselves constitute grounds for applying the proviso.[58] These requirements are central to the protection afforded to individuals by Article 48(3) and Directive 64/221, as *Bonsignore v. Oberstadt-direktor Cologne*[59] illustrates. Carmelo Bonsignore, an Italian worker resident in the Federal Republic, unlawfully acquired a Beretta pistol, with which he accidentally shot his younger brother Angelo. He was fined for unlawful possession of a firearm, and deportation was ordered by the Chief Administrative Office of the City of Cologne. A reference to the Court of Justice sought a ruling on the question whether Article 3(1) and (2) of the Directive was to be interpreted as excluding deportation of a national of a Member State for the purpose of deterring other foreign nationals from such offences, or whether expulsion was only permissible when there were clear indications that an EEC national, who had been convicted of an offence, would himself commit further offences or in some other way disregard public security or public policy. "As departures from the rules concerning the free movement of persons constitute exceptions which must be strictly construed," declared the Court, "the concept of 'personal conduct' expresses the requirement that a deportation order may only be made for breaches of the peace and public security which might be committed by the individual affected."[60] In *R. v. Bouchereau*,[61] however, Advocate General Warner expressed agreement with the Government of the United Kingdom that "cases do arise, exceptionally, where the present conduct of an alien has been such that, whilst not necessarily evincing any clear propensity on his part [to indulge in future misbehaviour], it has caused such deep public revulsion that public policy requires his departure."[62] The Court apparently took a similar view. While emphasising that "The existence of a previous criminal conviction can therefore only be taken into account insofar as the circumstances which gave rise to that conviction are evidence of personal conduct constituting a present threat to the requirements of public policy," and admitting that, "in general, a finding that such a threat exists implies the existence in the individual concerned of a propensity to act in the same way in the future," the Court added that "it is possible that past conduct alone may constitute such a threat to the requirements of public policy."[63] It was for the national authorities, and, where appropriate, national courts, to consider each individual case in the light of the legal position of persons subject to Community law and the fundamental nature of the principle of the free movement of persons. It

---

[57] Art. 3(1).
[58] Art. 3(2). The word "measure" in Art. 3(1) and (2) includes a recommendation for deportation under the Immigration Act 1971: Case 30/77, *R. v. Bouchereau* [1977] E.C.R. 1999.
[59] Case 67/74 [1975] E.C.R. 297.
[60] [1975] E.C.R. 297 at p. 307.
[61] Case 30/77 [1977] E.C.R. 1999.
[62] [1977] E.C.R. 1999 at p. 2022.
[63] [1977] E.C.R. 1999 at p. 2012. For possible circumstances when past conduct may justify deportation, see Wyatt, (1978) 15 C.M.L.Rev. 221 at pp. 224, 225.

seems clear, as Advocate General Warner notes, that it will only be in the most exceptional cases that past conduct will of itself be capable of justifying deportation.

The Directive explicitly provides that expiry of an identity card or passport used to enter the host country and obtain a residence permit shall not justify expulsion, and furthermore, that the State which issued such travel documents should allow the holder to re-enter its territory without formality even if the document is no longer valid, or the nationality of the holder is in dispute.[64]

Grounds of "public health," as well as "public policy" and "public security," justify recourse to the proviso. The fourth recital to the preamble to the Directive declares that it would be of little practical use to compile a list of diseases and disabilities which might endanger public health, public policy or public security, and that it is sufficient to classify such diseases and disabilities in groups. The result is an Annex to the Directive, comprising a Group A—diseases and disabilities which might threaten public health (infectious diseases), and a Group B—diseases and disabilities which might threaten public policy or public security (such as drug addition or mental illness). Article 4 of the Directive provides that the only diseases or disabilities justifying refusal of entry into a territory or refusal to issue a first residence permit are those listed in the Annex. Diseases or disabilities occurring after a first residence permit has been issued do not justify refusal to renew the residence permit or expulsion from the territory.[65]

In addition to the substantive safeguards referred to above, the Directive also provides a number of procedural safeguards.

Decisions to grant or refuse a first residence permit must be taken as soon as possible and in any event not less than six months after the date of application for the permit, and the worker is entitled to remain in the territory of the host State pending a decision in his particular case.[66] Although a Member State may, if it thinks essential, request the Member State of origin of the applicant for details of any criminal record, and the latter State is obliged to respond within two months, such inquiries must not be made as a matter of routine.

The individual concerned must always be officially notified of any decision to[67] refuse the issue or renewal of a residence permit, or to expel him from the territory, and of the time allowed him to leave. Save in cases of urgency, this period must not be less than 15 days where the person has not yet been granted a residence permit, and not less than a month in all other cases.[68]

In order to allow workers an opportunity to safeguard their rights, Article 6 of the Directive provides that in all cases the individual concerned is entitled to be informed of the grounds of public policy, public security or

---

[64] Art. 3(3), (4).
[65] Art. 4(2).
[66] Art. 5.
[67] Art. 5.
[68] Art. 7.

public health upon which the decision taken in his case was based, unless to do so would be contrary to the interests of the security of the State involved.

With respect to decisions relating to entry, the refusal to issue or renew a residence permit, or expulsion, the person concerned is entitled to the same legal remedies as are available to nationals of the State concerned in respect of acts of the administration.[69]

There are three types of case in which a decision refusing renewal of a residence permit or ordering the expulsion of the holder of a residence permit must not be taken—save in cases of urgency—until an opinion has been obtained from a competent authority of the host country before which the person concerned enjoys such rights of defence and representation as are provided by domestic law.[70] These three types of case are: (i) where there is no right of appeal to a court of law; (ii) where such an appeal lies only in respect of the legal validity of the decision; (iii) where the appeal cannot have suspensory effect. The purpose of recourse to the "competent authority"[71] is, in the first case, to compensate for the absence of a right of appeal to the courts; in the second case to enable a detailed examination to be made of the situation of the person concerned, including the appropriateness of the measure contemplated, before the decision is finally taken; and in the third case to permit the person concerned to request and to obtain, if appropriate, a stay of the execution of the measure envisaged in such a way as to compensate for the absence of a right to obtain a stay of execution from the courts.

The "competent authority" referred to in Article 9 of Directive 64/221 must not be the same as that empowered to take the decision refusing renewal of the residence permit or ordering expulsion.[72] It must be independent of the administration, but Member States are given a margin of discretion as to the nature of the authority.[73] Thus it has been held that a recommendation for deportation made by a criminal court at the time of conviction may constitute an opinion of competent authority within the meaning of Article 9 of the Directive.[74] However, such an opinion must be sufficiently proximate in time to the decision ordering expulsion to ensure that there are no new factors to be taken into account occurring between the opinion and the decision, liable to deprive the opinion of its useful effect.[75]

Where a decision is taken refusing the issue of a first residence permit, or ordering expulsion of the person concerned before the issue of the permit, the worker must be entitled to refer the decision for reconsideration by the competent authority referred to above, where he can submit his defence in person.[76]

The Court of Justice considered Articles 6, 8 and 9 of the Directive in

---

[69] Art. 8. The Article is directly effective: Case 131/79, *Santillo* [1980] E.C.R. 1585.
[70] Art. 9(1). Art. 9 is directly effective: Case 131/79, *Santillo* [1980] E.C.R. 1585.
[71] Case 98/79, *Pecastaing* [1980] E.C.R. 691.
[72] Art. 9(1).
[73] Case 131/79, *Santillo* [1980] E.C.R. 1585, para. 15 of judgment; Cases 115 and 116/81, *Adoui* [1982] E.C.R. 1665.
[74] *Santillo*, para. 17 of judgment.
[75] *Santillo*, but see [1981] 2 All E.R. 897, C.A.
[76] Art. 9(2).

Rutili v. *French Minister of the Interior*,[77] and concluded that any person enjoying the protection of these provisions was entitled to a double safeguard comprising notification to him of the grounds on which any restrictive measure had been adopted and the availability of a right of appeal. The Court added that all steps should be taken by Member States to ensure that the double safeguard was in fact available to anyone against whom a restrictive measure had been adopted. "In particular," declared the Court, "this requirement means that the State concerned must, when notifying an individual of a restrictive measure adopted in his case, give him a precise and comprehensive statement of the grounds for the decision to enable him to take effective steps to prepare his defence."[78]

The question of the relationship between Articles 8 and 9 of the Directive arose in *Procureur du Roi* v. *Royer*,[79] in which the Tribunal de Première Instance of Liège sought a ruling from the Court of Justice on the question, *inter alia*, whether a decision ordering expulsion or a refusal to issue a residence permit would give rise to immediate measures of execution or whether such a decision could only take effect after the exhaustion of national remedies. The Court held that in the case of the remedies referred to in Article 8 of Directive 64/221, the person concerned must at least have the opportunity of lodging an appeal and thus obtaining a stay of execution before the expulsion order was carried out. If no remedy was available, or if it was available, but did not have suspensive effect, the decision could not be taken—save in cases of urgency which had been properly justified—until the party concerned had had the opportunity of appealing to the competent authority referred to in Article 9 of the Directive, and until this authority had reached a decision. Referring to the right of appeal provided for in Articles 8 and 9 of the Directive, the Court declared that "this guarantee would become illusory if the Member State could, by the immediate execution of a decision ordering expulsion, deprive the person concerned of the opportunity of effectively making use of the remedies which he is guaranteed by Directive No. 64/221."[80]

The Court returned to the relationship between Articles 8 and 9 in *Pecastaing*.[81] In its view Article 9 would be rendered nugatory unless expulsion were suspended pending the giving of the opinion of the competent authority (save, that is, in cases of urgency). But there was no analogous requirement in the case of Article 8. While a decision ordering expulsion could not be executed (save in cases of urgency) before the party concerned was able to complete the formalities necessary to avail himself of the national remedy contemplated by Article 8, it could not be inferred from that provision that the person concerned was entitled to remain on the territory of the State concerned throughout the proceedings initiated by him.

---

[77] Case 36/75 [1975] E.C.R. 1219.
[78] [1975] E.C.R. 1219 at 1233.
[79] Case 48/75 [1976] E.C.R. 497.
[80] [1976] E.C.R. 497 at p. 516.
[81] Case 98/79 [1980] E.C.R. 691.

In the case of decisions concerning entry, it will be noted that Article 8 is applicable, but that Article 9 is not, since the latter provision conspicuously omits such decisions.

The area of discretion left to national authorities under Article 48(3)

The area of discretion left to national authorities in the application of Article 48(3) has been clarified in a number of decisions of the Court of Justice, in particular *Van Duyn*,[82] *Rutili*,[83] *Bouchereau*,[84] and *Adoui*.[85]

Miss Van Duyn was a Dutch national who had been offered employment as a secretary with the Church of Scientology at its College at East Grinstead. Since the United Kingdom Government regarded Scientology as objectionable, socially harmful, and damaging to the health of its practitioners, it had announced its intention in 1968 of taking all steps within its power—short of legal prohibition—to curb its growth. Accordingly, Miss Van Duyn was refused leave to enter the United Kingdom. Alleging violation of her rights as a Community national under Article 4 of the Treaty, and Article 3 of Directive 64/221, she sought a declaration in the High Court to the effect that she was entitled to enter the United Kingdom to take up her employment at East Grinstead. The High Court posed the question, *inter alia*, whether:

> "a Member State, in the performance of its duty to base a measure taken on grounds of public policy exclusively on the personal conduct of the individual concerned is entitled to take into account as a matter of personal conduct:
> (a) the fact that the individual is or has been associated with some body or organisation whose activities the Member State considers contrary to the public good but which are not unlawful in that State;
> (b) the fact that the individual intends to take employment in the Member State with such body or organisation, it being the case that no restrictions are placed upon nationals of the Member State who wish to take similar employment with such body or organisation."

On the first point the Court, acknowledging that a person's past association could not, in general, justify refusal of entry, declared that nevertheless present association, reflecting participation in the activities of the organisation as well as identification with its aims or designs, could be considered as a voluntary act of the person concerned and, consequently, as part of his personal conduct within the meaning of the Article cited. As to the fact that the United Kingdom authorities had not prohibited the practice of Scientology, the Court took the view that although Article 48(3), as an exception to a fundamental freedom under the Treaty, must be interpreted

---

[82] Case 41/74 [1974] E.C.R. 1337.
[83] Case 36/75 [1975] E.C.R. 1219.
[84] Case 30/77 [1977] E.C.R. 1999.
[85] Cases 115 & 116/81 [1982] E.C.R. 1665.

strictly, nevertheless the Member States were allowed a margin of discretion, inasmuch as the particular circumstances justifying recourse to the concept of public policy might vary from one country to another and from one period to another. "It follows," the Court said, ". . . that where the competent authorities of a Member State have clearly defined their standpoint as regards the activities of a particular organisation and where, considering it to be socially harmful, they have taken administrative measures to counteract these activities, the Member State cannot be required, before it can rely on the concept of public policy, to make such activities unlawful, if recourse to such a measure is not thought appropriate in the circumstances."[86] The fact that the result of the policy of the United Kingdom authorities was to bar employment to non-national Community workers while allowing similar employment to United Kingdom nationals seemed to raise no further issue of principle for the Court. The very essence of the exception was that it enabled national authorities to treat non-nationals in a discriminatory fashion. "It follows," declared the Court, "that a Member State . . . can, *where it deems necessary* [emphasis added], refuse a national of another Member State the benefit of the principle of freedom of movement for workers . . . where such a national proposes to take up a particular offer of employment even though the Member State does not place a similar restriction upon its own nationals."[87]

The Court's decision in *Van Duyn* introduces a subjective element into the application of Article 48(3) that is apparently at odds with its statement that "its scope cannot be determined unilaterally by each Member State without being subject to control by the institutions of the Community."[88] But it must be remembered that the Court was faced with a very limited question—whether or not, *in principle*, a State was entitled to take into account the factors indicated. This question is answered in the affirmative. It did not have to examine the circumstances in which such factors could justify an exclusion in a particular case. Such a question was posed to the Court in *Rutili* v. *French Minister of the Interior*.

The plaintiff in the main suit was an Italian resident in France, who had incurred the displeasure of the French authorities as a result of political, and allegedly subversive, activities. He was issued with a residence permit subject to a prohibition on residence in certain departments. Mr. Rutili brought proceedings before the Tribunal Administratif for the annulment of the decision limiting the territorial validity of his residence permit. During the proceedings before the Tribunal, the argument was advanced that Mr. Rutili's presence in the departments prohibited to him was "likely to disturb public policy." Two questions were referred to the Court for a preliminary ruling. The first asked whether the expression "subject to limitations justified on grounds of public policy" in Article 48(3) of the Treaty concerned merely legislative decisions of the Member States, or whether it concerned also individual decisions taken in application of such legislative

---

[86] [1974] E.C.R. 1337 at p. 1350.
[87] [1974] E.C.R. 1337 at p. 1351.
[88] [1974] E.C.R. 1337 at p. 1350.

decisions. The second question sought the precise meaning to be attributed to the word "justified."

On the first question, the Court held that inasmuch as the object of the provisions of the Treaty and of secondary legislation was to regulate the situation of individuals and to ensure their protection, it was also for the national courts to examine whether individual decisions were compatible with the relevant provisions of Community law.

The Court then considered the meaning to be given to the word "justified" in Article 48(3). Since the exception was a derogation from a fundamental freedom granted by the Treaty, and must be interpreted strictly, it followed, argued the Court, that "restrictions cannot be imposed on the right of a national of any Member State to enter the territory of another Member State, to stay there and to move within it unless his presence or conduct constitutes a genuine and sufficiently serious threat to public policy (emphasis added)."[89] The Court concluded:

> "Taken as a whole, these limitations placed on the powers of Member States in respect of control of aliens are a specific manifestation of the more general principle, enshrined in Articles 8, 9, 10 and 11 of the Convention for the Protection of Human Rights and Fundamental Freedoms, signed in Rome on November 4, 1950, and ratified by all the Member States, and in Article 2 of the Protocol No. 4 of the same Convention, signed in Strasbourg on September 16, 1963, which provide, in identical terms, that no restrictions in the interests of national security or public safety shall be placed on the rights secured by the above-quoted articles other than such as are necessary for the protection of those interests in a democratic society."[90]

The Court thus makes explicit the test of "proportionality" in the judicial review of individual decisions taken on the basis of Article 48(3). The principle of "proportionality"—whereby legal authorisation of legislative or administrative action to a particular end extends only to those measures which, being apt to achieve the permitted end are, objectively speaking, least burdensome to those subject to the law—is well established in the jurisprudence of the Court of Justice. The principle may be invoked as a result of the express wording of the Treaty or implementing legislation, or as one of the basic principles of law which the Court of Justice is bound to safeguard.[91]

In *R. v. Bouchereau*, the Court added a glass to its statement in *Rutili*. Not only must the threat to the requirements of public policy be "genuine and sufficiently serious," but the requirements invoked must affect "one of the fundamental interests of society."[92]

The *Van Duyn*[93] decision seems in retrospect to have formulated

---

[89] [1975] E.C.R. 1219 at p. 1231.
[90] [1975] E.C.R. 1219 at p. 1232.
[91] Case 11/70, *International Handelsgesellschaft* [1970] E.C.R. 1125.
[92] Case 30/77 [1977] E.C.R. 1999 at 2014, para. (35).
[93] Case 41/74 [1974] E.C.R. 1337.

somewhat generous criteria for the exercise of national discretion under Article 48(3). In *Adoui*[94] the Court stressed that while Article 48(3) allowed different treatment for aliens than for its own nationals (since Member States could not expel their own nationals), it did not authorise measures which discriminated against nationals of other Member States on arbitrary grounds. The Court amplified its reference in *Bouchereau*[95] to "a genuine and sufficiently serious threat affecting one of the fundamental interests of society," as follows:

> "Although Community law does not impose upon the Member States a uniform scale of values as regards the assessment of conduct which may be considered as contrary to public policy, it should nevertheless be stated that conduct may not be considered as being of a sufficiently serious nature to justify restrictions on the admission to or residence within the territory of a national of another Member State in a case where the former Member State does not adopt, with respect to the same conduct on the part of its own nationals, repressive measures or other genuine and effective measures to combat such conduct."[96]

It is clear that the national judge, in assessing the legality of action by national authorities under Article 48(3), must decide whether such action is "excessive" with regard to the threat to public policy posed by the individual concerned. In making such an assessment, he must take as his yardstick the view which the national authorities take of such conduct when engaged in by nationals, for although Article 48(3) by its nature permits discrimination, such discrimination must not be arbitrary.

It is interesting to note that the Court refers in *Rutili* to the European Convention on Human Rights, ratified, as the Court points out, by all the Member States. The Court's concern for the maintenance of basic rights within the sphere of operation of the Treaty has been expressed on several occasions, but generally as a constraint of Community action. The Court's judgment in *Rutili* was an early indication that Treaty provisions binding on the Member States will be interpreted by the Court in the light of the fundamental freedoms guaranteed by the European Convention.[97] If *Van Duyn* supports the proposition that the "categories" of national interest which are eligible for protection under the proviso may vary in time and space[98] without prejudicing the uniform application of Community law, *Rutili* and subsequent cases emphasise that the extent to which such interests may be safeguarded will be subject to strict judicial control.

Naturally, each Member State has its own rules for controlling the entry of aliens and their residence in national territory. The decision of the Court in *Royer*[99] makes it clear that failure to comply with national immigration formalities cannot of itself provide grounds for expulsion under Article

---

[94] Cases 115 & 116/81 [1982] E.C.R. 1665.
[95] Case 30/77 [1977] E.C.R. 1999.
[96] Cases 115 & 116/81 [1982] E.C.R. 1665, para. 8 of judgment.
[97] See *supra* at p. 100.
[98] *Adoui* reaffirms this proposition: see note 96.
[99] Case 48/75 [1976] E.C.R. 497.

48(3). Mr. Royer, a Frenchman, had been expelled from Belgium for failing to comply with national formalities concerning the residence of aliens. He returned to Belgium, and was tried for the offence of illegal residence in the Kingdom. The Tribunal de Première Instance of Liège sought a ruling from the Court on the question, *inter alia*, whether the mere failure of an EEC national to comply with local entry formalities could provide a ground for expulsion under Article 48(3). The Court replied in the negative. While Community law did not prevent Member States providing sanctions for breaches of national law relating to the control of aliens, such sanctions could not include expulsion. "Since it is a question of the exercise of a right acquired under the Treaty itself," said the Court, "such conduct cannot be regarded as constituting in itself a breach of public policy or public security."[1] The view of the Court accords with the principle enunciated in *Schluter & Maack* v. *Hauptzollamt Hamburg-Jonas*[2]—national requirements may be attached to rights arising under Community law, but not as a precondition to their exercise. Any other solution would prejudice the uniform application of Community law. From another perspective, it could simply be said that such minor infringements as those in issue could never amount to the genuinely and sufficiently serious threat to public policy required by the terms of Article 48(3).

THE PUBLIC SERVICE PROVISO

Article 48(4) of the Treaty declares that the "provisions of this Article shall not apply to employment in the public service." The provision does not apply to all employment in the public service, nor does it allow discrimination in the terms and conditions of employment once appointed. This much is clear from the judgment of the Court in *Sotgiu* v. *Deutsche Bundespost*,[3] in which the Bundesarbeitsgericht sought a ruling from the Court on the question whether or not Article 7 of Regulation 1612/68 was applicable to employees in the German postal service in view of this proviso. The Court replied that since the exception contained in Article 48(4) could not be allowed a scope extending beyond the object for which it was included, the provision could be invoked to restrict the admission of foreign nationals to certain activities in the public service, but not to justify discrimination once they had been admitted.[4]

The Court further clarified the scope of Article 48(4) in *Commission* v. *Belgium* (Case 149/79, No. 1), holding that that Article:

". . . removes from the ambit of Article 48(1)–(3) a series of posts which involve direct or indirect participation in the exercise of powers conferred by public law and duties designed to safeguard the general interests of the State or of other public authorities. Such posts in fact

---

[1] [1976] E.C.R. 497 at 513.
[2] Case 94/71 [1972] E.C.R. 307.
[3] Case 152/73 [1974] E.C.R. 153.
[4] See Case 225/85, *Commission* v. *Italy* [1987] E.C.R. 2725, and Cases 389 & 390/87, *Echternach* [1987] E.C.R. 723.

presume on the part of those occupying them the existence of a special relationship of allegiance to the State and reciprocity of rights and duties which form the foundation of the bond of nationality."[5]

Thus not all posts in the public service fall within the public service proviso. In the Court's view, to extend Article 48(4) to posts which, while coming under the State or other organisations governed by public law, still do not involve any association with tasks belonging to the public service properly so-called, would be to remove a considerable number of posts from the ambit of the principles set out in the Treaty and to create inequalities between the Member States according to the different ways in which the State and certain sectors of economic life are organised.

Nevertheless, classification of particular posts can cause difficulty. In *Commission* v. *Belgium* (Case 149/79, No. 2),[6] the Courts approved the Commission's concession that the following posts fell within the ambit of Article 48(4): head technical office supervisor, principal supervisor, works supervisor, stock controller, and nightwatchman, with the Municipalities of Brussels and Auderghem. The Court also upheld the Commission's view that a number of other jobs with Belgian National Railways, Belgian Local Railways, the City of Brussels, and the Commune of Auderghem, fell outside Article 48(4). These jobs included railway shunters, drivers, platelayers, signalmen and nightwatchmen, and nurses, electricians, joiners and plumbers employed by the Municipalities of Brussels and Auderghem.

Whereas access to the posts in question will often be direct, it might also be by promotion from other posts which could not be classified along with those "certain activities" to which access may be limited. It would seem to follow that Article 48(4) should be read as permitting discrimination against Community nationals already holding posts in the public service, insofar as promotion to "sensitive" posts is concerned. This consideration was argued by the German Government in *Commission* v. *Belgium*[7] to militate against construing Article 48(4) as only applying to certain posts within the public service, rather than to the public service at large. The Court's reply was that applying Article 48(4) to all posts in the public service would impose a restriction on the rights of nationals of other Member States which went further than was necessary to achieve the aims of the proviso.

The Court has held that the following posts do not qualify for application of the public service proviso: a nurse in a public hospital,[8] a trainee teacher,[9] and a foreign language assistant at a university.[10]

---

[5] Case 149/79 [1980] E.C.R. 3881.
[6] Case 149/79 [1982] E.C.R. 1845.
[7] Case 149/79 [1980] E.C.R. 3881.
[8] Case 307/84, *Commission* v. *France* [1986] E.C.R. 1725.
[9] Case 66/85, *Lawrie-Blum* [1986] E.C.R. 2121.
[10] Case 33/88, *Allue and Coonan* [1989] E.C.R. 1591.

RIGHT OF RESIDENCE FOR PERSONS OTHER THAN THE ECONOMICALLY ACTIVE

It is appropriate to refer to three other Directives which bestow rights of residence upon individuals, subject to certain conditions. The first is Directive 90/365,[11] on the right of residence for employees and self-employed persons who have ceased their occupational activity. The second is Directive 90/366,[12] on the right of residence of students enrolled on vocational training courses. The third is Directive 90/364,[13] on the right of residence of those persons who do not enjoy this right under any other provision of Community law.

CITIZENSHIP OF THE UNION

Article 8 of the Treaty, as amended by the Treaty on European Union provides that every person holding the nationality of a Member State shall be a citizen of the Union, and that citizens of the Union shall enjoy the rights conferred by the Treaty and shall be subject to the duties imposed thereby. Article 8a(1) provides that every citizen of the Union shall have the right to move and reside freely within the territory of the Member States, subject to the limitations and conditions laid down in the Treaty and by the measures adopted to give it effect. Under Article 8a(2) the Council may adopt provisions with a view to facilitating the exercise of the rights referred to in Article 8a(1), and save as otherwise provided in this Treaty, the Council shall act unanimously on a proposal from the Commission and after obtaining the assent of the European Parliament.

---

[11] O.J. 1990 L180/28.
[12] O.J. 1990 L180/30. The Directive was based on Art. 235 and the Parliament challenged the legal basis, alleging that it should have been based on Art. 7: Case C–295/90, *Parliament* v. *Council*, judgment of July 7, 1992. For vocational training, see Chap. 22.
[13] O.J. 1990 L180/26.

CHAPTER 10

THE RIGHT OF ESTABLISHMENT AND THE FREEDOM TO PROVIDE SERVICES

INTRODUCTION

As well as ensuring the free movement of workers, the Treaty guarantees the right of establishment, and the freedom to provide services between Member States: what Article 48 provides for the employee, Articles 52 and 59 provide for the employer, the entrepreneur and the professional.

The right of establishment is the right of a natural person or a company to settle in a Member State and to pursue economic activities therein.[1] It involves "the actual pursuit of an economic activity through a fixed establishment in another Member State for an indefinite period."[2] It includes the right to take up and pursue an occupation in a self-employed capacity, and to set up and manage undertakings.[3]

The right of establishment is to be contrasted with the freedom to provide services. The former entails settlement in a Member State for economic purposes, and connotes permanent integration into the host State's economy. The latter entails a person established in one Member State providing services in another, as in the case of a doctor established in France visiting a patient in Belgium. The distinction may not always be clear-cut, because the provision of services may involve temporary residence in the host State, as in the case of a German firm of business consultants which advises undertakings in France, or a construction company which erects buildings in a neighbouring country. As long as such residence is temporary the activities in question will fall within the ambit of Articles 59–66, on freedom to provide services[4]; if it is permanent, they will be regulated by the provisions governing the right of establishment. It is evident that the provision of services from one State to another on a regular basis, accompanied by temporary residence in the host State, may shade imperceptibly into establishment. The separate legal treatment of these related concepts has been criticised. Not only is it said to be somewhat arbitrary from an economic standpoint, but it is alleged to lead to

---

[1] Brita Sundberg-Weitman, *Discrimination on Grounds of Nationality* (1977), p. 179; W. van Gerven, (1966) 3 C.M.L.Rev. 344

[2] Case C–221/89, *Factortame* [1991] E.C.R. I–3905 at para. 20. Registration of a vessel does not necessarily involve establishment, but it may be impossible to dissociate such registration from establishment, [1991] E.C.R. I–3905 at paras. 21, 22.

[3] Art. 52, second para. Case 182/83, *Fearon* [1984] E.C.R. 3677.

[4] Art. 60, third para. provides: "Without prejudice to the provisions of the Chapter relating to the right of establishment, the person providing a service may, in order to do so, temporarily pursue his activity in the State where the service is provided, under the same conditions as are imposed by that State on its own nationals. Where the activities of a person established in one Member State are directed principally towards the territory of another, the rules relating to establishment rather than services may apply": Case 33/74, *Van Binsbergen* [1974] E.C.R. 1299 at p. 1309, para. 13.

unnecessary difficulties of classification.[5] Nevertheless, while the legal and factual obstacles to a non-national establishing himself in the host State may in many cases be the same as those confronting persons established in one Member State and seeking to provide services in another, some problems are specific to each category. In particular, Article 52 seeks principally to guarantee national treatment to non-nationals established within the host State.[6] Article 59 allows non-national undertakings to do business in a Member State without setting up an establishment there, and without necessarily being subject to all the rules which apply to undertakings established in that Member State.[7]

Certain occupational activities, on the other hand, appear to fall within the ambit of neither Article 52 nor Article 59. How, for instance, would one classify the activities of a British camera crew filming scenes in France and Germany? On a strict construction of Articles 52 and 59, taking each Article individually, the crew would seem to be neither establishing themselves, nor providing or receiving services. Such a conclusion—that there may be "gaps" between the scope of Article 52 and Article 59—would seem to conflict with the object of the Treaty to create a single market between the Member States. A more satisfactory solution would be to consider Articles 52 and 50 as a whole, and in the light of the object and purpose of the Treaty. On this view, the chapters on establishment and freedom to provide services would be interpreted as requiring the fullest possible freedom of movement for self-employed persons wishing to engage in economic activities, regardless of the stage of provision or distribution of the service involved. The British film crew would be entitled to entry into and residence in France and Germany on the basis of Article 59 of the Treaty, since their activities would be a step in the provision of services.[8] Articles 52 and 59 are intended to safeguard the rights of self-employed persons to pursue occupational activities throughout the Community regardless of the location of their place of business—not to differentiate between various stages of the economic process. Signs of a broad approach on the part of the Court may be detected in the *Coenen*[9] and *Koestler*[10] cases. It may be that the Court has already taken this step, in *Luisi*, when it says that persons travelling for the purpose of business are to be regarded as recipients of services,[11] though the context

---

[5] Dr. Ulrich Everling, *The Right of Establishment in the Common Market* (1964), p. 51; Kapteyn and Verloren van Themaat, *Introduction to the Law of the European Communities* [1973], p. 213. See Case 39/75, *Coenen* [1975] E.C.R. 1547, decided on the basis of Art. 59, concerned an individual apparently established in the same state as the recipients of the services in question; it was his personal residence outside that State that was held against him.

[6] Case 221/85, *Commission* v. *Belgium* [1987] E.C.R. 719.

[7] Case 205/84 *Commission* v. *Germany* [1986] E.C.R. 3755 at p. 3802, para. 26, and p. 3808, paras. 48, 49. Case C–76/90, *Sager* [1991] E.C.R. I–4221 at para. 12.

[8] Everling, *op. cit.* pp. 51, 52 and 165, 166. Art. 48 would not provide an independent ground for such activity, even if the camera crew in the hypothetical situation postulated in the text were employed persons: what is in issue is not the right of the worker to take up or maintain an employment relationship, but the right of the employer to carry on economic activities in the host State. *Cf.* Cases 262 and 263/81, *Seco* [1982] E.C.R. 223.

[9] Case 39/75 [1975] E.C.R. 1547.

[10] Case 15/78 [1978] E.C.R. 1971; see *infra* at p. 218.

[11] Case 286/82 and 26/83 [1984] E.C.R. 377 at p. 403, para. 16.

seems to assume that the persons in question would actually receive a service in the host State.

THE RIGHT OF ESTABLISHMENT

Scope of freedom of establishment

Freedom of establishment includes a number of distinct rights. The first is the right of a natural or legal person to leave his or its Member State of origin or establishment in order to accomplish a shift in primary establishment, or to set up a secondary establishment, in another Member State.[12] The second is the right in principle to have more than one place of business in the Community.[13] The third is the right to carry on business under the conditions laid down for its own nationals by the law of the host Member State.[14] It should be added that Article 52 can have no application in a situation which is purely internal to a Member State.[15]

Establishment of natural persons

Article 52 draws a distinction between nationals[16] of Member States *simpliciter*, and those already established in the territory of a Member State. The former are entitled to establish themselves in any Member State, the latter are entitled to set up agencies and branches.

The right to set up agencies and branches has been described by the Court as a specific statement of a general principle, applicable equally to the liberal professions, according to which the right of establishment includes the freedom to set up and maintain, subject to observance of the professional rules of conduct, more than one place of work within the Community.[17] Thus Articles 52 *et seq.* of the Treaty have been held to preclude the denial to a national of another Member State the right to enter and to exercise the profession of advocate solely on the ground that he maintains chambers in another Member State.[18] It has also been held that a non-discriminatory measure may infringe Article 52 where its effect is to disadvantage those with more than one place of business within the Community.[19] Article 52 thus prohibits not only measures which discriminate on grounds of nationality, but those which discriminate against a person for having more than one place of business. The existence of such a disadvantage must

---

[12] *Infra*, pp. 282 & 298.
[13] *Infra*, p. 280.
[14] *Infra*, p. 284.
[15] Case 204/87, *Bekaert* [1988] E.C.R. 2029; Cases C–54/88 *et al.*, *Nino* [1990] E.C.R. I–3537.
[16] For the position of nationals of the countries and territories listed in Annex IV to the Treaty, see Sundberg-Weitman, *op. cit.* p. 186.
[17] Case 107/83, *Klopp* [1984] E.C.R. 2971.
[18] *Ibid.* Similarly, it is not permissible to make practice as a doctor or dentist in one Member State conditional on cancellation of registration in another: see Case 96/85, *Commission* v. *French Republic* [1986] E.C.R. 1475.
[19] Case 143/87, *Stanton* [1988] E.C.R. 3877; Cases 154 & 155/87, *Wolf* [1988] E.C.R. 3897.

nevertheless be assessed by reference to a national with a single place of business in the host Member State.

The distinction between the right to establish oneself, and the right, once initially established in the territory of Member State, to establish agencies, branches and subsidiaries, may be significant in relation to the establishment of companies, and will be considered later.[20]

The Treaty provides for the abolition of restrictions on freedom of establishment in progressive stages during the transitional period. Such abolition was to be facilitated by secondary legislation prohibiting discrimination on grounds of nationality, ensuring the mutual recognition of "diplomas and certificates, and other evidence of formal qualifications,"[21] and co-ordinating national requirements governing the pursuit of non-wage-earning activities.[22] Legislation on the abolition of restrictions was to be preceded by a General Programme, which was to be drawn up by the Council before the end of the first stage. The Programme[23] was adopted in December 1961,[24] and provided the basis for the Council's subsequent legislative activities in this area.

Entry and residence

Title II of the Council's General Programme sought the adjustment of the legislative and administrative requirements in the Member States governing entry and residence, to the extent that such requirements might impair the access of nationals of other Member States to non-wage-earning activities. Directive 64/220 of February 25, 1964 followed,[25] providing for the abolition of restrictions on movement and residence within the Community, and applied, like many other instruments in this area, to the provision of services as well as to the right of establishment. It was superseded by Directive 73/148,[26] which brought the law governing the entry and residence of the self-employed into line with that applying to employees, and indeed, it follows closely the pattern of Directive 68/360,[27] which has been considered in detail in the context of the free movement of workers.[28]

Directive 73/148, like its predecessor, applies to both the right of establishment and to the provision of services. Its beneficiaries are described in Article 1(1) as:

"(a) nationals of a Member State who are established or who wish to establish themselves in another Member State in order to pursue

---

[20] *Infra*, p. 299.
[21] Art. 57(1).
[22] Art. 57(2).
[23] It constitutes neither a Regulation, Directive nor Decision within the meaning of Art. 189 of the Treaty. For the view that it bound the Community institutions, but not the Member States, see van Gerven (1966) 3 C.M.L.Rev. 344 at p. 354. There seems to be no reason why it could not bind the Member States: see Case 22/70, *E.R.T.A.* [1971] E.C.R. 263.
[24] O.J. 1974, Sp.Ed., Second Series, XI, p. 7. The Court has referred to the General Programme in Case 7/76, *Thieffry* [1977] E.C.R. 765; Case 136/78, *Auer* [1979] E.C.R. 452; Case 182/83, *Fearon* [1984] E.C.R. 3677; Case 107/83, *Klopp* [1984] E.C.R. 2971.
[25] J.O. 1964, 845.
[26] O.J. 1973 L172/14.
[27] J.O. 1968 L257/13.
[28] *Supra*, p. 242.

activities as self-employed persons, or who wish to provide services in that State;

(b) nationals of Member States wishing to go to another Member State as recipients of services;

(c) the spouse and the children under 21 years of age of such nationals, irrespective of their nationality;

(d) the relatives in the ascending and descending lines of such nationals and of the spouse of such nationals, which relatives are dependent on them, irrespective of their nationality."

Following the pattern of Directive 68/360, Directive 73/148 bestows the following rights on the above persons:

— the right to be allowed to leave national territory, and to be issued with an identity card or passport (Art. 2);

— the right to be allowed to enter the territory of the Member States merely on production of a valid identity card or passport (Art. 3).

A distinction is drawn between the right of residence of a person exercising the right of establishment, and the right of a person providing services. In the former case, Article 4(1) applies, requiring each Member State to "grant the right of permanent residence to nationals of other Member States who establish themselves within its territory in order to pursue activities as self-employed persons." This right is evidenced by a "residence Permit for a National of a Member State of the European Communities," which must be valid for not less than five years and be automatically renewable.[29] In the case of the provision of services, the Directive declares that "the right of residence for persons providing and receiving services shall be of equal duration with the period during which the services are provided."[30] Where such periods exceed three months, the Member State in whose territory the services are performed must issue a "right of abode" as proof of residence.[31] An applicant for a residence permit or right of abode is only required to produce: (a) the identity card or passport with which he or she entered the territory in question; and (b) proof that he or she comes within the protection of the Directive.[32]

Whereas Directive 68/360 is ambiguous as to the rights of entry and residence of dependent relatives other than children or those in the ascending line, and relatives living under the worker's roof in the country whence they came,[33] Directive 73/148 contains no such ambiguity in the case of the relatives of the self-employed. Article 1 of the Directive makes it clear that such persons do not enter and reside as of right, though Member States "shall favour" their admission. As indicated earlier,[34] it is believed that such differentiation between dependent relatives is capable of constituting an

---

[29] Art. 4(1), second sub-para.
[30] Art. 4(2), first sub-para.
[31] Art. 4(2), second sub-para.
[32] Art. 6.
[33] *Supra*, p. 246.
[34] *Supra*, p. 246.

obstacle to the free movement of persons, and accordingly be contrary to Articles 7, 48, 52 and 59 of the Treaty.

Where a national of one Member State who has worked in another returns to the first Member State to pursue self-employed activities there, the latter Member State must grant entry and residence to the spouse of such person.[35]

The right to remain in the territory of a Member State after having been self-employed there

The Court has on several occasions stressed the parallels between Articles 48, 52 and 59,[36] and indeed, they comprise an integrated whole embracing all economic activities,[37] whether carried on by the employed or the self-employed, regardless of the stage of production, distribution or provision of services concerned, and, apart from the case of activities confined to a single Member State, irrespective of the place of business of a supplier undertaking relative to that of its customers. Nevertheless, there are substantial differences in the scheme and text of these various provisions, not least in the omission of any explicit authority in Articles 52–58: (i) to make provisions for the social security rights of the self-employed,[38] and (ii) to safeguard the position of self-employed persons who may wish to remain in the territory of the Member States after terminating their business activities. It is as a result of the latter omission that Directive 75/34[39] on the right of self-employed persons to remain in Member States, *inter alia*, after retirement is based on Article 235, the third recital to its preamble acknowledging the absence of authority in Article 54(2). The rights of the self-employed enumerated in the Directive are identical to those bestowed upon workers in Regulation 1251/70,[40] and permit retired and incapacitated persons to remain in a Member State where they have previously been self-employed. For the details of these provisions, the reader is referred to the treatment of Regulation 1251/70 in the chapter on the free movement of workers.[41]

Oddly enough, in the case of the self-employed, the Council proceeded by Directive, although a Regulation could have been adopted under Article 235, which authorises "appropriate measures." This is somewhat puzzling, since the Council adopts an almost identical text to that of Regulation 1251/70. Workers may clearly rely on the latter instrument; its provisions are directly applicable and hence capable by their very nature of producing direct effects. Article 8(2) in both the Regulation and the Directive may lack the clarity and the precision characteristic of a directly effective provision, but this cannot be said of the principal rights enumerated in each instrument: they clearly give rise to rights in individuals which national courts are bound

---

[35] Case C–370/90, *Surinder Singh*, judgment July 7, 1992.
[36] See *infra*, p. 288.
[37] Subject to Arts. 60 and 61 of the Treaty.
[38] Reg. 1408/71, on the application of social security schemes to employed persons, is extended to self-employed persons by Reg. 3795/81, O.J. 1981 L378/1. See *infra* at p. 316.
[39] O.J. 1975 L14/10.
[40] *Supra*, p. 262.
[41] *Supra*, p. 262.

to safeguard.[42] This being the case, it would seem that both employed and self-employed persons may invoke in national courts the right to remain in a Member State after having pursued economic activities therein. Nevertheless, the adoption of a Regulation in one case renders otiose and impermissible in principle any national legislative duplication of the provisions in question,[43] while the adoption of a Directive in the other invites national implementation, notwithstanding the apparent direct effect of its provisions. Such legislative inconsistency on the part of the Council can only give rise to needless difficulty.

Abolition of discriminatory restrictions and application of the national standard

Title III of the General Programme called for the abolition of discriminatory measures which might impair access to the non-wage-earning activities of nationals of the Member States, such as measures which:

— conditioned the access to or exercise of a non-wage-earning activity on an authorisation or on the issuance of a document, such as a foreign merchant's card or a foreign professional's card;
— made the access to or exercise of a non-wage-earning activity more costly through the imposition of taxes or other charges such as a deposit or surety bond paid to the receiving country;
— barred or limited membership in companies, particularly with regard to the activities of their members.

In addition to measures primarily likely to discriminate against nationals of the Member States with respect to access to non-wage-earning activities, the General Programme condemned specific national practices discriminating against such persons in the exercise of these activities, such as those limiting the opportunity:

— to enter into certain types of transaction, such as contracts for the hire of services or commercial and farm leases;
— to tender for bids or to participate as a co-contractor or sub-contractor in public contracts or contracts with public bodies[44];
— to borrow and to have access to various forms of credit;
— to benefit from aids granted by the State.

Subsequently, the Council issued a series of Directives implementing the General Programme, and dealing with the right of establishment in a wide variety of commercial callings, from the wholesale trade to the provision of electricity, gas, water and sanitary services![45] Many such Directives are

---

[42] For direct effect, see *supra*, p. 53.
[43] *Supra*, p. 68.
[44] See in particular Dir. 71/305, O.J. 1971 L185/5, as amended, on the co-ordination of procedures for the award of public works contracts; and Dir. 77/62, O.J. 1977 L13/1, as amended, co-ordinating procedures for the award of public supply contracts. The Court has held that the criteria in Dir. 71/305 for the eligibility of contractors are exhaustive, and cannot be supplemented by national requirements: Case 76/81, *Transporoute* [1982] E.C.R. 417. See also Case 274/3, *Commission* v. *Italian Republic* [1985] E.C.R. 1077.
[45] The Directives are too numerous to list. For the collected texts, see the *Encylopaedia of European Community Law*, Vol. CIV, Part C12.

applicable to both establishment and the provision of services, emphasising again the close practical relationship between the two. Directive 64/223,[46] concerning the attainment of freedom of establishment and freedom to provide services in respect of activities in the wholesale trade, may be considered for illustrative purposes. Under the Directive Member States are required to abolish the restrictions itemised in Title III of the General Programmes with respect to the commercial activities concerned. Specific legislative provisions in effect in the Member States are singled out for prohibition, such as the obligation under French law to hold a carte d'identité d'étrangère commerçant,[47] while Member States are obliged to ensure that beneficiaries of the Directive have the right to join professional or trade organisations under the same conditions, and with the same rights and obligations, as their own nationals.[48] Where a host State requires evidence of good character in respect of its own nationals taking up the commercial activities concerned, provision is made for accepting appropriate proof from other Member States, and for the taking of a solemn declaration by self-employed persons from such States, where the State in question does not issue the appropriate documentation.[49]

Although Article 53 of the Treaty, prohibiting Member States from introducing any new restrictions on the right of establishment of nationals of other Member States, was held by the Court to be directly applicable in *Costa* v. *ENEL*,[50] the Council's extensive legislative scheme, based on the General Programme, was clearly adopted on the basis that the prohibition of discrimination contained in Article 52 was ineffective in the absence of implementation. That this was not the case was made clear by the Court of Justice in *Reyners* v. *Belgian State*.[51] The plaintiff in the main suit was a Dutch national resident in Belgium. He had been born in Belgium, educated there, and taken his docteur en droit belge, only to be finally refused admission to the Belgian bar on the ground of his Dutch nationality. On a reference for a preliminary ruling, the Court held that the prohibition on discrimination contained in Article 52 was directly applicable as of the end of the transitional period, despite the opening words of the text of that Article, which referred to the abolition of restrictions "within the framework of the provisions set out below." These provisions—the General Programme and the Directives provided for in Article 54—were of significance "only during the transitional period, since the freedom of establishment was fully attained at the end of it." According to the Court, the aim of Article 52 was intended to be facilitated by the Council's legislative programme, but not made dependent upon it.

The Court's decision had immediate repercussions. The Commission

---

[46] J.O. 1964, 863.
[47] Art. 3.
[48] Art. 4.
[49] Art. 6.
[50] Case 6/64 [1964] E.C.R. 585.
[51] Case 2/74 [1974] E.C.R. 631. For a discriminatory provision remaining on the Statute Book contrary to Art. 52, see Case 159/78, *Commission* v. *Italy* [1979] E.C.R. 3247. And see Case 38/87, *Commission* v. *Hellenic Republic* [1988] E.C.R. 4415. For discriminatory conditions of tender contrary to Art. 52, see Case 197/84, *Steinhauser* [1985] 1819.

undertook, at a meeting of the Permanent Representatives, to report to the Council its view of the implications of the *Reyners* case for the implementation of the right of establishment. In its promised memorandum,[52] the Commission expressed the view that all the rules and formalities cited in the Directives on the abolition of restrictions were no longer applicable to nationals of the Member States, though, in the interests of legal security, the Member States should formally bring their legislation into line with the requirements of Article 52. In view of this, the Commission considered that it was no longer necessary to adopt Directives on the abolition of restrictions, and furthermore, since Directives were by their nature constitutive, that the adoption of such instruments having only declaratory effect would create confusion and protract the work of the Council unnecessarily. With respect, the latter view is open to question. Several Directives in the field of free movement of persons have been stated by the Court to give rise to no new rights, but merely to give closer articulation to rights bestowed directly by the Treaty.[53] This would also appear to be the case with Directive 75/117 on equal pay, which clarifies but does not add to the material scope of Article 119. It was on this ground that Advocate General VerLoren van Themaat urged the Court to hold a Member State in breach of Article 119, rather than the Directive, in proceedings brought by the Commission under Article 169 EEC. The Court nonetheless held the Member State in default for failing to implement the Directive.[54] As the Court commented in *Reyners* itself, Directives already issued under Article 54(2) would not lose all interest, since they would "preserve an important scope in the field of measures intended to make easier the effective exercise of the right of freedom of establishment."[55] The Court was no doubt mindful of the value to the individual litigant before a national tribunal of some more precise formulation of his rights than the general prohibitions of the Treaty. In any event, the Commission formally withdrew a large number of proposed Directives on abolition of restrictions on freedom of establishment.

The prohibition in Article 52 of discrimination on grounds of nationality is not concerned solely with the specific rules on the pursuit of occupational activities but also with the rules relating to the various general facilities which are of assistance in the pursuit of those activities, including access to housing, and to the facilities provided by national authorities to alleviate the financial burden of acquiring housing.[56]

The guarantee of equal treatment for non-nationals under Article 52 is the essence of freedom of establishment, but it is important to emphasise the other side of the coin—that Member States remain free to lay down the conditions for the exercise of a trade or profession, providing that those conditions apply without discrimination to nationals and non-nationals

---

[52] Commission Communication, S.E.C. (74) Final, Brussels.
[53] Case 48/75, *Royer* [1976] E.C.R. 497.
[54] Case 58/81, *Commission* v. *Luxembourg* [1982] E.C.R. 2175.
[55] [1974] E.C.R. 631 at 652.
[56] Case 63/86, *Commission* v. *Italy* [1988] E.C.R. 129; Case 305/87, *Commission* v. *Hellenic Republic* [1989] 1461.

alike. In *Gullung*,[57] a lawyer of dual French and German nationality registered as a Rechtsanwalt in Germany sought to rely on Article 52 in order to practise at the Bar in France, although he had been refused admission to the Bar in France on grounds connected with his character. The Court stated:

> "... in the absence of specific Community rules in the matter each Member State is, in principle, free to regulate the exercise of the legal profession in its territory. It should be added that the requirement that lawyers be registered at a bar laid down by certain Member States must be regarded as lawful in relation to Community law provided, however, that such registration is open to nationals of all Member States without discrimination. The requirement seeks to ensure the observance of moral and ethical principles and the disciplinary control of the activity of lawyers and pursues an objective worthy of protection."[58]:

It follows that while a national of one Member State establishing himself in the territory of another may claim the same treatment as a national established in that State, he cannot resist the application to him of those rules which apply to nationals established in that State.[59] The point is worthy of emphasis since, as is explained below,[60] the position is different for the provision of services under Article 59; in the latter case the provider of services may be entitled to resist the application of rules applicable to nationals established in the host Member State if those rules place unnecessary restrictions on the provision of services. In *Commission* v. *Belgium*[61] the Commission alleged that non-discriminatory Belgian rules governing the activities of clinical biology laboratories were incompatible with Article 52, on the ground that the latter article prohibited not only discriminatory measures, but also "measures which apply to both nationals and foreigners without discrimination where they constitute an unjustified constraint for the latter." The Court repeated this "services" approach to establishment, emphasising that the text of Article 52 guaranteed equality of treatment for nationals and non-nationals, and stating:

> "provided that such equality of treatment is respected, each Member State is, in the absence of Community rules in this area, free to lay down rules for its own territory governing the activities of laboratories providing clinical biology services."[62]

The Commission's application under Article 169 of the EEC Treaty was accordingly dismissed.

---

[57] Case 292/86 [1988] E.C.R. 111.
[58] [1988] E.C.R. 111 at p. 139, paras. 28, 29. The reference to "an objective worthy of protection" implies that national rules, unjustified by considerations of public interest, might infringe Article 52.
[59] Though if the rules disadvantage persons with more than one place of business in the Community the applicable national standard is that of a national with a single place of business in the host State, *supra*, p. 280.
[60] *Infra*, p. 309.
[61] Case 221/85 [1987] E.C.R. 719.
[62] [1987] E.C.R. 719 at p. 737.

Relationship between Article 7 of the Treaty and Articles 52 and 59

Article 7 of the EEC Treaty prohibits discrimination on grounds of nationality within the sphere of operation of the Treaty. This general prohibition of discrimination has been implemented as regards freedom of establishment and the provision of services by Articles 52 and 59 of the Treaty. The Court has said that any rules incompatible with the latter Articles are also incompatible with Article 7.[63] However, non-discriminatory rules which disadvantage a person by virtue of the fact that he has more than one place of business within the Community may be consistent with Article 7 but inconsistent with Article 52.[64] And non-discriminatory rules which amount to restrictions on the provision of services would be incompatible with Article 59, but consistent with Article 7.[65] It follows that a more appropriate formulation is that any rules which discriminate on grounds of nationality which infringe Articles 52 and 59 are also inconsistent with Article 7.

Parallel interpretation of Articles 48, 52 and 59 in appropriate cases

Theoretically, problems may arise in differentiating between the employed and the self-employed, and between instances of establishment and provision of services, but it will in many cases be unnecessary to make any hard-and-fast classification, because the applicable principles will be the same in any event. Thus, in *Procureur du Roi* v. *Royer*,[66] the Court of Justice, considering a request for a preliminary ruling from a national court which was uncertain whether the subject of the proceedings before it was to be considered as falling within Article 48, Article 52 or Article 59, observed:

> ". . . comparison of these different provisions shows that they are based on the same principles both in so far as they concern the entry into and residence in the territory of Member States of persons covered by Community law and the prohibition of all discrimination between them on grounds of nationality."[67]

An important corollary is that Article 52, like Article 48, must be construed as prohibiting discrimination by private parties as well as by public authorities.[68] In *Walrave* v. *Union cycliste internationale*,[69] the Court expressed the opinion that Article 48 of the Treaty extended to agreements and rules other than those emanating from public authorities, citing in

---

[63] Case 90/76, *Van Ameyde* v. *UCI* [1977] E.C.R. 1091 at p. 1126, para. 27; Case 305/87, *Commission* v. *Hellenic Republic* [1989] E.C.R. 1461 at p. 1476, para. 12.
[64] Case 143/87, *Stanton* [1988] E.C.R. 3877; Cases 154 and 155/87, *Wolf* [1988] E.C.R. 3897.
[65] For the scope of Article 59, see *infra*, p. 302.
[66] Case 48/75 [1976] E.C.R. 497. And see Case 118/75, *Watson & Belmann* [1976] E.C.R. 1185.
[67] [1976] E.C.R. 497 at 509.
[68] Sundberg-Weitman, *op. cit.* p. 203.
[69] Case 36/74 [1974] E.C.R. 1405.

support of its view the text of Article 7(4) of Regulation 1612/68, which nullifies discriminatory clauses in individual or collective employment agreements. A similar conclusion was justified in the case of Article 59, since the activities referred to therein were "not to be distinguished by their nature from those in Article 48, but only by the fact that they are performed outside the ties of a contract of employment."[70] It follows that Article 52 has a similar ambit.

Reference has already been made to the similarity between the legislative provisions governing both the entry and residence of employed and self-employed persons, and the right to remain in the territory of a Member State, having been employed therein.[71] But it has also been noted that the respective scope of Article 52 and Article 59 is not identical in all respects. In particular, whereas Article 52 accords to non-nationals the conditions of doing business which apply to nationals, Article 59 may in certain cases place a provider of services in a different and even more favourable position than a national established in the host Member State.[72] As between Articles 48 and 52 on the one hand, and Article 59 on the other, a further difference is that whereas Article 59 may be invoked by a national against the *host* State even where that State is his own,[73] such a possibility arises only exceptionally under Articles 48 and 52, and in particular where the position of a national is assimilated to that of a non-national under Community rules.[74] Thus in the *Auer* case,[75] in which a French national alleged that the refusal of the French authorities to recognise an Italian veterinary qualification amounted to an obstacle to his freedom of establishment in France, contrary to Article 52, the Court declared that the latter article could, by virtue of its wording, concern only, in each Member State, nationals of other Member States. However, in *Knoors*,[76] the Court held that a national of a Member State could rely upon a period of professional activity undertaken in another Member State where a Directive designed to facilitate freedom of establishment so provided. The Court stated:

> "Although it is true that the provisions of the Treaty relating to establishment and the provision of services cannot be applied to situations which are purely internal to a Member State, the position nevertheless remains that the reference in Article 52 to 'nationals of a

---

[70] [1974] E.C.R. 1405 at 1419.
[71] *Supra*, pp. 281, 283.
[72] *Infra*, p. 309.
[73] The *locus classicus* on the interpretation of Art. 59 involved a plea raised in a Netherlands court by a Netherlands national challenging the compatibility of Netherlands law with the Treaty: Case 33/74, *Van Binsbergen* [1974] E.C.R. 1299. Similarly, Case 39/75, *Coenen* [1975] E.C.R. 1547, arose from national proceedings in which an individual invoked Art. 59 against his own State.
[74] The right of exit can be claimed by a national against his own national authorities under Articles 48 and 52, as well as Article 59: see *supra* at pp. 243 and 282. And restrictions by a Member State on its own nationals having more than one place of business in the Community would amount to a restriction on the right of exit. See also Case 79/85, *Segers* [1986] E.C.R. 2375 at 2380 on a national measure discouraging nationals of that Member State establishing themselves in another. See also Case C–370/90, *Surinder Singh*, judgment of July 7, 1992, *supra*, p. 242.
[75] Case 136/78 [1979] E.C.R. 437.
[76] Case 115/78 [1979] E.C.R. 399.

Member State' who wish to establish themselves 'in the territory of another Member State' cannot be interpreted in such a way as to exclude from the benefit of Community law a given Member State's own nationals when the latter, owing to the fact that they have lawfully resided on the territory of another Member State and have there lawfully acquired a trade qualification which is recognised by the provisions of Community law, are, with regard to their State of origin, in a situation which may be assimilated to that of any other persons enjoying the rights and liberties guaranteed by the Treaty."[77]

Direct and indirect discrimination

Article 52 prohibits both direct and indirect discrimination on grounds of nationality. Examples of direct discrimination are:

— a requirement that nationals of other Member States set up a company incorporated in the host State before obtaining a licence to fish at sea[78];
— a requirement that in order for a ship to qualify for the nationality of a member State, it must be owned by nationals of that Member State.[79]

The Court has held that Article 52 prohibits not only overt discrimination by reason of nationality but also all covert forms of discrimination which, by the application of other criteria of differentiation, lead in fact to the same result.[80] A national measure providing that only companies in which all or a majority of the shares are either directly or indirectly in public or state ownership may conclude agreements for the development of data-processing systems for public authorities has been held to be contrary to Article 52.[81] The Court held that although the rules in issue applied without distinction to all companies, they essentially favoured domestic companies, and observed that no data-processing companies from other Member States qualified under the criteria in question at the material time.[82]

However, indirect differentiation on objective grounds consistent with the Treaty does not amount to prohibited discrimination. Although residence requirements may amount in certain cases to indirect discrimination,[83] the Court has held that a national law exempting rural land from compulsory acquisition if the owners have lived on or near the land for a specified period is consistent with Article 52, where the purpose of the law is to ensure as far as possible that rural land belongs to those who work it, and where the law applies equally to its own nationals and to the nationals of other Member States.[84] Again, in *Commission* v. *French Republic* the Court

---

[77] [1979] E.C.R. 399 at p. 410, para. 24
[78] Case C–93/89, *Commission* v. *Ireland*, judgment of October 4, 1991.
[79] Case C–221/89, *Factortame* [1991] E.C.R. I–3905. Though it is not contrary to Community law for a Member State to stipulate as a condition for the registration of a fishing vessel in its national register that it be managed and its operation directed and controlled from within that Member State, *ibid.* at para. 36.
[80] Case C–3/88, *Commission* v. *Italian Republic* [1989] E.C.R. 4035.
[81] Note 79.
[82] [1989] E.C.R. at p. 4059, paras. 9 and 10.
[83] Case 152/73, *Sotgiu* [1974] E.C.R. 153.
[84] Case 182/83, *Fearon* [1984] E.C.R. 3677.

acknowledged the possibility that a distinction based on the location of the registered office of a company or the place of residence of a natural person might under certain conditions be justified in an area such as tax law.[85]

Exception in the case of activities connected with the exercise of official authority

Article 55 provides that the provisions of Chapter 2 shall not apply, "so far as any given Member State is concerned, to activities which in that State are connected, even occasionally, with the exercise of official authority." This exception constitutes a derogation from a fundamental Treaty rule, and must be interpreted strictly, so as not to exceed the purpose for which it was inserted.[86]

The notion of "official authority" is not defined in the Treaty. In *Reyners* v. *Belgian State*,[87] it was argued that the profession of avocat was exempted from the chapter on establishment because it involved the exercise of official authority. The Court, while tacitly acknowledging that the occasional exercise of judicial power by an avocat would amount to the exercise of official authority, declared that this would not be the case with respect to the advocat's other responsibilities:

"Professional activities involving contacts, even regular and organic, with the courts, including even compulsory co-operation in their functioning, do not constitute, as such, connexion with the exercise of official authority.

The most typical activities of the profession of avocat, in particular, such as consultation and legal assistance and also representation and the defence of parties in court, even when the intervention or assistance of the avocat is compulsory or is a legal monopoly, cannot be considered as connected with the exercise of official authority."[88]

The Commission argued in its observations that the exercise of official authority involved the exercise of "prerogatives outside the general law,"[89] and the Advocate General agreed, describing official authority as "that which arises from the sovereignty and majesty of the State; for him who exercises it, it implies the power of enjoying the [*sic*] prerogatives outside the general law, privileges of official power and powers of coercion over citizens."[90] This definition is consistent with the views of commentators, and would include the exercise of law-making or judicial authority.[91]

Reference by analogy to *Commission* v. *Belgium*[92] on the ambit of Article 48(4) would seem to be permissible, since that Article pursues the same aim

---

[85] Case 270/83 [1986] E.C.R. 273 at p. 304, para. 19.
[86] Case 2/74, *Reyners* [1974] E.C.R. 631; Case 152/73, *Sotgiu* [1974] E.C.R. 153.
[87] Case 2/74, *Reyners* [1974] E.C.R. 631.
[88] [1974] E.C.R. 631 at 655.
[89] [1974] E.C.R. 631 at 640.
[90] [1974] E.C.R. 631 at 664. And see Case 147/86, *Commission* v. *Hellenic Republic* [1988] E.C.R. 1637.
[91] Everling, *op. cit.* 85, 86; Sundberg-Weitman, *op. cit.* 206, 207; Smit and Herzog, 2–605.
[92] Case 149/79 [1980] E.C.R. 3881. On Article 48(4), see p. 275, *supra*.

as Article 55. Possible examples of activities falling within Article 55 would be the carrying out of certain functions by notaries public,[93] or the issuing of death certificates by doctors.[94]

Article 55 refers to "activities" connected with the exercise of official authority, rather than "to professions." The Court in *Reyners* made it clear that while certain "activities" forming part of a particular profession might fall within Article 55, the profession as a whole might nevertheless be subject to the right of establishment. This would be the case wherever the activities could be "severed" from the profession concerned, as they could be so severed, it seems, in the case of the avocat called upon to perform occasional judicial functions. The Court took the view that the exception allowed by Article 55 could only be extended to a whole profession where the activities in question "were linked with that profession in such a way that freedom of establishment would result in imposing on the Member State concerned the obligation to allow the exercise, even occasionally, by non-nationals of functions appertaining to official authority."[95] In the final analysis the relevant question must be whether it is reasonable to regard particular activities as constituting an essential aspect of a particular profession considered as a whole.[96]

In view of the Court's decision in *Sotgiu* v. *Deutsche Bundespost*,[97] it would seem that Article 55 should be interpreted as applying only to access to activities connected with the exercise of official authority; not as authorising discriminatory conditions of work once a person had been allowed to take up such activities.

The second paragraph of Article 55 provides that the Council may rule "that the provisions of this Chapter shall not apply to certain activities." It seems that these words must be construed subject to the text of the previous paragraph, *i.e.* as involving activities connected with the exercise of official authority. The authority bestowed thereby upon the Council is extremely limited, and has not, so far, been exercised. In applying Article 55 to a particular profession, it will be necessary to establish the ambit of the "activities" which "taken on their own, constitute a direct and specific connexion with the exercise of official authority."[98] While the "exercise of official authority" is a concept of Community law, the question of "direct and specific connexion" with such exercise is one of fact which, unresolved, can lead to uncertainty on the part of those subject to the law. It is submitted that the Council's function is limited to finding, as a fact, that certain activities do indeed have a "direct and specific connexion" with the exercise of official authority.

---

[93] Everling, *op. cit.* 86, note 20; Sundberg-Weitman, *op. cit.* p. 207; Smit and Herzog, 2–608; Lipstein, *The Law of the European Economic Community*, pp. 132, 133.
[94] Sundberg-Weitman, *op. cit.* p. 207; Smit and Herzog, *op. cit.* p. 209.
[95] [1974] E.C.R. 631 at p. 654.
[96] See Everling, *op. cit.* p. 87, ". . . a substantial part of the economic activity which cannot be separated from its other parts."
[97] Case 152/73 [1974] E.C.R. 153.
[98] [1974] E.C.R. 631 at p. 654.

Article 56—the public policy proviso

Article 56 declares that "The provisions of this Chapter and measures taken in pursuance thereof shall not prejudice the applicability of provisions ... providing for special treatment for foreign nationals on grounds of public policy, public security or public health." The integrated scheme of Articles 48 to 66, the parallel interpretation given to these provisions in relation to discrimination, entry and residence,[99] and the fact that the public policy provisos of Article 48(3) and Article 56 are given "closer articulation" in one and the same Directive—Directive 64/221 of February 25, 1964[1]—compels the conclusion that the text of Article 56 is to be interpreted in an identical manner to that of Article 48(3). Thus, for instance, Article 56 must be interpreted as permitting derogation from the chapter on establishment only in respect of entry and residence—not in respect of the terms and conditions under which occupational activities are carried on.[2] For a detailed analysis of the terms of Directive 64/221, and an examination of the Court's jurisprudence on the public policy proviso in Article 48(3), the reader is referred to the chapter on freedom of movement for workers.[3]

While the need to combat fraud may justify a difference in treatment on grounds of nationality in certain circumstances,[4] the mere risk of tax avoidance cannot justify discriminatory treatment.[5] Article 56 permits derogation from the right of establishment in the case of foreign nationals. The chapter may be subject to further implicit requirements of national law (*cf.* Articles 30 and 59) which can be invoked also against a State's own nationals seeking to establish themselves in another Member State.[6] But discriminatory restrictions can only be justified in this context on the basis of the express derogation contained in Article 56 of the Treaty.[7]

Mutual recognition of diplomas and the co-ordination of national qualifications

Paragraphs (1) and (2) of Article 57 provide, respectively, for the "mutual recognition of diplomas, certificates, and other evidence of formal qualifications," and for "the co-ordination of the provisions laid down by law, regulation or administrative action in Member States concerning the taking up and pursuit of activities as self-employed persons."

The General Programme contemplated transitional measures, where access to non-wage-earning activities might be allowed on proof of "actual

---

[99] *Supra,* p. 288.
[1] J.O. 1964, 850, as amended by Dir. 75/35, O.J. 1975 L14/14, which provides that Dir. 64/221 shall apply to nationals of Member States and members of their families benefiting from the provisions of Dir. 75/34: see *supra,* p. 266.
[2] Case 152/73, *Sotgiu* [1974] E.C.R. 153; Case 15/69, *Ugliola* [1969] E.C.R. 363, *supra,* p. 254.
[3] *Supra,* p. 266.
[4] Case 79/85, *Segers* [1986] E.C.R. at p. 2388, para. 17.
[5] Case 270/83, *Commission v. French Republic* [1986] E.C.R. 273 at p. 306, para. 25
[6] See *supra* at p. 225, and *infra* at p. 311.
[7] Case 352/85, *Bond van Averteerders* [1988] E.C.R. 2085.

and legitimate exercise of the activity in the country of origin."[8] An example of such a transitional regime is provided by Directive 75/369, dealing with the activities of itinerant tradespeople, such as fairground operators.[9] The Directive provides that where, in the case of its own nationals, a Member State requires documentary evidence of good repute, or of never having been declared bankrupt, it must accept, in the case of nationals of other Member States, appropriate equivalent documentation issued in their country of origin.[10] Where no such documentation is issued, the host State must accept a declaration on oath, or a solemn declaration, made before, and duly certified by, a competent judicial or executive authority in the appropriate country of origin.[11] Where in a Member State the pursuit of the activities in question is subject to the possession of "general, commercial or professional knowledge and ability," that Member State must accept as sufficient evidence of such knowledge and ability the fact that the activity in question has been previously carried on in another Member State.[12] The period required is either two or three years, depending on whether it was completed in an employed or self-employed capacity, and on whether or not the relevant experience was preceded by a course of training.[13]

The Directive applies also to employees,[14] no doubt because differences in national vocational requirements are as capable of constituting an obstacle to the free movement of workers as they are of hindering the peregrination of the self-employed.

Progress under Article 57 in ensuring freedom of establishment for the learned professions has predictably been slow. Nevertheless, the adoption of Directives 75/362 and 75/363[15] of June 16, 1975, on the mutual recognition of medical diplomas and the co-ordination of national medical qualifications, must be regarded as a breakthrough. In the case of non-specialist medicine, the Directives require[16] that each Member State recognise diplomas awarded to nationals of the Member States by other Member States[17] on condition that the diplomas comply with the requirements specified in Article 1 of Directive 75/363. This Article provides that diplomas awarded in the Member States must guarantee that a doctor, during his training period, has acquired:

"(a)   adequate knowledge of the sciences on which medicine is based and
         a good understanding of the scientific methods including the

---

[8] Title IV, O.J. 1974 Sp.Ed., Second Series, IX, p. 10.
[9] O.J. 1975 L167/29.
[10] Art. 3(1), (92).
[11] Art. 3(3).
[12] Art. 5(1).
[13] Art. 5(1).
[14] Art. 1(2).
[15] O.J. 1975 L167/1, 14. Supplemented or amended by, *inter alia*, Dir. 81/1057, O.J. 1981 L385/25; Dir. 82/76, O.J. L43/21; Dir. 89/594, O.J. 1989 L341/19; Dir. 90/658, O.J. 1990 L353/73 (unification of Germany); see in general Sweet and Maxwell's *Encyclopedia of European Community Law*, C12 at 932 *et seq.*
[16] Dir. 75/362, Arts. 2 and 3; Dir. 75/363, Art. 1.
[17] Note that the Directive does not cover qualifications awarded in third countries and recognised in Member States.

principles of measuring biological functions, the evaluation of scientifically established facts and the analysis of data;

(b) sufficient understanding of the structure, functions and behaviour of healthy and sick persons, as well as relations between the state of health and the physical and social surroundings of the human being;

(c) adequate knowledge of clinical disciplines and practices, providing him with a coherent picture of mental and physical diseases, of medicine from the point of view of prophylaxis, diagnosis and therapy and of human reproduction;

(d) suitable clinical experience in hospital under appropriate supervision."

In addition, a course in medical training must comprise at least a six-year course or 5,500 hours of theoretical or practical instruction given in a university or under the supervision of a university.[18]

The requirements specified above are of a somewhat general nature, and no doubt reflect the conviction that standards of medical education in the Member States are, on the whole, comparable. That is not to say the the various qualifications are equivalent, and Directive 75/362 admits as much.[19] Thus a doctor of one Member State established in another may use the professional title customary therein, but the host State may require that his academic title be expressed in the language of his country of origin,[20] and be followed by the "name and location of the establishment or examining board which awarded it."[21]

Even in the case of medical diplomas which do not conform with the requirements specified in Article 1 of Directive 75/362, recognition will still be accorded if they were awarded by a Member State before the implementation of Directive 75/363, and they are accompanied by a certificate stating that the doctor in question has been "effectively and lawfully" engaged in his profession for at least three consecutive years during the five years prior to the date of the issue of the certificate.[22]

Similar provision is made with respect to qualifications in specialist medicine.[23] Both Directives apply to employed persons, as well as to the self-employed.[24] In the event of difficulties arising in the implementation of the Directive, two Committees, established by Council Decision, have the responsibility of considering such matters, and making recommendations as to, for example, the necessity for amending the present arrangements.[25]

Whereas under the above-mentioned Directives additional requirements

---

[18] Dir. 75/363, Art. 1(2).
[19] Second recital to the preamble to Dir. 75/362.
[20] Dir. 75/362, Art. 10(1), is ambiguous on this point, but the seventh recital to the preamble is not.
[21] Art. 10(1).
[22] Art. 9. And see Dir. 81/1057, O.J. 1981 L385/25, by virtue of which the provision also applies to training commenced before implementation, and finishing afterwards.
[23] Dir. 75/362, Chaps. III and IV; Dir. 75/363, Art. 6.
[24] Dir. 75/362, Art. 24; Dir. 75/363, Art. 6.
[25] See Council Dec. 75/364 and 75/365, establishing, respectively, an Advisory Committee on Medical Training, and a Committee of Senior Officials on Public Health, and defining their functions: see Dir. 75/362, Art. 26; Dir. 75/363, Art. 12.

may be imposed in the case of specialists, this is not permitted in the case of general practitioners. General practitioners came to be regarded as specialists in their own right in the Netherlands, and in that country a year's professional training after qualification was laid down for all nationals. The requirement was not made of nationals of other EEC countries, since the Netherlands authorities accepted that such persons were entitled to rely on the Directives. The Court of Justice held that a Netherlands national who had qualified in Belgium was equally entitled to rely on the Directives, and to avoid the additional year's professional training.[26] This situation—that a Member State may impose additional requirements upon the holders of its own general medical qualifications, but not upon the holders of those of other Member States—is clearly anomalous. It is remedied by Directive 86/457 on specific training in general medical practice,[27] which provides that each Member State which dispenses the complete training referred to in Article 1 of Directive 75/363 within its territory shall institute specific training in general medical practice.[28] From January 1, 1995, and subject to acquired rights it has recognised, each Member State shall make the exercise of general medical practice under its national social security scheme conditional on evidence of such specific training.[29] Directive 85/432 on the free movement of pharmacists was amended in draft to avoid the difficulty by providing that a Member State may, where appropriate, require "additional professional experience" of practitioners.[30]

The Directives referred to above concerning the medical profession provide for mutual recognition on the basis of a certain degree of harmonisation of training requirements. Directive 89/48 on a general system for the recognition of higher education diplomas awarded on completion of professional education and training of at least three years' duration adopts a different approach—the mutual recognition of diplomas without harmonisation, but accompanied by the safeguards of adaptation periods or aptitude tests in the host State.[31] In principle the choice between adaptation period and aptitude test is left to the migrant, but an exception is made for law, where an aptitude test may be required.[32]

Even in the absence of Directives under Article 57, recognition of foreign diplomas may be required under Article 52, prohibiting discrimination on grounds of nationality, as *Thieffry* v. *Paris Bar Council*[33] shows. A Belgian national held a Belgian law degree recognised by the University of Paris as equivalent to a French law degree. He acquired the qualifying certificate for the profession of advocate, but the Paris Bar Council refused to allow him to undergo practical training on the ground that he did not possess a French law

---

[26] Case 246/80, *Broekmulen* [1981] E.C.R. 2311.
[27] O.J. 1986 L267/26.
[28] *Ibid* Art. 1.
[29] *Ibid* Art. 7.
[30] O.J. 1985 L253/34. Watson, (1983) 20 C.M.L. Rev. 767, 784. And see Dir. 85/433, O.J. 433, O.J. 1985 L253/37.
[31] O.J. 1989 L19/16. See Wallace, (1989) N.L.J. 1004.
[32] See in particular Art. 4.
[33] Case 71/76 [1977] E.C.R. 765. See Case 11/77, *Patrick* [1977] E.C.R. 119; and Case 65/77, *Razanatsimba* [1977] E.C.R. 2229 (Lomé Convention, Art. 62).

degree. The Court of Justice held that such a refusal could amount to indirect discrimination prohibited by Article 52 of the Treaty. As the General Programme for the abolition of restrictions on freedom of establishment made clear in Title III(B), the Council proposed to eliminate not only overt discrimination, but also any form of disguised discrimination, including "Any requirements imposed . . . in respect of the taking up or pursuit of an activity as a self-employed person where, although applicable irrespective of nationality, their effect is exclusively or principally to hinder the taking up or pursuit of such activity by foreign nationals."[34] It would be for the competent national authorities, taking account of the requirements of Community law, to judge whether a recognition granted by a university authority could, in addition to its academic effect, constitute valid evidence of a professional qualification. The Court has subsequently emphasised that a Member State, dealing with a request for authorisation to practise a profession access to which is under national legislation subject to the holding of a diploma or professional qualification, is obliged to take into account qualifications acquired in another Member State, by carrying out a comparison between the skills evidenced by those diplomas and the knowledge and qualifications required by national rules.[35] In the context of that review a Member State might take into consideration objective differences relating to the legal context of the profession concerned in the Member State of origin and its field of activity.[36] If such a comparison indicates the possession of a qualification equivalent to that required by the national law of the host State, the Member State is bound to accept the person concerned as being qualified. If the comparison shows only partial equivalence, the host State has the right to require that the person concerned should demonstrate that he has acquired the additional knowledge and qualifications needed.[37] Comparison of the national qualifications must be carried out according to a procedure complying with the requirements of Community law relating to the effective protection of fundamental rights conferred by the Treaty on nationals of Member States.[38] It follows that it must be possible for any decision to be made the subject of judicial proceedings in which its legality under Community law can be reviewed and it must be possible for the person concerned to ascertain the reasons for the decision.[39]

Establishment of companies

The right of establishment is enjoyed by companies and firms, as well as by natural persons. Article 58 provides:

---

[34] O.J. 1974, English Sp.Ed., Second Series, IX, p. 8.
[35] Case 222/86, *UNECTEF* v. *Heylens* E.C.R. 4097; Case C–340/89, *Vlassopoulou* [1991] E.C.R. I–2357.
[36] Case C–340/89, note 34.
[37] *Ibid.*
[38] *Ibid.*
[39] *Ibid.* and Case 222/86, note 34.

"Companies or firms formed in accordance with the law of a Member State and having their registered office, central administration or principal place of business within the Community shall, for the purposes of this Chapter, be treated in the same way as natural persons who are nationals of Member States.

'Companies or firms' means companies or firms constituted under civil or commercial law, including co-operative societies, and other legal persons governed by public or private law, save for those which are non-profit making."

While Article 1 of Directive 73/148 confirms the right of natural persons who are nationals of one Member State to leave that Member State in order to establish themselves in another, that provision does not apply by analogy to corporate persons.[40] However, the Court has said of Articles 52 and 58:

"Even though those provisions are directed mainly at ensuring that foreign nationals and companies are treated in the host Member State in the same way as nationals of that State, they also prohibit the Member State of origin from hindering the establishment in another Member State of one of its nationals or of a company incorporated under its legislation which comes within the definition contained in Article 58."[41]

As the Court has observed:

"In the case of a company, the right of establishment is generally exercised by the setting up of agencies, branches or subsidiaries, as is expressly provided for in the second sentence of the first paragraph of Article 52."[42]

An undertaking of one Member State which maintains a permanent presence in another "comes within the scope of the provisions of the Treaty on the right of establishment, even if that presence does not take the form of a branch or agency, but consists merely of an office managed by the undertaking's own staff or by a person who is independent but authorised to act on a permanent basis for the undertaking, as would be the case with an agency."[43]

The Court has held that to allow a Member State in which a company carried on its business to treat that company in a different manner solely because its registered office was in another Member State would render Article 58 nugatory.[44] Furthermore, discriminatory tax treatment as between companies of the host Member State and branches of companies registered in other Member States is contrary to Article 52, and such discrimination cannot be justified on the ground that companies registered in other Member States are at liberty to establish themselves by setting up a

---

[40] Case 81/87, *Ex p. Daily Mail and General Trust plc* [1988] E.C.R. 5483
[41] [1988] E.C.R. 5483 at p. 5510, para. 16.
[42] [1988] E.C.R. 5483 at p. 5511, para. 17.
[43] Case 205/84, *Commission v. Germany* [1986] E.C.R. 3755, at p. 3801, para. 21.
[44] Case 79/85, *Segers* [1986] E.C.R. 2375.

subsidiary in order to have the benefit of the tax treatment in question.[45] As the Court has emphasised:

> "The second sentence of the first paragraph of Article 52 expressly leaves traders free to choose the appropriate legal form in which to pursue their activities in another Member State and that freedom of choice must not be limited by discriminatory tax provisions."[46]

The definition of "companies or firms" is framed so as to encompass the widest possible circle of beneficiaries.[47] The reference to "other legal persons" might suggest that the entities concerned must possess full "legal personality," *i.e.* must, in addition to the capacity to bring and defend actions, enjoy the capacity to possess goods and to enter into other legal transactions.[48] On the other hand, the (as yet unratified) Convention on the Mutual Recognition of Companies and Legal Persons, drawn up to provide for the mutual recognition of "companies or firms within the meaning of the second paragraph of Article 58," declares in its opening Article that "Companies . . . established in accordance with the law of a Contracting State which grants them the capacity of persons having rights and duties . . . should be recognised as of right." Goldman concludes that "[i]t follows . . . that if a company is given by the law under which it was formed the capacity to bring or defend actions in its own name, but not that of being owner . . . that will suffice for it to be recognised."[49] Other commentators take a similar view.[50] A partnership under English law, capable of suing and being sued in its own name, would seem to be included in the definition contained in the second paragraph of Article 58.

The exclusion of non-profit-making companies from the bodies entitled to claim the right of establishment is not intended to exclude subsidised public enterprises[51] and the purpose of the clause seems to be to exclude organisations of a political, cultural, religious, social or charitable nature, which are unconnected with the economic objectives of the Treaty.[52] Nevertheless, the economic activities of a religious community may bring it within the sphere of application of the Treaty.[53]

A company formed in accordance with the law of a Member State is entitled to exercise the right of establishment if it has either its registered office, its central administration, or its principal place of business within the Community. As indicated at the beginning of the present chapter, Article 52 draws a distinction between transferring a primary establishment to another Member State and setting up a secondary establishment, in the form of a branch or a subsidiary. In the former case the only qualifying characteristic is the nationality of a Member State, while in the latter there must be an

---

[45] Case 270/83 [1986] E.C.R. 273.
[46] [1986] E.C.R. 273 at p. 305, para. 22.
[47] Everling, *op. cit.* p. 69. Sundberg-Weitman, p. 189.
[48] Goldman, 6 C.M.L.R. Rev. 1969 at p. 116.
[49] Goldman, *loc. cit.* p. 113.
[50] Everling, *op cit.* p. 68; Sundberg-Weitman, p. 190.
[51] Smit and Herzog, 2–642.
[52] Everling, *op. cit.* p. 69.
[53] See Case 196/87, *Steymann* [1988] E.C.R. 6159.

existing establishment in one of the Member States. The General Programme construed this qualification as requiring, in the case of companies having only the seat prescribed by their statutes in the Community, a "real and continuous link with the economy of a Member State."[54] In the *Segers* case the Court of Justice regarded a company registered in one Member State and undertaking *all* its business through an agency in another Member State as entitled to exercise its right of establishment in the second Member State.[55] Thus registration of a company in a Member State of itself amounts to establishment in that State, even if the company does no business in that Member State, and all its shareholders are nationals of the Member State in which it transacts all business through a branch or agency (for this was the position in *Segers*).

Article 54(3)(f) of the Treaty provides for the abolition of restrictions on the transfer of personnel from the main establishment to managerial or supervisory posts in its branches or subsidiaries.[56] In the event of such personnel holding the nationality of a Member State, they will, of course, be entitled to assert an independent right of entry and residence under the provisions of the Treaty guaranteeing freedom of movement for workers.[57] The implication is that certain senior personnel may be transferred under Article 54(3)(f) who would not otherwise be entitled to a right of residence under the Treaty. The principal reason for such lack of entitlement is likely to be that they are nationals of third countries. An undertaking providing services in another Member State may bring its workforce with it, irrespective of whether the employees concerned enjoy an independent right of free movement.[58] It seems that a national of a third country may be posted from the main establishment to a *senior* post in a branch or subsidiary in another Member State, and that workers employed by an undertaking established in a Member State may, *irrespective of status*, be posted on a temporary basis to another Member State under Article 59. This distinction between the scope of Articles 52 and 59 as regards the status of employees who may be entitled to residence as a result of a posting may reflect the permanent nature of establishment as against the temporary and sporadic nature of the provision of services, and the intent of the draftsman of the Treaty to limit the duty of Member States to grant a right of residence to nationals of third countries.

A change of primary establishment involving a transfer of company headquarters may be hindered by national legal provisions to the effect: (a) that a company transferring its executive offices out of the jurisdiction loses its corporate personality; or (b) that a company wishing to establish its executive offices within the jurisdiction must be newly constituted there.[59] These requirements amount to a refusal to recognise the legal personality of a company incorporated in a Member State other than where its central

---

[54] Title I, O.J. 1974 Sp.Ed., Second Series, IX, p. 7.
[55] Case 79/85, *Segers* [1986] E.C.R. 2375.
[56] And see the General Programme, Title III, A, final paragraph, *loc. cit.* p. 8.
[57] *Supra*, p. 237.
[58] Case C–113/89, *Rush Portugesa Ldc* [1990] E.C.R. I–1417.
[59] Smit and Herzog, 2–647.

administration is located. It may be that to deny recognition to a company satisfying the requirements of the first paragraph of Article 58 amounts to a denial of that company's right of establishment.[60] However, in *ex parte Daily Mail and General Trust Plc* the Court held that the differences in national legislation concerning the required connecting factor between a company and the Member State under which it is incorporated and the question whether—and if so how—the registered office or real head office of a company incorporated under national law may be transferred from one Member State to another were problems which were not resolved by the Treaty rules concerning the right of establishment but were to be dealt with by future legislation or Conventions.[61] It followed that Articles 52 and 58 of the Treaty could not be interpreted as conferring on companies incorporated under the law of a Member State a right to transfer their central management and control and their central administration to another Member State while retaining their status as companies incorporated under the legislation of the first Member State.[62] While this result may be reasonable where the national law of incorporation does not permit a transfer of central administration, it is less so where the law of incorporation does so allow and the host State recognises that fact. If a British company with a central administration located in a municipally owned office block in another Member State were charged a higher rent chargeable to foreign companies, does it follow from the *Daily Mail* decision that Articles 7 and 52 could not be invoked by the company? The result in this context seems anomalous. It may be that the *Daily Mail* ruling is strictly confined to claims to exercise the right of free movement and that once the transfer of central administration is achieved in accordance with the applicable national law Article 52 can be invoked to guarantee equal treatment in the host State.

The position would be clarified if the Member States ratified the 1968 Convention on the Mutual Recognition of Companies and Legal Persons, which seeks to resolve the difficulties which arise from the existence of different national rules relating to the recognition of foreign companies.

The prospect of firms incorporated under the law of one Member State being free to establish themselves in another led the drafters of the Treaty to insert Article 54(3)(g), which requires the co-ordination of the provisions of national company law which safeguard the position of investors and "others." The rationale of such harmonisation is that in its absence the existence of different national rules could discourage the exercise of the right of establishment. For example, in the *Daily Mail* case the Court observed:

> "A company may also exercise its right of establishment by taking part in the incorporation of a company in another Member State, and in that regard Article 221 of the Treaty ensures that it will receive the same

---

[60] Everling, *op. cit.* p. 71.
[61] Case 81/87 [1988] E.C.R. 5483 at p. 5512, para. 23.
[62] [1988] E.C.R. at p. 5512, para. 24.

treatment as nationals of that Member State as regards participation in the capital of the new company."[63]

Yet such equality of treatment might fail to win the confidence of a company contemplating the incorporation of a subsidiary under the law of a Member State offering legal protection to shareholders different from or inferior to that available in the Member State of primary establishment. Equally, third parties dealing with an agency or branch of a company established in another Member State might hesitate to place their trust in the guarantees of a corporate law system of another Member State with which they might be unfamiliar. These considerations are considerations of *principle*, and the company law harmonisation programme does seem to have been based to any great extent on an empirical assessment of the extent to which differences in national company law actually do restrict the exercise of the right of establishment by corporate persons.[64]

Obstacles to the freedom of corporate establishment and indeed the provision of services may arise from differences between regulatory régimes in different Member States. For example, if one Member State requires an insurance undertaking to have a particular management and capital structure if it is to carry on insurance business, and another Member State has different requirements in this regard, it may be impossible for undertakings established in either Member State to sell insurance in the other either through agencies or branches or by way of the provision of services. In such cases the problems of doing business in the single market are clearly not theoretical and the solutions provided by the Treaty are to be welcomed. It will be recalled that Article 57(2) of the Treaty provides that in order to make it easier for persons (including corporate persons) to take up and pursue activities as self-employed persons the Council shall issue Directives for the co-ordination of national laws in this respect. It must suffice for present purposes simply to make reference to the growing corpus of important legislation relating to activities by firms and companies enacted by the Community under *inter alia* this provision, in particular in the fields of banking and insurance.[65]

THE FREEDOM TO PROVIDE SERVICES

Article 59 of the Treaty provides that "[w]ithin the framework of the provisions set out below, restrictions on freedom to provide services within the Community shall be progressively abolished during the transitional period in respect of nationals of Member States who are established in a State of the Community other than that of the person for whom the services are intended." It will be noted that in order to invoke this provision, nationals must be "established" in a Member State. In the case of companies

---

[63] Case 81/87 [1988] E.C.R. 5483 at p. 5511, para. 17.
[64] For a survey of the company law tax harmonisation programme, see Dine, *The Harmonisation of Company Law in the European Community* (1989) 9 Y.E.L. 93.
[65] For legislation see in general Sweet and Maxwell, *Encyclopedia of European Community Law*, C12.

whose registered office is situated inside the Community, but whose central management or principal place of business is not, this requirement is satisfied by their activities having "a real and continuous link with the economy of a Member State, excluding the possibility that this link might depend on nationality, particularly the nationality of the partners or the members of the managing or supervisory bodies, or of persons holding the capital stock."[66] It has already been noted that a company registered in a Member State is established in that State even if it conducts all its business through an agency in another Member State.[67]

"Services" are defined in Article 60, and are considered as such when they are "normally provided for remuneration." One would expect the remuneration to be normally provided by the receiver of the services, but this is not essential. In the *Debauve* and *Coditel* cases,[68] Advocate General Warner expressed the opinion that the purpose of the definition of "services" in Article 60 was to exclude those that are normally provided gratuitously. Television broadcasting thus in his view fell within the definition whether it was financed by licence fee or by advertising. The decisive factor was that the broadcasting was remunerated in one way or another. *Bond van Averteerders*[69] concerned *inter alia* the provision of services by cable television operators in one Member State to broadcasters in another by relaying to network subscribers in the first Member State television programmes transmitted to them by the broadcasters. The Court held that these services were provided for remuneration. The cable network operators were paid, in the form of the fees which they charged their subscribers for the service which they provided to the broadcaster, and it was irrelevant that the broadcasters generally did not themselves pay the cable network operators for relaying their programmes.[70]

A non-exhaustive list of services in Article 60 specifies activities of an industrial character, activities of a commercial character, activities of craftsmen, and activities of the professions. Where a particular activity falls within the provisions of the Treaty relating to the free movement of goods, capital or persons, however, these latter provisions govern. The Court has held that tourism, medical treatment, and education are covered by the freedom to provide services.[71]

Without prejudice to the right of establishment, a person providing a service may, in order to do so, "temporarily pursue his activity in the State where the service is provided, under the same conditions as are imposed by that State on its own nationals."[72] The Court of Justice has concluded from these words that:

"Articles 59 and 60 of the Treaty therefore preclude a Member State

---

[66] General Programme (Services), O.J. 1974, Sp.Ed., 2nd Series, IX, p. 3.
[67] Case 79/85, *Segers* [1986] E.C.R. 2375, *supra*, p. 300.
[68] Case 52/79, *Debauve* [1980] E.C.R. 833; Case 62/79, *Coditel* [1980] E.C.R 881; Opinion at p. 876.
[69] Case 352/85 [1988] E.C.R. 2085.
[70] [1988] E.C.R. 2085 at p. 2131, para. 16.
[71] Cases 286/82 and 26/83, *Luisi* [1984] E.C.R. 377 at p. 403, para. 16.
[72] Art. 60, third para.

from prohibiting a person providing services established in another Member State from moving freely in its territory with all his staff and preclude that Member State from making the movement of staff in question subject to restrictions such as a condition as to engagement *in situ* or an obligation to obtain a work permit. To impose such conditions on the person providing services established in another Member State discriminates against that person in relation to his competitors established in the host country who are able to use their own staff without restrictions, and moreover affects his ability to provide the service."[73]

As observed above, the pursuit of economic activities on a permanent basis would amount to establishment in the host State.[74] As the Court explained in *Steymann*:

"It is clear from the actual wording of Article 60 that an activity carried out on a permanent basis or, in any event, without a foreseeable limit to its duration does not fall within the Community provisions concerning the provision of services. On the other hand, such activities may fall within the scope of Articles 48 to 51 or Articles 52 to 58 of the Treaty, depending on the case."[75]

While the transfrontier provision of services is generally governed by Article 59 of the Treaty, this will not be so in exceptional cases. The Court has held that:

". . . a Member State cannot be denied the right to take measures to prevent the exercise by a person providing services whose activity is entirely or principally directed towards its territory of the freedom guaranteed by Article 59 for the purpose of avoiding the professional rules of conduct which would be applicable to him if he were established in that State. Such a situation may be subject to judicial control under the provisions of the chapter relating to the right of establishment and not that on the provision of services."[76]

A literal interpretation of Articles 59 and 60 would guarantee freedom to provide services in the following circumstances:

— freedom to provide services across national frontiers, where provider and recipient remain in their respective Member States, as in the case of financial advice from United Kingdom advisers to French clients;
— freedom to provide services *in situ*, where the provider of a service visits temporarily the recipient in the latter's Member State as in the case of a United Kingdom doctor visiting a French patient.

As indicated at the beginning of the chapter, however,[77] it is important to

---

[73] Case C–113/89, *Rush Portuguesa Ldc* [1990] E.C.R. I–1417 at p. 1443, para. 12.
[74] *Supra*, p. 6173.
[75] Case 196/87 [1988] E.C.R. 6159 at p. 6173, para. 16.
[76] Case 33/74, *Van Binsbergen* [1974] E.C.R. 1299; Case 205/84, *Commission* v. *Germany* [1986] E.C.R. 3755 at p. 3801, para. 22.
[77] *Supra*, p. 278.

consider the provisions of Articles 52 and 59 as a whole, and in the light of the object and purpose of the Treaty, which is to ensure the fullest possible freedom to engage in economic activities in the territory of the Member States, regardless of the stage of provision or distribution of the services involved.

The Court's case law leaves scope for such an approach. In *Coenen*,[78] the Court held that Article 59 applied to a Netherlands national resident in Belgium who was providing services as an insurance intermediary through an office in the Netherlands, on the ground that the precise object of that Article was to abolish restrictions on freedom to provide services imposed on persons "who do not reside in the State where the service is to be provided." It will be recalled that Article 59 contemplates establishment in a State different from that of the receiver of the services. It is not clear whether Mr. Coenen was established in his own right in Belgium or not, and the Court does not seem to think it material. In truth, Mr. Coenen does seem to have been established in the Netherlands, and the Court's ruling prevented his personal residence in Belgium from being held against him in the former country. Perhaps nowadays such a situation would be considered as amounting to indirect discrimination on grounds of nationality contrary to Article 52 of the EEC Treaty, rather than as a situation governed by Article 59. In *Koestler*[79] contractual relations between a French bank and a German national resident in France were held to fall within Article 59 because the German national returned to Germany without having paid his debts. If the latter case decides that the residence of the recipient and the establishment of the provider in different States need not be contemporaneous with the actual provision of services, and *Coenen* decides that the personal residence of the provider may be an equivalent disability to that of establishment for the purposes of defining the mischief at which Article 59 is aimed, the way is open to the Court to hold that a visit by an English journalist to France to write a news story on a French election for an English newspaper is a step in the provision of services which falls within the ambit of Article 59, quite apart from the position of the journalist as a recipient of various services during his visit to France.[80]

The entry and residence of self-employed persons under Article 59 of the Treaty is governed by the same secondary legislation as entry and residence under Article 52, on the right of establishment, and the reader is referred accordingly to the treatment of Directive 73/148 found earlier in this chapter.[81] Although Article 59 only explicitly refers to the freedom to provide services, it will be recalled that Article 1(1)(b) of Directive 73/148 includes among its beneficiaries "nationals of Member States wishing to go to another Member State as recipients of services." In *Luisi*,[82] the Court held that the freedom to provide services included the freedom, for the recipients

---

[78] Case 39/75 [1975] E.C.R. 1555.
[79] Case 15/78 [1978] E.C.R. 1971.
[80] See *infra*, p. 306.
[81] *Supra*, p. 281.
[82] Cases 286/82 and 26/83 [1984] E.C.R. 377.

of services, to go to another Member State in order to receive a service there, without being obstructed by restrictions, and that tourists, persons receiving medical treatment and persons travelling for the purpose of education or business were to be regarded as recipients of services. An example of a tourist invoking the provisions of Article 59 is provided by the *Cowan* case.[83] Mr. Cowan, a citizen of the United Kingdom, made a brief visit to Paris, and was assaulted at the exit of a metro station. His attackers could not be identified, and he applied to the French authorities for compensation, under French law which provided for compensation in such circumstances. Mr. Cowan was refused compensation however, on the principal ground that he was not a French national. He challenged this refusal before a French court. On a reference for a preliminary ruling, the Court of Justice upheld his claim in the following terms:

> "When Community law guarantees a natural person the freedom to go to another Member State the protection of that person from harm in the Member State in question, on the same basis as that of nationals and persons residing there, is a corollary of that freedom of movement. It follows that the prohibition of discrimination is applicable to recipients of services within the meaning of the Treaty as regards protection against the risk of assault and the right to obtain financial compensation provided for by national law when that risk materializes."[84]

Abolition of restrictions

Like Article 54, Article 63 provides for the drawing up of a General Programme for the abolition of restrictions on freedom to provide services within the Community. The Programme was adopted in December 1961,[85] and closely resembles the General Programme for the abolition of restrictions on the right of establishment. Thus, for example, Title III calls for the abolition of restrictions such as those which "condition the provision of services on an authorisation or on the issuance of a document, such as a foreign merchant's card or a foreign professional's card."[86] As indicated earlier, most of the Directives issued to abolish restrictions on the right of establishment apply in addition to freedom to provide services. Thus Directive 64/223, used for illustrative purposes in the context of establishment,[87] also applies, in relation to the wholesale trade, to freedom to provide services. Furthermore, Article 57(2) of the Treaty, which provides for the harmonisation of national rules governing the pursuit of

---

[83] Case 186/87 [1989] E.C.R. 195.
[84] [1989] E.C.R. 195 at p. 221, para. 17. The Court's ruling refers "in particular" to Art. 7, and the judgment is based on the guarantee of equal treatment laid down generally in Art. 7 and more specifically in Art. 59: see [1989] E.C.R. at p. 220, paras. 14 and 15.
[85] O.J. 1974, Sp.Ed., 2nd Series, IX, p. 3. The Programme has been referred to by the Court in Case 15/78, *Koestler* [1978] E.C.R. 1971; Case 136/78, *Auer* [1979] E.C.R. 452; Cases 286/82 and 26/83, *Luisi* [1984] E.C.R. 377; Case 63/86, *Commission* v. *Italy* [1988] E.C.R. 29; Case 305/87, *Commission* v. *Hellenic Republic* [1989] E.C.R. 1461.
[86] O.J. 1974, *loc. cit.* p. 4.
[87] *Supra*, p. 285.

self-employed activities, is applied to the chapter on services by Article 66. Further reference is made to this below.[88]

Just as the Court's decision in *Reyners* v. *Belgian State*[89] on the direct applicability of Article 52 reduced significantly the importance of Directives requiring the abolition of particular discriminatory restrictions, so its later decision in *Van Binsbergen* v. *Bedrijfsvereniging Metaalnijverheid*,[90] upholding the direct effect of Articles 59, first paragraph and 60, third paragraph entailed similar consequences for the provisions of Directives concerned with the abolition of restrictions on the supply of services.[91] Thus, where discrimination is concerned, individuals and enterprises alike are entitled to rely directly on the Treaty, irrespective of national implementation of particular Directives, and regardless of whether or not Directives have even been adopted in the field in question.

It is to be noted that Article 59, like Article 52,[92] is concerned not only with the specific rules on the pursuit of occupational activities but also with the rules relating to the various general facilities which are of assistance in the pursuit of those activities, including the right to equal access to housing, and financial facilities to acquire housing.[93]

Restrictions in respect of non-residence, nationality, or otherwise

It is proposed to deal first with restrictions which are in principle contrary to Article 59, and to deal later with possible justifications for such restrictions. In *Van Binsbergen*, the Court stated that:

> "The restrictions to be abolished pursuant to Articles 59 and 60 include all requirements imposed on the person providing the service by reason in particular of his nationality or of the fact that he does not habitually reside in the State where the service is provided, which do not apply to persons established within the national territory or which prevent or otherwise obstruct the activities of the person providing the service."[94]

In *Commission* v. *Germany* the Court described the requirement of a permanent establishment as "the very negation" of freedom to provide services. "It has," said the Court, "the result of depriving Article 59 of the Treaty of all effectiveness, a provision whose very purpose is to abolish restrictions on the freedom to provide services of persons who are not established in the State in which the service is to be provided."[95]

---

[88] *Infra*, p. 309.
[89] Case 2/74 [1974] E.C.R. 631.
[90] Case 33/74 [1974] E.C.R. 1299; and see Case 36/74, *Walrave* [1974] E.C.R. 1405; Case 13/76, *Dona* v. *Mantero* [1976] E.C.R. 133; Cases 110 and 111/78, *Van Wesemael* [1979] E.C.R. 35
[91] See Commission Communication to the Council, SEC(74) 4024 Final, Brussels.
[92] *Supra*, p. 284.
[93] Case 63/86, *Commission* v. *Italy* [1988] E.C.R. 29; Case 305/87, *Commission* v. *Hellenic Republic* [1989] E.C.R. 1461.
[94] Case 33/74 [1974] E.C.R. 1299 at p. 1309, para. 10.
[95] Case 205/84, *Commission* v. *Germany* [1988] 3755 at p. 3809, para. 52, citing Case 39/75, *Coenen* [1975] E.C.R. 1547, and Case 76/81, *Transporoute* [1982] E.C.R. 417.

The Court has held incompatible with Article 59 a national requirement that a legal representative before a tribunal before which representation by a qualified lawyer is not obligatory be established in the Member State in which the tribunal is located.[96] Again, the Court has held incompatible with Article 59 a national requirement of one Member State that an insurance undertaking established in another Member State maintain a permanent establishment in the first Member State as a condition of carrying on insurance business in that State.[97]

It is also clear that Article 59 prohibits both direct and indirect discrimination on grounds of nationality. An example of a discriminatory restriction on the provision of services is considered in the *Bond van Averteerders* case.[98] Netherlands law prohibited cable network operators relaying programmes received via satellite from broadcasters in other Member States if they contained advertisements intended especially for the public in the Netherlands. The Court held that these rules amounted to restrictions on the provision of services in two respects. First, cable network operators were prevented from relaying television programmes supplied by broadcasters established in other Member States. Secondly, those broadcasters were prevented from scheduling advertisements for advertisers in the Member State where the programmes were received. Furthermore, these restrictions were discriminatory, since the Netherlands rules permitted the broadcasting of advertisements on national television stations for the benefit of all the national broadcasting organisations.

National measures may be indirectly discriminatory if they impose requirements which duplicate requirements complied with within the Member State of establishment. Thus, requiring an undertaking already licensed in the Member State of establishment to take out a similar licence in the State where the services are provided has been held to constitute a restriction contrary to Articles 59 and 60.[99] As has a provision of national law requiring the employers of short-stay workers to pay social security contributions in respect of workers still affiliated to the scheme of another Member State and accordingly themselves (the workers) exempted from the scope of the rules of the temporary host state.[1]

Differentiation which *prima facie* amounts to indirect discrimination on grounds of nationality will not amount to discrimination contrary to Article 59 where it is objectively justified. Thus, an insurance scheme in the Federal Republic of Germany under which no-claims bonuses were not granted to owners of vehicles bearing customs registration plates has been held to be compatible with Articles 7 and 59 of the EEC Treaty where it was based exclusively on objective actuarial factors and the objective criterion of registration under customs plates. The fact that it affected mainly the nationals of other Member States did not condemn the scheme, since it was

---

[96] Case 33/74, *Van Binsbergen* [1974] E.C.R. 1299.
[97] Case 205/84, *Commission* v. *Germany* [1986] E.C.R. 3755.
[98] Case 352/85 [1988] E.C.R. 2085.
[99] Cases 110 and 111/78, *Van Wesemael* [1979] E.C.R. 35; Case 249/80, *Webb* [1981] E.C.R. 3305.
[1] Cases 62 and 63/81, *Seco* [1982] E.C.R. 223.

also capable of affecting nationals of the Federal Republic in certain circumstances.[2]

Exceptionally, it seems that even direct discrimination on grounds of nationality may be justified on objectives consistent with the Treaty. This is probably the explanation of *Dona* v. *Mantero*,[3] in which the Court of Justice held that while the activities of semi-professional or professional footballers in the nature of gainful employment or remunerated service amounted to economic activity within the scope of the Treaty, the exclusion of foreign players from participation in certain matches, such as matches between national teams, would be consistent with the Treaty.

National measures which neither impose a residence requirement nor discriminate directly or indirectly on grounds of nationality will nevertheless be contrary to Article 59 if they amount to an unnecessary burden on the provision of services. Thus in *Sager*,[4] the Court considered national rules prohibiting a company established in another Member State from providing patent owners in the first Member State with a service for monitoring patents, on the ground that such activities in that State were reserved to persons holding a special professional qualification. The company did not comply with the rules in question. The Court held that such rules were a restriction on the provision of services contrary to Article 59. The Court emphasised that Article 59 required not only the elimination of all discrimination on grounds of nationality, but also the elimination of any restriction, even one applying equally to nationals and non-nationals alike, which might prohibit or restrict the activities of a provider of services established in another Member State, where that provider lawfully provided the services in question.[5]

Mutual recognition of diplomas and the co-ordination of national rules

The mutual recognition of professional qualifications and the co-ordination of national rules governing self-employed activities is as crucial to securing the free provision of services as it is to facilitating the right of establishment, and Directives 75/362 and 363, on the mutual recognition of medical diplomas, and the co-ordination of national medical qualifications, considered in the context of the latter[6] are equally applicable to the former, as is Directive 89/48 on the recognition of higher education diplomas.[7] In order to facilitate the provision of services, medical practitioners established outside the host State are relieved of the obligation to register with professional organisations or bodies therein though they are subject to the applicable national rules of professional conduct.[8]

---

[2] Case 251/83, *Eberhard Haug-Adrion* [1984] E.C.R. 4277.
[3] Case 13/76 [1976] E.C.R. 113.
[4] Case C–76/90 [1991] E.C.R. I–4221.
[5] [1991] E.C.R. I–4221 at para. 12.
[6] *Supra*, pp. 294, 295.
[7] O.J. 1989 L19/16.
[8] Dir. 75/362, Art. 16.

Progress has been less dramatic in the case of lawyers than of doctors, in view of the different legal systems in the Member States. Thus Directive 89/48 allows Member States to decide between an adaptation period and an aptitude test in the case of lawyers seeking recognition of their qualifications in another Member State.[9] However, specific provision is made for the provision of services by lawyers in Directive 77/249.[10] Under the Directive, Member States must recognise designated legal practitioners[11] as "lawyers" for the purpose of pursuing "the activities of lawyers pursued by way of provision of services."[12] Since the substantive content of legal training differs in the Member States, and the Directive contains no provisions for the mutual recognition of diplomas, a designated legal practitioner must adopt the professional title used in the Member State from which he comes, expressed in the language of that State, and with an indication of the professional organisation by which he is authorised to practise.[13] When representing a client in legal proceedings, a lawyer must comply with the conditions laid down for lawyers in the host State, except for conditions requiring residence, or registration with a professional organisation in that State,[14] and the host State may further require him:

"— to be introduced, in accordance with local rules or customs, to the presiding judge and, where appropriate, to the President of the relevant Bar in the host Member State;
— to work in conjunction with a lawyer who practises before the judicial authority in question and who would, where necessary, be answerable to that authority . . ."[15]

The Court has held that the purpose of the requirement that a lawyer providing services "work in conjunction with" a local lawyer is intended to provide him with the support necessary to enable him to act within a judicial system different from that to which he is accustomed and to assure the judicial authority concerned that the lawyer providing services actually has that support and is thus in a position fully to comply with the procedural and ethical rules that apply.[16] But national implementing measures must not lay down disproportionate requirements in this regard, such as a requirement that a local lawyer be present throughout the oral proceedings, or a requirement that the local lawyer be the authorised representative or defending counsel.[17]

---

[9] *Supra*, p. 296.
[10] O.J. 1977 L78/17. Annotated by H. Bronkhorst in (1977) 2 E.L.Rev. 224. And see D. B. Walters, (1978) 3 E.L.Rev. 265.
[11] Art. 1(2).
[12] Art. 2.
[13] Art. 3.
[14] Art. 4(1).
[15] Art. 5
[16] Case 427/85, *Commission* v. *Germany* [1988] E.C.R. 1123.
[17] *Ibid.* And see Case C–294/89, *Commission* v. *French Republic* [1991] E.C.R. I–3591.

Public policy and reasonable restrictions in the general interest

Article 59 is subject to express exceptions under Articles 55, 56 and 66 of the EEC Treaty, and to implied exceptions in the case of non-discriminatory restrictions which are reasonable and in the general interest. Case law on Articles 55 and 56 is thus applicable *mutatis mutandis*. Article 56 allows derogation from Article 52 by way of special treatment for foreign nationals on grounds of public policy, public security or public health, and Article 66 applies this provision to the chapter on services. The Court has held that *discriminatory* restrictions can only be compatible with Community law if they can be brought within the scope of an express derogation such as those provided under Articles 56 and 66.[18] Furthermore, economic aims cannot constitute grounds of public policy within the meaning of Article 56.[19] In any event, measures taken by virtue of that Article must not be disproportionate to the intended objective.[20]

A State may impose a residence requirement if it is strictly necessary to do so in order to prevent the evasion, by those resident outside its borders, of professional rules applicable to the pursuit of a particular activity.[21] Needless to say, such a requirement cannot be considered necessary if the provision of certain services in a Member State is "not subject to any sort of qualification or professional regulation and when the requirement of habitual residence is fixed by reference to the territory of the State in question."[22] Even if professional rules are applicable to a particular activity, a requirement that practitioners maintain a personal residence within the jurisdiction will not normally be justified in the case of those who maintain a bona fide place of business therein.[23] An example of a permissible residence requirement given by the Court was the rule that "persons whose functions are to assist in the administration of justice must be permanently established for professional purposes within the jurisdiction of certain courts or tribunals,"[24] though this statement must not be read in the light of Article 4(1) of Directive 77/249, on the freedom to provide legal services.[25]

The Court has held that Article 59 does not preclude the enforcement of national rules for the protection of intellectual property, save where such application constitutes a means of arbitrary discrimination or a disguised restriction on trade between Member States.[26] Likewise, it does not preclude national rules prohibiting the transmission of advertisements by cable television, if these rules are applied without distinction as regards the

---

[18] Case 352/85, *Bond van Averteerders* [1988] E.C.R. 2085 at p. 2134, paras. 32, 33.
[19] *Ibid.* para. 34.
[20] *Ibid.* para. 36.
[21] Case 33/74, *Van Binsbergen* [1974] E.C.R. 1299; Case 39/75, *Coenen* [1975] E.C.R. 1547.
[22] Case 33/74, *Van Binsbergen* [1974] E.C.R. 1299 at p. 1310.
[23] Case 39/75, *Coenen* E.C.R. 1547. Yet where there is an establishment within the host State, Art. 52 rather than Art. 59 would seem to apply, see Case 205/84, *supra*, note 42; Case 196/87, *supra*, note 74.
[24] Case 33/74, *Van Binsbergen* [1974] E.C.R. 1299 at p. 1310.
[25] O.J. 1977 L18/17.
[26] Case 62/79, *Coditel* [1980] E.C.R. 881.

origin, whether national or foreign, of those advertisements, the nationality of the person providing the service, or the place where he is established.[27]

The categories of general interest are not closed. Thus the public interest in promotion and conservation of historical, artistic and archaeological treasures could constitute an imperative reason justifying a restriction on the freedom to provide services.[28] Furthermore, cultural policy might afford an imperative reason of public interest justifying a restriction on the freedom to provide services.[29]

TRANSPORT, BANKING AND INSURANCE

The scope of Articles 59 to 66 on the provision of services is subject to certain derogations and exceptions in favour of other Articles of the Treaty, such as the provisions relating to the movement of goods, capital and persons.[30] Similarly, freedom to provide services in the field of transport is governed by the provisions of Title IV of Part Two of the Treaty, relating thereto,[31] while the liberalisation of banking[32] and insurance[33] services connected with the movement of capital is to be effected in step with the progressive liberalisation of the latter.[34]

---

[27] Case 52/79, *Debauve* [1980] E.C.R. 833.
[28] Case C-154/89, *Commission* v. *French Republic* [1991] E.C.R. I-659.
[29] Case C-353/89, *Commission* v. *Netherlands* [1991] E.C.R. I-4069.
[30] Art. 60, first para.
[31] Art. 61(1). For Transport, see Arts. 74-84, and for secondary legislation, see Sweet and Maxwell's *Encyclopedia of European Community Law*, Vol. C, Pt. C16.
[32] Art. 61(2). See Case 267/86, *Van Eycke* [1988] E.C.R. 4769. For legislation on banks and credit institutions, see Sweet and Maxwell's *Encyclopedia of European Community Law*, Vol. C, Pt. C12. And see Strivens, (1992) 29 C.M.L. Rev. 283.
[33] Art. 61(2). For legislation on insurance, see Sweet and Maxwell's *Encyclopedia of European Community Law*, Vol. C, Part C12. And see See Poole, (1984) 21 C.M.L. Rev. 123; Chappatte, (1984) 9 E.L. Rev. 3; Ottow, (1992) 29 C.M.L. Rev. 511.
[34] Art. 61(2). For the free movement of capital, see Arts. 67-73; Sweet and Maxwell's *Encyclopedia of of European Community Law*, Vol. IV, Pt. C5-013 *et seq.* And see Oliver, (1984) 9 E.L. Rev. 401.

CHAPTER 11

SOCIAL SECURITY FOR MIGRANTS

The territorial limitations of national social security law

Articles 48 and 49 of the Treaty, and the secondary legislation made thereunder, grant to employed persons the right to seek and to take up employment throughout the Community, without discrimination on grounds of nationality. Articles 52 and 59 of the Treaty, implemented by the applicable secondary legislation, make analogous provision for the self-employed. Such rights, while of the utmost importance, cannot of themselves secure genuine freedom of movement, in view of the territorial limitations of the national social security systems. Such limitations are capable of constituting an obstacle to the free movement of employed and self-employed persons in several respects. First, both entitlement to benefit and the amount of benefit payable may depend on the claimant's having paid, or having been credited with, social security contributions. And yet contributions in one Member State may not give rise to a right to benefit under the national law of another. A hypothetical example is illustrative. Suppose an employed or self-employed person works for five years, paying social security contributions in one Member State, and then moves to another, where he takes up wage-earning or self-employed activities. Suppose that after six months he becomes ill, and claims sickness benefit from the social security authorities of his State of residence. Although our employed or self-employed person has been insured continuously for five and a half years, he will receive benefit exclusively on the basis of his contributions in the State where he is now employed, *i.e.* on the basis of six months' contributions.[1] The reasons for this are perfectly understandable, but the practical effect is that he has forfeited his insurance contribution record in one State by taking up employed or self-employed activities in another.

National social security schemes may place the migrant at a further disadvantage if his wife and family have remained for the time being in his country of origin. Although the law of the host State may provide for an increased rate of benefit to be payable in respect of a claimant's dependants, it may also condition such increased payment on the presence of said dependants in national territory. Although not the object of formal discrimination on grounds of nationality, the migrant is undoubtedly placed at a disadvantage compared to the indigenous wage-earning or self-employed worker.

Again, national authorities may refuse to pay benefit to a claimant outside the jurisdiction, even if he otherwise satisfies the contribution conditions

---

[1] Unless the Member States in question have otherwise agreed in bilateral or multilateral agreements.

313

required under national law. Thus a migrant who has acquired a right to an old-age pension under the law of the host State, but returns to his country of origin on retirement, may find himself denied advantages accorded to workers remaining within the territory of the host State. Although an employed or self-employed person who has acquired a right to a pension under national law may be allowed to "export" the right abroad, he may thereby disentitle himself to any subsequent cost-of-living increases which would be payable were he to remain within the jurisdiction.

The solution prescribed by Community law

It was with these problems in mind that the signatories of the Treaty declared, in Article 51, that the Council should adopt such measures in the field of social security as would be necessary to provide freedom of movement for workers. To this end, the Council was instructed to make arrangements to secure for migrant workers and their dependants:

"(a) aggregation, for the purpose of acquiring and retaining the right to benefit and of calculating the amount of benefit, of all periods taken into account under the laws of the several countries;
 (b) payment of benefits to persons resident in the territories of Member States."

These aims are realised in the text of Regulation 1408/71,[2] which, *inter alia*, remedies for the employed person the territorial limitations of national law described above. That Regulation does not aim to harmonise the social security systems of the Member States but rather to co-ordinate them so that they interact to provide the migrant worker with constant social security protection wherever he moves within the Community. Apart from removing the territorial barriers inherent in national social security systems, Regulation 1408/71 does not alter those systems in any way: conditions of affiliation and entitlement to benefits and the range and level of benefits are matters to be decided by each Member State.[3] Co-ordination involves two processes: aggregation and proraterisation. The process of aggregation ensures for the worker who pursues employment in several Member States a continuous contribution record. Thus, in the case of sickness and maternity benefits, the Regulation requires that the authorities of a Member State whose legislation makes the "acquisition, retention or recovery of the right to benefits" conditional upon the completion of insurance periods "take account of periods of insurance . . . completed under the legislation of any other Member State as if they were periods completed under the legislation

---

[2] J.O. 1971 L149/1, J.O.Sp.Ed., 1971 (I), p. 416: as amended and updated (and in effect consolidated) in Reg. 2001/83, O.J. 1983 L230/6. Reg. 1408/71 is implemented by Reg. 547/72, J.O. 1972 L74/1, also amended and updated and consolidated in Reg. 2001/83, *supra*. With respect to Spain and Portugal, see Arts. 60 and 220 respectively of the 1985 Act of Accession, and Annex I, VIII, 1. For a comprehensive treatise, see Watson, *Social Security Law of the European Communities*.
[3] Case 266/78, *Brunori* 1979 E.C.R. 2705; Case 110/79, *Coonan* 1980 E.C.R. 1445; Case 70/80, *Vigier* 1981 E.C.R. 229; Case 29/88, *Schmitt* 1989 E.C.R. 581. Watson, (1981) 6 E.L.Rev. 41, (1989) 14 E.L.Rev. 350.

which it administers."[4] Similar provisions ensure aggregation in the case of invalidity, old-age and death pensions, death grants, unemployment benefits, and family benefits and allowances.[5] Proraterisation ensures, particularly in the case of pensions which are paid out over a lengthy period of time, the equitable distribution of the cost of benefits between the Member States in which a claimant has been insured. Essentially each Member State is required to pay benefits in proportion to the length of time the claimant has been insured in that Member State.

Whereas a claimant may only be entitled to a higher rate of benefit under national law in respect of members of his family who are to be found within the jurisdiction, the Regulation requires that national authorities "take into account the members of the family of the person concerned who are resident in the territory of another Member State as if they were resident in the territory of the competent State."[6] Furthermore, in accordance with paragraph (b) of Article 51 of the Treaty, provision is made for the payment of cash benefits to claimants absent from the territory of the competent State. Thus in the case, *inter alia*, of old-age pensions, Member States are precluded from withdrawing or reducing benefit on the ground that the recipient is resident in a Member State other than that whose institution is responsible for payment.[7]

Whereas Article 51 of the Treaty provides for Community measures designed to safeguard the social security rights of employed persons, the Treaty makes no specific provision for the social security rights of the self-employed. In the first instance, Regulation 1408/71, based on Articles 2, 7 and 51 of the Treaty, was limited in its application to the social security rights of employed persons. Regulation 1390/81,[8] based on Articles 2, 7, 51 and 235[9] of the Treaty, extended the provisions of Regulation 1408/71 to the self-employed.

Although Regulation 1408/71 superseded its predecessor, Regulation 3,[10] on October 1, 1972, the latter Regulation may still be applicable to persons who acquired rights thereunder. Thus Article 94(5) of Regulation 1408/71 provides that "persons whose pension rights[11] were determined before the entry into force of this Regulation . . . may apply for such pension rights to be

---

[4] Reg. 1408/71, Art. 18(1).

[5] Arts. 38, 45, 64, 67, 72. But it should be noted that aggregation can only be relied upon to establish qualifying periods; not to establish affiliation to a national system. Note 3.

[6] Art. 23(3), relating to sickness and maternity benefit. Arts. 68(2) and 73, 74 make similar provision in respect of unemployment and family benefits respectively. Art. 39(4) provides for the taking into account of members of the family other than children in the case of invalidity pensions; for the position of children in the case of old-age, invalidity and occupational pensions, see Chap. 8 of the Regulation.

[7] Art. 10(1).

[8] O.J. 1981 L143/1.

[9] Art. 235 provides: "If action by the Community should prove necessary to attain, in the course of the operation of the common market, one of the objectives of the Community and this Treaty has not provided the necessary powers, the Council shall, acting unanimously on a proposal from the Commission and after consulting the Assembly, take the appropriate measures."

[10] J.O. 1958, 561. Implemented by Reg. 4, J.O. 1958, 597.

[11] See Art. 1(t) of Reg. 1408/71. The pensions referred to are not simply those in respect of old age, but include invalidity and survivor's benefits, and benefits payable in respect of accidents at work.

reviewed, taking account of the provisions of this Regulation." The Court explained in *Alfonsa Reale* v. *Caisse de compensation des allocations familiales* that the paragraph was based on the principle "that benefits awarded under Regulation No. 3 which are more favourable than those payable under the new Regulation shall not be reduced."[12]

It has been noted that Regulation 1390/81 extended the application of Regulation 1408/71 to the self-employed. The former Regulation, however, does not affect any rights acquired, prior to its entry into force, under Regulation 1408/71.[13] With respect to self-employed persons, no right may be acquired under Regulation 1408/71, as amended by Regulation 1390/81, in respect of a period prior to July 1, 1982.[14] All insurance periods and, where appropriate, all periods of employment, of self-employment or of residence completed under the legislation of a Member State before July 1, 1982 shall be taken into consideration for the determination of the rights of the self-employed to benefits under Regulation 1408/71.[15] Subject to the exclusion of rights arising from July 1, 1982, rights may nevertheless be acquired relating to contingencies which materialised prior to that date.[16] The rights of a self-employed person to whom a pension was awarded prior to July 1, 1982, may, on the application of the person concerned, be reviewed, taking into account the provisions in Regulation 1408/71, as amended.[17]

Persons to whom Regulation 1408/71 applies

Article 2(1) of Regulation 1408/71 provides that it shall apply to "employed or self-employed persons who are or have been subject to the legislation of one or more Member States and who are nationals[18] of one of the Member States ... also to the members of their families and their survivors."[19]

Employed and self-employed persons

One might expect that the "employed persons" (formerly "workers" before Regulation 1408/71 was extended to cover the self-employed) referred to in Article 2(1) of Regulation 1408/71 would be none other than the "workers" referred to in Article 48 of the Treaty, but this is not precisely

---

[12] Case 23/76 [1976] E.C.R. 1523 at p. 1531.
[13] Reg. 3795/81, O.J. 1981 L378/1, Art. 3. And see Case 32/76, *Reale* [1976] E.C.R. 1523.
[14] Reg. 1408/71, Art. 95. This date is the date of the entry into force of Reg. 1390/81; see Reg. 1390/81, Art. 4, and Reg. 3795/81, O.J. 1981 L378/1, Art. 5.
[15] Reg. 1408/71, Art. 95(2).
[16] Reg. 1408/71, Art. 93(3).
[17] Reg. 1408/71, Art. 95(5). *N.B.* Reg. 3795/81, Art. 3; and Case 32/76, *Reale* [1976] E.C.R. 1523.
[18] Nationality of a Member State at the time of the completion of insurance periods has been held to be decisive, even if such nationality was lacking at the time the claim was made: Case 10/78, *Belbouab* [1978] E.C.R. 1915. See Watson, (1979) 4 E.L.Rev. 106.
[19] Stateless persons and refugees resident within the territory are also covered, as are civil servants. But see Art. 4(4) of Reg. 1408/71, which excludes special schemes for civil servants from the ambit of the Community rules: Case C–245/88, *Daalmeijer* 1991 E.C.R. 1–555.

the case. The discrepancy is best understood in the light of the provisions of Regulation 3, predecessor of Regulation 1408/71, and the case-law of the Court thereon. Article 4(1) of the latter Regulation declared it to be applicable to "wage-earners and comparable workers."[20] The Court held in *Hoekstra (nee Unger)*[21] that this category included persons compulsorily insured in the first place as workers who continued to make contributions on a voluntary basis after ceasing employment. In the Court's view it was the intention of the Treaty and the Regulation to protect those who had terminated their employment as well as those actually employed—this followed from the text of Article 48(3) of the Treaty, which referred to persons likely "to remain in the territory of a Member State after having been employed in that State," and from the definition in Article 4 of Regulation 3, which embraced wage-earners who were or had been subject to the legislation of one or more of the Member States.

Although the Court in *Hoekstra* defined the ambit of Regulation 3 primarily by reference to Article 48 of the Treaty, later decisions were to define the concept of "travailleurs assimiles" by reference to the national social security systems. In *De Cicco*,[22] the question arose as to whether a self-employed artisan could be regarded as a "comparable worker" within the meaning of Regulation No. 3, the Court held such persons were to be considered as assimilated to wage-earners "to the extent to which, by virtue of the provisions of national legislation, they are protected against one or more risks by extension of a scheme organised for the benefit of the generality of workers."[23]

The fourth recital to the preamble to Regulation 1408/71 recorded that considerable differences in the categories of persons to whom the national legislations applied made it preferable to establish the principle that the Regulation applies to all nationals of Member States insured under social security schemes for employed persons. The same principle was applied to extend the application of Regulation 1408/71 to the self-employed. Article 1(a) of the Regulation classifies employed and self-employed persons, not by reference to Articles 48, 52 and 59 of the Treaty, but according to the provision of the national social security schemes applicable to them: a person insured as an employed or self-employed person under the social security system of a Member State is to be considered as an insured person for the purposes of Regulation 1408/71. Thus, under sub-paragraph (i) of Article 1(a) an employed or self-employed person is so classified because he is insured under a scheme established to benefit employed or self-employed persons.[24] Under sub-paragraph (ii) a claimant who is affiliated to a scheme established to benefit the whole working population, or all residents, may be

---

[20] "Travailleurs salariés ou assimilés."
[21] Case 75/63 [1964] E.C.R. 177.
[22] Case 19/68 [1968] E.C.R. 473.
[23] [1968] E.C.R. 473 at p. 481.
[24] Art. 1(a)(i) provides that "employed person" and "self-employed person" mean respectively "any person who is insured, compulsorily or on an optional continued basis, for one or more of the contingencies covered by the branches of a social security scheme for employed or self-employed persons." It will be noted that a person is covered by this provision even if he is not in fact insured, as long as he ought to be insured: see Case 39/76, *Mouthaan* [1976] E.C.R.

classified as an employed or self-employed person, *inter alia*, (a) by virtue of the method by which the scheme is administered or financed, or (b) as a result of simultaneous affiliation to a scheme for employed or self-employed persons, albeit in respect of risks other than those covered by Regulation 1408/71.[25]

The Regulation itself is silent as to the modes of administration or financing ((a) above) which permit the identification as "employed or self-employed persons" of claimants covered by general schemes. In the *Brack* case[26] the Court acknowledged that Article 1(a)(ii) of Regulation 1408/71 (at that time applicable only to "workers") might cover both self-employed persons who had formerly been employed persons, and those self-employed persons who were nevertheless treated as employed persons by the national social security systems. Thus even before Regulation 1408/71 was extended to the self-employed, it already covered certain categories of such persons, as was acknowledged by the sixth recital to Regulation 1390/81.

In *van Roosmalen*[27] the Court ruled upon the meaning of "self-employed person." The case concerned a missionary priest who had worked from 1955 to 1980 in the Belgian Congo, which became Zaire in 1960. He was not paid by the religious order of which he was a member but was maintained by his parishioners. The question arose as to whether he was to be considered a self-employed person within the meaning of the Regulation. The Court held that the concept of a self-employed person encompasses any person who pursues, other than under a contract of employment, the exercise of an independent trade or profession in respect of which he receives income permitting him to meet some or all of his needs: it is of no importance that that income may be supplied by a third party (in this case the parishioners of the claimant).

Annex I, L, entitled "Employed persons and/or self-employed persons (Article 1(a)(ii) and (iii) of the Regulation)," states under heading L, United Kingdom,

> "Any person who is an 'employed earner' or a 'self-employed earner' within the meaning of the legislation of Great Britain or of the legislation of Northern Ireland shall be regarded respectively as an

---

1901. The formulation covers those who are no longer economically active: Case 182/78, *Pierik* [1978] E.C.R. 1971.

[25] Art. 1(a)(ii) refers to "any person who is compulsorily insured for one or more of the contingencies covered by the branches of social security dealt with in this Regulation, under a social security scheme for all residents or for the whole working population, if such person:— can be identified as an employed or self-employed person by virtue of the manner in which such scheme is administered or financed, or—failing such criteria, is insured for some other contingencies specified in Annex I under a scheme for employed or self-employed persons, or a scheme referred to in (iii), either compulsorily or on an optional continued basis or, where no such scheme exists in the Member State concerned, complies with the definition given in Annex I."
Art. 1(a)(iii) refers to a person "who is compulsorily insured for several of the contingencies covered by the branches dealt with in this Regulation, under a standard social security scheme for the whole rural population in accordance with the criteria laid down in Annex I."
[26] Case 17/76 [1976] E.C.R. 1429.
[27] Case 300/84 1986 E.C.R. 3095.

employed person or a self-employed person within the meaning of Article 1(a)(ii) of the Regulation."[28]

The Court held in *Walsh*[29] that a person who is entitled under the legislation of a Member State to benefits covered by Regulation 1408/71 by virtue of contributions paid compulsorily does not lose his status as a "worker" under Article 1(a)(ii) by reason only of the fact that at the time when the contingency occurred he was no longer paying contributions and was not bound to do so.

Article 1 of Regulation 1408/71 includes in the categories of "employed person" and "self-employed person" anyone who is voluntarily insured for one or more of the contingencies covered by the branches of social security dealt with in the Regulation, under a social security scheme of a Member State for employed or self-employed persons, or for all residents, or for certain categories of residents, provided that certain conditions are satisfied. These are that such a person carries on an activity as an employed or self-employed person, or has previously been compulsorily insured for the same contingency under a scheme for employed or self-employed persons of the same Member State.

Who are or have been subject to the law of one or more Member States

An employed or self-employed person may be entitled to rely on Regulation 1408/71, although he pursues his occupation in his country of origin, always has done, and has never been subject to the legislation of another Member State. This results from the wording of Article 2(1), which provides that the Regulation shall apply to workers who are or have been subject to the legislation of one or more Member States.

Thus a worker subject to Netherlands social security legislation who fell ill during a visit to her parents in Germany was entitled to claim for the cost of treatment received in that country on her return.[30] Furthermore, in the *Laumann*[31] case, the Court held that the right to orphan's benefits in respect of the children of a worker who had never moved between Member States fell within the ambit of Regulation 1408/71 as a result of the children's change of residence to another Member State.

---

[28] It is also provided that "Any person in respect of whom contributions are payable as an 'employed person' or a 'self-employed person' in accordance with the legislation of Gibraltar shall be regarded respectively as an employed person or a self-employed person within the meaning of Article 1(a)(iii) of the Regulation."

[29] Case 143/79 [1980] E.C.R. 1639. On the definition of "worker" under Art. 1(a)(ii); see also Case 84/77, *Tessier* [1978] E.C.R. 7; Wyatt, (1978) 3 E.L.Rev. 391; Case 99/80, *Galinsky* [1981] E.C.R. 941; Watson, (1982) 7 E.L.Rev. 126.

[30] Case 75/63, *Hoekstra (née Unger)* [1964] E.C.R. 177.

[31] Case 115/77 [1978] E.C.R. 805; (1979) 4 E.L.Rev. 371.

The scope of Regulation 1408/71 *ratione personae* and the governing Treaty provisions

It is apparent from the foregoing that Regulation 1408/71 is applicable, not only to migrants subject to the legislation of several Member States, but also to persons who have never pursued occupational activities in more than one country nor been subject to the social security legislation of more than one Member State. This may seem surprising, since Article 51 of the Treaty, the legal basis for Regulations 3 and 1408/71, merely authorises the Council to adopt such measures in the field of social security as are necessary to provide freedom of movement for workers. Article 235, one of the Treaty Articles upon which Regulation 1390/81 is based, is invoked in conjunction with Article 51, and apparently to similar effect with respect to the self-employed.

The purpose of the latter Articles, read in conjunction with the texts of Articles 48, 52 and 59, would seem to suggest that the only persons entitled to take advantage of the Community provisions co-ordinating the national social security systems are migrants seeking employment or self-employment, engaged in employment or self-employment, or remaining in a Member State after cessation of employment or self-employment under the conditions specified in Regulation 1251/70[32] or Directive 75/34.[33] The Court however, recognising the practical difficulties of co-ordinating diverse systems of social security legislation, has allowed the Council a margin of discretion in its implementation of Article 51 of the Treaty. The *Maison Singer*[34] case is illustrative. A German national holidaying in France was killed in a collision between his motorcycle and a livestock van belonging to Maison Singer and driven by one of its employees. The Hessische Knappschaft paid benefits to the dependants of the deceased, and sued in a French court for reimbursement from Maison Singer on the ground that, under French law and Article 52 of Regulation 3, it was subrogated to the rights of the dependants. The Court held that it would be impracticable to confine the application of Article 51 and Regulation No. 3 to migrant workers *stricto sensu* or to workers who moved for the purpose of their employment.

The Court's reasoning is based on two propositions: the first is that freedom of movement for workers is a right which is not strictly limited by the economic requirements of a common market[35]; the second is that a permissible method of facilitating such freedom of movement is the removal of territorial limitations on the application of the various social security systems. This reasoning is equally applicable to sustain the amendments to Regulation 1408/71 made to extend its operation to the self-employed. In the process of removing the territorial limitations on the application of the national social security systems, benefits will inevitably accrue to employed

---

[32] O.J.Sp.Ed. 1970 (II), p. 42: see *supra* at p. 182.
[33] O.J. 1975 L14/10, *supra* at p. 202.
[34] [1965] E.C.R. 965 at p. 971.
[35] See *supra*, at p. 238.

and self-employed persons who are not migrants, and to members of their families, and may even accrue to persons who are not employed or self-employed persons at all, but are treated as such by the applicable social security systems.

Members of workers' families, and survivors

Article 51 of the Treaty refers to the need to ensure social security coverage for workers' dependants, and Regulation 1408/71 provides accordingly for the families of employed persons, and, more latterly, for the families of the self-employed. A "member of the family" is any person defined or recognised as a member of the family or designated as a member of the household by the legislation under which benefits are provided.[36] Members of the family may only claim such rights as are derived under national law from the family relationship with the employed or self-employed person.[37] Where national law regards as a member of the family only a person living under the same roof as the employed or self-employed person, this condition is considered satisfied if the person in question is mainly dependent on that person.[38] Regulation 1408/71 vests rights to sickness and maternity benefits directly in members of the family of an employed or self-employed person visiting another Member State.[39] In such a case the classification of members of the family is in accordance with the law of the Member State of residence of the person in question.[40] Furthermore, it is not necessary in this case that the applicable national legislation provides benefits derived from the family relationship with the employed or self-employed person.[41] An exception to this general rule has been recently introduced in the case of disablement benefits, by virtue of Regulation 1247/92,[42] amending Article 1(f) of Regulation 1408/71, in the case of benefits for disabled persons granted under the legislation of a Member State to all nationals of that State who fulfil conditions for entitlement. In such cases the term "members of the family" means the spouse of an employed or self-employed person and the children of such persons who are either minors or who are dependants.

Regulation 1408/71 applies also to the survivors of employed or self-employed persons.[43] A "survivor" means any person defined or recognised as such by the legislation under which the benefits are granted.[44] Where that

---

[36] Reg. 1408/71, Art. 1(f).
[37] Case 40/76, *Kermaschek* [1976] E.C.R. 1669; Case 157/84, *Frascogna* 1985 E.C.R. 1739; Case 94/84, *Deak* 1985 E.C.R. 1873. Case C–243/91, *Belgian State* v. *Taghavi*, Judgment of July 8, 1992; Case 7/75, *Mr. and Mrs. F.* [1975] E.C.R. 679, which allows the dependent child of a worker to claim a benefit for the handicapped in his own right under Reg. 1408/71, is inconsistent with the above cases. The deficiencies of Reg. 1408/71 are largely remedied by Art. 7(2) of Reg. 1612/68, see *supra* at p. 179, (1985) 10 E.L.Rev. 343.
[38] Reg. 1408/71, Art. 1(f).
[39] Art. 22(3).
[40] Reg. 1408/71, Art. 1(f).
[41] The Court's case law referred to in note 37 would seem to have no relevance to a case where the Reg. vests rights directly in members of the family.
[42] O.J. 1992 L136/1.
[43] Art. 2(1). See, *e.g.* Art. 44(1).
[44] Art. 1(g).

legislation regards as a survivor only a person who was living under the same roof as the deceased, this condition shall be considered satisfied if such person was mainly dependent on the deceased.[45]

Refugees and stateless persons

Refugees and stateless persons are also covered by Regulation 1408/71. The meaning to be given to these concepts is that accorded to them in the Convention on Status of Refugees signed in Geneva on July 28, 1951 and the Convention on the Status of Stateless Persons signed in New York on September 28, 1954 respectively.[46]

Social security benefits falling within the ambit of Regulation 1408/71

National legislation concerning the following branches of social security falls within the ambit of the Regulation[47]:
— sickness and maternity benefits;
— invalidity benefits;
— old-age benefits;
— survivors' benefits;
— benefits in respect of accidents at work and occupational diseases;
— death grants;
— unemployment benefits;
— family benefits.

Article 1(j) of the Regulation provides:

" 'legislation' means in respect of each Member State statutes, regulations and other provisions and all other implementing measures, present or future, relating to the branches and schemes of social security covered by Article 4(1). . . ."

Despite the reference to provisions "present and future" the Court has held that the formulation in Article 1(j) embraces national legislation previously in force but which had ceased to exist when the Community social security regulations were adopted.[48]

The term "benefits" used in Article 4(1) of the Regulation is defined in Article 1(t) as including all elements payable out of public funds, as well as all revalorisation increases and supplementary allowances.

---

[45] Reg. 1408/71, Art. 1(g).
[46] Art. 1(d), (e).
[47] Art. 4(1).
[48] Case 109/76, *Blottner* [1977] E.C.R. 1141; Wyatt, (1978) 3 E.L.Rev. 46; Case 285/82, *Derks* [1984] E.C.R. 433. For "legislation" governing the social security rights of workers in the Belgian Congo, see Case 87/76, *Bozzone* [1977] E.C.R. 687; Case 150/79, *Commission* v. *Belgium* [1980] E.C.R. 2621.

Article 4(2)(a)[49] provides that the Regulation shall apply to all general and special social security schemes, whether contributory or non-contributory. Article 4(2)(a) inserted into Regulation 1408/71 by Regulation 1247/92 extends the scope of the Regulation to special non-contributory benefits which are provided under legislation other than that covered by Article 4(1) where such benefits (i) act as a supplement to, or a substitute for, the social security benefits covered by the Regulation; or (ii) are intended solely for the protection of the disabled; or (iii) are intended to guarantee a minimum income.

Three categories of benefits are excluded from the scope of the Regulation by Article 4(4). These are:

— social and medical assistance;
— benefit schemes for victims of war or its consequences;
— special schemes for civil servants and persons treated as such.[50]

The Regulation contains no criteria for differentiating between "social security" and "social assistance" but the Court has ruled on the matter on several occasions.[51] From that case-law it is clear that benefit which is in the nature of social assistance must satisfy two criteria to come within the scope of the Regulation. First, the legislation under which the benefit is granted must place claimants in a legally defined position as a result of which they have an absolute right to benefits as opposed to a conditional right dependent upon the exercise of a discretionary power in their favour. Secondly, the benefit must cover one of the risks enumerated in Article 4(1) of Regulation 1408/71. To a large extent the problems which have arisen in the past due to the exclusion of social assistance from the scope of the Regulation have now been resolved as a result of the extension of the scope of Regulation 1247/92 to cover a wide range of non-contributory social security benefits.

Even if a benefit falls to be classified as social "assistance" rather than social "security," and so falls outside the scope of Regulation 1408/71 it may well be embraced by the terms of Article 7 of Regulation 1612/68.[52] Nevertheless, there will be occasions when the distinction may be significant, for example when a claimant seeks to invoke Article 10(1) of the Regulation, which prohibits the reduction of benefit for the sole reason that the beneficiary has transferred his residence to another Member State.[53]

The exclusion of benefit schemes for victims of war or its consequences has been held to apply to a scheme for early payment of old-age pensions at

---

[49] O.J. 1992 L136/1.
[50] Case 129/78, *Lohmann* [1979] E.C.R. 853.
[51] Apart from the decisions cited in the text, see Case 1/72, *Frilli* [1972] E.C.R. 457; Cases 14, 15 & 16/72, *Heinze* [1972] E.C.R. 1105; Case 24/74, *Biason* [1974] E.C.R. 999; Case 79/76, *Fossi* [1977] E.C.R. 667; Case 9/78, *Gillard* [1978] E.C.R. 1661; Case 139/82, *Piscitello* [1983] E.C.R. 1427; Watson, (1985) 10 E.L.Rev. 335.
[52] Workers entitled to same "social and tax advantages" as national workers. Case 63/76, *Inzirillo* [1976] E.C.R. 2057; Case 122/84, *Scrivner* [1985] E.C.R. 1027; Case 249/83, *Hoeckx* [1985] E.C.R. 973. See *supra* at p. 257.
[53] Case 24/74, *Biason*, note 51.

full rate to former prisoners of war,[54] and to a scheme for early retirement on full pension for those in receipt of war service invalidity pensions.[55]

The Member States are obliged to specify the legislation and schemes referred to in Article 4(1) and 4(2) in declarations which are to be notified to the Council and published in the *Official Journal*.[56] Failure of a Member State to specify particular benefits is not of itself conclusive evidence that the law or Regulation in question does not fall within the application of Regulation 1408/71, but the fact that a Member State has specified particular benefits in a declaration is conclusive.[57]

Prohibition of discrimination on grounds of nationality

Persons to whom Regulation 1408/71 applies who are resident in the territory of one of the Member States "shall be subject to the same obligations and enjoy the same benefits under the legislation of any Member State as the nationals of that State,"[58] subject only to the special provisions of the Regulation itself. This guarantee prohibits indirect or covert discrimination, which although based on criteria other than nationality or residence has the same effect, as well as direct or overt discrimination. The point is well illustrated in the *Palermo* case[59] which concerned a claim by an Italian woman to an allowance payable under the French Social Security Code to French women of at least 65 years and insufficient means, who were married and who had brought up at least five dependent children of French nationality during a period of at least nine years before their sixteenth birthday. The French authorities waived the nationality requirement in the case of the woman herself, but refused benefit on the ground that five of her seven children were Italian, and not French. The Court held that the granting of benefit could not be made dependent either on the nationality of the claimant or that of her children, provided both had the nationality of a Member State. Consequently Mrs. Palermo could not be denied the allowance in question because some of her children were not French.

In the field of social security, equality of treatment between nationals means that employed and self-employed persons must be given the same treatment under the social security system of the Member State to which he is affiliated as those persons who have lived and worked in that State all their lives. His social security contributions must be calculated in the same way as

---

[54] Case 9/78, *Gillard* [1978] E.C.R. 1661; Wyatt, (1979) 4 E.L.Rev. 369. It was not argued that Art. 7(2) of Reg. 1612/68 applied to such a benefit as one of the "social and tax advantages" which must be accorded to workers without discrimination on grounds of nationality.

[55] Case 207/78, *Even* [1979] E.C.R. 2019; Wyatt, (1981) 6 E.L.Rev. 42. The Court held that such a benefit did not amount to a social or tax advantage within the meaning of Art. 7(2) of Reg. 1612/68. A German scheme providing for reparation to victims of Nazi persecution by allowing the retroactive payment of social security contributions, and which supplemented the general provisions of German social security law, has been held to fall within Reg. 1408/71: Case 70/80, *Vigier* [1981] E.C.R. 229.

[56] Arts. 5 & 97.

[57] Case 35/77, *Beerens* [1977] E.C.R. 2249; Case 237/78, *Palermo* [1979] E.C.R. 2645; Case 70/80, *Vigier* [1981] R.C.R. 229.

[58] Art. 3(1).

[59] Case 237/78 [1979] E.C.R. 2645; Wyatt, (1981) 6 E.L.Rev. 42, 44.

those of nationals and he must receive the full range of benefits available under that system. In *Allue and Coonan*[60] the Court held that Article 3(1) of Regulation 1408/71 was violated when a determined class of workers, mainly nationals from other Member States, are excluded from the social security system of a Member State. In that case, which involved two United Kingdom nationals teaching in the University of Venice, Italian legislation, in effect, provided that foreign language lecturers—who were predominantly non-Italian—were obliged to pay their own social security contributions whereas in the case of normal salaried employment the employer paid the greater part of these contributions in addition to the salary. Foreign language lecturers therefore, being obliged to bear the full burden of social security contributions, received a much lower salary than other university lecturers. This practice the Court considered to be contrary to the principle of equality of treatment.

Similarly in *Ursaff* v. *Société à Responsabilité Limitée Hostellerie Le Manoi*[61] the Court held that the prohibition on any discrimination based on nationality:

"... precluded national rules which require a body responsible for recovering social security contributions to take into account, for a trainee worker who does not come under a national educational system, a basis for calculating employers' social security contributions which is less favourable than that applied in respect of a trainee worker who comes under the national educational system."

The concept of indirect discrimination covers situations in which, in spite of the apparent equal treatment of nationals and non-nationals before the law, non-nationals are exclusively or mainly prejudiced against.

Consequently the possibility of exemption from the payment of social security contributions or taxes on a Member State must be made available to non-nationals on the same terms as nationals with the result that social security contributions paid in one Member State must be assimilated to social security contributions paid in another Member State when assessing in the latter liability to social security charges or taxation.[62]

It is not entirely clear whether the effect of Article 3(1) of Regulation 1408/71, in conjunction with Articles 7, 48, 52 and 59 of the Treaty, prohibits reverse discrimination, that is to say, discrimination by national authorities against their own nationals and in favour of migrants. The question arose in the *Kenny*[63] case, in which an Irish national had claimed sickness benefit in the United Kingdom for a period during which he was serving a prison sentence in Ireland. Under the applicable British rules, he would have been disqualified for benefit had he served a prison sentence in the United Kingdom. The social security authorities refused benefit, arguing that the

---

[60] Case 33/88 1989 E.C.R. 1591, Watson, 1989 14 E.L.Rev. 419.
[61] Case C–27/91 1991 E.C.R. I-5531.
[62] Case 143/87, *Stanton* v. *INASTI*, 1988 E.C.R. 3877; Case 204/90, *Bachmann* v. *Belgian State*, Judgment of January 28, 1992; Case C–300/90, *Commission* v. *Belgium*, Judgment of January 28, 1992.
[63] Case 1/78 [1978] E.C.R. 1489; Wyatt, (1978) 3 E.L.Rev. 488.

British rules on their true construction also applied to imprisonment outside the United Kingdom, and that Articles 7 and 48 of the EEC Treaty in any event required that they be so construed, since otherwise they would have the effect of discriminating against British nationals. This discrimination would result from the fact that migrants would be more likely than British nationals to serve prison sentences outside the United Kingdom. The Court's judgment does not clearly indicate whether reverse discrimination of the kind alleged is consistent with the Treaty or not. On the one hand, the Court asserts that the laws of the various Member States "must affect all persons subject to them in accordance with objective criteria and without regard to their nationality."[64] On the other hand, the Court refers to discrimination against nationals of "the other Member States,"[65] though the Court goes on to say that its reply applies "to the same extent to cases in which the worker concerned is a national of the Member State to which the competent institution belongs."[66] The circumstances in which Articles 48, 52 and 59 of the Treaty may be invoked by an employed or self-employed person against his own State has already been considered.[67] In our view, since discrimination on grounds of nationality is prohibited primarily in order to remove obstacles to the free movement of persons, it would seem to follow that Articles 7, 48, 51, 52 and 59, and Regulation 1408/71, are intended to ensure that workers be free to move as they please between the Member States, without being either advantaged or disadvantaged by the territorial application of the national social security systems. It is the aim of the Treaty that national rules, supplemented by Community regulations, be neutral in their effect on free movement. It need hardly be added that freedom of movement includes the freedom not to migrate, as well as the right to do so. Reverse discrimination in the administration of national social security rules should in our view be regarded as incompatible with the Treaty.

The principle of non-discrimination operates as a constraint not only upon national authorities in the formulation and implementation of national rules, but upon the Council in framing the Community rules which co-ordinate the national social security systems, as the *Pinna* case[68] demonstrates.

Article 73(1) of Regulation 1408/71 provides that family benefits are to be provided under the law of the Member State of employment. Article 73(2) provided at the relevant time that where the Member State of employment was France, however, the level of available allowances was determined by the law of the State in which the members of the family resided. Mr. Pinna, an Italian national resident in France, was refused family allowances under French law for periods when his two children were visiting Italy. He challenged Article 73(2) of Regulation 1408/71 before a French court,

---

[64] Judgment, para. 18.
[65] Judgment, para. 20.
[66] Judgment, para. 21.
[67] *Supra* at p. 206.
[68] Case 41/84 1986 E.C.R. 1; Case 359/87, *Pinna* II 1989 E.C.R. 585; Watson, (1989) 14 E.L.Rev. 346.

arguing that its effect was to discriminate in two respects against non-French nationals subject to French legislation. First, such workers were treated less favourably than French workers; and secondly, they were treated less favourably than workers subject to the legislation of any Member State other than France. Article 73(2) therefore infringed Articles 7, 48 and 51 of the EEC Treaty.

The Court of Justice considered first the alleged discrimination in Article 73 between migrant workers employed in France, and migrant workers employed in the other Member States. The Court acknowledged that Article 51 of the Treaty provided for the co-ordination of the legislation of the Member States, rather than for their harmonisation, thus leaving intact the differences between the national social security systems. This resulted in migrants enjoying different social security rights according to the law of their State of employment. However, in the Court's view securing freedom of movement for workers would be made more difficult if avoidable differences between the social security entitlements of migrants were actually introduced by Community law. It followed that Community social security rules made under Article 51 of the Treaty must not add to those differences which already resulted from the lack of harmonisation of the national systems.

Article 73, held the Court, created two different systems for migrant workers, one for migrant workers subject to the law of France, and one for workers subject to the legislation of the other Member States. In this way it added to the disparities intrinsic in the existence of the different national systems, and impeded the purposes of Articles 48 to 51 of the Treaty.

The Court next considered the allegation that Article 73(2) discriminated between migrant workers employed in France, and French workers employed in France. The Court recalled that the principle of non-discrimination prohibited not only overt discrimination, based on nationality, but also all forms of covert discrimination which, by the application of criteria other than nationality, led in fact to the same result. Yet this was the very effect of the criterion—residence of members of the family in a Member State other than France—adopted in Article 73(2) to determine the legislation under which family benefits were payable. Although French workers employed in France whose families were resident in other Member States were treated no more favourably than migrant workers employed in France whose families were resident in other Member States, it was likely to be migrant workers, rather than French workers, who had families resident in other Member States. Thus the criterion of residence of members of the family in a Member State other than France was not appropriate to secure the equality of treatment prescribed by Article 48 of the Treaty and it could not properly be used as a means of co-ordinating the national social security systems for the purpose of promoting the free movement of workers in the Community. Article 73 was subsequently amended by Regulation 3427/89.[69]

---

[69] O.J. 1989 L331.

Payment of benefit to recipients in other Member States

It is not uncommon for an employed or self-employed migrant to return with his family to his country of origin at the end of his working life, or if an accident incapacitates him for work. It would cause grave hardship to migrants and their dependants if such a person or the members of his family were forced to forgo the right to benefits acquired under the law of the Member State (or Member States) where he had been employed, simply because of such a change of residence. Article 10(1) of Regulation 1408/71 provides accordingly:

> "Save as otherwise provided in this Regulation, invalidity, old-age or survivors' cash benefits, pensions for accidents at work or occupational diseases and death grants acquired under the legislation of one or more Member States shall not be subject to any reduction, modification, suspension, withdrawal or confiscation by reason of the fact that the recipient resides in the territory of a Member State other than that in which the institution responsible for payment is situated."

The "legislation" under which the right to benefits is acquired under Article 10(1) is national legislation modified by the provisions of Community law. As the Court explained in *Smieja*:

> "The aim of this provision is to guarantee the party concerned his right to have the benefit of such payments even after taking up residence in a different Member country, *e.g.* his country of origin.
>
> The rights under discussion often derive, not from national legislation alone, but from that legislation combined with the principle of non-discrimination on the basis of nationality set out in Article 8 of Regulation 3 and Article 3(1) of Regulation No. 1408/71.
>
> In the event of the party's rights deriving from the legislation of several Member States—a possibility expressly foreseen in Article 10—payment is always made according to the provisions in the regulation.
>
> It may therefore be concluded that the phrase 'legislation of one or more Member States' in Article 10(1) must be interpreted as embracing the relevant provisions of Community law."[70]

The scope of Article 10(1) is not confined to the right to export benefits once they have been acquired under the social security system of a Member State. It also prohibits national law from making the acquisition of benefits dependent upon residence in a Member State.

This principle was confirmed in *Carraciolo*,[71] in which a claim to invalidity benefit under Belgian law was made by a person resident in Italy. Benefit was refused because the claimant was not present in Belgium. The Court of Justice, referring to its previous ruling in *Smieja*, declared that:

---

[70] Case 51/73 [1973] E.C.R. 1213 at pp. 1221, 1222.
[71] Case 92/81 [1982] E.C.R. 2213; Watson, (1984) 9 E.L.Rev. 113.

"... the aim of the provision contained in Article 10 is to promote the free movement of workers by insulating those concerned from the harmful consequences which might result when they transfer their residence from one Member State to another. It is clear from that principle not only that the person concerned retains the right to receive pensions and benefits acquired under the legislation of one or more Member States even after taking up residence in another Member State, but also that he may not be prevented from acquiring such a right merely because he does not reside in the territory of the State in which the institution responsible for payment is situated."[72]

Selection of national legislation applicable to migrants[73]

Articles 13 and 14 of Regulation 1408/71 lay down rules for determining which national social security system applies to an employed or self-employed person at any given time. Special provisions regarding the various categories of benefits are laid down in Title III of the Regulation.[74] The general rule is that a person is subject to the law of the Member State in which he is employed or self-employed: his place of residence or the place of establishment of his employer is irrelevant.[75] The fact that a national system is applicable by virtue of Regulation 1408/71 does not mean that a person has an absolute right to become affiliated to that system: affiliation is dependent upon the fulfilment of conditions laid down by national law.[76] However, if the Community choice rules specify a social security regime as being applicable, it would be incompatible with the Regulation for the national system to deny affiliation to an employed or self-employed person on the ground that the migrant is insured under the law of another Member State.[77] A contrary conclusion would allow the substitution of national choice rules for those laid down in the Regulation.

Where an employed person is resident in one Member State and employed in another—Article 13(2)(a) of Regulation 1408/71

A worker resident[78] in one Member State and employed in another is subject to the social security legislation of the latter, even if the registered office or place of business of his employer is situated in the territory of another Member State. The aim of this provision was described by the Court in *Massonet* as being

---

[72] Judgment, para. 14.
[73] Arts. 13 and 14 of Reg. 1408/71, some of the provisions of which are discussed in the text, are applicable to schemes of compulsory insurance. For optional insurance, see Art. 15.
[74] Case 227/81, *Aubin* [1982] E.C.R. 1991.
[75] Case C–2/89, *Kits van Heijningen* 1990 E.C.R. 1753.
[76] Case 275/81, *Koks* [1982] E.C.R. 3013, referring to Case 110/79, *Coonan* [1980] E.C.R. 1445. See Watson, (1984) 9 E.L.Rev. 428.
[77] Case 276/81, *Kuijpers* [1982] E.C.R. 3027; Watson, (1984) 9 E.L.Rev. 428.
[78] Art. 1(h) of Reg. 1408/71 provides that "residence" means "habitual residence." See Case 13/73, *Hakenberg* [1973] E.C.R. 935.

"to avoid any plurality or purposeless overlapping of contributions and liabilities which would result from the simultaneous or alternate application of several legislative systems and, moreover, preventing those concerned, in the absence of legislation applying to them, from remaining without protection in the matter of social security."[79]

This explanation of the principle underlying Article 13(2)(a) is in fact the justification for including choice of law rules in Regulation 1408/71 in the first place. The normal subject of national social security legislation is the worker both employed and resident in national territory. When workers take to residing in one Member State and working in another—or several others—they run a twofold risk: on the one hand they may find themselves unprotected by any scheme at all, and on the other hand they may find themselves bound to contribute to several systems simultaneously.

Where a self-employed person is resident in one Member State and self-employed in another—Article 13(2)(b)

What Article 13(2)(a) provides for the employed worker, Article 13(2)(b) provides for the self-employed: a person who is self-employed in the territory of one Member State is subject to the legislation of that State even if he resides in the territory of another.

Logical as the general rule may be, to the effect that the governing legislation is that of the Member State of employment or self-employment, its invariable application would itself give rise to anomalies. The subsequent provisions of the Regulation thus contain certain exceptions.[80]

Where a worker normally engaged in one Member State is posted temporarily to another—Article 14(1)(a)

Article 14(1)(a) of the Regulation provides as follows:

"(i) a person employed in the territory of a Member State by an undertaking to which he is normally attached who is posted by that undertaking to the territory of another Member State to perform work there for that undertaking shall continue to be subject to the legislation of the first Member State, provided that the anticipated duration of that work does not exceed 12 months and that he is not sent to replace another worker who has completed his term of posting."[81]

In the absence of such an exception, application of the general rule would require an undertaking established in the territory of one Member State to

---

[79] Case 50/75 [1975] E.C.R. 1473 at p. 1482. The concept of a worker employed in a Member State includes a worker last employed in that State: Case 150/82, *Coppola* [1983] E.C.R. 43.

[80] In addition to the exceptions in the text, special provision is made in the case of those employed in international transport, as diplomats, etc.

[81] Art. 14(1)(b) provides for an extension of the application of the law of the original State for a further 12 months, subject to the consent of the authorities of the State of temporary employment.

register its workers, usually subject to the social security legislation of that State, with the social security system of the Member State where they were sent to perform short-term jobs of work: the result would be administrative complications for workers, undertakings, and social security institutions.[82]

The scope of this provision is well illustrated by two decisions of the Court of Justice on the analogous terms of Article 13(1)(a) of Regulation 3[83]:

Manpower[84] and *Hakenberg*[85]

Manpower, an employment agency specialising in short-term placements, posted a French skilled worker to Germany for three days in 1969. On arrival, he sustained an accident on the site, received medical treatment, and later sought reimbursement of the cost from the French social security authorities. The Court of Justice rejected the argument that a posting such as that in issue fell outside the ambit of Article 13(1)(c) of Regulation 3 merely because the object of *Manpower* was not to perform work, but to place workers at the disposal of other undertakings. The crucial factors in such a case were (a) whether or not the worker in question was attached to an undertaking established in one Member State, and (b) whether or not he remained in the employment of such undertaking for the duration of his posting. This latter requirement would be satisfied at any rate where the undertaking paid the worker's wages and retained the right of dismissal.

It seems that the terms of the provisions in question cannot be applied to the case of a commercial traveller, paid by commission, who represents undertakings established in one Member State, and spends nine months of each year canvassing for orders in another. Such was the view of the Court in the *Hakenberg* case, reasoning that Article 13(1)(a) applied to wage-earners employed on a regular basis rather than business representatives paid by commission, and that "the strict time limits laid down . . . are not compatible with working activities which involve making regular business-canvassing tours in the territory of a Member State, in the interests of undertakings situated in another Member State."[86]

Where a person normally self-employed in one Member State performs work in another

A person who is normally self-employed in the territory of one Member State who performs work in the territory of another shall continue to be subject to the legislation of the former Member State, provided that the anticipated duration of the work does not exceed 12 months.[87]

---

[82] Case 35/70 [1970] E.C.R. 1251.
[83] As amended by Art. 1 of Reg. 24/64, J.O. 1964, 746.
[84] Case 35/70 [1970] E.C.R. 1251.
[85] Case 13/73 [1973] E.C.R. 935.
[86] [1973] E.C.R. 935 at p. 948.
[87] Art. 14a(1)(a). Art. 14a(1)(b) provides for an extension of the application of the law of the original State for a further 12 months, subject to the consent of the authorities of the State of temporary self-employment.

Where a worker is normally employed in several Member States—Article 14(2)

Article 14(2) of the Regulation provides as follows:

"A person normally employed in the territory of two or more Member States shall be subject to the legislation determined as follows:

(b) ...
(i) to the legislation of the Member State in whose territory he resides, if he pursues his activity partly in that territory or if he is attached to several undertakings or several employers who have their registered offices or places of business in the territory of different Member States[88];
(ii) to the legislation of the Member State in whose territory is situated the registered office or place of business of the undertaking or individual employing him, if he does not reside in the territory of any of the Member States where he is pursuing his activity."[89]

The purpose of these exceptions to the general rule is to avoid the simultaneous application of the laws of the several Member States where the worker is employed. Since this is the case, the Court had held that it is a prerequisite for the application of Article 13(1)(c), first sentence, of Regulation 3 (the sense of which provision is incorporated into the text of Article 14(1)(c)(i) that the worker be indeed affiliated to a social security institution in the State where he has his permanent residence. Otherwise, the general rule is applicable, and the law of the State of employment applies.[90]

Although the text of Article 14 refers to workers who normally carry out their activities on the territory of several Member States, the Court has made it clear that a worker who is occasionally employed in a Member State other than that of his permanent residence is not thereby excluded.[91]

Where a person is normally self-employed in several Member States—Article 14a(2)

Once again, a similar choice rule is applicable to the self-employed as to the employed in analogous circumstances. A person normally self-employed in the territory of two or more Member States is subject to the legislation of the Member State in whose territory he resides if he pursues any part of his activity in the territory of that Member State. If he does not pursue any activity in the territory of the Member State in which he resides, he is subject

---

[88] Reproducing the sense of the first and third sentences of Art. 13(c) of Reg. 3, as amended by Reg. 24/64.
[89] Reproducing the sense of the second sentence of Art. 13(c) of Reg. 3.
[90] Case 8/75, *Association du foot-ball club d'Andlau* [1975] E.C.R. 739.
[91] Case 8/75, note 88.

to the legislation of the Member State in whose territory he pursues his main activity.[92]

Whether national law applicable under Articles 13 and 14 of Regulation 1408/71 is exclusively so

The foundation of the choice rules of Regulation 1408/71 is the rule that the applicable law is that of the State of employment; this general rule is only modified where its application would lead to administrative inconvenience, or the cumulative application of the legislation of several Member States. Thus Community law, in general, requires the application of the law of a single State.

But it will be recalled that the Community system of choice rules was adopted to ensure not only that at any given time at least one national legal system would be applicable, but also to prevent the purposeless cumulation of national social security legislation.

The Court, in its decision on the interpretation of Regulation 3, has been somewhat ambivalent as to the extent to which the law required by the Community choice rules is exclusively applicable. In two decisions, *Nonnenmacher*[93] and *Van der Vecht*,[94] the Court held that Article 12 of Regulation 3 (equivalent to Article 13(2)(a) of Regulation 1408/71) only prohibited Member States other than that in whose territory the worker was carrying out his duties from applying their social security legislation if this would lead to additional contributions on the part of the worker or his employer without a corresponding increase in social security benefits. The basis of these decisions was the objective of Articles 48 to 51 of the Treaty; to protect migrant workers from legal detriments, without withdrawing from them the protection of national rules which would be in any event applicable. Such reasoning suggests that although the choice rules of Regulation 3 require the application of at least one national system at any given time, they do not rule out the concurrent application of other systems, providing that workers are entitled to additional benefits for any additional contributions which they are required to make.

Regulation 1408/71 clarifies the position somewhat. Article 13(1) of Regulation 1408/71 provides that "A worker to whom this Regulation applies shall be subject to the legislation of a single Member State only. That legislation shall be determined in accordance with the provisions of this Title." (Emphasis added.) However, the Court in *Nonnenmacher* based its reasoning in part on Articles 48 to 51 of the Treaty, holding that these Articles, being calculated to protect the worker, were inconsistent with an

---

[92] Art. 14a(2). The criteria used to determine the principal activity are laid down in Art. 12a(5)(d) of Reg. 547/72, according to which account shall be taken first and foremost of the locality in which the fixed and permanent premises from which the person concerned pursues his activity is situated, and failing that, account shall be taken of criteria such as the usual nature or the duration of the activities pursued, the number of services rendered and the income arising from those activities.

[93] Case 92/63 [1964] E.C.R. 281.

[94] Case 19/67 [1967] E.C.R. 345.

interpretation of Regulation 3 whereby a State would be prohibited from extending supplementary social protection to members of its population employed in another Member State. This reading of the Treaty underlies the Court's oft-repeated view that the Community's social security rules should only be applied so as to improve the lot of the migrant, not so as to diminish rights acquired under national legislation independently of Community law.[95] The argument could thus be adduced that Article 13(1) of Regulation 1408/71 is inconsistent with the Treaty to the extent that it excludes the concurrent application of the legislation of a Member State other than that applicable under the Regulation's choice rules, where such legislation provides additional protection in return for additional contributions.

In the *Perenboom*[96] and *Kuijpers*[97] cases, the Court applied Article 13(1) of Regulation 1408/71, but without excluding the possibility that national legislation other than that applicable by virtue of the Community choice of law rules might also be applicable where that legislation provided additional social protection for workers.

Subsequently in the *Ten Holder*[98] case, the Court placed the matter beyond dispute, holding that the provisions of Title II of Regulation 1408/71 constitute a complete system of conflict rules the effect of which is to divest the legislature of each Member State of the power to determine the ambit and the conditions for the application of its national legislation so far as the persons who are subject thereto and the territory within which the provisions of national law take effect are concerned.[99] The Court stressed that the rule was not at variance with its decisions[1] to the effect that the application of Regulation 1408/71 cannot entail the loss of rights acquired exclusively under national legislation; that principle applies not only to rules for determining the legislation applicable but to the rules of Community law on the overlapping of benefits provided for by different national legislative systems.[2] The Court's judgment is to be welcomed, but the distinction it draws between the immunity of rights acquired under national law from the operation of the Community rules against overlapping, and the ousting of rights which would be enjoyed under national law but for the Community choice of law rules, is, it is submitted, a distinction without substance. Indeed, the principle which protects rights acquired under national law alone from the operation of the Community rules against overlapping is itself anomalous, and ripe for reconsideration by the Court.

---

[95] See, *e.g.* Case 191/73, *Niemann* [1974] E.C.R. 571 on Reg. 3, Arts. 27 and 28; Case 24/75, *Petroni* [1975] E.C.R. 1149 on Reg. 1408/71, Art. 46(3); Case 27/75, *Bonaffini* [1975] E.C.R. 971 on Reg. 1408/71, Art. 69; Case 69/79, *Jordens-Vasters* [1980] E.C.R. 75.
[96] Case 102/76 [1977] E.C.R. 815.
[97] Case 276/81 [1982] E.C.R. 3027.
[98] Case 302/84 1986 E.C.R. 1821. See also Case 60/85, *Vermoolen* 1986 E.C.R. 2365.
[99] *Ibid.* para. 21 of judgment.
[1] The Court cites Case 24/75, *Petroni* [1975] E.C.R. 1149. And see cases at note 93, and *infra* at p. 258.
[2] *Ibid.* at para. 22 of judgment.

Exception—pensioners

In the case of *Noij*[3] the Court ruled that a person who had worked as an employed person on the territory of a Member State and had as a result of this activity become entitled to a pension and who had subsequently taken up residence in another Member State could be subject to the social security legislation of that Member State. However, such a person could not be required to pay, on a compulsory basis, contributions in respect of benefits for which he was insured in another Member State.

Following that judgment the Council amended Regulation 1408/71.[4] Article 17(a) of that Regulation now provides that the recipient of a pension due under the legislation of a Member State or of pensions due under the legislation of several Member States who resides in the territory of another Member State may, at his request, be exempted from the legislation of the latter State provided he is not subject to that legislation because of the pursuit of an occupation. The purpose of this provision is primarily to ensure that pensioners are not subject, on a compulsory basis, to medical insurance both in the Member State or States from which they receive their pension and in their Member State of residence.

Exceptions to the normal choice rules by agreement between Member States—Article 17

It is provided in Regulation 1408/71 that two or more Member States or the competent authorities of those States may, by common agreement, provide for exceptions to the choice rules normally applicable under the provisions discussed above, in the interest of certain workers or categories of workers.[5]

The *Brusse* case[6] is illustrative. The proceedings in the national court involved a Netherlands national who had originally worked in the Netherlands, but been employed and resident in the United Kingdom since 1964. Under the applicable choice of law rule he should have been subject to the social security legislation of the United Kingdom, but in fact he had remained affiliated to, and paid, voluntary contributions to the Netherlands scheme. The irregularity was discovered in 1977. The competent authorities decided to conclude an agreement under Article 17, whereby the person concerned was to be regarded as subject to the Netherlands social security scheme for the period ending on December 31, 1977, and thereafter regarded as being subject to the legislation of the United Kingdom.

On the basis of this agreement, the person concerned claimed family allowances under the law of the Netherlands for periods prior to December 31, 1977. Benefits were refused on the ground that it was not open to Member States to specify by agreement, with retroactive effect, the

---

[3] Case C–140/88 1991 E.C.R. 387.
[4] O.J. 1991 L206/2.
[5] Art. 17.
[6] Case 101/83, *Brusse* [1984] E.C.R. 2223. Watson, 9 E.L.Rev. 437.

application of national legislation other than that stated to be applicable under the Community choice rules.

The Court of Justice held, however, that it was indeed open to the national authorities to derogate by agreement from the normally applicable choice rules, provided that the agreement was in the interest of the worker concerned. Furthermore, it followed in the Court's view from the spirit and scheme of Article 17 that an agreement made thereunder must be capable of covering past periods, in order to remedy an existing situation the injustice of which appeared only after it had arisen. In view of the time needed for two or more Member States to reach agreement as to whether it was appropriate to derogate from the normal rules, Article 17 would be deprived of much of its meaning if the agreement could have only prospective effect.

Title III of Regulation 1408/71—special provisions relating to the various categories of benefits

Title III of Regulation 1408/71 contains eight chapters which lay down the special provisions applicable to the various categories of benefits listed in Article 4. The rules are somewhat complex, and must be read in the light of the implementing provisions of Regulation 574/72.[7] It is proposed to illustrate the operation of the Community rules by reference to three categories of benefits: sickness and maternity benefits, unemployment benefits, and old-age pensions.

Chapter 1 of Title III (Articles 18 to 36)—sickness and maternity benefits

Although the provisions of Chapter 1 are detailed, certain governing principles may be identified. The first is that of aggregation, whereby, according to Article 18(1) of the Regulation: "The competent institution of a Member State whose legislation makes the acquisition, retention or recovery of the right to benefits conditional upon the completion of insurance periods ... shall, to the extent necessary, take account of insurance periods ... completed under the legislation of any other Member State as if they were periods completed under the legislation which it administers."[8] The worker who is employed in several Member States may thus retain a continuous contribution record.

A further principle is that the provision of health and welfare services, for reasons of practicality, must be undertaken by the social security authorities of the country of residence of the worker, despite the fact that he may be affiliated to a social security institution in another Member State, where he is employed.

A third principle is that a worker should not be precluded from making claims for cash benefits against an insurance institution simply because he is

---

[7] J.O. 1983 L230/6.
[8] See Art. 16 of Reg. 574/72, providing for certification of insurance periods by relevant social security institutions.

resident in another Member State, and a fourth that the social security institution to which a worker is presently affiliated is in general liable for the costs of benefits provided to that worker, even if such benefits are in fact provided on its behalf by the social security authorities of another Member State.

Residence in a Member State other than that of social insurance affiliation

The application of the rules of Chapter 1 may be illustrated by reference to a hypothetical situation. Suppose a worker, a citizen of the United Kingdom and Colonies, is employed in the United Kingdom, and insured there as an employed person. He takes up permanent residence in Belgium, but is employed in France, returning home, on average, less than once a week (were he to return home every day, or on average once a week, he would be known as a "frontier worker").[9] In accordance with Article 13(2)(c) of the Regulation, he is subject to the social security legislation of France, and is insured thereunder as an employed person. The social security institution with which he is insured is termed, for the purposes of the Regulation, the "competent institution,"[10] and France, as the Member State in whose territory the competent institution is situated, is termed the "competent State."[11]

Suppose our hypothetical worker becomes ill, and is unable to work. He consults a doctor in Belgium, and is shortly afterwards admitted to hospital for a minor operation. His legal position under Regulation 1408/71 is as follows. His entitlement to benefit is governed by the legislation of the competent State (France). In the application of this legislation the competent institution will be obliged to take into account, to the extent necessary, any insurance periods completed under the legislation of any other Member State (the United Kingdom) as if they were periods completed under its own legislation. If the claimant satisfies the conditions imposed by French legislation to qualify for benefit, he will be entitled to receive, in the State in which he is resident (Belgium) the following[12]:

"(a) benefits in kind provided on behalf of the competent institution by the institution of the place of residence in accordance with the provisions of the legislation administered by that institution as though he were insured with it;

(b) cash benefits provided by the competent institution in accordance with the legislation which it administers. However, by agreement between the competent institution and the institution of the place or residence, such benefits may be provided by the latter institution on

---

[9] Art. 1(b) of Reg. 1408/71.
[10] Art. 1(o) of Reg. 1408/71.
[11] Art. 1(q) of Reg. 1408/71.
[12] Art. 19(1) of Reg. 1408/71.

behalf of the former, in accordance with the legislation of the competent State."

The distinction between benefits "in kind" and "cash benefits" requires explanation. The former benefits comprise not only health and welfare services administered under the terms of the relevant legislation, but also cash payments payable to reimburse the cost of such services for which the claimant has already been charged. "Cash benefits" are benefits payable to compensate for loss of earnings resulting from incapacity.[13]

The result of the application of the terms of Article 19 of the Regulation is thus that the claimant is entitled to such cash benefits as are provided under French law, from the institution of the competent State (France),[14] and to reimbursement, from the relevant Belgian institution, of the costs of medical care received. Such benefits "in kind" awarded by the Belgian institution must in turn be reimbursed by the competent French institution, unless there exists a reciprocal agreement between France and Belgium to waive such refunds.[15] Members of the worker's family resident in Belgium would have an equal right to claim reimbursement of medical costs against the relevant Belgian institution,[16] again subject to reimbursement by the French institution.

It will be recalled that our hypothetical worker was accustomed to return home, on average, less than once a week. Were he to return daily, he would be classed as a frontier worker, and would have the right, in urgent cases, to claim benefits in the territory of the competent State, as would members of his family.[17]

The above legal position would be identical if our hypothetical migrant were self-employed.

Medical care and benefits during a visit to another Member State and visits for the purpose of medical treatment

In two cases sickness and maternity benefits may be claimed by an employed or self-employed person or a member of his family during a visit to a Member State other than the competent State or State of residence. First, where the condition of such a person or a member of his family necessitates immediate benefits during a stay in the territory of another Member State.[18]

---

[13] Case 61/85, *Vaassen* [1966] E.C.R. 261 at p. 278. Health benefits in kind calculated to improve or restore capacity to work have been classified as sickness benefits, rather than invalidity benefits: Case 69/79, *Jordens-Vosters* [1980] E.C.R. 75.

[14] Art. 18(8) of Reg. 574/72 provides: The competent institution shall pay cash benefits by the appropriate method, in particular by international money order, and shall inform the institution of the place of residence and the person concerned accordingly. Where cash benefits are paid by the institution of the place of residence on behalf of the competent institution the latter shall inform the person concerned of his rights and shall notify the institution of the place of residence of the amount of the cash benefits, the dates of payment, and the maximum period during which they should be granted, in accordance with the legislation of the competent State.

[15] Art. 36 of Reg. 1408/71.

[16] Art. 19(2) of Reg. 1408/71.

[17] Art. 20 of Reg. 1408/71. An odd result. Our worker's connection with the competent State is closer.

[18] Art. 22(1)(a); Art. 22(3). Benefits in kind and cash benefits are covered.

Secondly, where an employed or self-employed person or a member of his family is authorised by the competent institution to go to the territory of another Member State to receive treatment appropriate to his condition.[19]

It is the first provision which enables employed and self-employed persons and members of their families to claim the benefit of the various health services of the Member States while on holiday, despite the fact that their travel is quite unconnected with the employment of a worker or the professional or trade activities of a self-employed person.

Further consideration is necessary of the circumstances in which a person may be authorised to go to another Member State to seek medical treatment. Article 22(1) provides that an employed or self-employed person who satisfies the conditions of the legislation of the competent State for entitlement to benefits, taking into account where appropriate the provisions of Article 18 (which deals with the aggregation of insurance periods) and

"(c) who is authorised by the competent institution to go to the territory of another Member State to receive there treatment appropriate to his condition, shall be entitled:

(i) to benefits in kind provided on behalf of the competent institution by the institution of the place of stay or residence in accordance with the provisions of the legislation which it administers, as though he were insured with it; the length of the period during which benefits are provided shall be governed, however, by the legislation of the competent State;

(ii) to cash benefits provided by the competent institution in accordance with the provisions of the legislation which it administers. However, by agreement between the competent institution and the institution of the place of stay or residence, such benefits may be provided by the latter institution on behalf of the former, in accordance with the provisions of the legislation of the competent State."

The Court has had occasion to rule on the scope of Article 22(1)(c) in the two *Pierik* cases.[20] In the first case the Court described Article 22 as "one of the measures intended to permit a worker [self-employed persons are of course now included] who is a national of a Member State of the Community, without regard to the national institution to which he is affiliated or the place of his residence, to receive benefits in kind provided in any other Member State."

The Court in the first *Pierik* case clarified the scope of Article 22(1)(c) as follows:

— the benefits in kind referred to covered all treatment calculated to be effective for the sickness or disease from which the person concerned suffered;

---

[19] Art. 22(1)(c); Art. 22(3). Benefits in kind and cash benefits are covered.
[20] Case 117/77 [1978] E.C.R. 825; Wyatt, (1978) 3 E.L.Rev. 394; Case 182/78 [1979] E.C.R. 1977; Wyatt, (1981) 6 E.L.Rev. 47.

— a person was not restricted to those benefits in the State to which he went for treatment to which he was entitled in the State in which he was insured;

— the costs relating to benefits in kind provided on behalf of the competent institution by the institution of the place of stay were to be fully refunded, in accordance with Article 36(1) of Regulation 1408/71.[21]

At the time of the first *Pierik* ruling, Article 22(2) provided that the authorisation referred to above might not be refused where the treatment in question could not be provided for the person concerned within the territory of the Member State in which he resided. Also in issue in the *Pierik* case were the circumstances in which authorisation might be refused by the competent institution.

The Court held that the power to refuse authorisation to a worker to receive treatment abroad was limited by the requirement that the person concerned should be guaranteed the opportunity of receiving treatment appropriate to his state of health provided in any Member State, whatever the place of his residence or the Member State to which the social security institution to which he was affiliated belonged. Thus the provision that authorisation be not refused where the treatment in question was unavailable in the State of residence implied that the authorisation might similarly not be refused in cases in which the treatment was less effective than that which the person concerned could receive in another Member State. This principle is reinforced by the current text of Article 22(2), second sub-paragraph, which provides that the authorisation required under paragraph (1)(c):

"may not be refused where the treatment in question is among the benefits provided for by the legislation of the Member State on whose territory the person concerned resides and where he cannot be given such treatment within the time normally necessary for obtaining the treatment in question in the Member State of residence taking account of his current state of health and the probable course of the disease."

In the second *Pierik* case the Court was asked whether Article 22(1)(c) also covered cases in which the treatment requested was excluded from the scheme of benefits in kind available under the legislation of the competent State on medical, medical-ethical or financial grounds. The Court noted that its decision in the first *Pierik* case implicitly acknowledged that it was for the competent institution objectively to assess the medical grounds for granting or refusing authorisation, having regard *inter alia* to the state of health of the person concerned, the seriousness of his sickness or disease and the effectiveness of the treatment in question. Financial considerations, it seems, do not enter into the question.

---

[21] Art. 36(1) provides that "benefits in kind provided in accordance with the provisions of this Chapter by the institution of one Member State on behalf of the institution of another Member State shall be fully refunded."

The Court was also asked in the second *Pierik* case whether the right to an authorisation by the competent State, and the right to treatment in the Member State of ensuing temporary residence, only applied to benefits to which there was a right under the latter State's social security rules, or if it was enough that there was a discretion to grant it. The Court emphasised that the competent institution was bound to refund the costs of treatment in the Member State of stay. Since the costs relating to the treatment in question were chargeable to the competent institution which granted the authorisation, the institution of the Member States to which the person concerned went to receive the treatment was required to provide it upon presentation of such an authorisation, even if, under the legislation which it administered, it did not have a duty, but only a power, to grant it.

The Court's ruling on this final point is clearly open to some implicit qualification. The United Kingdom Government, in the course of proceedings before the European Court, observed that Article 22(1)(c) did extend to discretionary benefits in the second State, but argued that the institution in question would have the discretion to grant or withhold the treatment in question, so long as it acted on the same basis as it would in deciding whether or not to grant such treatment to a national of its own Member State insured with that institution. The Commission concurred, expressing the view that the institution must apply the same criteria to workers and their families from other Member States as to workers insured with it, for example the criteria of urgency, or placing on a waiting list.

Calculation of cash benefits

The social security authorities of the competent State, in applying its legislation, are required to take into account insurance periods completed under the legislation of other Member States.[22] However, if its legislation provides for the calculation of cash benefits on the basis of average earnings or average contributions, such average earnings or contributions shall be determined exclusively by reference to earnings or contributions under its legislation.[23] Again, if its legislation provides that the calculation of cash benefits shall be based on standard earnings, it must take account exclusively of the standard earnings, or where appropriate, the average of standard earnings for the periods completed under its legislation.[24]

Where the cash benefits vary with the number of members of the family, the social security authorities of the competent State must take into account members of the employed or self-employed person's family resident in the territory of other Member States.[25]

---

[22] Art. 18 of Reg. 1408/71.
[23] Art. 23(1).
[24] Art. 23(2).
[25] Art. 23(3).

Chapter 3 of Title III (Articles 44 to 51)—old-age and death pension)

Aggregation and apportionment

The provisions of Regulation 1408/71 dealing with pension entitlement are based on the principle of aggregation and apportionment. The principle of aggregation is by now familiar, and requires the social security authorities of one Member State to take into account periods of insurance completed under the legislation of another.[26] Apportionment is the other side of the coin: the rights acquired under successive social security schemes are rights against the social security institutions under whose law insurance periods were in fact completed. The rationale of aggregation is that without it the migrant's contribution record might be inadequate to sustain a right to a pension; the rationale of apportionment that the cost of pensions be borne proportionately to contributions received.

Once again, a hypothetical example is illustrative. Suppose a migrant is employed in France, and then in Germany, where he retires, having completed insurance periods in both countries. He presents a claim to the relevant social security institution in each country, and each institution proceeds as follows.[27] First, it calculates the total number of insurance periods completed by the worker in France and Germany, and estimates the amount of benefit to which he would have been entitled had he completed all such periods under its law. Secondly, it determines what proportion of the total insurance periods completed in both Member States constituted insurance periods completed under its legislation. Finally, it awards a pension equal to the proportion so determined of the total benefit which would have been payable had all periods in fact been completed under its legislation. To put the most simple case, suppose our migrant had been employed for 10 years in France, and for 10 years in Germany. The relevant institution in each Member State would calculate the pension payable under its law to a claimant who had contributed for 20 years, and award a pension equal to half that amount.

Sanctity of pension rights acquired under national law

Although the object of aggregation and apportionment is to improve the lot of the migrant, it could on occasion lead to his receiving a smaller pension from a particular institution than would in any event be payable under national law alone, independently of Community rules. This can happen, for example, when a pension is calculated on the basis of a basic rate plus a sliding scale graduated according to contributions paid. The Court, in a

---

[26] Art. 45 contemplates aggregation of insurance periods only for the purpose of the acquisition, retention or recovery of the right to benefits. As such it does not deal with affiliation to social security schemes, which is governed by national law: Case 266/78, *Brunori* [1979] E.C.R. 2705; Wyatt, (1981) 6 E.L.Rev. 41; Case 110/79, *Coonan* [1980] E.C.R. 1445; Watson, (1980) 5 E.L.Rev. 229.

[27] Arts. 27 and 28 of Reg. 3, and Arts. 45 and 46 of Reg. 1408/71. All claims may be submitted via the institution of the place of residence: see Art. 36 of Reg. 574/72.

series of decisions on the application of Regulation 3,[28] held the process of aggregation and apportionment to be impermissible in such circumstances.[29]

The detailed scheme of Regulation 1408/71

The rules relating to the claiming and calculation of pensions have been the subject of a considerable body of case-law. In order to take account of this, and the administrative difficulties encountered by national social security authorities in implementing those rules, the pensions chapter of Regulation 1408/71 was amended extensively by Regulation 1248/92.[30] The current rules will be summarised below.

There are two sets of rules for the calculation of pensions set out in Article 46: the first applies where a claimant is not entitled to a pension by virtue of the legislation of any one Member State to which he has been subject, the second governs the converse situation, that is where a claimant who has been insured in several Member States is entitled to benefit by virtue of the law of one of those Member States.

Entitlement to benefit on the basis of insurance periods completed in more than one Member State.

Where an employed or self-employed person is not entitled to a pension under the legislation of any one Member State in which he has been insured his pension is calculated as follows:

(i) The institution calculates the amount of benefit to which the claimant would have been entitled if all insurance periods or periods of residence completed by him under the legislation of all the Member States to which he has been subject had been completed in the competent Member State (Article 46(2)(a)) The result of this calculation is known as the "theoretical amount."

(ii) The institution then establishes *pro rata* with the length of insurance periods or periods of residence completed under the legislation of the competent Member State as compared with the total length of periods of insurance or residence completed under the legislation of any one Member State. Where this is longer than the maximum required by the legislation of any one of those Member States the responsible institution shall only consider the maximum period required and not the total length of insurance or residence of the claimant.

Entitlement to benefit on the basis of insurance periods completed in one Member State

Where a claimant has worked in more than one Member State but is entitled to a pension by virtue of the law of one of those Member States, the competent institution considers the claimant's entire insurance record in

---

[28] See, *e.g.* Case 1/67, *Ciechelski* [1967] E.C.R. 181; Case 2/67, *de Moor* [1967] E.C.R. 197; Case 22/67, *Goffart* [1967] E.C.R. 321; Case 140/73, *Mancuso* [1973] E.C.R. 1449.
[29] Case 191/73, *Niemann* [1974] E.C.R. 571.
[30] O.J. 1992 L136/7.

every Member State. It then completes the process of aggregation and proraterisation set out above as if the claimant was not entitled to a pension by virtue of national law alone. The amounts produced as a result of this calculation are compared and the highest is paid out (Article 46(1)(a)(ii)).

In making this calculation account should be taken of the application of national provisions concerning reduction, suspension or withdrawal of benefits.[31] Where such provisions are applied the comparison to be carried out must relate to the amounts determined after the application of such provisions.

Where the calculation of a pension on the basis of the claimant's entire insurance record would lead to an amount equal to that payable to him under the law of the competent State, that Member State may grant the claimant a pension on the basis of its law alone. There is no obligation to calculate the amount due under the laws of all the Member States where the claimant has been insured. Annex VI, Part C of Regulation 1408/71 lists for each Member State the cases where the two calculations would lead to an equal amount of money.[32]

Just as application of the process of aggregation and apportionment can in some cases lead to reduction of a pension payable in any event under national law, so it has the effect in others of entitling a migrant to several pensions, payable by the institutions of several Member States, which exceed in total the amount which would have been payable had the worker spent his entire working life in any one of the countries concerned! In order to counter this "new discrimination" Article 46(a) contains four rules relating to the reduction or suspension of benefits of the same kind which overlap, that is which are calculated or provided on the basis of periods of insurance and/or residence completed by one and the same person. These rules specify the benefits or other income acquired under the law of another Member State which may be taken into account by the competent Member State in assessing the rate of pension payable under its law. Account may not be taken of benefits awarded on the basis of voluntary insurance or continued optional insurance and no account may be taken of any benefits or income arising in another Member State unless the law of the competent Member State so provides. Moreover, the provisions on the reduction, suspension or withdrawal of benefits laid down by the legislation of a Member State do not apply to a benefit calculated in accordance with Article 46(2), that is by means of aggregation and proraterisation. Where a benefit is calculated in accordance with Article 46(1)(a)(i), that is in accordance with national law alone, rules relating to suspension or reductions are applicable where the amount of pension does not depend upon the length of periods of insurance or of residence or where the amount of benefit is determined on the basis of credited periods of insurance. There are exceptions to this rule.[33]

---

[31] Art. 46(3).
[32] Art. 46(1)(b).
[33] Art. 46(b)(2).

Maximum benefit

In order to avoid the unjustified cumulation of a series of benefits acquired under the national law, Article 46(c) sets out the circumstances in which reduction in benefit may be made where there is overlapping of one or more such benefits.

Minimum benefit

The Regulation places an additional responsibility on the authorities of the State of residence, over and above that to pay an apportioned pension under the provisions of Articles 45 and 46. If a migrant resides in the territory of a Member State, and is in receipt of a pension under its legislation, the social security authorities of that State must ensure that the total benefits received under the provisions of Articles 45 and 46 amount to no less than the minimum pension prescribed by national law for insurance periods equal to all the insurance periods taken into account for the purposes of aggregation. The social security authorities must pay, if necessary, a supplement equal to the difference between the total of the benefits due under Articles 45 and 46, and the amount of the minimum benefit.[34]

The minimum pension referred to is a benefit which amounts to a specific guarantee the object of which is to ensure for recipients of social security benefits a minimum income which is in excess of the amount of benefit which they may claim solely on the basis of their periods of insurance and contributions.[35]

Revalorisation and recalculation of pension

If, in a Member State paying a pension under Articles 45 and 46, the rules governing the method of calculating pension entitlement are changed, a recalculation of the pension payable must be made on the basis of Article 46.[36] However, if benefits are simply increased by a fixed percentage or amount, to compensate for cost-of-living increases or changes in the level of wages or salaries or the like, this increase must be applied directly to the benefits determined under Article 46 without the need for a recalculation.[37]

The purpose of these provisions is to exclude a fresh calculation (and thereby reduce the burden upon the administration) when the alterations in benefits result from events which are unconnected with the personal circumstances of the insured person and are the consequences of the "general evolution of the economic and social situation."[38] But such exclusion may not be extended to changes in the personal circumstances of the insured person, such as the fact that his spouse is now earning, so as to require reduction of his pension to the "single" rather than "household" rate.[39]

---

[34] Art. 50 of Reg. 1408/71. See Case 64/77, *Torri* [1977] E.C.R. 2299.
[35] Case 22/81, *Browning* [1981] 3357.
[36] Art. 51(2) of Reg. 1408/71.
[37] Art. 51(1) of Reg. 1408/71.
[38] Case 7/81, *Sinatra* [1982] E.C.R. 137, para. 10.
[39] Case 7/81, note 38.

By the same token, a recalculation of a pension payable in one Member State is not necessary in order to take account of a cost-of-living increase in a benefit—even of a different type—in another Member State, the level of which influenced the amount at which the pension was originally fixed, by virtue of the application of the national rules against overlapping.[40]

Chapter 6 of Title III (Articles 67 to 71)—unemployment

Aggregation

Where the law of the competent State conditions benefits on the completion of periods of insurance, the competent institution shall take into account:

— periods of insurance completed under the law of any other Member State;
— periods of employment completed under the legislation of any other Member State and treated as periods of insurance under that legislation;
— periods of employment completed under the legislation of any other Member State, and treated as such under that legislation, provided that such periods are recognized as insurance periods under the law of the competent State.[41]

Where the legislation of the competent State conditions benefits on the completion of periods of employment, it shall take into account periods of insurance or employment completed as an employed person under the legislation of any Member State, as though they were periods of employment completed under the legislation which it administers.[42]

Unemployed persons going to a Member State other than the competent State

Articles 69 and 70 of the Regulation provide an invaluable corollary to the right of a worker to enter the territory of a Member State in order to seek employment therein: the right to receive unemployment benefit during his stay.

A worker who is wholly unemployed and who satisfies the conditions of the legislation of a Member State for entitlement to benefits, and who goes to one or more other Member State seeking employment, retains his right to benefit, providing that he complies with certain requirements. Before leaving the competent State, he must have been registered with the employment services therein, and have remained available for work for at least four weeks after becoming unemployed.[43] Upon registration with the employment services of another Member State, in which he is seeking employment, the worker is entitled to receive benefits from the relevant

---

[40] Case 104/83, *Cinciuolo* [1984] E.C.R. 1286.
[41] Art. 67(1) of Reg. 1408/71; Case 126/77, *Frangiamore* [1978] E.C.R. 725.
[42] Art. 67(2) of Reg. 1408/71.
[43] Unless this requirement is waived by the authorities of the competent State; Art. 69(1)(a).

social security authorities.[44] These benefits must be reimbursed by the authorities of the State where the worker was last employed, unless the State providing benefits waives such reimbursement.[45] Benefit is payable for a period of three months from the date when the worker concerned ceased to be available to the employment services of the State under the law of which he was originally entitled to benefit, provided that he does not receive benefits for a longer period than that during which he would have been entitled had he remained in that State.[46] If a worker returns to the competent State within three months, he maintains his entitlement in that State.[47]

The Court has held that these provisions have no application to an unemployed person who has never been in employment and never been treated as an unemployed person under the relevant national legislation.[48]

The State to which an unemployed worker goes seeking work, and where he is entitled to unemployment benefits under national law alone, independently of the Community rules, may not deny him benefit on the ground that he has not complied with the procedures referred to above.[49]

An unemployed worker who fails to return to the competent State before the expiry of the period during which he is entitled to benefits "shall lose all entitlement to benefits under the legislation of the competent State. . . . In exceptional cases, the time limit may be extended by the competent services or institution."[50]

In *Coccioli*[51] the Court held that "exceptional cases" might be of such a nature as to prevent not only the return of the worker but also the lodging of a request for benefit. In the Court's view national authorities were free to take into account all relevant factors in assessing "exceptional cases," and it was quite permissible to consider a request for an extension made after the expiry of the period referred to above.

The Court has held in a number of cases, notably the *Petroni* case,[52] that it would be inconsistent with Articles 48 to 51 of the Treaty for Regulation 1408/71 to diminish rights acquired under national law and independently of the Community rules. In *Testa*,[53] the question arose whether Article 69(2) was on this ground inconsistent with the Treaty. Workers in receipt of unemployment benefit in Germany went to Italy to seek work, but returned to Germany after the expiry of the applicable three-month period. Under German law they were still entitled to benefit, but benefit was refused on the basis of Article 69(2) of Regulation 1408/71. In reply to a question concerning the validity of Article 69(2), the Court of Justice upheld that

---

[44] Art. 69(1)(b). The worker is considered registered for the period prior to registration provided he registers within seven days of his ceasing to be available to the employment services of the State which he left.

[45] Art. 70(1), (3), of Reg. 1408/71.

[46] Art. 69(1)(c) of Reg. 1408/71.

[47] Art. 69(2).

[48] Case 66/7, *Kuyken* [1977] E.C.R. 2311; cited in Case 238/83, *Meade* [1984] E.C.R. 2631, para. 9 of judgment.

[49] Case 27/75, *Bonaffini* [1975] E.C.R. 971.

[50] Art. 69(2) of Reg. 1408/71.

[51] Case 139/78 [1979] E.C.R. 991; Watson, (1979) 4 E.L.Rev. 367.

[52] Case 24/75 [1975] E.C.R. 1149: see *supra* at p. 258.

[53] Cases 41/79, 121/79, 769/79 [1980] E.C.R. 1979.

provision, and distinguished the *Petroni* case. Article 69, held the Court, conferred on a person availing himself of that provision an advantage as compared with a person who remains in the competent State. He is freed for a period of three months of the duty to make himself available to the employment services of the competent State and be subject to the control procedure organised therein, even though he must register with the employment services of the Member State to which he goes. The Court concluded:

> "As part of a special system of rules which give rights to workers which they would not otherwise have, Article 69(2) cannot therefore be equated with the provisions held invalid by the Court in . . . *Petroni* . . . to the extent to which their effect was to cause workers to lose advantages in the field of social security guaranteed to them in any event by the legislation of a single Member State."[54]

In *Varhaeren*[55] the Court seemed to move away from the strict approach it adopted in *Testa*. Mrs. Varhaeren was employed in Belgium where she received unemployment benefits. She then settled in Germany where she received unemployment benefits in accordance with Article 69(1) for a period of three months after her departure from Belgium. For a time she was employed in Germany but later returned to Belgium where she claimed unemployment benefits. In these circumstances the Court held that Article 69(2) and (4) did not apply with the result that Mrs. Varhaeren could claim unemployment benefit in Belgium for the remaining period of her entitlement under Belgian law.

Unemployed persons resident in the territory of a Member State other than the competent State during last employment

A wholly unemployed worker who is resident in a State other than the competent State has an option open to him. If he remains available to the employment services in the competent State, he is entitled to receive unemployment benefit in accordance with its law, at its expense, as though he were residing there.[56] If, on the other hand, he makes himself available for work to the employment services of the State in which he resides, he is entitled to receive benefits in accordance with the legislation of that State, at its expense, as if he had last been employed there.[57]

However, if such a worker has acquired a right to benefits in the competent State, his rights in the State of residence are governed by Article 69 of the Regulation, and any right to benefit under the legislation of the State of residence is suspended as long as he is so entitled.[58]

The Court has held that Article 71(1)(b)(ii) of Regulation 1408/71, which

---

[54] Case C–62/91 judgment of April 8, 1992.
[55] Cases 41/79, etc. [1980] E.C.R. 1979 at para. [15] of judgment.
[56] Art. 71(1)(b)(i) of Reg. 1408/71.
[57] Art. 71(1)(b)(ii) of Reg. 1408/71. The worker is bound by this election and may not claim benefit in the competent State on the basis of registration as an employed person in the State of residence: Case 227/81, *Aubin* [1982] E.C.R. 1991.
[58] Art. 71(1)(b)(ii).

allows workers to claim benefits in their State of residence rather than of last employment, must be interpreted strictly, as an exception to the general rule that workers are entitled to claim unemployment benefit exclusively from the authorities of the Member State in which they were last employed. Transfer of liability to the Member State of residence is justified only where the worker has retained close ties with the country where he is settled and habitually resident. For the purpose of applying the provision in question, account must be taken of the length and continuity of a worker's residence, the length and purpose of his absence in the State of employment, the nature of his occupation and "the intention of the person concerned as it appears from all circumstances." Whenever a worker has stable employment in a Member State there is a presumption that he resides there, even if he has left his family in another State. It is for the national authorities concerned to locate the "habitual centre of his interests."[59]

Frontier workers, it will be recalled, are those employed in one Member State and residing in another, returning as a rule daily, or at least once a week. If such a worker is wholly unemployed, he is entitled to receive benefits in accordance with the legislation of the State where he resides, at its expense, as though he had been subject to that legislation while last employed.[60]

An unemployed worker entitled to benefits under Article 71 in the State of residence may not rely on Article 69 of Regulation 1408/71 so as to claim unemployment benefit in the State where he was last employed. Article 69 only applies to persons going to a Member State other than the competent State, and the Member State of last employment is still the competent State in this context, despite the entitlement of the unemployed person to benefit in the State of residence.[61]

Calculation of benefits

If the legislation of a Member State provides that benefits should be calculated on the basis of a worker's previous earnings, the previous earnings which must be taken into account are those received by the person concerned in respect of his last employment in that State. If the worker has been employed there for less than four weeks, benefits must be calculated on the basis of the normal wage in the place of residence for work similar to that of his last employment in another Member State.[62]

The above-mentioned provisions have no application to a frontier worker, in whose case the competent institution should take into account the salary earned in the Member State where he was last employed.[63]

Where the legislation of a Member State provides that the amount of

---

[59] Case 76/76, *Di Paolo* [1977] E.C.R. 315.
[60] Art. 71(1)(a)(ii) of Reg. 1408/71. The unemployed person may claim only in the Member State of residence even if entitled under the legislation of the reference Member State of last employment. However, if he has maintained links favouring his employment prospects in the Member State where he was last employed, he must not be regarded as a frontier worker, and Art. 71(1)(b) applies: Case 1/85, *Miethe* 1986 E.C.R. 1837.
[61] Case 145/84, *Cochet* [1985] E.C.R. 2801.
[62] Art. 68(1) of Reg. 1408/71.
[63] Case 67/79, *Fellinger* [1980] E.C.R. 535.

benefits should vary with the number of members of the family, the social security authorities must take into account any members of the family who are residing in other Member States. An exception is made where another person is entitled to unemployment benefits in respect of the same members of the family in their country of residence.[64]

Overlapping of benefits

The purpose of Regulation 1408/71 is to ensure that employed and self-employed persons are not prejudiced by exercising their right of free movement; it is not to ensure that they are placed in a more favourable position.

Accordingly, Article 12(1) of the Regulation provides:

> "This Regulation can neither confer nor maintain the right to several benefits of the same kind for one and the same period of compulsory insurance. However, this provision shall not apply to benefits in respect of invalidity, old-age, death (pensions) or occupational disease which are awarded by the institutions of two or more Member States, in accordance with the provisions of Arts. . . . . 46 etc."

In the case of pensions, the overlapping which would arise from simple aggregation is qualified by apportionment, though the migrant may nevertheless acquire a right to several pensions under the law of several Member States, which exceed in sum the total pension which would have been payable had he spent his entire working life in any one Member State. This is a form of "overlapping"; the migrant is in effect being credited with fictional insurance periods under one legislation while actual periods were in fact completed under another.[65] It was to consider such overlapping that the Council adopted Article 46(3) of Regulation 1408/71. As we have seen, however, it is only applicable to the extent that it operates to diminish rights acquired under the Regulation—not to diminish rights acquired under national law independently of the Community rules.

National legislation may contain rules designed to reduce benefits paid under national law to take account of (a) other benefits paid under national law (so-called internal rules against overlapping), or (b) benefits paid under the laws of other countries (so-called external rules against overlapping). Article 12(2) of Regulation 1408/71 accordingly provides:

> "Save as otherwise provided in this Regulation the provisions of the legislation of a Member State governing the reduction, suspension or withdrawal of benefits in cases of overlapping with other social security benefits or any other form of income may be revoked even where such benefits or income was acquired in the territory of another Member

---

[64] Art. 68(2) of Reg. 1408/71.
[65] On the assumption that a full pension represents a lifetime's deferred earnings which may, for reasons of equity, be paid to a worker who has completed insurance periods for only a fraction of his working life.

State or where income was acquired in the territory of another Member State."

Articles 46(a), 46(b), 46(c), and 60 provide for exceptions to this rule.

It follows from these exceptions that in calculating the amount of pension payable under national law for the purposes of Article 46(1) of Regulation 1408/71, national rules for the reduction of a pension to take account of a pension arising in another Member State are to be left out of account.[66]

The Court has held that a national provision which reduces notional additional years of employment normally accredited to a worker by the number of years in respect of which he may claim a pension in another Member State constitutes a provision for the reduction of benefit within the meaning of Article 12(2) which, by virtue of the second sentence of that Article, must not be applied when the amount of pension is calculated under Article 46(1) of Regulation 1408/71.[67]

It is always open to a migrant, however, to opt for a pension payable under national law alone, including national rules against overlapping, where that pension is greater than that which would be payable under the provision of Article 46 of Regulation 1407/71.[68] Thus it may be advantageous to a migrant to opt for a pension payable under national law alone, and subject to a deduction under national overlapping rules, rather than for a higher pension payable under the rules for aggregation and apportionment, the advantage of which in the particular case is eliminated by the application of Article 46(3) of Regulation 1408/71.

It may sometimes be a matter of some difficulty to determine whether benefits are indeed of the same kind for the purposes of the second sentence of Article 12(2).[69] The Court has considered this nebulous question on a number of occasions. Article 12(2) has recently been simplified.

The first sentence of Article 12(2) has the effect of allowing the national authorities of a Member State to rely on an internal rule against overlapping (that is to say, a rule calculated to suspend or reduce one national benefit to take account of another) in a case where the second benefit or income arises under the law of another Member State. However, Article 12(2) can only be invoked to "transform" an internal overlapping rule into an external rule (that is to say, a rule calculated to suspend or reduce a national benefit to take account of a benefit arising under the law of another country) where the benefit to be suspended or reduced arises as a result of the operation of the Community rules.[70] In cases where the benefit to be suspended or reduced arises under national law independently of the Community rules, Article

---

[66] See, e.g. Cases 116, etc./80, *Celestre* [1981] E.C.R. 1737.

[67] Case 58/84, *Romano* 1985 E.C.R. 1679.

[68] See, e.g. Case 236/78, *Mura* E.C.R. 1819.

[69] Case 4/80, *D'Amico* [1980] E.C.R. 2951 (invalidity benefits converted into old-age pensions and unconverted invalidity benefits of same kind); Case 17/81, *Valentini* [1983] E.C.R. 2157 (guaranteed income allowances not of same kind as old-age pension, and national rules against overlapping apply).

[70] Case 184/73, *Kaufmann* [1974] E.C.R. 517. A decision on the scope of Art. 11(2) of Reg. 3. It is immaterial whether the benefit of which account is taken arises under national law or under the Community rules, *per* Advocate General Warner at p. 531.

12(2) cannot be relied upon to transform an internal rule against overlapping into an external rule.[71]

However, although the Court has consistently held that limitations may be imposed on migrant workers to balance the social security advantages which they derive from the Community regulations and which they could not obtain without them, the aim of Articles 48 to 51 of the Treaty would not be attained if the social security advantages which a worker may derive from the legislation of a single Member State were to be withdrawn or reduced as a result of the application of those regulations.[72]

However, where a national external overlapping rule is concerned, a benefit acquired under national law alone may, consistently with the first sentence of Article 12(2) of Regulation 1408/71, be suspended or reduced to take account of benefits arising under the laws of other Member States.[73]

Social security authorities are furthermore entitled to invoke provisions of national law for the reduction, suspension or withdrawal of benefit in the case of persons in receipt of invalidity benefits or anticipatory old-age benefits who are pursuing a professional or trade activity, even though they are pursuing such activity in another Member State.[74]

Subrogation

Article 93(1) of Regulation 1408/71[75] provides that if a person is in receipt of benefit under the legislation of one Member State in respect of an injury in another, and is entitled to claim compensation for that injury from a third party in the latter State's territory, any right of subrogation vested in the institution[76] liable for payment of benefit under the law applicable to it shall be recognised in the other Member States. Thus if a worker is killed in France by the negligence of a third party, and as a result his widow receives a pension from a German social security institution, the latter may be subrogated, in accordance with German law, to the widow's rights against the tortfeasor in France. These were indeed the facts of the *Topfer* case,[77] in which the widow received a pension from the German social security institution, and was subsequently successful in her claim in France against the tortfeasor and his insurance company.

---

[71] Case 34/69, *Duffy* [1969] E.C.R. 597 (a decision on Art. 11(2) of Reg. 3); Case 279/82, *Jerzak* [1983] E.C.R. 2603.
[72] Case 279/82 [1983] E.C.R. 2603 at paras. 10 to 12 of the judgment.
[73] Case 171/82, *Valentini* [1983] E.C.R. 2157.
[74] Art. 12(3) of Reg. 1408/71.
[75] Superseding Art. 52 of Reg. 3. On the interpretation of Art. 52, see Case 31/64, *Bertholet* [1965] E.C.R. 81; Case 33/64, *van Dijk* [1965] E.C.R. 97; Case 44/65, *Maison Singer* [1965] E.C.R. 965; Case 27/69, *Assurance generale* [1969] E.C.R. 405; Case 78/82, *de Waal* [1973] E.C.R. 499.
[76] The term "institution" in Art. 93 means the body or social security authority responsible for administering all or part of a Member State's social security legislation, and it does not include a private insurance company which has indemnified an assured under an ordinary insurance policy: Case 313/82, *NV Tiel Utrecht* [1984] E.C.R. 1389.
[77] Case 72/76 [1977] E.C.R. 271.

CHAPTER 12

THE COMPLETION OF THE INTERNAL MARKET[1]

Background

As previous chapters will have made clear, when the 12-year transitional period for the establishment of the common market ended on December 31, 1969, "the elimination of all obstacles to intra-Community trade in order to merge the national markets into a single market bringing about conditions as close as possible to those of a genuine internal market"[2] was still far from having been achieved. The rapid development of the case law of the Court of Justice on the scope and the direct effect of the prohibitions contained in such provisions of the EEC Treaty as Articles 30, 48, 54 and 59 allowed a great variety of discriminatory or otherwise unjustifiable interferences with freedom of movement to be challenged successfully, but the completion of the internal market could not be achieved by judicial action alone. A major legislative effort was needed, and this was finally set in train by the Commission which took office in January 1985 under the Presidency of Mr. Jacques Delors.

Responding to an invitation issued at the Brussels meeting of the European Council in March 1985, the Commission prepared a White Paper[3] on completing the internal market, which it presented at the Milan meeting in June of that year. The White Paper set out a detailed legislative programme for the unification of the market, focusing on the removal of the remaining physical, technical and fiscal barriers to freedom of movement for goods, persons, services and capital. Annexed to the programme was a timetable for the adoption of the specific measures the Commission considered necessary to achieve the desired unification. The deadline fixed for the final establishment of the internal market was December 31, 1992, which gave a period of some eight years (corresponding to two Commission terms of office), for the enactment of the necessary measures.

The European Council welcomed the Commission's White Paper and instructed the Council to initiate a precise programme of action based upon it, which was to give high priority to the following:

(i) the removal of physical barriers to the free movement of goods within the Community;

(ii) the removal of technical barriers to the free movement of goods

---

[1] The present chapter is in large part a reworking of a report by Alan Dashwood on research carried out within the Centre for Studies and Research of The Hague Academy of International Law at its 1991 session: see *The Legal Implications of 1993 for Member and Non-Member Countries of the EEC* (1992, Martinus Nijhoff), pp. 91 *et seq.* The authors express their thanks to the Curatorium of the Academy for their kind permission to draw on that report.

[2] Case 15/81, *Schul* v. *Inspecteur de Invoerrechten en Accijnzen* [1982] E.C.R. 1409 at pp. 1431 to 1432.

[3] COM(85)310.

within the Community (in particular the adoption of common or compatible standards for major new technologies in order to open up public purchasing and satisfy the needs of the economy);

(iii) the creation of a free market in the financial services and transport sectors;

(iv) the creation of full freedom of establishment for the professions;

(v) the liberalisation of capital movements.[4]

New legal machinery for the attainment of the political objectives stated in the White Paper and endorsed by the European Council was included in the S.E.A. which represented the outcome of inter-governmental negotiations undertaken in the light of the conclusions reached at the Milan meeting. The S.E.A. was signed on February 17, 1986, and entered into force, after ratification by the Member States on July 1, 1987. The provisions relating to the internal market which the S.E.A. added to the EEC Treaty were broadly of two kinds: general principles defining the project to be implemented by the end of 1992, which are to be found, notably, in Article 8a; and new or modified legal bases for the enactment of internal market legislation by the co-operation procedure, notably Article 100a which applies where measures are needed for the approximation of provisions laid down by law, regulation or administrative action in Member States.[5] In the present chapter we examine that legal machinery and its functioning over the period of some five years since it became operational.

Article 8a: the internal market project

Article 8a EEC (which under the T.E.U. will become Article 7a, without any change of content) provides as follows:

"The Community shall adopt measures with the aim of progressively establishing the internal market over a period expiring on December 31, 1992, in accordance with the provisions of this Article and of Articles 8b, 8c, 28, 57(2), 59, 70(1), 84, 99, 100a and 100b and without prejudice to the other provisions of this Treaty.

The internal market shall comprise an area without internal frontiers in which the free movement of goods, persons, services, and capital is ensured in accordance with the provisions of this Treaty."

The first paragraph of the Article creates an obligation for "the Community" to achieve a specified object (the establishment of the internal market) within a specified time limit (December 31, 1992) and by specified means (the adoption of "measures" in accordance with certain Articles of the EEC Treaty but without prejudice to its other provisions). The second paragraph defines the notion "internal market." Although, for convenience in

---

[4] Conclusions on the completion of the internal market, point 1.
[5] For a full analysis of the background to the S.E.A. and of its provisions, see J. De Ruyt, *L'Acte unique européen* (1987, Editions de l'Université de Bruxelles). On the internal market aspects of the S.E.A., see A. Mattera, *Le marché unique européen*, (2nd ed., 1990, Jupiter).

presentation, we examine the two paragraphs separately, it is important to stress that the Article must be read as a whole, the second paragraph merely clarifying the object to be achieved within the deadline, and by the means, laid down in the first paragraph.

The obligation in the first paragraph

The obligation imposed on "the Community" binds its institutions to use their respective powers under the Treaty to adopt the measures necessary for the completion of the internal market before 1993. Article 8a does not directly address the Member States but they are bound, pursuant to Article 5 EEC, to co-operate fully in the internal market project.[6] The nature and scope of the obligation falling on the Member States will be examined more fully below.

The Community institutions are to carry out their task under Article 8a, first paragraph, in accordance with the following specified provisions of the EEC Treaty: Article 8a, 8b and 8c (general principles relating to the establishment of the internal market); Article 28 (autonomous alteration or suspension of duties under the common customs tariff); Article 57(2) (co-ordination of provisions concerning the taking up and pursuit of self-employed activities); Article 59 (abolition of restrictions on freedom to provide services); Article 70(1) (co-ordination of exchange policies in respect of the movement of capital between Member States and third countries); Article 84 (legislation relating to sea and air transport); Article 99 (harmonisation of indirect taxation); Article 100a (the general legal basis for approximation measures having as their object the establishment or functioning of the internal market); and Article 100b (the legal basis for measures to be adopted in the final phase of the establishment of the internal market, requiring mutual recognition of the equivalence of standards that have not been harmonised). All of those provisions were either introduced or amended by the S.E.A.

However, it is expressly stipulated that the list of provisions in Article 8a is without prejudice to the other provisions of the Treaty. This is important for two reasons.

First, by no means all of the legal bases central to the internal market project are mentioned in the list. For example, veterinary and plant health measures, necessary for the removal of obstacles to trade in live animals and plants and in the whole range of animal and plant products, falls within the purview of Article 43 EEC, the general basis of legislation for the purposes of the common agricultural policy.[7] Similarly, the liberalisation of transport services by rail, road or inland waterway has been pursued on the basis of Article 75 EEC.

Secondly, Article 8a does not derogate from Article 36 or from other

---

[6] On the principle of loyal co-operation in Art. 5 EEC, see de Cockborne *et al.*, *Commentaire Mégret*, (2nd ed., 1992, Éditions de l'Université de Bruxelles), Vol. 1, Chap. II.
[7] See the discussion of Art. 43 as a basis for internal market legislation, *infra*.

similar provisions of the Treaty allowing freedom of movement to be restricted for certain narrowly-defined, non-economic reasons.[8] Nor does it modify the rule, which was confirmed by the *Cassis de Dijon* line of authority, that the Treaty does not prohibit the non-discriminatory application of national provisions that are necessary to serve important purposes of public interest, even where, owing to disparities between the legal solutions adopted by different Member States, such application may result in impediments to free movement.[9] Thus a major part of the task for the Community institutions consisted of removing the justifications hitherto available to Member States under the Treaty for maintaining restrictive national provisions, through the enactment of harmonised rules or of measures for the mutual recognition of standards and qualifications that would adequately protect the interests in question.

The definition in the second paragraph

The definition of the internal market in the second paragraph of Article 8a comprises two elements—absence of internal frontiers and the free movement of goods, persons, services and capital. Those elements may be contrasted in terms of their relative precision and scope.

The first element, a space without internal frontiers, sets the Community institutions the measurable objective of securing the abolition of all frontier controls on goods or persons moving between the Member States. As long as any such controls remain in place, it will be clear that the objective has not been achieved. The second element, consisting of the realisation of the four freedoms, is more elusive: there is simply no way of identifying the exact moment at which the requisite degree of liberalisation will have been attained.

On the other hand, for all its psychological importance, the complete removal of physical frontiers will not, in itself, ensure freedom of movement. For instance, divergent national rules on such things as maximum levels of food additives or the labelling of foodstuffs, could be enforced, even in the absence of frontier controls, by inspection at the retail stage of distribution. Similarly, immigration controls are not the only way of restricting the entry and residence of non-nationals (although perhaps a uniquely effective one in the case of the insular Member States). Control can

---

[8] *Cf.* proviso to Art. 48(3) and Art. 48(4) (workers); Art. 56(1) (establishment and services). Such exceptions to fundamental Community principles are very narrowly construed. As to goods, see Case 46/76 [1977] E.C.R. 5; Case 252/78, *Denkavit Futtermittel* [1979] E.C.R. 3369. As to persons, see Case 30/77, *Bouchereau* [1977] E.C.R. 1999.

[9] The abundant case law on the limits of the directly effective prohibitions imposed by the relevant Treaty Articles has been analysed in previous chapters of this book. As to Art. 30 (goods), leading cases are Case 8/74, *Procureur du Roi* v. *Dassonville* [1974] E.C.R. 837; Case 120/78, *Rewe-Zentral* v. *Bundesmonopolverwaltung für Branntwein* ("*Cassis de Dijon*") [1979] E.C.R. 649. As to establishment and services (Arts. 52 and 59), leading cases are Case 2/74 E.C.R. 1299, Case 39/75, *Coenen* [1975] E.C.R. 1547. See the discussion of "indistinctly applicable" measures in P. Oliver, *Free Movement of Goods in the EEC*, pp. 82 *et seq.* As to capital (Art. 67), the requirement was only to liberalise "to the extent necessary to ensure the proper functioning of the common market." However, Art. 73b of the EC Treaty, as amended by the T.E.U., contains a prohibition against *all* restrictions on capital movements between Member States and between Member States and third countries.

be exercised, for example, through hotels or lodging houses, through employers or by spot checks in public places.

Indeed, for certain kinds of restriction on freedom of movement, the abolition of physical frontiers would have little or no impact. An example, of the greatest importance for the internal market in goods and, to some extent, in services, is the protection of intellectual property rights, still largely organised at the level of individual Member States[10]: such protection is achieved not by checks on imports but by infringement proceedings brought by interested parties in national courts. Another, very obvious, example, affecting the free movement of persons, is that of differences between Member States as to professional qualifications or the conditions of access to business activities, where impediments can only be removed by harmonisation or mutual recognition.[11]

A question that arises is whether the unqualified reference in the second paragraph of Article 8a to the free movement of *persons* can be taken at face value, or whether it must be interpreted in the sense of Title III of Part Two of the Treaty, as relating only to Community nationals who travel to another Member State to carry on employed or self-employed activities, or as providers or recipients of services. It is submitted that the wider interpretation is the correct one. Not only does it correspond to the letter of Article 8a (as well as to that of Article 3(c)) but it is also necessary to ensure the *effet utile* of the removal of internal frontiers since, if controls are retained for any categories of travellers, they are liable to be applied to all.

The four freedoms are to be ensured "in accordance with the provisions of this Treaty." This confirms the point made in relation to the first paragraph that Article 8a does not derogate from the provisions under which certain justified restrictions are tolerated by the Treaty, despite their incompatibility with a single market. The strategy of the Article is to implement a legislative programme removing any such justification, thereby enabling the basic Treaty provisions on freedom of movement to apply with full effect.[12]

A final question is how the notion of the internal market, as defined by Article 8a, relates to that of the common market with which it has co-existed in the EEC Treaty since the S.E.A. (and will continue to do so under the

---

[10] See Chap. 20, *infra*. The European Patent Convention, which entered into force on October 7, 1977, enables a European patent to be obtained which has the effect of a national patent in all the contracting States in which protection is granted. The Community Patent Convention, when it comes into force, will enable a unitary patent to be obtained for the whole of the common (internal) market. A proposal for a regulation on a Community trade mark is currently before the Council. However, none of these measures preclude the continued existence of separate national systems of protection.

[11] The report of the *ad hoc* Committee for a People's Europe ("Adonnino Report"), which was submitted to the European Council in March 1985, recommended a new approach to the implementation of the Treaty provisions on freedom of establishment, based on mutual trust and the assumption that qualifications awarded in different Member States are broadly equal. That was the approach adopted by the White Paper, which led to the enactment of a general system for the mutual recognition of higher education diplomas awarded on completion of professional education and training of at least three years' duration: see Council Dir. 89/48 of December 31, 1988, O.J. 1989 L19/16. For a full analysis of the background to the Dir. and its provisions, see J. M. Laslett, *Legal Issues of European Integration*, 1990/91, p. 1; A. Carnelutti, *Revue du Marché unique*, No. 1–1991, p. 1.

[12] On the same lines, see de Cockborne *et al.*, *op. cit.* note 6, *supra*, pp. 20 *et seq.*

regime of the T.E.U.). It would be confusing if, as is sometimes said, the two notions were simply interchangeable. "Common market" is nowhere defined in the Treaty but its primary meaning can be gathered from Article 2 which speaks of the establishment of a common market as one of only two means—the other being the progressive approximation of the economic policies of Member States—by which the Community is to carry out its task of pursuing the objectives specified in that Article. Here "common market" is used as a term of art, covering the whole range of Community activities other than those connected with the approximation of economic policies; and legislative practice over the years suggests that a similarly broad meaning has been given to the term in Article 100 and Article 235. The internal market should, therefore, be regarded as the more specific notion, introduced to provide a sharper focus for the project that was set in motion by the 1985 White Paper.

The legal effects of Article 8a

Effects for the Community institutions

Does Article 8a impose on the Community institutions involved in the legislative process a *legally* binding obligation? Or is the commitment expressed in the Article to the task of establishing the internal market before the deadline of December 31, 1991 purely political?

The Declaration on Article 8a annexed to the Final Act of the S.E.A. might seem to indicate the latter, since it states:

> "The Conference wishes by means of the provisions in Article 8a to express its firm political will to take before January 1, 1993 the decisions necessary to complete the internal market defined in those provisions, and more particularly the decisions necessary to implement the Commission's programme described in the White Paper on the Internal Market.
>
> Setting the date of December 31, 1992 does not create an automatic legal effect."

However, it is thought the Declaration does not express any view as to the nature of the obligation resulting from the Article *for the Community institutions*. The reference in the final sentence to the date of December 31, 1992 as not creating "an automatic legal effect" suggests that the issue the Conference intended to address was that of the possible direct effect of the Article, if the necessary legislation had not been enacted by that date. This is an altogether different issue, to which we return when we examine the effects for the Member States.

It is, therefore, submitted that the mandatory language of the first paragraph of Article 8a ("The Community *shall* adopt . . .") must be given its plain meaning.

The further question then arises: if, in breach of the obligation imposed by Article 8a, the Commission fails to propose, or the Council to adopt, measures necessary for the establishment of the internal market before December 31, 1992, would this constitute a failure to act within the meaning of Article 175 EEC, providing grounds for an action against the responsible institution?

The answer to that question depends on the test that was formulated by the Court of Justice in Case 13/83, where proceedings under Article 175 were brought against the Council by the European Parliament in respect of the failure to introduce a common transport policy before the end of the transitional period.[13] According to that test, the measures which are the subject of the allegation of a failure to act must be defined with sufficient precision for them to be identified individually, and adopted in compliance with the Court's judgment, pursuant to Article 176 EEC. This cannot be the case where discretionary power is given to the institution concerned, allowing it to make policy choices the content of which is not specified by the Treaty.

In applying the test laid down in the *Transport* case to Article 8a, it is useful to recall what was said in the previous section about the two elements of the definition of the internal market in the second paragraph of the Article.

Ensuring the free movement of goods, persons, services and capital, with all that implies in terms of the harmonisation or mutual recognition of standards, qualifications and control procedures, is too general an objective, and its attainment too fraught with policy choices, to be the subject of proceedings under Article 175: it would not be possible, if the Court found there had been a failure to act, to specify the legislative steps that would have to be taken to comply with the judgment.

A different question is whether there may be a risk of liability for the Council if it fails to adopt before the end of 1992 aspects of the legislative programme for completing the internal market that have been the subject of specific proposals by the Commission. That question can only be answered on a case by case basis, having regard to such matters as the date when the proposal was received by the Council and its centrality to the 1993 project.

Turning to the other element of the definition, the absence of internal frontiers, a further distinction needs to be drawn—between controls on goods and controls on persons. On the one hand, the Commission was able to spell out with reasonable precision the measures necessary to allow the removal of internal physical frontiers in respect of goods[14] (which is not the same as saying that the adoption of such measures has been politically a straightforward matter). The measures in question relate essentially to the administration of systems of indirect taxation, commercial policy matters affecting Member States individually, human, animal and plant health, the requirements of transport policy and the collection of statistics. On the other hand, the abolition of frontier controls on persons can finally be achieved only when a whole range of matters relating to the entry and residence of third country nationals—among other things, visa policy and the right of

---

[13] *European Parliament* v. *Council* [1985] E.C.R. 1583. See, more particularly, pp. 1592 to 1593 and 1596 to 1597.
[14] White Paper, points 24 to 56.

asylum—have been regulated.[15] Decisions on these matters, whether adopted by the Community institutions under powers conferred by the Treaty or by way of conventions between the Member States, clearly involve discretionary choices.

It seems, therefore, that failure to adopt the legislation necessary to allow the complete removal of frontier controls on goods would carry a greater risk of an adverse ruling under Article 175 than would such failure in respect of controls on persons.

Effects for the Member States

Here the main question is whether, or to what extent, Article 8a may be directly effective.[16] Supposing the legislative programme laid down by the White Paper has not been fully implemented by the end of 1992, will it still be possible for a Member State to apply its national rules in areas where internal market legislation is not yet in place or where it has not yet been fully implemented, despite the tendency of such rules to restrict the free movement of goods, persons, services or capital? Or would individuals affected by those rules have the right, pursuant to Article 8a, to resist their continued application, and would national courts be required to recognise and give effect to that right?

The conditions under which provisions of the EEC Treaty and of acts of the institutions produce direct effects for the subjects of the Community legal order, as established in the case law of the Court of Justice, were discussed in Chapter 4, above. To summarise: the provision in question must be clear and unconditional; and it must also be complete, in the sense of being immediately usable by the Court of Justice or by national courts in determining the rights and obligations of individuals, without any need for further definition of those rights and obligations by the legislator.

Article 8a would not seem to fulfil those conditions since, as we have seen, the creation of an area without internal frontiers in which the four freedoms are ensured *in accordance with the provisions of the Treaty* requires the enactment of Community measures making recourse to restrictive national provisions, in the cases allowed by the Treaty, no longer justifiable. Given

---

[15] The various measures essential for the abolition of frontier controls on individuals were set out in the so-called "Palma document" which was approved by the European Council in Madrid in June 1989. Inter-governmental activity with a view to implementing the Palma document has already borne fruit. A Convention determining the State responsible for examining applications for asylum was signed in Dublin in June 1990 by all the Member States other than Denmark. Since then, Denmark has both signed and ratified the Convention, which has also been ratified by Greece and by the United Kingdom. At the time of writing, ratifications by Ireland and Portugal were expected shortly. A second Convention, on the management of the external borders of the Community, is ready for signature, but this has been delayed owing to a dispute between Spain and the United Kingdom over its application to Gibraltar. Title VI of the Treaty on European Union provides a new framework for action in this area. A further step forward has been taken by the Member States which are parties to the Schengen Agreement of 1985 and the Convention of 1990 for the application of that Agreement. On the relationship between the Dublin and Schengen Conventions of 1990, see J. J. Bolten, *Nederlands Juristenblad* (1991), p. 165. See also P. Weckel, *Revue générale de Droit international public* (1991/92), p. 405.

[16] On the doctrine of direct effect in Community law, see Chap. 4, *supra*. See also J. Winter, (1972) 9 C.M.L.Rev. 425; A. Dashwood, (1978) J.C.M.S. 229; P. Pescatore, (1983) 8 E.L.Rev. 155.

the need for such legislation, until this is fully in place certain impediments to freedom of movement, resulting from the application of national provisions, will continue.

That analysis is confirmed by the Declaration to Article 8a, cited above, in which it was stated that the setting of the end of 1992 deadline "does not create an automatic legal effect." While the case law of the Court of Justice casts doubt on the interpretative value of statements entered in the minutes of the Council,[17] a published declaration of a negotiating conference is in a quite different category. The Declaration in question made manifest the intention of the Conference of the Representatives of the Government of the Member States, at the time of signing the S.E.A., to avoid the result that, independently of the state of implementation of the White Paper, complete freedom of movement might be legally a *fait accompli* after December 31, 1992.[18]

A controversial question is whether the maintenance of controls at the internal frontiers of the Community will be absolutely prohibited after December 31, 1992. The Commission seems to believe that Article 8a, taken together with Article 5, imposes such a prohibition.[19] If that were correct, any Member State which had not dismantled internal frontier controls by the end of 1992 would be in breach of the Treaty and liable to be condemned in enforcement proceedings under Article 169 or Article 170; and it would also run the risk of having to pay compensation to undertakings or individuals suffering loss as a result of the failure to abolish controls.[20]

However, as the foregoing analysis will have made clear, the matter is rather more complicated. Frontier controls on movement between Member States will be illegal after 1992 if, but only if, they are no longer necessary to safeguard interests recognised as legitimate by the Treaty. That will obviously be the case where harmonised rules, standards or qualifications are *fully* in place. It is further submitted that, even where the legislative framework remains incomplete, the combined effect of Article 8a and the obligation of loyal co-operation in Article 5 will prevent Member States from having recourse to frontier controls, if the interests in question could be protected by some other means. The principle of proportionality, too, would seem to require, in the conditions of the internal market, that frontier controls be retained only where they are truly indispensable.[21] So, while there is no automatic obligation to abolish all controls at the Community's internal frontiers before January 1, 1993, as from that date the burden of proof will be on Member States to justify the retention of such controls.

---

[17] Case 38/69, *Commission* v. *Italy* [1970] E.C.R. 47; Case 237/84, *Commission* v. *Belgium* [1986] E.C.R. 1247. More recently in Case C–292/89, *Antonissen* [1991] E.C.R. 745 at p. 778, the Court said: " . . . a declaration cannot be used for the purpose of interpreting a provision of secondary legislation where, as in this case, no reference is made to the content of the declaration in the wording of the provision in question."

[18] On the effect of the Declaration, see the article by Judge F. Schokweiler, R.M.C. 1991, p. 882.

[19] See the Commission's Communication of May 18, 1992 (SEC(92) 877 final). See also the remarks by Vice-President Bangemann reported in *Agence Europe*, February 26, 1992, pp. 9 and 10.

[20] Joined cases C–6 and 9–90, *Francovich*, judgment of November 19, 1991 (not yet reported).

[21] See the discussion of the proportionality principle at pp. 89 *et seq.*, *supra*.

So far as concerns the movement of goods, recent progress made in the difficult areas of veterinary and plant health legislation and of the harmonisation of indirect taxation give grounds for hope that the conditions for the abolition of internal frontier controls will be realised in time for 1993. Thus a legislative framework is now substantially in place that will allow livestock, meat and meat products, as well as plants and plant products, to circulate freely within the Community. The general principle is that health controls should normally be carried out in the Member State of production or of first importation from a third country: where harmonised rules exist, the Member State of origin must apply those rules; in the absence of such rules, it must apply the rules of the Member State of destination.[22] The legislation seeks to reconcile the aim of unifying the market with that of effectively preventing the spread of animal and plant diseases: it includes new rules on the controversial issue of anti-rabies controls which will allow the requirement of quarantine to be dispensed with under certain very stringent conditions (and not in the case of domestic pets).[23] As for the abolition of fiscal frontiers, the transitional VAT-regime has now been formally adopted,[24] as well as the Regulation on administrative co-operation.[25] There are also Directives on the general arrangements for products subject to excise duty and on the holding, movement and monitoring of such products,[26] as well as on the approximation of VAT rates and of excises on specific products.[26a] In view of these developments, the Court of Justice will surely take a good deal of convincing that frontier controls in respect of goods are still justifiable after 1992.

So far as concerns the movement of persons, whether 1993 will bring the obligation for Member States to abolish all internal frontier controls seems more doubtful. It is arguable that systematic frontier controls are necessary in the fight against terrorism, drug trafficking and other forms of serious

---

[22] See, in particular, Council Dir. 89/662 of December 11, 1989, concerning veterinary checks in intra-Community trade with a view to the completion of the internal market, O.J. 1989 L395/13; Council Dir. 90/425 of June 16, 1990, concerning veterinary and zoological checks applicable in intra-Community trade in certain live animals and products with a view to the completion of the internal market, O.J. 1990 L224/29; Council Dir. 90/675 of December 10, 1990, laying down the principles governing the organisation of veterinary checks on products entering the Community from third countries, O.J. 1990 L373/1; Council Dir. 91/497 of July 29, 1991, amending and consolidating Dir. 64/433 on health problems affecting intra-Community trade in fresh meat to extend it to the production and marketing of fresh meat, O.J. 1991 L268/69; Council Dir. 91/682 of December 19, 1991, on the marketing of ornamental plant propagating material and ornamental plants, O.J. 1991 L376/21; Council Dir. 91/683 of December 19, 1991, amending Dir. 77/93 on protective measures against the introduction into the Member States of organisms harmful to plants and plant products, O.J. 1991 L376/29; Council Dir. 92/5 of February 10, 1992, amending and updating Dir. 77/99 on health problems affecting intra-Community trade in meat products and amending Dir. 64/433, O.J. 1992 L57/1; Council Dir. 92/33 of April 28, 1992, on the marketing of vegetable propagating and planting material other than seed, O.J. 1992 L157/1; Council Dir. 92/34 of April 28, 1992, on the marketing of fruit plant propagating material and fruit plants intended for fruit production, O.J. 1992 L157/10.

[23] Council Dir. 92/65 of July 13, 1992, laying down animal health requirements governing trade in and imports into the Community of animals, semen, ova and embryos not subject to animal health requirements laid down in specific community rules referred to in Annex A(I) to Dir. 90/425. Special rules relating to Ireland and the United Kingdom are found in Art. 10(3) and (4) of Dir. 92/65.

[24] Council Dir. 91/680 of December 16, 1991, O.J. 1991 L376/1.

[25] Council Reg. 218/92 of January 27, 1992, O.J. 1992 L24/1.

[26] Council Dir. 92/12 of February 25, 1992, O.J. 1992 L76/1.

[26a] See the Directives published in O.J. 1992 L316.

international crime, and that Member States should not be deprived of this defence at the present early stage of co-operation in judicial and police matters.[27] Moreover, the complete abolition of controls on Community nationals depends on the adoption of harmonised rules on the entry, movement and residence of nationals of third countries: here much remains to be done, although there has been significant progress, notably through the signature of a Convention determining the State responsible for examining applications for asylum, and by the preparation of the Convention on the management of the external borders of the Community, which has yet to be signed.[28] A fundamental difference between the legal position in respect of persons and that in respect of goods is that, for persons, there is no legislation equivalent to the Common Customs Tariff, nor any principle of the Treaty corresponding to that of the free circulation of third country products once these have cleared customs.[29] It is thought, therefore, that the task of justifying the maintenance, for the time being, of internal frontier controls on persons should not prove insuperable for Member States.

Article 100a: approximation by qualified majority

It has been said that the central idea which dominated the inter-governmental negotiations leading to the signature of the S.E.A. was that wider recourse to the qualified majority was essential for the attainment of the objective of completing the internal market before January 1, 1993.[30] The most significant of the amendments to the EEC Treaty giving effect to that idea was the introduction of Article 100a as a general legal basis for the adoption, under the co-operation procedure, of "measures for the approximation of the provisions laid down by law, regulation or administrative action in Member States which have as their object the establishment and functioning of the internal market."

Article 100a operates by way of derogation from Article 100 which enables the Council, acting *unanimously*, to issue directives for the approximation of national provisions directly affecting the establishment or functioning of the common market.[31] Article 100 has thus been reduced to a residual role. It is available, for example, in the cases expressly excluded by paragraph (2) of Article 100a from the scope of that Article (see below), as

---

[27] See Treaty on European Union, Art. K.1.(7) and (9). It is worth noting that neither of these are matters in respect of which the new Art. 100c could be applied, pursuant to Art. K.9.

[28] See note 15, *supra*. The Commission has conceded that, unless the problem that had prevented the signing of the latter Convention is resolved, "the abolition of internal frontier controls in accordance with Article 8a will not be able to take place under satisfactory conditions owing to deficiencies in the administration of external frontiers": see seventh annual report on the implementation of the White Paper, COM(92) 383 final, point 58.

[29] See Arts. 9(2) and 10 EEC.

[30] See J.-L. Dewost in Capotorti *et al.* (eds.), *Du droit international au droit communautaire, Liber amicorum Pierre Pescatore* (1988, Nomos), pp. 167 *et seq.*

[31] On the approximation of laws pursuant to Art. 100, see Mégret *et al.*, *Le droit de la CEE* (1973, Editions de l'Université de Bruxelles), Vol. 5, pp. 152 *et seq.*; A. Dashwood in Wallace, Wallace and Webb. (eds.), *Policy-making in the European Community* (2nd ed., 1983, John Wiley & Sons), Chap. 6.

well as in respect of matters not linked with the establishment or functioning of the internal market but covered by the broader notion of the common market.

In its turn, Article 100a is a residual provision, since it applies "save where otherwise provided in this Treaty." This means that the specific legal bases provided by the Treaty in areas such as the common agricultural policy, the right of establishment, freedom to provide services and the common transport policy,[32] should be used, in preference to Article 100a, for the adoption, in those areas, of legislation having as its object the establishment and functioning of the internal market. Some problems of choosing between Article 100a and other available legal bases are discussed in the next section of this chapter.

The reference to "measures" in Article 100a(1) leaves the institutions the choice as to the particular form of act appropriate in a given case, in contrast to Article 100 which only allows the adoption of directives. In practice, however, the Council has shown a clear preference for using directives for the enactment of approximation measures under Article 100a, even in cases where an act in the form of a regulation has been proposed by the Commission.

The prospect of having approximation measures adopted by majority decision prompted concerns among the different Member States, which could only be assuaged by subjecting the power created by Article 100a(1) to a number of qualifications. Thus it is expressly provided by paragraph (2) of the Article that paragraph (1) does not apply to fiscal provisions or to provisions relating to the free movement of persons or to the rights and interests of employed persons. By paragraph (3) the Commission is required, in the proposals it makes concerning health, safety, environmental protection and consumer protection, to take as a base a high level of protection. In paragraph (5) it is recalled that harmonisation measures may include safeguard clauses authorising Member States "to take, for one or more of the non-economic reasons referred to in Article 36, provisional measures subject to a Community control procedure." However, it is paragraph (4) of the Article that claims our particular attention, since it became the focus of fierce criticism which proved, in the event, to have been misconceived.

Paragraph (4) of Article 100a provides:

"If, after the adoption of a harmonisation measure by the Council acting by a qualified majority, a Member State deems it necessary to apply national provisions on grounds of major needs referred to in Article 36, or relating to protection of the environment or the working environment, it shall notify the Commission of these provisions.

The Commission shall confirm the provisions involved after having verified that they are not a means of arbitrary discrimination or a disguised restriction on trade between Member States.

---

[32] Respectively, Arts. 43, 54, 57, 75 and 84(2).

By way of derogation from the procedure laid down in Article 169 and 170, the Commission or any Member State may bring the matter directly before the Court of Justice if it considers that another Member State is making improper use of the powers provided for in this Article."

Essentially, this allows an escape route for a Member State which considers that harmonised rules, adopted under Article 100a by a qualified majority, do not constitute a sufficient guarantee of attaining certain public interest objectives. When it is properly invoked, paragraph (4) prevents the operation, in respect of the Member State concerned, of the general rule of Community law that, once the standards protecting the interests in question have been harmonised, recourse to national provisions previously allowed under the Treaty despite potential interference with freedom of movement, can no longer be justified.[33]

According to the paragraph, when a measure has been adopted under Article 100a by a qualified majority, a Member State which "deems it necessary to apply national provisions on grounds of major needs referred to in Article 36, or relating to the protection of the environment or the working environment" should notify those provisions to the Commission, which must verify that they are not a means of arbitrary discrimination or a disguised restriction on trade between Member States, before confirming them. If a Member State abuses this possibility, the matter can be brought directly before the Court of Justice by a special remedy which omits the administrative phase of enforcement proceedings under Article 169 or Article 170 EEC.[34]

It is clear that the escape clause applies only when a measure has actually been adopted by a qualified majority and not when the compromise solution finally arrived at is one that commands unanimous support. Some commentators have drawn the conclusion that the paragraph can only be invoked by Member States forming part of the minority that was outvoted.[35] However, the benefit of paragraph (4) is not expressly restricted in this way, and such a restriction would detract from the *effet utile* of a provision designed to facilitate the formation of qualified majorities, since a Member State, wanting to have the right to apply its national rules but otherwise perfectly willing for a given measure to be passed, would be forced to join with those irreconcilably opposed to the measure in voting it down. The better view is, therefore, that absence of unanimity opens the way for any Member State to rely on paragraph (4), provided that the substantive and procedural requirements imposed by the paragraph are complied with.

The justification for applying national measures has to be found among

---

[33] On the background to the inclusion of para. (4) in Art. 100a, see De Ruyt, *op. cit.* note 5, *supra*, pp. 170 *et seq.*

[34] On enforcement proceedings, see Chap. 6, *supra*. See also A. Dashwood and R. White, (1989) 14 E.L.Rev., p. 388. An abbreviated procedure is similarly provided by Art. 93(2) EEC in the event of non-compliance by a Member State with a decision by the Commission finding a state aid incompatible with the common market.

[35] *Cf.* De Ruyt, *op. cit.* note 5, *supra*, pp. 171 and 174.

the "major needs" (*exigences importantes*) mentioned in Article 36 of the Treaty, to which are added the protection of the environment and of the working environment. That list is evidently intended to be exhaustive, unlike the open-ended list of "mandatory requirements" which, according to the *Cassis de Dijon* line of authority, may justify the application of disparate national provisions until harmonised rules have been adopted.[36]

A disputed issue is whether the national provisions whose application it is sought to justify under paragraph (4) must already have been in force at the time when the harmonisation measure in question is adopted under Article 100a. It is submitted that there is no such requirement, since the text speaks of applying, not of *continuing* to apply, national provisions.

The procedure laid down by paragraph (4) requires notification of the national provisions in question to the Commission, which must then proceed to verify that they are not a means of arbitrary discrimination or a disguised restriction on trade between Member States. The Commission is thus given the task of ensuring that notified provisions comply, in the new situation created by the adoption of the approximation measure, with the conditions laid down by the proviso to Article 36. That task necessarily involves the exercise of judgment, particularly as to whether any interference with freedom of movement resulting from the application of the provisions would be proportional to the "major need" being served. It does not, therefore, seem possible to share the interpretation enshrined in a unilateral Declaration on paragraph (4) by the Danish Government and suggesting that, when a Member State is of the opinion that measures adopted under Article 100a do not safeguard higher national requirements, confirmation by the Commission of the relevant national provisions is a pure formality. Of course, refusal of confirmation would be an act of the Commission within the meaning of Article 173 and could, therefore, be the object of annulment proceedings brought by the Member State concerned. If, in spite of being refused confirmation, the Member State concerned went ahead and applied the notified provisions, an enforcement action could be brought against it under the accelerated procedure provided for by the third sub-paragraph of paragraph (4). In such circumstances, the Court of Justice might also be persuaded to issue an interim order prohibiting the application of the provision pending the outcome of the proceedings.[37]

Critics of the S.E.A.[38] have argued that paragraph (4) undermines the case law of the Court of Justice on Article 36 of the Treaty. That criticism is misconceived, insofar as it implies that paragraph (4) represents a step backwards from the legal position which had been reached before the entry into force of the S.E.A. As we have seen, paragraph (4) is only available where an approximation measure has been adopted by a qualified majority which, prior to the S.E.A., would not have been possible: when the Council

---

[36] See Chap. 8, *supra*.
[37] Art. 186 EEC. See, *e.g.* Cases 31/77R and 53/77R, *Commission* v. *United Kingdom* [1977] E.C.R. 921. On interim measures, see Chap. 6, *supra*.
[38] Notably P. Pescatore in J.-V. Louis (ed.), *L'acte unique européen* (Journée d'études, Bruxelles, March 1, 1986), pp. 39 *et seq.; contra*, H.-J. Glaesner, R.M.C. 1986, p. 321.

acts unanimously, the rule is the same now, as before, that the harmonised standards apply and the protection of Article 36 is no longer available.

It is true that, if one or other of the Member States regularly resorted to paragraph (4), the effectiveness of Article 100a as an instrument for carrying out the work of approximation which is necessary in order to realise the objectives of Article 8a would have been seriously compromised.[39] However, in practice this has simply not happened. Indeed, in the five years since the S.E.A. came into force there have been only two occasions when Member States have given notice to the Commission, following the adoption by a qualified majority of a common position in respect of an approximation measure, of an intention of applying stricter national standards—in 1987 in respect of Directives relating to emissions from motor vehicles[40] and in 1991 in respect of an amendment to the Directive on the marketing and use of dangerous substances;[41] and only in the latter case was the procedure carried through to the stage of formal confirmation of the national provisions in question by the Commission. Experience to date can thus be regarded as reassuring.

Why should the dire predictions of eminent commentators have proved so wrong? Three reasons may be hazarded. First, the common political will to complete the internal market within the time limit set by Article 8a must have helped to overcome inhibitions. Secondly, Member States which may have hoped to use paragraph (4) to protect the high health status of their livestock industries have been prevented from doing so by the evolution of the case law on Article 43 which has shown that Article to be the appropriate legal basis for internal market legislation in the veterinary field.[42] Thirdly, the obligation imposed on the Commission by Article 100a(3) to propose high common standards of consumer and environmental protection may have helped to deter Member States from having recourse to paragraph (4), as it was clearly intended to do.

A final question is how paragraph (4) relates to the practice known as "minimal harmonisation." The latter occurs when Community legislation lays down certain minimum standards which must be observed in all the Member States, while authorising any Member State that so wishes to apply stricter standards in respect of the same matters.[43] The answer to the question is that paragraph (4) only comes into play once the rules relating to the matters in question have been fully harmonised: minimal harmonisation represents a step in a process which remains incomplete, leaving it open for Member States to invoke, as the case may be, Article 36 or one of the "mandatory requirements" recognised under the *Cassis de Dijon* doctrine. Step by step harmonisation is, in principle, a legitimate strategy for the

---

[39] De Ruyt, *op. cit.* note 5, *supra*, p. 174.
[40] Council Dir. 88/76 of December 3, 1987, O.J. 1988 L36/1; Council Dir. 88/77 of December 3, 1987, O.J. 1988 L36/33.
[41] Council Dir. 91/173 of March 21, 1991, O.J. 1991 L85/34. The substance in question was pentachlorophenol (P.C.P.).
[42] See the cases cited in note 49, *infra*.
[43] An example of a minimal harmonisation measure adopted on the basis of Art. 100a is Council Dir. 90/31 on package holidays, O.J. 1990 L158/59. See also Council Dir. 91/477 of June 18, 1991 on the acquisition and detention of weapons, O.J. 1991 L256/51.

Community legislator to adopt,[44] bearing in mind, however, the time limit fixed by Article 8a for the completion of the internal market.

Mutual recognition in default of harmonisation

A procedure enabling the Council to require the mutual recognition of national rules and standards which have not been the subject of harmonisation measures pursuant to Article 100a is laid down by Article 100b. That Article provides:

> "1. During 1992, the Commission shall, together with each Member State, draw up an inventory of national laws, regulations and administrative provisions which fall under Article 100a and which have not been harmonized pursuant to that Article.
>
> The Council, acting in accordance with the provisions of Article 100a, may decide that the provisions in force in a Member State must be recognized as being equivalent to those applied by another Member State.
>
> 2. The provisions of Article 100a(4) shall apply by analogy.
>
> 3. The Commission shall draw up the inventory referred to in the first subparagraph of paragraph 1 and shall submit appropriate proposals in good time to allow the Council to act before the end of 1992."

Article 100b, therefore, creates a convenient mechanism for a sweeping up operation covering any unfinished elements of the legislative programme contained in the White Paper of 1985. A question that arises is whether the Article makes mutual recognition the only available option in any case where harmonisation cannot be completed by the 1993 deadline. That, it is submitted, is not the meaning of the Article, since the Council is only given a power to act ("The Council . . . may decide . . ."): nor is there anything in the wording of Article 100a itself to suggest that Article will no longer be usable after the end of 1992; indeed, the reference in paragraph (1) of Article 100a to the *functioning* of the internal market, as distinct from its establishment, is a clear indication that the Council will continue to have the option of adopting approximation measures after the end of 1992.

Despite the mandatory language of the third paragraph of Article 100b, no proposal for making use of the power conferred by the Article had been placed on the Council's table by the autumn of 1992. That made it highly unlikely that the Council would be in a position to act under the Article before the end of 1992, since it would be required to do so, "in accordance with the provisions of Article 100a," *i.e.* by the co-operation procedure.

---

[44] See Case 215/87, *Heinz Schumacher* v. *HZA Frankfurt-am-Main* [1989] E.C.R. 638; Case C–42/90, *Bellon* [1990] E.C.R. 4863.

Legal bases for internal market legislation

Choice of legal bases

The issue addressed in this section is that of the selection of the correct legal basis for a given piece of internal market legislation. In practice, disputed choices are generally between Article 100a and some other provision of the EEC Treaty. Preferences are liable to be influenced by the perception of political advantage (or disadvantage) in the procedure for the adoption of harmonisation measures by the Council acting by a qualified majority in co-operation with the European Parliament, in the one hand, or in the escape route paragraph (4) of the Article may offer from the consequences of such measures, on the other. Disputes may arise between different Community institutions, especially where the Council has amended by unanimity the legal basis proposed by the Commission, or between the Council and one or more of the Member States, when a proposal has been adopted in the face of minority opposition.

General principles governing the choice of the legal basis of Community acts have been laid down by the Court of Justice. According to those principles, the choice must be made in the light of objective factors capable of being the subject of judicial review,[45] in particular the aim and content of the act.[46] Where examination of the relevant factors shows that the act is concerned with two or more distinct matters which are dealt with in separate provisions of the EEC Treaty, a dual or multiple legal basis may be required.[47] However, legal bases must not be combined if the procedures which they prescribe are incompatible. Thus the Court has held that it is impossible for an act to be based on Treaty Articles one of which provides for the co-operation procedure, while the other requires the Council to act unanimously after simple consultation of the European Parliament.[48] In such cases, it seems, preference should be given to the former legal basis, as providing a reinforced rôle for the European Parliament on the legislative process, so long has the different objectives of the proposal are capable of being furthered by legislation based on the Article in question.

The choice between Article 100a and Article 43

The leading cases concern legislation pre-dating the S.E.A., when the disputed demarcation was between Article 43 and Article 100. However, the lessons to be drawn from those cases are equally applicable to the demarcation between Article 43 and Article 100a.

Article 43 does not prescribe the co-operation procedure but the Council acts by a qualified majority, so the choice of legal basis does not affect the voting rule. More significant is the possibility of invoking paragraph (4) of Article 100a, which has no equivalent in Article 43. Delegations wishing to maintain national rules guaranteeing, as they claim, a higher health status

---

[45] Case 45/86, *Commission* v. *Council* [1987] E.C.R. 1493.
[46] Case C–300/89, *Commission* v. *Council (Titanium Dioxyde Waste)* [1991] E.C.R. 2867.
[47] Case 165/87, *Commission* v. *Council* [1988] E.C.R. 5545.
[48] Case C–300/89, note 45, *supra*.

for their countries than harmonised rules which it is proposed to adopt on veterinary or plant health matters, may accordingly press for the proposal to be based on Article 100a.

The cases establish that Article 43 is the correct legal basis for legislation satisfying two conditions: it must relate to the production or marketing of the agricultural products listed in Annex II to the EEC Treaty; and it must contribute to the attainment of one or more of the objectives of the common agricultural policy set out in Article 39 of the Treaty.[49] It has further been held that, where the bulk of the products to which legislation applies are Annex II products, the fact that the legislation may also apply, in an accessory way, to certain non-Annex II products does not take it outside the scope of the common agricultural policy[50]; nor does the fact that the legislation pursues, at the same time, certain general aims, such as the protection of health.[51]

Applying those principles, the Court has found that Article 43 was the correct legal basis for a ban on the administration of growth hormones to livestock,[52] a directive laying down conditions for the treatment of battery hens,[53] a directive relating to the importation of animal glands and organs for use by the pharmaceutical industry,[54] and a directive on undesirable substances in animal feedingstuffs.[55]

On the other hand, where internal market measures apply equally to certain agricultural and non-agricultural products, a dual legal basis, Article 43 together with Article 100a, seems both desirable and possible, since there is no problem of procedural incompatibility.

The choice between Article 100a and Article 130s

A new Title VII on the Environment, comprising Articles 130r to 130t was added to Part Three of the EEC Treaty by Article 25 of the S.E.A. Article 130r defines the objectives and the general principles of action by the Community relating to the environment. It is provided that the Community shall take action to the extent to which objectives can be attained better at its level than at the level of individual Member States, an application of the subsidiarity principle which has been given a much more prominent place in the Treaty on European Union.[56] The legal basis for Community action in relation to the environment is Article 130s under which the Council acts by unanimity after consulting the European Parliament and the Economic and Social Committee. The Council is empowered to define, by the same procedure, matters on which decisions may be taken by a qualified majority but has not so far taken advantage of this possibility. Finally, Article 130t

---

[49] See, in particular, Case 68/86, *United Kingdom* v. *Council* [1988] E.C.R. 855; Case 131/86, *United Kingdom* v. *Council* [1988] E.C.R. 905; Case 13/87, *Commission* v. *Council* [1989] E.C.R. 3743; Case 11/88, *Commission* v. *Council* [1989] E.C.R. 3799.
[50] Case 11/88, *loc. cit.* note 49, *supra.*
[51] See cases cited in note 48, *supra.*
[52] Council Dir. 87/519 of October 19, 1987, O.J. 1987 L304/38.
[53] Council Dir. 86/113 of March 25, 1986, O.J. 1986 L95/45.
[54] Council Dir. 87/64 of December 30, 1986, O.J. 1987 L34/52.
[55] Council Dir. 87/519 of October 19, 1987, O.J. 1987 L304/38.
[56] See the discussion of the new Art. 3b of the EC Treaty, as amended, in Chap. 23, *supra.*

reserves for the Member States the right to maintain or introduce more stringent protective measures which must, however, be compatible with the Treaty.

The last sentence of Article 130r(2) says that environmental protection requirements shall be a component of the Community's other policies. However, it does not follow that Article 130s must be regarded as a residual legal basis to which resort can only be had where no other basis for action is available under the Treaty.[57] The new Articles 130r to 130t were clearly intended to provide a coherent framework for organising a Community environmental policy. Like regional policy or social policy, this is a Community policy applying in an area where the Member States enjoy concurrent competence. It is to be contrasted with the common policies in the fields of agriculture and transport, where Community competence is potentially exclusive, and actually so, once it has been exercised.

However, it is equally clear that Article 100a was intended to serve as the legal basis of measures for the approximation of national provisions on the protection of the environment, where such measures have as their object the establishment or functioning of the internal market. This follows from the reference in Article 100a(3) to Commission proposals "concerning . . . environmental protection." There is a fine dividing line between such harmonisation measures and the "specific Community action in relation to the environment" which is the province of Article 130s.

An uncontroversial example of the use of Article 100a would be the harmonisation of legislation laying down technical specifications, with a view to the protection of the environment, for certain manufactured products which are traded within the internal market. By removing disparities between national provisions, while guaranteeing a high level of environmental protection throughout the Community, the harmonising measure would obviously contribute towards ensuring the free movement of the products in question. Article 100a was thus correctly chosen as the legal basis for Community measures in relation to the control of emissions from motor vehicles.[58]

A more difficult case is that of Community measures designed to protect the environment against the harmful consequences of industrial processes, such as legislation on the disposal of industrial waste. Such measures cannot be regarded as removing impediments to the free movement of goods within the internal market. However, since pollution control is expensive for the undertakings concerned, disparities between the levels of protection prescribed by the legislation of different Member States may result in distortions of competition, which the harmonisation of national provisions would help to remedy. The Court of Justice has said that action by the Community for the approximation of national rules relating to conditions of

---

[57] *Cf.* the second sentence of the new Article 130b to be inserted into the European Community Treaty by the Treaty on European Union which requires the objectives of economic and social cohesion to be taken into account in the formulation and implementation of the Community's policies and actions and of the internal market. This was obviously not intended to reduce to a residual rôle the legal bases provided by Arts. 130d and 130e.

[58] See note 40, *supra.*

production in a given industrial sector, with a view to eliminating distortions of competition in that sector, is capable of contributing to the attainment of the internal market and, accordingly falls within the purview of Article 100a.[59] On the other hand, if that logic is pressed too far, it would completely exclude Article 130s as a basis for legislation on such matters as the control of industrial pollution, which lie at the very heart of any policy on the protection of the environment. This seems inconsistent with the letter and spirit of the new Treaty Articles introduced by the S.E.A. and even more so with the amendments to Article 130s provided for in the Treaty on European Union.[60]

The choice between Article 100a and Article 130s was the subject of the litigation in Case C–300/89 concerning the Council Directive of June 21, 1989, on the harmonisation of national programmes for the reduction, with a view to its elimination, of pollution caused by the titanium dioxyde waste industry.[61] The Directive was annulled by the Court on the ground that Article 100a, as proposed by the Commission, and not Article 130s, substituted by the Council, was the correct legal basis. Analysis of the aim and content of the Directive led the Court to conclude that it was a measure with the dual object of protecting the environment and removing distortions of competition, which seemed to point to the requirement of a dual legal basis. However, that solution had to be rejected since, in the Court's view, the unanimity rule in Article 130s, was incompatible with the co-operation procedure prescribed by Article 100a. A choice had, therefore, to be made, and the Court opted for Article 100a, apparently because it considered both the objects of the Directive could effectively be pursued on that legal basis, although the judgment does not explain why they could not be pursued, as effectively and appropriately, on the basis of Article 130s.

It would be premature to conclude from the *Titanium Dioxyde Waste* judgment that any Community measure for the protection of the environment which has a tendency to equalise conditions of competition must, for that reason, be based on Article 100a. The judgment may be explained by the drafting of the Directive in question which emphasised its dual object. The position will be clearer once the Court has given judgment in a pending case which concerns a Directive amending the general Directive on waste disposal.[62] That case is likely to decide whether it will be possible in future to develop and overall Community approach to pollution control on the basis of Article 130s.

---

[59] Case C–300/89, note 46, *supra*, at point 23.
[60] The amended Art. 130s provides for the adoption, under the new procedure laid down by Art. 189b, of general action programmes setting out priority objectives to be attained (para. (3)). Action on the environment is generally to be taken under the procedure laid down by Art. 189c, the present co-operation procedure (para. (2)). However, on certain matters, the existing procedure, with the Council acting by unanimity, is retained (para. (2)). "Waste management" is specifically mentioned in the amended Art. 130s(2) as an aspect of land use that will fall to be regulated under the co-operation procedure.
[61] O.J. 1989 L201/6.
[62] Council Dir. 91/156 of May 18, 1991, O.J. 1991 L78/32, amending Council Dir. 75/442 of March 15, 1975, O.J. 1975 L194/39.

Other cases

The exclusions in paragraph (2) of Article 100a may sometimes give rise to difficult borderline cases.

For instance, it was a question whether the Regulation on the elimination of controls and formalities applicable to the cabin and hold baggage of persons taking an intra-Community flight and the baggage of persons making an intra-Community sea crossing should have been based on Article 100a, as a measure facilitating the movement of goods, or on Article 100, as a measure facilitating the movement of persons.[63] The choice of Article 100a seems correct, since the provisions of the Regulation apply specifically to controls on baggage. The fact that baggage is accompanied by its owner when frontiers are crossed does not prevent it from being regarded as "goods" within the meaning of the Treaty. Similar reasoning justified the choice of Article 100a as the legal basis for the Directive on the acquisition and detention of weapons.[64]

A different position was taken by the Council in the case of the Regulation on co-operation between tax authorities, the aim of which was to ensure the effective collection of revenue, while avoiding interference with the free movement of goods.[65] Since the administrative arrangements in question were ancillary to the objective of levying taxation, the right legal basis for the measure was thought to be Article 99 EEC.

A limitation on the scope of Article 100a that must not be forgotten is that it only applies to measures for the approximation of national provisions. That makes it hard to understand the view of the Commission that the proposed regulation on the European Company could be based on Article 100a.[66] The object of the proposal is the creation of a new company form that would exist only in Community law. This is altogether different from, say, a directive requiring all the Member States to introduce a uniform company statute into their national law, a genuine case of harmonisation, which could be achieved by means of a directive based on Article 54(2) of the Treaty. Since the object of the proposed regulation is something that could not be done under the law of any individual Member State, there can be no question of approximating national provisions, even by anticipation. Therefore, it is thought, the only possible legal basis for the European company regulation is Article 235 EEC.

The balance sheet

The Commission was required by Article 8b EEC[67] to report to the Council at the end of 1988, and again at the end of 1990, on the progress

---

[63] See Council Reg. 3925/91 of December 19, 1991, O.J. 1991 L374/4. This has been supplemented by Commission Reg. 1823/92 of July 3, 1992 laying down detailed rules.

[64] Council Dir. 91/477 of June 18, 1991 L256/51.

[65] Council Reg. 218/92 of January 27, 1992, O.J. 1992 L24/1.

[66] See O.J. 1989 C263/41. The proposed regulation would be accompanied by a directive, based on Art. 64(2), concerning worker participation. This element had to be excluded from the proposal based on Art. 100a because of the express reference in para. (2) of the Article to "provisions . . . relating to the rights and interests of employed persons."

[67] Introduced into the EEC Treaty by S.E.A., Art. 14.

made towards achieving the internal market within the time limit fixed by Article 8a.[68] Besides these periodic stocktakings, it has submitted annual progress reports to the Council and the European Parliament.[69] Since 1989 the annual reports have been supplemented by a report dealing with the implementation of the measures for completing the internal market by Member States and by the Commission itself.[70] The series of reports has presented a generally satisfactory picture, keeping alive the expectation that the great bulk of the legislative programme in the White Paper would be enacted by the end of 1992.

The seventh, and last, annual report,[71] which was presented by the Commission in September 1992, appeared to confirm that expectation. The report noted that, of the 282 measures proposed in the White Paper, 32 remained to be adopted by the Council; nine of these were of low priority, not being linked to the removal of frontier controls, so that there were only 23 measures which, in the Commission's view, the Council needed to tackle as a matter of urgency, if necessary by holding special meetings.[72] As for the rate of transposition of directives by the Member States, this was estimated by the Commission as 75 per cent. (89 per cent. in the case of directives that were in force in June 1991).[73]

The Commission's overall assessment was that "in view of the decisions already in force, the economic framework for the single market is now in place, with people, goods, capital and services able to move around freely either on the basis of harmonised or common rules or on the basis of mutual recognition."[74]

---

[68] The reports were published as, respectively, COM(88) 650 and COM(90) 552. See also the detailed survey of the progress made up to the end of 1990 by M. Ayral in *Revue du marché unique*, No. 2–1991, p. 101.

[69] See, *e.g.* the seventh report, COM(92) 383 final.

[70] See, *e.g.* the report dated December 19, 1991, SEC(91) 2491 final.

[71] See note 69, *supra*.

[72] Seventh report, points 17 to 19.

[73] *Ibid.* point 11.

[74] *Ibid.* point 1. See also the optimistic prognosis of Vice-President Bangemann that the 1993 deadline will be met, as reported, in *Agence Europe*, September 3, 1992, p. 7. While the Commission maintains its interpretation of Art. 8a, it seems likely that a practical solution will be found enabling Member States that wish to maintain internal frontier controls on persons, notably the United Kingdom, to require nationals of Member States to identify themselves as such: see *ibid.* pp. 7–8.

PART IV: POLICIES OF THE COMMUNITY

CHAPTER 13

INTRODUCTION TO THE RULES ON COMPETITION

Competition and the common market

The list of "activities of the Community" in Article 3 EEC includes "the institution of a system ensuring that competition in the common market is not distorted."[1] There are two main reasons why competition policy was singled out in this way as a key factor in the pursuit of the broad objectives laid down for the Community in Article 2.

In the first place, a conscious choice was made by the authors of the Treaty, and by those who have since adhered to it, not only of an economic life in common but of a way of life in which the market plays a central, though not necessarily an exclusive, role. Competition is an essential aspect of the market mechanism because the availability of choice between goods and services establishes a link between the success of an undertaking and its ability to satisfy customers' wishes. The phrasing of Article 3 is, perhaps, not altogether happy, since the idea of "distortion" implies deviation from a state of perfect competition. That, of course, is unrealistic. What is needed is the preservation of *effective* competition, *i.e.* a level of challenge from other operators sufficient to make efficiency and innovation a condition of ultimate survival as a market participant. In the introduction to its *First Report on Competition Policy* the Commission wrote:

> "Competition is the best stimulant of economic activity since it guarantees the widest possible freedom of action to all. An active competition policy pursued in accordance with the provisions of the Treaties establishing the Communities makes it easier for the supply and demand structure continually to adjust to technological development. Through the interplay of decentralized decision-making machinery, competition enables enterprises continuously to improve their efficiency, which is the *sine qua non* for a steady improvement in living standards and employment prospects within the countries of the Community. From this point of view, competition policy is an essential means for satisfying to a great extent the individual and collective needs of our society."[2]

Thus competition policy is seen as ensuring that the common market envisaged by the Treaty functions as a genuine *market*.

Secondly, competition policy contributes to the creation and preservation of a market that is *common*, since it reinforces the provisions of the Treaty aiming at the removal of barriers between the economies of the Member

---

[1] For an account of EEC competition policy and its relationship with industrial policy in the strategy for the creation of a genuine internal market in goods and services, see Dennis Swann, *Competition and Industrial Policy in the European Community* (1983).
[2] Comp. Rep. 1971, p. 11. See also Comp. Rep. 1979, pp. 9–11.

States. It would be futile to attempt to create a single market without internal frontiers in goods, persons, services and capital, as required by Article 8a EEC, if the isolation of national markets could effectively be maintained by restrictive practices on the part of undertakings, or by State aid policies giving competitive advantages to the national industries. As we shall see, for an agreement or practice to have the object or effect of dividing the common market involves a particularly serious infringement of the rules on competition. Those rules, accordingly, by opening up possibilities for competition on a Community-wide scale, both supplement the provisions of Pa.t Two of the Treaty and assist in the attainment of the greater prosperity mentioned in Article 2 through the operation of economics of scale.

The EEC Treaty provisions on competition

The preamble to the Treaty and the general provisions of Articles 2 and 3 have played a significant part in the development of the case-law on competition.[3] However, the primary Treaty provisions in which the substantive law on the topic is to be found are Articles 85 to 94.

So far as the behaviour of undertakings is concerned, the Treaty adopts a distinction which is familiar in competition law (or, to use the American term, " antitrust law"[4]) between two types of problem that may arise.[5] The first concerns restrictive agreements or practices involving a degree of collusion between undertakings that are economically independent of each other. Such combinations in restraint of trade are sometimes referred to as "cartels." An example would be an agreement between trade associations representing French and German manufacturers of garden gnomes that each group would refrain from selling its products on the other's market. Article 85 of the Treaty is designed to deal with such a situation. It is considered in Chapter 14, *infra*. The second type of problem arises where a single undertaking or a group of undertakings has reached a position of such strength on a given market that the normal constraints of the competitive process no longer apply to it. Community law calls that a "dominant position" and English law a "monopoly situation." Dominant undertakings represent a danger to other operators on the same market and to their customers or suppliers. They may, for example, drive the remaining participants in the same market out of business or charge unreasonably high prices for their products. One way of averting this danger is to attack the fact of dominance itself, by seeking to prevent the growth of undertakings beyond a certain point, and by taking power to break up any that may succeed in doing so. An alternative approach is to attempt to regulate the behaviour of dominant undertakings. Here public power is used as a

---

[3] See, *e.g.* Case 32/65, *Italy* v. *Council and Commission* [1966] E.C.R. 389 at p. 405; Case 6/72, *Europemballage and Continental Can* v. *Commission* [1973] E.C.R. 215 at pp. 243–244.

[4] In the nineteenth century anti-competitive arrangements were often carried out in the USA through trusts, hence this term. For an introduction to US antitrust law, see Raybould and Firth, *Law of Monopolies* (1991).

[5] On the nature of the problems, and the different solutions adopted in United Kingdom and Community law, see Whish, *Competition Law* (2nd ed., 1989).

constraining influence, to compensate for the absence of effective competition. Initially the latter approach was adopted by the EEC Treaty which in Article 86 outlaws the "abuse" of dominant positions.[6] Subsequently the European Court held that, in certain circumstances, a further accretion of market power to a dominant undertaking may, in itself, constitute an abuse. Now, the former approach has been adopted in the merger regulation which is considered in Chapter 20, *infra*.

Provision for the application of the substantive rules in Articles 85 and 86 is made by Articles 87 to 89 of the Treaty. Article 87 empowers the Council, acting by a qualified majority on a proposal from the Commission and after consulting the European Parliament, to adopt implementing regulations or directives. This power has been used for the enactment of, *inter alia*, Regulation 17, which established the basic machinery for the execution of EEC competition policy, giving primary responsibility to the Commission.[7] Articles 88 and 89 contain transitional provisions applicable in the absence of such special machinery,[8] but since all sectors of the economy are now covered by such machinery, then these provisions are only of importance where there are lacunae.[9] Regulation 17 covers all sectors of the economy except where other provisions have been made. The most important of these cover merger control[10]; rail, road and inland waterway transport[11]; maritime transport[12]; and air transport.[13]

Problems arising from the relationships between governments, on the one hand, and public undertakings or undertakings which have been entrusted with the performance of certain tasks in the public interest, on the other, are the subject of Article 90. This relationship, although clearly liable to affect the conditions of competition, has a wider significance for the operation of the common market. It is discussed in Chapter 19, *infra*.

Article 91 laid down procedures to be followed if dumping should take place within the common market during the transitional period of the Community as originally constituted.[14] "Dumping" is a species of unfair competition which consists of selling goods on an export market below their "normal value." There are various ways of establishing the normal value of a product, the most straightforward being the price charged on the domestic market. The provision was limited to the transitional period since, once barriers to internal trade had come down, dumped products could be

---

[6] On the variety of approaches adopted by national authorities, see Von Kalinowski, *Overview, World Law of Competition* (looseleaf), Chap. 1.
[7] J.O. 1962, 204; O.J. 1959–1962, 87. The section of the Commission responsible for competition law and policy is Directorate-General IV, usually abbreviated to DGIV.
[8] On the application of the competition rules to air transport, see Joined Cases 209 to 213/84, *Ministère Public* v. *Asjès and Others* [1986] E.C.R. 1425.
[9] For example, in air transport, the relevant machinery only covers agreements relating to flights between different EEC states and so does not cover agreements relating to domestic flights or to flights to non-EEC destinations. In such cases, Articles 88 and 89 remain applicable.
[10] Regulation 4064/89, for which see Chap. 17, *infra*.
[11] Regulation 1017/68 O.J. 1968 L175/1.
[12] Regulation 4056/86 O.J. 1986 L378/4.
[13] Regulations 3975/87 O.J. 1987 L374/1, and 82/91, 83/91 & 84/91 O.J. 1991 L10/7 *et seq*.
[14] Anti-dumping measures against third countries are an aspect of the Common Commercial Policy. See Art. 113 EEC and Reg. 2176/84, O.J. 1984 L201/1.

re-exported to the country of origin, where they could be sold at a price that would undercut the price prevailing there. The Article itself is, therefore, of mainly historical interest, though equivalent provisions are found in the accession arrangements with new Member States.[15]

Under Articles 92 to 94 the Community institutions, and in particular the Commission, have supervisory powers over the granting of aids to industry in the various Member States. The general principle is that aid must not be granted if it distorts or threatens to distort competition by favouring certain undertakings or forms of production, in so far as trade between Member States may be affected. However, wide exceptions are permitted, enabling the Commission to take account of the economic and social pressures to which the Member States are subject. These provisions are discussed in Chapter 18, *infra*.

Other sources of EEC competition law

Besides the EEC Treaty itself, the principal sources of EEC competition law are regulations pursuant to Article 87, the case law of the Court of Justice and the Court of First Instance, and the administrative practice of the Commission.

Regulations on competition have been adopted by both the Council and the Commission, the latter acting under delegated powers. Regulation 17,[16] the general implementing measure, has already been mentioned. This is supplemented by various measures governing more detailed matters, such as Regulation 99[17] on the conduct of hearings and Regulation 2988/74[18] on periods of limitation. There is also a growing body of regulations granting "block" exemptions under Article 85(3) in respect of categories of agreements (for example exclusive distribution agreements, exclusive purchasing agreements, franchising agreements) which would otherwise be liable to prohibition under Article 85(1).[19]

The Court of Justice has played a vital part in the development of the rules on competition, as of other areas of Community law. Competition matters normally come to the courts by way of proceedings under Article 173 EEC for the review of decisions of the Commission applying the rules, or of references under Article 177 from national courts before which the rules have been invoked. In addition, Regulation 17 has conferred on the Court unlimited jurisdiction as provided by Article 172 EEC, to hear appeals against the imposition by the Commission of fines for infringements of the rules.[20] Since its establishment[21] proceedings under Article 173 relating to the implementation of the competition rules of the EEC must be brought

---

[15] See Act of Accession, Denmark, Ireland and United Kingdom, Art. 136; Greece, Art. 131; Spain and Portugal, Art. 380.
[16] *Loc. cit.* note 7, *supra.*
[17] J.O. 1963, 2268; O.J. 1963–64, 47.
[18] O.J. 1974 L319/1.
[19] See the discussion, pp. 426 *et seq., infra.*
[20] See Reg. 17, Art. 17.
[21] Council decision 88/591 Establishing an EC Court of First Instance O.J. 1988 L319/1.

before the Court of First Instance.[22] Appeal lies to the Court of Justice from the Court of First Instance only on points of law.[23] In interpreting the competition provisions of the Treaty and of regulations the Court has followed its usual approach of giving weight, as appropriate, to their wording, their legal content and their objectives, as well as to the wider objectives of the Community. A bold example of the application of the principle of effectiveness was the decision in *Camera Care*[24] that the Commission has power to adopt interim measures in competition proceedings, despite the silence of Regulation 17 on this point. The technique of comparative analysis of national laws, including United States antitrust law, has also proved fruitful.[25]

As we have seen, the Commission is the authority charged with the administration of the competition system at Community level. For this purpose it has been empowered to take decisions, *inter alia*, ordering the termination of infringements,[26] granting exemption under Article 85(3)[27] and imposing fines[28] or periodic penalty payments.[29] The competition decisions of the Commission are the best guide to the practical working of the rules. Further guidance may be obtained from the press releases the Commission issues when it terminates a proceeding without a formal decision and from the Annual Reports on Competition Policy annexed to its General Report to the European Parliament. The Commission has also published a series of Notices setting forth its views on a variety of issues.[30] The Notices have made a useful contribution to general understanding of the law but they may not give reliable guidance in individual cases.

Finally, it may be noted, the directly effective provisions of Article 85 and Article 86 are being applied with increasing frequency by the courts of the Member States. The resulting case law is an additional source of persuasive authority on the interpretation of those provisions.

The scope of the EEC rules on competition

Personal scope

The rules in Article 85 and Article 86 apply to "undertakings." No definition of this concept for the purposes of competition law is provided by the EEC Treaty.[31] It has been described as much wider and looser than the

---

[22] Council decision 88/591, *loc. cit.* Art. 3(1)(c).
[23] Art. 51 Statute of Court of Justice as amended by Art. 7 Council decision 88/591, *loc. cit.*
[24] Case 792/79R, *Camera Care* v. *Commission* [1980] E.C.R. 119; [1980] 1 C.M.L.R. 334.
[25] The actual analysis is normally to be found in the opinion of the Advocate General in the case. See, *e.g.* Case 48/69, *ICI* v. *Commission (Dyestuffs)* [1972] E.C.R. 619; [1972] C.M.L.R. 557; Case 155/79, *A. M. & S. Europe* v. *Commission* [1982] E.C.R. 1575; [1982] 2 C.M.L.R. 264.
[26] Reg. 17, Art. 3(1).
[27] Reg. 17, Art. 9(1).
[28] Reg. 17, Art. 15.
[29] Reg. 17, Art. 16.
[30] Some of the more important notices are: agreements with commercial agents, J.O. 1962, 2921; co-operation agreements, J.O. 1968 C75/3; agreements of minor importance, O.J. 1986 C231/2 (replacing a Notice of 1977); subcontracting agreements, O.J. 1979, C1/2.
[31] *Cf.* the definitions in Art. 80 ECSC and Art. 196 Euratom. See also the partial definition in Art. 52 EEC for the purposes of the provisions on freedom of establishment.

concept of "persons"[32] and seems to extend to any entity carrying on economic activities.[33] A rough synonym would be a "business concern."

The requirement of participation in economic activities must be understood in a wide sense. It covers not only the production and distribution of goods but also the provision of services.[34] A body that exists for a non-economic purpose but engages in certain operations of a commercial nature will be, to that extent, an undertaking[35]: for example a public service broadcasting establishment when it licenses the manufacture of toys based on a popular children's series.[36] Nor is there any need for the body in question to be motivated by the pursuit of profits. Thus societies that manage the rights of authors and performing artists on a non-profit making basis qualify as undertakings because they provide a commercial service.[37]

The entities accepted as undertakings by the Court of Justice and the Commission exhibit a wide range of legal forms. They include companies, partnerships,[38] co-operatives[39] and even the mutual marine insurance associations known as "P and I Clubs."[40] Individuals may be undertakings, for example, an inventor who grants licences for the use of patents he has taken out[41] or opera stars who contract to perform for a television company.[42] At the opposite end of the spectrum are nationalised industries and the other kinds of public corporation.[43] The Commission regards as undertakings the foreign trade organisations of countries, even if under their domestic law they have no identity separate from the state.[44] A similar view would, it is submitted, be taken of a Member State, or of a subdivision of the state such as a local authority, engaging directly in commercial activity.[45] The Court of Justice in the *Bodson* case[46] has drawn a distinction between a

---

[32] By Ad. Gen. Warner in Joined Cases 6 and 7/73, *Commercial Solvents Corporation* v. *Commission* [1974] E.C.R. 223 at p. 263.

[33] See the definition offered by Ad. Gen. Roemer in Case 32/65, *Italy* v. *Council and Commission* [1966] E.C.R. at p. 418.

[34] Case 155/73, *Sacchi* [1974] E.C.R. 409; [1974] 2 C.M.L.R. 177.

[35] *Ibid.*

[36] *Re BBC* [1976] 1 C.M.L.R. D89. The same would be true of sports clubs: see *Re English Football League* Comp. Rep. 1979, points 116–117.

[37] Case 127/73, *BRT* v. *SABAM* [1974] E.C.R. 51 and 313; [1974] 2 C.M.L.R. 238; Case 7/82, *GVL* v. *Commission* [1983] E.C.R. 483; [1983] 3 C.M.L.R. 645.

[38] *E.g. Re William Prym-Werke* J.O 1973 L296/24; [1973] C.M.L.R. D 250.

[39] *E.g. Re Rennet* O.J 1980 L51/19; [1980] 2 C.M.L.R. 402. The decision was upheld by the Court in Case 61/80, *Co-operatieve Stremsel-en-Kleurselfabriek* v. *Commission* [1981] E.C.R. 851; [1982] 1 C.M.L.R. 240. See also *Re Milchförderungsfonds* O.J. 1985 L35/35; [1985] 3 C.M.L.R. 101.

[40] See *Re P and I Clubs* O.J. 1985 C 9/11. The Clubs are groupings of shipowners, charterers, and operators who agree to share certain liabilities, in particular contractual and third party liabilities, on a non-profit making basis. Risks in excess of certain agreed thresholds are often shared between "pools" of P and I Clubs.

[41] See, *e.g. Re AOIP/Beyrard* O.J. 1976 L6/8; [1976] 1 C.M.L.R. D14; *Re Vaessen/Moris* O.J. 1979 L19/32; [1979] 1 C.M.L.R. 511.

[42] *Re Unitel* O.J. 1978 L157/39; [1978] 3 C.M.L.R. 306.

[43] *E.g. Re British Telecom* O.J. 1982 L360/36; [1983] 1 C.M.L.R. 457. The decision was upheld by the Court in Case 41/83, *Italy* v. *Commission* [1985] 2 C.M.L.R. 368. See also *Re Federacion Nacional de Cafeteros de Colombia* O.J. 1982 L360/31; [1983] 1 C.M.L.R. 703.

[44] *Re Aluminium Imports from Eastern Europe* O.J. 1985 L92/1.

[45] But see Bellamy and Child, *Common Market Law of Competition* (3rd ed., 1987, 1st supplement 1991) at para. 2–011 where it is argued that a clear distinction is drawn throughout the Treaty between Member States and undertakings.

[46] Case 30/87, *Bodson* v. *Pompes Funèbres des Regions Libérées SA* [1988] E.C.R. 2479; *see also* Case C–41/90, *Hofner* v. *Macroton GmbH*, April 23, 1991, not yet reported.

public body acting in a public capacity and such a body engaging in commercial activity, holding that only in the latter case does it qualify as an undertaking.

In applying the rules on competition to groups of companies the Court of Justice does not hesitate to go behind the facade of separate corporate identity. This pragmatic approach is illustrated by the *Hydrotherm* case[47] which concerned the block exemption granted by Regulation 67/67[48] to certain categories of exclusive dealing agreements. The exemption was expressly limited to agreements "to which only two undertakings are party."[49] That condition was held to be fulfilled where the parties to a contract were, on the distribution side, a German company, and on the manufacturing side, the Italian developer of a product and two legally independent firms controlled by him. The Court explained that "In competition law, the term 'undertaking' must be understood as designating an economic unit for the purpose of the subject-matter of the agreement in question even if in law that economic unit consists of several persons, natural or legal."[50] In practice, the main impact of the "enterprise entity" doctrine has been on two issues: the assertion of jurisdiction against a parent company established in a third country which has subsidiaries within the common market; and the application of Article 85 to agreements and practices between parent companies and subsidiaries. These issues are further examined below.[51]

Material scope

The EEC rules on competition apply generally, to all sectors of the economy, except where express derogations are provided in other Articles of the Treaty.[52]

The main sectors falling outside the rules are coal and steel, which are governed by the ECSC Treaty.[53] However, where an ECSC undertaking deals in goods other than those defined in Annex I to the ECSC Treaty, the EEC rules will apply to it.[54] When the ECSC Treaty expires in 2002 it seems that these sectors will become subject to the normal EEC Treaty rules.

By Article 42 EEC the extent to which the competition provisions should apply to agricultural products was made a matter for the discretion of the Council. In exercising its discretion the Council differentiated between the rules applicable to undertakings in Articles 85 to 90 and the rules on state aids in Articles 92 to 94. The former Articles were extended to agricultural products by Regulation 26,[55] subject to an exemption from the prohibition in Article 85(1) for the benefit of agreements that form an integral part of a

---

[47] Case 170/83, *Hydrotherm Gerätebau* v. *Andreoli* [1984] E.C.R. 2999.
[48] J.O. 1967, 849; O.J. 1967, 10. This was replaced by Reg. 1983/83 (exclusive distribution) O.J. 1983 L173/1 and Reg. 1984/83 (exclusive purchasing) O.J. 1983 L173/5: see Chap. 14, *infra*.
[49] Reg. 67/67, Art. 1(1).
[50] [1984] E.C.R. at p. 3016.
[51] See, respectively, pp. 384 *et seq.* and pp. 385–386, *infra*.
[52] Joined Cases 209 to 213/84, *Ministère Public* v. *Asjès and others* [1986] E.C.R. 1425.
[53] See Art. 232 EEC.
[54] Case 1/59, *Macchiorlatti Dalmas* v. *High Authority* [1959] E.C.R. 199.
[55] J.O. 1962, 993; O.J. 1959–1962, 129.

national market organisation or that are necessary for the attainment of the objectives of the Common Agricultural Policy set out in Article 39 EEC. The exception has been narrowly interpreted and is of limited practical significance.[56] In the case of state aids, effect has been given to the relevant provisions of the EEC Treaty by the basic regulations of the various common organisations of national markets.

One other economic sector that should perhaps be mentioned is that of transport. The Court of Justice has held that the Treaty provisions on competition apply to transport.[57] However, separate arrangements have been made for the implementation of the rules in this sector.[58]

Territorial scope[59]

The prohibition in Article 85 applies to arrangements between undertakings "which may affect trade between Member States and which have as their object or effect the prevention, restriction or distortion of competition within the common market", and that in Article 86 to any abuse of a dominant position "within the common market or in a substantial part of it . . . in so far as it may affect trade between Member States." This wording makes it clear that the target of the prohibitions is behaviour having an actual or intended impact on the conditions of competition in the territory over which the common market extends, *i.e.* the territory of the Community as defined by Article 227 EEC.

It follows that undertakings carrying on business in the Community are free under the EEC rules on competition to participate in agreements or practices that may interfere with the functioning of the market mechanism in third countries, so long as the consequences are unlikely to spill back into the common market.[60] Thus in its *VVVF* Decision[61] the Commission allowed a Dutch association of paint and varnish manufacturers to continue a system of minimum prices and uniform conditions of sale in respect of exports by its members outside the common market, after securing the abolition of the system in respect of intra-Community trade.

---

[56] The first limb of the exception ceases to be available once a common organisation of the market has been established in respect of the product in question: Case 83/78, *Pigs Marketing Board* v. *Redmond* [1978] E.C.R. 2347 at pp. 2369–2370; [1979] 1 C.M.L.R. 177. Most sectors of agriculture are now covered by such common organisation. To satisfy the second limb of the exception, an agreement must be shown to be necessary for the attainment of all five of the objectives in Art. 39 EEC: Case 71/74, *FRUBO* v. *Commission* [1975] E.C.R. 563 at pp. 582–583. So far there have been no cases where this second limb has been found to be satisfied.

[57] Joined Cases 209 to 213/84, *Ministère Public* v. *Asjès and others* [1986] E.C.R. 1425.

[58] See p. 379 and notes 10–13.

[59] For a detailed examination of this topic, see Barack, *The Application of the Competition Rules (Antitrust Law) of the European Economic Community to Enterprises and Arrangements External to the Common Market* (1981) and Neale and Stephens, *International Business and National Jurisdiction* (1988). There are excellent shorter accounts in Kerse, *EEC Antitrust Procedure* (2nd ed., 1987), pp. 237 *et seq.*, and Whish, *Competition Law* (2nd ed., 1989), Chap. 11.

[60] Community law is not alone in tolerating anti-competitive behaviour when its effects are limited to export markets. *Cf.* the Webb-Pomerene Act in the United States and the approach adopted under the Restrictive Trade Practices Act 1976 in the United Kingdom. See Whish, *op. cit.* note 59, *supra*, pp. 187–188.

[61] J.O. 1969 L168/22; [1970] C.M.L.R. D 1.

The converse case is where undertakings not physically present on Community territory behave in ways that are liable to affect competition on the common market. How far does the Community claim extraterritorial jurisdiction in competition matters? In addressing this question it is useful to bear in mind the distinction drawn by international lawyers between "prescriptive jurisdiction" (the power to make rules and to take decisions under them) and "enforcement jurisdiction" (the power to give effect to such rules or decisions through executive action).[62] The assertion of either form of jurisdiction, but especially the latter, against an undertaking located on another state's territory raises legal and political issues of some delicacy. Three possible bases for the application of the EEC rules in such cases fall to be considered.

First, it is generally accepted in international law that a state is entitled to jurisdiction where activity which was commenced abroad is brought to consummation on its territory. This is known as the "objective territorial principle."[63] It would, for example, allow the Commission to apply Article 85 to a contract made in a third country but substantially performed, at least on one side, within the Community.

Secondly, and more controversially, the Court of Justice has developed a doctrine of enterprise entity as a basis of jurisdiction against a parent company which has subsidiaries inside the Community, though situated itself on the outside. Under the doctrine, where material aspects of the subsidiary's commercial policy are controlled by the parent company, behaviour of the former in contravention of the rules on competition may be imputed to the latter. The leading case is *Dyestuffs*,[64] which concerned a decision by the Commission that a group of major manufacturers of aniline dyes had been guilty on three separate occasions of concerted price fixing. The addresses of the decision included ICI (this was prior to British accession) and certain Swiss companies. Objections by these companies to the jurisdiction of the Commission were dismissed by the Court on the ground that all of them had subsidiaries within the common market for whose decisions on pricing they could be held responsible.[65] In a later case, *Commercial Solvents Corporation*,[66] Advocate General Warner suggested that a subsidiary should be presumed to act in accordance with its parent's wishes; and that the assumption should be rebuttable only by affirmative proof that the subsidiary carried on its business autonomously.[67] The Court

---

[62] See Ch. XIV, "Jurisdictional Competence," in Brownlie, *Principles of Public International Law* (4th ed., 1990).

[63] *Ibid.* pp. 300–303. Under the "subjective territorial principle" jurisdiction may be asserted where activity commenced in the state in question is consummated abroad.

[64] There was, in fact, a group of cases brought by different addressees of the decision in question, to which this collective designation is given. See, in particular, Case 48/69, *ICI* v. *Commission*, *loc. cit.* note 25, *supra*.

[65] See, besides the *ICI* case, *supra*, Case 52/69, *Geigy* v. *Commission* [1972] E.C.R. 787 and Case 53/69, *Sandoz* v. *Commission* [1972] E.C.R. 845.

[66] Joined Cases 6 and 7/73, *Commercial Solvents Corporation* v. *Commission, loc. cit.* note 32, *supra*.

[67] [1974] E.C.R. at p. 264.

did not adopt this suggestion but it seems willing to infer from fairly slender evidence that a sufficient degree of practical control is exercised by the parent company.[68] The main indicators of control are a majority (or larger) shareholding in the subsidiary, representation on its board of directors and other organs, general ability to influence its business decisions and any evidence of specific instructions having been given to it.[69]

The enterprise entity doctrine has been used by the Court and the Commission to found not only prescriptive but also enforcement jurisdiction. Thus competition proceedings may be validly initiated against the foreign parent of a Community subsidiary by sending it a statement of objectives through the post,[70] and the final decision finding the company guilty of an infringement of the rules may be similarly served.[71] A fine may be imposed on the parent company for the infringement, and it may be ordered to take remedial action. In *Commercial Solvents Corporation*,[72] for example, an American multi-national company was found to have infringed Article 86 by refusing, through its Italian subsidiary, to supply a customer with a product in which it held the world monopoly. The Court did not question the power of the Commission, besides fining Commercial Solvents, to require it to make an immediate delivery of a specified quantity of the product in question to the customer and to submit proposals for longer term supply arrangements.[73] Of course, if fines are not paid, they can only be enforced by levying execution on property of the parent or subsidiary which is on the territory of a Member State.[74]

A third, and still more controversial, basis for the extra-territorial application of competition law is the so-called "effects doctrine." Broadly, the doctrine holds that a state is entitled to assert jurisdiction in respect of activities by non-nationals abroad, where these produce effects felt within the state's own territory. A strong lead in asserting jurisdiction on the ground of the anti-competitive effects of conduct in other countries has been given by courts in the United States.[75] Their readiness not only to find that such conduct infringes United States antitrust law but to issue orders requiring, for example, the production of documents or the disposal of

---

[68] See, *e.g.* the *ICI* case, *loc. cit.* note 25, *supra* and *Commercial Solvents Corporation, loc. cit.* note 32, *supra*. See the critical comments by Mann (1973) 22 I.C.L.Q. 35.

[69] Barack, *op. cit.* note 59, *supra*, pp. 53 *et seq.*

[70] See, *e.g.* Case 52/69, *Geigy* v. *Commission loc. cit.* note 65, *supra*.

[71] Case 6/72. *Europemballage and Continental Can* v. *Commission, loc. cit.* note 3, *supra*. An alternative would be to serve the decision on the Community subsidiary, as the Commission did in *Dyestuffs*.

[72] Joined Cases 6 and 7/73 *loc. cit.* note 32, *supra*.

[73] *Cf.* the narrower view taken by Adv. Gen. Mayras in *Dyestuffs* as to the scope of enforcement jurisdiction based on the "effects doctrine": [1972] E.C.R. at pp. 694–695.

[74] See Art. 192 EEC.

[75] See the statement of Judge Learned Hard in *United States* v. *Aluminium Company of America* that ". . . it is settled law . . . that any state may impose liabilities, even upon persons not within its allegiance, for conduct outside its borders that has consequences within its borders": 148 F. 2d. 416 (2d Cir. 1945) at p. 444. For a critical view, see Jennings (1957) BYBIL 146.

patent rights held by foreign companies,[76] has provoked some states, including the United Kingdom, into taking defensive measures.[77]

How far the effects doctrine has been received into the competition law of the EEC remains uncertain. In the *Dyestuffs* case Advocate General Mayras gave his support to a moderate form of the doctrine according to which the EEC rules may be applied where agreements or practices outside the Community have effects inside its territory that are direct, reasonably forseeable and substantial.[78] The Commission also accepts, and has acted on, the doctrine.[79] On the other hand it has never yet been applied by the Court of Justice. Thus in *Dyestuffs,* contrary to the opinion of its Advocate General, the Court opted for enterprise entity as the basis of jurisdiction against the British and Swiss addressees of the decision. In the *Béguelin* case,[80] which arose out of the appointment of a Belgian firm by a Japanese manufacturer as the exclusive distributor of its products in Belgium and France, the Court said "The fact that one of the undertakings which are parties to the agreement is situate in a third country does not prevent application of that provision *since the agreement is operative in the territory of the common market*" (emphasis added).[81] The italicised phrase has sometimes been taken as indicating acceptance of the effects doctrine, but this seems misconceived. The Court was surely making the point that the actual performance of the contract was to take place within the Community.

The leading case on the status of the effects doctrine in Community law is now the *Wood Pulp* case.[82] There the Commission found that a concerted practice had existed for a number of years between North American and Scandinavian producers of wood pulp as to the prices at which they supplied the paper industry in the common market. The activities regarded by the Commission as amounting to concertation took place in the producers' home countries, and several of those involved had no establishment and no subsidiaries within the Community.

The Commission had held in its decision that the effects doctrine should be applied. On appeal, Advocate General Darmon concluded that a qualified effects doctrine was appropriate, limiting jurisdiction to cases only where the effects were direct, substantial and forseeable. The Court did not expressly follow either. Instead, it developed a new formulation of the test for jurisdiction: the implementation doctrine. It held that "the decisive

---

[76] For notorious examples of the assertion of enforcement jurisdiction, see *United States* v. *ICI* 145 F.Supp. 215 (S.D. N.Y. 1952); *United States* v. *The Watchmakers of Switzerland Information Centre* 1963 Trade Cases para. 70.600 (S.D. N.Y. 1962). In more recent decisions there is recognition of the constraints imposed on the effects doctrine by international law and comity. See, in particular, *Timberlane Lumber Company* v. *Bank of America* 49 F. 2d. 597 (9th Cir. 1976); *Mannington Mills* v. *Congoleum Corporation* 595 F. 2d. 1287 (3d. Cir. 1979).

[77] *E.g.* Protection of Trading Interests Act, 1980.

[78] Case 48/69 [1972] E.C.R. at pp. 687–697.

[79] See, *e.g.* Decs. of the Commission in *Re Aniline Dyes Cartel* J.O. 1969 L195/11; [1969] C.M.L.R. D 23; *Re Wood Pulp* O.J. 1985 L 85/1. See also the statement in Comp. Rep. EC 1981, points 34–42. The Commission's approach is fully analysed by Barack, *op. cit.* note 59, *supra* at pp. 98 *et seq.*

[80] Case 22/71, *Béguelin Import* v. *GL Import Export* [1971] E.C.R. 949; [1972] C.M.L.R. 81.

[81] [1971] E.C.R. at p. 959.

[82] Cases 89, 104, 114, 116, 117, 125–129/85, *Ahlstrom* v. *Commission* [1988] E.C.R. 5193.

factor is . . . the place where [the agreement] is implemented." The Court had jurisdiction because the wood pulp producers "had implemented their pricing agreement within the Common Market."[83] The Court did not explain whether there was any difference between this test of jurisdiction and the qualified effects doctrine suggested by the Advocate General, and commentators remain divided on this point.[84]

Ultimately, the issue is one which calls for international co-operation over the allocation of jurisdiction, rather than unilateral assertions of extensive jurisdiction. The first step towards this has been taken by the competition authorities of the EEC and the United States who have concluded the "Competition laws co-operation agreement 1991." This has the purpose of promoting co-operation and co-ordination in the application of their respective competition laws, largely through the timely disclosure of information between them.[85] As yet though, such co-operation has not led to any changes to the substantive law of either the EEC or the United States.

Temporal scope

The rules on competition came into force under the EEC Treaty with effect from January 1, 1958. An agreement completely performed before that date would not be caught by the rules; but if the objects of the agreement were still being pursued by means of a concerted practice, the latter might fall within Article 85.[86]

Each time the Community has been enlarged, a new range of agreements and practices has been brought within the purview of the competition rules from the date of accession. It must, however, be remembered that undertakings established on the territory of a new Member State may have been subject to the rules even prior to accession, for example as parties to an agreement to be performed in the EEC or because they had subsidiaries there.[87]

The prohibitions in Article 85(1) and Article 86 began to have direct effect for the general class of agreements and practices from the date when Regulation 17 with its implementing machinery came into force, viz. March 13, 1962.[88]

---

[83] Cases 89, 104, 114, 116, 117, 125–129/85, Ahlstrom v. Commission [1988] E.C.R. 5193, 5243.
[84] Mann, (1989) 38 I.C.L.Q. 375 argues that this test is more extensive than the effects doctrine; Lange and Sandage, (1989) 26 C.M.L.Rev. 137 interpret the judgment as establishing a test similar to, if not the same as, the qualified effects doctrine.
[85] Agreement dated September 23, 1991 [1991] 4 C.M.L.R. 823.
[86] Case 51/75, EMI v. CBS United Kingdom [1976] E.C.R. 811 at pp. 848–849. In Case 40/70, Sirena v. Eda [1971] E.C.R. 69 at p. 83 the Court had used language which might have been taken to imply that Art. 85 could be invoked where the effects of an agreement were still being felt, even in the absence of a continuing understanding between the parties. See Chap. 20 infra.
[87] As in the Dyestuffs case.
[88] Case 13/61, Bosch v. de Geus [1962] E.C.R. 45; [1962] C.M.L.R. 1.

CHAPTER 14

RESTRICTIVE PRACTICES

Article 85 EEC

Article 85 addresses the problem of interference with the play of competition on the common market resulting from collusion between market participants over their business decisions. The strategy of the Article is to prohibit such interference prima facie, while providing an avenue of escape for arrangements which, in spite of their anti-competitive character, are found to be, on balance, economically beneficial.

The Article provides:

"1. The following shall be prohibited as incompatible with the common market: all agreements between undertakings, decisions by associations of undertakings and concerted practices which may affect trade between Member States and which have as their object or effect the prevention, restriction or distortion of competition within the common market, and in particular those which:

    (a) directly or indirectly fix purchase or selling prices or any other trading conditions;

    (b) limit or control production, markets, technical development, or investment;

    (c) share markets or sources of supply;

    (d) apply dissimilar conditions to equivalent transactions with other trading parties, thereby placing them at a competitive disadvantage;

    (e) make the conclusion of contracts subject to acceptance by the other parties of supplementary obligations which, by their nature or according to commercial usage, have no connection with the subject of such contracts.

2. Any agreements or decisions prohibited pursuant to this Article shall be automatically void.

3. The provisions of paragraph 1 may, however, be declared inapplicable in the case of:

    — any agreement or category of agreements between undertakings;

    — any decision or category of decisions by associations of undertakings;

    — any concerted practice or category of concerted practices;

    which contributes to improving the production or distribution of goods or to promoting technical or economic progress, while allowing consumers a fair share of the resulting benefit, and which does not:

    (a) impose on the undertakings concerned restrictions which are not indispensable to the attainment of these objectives;

    (b) afford such undertakings the possibility of eliminating

389

competition in respect of a substantial part of the products in question."

The generality of the prohibition in paragraph (1) has been remarked upon.[1] Some guidance is given as to the kinds of arrangement that are liable to fall within the paragraph, but the list of examples has proved to be of limited practical importance. Paragraph (2) withdraws the support of national law from arrangements intended to have binding effect which are caught by the prohibition. Paragraph (3) sets out the criteria that must be met by arrangements prima facie within paragraph (1), in order to benefit from a declaration of the inapplicability of the paragraph. As we shall see, power to grant exemption under Article 85(3) has been reserved by Regulation 17 to the Commission.[2]

CRITERIA OF PROHIBITION

Co-operative market behaviour

The target of the prohibition in Article 85(1) is co-operative market behaviour. The EEC Treaty assumes that an undertaking acting unilaterally cannot threaten competition, unless it occupies a dominant position within the meaning of Article 86.

Acts in furtherance of a contract do not escape prohibition under Article 85(1) merely because they are performed by a single party. In the *AEG* case[3] the Court of Justice was called upon to assess the compatibility with Article 85 of a system of selective distribution. Under such a system the resale of goods is limited to a network of "approved" dealers.[4] One of the arguments put forward by AEG was that refusal to admit prospective dealers to its network was a unilateral act and therefore not within the scope of the prohibition. The argument was rejected by the Court on the ground that refusals of approval were acts performed in the context of AEG's contractual relations with approved dealers.[5]

It is settled law that Article 85 does not apply to an agreement between a parent company and a subsidiary where the latter enjoys no real freedom to determine its course of action on the market.[6] Nor does the Article apply to

---

[1] See Korah, *Competition Law of Britain and the Common Market* (3rd ed., 1982, Marthinus Nijhoff), p. 198.
[2] The machinery for the implementation of Art. 85 is discussed in Chap. 16 *infra*.
[3] Case 107/82, *AEG* v. *Commission* [1983] E.C.R. 3151; [1984] 3 C.M.L.R. 325.
[4] On the application of Art. 85 to selective distribution systems, see pp. 408–410, *infra*.
[5] See also Joined Cases 25 and 26/84, *Ford* v. *Commission* [1985] E.C.R. 2725; [1985] 3 C.M.L.R. 528.
[6] Case 22/71, *Béguelin Import* v. *G.L. Import Export* [1971] E.C.R. 949 at p. 959; [1972] C.M.L.R. 81; Case 15/74, *Centrafarm* v. *Sterling Drug* [1974] E.C.R. 1147 at p. 1167; [1974] 2 C.M.L.R. 480; Case 16/74, *Centrafarm* v. *Winthrop* [1974] E.C.R. 1183 at p. 1198; Case 30/87, *Bodson* v. *Pompès Funebres* [1988] E.C.R. 2479; [1989] 4 C.M.L.R. 984. For an example of an agreement of a classic anti-competitive type (market sharing) which the Commission found unobjectionable because the parties were a parent company and its subsidiary, see *Re Christiani & Nielsen* J.O. 1969 L165/12; [1969] C.M.L.R. D36. The corollary is the imputation to parent companies of infringements of the competition rules by subsidiaries; see the discussion at pp. 385–386, *supra*. Cf. *Re Peroxygen Products*, where the Commission was not willing to regard the Interox grouping as an undertaking with an identity

the relationship *inter se* of a group of subsidiaries which operate under the tight control of their parent.[7] In such cases the element of consensus between independent market participants (in the language of the Article, "undertakings") is missing.[8] The "agreement" amounts in effect to a "distribution of tasks within a single economic entity."[9]

A similar analysis has been adopted in the case of agreements within a pure agency relationship, where the agent acts in the name and for the account of his principal, taking none of the risks of a transaction upon himself.[10] Such an agent, the Court of Justice has said, when working for his principal can be regarded "as an auxiliary organ forming an integral part of the latter's undertaking bound to carry out the principal's instructions and thus, like a commercial employee, forms an economic unit with this undertaking."[11] An agreement by the agent not to trade in goods competing with the products of his principal would not in these circumstances fall within Article 85(1).[12]

Forms of co-operation

Article 85(1) refers to three forms of co-operation on which the prohibition may bite—agreements between undertakings, decisions of associations of undertakings and concerted practices. Something will be said about each of these forms, although the lines of demarcation between them are of mainly theoretical interest.[13] The Commission will sometimes leave open the classification of an arrangement, saying that it amounts "if not to an agreement properly so called, at least to a concerted practice."[14]

---

sufficiently distinct from its parent companies, Solvay and Laporte, to absolve them from liability under Art. 85: O.J. 1985 L35/1; [1985] 1 C.M.L.R. 481.
[7] See *Re Kodak* J.O. 1970 L147/24; [1970] C.M.L.R. D19.
[8] There was formerly some doubt as to the correctness of this rationale because of references in Case 15/74, *Centrafarm* v. *Sterling Drug* and Case 16/74, *Centrafarm* v. *Winthrop* to both the parent company and the subsidiary as "undertakings." That doubt has been put to rest by the clear statement in Case 170/83, *Hydrotherm Geraetebau* v. *Andreoli* [1984] E.C.R. 2999 at p. 3016, cited at p. 383, *supra*. An alternative rationale, adopted by the Commission in *Re Christiani & Nielsen loc. cit.* note 6, *supra*, and by the Court in Case 22/71, *Béguelin Import* v. *G.L. Import Export loc. cit.* note 6, *supra*, is that, as between a parent company and a subsidiary, there can be no competition for any agreement to restrict. The rationale is less satisfactory, because it does not cover the possibility that an agreement may restrict competition between one of the parties *and a third party* (see *infra*).
[9] This was the Commission's description in *Re Christiani & Nielsen* [1969] C.M.L.R. at p. D39. In *Centrafarm* v *Sterling Drug loc. cit.* note 8, *supra*, the Court seems to say in para. 41 of its judgment that such agreements will fall outside Art. 85(1) only if they are concerned merely with the internal allocation of tasks, leaving open the possibility that there could be agreements going further than internal allocation which would be caught by Art. 85(1).
[10] Joined Cases 40–48, 50, 54–56, 111, 113 and 114/73, *Suiker Unie and others* v. *Commission (Sugar)* [1975] E.C.R. 1163; [1976] 1 C.M.L.R. 295.
[11] [1975] E.C.R. at p. 2007.
[12] *Ibid.* In the instant case the relationship between a German sugar producer and its trade representatives was found not to be such as to escape the prohibition in Art. 85(1).
[13] The view of some commentators that, unlike an agreement, a concerted practice is only caught by Art. 85(1) once the anti-competitive object has been put into effect does not seem compatible with the definitions in the *Sugar* and *Bank Charges* cases which are discussed *infra*, pp. 394–395. A similar point is made by Bellamy and Child, *Common Market Law of Competition* at paras. 2–033 *et seq.* (3rd ed., 1987, 1st Supplement 1991) and by Whish, *Competition Law* (2nd ed., 1989) at p. 230.
[14] See, *e.g.* *Re Peroxygen Products* O.J. 1985 at L35/14.

Agreements between undertakings

Must agreements for the purposes of Article 85(1) be intended by the parties to have binding legal force? The Commission considers that they need not,[15] and the Court of Justice appears to share this view.

In the *Quinine* cases,[16] for instance, the Court had to consider the application of Article 85(1) to arrangements between European producers of quinine and quinidine contained in an "export agreement" and a "gentlemen's agreement": the former, which was signed and made public, purported to apply only to trade with third countries but its provisions were extended by the latter, which remained unsigned and secret, to trade within the EEC. In view of its clandestine character, let alone its name, the gentlemen's agreement cannot have been intended to be legally enforceable. The parties had, however, made clear that it faithfully expressed their joint intention as to their conduct on the common market and that they considered themselves no less bound by it than by the export agreement. The Court, therefore, accepted it as an agreement within Article 85(1).

A further illustration can be found in the *BMW* case.[17] This concerned an attempt by BMW's subsidiary in Belgium to discourage dealers in that country from selling cars for export to other Member States. A circular condemning such sales had been sent by BMW Belgium to the dealers, who were asked to indicate assent by returning a signed copy, and this was accompanied by a circular in similar vein from a representative body, the "Dealers' Advisory Committee." BMW Belgium, the Advisory Committee and dealers who had given their consent were held to have entered into an "agreement" the detailed content of which was determined by the two circulars, though it is clear there was no intention to create binding legal relations.

It is submitted, therefore, that "agreements" in Article 85(1) covers any kind of arrangement under which an intention to co-ordinate market behaviour is manifested in the explicit acceptance of obligations, whether legal or moral, by one or more of the parties.

Decisions of associations of undertakings

A typical example would be a resolution of a trade association laying down standard terms on which its members are required to do business. An express reference to "decisions of associations of undertakings" in Article 85(1) may not have been strictly necessary.[18] Such decisions, if they fulfil the

---

[15] See, *e.g. Re Quinine* J.O. 1969 L192/5; [1969] C.M.L.R. D41; *Re Franco-Japanese Ballbearings Agreement* O.J. 1974 L34/19; [1975] 1 C.M.L.R. D8; *Re Preserved Mushrooms* O.J. 1975 L29/26; [1975] 1 C.M.L.R. D83; *Re Stichting Sigarettenindustrie Agreements* O.J. 1982 L232/1; [1982] 3 C.M.L.R. 702.

[16] See Cases 41, 44 and 45/69, *ACF Chemiefarma and others* v. *Commission* [1970] E.C.R. 661.

[17] Joined Cases 32/78 and 36–82/78, *BMW Belgium and others* v. *Commission* [1979] E.C.R. 2435; [1980] 1 C.M.L.R. 370.

[18] Whish, *op. cit.* note 13, *supra*, discusses the point at pp. 220–221.

other criteria in the paragraph, are likely to be caught by the prohibition, either as representing the consequence of an agreement (the association's constitution) or as providing the basis for a concerted practice between the members. The reference, however, enhances legal certainty and makes it possible, in an appropriate case, for the Commission to impose a fine on the trade association itself.[19]

The Court of Justice is inclined to brush aside technical arguments about the precise legal character of acts of trade associations. Its attitude is summed up by the remark in the *FRUBO* judgment[20] that "Article 85(1) applies to associations in so far as their own activities or those of the undertakings belonging to them are calculated to produce the results to which it refers."[21] For instance, the constitution of an association has sometimes been treated as a decision[22] and sometimes as an agreement.[23]

There is no more need for "decisions" than for "agreements" to be legally binding. In *Re Fire Insurance*[24] the Commission applied Article 85 to a "recommendation" by an association of insurers in Germany that premiums for various classes of policy be raised by a stipulated percentage. Although described in its title as "non-binding" the recommendation was found to constitute a decision within the meaning of the first paragraph. "It is sufficient for this purpose," the Commission said, "that the recommendation was brought to the notice of members as a statement of the association's policy provided for, and issued in accordance with, its rules."[25] In other cases a pattern of past compliance with recommendations has been emphasised.[26] The conclusive factor, it is submitted, is the ability of the association, in fact if not in law, to influence its members' conduct.

It is common for a number of trade associations to be grouped together in a wider association, for example the national associations of manufacturers of textile machinery belonging to CEMATEX, which existed for the purpose of organising periodic trade fairs.[27] The decisions of such groupings count as decisions of associations of undertakings for the purpose of Article 85(1).

The fact than an association has its chairman and members appointed by a government minister and that it is entrusted with certain public functions will not prevent its decisions on commercial policy from being caught by

---

[19] See, *e.g. Re AROW/BNIC* O.J. 1982 L379/1; [1983] 2 C.M.L.R. 240.
[20] Case 71/74, *FRUBO* v. *Commission* [1975] E.C.R. 563; [1975] 2 C.M.L.R. 123.
[21] [1975] E.C.R. at p. 583.
[22] *Re ASPA* [1970] J.O. L148/9; [1970] C.M.L.R. D25. A similar view was taken of an association's general regulations in *Re Centraal Bureau voor de Rijwielhandel* O.J. 1978 L20/18; [1978] 2 C.M.L.R. 194.
[23] *Re Nuovo CEGAM* O.J. 1984 L99/29; [1984] 2 C.M.L.R. 484.
[24] O.J. 1985 L35/20. The Dec. was upheld by the Court of Justice in Case 45/85, *Verband der Sachversicherer* [1987] E.C.R. 405.
[25] O.J. 1985 at L35/24.
[26] See, in particular, Joined Cases 209–215 and 218–78, *Van Landewyck* v. *Commission (FEDETAB)* [1980] E.C.R. 3125; [1981] 3 C.M.L.R. 134; Joined Cases 96–102, 104, 105, 108 and 110/82, *IAZ* v. *Commission* [1983] E.C.R. 3369; [1984] 3 C.M.L.R. 276.
[27] *Re CEMATEX (No. 1)* J.O. 1971 L227/26; [1973] C.M.L.R. D135; (No. 2) O.J. 1983 L140/27; [1984] 3 C.M.L.R. 69. See also *Re CECIMO* J.O. 1969 L69/13; [1969] C.M.L.R. D1; *Re AROW/BNIC loc. cit.* note 19, *supra; Re Milchförderungsfonds* O.J. 195 L35/35; [1985] 3 C.M.L.R.

Article 85(1).[28] Similarly, a decision fixing minimum prices for a product will not escape prohibition merely because its binding effect has been extended to non-members of the association by an official act.[29]

Concerted practices

The concept of a concerted practice

The Court of Justice has defined a concerted practice as "a form of co-ordination between undertakings which, without having reached the stage when an agreement properly so called has been concluded, knowingly substitutes practical co-operation between them for the risks of competition."[30] That definition was first offered in the *Dyestuffs* case, where the Court upheld a Decision of the Commission that concertation had taken place between the principal suppliers of aniline dyes in the EEC over price rises effected in 1964, 1965 and 1967. The adequacy of the evidence of "practical co-operation" accepted by the Court on that occasion is considered below.

Further light was shed on the concept in the *Sugar* case[31] where one of the infringements found by the Commission related to a concerted practice protecting sugar producers in the Netherlands against imports from Belgium.[32] The finding was contested by the Belgian and Dutch producers on the ground, *inter alia*, that a concerted practice presupposes a plan and the aim of removing any doubt as to the future conduct of competitors, which the evidence produced against them did not support. The Court responded that the criteria of co-ordination did not require the working out of an actual plan. The key to understanding the criteria was the principle underlying the EEC rules on competition that "each economic operator must determine independently the policy which he intends to adopt on the common market . . ."[33] The Court went on:

> "Although it is correct to say that this requirement of independence does not deprive economic operators of the right to adapt themselves intelligently to the existing and anticipated conduct of their competitors, it does however strictly preclude any direct or indirect contact between such operators, the object or effect whereof is either to influence the conduct on the market of an actual or potential competitor or to disclose to such a competitor the course of conduct which they themselves have decided to adopt or contemplate adopting on the market."[34]

---

[28] *Re Pabst and Richarz/BNIA* O.J. 1976 L231/24; [1976] 2 C.M.R. D63.
[29] *Re AROW/BNIC loc. cit.* note 19, *supra*.
[30] Case 48/69, *ICI* v. *Commission* [1972] E.C.R. 619 at p. 655; [1972] C.M.L.R. 557. See the identical definitions in Cases 49 and 51–57/79, [1972] E.C.R. at pp. 733, 773, 828, 875, 915 and 952. See also Joined Cases 40–48, 50, 54–56, 111, 113 and 114/73, *Suiker Unie and others* v. *Commission (Sugar) loc. cit.* note 10, *supra* at p. 1916; Case 172/80, *Zuchner* v. *Bayerische Vereinsbank (Bank Charges)* [1981] E.C.R. 2021 at p. 2031; [1982] 1 C.M.L.R. 313.
[31] *Loc. cit.* note 10, *supra*.
[32] *Ibid.* Chap. 8.
[33] [1975] E.C.R. at p. 1942.
[34] *Ibid.* The view expressed here was foreshadowed in *Dyestuffs*: see [1972] E.C.R. at p. 660.

The definition in *Dyestuffs* and the gloss put on it in *Sugar* were quoted in the *Bank Charges* judgment[35] as part of the advice given to a German court in proceedings under Article 177 EEC concerning the application of Article 85 to the uniform service charges imposed by banks in respect of transfers of funds by cheque from one Member State to another. Together they form a coherent statement of the Court's considered view as to the nature of a concerted practice.

On that view, the subjective content of the concept falls well short of agreement even in the extended sense discussed above. A meeting of minds must take place but nothing need be put into words. Nor need there be any guarantee, however loose or informal, as to future conduct. The minimum of mutuality that will bring a relationship within the purview of Article 85(1) is "contact," which would normally connote a conscious act of communication. If that is the sense of "contact" in *Sugar* and *Bank Charges* it would not be sufficient that a course of conduct voluntarily undertaken was likely to increase the transparency of dealings between the parties: one of them must be shown to have intended specifically to impart information to the other, who must have been aware that the information was aimed at him. There would be contact in the required sense if X notified a business decision to Y, an individual competitor, or to their trade association; and perhaps also if he were identifiable as the source of information published in a specialised trade journal.[36] On the other hand, the fact that X and Y have a number of common customers may mean that each will quickly get to know, in the course of bargaining, what terms the other one is offering. This, it is submitted, would not amount to "contact" between X and Y, unless positive proof could be found that they were using their customers as a conduit for the exchange of information.

The Court of First Instance has now had the opportunity to review what conduct will constitute a concerted practice in its judgments in the *Polypropylene* cases.[37] The applicant took part in meetings in which it disclosed price and production figures to its competitors. The Court endorsed the Commission's view that these meetings had the purpose of influencing conduct on the market. The Court noted in particular[38] that mere attendance at such meetings would be proof of participation in a concerted practice since an undertaking "could not fail to take into account, directly or indirectly, of the information obtained during the course of those meetings." To this extent, therefore, there is room for the view that the type of contact

---

[35] [1981] E.C.R. at pp. 2031–2032. The passage from *Sugar* was reformulated by the Court in terms relating less specifically to the context of that case. The Court spoke of "contact . . . the object or effect of which is to create conditions of competition which do not correspond to the normal conditions of the market in question, regard being had to the nature of the product or services offered, the size and number of the undertakings and the volume of the said market."

[36] See *Re. Wood Pulp* which refers to the giving of prices to the trade press as a form of indirect exchange of information: O.J. 1985 L85/1 at para. 108. See also *Polypropylene cartel* O.J. 1986 L230/1, [1988] 4 C.M.C.R. 347; *PVC cartel* O.J. 1989 L74/1, [1990] 4 C.M.L.R. 345; *LdPE cartel* O.J. 1989 L74/21; [1990] 4 C.M.L.R. 382.

[37] Cases T–1 – T–8/89 *Rhone Poulenc and others* v. *Commission*, not yet reported in full.

[38] See, *e.g.* Case T–7/89, *Hercules Chemicals* [1992] 4 C.M.L.R. 84, 312 at para. 260.

required is merely passive, if the effect of that conduct is that market behaviour will be affected.

Moreover, in the absence of proof of sufficient contact, then it still may be possible that the conduct will be caught as an abuse of a jointly or collectively held dominant position, a concept which is discussed in the next chapter.[39]

It is not altogether clear whether the Commission regards an intention to communicate as an essential ingredient of "contact." One aspect of the concerted practice condemned in the *Wood Pulp* Decision[40] was found to consist of the "system" of calendar quarterly price quotation which was an old-established custom of the pulp trade. Prices were fixed on a quarterly basis and customers were notified of those applicable during a given quarter some little time before the end of the previous one. The timing of the notifications was considered by the Commission to be an important cause of the rapid spread of information about prices among the producers. The Decision states that "The system of quarterly price announcements, which the firms voluntarily chose, constituted in itself, at the very least, an indirect exchange of information on future market conduct."[41] This suggests the Commission may have taken the view that, by its very nature, a practice of the kind in question involved "contact" between the parties, irrespective of their motives for adopting it.[42] However, an alternative interpretation is possible—that the Commission concluded, in the light of all the circumstances, that the price announcement "system" was consciously exploited by the producers as a medium of communication.[43]

Evidence of concertation

Proving that a concerted practice exists may be a delicate task. Care has to be taken to preserve the distinction, which we have seen may be a fine one, between co-ordinated market behaviour and parallel behaviour resulting from decisions by traders which have been independently arrived at. Such innocent parallelism may, in particular, entail the exercise of the right, acknowledged by the Court in *Sugar* and *Bank Charges*, to "adapt intelligently" to the decisions of competitors, of which a trader has become aware in the ordinary course of his business.

Direct evidence of relevant contact between the parties may be available in the form of letters, telexes or records of telephone conversations or meetings. For instance, the concerted practice between the Belgian and Dutch sugar producers dealt with in Chapter 2 of the *Sugar* judgment was proved by a wealth of documentation discovered during the Commission's investigation.[44] This consisted in the main of correspondence between a major Belgian producer and a Belgian sugar dealer, and the Dutch

---

[39] Chap. 15, *infra*.
[40] *Ibid.*
[41] *Ibid.*
[42] See also para. 86 of the Dec. where calendar quarterly price quotation is said not to be "necessitated by objective market conditions."
[43] There is support for this interpretation in the allegation that common selling agents, as well as the trade press, were used by the producers to transmit information: see para. 108.
[44] *Loc. cit.* note 10, *supra* at pp. 1924 *et seq.*

producers contested its admissibility as evidence against them. The Court, however, agreed with Advocate General Mayers that such evidence must be treated on its merits. In case any misgivings may be felt about the use of hearsay evidence in competition proceedings, it is worth pointing out that the fines that may be imposed are expressly declared by Regulation 17 "not to be of criminal law nature."[45]

Where direct evidence of concertation is lacking or inconclusive, the Commission has to rely on circumstantial evidence, *i.e.* on the inferences that can be drawn from the behaviour of the alleged parties, in the light of an analysis of conditions on the market in question.[46] In such cases the Commission, and ultimately the Court, must be satisfied that there can be no reasonable explanation of the parties' behaviour other than the existence of a concerted practice between them.

The point is well illustrated by the *Zinc Products* case,[47] The concerted practice in issue was allegedly designed to protect the German market for rolled zinc products, where prices were higher than elsewhere in the Community, against parallel imports. A French producer, CRAM,[48] and a German producer, Rheinzink, had delivered quantities of zinc products to a Belgian dealer, Schiltz, under contracts which stipulated that the products be exported to Egypt. Schiltz, however, relabelled them and sent them back to Germany, where they were sold below the normal price. It was common ground that employees of Rheinzink found out about the reimports towards the end of October 1976 and that CRAM and Rheinzink discontinued their deliveries to Schiltz on, respectively, 21st and 29th of that month. In its Decision[49] the Commission had taken the view that the cessation of deliveries by CRAM and Rheinzink could only be explained as the result of an exchange of information for the purpose of preventing imports into Germany. "Faced with such an argument," the Court said, "it is sufficient for the applicants to prove circumstances which cast the facts established by the Commission in a different light and which thus allow another explanation of the facts to be substituted for the one adopted by the contested decision."[50] In the event, CRAM was able to point to two such circumstances: the fact that, when it ceased deliveries on October 21, it had completed a particular order from Schiltz; and the fact that there had been difficulties over obtaining payment for products supplied to Schiltz in September (and there were similar difficulties in respect of the October delivery). The Court concluded that the Commission had failed to provide "sufficiently precise and coherent proof" of a concerted practice.[51]

Whether the Commission has discharged its burden of proof is sometimes

---

[45] J.O. 1962, 204; O.J. 1959–69, 87. See Art. 15(3).
[46] Case 48/69, *ICI* v. *Commission* [1972] E.C.R. at p. 655; Joined Cases 40–48, 50, 54–56, 111, 113 and 114/73, *Suiker Unie and others* v. *Commission (Sugar)* [1975] E.C.R. at p. 1916.
[47] Joined Cases 29 and 35/83, *CRAM and Rheinezink* v. *Commission* [1984] E.C.R. 1679; see also the Commission decisions cited note 37, *supra*. [1985] C.M.L.R. 688.
[48] Compagnie Royale Asturienne des Mines SA.
[49] *Re Rolled Zinc Products and Zinc Alloys* O.J. 1982 L362/40; [1983] 2 C.M.L.R. 285. Another aspect of the case is discussed at p. 400, *infra*.
[50] [1984] E.C.R. at p. 1702.
[51] *Ibid.*

a matter of nice judgment over which lawyers, not to mention economists, may differ. A leading example is the *Dyestuffs* case,[52] long the subject of controversy.[53] The case arose, it will be remembered, out of the imposition on three separate occasions of uniform price rises in respect of a range of aniline dyes. The first price rise was announced in January 1964 (with immediate effect), the announcements by different producers following each other on the various national markets at very short intervals. In the case of the second price rise announcements were made in advance, between October and December 1964, to take effect on January 1, 1965. Similarly, in 1967 announcements were made in August and September and came into effect on October 16. The producers sought to explain their behaviour as conscious parallelism typical of a market comprising a small number of large firms, which is known as an "oligopoly." In such a market any significant increase in a firm's sales is liable to be made at the expense of the other participants.[54] This results in a situation where, in the words of Advocate General Mayras, "the producers are closely interdependent so that none can take a decision concerning competition, particularly as regards prices, without the others' being immediately affected, being aware that this is the case and being bound to do something about it."[55] Thus if one oligopolist lowers his prices, the others may be compelled to lower theirs; while no one may feel able to raise his prices unless he is reasonably sure that his competitors are ready to make a similar move. That line of argument was rejected by the Court in a very few words. The dyestuffs market, it held, was not in the strict sense an oligopoly in which price competition could no longer play a substantial role. The producers were sufficiently powerful and numerous for there to be a real possibility that some might resist the pressure to follow prices upwards and try instead to increase their market share. For the Court, the main indicator of concertation between the dye producers seems to have been the fact that the increases of 1965 and 1967 were made public well in advance of the date when they were to be applied.[56] "By means of these advance announcements," the Court said, "the various undertakings eliminated all uncertainty between them as to their future conduct and, in doing so, also eliminated a large part of the risk usually inherent in any independent change of conduct on one or several markets."[57] A further consideration was the division of the common market, in practice, into five national markets which had different price levels and structures. The Court found it hardly conceivable "that the same action could be taken spontaneously at the same time on the same national markets and of the same range of products."[58] On the other hand, curiously little is made in the judgment of the direct evidence of concertation that was before the Court.

---

[52] *Loc. cit.* note 30, *supra.*
[53] For critical comments, see Mann, (1973) 22 I.C.L.Q. 35; Korah, (1973) 36 M.L.R. 220 and *op. cit.* note 1, *supra,* at pp. 201 *et seq.*
[54] The notion is clearly explained by Korah *op. cit.* note 1, *supra,* at p. 8.
[55] [1972] E.C.R. at p. 677.
[56] *Cf.* the situation in *Re Wood Pulp loc. cit.* note 36, *supra,* where the timing of price announcements could be explained as a custom of the trade.
[57] [1972] E.C.R. at p. 659.
[58] *Ibid.*

This included evidence of a meeting of producers in Basle in August 1967 where one of the firms announced an intention to increase its prices, apparently by the precise amount, and on the precise date, of the rise that subsequently took place.[59] There was also the fact that notification of the price rise in 1964 had been given by several of the producers to their subsidiaries and agents in language so similar as to suggest a common origin.[60] The Court's almost total reliance on general economic arguments, stated in a summary way that makes it hard to assess their force, helps to explain why some commentators have found the judgment unsatisfactory.

Parallel behaviour may be the outcome of collusion between certain traders and of independent adaptation by others to that state of affairs, which they encounter as an objective condition of the market. It follows that direct evidence of concertation between X and Y will not serve as corroboration that Z, whose conduct was parallel to theirs, colluded with them. Any explanation offered by Z must be examined by the Commission on its individual merits. If this were not so, the concept of a concerted practice would be deprived of even the vestigial element of mutuality surviving in the requirement that "contact" must have taken place between the undertakings in question.[61]

Where, however, a contractual network, such as a distribution system, already exists, and some of the members can be shown to have taken part in a concerted practice, not much evidence may be needed to convince the Court that other members were involved. This is especially true of the distributor himself, since he stands at the heart of the network. In *Musique Diffusion Française* v. *Commission*[62] the annulment was sought of a Decision that the European subsidiary of the Japanese Pioneer company and the exclusive distributors of Pioneer hi-fi equipment in France, Germany and the United Kingdom had collaborated in attempts to prevent parallel imports from reaching the French market on which prices were relatively high. In confirming that Pioneer (Europe) had been implicated in the prohibited conduct, the Court said that "on account of its central position, it was obliged to display particular vigilance in order to prevent concerted efforts of that kind from giving rise to practices contrary to the competition rules."[63]

---

[59] Described by A. G. Mayras at [1972] E.C.R. pp. 679–680.
[60] *Ibid* at p. 681.
[61] In *Re Wood Pulp loc. cit.* note 36, *supra*, the Commission treated direct evidence against certain of the producers as confirming the existence of a concerted practice involving all those whose pricing was parallel. Whether it was right to do so may become clear in Cases 89, 104, 114, 116, 117 and 125–129/85, *Ahlstrom* v. *Commission*, pending before the Court of Justice.
[62] Joined Cases 100–103/80, *Musique Diffusion Française* v. *Commission (Pioneer)* [1983] E.C.R. 1825; [1983] 3 C.M.L.R. 221.
[63] [1983] E.C.R. at p. 1898. See also Case 86/82, *Hasselblad* v. *Commission* [1984] E.C.R. 883; [1984] 1 C.M.L.R. 559.

Competition

Article 85(1) refers to agreements, etc.[64] "which have as their object or effect the prevention, restriction or distortion of competition within the common market."

Object or effect

The phrase "object or effect" must be read disjunctively.[65] The precise purpose of the agreement must first be ascertained by examining its terms in the particular context in which they will have to be performed. Where it can be seen that the purpose, if achieved, will entail the prevention, restriction or distortion of competition to an appreciable degree,[66] there will be no need to go on and show that such has in fact been the outcome. Where, however, the implications an agreement may have for competition are less clear-cut, it will be necessary to undertake an analysis of economic conditions on the relevant market to assess the actual extent of any adverse impact.[67]

An example of contractual terms found by the Court of Justice to be anti-competitive in their object can be seen in the *Zinc Products* case.[68] It will be remembered that the Belgian dealer, Schiltz, was put under an obligation to export to Egypt the rolled zinc products delivered under its contracts with CRAM and Rheinzink. The obligation had been accepted by Schiltz after CRAM had queried its first order on the ground that products with the dimensions in question, although widely sold in France and Germany, were not in demand in Belgium. However, despite the purported destination of the goods, the prices at which they were supplied to Schiltz by CRAM and Rheinzink were identical with, or closely similar to, those charged for goods intended for the Belgian market. "In those circumstances," the Court said, "the conclusion cannot be avoided that the export clauses were essentially designed to prevent the re-export of the goods to the country of production so as to maintain a system of dual prices and restrict competition within the common market."[69]

The case showed that an agreement may have as its object the restriction of competition without this necessarily representing the common intention of the parties. In the words of the Court, "It is rather a question of examining the aims pursued by the agreement as such, in the light of the economic context in which the agreement is to be applied."[70] Regard must also be had to the legal context. In *Consten and Grundig* v. *Commission*[71] certain of the terms of an agreement creating an exclusive distributorship were held to

---

[64] References hereinafter to "agreements" should be understood as applying also to decisions and concerted practices unless the context indicates otherwise.

[65] Case 56/65, *Société Technique Minière* v. *Maschinenbau Ulm* [1966] E.C.R. 235; [1966] 1 C.M.L.R. 357.

[66] On the *de minimis* rule, see pp. 415–417, *infra*.

[67] [19766] E.C.R. at p. 249.

[68] *Loc. cit.* note 49, *supra*. For another well known example, see Joined Cases 56 and 58/64, *Consten and Grundig* v. *Commission* [1966] E.C.R. 299; [1966] C.M.L.R. 418.

[69] [1984] E.C.R. at p. 1704.

[70] *Ibid.*

[71] *Loc. cit.* note 68, *supra*.

have the object of restricting competition. Consten had been given the sole right to sell Grundig products in France and an attempt had been made to provide it with "absolute territorial protection," *i.e.* to prevent the contract products from being brought into the country by any other importer. The desired level of protection was to be achieved in two ways. First, Grundig undertook not to deliver the contract products, even indirectly, to other traders for export to France. Secondly, Consten was authorised to register in France the trade mark GINT (standing for "Grundig International") which was affixed to all Grundig products. This would enable it to oppose the sale of any parallel imports reaching the French market, as an infringement of its trade mark right.[72] The point that concerns us here is that the contract with Consten was one of a network of contracts with Grundig customers and exclusive distributors in other territories, all prohibiting the exportation of the products to be supplied. Those agreements were not themselves in issue in the case but they were relevant to an assessment of the aims of the Grundig/Consten agreement, since they contributed to the isolation of the French market for Grundig products. The legal context may be similarly relevant when it is not the object but the practical effects of an agreement that are being considered.[73]

Prevention, restriction or distortion

Nothing turns on the distinction between "prevention," "restriction" and "distortion" of competition. The *Consten and Grundig* judgment, for instance, describes the agreement in question as being "such as to *distort* competition in the common market," while a few lines later it refers to "the above-mentioned *restrictions*"[74] (emphasis added). The three terms express, with varying emphasis, the basic idea of a change in the state of competition.

No competition to restrict

The starting point for an inquiry on the implications of an agreement for competition is the situation as it would have been if the agreement did not exist.[75] Without some competition capable of being restricted by the agreement, there can be no infringement of Article 85. In *Re Cement Makers Agreement*,[76] for example, the Commission gave negative clearance to an agreement between an association of manufacturers of Portland cement in Belgium and a number of lime-burning companies which produced "natural" cement. In consideration of the payment to them of an indemnity the lime burners had undertaken, *inter alia*, to refrain from manufacturing Portland cement; but the Commission found they would not have been able,

---

[72] The use of rights of intellectual property so as to impede the movements of goods between Member States is discussed in Chap. 20, *infra*.
[73] See, *e.g.* Case 23/67 *Brasserie de Haecht* v. *Wilkin (No. 1)* [1967] E.C.R. 407; [1968] C.M.L.R. 26 and Case 234/89, *Delimitis* v. *Henninger Brau* [1992] 5 C.M.L.R. 210.
[74] [1966] E.C.R. at p. 343.
[75] Case 56/65, *Société Technique Minière* v. *Maschinhenbau Ulm* [1966] E.C.R. at p. 250.
[76] [1969] C.M.L.R. D15.

anyway, to finance a change in their production. Lack of competition in a market may also be the result of government intervention. In Chapter 2 of the *Sugar* judgment[77] the Court of Justice held that measures taken to regulate the market in Italy had fundamentally restricted the scope for competition between sugar producers. The Commission's finding of an infringement of Article 85 was, therefore, quashed, although it was manifest that concertation had taken place between the Italian producers and exporters from other Member States.

Where, however, despite intervention by the public authorities, some room remains for competitive pressures to influence the decisions of market participants, further restriction of competition through an agreement between undertakings is liable to fall foul of Article 85(1). Indeed, the Commission contends that in such circumstances the anti-competitive effects of private arrangements are all the more significant.[78] A central issue in the *Van Landewyck* case was whether competition had effectively been banished from the Belgian market for tobacco products as a result of the system of levying excise duties on those products, combined with legislation imposing price controls.[79] The Court of Justice accepted that in the circumstances it was practically impossible for manufacturers and importers to compete in such a way as to affect the level of retail selling prices. However, there did still appear to be a possibility of competition in respect of the profit margins allowed to wholesalers, which could have provided an incentive for the latter to pursue a sales policy beneficial to the producers or importers willing to treat them more generously. That kind of competition had been prevented from developing because of the agreement between the tobacco manufacturers and importers relating to the size of the margins and bonuses allowed to traders, which accordingly amounted to a restriction within the meaning of Article 85(1).

Horizontal and vertical agreements

Article 85 applies both to agreements between undertakings operating at the same level in the process of production and distribution, which are known as "horizontal" agreements, and to agreements between undertakings operating at different levels, known as "vertical" agreements.

The classic forms of cartel are horizontal agreements restricting actual or potential competition between the parties themselves. Examples can be seen in the first three items on the list in Article 85(1), *viz.* agreements whereby traders co-ordinate the prices and other conditions they will apply in purchasing or selling goods or services, agreements to limit production, markets, technical development or investment and agreements sharing out markets or sources of supply. In some of the major cartels dealt with under

---

[77] Joined Cases 40–48, 50, 54–56, 111, 113 and 114/73, *Suiker Unie and others* v. *Commission loc. cit.* note 10, *supra*, at pp. 1916 *et seq.*
[78] See, *e.g. Re Stichting Sigarettenindustrie Agreements loc. cit.* note 15, *supra*. The point is mentioned in Joined Cases 209–215 and 218–78, *Van Landewyck v. Commission loc. cit.* note 26, *supra* at p. 3261.
[79] *Loc. cit.* note 26, *supra.* at pp. 3251–3265.

Article 85 several of these objectionable features have been present together. One such agreement was the subject of the Decision of the Commission in *Re Zinc Producer Group*.[80] The Group comprised the main Western zinc mining and smelting companies, apart from those based in Japan. The members agreed to establish a common "producer price" for zinc and to apply it instead of the price on the London Metal Exchange, where they would no longer sell their zinc. They also agreed to support the zinc price on the London Metal Exchange by intervention buying and, where necessary, to limit their production and sales. Zinc was to be supplied only to bona fide customers for their own consumption and subject to a prohibition against resale. Regular exchanges of information took place, including information about individual firms' investment plans. Finally, there was an agreement to sell only specified quantities of zinc in fellow producers' traditional markets. Price fixing, limitation of output and investment and the sharing of markets were just some of the ways in which, it was found, the parties had sought to manipulate competition in the EEC.[81]

It used to be argued by some commentators that the prohibition in Article 85(1) did not apply to vertical agreements.[82] That view was firmly rejected by the Court in its *Consten and Grundig* judgment[83] and in another judgment delivered the same day in a case brought by Italy for the annulment of Regulation 19/65, which authorised the Commission to grant block exemptions pursuant to Article 85(3) in respect of certain types of agreement, among them exclusive dealing agreements.[84] The Court pointed out that there was nothing in the wording of Article 85 to limit its scope to horizontal restraints.[85] Nor was it an argument against applying the Article to exclusive dealing agreements that the parties to such agreements were not themselves competitors. "Competition," the Court said, "may be distorted within the meaning of Article 85(1) not only by agreements which limit it as between the parties, but also by agreements which prevent or restrict the competition which might take place between one of them and third parties."[86] A related point, which *Consten and Grundig* also makes clear, is that the "competition" referred to includes, as well as competition between products of different brands ("inter-brand competition"), that between distributors of products of the same brand ("intra-brand competition"). The Court considered the absolute territorial protection aimed at by the parties unacceptable, because some competition from parallel imports was needed to spur dealers on the greater efforts and to prevent them from charging unduly high prices.[87]

---

[80] O.J. 1984 L220/27; [1985] 2 C.M.L.R. 108.
[81] See also, among many examples, the *Quinine* cases *loc. cit.* note 15, *supra* (price fixing, market sharing, export quotas, limitation of production of quinidine); *Re Flat Glass*, O.J. 1984 L212/13; [1985] 2 C.M.L.R. 350 (price fixing, market sharing, exchange of information); *Re Peroxygen Products loc. cit.* note 6, *supra* (rice fixing, market sharing).
[82] See, *e.g.* Morera, (1964) *Rivista di Diritto Industriale* 52.
[83] *Loc. cit.* note 68, *supra.*
[84] Case 32/65, *Italy* v. *Council and Commission* [1966] E.C.R. 389.
[85] Korah, *op. cit.* note 1, *supra*, p. 207, points out that the last two items on the list in Art. 85(1) presuppose more than one level of trade.
[86] [1966] E.C.R. at p. 339.
[87] See the discussion at [1966] E.C.R. 343.

Consten and Grundig laid the foundation of what has become an extensive structure of case law and legislation on the application of Article 85 to various kinds of vertical agreements, notably systems of exclusive and selective distribution.[88] In recent years, however, there has been criticism of the Community authorities for exaggerating the anti-competitive effects of such agreements. The current orthodoxy in the United States appears to be that vertical restraints, such as the limitation of outlets for a product to a number of specialised wholesale and retail traders, are normally imposed by businesses not in order to fetter competition but in the hope of competing more effectively, thereby increasing their sales—and that they are in the best position to make a judgment about this. Competition authorities are, accordingly, only justified in taking action where vertical restraints are the consequence of *horizontal* agreements between either producers or distributors.[89] This analysis may be persuasive in relation to the American market, but its extension to the common market seems to us to be misconceived. It was grasped by the Commission and the Court of Justice at an early stage that vertical agreements represent a serious threat to the unification of the market, because they often involve limiting distribution rights to a particular territory. As the Court remarked in the case on Regulation 19/65, "An agreement between producer and distributor intended to restore national partitioning in trade between Member States would be such as to run counter to the most fundamental objectives of the Community."[90] This is a valid concern in the application of Article 85, since continuing compartmentalisation of the market is a major cause of the distortion of competition in the EEC.

The rule of reason

In the United States the rigour of the prohibition in section 1 of the Sherman Act against contracts in restraint of trade has been mitigated by the development in the case law of the so-called "rule of reason."[91] The rule applies to agreements other than those, such as horizontal price-fixing agreements, which are treated by the American courts as illegal *per se*. Essentially, a court is required under the rule to consider the overall impact of the agreement in question on competition within the relevant market. This involves, in particular, identifying any pro-competitive effects the agreement may have and weighing them against its anti-competitive effects. A straightforward example would be a promise by the seller of a business not

---

[88] On selective distribution agreements, see pp. 408–410, *infra*.
[89] See, in particular, Bork, *The Antitrust Paradox* (1978); Chard, (1980) *Antitrust Bulletin* 405; Posner, (1981) 48 *University of Chicago Law Review* 6; Baxter, *Journal of Reprints for Antitrust Law and Economics*, Vol. XV, No. 2 for the contrary view, see Comanor, (1984–85) 98 Harvard Law Review 983; Waelbroeck, (1985) 25 Swiss Review of International Competition Law.
[90] Case 32/65, *Italy v. Council and Commission* [1966] E.C.R. at p. 408. See the equivalent passage in *Consten and Grundig* where, however, "objectives" is misprinted "objections": [1966] E.C.R. at p. 340.
[91] For a fuller account of the rule of reason in American antitrust law, see Neale and Goyder, *The Antitrust Laws of the USA* (3rd ed., 1980). The rule is summarised by Whish and Sufrin (1987) 7 YEL 1 at pp. 4–12.

to compete with the buyer for a reasonable price. Without protection of this kind for the buyer, the goodwill of the business might have been worth a great deal less, or have been unsaleable. The pro-competitive effect of permitting the disposal of a going concern may be regarded as outweighing the temporary restriction of competition between the buyer and the seller.[92] However, it must be emphasised that the rule of reason cannot be used to *justify* behaviour that restricts competition.[93] Its importance in American antitrust law is, indeed, explained by the absence of any "gateway" through which a restrictive agreement which is felt, nevertheless, to be economically beneficial may escape prohibition. Where application of the rule leads to a favourable assessment of an agreement under the Sherman Act, that will be because the agreement is judged, on balance, not to be restrictive of competition.

In EEC law, on the other hand, an agreement that restricts competition within the meaning of Article 85(1) may still qualify for exemption under Article 85(3). Where pro-competitive aspects of an agreement are not regarded as tipping the scales against a finding that it is restrictive, they may be taken into account in assessing the economic benefits that may justify a grant of exemption. Does it then matter under which paragraph of the Article such aspects fall to be considered? The answer is that it does matter because, while Article 85(1) may be applied by courts in the Member States, the power to grant exemption under Article 85(3) is reserved exclusively to the Commission. If a national court finds that a contract falls within Article 85(1), its only options are to hold the contract void or to adjourn the proceedings pending a decision by the Commission. Proponents of the rule of reason point out that the Commission has found it impossible in practice to deal on an individual basis with more than a fraction of the notifications made with a view to obtaining exemption and that uncertainty as to the status of agreements may last for years. Thorough-going application of the rule would widen the range of cases that could be disposed of under Article 85(1). This, it is argued, would enable national courts to play a more active part in the application of EEC competition law, leaving the Commission free to concentrate its limited resources on cases of strategic importance.[94]

There is evidence of cautious acceptance by the Court of Justice of the utility of a rule of reason approach to the analysis of cases under Article 85, though within rather narrow limits. The Commission has shown some

---

[92] See *National Society of Professional Engineers* v. *United States* 435 U.S. 679 at p. 689. The example is cited by Steindorff (1984) 21 C.M.L.R. 639 at p. 643. On the position in EEC law, see *infra*.

[93] See Steindorff, *op. cit.* note 92, *supra* at pp. 640–641.

[94] On the need for a rule of reason in EEC competition law see, in particular, Joliet, *The Rule of Reason in Antitrust Law* (1967); Korah, (1981) 3 *New Journal of International Law and Business* 320; Schechter, (1982/3) LIEI 1; Joliet, (1984) 20 RTDE 1; Forrester and Norrall, (1984) 21 C.M.L. Rev.11. More qualified support is given by Steindorff, *op. cit.* note 92, *supra*. Whish and Sufrin, *op. cit.* note 91, *supra*, support the Court and Commission's approach to date.

reluctance to follow the Court down this road.[95] The rule can be seen at work in the case law in three ways.

First, in a growing number of cases the Court has held that contractual provisions giving a measure of protection against competition do not fall within Article 85(1) if they are genuinely necessary to enable a partner to be found in a business transaction.[96] The earliest reference to this "indispensable inducement" rationale is in *Société Technique Minière* v. *Maschinenbau Ulm*[97] which concerned an exclusive distribution agreement. Under the agreement the supplier promised not to appoint another distributor in the concession territory or to sell the goods there himself, but no protection was provided against parallel imports. The Court said that "it may be doubted whether there is an interference with competition if the said agreement seems really necessary for the penetration of a new area by an undertaking."[98] The case is distinguishable from *Consten and Grundig*,[99] where the absolute territorial protection sought by the parties could not be regarded as "really necessary" to secure access for Grundig products to the French market.[1] In the *Maize Seeds* case[2] the analysis was applied to a licensing agreement for the exploitation of plant breeders' rights. An "open" exclusive licence, which would not impede parallel imports, was held compatible with Article 85(1), since without some protection against competition no one might have been willing to take the risk of introducing previously unknown crop varieties onto the market in question.[3] In *Pronuptia*,[4] on the other hand, exclusivity provisions in a franchising agreement were found to be within Article 85(1) because the franchisor's trade mark was already widely known.[5] The novelty of the product, or at least of the brand, may thus be of crucial significance where the territorial protection of distributors is in issue. A last example to mention is *Remia*[6] where the Court accepted that the seller of a business could be put under an obligation not to compete with the buyer, while emphasising that "such clauses must be necessary to the transfer of the undertaking concerned and their duration and scope must be strictly limited to that purpose."[7] The

---

[95] On the contrasting approaches of the Court and the Commission, see Whish and Sufrin, *op. cit.* note 91, *supra* at pp. 30–36. The contrast comes out especially clearly in respect of agreements for the exclusive licensing of intellectual property rights: see Chap. 20, *infra*.

[96] See Steindorff, *op. cit.* note 92, *supra* at p. 646.

[97] Case 56/65, *loc. cit.* note 65, *supra*.

[98] [1966] E.C.R. at p. 250. The lack of further authority on "indispensable inducement" in respect of exclusive distribution agreements is due, presumably, to the enactment of a block exemption regulation soon afterwards: see Reg. 67/67, O.J. 1967, 10.

[99] Joined cases 56 and 58/64, *loc. cit.* note 68, *supra*.

[1] A similar point is made in Halsbury, *Laws of England*, Vol. 52, p. 889.

[2] Case 258/78, *Nungesser* v. *Commission* [1982] E.C.R. 2105; [1983] 1 C.M.L.R. 278. The case is more fully discussed in Chap. 20, *infra*.

[3] See also Case 262/81, *Coditel* v. *Cine Vog Films* [1982] E.C.R. 3381; [1983] 1 C.M.L.R. 49. The case concerned an exclusive licence of the performing rights in a film. See Chap. 20, *infra*.

[4] Case 161/84, *Pronuptia de Paris* v. *Schillgalis* [1986] E.C.R. 353; [1986] 1 C.M.L.R. 414.

[5] The relevant passage of the judgment is far from clear. However, the court appears to have contemplated that absolute territorial protection of the members of the network might have been acceptable, if the franchisor had been a new market entrant. On this, see Venit, (1986) 11 E.L.Rev. 213 at p. 218.

[6] Case 42/84, *Remia* v. *Commission* [1985] E.C.R. 2545; [1986] 1 C.M.L.R. 414.

[7] See para. 20 of the judgment.

Court refused to interfere with the Commission's finding that four years' protection for the buyer of a sauce-manufacturing business would have been enough to cover the introduction of a new trade mark and to win customer loyalty, instead of the 10-year period which had been agreed.

Secondly, in its *Pronuptia*[8] judgment the Court held that various provisions in an agreement forming part of a distribution franchise system did not restrict competition within the meaning of Article 85(1) because they were necessary to the successful functioning of the system. Its approach has been described as amounting to the application of a doctrine of "ancillary restraints" similar to that developed in American antitrust law.[9] This goes beyond the simple "but for" analysis of the cases referred to in the previous paragraph: the issue is not whether, a part from the provisions in question, a bargain could have been struck but whether the essential aims of the transaction (considered to be one that competition law ought not to disfavour) could have been realised. As applied by the Court the analysis comprises four logical steps: (i) definition of the salient features of the transaction; (ii) finding that the transaction is not in itself restrictive of competition; (iii) identification of the conditions that have to be met to enable such a transaction to be satisfactorily performed; (iv) identification of the contractual terms indispensable to the fulfilment of those conditions. Distribution franchising,[10] the Court explained, is a marketing system under which an established distributor whose success is associated with a certain trade mark and certain commercial methods (the franchisor) puts his mark and methods at the disposal of independent traders (the franchisees) in return for the payment of a royalty. This has the advantage to the franchisor of enabling him to exploit his know-how without having to commit his own capital; and to the franchisees of giving them access to methods they could otherwise only have acquired through prolonged effort and research, while also allowing them to profit from the reputation of the mark. The success of such a system depended on two things: the franchisor must be able to communicate his know-how to the franchisees and help them in putting his methods into practice without running the risk that his competitors might benefit, even directly; and he must be able to take appropriate measures to preserve the identity and reputation of the network symbolised by the mark. Under the agreement in question the franchise had undertaken not to open a shop selling competing goods and not to dispose of the franchise premises except with the prior consent of the franchisor. These terms imposed quite severe restraints on the running of the franchisee's business but they were found to be indispensable to the fulfilment of he first condition and so outwith Article 85(1). Among the terms excluded from Article 85(1) by the second condition was the franchisee's obligation to obtain stock only from the franchisor or from suppliers chosen by him. This helped to protect the

---

[8] Case 161/84, *loc. cit.* note 4, *supra*.
[9] The suggestion was made by Venit, *op. cit.* note 5, *supra* at p. 406.
[10] The case was confined to this form of franchise agreement. Other forms are service franchise agreements and production franchise agreements: see [1986] 1 C.M.L.R. at p. 442.

reputation of the network by ensuring that the public would find goods of uniform quality in all Pronuptia shops. Given the character of the franchise products (wedding dresses and formal wear) it would, in the Court's view, have been impossible to achieve that result by formulating a set of objective quality specifications. The Court has been criticised, however, for holding that terms in the agreement giving members of the network a measure of territorial protection were contrary to Article 85(1).[11] In a system of uniform business-format franchising like that of Pronuptia a particular area may, in practice, be able to support no more than one outlet. Depending on the size of territories, exclusivity could, it is argued, be an indispensable element in a well-functioning franchise system.

Thirdly, it is well established that a system of selective distribution based on objective qualitative criteria which are applied in a non-discriminatory way may be compatible with Article 85(1).[12] Under such a system, for example, a manufacturer may limit the outlets for a product which is expensive and technically complex to dealers able and willing to promote it effectively and to provide pre-sales advice, and an after-sales maintenance and repair service, for customers.[13] Selectivity is likely, on the one hand, to result in higher prices. As the Court itself has pointed out, "prices charged by specialist traders necessarily remain within a much narrower span than that which might be envisaged in the case of competition between specialist and non-specialist traders.[14] On the other hand, opportunities are created for competition between manufacturers in respect of the customer services associated with their brands. The issue was first addressed by the Court in *Metro* v. *Commission (No. 1).*[15] The background to the case was the refusal by SABA, a manufacturer of electronic goods such as television sets, radios and tape recorders, to admit the cash and carry wholesalers, Metro, to its distribution network. The Court upheld the decision of the Commission that the central features of the Metro system of selective distribution did not infringe Article 85(1), whilst other features were eligible for exemption under Article 85(3).[16] The starting point of the Court's analysis was the concept of "workable competition" defined as "the degree of competition

---

[11] See Venit, *op. cit.* note 5, p. 406, *supra* at pp. 220–221. The relevant provisions were given exemption under Art. 85(3): see *Re Pronuptia* O.J. 1987 L13/39.

[12] See, in particular, Case 26/76, *Metro* v. *Commission (No. 1)* [1977] E.C.R. 1875; [1978] 2 C.M.L.R. 1; Joined Cases 253/78 and 1–3/79, *Guerlain, Rochas, Lanvin and Nina Ricci (Perfumes)* [1980] E.C.R. 2327; [1981] 2 C.M.L.R. 99; Case 99/79, *Lancôme* v. *Etos (Perfumes)* [1980] E.C.R. 2511; [1981] 2 C.M.L.R. 164; Case 31/80, *L'Oreal* v. *De Nieuwe AMCK (Perfumes)* [1980] E.C.R. 3775; [1981] 2 C.M.L.R. 235; Case 86/82, *Hasselblad* v. *Commission* [1984] E.C.R. 883; [1984] C.M.L.R. 559; Case 107/82, *AEG* v. *Commission* [1983] E.C.R. 3151; [1984] 2 C.M.L.R. 325; Case 243/83, *Binon* v. *Agence et Mesageries de la Presse* [1985] E.C.R. 2015; [1985] 3 C.M.L.R. 800; Case 75/84, *Metro* v. *Commission (No. 2)* [1986] E.C.R. 3021; [1987] 1 C.M.L.R. 118. See also, among numerous Decs. of the Commission, *Re Omega*, J.O. 1970 L242/22; [1970] C.M.L.R. D49; *Re BMW*, J.O. 1975 L29/1; [1975] 1 C.M.L.R. D44; *Re Junghans* J.O. 1977 L30/10; [1977] 1 C.M.L.R. D82; *Re Murat* J.O. 1983 L348/20; [1984] 1 C.M.L.R. 219.

[13] The *Perfumes* cases, *loc. cit. supra*, illustrate selective distribution of another kind of product thought to require special handling, *viz.* luxury items.

[14] Case 107/82, *AEG* v. *Commission* [1983] E.C.R. at pp. 3196–3197.

[15] Case 26/76, *loc. cit. supra.*

[16] The Dec. of the Commission to similar effect in respect of a subsequent version of the SABA system was upheld by the Court in *Metro* v. *Commission (No. 2)* [1986] E.C.R. 3021; [1987] 1 C.M.L.R. 118.

necessary to ensure the observance of the basic requirements and the attainment of the objectives of the Treaty, in particular the creation of a single market achieving conditions similar to those of a domestic market."[17] In accordance with that concept, the nature and intensity of competition might vary to an extent dictated by the products and services in question and the economic structure of the market. The Court went on:

> "In the sector covering the production of high quality and technically advanced consumer durables, where a relatively small number of large and medium-scale producers offer a varied range of items which, or so consumers may consider, are readily interchangeable, the structure of the market does not preclude the existence of a variety of channels of distribution adapted to the peculiar characteristics of the various producers and to the requirements of the various categories of consumers.
>
> On this view the Commission was justified in recognizing that selective distribution systems constituted, together with others, an aspect of competition which accords with Article 85(1), provided that resellers are chosen on the basis of objective criteria of a qualitative nature relating to the technical qualifications of the reseller and his staff and the suitability of his trading premises and that such conditions are laid down uniformly for all potential resellers and are not applied in a discriminatory fashion."[18]

The rationale was spelt out even more clearly in the subsequent *AEG* case which also concerned a system of selective distribution for electronic equipment. The Court said:

> "...there are legitimate requirements, such as the maintenance of a specialist trade capable of providing specific services as regards high-quality and high-technology products, which may justify a reduction of price competition in favour of competition relating to factors other than price. Systems of selective distribution, in so far as they aim at the attainment of a legitimate goal capable of improving competition in relation to factors other than price, therefore constitute an element of competition which is in conformity with Article 85(1)."[19]

The analytical method in such cases consists of weighing the pros and cons of different forms of competition against each other. This rather sophisticated application of the rule of reason has not been extended to other terms that may be found in selective distribution agreements, for example the limitation of outlets on a *quantitative* basis, resale price maintenance and export bans.[20] The unwillingness of the Court and the Commission to recognise such terms as being "capable of improving competition," thus

---

[17] [1977] E.C.R. at p. 1904.
[18] *Ibid.*
[19] Case 107/82 [1983] E.C.R. 3151 at p. 3194.
[20] Quantitative criteria, though not resale price maintenance provisions or export bans, have a good prospect of exemption under Art. 85(3): see *Re Omega loc. cit.* note 12, p. 408, *supra.*

eluding Article 85(1), has brought accusations of inconsistency, since the purpose of their inclusion in the agreement may be to ensure a sufficient turnover for the dealer to support the desired range of customer services.[21] They might, in other words, constitute "ancillary restraints," indispensable to the selective method of marketing judged appropriate for goods of the kind in question.

Some critics of the approach adopted by the Court and the Commission to Article 85(1) may be guilty of neglecting the definition of "workable competition" in *Metro* v. *SABA (No. 1)*[22] with its stress on the objective of creating a single internal market. An Ariadne thread running through the case law is a very strong presumption that contractual provisions tending to preserve or reinforce the division of the market along national lines are anti-competitive. This explains, for example, the difference in the treatment of qualitative criteria of selective distribution, as compared with quantitative criteria, resale price maintenance terms and export bans: the latter, but not the former, are all liable, in their different ways, to have market-splitting effects. Although lines are sometimes difficult to draw, the presumption has been applied with reasonable consistency, the Court showing more readiness than the Commission to accept evidence in rebuttal.[23] The practical consequence has been that, to escape prohibition, any agreement that might have an adverse impact on the unity of the market, has had to be brought specifically to the attention of the Commission under the procedure for obtaining exemption. That a presumption of this kind was thoroughly justified in the economic, political and legal circumstances of a common market in the course of evolution seems undeniable. The only question is whether the EEC has now reached a stage in its development where some relaxation of the presumption, allowing further devolution of enforcement to the national level, has become desirable.

Permissible co-operation

There are many forms of co-operation between undertakings that offer no threat to the maintenance of effective competition, while they may bring a variety of economic benefits such as the pooling of experience or the reduction of costs. It would be unfortunate if undertakings, especially small and medium sized ones, were to be deterred from such activities by ungrounded fears of infringing Article 85. To avoid this, the Commission issued in 1968 a "Notice on Co-operation Agreements" setting out the considerations by which it would be guided in applying Article 85(1) to such agreements and identifying the categories it considered did not fall within the provisions of the paragraph.[24]

Eight categories of co-operative activity are listed in the Notice:

---

[21] See the very full analysis by Chard, (1982) 7 E.L.Rev. 83.
[22] Case 26/76, *loc. cit.* note 12, p. 408, *supra*.
[23] See the cases discussed at p. 406, *supra*.
[24] Notice of July 29, 1968 on Co-operation Agreements, J.O. 1968 C75/3; [1968] C.M.L.R. D5.

— exchanges of information and joint information gathering, for example through market research, comparative studies of enterprises or industries and preparation of statistics and calculation models, but not where these lead to co-ordination of market behaviour[25];
— financial co-operation (in accountancy, the provision of credit guarantees, debt collection and consultancy facilities on business and tax matters);
— joint research and development up to the stage of industrial application, but not where the partners enter into commitments which restrict their own research and development activity or the exploitation of the results of their joint efforts[26];
— sharing of production, storage and transport facilities;
— co-operation in the execution of orders, where either the parties are not in competition with each other or, although competitors, they would not be able individually to execute a given order;
— joint selling or the joint provision of after-sales services, where the partners are not competitors[27];
— joint advertising, but not where the partners are prevented from advertising individually[28];
— use of a common label indicating a certain quality, where the label is available to all competitors on the same condition.[29]

The Notice is useful but undertakings relying on it need to be warned that its terms are narrowly construed by the Commission. This has been seen especially in relation to research and development agreements. In *Re Henkel/Colgate*[30] the Commission found that an agreement between two major manufacturers of detergents setting up a joint subsidiary to carry out research fell within Article 85(1). Under the agreement the partners were free to continue their independent research but were required to make the results known to the joint subsidiary. This, in the view of the Commission, made it very unlikely in practice that such research would take place, since the party concerned could obtain no competitive advantage from it. Thus the effect of the agreement, though not its express provisions, took it outside the scope of the Notice.[31] It must be added that the Notice is without prejudice to the interpretation of Article 85(1) by the Court of Justice.

---

[25] For an example of an exchange of information considered acceptable by the Commission, see *Re Department Stores* Comp.Rep. 1979, p. 62. For references showing the limits of acceptability, see note 40, *infra*.
[26] See the discussion of the block exemption Reg., *infra*, pp. 433–434.
[27] E.g. *Re Wild/Leitz* J.O 1972 L61/21; [1972] C.M.L.R. D36. For examples of joint sales agencies outside the Notice, see note 39, *infra*.
[28] E.g. *Re Association pour la promotion du tube d'acier soundé electriquement* J.O. 1970 L153/14; [1970] C.M.L.R. D31.
[29] *Ibid.*
[30] J.O. 1972 L14/14.
[31] See also *Re Research and Development* [1971] C.M.L.R. D31; *Re Beecham/Parke Davis* O.J. 1979 L70/11; [1979] 2 C.M.L.R. 157.

An Article 85(1) checklist

Examples of agreements especially likely to restrict competition are given in Article 85(1) itself. However, it will be clear from the discussion so far that, depending on the circumstances and the particular combination of terms, many agreements other than those expressly mentioned may be caught by the paragraph. A list of such agreements, which does not purport to be exhaustive, is given below. The items on the list are commercially important transactions which, experience shows, are liable, either in themselves or because of terms commonly associated with them, to attract the unwelcome attention of the Commission. Before entering into one of these transactions firms should consider carefully any possible incompatibility with Article 85(1), the relevance of any of the block exemption regulations and the advisability of seeking individual exemption.

The list comprises:

— exclusive distribution agreements[32];
— exclusive purchasing agreements (including "tied house" and garage "solus" agreements)[33];
— exclusive licences of intellectual property rights (patents, trade marks, copyright, etc.)[34];
— selective distribution agreements[35];
— franchise agreements[36];
— research and development agreements[37];
— joint ventures (firms collaborating on a particular project, often one they would not have had the financial or technical resources to undertake individually)[38];
— joint sales and buying agencies[39];
— information agreements (concerning matters normally kept confidential from competitors)[40];

---

[32] See the discussion of the block exemption Reg., *infra*, pp. 426–428.
[33] See the discussion of the block exemption Reg., *infra*, pp. 428–431.
[34] See Chap. 20, *infra*.
[35] See the discussion, *supra*.
[36] See the discussion of the block exemption reg., *infra*, pp. 434–436.
[37] See the Notice on Co-operation Agreements, *supra*, and the discussion of the block exemption Reg., *infra*, pp. 433–434.
[38] For recent examples, see *Optical Fibres* O.J. 1986 L236/30; noted by Korah, (1987) 12 E.L.Rev. 18; *Re Continental/Michelin* O.J. 1988 L305/33; [1989] 4 C.M.L.R. 920; *Re Elopak/ Metal Box (ODIN)* O.J. 1990 L209/15. See also the statements of the Commission's policy in relation to joint ventures, Comp.Rep. 1974, pp. 25–27; Comp.Rep. 1976, pp. 389–41; Comp.Rep. 1983, pp. 50–52. Now that some "concentrative" joint venture dealt with under the Merger Regulation (see Chap. 17, *infra*), the Commission is preparing a Notice on joint venture to set out how the Commission applies Arts. 85(1) and 85(3); see [1992] 4 C.M.L.R. 504 for draft Notice.
[39] See, *e.g. Re CFA* J.O. 1968 L276/29 [1968] C.M.L.R. D57; *Re Supexie* J.O. 1971 L10/12; [1971] C.M.L.R. D1; *Re Centraal Stikstof Verkoopkantoor* O.J. 1978 L242/15; [1979] 1 C.M.L.R. 11; *Re Floral* O.J. 1980 L39/51; [1980] 2 C.M.L.R. 285; *Re Italian Flat Glass* O.J. 1981 L326/32; [1982] 3 C.M.L.R. 366. See also Comp.Rep. 1971, pp. 31–35 and 52–53.
[40] See *Re COBELPA/VNP* O.J. 1977 L242/10; [1977] 2 C.M.L.R. D28; *Re Italian Cast Glass* O.J. 1982 L383/19; [1982] 2 C.M.L.R. 61; *Re Zinc Producer Group loc. cit.* note 80, p. 403, *supra*.

— trade fairs (where participation is often conditional or not exhibiting at other fairs in a given period).[41]

Effect on trade between Member States

The purpose of the condition in Article 85(1) relating to the effect of an agreement on trade between Member States is, in the words of the Court of Justice, "to define, in the context of the law governing competition, the boundary between the areas respectively covered by Community law and the law of the Member States."[42] Where behaviour may have implications for competition in more than one of the Member States, the EEC rules apply: where its effects are confined to a single Member State, the matter is one exclusively for national law. The line of demarcation is the same under both Article 85 and Article 86.[43]

The concept of the common market determines where that line is to be drawn. "Community law," the Court has said, "covers any agreement or any practice which is capable of constituting a threat to freedom of trade between Member States in a manner which might harm the attainment of a single market between the Member States, in particular by partitioning the national markets or by affecting the structure of competition within the common market."[44] As the passage indicates, the question whether an agreement represents a threat to the unity of the market may be approached in more than one way.

The approach normally adopted by the Court and the Commission is to examine the effect of an agreement on the flow of goods and services between Member States.[45] The test, first formulated in *Société Technique Minière*, is that "it must be possible to foresee with a sufficient degree of probability on the basis of a set of objective factors of law or of fact that the agreement in question may have an influence, direct or indirect, actual or potential, on the pattern of trade between Member States."[46] The crucial element is the diversion of trade flows from the pattern they would naturally follow in a unified market. Where trade has been so diverted, it is immaterial that the agreement may have led to an increase in the volume of goods or services reaching the market in other Member States. Thus in *Consten and Grundig*[47]; trade was held to be affected in the necessary sense, regardless of any increase in imports of Grundig products into France, because not only were all such imports to be channelled through Consten but their re-exportation to the Member States was prohibited.

In practice, the requirement of a direct or indirect, actual or potential

---

[41] See, *e.g. Re CECIMO* J.O. 1969 L69/13; [1969] C.M.L.R. D1; *Re CEMATEX loc. cit.* note 27, p. 393, *supra; Re UNIDI (No. 1)* O.J. 1975 L228/14; [1975] 2 C.M.L.R. D51; (No. 2) O.J. 1984 L322/10; [1985] 2 C.M.L.R. 38.

[42] Case 22/78, *Hugin* v. *Commission* [1979] E.C.R. 1869 at p. 1899; [1979] 3 C.M.L.R. 345.

[43] [1979] E.C.R. at p. 1899.

[44] *Ibid.*

[45] See Bellamy and Child at para. 2–116, *op. cit.* note 13, p. 391, *supra*; Whish, *op. cit. ibid.* pp. 242–250.

[46] Case 56/65 [1966] E.C.R. at p. 249.

[47] Joined Cases 56 and 58/64 *loc. cit.* note 68, *supra*.

influence on the pattern of trade does not usually present a serious obstacle to establishing an infringement of Article 85(1). Trade is liable to be affected directly by, for instance, the grant of an exclusive distributorship or an exclusive patent licence in respect of a Member State's territory. An example of indirect effect would be where the product covered by an agreement is not itself exported to other Member States but a product derived from it is exported. Thus in *BNIC* v. *Clair*[48] it was pointed out that the product in question, potable spirits used in the manufacture of cognac, was not normally sent outside the Cognac region of France. The Court responded that "any agreement whose object or effect is to restrict competition by fixing minimum prices for an intermediate product is capable of affecting intra-Community trade, even if there is no trade in that intermediate product between the Member States, where the product constitutes the raw material for another product marketed elsewhere in the Community."[49] An agreement between parties in the same Member State and relating to sales of domestic products within that State may affect trade indirectly, for example by making it harder for imports to penetrate the market, especially where it extends over the whole national territory. For example, in *Cementhandelaren* v. *Commission*[50] an agreement setting target prices for cement throughout the Netherlands was found capable of affecting trade, although it did not apply to imports or exports. Such an agreement, the Court said, "by its very nature has the effect of reinforcing the compartmentalisation of markets on a national basis, thereby holding up the economic interpenetration which the Treaty is designed to bring about and protecting domestic production."[51] Since a potential effect on trade will suffice, there is no need for the Commission to produce statistical evidence showing that, as a result of the agreement, trade has actually begun to flow through different channels. Nor does the absence for the time being of concrete effects necessarily provide an answer to objections raised against an agreement, if there is a reasonable expectation that things may be different in the future. In *AEG* v. *Commission*[52] it was argued, *inter alia*, by the company that the operation of its selective distribution system could not create appreciable obstacles to trade between Member States because the dealers concerned did not, in fact, engage in such trade or were not in a position to do so. Citing its *Miller* judgment,[53] the Court remarked;

> "... the mere fact at a certain time traders applying for admission to a distribution network or who have already been admitted are not engaged in intra-Community trade cannot suffice to exclude the possibility that restrictions on their freedom of action may impede intra-Community trade, since the situation may change from one year

[48] Case 123/83, *BNIC* v. *Clair* [1985] E.C.R. 402; [1985] 2 C.M.L.R. 430.
[49] [1985] E.C.R. at p. 425.
[50] Case 8/72 [1972] E.C.R. 977; [1973] C.M.L.R. 7.
[51] [1977] E.C.R. at p. 991. See also Case 126/80, *Salonia* v. *Poidomani* [1981] E.C.R. 1563; [1982] 1 C.M.L.R. 64; Case 42/84, *Remia* v. *Commission* [1985] E.C.R. 2545; [1986] 1 C.M.L.R. 414.
[52] Case 107/82, *loc. cit.* note 19, p. 409, *supra*.
[53] Case 19/77, *Miller* v. *Commission* [1978] E.C.R. 131; [1978] 2 C.M.L.R. 334.

to another in terms of alterations in the conditions or composition of the market both in the common market as a whole and in the individual national markets."[54]

An alternative approach has been adopted by the Court of Justice in some cases under Article 86. Attention is focused not on any change in the pattern of imports or exports but on the consequences of the behaviour in question for the structure of competition within the common market. The leading case is *Commercial Solvents Corporation* v. *Commission*.[55] Commercial Solvents was found to have abused its dominant position (amounting to a world monopoly) in respect of a product used as a raw material in the manufacture of a medicinal drug, by refusing to supply the product to an Italian company, Zoja. Since there was no other source of supply, Zoja was liable to be driven out of business as a manufacturer of the drug. The argument that trade between Member States could not be affected, since Zoja sold almost all of its production outside the common market, was rejected by the Court. The requirement of an effect on trade would, it was held, be satisfied by the impairment of the competitive structure caused by the elimination of a major EEC producer. This structural test is less likely to be relevant in cases under Article 85, where the starting point is not, as it is under Article 86, the existence of a dominant position.[56] However, the Court considers the test to be available in such cases,[57] and it has occasionally been applied by the Commission. Thus in *Re Wood Pulp*[58] trade between Member States was said to have been affected owing to the impairment of competition throughout the Community by the creation of an artificially uniform price level.

The de minimis rule

For Article 85(1) to apply, the agreement in question must have the object or effect of restricting competition, and an actual or potential impact on trade between Member States, to a degree that is appreciable. This *de minimis* rule is a specialised aspect of the rule of reason. It was laid down by the Court of Justice in *Völk* v. *Vervaecke*[59] where the agreement in question was for the grant of an exclusive distributorship with absolute territorial protection. Such an agreement would, following *Grundig and Consten*,[60] normally be considered to be restrictive in its object. However, in the instant

---

[54] [1983] E.C.R. at p. 3201.
[55] Joined Cases 6 and 7/73 [1974] E.C.R. 223; [1974] 1 C.M.L.R. 309. See also Case 22/79, *Greenwich Film Production* v. *SACEM* [1979] E.C.R. 3275; [1980] 1 C.M.L.R. 629, Case 7/82, *GVL* v. *Commission* [1983] E.C.R. 483; [1983] 3 C.M.L.R. 645.
[56] See, in the same sense, Bellamy and Child at para. 2–118, *op. cit.* note 13, p. 391, *supra*; Whish, *op. cit. ibid.* p. 248.
[57] This is clear from the reference to Arts. 85 and 86 in the passage in the *Hugin* judgment concerning the purpose of the requirements of an effect on inter-Member State trade: Case 22/78 [1979] E.C.R. at p. 1899.
[58] *Loc. cit.* note 36, p. 395, *supra* at para. 137. See also *Re Vacuum Interrupters (No. 1)* O.J. 1977 :48/32; [1977] 1 C.M.L.R. D67.
[59] Case 5/69, *Völk* v. *Vervaecke* [1969] E.C.R. 295; [1969] C.M.L.R. 273.
[60] Joined Cases 56 and 58/64 *loc. cit.* note 68, *supra*.

case the manufacturer had a minute share of the market in the contract products.[61] The Court said that the conditions in Article 85(1) relating to competition and inter-State trade must be understood by reference to the actual circumstances of the agreement. "Consequently an agreement falls outside the prohibition in Article 85 when it has only an insignificant effect on the market, taking into account the weak position which the persons concerned have on the market of the product in question."[62]

Guidance as to whether an agreement is capable of having an appreciable impact on market conditions was provided by the Commission's Notice Concerning Agreements of Minor Importance, the most recent version of which was published in 1986.[63] The test of appreciability offered in the Notice consists of two criteria: the products which are the subject of the agreement and other products of the participating undertakings[64] considered by users to be equivalent in view of their characteristics, price or use must not represent in the affected part of the common market more than 5 per cent. of the total market for such products; and the aggregate annual turnover of the participating undertakings must not exceed 200 million ECUs. As Advocate General Warner pointed out in the *Miller* case,[65] the test appears to have been formulated with horizontal agreements in mind: it is difficult to see how the criterion relating to aggregate annual turnover can be applied to vertical agreements. At all events, the Notice stresses that the test is purely indicative and it is, again, without prejudice to the interpretation of Article 85 by the Court of Justice.[66]

The *de minimis* arguments appears to have swayed the Commission in a number of cases relating to joint sales or buying agencies formed by very small undertakings to enable them to compete more effectively. In *Re SAFCO*,[67] for example, an agency in France for the exportation of vegetable preserves, accounting for only 1 to 2 per cent. on average of consumption of those products in Germany, its principal export market, was found not to constitute a restriction of competition.[68] This may be contrasted with *Re Floral*[69] which concerned an agency set up by three French fertiliser manufacturers to handle their exports to Germany. The quantities exported

---

[61] The agreement was for the supply of washing machines manufactured in Germany to a Belgian dealer. The manufacturer's share of the German market was between 0.2 and 0.05 per cent. The volume represented by this share was also very small—between 2361 and 861 units.

[62] [1969] E.C.R. at p. 302. See also Case 1/71, *Cadillon* v. *Hoss* [1971] E.C.R. 351; [1971] C.M.L.R. 420.

[63] O.J. 1986, C231/2. This replaced a Notice of 1977, itself replacing one of 1970.

[64] The Notice defines "participating undertakings" so as to cover, as well as the parties themselves, undertakings controlling or controlled by them.

[65] Case 19/77, *Miller* v. *Commission* [1978] E.C.R. at pp. 157–158.

[66] On two occasions when the Notice has been cited to the Court, Adv. Gen. Dutheillet de Lamothe made the point that, because of peculiarities in the market in question, even an agreement meeting the criteria laid down by the Commission might be caught by Art. 85(1): see Case 1/71, *Cadillon* v. *Hoss* [1971] E.C.R. at p. 361; Case 22/71, *Béguelin Import* v. *GL Import Export* [1971] E.C.R. 949 at p. 968; [1972] C.M.L.R. 81.

[67] J.O. 1972 L13/14; [1972] C.M.L.R. D83.

[68] See also *Re Alliance de Constructeurs Français de Machines-Outils* J.O. 1968 L201/1; [1968] C.M.L.R. D23; *Re SOCEMAS* J.O. 1968 L201/4; [1968] C.M.L.R. D28; *Re Intergroup Trading (Spar)* O.J. 1975 L212/23; [1975] 2 C.M.L.R. D14.

[69] *Loc. cit.* note 39, p. 412, *supra.*

through the agency represented only 2 per cent. of the German fertiliser market but the Commission decided that the case fell within Article 85(1) owing to the size of the undertakings concerned (their combined share of the EEC market was 10 per cent.) and the fact that the uniform supply terms made an already oligopolistic market structure even tighter.[70]

In applying the rule, the Court of Justice has regard, in particular, to the size of the parties to the agreement, their market shares and those of their competitors, their absolute turnover figures and any effect on the structure of the market. In *Distillers Company* v. *Commission*,[71] for example, it was held that an agreement concerning the terms of supply of Pimms was not covered by the rule, although sales of the drink outside the United Kingdom were minimal as compared with those of other spirits. This was due to the importance of Distillers, the sole producer of Pimms, on the market for alcoholic drinks.[72] In *Pioneer*[73] the Court found that the market in hi-fi products in the Member States where a concerted practice had occurred was extremely fragmented. The fact that the shares held by the parties, though small, exceeded those of most of their competitors, taken together with their absolute turnover figures, made it impossible to regard the practice as insignificant.[74]

A necessary step in assessing the significance of an agreement is the definition of the relevant market. This was an issue between the parties in *Pioneer* where the Court admitted that there was no generally agreed conception of "hi-fi products." It was, however, unnecessary on that occasion to resolve the issue, since the estimates of their market shares put forward by the parties to the concerted practice themselves were sufficient for the purposes of Article 85(1).[75] In the *Hasselblad* case[76] the Court accepted the view of the Commission that the relevant market was that of medium format reflex cameras, which excluded all 35 mm cameras. Because of their particular characteristics (format, quality of reproduction, handiness and range of accessories) Hasselblad cameras were found to be "virtually indispensable for a large number of users in the various Member States of the Community."[77]

---

[70] See also *Re Toltecs and Dorcet (Trade Marks)* O.J. 1982 L379/19; [1983] 1 C.M.L.R. 412. This was the Dec. reviewed in Case 35/83, *BAT Cigaretten-Fabriken* v. *Commission* [1985] E.C.R. 363; [1985] 2 C.M.L.R. 470 where, however, the *de minimis* issue was not addressed by the Court.

[71] Case 30/78 [1980] E.C.R. 2229; [1980] 3 C.M.L.R. 121.

[72] [1980] E.C.R. at p. 2265. See also Case 19/77, *Miller* v. *Commission, loc. cit.* note 53, p. 414, *supra*; Joined Cases 29 and 30/83, *CRAM and Rheinzink* v. *Commission, loc. cit.* note 47, p. 397, *supra*.

[73] Joined Cases 100–103/80 *Musique Diffusion Française* v. *Commission, loc. cit.* note 62, p. 399, *supra*.

[74] [1983] E.C.R. at pp. 1899–1901. See also the Opinion of Adv. Gen. Sir Gordon Slynn in that case: [1983] E.C.R. at pp. 1942–44.

[75] [1983] E.C.R. at p. 1900.

[76] Case 86/82, *Hasselblad* v. *Commission* [1984] E.C.R. 883; [1984] 1 C.M.L.R. 559.

[77] [1984] E.C.R. at p. 902. See the definition of the relevant product and geographic market in the 1986 Notice.

CRITERIA OF EXEMPTION

Agreements that appreciably restrict competition may nevertheless bring significant economic advantages. Some systems of competition law, accordingly, provide "gateways" through which a restrictive agreement serving certain important objectives of public policy may escape prohibition.[78] The function of Article 85(3) is to enable a balance to be struck between the maintenance of effective competition and other aspects of the Community's task as defined in Article 2 EEC.

Pursuant to Article 85(3) the provisions of Article 85(1) may be declared inapplicable to "any agreement or category of agreements." It has already been noted that the power to grant exemption in respect of individual agreements is reserved by Regulation 17 to the Commission. The procedure for obtaining individual exemption by notification of the agreement in question is described in Chapter 16, below. "Block" exemption of categories of agreements is given by regulations of the Commission which are adopted under powers delegated by the Council in accordance with Article 87 EEC. The block exemption regulations so far enacted relate to agreements for exclusive distribution, exclusive purchasing, patent licensing, motor vehicle distribution and servicing, specialisation, research and development, franchising and know-how licensing.[79] Their scope and effect are examined in the final section of this chapter.

In the present section we consider the criteria in Article 85(3) that must be met by agreements in order to qualify for exemption. There are two positive criteria and two negative ones.

Economic benefit

The first of the positive criteria identifies in broad terms a number of economic benefits that provide the rationale for refraining from applying Article 85(1). The agreement must contribute "to improving the production or distribution of goods or to promoting technical or economic progress." It may be found that a given agreement helps to further more than one, or even all, of these objects.

The basic target of the Commission in applying the criterion of economic benefit is that the gain to welfare must exceed what could have been achieved without any restriction of competition. As the Commission has stated:

> "For the agreements to contribute to the improvement of production or distribution, or to promote technical or economic progress, they must objectively constitute an improvement on the situation that would otherwise exist. The fundamental principle in this respect, established

---

[78] *Cf.* the provisions of ss.10 and 19 of the Restrictive Trade Practices Act 1976. See the discussion in Whish, *op. cit.* note 13, p. 391, *supra* at pp. 179 *et seq.*

[79] These Regs. were adopted by the Commission pursuant to Council Reg. 19/65 (J.O. 1965, 533; O.J. 1965–66) except for the specialisation and research and development Regs. which were adopted pursuant to Council Reg. 2821/71 (J.O. 1971 L285/46; O.J. 1971, 1032).

at the time the Common Market was formed, lays down that fair and undistorted competition is the best guarantee of regular supply on the best terms. Thus the question of a contribution to economic progress within the meaning of Article 85(3) can only arise in those exceptional cases where the free play of competition is unable to produce the best result economically speaking."[80]

The matter is to be judged in the light of the general interest in a well functioning market. It is not sufficient merely that the parties themselves may secure advantages in their production and distribution activities.[81]

Re VBBB/VBVB[82] provides an example of an agreement which was found not to have objective advantages outweighing the disadvantage of its restrictive effect on competition. The agreement, which was between associations of booksellers and publishers in the Netherlands and in Belgium, established a system of collective resale price maintenance for trade between the two countries in books in the Dutch language. The main grounds relied on to justify this system were that it made possible the cross-subsidisation of less popular titles by more popular ones and also helped to ensure the survival of small book shops. The Commission did not deny the worthiness of these objectives but took the view that their dependence on the disputed system had not been demonstrated. Cross-subsidisation could have been achieved by individual publishers' decisions on pricing, while the number of specialised booksellers had declined sharply, despite resale price maintenance, owing in part to the rise of self-service shops and the activities of book clubs. On the debit side, by excluding price competition in respect of a given title, the agreement removed an important means of rationalising and improving the system of book distribution.[83]

The balance of advantage and disadvantage may go against an agreement because of the way in which it is applied in practice. In *Re Ford Werke*[84] the Commission considered the compatibility with Article 85 of the standard form agreement concluded between Ford Germany and its main dealers. Essentially, a dealer would be given an exclusive right to distribute and service Ford vehicles within an allotted territory, while undertaking not to sell vehicles of other makes. The agreement was caught by Article 85(1), since it affected the intensity of competition within the distribution network, as well as limiting the outlets available to other car manufacturers, but might have been expected, on its terms, to qualify for exemption under Article 85(3). Exemption was, however, refused by the Commission on the ground that Ford Germany had cut off supplies of right hand drive vehicles to its dealers. The purpose of this action was to staunch the flow of parallel imports into the United Kingdom where local Ford prices were significantly

[80] *Re Bayer/Gist-Brocades* O.J. 1976 L30/13; [1976] 1 C.M.L.R. D98. See para. 57 of the Dec.
[81] Joined Cases 56 and 58/64, *Consten and Grundig* v. *Commission* [1966] E.C.R. at p. 348.
[82] O.J. 1982 L54/36; [1982] 2 C.M.L.R. 344.
[83] The Dec. was upheld by the Court of Justice in Joined Cases 43 and 63/82 [1984] E.C.R. 19; [1985] 1 C.M.L.R. 87. See also Case T–66/89, *Publishers' Association* v. *Commission* [1992] 4 All E.R. 70.
[84] O.J. 1983 L327/31; [1984] 1 C.M.L.R. 596.

higher than in Germany. Ford's argument that it had acted purely unilaterally, and therefore outside Article 85, was rejected by the Commission and subsequently by the Court of Justice.[85] The Court held that the refusal to supply formed part of the contractual relationship between Ford and its dealers, whose admission to the network implied acceptance of the company's policy regarding the models to be delivered to the German market. It could, therefore, properly be taken into account in assessing the eligibility of the agreement for exemption.

In preserving the delicate balance between the benefits claimed to flow from an agreement and the need to maintain effective competition, an important part is played by the time limits and conditions imposed pursuant to Article 8(1) of Regulation 17. Time limits are at the discretion of the Commission. Agreements are generally given a period of five to ten years to produce the hoped-for result but, in the case of research and development agreements and manufacturing joint ventures relating to products not yet established on the market, 15 years may be judged appropriate.[86] Despite their limited period of validity, many exemptions will produce permanent changes in the structure of the market concerned: thus specialisation agreements by their very nature entail a decisive shift in the business activities of the parties. In addition, where a period of exemption has elapsed it may be renewed by the Commission, although not necessarily on the same terms.[87] The conditions attached to a grant of exemption will be designed to ensure that benefits really are obtained and competition is not unduly prejudiced. An example would be an obligation to report from time to time on the progress made in implementing the agreement.[88]

As might be expected, improvements in production have frequently been found to result from agreements which enable the parties to specialise in particular areas of production[89] or which provide for collaboration in research and development.[90] Typical of such improvements would be: a reduction in costs or an increase in productivity, thanks to economies of scale; enhancement of output or the quality and range of goods, through the modernisation of plant or the centralisation of production and planning; and avoidance of duplication in research and development projects, giving a better chance of obtaining a useful result and reducing the time needed to do so. Patent and know-how licensing agreements[91] and manufacturing joint

---

[85] Joined Cases 25 and 26/84, *Ford* v. *Commission* [1985] E.C.R. 2725; [1985] 3 C.M.L.R. 528.

[86] See, *e.g. Re United Reprocessors* O.J. 1976 L51/7; [1976] 2 C.M.L.R. D1. In *De Laval/Stork* O.J. 1988. L59/32 an initial nine-year exemption was renewed for a further 20 years.

[87] See, *e.g. Re Transocean Marine Paint Association (No. 2)* O.J. 1974 L19/18; [1974] 1 C.M.L.R. D11; *Re Jaz/Peter (No.2)* O.J. 1978 L61/17; [1978] 2 C.M.L.R. 186; *Re Vacuum Interrupters (No. 2)* O.J. 1980 L383/1; [1981] 2 C.M.L.R. 217.

[88] See, *e.g. Re Bayer/Gist-Brocades loc. cit.* note 80, p. 419, *supra*.

[89] See, *e.g. Re Jaz/Peter (No. 1)* J.O. 1969 L195/5; [1970] C.M.L.R. 129; *Re Lightweight Paper* J.O. 1972 L182/24; [1972] C.M.L.R. D94; *Re Prym/Beka* O.J. 1973 L296/24; [1973] C.M.L.R. D250; *Re Bayer/Gist-Brocades loc. cit., supra*. See also the discussion of Reg. 417/85, *infra*.

[90] See, *e.g. Re United Reprocessors loc. cit., supra; Re Vacuum Interrupters (No. 1) loc. cit.* note 58, p. 415, *supra*; [1977] 1 C.M.L.R. D67; *Re Beecham/Parke Davis loc. cit.* note 31, p. 411, *supra; Re BP/Kellogg* O.J. 1986 L369/6; [1986] 2 C.M.L.A. 619. See also the discussion of Reg. 418/85, *infra*.

[91] See Chap. 20, *infra*.

ventures[92] may contribute to improving production by allowing inventions and processes to be more widely exploited. A consideration of particular importance may be the facilitation of the transfer of new technology to EEC companies.[93] Distribution agreements have also on occasion been seen as beneficial to production, for example where there was provision for exchanges of information between the manufacturer and the distributors, which might lead to improvements in design.[94]

Common examples of arrangements bringing improvements in distribution are exclusive distributorships,[95] selective dealer networks[96] and trade fairs.[97] In the case of exclusive distribution agreements, recognised advantages are the easier penetration of markets (especially foreign ones), continuity of supply, more effective promotion of the goods, maintenance of adequate stocks and the organisation of after-sales services.[98] These factors have also been cited in justification for limiting the outlets for certain types of product on a quantitative basis under systems of selective distribution.[99] Rationalisation of participation in trade fairs may improve distribution by periodically bringing together the complete range of products on offer in a given sector, thereby providing an overview and saving manufacturers the heavy costs involved in exhibiting at a series of smaller events.[1] Despite the wording of Article 85(3), account is taken of improvements in the distribution of *services*. Thus in *Re ABI*[2] agreements restricting competition in respect of the charges imposed for their services by banks in Italy were given exemption because they made possible the standardisation and simplification of banking procedures. Exceptionally, a market sharing agreement has been regarded as improving distribution, where it allowed a number of small or medium sized undertakings to compete with much larger rivals in the supply of marine paint, through the establishment of a worldwide network.[3]

The promotion of technical progress is often linked by the Commission with improvements in production, and the range of agreements it may be invoked to justify is similar. Instances of technical progress mentioned in the Decisions include the discovery and application of new technology, the development of new products and the improvement of existing ones, better standards of safety for consumers and the public and the saving of energy.[4] In *Re X/Open Group*[5] exemption was granted in respect of an agreement

---

[92] See, joint ventures listed at note 38, p. 412, *supra*.
[93] *Ibid.* 20 C.M.L.R. 619 para. 59.
[94] *Re BMW loc. cit.* note 12, p. 408, *supra*. See also *Re Pronuptia loc. cit.* note 11, p. 408, *supra*.
[95] See the discussion of Reg. 1983/83, *infra*.
[96] See the cases cited in note 12, p. 408, *supra*.
[97] See, *e.g. Re CECIMO loc. cit.* note 27, p. 393, *supra; Re CEMATEX ibid.; Re UNIDI* O.J.1975 L228/14; [1975] 2 C.M.L.R. D51.
[98] See the 6th recital to Reg. 1983/83.
[99] *Re Omega loc. cit.* note 12, p. 408, *supra; Re BMW ibid.*
[1] See, *e.g.* the reasoning in *Re CECIMO loc. cit., supra*.
[2] O.J. 1987 L43/51.
[3] *Re Transocean Marine Paint Association (No. 1)* J.O. 1967, 163; [1967] C.M.L.R. D9. This exemption was most recently renewed until the end of 1998: *Re Transocean Marine Paint Association (No. 5)* O.J. 1988 L351/40; [1989] 4 C.M.L.R. 621.
[4] See the cases cited in note 90, p. 420, *supra*.
[5] O.J. 1987 L35/36.

between a number of substantial computer manufacturers having as its object the establishment of a standard interface for an operating system which it was possible to use on a wide variety of machines. An "open industry standard" would extend the availability of software and increase the opportunities for users to switch between hardware and software from different sources. This, it was found, would contribute to promoting technical progress by enabling software houses, and conceivably members of the Group as well, to develop application programmes for which there might not otherwise have been a market.

"Economic progress" *might* be viewed as a "catch-all" term, to fall back on when it is desired to exempt an agreement which does not clearly fulfil any other positive requirement. It has been invoked in the case of trade fairs, where the co-ordination of supply and demand was improved.[6] From these decisions, however, it can be deducted that the Commission is here looking at improvements in the way the *market operates*. In other cases economic progress has been found because of improvements in the *structure* of a particular industry. Thus in *Davidson Rubber Company*,[7] a patent licence agreement led to economies of scale; and in *Kabelmetal*,[8] which again concerned a patent licence, the agreement was justified because it brought a better return on investment. The introduction of new goods or processes might amount to "economic progress."[9] This is also the heading that seems most apt for dealing with "crisis cartels," formed to enable an industry to adapt in an orderly way to adverse economic conditions such as a decline in the overall market for its products. There is a long-running controversy as to whether Article 85(3) can be used to sanction such cartels.[10] The view of the Commission is that it can be, where the purpose is to achieve a co-ordinated reduction of overcapacity and the commercial freedom of the participants is not restricted.[11] Thus in *Re Synthetic Fibres*[12] an agreement providing for joint measures to cut capacity, in an industry where the trend in demand had not kept pace with increased output resulting from rapid technical advances, was considered eligible for exemption. The advantages identified by the Commission included the shedding of the financial burden of keeping under-utilised capacity open, the achievement of optimum plant size and specialisation in the development of products adapted to user's requirements. "The eventual result," the Commission said, "should be to raise the profitability and restore the competitiveness of each party."[13]

Another controversial issue is whether it is proper for the Commission to take social advantages, into account in applying Article 85(3). Among the factors mentioned in support of the *Synthetic Fibres* exemption was the possibility of cushioning the social effects of restructuring by making

---

[6] *Re CECIMO loc. cit.* note 27, p. 393, *supra.*
[7] J.O. 1972 L143/31; [1972] C.M.L.R. D52.
[8] *Re Kabelmetal/Luchaire* O.J. 1975 L272/34; [1975] 2 C.M.L.R. D40.
[9] *Re Bronbemaling/Heidemaatschappij* O.J. 1975 L249/27; [1975] 2 C.M.L.R. D67.
[10] See the references cited by Faull at (1986) 11 E.L. Rev. 64.
[11] See Comp.Rep. 1982, pp. 43–45; Comp. Rep. 1983, pp. 53–54; Comp.Rep. 1984, pp. 69–72.
[12] O.J. 1984 L207/17; [1985] 1 C.M.L.R. 787.
[13] *Ibid* at para. 36.

suitable arrangements for the retraining and redeployment of redundant workers. In our submission, the right approach in such cases is that indicated by the Court of Justice in *Metro (No. 1)*[14] concerning the obligation of SABA distributors to enter into six-monthly supply contracts based on forecasts of the probable growth of the market. The establishment of such forecasts, the Court said, "constitutes a stabilising factor with regard to the provision of employment which, *since it improves the general conditions of production*, especially when market conditions are unfavourable, comes within the framework of the objectives to which reference may be had pursuant to Article 85(3)" (emphasis added).[15] As the italicised phrase makes clear, the Court was here treating stability of employment not as a purely social objective but as a matter going to the economic well being of the sector in question.

Benefit to consumers

The second positive criterion is that consumers must receive a fair share of the benefit resulting from the restriction of competition. At first sight, the use of the term "consumer" suggests that only the consuming public, or end consumer, is meant. Such a construction, however, would have the effect of severely limiting the scope of possible exemptions, because in many cases the parties to the agreement cannot by themselves do anything to ensure that the condition is met. For instance, manufacturers often, and if small usually, sell through middlemen; they could not guarantee that these middlemen will pass on the benefits of the agreement, even if they themselves do so. It is not therefore surprising that the Commission has taken the view that consumers include persons at intermediate stages in the marketing process. For example, in *Re ACEC/Berliet*[16] the agreement in question was one concerning the development and ultimate marketing of buses equipped with an electrical transmission system invented by one of the parties. Here the consumer likely to benefit were operators of bus companies. The term "consumer" in English may, besides, have a narrower connotation than the term used in other language texts: the French text uses the term *utilisateur*.

The requirement of a "fair share of the resulting benefit" involves two considerations: what is a benefit, so far as the consumer is concerned; and how can the Commission be sure that the consumer will receive it? The first consideration is closely related to the type of improvement at which the agreement is aiming. Improvements in production or the promotion of technical progress will usually result in a cheaper and/or better product. Improvements in distribution and the promotion of economic progress will usually result in better supply and greater choice of product. The second consideration depends on the pressures on the undertakings to pass on the benefits. The Commission has generally been content to establish that the parties will continue to be subject to lively competition from other

---

[14] *Loc. cit.* note 12, p. 408, *supra*.
[15] [1977] E.C.R. at p. 1916.
[16] J.O. 1968 L201/7; [1968] C.M.L.R. D35.

competitors.[17] Where the agreement concerns research and development there may be no other likely competition than that between the parties once the project is completed, but here the Commission may have regard to the power of purchasers[18] or to its own conditions.[19]

No restrictions that are not indispensable

The first negative criterion is that exemption cannot be given to restrictions of competition going beyond what is absolutely necessary to achieve the objectives regarded as beneficial.

For the commoner forms of restrictive agreement it has long been clear whether a given term is likely to be considered essential or non-essential. The protection against direct competition from the supplier himself or from other distributors appointed within the concession territory is accepted as the price for securing the wholehearted performance of his obligations by an exclusive distributor. On the other hand, since *Consten and Grundig*[20] the chances of establishing the indispensability of absolute territorial protection have been minimal. Quantitative criteria in a selective distribution system may be recognised as indispensable where, without the guarantee of a minimum turnover, dealers would not be in a position to provide the pre- and post-sales service appropriate to the marketing of certain classes of goods.[21] In a specialisation agreement an obligation to purchase exclusively from the other party will normally only pass the test if it is open to the purchaser to accept more favourable offers from third parties.[22] As for research and development agreements, the delicacy of the relationship between the partners may justify a wide variety of restrictions, including the obligation not to carry on the activity in question either independently or with a third party.[23]

The indispensability requirement is of great practical significance, since the Commission is in a position to insist that certain of the provisions in an agreement be dropped before it will grant exemption. Revision of an agreement carried out under the threat of a refusal of exemption, and hence of automatic nullity, may sometimes be far-reaching. For example, under the joint venture arrangements in *Re Optical Fibres*,[24] as they were originally conceived, the technology provider (the American firm, Corning) had a share of the equity giving it effective control over production and marketing policies. This, it was feared, might enable Corning to prevent the joint ventures from competing actively with each other. The Commission,

---

[17] See, *e.g. Re Rank/Sopelem* O.J. 1975 L29/20; [1975] 1 C.M.L.R. D72.
[18] In *Re United Reprocessors loc. cit.* note 86, p. 420, the primary consumers of reprocessing services were the electricity monopolies in the Member States. See also the *Davidson Rubber Company loc. cit.* note 7, p. 422, *supra.*
[19] *Re KEWA* O.J. 1976 L51/15; [1976] 2 C.M.L.R. D15; *Re United Reprocessors loc. cit.* note 86, p. 420, *supra.*
[20] Joined Cases 56 and 58/64, *loc. cit.* note 68, p. 400, *supra.*
[21] *Re Omega loc. cit.* note 12, p. 408, *supra.*
[22] *Re Clima Chappée* J.O. 1969 L195/1; [1970] C.M.L.R. D7. See also Reg. 417/85, Art. 2(1)(*a*), *infra.*
[23] See the cases cited in note 90, p. 420, *supra.* See also Reg. 418/85, Arts. 2 and 4, *infra.*
[24] *Loc. cit.* note 38, p. 412, *supra.*

therefore, persuaded the parties to reduce Corning's voting rights to below the level that could give it a veto over decisions at shareholder's meetings, while also curbing its influence over day-to-day management. It has been argued[25] that intervention by the Commission in cases of this kind may compel parties to renegotiate an agreement after there has been a shift in their relative bargaining power. The risk of such an outcome may deter overseas providers of technology from entering into arrangements particularly beneficial to the European economy.

No possibility of eliminating competition

The final criterion is that the agreement must not afford the parties the possibility of eliminating competition in respect of a substantial part of the product in question. There is thus, in principle, a limit beyond which considerations of general economic policy cannot be allowed to prevail over the maintenance of effective competition in the common market.

Here, as in the application of the *de minimis* rule, the Commission has the task of defining the relevant market.[26] This is done by identifying the range of products competing with those affected by the contract, taking into account the geographic scope of offers, and on occasion also their timing. In *Kali und Slaz*[27] a Decision of the Commission refusing exemption to an agreement for the exclusive sale of "straight" potash fertiliser was annulled by the Court on the ground, *inter alia*, that the relevant product market had been wrongly defined. The Commission had taken the view that the agreement was liable to result in the substantial elimination of competition because between them the parties accounted for the whole production of "straight" potash fertiliser in the Federal Republic of Germany. However, the Commission's own reasoning showed there was competition between the product and "compound" potash fertiliser, which ought therefore to have been regarded as belonging to the same market. In some cases, especially where a vertical agreement is in question, it may be appropriate to limit consideration to the territory of the Member State in which the performance takes place,[28] while in other cases the Commission may have regard to the existence of lively competition on the common market as a whole,[29] or even on the world market.[30] The time factor may be relevant where, for example, it is anticipated that the parties to a research and development agreement will become competitors when the stage of exploiting their final product is reached.[31]

Experience suggests that an agreement which clearly satisfies the other criteria in Article 85(3) is unlikely to fail under this one.

---

[25] By Korah, *op. cit. ibid.*
[26] See p. 417, *supra*. See also the discussion of this issue in the context of Art. 86.
[27] Joined Cases 19 and 20/74, *Kali und Salz* v. *Commission* [1975] E.C.R. 499; [1975] 2 C.M.L.R. 154.
[28] Joined Cases 209–215 and 218/78, *Van Landewyck* v. *Commission loc. cit.* note 26, p. 393, *supra*.
[29] *E.g., Re Lightweight Paper loc. cit.* note 89, p. 420, *supra*.
[30] *E.g., Re Vacuum Interrupters (No. 1) loc. cit.* note 58, p. 415, *supra*.
[31] *Re United Reprocessors loc. cit.* note 86, p. 420, *supra*.

BLOCK EXEMPTION

An agreement that would otherwise be liable to prohibition under Article 85(1) will automatically escape this fate if it fulfils the terms of a block exemption regulation. The parties to qualifying agreements are saved the uncertainty and delay of seeking individual exemption, although that route would remain open where none of the regulations applied. The gain in terms of legal certainty, it has been pointed out,[32] is paid for in the acceptance of a degree of dirigisme, since the parties to a prospective agreement are inevitably under pressure to order their affairs so as to attract block exemption, if it should be available.

A standard approach is discernible in the drafting of the regulations. The category of agreements to which the regulation applies is identified in broad terms and lists are then given of specific obligations which may or may not be included without forfeiting the benefiting of the block exemption. These are sometimes referred to as, respectively, the "white" and "black" lists. Provision will be made for the withdrawal of the exemption by the Commission if it finds that, despite compliance with the regulation, an agreement has certain effects that do not satisfy the criteria in Article 85(3). There will also be transitional provisions, and the duration of the regulation will be specified. Some of the regulations have introduced an "opposition procedure" which expedites the process of obtaining exemption on an individual basis. An agreement not covered by the regulation may be notified to the Commission which is given a period (normally six months) to express its opposition. If the agreement is not opposed by the Commission within the prescribed period, it is brought within the scope of the block exemption.

In the remainder of this section we examine the main features of the block exemption regulations in force at the time of writing, with the exception of the regulations on patent and know-how licensing agreements which are treated in Chapter 20, below.

Exclusive distribution agreements

The earliest of the block exemption measures was Regulation 67/67[33] which covered exclusive distribution, exclusive purchasing and combinations of the two. This has been replaced by two regulations, which came into force on July 1, 1983. Exclusive distribution agreements are dealt with in Regulation 1983/84.[34] Its companion, Regulation 1984/84,[35] which deals with exclusive purchasing, is considered below.

Under an exclusive distribution agreement one party (the supplier)

---

[32] By Whish, *op. cit.* note 13, p. 391, *supra* at p. 263.
[33] J.O. 1967, 849; O.J. 1967, 10. This was amended, and its period of validity was extended, by Reg. 2591/72 (O.J. 1982 L276/15) and Reg. 3577/82 (O.J. 1982 L373/58). It expired on June 30, 1983.
[34] O.J. 1983 L173/1. The Reg. and its companion were the subject of an explanatory Notice: O.J. 1984 L101/2.
[35] O.J. 1983 L173/5.

allocates to the other party (the distributor) a defined territory in which the distributor is required to concentrate his sales effort. In return, the supplier undertakes not to deliver the contract products to other resellers within the concession territory. We have seen in the discussion of Article 85(3) what advantages marketing systems of this kind may bring. However, like its predecessor, Regulation 1983/83 reflects the view in the case law that absolute territorial protection cannot be regarded as essential to enable the distributor to work the market intensively.[36]

The general class of agreements to which Regulation 1983/83 applies is defined in Article 1 as "agreements to which only two undertakings are party and whereby one party agrees with the other to supply certain goods for resale within the whole or a defined area of the common market only to the other." Although the block exemption is thus confined to bilateral agreements,[37] it can be seen from the case law on Regulation 67/67 that agreements in a distribution network will be covered.[38] On the other hand, an agreement between two trade associations, both of which have a large membership, will not be.[39] The contract must be supplied "for resale" and not, for instance, for further processing or consumption. The Article makes clear, as the equivalent provision of Regulation 67/67 did not, that a concession territory consisting of the whole of the common market may qualify for exemption.[40]

The Regulation's "white" list of contractual provisions is found in Article 2. Apart from his obligation pursuant to Article 1 not to appoint other distributors in the concession territory, the only restriction on competition that may be imposed on the supplier is the obligation not to sell the contract product there himself. Allowable restrictions on the distributor are listed in the second paragraph. He may be required to refrain from manufacturing or distributing competing products, to purchase the contract products exclusively from the supplier and to refrain from pursuing an active sales policy outside the concession territory (though not from responding to orders). The third paragraph sets out a number of positive obligations, designed to ensure the effective marketing of a contract product, that may be accepted by the reseller, such as the purchasing of complete ranges of goods, advertising or the provision of customer and guarantee services.

Article 3 excludes the block exemption in two important kinds of case. The first is that of exclusive distribution agreements, whether reciprocal or otherwise, between competing manufacturers. However, for the sake of small manufacturers, who may be dependent on agreements with larger competitors to increase distribution of their products, the block exemption may apply to non-reciprocal agreements, where one of the parties has a total

---

[36] The leading authority is Joined Cases 56 and 58/64, *Consten and Grundig* v. *Commission loc. cit.* note 68, p. 400, *supra.*

[37] On the meaning of "agreements to which only two undertakings are party," see Case 170/83, *Hydrotherm Geraetebau* v. *Andreoli loc. cit.* note 8 p. 391, *supra.*

[38] Case 1/70, *Parfums Marcel Rochas* v. *Bitsch* [1970] E.C.R. 515; [1971] C.M.L.R. 104.

[39] Case 126/80, *Salonia* v. *Poidomani* [1981] E.C.R. 1563; [1982] 1 C.M.L.R. 64.

[40] For an example of an agreement relating to the whole common market, see *Re Duro-Dyne/ Europair* O.J. 1975 L29/11; [1975] 1 C.M.L.R. D62.

annual turnover of no more than 100 million ECUs.[41] The second kind of case involves absolute territorial protection. Particular attention is drawn to the use of intellectual property rights in order to prevent parallel imports. However, the Article makes clear that the benefit of the block exemption will be lost even where absolute territorial protection is not the result of active steps taken by either party. Action to prevent imports from third countries will cause loss of the exemption, if there is no alternative source of supply within the common market. The Regulation expires at the end of 1997.

Exclusive purchasing agreements

Under an exclusive purchasing agreement goods are supplied to a reseller who undertakes to obtain his requirements exclusively from the supplier. In contrast to exclusive distribution agreements, there is no obligation on the supplier to refrain from delivering the contract product to other resellers in the same area and at the same level of distribution. The incentive for the reseller lies in security of supply, which may be reinforced with various forms of help in equipping or running his business. Arrangements of this kind may streamline distribution, though they carry a danger of shutting other suppliers who are potential competitors out of the market. The approach adopted by the Commission in Regulation 1984/83 was to lay down conditions for the block exemption of exclusive purchasing agreements in general, while making specific provision, in the light of investigations of the sectors concerned, in relation to beer supply (or "tied house") agreements and service station (or "solus") agreements.

The general provisions of the Regulation are found in Title I. Under Article 1, block exemption is granted in respect of "agreements to which only two undertakings are party and whereby one party, the reseller, agrees with the other, the supplier, to purchase certain goods specified in the agreement for resale only from the supplier or from a connected undertaking or from another undertaking which the supplier has entrusted with the sale of his goods." The only restriction of competition Article 2 allows to be imposed on the supplier without loss of exemption is the obligation not to compete directly with the reseller in his principal sale area: the supplier cannot be prevented from appointing other resellers in that area. The reseller may be required not to manufacture or sell goods competing with the contract goods and he may accept marketing obligations similar to those allowed under the exclusive distribution Regulation. Article 3 excludes the block exemption in the case of agreements between competing manufacturers (subject again to the turnover threshold of 100 million ECUs if the agreement is non-reciprocal) and of agreements that involve "tying."[42] It also imposes a limit of five years on the duration of agreements qualifying for exemption.

---

[41] The turnover threshold is further defined by Art. 5.
[42] The language of Art. 3(c) reflects that of Art. 85(1)(e) EEC. See the discussion of tying in the context of Art. 86, *infra*.

Title II contains the special provisions for beer supply agreements. These are defined by Article 6(1) as "agreements to which only two undertakings are party and whereby one party, the reseller, agrees with the other, the supplier, in consideration for according special commercial or financial advantages, to purchase only from the supplier . . . certain beers, or certain beers and certain other drinks, specified in the agreement for resale in premises used for the sale and consumption of drinks and designated in the agreement." The subject-matter of agreements eligible for exemption may, therefore, either be beers, specified by brand or type in the agreement, or beers together with other specified drinks: exclusive purchasing agreements relating, for example to spirits but not to beer are not covered. Examples of "special commercial or financial advantages" accorded in consideration of an exclusive purchasing obligation would be a loan on favourable terms, or the provision of business premises, equipment or fittings.[43] The description of the resale premises would cover a public house, club or restaurant but an agreement between a supplier and an off-licence retailer would fall under Title I. Article 6(2) extends the scope of the exemption to, *inter alia*, agreements providing for the transmission of an exclusive purchasing obligation from the owner of licensed premises to his tenant or from an owner or tenant to his successor in title. Restrictions on competition additional to the exclusive purchasing obligation, which may be imposed on the reseller without loss of the block exemption, are set out in Article 7. He may, in particular, be put under an obligation not to sell beers or other drinks supplied by other undertakings which are of the same type as those supplied under the agreement. The sale of draught beers of a different type to those specified in the agreement may also be restricted, but not where the sale of such beers in draught form is customary or where there is sufficient consumer demand for it. Any other curb on the freedom of the reseller to choose his suppliers will bring denial of exemption under Article 8. The Article places a limit of five years on the duration of qualifying agreements where the exclusive purchasing obligation relates to specified beers and other drinks and of 10 years where it relates to beers only. However, where the reseller occupies the designated premises under a lease or licence from the supplier, the time limit is extended for as long as he carries on business there. Because of the reseller's special vulnerability to pressure in such circumstances, in order to qualify for exemption the agreement must expressly preserve his right to obtain drinks other than beer from other sources, where the supplier does not match their terms or deal in the brands that are on offer.

Title III provides in a similar way for solus agreements. According to Article 10, the subject-matter of the agreement in question may be either "certain petroleum-based motor vehicle fuels," such as petrol, diesel and LPG, or those fuels together with "other fuels," such as heating oil, bottled gas and paraffin. Article 11 permits a ban on the sale of competing fuels, and also on the use of competing lubricants, though as to the latter only where

---

[43] See the 13th recital to the Reg.

the supplier has made available or financed a lubrication bay or other equipment. In Article 12, as in Article 8, an attempt is made to preserve the freedom of the reseller, apart from the exclusive purchasing obligation and any ban on dealing in competing products, to obtain goods and services where he chooses. The maximum duration of exempted agreements is 10 years, except that, once again, the time limit does not apply where the designated premises are operated by the reseller under a lease or licence from the supplier. This regulation, too, expires at the end of 1997.

Motor vehicle distribution and servicing agreements

Exclusive dealing agreements in the motor vehicle sector may be eligible for exemption under the general regulations on exclusive distribution and exclusive purchasing agreements. However, the Commission took the view that certain restrictions not covered by those Regulations may be acceptable in the special circumstances of the motor trade. In particular, given the nature of motor vehicles as consumer durables requiring expert maintenance, not always in the same location, throughout their useful lives, consumers may benefit from close co-operation between a manufacturer and his dealers, which guarantees specialised servicing. Regulation 123/85[44] on motor vehicle distribution and servicing agreements was accordingly adopted, though it is expressly provided that the Regulation shall not apply where the scope of the block exemption in Regulation 1983/83 or Regulation 1984/83 is wider.

The class of agreements to which the new block exemption applies is defined in Article 1 of the Regulation. It consists of bilateral agreements under which one party undertakes to supply exclusively to the other party (or to that party and a specified number of other undertakings within the distribution system) for resale "certain motor vehicles intended for use on public roads and having three or more road wheels, together with spare parts therefor." Article 2 allows the supplier to be put under an additional obligation not to sell contract goods to final consumers or to provide them with servicing for such goods within the contract territory.

The various restrictions and obligations that may be imposed on dealers in a distribution network are set out in Articles 3 and 4. Dealers may be required, *inter alia*: not to sell new vehicle or spare parts from another manufacturer which compete with contract goods; not to conclude with third parties distribution or servicing agreements for competing goods; to impose similar conditions on their subcontractors; not to maintain a branch or depot or to seek customers for contract goods outside the contract territory nor to subcontract distribution or servicing outside the territory; not to supply contract goods to dealers outside the network. Obligations to ensure the provision of customer services and active exploitation of the market include: observance of minimum standards with regard to equipment, technical facilities, staff training, advertising and the collection, storage, delivery and

---

[44] O.J. 1984 L15/16. An explanatory Notice was provided: O.J. 1985 L17/4.

servicing of contract goods; endeavouring to meet a minimum sales quota; keeping stocks at an appropriate level; and performing guarantee work.

Of considerable interest are the conditions in Article 5 which have to be satisfied before the benefit of the Regulation can be claimed. These are designed to prevent competition from being unduly restricted and, more especially, to avoid compartmentalisation of the common market. Dealers are required to undertake to honour guarantees and carry out servicing on contract goods supplied anywhere in the common market by or with the consent of the manufacturer.[45] The Decision in *Re Ford Werke*[46] is reflected in the requirement that the manufacturer "supply to the dealer, for the purpose of performance of a contract of sale concluded between the dealer and a final consumer in the common market, any passenger car which corresponds to a model within the contract programme and which is marketed by the manufacturer or with the manufacturer's consent in the Member State in which the vehicle is to be registered." This should serve as a deterrent to refusals to supply by manufacturers wishing to protect their dealers in high priced markets against competition from individual imports. To ensure the effectiveness of the provision, while the consent of the manufacturer to the modification of the contract goods may generally be required, a dealer may not be prevented from modifying a particular vehicle (for example from left hand to right hand drive) which has been purchased by a final consumer.[47]

Article 6 denies block exemption where the parties to the agreement are both motor vehicle manufacturers; as also where a dealer is under an obligation to apply minimum resale prices or maximum trade discounts.

Circumstances in which the benefit of the Regulation may be withdrawn from otherwise qualified agreements are identified in Article 10. Two such circumstances deserve special mention: where a manufacturer or dealer makes strenuous efforts, by means not allowed under the Regulation, to hinder final consumers from purchasing, or obtaining servicing for, contract goods within the common market; and where, over a considerable period, prices and conditions of sale vary substantially between different Member States, and this is chiefly due to obligations covered by the block exemption.[48] The Regulation expires on June 30, 1995.

Specialisation agreements

Under a typical specialisation agreement each party will give up the

---

[45] *Cf. Re Fiat* [1984] 2 C.M.L.R. 497 (Press Release). To obtain a refund under Fiat's guarantee system, the vehicle had to be presented for examination by the dealer who originally supplied it. This obviously created difficulties for customers who bought vehicles in other Member States. The system was changed, following intervention by the Commission.
[46] *Loc. cit.* note 84, p. 419, *supra*.
[47] Art. 3(1).
[48] In its Notice the Commission announced that it did not intend to take action where the difference in list prices for similar vehicles did not exceed 12 per cent. of the lower price over a period of a year or 18 per cent. over a lesser period; where the difference affected an insignificant number of the vehicles covered by the agreement; or where it was attributable to the levels of national taxation or price controls.

manufacture of specified products, leaving the other to concentrate his efforts in that field. Mutual renunciation of activities is often accompanied by arrangements for mutual exclusive dealing, so that the parties will have an assured outlet for, and an assured supply of, their respective specialities. The likely benefits of specialisation in terms of improved efficiency have to be weighed against the consequences of the agreed cessation of competition between the parties. The more powerful the parties, and the larger the share of the market affected, the more serious those consequences are liable to be. The broad policy of Regulation 417/85,[49] like that of the original measure which it replaces,[50] is to grant block exemption to specialisation agreements on terms that are fairly generous, subject to specified thresholds designed to prevent the elimination of competition in respect of a substantial part of the products in question.

According to Article 1, the block exemption applies to agreements under which the parties "accept reciprocal obligations: (a) not to manufacture certain products or to have them manufactured, but to leave it to other parties to manufacture the products or have them manufactured; or (b) to manufacture certain products or have them manufactured only jointly." A non-reciprocal obligation to cease production is not within the Regulation.[51] A line may have to be drawn between specialisation and market sharing. In *Re Italian Cast Glass*[52] arrangements fixing quotas for sales in Italy of certain types of cast glass were found not to constitute genuine specialisation. The Commission noted, *inter alia*, that the arrangements could not be justified with reference to objective criteria such as the parties' production facilities or the intrinsic characteristics of the product; and they applied only to output destined for the Italian market.

Article 2 allows the inclusion of an obligation not to enter into specialisation agreements with third parties relating to identical or competing products, and of exclusive purchasing and exclusive distribution provisions.[53] It is also permissible to require one of the parties to supply the others with products which are the subject of specialisation and to maintain minimum stocks of, and provide customer and guarantee services for, such products.

The thresholds governing the availability of the block exemption are found in Article 3. In the first place, the products which are the subject of specialisation, and other competing products of the participating undertakings, must not represent more than 20 per cent. of the market for such products in a substantial part of the common market. Secondly, the aggregate annual turnover of all the participating undertakings must not

---

[49] O.J. 1985 L53/1.
[50] Reg. 2779/72, O.J. L292/23. Amended and extended by Reg. 2903/77, O.J. 1977 L338/14.
[51] *Re Prym/Beka loc. cit.* note 89, p. 420, *supra.*
[52] *Loc. cit.* note 40, p. 412, *supra.*
[53] Exemption in the case of an exclusive purchasing obligation is subject to the proviso that the purchaser must be free to accept more favourable terms offered by a third party which the party charged with manufacturing the contract product is unwilling to match: see Art. 2(1)(b).

exceed 500 million ECUs. The thresholds may be exceeded by up to 10 per cent. in any two consecutive financial years without the loss of exemption.

An opposition procedure is provided under Article 4, where the turnover threshold (but not the market share threshold) is exceeded. The Regulation expires at the end of 1997.

Research and development agreements

Agreements on joint research and development up to, but not including, the stage of industrial application are among the forms of permissible co-operation recognised by the Commission's Notice of 1968.[54] However, as we have seen, the Notice is narrow in scope and does not apply, for example, where the object or effect of an agreement is to prevent the parties from carrying on independent research. In practice, the Commission has usually found that research and development agreements are liable to restrict competition and affect trade between Member States, at least potentially, but has been willing to grant them exemption in view of their expected contribution towards improving production and promoting technical and economic progress. Experience gained over the years in dealing with individual notifications have now made possible the grant of a block exemption by Regulation 418/85.[55]

Article 1 of the Regulation confers exemption on three classes of agreements: those for joint research and development of products or processes and joint exploitation of the result; those for joint exploitation of the results of research and development jointly carried out under a prior agreement between the parties; and those for joint research and development, without subsequent exploitation (insofar as they fall within Article 85(1)).[56] As defined in the Article, "exploitation" includes the manufacture of products, the application of processes and the assignment or licensing of intellectual property rights but not, it seems, distribution or selling. This is consistent with the practice of the Commission, which has been ready to acknowledge the advantage of joint production, such as the possibility of achieving economies of scale, while treating collaboration at the marketing stage with much greater reserve.[57]

Article 2 lays down conditions that must be satisfied if the exemption is to apply. The joint research and development work must be carried out under a programme defining its objectives and the relative field. All parties must have access to the results of the work and, if there is not to be joint exploitation, each of them must be free to exploit the results independently. Any joint exploitation must be limited to results which are protected by

---

[54] Discussed at pp. 410–411, *supra*.

[55] O.J. 1985 L53/5. For joint venture agreements not within its terms and most in practice are not due to its limited ambit, the Commission has indicated that it will issue a Notice to give guidance. See note 38, p. 412, *supra*.

[56] In *Re BP/Kellog loc. cit.* note 90, p. 420, *supra*, an agreement was found not to be within the block exemption because the restrictions imposed on the parties extended to products and processes they had not developed together. However, individual exemption was granted.

[57] E.g. *Re Henkel/Colgate loc. cit.* note 30, p. 411, *supra*.

intellectual property rights or which constitute know-how; and the result must be decisive for the manufacture of the contract product or the application of the contract processes. Finally, any joint venture or third party charged with manufacture of the products must be required to supply them exclusively to the parties, while undertakings charged with manufacture by way of specialisation must be required to fulfil orders from all of the parties.

The provisions of Article 3 aim to prevent the substantial elimination of competition as a result of the agreement. Where two or more of the parties are competing manufacturers of products which may be improved or replaced by the contract products, block exemption is only available if their combined share of the market does not exceed 20 per cent. The Article also seeks to limit the duration of joint exploitation. Whether the parties are competitors or not, exemption will be lost five years after the contract products are first put on to the common market, if by then output of those products, together with the parties' combined output of competing products, exceeds 20 per cent. of the total market for such products in a substantial part of the common market.

The "white" list of restrictions in Article 4 includes an obligation not to carry out independent research and development in the field to which the programme relates and an obligation to procure the contract product exclusively from other parties, a joint venture or third parties. This is supplemented by the list in Article 5 containing obligations not thought to fall within Article 85(1), but which are mentioned in case exceptionally they should require exemption, for example an obligation to protect intellectual property rights and know-how. The "black" list in Article 6 of terms that exclude the block exemption reflect two main preoccupations of the Commission: that restrictions should not be allowed to extend into fields unconnected with the programme, or beyond the date of its completion; and that the parties should be free to compete at the marketing stage.

Article 7 provides an opposition procedure for agreements within Article 1, which fulfil the conditions in Articles 2 and 3 and are not caught by Article 6.

Under Article 10 the Commission has the usual power to withdraw exemption in respect of individual agreements, for example where, without any objectively valid reason, the parties do not exploit the results of the joint research and development. The Regulation expires at the end of 1997.

Franchising agreements

The Court's decision in *Pronuptia*[58] has already been discussed in the context of the rule of reason debate.[59] In the light of the guidance given by the Court in that case and following a number of decisions in which the Commission had clarified its own views about the compatibility of

---

[58] Case 161/84, *loc. cit.* note 4, p. 406, *supra.*
[59] Pp. 404–410, *supra.*

franchising with Article 85,[60] the Commission issued a block exemption on franchise agreements at the end of 1988.[61] It came into force on February 1, 1989 and expires on December 31, 1999.

The block exemption only applies to distribution franchises, not to wholesale or manufacturing franchise agreements. Such agreements might, however, be exempt under another block exemption. For example, the patent and know-how licensing block exemptions might apply to a manufacturing franchise. Only bilateral agreements are covered, including master franchise agreements in which a franchisor grants permission to a master franchisee to develop its franchises in a particular area.

Article 1 exempts franchise agreements pursuant to Article 85(3) and then goes on to define franchise agreements for these purposes. The essence is that the franchise must relate to the marketing of goods or services in which the franchisee pays the franchisor for the right to use the franchisor's know-how (which must be secret, substantial and identified) and to receive continuing commercial or technical assistance. In return the franchisee must at least be required to use a common business format.

Article 2 sets out permissible restrictions considered to fall within Article 85(1) but which are exempted, and Article 3 then sets out lesser restrictions probably beyond the scope of Article 85(1) but exempted nonetheless for the sake of certainty. Together they form the "white list" of restrictions which may be included in a franchise agreement without prejudicing the application of the block exemption. Further restrictions not listed may be included provided they are not specifically excluded from the block exemption and the agreement submitted for individual clearance under Article 6's opposition procedure.[62]

However, it is also necessary to ensure compliance with Article 4 which sets out three conditions for the applicability of the block exemption. These are that the franchisee is free to obtain goods sold through the franchise network from any other franchisee or authorised distributor, that guarantees for goods are honoured throughout the Community irrespective of which outlet supplied the goods and that the franchisee indicates its separate legal status from that of the franchisor. The first two conditions are an attempt to prevent franchise networks maintaining price differentials either directly or indirectly between different Member States. The latter's objective is consumer protection in that a consumer should appreciate that the business supplying the goods while part of a larger network is itself an independent legal entity and therefore contracts are made with it, not with its franchisor.[63]

Article 5 sets out a black list of impermissible restrictions, covering those

---

[60] *Yves Rocher* O.J. 1987 L8/49; [1988] 4 C.M.L.R. 592; *Pronuptia* O.J. 1987 L13/39; [1988] 4 C.M.L.R. 355; *Computerland* O.J. 1987 L222/12; [1988] 4 C.M.L.R. 259; *Service Master* O.J. 1988 L322/38; [1989] 4 C.M.L.R. 581.

[61] Commission Regulation 4087/88 of November 30, 1988 on the application of Article 85(3) of the Treaty to categories of franchise agreements O.J. 1988 L359/46; [1988] 4 C.M.L.R. 387, annotated by Korah.

[62] See p. 433, *supra*.

[63] This does not rule out the possibility of a national legal system declaring a franchisor to be liable, in tort for example, for the acts of a franchisee.

which are more than ancillary to the operation of a franchise network, or which more blatantly attempt to divide the common market territorially further than to the limited degree of territorial exclusivity allowed under the white-listed clauses. As with other block exemptions, the Commission reserves the right in Article 8 to withdraw its benefit from an agreement to which it would otherwise apply if, whatever the intent, the effect of the agreement is to give a franchisee absolute territorial protection.

CHAPTER 15

ABUSE OF A DOMINANT POSITION

Introduction

The Court of Justice has said that "Articles 85 and 86 seek to achieve the same aim on different levels, *viz*. the maintenance of effective competition within the common market."[1] The "level" at which Article 86 operates is that of seeking to neutralise the adverse consequences of an absence of effective competition.

Dominant undertakings may conduct their business efficiently, keeping down prices and maintaining or improving the quality of their product; indeed, the existence of a dominant position may have positive economic advantages, for example enabling the undertaking in question to pursue an adventurous research and development policy. On the other hand, insulation from competitive pressure is liable to encourage bad habits: for example an undertaking may choose to limit its output and charge high prices rather than to increase its output and charge lower prices. The function of Article 86 is to ensure that the market conduct of dominant undertakings remains consistent with the objectives of the EEC Treaty. As the Court explained in the *Michelin* case:

> "A finding that an undertaking has a dominant position is not in itself a recrimination but simply means that, irrespective of the reasons for which it has such a dominant position, the undertaking concerned has a special responsibility not to allow its conduct to impair genuine undistorted competition on the common market."[2]

Dominant undertakings are thus subject to legal obligations which are not incumbent on those with less economic power.

Article 86 provides:

> "Any abuse by one or more undertakings of a dominant position within the common market or in a substantial part of it shall be prohibited as incompatible with the common market in so far as it may affect trade between Member States. Such abuse may, in particular, consist in:
>
> (a) directly or indirectly imposing unfair purchase or selling prices or other unfair trading conditions;
> (b) limiting production, markets or technical development to the prejudice of consumers;
> (c) applying dissimilar conditions to equivalent transactions with

---

[1] Case 6/72, *Europemballage and Continental Can* v. *Commission* [1973] E.C.R. 215 at p. 244; [1973] C.M.L.R. 199.
[2] Case 322/81, *NV Nederlandsche Banden-Industrie Michelin* v. *Commission* [1983] E.C.R. 3461 at p. 3511.

other trading parties, thereby placing them at a competitive
disadvantage;

(d) making the conclusion of contracts subject to acceptance by the
other parties of supplementary obligations which, by their nature
or according to commercial usage, have no connection with the
subject of such contracts."

The concept of a dominant position

The EEC Treaty does not define a dominant position,[3] but the meaning
and scope of the concept have been clarified by the practice of the
Commission and the case-law of the Court of Justice.

In a famous passage of its *Continental Can* Decision the Commission
identified as the hallmark of dominance overall independence of behaviour
on the market. The Commission stated:

"Undertakings are in a dominant position when they have the power to
behave independently, which puts them in a position to act without
taking into account their competitors, purchasers or suppliers. That is
the position when, because of their share of the market, or of their share
of the market combined with the availability of technical knowledge,
raw materials or capital, they have the power to determine prices or to
control production or distribution for a significant part of the products
in question. This power does not necessarily have to derive from an
absolute domination permitting the undertakings which hold it to
eliminate all will on the part of their economic partners, but it is enough
that they be strong enough as a whole to ensure to those undertakings
an overall independence of behaviour, even if there are differences in
intensity in their influence on the different partial markets."[4]

This formulation was described by Advocate-General Roemer in his
Opinion relating to the *Continental Can* case as being "obviously in
agreement with the prevailing opinion and with tests legally laid down."[5]

The definition of a dominant position which has become the standard one
was first put forward by the European Court in *United Brands*.[6] According

---

[3] *Cf.* Art. 66(7) ECSC which speaks of undertakings holding or acquiring in the market for one
of the products within the jurisdiction of the High Authority (now the Commission) "a
dominant position shielding them against effective competition in a substantial part of the
common market." The importance not only of this provision, but of Arts. 65 and 66 ECSC as
a whole, in the interpretation of Art. 86 has been stressed by Schröter in Van Damme,
Regulating the behaviour of monopolies and dominant undertakings in Community law at pp.
446 *et seq.*

[4] J.O. 1972 L7/25 at L/35. Tr. from [1972] C.M.L.R. D11 at D35. In a Memorandum published
on December 1, 1965, the Commission had put forward a wider definition of a dominant
position, emphasising the ability of the undertaking or undertakings concerned to influence
the behaviour of other operators in a substantial and foreseeable way: see EEC, Serie
Concurrence 3, *Le Problème de la concentration dans le marché commun* (Brussels, 1966).
Cf. the definition suggested by the group of professors which the Commission had appointed
in 1963 to advise it on the interpretation of Art. 86, *ibid.*

[5] [1973] E.C.R. at p. 257.

[6] Case 27/76, *United Brands Company* v. *Commission* [1978] E.C.R. 207 at p. 277; [1978] 1
C.M.L.R. 429.

to this definition, as formulated in the Court's *Michelin* judgment, a dominant position consists of

> "a position of economic strength enjoyed by an undertaking which enables it to hinder the maintenance of effective competition on the relevant market by allowing it to behave to an appreciable extent independently of its competitors and customers and ultimately of consumers."[7]

The concept, therefore, refers to the economic power of the undertaking concerned, which frees it from the constraints normally imposed by dealing at arms length on a competitive market. This liberation is qualified: in *Continental Can* the Commission used the phrase "*overall* independence of behaviour,"[8] while the Court speaks of "power to behave *to an appreciable extent* independently" (emphasis added). So understood, a dominant position is compatible with the survival of some competition.[9] It will be sufficient if the undertaking in question is able "at least to have an appreciable influence on the conditions under which that competition will develop, and in any case to act largely in disregard of it so long as such conduct does not operate to its detriment."[10]

Thus in the *United Brands* case it was admitted that UBC encountered very lively competition in Denmark and Germany during 1973 when other banana suppliers had mounted advertising and promotional campaigns and had cut their prices; while in the Netherlands competition had pushed banana prices below those in Germany, which was traditionally a lower priced market. Indeed, the European Court seems to have accepted, for the sake of argument, UBC's claim that its banana division had made a loss over several years. However, not only was the competition limited in its duration and its geographical scope, it was also finally ineffective: UBC had suffered no significant reduction of its market share, while remaining the highest priced supplier. Of course, if UBC had been forced by the tactics of its competitors to sustain continuing losses over a long period, at some point its "overall independence of behaviour" would have been put in question.[11]

In some of the case law, the concept of dominance has been expressed in terms of the dependence of the customer rather than the independence of

---

[7] [1984] E.C.R. at p. 3503. See also Case 85/76, *Hoffmann-La Roche* v. *Commission* [1979] 461 at p. 520; Case 31/80, *NV L'Oreal und SA L'Oreal* v. *PVBA De Nieuwe AMCK* [1980] E.C.R. 3775 at p. 3793; Case 311/84, *Centre Belge d'Etudes de Marché—Télé-marketing SA* v. *Commission* [1985] E.C.R. 3261; [1986] 2 C.M.L.R. 558. The definition echoes references in earlier judgments of the Court to "the power to impede the maintenance of effective competition," see Case 40/70, *Sirena* v. *Eda* [1979] E.C.R. 69 at p. 83; [1971] C.M.L.R. 260; Case 78/70, *Deutsche Grammophon* v. *Metro* [1971] E.C.R. 487 at p. 501; [1971] C.M.L.R. 631; Joined Cases 40–48, 50, 54 to 56, 111, 113 and 114/73, *Suiker Unie and Others* v. *Commission (Sugar)* [1975] E.C.R. 1663 at pp. 1978 and 1994; [1976] 1 C.M.L.R. 295.

[8] In its *BP* Decision the Commission referred to the ability of a firm "to act *fully* independently" (emphasis added): see O.J. 1977 L117/1. However, it is thought this apparent adoption of an absolutist standard should be attributed to defective drafting.

[9] Case 85/76, *Hoffmann-La Roche* v. *Commission* [1979] E.C.R. at p. 520.

[10] *Ibid.*

[11] In the *Michelin* case the Court similarly brushed aside the argument that NBIM had been incurring losses, remarking that "*temporary* unprofitability or even losses are not inconsistent with the existence of a dominant position" (emphasis added): [1983] E.C.R. at p. 3511.

the dominant party. Thus, in *Hugin*[12] the dependence of repairers was created by the uniqueness of the firm's own spare parts for its cash registers. In the *BP* case[13] the Commission argued that the oil companies acquired temporary dominance because their customers became completely dependent upon them in a time of shortages.[14] The clearest example of dependence being used to confirm dominance can be seen from the cases relating to the refusal by television broadcasting companies to allow publication of their weekly listings of programmes by outsiders.[15] This monopoly was rooted in the copyright attaching to the listings, which meant that publishers had to obtain listings from the broadcasting companies themselves. The result, according to the Court of First Instance, was that "Third parties ... were in a situation of economic dependence on the applicant, which was thus in a position to hinder the emergence of any effective competition on the market for information on its weekly programmes."[16]

This approach carries with it the danger that one characteristic effect of dominance is used to embody the concept as a whole. It is suggested that the use of dependency as a mirror-image to reflect dominance diverts attention from the task of ascertaining all the features of economic strength which might be relevant to measure dominance.[17]

Although dominant positions more often relate to the supply of goods or services, it must not be forgotten that they may also exist on the demand side. For instance Eurofima,[18] an agency set up by a number of national railway administrations to supply them with rolling stock of standard design, was regarded by the Commission as a dominant customer for a new form of passenger carriage for which tenders had been invited. The terms offered by Eurofima, which appeared to the Commission to be extremely harsh, were amended without a formal decision being necessary. Another example of dominance as a purchaser would be that of companies with the exclusive right to provide television services in a Member State, in respect of the market for materials for broadcasting.[19]

The existence of a dominant position[20]

It now seems to be well-established in Community law that the process of determining the existence of a dominant position in a particular case should

---

[12] Case 27/28, *Hugin Kassaregister AB* v. *Commission* [1979] E.C.R. 1869; [1979] 3 C.M.L.R. 345.
[13] Case 77/77, *BP* v. *Commission* [1978] E.C.R. 1511.
[14] This point was not pursued by the Court, which concentrated upon the question of abuse.
[15] Case T–69/89, *RTE* v. *Commission* [1991] 4 C.M.L.R. 586, Case T–70/89, *BBC* v. *Commission* [1991] 4 C.M.L.R. 669 and Case T–76/89, *ITP* v. *Commission* [1991] 4 C.M.L.R. 745.
[16] Case T–76/89, *ITP* v. *EC Commission* [1991] 4 C.M.L.R. 745, para. 49.
[17] See *infra*, p. 450 *et seq.*
[18] [1973] C.M.L.R. D217. See also Comp.Rep. 1973, p. 60.
[19] See, *e.g.* the complaint that was the subject of the proceedings in Case 298/83, *C.I.C.C.E.* v. *Commission* [1985] E.C.R. 1105; [1986] 1 C.M.L.R. 486.
[20] For a critical view of the Court's analysis of the existence of a dominant position, see Baden Fuller, (1979) 4 E.L.Rev. 423. See also Gyselen and Kyriazis, (1986) 11 E.L.Rev. 134 and B. Hawk, *United States, Common Market and International Antitrust*, Vol. II, pp. 796–825.

normally comprise two distinct stages: first the definition of the relevant market; and secondly, the assessment of the strength of the undertaking in question on that market.[21]

The relevant market

This expression is used to designate the field of competitive forces within which the undertaking operates in either satisfying, or obtaining satisfaction of a certain demand. The aim of defining the relevant market is to differentiate between those performances of other undertakings which must be taken into account in evaluating the position of the undertaking subject to the investigation, and those which can safely be left out of account for this purpose. The two main questions to be answered are how wide a range of products, and what geographical distribution of offers, should be covered by the evaluation. The timing of the offers is also likely to be significant. These three criteria of relevance—material, geographic and temporal—will be examined separately.

(i) *The material criterion or product market.* The definition of the product market is not always an easy matter because, on the one hand, things which are physically dissimilar may be in competition with regard to a particular application (for example, oil and gas domestic heating systems) while on the other hand, things which are physically similar may not be in competition (for example, tyres for heavy vehicles and tyres for vans or motor cars).[22] It will usually be an advantage for the undertaking in question to have the product market defined as widely as possible, since the greater the variety of products involved, the more difficult it will be to make out the existence of a dominant position.

Various tests to help in the delineation of product markets have become part of the common currency of competition jurisdictions.[23] The fundamental test is that of the interchangeability of product X and product Y as to their end uses.[24] In the words of the European Court,

> ". . . the possibilities of competition must be judged in the context of the market comprising the totality of the products which, with respect to their characteristics, are particularly suitable for satisfying constant needs and are only to a limited extent interchangeable with other products."[25]

---

[21] See the structure of the judgments in Case 27/76, *United Brands, loc. cit.* note 6, *supra*; Case 85/76, *Hoffmann-La Roche, loc. cit.* note 7, *supra*; Case 322/81 *Michelin, loc. cit.* note 2, *supra*. See also the strong statement by the Court in Case 31/80 *L'Oreal, loc. cit.* note 7, *supra* at p. 3793.

[22] See Case 322/81 *Michelin, loc. cit.* note 2, *supra* and the discussion, *infra*, of the issue of the relevant product market in that case.

[23] The American experience has been particularly influential. See the useful discussion by Holley in Van Damme, *op. cit.* note 3, *supra*, p. 201.

[24] A well known example from the United States is the *Du Pont* case where there was held to be competition as to end use, and hence a single market, between cellophane and other flexible packaging materials: see *United States* v. *Du Pont de Nemours*, 1956 Trade Cases s.68, 369 (Sup.Ct.) discussed by Holley, *loc. cit.* note 23, *supra* at pp. 147–149.

[25] Case 31/80, *L'Oreal* [1980] E.C.R. at p. 3793; Case 322/81, *Michelin* [1983] E.C.R. at p. 3505.

The Court has stressed, however, that examination should not be limited to the objective characteristics of the products in question: "the competitive conditions and the structure of supply and demand on the market must also be taken into consideration."[26] A test which sometimes proves useful, since it focuses on the real reactions of consumers, is "cross-elasticity of demand." By this is meant the degree to which sales of X increase in response to an increase in the price of Y; high elasticity, *i.e.* a substantial increase in the quantity of X sold when the price of Y rises only slightly, provides a clear indication of competition between the products. There is also the narrower test of "peculiar characteristics and uses," which makes the common sense point that highly specialised products are likely to be found on a separate market.[27] It must, though, be stressed that these and similar tests are only capable of guiding analysis in a rough and ready way. Ultimately, market definition is a matter for legal judgment rather than a description of economic fact.

The operation of the test of limited interchangeability may be illustrated by the *United Brands*[28] case on the supply of bananas to certain of the Member States. The proceedings arose out of the condemnation of the supplier concerned, the United Brands Company (UBC), by the Commission on four counts of abusive conduct contrary to Article 86. According to the Commission, the product market consisted of "bananas of all varieties, where branded or unbranded." On the other hand, UBC argued that bananas formed part of the general market for fresh fruit: in other words, customers make their choice freely between bananas and other varieties of fruit on the basis of availability and relative prices. If this were so, even a very large supplier of bananas like UBC would not be at liberty to set prices within a wide range, since allowance would have to be made for the risk of potential customers altering their preferences (assuming of course that the same company did not control the supply of other fruits). The Court said that:

> "For the banana to be regarded as forming a market which is sufficiently differentiated from other fruit markets it must be possible for it to be singled out by such special features distinguishing it from other fruits that it is only to a limited extent interchangeable with them and it is only exposed to their competition in a way that is hardly perceptible."[29]

In the Court's view, the test was satisfied. It noted, in particular, the year-round excess of banana supplies over demand, which enabled marketing to be adapted to the seasonal fluctuations of other fruits. There was no evidence of "significant long term cross-elasticity," nor of "seasonal substitutability in general between the banana and all the seasonal fruits," the latter occurring only in Germany in respect of peaches and table grapes.

---

[26] Case 322/81, *Michelin, ibid.*
[27] *e.g.* the different groups of vitamins in Case 85/76, *Hoffmann-La Roche* v. *Commission, loc. cit.* note 7, *supra.*
[28] Case 27/76, *United Brands Company* v. *Commission, loc. cit.* note 6, *supra.* See also the Dec. of the Commission (entitled *Chiquita*), O.J. 1976 L95/1; [1976] 1 C.M.L.R. D28.
[29] [1978] E.C.R. at p. 272.

Bananas, also, had characteristics enabling them to play an important part in the diet of a large section of the population comprising the very old, the very young and the sick. The constant needs of such consumers, and the limited and sporadic nature of the competition, justified recognition of the separate entity of the banana market.

The question arises whether perhaps, the relevant market in this case ought to have been defined still more narrowly, in terms of a separate market for the "Chiquita" brand of UBC. Such fragmentation of the market might be the result of building up consumer preferences for the branded fruit by advertising and by maintaining a consistently high quality. That some development of this kind had taken place is suggested by the difference of 30 to 40 per cent. between the prices of UBC's branded and unbranded bananas.[30] The Commission, however, did not examine this possibility in its Decision (so that there was no call for the Court to do so), presumably because it felt sufficiently confident of proving the dominance of UBC on the general banana market; had there been any doubt on the matter it might have seemed worthwhile to establish the independence of the narrower market.

Interchangeability must be considered on the supply side of the market as well as on the demand side. This was brought home by the quashing of the Decision of the Commission in *Continental Can Company*.[31] The Commission had found that the acquisition of a Dutch packaging firm, Thomassen en Drijver-Verblifa (TDV), by the Continental Can subsidiary, Europemballage Corporation, amounted to an abuse of the dominant position which the American firm enjoyed, through its German subsidiary, Schmalbach-Lubecke-Werke (SLW) on the market in Germany for meat tins, fish tins and metal closures for glass jars; the abuse consisting of an unacceptable strengthening of SLW's position on the markets concerned since, in the Commission's view, TDV had been a potential competitor of SLW. The main ground for the annulment of the Decision was that the Commission had not shown convincingly why manufacturers, for example of tins for vegetables, condensed milk, olive oil or fruit juice could not, by making some adaptation to their product, enter the field as serious competitors to SLW, if the latter raised its prices unduly. The Commission was also criticised for not dealing adequately with the possibility that SLW's major customers might begin to manufacture the relevant types of container themselves. The essence of these objections was that potential competition from new products or new producers ("elasticity of supply") had not been ruled out.

In the *Michelin*[32] case analysis of the structure of both supply and demand contributed crucially to the definition of the product market. The case concerned a decision of the Commission that NBIM, the Dutch subsidiary of the Michelin tyre group, was guilty of infringing Article 86 because of certain terms included in the contracts under which it supplied dealers. The Court of

---

[30] See the note by Korah on the Dec. of the Commission, (1975–76) 1 E.L.Rev. 322 at p. 324.
[31] Case 6/72, *Europemballage and Continental Can* v. *Commission, loc. cit.* note 1, *supra.*
[32] Case 322/81, *loc. cit.* note 2, *supra.*

Justice approved the Commission's definition of the market as that in new "replacement" tyres for heavy vehicles. This market was distinguishable from: (a) the market in "original equipment" tyres; (b) the market in tyres for cars and light vans; and (c) the market in retreads. As to (a), it was common ground that the structure of demand for replacements was entirely different from that for original equipment tyres, although they were identical products: while the former were supplied to dealers for retail sale, the latter were supplied to manufacturers to be fitted to new vehicles. As to (b), besides the lack of interchangeability at user level between car and van tyres and heavy vehicle tyres, there was again a difference of demand structures. For car and van drivers the purchase of tyres was an occasional event; whereas buyers of heavy vehicle tyres were normally haulage undertakings for which tyres represented an important business cost and which expected specialised advice and services from dealers. Nor was there elasticity of supply between tyres for light and heavy vehicles: the time and expenditure needed to switch production from one to the other made this impracticable as a way of responding to fluctuations in demand.[33] As to (c), the Court acknowledged that retreads were to some extent interchangeable, and hence in competition, with new tyres, but not sufficiently to undermine a dominant position on the market for the latter. Some consumers had reservations, whether rightly or wrongly, about the safety and reliability of retreads. In addition, a significant proportion of retreads used by transport undertakings were made to order from their own tyre carcasses. These would not compete with new tyres, since their production involved the provision of a service directly by retreading firms to the tyre owners. A further consideration was the dependence of the market for retreads, with respect to price and supply, on the market for new tyres. Every retread must have started life as a new tyre; and there was a limit to the number of times retreading could be done. So a dominant supplier of new tyres would have a privileged position *vis-à-vis* retreading undertakings. On an opposite tack, NBIM had suggested that the various types and sizes of tyres for heavy vehicles could be regarded as belonging to separate markets, because from a user's point of view they were not interchangeable. That suggestion was rejected by the Court on the ground that dealers had to be ready to meet demand from their customers for the whole range of such tyres. Also, in the absence of specialisation on the part of the undertakings concerned, the similarity between heavy vehicle tyres of different types and sizes and the way in which they complemented one another at the technical level meant they were subject to the same conditions of competition on the market.

Prior economic choices by a consumer may narrow the range of offers from which future demands have to be met. This phenomenon is sometimes

---

[33] The Court noted that in 1977, when there was a shortfall in the supply of heavy vehicle tyres, NBIM chose to grant an extra bonus rather than use surplus car tyre capacity to meet demand: [1983] E.C.R. at p. 3506. *Cf.* the *Continental Can* case, *loc. cit.* note 1, *supra*, where the Dec. of the Commission adverted to the barriers to market entry confronting possible competitors, notably the size of the necessary investments, but the Court did not think the burden of proof had been discharged.

referred to as "lock-in."[34] It operates where the opportunity cost of reversing a choice is felt to outweigh the advantages in the longer term of doing so. For instance, oil, gas and other domestic fuels may form a single market from the point of view of a person contemplating the installation of a new central heating system, but not after one or other system has been installed. Similar reasoning may apply where spare parts for a consumer durable are available only from the manufacturer. In *Hugin*[35] the Court found that most of the spare parts for Hugin cash registers were not interchangeable with parts made to fit any other type of machine, so that the operator of an independent maintenance, repair or reconditioning business, was entirely dependent on Hugin for supplies. The relevant market was, accordingly, that for Hugin spare parts required by such businesses. This was a crucial issue in the case, since the share held by Hugin of the market for cash registers as such was very modest.[36]

Another way of limiting the relevant market adopted by the Commission has been to identify targetable submarkets. Thus in *Napier Brown/British Sugar*[37] the Commission was able to distinguish retail and industrial customers as submarkets for granulated sugar. The Court of First Instance also accepted the notion of submarkets in litigation arising from television programme listings,[38] holding that markets for weekly programme listings of television broadcasts and the magazines in which they were published constituted distinct submarkets within the market for television programme information in general.

A different issue in *Commercial Solvents Corporation*[39] was whether the market for a raw material (or base or intermediate product) may be considered separately from the market for the end product. The case arose from a complaint to the Commission by the Italian pharmaceutical firm, Zoja, that CSC, through its Italian subsidiary, Istituto, had refused to supply it with aminobutanol, the base product for the manufacture of the drug ethambutol, which was used in the treatment of tuberculosis. CSC contended, *inter alia*, that the relevant market could not be that for aminobutanol, on which its dominance was relatively easy to prove, since the derivative, ethambutol, formed part of a wider market for anti-tubercular drugs. With this the Court disagreed:

"Contrary to the arguments of the applicants it is in fact possible to

---

[34] See the discussion of lock-in by Gyselen and Kyriazis, *op. cit.* note 20, *supra* at pp. 143–144.
[35] Case 22/78, *Hugin Kassaregister AB* v. *Commission* [1979] E.C.R. 1869; [1979] 3 C.M.L.R. 345. For the Dec. of the Commission, see O.J. 1978 L22/23; [1978] 1 C.M.L.R. D19. But see the criticism of Baden Fuller, *op. cit.* note 20, *supra* at pp. 426–427.
[36] Hugin had a market share of 12 per cent. in the common market as a whole and 13 per cent. in the U.K. Its largest competitor, the American company, National Cash Register had shares of 36 per cent. and 40 per cent. respectively.
[37] O.J. 1988 L284/41, [1990] 4 C.M.L.R. 196.
[38] Case T–69/89, *RTE* v. *Commission* [1991] 4 C.M.L.R. 586, Case T–70/89, *BBC* v. *Commission* [1991] 4 C.M.L.R. 669 and Case T–76/89, *ITP* v. *Commission* [1991] 4 C.M.L.R. 745.
[39] Commission: J.O. 1972 L299/51, [1973] C.M.L.R. D50. Court: Cases 6 and 7/73, *Istituto Chemioterapico Italiano and Commercial Solvents Corporation* v. *Commission* [1974] E.C.R. 223; [1974] 1 C.M.L.R. 309. *Cf.* Case 311/84, *Télémarketing, loc. cit.* note 7, *supra*, which concerned related markets for the provision of services.

distinguish the market in raw material necessary for the manufacture of a product from the market on which the product is sold. An abuse of a dominant position on the market in raw materials may thus have effects restricting competition in the market on which the derivatives of the raw material are sold and these effects must be taken into account when considering the effects of an infringement, even if the market for the derivative does not constitute a self-contained market."[40]

Thus, according to the Court, the raw material may constitute a relevant market in its own right; but it may still be valid, in determining whether a dominant position on that market has been abused, to take into account any anti-competitive effects which may have been felt on the market for the derivative. This problem of the relevance of potentially separate markets is especially acute in the context of vertically integrated organisations, whose behaviour in one market may produce or be directed towards effects in others. In *ECS/AKZO*[41] the abuse in the benzoyl oxide market occurred as a result of predatory pricing in the flour additives market.

(ii) *The geographic criterion.* The geographic distribution of producers and consumers may prevent effective competition from taking place between goods or services which in other circumstances would be readily interchangeable. For instance, a motorway café may be able to set its prices within a very wide range, because travellers are unwilling to make a detour in search of equivalent services offered by other establishments in the neighbourhood. It is, therefore, necessary in defining a relevant market for the purpose of Article 86 to identify the specific territory within which the interplay of supply and demand is to be considered. The starting point will normally be the sales area of the undertaking concerned, and the question will be whether the geographic market is co-terminous with that area, or wider or narrower in extent.

Factors obviously tending to promote geographic isolation would be a lack of transport facilities, or the cost of transportation relative to the value of a product, giving an unchallengeable advantage to local producers. The cost factor has been mentioned by the European Court as being of particular relevance in the case of the sugar market.[42] In other cases, the separation of a market may be due to government action, for example, the Dutch price controls which, according to the Commission, during the oil supply crisis of November 1973 to March 1974 helped to create a separate market for petrol refined in the Netherlands.[43] Habit and commercial convenience may also

---

[40] *Ibid.* pp. 249–250.
[41] O.J. 1985 L374/1.
[42] Joined Cases 40–48, 50, 54–56, 111, 113 and 114/73, *Suiker Unie and others* v. *Commission*, *loc. cit.* note 7, *supra*. See also *Napier Brown/British Sugar*, *loc. cit.* note 37, *supra*, where the Commission found that cost of freight and the presence of the English Channel combined to keep the United Kingdom as a separate market.
[43] The price controls made it impractical for Dutch distributors to buy motor spirit on the world market, so that they were entirely dependent on local refiners: see O.J. 1977 L117/1. The Decision of the Commission was annulled by the European Court: see Case 77/77, *B.P.* v. *Commission* [1978] E.C.R. 1511. On the reasons for the annulment, see *infra*. For a

play a part. In *Michelin*[44] the Court found that tyre companies operated on the Dutch market through local subsidiaries, to which local dealers looked for their supplies. The Commission had, therefore, been right in regarding the Netherlands as the area from which the competition facing NBIM mainly came.[45]

The chosen area must be one "where the conditions of competition are sufficiently homogeneous for the effect of the economic power of the undertaking to be able to be evaluated."[46] In *United Brands* it was held that the Commission had been right to exclude France, Italy and the United Kingdom from the relevant market because, for historical reasons, each of these Member States applied a different preferential system in respect of banana imports (for example, Commonwealth preference in the United Kingdom). On the other hand, a system of free competition was common to the six Member States included in the market.[47] It is possible for there to be a Community-wide market even though there is varying demand within different Member States.[48]

The market territory must also satisfy a *de minimis* rule which is implicit in the reference in Article 86 to "a dominant position within the common market or in a substantial part of it." The test of "a substantial part" is not the geographic extent of the territory in question but the economic importance of the market situated there. This was made clear in the *Sugar* judgment where the Court said:

> "For the purpose of determining whether a specific territory is large enough to amount to 'a substantial part of the common market' within the meaning of Article 86 of the Treaty the pattern and volume of the production and consumption of the said product as well as the habits and economic opportunities of vendors and purchasers must be considered."[49]

And after mentioning figures for sugar production and consumption in Belgium and in the whole Community between the marketing years 1968–69 and 1971–72, it concluded:

> "If the other criteria mentioned above are taken into account these market shares are sufficiently large for the area covered by Belgium and Luxembourg to be considered, so far as sugar is concerned, as a substantial part of the common market in this product."[50]

---

comment on the Decision, see Williams, (1977) 2 E.L.Rev. 294; and on the judgment, see Laddie, (1978) 3 E.L.Rev. 501.

[44] Case 322/81, *loc. cit.* note 2, *supra*.

[45] It was, of course, open to the Commission, in assessing the position of NBIM on the Netherlands market, to take into account the strength of the Michelin group as a whole: see *infra*.

[46] See Case 27/76, *United Brands* v. *Commission* [1978] E.C.R. at p. 270.

[47] The Court noted that in the six Member States concerned it had been possible for UBC to adopt an integrated marketing policy, centred on its Dutch subsidiary, United Brands Continentaal: *ibid.* at pp. 273–276.

[48] *Tetra Pak I* O.J. 1988 L272/27, [1990] 4 C.M.L.R. 47.

[49] Joined Cases 40–48, 50, 54–56, 111, 113 and 114/73, *Suiker Unie and others* v. *Commission*, [1975] E.C.R. at p. 1977.

[50] *Ibid.*

From the criteria cited, it can be seen that the Court was dealing in one breath with the two separate issues of the territorial extent of the relevant market, and the substantiality of that market. In determining the latter, the crucial consideration was the relative size of the Belgo-Luxembourg sugar market, as compared with the size of the sugar market in the whole Community.

Two comments seem called for on this *de minimis* rule. In the first place, because it is based on a principle of relativity, it is capable of being satisfied by markets which are, in absolute terms, extremely small, if the common market in the product concerned is itself small. For instance, the rule provided no impediment to the Commission's Decision in *General Motors Continental*: the product market was that for inspections, to ensure conformity with technical standards, of Opel vehicles imported into Belgium, a specialised service which by definition could be offered only in that country.[51] Secondly, it may be that the importance of the market should not be assessed with regard to purely quantitative criteria. In *BP*[52] the Advocate-General, Mr. Warner, found that on the Commission's reasoning as to the existence of a dominant position between the major oil companies and their customers during the supply crisis, the relevant market must have been the market for motor spirit among BP's regular customers, or at most, among its customers generally in the Netherlands. On BP's estimate that the Dutch market represented 4.8 per cent. of the common market for motor spirit, and given that BP held 10 per cent. of the Dutch market, the relevant share of the common market could not have exceeded 0.48 per cent. Could a market below 0.5 per cent. be regarded as sufficiently substantial? Mr. Warner was prepared to accept as tenable the view that it could not be, but warned against focusing attention exclusively on percentages. He went on:

> "The opposite of 'substantial' is 'negligible,' and what may seem negligible when looked at in terms of a percentage may seem otherwise when looked at in absolute terms. The population of Luxembourg is, I believe, about .23 per cent. of the population of the whole Community. I would however shrink from saying that one who had a monopoly, or near monopoly, of the Luxembourg market for a particular product was exempt from the application of Article 86. Similarly I would shrink from holding that BP's share of the Dutch market for motor spirit was negligible."[53]

---

[51] Commission: O.J. 1975 L29/14; [1975] 1 C.M.L.R. D20. Court: Case 26/75, *General Motors Continental* v. *Commission* [1975] E.C.R. 1367; [1976] 1 C.M.L.R. 95. Under the relevant Belgian legislation responsibility for carrying out inspections and issuing certificates of conformity was delegated to the sole authorised agent of any foreign manufacturer in the case of new cars and cars imported into Belgium after being registered abroad for less than six months. Similar arrangements in the U.K. were the subject of the Commission's *BL* Dec., O.J. 1984 L207/11. See Case 226/84, *British Leyland* v. *Commission* [1986] E.C.R. 3263; [1987] 1 C.M.L.R. 184, when the Decision of the Commission was upheld.

[52] Case 77/77, *B.P.* v. *Commission, loc. cit.* note 43, *supra*. The Commission had actually stated in its Decision that the relevant market was that for petroleum spirit in the Netherlands. However, dominance on this *general* market could not have been explained by the relationship of dependence between *particular* suppliers and their customers.

[53] [1978] E.C.R. at p. 1537. See also Case 30/87, *Bodson* v. *SA Pompes funèbres des regions liberées* [1988] E.C.R. 2479.

At one time it used to be debated whether the territories of some of the smaller Member States would be large enough to satisfy the *de minimis* rule, or whether, for example, the Benelux countries should be grouped together for this purpose.[54] What has been said above, shows that this debate was misconceived: a market amounting to a substantial part of the common market may cover a number of Member States or a single Member State or parts of one or more Member States. In fact, although relevant markets have been found more often than not to coincide with the territories of States, this is a tendency which should decline with the achievement of the single internal market. An issue which has not yet received the attention of the Court is whether a relevant market may extend beyond Community territory. In principle, it is thought that, if the concept of the relevant market is applied at all, it must relate to the actual supply/demand situation in which an undertaking finds itself; where this overlaps with third States, dominance under Article 86 will have to be assessed in relation to the wider area. However, this would be subject to the condition that the part of the market which is located within the Community amounted to a substantial part of the common market.

(iii) *The temporal criterion.* The market on which an undertaking operates may fluctuate from time to time with respect both to the range of products and the geographical area covered. For example, if the view had been taken in *United Brands* that the demand for bananas was seriously affected by the availability of various seasonal fruits, it might have concluded that bananas formed part of a series of different markets at different times of the year; and it would have followed that the position of UBC must be examined in relation to each of these markets. Another example is provided by *Commercial Solvents Corporation.* It had been argued by CSC that the manufacture of ethambutol was possible by processes other than that involving aminobutanol. However, the Court held that the processes in question were still of an experimental nature and incapable at the material time of being used for production on an industrial scale. They, therefore, did not constitute a realistic alternative for the customer, Zoja.[55]

Market power will only give a dominant position if it is capable of enduring for a considerable time. The prospect of substitutes becoming available in the short run limits freedom of action because of the risk of future defections by customers.[56] Thus in *BP* Mr. Warner contested the Commission's view that, because there was no petrol available from other sources, the oil companies occupied a dominant position in respect of their customers during the crisis of 1973 to 1974. He pointed out that in a *temporary* supply crisis, a trader cannot determine his distribution policy without having regard to his customers. "He must have it in mind that, once

---

[54] The Commission itself flirted with this idea: see the proposal sent to the Council on May 29, 1970 (J.O. 1970, C92/14).

[55] [1973] E.C.R. at p. 248.

[56] Gyselen and Kyriazis, *op. cit.* note 20, *supra* stress that market power only gives cause for concern if it is a long-run phenomenon.

the emergency is over, they will have memories of the way in which they were treated by him during the period of scarcity."[57]

The criteria of dominance

A variety of factors may point to the conclusion that a dominant position exists on a given market. In each case it is necessary to consider whether the particular combination of factors which is found to be present confers the requisite degree of power upon the undertaking in question.

(i) *Market share.* The most important factor is the size of the undertaking's share of the relevant market. In assessing this any part of production which is transported outside the relevant market must be left out of account. The European Court has said that, allowing for exceptional circumstances, extremely large market shares may be regarded as constituting in themselves proof of the existence of a dominant position.[58] Where the share of the market held by the undertaking is smaller, other factors take on increased significance.

In a number of cases Article 86 has been applied in relation to undertakings enjoying a more or less complete monopoly. For instance, in *Commercial Solvents Corporation*[59] the Commission found that CSC had a "world monopoly" in the production and sale of the base products used in the manufacture of the anti-tubercular drug, ethambutol. The European Court, without itself adopting the Commission's phrase, appears to have been satisfied that the CSC group was the only practical source of materials for the manufacture of ethambutol on an industrial scale, alternative sources, suggested by CSC, being either of an experimental nature or of limited capacity. In a later case, the Court confirmed the Commission's finding that GVL had a *de facto* monopoly on the market in Germany in services relating to the management of performing artists' rights of "secondary exploitation."[60] It makes no difference to the application of the Article that a monopoly position may have been created by statute.[61]

Even in cases where control has been less complete, market shares have normally been high. For example, according to the Commission's figures in *Continental Can Company*[62] SLW accounted for 70 to 80 per cent. of the

---

[57] Case 77/77, *B.P.* v. *Commission*, [1978] E.C.R. at p. 1538.

[58] Case 85/76, *Hoffmann-La Roche* v. *Commission* [1979] E.C.R. at p. 521. This was repeated by the Court in Case 62/86, *AKZO Chemie BV* v. *Commission* (not yet reported) and adopted by the Court of First Instance in Case T–30/89, *Hilti AG* v. *Commission* [1992] 4 C.M.L.R. 16 at p. 43. A figure of 90 per cent. was suggested by Judged Learned Hand in *United States* v. *Aluminium Co. of America* 1945 Trade Cases, s.57, 342 (2d. Cir.) at s.57, 679. See the discussion in Holley, *loc. cit.* note 23, *supra*, pp. 174 *et seq.*

[59] Joined Cases 6 and 7/73, *loc. cit.* note 39, *supra*.

[60] Case 7/82, *GVL* v. *Commission* [1983] E.C.R. 483. "Secondary exploitation" occurs where a performance which has previously been recorded is broadcast or disseminated to the public in some other manner. See also the Commission's *GEMA* Dec. concerning a monopoly in the management of musical authors' rights: J.O. 1971 L134/15; [1971] C.M.L.R. D35; (No. 2) J.O. 1972 L166/22.

[61] See Case 26/75, *General Motors Continental* v. *Commission*, *loc. cit.* note 51, *supra*; Case 13/77, *INNO* v. *ATAB* [1977] E.C.R. 2115; Case 41/83, *Italy* v. *Commission (British Telecom)* [1985] E.C.R. 873, [1985] 2 C.M.L.R. 368; Case 311/84, *Télémarketing, loc. cit.* note 7, *supra*.

[62] Case 6/72, *loc. cit.* note 1, *supra*. The figures were disputed by Continental Can.

market in Germany for meat tins, 80 to 90 per cent. of the market for fish tins and 50 to 55 per cent. of the market for metal closures for glass jars. And in *Hoffmann-La Roche* the shares held by Roche on three of the seven vitamin markets considered by the Court amounted to more than 80 per cent.[63] Comparatively low for an undertaking which has been held to occupy a dominant position was the 45 per cent. share of the banana market in six Member States attributed to UBC by the Commission. UBC contended that its share had dropped to 41 per cent. by 1975, and the European Court was content to accept the figure of "more than 40 per cent. and nearly 45 per cent." In *Michelin*[64] NBIM's share of the relevant market was somewhat higher, varying between 57 and 65 per cent. during the reference period of 1975–80. The Commission has expressed the view that a dominant position will usually be found once a market share of the order of 40 to 45 per cent. is reached; and that the existence of such a position cannot be ruled out in respect of shares between 20 and 40 per cent.[65]

The *United Brands* Judgment contained the rather surprising statement that:

"A trader can only be in a dominant position on the market for a product if he has succeeded in winning a large part of this market."[66]

This suggests that the existence of an important market share is not only a more or less reliable indicator, but a *necessary* (though not a *sufficient*) condition of dominance. However, such a condition would not be consistent with the essentially dynamic concept of a dominant position which both the Court and the Commission employ. As the Commission has written:

"An undertaking which is able, when it so wishes, to eliminate the other competing undertakings from the market may already enjoy a dominant position and decisively determine the behaviour of the other undertakings even if its own share of the market is still relatively weak."[67]

The impression created by the passage quoted from *United Brands* was corrected by the court in the *Hoffmann-La Roche* judgment, where it said:

"A substantial market share as evidence of the existence of a dominant position is not a constant factor and its importance varies from market to market according to the structure of these markets, especially as far as production, supply and demand are concerned."[68]

---

[63] Case 85/76, *loc. cit.* note 7, *supra*. The figures for the seven markets were: Vitamin A, 47 per cent.; Vitamin B2, 74.8–87 per cent.; Vitamin B3, 18.9–51 per cent.; Vitamin B6, 83.9–90 per cent.; Vitamin C, 63–66.2 per cent.; Vitamin E, 50–64 per cent.; Vitamin H, 93–100 per cent. (lowest and highest figures for value or quantity). Roche was held to be dominant, on account of its market share alone or in combination with other factors, on all the markets except that for Vitamin B3.
[64] Case 322/81, *loc. cit.* note 2, *supra*.
[65] Comp.Rep. 1980, point 150.
[66] [1978] E.C.R. at p. 282.
[67] Authors' translation. See Memorandum, *loc. cit.* note 4, *supra*.
[68] [1979] E.C.R. at p. 520. For the interplay between market share and geographical issues, see Case 247/86, *Alsatel* v. *Novosam* [1988] E.C.R. 5987, [1990] 4 C.M.L.R. 434.

(ii) *Shares of other market participants.* It may be helpful to compare the size of the market share under investigation with the size of the shares held by other operators on the relevant market. An undertaking with a relatively low market share, for example, 30 to 40 per cent., may still be in a dominant position if the rest of the market is highly fragmented, so that none of the other participants constitutes a serious threat to its independence. Thus in *United Brands* the European Court cited as a consideration affording evidence of "preponderant strength" the fact that UBC's percentage of the market was several times greater than that of Castle and Cooke (16 per cent.) which was its nearest competitor, with the remaining market participants well behind.[69] The gap in *Michelin* was even wider, the shares of NBIM's main competitors amounting only to between 4 and 8 per cent.[70] On the other hand, in an oligopoly where, for example, three operators divide a market more or less evenly between them no single undertaking will be able to act without taking the reactions of the others into account. None of them can, therefore, be regarded as individually occupying a dominant position, although they might do so as a group.[71]

(iii) *The conditions of market entry.* Even a very large market share can be rapidly eroded when the market is penetrated by lively new competitors. An example is provided by the lamentable decline in the British motor cycle industry, which in the 1950s accounted for 70 per cent. of the world market but was unable to withstand competition from Continental and Japanese manufacturers, responding to the demand for smaller motor cycles.[72] A careful analysis of a dominant position should, therefore, refer to any advantages enjoyed by the undertaking in question, or to any difficulties in the way of potential market entrants, making it unlikely that the structure of the market will change radically in the shorter run.

This might be the case, for example, because the undertaking controls essential patents or know-how; or because, like UBC, it is vertically integrated, with privileged access to supplies, means of transport and distribution outlets[73]; or because, like Michelin, it has a well developed network of commercial representatives providing continuous contact with customers[74]; or because of its technical superiority, sustained by a continuous programme of research and development and the resulting scope of its product range.[75] Another factor which may be influential is "product differentiation." By this is meant the phenomenon of consumer preference

---

[69] [1978] E.C.R. at pp. 282–283. See also Case 85/76, *Hoffmann-La Roche* v. *Commission*, where the smallness of its competitors' market shares helped to establish the dominance of Roche on the markets for Vitamins A, C and E.

[70] [1983] E.C.R. at pp. 3509–3510.

[71] On collective dominant positions see further, *infra.*

[72] The story is related in Bruce-Gardyne, *Meriden: Odyssey of a Lame Duck*, published by The Centre for Policy Studies.

[73] Case 27/76 [1978] E.C.R. at pp. 278–280.

[74] Case 322/81 [1983] E.C.R. at p. 3511. See also the reference to "a highly developed sales network" in Case 85/76, *Hoffmann-La Roche* [1979] E.C.R. at p. 524.

[75] This was referred to as a relevant factor in Case 27/76, *United Brands* [1978] E.C.R. at p. 279; Case 85/76, *Hoffmann-La Roche* [1979] E.C.R. at p. 524; Case 322/81, *Michelin* [1983] E.C.R. at p. 3510.

becoming attached to a particular brand of goods to an extent which cannot be justified by the specific properties of the goods as compared with available substitutes. Such a preference may have been built up by a protracted advertising campaign.

From the point of view of a potential competitor the chief difficulty in overcoming such advantages would be that of cost. Very large resources may be needed, for instance, to finance independent research or countervailing advertising. The crucial consideration will be the range within which the undertaking is free to fix its prices without making it commercially attractive for others to risk the investment required in order to mount a challenge. Also in the present context it is important to bear in mind the time factor. The possibility that, at the end of a very long period of development, another undertaking may succeed in establishing itself as a serious competitor would not normally be sufficient to impair an existing dominant position.[76]

The advantages helping to reinforce the market strength of an undertaking may be wholly attributable to its business initiative. Could it then be argued that taking them into account in deciding whether the undertaking fulfils the conditions for the application of Article 86, would be to put a premium on enterprise and efficiency? It is thought that such an objection would be misplaced. Whether or not an undertaking occupies a dominant position is a question which has to be determined irrespective of the means, fair or foul, by which the position was attained. It is at a later stage, when it has to be decided whether the dominant position has been abused, that the efficiency of the undertaking may become relevant.

(iv) *Financial resources.* The ability of an undertaking to command finance is bound to enhance its freedom of action. In particular, it will allow the undertaking to keep abreast of the latest developments in technology, to adapt rapidly to changes in the pattern of demand and to expand its operation, either vertically or horizontally. Thus in *Continental Can Company*[77] the Commission drew attention to the fact that Continental Can, because of its large size, was able to resort to the international capital market; and that it had done so in 1969 to finance the acquisition of an additional 60 per cent. participation in SLW with loans in Eurodollars and Deutsche Marks. The concept of parent companies and their subsidiaries all forming part of the same undertaking is important in the present context.[78] Its consequences may be particularly striking where the undertaking concerned is a conglomerate, *i.e.* a business group having interests in a wide variety of separate economic sectors.

(v) *Conduct and performance of the undertaking.* The criteria examined so

---

[76] See the very full analysis of those features of UBC's banana operation which the European Court regarded as contributing to its retention of a large market share: Case 27/76 [1978] E.C.R. at pp. 278–281.
[77] *Loc. cit.* note 4, *supra.*
[78] See the discussion, *supra*, Chap. 13.

far have related to the structure of the market,[79] *i.e.* the reasonably stable features of the competitive environment within which the undertaking operates and to which accordingly its decisions must be adjusted, and of the undertaking itself, *i.e.* its general organisation and resources both for the purposes of the particular line of business in question and for any other purpose having a bearing on that business. It remains to say something about the behavioural criteria of dominance, consisting of the conduct and performance of the undertaking on the relevant market. Roughly speaking, by "conduct" is meant the activities pursued by the undertaking in the course of its business, for example, its policies on pricing, output and sales promotion[80]; and by "performance" is meant the result of these activities, for example, the level of profits, the efficiency of production or the quality and range of the goods produced.[81]

It might be thought that the actual conduct or performance of an undertaking would provide the best possible evidence of the existence or otherwise of a dominant position. If an undertaking is able to behave in a manner, or to achieve results, which would not be expected under conditions of effective competition, the inference is surely legitimate that competitive restraints are, in fact, absent. However, writers have warned of the equivocality of such evidence.[82] Given that in practice the competitive process works more or less imperfectly, it may be possible for an undertaking to make very large profits, to limit its output or to impose discriminatory prices, although it does not enjoy market power amounting to dominance; while, on the other hand, it has been pointed out that a monopolist wishing to safeguard his long term position may treat his customers relatively benignly.[83] Predatory practices such as local price cutting may be an indication of a wish to acquire a dominant position, rather than of dominance already achieved.[84] The better view is, therefore, that behavioural evidence should not normally be treated as sufficient in itself to establish the existence of a dominant position. However, it may be invoked to corroborate the evidence resulting from a structural analysis. It will be more persuasive, the longer the conduct or performance in question is found to have continued.

In *United Brands* the European Court was faced with a choice between two performance criteria: the loss which UBC claimed that its banana division had suffered from 1951 to 1976; and the success of UBC in retaining its share of the banana market against vigorous competition. Because it accorded with the impression of overall strength gained from a structural analysis of the relevant market, the Court gave greater weight to the latter.[85]

---

[79] This definition is culled from the definitions discussed by Joliet in *Monopolization and Abuse of Dominant Position* (Nijhoff, 1970), pp. 25–26.
[80] See *ibid.* pp. 27–28.
[81] See *ibid.* pp. 29–30.
[82] See *ibid.* pp. 96 *et seq.* and references. See also Gyselen and Kyriazis, *op. cit.* note 20, *supra* at pp. 135–137.
[83] By Edwards in *Maintaining Competition* (1949), p. 125, cited by Joliet, *op. cit.* (note 79), *supra*, pp. 97–98.
[84] See *ibid.* p. 127.
[85] [1978] E.C.R. at p. 284–285.

One or more undertakings

The concept of an undertaking was examined in Chapter 13.[86] It will be remembered that legally distinct companies may be regarded as forming a single undertaking, if in practice they are subject to common control. The importance of this principle in the context of Article 86 is that, in determining whether the conduct of one member of a group constitutes an abuse of a dominant position on a relevant market within the common market, it may be possible to take into account the economic strength of other members of the group, some or all of them established in third countries. For example, in *Continental Can Company*[87] the dominant position on which the Commission relied was that of SLW on the German market, while the alleged abuse had been committed by Europemballage through its acquisition of TDV; and this conduct was attributable to the parent company, Continental Can. In the same way, in *Commercial Solvents Corporation*[88] it was CSC's control over world supplies of aminobutanol that gave Istituto a dominant position on the common market; CSC was legally answerable for Istituto's refusal to supply Zoja.[89]

A more controversial use of the phrase "one or more undertakings" involves its attachment to so-called joint dominance by non-connected firms. In *Hoffmann-La Roche* the Court appeared to resist the application of Article 86 to this situation by stating that:

"a dominant position must be distinguished from parallel courses of conduct which are peculiar to oligopolies in that in an oligopoly the courses of conduct interact, while in the case of an undertaking occupying a dominant position the conduct of the undertaking which derives profits from that position is to a great extent determined unilaterally."

However, the Commission has since tried on several occasions to establish that collective dominance can be regulated by Article 86. Its Sixteenth Report on Competition Policy[90] pointed to the risks of shared dominance in the following terms:

"In the case of a tight oligopoly, the reduction in the intensity of competition does not necessarily lead to the appearance of tacit collusion. Tacit collusion may, however, arise from the fact that members of the oligopoly become aware of their interdependence and of the probably unfavourable consequences of adopting a competitive attitude."

These arguments were applied by the Commission in the *Italian Flat Glass* case[91] where it issued a decision against the three main producers of flat glass

---

[86] See p. 381, *supra*.
[87] *Loc. cit.* note 1, *supra*.
[88] *Loc. cit.* note 39, *supra*.
[89] See also Case 322/81, *Michelin*, *loc. cit.* note 2, *supra*.
[90] [1986], p. 231.
[91] [1989] O.J. L33/44; [1990] 4 C.M.L.R. 535.

on the basis of infringements of both Articles 85 and 86. In language closely following its stance taken in the Sixteenth Report the Commission referred to the tight oligopoly of the market and identified a "marked degree of interdependence with regard to prices, terms of sale, relations with customers and business strategies." The alleged abuses related to identical pricing, discounts and other practices. However, no fines were imposed for the breaches of Article 86 since this was the first occasion on which the Commission had relied upon collective dominance.

The exact scope for applying Article 86 on this issue still remains unclear[92] since the Court was able to avoid ruling upon it in *Alsatel*.[93] In the course of a reference under Article 177 the Commission submitted observations whether parallel behaviour on the part of several independent undertakings which does not leave their customers any possibility of negotiating the terms of the contracts to be concluded might place those undertakings collectively in a dominant position. However, the Court refused to respond to this argument, noting that it was unconnected with the facts before the national court and was based on information in the Commission's possession which, on its own admission, was insufficiently precise.

The concept of an abuse

The wording of Article 86 indicates that the existence of a dominant position does not in itself attract the prohibition contained in the Article. Nevertheless, aggrieved parties seeking the protection of the provision have become more adventurous in their attempts to push back the limits of the notion of abuse. For example, in the *Macrotron* case[94] it was argued that the exclusive right to provide employment agency services granted by a German statute to the Federal Labour Office was itself abusive. Although the Court affirmed its view that more than dominance was needed to constitute a breach of Article 86, it went on to state that there would be an abuse where a party holding such a position manifestly failed to meet market demand. More cases are needed to refine this approach, particularly as to the extent to which a simple failure to satisfy the market place could infringe the provision.

But whilst not unlawful, it is clear that dominance creates special obligations for the undertakings concerned.[95] There is no definition of abuse in the EEC Treaty, and guidance in interpreting the concept must be sought from the objects and general principles set out in the Preamble to the Treaty and in Articles 2 and 3, especially Article 3(f)[96] and from the case-law.

In its *Hoffmann-La Roche* judgment the Court of Justice said:

> "The concept of abuse is an objective concept relating to the behaviour

---

[92] See Schodermeier [1990] 1 E.C.L.R. 28.
[93] Case 247/86, *Alsatel Societé Alsacienne et Lorraine de Telecommunications et d'Electronique* v. *Novasam SA* [1988] E.C.R. 5987; [1990] 4 C.M.L.R. 434.
[94] Case C–41/90, *Höfner and Elser* v. *Macrotron* (not yet reported).
[95] See the passage quoted from para. 3511 of the *Michelin* judgment at the start of this chapter.
[96] Redesignated as Art. 3(g) on ratification of the Maastricht Treaty on European Union.

of an undertaking in a dominant position which is such as to influence the structure of a market where, as a result of the very presence of the undertaking in question, the degree of competition is weakened and which, through recourse to methods different from those which condition normal competition in products or services on the basis of the transactions of commercial operators, has the effect of hindering the maintenance of the degree of competition still existing in the market or the growth of that competition."[97]

The definition confirms the answer given in *Continental Can Company*[98] to two important questions about the meaning of "abuse" in Article 86.

The first question was whether the concept was confined to unfair and oppressive behaviour towards suppliers and consumers, or included behaviour towards actual or potential competitors tending to protect or reinforce the dominant position. This question reflects the distinction which is sometimes drawn between two broad approaches to the control of market power, one aiming to ensure the good behaviour of the undertaking concerned, and the other to limit the power itself by seeking to preserve effective competition.[99] It has been noted that the two approaches tend in practice to converge[1] and in this respect Community competition law has proved no exception. From the definition in *Hoffmann-La Roche* it seems the Court regards anti-competitive behaviour as the primary target of Article 86; but it is equally clear that exploitative behaviour, such as imposing excessive prices or other unfair teaching conditions, may be caught by the Article.[2]

The second question was whether a causal link must exist between the dominant position and the behaviour constituting an abuse. In other words, was full value to be given to the notion of "exploiting" a dominant position, so that the undertaking in question must have used its power as the means of achieving the result which is regarded as objectionable? One of the arguments put forward by Continental Can had been precisely that that there was no causal connection between its acquisition of a controlling participation in TDV and its position on the German market which, through SLW, it was alleged to dominate. However, the Court held that, if a merger had the effect of substantially fettering competition, "the question of the link of causality raised by the applicants which in their opinion had to exist between the dominant position and its abuse, is of no consequence, for the strengthening of the position of an undertaking may be an abuse and prohibited under Article 86 of the Treaty, regardless of the means and procedure by which it is achieved. . . ."[3] A similar line of argument was rejected by the Court in *Hoffmann-La Roche*.[4] The idea that abusive

---

[97] Case 85/76 [1979] E.C.R. at p. 541.
[98] Case 6/72, *loc. cit.* note 1, *supra*.
[99] See the clear account in Joliet, *op. cit.* note 79, *supra*, pp. 8 *et seq.*
[1] See Waelbroeck in Van Damme, *op. cit.* note 3, *supra*, pp. 111–112.
[2] See Art. 86(*a*) and the examples of abuses discussed, *infra*.
[3] Case 6/72 [1973] E.C.R. at p. 245. See the criticism by Focsaneanu in Van Damme, *op. cit.* note 3, *supra*, pp. 324 *et seq.*
[4] Case 85/76 [1979] E.C.R. at p. 541.

behaviour consists of obtaining advantages which would not have been obtainable under conditions of effective competition is thus seen to be too restrictive.[5] A dominant undertaking may be prohibited from taking action which would be possible and permissible for an undertaking having less market power, because of the adverse consequences that are liable to ensue for the competitive structure of the market.

Article 86 does not contain any provision like Article 85(3) expressly providing an escape from the broad prohibition which it imposes.[6] However, in practice the operation of the two Articles is rather similar, owing to the flexibility of the concept of an abuse. Behaviour which might appear to be prima facie abusive, for example, because it falls within one of the categories mentioned in Article 86, may nevertheless escape prohibition if in the circumstances it is found to be objectively justified. This can be seen, for example, in the cases relating to refusals to deal, which are discussed *infra*.[7]

The Commission regards the occurrence of an abuse as an objective matter: there is no need for the undertaking to have intended to cause harm, nor for its behaviour to have been morally reprehensible. Thus the Commission rejected as immaterial the argument put forward by GEMA[8] that it had not been aware of the discriminatory consequences of its activities. Intention or negligence only become relevant if the Commission sees fit to impose a penalty under Article 15(2)(*a*) of Regulation 17. The definition of "abuse" in *Hoffmann-La Roche* supports that view.[9]

The fact that an abuse of a dominant position may have been encouraged by national legislative provisions does not provide any justification for the undertaking concerned.[10] However, some element of free will on the part of the undertaking is required. If it acts under legal constraint there will be no direct infringement of Article 86, but the Member State responsible will be in breach of its general duty under the second paragraph of Article 5 to abstain from any measure capable of jeopardising the attainment of the objectives of the Treaty.[11]

Member States acting in the exercise of their sovereign powers may interfere with the normal functioning of the competition system, for

---

[5] This was the definition suggested by the group of professors appointed in 1963 to advise the Commission on the interpretation of Art. 86. It is quoted in the Memorandum cited in note 4, *supra*.

[6] Case 66/86, *Ahmed Saeed Flugreisen and Silver Line Reisebüro* v. *Zentrale Zur Bekämpfung Unlauteren Wettbewerbs* [1989] E.C.R. 803; [1990] 4 C.M.L.R. 102, para. 32.

[7] See also the part of the *United Brands* judgment dealing with the clause in UBC's sales contracts prohibiting the resale of green bananas. UBC had argued that the sole purpose of the clause was to protect the "Chiquita" brand name, and ultimately the consumer, by ensuring that bananas were of consistently high quality; and this could only be done by reserving supplies for ripeners with proper equipment and expertise. The Court took the view that, as a quality control the blanket prohibition on resales was unduly restrictive. However, it is implicit in the judgment that a clause limiting resales to approved "Chiquita" ripeners, although restrictive of competition because excluding non-approved ripeners from this activity, would have escaped censure: Case 27/76 [1978] E.C.R., pp. 285 *et seq.*

[8] *Loc. cit.* note 60, *supra*. But see Case 26/75, *General Motors Continental* v. *Commission, loc. cit.* note 51, *supra* where the Court appeared to give weight to subjective factors in deciding that no abuse had been committed.

[9] Case 85/76, *loc. cit.* note 95, *supra*.

[10] Case 13/77, *INNO* v. *ATAB* [1977] E.C.R. at p. 2144.

[11] *Ibid.* If a public or privileged undertaking is concerned, there will be an infringement of Art. 90(1): see Chap. 19, *infra*.

example, by imposing a parafiscal charge on certain products in order to finance an aid to the domestic industry. Article 86 (and, indeed, Article 85) will not apply in such cases, even if the task in question has been assigned to a legally autonomous public body.[12] However, this does not mean that the Member State in question will get off scot free, since a number of other Treaty provisions may be relevant.[13]

Examples of abuses

Examples of behaviour which has been, or is likely to be, held abusive under Article 86 are discussed below. The list of possible abuses contained in the Article, like that of possibly restrictive agreements in Article 85, is purely illustrative. The list will not be analysed as such, but examples appearing under its various items will be considered either individually or in the particular forms of behaviour in which they most frequently manifest themselves.

(1) *Unfair prices*

(a) *Excessively high prices exacted by dominant sellers.* This is probably the first example of an abuse of a dominant position which would occur to most people, because of the direct impact felt by consumers. However, it is not easy to formulate theoretically adequate and practically useful criteria for determining where the line between fair and unfair prices should be drawn in a given case.[14]

The European Court in its *United Brands*[15] judgment, echoing its earlier judgment in *General Motors Continental*,[16] spoke of a price being excessive "because it has no reasonable relation to the economic value of the product supplied." It went on to approve as one test of excess over economic value, a comparison between the selling price of a product and its cost of production, which would disclose the size of the profit margin. As the Court said, the question was "whether the difference between the costs actually incurred and the price actually charged is excessive"; and if so, "whether a price has been imposed which is either unfair in itself or when compared to competing products."[17]

Such a test may attract criticism. Thus it has been pointed out[18] that high profits may be the result of a firm's efficiency which deserves to be rewarded (although it is reasonable to require some element of cost saving to be handed on to consumers); while low profits may be the result of inefficiency, in which case prices may still be excessive. The task of assessing how efficiently a dominant undertaking employs it resources is likely to be a

---

[12] Case 94/74, *IGAV* v. *ENCC* [1975] E.C.R. 699 at p. 714; [1976] 2 C.M.L.R. 37.
[13] Those mentioned by the European Court, *ibid.* were Arts. 37, 90, 92–94, 101 and 102.
[14] The problem is very fully analysed by Schwarz in Van Damme, *op. cit.* note 3, *supra*, pp. 381 *et seq.*
[15] Case 27/76 [1978] E.C.R. at p. 301.
[16] Case 26/75, *loc. cit.* note 51, *supra*.
[17] *Loc. cit.* note 13, *supra*.
[18] By Korah in Van Damme, *op. cit.* note 3, *supra* at p. 237.

formidable one. There is also the question of the proportion of indirect costs and general expenditure which should be allocated to the cost of putting a particular product on the market. And the structure of the undertaking, the number of subsidiaries and their relationship with each other and with their parent company, may cause further complications. However, it is clear that the Court was aware of these problems and intended the test to be applied sensitively, with due regard to its limitations. In the case of the banana market, the Court was of the opinion that a satisfactory estimate could have been arrived at.

The Commission in its *United Brands* Decision[19] sought to avoid the pitfalls of comparing production costs and prices by offering indirect evidence of unfair pricing. This took the form of comparisons between the prices charged by UBC for "Chiquitas" destined, respectively, for the Irish and Continental markets, between UBC's prices for "Chiquitas" and the prices of other branded bananas of similar quality and between the prices of "Chiquitas" and UBC's unbranded bananas. The Court took the Commission to task for not having at least required UBC to give particulars of its production costs, but did not dispute the relevance of the indicators actually referred to in the Decision: it was the lack of supporting evidence which led to the annulment of this head of abuse.[20]

From *United Brands* it seems that, in seeking to establish an abuse in the form of unfairly high prices, the Commission should normally proceed by way of an analysis of the cost structure of the undertaking concerned. However, other methods of proving unfairness will continue to be acceptable, if the Court is satisfied of their appropriateness in the specific circumstances of the case.[21] For example, in *Bodson*[22] the Court noted that since more than 30,000 communes in France had not passed the relevant funeral services over to undertakings, there would be comparisons available to provide a basis for assessing whether the prices charged by the concession holders were indeed excessive.[23]

(b) *Excessively low prices exacted by dominant buyers.* A dominant buyer may be successful in obtaining the reduction of prices to an unreasonable extent. Possible objections are that the profitability of the supplier, and his capacity to expand production or improve his product, may be jeopardised; and that other operators at the same market level as the buyer may be put at a competitive disadvantage, for reasons which have nothing to do with the buyer's efficiency.

---

[19] *Loc. cit.* note 28, *supra.*
[20] See the reasoning of the Court at [1978] E.C.R. pp. 299–303.
[21] The Court did not question the Commission's finding in *General Motors Continental* that the fee for conformity inspections of parallel imports from other European countries was excessive, while holding on other grounds that no abuse had been committed: see Case 26/75, *loc. cit.* note 51, *supra.* See also the *BL* Dec. *loc. cit.* note 51, *supra.*
[22] *Supra*, note 53.
[23] See also Case 395/87, *Ministère Public* v. *Tournier* [1989] E.C.R. 2521 and Cases 110/88 and 241–242/88, *Lucazeau* v. *SACEM* [1989] E.C.R. 2811 at paras. 38 and 25 respectively of the Court's judgments.

The proceedings in *CICCE* v. *Commission*[24] concerned a complaint that television companies in France would only pay very low fees for broadcasting films originally made for the cinema. The Commission, while accepting that a dominant purchaser may commit an abuse within the meaning of Article 86 by imposing an unfair price for a service, rejected the complaint on account of its generality. The reasonableness of the broadcasting fee could, in the view of the Commission, be judged only in respect of the value of individual films, which was very variable.[25]

(c) *Predatory price cutting.* A dominant seller may adopt a tactic of pricing his goods very low, or even below cost, in order to drive out of business competitors with more limited resources who cannot for long sustain the losses occasioned by matching the terms he is offering. Consumers, of course, benefit from price reductions in the short run but risk finding themselves even more at the mercy of the dominant undertaking after it has captured a larger share of the market.

The application of Article 86 to predatory price cutting is illustrated by the *AKZO* litigation. AKZO is the EEC's major supplier of a chemical substance, benzoyle peroxide, which is used in the manufacture of plastics and in the blanching of flour.[26] The Commission found that, in order to deter ECS, a small competitor in the market in flour additives, from expanding its business into the market in organic peroxides for plastics, AKZO had first threatened and later implemented a campaign of price cuts aimed at important customers of ECS in the former market. If successful, the campaign would not only have eliminated ECS as a competitor in the supply of organic peroxides; it would also have discouraged other potential challenges to AKZO's established position. AKZO's appeal[27] against the Commission's decision was dismissed.[28] The Court observed[29]:

"Prices lower than the average variable costs by which a dominant undertaking seeks to eliminate a competitor must be regarded as an abuse. A dominant undertaking has no interest in offering such prices except to eliminate its competitors in order then to raise its prices again on the basis of its monopolistic position, since every sale involves it in a loss, namely all the fixed costs and at least a part of the variable costs relating to the unit produced.

Moreover, prices less than the average total costs, which include fixed costs and variable costs, but greater than the average variable

---

[24] Case 298/83, *Comité des Industries Cinématographiques des Communantés Européennes* v. *Commission* [1985] E.C.R. 1105. The action was brought in respect of the Commission's Dec. not to proceed with the complaint lodged by the CICCE.
[25] The Court held that in the circumstances the Commission had been justified in not taking the matter further.
[26] AKZO estimated its share of the relevant market as 50 per cent. or more. It was equivalent to those of all the remaining producers together.
[27] Case C–62/86, judgment of July 3, 1991 (not yet reported).
[28] Although the fine was reduced for several reasons, and allegations of discrimination were held to be unfounded.
[29] Taken from bulletin version of judgment issued in Proceedings of the Court of Justice No. 17/91.

costs must be regarded as an abuse where they are fixed as part of a plan to eliminate a competitor. Such prices can remove from the market undertakings which are perhaps as effective as the dominant undertaking but because of their lesser financial capacity are unable to resist the competition to which they are subject."

(ii) *Discriminatory prices*

A dominant undertaking may fall foul of Article 86 by charging different prices in respect of equivalent transactions without objective justification. If the customers concerned are "trading parties," *i.e.* the purchase is made for the purposes of a economic activity in which they are engaged, the objectionable feature of such a pricing policy is found in the competitive disadvantage suffered by those called upon to pay the higher prices, and the case falls precisely within Article 86(*c*). However, even in transactions with ultimate consumers, discriminatory pricing may be abusive, if it is incompatible with any aims of the Treaty.

An abuse may take the form of discriminating between customers within the same market or of following different pricing policies on different markets, although in the latter case objective justification may be more readily available. It should be noted that the customers concerned need not be in competition with each other: the one paying the higher price suffers a "competitive disadvantage" simply because he is, to that extent, less well equipped to meet competition, whichever quarter it may come from.

The *United Brands* case highlighted the particular problem of how far it is permissible for dominant undertakings to adapt their pricing policies to take account of the diversity of marketing conditions in the various Member States.[30] For instance, there may be significant disparities in rates of taxation, freight charges or the wages paid to workers for assembling or finishing the product, which may influence costs; or in other factors relevant to a marketing strategy, such as consumer preferences or the intensity of competition. In addition, price differences may result from government action over which a supplier has no control, for example, the alteration of exchange rates or the imposition of a price freeze. Some convergence of these conditions may be expected as the common market develops, but markets within the Community are bound to retain a degree of territorial specificity (although not necessarily along national lines) due, for example, to climate, geography and cultural differences.

UBC had put forward, as objective justification for its policy of charging different prices for its bananas, depending on the Member State where the ripened fruit was to be sold, the continuing division of the market for bananas along national lines. Each of the national markets had its own internal characteristics, and accordingly different price levels; and the prices to the ripener/distributors in a given week were intended to reflect as accurately as possible the prices which ripened bananas were expected to

---

[30] Case 27/76 [1978] E.C.R., pp. 294 *et seq.* The Commission found that UBC's differential pricing policy amounted to a separate head of abuse, and this part of the Dec. was upheld by the Court of Justice.

fetch on the individual markets during the following week. The defect which the European Court found in this argument was that UBC did not operate directly on the retail markets. It was not, therefore, entitled to take account of market pressures which only made themselves felt at the retail stage.

The view of the European Court is evidently that a dominant undertaking may charge different prices for the same product in different Member States, where this represents to real market pressures operating on it. For instance, there would have been no objection to UBC's adopting lower prices in relation to a certain national market where a price war was raging, if pressure to do so had been exerted by the relevant ripener/distributors in the course of a genuine bargaining process. On the other hand, there may be a case of abusive discrimination if the aim of the undertaking is simply to obtain maximum profits by setting its prices at the highest level which each of the markets will bear, especially since, in order for this policy to be effective, measures will probably be necessary to maintain the isolation of the markets from each other.[31]

(iii) *Unfair trading conditions*

Apart from determining the level of prices, a dominant undertaking may be able to compel its trading partners to accept other terms which are unreasonably onerous.

For instance, a number of the conditions of membership of the German copyright society, GEMA, were condemned by the Commission as unfair[32]; and subsequently in *BRT* v. *SABAM*[33] which arose out of proceedings involving GEMA's sister society in Belgium, the European Court was asked whether it might be abusive for such a body, occupying a dominant position, to demand a global assignment of copyrights, without making any distinction between specific categories of rights, and one which would apply to both present and future rights. The Court's answer was that a balance must be struck between allowing authors, composers and publishers maximum freedom, and enabling the society to manage their rights effectively. The crucial issue was whether the conditions imposed by a copyright society were absolutely necessary to enable it to carry out its task. If not, the encroachment on members' freedom could constitute an abuse.

An example of the use of purchasing power to impose unfair conditions on a seller was provided by the tender which the Commission examined in *Eurofima*.[34] The term to which the Commission took exception would have required the manufacturers of the rolling stock to cede to the purchasing organisation an unlimited right to the use of patents resulting from the development, including a right to grant licences under future patents to third parties, without consulting the manufacturers or paying compensation. The contract was revised so as to limit the use of the right to Eurofima's own

---

[31] In *United Brands* the clause prohibiting the resale of green bananas was capable of having such an effect, since the exportation of ripened bananas would be impracticable.
[32] *Loc. cit.* note 60, *supra.*
[33] Case 127/73 [1974] E.C.R. 313; [1974] 2 C.M.L.R. 238.
[34] *Loc. cit.* note 18, p. 440, *supra.*

needs. The granting of licences to third parties was to require the consent of the manufacturers, and further payment.

(iv) *Exclusive rights of supply*

Purchasers may become bound to a particular supplier either by accepting a direct obligation to obtain all or most of their requirements of goods of a certain description from him[35] or through the pressure exerted by "loyalty" or "target" discounts.

A loyalty discount[36] consists of a reduction in the price of a product which is granted on condition that the purchaser obtain a specified proportion (normally very high) of his requirements of the product from the supplier granting the discount. The usual arrangement will be for the discount to be paid as a rebate at the end of, say, a year, and entitlement will be lost in respect of the whole period, if the limit agreed for procurements from third parties is exceeded. This means that a competing supplier will have to pitch his offer at a level that takes into account not only the rebate on the particular quantity ordered but also the higher price the customer will have to pay for the remainder of the goods purchased from the first supplier.[37]

In the case of a target discount the price reduction is conditional on the purchasing of an agreed quantity of products from the supplier in question during the reference period. The target is not linked to any specific proportion of the customer's requirements but is likely in practice to be set at a level that will lead to the loss of the discount if substantial purchases are made from third parties. To win orders from the customer, therefore, competing suppliers must, again, be prepared to cover that loss.[38]

Loyalty and target discounts are to be distinguished from "quantity" discounts, where the reduction in the price is determined by the actual volume of goods purchased from the supplier. Quantity discounts are not considered anti-competitive, because of the correlation between cost savings to the supplier and the lower price paid by the purchaser.[39]

On the other hand, an exclusive or preferential right of supply, whether it operates directly or through a discount system, is very likely to infringe Article 86 if the supplier enjoys a dominant position on the market in question. Such arrangements, the European Court has said,[40] are incompatible with the objective of undistorted competition because, except in circumstances of the kind that might lead to a grant of exemption under Article 85(3), they have no economic justification but are designed to deprive the customer of any choice of his sources of supply, or at least to restrict his choice, and to deny other producers access to the market. The effect will be further to strengthen the position of the dominant supplier.

---

[35] On the application of Art. 85 to exclusive supply agreements, see Chap. 14, *supra*.
[36] Also known as a "fidelity" discount.
[37] See the analysis of loyalty discounts in Case 85/76, *Hoffmann-La Roche* v. *Commission* [1979] E.C.R. at pp. 539–541.
[38] See the analysis of target discounts in Case 322/81, *Michelin* v. *Commission* [1983] E.C.R. at pp. 3514–3515.
[39] Case 85/76, *Hoffmann-La Roche* v. *Commission* [1979] E.C.R. at p. 540.
[40] *Ibid.*

Another possible objection, when loyalty or target discounts are involved, is that charging two customers different net prices for the same quantity of goods, because of purchases made or not made on other occasions, amounts to discrimination contrary to Article 86(c).

In *Hoffmann-La Roche* the Commission condemned the provisions giving Roche a more or less exclusive right of supply, usually in combination with loyalty rebates, which were contained in agreements with a number of important bulk purchasers of vitamins. Under the so-called "English clause" which was generally included in the agreements, customers were required to notify Roche if they received more favourable offers from other manufacturers; and if Roche then chose not to match the offers, these could be accepted without the loss of any rebate entitlement. However, the Commission regarded the clause as mitigating the exclusive supply system only slightly, because it left the decision to Roche whether the customer in question should be free to purchase from the third party; and anyway, the clause was usually restricted to offers coming from "reputable" manufacturers in the customer's own territory, and was therefore of limited effect. The Court upheld the decision of the Commission as to the abusive nature of the contractual provisions in question.[41]

The *Michelin* case illustrates the application of Article 86 to a system of target discounts. An "annual variable discount," based on the previous year's turnover in Michelin tyres of all types, and a sales target for heavy vehicle tyres were fixed at the beginning of each year by discussion between a commercial representative of NBIM and individual dealers. The system allowed a proportion of the discount to be paid as an advance but the full amount would only be rebated if the sales target for the year was reached. The European Court found that the variation dependent on the attainment of the target was a mere 0.2 to 0.4 per cent. Nevertheless, it was held, even quite a slight variation could exert significant pressure on a dealer towards the end of a relatively long reference period, when the chance of earning the discount might turn on a single order. Other factors tending to accentuate the pressure on the dealers were: the difference between NBIM's market share and those of its main competitors, which made it hard for the latter to offer inducements sufficient to compensate dealers risking the loss of the target discount; the lack of transparency of the discount system as a whole and the fact that particular traders' discounts and sales targets were never confirmed by the company in writing, which left them in a state of uncertainty; and the existence of a network of NBIM representatives to remind dealers of their situation and encourage them to place further orders. The result was "to prevent dealers from being able to select freely at any time in the light of the market situation the most favourable of the offers made by the various competitors and to change supplier without suffering

---

[41] [1979] E.C.R. at pp. 544–546. See also *Sugar* where SZV was found guilty of an abuse for having inserted into its sales contracts a clause allowing an annual rebate of 0.30 Deutsche Marks per 100 kg to customers who had purchased exclusively from members of SZV: Joined Cases 40–48, 50, 54 to 65, 111, 113 and 114/73, *Suiker Unie and Others* v. *Commission*, *loc. cit.* note 7, p. 439, *supra.*

any appreciable economic disadvantage."[42] That loss of independence on the part of the dealers could not be justified by the interest of NBIM in selling more tyres and planning its production more evenly. The discount system, therefore, amounted to an abuse of NBIM's dominant position on the Dutch market.

(v) *Restrictions on distribution*

Various types of obligation which suppliers commonly impose on the distributors of their products have already been discussed in connection with Article 85.[43] If the supplier concerned is a dominant undertaking, it may also be necessary to consider whether the obligations fall within the purview of Article 86.[44]

Export bans and other devices for restricting the distribution of goods to a certain geographical area are liable to be considered serious infringements of Article 86, as of Article 85. For instance, in *Sugar*[45] the Court upheld the Commission's finding that the Belgian producer RT had abused its dominant position by bringing pressure to bear on sugar dealers in Belgium to fall in with its export policy in relation to the Netherlands and the western part of the Federal Republic. The pressure took the form of threatening to cut off supplies of sugar; and the policy, that of selling sugar only to the Dutch and German producers themselves, or selling for specified purposes, for example, milk processing but not sweet manufacture. In the Court's view, the behaviour of RT in restricting the outlets of the dealers and indirectly of ulterior purchasers fell within the terms of Article 86(*b*). Similarly, in *United Brands*[46] the prohibition against the resale of green bananas which UBC imposed on its ripener/distributors was condemned as limiting markets to the prejudice of consumers. Given the perishable nature of ripened bananas, the clause had the effect, *inter alia*, of partitioning national markets.

(vi) *Refusal to deal*

There is a well developed case law on the circumstances in which a refusal by a dominant undertaking to deal, in the ordinary course of its business, with another undertaking—especially to supply goods or services or to supply them in the desired quantity—may amount to an abuse. Such conduct is liable to conflict with the objective of undistorted competition in Article 3(*f*), and more particularly to fall within the terms of Article 86(*b*) and (*c*), involving the limitation of markets and discrimination.[47] Whether it does so may require a nuanced decision, taking account of, *inter alia*, the relationship between the parties, the nature of the order which has been refused, the effect of the refusal and reasons for the refusal.

The earliest case on refusal to deal was *Commercial Solvents*

---

[42] Case 322/81, *Michelin* v. *Commission* [1983] E.C.R. at p. 3518.
[43] See Chap. 14, *supra*.
[44] See Case 126/80, *Salonia* v. *Poidomani* [1981] E.C.R. 1563.
[45] Joined Cases 40–48, 50, 54 to 56, 111, 113 and 114/73, *loc. cit.* note 7, p. 439, *supra*.
[46] Case 27/76 [1978] E.C.R., pp. 285 *et seq.*
[47] Case 27/76 [1978] E.C.R. at p. 292.

Corporation.[48] The refusal from the end of 1970 to supply Zoja with aminobutanol required for the manufacture of the derivative, ethambutol, was the result of a policy decision by the CSC Group to manufacture and sell the derivative on its own account. Upholding the Decision of the Commission that CSC had been guilty of an abuse, the Court said:

> "... an undertaking being in a dominant position as regards the production of raw material and therefore able to control the supply to manufacturers of derivatives, cannot, just because it decides to start manufacturing these derivatives (in competition with its former customers) act in such a way as to eliminate their competition which in the case in question, would amount to eliminating one of the principal manufacturers of ethambutol in the common market."[49]

Three main points emerge from this passage. In the first place, Zoja was an established customer of CSC. Admittedly, at the beginning of 1970 Zoja had cancelled its orders under the current supply contract, but the Court regarded this as irrelevant because CSC had anyway decided to cut off the supplies once deliveries under the contract had been completed. Secondly, the effect of withholding supplies of the raw material was likely to be serious, namely the elimination of a major producer from the market for the derivative. Thirdly, the reason for driving Zoja out of the market was to smooth CSC's own entry. The Court made it clear that the conduct in question could not be justified as a legitimate competitive tactic.

The *United Brands* judgment contains an even more forthright condemnation of refusal to supply:

> "... it is advisable to assert positively from the outset that an undertaking in a dominant position for the purpose of marketing a product—which cashes in on the reputation of a brand name known to and valued by the consumers—cannot stop supplying a long standing customer who abides by regular commercial practice, if the orders placed by that customer are in no way out of the ordinary."[50]

The victim was the Danish ripener/distributor, Olesen, which UBC has refused to supply with "Chiquitas" after it had taken part in a sales campaign mounted by the rival supplier, Castle and Cooke. That collaboration was not regarded by the Court as justifying the refusal. Even a dominant undertaking may act in defence of its commercial interests, but such action must be reasonable and proportional to the threat, which that taken against Olesen had not been.

Refusal to supply a service may be illustrated by the *Tele-marketing* case.[51] "Tele-sales" or "tele-marketing" is a technique whereby an advertisement in the media includes a telephone number which the public are invited to call in

---

[48] Joined Cases 6 and 7/73, *loc. cit.* note 39, *supra.*
[49] [1974] E.C.R. at pp. 250–251.
[50] [1978] E.C.R. at p. 292.
[51] Case 311/84, *loc. cit.* note 7, p. 439, *supra.* For another example, see Case 7/82, *GVL* v. *Commission, loc. cit.* note 60, *supra.*

order to obtain further information or to respond in some other way. The proceedings arose from the fact that the company which operates the RTL television station in Luxembourg would only sell advertising time for telephone marketing if the number used was that of an agency, Information Publicité, which belonged to the same group.[52] Such behaviour, it was held, was tantamount to a refusal to provide the services of a broadcasting station to other tele-marketing undertakings. If the purpose of the refusal were to reserve the downstream market in tele-sales operations for an affiliated agency, and the other conditions of Article 86 were satisfied, there would be an infringement of the Article analogous to that in *Commercial Solvents Corporation*.

The apparent importance of distinguishing carefully between different categories of customer was highlighted by the *BP*[53] judgment, in which the Court annulled the Decision of the Commission that BP had abused the dominant position which it enjoyed in relation to its Dutch customers during the oil supply crisis of November 1973 to March 1974 by reducing deliveries of motor spirit to a particular customer, ABG, more drastically than to others. The Court found that BP had given notice of the termination of its supply contract with ABG in November 1972, and that at the time when the crisis broke, ABG's relationship with BP, so far as concerned supplies of motor spirit, was that of a casual customer. BP could not, therefore, be blamed for treating ABG less favourably than its regular customers, since the latter would have received a substantially smaller quantity than they were entitled to expect, if a standard rate of reduction had been applied.[54]

It might be assumed from these cases that a pre-existing relationship between the parties is required before a later refusal to deal can constitute an abuse. Certainly, a refusal by a dominant undertaking to supply a regular customer placing an unexceptional order will amount to an abuse unless the refusal can be objectively justified. However, there is some evidence from cases involving intellectual property that the inroads made by Article 86 into the commercial choices available to dominant firms may go even further.

At one point it seemed clear that the Court believed that a refusal to grant a licence of an intellectual property right could not *per se* amount to abusive behaviour. This was the view expressed in the context of registered designs in *Volvo*.[55] But it is difficult to reconcile this stance with the position adopted more recently by the Court of First Instance in the television listings cases. It held that the companies in question used their copyright in listings produced as part of the activity of broadcasting in order to secure a monopoly in the derivative market of weekly television guides. This, according to the Court of First Instance, went beyond the essential function of copyright.[56] If there

---

[52] The case came to the Court of Justice by way of a reference for a preliminary ruling under Art. 177. The Court was, therefore, able to rule only in general terms.

[53] Case 77/77, *loc. cit.* note 57, *supra.*

[54] As Adv.-Gen. Warner pointed out, a legal and moral right to security of supplies is the counterpart, for a contractual customer, of his loss of freedom to seek the best available bargain at a given moment, and the loyalty of regular, though non-contractual, customers also merits special consideration: [1978] E.C.R. at p. 538.

[55] Case 238/87, *AB Volvo* v. *Erik Veng (UK)* [1988] E.C.R. 6211. See also Case 53/87, *Maxicar* v. *Renault* [1988] E.C.R. 6039.

[56] Discussed further in Chap. 20 below.

is any analogy to be drawn between a refusal to supply a customer with a product and a refusal to issue intellectual property licences, then the notion of any need to have a pre-existing relationship with the "victim" disappears.

The best explanation of this change, if it is confirmed, is perhaps in terms of the objectives to be served. Putting the focus on pre-existing relationships tends to emphasise the unfairness of behaviour in the context of the bargaining relationship between abuser and abused. On the other hand, if market integration is the uppermost consideration, the character of abuse does not require unfairness to exist, only anti-competitiveness. The climate induced by the pursuit of the "1992" programme may therefore have fed the latter approach.

(vii) *Acquisition of exclusive access to new technology*

The special responsibilities attaching to dominant undertakings inhibit their freedom to reinforce market strength. Acquisition of competitors has been held to fall foul of Article 86[57]; so too may the purchase of intellectual property rights which seal off or delay the entry of competitors into the market. This issue was confronted in *Tetra Pak*.[58]

Tetra Pak acquired a group which held an exclusive patent licence for new and important technology relating to the sterilisation of milk cartons. This was held to be an abuse of Tetra Pak's existing dominance in the market for liquid food packaging. In its Decision, the Commission observed that the right to use the patented technology was "alone capable of giving an undertaking the means of competing effectively with [Tetra Pak]." The Court of First Instance[59] rejected Tetra Pak's appeal. Although an exclusive licence was not *per se* an abuse, the circumstances surrounding the acquisition of it in this case constituted an unlawful barrier to entry. As discussed elsewhere,[60] the Court of First Instance emphasised that the fact that the licence fell within block exemption 2349/84 for the purposes of Article 85(3) did not preclude the application of Article 86 to its subsequent acquisition by Tetra Pak.

(viii) *Tying*

The example in Article 86(*d*) covers all kinds of "tying" arrangements, where a person is required to accept, as a condition of entering into a contract, "supplementary obligations which, by their nature or according to commercial usage, have no connection with the subject of such contracts." For instance, the purchase of a freezer may entail an obligation to receive monthly packages of frozen food for the first year of ownership (product tied to product)[61]; or the purchase of a heating system, the obligation to enter into a five-year service contract (product tied to service). On the other hand,

---

[57] See Chap. 17, *infra*.
[58] O.J. 1988 L317/47.
[59] Case T–51/89, *Tetra Pak Rausing SA* v. *Commission* [1991] 4 C.M.L.R. 334.
[60] See Chap. 20, *infra*.
[61] See also the allegations of "memory bundling" and "software bundling" in the Commission's Statement of Objections against IBM, which are summarised in the account of the settlement of the case: Comp.Rep. 1984, point 94.

the inclusion of a meal in the price of an airline ticket has been cited[62] as a possible example of tying sanctioned by commercial usage.

The main objection to tying is that it enables a dominant position on market A to be used in order to gain a competitive advantage on market B, by reducing the outlets for third parties operating on that market. It may also be directly oppressive to consumers on market A. Thus, in *Hilti*,[63] the Court of First Instance affirmed the Commission's decision that it was an abuse for Hilti to require users of its patented nail cartridges to buy nails from them as well. The arguments raised by Hilti concerning safety standards and the protection of users against injury were not accepted as sufficient to provide objective justification for the conduct.

(ix) *Mergers*

The impression that may have originally been given by Article 86 that it only applied to behaviour was sharply changed by the Court's ruling in *Continental Can* that the acquisition of a competitor was capable of constituting an abuse. The advent in 1990 of a Community framework for the regulation of mergers has significant implications for the future application of Article 86 in this context. These issues are treated more fully in Chapter 17, *infra*.

Effect on trade between Member States

An abuse of a dominant position only attracts the prohibition in Article 86 if it is capable of affecting trade between Member States.

As we have seen, the same condition applies under Article 85, and the general principles relating to its operation were discussed in Chapter 14, *supra*,[64] including those established in cases which have arisen under Article 86.[65] It was noted, in particular, that the Court of Justice considers the purpose of the condition to be that of defining the boundary between the EEC rules on competition and the competition laws of Member States. The test is whether the agreement or practice in question constitutes a threat to freedom of trade between Member States in a way that might harm the attainment of the objectives of a single Member State. The Court has also made clear that the condition may be satisfied in different ways: through the diversion of the flow of goods or services from its normal channels; or through the modification of the structure of competition within the common market.

The application of the condition in the context of Article 86 was substantially developed in *Hugin*.[66] The abuse found by the Commission

---

[62] By Siragusa in Van Damme, *op. cit.* note 3, p. 438, *supra* at p. 412.
[63] Case T–30/89, *Hilti AG* v. *Commission* [1992] 4 C.M.L.R. 16.
[64] At p. 413.
[65] See, in particular, Joined Cases 6 and 7/73, *Commercial Solvents Corporation*, *loc. cit.* note 39, p. 404, *supra*; Case 22/78, *Hugin*, *loc. cit.* note 12, p. 440, *supra*; Case 22/79, *Greenwich Film Production* v. *SACEM* [1979] E.C.R. 3275.
[66] Case 22/78, *loc. cit.* note. 35, p. 445, *supra*. See the discussion at [1979] E.C.R., pp. 1898–1901.

against the Swedish manufacturer of cash registers, Hugin, was that it had refused to supply spare parts for its machines to a London firm, Liptons, and had prohibited its subsidiaries and distributors in the common market from selling spare parts outside its distribution network. The business of Liptons was the maintenance and repair of cash registers and the renting-out or sale of reconditioned machines. The supply of spare parts from Sweden to the United Kingdom would not entail trade between Member States, but there were two ways in which the condition might have been satisfied. One was that the withholding of the parts might have interfered with the commercial activities of Liptons in other Member States. However, the Court of Justice was satisfied that the firm had never extended its activities outside the United Kingdom; indeed, its business was of a kind that could only be carried on profitably within a local area. The second possibility was that Hugin's policy of not supplying spare parts outside its distribution network restricted intra-Community trade in the parts. This, too, was rejected. The Court pointed out that the value of the articles was small and that anyone needing a part which the local Hugin subsidiary could not supply would normally address its request directly to the parent company. Hugin had not, therefore, been guilty of diverting trade from channels it would otherwise have followed. The Court regarded cases like that of Liptons, which had attempted to obtain Hugin spare parts in other Member States, as exceptional and, therefore, it seems, covered by the *de minimis* principle.[67]

The effect on trade was also important in the *Bodson* case.[68] Both the French Government and the Commission took the view that the concessions relating to the provision of local funeral services did not affect trade between Member States. The only goods involved were coffins and a monopoly only existed in 14 per cent. of the communes in France. In two-thirds of these the concession was held by a single group of undertakings. This same group provided funeral services in other Member States, especially the Netherlands, United Kingdom and Germany. In its reply to the reference under Article 177 by the Cour de Cassation, the Court observed that the inter-state trade requirement demanded account to be taken of the consequences for the effective competitive structure in the common market. With regard to services, the Court attached particular importance to the risk of partitioning markets. It therefore left it to the national court to consider whether the conduct of the concessionaires affected the importation of goods from other Member States or the possibility of competing undertakings established in other Member States to provide services in the original State.

---

[67] See Case 56/65, *La Technique Minière* v. *Maschinenbau Ulm* [1966] E.C.R. 235; [1966] C.M.L.R. 357; Case 5/69, *Volk* v. *Vervaecke* [1969] E.C.R. 295; [1969] C.M.L.R. 273. See also the discussion of the principle in Chap. 14, *supra*.
[68] See note 53, p. 448, *supra*.

CHAPTER 16

APPLICATION OF ARTICLES 85 AND 86

Introduction

Articles 87 to 89 EEC contain provisions relating to the implementation of the substantive rules on competition in Article 85 and Article 86. Under Article 87 the Council is empowered to enact "any appropriate regulations or directives" for this purpose. Pending the exercise by the Council of its powers under Article 87, a transitional regime is provided by Articles 88 and 89. The task of applying the competition rules in individual cases, including the granting of exemption under Article 85(3), is given by Article 88 to "the authorities in Member States." The Commission is required under Article 89 to investigate cases of suspected infringement and, where it finds an infringement has occurred, to propose measures for bringing it to an end. If this does not produce the desired result, the Commission must record the infringement in a reasoned decision, which may be published; and it may authorise Member States to take the steps needed to remedy the situation. However, it has no powers that can be used directly against offending undertakings.

The principal measure enacted by the Council under Article 87 is Regulation 17, which came into force on March 13, 1962.[1] The Regulation has been amended from time to time[2] but the legal machinery established by it remains substantially in place. This has been supplemented by further Council regulations[3] and by regulations adopted by the Commission under delegated powers.[4] On its own terms Regulation 17 is of general application but the transport sector was removed from its scope by Regulation 141.[5] Special competition measures for transport and merger control have now been put in place.[6]

The present chapter is concerned mainly with the system for the administration of the EEC rules on competition developed on the basis of Regulation 17. Under this system the Commission wields real executive powers, subject to judicial control by the Court of Justice and the Court of First Instance. We examine the central functions of the Commission in the machinery and the ancillary rôle reserved for national competition authorities. We also discuss briefly the application of the competition rules,

---

[1] J.O. 1962, 204; O.J. 1959–62, 87.
[2] Most recently by the 1985 Act of Accession of the Kingdom of Spain and the Portuguese Republic.
[3] See, in particular, those empowering the Commission to adopt block exemption regs., Chap. 14, *supra*.
[4] Notably Reg. 99/63 on the hearings provided for in Art. 19(1) and (2) of Reg. 17: (J.O. 1963 2268; O.J. 1963–64, 47).
[5] J.O. 1962, 2751.
[6] See notes 10–13 p. 379, Chap. 13, *supra*.

in so far as they are directly effective, by the ordinary courts in the Member States.[7]

First steps

Proceedings for the application of Article 85 or Article 86 may be started by the Commission on its own initiative[8] or in response to an application for negative clearance[9] and/or the notification of an agreement[10] or to a complaint.[11]

(i) *Action by the Commission*

Where the Commission itself takes the initiative in a competition matter it is said to act *ex officio*. It may be prompted to do so by various factors for example newspaper reports, the results of studies or unofficial representations.

(ii) *Action by the parties to a possible infringement*

A feature of Regulation 17 is the encouragement given to the parties to a possible infringement of the competition rules to bring the matter themselves to the attention of the Commission, through the negative clearance and notification procedures.

The purpose of an application for negative clearance is to enable undertakings to ascertain whether the Commission considers any aspects of an agreement to which they are party, or of their business conduct, to fall within Article 85(1) or Article 86.[12] A formal grant of clearance consists of a decision by the Commission certifying that, on the basis of the facts in its possession, there are no grounds under those provisions for action to be taken in respect of the agreement or conduct in question. An application will only have point where infringement of Article 85 or Article 86 seems a genuine possibility. Undertakings that feel any doubts about an agreement should consider, in particular, whether it may be covered by a block exemption regulation or by one of the Commission's Notices.

With the adoption of Regulation 17 the national competition authorities lost their transitional power under Article 88 to declare the prohibition in Article 85(1) inapplicable to agreements which fulfil the criteria of Article 85(3). Article 9(1) of the Regulation confers that power exclusively upon the Commission. Notification of an agreement to the Commission is made for the purpose of seeking exemption, either by an individual grant or under the opposition procedure of a block exemption regulation.[13] Where there are

---

[7] The subject-matter of this chapter is covered in greater depth by Kerse in his excellent treatise, *EEC Antitrust Procedure* (2nd ed. 1987).
[8] Reg. 17, Art. 3(1).
[9] Reg. 17, Art. 2. See *infra*.
[10] Reg. 17, Arts. 4(1) and 5(1). See *infra*.
[11] Reg. 17, Art. 3(1) and (2).
[12] See the Complementary Note to Commission Reg. 2526/85, O.J. 1985 L240/1 at p. 6. The Reg. amended Reg. 27 on the form to be used in applying for negative clearance or notifying an agreement (see *infra*).
[13] *Ibid* at p. 7. On the opposition procedure, see Chap. 14, *supra*.

grounds for believing that an agreement may be caught by Article 85(1), Regulation 17 provides powerful incentives for the parties to notify punctually.

In the first place, Article 4(1) of the Regulation lays down the general rule that, until agreements have been notified to the Commission, they cannot be the subject of a decision in application of Article 85(3). This is so, even if the agreement in question manifestly satisfies the criteria of exemption in the paragraph. Certain categories of agreements are, however, excused notification, as a matter of administrative convenience, because they pose no very serious threat to competition and are considered particularly likely to qualify for exemption.[14] The list, which is to be found in Article 4(2), comprises: (1) agreements between parties from the same Member State which do not relate either to imports or to exports between Member States, for example a tied house agreement with a local brewery[15]; (2) agreements between two parties which *only*: (a) restrict the freedom of one party to determine the prices or conditions of business on which goods obtained from the other party may be resold; or (b) impose restrictions on the exercise of the rights of an assignee or user of industrial property rights or of know-how[16]; (3) agreements which have as their *sole* object: (a) the development or uniform application of standards or types; or (b) joint research and development; or (c) specialisation in the manufacture of products including agreements necessary for the achievement thereof, subject to a market share threshold of 15 per cent. and an aggregate turnover threshold of 200 million units of account. The categories in Article 4(2) are narrowly drawn and the paragraph has been largely superseded by the block exemption Regulations[17] in whose provisions, it has been pointed out, there lies greater legal security.[18]

Secondly, the date of notification determines how far a grant of exemption may be made retrospective. For this purpose Regulation 17 draws a distinction between agreements which have been entered into since the date when it came into force, known as "new agreements," and agreements then already in existence, known as "old agreements." Under Article 6(1) in the case of new agreements exemption cannot be granted from a date earlier than that of notification. In respect of any period which may have elapsed

---

[14] Case 63/75, *Fonderies Roubaix-Wattrelos* v. *Fonderies A. Roux* [1976] E.C.R. 111; [1976] 1 C.M.L.R. 538.

[15] See Case 43/69, *Bilger* v. *Jehle* [1970] E.C.R. 127; [1974] 1 C.M.L.R. 382. The Court said in that case that the phrase "relate to imports or exports" was narrower than the phrase "affect trade between Member States" in Art. 85(1). See also Case 63/75, *Fonderies Roubaix-Wattrelos* v. *Fonderies A. Roux, loc. cit.* note 14, *supra*, where it was held that agreements between undertakings from the same Member State granting exclusive sales concessions in that State need not be regarded as relating to imports within the meaning of Art. 4(2)(1) merely because the goods in question came originally from another Member State. *Cf.* Joined Cases 209–215 and 218/78, *Van Landewyck* v. *Commission* [1980] E.C.R. 3125; [1981] 3 C.M.L.R. 134; Joined Cases 96–102, 104, 105, 108 and 110/82, *IAZ* v. *Commission* [1983] E.C.R. 3369; [1984] 3 C.M.L.R. 276.

[16] Art. 4(2)(2)(*b*) has been very strictly construed by the Commission: see *Re. Vaessen/Moris* 1979 O.J. L19/32; [1970] 1 C.M.L.R. 511. On patent licensing agreements, see Chap. 20, *infra*.

[17] See Chap. 14, *supra*.

[18] By Kerse, *op. cit.* note 7, *supra* at pp. 50–51.

between its making and notification, a new agreement caught by Article 85(1) is irretrievably void pursuant to Article 85(2). Old agreements, on the other hand, benefit from transitional arrangements. If notified by the dates specified in Article 5(1) of Regulation 17,[19] they are eligible for exemption extending back to the date when Article 85(1) first applied to them. In addition, if there are clauses in a duly notified old agreement which are ineligible for exemption, the Commission has power under Article 7(1) to grant retrospective validation to the agreement as a whole, provided that the offending clauses are amended or abandoned for the future. Similar arrangements have been made to cater for agreements brought within the scope of the competition rules as a result of successive enlargements of the Community ("accession agreements").[20] The period of grace for the notification of such agreements is six months from the date of accession.[21]

Thirdly, where activity takes place under an agreement which has been notified, the parties are protected by Article 15(5) of Regulation 17 against the imposition of fines for the infringement of Article 85. However, the Commission may put an end to that immunity by informing the parties that, in the light of a preliminary examination, it has formed the view that Article 85(1) applies to the agreement and exemption under Article 85(3) is not justified.[22] The intimation of such an assessment is an act reviewable under Article 173, since it alters the legal position of the parties to the agreement.[23]

A final incentive to notify, which applies only to old agreements, is found in the doctrine of provisional validity. We return to the topic of provisional validity in the section dealing with the application of the EEC competition rules in the national courts.

For Article 86 there is, of course, no equivalent to the procedure for notifying agreements with a view to obtaining exemption under Article 85(3).

A special form, known as Form A/B, has been provided for applications for negative clearance in respect of Article 85(1) and for notifications,[24] and its use is compulsory.[25] There is no such requirement in the cases of applications for negative clearance in respect of Article 86. In all cases the relevant facts must be fully and accurately disclosed to the Commission.[26] A decision granting negative clearance on the basis of incomplete or incorrect information could be without effect, and one granting exemption could be revoked. The Commission also has power under Article 15(1)(a) of Regulation 17 to impose fines on undertakings that intentionally or negligently supply incorrect or misleading information.

---

[19] February 1, 1963 for bilateral agreements, otherwise November 1, 1962.
[20] Reg. 17, Art. 25.
[21] *Ibid* para. (2).
[22] Reg. 17, Art. 15(6).
[23] Joined Cases 8–11/66, *Cimenteries* v. *Commission* [1967] E.C.R. 75; [1967] C.M.L.R. 77.
[24] The latest version of Form A/B was annexed to Reg. 2526/85, *loc. cit.* note 12, *supra*.
[25] Reg. 27, Art. 4. See Case 30/78, *Distillers Company* v. *Commission* [1980] E.C.R. 2229; [1980] 3 C.M.L.R. 121; Joined Cases 209–215 and 218/78, *Van Landewyck* v. *Commission* *loc. cit.* note 15, *supra*.
[26] See Complementary Note to Reg. 2526/85, *loc. cit.* note 12, *supra*.

(iii) *Complaints*

Article 3(2) of Regulation 17 provides that those entitled to make application to the Commission to set infringement proceedings in motion are Member States and "natural or legal persons who claim a legitimate interest." The practice of the Commission indicates that complaints will be accepted from persons with a plausible claim to have suffered as a result of an alleged infringement of the competition rules or from a body representing such persons. There is a form for the submission of complaints (Form C) but its use is optional. To maximise the chance that action will be taken by the Commission, an attempt should be made in the complaint to demonstrate, with as much detailed information as possible, that each of the criteria of prohibition in Article 85 and/or Article 86 is satisfied and, where relevant, the exemption under Article 85(3) is not available.

A complainant has no right to insist that the Commission adopt a final decision as to the existence or otherwise of an alleged infringement.[27] On the other hand, he is entitled to have his complaint taken seriously. Where the Commission does not propose to initiate infringement proceedings, it is required by Article 6 of Regulation 99/63 to inform any complainants of its reasons and to fix a time limit within which they may submit further comments in writing. A letter sent in response to such further comments, which finally rejects the complaint, may be the subject of an action for annulment under Article 173 even if it is not signed by a member of the Commission but by the Director-General for Competition.[28] Moreover, it has been clear since *Metro (No. 1)*[29] that a complainant whose interests are affected by a grant of exemption under Article 85(3) has *locus standi* to bring annulment proceedings.

Fact-finding

Where fact-finding is necessary, the Commission has important powers under Article 11 and Article 14 of Regulation 17.

Article 11 enables the Commission to obtain "all necessary information from the Governments and competent authorities of the Member States and from undertakings and associations of undertakings." For seeking information from undertakings a two-stage procedure is laid down. The first stage consists of an informal request for specified information to be given by a certain date.[30] If the information requested is not forthcoming, the procedure enters its second, formal stage with the adoption by the Commission of a decision ordering that it be supplied.[31] Failure to comply

---

[27] Case 125/78, *GEMA* v. *Commission* [1979] E.C.R. 3173; [1980] 2 C.M.L.R. 177.
[28] Case 298/83, *CICCE* v. *Commission* [1985] E.C.R. 1105; [1986] 1 C.M.L.R. 486. See also Case 210/81, *Demo-Studio Schmidt* v. *Commission* [1983] E.C.R. 3045; [1984] 1 C.M.L.R. 63.
[29] Case 26/76, *Metro* v. *Commission (No. 1)* [1977] E.C.R. 1875; [1978] 2 C.M.L.R. 1.
[30] Reg. 17, Art. 11(3). An incorrect response will attract a fine under Art. 15(1)(*b*) of the Reg. See, *e.g.* Re Telos O.J. 1982 L58/19; [1982] 1 C.M.L.R. 267.
[31] Reg. 17, Art. 11(5). See, *e.g.*, *Re. UNITEL* O.J. 1978 L157/39; [1978] 3 C.M.L.R. 306. The Court of Justice has stressed that it is for the Commission to assess what information is necessary, but that the Commission cannot require an undertaking to give self-incriminating

with such a decision may result in the imposition of a fine under Article 15(1)(*b*) or of a periodic penalty payment under Article 16(1)(*c*).

Under Article 14 the Commission is empowered to enter the premises of undertakings,[32] to examine and take copies of, or extracts from, books and business records and to ask for oral explanations on the spot. Inspections may take place on the basis of an authorisation in writing pursuant to paragraph (2) of the Article or of a Commission decision pursuant to paragraph (3). In neither case need any advance warning be given.[33] Where the Commission's inspectors are armed merely with a written authorisation, the undertaking concerned may refuse to submit to investigation; but once it has agreed, there is an obligation to co-operate fully. Refusal of an investigation ordered by a decision may attract a fine under Article 15(1)(*c*) or a periodic penalty payment under Article 16(1)(*d*). In *National Panasonic*[34] the Court rejected the argument that Article 14 envisages a two-stage procedure, like that of Article 11, under which a binding decision may be adopted only after an attempt to carry out an investigation on the basis of a written authorisation has proved unsuccessful. The Court took the view that, on a true construction of the Article, the Commission has a choice between two possible methods of proceeding.

The decision authorising an investigation under Article 14(3) must set out the subject-matter and the purpose of an investigation, this being held by the Court of Justice in *Hoechst*[35] to be essential so that the undertakings concerned are informed about the matters being investigated. In this case, the Court observed that the statement of reasons, although it could have been more precise, contained sufficient detail in that it specified the products (PVC and low density polyethylene) in which there was a suspected cartel contrary to Article 85(1) and that the cartel was suspected to concern prices, quantities or sales targets for those products.

The Commission may be denied access to documents protected by the principle of the confidentiality of communications between lawyer and client. The principle, which is narrower in scope than the legal professional privilege of English law, was recognised by the Court of Justice in the *AM & S* case.[36] Protection of confidentiality was held to be subject, in effect, to three conditions. First, the communication must be "made for the purposes and in the interests of the client's rights of defence." That extended, in particular, to "all written communications exchanged after the initiation of the administrative procedure under Regulation No.17 which may lead to a

---

answers to questions (as opposed to supplying relevant information): Case 374/87, *Orkem* v. *Commission* [1989] E.C.R. 3283; [1991] 4 C.M.L.R. 502; para. 15 of the judgment; see also Case 27/88, *Solvay* v. *Commission* [1989] E.C.R. 3255; [1991] 4 C.M.L.R. 502.

[32] The Commission may not, however, investigate at an individual's private home: Joined Cases 46/87 & 227/88, *Hoechst* v. *Commission* [1989] E.C.R. 2859; [1991] 4 C.M.L.R. 410; see para. 17 of the judgment.

[33] Case 136/79, *National Panasonic* v. *Commission* [1980] E.C.R. 2033; [1980] 3 C.M.L.R. 169.

[34] *Ibid.*

[35] Joined Cases 46/87 & 227/88, *Hoechst* v. *Commission* [1989] E.C.R. 2859; [1991] 4 C.M.L.R. 410; see also Cases 85/87, *Dow Benelux* v. *Commission* [1989] E.C.R. 3137 and 97–99/87, *Dow Chemical Iberica* v. *Commission* [1989] E.C.R. 3165, both also reported at [1991] 4 C.M.L.R. 410.

[36] Case 155/79, *A.M. & S.* v. *Commission* [1982] E.C.R. 1575; [1982] 2 C.M.L.R. 264.

decision on the application of Articles 85 and 86 of the Treaty or to a decision imposing a pecuniary sanction on the undertaking,"[37] as well as to "earlier written communications which have a relationship to the subject-matter of that procedure."[38] Secondly, the communication must "emanate from independent lawyers, that is to say, lawyers who are not bound to the client by a relationship of employment."[39] Thirdly, the lawyers in question must be entitled to practise their profession in one of the Member States. Communications with two classes of lawyers are accordingly outwith the privilege, *viz.* in-house lawyers, even in those Member States where they are subject to professional ethics and discipline, and lawyers from non-EEC countries.[40] Where the status of a document is disputed, the Commission may adopt a decision ordering its disclosure, which may then be challenged in proceedings under Article 173. Such proceedings would not automatically have suspensory effect, although suspension of the application of the decision, or any other interim measures, could be ordered in an appropriate case.[41]

Positive reactions

(i) *General*

Once the relevant facts have been found, the Commission will consider the legal position and, if it seems likely that in infringement of Article 85 and/or Article 86 has occurred, proceedings may be initiated by sending the undertaking or undertakings concerned a statement of objections. Infringement proceedings are discussed in the next section of this Chapter. Where, on the other hand, Article 85(1) or Article 86 are thought not to apply, or exemption under Article 85(3) is available, a positive reaction will be prepared. To elicit such a reaction from the Commission it may have been necessary for parties to modify or abandon aspects of an agreement or business practice.[42] In some cases a decision of the Commission formally granting negative clearance or exemption may be considered necessary. Most proceedings, however, are brought to an end by a letter from the Directorate-General for Competition (DGIV) informing the parties that the file in the case is to be closed. These are known colloquially as "comfort letters."

(ii) *Negative clearance*

We have seen that negative clearance is a certification by the Commission that the facts in its possession provide no grounds under Article 85 or Article 86 for intervention. The value of the assurance given is proportional to the

---

[37] [1982] E.C.R. at p. 1611.
[38] *Ibid.*
[39] *Ibid.*
[40] The Commission sought unsuccessfully a mandate from the Council to negotiate agreements with certain third countries for the purpose of extending the principle of confidentiality to communications with lawyers from those countries. See Faull, (1985) 10 E.L.Rev. 119.
[41] See Arts. 185 and 186 EEC.
[42] See, *e.g.* the far-reaching modifications required by the Commission in *Re Optical Fibres* O.J. 1986 L236/30.

completeness of the disclosure made to the Commission. A decision granting negative clearance is probably not binding on national courts which derive jurisdiction to apply Article 85(1) or Article 86 from the direct effect of those provisions though it is likely to have considerable persuasive authority. Where the Commission intends to grant negative clearance, it is required by Article 19(3) of Regulation 17 to publish in the *Official Journal* a summary of the relevant application and invite all interested third parties to submit their observations within a specified time limit, which may not be less than a month. The final decision must also be published.[43]

(iii) *Individual exemption*

A decision of the Commission granting individual exemption pursuant to Article 85(3) declares the prohibition in Article 85(1) inapplicable to the agreement in question. The extent to which exemption may be made retrospective was considered above. Under Article 8 of Regulation 17 exemption is granted for a fixed period and may be subjected to conditions. Before imposing an onerous condition the Commission must inform the parties of what it has in mind and give them an opportunity of making representations.[44] That right is not derived from the provisions of Regulation 99/63 on hearings in competition matters but from general principle. Exemption may be revoked pursuant to Article 8(3) where there has been a material change in the facts, where an obligation attached to the grant has been breached, where the decision was based upon incorrect information or induced by deceit or where the exemption has been abused by the parties. In the last three cases, the revocation may be made retroactive. As with negative clearance, the Commission must publish an Article 19(3) notice before adopting a final decision; and the latter must be published also.[45]

(iv) *Block exemption*

(a) *Conformity.* Where a notified agreement is found to be in conformity with a block exemption Regulation, the parties will be so informed by letter. Such letters merely state a view as to the applicability of directly effective provisions of Community law.

(b) *"No opposition"* or *"withdrawal of opposition."* Where the Commission expresses no opposition to a notified agreement within the period stipulated in a block exemption regulation (normally six months), or withdraws its opposition, the effect is to trigger the Regulation in respect of the agreement.[46] Since it alters the legal situation, the decision not to oppose

---

[43] Reg. 17, Art. 21(1).
[44] Case 17/74, *Transocean Marine Paint* v. *Commission* [1974] E.C.R. 1063; [1974] 2 C.M.L.R. 459.
[45] Reg. 17, Art. 21(1).
[46] See D. Waelbroeck, (1986) 11 E.L.Rev. 268. *Cf.* Venit, (1985) 22 C.M.L.Rev. 167. In *Odin Developments* O.J. 1990 L209/15; [1991] 4 C.M.L.R. 832 negative clearance was granted to a joint venture agreement under Reg. 17, Art. 2 following the Commission's opposition under Reg. 418/85, Art. 7.

or to withdraw opposition must, it is submitted, be susceptible of review under Article 173.

(v) *Comfort letters*

These are, in the phrase used by the Court of Justice in the *Perfumes* cases,[47] "merely administrative letters" signed by a official of DGIV, usually of the rank of Director. Comfort letters may be used to indicate either that there are no grounds for applying Article 85(1) or Article 86 (in other words, as an informal negative clearance) or that an agreement falling within Article 85(1) is considered eligible for exemption under Article 85(3).[48] They state that the file will be closed, with the proviso that it may be re-opened if material legal or factual circumstances change. Dealing with a case in this way has the great advantage of simplifying and shortening the proceedings: a disadvantage is that the legal consequences of comfort letters remain somewhat uncertain.

For the addressee, it is submitted, a comfort letter gives rise to the legitimate expectation that, unless there is a material change of circumstances, no further action will be taken by the Commission on the file that has been closed.[49] If, without any change of circumstances, a decision inconsistent with a comfort letter were subsequently adopted, there would be grounds for seeking its annulment under Article 173. The Court of Justice has said that comfort letters are not binding on national courts; but a court may properly take into account the opinion contained in such a letter in reaching its own conclusion on the applicability of Article 85(1) or Article 86.[50] It has also been held that comfort letters bring to an end the provisional validity enjoyed by duly notified old agreements.[51] The Commission is not legally bound to publish a notice under Article 19(3) of Regulation 17 before disposing of a case by comfort letter but in the *Eleventh Report on Competition Policy* it announced that, where appropriate, it would do so.[52] By allowing interested third parties to make representations, a more rounded picture of a case may be obtained and the danger that facts may

---

[47] Joined Cases 253/78 and 1–3/79, *Procureur de la Republique* v. *Giry and Guerlain* [1980] E.C.R. 2327; [1981] 2 C.M.L.R. 94; Case 99/79, *Lancome* v. *Etos* [1980] E.C.R. 2511; [1981] 2 C.M.L.R. 164; Case 31/80, *L'Oreal* v. *De Nieuwe AMCK* [1980] E.C.R. 3775; [1981] 2 C.M.L.R. 235. See Korah, (1981) 6 E.L.Rev. 14.

[48] On the extension of the use of comfort letters from the application of Art. 85(1) to that of Art. 85(3), see Comp.Rep. 1983 pp. 61–62.

[49] In *L'Oreal* v. *De Nieuwe AMCK* Advocate General Reischl said "... having regard to the principle that legitimate expectations must be upheld, the Commission may depart from the judgment arrived at by its officers only if the factual circumstances change or if its finding was reached on the basis of incorrect information": [1980] E.C.R. at p. 3803. See also the views expressed extra-judicially by Lord Mackenzie Stuart, 1983/1 LIEI 64. The crucial issue is whether a comfort letter can be regarded as an expression of intention by the Commission itself. D. Waelbroeck, *op. cit.* note 46, *supra.* recalls the strict requirements of a valid delegation of authority laid down by the Court in Case 9/56, *Meroni* v. *High Authority* [1957–58] E.C.R. 133. The Court refused in Case 71/74, *FRUBO* v. *Commission* to treat as binding upon the Commission a statement by an official that a certain amendment to an agreement would enable it to qualify for exemption: [1975] E.C.R. 563; [1975] 2 C.M.L.R. 123. That case is, in our view, distinguishable, since a comfort letter purports to dispose of the matter in question, albeit provisionally.

[50] See *Perfumes, loc. cit.* note 47, *supra.*

[51] Case 99/79, *Lancome* v. *Etos, loc. cit.* note 47, *supra.*

[52] See Comp.Rep. 1981 pp. 27–28; Comp.Rep. 1982, p. 83.

subsequently come to light that call for the re-opening of the file is reduced. In our view, the security provided by a comfort letter following the publication of an Article 19(3) notice is not markedly inferior in practice to that provided by a decision granting negative clearance. However, where exemption is required, the use of comfort letters may be less satisfactory. The letter will state the Commission's view that the criteria in Article 85(3) are fulfilled but will do nothing to lift the prohibition in Article 85(1). Faced with evidence that an agreement falls within Article 85(1), and incapable itself of applying Article 85(3), a national court may feel justified in holding the agreement void pursuant to Article 85(2); though a better course would be to suspend proceedings and invite the Commission to adopt a formal decision granting exemption.[53] Form A/B asks notifying firms to indicate whether closure of the proceedings by a comfort letter would be acceptable to them. It seems wise advice to say no to this, if there is any risk at all that the validity of the agreement in question may be contested in proceedings before a national court.

A complainant dissatisfied with the closure of proceedings by a comfort letter faces the difficulty that the latter itself probably does not constitute an act susceptible of review under Article 173. However, from the Court's repeated statements about the need to safeguard the legitimate interests of complainants, it is impossible to believe no remedy would be available.[54] The right approach, it is submitted, is to challenge the legality of the decision rejecting the complaint.

Infringement proceedings

(i) *The right to a hearing*

(a) *Legal basis.* Before it adopts a decision applying Article 85 or Article 86 the Commission ie required, pursuant to Article 19 of Regulation 17, to give the undertakings concerned the opportunity of being heard on the matters to which the Commission has taken objection. Other natural or legal persons, if they can show a sufficient interest, will also be entitled to a hearing. Detailed provisions on hearings were laid down by the Commission in Regulation 99/63.

Those provisions implement in the sphere of competition the general principle of law that a person whose interests are liable to be adversely affected by an individual decision of a public authority has a right to make his views known to the authority before the decision is taken. In cases to which Regulation 99 does not apply, it may be possible to invoke the general principle directly.[55]

(b) *The statement of objections.* In order for a person effectively to

---

[53] It may be that a Court is obliged under Art. 5 EEC to do so, as part of the reciprocal duty of co-operation which has been held to exist between national authorities and Community institutions in Case C–2/88, *Zwartweld* [1990] 3 C.M.L.R. 45. See *Draft Notice on the application of Articles 85 and 86 of the EEC Treaty by national courts* [1992] 4 C.M.L.R. 524.
[54] See the cases cited in notes 28 and 29, *supra.*
[55] Case 17/74, *Transocean Marine Paint* v. *Commission, loc. cit.* note 44, *supra.*

exercise his right to a hearing, he must be informed of the facts and considerations on the basis of which the responsible authority is minded to act.[56] Article 2(1) of Regulation 99 accordingly places the Commission under a duty to inform undertakings in writing of the objections raised against them. The issuing of a "statement of objections" marks the formal initiation of proceedings that may culminate in a finding that Article 85 or Article 86 has been infringed. Under Article 2(3) of the Regulation a fine or periodic penalty payment may only be imposed on an undertaking where objection has been notified in the requisite manner; while Article 4 provides that the Commission in its decisions shall deal only with objections on which undertakings have been afforded an opportunity of making their views known.

The Court of Justice has repeatedly affirmed that the statement of objections must set forth clearly all the essential facts upon which the Commission relies against the respondent undertakings.[57] A fairly succinct summary may be judged adequate for this purpose.[58] The final decision need not be an exact replica of the statement, since the Commission must take into account factors which emerge during the administrative proceedings: some objections may be abandoned altogether; and different arguments may be put forward in support of those which are maintained.[59] Where, however, the Commission wishes to introduce fresh objections, a supplementary statement should be sent to the respondents.[60]

In the *IBM* case[61] the Court upheld an objection to the admissibility of an action under Article 173 for the annulment of the decision to initiate competition proceedings against the applicants and of the statement of objections setting out the grounds on which the Commission considered they had violated Article 86. These, in the Court's view, were not acts within the meaning of the first paragraph of Article 173 but merely preparatory steps that might lead to the adoption of a reviewable act. In particular, the Court pointed out that a statement of objections does not place the undertaking concerned under any obligation to alter its business practices or deprive it of any protection it may enjoy against the imposition of fines. To review the legality of the measure in question would, the Court thought, be incompatible with the division of competences between itself and the Commission. Nevertheless, care was taken in the judgment not to exclude

---

[56] See the principle enunciated by Advocate General Warner in Cases 113 and 118–121/77, *NTN Toyo Bearing Company and others* v. *Council and Commission (Ballbearings)* [1979] E.C.R. 1185 at p. 1261; [1979] 2 C.M.L.R. 257. This was in the context of anti-dumping proceedings but the Advocate General clearly regarded the principle as applying generally in Community law.

[57] See Case 45/69, *Boehringer Mannheim* v. *Commission* [1970] E.C.R. 769; Case 85/76, *Hoffmann-La Roche* v. *Commission* [1979] E.C.R. 461; [1979] 3 C.M.L.R. 211; Joined Cases 100–103/80, *Musique Diffusion Francaise* v. *Commission (Pioneer)* [1983] E.C.R. 1825; [1983] 3 C.M.L.R. 221; Joined Cases 43 and 63/82, *VBVB and VBBB* v. *Commission* [1984] E.C.R. 19; [1985] 1 C.M.L.R. 27.

[58] *Ibid.*

[59] Joined Cases 100–103/80, *Pioneer loc. cit.* note 57, *supra*; Joined Cases 209–215 and 218/78, *Van Landewyck* v. *Commission loc. cit.* note 15, *supra*.

[60] Case 54/69, *Francolor* v. *Commission* [1972] E.C.R. 851; [1972] C.M.L.R. 557.

[61] Case 60/81, *IBM* v. *Commission* [1981] E.C.R. 2639; [1981] 3 C.M.L.R. 635.

altogether the possibility of bringing an action under Article 173 to challenge measures still only at a preparatory stage, where the illegality is manifest.

(c) *Access to the file.* The Commission is not legally obliged to give respondent undertakings access to the whole of its file in a case.[62] In *Hoffmann-La Roche* the Court said that undertakings "must have been afforded the opportunity during the administrative procedure to make known their views on the truth and relevance of the facts and circumstances alleged and on the documents used by the Commission to support its claim that there has been an infringement . . ."[63] The duty of disclosure is thus confined to documents specifically relied upon in constructing the case against a given respondent. However, the current practice of the Commission is more liberal than the law requires. Once a statement of objections has been issued, the respondent is allowed to examine and copy all the contents of the file, with the exception of "internal documents" and documents containing "business secrets."[64]

An example of an internal document would be the final assessment report of the inspectors who have conducted an investigation (as distinct from a clearly factual account of an inspection visit or a minute of statements by employees or officers of the undertaking concerned).[65] More difficult to classify are working documents produced by the Commission which constitute a vital element in the proof of the alleged infringement, for example, a comparative study of the prices charged by a group of competing undertaking for which the existence of a concerted practice has been inferred. Subject to what is said below about the protection of business secrets, it is submitted that access ought to be given to such documents, where this is necessary to enable an undertaking fully to grasp the case it has to answer.

Article 20(1) provides that information required pursuant to the Commission's powers under Regulation 17 shall be used only for the purposes of the relevant investigation. This precludes its use, for instance, in civil proceedings before a national court.[66] By Article 20(2) the Commission is forbidden to divulge information so acquired which is "of the kind covered by the obligation of professional secrecy." That duty is, however, expressed to be without prejudice to the provisions of Article 19 of the right to a hearing and of Article 21 on the publication of decisions. It follows that certain information within the protection of Article 20 may properly be disclosed to an undertaking to enable it to answer objections that have been raised against it. However, there is a duty, deriving not from Regulation 17

---

[62] Joined Cases 56 and 58/64, *Consten and Grundig* v. *Commission* [1966] E.C.R. 299; [1966] C.M.L.R. 418; Joined Cases 43 and 63/82, *VBVB and VBBB* v. *Commission loc. cit.* note 57, *supra.*

[63] [1979] E.C.R. at p. 512.

[64] See Comp.Rep. 1981; p. 30; Comp.Rep. 1982, pp. 40–41; Comp.Rep. 1983, pp. 63–64. See also Joshua, (1986) 6 E.L.Rev. 409.

[65] Comp.Rep. 1983, pp. 63–64.

[66] The same restriction applies to the use of such information by national competition authorities; see Case C–67/91, *DGDC* v. *AEB*, judgment of the Court of Justice of July 16, 1992 (not yet reported).

but from general principle, against the disclosure of business secrets.[67] What amounts to a business secret has yet to be clarified fully but the notion would presumably cover such things as turnover figures, customer lists, investment plans and technical or commercial know-how. The Commission is not allowed to use against an undertaking documents which it is prevented from disclosing because they contain other firms' business secrets, where the withholding of the documents would adversely affect the ability of the respondent to express its views on them.[68] To avoid such an outcome, the Commission may seek the permission of the undertakings concerned (which are likely to be competitors or customers of the respondent) to the disclosure of their secrets. Or it may offer the respondent an edited version of the documents.

The Commission takes the view that the complainant in a case is not automatically entitled to see the file.[69] However, it will normally provide him with at least an edited version of the reply received from the undertaking complained against; and, it may invite his comments, where relevant, on certain evidence, for example documents discovered in the course of an investigation under Article 14. If the respondent asserts that documents the Commission is proposing to hand over to the complainant contain business secrets, it must be given an opportunity to challenge the decision rejecting that claim, before the delivery take place.[70]

(d) *Hearing the parties.* The letter under cover of which the statement of objections is sent will invite the respondent undertaking to make known in writing its views on the objections within a specified period (normally three months). The undertaking will also be informed that it may include in its written comments a request for an opportunity to put forward its arguments orally. Under Article 7 of Regulation 99/63 the Commission is bound to accede to a request for an oral hearing, where a sufficient interest is shown or where it is proposing to impose a fine or periodic penalty payment. The complainant in a case will usually be invited to the oral hearing.

The purpose of the oral hearing is to enable the parties further to develop their written submissions. The procedure is administrative in character and parties are not allowed to question the Commission. To reassure parties that they would be given a fair opportunity to state their case and that due account would be taken of their submissions at the decision-making stage, the post of "Hearing Officer" was created in 1982.[71] The Hearing Officer has nothing to do with preparing or bringing home the allegation that the rules on competition have been infringed. He presides at the oral hearing and his views on the case are made known to the member of the Commission

---

[67] Case 53/85, *AKZO* v. *Commission* [1986] E.C.R. 1965; [1987] 1 C.M.L.R. 231.
[68] Case 85/76, *Hoffmann-La Roche* v. *Commission loc. cit.* note 57, *supra.*
[69] Comp.Rep. 1983, p. 64. See also Joshua, *op. cit.* note 64, *supra*, pp. 419–423. In Joined Cases 209–215 and 218/78, *Van Landewyck* v. *Commission loc. cit.* note 15, *supra*, the Court said Art. 19(2) of Reg. 17 gives complainants "a right to be heard and not a right to receive confidential information": [1980] E.C.R. at p. 3239.
[70] Case 53/85, *AKZO* v. *Commission* [1986] E.C.R. 1965; [1987] 1 C.M.L.R. 231.
[71] Comp.Rep. 1982, 41–42. The Hearing Officer's terms of reference were published as an annex to the *Thirteenth Report on Competition Policy* (1983).

responsible for competition, to whom he has a right of direct access. His opinion is not, however, disclosed to the parties.

(ii) *Final decision*

In making a formal decision under Regulation 17, the Court of First Instance has held in the *PVC Cartel* case[72] that strict adherence by the Commission to formal procedural requirements is essential. In this case, the Commission's decision to fine several chemicals producers for operating a cartel in PVC was declared non-existent and thus effectively set aside for two principal reasons. First, there were discrepancies between the text of the decision adopted by the Commission and the texts in the various official languages notified to the companies involved. Secondly, the decision had not been authenticated as required by the Commission's Rules of Procedure by the signatures of both the President and Executive Secretary of the Commission, and indeed the Commissioner responsible for competition matters who had purported to issue the decisions had left office several days prior to the final texts of the decisions being settled. It should be noted that, although the textual differences were not insignificant in all cases, there was no suggestion that any of the addressees of the decision had suffered material prejudice as a result. The Court justified its approach as being necessary to guarantee "observance of the principles of legality, legal certainty and sound administration."[73]

The implication of the finding of non-existence, as opposed to annulment under Article 173 of the Treaty, is that every Commission decision taken where similar discrepancies or procedural failures exist is susceptible to being set aside, for there is no equivalent to Article 173's two months deadline for bringing a claim of non-existence. The case is being appealed by the Commission to the Court of Justice, which may consider that the Court of First Instance's judgment was disproportionately severe given the relatively minor effect of the Commission's transgressions. It if does so, it may well find instead that the decision is subject to annulment, either in whole or in part, rather than a finding of non-existence in order that the two month limitation period applies.

(a) *Order to terminate infringement.* Article 3(1) of Regulation 17 provides that, where the Commission finds that there is an infringement of Article 85 or Article 86, it may by decision order this to be brought to an end. Termination may involve positive action on the part of the addressee or addressees, and the decision may specify the steps to be taken. Thus in *Commercial Solvents Corporation*[74] the Commission imposed on CSC and Instituto an obligation to deliver an initial quantity of aminobutanol to Zoja

---

[72] Joined Cases T–79, 84–86, 89, 91, 92, 94, 96, 98, 102 & 104/89, *BASF and others* v. *Commission*, Judgment of Court of First Instance (Second Chamber) of February 27, 1992.

[73] Joined Cases T–79, 84–86, 89, 91, 92, 94, 96, 98, 102 & 104/89, *BASF and others* v. *Commission*. Judgment of Court of First Instance (Second Chamber) of February 27, 1992 at para. 76. See Editorial [1992] E.C.L.R. 143.

[74] Joined Cases 6 and 7/73, *Commercial Solvents Corporation* v. *Commission* [1974] E.C.R. 223; [1974] 1 C.M.L.R. 309.

within 30 days and to submit within two months a plan for making supplies available in the longer term. The order was upheld by the Court of Justice which said of Article 3:

> "This provision must be applied in relation to the infringement which has been established and may include an order to do certain acts or provide certain advantages which have been wrongly withheld as well as prohibiting the continuation of certain action, practices or situations which are contrary to the Treaty."[75]

A periodic penalty payment may be attached to the order to ensure that it is complied with.

It was argued, *inter alia*, in the *G.V.L.*[76] case that the Commission had no power under Regulation 17 to adopt a decision recording an infringement which had already been brought to an end. The Court of Justice held that the Commission might well have a legitimate interest in taking such a decision, where it was necessary to clarify the legal position in order to prevent a repetition of the infringement.[77]

(b) *Fines.* For negligent or intentional infringements of Article 85 or Article 86 the Commission has power under Article 15(2) of Regulation 17 to impose fines of between 1,000 and 1,000,000 ECUs, or a greater sum not exceeding 10 per cent. of the turnover in the previous business year of each of the participating undertakings. In fixing the amount of fines regard must be had to the gravity and the duration of the infringement.

The power to fine is not only a means of punishing individual infringements: it is one of the policy instruments given to the Commission to enable it to apply in the sphere of competition the principles laid down by the EEC Treaty. An argument put forward by the applicants in the *Pioneer* case[78] was that the level of the fines imposed on them had been determined not by the gravity or duration of their particular conduct but by a change of policy on the part of the Commission. The Court of Justice held that it was open to the Commission to adopt a change of policy involving an increase in the fines imposed, where this was necessary to reinforce their deterrent effect.[79]

The gravity of an infringement is to be appraised, the Court has said, "by taking into account in particular the nature of the restrictions on competition, the number and size of the undertakings concerned, the respective proportions of the market controlled by them within the Community and the situation in the market where the infringement was committed."[80] Also relevant is the fact that agreements or conduct of the

---

[75] [1974] E.C.R. at p. 255.
[76] Case 7/82, *GVL* v. *Commission* [1983] E.C.R. 483; [1983] 3 C.M.L.R. 645.
[77] No dec. is necessary to bring the prohibition in Art. 85(1) or Art. 86 into force. See Reg. 17, Art. 1.
[78] Joined Cases 100–103/80, *loc. cit.* note 57, *supra.*
[79] See the statement on the Commission's fining policy, Comp.Rep. 1983, pp. 56–58. The largest fine to date was one of 75 million ECUs (approx. £50 million) imposed on Tetrapak for breaches of Article 86; O.J. 1992 L72/1; [1992] 4 C.M.L.R. 551. The decision imposing this fine is being appealed to the Court of First Instance.
[80] Case 41/69, *ACF Chemiefarma* v. *Commission* [1970] E.C.R. 661 at p. 701.

kind in question have been found in the past to be incompatible with the common market. Infringements the Commission considers particularly susceptible to heavy fines are, in respect of Article 85, export bans, market sharing and horizontal or vertical price-fixing and, in respect of Article 86, refusals to supply, price discrimination, exclusive or preferential long term supply arrangements and loyalty rebates.[81]

Where an undertaking co-operates with the Commission in the investigation of an infringement, this may be reflected in the level of the fine imposed on it. Another mitigating factor may be willingness to give certain undertakings as a guarantee against the recurrence of the infringement. In *Wood Pulp*[82] the fines on some of the respondents were reduced by 90 per cent. in consideration of an undertaking to market a proportion of their products in local EEC currencies instead of in United States dollars, which it was thought would make concerted price-fixing more difficult. The text of the undertakings was annexed to the decision.

The Commission will refrain from taking steps to collect a fine pending the outcome of review proceedings in the Court of Justice, if two conditions are met. These are the agreement of the undertaking concerned to pay interest in respect of any fine to which it is held liable by the Court and the provision of a bank guarantee covering the interest as well as the principal sum. The practice received the approval of the Court in the *A.E.G.* case.[83] The amount of interest normally charged by the Commission is the local bank rate plus 1 per cent.

The Commission's power to adopt interim measures

Regulation 17 does not expressly empower the Commission to adopt interim measures in respect of behaviour which is the subject of proceedings for the infringement of Article 85 or Article 86. The drafting of Article 3 of the Regulation in particular, seems to assume that, before a binding order is made, the Commission must have found that an infringement exists. However, in the *Camera Care* case[84] the Court of Justice held that a power to adopt interim measures is impliedly conferred on the Commission "to avoid the exercise of the power to make decisions given by Article 3 from becoming ineffectual or even illusory because of the action of certain undertakings."[85] According to the *Camera Care* judgment, the adoption of interim measures is subject to four conditions: that the case is urgent and the measures are needed to avoid a situation likely to cause serious and irreparable damage to the party seeking them, or one which is intolerable for the public interest; that the measures are of a temporary and conservatory nature and are restricted to what is necessary in the situation; that in adopting the measures the Commission maintains the essential safeguards guaranteed under Regulation 17, in particular by Article 19; and that the

---

[81] See Comp.Rep. 1983, p. 56.
[82] O.J. 1985 L85/1.
[83] Case 107/83, *AEG* v. *Commission* [1983] E.C.R. 3151; [1984] 3 C.M.L.R. 325.
[84] Case 792/79R, *Camera Care* v. *Commission* [1980] E.C.R. 119; [1980] 1 C.M.L.R. 334.
[85] [1980] E.C.R. at p. 131.

decision is made in a form that would enable it to be challenged before the Court.

The Court of First Instance has made it clear, in annulling a refusal by the Commission to order interim measures requiring the European Broadcasting Union to allow the French broadcasting company La Cinq access to Eurovision film (such as coverage of sporting events),[86] that a complainant is only required to demonstrate that there is a prima facie breach of the competition rules and need not also show that the breach is clear and flagrant. Moreover, the Commission had argued that the requirement that damage be serious and irreparable meant that it could only use its powers if the damage could not be remedied by a final decision. This was held to be too limited a view. The Commission must take into account the circumstances of the complainant. In this case, La Cinq held a licence to broadcast in France for a limited period only, and failure to secure access to Eurovision film might prejudice its chances of obtaining renewal. In effect, if required to wait until the Commission reached a final decision, La Cinq would run the risk of being refused the grant of a new licence and so going out of business in the interim, hence suffering serious and irreparable damage, whatever the outcome of the final decision.[87] This judgment is therefore likely to encourage more applicants to request the Commission to take interim measures.

In the *Ford* case[88] an interim decision of the Commission requiring Ford Germany to resume delivery of right hand drive vehicles to German dealers was annulled on the ground that the measure was not within the scope of the final decision that could be taken in the proceedings pending before the Commission. Those proceedings, it will be remembered, related to the standard form dealer agreement notified by Ford; and any decision under Article 3 would simply require the termination of the agreement. Even assuming (as was subsequently held)[89] that the refusal to supply right hand drive vehicles provided grounds for withholding exemption from the dealer agreement, the Commission could not by means of an interim decision adopt a separate enforceable order leaving Ford no option but to resume supplies.

Proceedings for the taking of interim measures will be suspended if satisfactory undertakings are obtained from the parties concerned.[90] For instance, in 1985 proceedings were started by the Commission in response to complaints from independent manufacturers that Ford was attempting to exclude them from the market for body panels in the United Kingdom by claiming copyright protection and refusing to grant licences on reasonable terms. The suspension of the proceedings followed an undertaking by Ford to offer licences immediately to its competitors in the United Kingdom for

---

[86] Case T–44/90, *La Cinq* v. *Commission*, judgment of January 24, 1992 (not yet reported).
[87] This argument mirrors that used successfully at the interim stage in the English House of Lords by the Spanish Fishermen who were able to secure an interim injunction in the *Factortame* litigation: *R.* v. *Secretary of State for Transport, ex p. Factortame Ltd. (No. 2)* [1991] 1 A.C. 603.
[88] Joined Cases 228 and 229/82, *Ford* v. *Commission* [1984] E.C.R. 1129; [1984] 1 C.M.L.R. 649.
[89] Joined Cases 25 and 26/84, *Ford* v. *Commission* [1985] E.C.R. 2725; [1985] 3 C.M.L.R. 528.
[90] See Comp.Rep. 1985, pp. 55–56.

the manufacture and sale of the body parts of certain models and an offer to settle copyright infringement proceedings pending before the English courts.

Review by the European Courts

Decisions of the Commission in the exercise of its powers in connection with the application of Articles 85 and 86 are subject to review by the Court of First Instance under Article 173 EEC. Appeal on points of law lies to the Court of Justice. We have seen that an action may lie in respect of decisions on ancillary matters such as an order to produce documents,[91] as well as of final decisions ordering the termination of infringements or granting negative clearance or exemption. The parties to an agreement or to conduct which is the subject of competition proceedings, and any complainants,[92] should have no difficulty in establishing *locus standi*. The four usual grounds of review apply: lack of competence; infringement of an essential procedural requirement; infringement of the Treaty or of any rule of law relating to its application; and misuse of powers. It has been made clear from the outset that, where complex economic evaluations are called for, the Court of First Instance will not substitute its own discretion for that of the Commission but will confine itself to an examination of the relevance of the facts and considerations taken into account, and of the conclusions drawn, in the decision.[93]

However, in reviewing a decision to impose a fine or periodic penalty payment, the Court of First Instance enjoys unlimited jurisdiction, pursuant to Article 17 of Regulation 17 and Article 172 EEC. This means that it is not required simply to quash a decision of which it disapproves but may determine for itself what the fine or penalty, if any, should be.

The role of national competition authorities

(i) *Application of the EEC rules on competition*

It was pointed out in the opening section of this chapter that the leading role given to national authorities under the transitional regime of Article 88 was lost to the Commission with the coming into force of Regulation 17. The authorities referred to in Article 88 are those responsible in the Member States for the application of domestic competition law, including courts specifically entrusted with this function, but not the ordinary courts before which directly effective Community provisions may be invoked.[94] Under Article 9 of Regulation 17 the national authorities have no power to apply Article 85(3); and their power to apply Article 85(1) and Article 86 is lost as soon as the Commission initiates any procedure under Article 2 (negative clearance), Article 3 (termination of infringements) or Article 6

---

[91] See, *e.g.* Case 53/85, *AKZO* v. *Commission* [1986] E.C.R. 1965; [1987] 1 C.M.L.R. 231.
[92] See the cases cited in notes 27 and 28, *supra*.
[93] Joined Cases 56 and 58/64, *Consten and Grundig* v. *Commission loc. cit.* note 62, *supra*.
[94] Case 127/73, *BRT* v. *SABAM* [1974] E.C.R. 51; [1974] 2 C.M.L.R. 238.

(exemption). One of the questions put to the Court of Justice in *Brasserie de Haecht (No. 2)*[95] was whether acknowledgement of the receipt of an application for negative clearance or of a notification amounted to the intitiation of a procedure for this purpose. The Court held that it did not. The reference in Article 9(3) concerned "an authoritative act of the Commission, evidencing its intention of taking a decision under the said Articles."[96]

The Commission is required to exercise its powers under Regulation 17 in close liaison with the national authorities.[97] They are sent all the important documents in a case and are represented on the Advisory Committee on Restrictive Practices and Monopolies which must be consulted before a decision is taken establishing an infringement of Article 85 or Article 86 or granting negative clearance or exemption. A report on the outcome of the consultation is annexed to the Commission's draft decision. The fact that the report is not made available to the undertakings concerned may represent a defect in the implementation of the right to a hearing.[98]

(ii) *Application of national competition law*

There is scope for conflict between the EEC rules of competition and the competition law of Member States but in practice this has not proved to be a serious problem. The general principle was laid down by the Court of Justice in *Wilhelm* v. *Bundeskartellamt*[99] which arose out of action by the German authorities overlapping that of the Commission in respect of the famous dyestuffs cartel. The principle is that, since their objectives are different, the national rules may be applied in parallel with those of the EEC; but not so as to prejudice the uniform application of the latter throughout the common market. The implications of the principle are not free from doubt but they may be summarised as follows. First, if behaviour is contrary to both sets of rules, it may be dealt with under both, though to avoid double jeopardy there should be a set-off of any pecuniary sanctions that may be imposed.[1] Secondly, behaviour prohibited by Article 85 or Article 86 but permissible under the competition rules of a given Member State, cannot be treated as lawful in that one State. Thirdly, behaviour which does not satisfy the criteria in Article 85(1) or Article 86, for example, because trade between Member States is not appreciably affected, may nevertheless be prohibited under national competition law.[2] Fourthly, a grant of exemption pursuant to Article 85(3) or a block exemption regulation probably overrides any conflicting rules of national competition law, since it represents a positive choice of policy by the Community authorities. Such would appear to be the view of the Commission,[3] though the view that exemption merely removes

---

[95] Case 48/72, *Brasserie de Haecht* v. *Wilkin (No. 2)* [1973] E.C.R. 77; [1973] C.M.L.R. 287.
[96] [1973] E.C.R. at p. 88.
[97] See in particular, Reg. 17, Arts. 10, 11(2) and 14(2), (4) and (5). See also Comp.Rep. 1983 pp. 66–67, and the remarks on the implications of Art. 5 EEC at note 53, *supra*.
[98] See the remarks on the Advisory Committee procedure by Advocate General Warner in Case 30/78, *Distillers Company* v. *Commission* [1980] E.C.R. at p. 2292.
[99] Case 14/68 [1969] E.C.R. 1; [1969] C.M.L.R. 100.
[1] *Ibid.*
[2] The Court of Justice so held in the *Perfumes* cases, *loc. cit.* note 47, *supra*.
[3] See Comp.Rep. 1974, p. 29.

the Community barrier to the enforcement of an agreement, leaving any national barrier in place, has had powerful advocates.[4]

The EEC rules on competition and the national courts

(i) *The direct effect of Article 85(1) and Article 86*

In *BRT* v. *SABAM* the Court of Justice said: "As the provisions of Articles 85(1) and 86 tend by their very nature to produce direct effects in relations between individuals, these Articles create direct rights in respect of the individuals concerned which the national courts must safeguard."[5] That broad statement of principle needs to be qualified in two ways. First, the provisions of Article 85(1) and Article 86 are only directly effective within the framework of implementing measures adopted under Article 87, such as Regulation 17 itself. Where there are no implementing measures, as with merger control where Regulation 17 is expressly disapplied,[6] the courts of Member States have no jurisdiction to apply those provisions in the absence of a relevant ruling by national competition authorities pursuant to Article 88 or of a decision by the Commission pursuant to Article 89(2).[7] Secondly, the doctrine of provisional validity, which is discussed below, prevents the application of the prohibition in Article 85(1) to, and consequential nullity of, certain agreements pending a decision by the Commission on the availability of exemption under Article 85(3).

We are concerned in this section with the ordinary national courts to which falls the task of safeguarding the rights (including privileges and immunities in the Hohfeldian sense)[8] conferred on individuals by Article 85(1) and Article 86, as by other directly effective provisions of Community law. They are to be distinguished from courts with special responsibilities in national competition matters whose authority to apply the EEC competition rules is derived from Article 88 and is subject to the limitation imposed by Article 9(3) of Regulation 17.[9]

(ii) *Nullity of prohibited agreements*

(a) *Euro-Defences*. So-called "Euro-Defences," based on the alleged infringement of Article 85 or Article 86, may be invoked in proceedings before national courts to cast doubt on the validity of transactions of which the enforcement is being sought. In the case of Article 85 the civil consequences of infringement are spelt out by the second paragraph which provides: "Any agreements or decisions prohibited pursuant to this Article shall be automatically void." The Court of Justice has stated that Article

---

[4] See Markert (1974) 11 C.M.L.Rev. 92; Kerse, *op. cit.* note 7, *supra* at pp. 329–331.
[5] Case 127/73, [1974] E.C.R. at p. 62.
[6] Reg. 4064/89, Art. 22(2).
[7] Cases 209–213/84, *Ministere Public* v. *Asjes* [1986] E.C.R. 1425; [1986] 3 C.M.L.R. 173. On the situation prior to the enactment of Reg. 17, see Case 13/61, *Bosch* v. *de Geus* [1962] E.C.R. 45; [1962] C.M.L.R. 1. For merger control, see Chap. 17, *infra*.
[8] Hohfeld, *Fundamental Legal Conceptions*. In Hohfeld's analysis "privilege" connotes the absence of duty (hence of a right vested in another) and "immunity" the absence of liability (hence of a power vested in another).
[9] Case 127/73, *BRT* v. *SABAM loc. cit.* note 94, *supra*.

85(2) is directly effective.[10] Article 86 contains no equivalent provision but it is clear from general principle that a national court would be required to refrain from giving effect to an agreement caught by the prohibition in the Article, for example one binding a purchaser to obtain all or most of his requirements of goods of a certain description from a dominant supplier.

(b) *Provisional validity*. We have seen that Article 9(1) of Regulation 17 empowers the Commission alone to grant exemption under Article 85(3): in other words, the paragraph is not directly effective. Where, therefore, a national court finds an agreement to be within Article 85(1), it cannot save the agreement from the automatic nullity prescribed under paragraph (2) of the Article by declaring the prohibition inapplicable pursuant to paragraph (3). This will not matter in cases where exemption is excluded in principle because the agreement is a notifiable one which has not been notified: even if it were subsequently notified and received exemption, the decision of the Commission could not be made retrospectively effective to the date of the national proceedings. It is different where the proceedings relate to an agreement which is non-notifiable or has been notified, and which may accordingly benefit from a retroactive grant of exemption at some future date. For the prohibition in Article 85(1) to be declared inapplicable to an agreement to which it has already been applied by a national court would be highly unsatisfactory.

That risk has been removed in respect of old agreements by the development of the doctrine of provisional validity. The doctrine has been explained by the Court of Justice as a compromise between the general principle of legal certainty, which underlies the power of retrospective validation in Article 7 of Regulation 17, and the intention of Article 85(2) "to attach severe sanctions to a serious prohibition."[11] In *Brasserie de Haecht (No. 2)* the Court said:

> "In the case of old agreements: the general principle of contractual certainty requires, particularly when the agreement has been notified in accordance with the provision of Regulation No. 17, that the Court may only declare it to be automatically void after the Commission has taken a decision by virtue of that Regulation.
>
> In the case of new agreements as the Regulation assumes that so long as the Commission has not taken a decision the agreement can only be implemented at the parties' own risk, it follows that notifications in accordance with Article 4(1) of Regulation No. 17 do not have suspensive effect."[12]

An old agreement which is non-notifiable or was notified by the dates specified in Article 5(1) of Regulation 17 must, therefore, be treated as valid in proceedings before a national court unless and until the Commission has

---

[10] Case 48/72, *Brasserie de Haecht* v. *Wilkin (No. 2) loc. cit.* note 95, *supra*.
[11] *Ibid* at p. 86.
[12] *Ibid* at pp. 86–87.

taken a decision refusing it exemption.[13] In the latter event, however, the agreement will be rendered void *ab initio*. The view has been expressed by the Commission[14] that the doctrine should be applied by analogy to accession agreements, and that, it is submitted, is likely to be the approach taken by the Court, if the issue is ever raised before it. On the other hand, new agreements, whether notifiable or not, do not enjoy provisional validity. According to the Court of Justice in *Brasserie de Haecht (No. 2)*, "Whilst the principle of legal certainty requires that, in applying the prohibitions of Article 85, the sometimes considerable delays by the Commission in exercising its powers should be taken into account, this cannot, however, absolve the Court from the obligation of deciding on the claims of interested parties who invoke the automatic nullity."[15] In such circumstances, the choices open to the national court are: to enforce the agreement, if it has no perceptible effect on competition or trade between Member States and is, therefore, clearly outwith Article 85(1); to treat the agreement as void if the Court considers it to be caught by Article 85(1) and to have no realistic hope of exemption under Article 85(3); otherwise, to suspend proceedings until the Commission has made up its mind.[16]

(c) *Severance.* In *Société Technique Minière* v. *Maschinenbau Ulm*[17] the Court of Justice declared that the automatic nullity in Article 85(2) "applies to those parts of the agreement affected by the prohibition, or to the agreement as a whole if it appears that those parts are not severable from the agreement itself."[18] Whether any offending clauses can be severed, leaving the main part of the agreement intact, falls to be determined under the law of the Member State concerned. In England it is not clear whether the doctrine of severance as applied in the field of covenants in restraint of trade is to be regarded as applying in the case of Article 85(1). In the *Chemidus Wavin*[19] case Buckley L.J. in the Court of Appeal indicated that he doubted whether the question was really one "of severance in the sense in which we in these courts are accustomed to use that term in considering whether covenants contained in contract of employment and so forth are void as being in restraint of trade." It appeared rather to be "whether, after the excisions required by the Article of the Treaty have been made from the contract, the contract could be said to fail for lack of consideration or any other ground, or whether the contract could be so changed in its character as not to be the sort of contract the parties intended to enter into at all."[20]

---

[13] This was confirmed in Case 59/77, *De Bloos* v. *Bouyer* [1977] E.C.R. 2359; [1978] 1 C.M.L.R. 511. See Faull and Weiler, (1978) 3 E.L.Rev. 116.
[14] Comp.Rep. 1973, p. 19.
[15] [1973] E.C.R. at p. 87.
[16] The topic of provisional validity has been much debated by commentators. See the full discussion, and references in Kerse, *op. cit.* note 7, *supra* at pp. 308–315.
[17] Case 56/65 [1966] E.C.R. 235; [1966] C.M.L.R. 357.
[18] [1966] E.C.R. at p. 250.
[19] *Chemidus Wavin* v. *TERI* [1978] 3 C.M.L.R. 514.
[20] [1978] 3 C.M.L.R. at p. 519.

(iii) *Civil remedies for infringements*

It seems clear in principle that the directly effective rights conferred upon individuals by Articles 85 and 86 should be exercisable offensively as well as defensively. The availability of remedies for their enforcement is, however, as normally under the EEC Treaty, a matter for national law. All Community law requires is that the conditions governing those remedies in a Community matter should be no less favourable than when they are used in purely national matters; and that the conditions should not make it impossible in practice to exercise rights which the national courts are called upon to safeguard.[21]

There is now authority in English law for the granting in appropriate cases of remedies by way of an injunction or damages to the victims of infringements of the EEC competition rules.[22] It was suggested by Lord Denning M.R. some years ago that special new torts had been created by Article 85 and Article 86 entitled, respectively "undue restriction of competition within the common market" and "abuse of dominant position with the common market,"[23] but this suggestion won little support.[24] The preferred approach of English courts appears to be to treat claims in such cases as arising out of a breach of statutory duty.[25] However, there is no reported case to date of such a claim for damages being successfully brought before the English High Court.

---

[21] See, *e.g.* Case 33/76, *Rewe* v. *Landwirtschaftskammer für das Saarland* [1976] E.C.R. 1989; [1977] 1 C.M.L.R. 533; Case 45/76, *Comet* v. *Produktschap voor Siergewassen* [1976] E.C.R. 2043; [1977] 1 C.M.L.R. 533; Case 61/79, *Denkavit* v. *Amministrazione delle Finanze* [1980] E.C.R. 1205; [1981] 3 C.M.L.R. 694; Joined Cases 66, 127 and 128/79, *Amministrazione delle Finanze* v. *Salumi* [1980] E.C.R. 1237; [1981] 1 C.M.L.R. 1; Case 826/79, *Amministrazione delle Finanze* v. *MIRECO* [1980] E.C.R. 2559; Case 199/82, *San Giorgio* [1983] E.C.R. 3595; [1985] 2 C.M.L.R. 65; Case 14/83, *Von Colson* [1984] E.C.R. 1891; [1986] 2 C.M.L.R. 430; Case C–213/89, *R.* v. *Secretary of State for Transport, ex p. Factortame* [1990] 3 C.M.L.R. 1, [1991] 1 A.C. 603.
[22] See, in particular, *Garden Cottage Foods* v. *Milk Marketing Board* [1984] A.C. 130. Noted by Jacobs, (1983) 8 E.L.Rev. 353.
[23] *Applications des Gaz S.A.* v. *Falks Veritas Ltd.* [1974] 3 All E.R. 51 at p. 58.
[24] See the reservations exposed by Roskill L.J. in *Valor International Ltd.* v. *Applications de Gas S.A. and EPI Leisure Ltd.* [1978] 3 C.M.L.R. 87.
[25] The various possible bases for damages in English law are fully discussed by Kerse, *op. cit.* note 7, p. 473, *supra* at pp. 315–322.

CHAPTER 17

THE CONTROL OF MERGERS

A merger takes place when two or more undertakings which were formerly independent are brought under common control.[1] There is a great variety of ways in which this may come about, most obviously where the company carrying on undertaking A acquires a controlling percentage of shares in the company carrying on undertaking B.[2] A merger between undertakings operating on totally unrelated markets may result in an accretion of economic power, through improved access to finance, entailing either the creation or the enhancement of a dominant position on one of the markets. However, the type of merger which is most likely to have an adverse effect on competition is one between undertakings which are actually or potentially competitors, or between an undertaking and its major supplier or consumer.

The EEC Treaty does not contain any explicit merger control provision equivalent to Article 66 ECSC, which requires the prior authorisation of the Commission for mergers involving coal or steel undertakings. Only since the adoption of Regulation 4064/89 ("the Merger Regulation")[3] has there been a specific Community law regime directed at significant mergers. However, during the prolonged gestation period of this secondary legislation the Commission took steps to apply the more general provisions of competition law under the Treaty to the mergers context. First, Article 86 was successfully invoked to challenge mergers that constituted abuses of existing dominance.[4] Then Article 85 was held to be capable of applying to acquisition agreements in some circumstances.[5] Nevertheless, it was always acknowledged that both these Treaty provisions had significant limitations and weaknesses as methods of merger supervision.[6]

The exact relationship between the Merger Regulation and Articles 85 and 86 still awaits definitive resolution, mainly on account of the compromise character of the Regulation. In the discussion that now follows, the original impact of the Treaty rules is examined first before analysing the scope and effects of the Regulation.

---

[1] This test forms the basis of the Merger Regulation, discussed below.
[2] For a discussion of the many techniques for achieving merger, see Weinberg and Blank, *Takeovers and Mergers*.
[3] 1989 O.J. L395/1: this is the revised text of the Regulation on the control of concentrations between undertakings, adopted on December 21, 1989, and which came into force on September 21, 1990.
[4] Case 6/72, *Europemballage and Continental Can* v. *Commission* [1973] E.C.R. 215, [1973] C.M.L.R. 199.
[5] Cases 142 and 156/84, *BAT Ltd. and R. J. Reynolds Inc.* v. *Commission and Philip Morris* [1987] E.C.R. 4487, [1987] 2 C.M.L.R. 551.
[6] Recital 6 to the Merger Regulation states that Articles 85 and 86 "are not . . . sufficient to control all operations which may prove to be incompatible with the system of undistorted competition envisaged in the Treaty."

Article 86[7]

The leading case on the application of this provision is *Continental Can*,[8] involving the acquisition by a dominant firm of a potential competitor in the packaging markets. Although the Commission's decision was annulled by the Court for lack of adequate analysis of the markets, the Court agreed that, in principle, Article 86 could apply to such acquisitions. This judgment was a landmark because it showed that an adverse effect on the competitive structure of a market could be sufficient in itself to attract the prohibition in Article 86. The Court rejected the claim that the provision could only govern market behaviour rather than structural measures, observing that "any structural measure may influence market conditions, if it increases the size and the economic power of the undertaking."[9]

However, as an instrument of merger control, Article 86 has serious drawbacks. Most importantly, it only applies to mergers which abuse existing dominance. The creation of a serious restriction or distortion of competition is not of itself enough to infringe Article 86. Moreover, this provision contains neither any advance notification procedure nor any system for exemption along the lines of Article 85. Evaluation of the competitive merits or disadvantages of a proposed merger is thus not an integral part of the machinery of Article 86. In the light of these difficulties, it is not surprising that the Commission made only modest use[10] of Article 86 in the wake of *Continental Can*.

Article 85[11]

In the early years of the Community, the Commission concluded that Article 85 did not apply to agreements whose purpose was the acquisition of total or partial ownership of enterprises or the reorganisation of the ownership of enterprises.[12] However, failure by the Member States to conclude specific legislation about mergers led to reconsideration by the Commission of the available Treaty tools. Leaving aside for the moment the subsequent impact of the Merger Regulation upon the current applicability of Article 85, the extent to which the latter applies to acquisitions must be seen against the judgment of the Court in the *BAT* case.[13] Some detailed background is necessary to establish the significance and scope of this ruling.

The case arose from agreements entered into by Rembrandt and Philip Morris, two leading tobacco companies. In April 1981 Rembrandt sold to

---

[7] See Chap. 15, *supra*.
[8] *Supra*, note 4.
[9] [1973] E.C.R. at 243.
[10] See Downes and Ellison, *The Legal Control of Mergers in the European Communities*, Chap. 1, esp. pp. 7–13.
[11] See Chap. 14, *supra*.
[12] *Memorandum on the problem of concentration in the common market*, Competition Series, No. 3, 1966, para. 58.
[13] *Supra*, note 5. The boundaries of this decision are examined by Korah and Lasok, (1988) 25 C.M.L.Rev. 333, Fine, (1987) E.C.L.R. 333, Strivens, (1988) E.I.P.R. 163. See also Downes, and Ellison, *op. cit., supra*, note 10, pp. 18–31.

Philip Morris a 50 per cent. equity interest in a previously wholly-owned subsidiary, Rothmans Holdings, and agreed that there should be joint management of it. Other companies, including *BAT*, complained to the Commission. As a result, a fresh arrangement was made, whereby Philip Morris relinquished its 50 per cent. equity in Rothmans Holdings and instead took a 30.8 per cent. stake in Rothmans International, a subsidiary of Rothmans Holdings. The voting rights were to be limited to 24.9 per cent. Other terms in the agreement between Rembrandt and Philip Morris included the right of first refusal in the event of disposal of the shareholdings in Rothmans International. Undertakings were given to the Commission that Philip Morris would not be represented in the management of Rothmans International. On this footing, the Commission accepted that the new agreement was compatible with Article 85(1). However, the two earlier complainant competitors still maintained their opposition. When the Commission formally rejected their complaints, they sought to have this act annulled in Article 173 proceedings.

The Court's ruling was controversial. In particular, it is not easy to reconcile the narrower and more expansive elements of the judgment. On the one hand, it stated[14]:

> "The main issue in these cases is whether and in what circumstances the acquisition of a minority shareholding in a competing company may constitute an infringement of Articles 85 and 86 of the Treaty. Since the acquisition of shares in Rothmans was the subject matter of agreements entered into by companies which have remained independent after the entry into force of the agreements, the issue must be examined first of all from the point of view of Article 85."

However, this limited view of the scope of the question must be seen against later paragraphs in the judgment where the Court observed[15]:

> "Although the acquisition by one company of an equity interest in a competitor does not in itself constitute conduct restricting competition, such an acquisition may nevertheless serve as an instrument for influencing the commercial conduct of the companies in question so as to restrict or distort competition on the market on which they carry on business.
>
> That will be true in particular where, by the acquisition of a shareholding or through subsidiary clauses in the agreement, the investing company obtains legal or *de facto* control of the commercial conduct of the other company or where the agreement provides for commercial cooperation between the companies or creates a structure likely to be used for such cooperation.
>
> That may also be the case where the agreement gives the investing company the possibility of reinforcing its position at a later stage and taking effective control of the other company. Account must be taken

---

[14] Paras. 30–31.
[15] Paras. 37–40.

not only of the immediate effects of the agreement but also of its potential effects and of the possibility that the agreement may be part of a long-term plan.

Finally, every agreement must be assessed in its economic context and in particular in the light of the situation pertaining on the relevant market . . ."

These comments omit the earlier references to minority acquisitions and maintaining independence after the agreement. Indeed, one of the problems to be examined in the light of the Merger Regulation is whether any regulatory "gap" exists between the notions of control employed by the Court in the *BAT* case and the tests to establish a concentration for the purposes of the Regulation.[16] Nevertheless, having established these potentially far-reaching points of principle, the Court took the view in *BAT* that the revised voting rights and the undertakings given about management representation meant that Philip Morris would not be in a position to restrict competition.[17] The complainants' claim against the Commission was therefore dismissed.

Developments since the *BAT* judgment have seen the application of Article 85 to other minority acquisitions[18] and to joint bids.[19] Article 85 has not been applied to open market purchases of shares, total mergers or passive minority investments. The arguments against using Article 85 in these situations (and, arguably, at all) point out the inappropriateness of the nullity sanction of Article 85(2), the repercussions of the revocability of exemptions under Article 85(3) and the adequacy of the evaluative criteria to be employed. From a business perspective, the "unspoken threat of an activist Commission"[20] intervening under either Article 85 or 86 in the middle of sensitive and delicately balanced negotiations probably constituted greater informal power in fact than might have been warranted by the narrowest construction of the decisions made by the Court.

In addition to the pressures of the "1992" programme, the somewhat open-ended possibilities surrounding the *BAT* judgment may have been partly responsible for the impetus given to negotiations over the Merger Regulation. In December 1989 the Member States finally reached agreement on the legislation, which took effect from September 21, 1990.[21]

THE MERGER REGULATION[22]

In broad terms, the Merger Regulation represents an attempt to provide a system of unitary control for mergers with a significant Community impact,

---

[16] Discussed further, *infra*.

[17] *Sed quaere*, see Fine, note 13, *supra*. The Advocate General in *BAT* would have held the Commission's decision to be defective for considering the cigarette market in isolation.

[18] See *Danish Fur Sales* [1989] 4 C.M.L.R. 353.

[19] See *Irish Distillers* (1988) 21 Bull. E.C. 7–8/34; *Plessey v. GEC and Siemens* [1992] 4 C.M.L.R. 471.

[20] Downes and Ellison, *op. cit.* note 10, p. 28, *supra*.

[21] The antecedents of the Regulation go back to 1973; see the first proposal published in 1973 O.J. C92/1.

[22] See Cook and Kerse, *EEC Merger Control*; Downes and Ellison, *op. cit.* note 10, *supra*; B. Hawk (ed.), *1990 Corporate Law Institute: International Mergers and Joint Ventures*. Of the

based on pre-notification to the Commission for evaluation and sanction. However, the political compromise[23] necessary to achieve the measure has also weakened its capacity to be a "one-stop" shop for merger supervision to the exclusion of national authorities and other provisions of the Treaty. These problems, together with doubts about the legal basis of the Regulation and the meaning of its central concepts, will be examined in the following stages: the qualifying conditions for notification, substantive appraisal by the Commission, the scope for application of national rules, the effect of the Regulation on other Treaty provisions and procedural matters.

Qualifying conditions

To trigger the application of the Merger Regulation there must be a concentration having a Community dimension. The former test is concerned with the structural alteration that is being achieved, whilst the latter is directed towards the economic significance and international character of the parties.

Concentration
This is defined in Article 3 of the Regulation and is deemed to arise where:

"(a) two or more previously independent undertakings merge, or
 (b) —one or more persons already controlling at least one undertaking, or
    —one or more undertakings
acquire, whether by purchase of securities of assets, by contract or by any other means, direct or indirect control of the whole or parts of one or more other undertakings."

Control is then further explained in paragraph 3 of Article 3 as constituted by rights, contracts or other means which confer the possibility of exercising decisive influence on an undertaking.[24]

It is not immediately apparent whether this test is different from the formulation adopted by the Court when interpreting Article 85 in the *BAT* case. "Decisive influence" is capable of being seen as a higher threshold to establish than "influence," so that some degree of investment or acquisition might be enough to fall within Article 85 but not constitute a concentration for the purposes of the Regulation.

The early case law of the Commission applying the control test demonstrates a flexible approach. In *Arjomari-Prioux/Wiggins Teape*,[25] for example, the Commission considered that the acquisition of a 39 per cent. stake gave the purchaser the ability to exercise decisive influence because

burgeoning periodical literature, see Venit, (1990) 27 C.M.L.Rev. 7; Siragusa and Subiotto, (1991) 28 C.M.L.Rev. 877; Kovar, (1990) 10 Yearbook of European Law 71.
[23] See Gardner, [1991] 4 I.C.C.L.R. 118; Elland, (1990) 3 E.C.L.R. 111.
[24] *Cf.* the test used under s.65 Fair Trading Act 1973 for mergers falling within domestic law, *i.e.* "materially to influence the policy of a body corporate."
[25] IV/M 025 1990 O.J. C321/16; [1991] 4 C.M.L.R. 8.

the remaining shares were widely dispersed among over 100,000 shareholders with no single member holding more than 4 per cent. Moreover, acquisition of minority holdings may give important rights of veto which will be sufficient to have the transaction classified as the creation of joint control. This has occurred in relation to the approval of annual budgets, strategic plans and financially important contracts.[26]

However, the Commission found in *Renault/Volvo*[27] that the proposed share swap of up to 25 per cent. in their car subsidiaries[28] did not give rise to the parties enjoying joint control over them. With no contractual provisions in place requiring co-decisions, the Commission pursued the circumstances of the deal to establish whether sufficient "commonality of interests" was present. It decided this question in the negative for several reasons,[29] principally that a "standstill" clause preventing either party from exceeding the 25 per cent. stake "secured the majority position of each party." The Commission was also of the view that it remained commercially feasible for each party to proceed independently in its car business, despite the co-operation agreement. For example, a Joint Car Committee had been established which could take decisions binding on both parties, so long as both parties agreed with those decisions. The practicality of this arrangement, according to the Commission, was that this provision formed a device to deny the Committee control over the car business of either party.

A special problem, expressly recognised in the Regulation, concerns the treatment to be given to joint ventures.[30] The Regulation distinguishes between concentrative joint ventures which will fall within its jurisdiction and co-operative joint ventures which are excluded.[31] According to Article 3(2) "an operation, including the creation of a joint venture, which has as its object or effect the coordination of the competitive behaviour of undertakings which remain independent shall not constitute a concentration." But on the other hand, "the creation of a joint venture performing on a lasting basis all the functions of an autonomous economic entity, which does not give rise to coordination of the competitive behaviour of the parties amongst themselves or between them and the joint venture, shall constitute a concentration." In an attempt to clarify the foreseeable difficulties arising from this demarcation, the Commission published a Notice[32] to explain the differences between concentrative and co-operative joint ventures.

There are two key elements which lead to a concentrative classification: performance of the functions of an autonomous economic entity and the

---

[26] See *Conagra/Idea* (IV/M010), 1991 O.J. C175/18, *Péchiney/Usinor-Sacilor* (IV/M097) 1991 O.J. C175/18) and *Lyonnaise des Eaux Dumez/Brochier* (IV/M076) 1991 O.J. C188/20. *Cf. Eridania/ISI* (IV/M062) 1991 O.J. C204/12.
[27] IV/M004 1990 O.J. C281/2, [1990] 4 C.M.L.R. 906.
[28] The 45 per cent. swap in bus and truck subsidiaries is discussed *infra*.
[29] Cook and Kerse, *op. cit.* note 22, suggest that the ghost of *BAT* may have loomed over the Commission in this case.
[30] See Sibree, (1992) 17 E.L.Rev. 91.
[31] These may be caught by Art. 85(1) if the tests of the *BAT* case, note 5, *supra*, are satisfied.
[32] *Commission Notice regarding concentrative and co-operative operations under Council Regulation 4064/89*, O.J. 1990 C203/10.

absence of co-ordination of behaviour by the undertakings. Both matters are highly delicate to evaluate, not least because the existence of mutual interests between parent companies is the very essence of a joint venture in the first place. The "autonomy" test is defined in both functional and decisional terms to accommodate the inevitable and legitimate concordance of interests in a joint venture.[33] Three criteria are especially significant to establish that a joint venture is functioning autonomously: i) that it acts as an independent supplier and purchaser on the market without remaining substantially dependent on its parents for the maintenance and development of its business, ii) that it has the human and material resources to ensure long-term independence and existence, and iii) that its business is not predicated upon facilities which remain economically integrated within the parents. In the context of decision-making, the relevant test is whether the joint venture is in a position to exercise its own commercial policy, based on the ability to plan, decide and act independently.[34]

The operation of the autonomy tests has emphasised the functional approach. In *Baxter/Nestlé/Salvia*,[35] for example, a combination of factors defeated any finding of autonomy. The necessary patent and know-how licences were only for a limited fixed term. Moreover, the parents still carried out research and development, and also continued as manufacturing sub-contractors whilst the joint venture was restricted to joint distribution. Conversely, in *Renault/Volvo*[36] a share swap between the two companies in relation to their bus and truck subsidiaries was accompanied by legally binding commitments to integrate the parties' development, production and purchasing operations, thereby creating a concentrative situation in which the parties would find it excessively costly to re-enter the market independently. Decisional criteria under the Notice seem to have been underplayed by the Commission, perhaps since it may be easier to assess policy freedom in the light of the co-ordination tests. However, the Commission tersely noted in *Mitsubishi/Union Carbide*[37] that a jointly owned subsidiary established on the basis of an agreement with no time limit was, on the facts, responsible for its own commercial policy. The matters on which the subsidiary was required to have the consent of the parents were all related to the need to protect the value of the shareholder's investment.

Whereas the criteria of autonomy appear to have been somewhat generously treated, the cases under the Regulation demonstrate a more exacting analysis of the co-ordination tests. The Notice postulates a range of situations, including joint ventures that undertake new activities on behalf of the parent companies, joint ventures that enter the parents' market, and those where they enter upstream, downstream or neighbouring markets.[38] Where the parents do not withdraw from the joint venture's market, or they are competitors in upstream or downstream markets, the Notice indicates

---

[33] *Ibid* at para. 23.
[34] *Ibid* at para. 18.
[35] IV/M058 O.J. 1990 C37/11, [1991] 4 C.M.L.R. 245.
[36] Note 27, *supra*.
[37] IV/M024 O.J. 1991 C5/7, [1992] 4 C.M.L.R. M50.
[38] Paras. 24–36 of the Notice.

that co-ordination will be either presumed or likely. However, not all decisions taken by the Commission seem consistent with this statement.[39] The risk of discriminatory treatment of joint ventures, depending on whether they fall within the Merger Regulation or Article 85(1), prompted the Commission to publish a discussion paper designed to ease the path for co-ordinating joint ventures under the latter regime.[40]

A Community dimension

The Regulation only applies to concentrations having "a Community dimension." This condition is satisfied if:

> "(a) the combined aggregate worldwide turnover of all the undertakings concerned is more than ECU 5,000 million; and (b) the aggregate Community-wide turnover of each of at least two of the undertakings concerned is more than ECU 250 million, unless each of the undertakings concerned achieves more than two-thirds of its aggregate Community-wide turnover within one and the same Member State."

It is thus size and Community impact of activity which combine to form the requisite significance of a concentration. The figures are the result of compromise in the Council, and a review procedure for the threshold was included in the Regulation.[41]

Calculation of turnover is set out in detail[42] in the Regulation. Essentially, it comprises the amounts derived by the undertakings concerned in the preceding financial year from the sale of products and the provision of services falling within the undertakings' ordinary activities after deductions of sales rebates and of value added tax and other taxes directly related to turnover, without taking into account intra-group transactions entered into by companies within the meaning of Article 5(4) of the Regulation. Special considerations apply to credit and financial institutions and insurance undertakings.[43] The proviso to the turnover thresholds, amounting to the "two-thirds" rule, is designed to prevent the Regulation from applying to concentrations in national markets. It, too, is subject to compulsory review.[44]

Less clear is the extent to which these threshold criteria amount to confirmation of the European Court's jurisprudence elsewhere on the scope of extraterritorial application of the Community's competition law rules.[45] It has been suggested[46] that the Regulation does not require the undertakings

---

[39] See *ABC/Compagnie Générale des Eaux/Canal +/W. H. Smith TV* (IV/M110) 1991 O.J. C244/5 and *Thomson/Pilkington* (IV/M086), discussed in Sibree, note 30, *supra*. *Cf.* the Commission's pre-Merger Regulation approach to Art. 85 displayed in *Mitchell Cotts/Sofiltra* 1986 O.J. L41/31.

[40] *Draft Co-Operative Joint Ventures (Antitrust) Guidelines* [1992] 4 C.M.L.R. 504.

[41] See Art. 3(3) providing for review before the end of the fourth year following adoption, by the Council acting by a qualified majority on a proposal from the Commission.

[42] Art. 5. See Cook and Kerse, *op. cit.* note 22, *supra*, Chap. 3.

[43] Art. 5(3).

[44] Art. 1(3).

[45] See joined Cases 89, 104, 114, 116, 117, 125–129/85, *Åhlstrom and others* v. *Commission (the "Woodpulp" case)* [1988] E.C.R. 5193. See Chap. 13, *supra*.

[46] Fine (1990) 2 E.C.L.R. 47.

concerned to have a legal presence in the Common Market. However, matters of substantive and enforcement jurisdiction are not expressly covered by the Regulation and caution should be exercised in canvassing any views which might extend the Court's rather restrictive view already taken in the context of Article 85.[47] Such references as obliquely exist in the Regulation incline towards assuming the presence of a territorial link of some sort with the Community. Recital 11, for example, after identifying the turnover basis constituting the necessary Community dimension, states:

"whereas that is also the case where the concentrations are effected by undertakings which do not have their principal fields of activities in the Community but which have substantial operations there."

Moreover, it might also be claimed that by dealing with matters of industrial structure, the control of concentrations is likely to be applied with greater restraint and sensitivity than in specific cases of market behaviour and effects, where a more adventurous approach to jurisdiction may produce less far-reaching consequences.[48]

Substantive appraisal of concentrations

The relevant criteria

The purpose of requiring notification of qualifying concentrations is to enable the Commission to establish whether they are compatible with the Common Market. According to Article 2(2) of the Regulation,

"A concentration which does not create or strengthen a dominant position as a result of which effective competition would be significantly impeded in the common market or in a substantial part of it shall be declared compatible with the common market."

Conversely, a concentration which does have such effects must be held incompatible with the common market. It may be noted immediately that this test goes further than the limits of *Continental Can*[49] relating to the application of Article 86 by contemplating that the *creation* of dominance is susceptible to control. In addition, the basic structure of Article 2 of the Regulation is neutral as to compatibility, leaving each case to be decided individually in the course of a single stage inquiry. As with Article 86, no exemption procedure as such is incorporated into the Regulation. However, although the language of Article 2 is obviously reminiscent of Article 86, it does not replicate it exactly and should be examined on its own merits.

The substance of the appraisal exercise is contained in Article 2, together with guidance from the Recitals to the Regulation. Article 2(1) provides:

"In making this appraisal, the Commission shall take into account:
(a) the need to maintain and develop effective competition within the common market in view of, among other things, the structure of all

---

[47] See Bourgeois (1990) 10 Yearbook of European Law 103.
[48] Lever and Lasok (1986) 6 Yearbook of European Law 121.
[49] Note 4, *supra*.

the markets concerned and the actual or potential competition from undertakings located either within or out-with the Community; (b) the market position of the undertakings concerned and their economic and financial power, the alternatives available to suppliers and users, their access to supplies or markets, any legal or other barriers to entry, supply and demand trends for the relevant goods and services, the interests of the intermediate and ultimate consumers, and the development of technical and economic progress provided that it is to consumers' advantage and does not form an obstacle to competition."

This competition-oriented evaluation must be set alongside the wider obligation of Recital 13, which states that the Commission "must place its appraisal within the general framework of the achievement of the fundamental objectives referred to in Article 2 of the Treaty, including that of strengthening the Community's economic and social cohesion, referred to in Article 130a."

Two recurring issues emerge from an examination of the application of the appraisal criteria. First, there is the question of how far the tests and considerations of the Article 86 case law may simply be imported into the assessments to be made under the Merger Regulation. In particular, attention should be paid to the methods of establishing the relevant product and geographical markets for the purpose of dominance. Secondly, the tension between competition and industrial or social criteria at least opens the possibility of inconsistent decision-making under the Regulation, even though the evidence at the moment may suggest that non-competitive criteria are not to the fore.

Market analysis

Article 2 of the Regulation refers to dominance, the result of which is a significant impediment to effective competition. It is suggested[50] that this is not a formal two-stage test, but instead a composite criterion which allows the Commission sufficient flexibility to depart from a mechanistic approach to dominance and its consequences. It enables other matters besides market share to be taken into account in measuring dominance and should ensure that a separate jurisprudence develops independently of the Article 86 case law.[51] By pursuing effective competition, the test also avoids the fruitless search for the perfect competition of economists' models.

The reference to significant impediment was originally seen by commentators as potentially a marked departure from Article 86. On one level the requirement could be construed as comparable to the *de minimis* rule which has long been recognised for the purposes of Article 85. This function seems compatible with the express statement in the Recitals to the Regulation that a market share not exceeding 25 per cent. either in the common market or in a substantial part of it would not be liable to impede

---

[50] Cook and Kerse, *op. cit.* note 22, *supra*, p. 68.
[51] Brittan, (1990) 15 E.L.Rev. 351.

effective competition.[52] Others have suggested[53] that the real contribution of the significant impediment requirement is that it focuses upon the dynamic nature of dominance, so that only real and lasting effects should be viewed with disfavour. However, the emerging case law under the Regulation suggests that the Commission has not been handicapped by the niceties of these possibilities. The emphasis of its decisions has been upon the creation or strengthening of dominance rather on measurement of the significance of the resulting impediment to effective competition.[54] Equally, the Commission has pursued examinations of concentrations which do not immediately create or strengthen dominance but which might do so in the future. Here the test appears to be whether such consequences are highly likely.[55]

In common with Article 86, the Regulation is predicated upon an analysis of the relevant markets before any existence or prospect of dominance can be established. With regard to product markets, some guidance is provided by the notification form used for qualifying concentrations, Form CO, which states that:

> "A relevant product market comprises all those products and/or services which are regarded as interchangeable or substitutable by the consumer, by reason of the products' characteristics, their prices and their intended use.... The product market will usually be the classification used by the undertaking in its marketing operations."

It has been noted[56] that this is a demand substitution test rather than one based on supply. Although supply factors have not been entirely overlooked,[57] the preponderance of the first decisions reveals reliance by the Commission upon the following[58]: the substitutability of products according to their end-use function,[59] the structure of demand leading to different competitive conditions[60] and the different categories of consumers or suppliers who might be affected by the concentration.[61]

Distinctions between the Regulation and Article 86 are more likely to arise in relation to the relevant geographical market. Again, some guidance is offered in Form CO, which provides:

> "The relevant geographic market comprises the area in which the

---

[52] Recital 15, although it should be noted that this figure seems remarkably high when set against the established *de minimis* jurisprudence under Article 85.

[53] Brittan, note 51, *supra*.

[54] *E.g. Alcatel/Telettra* (IV/M042) 1991 O.J. L122/48 [1991] 4 C.M.L.R. 405. See further Siragusa and Subiotto, *op. cit.* note 22, *supra*.

[55] *E.g. ATT/NCR* (IV/M050) 1991 O.J. C16/20 [1992] 4 C.M.L.R. M41 and *Matsushita/MCA* (IV/M 037) [1992] 4 C.M.L.R. M36.

[56] Siragusa and Subiotto, note 22, *supra*.

[57] *E.g. VIAG/Continental Can* (IV/M081) 1991 O.J. C156/10.

[58] Typology taken from Siragusa and Subiotto, *op. cit.* note 22, *supra*.

[59] As measured by price and/or other characteristics.

[60] Thus the presence of public procurement policies could be a distinguishing feature. *Cf. Renault/Volvo*, note 27, *supra*, where buses and coaches were distinguished on the footing that the former had purchasers in the public sector whilst the main purchaser for the latter was in the private sector.

[61] *E.g. Otto/Grattan* (IV/M070) 1991 O.J. C93/6, where mail order and other retail forms were examined for possible differences, although no distinction was ultimately found.

undertakings concerned are involved in the supply of products or services, in which the conditions of competition are sufficiently homogeneous and which can be distinguished from neighbouring areas because, in particular, conditions of competition are appreciably different in those areas.

Factors relevant to the assessment of the relevant geographic market include the nature and characteristics of the products or services concerned, the existence of entry barriers or consumer preferences, appreciable differences of the undertakings' market shares between neighbouring areas or substantial price differences."

Two complicating factors must be added here. First, the "1992" programme designed to secure the single internal market should carry with it an increasing view that the only relevant market for the purposes of the Regulation is Community-wide. Thus, in *ATT/NCR*[62] the Commission found a Community-wide market in financial and retail workstations (automatic cash dispensers and cash registers). Investors in such systems were guided by quality and accompanying service rather than national manufacturers. All the main players on the workstation markets could be found on almost all national markets. There was a substantial cross-border trade in such products and no unusually strong preference was present among end users for nationally manufactured products. Nevertheless, such cases are not the whole picture, and national markets continue to exist and to be assessed as such.[63]

Secondly, there is the express reference in the appraisal criteria of Article 2(1)(a) to:

"the structure of all the markets concerned and the actual or potential competition from undertakings located either within or out-with the Community."

This rather delphic statement raises the spectre of "Euro-champions" being defended through permitted dominance against American, Japanese or other rivals, and the possibility of evaluating concentrations against world markets rather than Community ones. As yet, the picture is not entirely clear, although Commissioner Sir Leon Brittan has forcefully rejected the first possibility, claiming that:

"our only concern is for competition within the Community and I reject the argument that a competitive world market may justify a dominant position in the Community.... There can be no trade-off between competition in the Community and competitiveness elsewhere. This would be economic nonsense and bad law ..."[64]

For political reasons, as well as competition ones, it is probably unrealistic to

---

[62] Note 55, *supra*.

[63] *E.g.* in insurance services (*AG/Amev* (IV/M018) 1990 O.J. C304/27 [1991] 4 C.M.L.R. 906), local food supermarkets (*Promodes/Dirsa* (IV/M027) 1990 O.J. C321/16, [1991] 4 C.M.L.R. 8), starter batteries (*Varta/Bosch* (IV/M012) April 12, 1991).

[64] *Op. cit.* note 51 *supra*, at p. 353. *Cf.* Elland, (1990) E.C.L.R. 111.

ignore the relevance of world implications for concentrations falling within the Regulation. But the scope for legal balancing of these considerations is controversial. The decision in *Aérospatiale/Messerschmitt-Bölkow-Blohm*[65] provides an illustration of the Commission's approach. The concentration arose from a joint venture between AS and MBB, respectively French and German helicopter manufacturers. The initial question as to the product market concerned the differences between civil and military markets. Although there was considerable interdependency between them, the Commission found that there were essential distinctions with regard to product characteristics, the structure of demand and the conditions of competition. In particular, the markets for military helicopters were in reality firmly drawn along national lines for those Member States who had their own helicopter industries (France, Germany, Italy and the United Kingdom). Given that AS and MBB held national monopolies, the Commission took the view that there would be no strengthening of dominance since there was no international competition between these States anyway. Moreover, competition in those Member States without national industries only amounted to 7 per cent. of the Community market in military helicopters. Therefore, according to the Commission, the concentration raised no problems of compatibility for this part of the market.

With regard to civil helicopters, the Commission concluded that the absence of barriers to entry and the mutual penetration of markets between the European Community, the United States of America and the rest of the world, meant that competition was world-wide. The proposed concentration would have given AS and MBB a combined share of just over 50 per cent. in the EC geographical market. The Commission cleared the proposal on the basis that the American competition potential was a sufficient guarantee to prevent the AS/MBB entity from being able to behave to an appreciable extent independently of its competitors and customers.[66] This was particularly likely given that American manufacturers were being faced with cuts in military budgets which would turn their attention to the civil market. In addition, AS and MBB had indicated that there would be no foreclosure of access by other manufacturers to technical co-operation and European development programmes as a result of the concentration. Finally, the Commission accepted that there would be little change in national civil markets apart from Germany, where AS had 40 per cent. and MBB 22 per cent. Here the Commission was satisfied that the total volume of trade was small and that the United States presence amounting to 33 per cent. was sufficient counterweight.

In other cases, the Commission's conclusions on the importance to be attached to world influences have not been free from criticism. Its findings in *Aérospatiale/Alenia-Aeritalia/de Havilland*,[67] for example, provoked

---

[65] IV/M017 [1992] 4 C.M.L.R. M70.
[66] This, of course, borrows the language of dominance embraced by the Article 86 case law, especially Case 322/81, *Michelin* [1983] E.C.R. 3461; see Chap. 15, *supra*.
[67] IV/M053 1991 O.J. L334/42, [1992] 4 C.M.L.R. M2.

considerable argument.[68] The case concerned the manufacture of regional turbo-prop aircraft, often undertaken by State-run enterprises. In its first ruling of incompatibility under the Regulation, the Commission identified three separate product markets based on seat capacity, and went on to find a world-wide geographical market with the exception of China and Eastern Europe. Its approach can be summarised by the reply later given by Sir Leon Brittan to a European Parliament question[69]:

> "The criteria for appraisal of concentrations under the Merger Regulation are the same for concentrations involving only European companies as for those involving also companies from outside the Community. Where a global market exists into which the Community market is fully integrated, the Commission takes this into account. In [this case], the Commission based its analysis on the world market for commuter aircraft in assessing the impact that the proposed concentration would have on the balance of competition in the Community."

This view may be contrasted with a minority opinion expressed within the Advisory Committee on Concentrations,[70] who did not accept the description or analysis of the market. In a strongly worded statement, the minority observed:

> "The Commission has chosen a methodology that gives the highest market shares possible to the parties ... not only is the Commission's approach to statistical analysis of the market flawed but ... the Commission has underestimated the strength of competitors and customers in the market, exaggerated the real strength of [de Havilland], ignored the history of competition in the market and the potential for new entrants. Further, this minority considers that the Commission is not so much protecting competition but rather protecting the competitors of the parties to this proposed concentration."

Whilst it must be recognised that all compatibility appraisals must be seen as case-specific, the conflicting views expressed here epitomise the tensions that are likely to arise even when the applicable criteria are themselves agreed.[71]

The finding of dominance

It is well established from the cases under Article 86 that market share is not the sole determinant of dominance.[72] This view applies with equal force

---

[68] See the editorial in (1992) 29 C.M.L.Rev. 1, drawing attention to the potential for conflict between the legal criteria of the Merger Regulation and the political character of the Commission as an institution.

[69] Question 2794/91, answer given February 10, 1992; see [1992] 4 C.M.L.R. 445.

[70] This must be consulted under Art. 19 of the Regulation (see procedures, *infra*); it consists of representatives of the authorities of the Member States.

[71] See also the minority opinion expressed in IV/M043, *Magneti Marelli/CEAc* [1992] 4 C.M.L.R. M61.

[72] See Chap. 15, and the discussion in Case 85/76, *Hoffman-La Roche* [1979] E.C.R. 461.

to the Merger Regulation. Various factors may offset or negate the significance of what might otherwise be considered powerful market shares. The presence of preponderant buyers,[73] the maturity or otherwise of the market,[74] the relative market shares of other players[75] and the range of opportunities for potential competitors to participate[76] may all contribute to the final assessment. It is clear that the Commission stresses the dynamics of the market and takes into account the fact that a competitor is particularly strong in the strategic parts of the overall market.[77]

Further clues as to the nature and purpose of the Commission's inquiry can be gleaned from the information required of notifying parties by Form CO.[78] It emphasises not just the product and geographical markets but the "affected markets" where the parties have horizontal[79] or vertical relationships.[80] Other required information concerns the general conditions in affected markets,[81] including views of the parties on the competitive environment, barriers to entry, research and development, as well as details of the parties' degree of vertical integration and participation in co-operative agreements in the affected markets.

An emerging issue, discussed already in the context of Article 86,[82] is the extent to which oligopolistic markets can given rise to collective dominance for the purposes of regulatory provision. The Merger Regulation appears no more equipped to deal with this problem than Article 86. A concentration in an oligopolistic market would not seem to satisfy the essential limb of Article 2 that it creates or strengthens dominance, even though there might be a distinct lessening of competition. The cases so far seem to suggest that the remaining market players following an oligopolistic concentration would be seen as providing countervailing strength.[83]

Compatibility of concentrations

Analysis of the markets and the degree of dominance resulting from the notified concentration will provide a competition-based view of its effects. But, as noted earlier, the overall compatibility of the concentration with the common market permits or, depending on view, demands some assessment

---

[73] E.g. Alcatel/Telettra note 54, supra, and Renault/Volvo, note 27, supra.
[74] Expressly considered in Mitsubishi/Union Carbide (IV/M024) [1992] 4 C.M.L.R. M50, para. 14 of the Commission's decision. See also para. 12 of Matsushita/MCA note 55, supra.
[75] See Magneti Marelli/CEAc note 71, supra, where the gap to the next largest competitor was 40 per cent. Also, ATT/NCR note 55, supra, Digital/Kienzle (IV/M057) 1991 O.J. C56/16, [1991] 4 C.M.L.R. 329.
[76] See Cargill/United Agricultural Merchanting (IV/M026) [1992] 4 C.M.L.R. M55.
[77] Aérospatiale/Alenia/de Havilland note 67, supra.
[78] Annex I to Commission Regulation 2367/90.
[79] Where two or more of the parties (including members of the same group) are engaged in business activities in the same product market or individual product group and where the concentration will lead to a combined market share of 10 per cent. or more.
[80] Where any of the parties (including undertakings belonging to the same group) is engaged in business activities in a product market which is upstream or downstream of a product market or individual product group in which any other party is engaged and any of their market shares is 10 per cent. or more, regardless of whether there is or is not any existing supplier/customer relationship between the parties concerned.
[81] Form CO, s.6.
[82] See Chap. 15, supra.
[83] See Renault/Volvo, note 27, supra. Cf. Fiat Geotech/Ford New Holland (IV/M009) 1991 O.J. C118/14, [1991] 4 C.M.L.R. 329.

of other factors. In addition to the economic and social cohesion reference made by Recital 13, there is also the Commission's observation[84] that account should be taken in particular of the competitiveness of undertakings located in regions which are greatly in need of restructuring owing *inter alia* to slow development.

Moreover, the criteria expressly set out in Article 2(1)(b) are not limited to matters of competition. The references to "economic and technical progress" and to the "interests of the intermediate and ultimate consumers" are reminiscent of the grounds listed for exemption in Article 85(3). The former, especially, could be construed as an invitation to examine matters of industrial policy. However, the proviso that technical and economic progress must not form an obstacle to competition appears to minimise any such possibility. Indeed, it may be difficult to see what function is left for this consideration since any concentration must satisfy the competition criteria to achieve compatibility. The task envisaged for technical and economic progress seems not one of balancing competing interests, but of reinforcing an already substantiated case.

The scope for application of national rules

The much-proclaimed attribute of the Regulation as it was being formulated was its capacity to become a "one-stop shopping" forum for the assessment of significant concentrations within the Community. However, the political compromises which shaped the final version of the legislation have left holes in the blanket coverage which was once intended.[85] Discussion of the scope for national authorities principally concerns Articles 9 (the so-called German clause) and 21(3). These cover distinct national markets and legitimate notifiable interests respectively.

Distinct Markets

Under Article 9(2) of the Merger Regulation, within three weeks of receiving its copy of a concentration notification,

> "a Member State may inform the Commission, which shall inform the undertakings concerned, that a concentration threatens to create or to strengthen a dominant position as a result of which effective competition would be significantly impeded on a market within that Member State, which presents all the characteristics of a distinct market, be it a substantial part of the common market or not."

If the Commission decides that such a distinct market and threat exist, it may either itself deal with the case or refer it to the competent authorities of the Member State concerned with a view to the application of that State's national competition law.[86] The Member State in the latter event may take only the measures strictly necessary to safeguard or restore effective

---

[84] *Accompanying statements entered in the minutes of the EC Council* [1990] 4 C.M.L.R. 314.
[85] See Bright, (1991) E.C.L.R. 139 and 184.
[86] Art. 9(3).

competition on the market concerned.[87] National authorities must decide the case within four months after referral by the Commission.[88] It has been seen as regrettable that no special procedure is provided to check the measures taken in such circumstances by the Member States.[89]

In a joint statement[90] concerning the use of Article 9, the Council and Commission indicated that the referral procedure should only be applied in exceptional cases where the interests in respect of competition of the Member State concerned could not be adequately protected in any other way. The first occasion on which the procedure was used concerned the notification in relation to bricks and clay tiles made by *Steetley/Tarmac*.[91] With regard to bricks, there were two local markets within the United Kingdom, the North-East and the South-West, where there was a threat of the creation of a dominant position if the proposed joint venture between the two companies went ahead. The position concerning clay tiles was different insofar as the relevant market was Great Britain as a whole. However, the key point was that the venture would give the new company a clear lead in what had hitherto been a highly concentrated market between three principal companies. This, together with significant entry barriers and little impact on any other part of the Community, led to the decision to send the matter back to the national authorities. A final consideration was that one of the parties was the target of a bid by a third party, although this transaction would not have crossed the turnover thresholds to trigger the Regulation.[92] Nevertheless, the Commission noted that it was better for related cases to be dealt with by one regulatory authority if at all possible.[93]

The proviso in Article 9 that a distinct market reference can be made whether it is a substantial part of the common market or not raises a potential difficulty in terms of the relationship between Article 9 and Article 2. It is clear enough that in a situation where the concentration affects a substantial part of the common market whilst still being a distinct national one, the Commission could choose to handle the case itself and proceed to a normal appraisal exercise. What is less obvious is the competence of the Commission to rule upon a case which did not comprise a substantial part of the common market since only concentrations with the latter quality fall within the scope of Article 2. To be able to handle such a case at all demands that Article 9 is given the status of a *lex specialis* in relation to Article 2. Such a step would also confer a greater jurisdiction upon the Commission than is present under Articles 85 and 86.

The other difficulty, which was overcome in the *Steetley/Tarmac* decision, is the extent to which a distinct market can be established in the light of

---

[87] Art. 9(8).
[88] Art. 9(6), *i.e.* the same as the comparable EC level machinery: see Art. 10(3).
[89] Kovar, *op. cit.* note 22, *supra* p. 97.
[90] Note 84, *supra*.
[91] IV/M180 1992 O.J. C50/25.
[92] Once the concentration was sent back under Art. 9, the Secretary of State announced the referral of the joint venture to the Monopolies and Mergers Commission. On the same day it was announced that the separate bid for Steetley would also be referred unless adequate undertakings were given. These were in fact obtained and the latter reference abandoned.
[93] [1992] 4 C.M.L.R. 343.

increasing homogeneity of market conditions. According to Article 9(7) such a distinct market must display conditions of competition which are "appreciably different" from neighbouring areas.

The converse of the "German" clause may be seen in the "Dutch" clause contained in Article 22(3) whereby a Member State may request the Commission to apply the Regulation to a concentration which does not have a Community dimension in relation to its own territory. This provision is intended to prevent lacunae arising where concentrations which fall beneath the Regulation's thresholds occur in Member States without merger controls. The need for some Community impact is nevertheless maintained by the requirement that the Commission's intervention is only possible at the request of the Member State concerned and if trade between Member States is affected. The appraisal under the Article 22(3) procedure seeks to examine whether effective competition will be significantly impeded within the territory of the Member State concerned.

An important potential scenario for conflict is provided by the observation in the interpretative statements[94] that the Dutch clause in no way prejudices the power of Member States, other than the one at whose request the Commission intervenes, to apply their national laws within their respective territories. In other words, any Member State having jurisdiction over a transnational concentration falling beneath the Regulation thresholds may intervene despite another State having requested Commission action. The resolution of this appears to lie in the approach taken elsewhere by the Court to matters of combined Community and national jurisdiction.[95]

The protection of legitimate interests

Article 21(2) of the Regulation baldly states that "No Member State shall apply its national legislation on competition to any concentration that has a Community dimension." However, this is qualified by paragraph (3), which provides that:

> "Member States may take appropriate measures to protect legitimate interests other than those taken into consideration by this Regulation and compatible with the general principles and other provisions of Community law.
>
> Public security, plurality of the media and prudential rules shall be regarded as legitimate interests within the meaning of the first subparagraph.
>
> Any other public interest must be communicated to the Commission by the Member State concerned and shall be recognised by the Commission after an assessment of its compatibility with the general principles and other provisions of Community law before the measures referred to above may be taken. The Commission shall inform the

---

[94] Note 84, *supra.*
[95] Case 14/68, *Walt Wilhelm* v. *Bundeskartellamt* [1969] E.C.R. 1.

Member State concerned of its decision within one month of that communication."

This provision, inserted at the request of several States as the price to be paid for giving up national control over concentrations, is likely to receive the strict interpretation that the European Court has always applied to derogations in Community measures. In its interpretative statement[96] on Article 21, the Commission has observed that it does not create any new rights for Member States, nor does it imply the attribution to them of any power to authorise concentrations which the Commission may have prohibited under the Regulation.

In the three specified cases, public security, plurality of the media and prudential rules, Member States may intervene as of right. The first of these concepts covers defence interests as interpreted in other areas of the Treaty by the Court.[97] Plurality of the media recognises the legitimate concern to maintain diversified sources of information for the sake of plurality of opinion and multiplicity of views. The prudential rules which form the third concrete interest relate to the surveillance of financial bodies and usually take the form of requirements as to the honesty of transactions, the good repute of individuals and rules governing solvency.

Any other interest which a Member State may wish to plead must be notified in advance. It does not have to relate to a particular concentration. Three limitations operate to prevent this becoming an open-ended escape route from the Community's jurisdiction. First, the terms of the provision make it clear that any legitimate interest must be beyond the matters already contained in the Regulation. It has been suggested[98] that the reference to technical and economic progress in Article 2 may play an important rôle here in excluding any further arguments by Member States on these grounds. Secondly, any pleaded interest must satisfy the general principles and other provisions of Community law. Thus well-established doctrines recognised by the Court, such as proportionality, may defeat overly extensive claims. Finally, although strictly no more than a specific allusion to one of the "other provisions" to be applied, the Commission has stated that it is essential that prohibitions or restrictions placed on the forming of concentrations should constitute neither a form of arbitrary discrimination nor a disguised restriction in trade between Member States.[99]

The Merger Regulation and other Community rules

Two questions are significant: the extent to which the Regulation has a secure legal base, and the remaining scope for the application of Articles 85 and 86 in the light of the purported exclusive jurisdiction of the Regulation.

---

[96] Note 84, *supra*.
[97] Thus embracing the approach taken in Case 72/83, *Campus Oil* [1984] E.C.R. 2727.
[98] Downes and Ellison, *op. cit.* note 10, p. 212, *supra*.
[99] *Accompanying Statements*, note 84, *supra*. This formula is taken from the proviso to Art. 36, allowing derogations from the free movement of goods rules.

Legal basis

The Recitals to the Regulation stress that it was introduced to meet the objective of Article 3(f) EEC as part of ensuring a system of undistorted competition. After noting that Articles 85 and 86 had not proved adequate for this task, it is stated that:

"a new legal instrument should therefore be created in the form of a Regulation to permit effective control of all concentrations from the point of view of their effect on the structure of competition in the Community and to be the only instrument applicable to such concentrations."[1]

Recital 9 then provides that the Regulation "should therefore be based not only on Article 87 but, principally, on Article 235 of the Treaty, under which the Community may give itself the additional powers of action necessary for the attainment of its objectives."

By acknowledging the deficiences of Articles 85 and 86 as instruments for merger control, the Regulation could hardly be exclusively based on Article 87, since the latter is concerned with the adoption of measures to implement those very provisions. As part of its rôle in giving effect to the principles of Articles 85 and 86, Article 87 also provides expressly for measures which determine the relationship between national laws and the competition part of the Treaty. The fact that Article 87 is the basis for implementing legislation such as Regulation 17[2] is also relevant to its inclusion as a basis for the Merger Regulation, since it is by disapplying that earlier legislation that the Merger Regulation seeks to remove the scope for use of Articles 85 and 86.

The effect on Articles 85 and 86

The objective of "one-stop shopping" assumes that the only regime for control of relevant concentrations should be at Community level through the Commission as adjudicator. However, the effect of the Merger Regulation on the application of Articles 85 and 86 is far from obvious. In part this is the result of internal inconsistencies within the Regulation. There are also difficulties relating to the status of secondary legislation in relation to substantive Treaty provisions. Finally, whatever impact the Regulation may have had on the application by the Commission of Articles 85 and 86, there remains a separate issue as to the use of the latter by individuals in accordance with the normal principles of direct effect.

Discussing these in turn, the purported aim of the Regulation is clouded by the difference between concentrations and those with a community dimension. Article 1(1) states that, without prejudice to Article 22, the Regulation applies to all concentrations with a Community dimension as defined in Article 1(2). However, Article 22(1) provides that "this Regulation alone shall apply to concentrations as defined in Article 3."

---

[1] Recital 8.
[2] Reg. 17/62, discussed more fully in Chap. 16, *supra.*

Article 22(2) goes on to disapply Regulation 17/62 and other implementing legislation in specific sectors[3] from all concentrations. The outcome at face value is that whilst only concentrations with a Community dimension are notifiable to the Commission for assessment against the compatibility criteria of the Regulation, all concentrations (*i.e.* including those without a Community dimension but which satisfy the control tests of Article 3) are removed from Community control other than the Regulation. Thus, the argument runs, "mere" concentrations escape Commission intervention altogether. It might still be possible to suggest that Article 85 could apply to *BAT*-type situations if the view were taken that the difference between "decisive influence" and "influence" meant that the latter failed to meet the definition of concentration in the first place, thereby escaping the exclusive net of the Regulation altogether.

Whether such exclusivity is in fact achieved by the Regulation is questionable. Certainly, scepticism should be applied to the pretensions of Article 22(1), since it cannot be within the powers of the Regulation to achieve directly what its declaration of exclusivity purports to do impliedly, that is to disapply Treaty provisions.

The other technique which is relied upon to achieve the same result is more plausible. By disapplying Regulation 17 from concentrations, the Commission appears to have given up its own rights to utilise the other competition provisions, other than through individual decisions under Article 89 of the Treaty. However, its stated view[4] is a little more cautious, noting that it does not "normally" intend applying Articles 85 and 86 to concentrations as defined in Article 3 of the Merger Regulation. It expressly reserves the right to take action under Article 89 with regard to concentrations not having a Community dimension, subject to a working *de minimis* threshold.[5]

The disapplication of Regulation 17 from concentrations reactivates Article 88 of the Treaty so far as national competition authorities are concerned, allowing them to take decisions on matters arising under Article 85, especially paragraph (3) exemptions, and Article 86.

From the different perspective of individual rights, the effect of the Merger Regulation also awaits definitive clarification. The consequences under Articles 85 and 86 seem distinguishable. In relation to the former, the effect of the disapplication of Regulation 17 is to remove the sanction of nullity available under Article 85(2). In a different context, the Court has already held[6] that in the absence of implementing legislation adopted under Article 87, agreements alleged before national courts to fall foul of Article 85 are deemed to be provisionally valid until such time as the Commission, acting under Article 89 or the Member State, invoking Article 88, has

---

[3] Reg. 4056/86 (maritime transport), Reg. 3975/87 (air transport), and Reg. 1017/68 (road transport).
[4] *Accompanying Statements*, note 84, *supra*.
[5] *I.e.* worldwide turnover of less than 2,000 million ECUs or below a minimum Community turnover of less than 100 million ECUs.
[6] Cases 209–213/84, *Ministère Public* v. *Lucas Asjes and others (Nouvelles Frontieres)* [1986] E.C.R. 1425.

established their illegality. It would therefore seem that if the disapplication of Regulation 17 is effective, the rights of individuals to use Article 85 with regard to any concentration as defined in the Merger Regulation have been removed.

It is this very outcome which may raise some doubts as to the vires of the Regulation. Indeed, it has been suggested[7] that the realignment of rôles between Community and Member States brings about a restriction of the previous scope of Community law and could not be characterised as satisfying the essential characteristics of action justified under Article 235 of the Treaty.

Recourse to Article 86, however, remains available for individuals. The Court's judgment in *Ahmed Saeed*[8] affirmed the direct effect of this provision, and held it to be fully applicable to the air transport sector even without the presence of implementing rules. Whereas the absence of such legislation under Article 85 gave rise to the possibility of national authorities or the Commission intervening to give exemptions under Articles 88 or 89 respectively, no such exemption considerations existed within Article 86. Its prohibition could therefore be applied by national courts. Translating this into the context of the Merger Regulation, the effect is that its disapplication of Regulation 17 has no impact on the applicability of Article 86 for individuals. This may not necessarily be of enormous practical value, in so far as the weaknesses of Article 86 as a tool for regulating mergers have already been explained.[9] Where a concentration has a Community dimension, the Regulation will, of course, be applicable. It has been suggested[10] that an attempt to seek redress from a national court on the basis of Article 86 in relation to a duly notified concentration would be regarded as frivolous.[11]

Procedures under the Merger Regulation

This chapter is not an appropriate place for the detailed explanation of the forms, time-limits, investigative powers and follow-up procedures which are essential to the practical application of the Regulation.[12] However, the following represents an overview of the key stages in the notification process. The relevant sources comprise the Merger Regulation itself, the Regulation on Notifications,[13] and the Notices on Ancillary Restrictions[14] and on Concentrations and Co-operative Operations.[15]

Within one month at most[16] from receipt of a concentration notification,

---

[7] Venit, (1990) C.M.L.Rev. 7 at 17. The author also suggests further arguments to challenge the vires of the Regulation.
[8] Case 66/86, *Ahmed Saeed* [1989] E.C.R. 838.
[9] *Supra*, p. 496.
[10] Cook and Kerse, *op. cit.* note 22, p. 140, *supra*.
[11] Although this would not affect the right to seek protection under Art. 7 of the Regulation suspending the implementation of concentrations with a Community dimension.
[12] See Cook and Kerse, *op. cit.* note 22, especially Chap. 5 and Appendix 8. See also Thieffry, Van Doorn and Nahmias, (1991) 25 The International Lawyer 615.
[13] Reg. 2367/90, 1990 O.J. L219/5.
[14] 1990 O.J. C203/5.
[15] 1990 O.J. C203/6.
[16] Merger Reg. Art. 10(1).

the Commission must decide whether it falls within the scope of the Merger Regulation and, if so, whether doubts are raised as to its compatibility with the common market. Discussion of the completeness of Form CO is likely to take place informally between the parties and the Merger Task Force set up within the Commission. Article 6(1) affords three actions to the Commission: (a) to issue a decision recording that the concentration is not caught by the Regulation; (b) to issue a non-opposition decision, on the basis that the concentration, whilst falling within the Regulation, does not raise serious doubts as to compatibility; or (c) to issue a decision initiating proceedings because of serious doubts raised as to compatibility.

If the Commission moves to initiate proceedings, the relevant procedures depend upon whether the serious doubts continue, are eliminated by undertakings of the parties or are removed in the course of further investigation. The latter two situations will result in a decision of compatibility under Article 8(2)(2) or 8(2)(1) of the Regulation. Where full investigation does not remove the serious doubts then a decision finding incompatibility will result under Article 8(3). For each of these decisions a preliminary draft decision must be put before the Advisory Committee on concentrations, constituted in accordance with Article 19, for an opinion. The Commission is obliged to "take the utmost account" of the opinion and has to inform the Committee of the manner in which this has been done.[17] The Committee may recommend publication of the opinion, in which case the decision to publish must take account of the undertakings' legitimate interests.

Mergers may not be put into effect either before notification or within the first three weeks following its notification.[18] The Commission is empowered to extend this period of suspension for the entire duration of its investigation. It is also given powers to obtain all necessary information from Governments and competent authorities of Member States, from persons in control within the meaning of Article 3(1)(b) and from undertakings and associations of undertakings.[19] Article 13 allows the Commission to undertake all necessary investigations, including rights of entry and examinations of books and records.[20]

Breaches of the notification requirements are enforceable by fines. This is a different regime from the rules laid down in Regulation 17 for competition policy generally.[21] Under Article 14 of the Merger Regulation, fines ranging from 1,000 to 50,000 ECUs may be levied for failing to notify or for submitting inaccurate or misleading information. Fines representing up to 10 per cent. of aggregate turnover of the undertakings may be imposed for failing to comply with decisions or going ahead with incompatible concentrations. Decisions to impose fines must go before the Advisory Committee.

---

[17] Art. 19(6).
[18] Art. 7(1).
[19] Art. 11(1).
[20] *Cf.* the powers conferred under Reg. 17.
[21] See Chap. 16, *supra*.

The processes of the Merger Regulation emphasise the need for the Commission to issue decisions at various stages. These must, of course, comply with the normal requirements of Community law.[22] Rights of challenge will therefore be governed by Article 173 and 175. It remains to be seen how judicial review will operate in the context of the Merger Regulation. In particular, the position of competitors may be threatened in cases where a non-opposition decision is issued under Article 6(1)(b), perhaps in response to caseload and political climate. It has been suggested[23] that a flexible approach to the *locus standi* requirements of Article 173(2) in such situations is needed to offset pressure on the Commission not to initiate investigation proceedings.

The Merger Regulation, itself the protracted result of political compromise, may thus prove the catalyst for important developments in refining the proper scope of the Commission's powers as a legal and political animal and the extent of individual protection. Meanwhile, at the functional level, the capacity of the Regulation to be used for social and economic cohesion purposes rather than narrower competition objectives remains untested.

---

[22] See Hartley, *The Foundations of European Community Law*.
[23] See editorial, (1992) 29 C.M.L.Rev. 1 at p. 4.

CHAPTER 18

STATE AIDS

State aids and the common market

The provision out of public funds of subsidies or other forms of aid to undertakings is generally considered a necessary instrument of government policy even in countries like the Member States of the EEC where free competition and the market mechanism continue to occupy a central place in the economic system. The purpose of such aid may be, for example, to attract investment into areas that are economically underdeveloped or where the existing industries are declining; or to enable the undertakings in a given industrial sector to improve their efficiency; or to encourage the development of new, high-technology industries requiring heavy expenditure on research and development. In particular, during a period of economic difficulty, such as that through which the Community and the other industrialised nations have been passing, there are strong social and political pressures for State aids to be used to preserve jobs, even where there is no real prospect of the undertakings in question returning to profitability.[1]

State aid is liable to cause serious difficulties in a system which has as its primary objective the creation and maintenance of a single internal market.

In the first place, by giving particular firms in a Member State an unearned competitive advantage over other providers of the goods or services in question, aid may interfere with the functioning of the market mechanism at the Community level. This may be so, whether the aided product is sold on the domestic market or exported to another Member State. In the former case, the aid may constitute an indirect barrier to trade by protecting the less efficient home industry against competition from imports. In the latter case, the aid may make it possible to penetrate an export market, threatening an industry in the State of importation which would otherwise be perfectly viable. Either situation is likely to give rise to pressure from the disadvantaged industry for its own government to provide compensatory aid, which makes no economic sense. There will also be temptation, when the threat comes from aided imports, for a government to take steps to keep them out, even at the risk of infringing Article 30 EEC. Thus massive French aid to the poultry industry in Brittany provided a spur to the illegal action by the Government of the United Kingdom in the *Turkey* case.[2]

Secondly, the dismantling of barriers between the national economies means that the aid policies of one Member State react on those of another, affecting both their cost and their prospects of success. As the Commission has written:

---

[1] An idea of the vast range of aids applied by the Member States can be obtained from the annual *Report on Competition Policy* produced by the Commission.
[2] Case 40/82, *Commission* v. *United Kingdom* [1982] E.C.R. 2793; [1982] 3 C.M.L.R. 497.

"Conflict between objectives and measures drawn up essentially within national contexts may very well result in a reciprocal neutralisation of national policies, or in a shifting of difficulties from one Member State to another, or even in new difficulties arising."[3]

Regional aids are a good example. Where governments bid against each other to attract investment funds, aid is liable to be fixed at a higher level than is warranted to compensate for the disadvantage of a given region; and resources may be diverted from those parts of the Community where they are needed most.

The express adoption of a policy of economic and social cohesion,[4] directed towards reduction in the disparities between the levels of development of the various regions and the backwardness of the least favoured regions, creates additional pressure upon the system of State aids supervision. Although the Commission has recognised the part to be played by aids in promoting cohesion,[5] commentators have claimed that a significant realignment will be required to counteract the previous heavy emphasis upon aid to large companies in central regions.[6]

State aids have thus always played a pivotal role in the common market, and will be especially controversial in the creation and maintenance of the single internal market. Their original inclusion in the EEC Treaty might have been as an element in a common industrial policy to be formulated at Community level. However, the only option that was politically feasible was to allow the Member States to continue granting aids but to establish a system of supervision by the Community institutions.

The relevant provisions of the Treaty are Articles 92 to 94.

The structure of Article 92 EEC

Article 92 EEC sets out the principles on the basis of which the compatibility of State aids with the common market is to be judged.[7]

Paragraph (1) of the Article lays down the general principle that State aids fulfilling certain broadly defined criteria are incompatible with the common market. The paragraph does not expressly declare incompatible aids to be prohibited (cf. the drafting of Articles 85 and 86 EEC) but the European Court has accepted that it contains an implied prohibition.[8]

The general principle in Article 92(1) is qualified by "exceptions *ipso jure*" listed in paragraph (2) and "discretionary exceptions" listed in paragraph (3). If an aid is found to be within one of the categories in paragraph (2), it

---

[3] Comp. Rep. 1971, point 133.
[4] Art. 130a EEC. See also the revised Art. 2 and Art. 3(j) of the EEC Treaty in the Maastricht agreement, as yet unratified.
[5] See Comp. Rep. 1990 point 169.
[6] See J. Gilchrist and D. Deacon in P. Montegnon (ed.), *European Competition Policy*, Chap. 3 esp. pp. 45–50. Also, Evans & Martin, (1991) 16 E.L.Rev. 79.
[7] On the interpretation of Art. 92 see further Schina, *State Aids under the EEC Treaty Articles 92 to 94*; Vaughan, *Law of the European Communities*, Vol. I, Pt. 7.
[8] See the references to "an aid which is prohibited" in Case 6/69, *Commission* v. *France* [1969] E.C.R. 523 and "the prohibition in Article 92(1)" in Case 78/76, *Firma Steinike und Weinlig* v. *Germany* [1977] E.C.R. 595; [1977] 2 C.M.L.R. 688.

must, as a matter of law, be regarded as compatible with the common market. On the other hand, the compatibility of aids falling within the categories in paragraph (3) is a discretionary matter, requiring an assessment of the positive and negative effects of the aid from the point of view of the Community as a whole. Under the machinery of Article 93 (see below) that discretion is exercised by the Commission, subject to reserve powers of the Council and the usual control by the European Court.

Article 92(1): aids incompatible with the common market

Article 92(1) provides:

> "Save as otherwise provided in this Treaty, any aid granted by a Member State or through State resources in any form whatsoever which distorts or threatens to distort competition by favouring certain undertakings or the production of certain goods shall, in so far as it affects trade between Member States, be incompatible with the common market."

A general definition of State aid for the purposes of the EEC Treaty was offered by the European Court in Case 61/79, *Amministrazione delle finanze dello stato* v. *Denkavit*,[9] where it said that paragraph (1) of the Article:

> "refers to the decisions of Member States by which the latter, in pursuit of their own economic and social objectives give, by unilateral and autonomous decisions, undertakings or other persons resources or procure for them advantages intended to encourage the attainment of the economic or social objectives sought."[10]

State aid is thus to be understood in terms of its function as an instrument of national economic and social policy involving the provision of some kind of tangible benefit for specific undertakings or individuals.

It is immaterial what form the benefit may take or what particular goal of policy it may be designed to serve. In Case 173/73, *Italy* v. *Commission*[11] the measure in question was a provision in an Italian statute reducing for a period of three years the contributions payable in respect of family allowances by employers in the textile industry. It had been argued, *inter alia*, on behalf of the Italian Government that this measure could not constitute an aid because it took the form of a reduction of tax liability and because the charge to which it applied was an instrument of social policy. In rejecting that argument, the Court said:

> "The aim of Article 92 is to prevent trade between Member States from being affected by benefits granted by the public authorities which, in

---

[9] [1980] E.C.R. 1205; [1981] 3 C.M.L.R. 694.
[10] [1980] E.C.R. at p. 1228; *cf.* the position under the ECSC Treaty, Case 30/59, *Steenkolenmijnen* v. *High Authority* [1961] E.C.R. 1 at p. 19; "An aid is a very similar concept [to a subsidy], which, however, places emphasis on its purpose and seems especially devised for a particular objective which cannot normally be achieved without outside help."
[11] [1974] E.C.R. 709; [1974] 2 C.M.L.R. 593.

various forms, distort or threaten to distort competition by favouring certain undertakings or the production of certain goods.

Accordingly, Article 92 does not distinguish between the measures of State intervention concerned by reference to their causes or aims but defines them in relation to their effects.

Consequently, the alleged fiscal or social aim of the measure in issue cannot suffice to shield it from the application of Article 92."[12]

A useful list of forms of aid was given by the Commission in reply to a Written Question in 1963,[13] comprising: direct subsidies; exemption from duties and taxes; exemption from parafiscal charges; preferential interest rates; guarantees of loans on especially favourable terms; making land or buildings available either gratuitously or on especially favourable terms; provision of goods or services on preferential terms; indemnities against operating losses; or any other measure of equivalent effect. This was further elaborated in a subsequent document[14] to include: reimbursement of costs in the event of success; State guarantees, whether direct or indirect, to credit operations; preferential rediscount rates; dividend guarantees; preferential public ordering; and deferred collection of fiscal or social contributions. The catalogue should not, of course, be regarded as exhaustive, although it covers the forms of aid most frequently granted by the Member States[15] The elasticity of the concept of aid is only matched by the difficulties in detecting it. To ameliorate this problem, the Commission embarked upon surveys of State aid in the Community which have given rise to two reports.[16] The picture which emerged was one of considerable variations in scale and type of aid within the Member States, confirming the seriousness of the threat to undistorted competition which aids present.

An issue which has recently come to the fore is the provision of aid through the purchase by the State of shares in a company. The *Intermills* case[17] concerned action taken by the authorities in Belgium for the benefit of a paper-making firm which was in financial difficulties. Loans had been made to the firm and there had been an injection of capital into it by the Walloon Regional Executive, giving the latter a controlling interest. The European Court held that no distinction could be drawn between aid granted in the form of loans and aid granted in the form of a holding acquired in the capital of a undertaking. This declaration that State participation can amount in principle to an aid has been consistently followed in a series of cases.[18] The test to be applied is whether the undertaking could have obtained the amounts in question on the capital market. Thus, if a

---

[12] *Ibid* pp. 718–719.
[13] J.O. 1963, 2235. See also Quigley, (1988) 13 E.L.Rev. 242.
[14] Doc. 20.502/IV/68 of December 1968, cited by Venceslai, (1969) Riv.Dir.Eur. 257 at p. 258.
[15] A catalogue of policy guidelines, aid codes and regulations relating to aids was published by the Commission in 1990, *Competition Law in the European Communities, Volume II: Rules applicable to State Aids.*
[16] *First Survey on State Aids, 1989. Second Survey, 1990.*
[17] [1984] E.C.R. 3809; [1986] 1 C.M.L.R. 614.
[18] See, *inter alia*, Joined Cases 296 and 318/82, *The Netherlands and Leeuwarder Papierwaren fabriek BV* v. *Commission* [1985] E.C.R. 809; [1985] 3 C.M.L.R. 380; Case 40/85, *Re Boch: Belgium* v. *Commission* [1986] E.C.R. 2321; [1988] 2 C.M.L.R. 301; Case C–142/87, *Re*

company's prospects of profitability are not such as to induce private investors operating under normal market economy conditions to subscribe, State intervention by equity or other support will be construed as an aid.[19] In *Re Boch*[20] the Court observed:

> "In the case of an undertaking whose capital is almost entirely held by the public authorities, the test is, in particular, whether in similar circumstances a private shareholder, having regard to the foreseeability of obtaining a return and leaving aside all social, regional policy and sectoral considerations, would have subscribed the capital in question."

The Commission has been sufficiently encouraged by the Court's support to assert these notions as the market economy investor principle.[21]

Attempts to question the appropriateness of the comparison with private investors have so far failed. It was suggested by the applicant in *Italy* v. *Commission*[22] that a private holding company might provide money to ailing subsidiaries for reasons other than profitability, such as the desire to maintain the group's image or to redirect its activities. The Court replied that capital provided by a public investor who is not interested in profitability, even in the long term, must be regarded as an aid for the purposes of Article 92. In another judgment on the same day,[23] the Court went further and held that the concept of the private investor, whilst not limited to one placing capital for a short- or medium-term profit, must at least relate to a private holding company or private group of undertakings carrying out a global structural policy or one limited to a particular sector which is guided by the prospects of profit in the longer term. On this test, therefore, the Commission was entitled to find that the capital contributions in question which had been made to car companies were beyond the contemplation of private investors and should be seen as solely designed to absorb the debts of the recipient undertaking in order to ensure that it survived.

Another way in which aid may be granted indirectly is through preferential pricing of energy supplies, whether these are used as a raw material input or as an energy source.[24] The Commission has, for example, persuaded the authorities in the Netherlands to amend the tariff system for natural gas supplied to the ammonia industry. Ammonia is the base product of nitrate fertilisers and the Commission considered that the previous tariff

---

Tubemeuse: Belgium v. *Commission* [1990] 1 E.C.R. 959; [1991] 3 C.M.L.R. 213; C–303/88, *Italy* v. *Commission*, judgment March 21, 1991 (not yet reported).

[19] See the detailed application of this in *Re Tubemeuse*, note 18, *supra*. More generally, see *The Measurement of the Aid Element of State Acquisitions of Company Capital—Evolution of Concentration and Competition*, EC Commission Document, 1987.

[20] Note 18, *supra*.

[21] Its most elaborate exposition of the idea can be seen in its Communication to Member States concerning the application of Articles 92 and 93 and the Transparency Directive 80/723 to public undertakings in the manufacturing sector, 1991 O.J. C273/2.

[22] Case C–303/88, note 18, *supra*.

[23] Case C–305/89, *Italy* v. *Commission*, (not yet reported).

[24] Comp. Rep. 1985, point 182.

gave a competitive advantage to Dutch fertiliser manufacturers.[25] The Commission's approach is that, where energy tariffs do not reflect supply economies to a given sector of industry, an element of State aid may be presumed to exist. However, the extent of that aid must be carefully analysed. It will not be adequate for the Commission simply to infer that the totality of any difference in tariff structures affecting classes of customer amounts to aid. There may be other savings accruing to the supplier with regard to the allegedly aided customer receiving the preferential tariff.[26]

The "benefit" conferred by an aid must be without any real counterpart on the side of the recipient.[27] Payment for goods or services or the reimbursement of losses due to decisions taken in the public interest, for example the fixing of rail or bus fares at unremunerative levels, would not amount to aids. However, the European Court has said that a measure does not lose the quality of a "gratuitous advantage" merely because it is wholly or partially financed out of contributions levied on the undertakings concerned.[28]

Aid within the meaning of Article 92(1) must be granted "by a Member State or through State resources." That must be taken to include grants by regional or local authorities as well as by central government.[29] Nor is it material whether the authorities choose to act directly or through the agency of some public or private body. Thus in a case concerning an aid system in Germany under which the proceeds of a levy were put at the disposal of a statutory body and used by it for market research and advertising both at home and abroad, in order to promote the sale of products of the German agricultural, food and forestry industries, the Court said:

> "In applying Article 92 regard must primarily be had to the effects of the aid on the undertakings or producers favoured and not the status of the institutions entrusted with the distribution and administration of the aid."[30]

On the other hand, the fixing of a minimum retail price for a product at the exclusive cost of consumers would not constitute an aid granted through State resources.[31]

The effects that render State aid incompatible with the common market

---

[25] Comp. Rep. 1983, point 235. The decision of the Commission closing the procedure it had initiated under Art. 93(2) was challenged in proceedings brought under Art. 173 EEC by competitors of the Dutch fertiliser manufacturers in France. See Case 169/84, *COFAZ* v. *Commission* [1986] E.C.R. 391; [1986] 2 C.M.L.R. 338 on admissibility. The merits were dealt with as *Société CdF Chimie Azote et Fertilisants SA and Another* v. *Commission* [1990] 1 E.C.R. 3083; [1992] 1 C.M.L.R. 177.

[26] *Ibid.* at para. 51 of judgment.

[27] See Mégret *et al.*, Le droit de la Communauté économique europeene, note 8, p. 380, *supra*.

[28] Case 78/76, *Firma Steinike und Weinlig* v. *Germany, loc. cit.* note 8, *supra*.

[29] *Cf.* the terms of the Transparency Directive 80/723, discussed in more detail in Chap. 19, *infra*.

[30] Case 78/76, *loc. cit.* note 8, *supra*. See also Case 173/73, *Italy* v. *Commission, loc. cit.* note 11, *supra*; Case 290/83, *Commission* v. *France* [1985] E.C.R. 439; [1986] 2 C.M.L.R. 546; Case 57/86, *Commission* v. *Greece* [1988] E.C.R 2855; Cases 67, 68 and 70/85, *Kwerkerij Gebroeders van der Kooy, Johannes Wilhelmus van Vliet, the Landbouwschap and Kingdom of the Netherlands* v. *Commission* [1988] E.C.R. 219; [1989] 2 C.M.L.R. 804.

[31] Case 82/77, *Openbaar Ministerie* v. *van Tiggele* [1978] E.C.R. 25; [1978] 2 C.M.L.R. 528.

are the actual or threatened distortion of competition "by favouring certain undertakings or the production of certain goods," where this has some impact on intra-Community trade.

A distinction is, therefore, drawn between general measures of economic policy, such as the devaluation of a currency or the easing of credit controls, which may very well improve the position of undertakings in the country concerned *vis-à-vis* their competitors elsewhere in the Community, and measures giving a competitive advantage to particular undertakings or industrial sectors. In Cases 6 and 11/69, *Commission* v. *France*[32] the European Court held that a preferential discount rate for exports must be regarded as an aid falling within Article 92(1), despite the fact that it applied to all national products without distinction. The explanation is that the possibility of obtaining credit more cheaply for export purposes was directly felt as a benefit by individual French manufacturers.

A case showing that the distinction may not always be easy to apply was raised by a Belgian member of the European Parliament in a Written Question in 1967.[33] It concerned Press reports of a change of plan by an American company as to the location of a new chemical factory, allegedly after it was informed by the authorities of the region ultimately chosen that a sewer was to be built there which would make it unnecessary for the company itself to provide for the purification of water used in its manufacturing processes. The Commission was asked whether public works undertaken in such circumstances were not caught by Article 92 EEC. In its Answer the Commission said that the provision by public authorities of infrastructures which are traditionally paid for out of State or local authority budgets would not normally constitute an aid within the meaning of the Article, but that it may do so if works are carried out specifically in the interest of one or more undertakings or of a certain type of product.

The favoured undertakings may be public or private, subject to the exception in Article 90(2) as regards entrusted undertakings and fiscal monopolies.[34] A politically delicate matter is the financing of public undertakings, which frequently contains an element of aid. For example, the waiver of interest on capital which the State makes available to a public undertaking may constitute an aid if a private investor in a comparable situation, acting from purely economic motives, would not have waived his rights, or would only have done so to a limited extent.[35] Part of the rationale behind the adoption of the Transparency Directive[36] was to respond to problems of detection and inadequate information in this area. In 1991 the Commission published a communication[37] to the Member States applying the requirements of this Directive to public undertakings in the manufacturing sector. The substance of the communication is to apply the

---

[32] [1969] E.C.R. 523.
[33] J.O. 1967, 2311.
[34] Case 78/76, *Steinike und Weinlig* v. *Germany, loc. cit.* note 8, *supra.*
[35] *Cf.* Case 323/82, *Intermills, loc. cit.* note 17, *supra*; Joined Cases 269/82 and 318/82, *Leeuwarder, loc. cit.* note 18, *supra.*
[36] Dir. 80/723, O.J. 1980 L195/35, as amended by O.J. 1985 L229. See further Chap. 19, *infra.*
[37] Note 20, *supra.*

market economy investor principle established in the equity participation cases[38] to public undertakings in all situations and all public funds covered by the Directive.

According to the European Court, ". . . in the application of Article 92(1) the point of departure must necessarily be the competitive position existing within the common market before the adoption of the measure in issue."[39] If the effect of the measure is to alter that position to the advantage of particular undertakings or products, there will be a distortion of competition within the meaning of the Article. It was, therefore, of no avail for the French Government in Cases and 11/69 to argue that its aim was merely to approximate the discount rates for exports to the lower discount rates generally applying in the other Member States; nor for the Italian Government in Case 173/73 to argue that the social charges devolving on employers in the textiles industry were heavier in Italy than elsewhere. As the Court said in the latter case:

> ". . . the unilateral modification of a particular factor of the cost of production in a given sector of the economy of a Member State may have the effect of disturbing the existing equilibrium. Consequently, there is no point in comparing the relative proportions of total production costs which a particular category of costs represents, since the decisive factor is the reduction itself and not the category of costs to which it relates.[40]

If the arguments of the French and Italian Governments had been accepted, the scope of Articles 92 to 94 would have been drastically reduced, pending the harmonisation under Articles 99 and 100 EEC of the factors influencing production costs in the Member States, since it would have been all too easy for a State to point to a particular high-cost factor as justifying a compensatory aid.

One of the questions in *Firma Steinike und Weinlig* asked, in substance, whether the effect on competition and trade of the activities of a State agency might not be mitigated by the fact that similar activities were carried on by similar bodies in other Member States. The Court replied that a breach of Article 92 by a Member State could not be justified by the fact that other Community partners were guilty of similar breaches. "The effects of more than one distortion of competition on trade between Member States do not cancel one another out but accumulate and its damaging consequences to the common market are increased."[41]

What kind of proof is needed to make out a case of actual or threatened distortion of competition affecting trade between Member States, such as to bring an aid within Article 92(1)? Does Article 92 include some kind of *de minimis* rule or requirement as to "appreciable effect" comparable to that

---

[38] Note 18, *supra.*
[39] Case 173/73, *Italy* v. *Commission, loc. cit.* note 11, *supra.*
[40] [1974] E.C.R. at p. 720.
[41] *Loc. cit.* note 8, *supra* at p. 612. The same point was made by the Commission in its decision on the subsidy on fuel oil given to French fishermen: see Case 93/84, *Commission* v. *France* [1985] E.C.R. 829; [1985] 3 C.M.L.R. 169.

embraced by Article 85? Numerous attempts have been made to persuade the Court that such a principle should be adopted, but, as yet, it has refused to impose onerous restraints on the Commission in this respect.

In *Philip Morris Holland* v. *Commission*[42] the Court came close to enunciating a *per se* rule as to the effect on inter-State trade which would result from aids designed to enable a cigarette manufacturer to close one of its two factories in the Netherlands and to expand production at the other. The reorganisation meant that Philip Morris would account for 50 per cent. of the cigarettes manufactured in the Netherlands, of which 80 per cent. would be exported. The Court said that:

> "When financial aid strengthens the position of an undertaking as compared with other undertakings competing in intra-Community trade the latter must be regarded as affected by that aid."[43]

In other cases, despite invitations to rule in principle against acknowledgment of a *de minimis* restriction,[44] the Court has limited itself to rejecting on the facts claims that an aid had insufficient impact to be caught by Article 92.[45] However, in *Re Tubemeuse*[46] the Court expressly rejected the contention put forward by the Belgian Government that the 5 per cent. principle adopted by the Commission in relation to competition matters generally should apply to State aids. Reaffirming *Philip Morris*, the Court observed that the relatively small amount of aid or the relatively small size of the undertaking which receives it does not as such exclude the possibility that intra-Community trade might be affected.[47] Advocate General Tesauro, in the same case, argued for a need to assess "in a dynamic perspective" whether a hindrance to trade exists, taking into account future foreseeable trends in the market.

The criterion of affecting inter-State trade thus appears to represent a conceptual rather than a practical requirement.[48] Its presence is legally important insofar as it requires the Commission to investigate the effect on trade and competition or face a challenge alleging inadequate reasoning under Article 190 of the Treaty. Nevertheless, the case law indicates that the evidence needed to satisfy the test will be minimal.[49] In practice, the Commission will not raise objections to minor aids but this does not relieve Member States from the duty to notify them.[50]

---

[42] Case 730/79 [1980] E.C.R. 2671; [1981] 2 C.M.L.R. 321.

[43] [1980] E.C.R. at pp. 2688–2689. This echoed the words of Adv. Gen. Capotorti: *ibid.* at p. 2697. See, in a similar sense, the opinion of Adv. Gen. Warner in Case 173/73, [1974] E.C.R. at p. 728.

[44] Notably Advocate General Lenz in Case 234/84, *Re Meura: Belgium* v. *Commission* [1986] E.C.R. 2263; [1988] 2 C.M.L.R. 331.

[45] See *ibid.* Also Case 310/85, *Deufil* v. *Commission* [1987] E.C.R. 901, [1988] 1 C.M.L.R. 553 and Case C–305/89, *Italy* v. *Commission*, note 22 *supra*.

[46] Case C–142/87, note 18, *supra*.

[47] Para. 43 of judgment. *Cf.* the rejection of *de minimis* by the Court in the context of Art. 30: Case 16/83, *Prantl* [1984] E.C.R. 1299.

[48] *Cf.* Evans & Martin, note 6, *supra*, whose analysis expresses it as a qualitative rather than quantitative factor.

[49] See Case 323/82 *Intermills, loc. cit.* note 13, *supra*; Joined Cases 296 and 318/82, *Leeuwarder, loc. cit.* note 14, *supra*.

[50] 1990 O.J. C40/2.

Article 92(2): exceptions *ipso jure*

Article 92(2) provides that the following categories of aid *shall* be compatible with the common market:

"(a) *aid having a social character, granted to individual consumers, provided that such aid is granted without discrimination related to the origin of the products concerned*"

An example would be the payment of a subsidy to manufacturers of a basic foodstuff, compensating them for any loss of profits resulting from a price freeze imposed in respect of sales to consumers. So long as it complied with the proviso that there must be no discrimination regarding the origin of the goods concerned, such aid would be unlikely to distort competition or affect trade at all, and so would fall outside the general principle in Article 92(1).[51] However, it might be caught by the principle if, for instance, the subsidised product were given a real competitive advantage over possible substitutes. In such a case the compatibility of the aid with the common market would be assured by the present exception.

"(b) *aid to make good the damage caused by natural disasters or exceptional occurrences*"

Aid to make good the damage caused by natural disasters is an obvious candidate for automatic exemption from the general principle in Article 92(1). Italian measures which the Commission has treated as falling under this heading were the assistance given in Liguria to repairs and reconstruction required as a result of the floods in 1977, and the provision in Friuli-Venezia Giulia of low interest loans and subsidies for the reconstruction of industrial plant destroyed by the earthquake in 1976.[52]

The notion of "exceptional occurrences" is very vague. The exception would, presumably, cover aid to repair business premises damaged by acts of political terrorism. Its applicability in the case of difficulties of an economic nature is more doubtful. The exceptional aid measures adopted by the Member States in the face of the serious recession which began to affect the Community from the second half of 1974 onwards were dealt with by the Commission under Article 92(3)(*b*) (see below).

---

[51] *E.g.* the Italian scheme under which hard wheat purchased by AIMA (the Intervention Agency for Agricultural Markets) was resold to manufacturers of pasta at prices well below the market rate, following the imposition of a freeze on the retail prices of pasta products. The Commission was satisfied that hard wheat benefiting from the subsidy was only used in the manufacture of pasta for domestic consumption and that imports into Italy of pasta made from hard wheat were insignificant: see Comp. Rep. 1975 points 126–129. In Case 40/75, *Produits Bertrand* v. *Commission* [1976] E.C.R. 1, an action for damages brought by a French pasta manufacturer against the Commission for its failure to prevent the granting of the aid was dismissed by the European Court on the ground that a causal connection between the behaviour complained of and the alleged damage had not been established.

[52] Comp. Rep. 1978, point 164.

"(c) *aid granted to the economy of certain areas of the Federal Republic of Germany affected by the division of Germany, in so far as such aid is required in order to compensate for the economic disadvantage caused by that division.*"

Following the unification of Germany in 1990[53] the State aids rules apply with full effect throughout the State. The Commission takes the view[54] that there is no longer any economic justification for continuing to subsidise the areas mentioned in Article 92(2)(c). It is therefore actively seeking the co-operation of the Federal authorities in achieving the elimination of such aid which, in any event, has hitherto been carried out as part of the principles applicable to regional aid.[55]

Article 92(3): discretionary exceptions

The discretion given to the Commission under Article 92(3) is a wide one. Advocate General Capotorti described it in *Philip Morris Holland* as "implying an assessment of an economic, technical and policy nature."[56] The Court said that the exercise of the discretion "involves economic and social assessments which must be made in a Community context."[57]

When applying the discretionary exceptions, the Commission seeks to ensure that aid measures are approved only if they both promote recognised Community objectives and do not frustrate the move towards the internal market.[58] The Commission only has power to authorise aids which are necessary for the furtherance of one of the objectives listed in paragraph (3). Since 1980 it has adopted the principle of compensatory justification; to gain approval, any aid proposal

"must contain a compensatory justification which takes the form of a contribution by the beneficiary of aid over and above the effects of normal play of market forces to the achievement of Community objectives as contained in derogations of Article 92(3) EEC."[59]

The Court upheld this principle in *Philip Morris Holland*, ruling that an aid purporting to be an incentive for investment that would have been made in any event was ineligible, on that ground alone, for exemption.[60]

The categories of aid that *may* be compatible with the common market are as follows[61]:

---

[53] Monetary union came into effect on July 1 and political union on October 3.
[54] See Comp. Rep. 1990, point 178.
[55] For an example of the use of Art. 92(2)(c), see Bull. EC 2, 65, Chap. III, point 18.
[56] [1980] E.C.R. at p. 2701.
[57] *Ibid* at p. 2691.
[58] Comp. Rep. 1990, point 169.
[59] Comp. Rep. 1980, point 213.
[60] For further discussion of compensatory justification, see Mortelmans, (1984) 21 C.M.L. Rev. 405; Schina, *op. cit.*, note 7, *supra*; Evans and Martin, note 6, *supra*.
[61] The Maastricht Treaty would add a further discretionary heading, namely aid to promote culture and heritage conservation where such aid does not affect trading conditions and competition in the Community to an extent that is contrary to the common interest.

"(a) *aid to promote the economic development of areas where the standard of living is abnormally low or where there is serious under-employment*"

The economic problem of the region in question must be more serious to attract this exception than to attract the general exception relating to sectoral and regional aids in sub-paragraph (3) (see below). The latter exception is, however, subject to the proviso that the aid "does not adversely affect trading conditions to an extent contrary to the common interest." No such limitation applies here, because the seriousness of the situation may justify exceptionally drastic measures.

The scope for invoking paragraph (*a*) is significantly restricted by the requirement that the assessment of socio-economic problems be made in a Community, not a national, context. In *Philip Morris Holland* it was claimed that in the Bergen-op-Zoom region, the location of the factory it was planned to enlarge, unemployment was higher, and *per capita* income lower, than the national average in the Netherlands. However, the Court supported the Commission's approach in taking the Community level as the appropriate yardstick.[62]

An example of aids authorised by the Commission under Article 92(30(*a*) was measures to promote the economic recovery of the sulphur-mining areas of Sicily.[63]

"(b) *aid to promote the execution of an important project of common European interest or to remedy a serious disturbance in the economy of a Member State*"

The exception applies to two completely different types of aid. Projects of common European interest were once thought to be confined to infrastructure activities or inter-State technological developments. The airbus venture, for example, received approved aid under this head.[64] Sub-paragraph (*b*) was also used by the Commission to authorise aid to develop a common standard for high-definition colour television.[65] More recently aids granted for environmental purposes[66] have been approved under this exception.[67] The Court has approved the Commission's approach in this area, noting that there will be no common European interest in a scheme "unless it forms part of a transnational European programme supported jointly by a number of Governments of the Member States, or arises from concerted action by a number of Member States to combat a common threat such as environmental pollution."[68] In any event, it is clear

---

[62] For other instances of failure to satisfy the stringent tests of paragraph (*a*), see Dec. 80/1157, *Re Investment Aids at Antwerp* O.J. 1980 L343/38; Joined Cases 296/82 and 318/82, *Leeuwarder, loc. cit.* note 18, *supra*.

[63] Comp. Rep. 1976, points 209–211.

[64] See Bull. E.C. 4/74, point 2112.

[65] Comp. Rep. 1989, point 151.

[66] One of the Community's horizontal policies, alongside research and development and support for small and medium-sized enterprises.

[67] See Comp. Rep. 1987 for the criteria adopted as guidelines by the Commission.

[68] Joined Cases 62/87 ad 72/87, *Executif Regional Wallon and Glaverbel* v. *Commission* [1988] E.C.R. 1573; [1989] 2 C.M.L.R. 771.

that the judgment as to whether aid serves the requisite common European interest is a matter for the Commission. The Court has indicated that research and development projects do not *per se* qualify, observing in the *Glaverbel* case that:

> "The mere fact that the investments envisaged enabled new technology to be used does not make the project one of common European interest; that certainly cannot be the case when . . . the products have to be sold on a saturated market."

As to the second category under Article 92(3)(*b*), serious disturbances, the Commission used it as a safety valve in the economic troubles besetting Member States which followed the energy crisis of 1974.[69] Disturbances must relate to the whole of a national economy, not just one region or sector.[70] In the latter case the appropriate tool is Article 92(3)(*a*) or (*c*).

"(c) *aid to facilitate the development of certain economic activities or of certain economic areas, where such aid does not adversely affect trading conditions to an extent contrary to the common interest. . . .*"

This is the most important of the exceptions to the general principle in Article 92(1). It enables the Commission to authorise aids to particular industrial sectors (for example, taking the headings under which national aids were discussed by the Commission in the *Fifteenth Report on Competition Policy*[71]: energy; shipbuilding and ship-repair; textiles and clothing; synthetic fibres; industrial investment; car and spare parts industries; information technologies and consumer electronics; household appliances; primary aluminium and semi-finished aluminium products; ceramics, glass, paper, wood and rubber) and aids to particular regions of a Member State.

The legal limits of the Commission's discretion are defined by the notion of facilitating the development of the industries or areas concerned and by the proviso that aid must not have an adverse effect on trading conditions "to an extent contrary to the common interest."

"Development" presupposes some improvement in economic performance or prospects. Thus aids of a purely conservatory nature, designed to prevent undertakings in a given industry or area from going out of business, thereby creating unemployment, do not fall within the exception.[72] Recipients of aid must be at least potentially competitive. It seems to follow that financial assistance to an undertaking should normally be temporary and given on a declining scale.

A crucial distinction between Article 92(3)(*a*) and (*c*) is that national yardsticks may be used as well as Community ones. In its *Eighteenth Report on Competition Policy*[73] the Commission noted:

---

[69] See Comp. Rep. 1975, point 133.
[70] See Schina, *op. cit.* note 7, *supra*, pp. 58–60.
[71] Comp. Rep. 1985, points 182 to 217.
[72] See the remarks of Adv. Gen. Sir Gordon Slynn in Case 84/82, *Germany* v. *Commission (Belgian Textile Aid)* [1982] E.C.R. 1505.
[73] Comp. Rep. 1989, point 147,

"Regions falling under Article 92(3)(c) are those with more general development problems in relation to the national as well as the Community situation. Often they suffer from the decline of traditional industries and are frequently located in the more central prosperous parts of the Community. In its Article 92(3)(c) method, the Commission has established a system which takes account of national regional problems and places them in a Community context . . . The better the position of a Member State relative to the Community situation, the wider must be the disparity of a region in order to justify the award of aid . . . the Commission does not in principle allow the award of operating aid in Article 92(3)(c) regions, and aid must be linked to initial investment and/or job creation."

The Court has approved this approach.[74]

The purpose of the aid must be the development of the sector or region in question and not of particular undertakings within it. In the *Belgian Textile Aid* case Advocate General Sir Gordon Slynn was of the opinion that the Commission ought not to have authorised grants to certain weak undertakings, given the relative strength of the market sector as a whole.[75]

The proviso imposes a limit, albeit a flexible one, on the extent to which disruption of the market mechanism may be tolerated for the sake of the socio-economic benefit sectoral or regional aids may bring. Its operation may be illustrated by Case 47/69, *France* v. *Commission*.[76] The aid in question took the form of contributions towards research and the restructuring of French textile undertakings, and seemed prima facie to be exactly the type of sectoral aid to which Article 92(3)(*c*) was intended to apply. However, the Commission objected to the fact that the aid was financed out of a parafiscal charge imposed both on textile products manufactured in France and on imports. The European Court agreed with the Commission that the method of financing an aid system was one of the factors to be taken into account in assessing its compatibility with the common market. It was capable of adding to the disturbance of trading conditions, thus rendering the system as a whole contrary to the common interest. That was the case here, because of the protective effect of applying the charge to imports. The amount of aid available increased automatically in proportion to any increase in revenue, so that the more undertakings from other Member States succeeded in making sales in France, the more they would have to contribute for the benefit of their French competitors, who might not have made similar efforts.

In that case the Court seems to have assessed the extent to which trading conditions were liable to be adversely affected independently of the benefits expected to flow from the aid.[77] Its approach was that, however worthwhile the objective being pursued, disruption of the market beyond a certain point

---

[74] Case 248/85, *Germany* v. *Commission* [1987] E.C.R. 4013.
[75] *Loc. cit.* note 71, *supra* at p. 1504.
[76] [1970] E.C.R. 487.
[77] The Court concluded that the Commission was justified in considering the aid system as contrary to the common interest "whilst acknowledging both the useful nature of the aid

must be judged contrary to the common interest. The Commission, on the other hand, has declared that it considers itself bound "to weigh the beneficial effects of the aid on the development of certain economic activities or of certain economic areas against its adverse effects on trading conditions and the maintenance of undisturbed competition."[78] That would allow greater interference with the play of market forces, the greater the importance of the Community interest an aid was thought to serve. The possible divergence in the approaches of the Court and the Commission was noted by Advocate General Sir Gordon Slynn in the *Belgian Textile Aid* case.[79]

In applying the proviso, account must be taken of any factors that may moderate the anti-competitive impact of an aid. In its *Intermills* judgment the Court said that "the settlement of an undertaking's existing debts in order to ensure its survival does not necessarily adversely affect trading conditions to an extent contrary to the common interest, as provided in Article 92(3), where such an operation is, for example, accompanied by a restructuring plan."[80] Failure to show that the possibly mitigating effects of restructuring had been adequately considered was one of the reasons for the annulment of the decisions of the Commission in the *Intermills* and *Leeuwarder* cases.[81]

"(d) *such other categories of aid as may be specified by decision of the Council acting by a qualified majority on a proposal from the Commission*"

A series of seven directives on aids to shipbuilding in the Member States has been adopted under this provision.[82] It was not possible to rely on Article 92(3)(*c*) because the measures included "production aids" which could not be regarded as facilitating "development."

It was assumed (correctly, it is submitted) that the term "decision" in this sub-paragraph is used in the general sense of Article 145 EEC to refer to a law-making act, as opposed to the sense of an "individual act" in Article 189 EEC.

The application of Article 92

We have seen that State aids meeting the criteria in Article 92(1) are not automatically to be regarded as incompatible with the common market, since they may fall within one of the excepted categories in paragraphs (2) and (3) of the Article. Moreover, the application, in particular, of Article 92(3) entails a complex appreciation of economic and social factors in the

---

properly so called and the fact that it conformed with 'the common interest' if the method whereby it was financed could be modified": see [1970] E.C.R. at p. 496.
[78] Comp. Rep. 1984, point 202.
[79] [1982] E.C.R. at pp. 1506–1507.
[80] [1984] E.C.R. at p. 3832.
[81] *Loc. cit.* notes 17 and 18, *supra*, respectively.
[82] The seventh Directive applies until December 31, 1993. See 1990 O.J. L380/27.

light of the overall Community interest. The approach adopted by the Treaty is, accordingly, to make the Community institutions responsible in the first instance for giving concrete effect to the principles of Article 92, and machinery has been provided for this purpose in Articles 93 and 94.

The corollary of the provision of special machinery at Community level is that courts in the Member States may not apply Article 92 independently of that machinery. In the words of the European Court, the parties concerned cannot:

> "... simply, on the basis of Article 92 alone, challenge the compatibility of an aid with Community law before national courts or ask them to decide as to any compatibility which may be the main issue in actions before them or may arise as a subsidiary issue. There is this right however where the provisions of Article 92 have been applied by the general provisions provided for in Article 94 or by specific decisions under Article 93(2)."[83]

In that sense, Article 92 is not directly effective. However, it does not follow that national courts may not sometimes have to interpret Article 92, for example to decide whether a measure introduced by a Member State without obtaining clearance under Article 93(3) constitutes "aid."[84] And in such a case the Court could obtain assistance in interpreting the Article by seeking a preliminary ruling under Article 177 EEC.[85]

The machinery in Articles 93 and 94 EEC[86]

Different treatment is accorded to "existing aids," *i.e.* aid systems which were already established when the EEC Treaty came into force (in new Member States, on the date of their accession) or which have been lawfully introduced since that date after passing through the clearance procedure under Article 93(3), and "plans to grant or alter aid," which are also referred to as "new aids."

The clearance procedure for new aids
Article 93(3) provides:

> "The Commission shall be informed, in sufficient time to enable it to submit its comments, of any plans to grant or alter aid. It it considers that any such plan is not compatible with the common market having regard to Article 92, it shall without delay initiate the procedure provided for in paragraph 2. The Member State concerned shall not put its proposed measures into effect until this procedure has resulted in a final decision."

---

[83] Case 78/76, *Firma Steinike und Weinlig* v. *Germany* [1977] E.C.R. at p. 609.
[84] See, *e.g. R.* v. *Attorney-General, ex p. ICI*; [1987] 1 C.M.L.R. 72 (C.A.) *Potato Marketing Board* v. *Robertsons* [1983] 1 C.M.L.R. 93 (Oxford County Court).
[85] Case 78/76, *Firma Steinike und Weinlig* v. *Germany, loc. cit.* note 8, *supra.*
[86] On this machinery, see further Schina, *op cit.* note 7, Chap. 11; Gilmour, (1981) 18 C.M.L.R. Rev. 63; Slot, (1991) 16 E.L.Rev. 38.

The paragraph establishes a system of prior control which is designed to prevent any aid incompatible with the common market from being introduced. Member States are required to notify the Commission of plans to grant or alter aid sufficiently in advance of the date set for their implementation to enable it to examine the plans and form a view as to whether the procedure under Article 93(2) should be initiated against them.

The last sentence of Article 93(3) imposes a "standstill" obligation upon the Member State proposing to introduce an aid.[87] This applies during the period of preliminary review by the Commission and, if the procedure under Article 93(2) is initiated, continues until a final decision is reached. *A fortiori*, a Member State is prohibited from putting an aid into effect without notifying it at all.

The Commission must be allowed sufficient time for its preliminary examinations of a notified aid project. However, it is required to act with due expedition, bearing in mind the interest of Member States in obtaining clarification in cases where there may be an urgent need to take action. The European Court has fixed on two months as a reasonable length of time for this purpose. If at the end of this period the Commission still has not defined its attitude towards the project, the Member State concerned may implement the aid but should, in the interests of legal certainty, give notice to the Commission of its intention of doing so.[88]

The outcome of the preliminary examination may be that the Commission finds the new aid compatible with the common market. This decision must be communicated to the Member State which made the notification and implementation of the aid may then go forward.[89]

However, should the Commission be left in any serious doubt as to the compatibility of the aid with the common market, it is bound to continue its examination within the framework provided by Article 93(2). The importance of the transition from the preliminary to the definitive phase in the examination of the aid is that only in the latter phase do interested parties other than the notifying State have a legal right to make their views known.[90] The issue was considered in the *Belgian Textile Aid* case,[91] where a decision of the Commission granting temporary approval to a scheme which had been the subject of negotiations lasting for 16 months was annulled by the Court. The Commission, it was held, being evidently dissatisfied with the scheme as originally notified, ought immediately to have initiated the procedure under Article 93(2) and formally invited comments from Member States and the textile trade, so that it would be fully informed of all the facts of the case before making up its mind.

Where an aid proposal is altered after having been notified to the

---

[87] Case 84/82, *Germany* v. *Commission* [1984] E.C.R. at p. 1488, which was foreshadowed in Case 120/73, *Lorenz* v. *Germany* [1973] E.C.R. 1471.
[88] *Ibid.* The two-month period was chosen by analogy with Arts. 173 and 175 EEC.
[89] *Ibid.* Once the project has been implemented it will be an "existing aid" subject to constant review pursuant to Art. 93(1). See *infra.*.
[90] The right is given by Art. 93(2), first sub-paragraph. See *infra.*
[91] [1984] E.C.R. at pp. 1488–1490. See the analysis of this case by Flynn at (1984) 9 E.L.Rev. 367.

Commission, the latter must be informed of the amendment, although this may be done in the course of consultations arising from the original notification.[92] Failure to bring amendments to the attention of the Commission will cause the standstill under Article 93(3) to remain in force against a scheme which has otherwise been found compatible with the common market. The only exception would be where the amendment could properly be regarded as a separate measure, examination of which was unlikely to have a bearing on the Commission's assessment of the notified plan.[93]

Effect of failure to notify

The prohibition against the implementation of new aids which have not been notified or which, during the preliminary stage following notification, are being investigated by the Commission or in respect of which proceedings under Article 93(2) are in progress has been held to be directly effective.[94] The criteria here have nothing to do with the incompatibility under Article 92 of the aid in question but are instead based on the failure to meet the clear, precise and unconditional procedures of Article 93(3). The consequences of this must be examined against the powers of the Commission as well as the rights of individuals before national courts.

In striving to balance the interests of Member States, beneficiaries, competitors and the Commission, the Court has been mindful of the difficulties which would arise if no sanction were attached to failure to notify. However, it has also sought to give effect to the clear procedures set out in the Treaty for the assessment of the compatibility of the alleged aid with the criteria of Article 92. In *Boussac*[95] the Commission had argued that failure to notify was itself a sufficiently serious default by a Member State to render an aid unlawful. The Court refused to accept this view, observing that:

> "Once it has established that aid has been granted or altered without notification, the Commission therefore has the power, after giving the Member State in question an opportunity to submit its comments on the matter, to issue an interim decision requiring it to suspend immediately the payment of such aid pending the outcome of the examination of the aid and to provide the Commission, within such period as it may specify, with all such documentation, information and data as are necessary in order that it may examine the compatibility of the aid with the common market."[96]

Where the Member State complies with the Commission's order, the latter is

---

[92] Joined Cases 91 and 127/83, *Heineken Brouwerijen* v. *Inspecteurs der Vernootschapsbelasting* [1984] E.C.R. 3435; [1985] 1 C.M.L.R. 389.
[93] *Ibid* at p. 3454.
[94] Case 72/72, *Capolongo* v. *Maya* [1973] E.C.R. 611; [1974] 1 C.M.L.R. 230; Case 120/73, *Lorenz* v. *Germany*, *loc. cit.* note 86, *supra*.
[95] Case 301/87, *France* v. *Commission* [1990] 1 E.C.R. 307; see Slot, note 85, *supra*.
[96] *Ibid*. para. 19 of the judgment. The same applies to aid which has been notified but implemented by the State without waiting for the procedure under Art. 93(2) and (3), *ibid* para. 20.

obliged to carry out an assessment of compatibility. If the Member State does not provide the information requested, the Commission at that point is empowered to terminate the procedure and make an assessment of compatibility on the basis of the information available to it. That decision may also call for the recovery of any aid that has already been paid.[97]

In contrast to the restraints imposed upon the Commission, individuals are entitled to effective protection against the consequences of a Member State's failure to notify aids. The question was raised in a request from the French Conseil d'État for a preliminary ruling on the effect of Article 93(3) in a case involving intervention in the sea fisheries sector.[98] The reply given by the Court stressed the fundamental difference between the central executive rôle performed by the Commission and the task of national courts. Whilst the Commission was required to examine the compatibility of the planned aid with the common market, even in cases where the Member State infringed the prohibition of implementing aid measures, national courts merely safeguarded, pending a final decision by the Commission, the rights of individuals against any disregard by the State authorities of the prohibition contained in the last sentence of Article 93(3). A decision in that regard by a national court did not amount to an adjudication on the compatibility of the aid with the common market. Nevertheless, the national court had to ensure that individuals were in a position to enforce rights of action in respect of any disregard of Article 93(3), from which all the proper consequences would follow, in accordance with their national law, both regarding the validity of acts involving the implementation of aid measures and the recovery of financial support granted in breach of that provision or of any provisional measures.

The Court has thus struck a careful balance between preserving the exclusive competence of the Commission to make reasoned assessments about aids and the rights of individuals in a single market. In an express attempt not to encourage disregard by Member States of the notification requirements, the Court ruled[99] that the Commission's final decision did not have the effect of regularising, *ex post facto*, implementing measures which were invalid for having been effected in breach of Article 93(3).

Review of existing aids

Article 93(1) provides:

> "The Commission shall, in co-operation with Member States, keep under constant review all systems of aid existing in those States. It shall propose to the later any appropriate measures required by the progressive development or by the functioning of the common market."

The Commission, in collaboration with the national authorities, is under a

---

[97] *Ibid.* paras. 21 and 22.
[98] Case C–354/90, *Federation Nationale du Commerce Exterieur des Produits Alimentaires* v. *France*, judgment November 21, 1991 (not yet reported).
[99] *Ibid.*

duty to keep existing aid systems under constant review and has the power to make any recommendations the progressive development or functioning of the common market may require. This supervision applies to all systems of aid in force, including those covered by the exception in Article 92(2). It enables the Commission to ensure that aids previously regarded as compatible with the common market do not change their character and are not applied abusively in particular cases. If a recommendation does not suffice to rectify the situation, the Commission may resort to the enforcement procedure under Article 93(2).

The special enforcement procedure for State aids

Article 93(2) provides:

> "If, after giving notice to the parties concerned to submit their comments, the Commission finds that aid granted by a State or through State resources is not compatible with the common market having regard to Article 92, or that such aid is being misused, it shall decide that the State concerned shall abolish or alter such aid within a period of time to be determined by the Commission.
>
> If the State concerned does not comply with the decision within the prescribed time, the Commission or any other interested State may, in derogation from the provisions of Articles 169 and 170, refer the matter to the Court of Justice direct . . ."

The first and second sub-paragraphs of Article 93(2) lay down a special procedure for securing the abolition or modification of an aid which is found on examination by the Commission to be incompatible with the common market.

The formal opening of the procedure is by the publication in the *Official Journal* of a notice inviting interested parties to submit their comments. The Commission is not obliged to give individual notice to firms in receipt of aid under the scheme which is being scrutinised.[1] Further examination may lead the Commission to drop its objections to the scheme; or it may do so in response to agreement by the awarding State to make substantial modifications. If, however, the Commission reaches the conclusion that the aid is incompatible with the common market or is being misused, it will adopt a decision requiring its abolition or alteration within a specified time. In the event of non-compliance with the decision, the Commission itself, or any interested Member State, may refer the matter to the European Court, by-passing the administrative phase of proceedings under Article 169 or Article 170 EEC. Direct referral to the Court is permitted because the parties have already been heard and the Commission has adopted a decision in which it has made known its views.

The procedure under Article 93(2) applies both to existing aids about which questions have been raised in the course of a review and to new aids.

---

[1] Case 323/82, *Intermills* v. *Commission, loc. cit.* note 17, *supra*. The Commission responded with various alterations in its practice under Art. 93(2) to encourage participation by interested third parties: Comp. Rep. 1985, point 171.

As to the latter, the drafting of Article 93(3) seems to assume that any plan in respect of which the Commission initiates the procedure will have been duly notified and subjected to a preliminary examination. However, the European Court has held that the procedure may also be invoked against unnotified aids, although here the Commission would have the option of taking action under Article 169 for infringement of the standstill obligation in Article 93(3).[2]

A decision by the Commission finding an aid incompatible with the common market and requiring its abolition or alteration will have a different effect in law depending on whether the aid in question is an existing or a new one. In the case of existing aids, the effect of the decision is clearly constitutive, bringing into force, from the date set for compliance by the Member State concerned, the implied prohibition in Article 92(1). Thereafter, the granting of the aid will be unlawful and it will be the duty of national courts to recognise the fact.[3] In the case of new aids, the measure will either not have been implemented at all or, if it has been implemented in breach of Article 93(3), it will already be unlawful. However, it may not be accurate to describe the effect of the decision here as purely declaratory. What it does is to transform a prohibition of a provisional nature, based on the procedural criteria of Article 93(3), into a prohibition based on Article 92(1) that will remain in force unless and until the Commission can be persuaded to revoke it, following a material change of circumstances. A practical consequence of the difference between the two cases is that when a new aid is in question the decision of the Commission does not have to specify any time-limit.[4]

It is of paramount importance that any decision by the Commission which amounts to the condemnation of an aid for incompatibility is based on completion of the procedure laid down by Article 93(2), which includes a hearing of the interested parties. Attempts by the Commission to adopt practices which might be more convenient for the purposes of enforcement action have been thwarted by the Court. The circumstances of the so-called *Sweeteners* case involving the United Kingdom Government's handling of the acquisition by British Aerospace of the Rover Group are particularly instructive. In 1988 the Commission issued a decision[5] approving a notified plan to grant £469 million aid to write off the debts of the Rover Group. The decision included conditions that the United Kingdom would not alter the

---

[2] See Case 173/73, *Italy* v. *Commission, loc. cit.* note 11, *supra*; Case 73/79, *Commission* v. *Italy* [1980] E.C.R. 1411; [1982] 1 C.M.L.R. 1. See the discussion of the latter case by Gilmour, *op. cit.* note 85, *supra*; and by Flynn, (1983) 8 E.L.Rev. 297. There is no such option where the compatibility of an aid scheme with the Common Market is in issue: Case 290/83, *loc. cit.* note 29, *supra*. See the discussion of this case by Flynn, (1987) 12 E.L.Rev. 124.

[3] There is a passage in the judgment in Case 70/72, *Commission* v. *Germany* [1973] E.C.R. 813 suggesting that a decision taken by the Commission under Art. 93(2) may have certain retrospective effects: [1973] E.C.R. at p. 829. See Bronkhorst, (1974) C.M.L.Rev. 206. However, in Case 177/78, *Pigs & Bacon Commission* v. *McCarren Ltd.* [1979] E.C.R. 3409; [1979] 3 C.M.L.R. 389 Adv. Gen. Warner pointed out that the Court's remark was made in the context of an aid introduced or continued in force in breach of the Treaty.

[4] Case 173/73, *Italy* v. *Commission, loc. cit.* note 11, *supra*.

[5] 89/58, 1989 O.J. L25/92.

terms of the sale of Rover as notified, and that no further aid would be granted to Rover. The Commission later discovered that a further £44 million of aid (the alleged "sweeteners") had been given. It issued a decision in 1990[6] which stated that the additional sum was an illegal aid paid in breach of Decision 89/58 and required the United Kingdom to recover it from the beneficiaries. British Aerospace and Rover sought to have this decision annulled.

The Court[7] took the view that the Commission had not followed the correct path in seeking to have the extra amounts recovered without re-examination. According to the Court, the Commission had two lawful choices at the point of the alleged failure by the United Kingdom to observe the conditions of Decision 89/58. It could either have referred the breach directly to the Court under the second sub-paragraph of Article 93(2) or it could have instituted the special procedure of the first sub-paragraph to investigate whether the new payments were an aid. It was not entitled simply to pursue recovery of the extra payments. The Court therefore annulled the 1990 decision. Nevertheless it repeated an earlier view[8] that when considering the compatibility of an aid with the common market, the Commission must take into account all relevant matters, including in appropriate cases the circumstances already considered in any previous decision and any obligations which that previous decision may have imposed on the Member State. The point for the Commission to adopt in future practice is that such examinations must be carried out in accordance with the procedures of Article 93(2), after advising and consulting the interested parties. The idea of establishing a new class of follow-up "implementing" decisions has been firmly rejected.

Recovery of unlawful aids

Although not spelt out in the Treaty, it has long been clear that the Commission is able to seek repayment of illegal aid.[9] Subject to the important procedural restraints explained above, recovery can be instituted against both notified (but wrongfully applied) and non-notified aids. The Court has taken a strict view as to the nature of the obligation to repay in a line of cases following *Commission* v. *Belgium*[10] where it emphasised the need to consider whether it was *impossible* for the Member State to comply with the Commission's decision. The mere fact that beneficiaries of the aid might suffer financial hardship from its revocation is not sufficient to thwart recovery.[11] Nor is conflict with national rules of company law in cases where undoing aid in the form of equity participation may run counter to existing principles about priorities between creditors and shareholders.[12] Apart from

---

[6] 1991 O.J. C21/2.
[7] Case C–292/90, *British Aerospace Plc and Rover Group Holdings Plc* v. *Commission* [1992] 1 C.M.L.R. 853.
[8] Case 261/89, *Italy* v. *Commission*, judgment October 3, 1991 (not yet reported).
[9] Case 70/72, *Commission* v. *Germany* [1973] E.C.R. 813.
[10] Case 52/84 [1986] E.C.R. 89; [1987] 1 C.M.L.R. 710.
[11] Case 63/87, *Commission* v. *Greece* [1988] E.C.R. 2875.
[12] See Case C–142/87, *Re Tubemeuse: Belgium* v. *Commission*, note 18, *supra*, discussed by Ross, (1989) 26 C.M.L.R. Rev. 167.

satisfying orthodox doctrine concerning the supremacy of Community law, this position also makes clear that repayment is not a matter of countering improper benefits but is an absolute consequence of infringement of the obligations under the aids system. Thus in *Re Tubemeuse*[13] the beneficiary was in liquidation, so that it was no longer able to take advantage of the unlawfully paid aid. Any repayment would in effect come from the company's other creditors, who would be disadvantaged *pro tanto* by the State's claim. The Court, citing previous authority,[14] ruled that:

> "recovery of unlawful aid is the logical consequence of finding that it is unlawful. Consequently, the recovery of State aid unlawfully granted for the purpose of re-establishing the previously existing situation cannot in principle be regarded as disproportionate to the objectives of the Treaty in regard to State aids."

One situation where it would seem impossible to recover aid is illustrated by the *Boussac* case.[15] The aid had consisted of capital injections, loans and reductions in employers' social security contributions. However, the Commission ruled out of account the sums paid out by Boussac to meet the cost of transferring certain production sites and employees to independent companies which had subsequently ceased production. These amounts were treated as lost and impossible to recover. The Court accepted this view and, moreover, cited the pursuit by the Commission of only partial repayment as an answer to the French Government's claim that the recovery of aid was disproportionate to the effect on competition. It is submitted that the statement of principle made in *Re Tubemeuse*, above, is better preserved if the *Boussac* observation is seen as a statement that the test of impossibility was satisfied, rather than one applying proportionality criteria. Impossibility is not for the State merely to assert; it must be demonstrated after an active search for a solution in the context of a dialogue between the Commission and the State concerned.[16]

Challenging the Commission's decision

Whether the procedure ends in a finding of compatibility or incompatibility with the common market, the decision of the Commission will be challengeable by an action under Article 173 EEC in the same way as any other institutional act capable of producing legal effects. Satisfying the conditions of admissibility in the second paragraph of the Article should present no problem to a direct recipient of the aid[17] or to an undertaking which responded to the Commission's invitation to submit comments and

---

[13] *Ibid.*
[14] Case 310/85, *Deufil* v. *Commission*, note 44 *supra.*
[15] Case C–301/87, *France* v. *Commission*, note 94, *supra.*
[16] Advocate General Darmon in Case C–5/89, *Re State aid to Bug-Alutechnik: Commission* v. *Germany* [1990] 1 E.C.R. 3437; [1992] 1 C.M.L.R. 117.
[17] Case 730/79, *Philip Morris Holland* v. *Commission, loc. cit.* note 41, *supra*; Case 323/82, *Intermills* v. *Commission, loc. cit.* note 17, *supra.*

which is able to produce prima facie evidence of substantial harm to its interests resulting from the granting of the aid to a competitor.[18]

The merits of an application under Article 173 must be based on the grounds listed therein. Of growing interest in the State aids field is the use of general principles by Member States and undertakings seeking to establish the infringement by the Commission of a rule of law of the Community. One example is the principle of legitimate expectations, recognised as part of Community law by the Court in *Deutsche Milchkontor* v. *Germany*.[19] In the *Bug-Alutechnik* case[20] the Court was asked to consider the German Government's claim that obtaining repayment of the aid concerned was absolutely impossible because of national laws relating to legitimate expectations demanding the weighing of the beneficiary's interests against those of the Community. The Court observed:

> "in view of the mandatory nature of the supervision of State aid by the Commission under Article 93 EEC, undertakings to which an aid has been granted may not, in principle, entertain a legitimate expectation that the aid is lawful unless it has been granted in compliance with the procedure laid down in that Article. A diligent businessman should normally be able to determine whether that procedure has been followed.
>
> In that regard, it must be pointed out that, by a communication published in the Official Journal . . ., the Commission informed potential recipients of State aid of the risk attaching to any aid granted them illegally, in that they might have to refund the aid.[21]
>
> It is true that a recipient of illegally granted aid is not precluded from relying on exceptional circumstances on the basis of which it had legitimately assumed the aid to be lawful and thus declining to refund that aid. If such a case is brought before a national court, it is for that court to assess the material circumstances, if necessary after obtaining a preliminary ruling on interpretation from the Court of Justice."[22]

Authorisation of aid by the Council "in exceptional circumstances"

The third and fourth sub-paragraphs of Article 93(2) provide:

> ". . . On application by a Member State, the Council may, acting unanimously, decide that aid which that State is granting or intends to grant shall be considered to be compatible with the common market, in derogation from the provisions of Article 92 or from the regulations provided for in Article 94, if such a decision is justified by exceptional circumstances. If, as regards the aid in question, the Commission has already initiated the procedure provided for in the first subparagraph of

---

[18] Case 169/84, *COFAZ and Others* v. *Commission*, note 24, *supra*.
[19] Case 205–215/82 [1983] E.C.R. 2633.
[20] Case C–5/89, note 15, *supra*.
[21] 1983, O.J. C318/3.
[22] Paras. 14–16; see also Case C–94/87, *Alcan: Commission* v. *Germany* [1989] E.C.R. 175, [1989] 2 C.M.L.R. 425.]

this paragraph, the fact that the State concerned has made its application to the Council shall have the effect of suspending that procedure until the Council has made its attitude known.

If, however, the Council has not made its attitude known within three months of the said application being made, the Commission shall give its decision on the case."

On application by the aid-awarding State, the Council, acting unanimously, has the power exceptionally to authorise an aid not falling within any of the categories in Article 92(2) or (3).[23] If the procedure under Article 93(2) has already been initiated in respect of such aid, the application to the Council has the effect of suspending it. However, if the Council has not made its attitude known within three months, the Commission may proceed to adopt a decision. Given the need for unanimity, and the fact that there will nearly always be at least one Member State whose producers may be adversely affected by the granting of the aid, the possibility of such applications succeeding must generally be regarded as poor.

Implementing regulations adopted by the Council

Article 94 provides:

"The Council may, acting on a qualified majority on a proposal from the Commission, make any appropriate regulations for the application of Articles 92 and 93 and may in particular determine the conditions in which Article 93(3) shall apply and the categories of aid exempted from this procedure."

The Council's power to adopt regulations under Article 94 covers the application of Article 92 as well as Article 93. However, the power has not hitherto been exercised.[24]

The relationship between Articles 92 to 94 EEC and other provisions of Community law

By virtue of Article 38(2) EEC the agricultural provisions of the Treaty contained in Articles 39 to 46 take precedence over Articles 92 to 94, as they do over the other rules laid down for the establishment of the common market.[25] In particular, the rules on State aids are among those the application of which Article 42 puts at the discretion of the Council. Provision was made in Article 4 of Regulation 26 for their application in the agricultural sphere, but only to a very limited extent. However, it has become customary for the basic regulations of the various common organisations of agricultural markets established under Article 40 EEC to

---

[23] For an example of the exercise of this power, see Comp. Rep. 1985, point 251.
[24] A Draft Regulation on the application of Art. 93 was submitted by the Commission to the Council in 1966 but has never been enacted. *Cf.* the powers of the Commission under Art. 90(3), discussed in Chap. 19, *infra.*
[25] See Case 83/78, *Pigs Marketing Board* v. *Redmond* [1978] E.C.R. 2347; [1979] 1 C.M.L.R. 177; Case 177/78, *Pigs & Bacon Commission* v. *McCarren Ltd.*, *loc. cit.* note 2, *supra.*

lay down that, "save as otherwise provided" in the regulation, Articles 92 to 94 are to apply *in toto* to the production of and trade in the products in question. Thus, in the case of goods covered by a common organisation of the market, Member States are required to observe the State aid provisions of the Treaty in the normal way, except where such observance would be incompatible with the rules of the common organisation.[26]

The European Court has had to deal with the question whether Articles 92 to 94 may have a similar pre-emptive effect to the Treaty provisions on agriculture (except, of course, in relation to those provisions). In other words, if a measure can be regarded as forming part of an aid system, does its compatibility with Community law fall to be determined exclusively on the basis of the State aid provisions? It would be convenient for the governments of Member States if this were so, because it would mean that such a measure could not be challenged before a national court unless the aid system in question had been the object of a decision under Article 93(2) or of a regulation under Article 94.[27]

The answer that emerges from the case law is definitely negative. Thus it was made clear in Case 73/79[28] that a measure of discriminatory taxation, which may be considered at the same time as forming part of an aid system covered by Article 92, remains nonetheless subject to the prohibition in Article 95. A similar approach was taken in Case 91/78, *Hansen* v. *Hauptzollamt Flensburg*[29] where one of the questions raised concerned the relationship between the State aid rules and Article 37 on State monopolies. The Court said:

> ". . . Article 37 of the Treaty constitutes in relation to Articles 92 and 93 a *lex specialis* in the sense that State measures, inherent in the exercise by a State monopoly of the commercial character of its exclusive right must, even where they are linked to grant of an aid to producers subject to the monopoly, be considered in the light of the requirements of Article 37."[30]

The relationship between the State aids rules and Article 30 has posed greater difficulties for the Court. Its original position was represented by *Iannelli* v. *Meroni*[31] where it said:

> "The aids referred to in Articles 92 and 93 of the Treaty do not as such fall within the field of application of the prohibition of quantitative restrictions on imports and measures having equivalent effect laid down by Article 30 . . ."

That is because, if the competitive edge that the granting of aid gives to

---

[26] Case 169/82, *Commission* v. *Italy* [1984] E.C.R. 1603; [1985] 3 C.M.L.R. 30; Case 114/83, *Société d'Initiatives et de Co-operation Agricoles and others* v. *Commission* [1985] 2 C.M.L.R. 767. See also Synder, *Law of the Common Agricultural Policy*, pp. 32–38.
[27] *E.g.* the arguments advanced in Case 177/78, *Pigs & Bacon, loc. cit.* note 2, *supra*.
[28] *Commission* v. *Italy, loc. cit.* note 1, *supra*. See also Case 17/81, *Pabst & Richarz* v. *Hauptzollamt Oldenburg* [1982] E.C.R. 1331; [1983] 3 C.M.L.R. 11.
[29] [1979] E.C.R. 935; [1980] 1 C.M.L.R. 162.
[30] [1979] E.C.R. at p. 953.
[31] Case 74/76 [1977] E.C.R. 557; [1977] 2 C.M.L.R. 688.

national products were treated as a measure having equivalent effect to a quantitative restriction, the directly effective prohibition in Article 30 would render the provisions of Articles 92 to 94 totally superfluous. However, the Court qualified its approach in *Iannelli* by introducing a "severability" test. According to this, some aspects of aid contravening specific Treaty provisions other than Articles 92–94 may be so indissolubly linked to the object of the aid that it would be impossible to evaluate them separately; but where a particular part of an aid system could be seen as not necessary for the attainment of its object or for its proper functioning, severance would be possible to enable directly effective provisions of the Treaty to operate.

Such a demarcation line is not always easy to draw. In *Commission v. Ireland ("Buy Irish")*[32] an advertising campaign inspired and financed by the Irish Government through the medium of a private company was held by the Court to fall within Article 30, contrary to the views of Advocate General Capotorti. The fact that Articles 92 and 93 might apply to the method of financing the operation did not mean that the campaign itself could escape the prohibition of Article 30. An even stronger affirmation of the role of Article 30 seemed to emerge in *Commission v. France*[33] concerning tax benefits to newspaper publishers on the basis that the publications were printed in France.[34] The Court stated that the mere fact that a national measure may be defined as an aid within the meaning of Article 92 was not an adequate reason for exempting it from the prohibition contained in Article 30.

Whether the "severability" test even exists any longer may be a matter of doubt in the light of the Court's approach in *Du Pont de Namours Italiana*.[35] Under Italian law, all public or semi-public bodies were required to obtain at least 30 per cent. of their purchases from companies operating in the Mezzogiorno region in the south of Italy where the goods had to be manufactured or transformed. An Article 177 reference arose when a firm not established in the Mezzogiorno challenged its exclusion from a tender list. The Court took the view that the requirements of the legislation restricted trade and thus fell within Article 30. The measures could not be justified under Article 36, and the mandatory requirements could not be applied since the measure was discriminatory.[36] Reiterating its statement in *Commission v. France*, the Court considered that the possible classification of the measure as an aid did not exempt it from the rules on goods. This seems to indicate a disposition towards giving Article 30 priority over Article 92 rather than an analysis of severability.

Thus, on the approach adopted by the European Court, the rules on State aids do not seem to present a serious threat to the protection against illegal action by Member States which the direct effect of much of Community law

---

[32] Case 249/81 [1982] E.C.R. 4005; [1983] 2 C.M.L.R. 99.
[33] Case 18/84 [1985] E.C.R. 1339; [1986] 1 C.M.L.R. 605.
[34] See also Case 103/84, *Commission v. Italy* [1986] E.C.R. 1759; [1987] 2 C.M.L.R. 825 on subsidies to agencies to buy vehicles of Italian origin.
[35] Case 21/88, *Du Pont de Namours Italiana v. Unita Sanitaria Locale No. 2 di Carrara* [1990] 1 E.C.R. 889; [1991] 3 C.M.L.R. 25.
[36] See Chap. 9, *supra.*

affords to the individual. However, this approach is not without its critics,[37] who argue that only the discretions and supervisory functions embodied in the Commission under Article 92 are appropriate to balance issues of social and economic cohesion against the creation and maintenance of the single market.

---

[37] See Fernandez Martin and Stehmann, (1991) 16 E.L.Rev. 216.

CHAPTER 19

PUBLIC UNDERTAKINGS

Public undertakings and the common market

The present chapter is concerned with Article 90 EEC. There is another provision of the Treaty, Article 37, which relates to a particular category of public undertakings, namely State monopolies of a commercial character.[1] However, since Article 37 constitutes a specialised regime for the removal of obstacles to the free movement of goods which may be associated with the arrangements under which such monopolies operate, it has been dealt with in Chapter 9.

An ever more conspicuous part is played in the economic life of the Community by undertakings which are State controlled or which enjoy a privileged legal status, normally in return for carrying out certain tasks deemed to be of public importance. Activities which are undertaken in this way in various Member States include the public utilities, railway and other transport services, broadcasting and some key industrial sectors such as the motor industry. The organisation of Member State participation may be at national, regional or local level.

The general approach of Community law to such undertakings is that, while there can be no objection in principle to their special relationship with the State,[2] whatever legal form this may take, their behaviour as market participants is governed by the same rules as those applicable to purely private undertakings, except where the Treaty itself specifically permits some derogation. The first limb of this proposition depends in part upon Article 222 EEC, preserving intact the systems of property ownership in the Member States, which are therefore free to determine the extent and internal organisation of their public sectors; and in part upon the clear inference to be drawn from Article 90(1) EEC that the conferment of special or exclusive rights upon an undertaking does not, in itself, constitute an infringement of any Treaty rule.[3] Nevertheless it is becoming increasingly clear that these basic assumptions are both coming under increasing scrutiny. For a long time the Court has been willing to recognise that the force of Article 222 is diminished where its strict application would prejudice

---

[1] Arts. 90 and 37 belong to a wider group of "provisions relating to infringements of the normal functioning of the competition system by actions on the part of the States": see Case 94/74, *IGAV* v. *ENCC* [1975] E.C.R. 699; [1976] 2 C.M.L.R. 37. The Court also mentioned in this connection Arts. 92 to 94 and Arts. 101 and 102.

[2] But see Deringer in *Equal Treatment of Public and Private Enterprises*, FIDE (1978), para. 36 to the effect that expansion of the public sector might be inconsistent with the mixed economy foundations of the Community.

[3] So held by the Court in Case 155/73, *Sacchi* [1974] E.C.R. 409; [1974] 2 C.M.L.R. 177. See also Case 311/84, *Centre Belge d'Etudes du Marché-Télé-marketing* v. *Compagnie Luxembourgeoise de Télédiffusion* [1985] E.C.R. 3261; [1986] 2 C.M.L.R. 558. The Court was still citing its *Sacchi* position in Case C–260/89, *E.R.T.* v. *Dimotiki*, judgment June 18, 1991 (not yet reported).

more fundamental principles of Community law.[4] More recently, the Court has implicitly acknowledged that Article 222 may take second place to the demands of provisions such as Article 5 of the Treaty. Member States must therefore observe all requirements of Community law when granting special or exclusive rights.[5]

Support for the second limb of the proposition can be found in the unqualified reference to "undertakings" in Articles 85 and 86, and in the limited exemption contained in Article 90(2) for the benefit of entrusted undertakings and fiscal monopolies (see below) which would have been formulated differently if the rules of the Treaty did not normally apply to public undertakings.

At the same time it had to be recognised that the close links existing between the State and certain undertakings entailed dangers for the proper functioning of the common market. For example, the authorities of a Member State would frequently be in a position to influence the appropriations policy of public undertakings, so as to give preference to domestic producers, although positive proof of an infringement of Article 30 might be very difficult to find. It was also necessary to take into account the importance attached by Member States to the use of undertakings as instruments of public policy, in particular for the performance of public service functions. These two considerations explain the inclusion of Article 90 in the Treaty, and its general shape.

Article 90 EEC

The Article provides as follows:

> "(1) In the case of public undertakings and undertakings to which Member States grant special or exclusive rights, Member States shall neither enact nor maintain in force any measure contrary to the rules contained in this Treaty, in particular to those rules provided for in Article 7 and Articles 85 to 94.
>
> (2) Undertakings entrusted with the operation of services of general economic interest or having the character of a revenue-producing monopoly shall be subject to the rules contained in this Treaty, in particular to the rules on competition, in so far as the application of such rules does not obstruct the performance, in law or in fact, of the particular task assigned to them. The development of trade must not be affected to such an extent as would be contrary to the interests of the Community.
>
> (3) The Commission shall ensure the application of the provisions of this Article and shall, where necessary, address appropriate directives or decisions to Member States."

---

[4] The clearest example concerns the free movement of goods, where balancing Art. 222 and the exercise of intellectual property rights has long occupied the Court; see Chap. 20, *infra*, and also Friden, (1989) 26 C.M.L.Rev. 193.

[5] Case C–202/88, *France* v. *Commission*, judgment March 19, 1991 (not yet reported), para. 22.

It can be seen that Article 90 has a dual function: to ensure that Member States conduct themselves towards public undertakings and undertakings which they have granted "special or exclusive rights" in a manner fully compatible with Community law[6]; and to define the privileged status in Community law of "undertakings entrusted with the operation of services of general economic interest or having the character of a revenue-producing monopoly." Paragraph (3) of the Article established machinery, on the one hand, for the enforcement of the obligation imposed on Member States by paragraph (1) and, on the other hand, for the retention within closely defined limits of the exception created by paragraph (2).

According to the Court of Justice, Article 90:

> "... concerns only undertakings for whose actions States must take special responsibility by reason of the influence which they may exert over such actions. It emphasises that such undertakings are subject to all the rules laid down in the Treaty, subject to the provisions contained in paragraph (2); it requires the Member States to respect those rules in their relations with those undertakings and in that regard imposes on the Commission a duty of surveillance which may, where necessary, be performed by the adoption of directives and decisions addressed to Member States."[7]

As the developing case law shows, the Court and the Commission have been concerned to prevent Article 90 from becoming a dangerous loophole in the system envisaged by the Treaty.[8]

Article 90(1): the responsibility of Member States for the conduct of public or privileged undertakings

Article 90(1) constitutes a particular application of the general principle contained in the second paragraph of Article 5 EEC that Member States are required to abstain from measures which are liable to jeopardise the attainment of the objectives of the Treaty.[9] The inclusion of a specific provision concerning the relationship between the State and public and privileged undertakings served both to highlight the particular seriousness of the problems which may arise, and to clarify the very extensive nature of the responsibility imposed upon Member States in this situation. It also enabled provision to be made in Article 90(3) (see below) for a more flexible and effective procedure than that of Article 169 in dealing with such cases.[10]

---

[6] Shindler points out that, since it imposes an obligation exclusively upon Member States, Art. 90 is misplaced in s. 1 of the Treaty chapter on competition, which is headed "Rules applying to undertakings": (1970) C.M.L.Rev. 57 at pp. 57–58.

[7] Cases 188–190/80, *France, Italy and the United Kingdom* v. *Commission* [1982] E.C.R. 2545; [1982] 3 C.M.L.R. 144.

[8] See Pappalardo, [1991] 1 E.C.L.R. 29. Earlier significant analyses include Page, (1982) 7 E.L.Rev. 19 and Marenco, (1983) C.M.L.Rev. 495.

[9] Case 13/77, *INNO* v. *ATAB* [1977] E.C.R. 2115 at pp. 2144–2145; [1978] 1 C.M.L.R. 283. Measures in relation to wholly private undertakings are within the scope of the general principle. See also Case C–202/88, *France* v. *Commission*, note 5, *supra*.

[10] The point is fully discussed by Pappalardo in Van Damme, *Regulating the behaviour of monopolies and dominant undertakings in Community law*, pp. 539 *et seq.*

The categories of undertaking in Article 90(1)

The concept of an undertaking as a body having legal capacity and carrying on economic (not necessarily profit-making) activities was discussed in relation to Articles 85 and 86,[11] but some nuances may be added in the context of Article 90. In the *Sacchi* case,[12] it was held by the European Court that, even where the primary objects of a body are non-economic, it will have the status of an undertaking to the extent that it engages in economic activity. Thus a broadcasting organisation may be entrusted with tasks of a cultural or informative nature; but it behaves as an undertaking, for example, when purchasing programmes or selling advertising time. The State itself and its regional or local subdivisions, it is thought, constitute undertakings when they participate in the production or distribution of goods or in the provision of services, but not when they act in the exercise of sovereignty or purely as consumers.[13] For instance, a local authority which had been empowered to carry on certain forms of retail business, and in the course of doing so had been guilty of predatory market practices, would risk attracting liability under Article 86 for itself and under Article 90(1) for the State to which it belonged. Where a local public authority assisted undertakings holding concessions relating to funeral services to charge unfair prices by imposing such prices as a condition for establishing the contract for the concession, this was held to be a situation clearly falling within Article 90(1).[14] On the other hand, a decision taken by a Minister under statutory powers, fixing maximum prices at a level which interfered with the free movement of goods, or the policy of a government department not to buy imported office equipment, would infringe Article 30, but not Article 90(1) since it would not involve entrepreneurial activity.[15]

There would be no consistency in the application of Article 90(1) if it were necessary to rely upon the widely varying classifications of undertakings as "public" or "private" in the national legal systems. Community law must, therefore, provide its own test of what constitutes a public undertaking, specifically adapted to the aims of Article 90(1). Although the Court of Justice has yet to define the concept exhaustively, in the *Transparency Directive* case[16] it approved the Commission's definition set out in the measure in question.[17] According to the Directive, which was adopted in 1980 and extended in 1985,[18] a public undertaking is:

> ". . . any undertaking over which the public authorities may exercise

---

[11] See Chaps. 14 and 15, *supra*.
[12] Case 155/73, *Sacchi, loc. cit.* note 3, *supra*. There are several further references to the case in this chapter, where the facts are presented more fully.
[13] See Deringer, *The Competition Law of the European Economic Community*, pp. 228–229. This view seems confirmed by Case 30/87, *Bodson* v. *SA Pompes funèbres des régions liberées* [1988] E.C.R. 2479.
[14] *Bodson*, note 13, *supra*.
[15] On problems of public procurement, see Weatherill, (1990) 10 *Yearbook of European Law*, p. 243.
[16] Joined Cases 188–190/80, *France, Italy and the United Kingdom* v. *Commission, loc. cit.* note 7, *supra*.
[17] Dir. 80/723 O.J. 1980 L195/35: see Page, (1980) 5 E.L.Rev. 492.
[18] O.J. 1985 L229.

directly or indirectly a dominant influence by virtue of their ownership of it, their financial participation therein, or the rules which govern it."

Article 2 of the Directive creates certain presumptions, so that a "dominant influence" will be taken to exist where the public authorities: hold the major part of the undertaking's subscribed capital; or control the majority of the votes attaching to shares issued by the undertaking; or can appoint more than half of the members of the undertaking's administrative, managerial or supervisory body.

The Court held that this definition of a public undertaking did not amount to an abuse by the Commission of its powers under Article 90(3), since the financial criteria which the Directive adopted reflected the substantial forms of influence exerted by public authorities over the commercial decisions of public undertakings and were thus compatible with the Court's view of Article 90(1). Of course, the Court remains free to provide an extended meaning of public undertaking for the purposes of the latter provision in the future.

"Public undertakings," therefore, include the following: the State and its subdivisions (see above); corporations established under public law, or in the United Kingdom statutory bodies such as British Coal; public services or authorities, for example a health authority with regard to the provision of private hospital treatment; and State-controlled undertakings operating under private law. With regard to the latter, and applying the criteria of the Transparency Directive, everything turns on whether the State exerts a dominant influence in such situations.

The category of undertakings to which Member States grant special or exclusive rights partially overlaps that of public undertakings. The rationale behind the category is the fact that the State has deliberately intervened to relieve the undertaking concerned either wholly or partially from the discipline of competition, and must bear responsibility for the consequences. A right conferred by national legislation upon those carrying on an economic activity which is open to anyone, who thus form an indefinite class, is unlikely to be regarded as "exclusive."[19] Similarly, undertakings which are licensed to engage in an activity on the basis of their fulfilment of certain objective conditions (for example the financial safeguards imposed in the public interest upon insurance businesses) would be excluded from the category. The mode of granting the right (whether by an act under public law, for example a statute, regulation or administrative order, or by a private contract) is immaterial, again because formal differences between the legal systems of the various Member States cannot be allowed to interfere with the operation of Article 90(1).

From the wording of Article 90(1) it may have been thought that the grantees of "special or exclusive" rights would comprise one homogeneous group. However, the decision of the Court in the *Telecommunications Terminal Equipment* case[20] cast doubt on this assumption. Article 2 of that

---

[19] See Case 13/77, *INNO* v. *ATAB*, *loc. cit.* note 9, *supra* at p. 2146.
[20] Case C–202/88, *France* v. *Commission* (not yet reported), note 5, *supra*.

Directive[21] required that Member States which had granted special or exclusive rights for the importation, marketing, connection, bringing into service of telecommunications terminal equipment and/or maintenance of such equipment had to ensure that those rights were withdrawn. Whilst fully upholding the Commission's application of the Directive to exclusive rights, the Court annulled the provision insofar as it related to special rights. Strictly speaking, the basis for this approach was that such rights had not been properly identified and explained in the Directive. However, the additional inference which could be drawn is that the Court sees some, as yet unexplained, distinction between special and exclusive rights.

It may be noted that in its later Directive 90/388 relating to competition in the markets for telecommunication services,[22] the Commission specifically included a provision defining special or exclusive rights as "the rights granted by a Member State or a public authority to one or more public or private bodies through any legal, regulatory or administrative instrument reserving them the right to provide a service or undertake an activity." Although greater reasoning is given here than in Directive 88/301, the fact that the definition jointly covers special and exclusive rights may not be enough to convince the Court. This Directive has been challenged by Belgium and Italy.[23]

Examples of undertakings falling within both the categories of Article 90(1) were found in the *Hein*[24] and *Sacchi*[25] cases. The former case raised the question of the compatibility with Community law of arrangements for the operation of river port facilities in Luxembourg by the Société du Port de Mertert. This company has close links with the State (including the right of the State to nominate half the members of the management and supervisory boards) and also enjoys certain privileges, *inter alia*, that of being consulted before permission is given for the development or operation of any other port or loading or unloading wharf on the Luxembourg bank of the Moselle. In *Sacchi* the relevant undertaking was the Italian broadcasting body, RAI, which was controlled by the State holding company, IRI. The State was also represented in its organs, and had powers of intervention in its operations. At the same time RAI enjoyed a statutory monopoly in the field of broadcasting. Examples of private undertakings which have been granted special or exclusive rights would be the commercial television companies in the United Kingdom or the companies taking part in the French petroleum import system.[26]

---

[21] 88/301 O.J. 1988 L131/73.
[22] O.J. 1990 L192/10.
[23] Cases C–281/90 and C–289/90.
[24] Case 10/71, *Ministère Public of Luxembourg* v. *Hein, née Muller* [1971] E.C.R. 723.
[25] Case 155/73, *loc. cit.* note 3, *supra*.
[26] Importation of petroleum products into France was carried out under specific State authorisation by a number of undertakings in competition with each other. See also the French system for the collection and disposal of waste oils which was the subject of Case 172/82, *Syndicat national des fabricants raffineurs d'huile de graissage* v. *Inter Huiles* [1983] E.C.R. 555; [1983] 3 C.M.L.R. 485. The Court, *ibid.*, merely said ". . . even if the approval granted by a Member State must be regarded as the grant of an exclusive right within the meaning of Art. 90(1) of the Treaty, that would not exempt the Member State from the

The scope of the obligation imposed on Member States

The phrase "shall neither enact nor maintain in force any measure" is wide enough to cover any forms of positive action by a Member State, or the failure to remedy such action previously taken. There is no reason to exclude from the category of "measures" general legislative acts (statutes or regulations): thus Deringer gives the example of a statutory provision requiring public utilities to obtain energy exclusively through a State purchasing agency.[27] However, a distinction must be drawn between legislation specifically relating to public or privileged undertakings, and legislation relating to such undertakings only among others,[28] for example an aid for nationalised industries, as opposed to a general regional aid system: the latter would not in itself constitute a measure for the purposes of Article 90(1), but its application in a particular case might do so. At the other end of the scale would be the exercise by the State of its rights as a shareholder, and the application to management of wholly informal pressures.

The first decision under Article 90(3) (see below) to challenge specific legislation of the type prohibited by Article 90(1) was issued by the Commission in 1985.[29] This related to a measure requiring all public property in Greece to be insured with a Greek State-owned insurance company, and also obliging State banks to recommend customers seeking a loan to take out associated insurance with a State-owned company. In the Commission's view,[30] the preferential treatment accorded to domestic State-owned companies had the effect of excluding from large sections of the Greek insurance market not only Greek private insurers but also insurance companies from other Member States with subsidiaries or branches in the country. The legislation thus amounted to a restriction on freedom of establishment, enacted by Greece in contravention of Article 90(1).

A literal view of Article 90(1) clearly embraces a standstill obligation upon Member States and the need to take positive action to undo prohibited measures. Additionally, the paragraph impliedly makes Member States accountable for the behaviour of public and privileged undertakings.[31] In other words, responsibility under Article 90(1) does not presuppose positive action by the Member State itself: it suffices merely that a public undertaking or an undertaking granted special or exclusive rights has been guilty of conduct which, on the part of the State, would have involved a Treaty violation. In such a situation the Member State is under an obligation to take any remedial steps which may be necessary; and if its existing legal

---

obligation to respect other provisions of Community law, particularly those relating to the free circulation of goods and those which result from Directive 75/439."
[27] *Op. cit.* note 13, *supra* at p. 240. See also Case 90/76, *Van Ameyde* v. *UCI* [1977] E.C.R. 1091; [1977] 2 C.M.L.R. 478. *Cf.* Case 72/83, *Campus Oil Ltd.* v. *Minister for Industry and Energy* [1984] E.C.R. 2727; [1984] 3 C.M.L.R. 544.
[28] The qualification is also made by Deringer, *op. cit.* note 13, *supra* at p. 240. The example has been slightly adapted.
[29] O.J. L152. See also Bull. EC 6–85, point 2.1.52.
[30] Comp.Rep. 1985, point 258.
[31] See Page, *op. cit.* note 8, *supra.*

powers are inadequate, it may be required by the Commission to equip itself with additional powers.

Interpreting the notion of maintaining a measure in force in this way is consistent with the obligation to take general and particular measures imposed on Member States by Article 5 and with the policy of Article 90(1). If State responsibility under this paragraph is derived, respectively, from the ability to influence public undertakings and from the assumption of the risk inherent in the deliberate distortion of competition by a grant of special or exclusive rights, it ought to make no difference whether the role of the State has been active, in imposing or encouraging certain behaviour, or passive, in failing to correct it. Furthermore, this view entirely reflects the steps already taken by the Court in relation to State directions or encouragement for enterprises to infringe Articles 85–86 in situations where no exclusive or special rights are involved.[32]

Article 90(1) refers, by way of example to Article 7 (the general prohibition against discrimination) and Articles 85 to 94 (the rules on competition including the machinery for the supervision of aids granted by Member States). Thus in *Van Ameyde* v. *UCI*[33] the European Court held that, in the context of the green card system of motor insurance, a measure giving a national insurance bureau sole responsibility for settling claims in relation to damage caused by foreign vehicles would not constitute an infringement of Article 90(1) in conjunction with Articles 85 and 86. The reservation of the *settlement* of claims to such a body, composed of insurance companies which had been subjected to the checks and guarantees required under national law, complied with one of the objectives of the green card system, namely that the interests of accident victims should be properly safeguarded. However, it is clearly implied that if the *handling and investigation* of claims had been similarly reserved, thereby excluding other types of undertaking, and notably loss adjusters, from this business, there might have been an infringement. Another provision of obvious importance in the present context is Article 30. Thus a government direction to a public undertaking instructing it to purchase its company cars from a nationalised car manufacturer would contravene the prohibition against measures having an equivalent effect to quantitative restrictions; and the discussion above suggests that it would make no difference from the point of view of Article 90(1) if the undertaking adopted such a policy spontaneously. The provisions of acts validly adopted by Community institutions would be covered by the phrase "the rules contained in this Treaty."

The responsibility of a Member State under Article 90(1) is entirely independent of any violation of Community law by the undertaking in question: it is not based upon a theory of imputation, like the joint liability of a parent company for infringements of the competition rules by a subsidiary which it controls.[34] For instance, the undertaking need not itself have acted

---

[32] Case 311/85, *Vereniging van Vlaamse Reisbureaus* [1987] E.C.R. 3801; [1989] 4 C.M.L.R. 213. See also Gyselen, (1989) 26 C.M.L.Rev. 33.

[33] Case 90/76, *loc. cit.* note 27, *supra*.

[34] See the discussion in Chapter 14, *supra*. See also Mathijsen, *op. cit.* note 27, *supra*, p. 11.3 to 4.

at all, if it is the recipient of an aid contrary to Article 92; or its own conduct may be unimpeachable: for example, it has been compelled by the State to enter a cartel, so that the element of agreement required by Article 85 is missing.[35] And in cases where the undertaking is guilty of infringing a rule, for example, abusing its dominant position on a relevant market by imposing unreasonable conditions on its trading partners, the position of the Member State falls to be determined not under the same provision, in this instance Article 86, but under Article 90(1).[36]

The most far-reaching emerging controversy about Article 90(1) is the extent to which the granting of exclusive or special rights can itself constitute a "measure" susceptible to challenge. In *Höfner* v. *Macrotron*[37] the Court was asked whether a national law conferring exclusive rights over the placement of business executives constituted an abuse under Article 86. It was acknowledged that in practice some competition in the market for business placements was tolerated despite the legal monopoly. Having prefaced its remarks with the observation that exclusive rights were not *per se* incompatible with Article 86, the Court observed that a Member State would infringe Article 90(1) if it placed an enterprise in a dominant position so that the mere exercise of its exclusive rights would be abusive. In its judgment:

> "A Member State created such a situation where the undertaking to which it entrusted an exclusive right, extending to the activity of placing business executives, was manifestly not in a position to satisfy the demand existing on the market for activities of that kind, where the effective exercise of those activities by private companies was rendered impossible by the keeping in force of a legal provision which prohibited such activities on pain of the contracts in respect thereof being rendered void and where those activities might extend to the nationals or territories of other Member States."

Effect of the obligation

It remains to consider whether the obligation in Article 90(1) is directly effective, enabling individuals to bring appropriate proceedings against Member States before their national courts. Since Article 90(1) is a reference provision, breach of it presupposes that some other Treaty rule has also been infringed. It is this complicating factor which led to some doubt in the provision's early untested years as to whether it could give rise to individual action. The Commission maintained that it was so in its submissions relating to *Hein*,[38] and there was distinguished support for this view in the literature.[39] The argument against direct effect, based upon the fact that special powers are given to the Commission under Article 90(3),

---

[35] *Cf.* Temple Lang, (1984) *Fordham Corporate Law Institute*, p. 543.
[36] Case 30/87, *Bodson*, note 13, *supra.*
[37] Case C–41/90, judgment April 23, 1991 (not yet reported). See Slot, (1991) 28 C.M.L.Rev. 964, esp. 972–977 and 980–988.
[38] Case 10/71, *loc. cit.* note 24, *supra.*
[39] See, *e.g.* Mégret *et al.*, *Le droit de la Communauté Economique Européenne*, Vol. 4 at pp. 86–87.

seems unconvincing: because there is a more than usually effective remedy at Community level, it does not follow that individuals should be deprived of the opportunity of enforcing the obligation. The answer, it is submitted, must be sought in the application to Article 90(1) of the three customary tests of direct effect, *i.e.* clarity, unconditionality and the absence of discretion in the course of implementation by the Community institutions or the Member States. These are liable to yield a different result, depending upon the particular rule of Community law which a measure is alleged to contravene. For example, the tests would presumably not be satisfied as regards a government direction to a publicly owned bank to grant low interest loans, since the determination whether this amounted to an illicit aid would be as much a matter for the judgment of the Commission under Article 92 as where a grant is made without the use of an intermediary. On the other hand, a direction to a publicly owned supplier of petroleum products to give preference to domestic customers in the event of a shortage would be readily identifiable as a measure contrary to Article 34 EEC. Thus the obligation in Article 90(1) may be directly effective, but only where it concerns the observance of Community provisions which are so effective.

For example, in *Merci Convenzionali Porto di Genova* v. *Siderurgica Gabriella*[40] Genoese port companies had been granted exclusive rights under Italian laws to load and unload all the ships in Genoa. The workers of these companies were required to be Italian nationals. In replying to a reference under Article 177, the Court pointed out that Article 90, in conjunction with Articles 30, 48 and 86, gave rise to individual rights which national courts must protect. Obviously, the reservation of nationality was a breach of Article 48. More controversially,[41] the Court observed that both Article 90 and Article 86 were infringed when the undertaking involved was caused, by the mere exercise of exclusive rights granted to it, to abuse its dominant position or when those rights were capable of creating a situation in which that undertaking was caused to commit such abuses. Most interesting of all, perhaps, was the Court's remark that a measure which facilitated an abuse of a dominant position would generally be incompatible with Article 30 to the extent that it had the effect of rendering more difficult and thus hindering imports of goods from other Member States. This observation may generate speculation as to the relationship between "measures" for the purposes of Articles 30 and 90(1). It also remains to be seen whether breach of Article 90(1) will give rise to actions for damages by individuals arguing from the basis of the tests laid down in *Francovich*.[42]

---

[40] Case C–179/90, judgment December 10, 1991 (not yet reported).
[41] See *Höfner* v. *Macrotron*, note 37, *supra*.
[42] Cases C–6/90 and 9/90, *Francovich and Bonifaci* v. *Italian Republic*, judgment November 19, 1991 (not yet reported) [1992] I.R.L.R. 84; discussed more fully in Chap. 5, *supra*. See Ross, (1993) 56 M.L.R. (forthcoming).

Article 90(2): the exception relating to entrusted undertakings[43] and fiscal monopolies

Article 90(2) is drafted in terms which first emphasise that "undertakings entrusted with the operation of services of general economic interest or having the character of a revenue-producing monopoly" are normally subject to the rules of the Treaty and then goes on to exclude the application of the rules where the performance of the particular tasks assigned to the undertakings is liable to be obstructed.[44] The exception is subject to a proviso designed to ensure that the disruption of the Community system will not be taken too far. The case-law of the Commission and Court has shown a marked disinclination to accept the application of the derogation. The continuing path towards deregulation of public undertakings in varying degrees may generate litigation to bring the scope of the exception into even sharper focus, especially where public utilities such as gas and electricity suppliers are concerned.[45]

The categories of undertaking in Article 90(2)

There is nothing in the text of the Article that would restrict the categories of undertakings in the second paragraph to those covered by the first. However, in practice it seems unlikely that undertakings would be called upon to perform services of the type envisaged by Article 90(2) unless they were either State controlled or given a *quid pro quo* in the form of special or exclusive rights.

The more important of the two categories in Article 90(2) is that of entrusted undertakings. Because of the possible derogation which may be involved, the European Court has said that the category must be strictly defined.[46]

It is immaterial whether the undertaking concerned is public or private, provided that the service has been entrusted to it "by an act of the public authority."[47] This does not imply that the act need be in any particular form, and references by Advocate General Mayras in *SABAM* to a "legislative" or "unilateral" act seem unduly restrictive.[48] The essential point is that the State must have taken legal steps to secure the provision of the service by the undertaking in question. Thus an undertaking created as a result of private initiative and managing the intellectual property rights of its members on an ordinary contractual basis, could not be an entrusted undertaking, even if it happened to serve public purposes.[49] The same is true where legislation only

---

[43] This convenient description is used by Deringer, *op. cit.* note 13, *supra*.
[44] The European Court may at one time have regarded Art. 90(2) as the source of obligations under the EEC Treaty for the categories of undertakings to which it relates. Its present view seems to be that the paragraph merely reaffirms the application of the general rules of the Treaty to such undertakings, while introducing a limited exception. See the discussion, *infra*.
[45] See Ehlermann, (1992) 29 C.M.L.Rev. 257.
[46] Case 127/73, *BRT* v. *SABAM*, [1974] E.C.R. 313; [1974] 2 C.M.L.R. 238.
[47] [1974] E.C.R. at p. 318.
[48] [1974] E.C.R. at p. 327.
[49] SABAM was such an undertaking. See also the Commission's Decision in *GEMA*; J.O. 1971 L134/15; [1971] C.M.L.R. D35.

authorises an undertaking to act, even though some supervision of those activities may be exercised by a public agency. Thus, in *GVL* v. *Commission*,[50] the Court held that the relevant German legislation did not confer the management of copyright and related rights on specific undertakings but defined in a general manner the rules applying to the activities of companies which intended to undertake the collective exploitation of such rights.

The phrase "operation of services" seems to have been chosen advisedly to indicate the organisation of some kind of regular performance, for example a public utility.[51] It is generally agreed that the definition of "services" in Article 60 EEC, as a residual concept relating to types of performance not governed by the provisions on the free movement of goods, persons or capital, does not apply in the context of Article 90(2).

A service will be "of general economic interest" where it involves economic activity (although its *aims* may, for example, be social) and is furnished in what the relevant authority of the Member State concerned believes[52] to be the interest of the general public (although the ultimate benefit of the service may be enjoyed by specific recipients).[53] Not surprisingly, telecommunications undertakings,[54] water supply companies[55] and electricity suppliers[56] have been treated as serving the general economic interest, although the derogation afforded by Article 90(2) remained inapplicable on other grounds in each case (see below). In *Ahmed Saeed*[57] the Court noted that Article 90(2) may be applied to airline carriers who may be obliged, by the public authorities, to operate on routes which are not commercially viable but which it is necessary to operate for reasons of the general interest. At the same time, however, the Court stressed that in the absence of effective transparency of the tariff structure it would be difficult, if not impossible, to assess the influence of the task of general interest on the application of the competition rules in the field of tariffs. In *Campus Oil Ltd.* v. *Minister for Industry and Energy*[58] the Court of Justice apparently did not

---

[50] Case 7/82 [1983] E.C.R. 483; [1983] 3 C.M.L.R. 645.

[51] The relevant phrase in the other official versions of the Treaty has been chosen with equal care to denote the conduct of a service rather than the provision of services: see the discussion in Deringer, *op. cit.* note 13, *supra* at p. 246; and Shindler, *op. cit.* note 6, *supra* at p. 70.

[52] The arguments are summarised by Page, *op. cit.* note 8, *supra* at p. 29.

[53] In Case 90/76, *Van Ameyde* v. *UCI* the Commission argued that the national insurers' bureau responsible for the settlement of claims in relation to damage caused by foreign vehicles in Italy did not qualify as an entrusted undertaking "since its activities do not benefit the whole of the national economy," but this view seems too restrictive: see [1977] E.C.R. 1091 at p. 1117. The Court seems to have taken for granted that the bureau would so qualify: *ibid.* at p. 1126.

[54] *Telespeed Services* v. *United Kingdom Post Office* [1982] O.J. L360/36; [1983] 1 C.M.L.R. 457. The Commission's Decision was unsuccessfully challenged in Case 41/83, *Italy* v. *Commission (British Telecom)* [1985] E.C.R. 873; [1985] 2 C.M.L.R. 368.

[55] *The Community* v. *ANSEAU-NAVEWA* [1982] 2 C.M.L.R. 193; challenged on other issues in Joined Cases 96–102, 104–105, 108 and 110/82, *IAZ International Belgium and others* v. *Commission* [1983] E.C.R. 3369; [1984] 3 C.M.L.R. 276.

[56] *IJsselcentrale and others* O.J. 1991 L28/32.

[57] Case 66/86, *Ahmed Saeed Flugreisen* v. *Zentrale zur Bekampfung unlauteren wettbewerbs* [1989] E.C.R. 803.

[58] Case 72/83, *loc. cit.* note 27, *supra*.

dispute the Greek Government's contention that a State-owned oil refinery could be an undertaking operating a service of general economic interest.[59]

On the other hand, a bank will not perform such a service when transferring customers' funds from one Member State to another.[60] Nor, it seems,[61] would the management company in the *GVL* case have fulfilled the criterion, since the collecting society was only engaged in the furtherance of the interests of private artistes. In *Merci Convenzionali Porto di Genova* v. *Siderurgica Gabriella*[62] the Court held that on the evidence submitted the port operations in question were not of general economic interest. Similar observations were made by the Court in the context of a monopoly granted under Belgian law for the establishment and running of the public telecommunications network. Although such a network was a service of general economic interest, the exclusion or restriction of competition by the monopoly holder refusing to allow other parties' equipment to be connected to it was not justifiable under the task of general interest.[63]

Writers have pointed to various other factors which may be helpful in determining whether "general economic interest" is present, notably: the fact that the provider of the service is subjected to positive duties which he may not vary unilaterally (Deringer cites as an example the duty to maintain a regular bus service); the vital character of the service, which means that it would have to be provided by the State if not entrusted to an undertaking; the granting of certain public law powers or of exclusive rights to an undertaking and, on the other hand, the retention of powers of intervention by the State with regard to the operation of the service; and the fact that the service is required to be available to all users under the same conditions.[64]

In the United Kingdom entrusted undertakings might include British Rail, British Airways, British Gas, regional Electricity Boards, the BBC and ITV companies, the Bank of England[65]; but not, it is submitted, British Coal or British Steel which are engaged in the production of commodities, rather than in the operation of services.

Undertakings "having the character of a revenue-producing monopoly," the second category in Article 90(2), are distinguished by the overriding purpose of raising revenue for the national exchequer through the exploitation of their exclusive right. They are normally combined with

---

[59] *Ibid* paras. 18–19 of the judgment. But note the strong statement that "Art. 90(2) does not, however, exempt a Member State which has entrusted such an operation to an undertaking from the prohibition on adopting, in favour of that undertaking and with a view to protecting its activity, measures that restrict imports from other Member States contrary to Article 30 of the Treaty."

[60] Case 172/80, *Zuchner* v. *Bayerische Vereinsbank (Bank Charges)* [1981] E.C.R. 2021; [1982] 1 C.M.L.R. 313. The bank was not viewed as "entrusted," either.

[61] *Per* Advocate General Reischl.

[62] Case C–179/90, note 40, *supra.*

[63] Case C–18/88, *Regie des Telegraphes et des Telephones* v. *GB-INNO-BM*, judgment December 13, 1991 (not yet reported).

[64] See Deringer, *op. cit.* note 13, *supra*, pp. 248–249. See also the comments by Advocate General Vilaca in *Bodson* (note 13, *supra*) as to the various obligations and burdens which might characterise a public service, *in casu* funeral services.

[65] The example is given by Lipstein in *The Law of the European Economic Community*, p. 241, note 3.

commercial monopolies, which causes problems in the application of Article 37 (see below).

In the discussion that follows references to entrusted undertakings should be understood to include fiscal monopolies, unless the context indicates otherwise.

The scope of the exception

The exception is capable of restricting the application of any Community provision, including Article 90(1). It makes no difference whether the rule in question is one designed primarily to influence the conduct of undertakings, for example Articles 85 or 86, or that of States, for example Articles 30 or 92.[66] Of interest in this connection is Article 37, which lays down certain rules for the adaptation of State monopolies of a commercial character to the requirements of a common market. To the extent that such monopolies perform the function of raising revenue, they fall within the second category of undertakings which may benefit from the exception; thus activities strictly related to this fiscal role would escape the effect of Article 37.[67] However, the protection of Article 90(2) would not extend to any other aspect of their activities, for example if maximum prices were fixed in respect of the goods marketed by a State monopoly, which had the effect of discouraging imports from other Community countries.

To benefit from the exception, an undertaking must show that application of the Treaty rules would obstruct the performance of the tasks assigned to it. Descriptions of that standard have varied. In the *British Telecom* case[68] the Court spoke of Italy's failure to prove that condemnation of British Telecom's behaviour as abusive within Article 86 would "prejudice" the accomplishment of the specific tasks assigned to that undertaking. The Decision of the Commission had considered whether application of the EEC's rules on competition would obstruct the performance by British Telecom of its duties "in an efficient and economic way."[69] These formulations may be contrasted with the approach adopted in the *Tobacco Margins* case[70] by Advocate General Rozès, who argued that the undertaking must have no choice but to infringe Treaty rules before the condition of Article 90(2) would be satisfied.[71] Similarly, the Commission in its *ANSEAU-NAVEWA* Decision stated:

> "It is not sufficient . . . that compliance with the provisions of the Treaty

---

[66] The possibility that Art. 90(2) may restrict the operation of Art. 92 was explicitly recognised by the European Court in Case 78/76, *Firma Steinike und Weinlig* v. *Germany* [1977] E.C.R. 595 at pp. 610–611.

[67] The relationship of Art. 90 and Art. 37 was discussed in some detail by Advocate General Rozès in Case 78/82, *Commission* v. *Italy (Tobacco Margins)* [1983] E.C.R. 1955. The Court found no breach of Art. 37 and did not discuss the exception.

[68] Case 41/83, *Italy* v. *Commission*, *loc. cit.* note 54, *supra*. Noted by Ross, (1985) 10 E.L.Rev. 457.

[69] *Telespeed Services* v. *Post Office*, *loc. cit.* note 54, *supra*.

[70] Case 78/82, *Commission* v. *Italy*, *loc. cit.* note 67, *supra*.

[71] But Madame Rozès herself used a less forceful phrase in Case 172/82, *Inter-Huiles*, *loc. cit.* note 26, *supra*, where she said that the privilege being claimed was unnecessary to enable the undertakings in question to accomplish their tasks "without compromising their profitability."

makes the performance of the particular task more complicated. A possible limitation of the application of the rules on competition can be envisaged only in the event that the undertaking concerned has no other technically and economically feasible means of performing its particular task."[72]

Finally, the European Court in *CBEM Télé-Marketing* v. *Compagnie Luxembourgeoise de Télédiffusion and Information Publicité Benelux*[73] reiterated the stance it had taken much earlier in *Sacchi*,[74] that rules of the Treaty continue to apply[75] so long as it is not shown that their prohibitions are "incompatible" with the performance of the undertakings' tasks.

In the light of these comments, and the normally strict construction to be given to any derogation from fundamental provisions of the Treaty, it is not easy to see how the "obstruction" condition in Article 90(2) can be satisfied. One example which has been suggested[76] is that of a fiscal monopoly imposing abusively high prices on its customers, but it is very doubtful whether Article 86 would be excluded in this case, unless the undertaking had been specifically charged to maximise revenue.[77] The exception is, perhaps, most likely to be successfully invoked in the field of State aids: for example, operating aids to bus or railway companies may be essential for the continued provision of a public transport service.

The wording of Article 90(2) indicates that recourse may only be had to the exception after the consequences of applying the normal rule to the case in point have become clear. It follows that the paragraph does not permit any relaxation of the procedural requirements connected with the application of the rule. Thus, for example, Member States are obliged to give the Commission advance notice of new or amended aids to entrusted undertakings, in accordance with Article 93(3)[78]: it is only when the Commission has found that the purposes of an aid do not fall within one of the categories in Article 92(2) or (3) and it is consequently liable to prohibition, that Article 90(2) comes into play. Any such aid, prematurely introduced, would be illegal. The only possible qualification is that the application of the rule in Article 93(3) itself might be excluded if the ability of the entrusted undertaking to perform its allotted task were dependent on the *immediate* introduction of the aid. The effect on the notification procedure under Regulation 17[79] may also be illustrated. Thus a notifiable new agreement, one of the parties to which is an entrusted undertaking, will not qualify for exemption under Article 85(3) if it has not been notified. Assuming that the agreement is caught by the prohibition in Article 85(1), it

---

[72] *Loc. cit.* note 55, *supra*. A similar formulation was approved by Advocate General Vilaca in *Bodson*, note 13, *supra*.
[73] Case 311/84, *loc. cit.* note 3, *supra*.
[74] Case 155/73, *loc. cit. ibid.*
[75] *In casu*, Art. 86.
[76] By Thiesing, cited by Deringer, *op. cit.* note 13, *supra* at p. 256, note 93.
[77] Even this task might itself be an infringement of the Treaty on the basis of the argument in *Merci* referred to above.
[78] See Chap. 18, *supra*.
[79] See Chap. 16, *supra*.

would normally be void under Article 85(2). But here the exemption intervenes, preserving the legality of the agreement, provided that it is essential to the task of the entrusted undertaking.

The proviso in the second sentence of Article 90(2) identifies the point at which it becomes necessary to apply the relevant provisions of Community law, even at the cost of preventing an entrusted undertaking or a fiscal monopoly from performing its allotted task. The phrase "the development of trade" refers to the process of establishing a common market (*cf.* the wider concept of affecting trade between Member States, which features in Articles 85, 86 and 92).[80] When interference with this process threatens the attainment of the Treaty objectives, the interests of individual Member States are subordinated to those of the Community. According to the Court:

> ". . . the application of Article 90(2) is not left to the discretion of the Member State which has entrusted an undertaking with the operation of a service of general economic interest. In fact, Article 90(3) confers on the Commission, subject to review by the Court, the task of ensuring application of the Article."[81]

Although made in the context of an argument relating to the *locus standi* of the Italian Government to challenge a decision addressed to British Telecom, these comments clearly reject the suggestion by Advocate General Darmon that the judgments to be made under Article 90(2) should be left in the hands of Member States.

Effect of the exception

The exception, in the rare cases where it might apply, only operates to relieve the undertakings in question. Accordingly, Member States remain fully exposed to any liability which might attach to their rôle under Article 90(1). As far as paragraph (2) is concerned, a difficult problem is the effect it has in proceedings before national courts. This may be formulated in terms of whether or not the paragraph is directly effective, but it must be kept firmly in mind that we are here concerned with a provision under which the scope of obligations imposed by the EEC Treaty is restricted in relation to certain categories of undertakings. The question is how far a claim that a matter falls within the exceptions of Article 90(2) will interfere with the application by a national court of Community provisions on which individuals would normally be entitled to rely.

The European Court recognises the competence of national courts to decide whether an undertaking falls into one of the categories which are eligible for exemption. In *SABAM*[82] a musical copyright society enjoying a *de facto* monopoly in Belgium had replied to an allegation of abusive conduct contrary to Article 86, *inter alia*, by claiming to be an entrusted undertaking within Article 90(2). In dealing with this aspect of the case the Court spoke of "the duty of the national court to investigate whether an

---

[80] See Advocate General Rozés in Case 78/82, *Commission* v. *Italy*, *loc. cit.* note 67, *supra*.
[81] In Case 41/83, *Italy* v. *Commission*, *loc. cit.* note 54, *supra*.
[82] Case 127/73, *BRT* v. *SABAM*, *loc. cit.* note 46, *supra*.

undertaking which invokes the provisions of Article 90(2) for the purpose of claiming a derogation from the rules of the Treaty has, in fact been entrusted by a Member State with the operation of a service of general economic interest."[83]

But what if the national court finds that the undertaking in question has been so entrusted? May it go on to apply the exception and, where appropriate, the proviso, to see whether they provide an escape from the consequences of the normal Community rule? After a period of considerable doubt and ambiguity in the case law, it now seems clear that a national court is fully competent to deal with the exception but that the matter of the proviso can only be handled by the Commission exercising its supervisory functions. The following discussion traces the evolution of the Court's position from its opaque stance in *Hein* through to its more recent acknowledgment of the competence of national courts.

The *Hein*[84] case originated in a prosecution in Luxembourg for the unauthorised use by the defendants of a wharf on the Moselle, in breach of legislation giving special rights and responsibilities in connection with the operation of river port facilities to the Société du Port de Mertert. The legislation was alleged by the defendants to contravene the EEC rules on competition and a reference was made for a preliminary ruling under Article 177, which the Court of Justice treated as a request for an interpretation of Article 90.[85] Having summarised the second paragraph of the Article, the Court went on:

> "An undertaking which enjoys certain privileges for the accomplishment of the task entrusted to it by law, maintaining for this purpose close links with the public authorities, and which is responsible for ensuring the navigability of the State's most important waterway, may fall within this provision.
>
> To answer the question referred, therefore, it is necessary to consider whether Article 90(2) is of such a nature as to create individual rights which the national courts must protect.
>
> Article 90(2) does not lay down an unconditional rule.
>
> Its application involves an appraisal of the requirements on the one hand, of the particular task entrusted to the undertaking concerned and, on the other hand, the protection of the interests of the Community.
>
> This appraisal depends on the objectives of general economic policy pursued by the States under the supervision of the Commission.
>
> Consequently, and without prejudice to the exercise by the Commission of the powers conferred by Article 90(3) Article 90(2) cannot at the present stage create individual rights which the national courts must protect."[86]

---

[83] [1974] E.C.R. at p. 318.
[84] Case 10/71, *loc. cit.* note 24, *supra*. The case is also frequently referred to as *Muller*.
[85] No EEC provisions were specified in the questions.
[86] [1974] E.C.R. at p. 730.

The tenor of the judgment is very clear. No interpretation is offered of Article 90(1) or of any other provision which might have given grounds for not applying the national legislation in question. The referring court is being advised that, because the legislation relates to an entrusted undertaking, the Community point raised by the defendants cannot affect the outcome of the national proceedings.[87] But why, it might be asked, does the Court say Article 90(2) cannot *create* individual rights, when what the paragraph does is to deprive individuals of rights they would otherwise have? *Page*[88] explains that the Court must have been thinking of the paragraph as a *lex specialis* for undertakings in the privileged categories: it must, in other words, have taken the view that, insofar as the Treaty imposed obligations on entrusted undertakings, this would be by virtue of Article 90(2) and not through its general provisions. And it must have concluded, in view of the exception and the proviso in the paragraph, that such obligations could not be directly effective. So interpreted, *Hein* conveys an uncompromising message: as against entrusted undertakings, Community provisions cannot be invoked by individuals in the national courts.[89]

However, by the time of *Sacchi*,[90] it seems, an evolution in the Court's thinking had taken place. The questions referred by a court in Italy concerned, *inter alia*, the compatibility with the Treaty of a measure extending the national broadcasting monopoly, RAI. Having held that, insofar as they engage in economic activities, broadcasting bodies fall within the provisions of Article 90(1), but that a further grant of exclusive rights to such a body would not, in itself, constitute an infringement of Article 86 taken together with Article 90, the Court continued:

> "Moreover, if certain Member States treat undertakings entrusted with the operation of television, even as regards their commercial activities, in particular advertising, as undertakings entrusted with the operation of services of general economic interest, the same prohibitions apply, as regards their behaviour within the market, by reason of Article 90(2), so long as it is not shown that the said prohibitions are incompatible with the performance of their tasks."[91]

As to whether certain practices allegedly entailed in the monopoly amounted to abuses within the meaning of Article 86, the Court said:

> "Such would certainly be the case with an undertaking possessing a monopoly of television advertising, if it imposed unfair charges or

---

[87] The formal ruling on the questions submitted under Art. 177 contained in the *dispositif* of the case simply reiterates the final paragraph of the quoted passage.

[88] *Op. cit.* note 8, *supra* at pp. 32–33. Strong approval of Page's approach is expressed by Marenco, *op. cit.* note 8, *supra*. *Cf.* the view of Smit that the Court was considering the individual rights not of the defendants in the national proceedings but of the Société du Port de Mertert. On his reading of the case, it is the special privilege created by Art. 90(2) for the benefit of entrusted undertakings which lacks direct effect. See Smit and Herzog, *The Law of the European Economic Community*, 3–361 to 3–363. That seems to us impossible to reconcile with what the Court actually *did* in *Hein*.

[89] This is the result attributed to the case by Mégret *et al.*, *op. cit.* note 39, *supra* at p. 88.

[90] Case 155/73, *loc. cit.* note 3, *supra*.

[91] [1974] E.C.R. at p. 430.

conditions on users of its services or if it discriminated between commercial operators or national products on the one hand, and those of other Member States on the other, as regards access to television advertising.

The national court has in each case to ascertain the existence of such abuse and the Commission has to remedy it within the limits of its powers.

Even within the framework of Article 90, therefore, the prohibitions of Article 86 have a direct effect and confer on interested parties rights which the national courts must safeguard."[92]

The two quoted passages seem calculated to correct the impression left by the *Hein* judgment that Article 90(2) creates a special set of truncated obligations for undertakings in the privileged categories. The paragraph is presented as reaffirming that the general rules of the Treaty apply to such undertakings, while creating a limited exception in their favour.[93] It is also explicitly stated that within the framework of Article 90(2) individuals enjoy Community rights which are enforceable in the national courts. The distinction rather obscurely drawn between the respective rôles of the national courts and the Commission need not be interpreted as denying the competence of the former to remedy an abuse once ascertained. It is probably just intended to underline the Commission's power under Art. 90(3) to take steps against the Member State concerned.[94]

Cases after *Sacchi* have confirmed the ability of national courts to apply the exception in Article 90(2). In *Ahmed Saeed*[95] the Court had implied this by its reference to the need for transparency in tariff structures to assist courts to whom tariff disputes might be referred to assess the needs of an entrusted task and their impact on the tariff arrangements. This view was made express in *ERT* v. *Dimotiki*[96] where the Court stated that the national judge could decide if particular behaviour by an undertaking infringed Article 86 and then also determine whether such an apparent breach could be justified by the need to perform the undertaking's entrusted task.[97] Thus, it is now clear that national courts can decide (with the help of a reference under Article 177 if appropriate) whether an undertaking is entrusted with services of general economic interest within the meaning of Article 90(2), and whether that undertaking is obstructed in the performance of that task by the application of the Treaty. Many cases involving directly effective rights in which an undertaking pleads the protection of Article 90(2) may

---

[92] *Ibid.*
[93] In Case 90/76, *Van Ameyde* v. *UCI, loc. cit.* note 27, *supra* at p. 1126 the Court spoke of "the prohibition contained in Article 90 of the Treaty in conjunction with Article 86." This suggests that Art. 90(2) (the provision which the Court must have in mind, since the passage concerns the behaviour of UCI) may itself impose a prohibition. However, it is submitted that the statement should be understood as a reference to the prohibition in Art. 86, as reaffirmed by Art. 90(2).
[94] See Page, *op. cit.* note 8, *supra* at p. 35.
[95] Note 57, *supra.*
[96] Case C–260/89, judgment June 18, 1991 (not yet reported).
[97] *Ibid* para. 34 of judgment.

therefore be fully disposed of where the national court forms the opinion that the limbs of the exception are not made out.

This therefore leaves the question of the application of the proviso to Article 90(2), namely that the development of trade must not be affected to such an extent as would be contrary to the interests of the Community. This tailpiece, reminiscent perhaps of the second sentence of Article 36, may well be seen as unsuitable for determination by national courts insofar as they will neither possess the information on which to take an overview of the Community's interests nor have the political legitimacy to determine the place at which the balance should be drawn. On this approach, national courts are not competent to apply the proviso for the benefit of entrusted undertakings.[98] The only way such undertakings can obtain exemption from the normal rules of the Treaty is by a decision of the Commission under Article 90(3). Unless and until such a decision is taken, the rules apply to them with full vigour. Article 90(2), therefore, functions similarly to Article 85(3), though without a formal system of notification to set the exemption process in motion.[99]

In its *IJsselcentrale* decision[1] the Commission briefly examined the proviso although it had already concluded that the arrangements between the electricity supply companies did not require absolute control of imports and exports in order to perform their entrusted tasks. Regarding the proviso, the Commission observed that the obstruction of imports and exports, intended under the co-operation agreement to continue for 25 years, could not be accepted in the context of the Community's efforts to achieve a single market in energy. The agreements accordingly fell foul of Article 85 and were not saved by Article 90(2).

To sum up, although it would be overstating matters to claim that the Court has "blue-pencilled" the provision, its interpretation of Article 90(2) has minimised its impact upon the protection of individual rights under the Treaty.

Article 90(3): the supervisory and legislative competence of the Commission

By Article 90(3) the Commission is both placed under an obligation to ensure the application of the Article and equipped with a special power to issue directives or decisions for this purpose. Directives or decisions under Article 90(3) can only be addressed to Member States. However, where appropriate the Commission may have recourse to other powers, for example, under Regulation 17 against the undertaking concerned. There is, of course, nothing in Article 90 to prevent the Commission, if it so chooses, from issuing non-binding recommendations.

---

[98] See Case 172/82, *Inter-Huiles*, note 26, *supra*, discussed more fully in the 2nd ed. of this work at pp. 532–533. Also Case 41/83, *Italy* v. *Commission*, note 54, *supra*.

[99] Smit, *op. cit.* note 88, *supra* at p. 3–363 points out that the Commission is the most appropriate body to be given the task of ruling on the permissibility of anti-competitive conduct within the Community system.

[1] Note 56, *supra*.

The problems which arise concern the relationship between measures adopted under Article 90(3) rather than other provisions of the Treaty, such as Article 100a or 94; the extent to which Article 90(3) and Article 169 represent enforcement choices; and the emerging distinction in the case law between the rules applicable under Article 90(3) to the adoption of directives and those applying to decisions.

Article 90(3) and other provisions of the Treaty

The Court's opportunities to explain the relationship between the supervisory function of the Commission and other legislative provisions in the Treaty have arisen principally in the context of the challenges made by Member States to the directives adopted by the Commission under Article 90(3). In the first of these[2] the Court was called upon to examine the validity of the so-called Transparency Directive.[3] This legislation seeks to ensure the transparency of financial relations between Member States and public undertakings, and requires Member States to keep available for five years relevant information and to supply it on request to the Commission.[4] The preamble to the Directive stresses the Commission's duty to ensure that Member States do not grant undertakings, public or private, aids incompatible with the common market, and the need for equal treatment of public and private enterprises. The complexity of financial relations between Member States and public undertakings hinders the achievement of that equality, and provides the rationale for the measure.

Part of the argument over competence before the Court concerned the relationship between Article 90(3) and Article 94.[5] The latter confers upon the Council power to determine the conditions in which Article 93(3), relating to notification of State aids, is to apply. The applicant Member States claimed that the Directive fell within the Council's competence under Article 94, rather than that of the Commission under Article 90(3). The Court replied, after contrasting the objectives of the two provisions:

"In comparison with the Council's power under Article 94, that which is conferred upon the Commission by Article 90(3) thus operates in a specific field of application and under conditions defined by reference to the particular objective of that Article. It follows that the Commission's power to issue the contested directive depends on the needs inherent in its duty of surveillance provided for in Article 90 and that the possibility that rules might be laid down by the Council, by virtue of its general power under Article 94, containing provisions impinging upon the specific sphere of aids granted to public undertakings does not preclude the exercise of that power by the Commission."

---

[2] Cases 188–190/80, *France, Italy and United Kingdom* v. *Commission* [1982] E.C.R. 2545.
[3] Note 17, *supra*.
[4] The Commission announced its application of the directive to public undertakings in the manufacturing sector in its Communication to Member States, O.J. 1991 C273/2.
[5] As to Art. 94, see Chap. 18.

The Commission's competence was thus confirmed, although it would seem that the Directive could have been adopted under either provision.

A challenge was also mounted, this time by France and supported by Italy, Belgium, Germany and Greece,[6] against the next principal Directive issued under Article 90(3), relating to telecommunications terminal equipment.[7] This measure provided, *inter alia*, that Member States which had granted special or exclusive rights for the importation, marketing, connection, bringing into service of telecommunications terminal equipment and/or the maintenance of such equipment were to ensure that those rights were withdrawn. One argument advanced to challenge the Commission's competence was that the provision constituted a normative act which could only properly belong under Articles 87 or 100a (thereby requiring Council action). Following its earlier reasoning in the *Transparency Directive* case, the Court ruled that the duty imposed upon the Commission under Article 90 was more specific than the general competence conferred on the Council under Articles 87 and 100a.

A further argument raised in the *Telecommunications Directive* case was the relationship between Article 90(3) and Article 169. It was argued by the French Government that the Directive amounted to a repressive act which could only be carried out by recourse to Article 169. According to the Court, Article 90(3) allows the Commission to define in a general way the obligations which the Treaty imposes upon Member States. By implication, therefore, this procedure is not available for the identification of specific situations existing in different Member States. However, since the Directive was treated by the Court as purely normative in nature it fell within the scope of the Commission's competence under Article 90(3). It is thus possible for the Commission to specify the obligations of Member States in the form of directives without going through the lengthier procedure of Article 169. But if a Member State does not comply, the default can then only be pursued by recourse to the latter.[8]

Directives and decisions distinguished

When the *Telecommunications Directive* judgment first appeared, it cast doubt upon the Commission's previous practice of using decisions under Article 90(3) to act as enforcement measures against Member States for specific infringements.[9] However, in an appeal from the case involving Netherlands express delivery services,[10] the Court has distinguished

---

[6] Case C–202/88, *France* v. *Commission*, March 19, 1991 (not yet reported).
[7] Directive 88/301, O.J. 1988 L131/73.
[8] As happened in the context of the Transparency Directive when Italy refused to supply requested information. See Case 118/85, *Re Amministrazione Autonama dei Monopoli di Stato: Commission* v. *Italy* [1987] E.C.R. 2599, [1988] 3 C.M.L.R. 255; see Ross, (1989) 26 C.M.L.Rev. 167 at pp. 189–192.
[9] Examples are: Decision 85/276, *Greek insurance arrangements* O.J. 1985 L152/25; Decision 87/359, *Spanish fare reductions* O.J. 1987 L194/28; Decision 90/16, *Dutch express delivery services* O.J. 1990 L10/47; Decision 90/456 *Spanish express courier services* O.J. 1990 L233/19.
[10] Cases C–48/90 and 66/90, *Netherlands, Koninklijke PTT Nederland NV and PTT Post BV* v. *Commission*, judgment February 12, 1992 (not yet reported).

directives from decisions in the context of the Commission's powers. According to the Court, the decision, which is adopted in view of the particular situation in one or more Member States, necessarily involves an assessment of that position from the point of view of Community law and determines the resulting consequences for the Member State concerned having regard to the requirements inherent in the fulfilment of a particular task imposed on an undertaking responsible for the management of services of a general economic interest. The Court went on to add that in order not to deprive of all useful purpose the power to adopt decisions under Article 90(3) it must be recognised that the Commission has power to find that a particular State measure is incompatible with the rules of the Treaty and to specify the measures which the addressee State must adopt in order to comply with its obligations under Community law. However, the Court then annulled the particular decision on the basis that the Commission had given neither the Netherlands Government nor the PTT a fair hearing.

It therefore appears that, where decisions are concerned, the Commission holds an enforcement power in derogation from Article 169.[11] The corresponding limitation placed upon the Commission would seem to be the establishment of defence rights. Directives will be lawful so long as they are normative and not repressive in nature. Although the Court has not allowed the Commission *carte blanche* to pursue Member States and public undertakings, it is clear that the special threat to competition which they pose constitutes the justification for upholding a particular regime of supervision and control alongside the protection of individual rights.

---

[11] *Cf.* Art. 93(2) which is specifically identified as a special procedure in the Treaty.

CHAPTER 20

INTELLECTUAL PROPERTY[1]

WHAT IS INTELLECTUAL PROPERTY?

The term "industrial property" is applied to certain valuable rights connected with the production and distribution of goods and the provision of services. A catalogue of such rights is found in the Paris Convention on the Protection of Industrial Property[2] which refers to "patents, utility models, industrial designs, trade marks, service marks, trade names, indications of source or appellations of origin, and the repression of unfair competition." Similar rights exist in relation to literary and artistic productions, the most important being copyright. "Intellectual property" is now widely accepted as a generic designation covering both industrial and artistic property, and this is the sense in which the term is used here.[3] It is not found in the EEC Treaty, where Article 36 speaks of "industrial and commercial property." As we shall see, that phrase has been widely interpreted by the Court of Justice.

A normal feature of intellectual property rights is their exclusiveness: they reserve to a particular person the enjoyment of some valuable advantage. Typically also, the rights have a territorial dimension. Thus a patentee (or his assignee or licensee) is the person solely entitled to manufacture and market the patented product within the territory of the State by which a patent is granted.[4] The sale within that State of any product covered by the patent specification would attract infringement proceedings.

The protection afforded to these rights is proprietary in nature, good against the world in general. Other exclusive rights closely associated with the main forms of intellectual property depend upon secrecy for the preservation of their commercial value. The guarantee of secrecy may be found in the law of contract or in rules on the confidentiality of information communicated by one party to another. An example of such a right is "know-how," consisting of specialised knowledge of industrial techniques and processes without which, for example, it may be impossible to exploit a patent properly.[5]

---

[1] For a full analysis of the United Kingdom law of intellectual property and its international (including its EEC) dimension, see Cornish, *Intellectual Property*, (2nd ed., 1989 Sweet & Maxwell). See also Whish, *Competition Law*, (2nd ed., 1989), Chap. 19.

[2] Convention of March 20, 1883. Most recently revised, Stockholm, July 14, 1967, Art. 1(2).

[3] The term is convenient, if not wholly appropriate, and received international recognition in the title of the World Intellectual Property Organisation. See Cornish, *op. cit.* note 1, *supra* at p. 3. See also Harris, (1975–76) 1 E.L.Rev. 515 at pp. 515–516.

[4] The State's legislation may make the granting of licences to work the patent compulsory in certain circumstances. The right of the patent holder will then be confined essentially to receiving a royalty. On the position in the United Kingdom, see the Patents Act 1977, ss. 48–54. See Cornish, *op. cit.* note 1, *supra* at pp. 205 *et seq.*

[5] On the status of know-how in English law, see *Handley Page* v. *Butterworth* (1935) 19 T.C. 328.

INTELLECTUAL PROPERTY AND THE COMMON MARKET

The main problem underlying the legal developments discussed in this chapter was neatly summarised by the European Court in the following passage from its judgment in *Parke, Davis* v. *Centrafarm*:

> "The national rules relating to the protection of industrial property have not yet been unified within the Community. In the absence of such unification, the national character of the protection of industrial property and the variations between the different legislative systems on this subject are capable of creating obstacles both to the free movement of the patented products and to competition within the common market."[6]

The co-existence of separate systems of protection for intellectual property rights in the different Member States is liable to conflict with the objective of creating a single market covering the whole Community. One aspect of the problem is that variations in the content of the rules relating to intellectual property between the Member States necessarily entail inequalities in the conditions of competition under which business is carried on. However, this is only one of a number of factors, such as differences in taxation systems or in the strictness of laws on the protection of the environment, contributing to such inequalities. More serious is the "national character" of intellectual property, the sheer fact that rights relating to the same subject-matter have an independent legal existence in each of the Member States where they are recognised. Given the exclusiveness of intellectual property rights and their territorial character, there is a danger that the market in goods or services covered by such rights may be divided up into more or less watertight national compartments. For example, X Ltd., the holder of a patent or trade mark right protected under the law of Member State A, may be entitled to oppose the importation into that State of an article manufactured under a parallel patent or bearing a parallel mark protected under the law of Member State B; and this may be so even if the holder of the patent or mark in Member State B is none other than X Ltd. itself or a subsidiary or licensee of X Ltd. It is obvious that such use of the patent or trade mark recognised by Member State A interferes with the free movement of goods and is liable to have a distorting effect on competition.

UNIFICATION OF LAWS ON INTELLECTUAL PROPERTY

The remedy hinted at by the Court in the passage quoted from *Parke, Davis* is that national rules on the protection of intellectual property rights should be unified.

In fact, since the judgment in that case an important step has been taken

---

[6] Case 24/67 [1968] E.C.R. 55 at p. 71.

towards the goal of unification through the signing of the Convention for
the European Patent for the Common Market (otherwise known as the
Community Patent Convention).[7] The Convention, signed on December
15, 1975, did not come into force. But on December 15, 1989 an Agreement
relating to Community patents made provision for the amendment of
the Community Patent Convention, and for that Convention to be
supplemented by three Protocols relating to: (i) the Settlement of Litigation
concerning the Infringement or Validity of Community Patents; (ii)
Privileges and Immunities of the Common Appeal Court; and (iii) the
Statute of the Common Appeal Court. A further Protocol provided for
possible modification of the conditions of entry into force of the Agreement
relating to Community Patents.[8] The general purpose of the Convention is
to introduce a unitary patent for the common market, within the framework
of the wider Convention on the Grant of European Patents,[9] and to lay down
the "common system of law" by which this patent is to be governed. Article 2
of the Convention provides:

"1. European patents granted for the Contracting States shall be called
Community patents.

2. Community patents shall have a unitary character. They shall have
equal effect throughout the territories to which this Convention applies
and may only be granted, transferred, revoked or allowed to lapse in
respect of the whole of such territories. The same shall apply *mutatis
mutandis* to applications for European patents in which the Contracting
States are designated.

3. Community patents shall have an autonomous character. They shall
be subject only to the provisions of this Convention and those
provisions of the European Patent Convention which are binding upon
every European patent and which shall consequently be deemed to be
provisions of the Convention."

An examination of the detailed provisions of the Convention and its
Protocols would fall outside the scope of this book. What concerns us is the
likely effect of the Convention on the problem of the partitioning of the
common market through the operation of national patents. Here the first
point to notice is that national patents will continue to exist side by side with
Community patents (although not in relation to the same inventions).
Where an inventor chooses to take out a Community patent, he will receive

---

[7] O.J. 1976 L17/1.
[8] As of May 18, 1992 only Germany had ratified the Agreement. Germany and the United
Kingdom had ratified the further Protocol referred to above.
[9] Or "European Patent Convention." This came into force on October 7, 1977. With the
accession of Ireland in 1992, all Member States are parties. The European Patent Office
which processes patent applications has been established in Munich, with a branch in The
Hague. An applicant for a European patent specifies the contracting States in which
protection is sought. If granted, the patent will have the same effect as a national patent in
each of those States. However, subject to transitional arrangements, once the Community
Patent Convention is in force the only available form of European patent for EEC members
will be a unitary Community patent.

protection on a Community-wide basis. There will thus be a single proprietor of the patent, whose rights will be exhausted by putting a protected product on to the market in one of the Member States. The possibility that the granting of licences limited to certain areas might be used as a means of splitting the common market has been provided against. Where an inventor prefers to take out a national patent, the situation will be much the same as before, except that Article 76 of the Convention provides a legislative basis for the exhaustion of rights principle developed by the Court in its case-law.[10] It may be concluded that the Community Patent Convention, when it comes into force, will go a considerable way towards reconciling the legitimate interests of patent holders with the requirements of a well-functioning common market; but areas of conflict will remain and the case-law of the Court, which is discussed below, has certainly not been superseded.

As for other types of intellectual property, significant steps have been taken in relation to trade marks and the protection of computer programmes. After earlier initiatives had come to nothing, a Memorandum on the creation of an EEC trade mark was published by the Commission in 1976.[11] This was followed in 1980 by the submission to the Council of a proposal for a directive to harmonise national trade mark laws and a proposal for a regulation on a Community trade mark.[12] Directive 89/104,[13] the First Council Directive on the approximation of the laws of the Member States relating to trade marks was to have been implemented in the Member States by December 28, 1991, but in accordance with its terms, implementation was deferred until December 31, 1992,[14] so that the date of putting into effect of national provisions applying the Directive would, as far as possible, be aligned with the date from which it would be possible for Community trade mark applications to be made. Council Directive 91/250 on the legal protection of computer programmes[15] provides that the expression of a computer programme (but not the ideas or principles which underlie any element of a programme) is to be protected by copyright.

A judicial solution—existence and exercise

The stark question for the Court of Justice has been how far it is bound to recognise the rights conferred by national laws on holders of intellectual

---

[10] Art. 81(1) provides:
"The rights conferred by a national patent in a Contracting State shall not extend to acts concerning a product covered by that patent which are done within the territory of that Contracting State after that product has been put on the market in any Contracting State by the proprietor of the patent or with his express consent, unless there are grounds which, under Community law, would justify the extension to such acts of the rights conferred by the patent."
On the relevant case-law, see *infra*.
[11] Bull. EC Supp. 8/76.
[12] O.J. 1980 C351 at, respectively, pp. 1 and 5. See Gormley, (1981) 6 E.L.Rev., pp. 385 and 463.
[13] O.J. 1989 L40/1.
[14] Dec. 92/10, O.J. 1992 L6/35.
[15] O.J. 1991 L122/42. The Directive is to be implemented in the Member States by January 1, 1993.

property where these allow activity, usually involving the exclusion from the market in question of imports from another Member State, which would normally be prohibited under Community law. The answer that effect must be given to all such rights might seem to follow from the provision of Article 222 EEC that:

> "This Treaty shall *in no way* prejudice the rules in Member States governing the system of property ownership" (emphasis added).

On the other hand, Article 36 EEC, which contains the only express derogation from the general rules of the Treaty for the benefit of intellectual property rights, provides in pertinent part:

> "The provisions of Articles 30 to 34 shall not preclude prohibitions or restrictions on imports, exports or goods in transit justified on grounds of ... the protection of industrial and commercial property. Such prohibitions or restrictions shall not, however, constitute a means of arbitrary discrimination or a disguised restriction on trade between Member States."

While restrictions on imports that are genuinely necessary for the protection of industrial and commercial property are here exempted from the prohibition in Article 30, it is made unequivocally clear in the second sentence of the Article that there may be circumstances where, regardless of rights existing under national law, the prohibition will apply.

The compromise enshrined in Article 36 pointed the way to a solution which has also been applied by analogy in the fields of competition and the provision of services. This was formulated in a leading case, *Terrapin* v. *Terranova*,[16] as follows:

> "... whilst the Treaty does not affect the existence of rights recognized by the legislation of a Member State in matters of industrial and commercial property, yet the exercise of those rights may nevertheless, depending on the circumstances, be restricted by the prohibitions in the Treaty. Inasmuch as it provides an exception to one of the fundamental principles of the common market, Article 36 in fact admits exceptions to the free movement of goods only to the extent to which such exceptions are justified for the purposes of safeguarding the rights which constitute the specific subject-matter of that property."[17]

The distinction drawn by the Court between the existence of rights and their exercise is evidently inspired by a wish to remain at least within the letter of Article 222. It invites the criticism that a form of property *is* the bundle of rights recognised by national law under a particular designation; and if Community law prevents any rights in the bundle from being exercised, the property is to that extent diminished. What the Court has done, in reality, emerges from the second sentence in the quoted passage. The derogation in

---

[16] Case 119/75 [1976] E.C.R. 1039; [1976] 2 C.M.L.R. 482. The formulation is found, with small verbal differences, in numerous judgments.
[17] [1976] E.C.R. at p. 1061.

Article 36 has been confined to rights which, the Court considers, constitute the essential core or "specific subject-matter" of the property in question.[18] The exercise of such rights is tolerated, even if it impedes trade or competition, because otherwise it would no longer be possible to say that the property was receiving protection. On the other hand, rights which the Court regards as merely incidental to the property are not allowed to interfere with the project of unifying the market.

The solution worked out in the Court's case-law on intellectual property is the fruit of teleological interpretation of the EEC Treaty. In *Polydor* v. *Harlequin*[19] the Court was invited to extend that interpretation to provisions in a free trade agreement with a third country which were similarly worded to Articles 30 and 36 EEC, but declined to do so. That was because the purpose of such agreements was less far-reaching than the purpose of the Treaty—"to create a single market reproducing as closely as possible the conditions of a domestic market."[20]

FREEDOM OF MOVEMENT—THE EXHAUSTION OF RIGHTS PRINCIPLE

The exclusive right of an owner of intellectual property to put into circulation for the first time goods that are subject to the property is likely to be understood in the law of the Member State concerned as applying to sales in that State's territory. Sales elsewhere will not count as an exercise of the right—in the jargon of the subject, they are considered not to "exhaust" it.[21] This means that, as a matter of national law, it will be open to the owner of the property to oppose the sale by other traders of imported products acquired in a Member State where they have been marketed by the owner himself. There would be an incentive for such "parallel" importing if, for some reason, the products in question were significantly cheaper in the State of initial distribution than in the one from which it was sought to exclude them.

On the other hand, the Court of Justice has repeatedly stated, as a general principle, that "the proprietor of an industrial or commercial property right protected by the legislation of a Member State may not rely on that legislation in order to oppose the importation of a product which has lawfully been marketed in another Member State by, or with the consent of, the proprietor of the right himself or a person legally or economically dependent on him."[22] Whatever the position in national law, the proprietor's exclusive right is deemed in Community law to be exhausted by

---

[18] The definitions the Court has given in its case-law of the "specific subject-matter" of various important forms of intellectual property are considered *infra*.

[19] Case 270/80 [1982] E.C.R. 329; [1982] 1 C.M.L.R. 677.

[20] [1982] E.C.R. at p. 349.

[21] On the exhaustion of patent rights in the law of the United Kingdom, see Cornish, *op. cit.* note 1, *supra* at pp. 200 *et seq*.

[22] See, among many instances, Case 144/81, *Keurkoop* v. *Nancy Kean Gifts* [1982] E.C.R. 2853 at p. 2873.

putting products into circulation anywhere within the common market. The rationale of the principle is to be found in the limitation of the exception in Article 36 by the notion of the specific subject-matter of property. Where exhaustion occurs it is because the right to exclude imports originally marketed in another Member State is not seen as part of the essential guarantee provided by the property in question. The exercise of the right would, therefore, not be "justified" within the meaning of Article 36 as being necessary for the protection of the property.[23]

The principle has now been applied by the Court of Justice to most of the important forms of intellectual property.[24]

Patents

The leading case on the application of the exhaustion of rights principle to patents is *Centrafarm* v. *Sterling Drug*.[25] Patents for a drug used in the treatment of urinary infections were held by Sterling Drug, an American company, in the United Kingdom and the Netherlands. The case originated in the proceedings brought for the infringement of the Dutch patent against Centrafarm, a company famous in the annals of the European Court as a parallel importer of pharmaceutical products.[26] Centrafarm's alleged infringement consisted of importing into the Netherlands and offering for sale there quantities of the patented product which had been lawfully marketed by licensees of Sterling Drug in the United Kingdom. This was commercially attractive for Centrafarm, since the price of the drug on the United Kingdom market was only about half the price on the Dutch market.

The Court of Justice defined the specific subject-matter of a patent as:

> ". . . the guarantee that the patentee, to reward the creative effort of the inventor, has the exclusive right to use an invention with a view to manufacturing industrial products and putting them into circulation for the first time, either directly or by the grant of licences to third parties as well as the right to oppose infringements."[27]

The essential function of a patent is here acknowledged to be the rewarding of (and hence encouragement to) creative effort. The reward comes from the patentee's ability to earn a monopoly profit through an exclusive right to manufacture the protected product and put it into circulation for the first time. That right may be exploited directly or by appointing licensees. It has, as a corollary, a right to oppose manufacturing or first marketing of the product by third parties.

---

[23] This analysis was applied by the Court for the first time in Case 78/70, *Deutsche Grammophon* v. *Metro* [1971] E.C.R. 487; [1971] C.M.L.R. 631. It is more fully worked out in Case 15/74, *Centrafarm* v. *Sterling Drug* [1974] E.C.R. 1147; [1974] 2 C.M.L.R. 480.

[24] There is a very full review of the case-law in Gormley, *Prohibiting Restrictions on Trade within the EEC*, T.M.C. Asser Instituut (1985), pp. 184 *et seq*. On the earlier cases, see Harris, *op. cit.* note 3, *supra*.

[25] *Loc. cit.* note 23, *supra*.

[26] There were parallel proceedings for the infringement of the Dutch trade mark: Case 16/74, *Centrafarm* v. *Winthrop* [1974] E.C.R. 1183; [1974] 2 C.M.L.R. 480, discussed *infra*.

[27] [1974] E.C.R. at p. 1162.

In the light of that definition the Court went on to consider the circumstances in which the use of a patent to block the importation of protected products from another Member State might be justified. Two cases of possible justification were mentioned: where the product is not patentable in the Member State of origin and has been manufactured there by a third party without the consent of the patentee in the Member State of importation[28]; and where a patent exists in each of the Member States in question but the original proprietors of the patents are legally and economically independent. On the other hand, there could be no justification for opposing importation "where the product has been put onto the market in a legal manner, by the patentee himself or with his consent, in the Member State from which is has been imported, in particular in the case of a proprietor of parallel patents."[29] If a patent could be used in this way, the patentee would be able to cordon off national markets, thereby restricting trade between Member States, "where no such restriction was necessary to guarantee the essence of the exclusive rights flowing from the parallel patents."[30] The objection that national patents were unlikely to be truly parallel, with the result that levels of protection would vary between Member States, was brushed aside. "It should be noted here," the Court said, "that, in spite of divergences which remain in the absence of any unification of national rules concerning industrial property the identity of the protected invention is clearly the essential element of the concept of parallel patents which it is for the courts to assess."[31] The conclusion was:

> ". . . that the exercise, by a patentee, of the right which he enjoys under the legislation of a Member State to prohibit the sale, in that State, of a product protected by the patent which has been marketed in another Member State by the patentee or with his consent is incompatible with the rules of the EEC Treaty concerning the free movement of goods within the common market."[32]

The basis of the ruling was not made altogether clear. On the one hand, it might be thought the existence of parallel patents was a crucial factor: a right to oppose the importation of protected products could be regarded as superfluous, because the patentee would already have received the monopoly profit, which was his due, in the Member State where the products were first put on the market. On the other hand, the general terms in which the ruling was expressed, taken with other hints in the judgment,[33] strongly suggested the principle of exhaustion would apply, even where the initial marketing occurred without the benefit of patent protection. If that were so, then the explanation could only lie in the patentee's consent to the

---

[28] This was the situation in Case 24/67, *Parke, Davis* v. *Centrafarm* [1968] E.C.R. 55; [1968] C.M.L.R. 47. The questions put to the Court were, however, formulated with reference to the competition rules.
[29] [1974] E.C.R. at p. 1163.
[30] *Ibid.*
[31] *Ibid.*
[32] *Ibid.*
[33] See, in particular, the reference *ibid.*, to non-patentable goods "manufactured by third parties without the consent of the patentee."

marketing. That such was indeed the Court's meaning was shown in the later case of *Merck* v. *Stephar*.[34]

The plaintiff in the national proceedings, Merck, was the holder in the Netherlands of patents relating to a drug used mainly in the treatment of high blood pressure. The proceedings arose because Stephar had imported the drug into the Netherlands from Italy where, although it was not patentable, it had been put into circulation by Merck. On Merck's behalf it was argued that the function of rewarding an inventor's creative effort would not be fulfilled if, owing to the impossibility of patenting a product, its sale in the Member State in question did not take place under monopoly conditions. To this the Court replied:

> "That right of first placing a product on a market enables the inventor, by allowing him a monopoly in exploiting his product, to obtain the reward for his creative effort without, however, guaranteeing that he will obtain such a reward in all circumstances.
>
> It is for the proprietor of the patent to decide, in the light of all the circumstances, under what conditions he will market his product, including the possibility of marketing it in a Member State where the law does not provide patent protection for the product in question. If he decides to do so he must the accept the consequences of his choice as regards the free movement of the product within the Common Market, which is a fundamental principle forming part of the legal and economic circumstances which must be taken into account by the proprietor of the patent in determining the manner in which his exclusive right will be exercised."[35]

The owner of a national patent, therefore, has a choice. He may decide to exploit his exclusive rights to the utmost, in which case he will have to stay out of markets in Member States where he has weaker protection or none at all. Or he may go into those other markets, at the cost of accepting a lower profit in his protected market. Whether it makes sense from an economic point of view for a patentee to be confronted with such a choice may be open to question; but for the Court the unity of the market takes precedence over conflicting considerations of economic policy.[36]

It used to be debated whether an owner of parallel national patents was entitled to resist the importation into one of the Member States concerned of products manufactured under a compulsory licence issued in respect of his patent in the other Member State.[37] The question received a clear affirmative answer in *Pharmon* v. *Hoechst*.[38] Parallel patents in a medicinal drug were owned by Hoechst in Germany, the Netherlands and the United Kingdom. A compulsory licence for the manufacture of the drug had been

---

[34] Case 187/80 [1981] E.C.R. 2063; [1981] 3 C.M.L.R. 463.

[35] [1981] E.C.R. at pp. 2081–2082.

[36] See Cornish, *op. cit.* note 1, *supra* at pp. 200 *et seq.*

[37] Under a system of compulsory licensing a patentee may be deprived of his monopoly by an official decision to grant licences to third parties in return for a reasonable royalty. See note 4, *supra.*

[38] Case 19/84 [1985] E.C.R. 2281.

obtained in the United Kingdom and Pharmon had purchased a consignment from the licensee with a view to selling it on the Dutch market. This Hoechst was anxious to prevent. Pharmon rested its case on the exhaustion of rights principle, arguing that Hoechst had entered the British market with its eyes open and must be taken to have accepted all the legal consequences flowing from the registration of a parallel patent. The passage quoted above from the judgment in *Merck* seemed to give force to that argument.[39] It was, however, rejected by the Court on the ground that the compulsory character of a licence meant the holder of the patent could not be regarded as having consented to the actions of the licensee. "Such a measure," the Court said, "deprives the patent proprietor of his right to determine freely the conditions under which he markets his products."[40] The provision of the Community Patent Convention excepting from the principle of exhaustion "the case of a product put on the market under a compulsory licence" has thus been shown to reflect the law of the EEC Treaty.[41]

Trade marks

Centrafarm v. *Sterling Drug*[42] had a companion case, *Centrafarm* v. *Winthrop*,[43] relating to the infringement of the trade mark, NEGRAM, under which the imported drug was sold. The plaintiff in the national proceedings was the Dutch subsidiary of Sterling Drug, Winthrop B.V., which owned the trade mark in the Netherlands. The United Kingdom mark was held by another Sterling subsidiary, Sterling Winthrop Group Ltd.

The European Court's conclusion was similar to that in the patent case and reached by a similar process of reasoning. The specific subject-matter of a trade mark was said to be:

> ". . . the guarantee that the owner of the trade mark has the exclusive right to use that trade mark, for the purpose of putting products protected by the trade mark into circulation for the first time, and is therefore intended to protect him against competitors wishing to take advantage of the status and reputation of the trade mark by selling products illegally bearing that trade mark."[44]

The emphasis here is on what makes a trade mark valuable—the reservation to the owner, through his exclusive right to put marked products into circulation, of the goodwill associated with the mark. Why such a right should be given (the question of the "essential function" of a trade mark) was not considered by the Court on this occasion.[45] The Court went on to

---

[39] [1981] E.C.R. at p. 2082.
[40] [1985] E.C.R. at 2298, para. 25.
[41] Community Patent Convention, Art. 76(3) (formerly 81(3)).
[42] *Loc. cit.* note 23, *supra.*
[43] Case 16/74, *loc. cit.* note 26, *supra.*
[44] [1974] E.C.R. at p. 1194.
[45] See Case 102/77, *Hoffmann-La Roche* v. *Centrafarm* [1978] E.C.R. 1139; [1978] 3 C.M.L.R. 217; Case 3/78, *Centrafarm* v. *American Home Products* [1978] E.C.R. 1823; [1978] 1 C.M.L.R. 326. The cases are discussed *infra.*

find that, where goods have been marketed by a trade mark owner or with his consent in another Member State "so there can be no question of abuse or infringement of the trade mark,"[46] their exclusion could not be justified as being necessary to guarantee the "essence" of the owner's right. The Court, accordingly, ruled:

> ". . . that the exercise, by the owner of a trade mark, of the right which he enjoys under the legislation of a Member State to prohibit the sale, in that State, of a product which has been marketed under the trade mark in another Member State by the trade mark owner or with his consent is incompatible with the rules of the EEC Treaty concerning the free movement of goods within the common market."[47]

This statement adopting consent to marketing as the criterion of the exhaustion of trade mark rights was seen to be in need of qualification in *Hoffmann-La Roche* v. *Centrafarm*[48] and *Centrafarm* v. *American Home Products*,[49] which came to the Court of Justice by way of references under Article 177 by courts in, respectively, Germany and the Netherlands. The background was, again, the resale by Centrafarm of pharmaceutical products it had purchased at the relatively low prices prevailing on the British market; however, a new feature of the cases was that Centrafarm has played a more active role in relation to the products than that of a mere importer. The product in the German case was the tranquilliser VALIUM, which had been marketed in the United Kingdom by the British subsidiary of Hoffmann-La Roche. The VALIUM was imported into the Netherlands where its original packaging was removed and it was put up into larger packages. On these Centrafarm placed the trade mark owned by Hoffmann-La Roche in Germany as well as a notice giving its own name and address as the vendor of the product. It then re-exported the VALIUM for sale on the German market. In the Dutch case Centrafarm had gone even further. The product there was a tranquilliser which was sold by American Home Products Corporation (AHPC) in various Member States under different trade marks. In the United Kingdom the mark used by AHPC was SERENID and in the Benelux countries it was SERESTA. Quantities of the tranquilliser which AHPC had put into circulation in the United Kingdom under the mark SERENID were imported into the Netherlands by Centrafarm and sold there after the original mark had been removed and the mark SERESTA substituted. The European Court was asked, in effect, by the referring courts whether Article 36 enabled Hoffmann-La Roche and AHPC to rely on their respective trade mark rights in Germany and the Netherlands to curb these activities. In both cases the answer given by the Court was in the form of statements of general principle, deduced from the first sentence of Article 36, subject to a qualification deduced from the second sentence of the Article.

---

[46] [1974] E.C.R. 1195.
[47] *Ibid.*
[48] *Loc. cit.* note 45, *supra.*
[49] [1978] E.C.R. at p. 1167.

In the German case the Court held that:

"The proprietor of a trade mark right which is protected in two Member States at the same time is justified pursuant to the first sentence of Article 36 of the EEC Treaty in preventing a product to which the trade mark has lawfully been applied in one of those States from being marketed in the other Member State after it has been repackaged in new packaging to which the trade mark has been affixed by a third party."[49]

It reached that conclusion in the light of the "essential function of the trade mark" which, it said, was "to guarantee the identity of the trade marked product to the consumer or ultimate user, by enabling him without any possibility of confusion to distinguish that product from products which have another origin."[50] There is a certain inelegance in juxtaposing this definition of *essential function* from the point of view of the consumer's interest in not being deceived with a definition of *specific subject-matter* from the point of view of the trade mark holder's interest in his goodwill. In the present context the Court took the view that the guarantee of origin meant "that the consumer or ultimate user can be certain that a trade marked product which is sold to him has not been subject at a previous stage of marketing to interference by a third person, without the authorisation of the proprietor of the trade mark, such as to affect the original condition of the product."[51] It followed that the right to prevent any dealing with the marked product which was likely to impair this guarantee formed part of the specific subject-matter of the trade mark right.

The Court then turned its attention to the proviso in Article 36 that the exercise of rights must not constitute "a disguised restriction on trade between Member States." It was held that such a restriction might arise if the variation of the packaging of the product in the different Member States formed part of a marketing strategy enabling the trade mark holder to compartmentalise the market. However, he would only be prevented from exercising his right against the seller of the imported product if three further conditions were satisfied. In the first place, the repackaging must have been carried out in a way which did not affect the original condition of the product. This might be the case, for example, where the product was marketed by the proprietor of the trade mark in a double packaging and the repackaging only affected the outer layer; or where the repackaging was inspected by a public authority. Secondly, the proprietor of the mark must be given prior notice of the marketing of the repackaged product. And thirdly, the new packaging must indicate the person by whom the operation has been performed. In this way the Court sought to reconcile, on the one hand, the legitimate interests of consumers and of the trade mark holder and, on the other hand, the principle of free internal trade, requiring that the

---

[50] [1978] E.C.R. at p. 1164.
[51] *Ibid.*

seller of the imported goods be given "a certain licence which in normal circumstances is reserved to the proprietor himself."[52]

In the Dutch case the Court rule that, in principle, the proprietor of a trade mark in one Member State was justified in opposing the sale by a third party of a product bearing that mark, even if the product had previously been marketed in another Member State under a different mark held by the same proprietor. Here too, the emphasis was in the essential function of a trade mark in providing a guarantee of a product's origin. The Court said that this guarantee would be compromised if anyone other than the trade mark owner were allowed to place the mark on the product. It was, therefore, consistent with the essential function of this type of property that, where a person held two or more trade marks in respect of the same product, national law should prevent any unauthorised third party from taking it upon himself to place one or other of the marks on any part of the production in question or to alter the marks placed by the holder on different parts of such production; the same would apply where the different parts of the production, bearing different marks, came from two different Member States.

As to the proviso in Article 36, the Court pointed out that there might be perfectly good reasons for using different trade marks in respect of the same products in different Member States. (An obvious case would be where it was impossible for the holder of a trade mark in State A to obtain registration of the mark in State B owing to its similarity to a mark of independent origin already protected in that State.) On the other hand, the proviso might apply if the trade mark rights were exploited for the purposes of a market-splitting strategy. It is, of course, for the national court to determine whether or not, in fact, the right is being legitimately exercised. Thus the derogation in Article 36 will not apply to a right the protection of which would otherwise be justified because it belongs to the specific subject-matter of the property in question, if the right is being exploited for an anti-competitive purpose.[53]

An ingenious parallel importer may find a way of repackaging marked products that does not compromise the guarantee of origin the trade mark represents to consumers. There was a good example in *Pfizer* v. *Eurim-Pharm*,[54] another case of alleged infringement of a German trade mark through the importation of pharmaceutical products first marketed in the United Kingdom. The packaging for the British market consisted of "blister strips," each containing five tablets, which were enclosed in an outer wrapping. The trade mark "VIBRAMYCIN PFIZER" was printed on the strips. After removing the outer wrapping, the importer, Eurim-Pharm, placed each strip in its own box, with an information leaflet as required by German legislation. The boxes had transparent windows through which the

---

[52] See [1978] E.C.R. at pp. 1165–1166.
[53] See the analysis by Judge Pescatore in a paper "Libre circulation des marchandises et droits de protection industrielle dans le marché commun" at the Institut Universitaire International, Luxembourg in July 1978.
[54] Case 1/81 [1981] E.C.R. 2913; [1982] 1 C.M.L.R. 406.

trade mark on the strip was plainly visible. On the back of the boxes the names and addresses of the manufacturer and the importer were given, and it was stated that the latter had been responsible for the packaging. Advance warning of its intentions had been given by Eurim-Pharm to Pfizer, the owner of the German mark and parent of the British company which had put the products into circulation.

Here, in contrast to *Hoffmann-La Roche* v. *Centrafarm*, nothing was done that might carry a risk of interference with the original condition of the products or of consumers' being misled as to their origin. The sealed inner packaging was left intact. The importer merely replaced the outer wrapping, exposing the mark affixed by the manufacturer himself. All the information needed by consumers was made available to them. In those circumstances, it was held, Article 36 could not be relied upon to prevent the sale of the imported products. The ruling was based on lack of justification—a right of the kind being claimed by Pfizer would not form part of the specific subject-matter of the trade mark. There was no need for Eurim-Pharm to fall back on the argument that the variation in packaging amounted to a market-splitting strategy, restricting trade between Member States contrary to the second sentence of the Article.

Copyright

The phrase "industrial and commercial property" in Article 36, while it clearly applies to patents and trade marks, is less apt as a description of artistic property.[55] Nevertheless, after some initial hesitation by the Court of Justice,[56] it is now beyond doubt that copyright and other rights protecting literary and artistic work are covered.

A right akin to copyright was the subject of *Deutsche Grammophon* v. *Metro*,[57] the earliest case in which the exhaustion of rights principle can be seen at work. Deutsche Grammophon (DG), the plaintiff in the national proceedings, supplied the records it manufactured to retailers in Germany under a retail price maintenance arrangement. It also exported records to France where they were marketed by its subsidiary, Polydor. Metro, the defendant, had succeeded in obtaining records originally sold in France by Polydor, which it then resold in Germany at prices well below the controlled price. DG sought to prevent these sales by invoking against Metro the exclusive right of distribution, akin to copyright, which manufacturers of sound recordings enjoy under German legislation. On a reference from the German court to which the case went on appeal, the European Court held that:

> "... it would be in conflict with the provisions prescribing the free movement of products within the common market for a manufacturer

---

[55] See the remarks by Advocate General Warner in his opinion relating to case 62/79, *Coditel* v. *Ciné Vog Films (No. 1)* [1980] E.C.R. at pp. 878–879.
[56] In the *Deutsche Grammophon* case, *infra*, the Court left open the question whether a record manufacturer's right analogous to copyright came within the scope of Art. 36.
[57] Case 78/70 [1971] E.C.R. 487; [1971] C.M.L.R. 631.

of sound recordings to exercise the exclusive right to distribute the protected articles, conferred upon him by the legislation of a Member State, in such a way as to prohibit the sale in that State of products placed on the market by him or with his consent in another Member State solely because such distribution did not occur within the territory of the first Member State."[58]

The conclusion is clear but the steps by which it was reached are less so. The judgment contains the first mention of the limitation of the derogation in Article 36 to measures justified for the safeguarding of rights which constitute the specific subject-matter of a form of intellectual property. However, the Court did not go on to define the specific subject-matter of a record manufacturer's exclusive right of distribution; nor did it rule that a right to oppose the sale of records marketed by a manufacturer or with his consent in another Member State could not be included in such subject-matter. It simply reasoned that the purpose of unifying the market could not be attained "if, under the various legal systems of the Member States, nationals of those States were able to partition the market and bring about arbitrary discrimination or disguised restrictions on trade between Member States."[59]

A decade later the fully-fledged principle was applied by the Court in *Musik-Vetrieb Membran* v. *GEMA*.[60] The case concerned the importation of records and cassettes into Germany from other Member States, one being the United Kingdom, where they had been manufactured and put on the market with the consent of the copyright owners. The copyright management society, GEMA, claimed the importation was in breach of the owners' rights in Germany. However, it did not seek to exclude the recordings from the German market but only to recover a sum representing any difference between the royalties payable in Germany and those paid in respect of the initial distribution. Three points in the case are of particular interest.

First, an attempt was made to establish a special status for copyright beyond the reach of the case-law on the exhaustion of rights. The French Government, which intervened on the side of GEMA, stressed the moral aspect of the protection given to authors, such as their right to object to any distortion, mutilation or alteration of their work or to any other action in relation to it that might prejudice their honour or reputation.[61] The Court of Justice readily conceded the special character of copyright but pointed out it was not the moral but the economic aspect of protection that was in issue. From the point of view of commercial exploitation, and the threat this might pose to the unity of the market, copyright was on all fours with other forms of intellectual property.

Secondly, GEMA relied on the fact that it was not actually opposing the

---

[58] [1971] E.C.R. at p. 500.
[59] *Ibid.*
[60] Joined Cases 55 and 57/80 [1981] E.C.R. 147; [1981] 2 C.M.L.R. 44.
[61] On the moral aspect of copyright, see Cornish, *op. cit.* note 1.

importation of the records. That, in the Court's view, was immaterial, since the society's royalty claim was based on the infringement of its members' exclusive rights of exploitation, which enabled it to interfere with the free movement of recordings. A further consideration was that individuals could not be allowed, in effect, to impose import levies on goods already in free circulation in the common market.[62]

Thirdly, it was argued that lower royalties in the United Kingdom, which encouraged exportation to Germany, were the product not of competition but of statutory intervention. Effectively, there was a ceiling on the remuneration a copyright owner could secure from a licensee, since anyone was entitled to reproduce a recording, once it had been put on the market with the author's consent, on payment of royalty of 6.25 per cent.[63] This was, in substance, the old argument that traders should be protected against distortions of competition resulting from continuing disparities between the legislation of Member States, and inevitably it failed.[64] The ground given by the Court for its ruling was that the exploitation of a copyright in a given market was a matter for the free choice of the owner. "He may," the Court said, "make that choice according to his best interests, which involve not only the level of remuneration provided in the Member State in question but other factors such as, for example, the opportunities for distributing his work and the marketing facilities which are further enhanced by virtue of the free movement of goods within the Community."[65] As a trader within the common market he must, in other words, abide by the consequences of his decisions.

GEMA has been distinguished in two subsequent cases. In *Warner Bros.* v. *Christiansen*[66] the plaintiff in the national proceedings was the owner in the United Kingdom of the copyright of the film "Never Say Never Again." The defendant, who managed a video shop in Copenhagen, purchased a copy of the film in London with a view to hiring it out in Denmark and imported it into Denmark for that purpose. Under Danish law the hiring out of a video-cassette was subject to the consent of the author or producer, even after the video-cassette had been marketed, whereas under the law of the United Kingdom, the author had no right to control hiring out after the initial sale of the video-cassette. On a reference to the Court of Justice by a Danish court[67] Warner Bros claimed that reliance on Danish law to restrict the hiring out of the video-cassette was justified under Article 36 of the Treaty. The defendant Christiansen relied upon GEMA arguing that if an author chose to market a video cassette in a country where national rules afforded no right to limit hiring out, he must accept the consequences of his choice and the exhaustion of his right to restrain the hiring out of that

---

[62] The point is only touched on briefly. However, it is clear the prohibition relates to the national legislation enabling private parties to levy charges on imports. This is, therefore, an Art. 30 not an Art. 9 matter.
[63] Pursuant to Copyright Act 1956, s. 8.
[64] *Cf.* the treatment of a similar argument relating to the price of pharmaceutical products in Case 15/74, *Centrafarm* v. *Sterling Drug* [1974] E.C.R. at pp. 1164–1165.
[65] [1981] E.C.R. at p. 165.
[66] Case 158/86 [1988] E.C.R. 2605.
[67] *Ibid.* at para. 18 of judgment.

video-cassette in any other Member State. The Court rejected this latter view, principally on the ground that it would render "worthless" the specific right to authorize hiring if that right were exhausted by sale in a Member State which afforded no specific protection for that right.

In *EMI Electrola* v. *Patricia*[68] the plaintiff in the national proceedings were assignees of the production and distribution rights in Germany of the musical works of Cliff Richard. The defendants sold in Germany sound recordings originating in Denmark which incorporated some of Cliff Richard's works, and resisted the plaintiff's action for an injunction on the ground that the recordings had been lawfully marketed in Denmark since the period during which exclusive rights were protected under Danish copyright law had expired. The Court distinguished GEMA on the ground that the marketing in Denmark was due, not to an act or the consent of the copyright owner or his licensee, but to the expiry of the protection period under the law of that Member State.

Copyright is a complex form of property, reflecting the diversity of the works to which it relates.[69] *Deutsche Grammophon* and *GEMA* concerned the aspect of copyright which protects an owner's interest in the reproduction and sale of material objects incorporating creative work, *in casu* sound recordings. That kind of interest is adequately served by the control the copyright owner enjoys over the initial marketing of protected products. There is, however, another aspect of copyright, namely the "performing rights" in a work such as a film or play, where exploitation takes place through public exhibitions which may be repeated an indefinite number of times. The principle of exhaustion obviously cannot apply to performing rights in the same way as it does to the marketing of goods. This was brought home in the earlier of two successive references to the Court of Justice arising out of copyright infringement proceedings in Belgium against the cable television undertaking, *Coditel*.[70]

The background to the case was as follows. The copyright in a film called "Le Boucher" was owned by a French company, Les Films la Boétie. The company granted Ciné Vog films an exclusive licence to exhibit "Le Boucher" in Belgium for a period of seven years. One of the conditions of the licence was that the film should not be broadcast on Belgian television until 40 months after its first cinema showing. A different licensee was appointed in Germany on terms which, it seems, allowed the television rights in the film to be exploited immediately. "Le Boucher" was accordingly shown in a dubbed version on German television more than two and a half

---

[68] Case 34/87 [1989] E.C.R. 79.
[69] See the discussion in Cornish, *op. cit.* note 1.
[70] Case 62/79, *Coditel* v. *Ciné Vog Films (No. 1)* [1980] E.C.R. 881; [1981] 2 C.M.L.R. 362. The reference was made by the Cour d'Appel of Brussels. On further appeal to the Cour de Cassation the need was felt for a reference on a different question of Community law: see Case 262/81, *Coditel* v. *Ciné Vog Films (No. 2)* [1982] E.C.R. 3381; [1983] 1 C.M.L.R. 49. As to the latter, see *infra* at p. 506, note 38. *Coditel* v. *Ciné Vog Films (No. 1)* was joined for the purposes of the oral procedure with another case involving Coditel companies, though originating in different proceedings, namely a prosecution for the infringement of the ban then in force on television advertising in Belgium. This was Case 52/79, *Procureur du Roi* v. *Debauve* [1980] E.C.R. 833; [1981] 1 C.M.L.R. 362.

years before it could have been broadcast in Belgium. That broadcast was picked up by Coditel on Belgian territory and relayed over its cable diffusion network. Under Belgian copyright law Coditel's action amounted to a "communication to the public" requiring the authorisation of the national licensee, Ciné Vog. In its defence Coditel argued, *inter alia*, that to prohibit the cable diffusion of a broadcast emanating from another Member State where it had been made with the consent of the copyright owner would be incompatible with Article 59 EEC on the freedom to provide services.

The EEC Treaty does not expressly exempt from the provisions of Article 59 restrictions on the provision of services justified for the protection of rights of intellectual property. Advocate General Warner, however, took the view that Article 36 applied by analogy in the present context and the Court, though it did not refer to the Article, seems to have agreed. The relevant passage of the judgment reads:

> "Whilst Article 59 of the Treaty prohibits restrictions upon freedom to provide services, it does not thereby encompass limits upon the exercise of certain economic activities which have their origin in the application of national legislation for the protection of intellectual property, save where such application constitutes a means of arbitrary discrimination or a disguised restriction on trade between Member States. Such would be the case if that application enabled parties to create artificial barriers to trade between Member States."[71]

The Court and the Advocate General were also at one as to the specific subject-matter of the performing right in a film. This consisted of the right of authorities to forbid each and every performance of the film, including the possibility of its being televised. The point is not fully developed in the judgment but its significance is apparent. Cable diffusion of a television broadcast constitutes a "performance" separate from the broadcast itself. The intervention by Coditel could not, therefore, be regarded as merely extending the performance covered by the German licence.[72] It was a fresh performance within the territory where Ciné Vog had been granted an exclusive right to exhibit "Le Boucher"; and the restriction claimed was necessary to guarantee the essence of that exclusive right. The only question was whether the strategy followed by Les Films la Boétie of appointing different licensees in different Member States might amount to an artificial barrier to trade. The Court decided in the circumstances it would not, since the strategy was objectively justifiable, owing to the organisation of television services on the basis of legal broadcasting monopolies. It, therefore, held:

> "... that the provisions of the Treaty relating to the freedom to provide services did not preclude an assignee of the performing right in a cinematographic film in a Member State from relying upon his right to

---

[71] [1980] E.C.R. at p. 903.
[72] It was assumed by the Court that Ciné Vog would have been bound by any authorisation given by the licensor, Les Films la Boétie, to its fellow licensee in Germany.

prohibit the exhibition of that film in that State, without his authority, by means of cable diffusion if the film so exhibited is picked up and transmitted after being broadcast in another Member State by a third party with the consent of the original owner of the right."[73]

Other property forms

In *Keurkoop* v. *Nancy Kean Gifts*[74] the Court of Justice had its first opportunity of considering the application of Article 36 to industrial designs. The case concerned the design of a ladies' handbag which had been registered under the Uniform Benelux Law on Designs by Nancy Kean Gifts. The registration had been effected without the consent of the American author of the design but this had no bearing on its validity in the Netherlands.[75] The reference to the Court was made in proceedings brought by Nancy Kean Gifts to prevent the sale on the Dutch market of handbags of the same design which had been imported by Keurkoop. It was held by the Court that industrial designs came with the protection afforded by Article 36 to "industrial and commercial property" since they had the aim of defining exclusive rights which was characteristic of such property. That protection enabled the owner of the right to a design in a Member State to prevent the sale of identical products imported from another Member State where they had been legally acquired by a third party—the situation described in the reference. However, the Court made it clear that the principle of the exhaustion of rights would apply if the products in question had been put on the market in the Member State of origin by or with the consent of the design owner in the Member State of importation or by a person legally or economically dependent on him.[76]

The leading case on plant breeders' rights, *Nungesser* v. *Commission (Maize Seeds)*[77] involved an attempt to obtain the annulment of a Decision applying Article 85 to a licensing agreement. However, underlying part of the applicant's case was the claim that breeders' rights enjoy a special status in Community law because of the role the owner is called upon to play in maintaining the stability of the plant variety.[78] Rejecting that argument, the Court said the object of such rights was not to substitute control by the owner for control by national authorities but to protect private interests. The owner's position was similar to that of a patentee or trade mark owner in respect of a product subject to strict public control, such as a medicinal drug.[79] "It is, therefore, not correct," the Court said, "to consider that

---

[73] [1980] E.C.R. at p. 904.
[74] Case 144/81 [1982] E.C.R. 2853; [1983] 2 C.M.L.R. 47.
[75] One of the questions put by the referring court to the Court of Justice was whether a rule giving an exclusive right to the first person to register a design, irrespective of its authorship, was compatible with Art. 36. The Court's response was that, in the absence of standardisation or harmonisation of laws on industrial designs, it was for national law to lay down the necessary conditions and procedures. See also Case 53/87, *CICRA* v. *Maxicar* [1987] E.C.R. 6039.
[76] [1982] E.C.R. at p. 2871.
[77] Case 258/78 [1982] E.C.R. 2015; [1983] 1 C.M.L.R. 278. See the discussion, *infra*.
[78] See [1982] E.C.R. at pp. 2060–2065.
[79] See Case 15/74, *Centrafarm* v. *Sterling Drug* and Case 16/74, *Centrafarm* v. *Winthrop* [1974] E.C.R. at, respectively, p. 1165 and p. 1196.

breeders' rights are a species of commercial or industrial property right with characteristics of so special a nature as to require, in relation to the competition rules, a different treatment from other commercial or industrial property rights."[80] Though expressed in relation to the competition rules that conclusion would, it is submitted, apply equally in the sphere of freedom of movement, including the limitation imposed on the exception in Article 36 by the exhaustion of rights principle.

Unfair competition laws, on the other hand, do not seem to be regarded by the Court as a species of intellectual property. Where such rules are invoked against imports, justification has to be sought in the public interest criteria of the *Cassis de Dijon* doctrine.[81] This can be seen in the *Beele*[82] case where the Court was asked, in effect, whether a product imported from Germany could be excluded from the Dutch market on the ground that, for no compelling reason, it was practically identical to, and thus liable to be confused with, a product which had long been sold in the Netherlands. Article 36 was specifically mentioned in the reference but was ignored by the Court. The judgment cited *Cassis de Dijon*[83] and *Irish Souvenirs*,[84] and the exclusion of imports in circumstances such as those of *Beele* was found to be justifiable, as meeting the "mandatory requirements" of consumer protection and the promotion of fair trading.[85]

What of the exhaustion of rights principle in such cases? The Court in *Beele* referred to the fact that there was no "dependence" between the producers involved,[86] implying that, if the manufacturer of the original product had consented to the marketing of the alleged imitation in Germany, he would not have been able to prevent its importation. It would, however, be misleading to attribute this outcome to the exhaustion of a private right belonging to the manufacturer, since it is not the function of the *Cassis de Dijon* doctrine to protect such rights. The explanation would lie in the absence of objective justification in the general public interest for keeping out authorised "imitations."

FREEDOM OF MOVEMENT—THE RISE AND FALL OF THE COMMON ORIGIN PRINCIPLE

A more controversial restriction on the use of intellectual property rights as a defence against parallel imports is the common origin principle.

---

[80] [1982] E.C.R. at p. 2065.
[81] The doctrine is examined *supra* at Chap. 8.
[82] Case 6/81, *Industrie Diensten Groep* v. *Beele* [1982] E.C.R. 707; [1982] 3 C.M.L.R. 102. See the discussion of the case by Gormley, *op. cit.* note 24, *supra* at p. 210. See also Whish, *op. cit.* note 1, *supra* at p. 381.
[83] Case 120/78, *Rewe-Zentralfinanz* v. *Bundesmonopolverwaltung für Branntwein* [1979] E.C.R. 649; [1979] 3 C.M.L.R. 337.
[84] Case 113/80, *Commission* v. *Ireland* [1981] E.C.R. 1625; [1982] 2 C.M.L.R. 706.
[85] The Court adopted a similar approach to the unfair competition point in Case 58/80, *Dansk Supermarked* v. *Imerco* [1981] E.C.R. 181; [1981] 3 C.M.L.R. 590. *Cf.* Case 144/81, *Keurkoop* v. *Nancy Kean Gifts*, *loc. cit.* note 74, *supra*, where the claim was also for the exclusion of an identical product but was based upon a proprietary right arising from registration. *Cf.* also Case 119/85, *Terrapin* v. *Terranova*, discussed *infra*, where the issue was the similarity of trade marks.
[86] [1982] E.C.R. at p. 717.

According to the principle, when trade marks held by different persons in different Member States had a common origin, the sale in a Member State of goods lawfully bearing one of the national marks could not be prevented merely because another of the marks is protected by the law of that State. It makes no difference whether the imported goods were sold by the proprietor of the mark himself or by some third party who has duly acquired them in the State of origin; or whether the fragmentation of the original trade mark was due to a voluntary act of parties or to an act of a public authority.

The source of the common origin principle was the decision of the European Court in *Van Zuylen* v. *Hag*.[87] The proceedings before the national court arose as a result of the importation into Luxembourg of decaffeinated coffee bearing the HAG trade mark which had been manufactured in Germany by Hag AG. In 1927 Hag AG had established a Belgian subsidiary to which it subsequently assigned its rights in the HAG trade mark for Belgium and Luxembourg. After the Second World War the subsidiary was sequestrated by the Belgian authorities as enemy property and was ultimately sold to the Van Oevelen family, who assigned the trade mark in 1971 to Van Zuylen Frères (VZ), the proprietor at the time when Hag AG commenced its deliveries to the Luxembourg market. The case, therefore, concerned a trade mark which was still held by the original common proprietor in the country from which the product was exported but which had come into the hands of an unrelated company through an act of the authorities in the country where it was sold.

The Court of Justice substantially repeated the statement it had made in *Deutsche Grammophon*[88] about the scope of the derogation in Article 36, adding that "the application of the legislation relating to the protection of trade marks at any rate protects the legitimate holder of the trade mark against infringement on the part of persons who lack any legal title." It then went on:

> "The exercise of a trade mark right tends to contribute to the partitioning off of the markets and thus to affect the free movement of goods between Member States, and all the more so since—unlike other rights of industrial and commercial property—it is not subject to limitations in point of time.
>
> Accordingly, one cannot allow the holder of a trade mark to rely upon the exclusiveness of a trade mark right—which may be the consequence of the territorial limitation of national legislations—with a view to prohibiting the marketing in a Member State of goods legally produced in another Member State under an identical trade mark having the same origin. Such a prohibition, which would legitimize the isolation of national markets, would collide with one of the essential

---

[87] Case 192/73 [1974] E.C.R. 731; [1974] 2 C.M.L.R. 127. The principle was foreshadowed in Case 40/70, *Sirena* v. *Eda* [1971] E.C.R. 69; [1971] C.M.L.R. 260. In that case, however, the reference was made and dealt with by the Court on the basis of the rules on competition. The facts of the case are given at p. 596, *infra*.

[88] Case 78/70 [1971] E.C.R. 487.

objects of the Treaty, which is to unite national markets in a single market.

Whilst in such a market the identification of origin of a product covered by a trade mark is useful, information to consumers on this point may be ensured by means other than such as would affect the free movement of goods."[89]

Three arguments are put forward in the quoted passage: that the exercise of the right claimed by VZ would have the effect of partitioning the market, thereby conflicting with one of the fundamental aims of the Treaty; that the effect would be all the more serious because of the indefinite duration of trade mark rights; and that the interests of consumers can be adequately safeguarded by means of supplementary designations of origin. These are powerful enough arguments in favour of the general proposition that a narrow view must be taken of the derogation in Article 36 so far as concerns trade marks. They do not, however, provide any clue as to why the Court attached special significance to the factor of a common origin. Thus it has been pointed out that the reasoning of the Court with regard to indefinite duration and the partitioning of the market would apply equally in the case of trade marks which were identical or similar although not of common origin.[90]

In *Terrapin* v. *Terranova*[91] the Court summed up its views on the interpretation of Article 36 as regards industrial property in general and clarified the scope of the principle enunciated in *Van Zuylen* v. *Hag.*

The case arose out of an attempt to prevent the marketing in Germany of a British-manufactured product bearing the trade mark TERRAPIN, on account of an alleged risk of confusion with a similar product bearing the locally protected mark TERRANOVA, which was also used as a business name. It was, of course, a matter for the national court whether any confusion between the names was likely to occur in practice. However, the European Court pointed out that in deciding this issue the national court must bear in mind that the protection which is accorded to industrial property rights cannot be permitted to constitute "a means of arbitrary discrimination or a disguised restriction on trade between Member States." It should, therefore, ascertain "whether the rights in question are in fact exercised by the proprietor with the same strictness whatever the national origin of any possible infringer."[92]

Three situations were identified by the Court where the derogation under Article 36 would not apply to the use of an industrial property right to prevent goods from being sold in the State protecting the right. The first was where the product had been lawfully marketed in another Member State by the holder of the right or with his consent—the exhaustion of rights principle; the second, where the right relied on was "the result of the

---

[89] [1974] E.C.R. at p. 744.
[90] See Johannes and Wright, (1975–76) 1 E.L.Rev. 230 at pp. 234–235.
[91] Case 119/75 [1976] E.C.R. 1039; [1976] 2 C.M.L.R. 482.
[92] [1976] E.C.R. at p. 1060.

subdivision, either by voluntary act or as a result of public constraint, of a trade mark right which originally belonged to one and the same proprietor"—the common origin principle[93]; and the third, where the rights in question belonged to different persons but their exercise was "the purpose, the means or the result of an agreement prohibited by the Treaty."[94] It is interesting to note the rationale which the Court provided for the common origin principle: "the basic function of the trade mark to guarantee to consumers that the product has the same origin is already undermined by the subdivision of the original right."[95] This completes the reasoning in the *Hag* case and serves as a basis for distinguishing it from the present case where marks of separate origin happened to possess a certain similarity.

The Court was quite clear that:

> ". . . in the present state of Community law an industrial or commercial property right legally acquired in a Member State may legally be used to prevent under the first sentence of Article 36 of the Treaty the import of products marketed under a name giving rise to confusion where the rights in question have been acquired by different and independent proprietors under different national laws. If in such a case the principle of the free movement of goods were to prevail over the protection given by the respective national laws, the specific objective of industrial and commercial property rights would be undermined. In the particular situation the requirements of the free movement of goods and the safeguarding of industrial and commercial property rights must be so reconciled that protection is ensured for the legitimate use of the rights conferred by national laws, coming within the prohibitions on imports 'justified' within the meaning of Article 36 of the Treaty, but denied on the other hand in respect of any improper exercise of the same rights of such a nature as to maintain or effect artificial partitions within the common market."[96]

The doctrine of common origin was not however to remain unchallenged. In 1979 the firm Van Zuylen Freres was purchased by a Swiss company called (subsequently) Jacobs Suchard AG. The firm was transformed into a wholly owned subsidiary of Jacobs Suchard AG trading under the name SA CNL-Sucal NV. In 1985 CNL-Sucal began to supply decaffeinated coffee under the HAG trade mark to the German market. Hag AG applied to the competent German court for an injunction restraining CNL-Sucal from infringing its trade mark. There followed a reference to the Court of Justice—*SA CNL-Sucal NV* v. *Hag GF AG*[97]—which raised *inter alia* the question whether doctrine of common origin established in *Van Zuylen* v. *Hag* (Hag I) was correct. Both the parties in the national proceedings

---

[93] [1976] E.C.R. at p. 1061.
[94] *Ibid.*
[95] *Ibid.*
[96] *Ibid* at pp. 1061–1062.
[97] Case C–10/89 [1990] E.C.R. I–3711.

alleged that it was. Hag AG argued that whereas CNL-Sucal derived their rights from parties (the Van Oevelen family and the Belgian Government) who had consented to the subdivision of the trade mark and who therefore could not oppose the marketing in Belgium and Luxembourg of coffee bearing the Hag mark affixed in Germany, they themselves, by way of contrast, had not consented to the subdivision of the mark, which had been compulsorily acquired. Hag AG concluded that whereas they might lawfully sell coffee under the Hag mark in Belgium and Luxembourg, CNL-Sucal could not lawfully sell coffee under the Belgium/Luxembourg mark in Germany. CNL-Sucal relied upon the ruling in *Hag I* for the proposition that holders of identical marks of common origin could not oppose the marketing of products bearing the mark affixed by another owner of the mark. The Court of Justice, stating at the outset that it was necessary to reconsider *Hag I* in light of subsequent case-law, effectively reversed the latter decision. In the first place, the Court emphasised the importance of trade mark rights in the scheme contemplated by the Treaty:

> "Trade mark rights are, it should be noted, an essential element in the system of undistorted competition which the Treaty seeks to establish and maintain. Under such a system, an undertaking must be in a position to keep its customers by virtue of the quality of its products and services, something which is possible only if there are distinctive marks which enable customers to identify those products and services. For the trade mark to be able to fulfil this role, it must offer a guarantee that all goods bearing it have been produced under the control of a single undertaking which is accountable for their quality."[98]

The Court of Justice regarded as a "determinant factor"[99] the absence of any consent on the part of the proprietor of the trade mark protected by national legislation to the putting into circulation in another Member State of similar products bearing an identical trade mark or one liable to lead to confusion, which are manufactured and marketed by an undertaking which is economically and legally independent of the trade mark proprietor. The Court added:

> "From the date of expropriation and notwithstanding their common origin, each of the marks independently fulfilled its function, within its own territorial field of application, of guaranteeing that the marked products originated from one single source.
>
> It follows from the foregoing that in a situation such as the present case, in which the mark originally had one sole proprietor and the single ownership was broken as a result of expropriation, each of the trade mark proprietors must be able to oppose the marketing, in the Member State in which the trade mark belongs to him, of goods originating from

---

[98] *Ibid.* at para. 13 of judgment.
[99] *Ibid.* at para. 15 of judgment.

the other proprietor, in so far as they are similar products bearing an identical mark or one which is liable to lead to confusion."[1]

The Court thus went out of its way to emphasise the demise of the common origin principle, as well as responding to the national court in terms appropriate to resolve the litigation pending before it.

Terrapin v. *Terranova* confirmed and explained the application of the common origin principle to trade marks but gave no guidance as to whether it applied to other forms of intellectual property. There were good reasons for believing that it did not. First, the rationale of the principle given in *Terrapin* v. *Terranova*—that the subdivision of a trade mark defeats the essential purpose of providing a guarantee of origin to consumers—cannot easily be adapted to property forms such as patents or copyright whose function is to reward creativity. Secondly, as the Court itself pointed out in the *Hag* case, partitioning of the market through the subdivision of a trade mark is an especially serious matter owing to the permanent character of the rights in question; whereas other property forms entail purely temporary monopolies. Thirdly, the Court had indicated that it considered trade marks to be, on the whole, less important, and less deserving of protection in derogation from the EEC rules on freedom of movement, than other intellectual property rights.[2] Fourthly, if the common origin principle were capable of applying to copyright, one would expect it to have been considered, and if necessary distinguished, in *Coditel* v. *Ciné Vog Films (No. 1)*; however, both the Advocate General and the Court approached the case from the point of view of the exhaustion of rights principle.[3] Finally, a principle which allows parallel imports without any previous marketing in another Member State is simply too wide for general application. It has been said that: "If the doctrine is sound, it is hard to see where the exhaustion principle can be used, since the owner of an intellectual property right could never impede the import of goods produced or marketed under a related right."[4]

One qualification is, perhaps, necessary. In *Keurkoop* v. *Nancy Kean Gifts*[5] the Court mentioned as one of the conditions enabling a design owner to oppose the importation of identical products "that the respective rights of the proprietors of the right to the design in the various Member States were created independently of one another."[6] This suggests that the common origin principle applies, at least, to registered industrial designs, a view which Advocate General Reischl appeared to share.[7] If that is so, the

---

[1] *Ibid.* at paras. 18 and 19 of judgment.
[2] See Case 40/70, *Sirena* v. *Eda loc. cit.* note 81, *supra* at p. 82. The point is not a strong one since there are trade marks, like the HAG mark itself, which are of vastly greater value than many of the gadgets for which patents can be obtained. And *Hag II* recognises this.
[3] The issue as to whether cable diffusion in Belgium constituted a "performance" separate from the broadcast in Germany would have been irrelevant if the common origin principle was being applied.
[4] By Whish, *op. cit.* note 1, *supra* at p. 382.
[5] Case 144/81, *loc. cit.* note 68, *supra.*
[6] [1982] E.C.R. at p. 2874.
[7] See [1982] E.C.R. at p. 2883. The relevant passage in Mr. Reischl's opinion is rather unclear. The *Sirena* and *Hag* cases are cited but the Advocate General speaks of design owners being

explanation would presumably be that the essential function of rights to industrial designs is considered, like that of trade mark rights, to be the provision of a guarantee of origin. *Hag II* presumably ends the debate.

Intellectual property rights and the rules on competition

General principles

The theoretical basis for the application of the rules on competition in respect of national rights of intellectual property is, once again, the distinction between the existence of such rights and their exercise. Indeed, the distinction was first developed by the Court of Justice in competition cases.[8] We have seen that in the *Maize Seeds* case an attempt to place plant breeders' rights beyond the scope of this compromise solution was decisively rejected.[9]

The Court has stressed that an intellectual property right, as a legal entity, does not in itself possess the elements that activate the prohibitions in Article 85(1) or Article 86 EEC.[10] The grant of protection by the authorities of a Member State is not the kind of collusive arrangement (agreement between undertakings, decision of an association of undertakings or concerted practice) to which Article 85(1) refers; nor does it automatically entail the existence of a dominant position within a substantial part of the common market.

The early case of *Parke, Davis* v. *Centrafarm*[11] provides an illustration. The background to the case, like that of *Merck*[12] some years later, was the absence of patent protection in Italy for medicinal drugs. Here, however, the complaint was of the importation, in contravention of patents held in the Netherlands, of a drug manufactured in Italy not by the patent owner himself but by a third party. Two questions were put by the referring court. The first question asked, in effect, whether the holder of a national patent was prevented by Articles 85 and 86 EEC "possibly considered in conjunction with the provisions of Articles 36 and 222" from using it to block imports from a country where they could be lawfully produced without a patent; and the second whether it was significant that the price of the patented product which was manufactured locally was higher than the price of the imported product. The Court replied:

"linked by legal or economic ties from which a single origin of the design may be inferred." Does this mean that, as between wholly independent owners, the common origin principle would not apply? In the instant case, the *designs* of the handbags may have had a common origin but the *rights* in those designs did not, since they were derived from registrations effected without the author's licence.

[8] See Joined Cases 56 and 58/64, *Consten and Grundig* v. *Commission* [1966] E.C.R. 299; [1966] C.M.L.R. 418; Case 24/67, *Parke, Davis* v. *Centrafarm* [1968] *loc. cit.* note 25, *supra*; Case 40/70, *Sirena* v. *Eda loc. cit.* note 87, *supra*. For the view of the Commission on the distinction between the existence of rights and their exercise as applied to competition matters, see Comp.Rep. 1974, p. 20.

[9] Case 258/78, *loc. cit.* note 77, *supra*.

[10] Case 40/70, *Sirena* v. *Eda* [1971] E.C.R. at p. 82; Case 51/75, *EMI* v. *CBS United Kingdom* [1976] E.C.R. at p. 848; Case 258/78, *Maize Seeds* [1982] E.C.R. at p. 2061.

[11] *Loc. cit.* note 28, *supra*.

[12] Case 187/80, *loc. cit.* note 34, *supra*.

"1. The existence of rights granted by a Member State to the holder of a patent is not affected by the prohibitions contained in Articles 85(1) and 86 of the Treaty.

2. The exercise of such rights cannot of itself fall either under Article 85(1), in the absence of any agreement, decision or concerted practice prohibited by this provision, or under Article 86, in the absence of any abuse of a dominant position.

3. A higher sale price for the patented product as compared with that of the unpatented product coming from another Member State does not necessarily constitute an abuse."[13]

The reply acknowledges that Article 85 or Article 86 may, in principle, be invoked to prevent the exercise of intellectual property rights, but only where additional factors, satisfying the criteria of prohibition in those provisions, are present; and of such factors there was no evidence before the Court.

In principle, therefore, the application of the rules on competition to an agreement respecting intellectual property rights should take place in two stages. The first stage involves considering whether particular provisions of the agreement go to the very existence of the property form in question (in other words, are necessary to safeguard its specific subject-matter) or merely regulate its exercise. If the former, the competition rules cannot be applied at all. If the latter, then the second stage—consideration of whether the provision is prohibited under Article 85 or Article 86—commences. In practice, however, the distinction between these two stages is not always clearly marked in the reasoning of the Commission or even of the Court.[14]

Assignment of intellectual property—"spent"[15] agreements

Where rights of intellectual property are assigned outright, as opposed to being licensed, the contract between the assignor and the assignee will be discharged by completion of performance. In such a case, will there be any consensual relationship to which the prohibition in Article 85 may attach? The question was first addressed by the European Court in *Sirena* v. *Eda*.[16] Under a contract concluded in 1937 the Italian rights to the trade mark PREP had been assigned to Sirena by an American company, Mark Allen. Sirena subsequently re-registered the mark in its own name, together with two other marks incorporating the word PREP. The right to use the mark in Germany had been granted by Mark Allen at some unspecified date to a German company and marked products manufactured by the latter were imported into Italy, where they were sold at much lower prices than Sirena's products. The national proceedings were brought by Sirena to prevent the infringement of its rights by the importer, a company called Novimpex.

The Italian Court referred the compatibility of the assignment with the

---

[13] [1968] E.C.R. at pp. 73–74.
[14] As an illustration of systematic application of the rules, see Case 198/83, *Windsurfing International* v. *Commission* [1986] 3 C.M.L.R. 489 at pp. 531–540. The case is more fully examined, *infra*.
[15] The term is used by Bellamy and Child, *Common Market Law of Competition* (3rd ed., 1987, 1st supplement, 1991) at para. 2–025.
[16] Case 40/70, *loc. cit.* note 87, *supra*.

competition rules to the European Court. It was stated by the Court that the exercise of a trade mark right "might fall within the ambit of the prohibitions contained in the Treaty each time it manifests itself as the subject, the means or the result of a restrictive practice."[17] The suggestion has been made, and it was evidently the view taken by the national court, that in fact, a concerted practice existed between Mark Allen and its assignees in the common market countries under which each respected the territorial rights of the others.[18] The Court contented itself with the statement that:

> "If the restrictive practices arose before the Treaty entered into force, it is both necessary and sufficient that they continue to produce their effects after that date."[19]

This indicates, mysteriously, that Article 85(1) can somehow be "applied" to a practice which ceased before the Article came into force.

The statement was qualified in *EMI* v. *CBS*,[20] the facts of which have already been given.[21] CBS' second main line of defence in the infringement proceedings brought by EMI was that the agreements for the assignment of the COLUMBIA trade mark were caught by the prohibition in Article 85(1) because they formed part of a complex of agreements the object of which had been to partition the world market. The agreements themselves had been terminated before the EEC Treaty came into force but CBS argued, with the support of the Commission, that the prohibition would apply so long as they continued to produce effects which were felt within the common market.

The Court held that an agreement between Community undertakings and their competitors in third countries which tended to isolate the common market from supplies of products originating in third countries and similar to products protected by trade marks in the Member States may adversely affect the competitive situation on the Community market; and where the proprietor of the disputed mark outside the Community has subsidiaries established in various Member States which would be capable of marketing the goods, trade between Member States may be affected.

On the question of "spent" agreements the Court said:

> "For Article 85 to apply to a case, such as the present one, of agreements which are no longer in force it is sufficient that such agreements continue to produce their effects after they have formally ceased to be in force.

---

[17] [1971] E.C.R. at p. 82.

[18] In his Opinion in *Van Zuylen* v. *Hag* Advocate-General Mayras suggested that the European Court may have acted on this assumption; see [1974] E.C.R. 731 at p. 750. For the view of the Tribunale of Milan, see [1975] 1 C.M.L.R. 409 at pp. 430–431.

[19] [1971] E.C.R. at p. 83.

[20] These proceedings involved references from trade mark infringement proceedings in courts in the United Kingdom, Denmark and Germany: Case 51/75, *EMI Records* v. *CBS United Kingdom* [1976] E.C.R. 811; [1976] 2 C.M.L.R. 235; Case 86/75, *EMI Records* v. *CBS Grammofon* [1976] E.C.R. 871; Case 96/75, *EMI Records* v. *CBS Schalplatten* [1976] E.C.R. 913.

[21] In each of these cases, the European Court was invited to consider whether EMI's use of its EC trade mark rights in the name COLUMBIA to restrain the importation and sale of records manufactured in the USA by CBS, who owned the COLUMBIA mark in the United States, was compatible with EC rules on free movement of goods and on competition.

> An agreement is only regarded as continuing to produce its effects if from the behaviour of the persons concerned there may be inferred the existence of elements of concerted practice and of coordination peculiar to the agreements and producing the same result as that envisaged by the agreement.
>
> This is not so when the said effects do not exceed those flowing from the mere exercise of the national trade mark rights."[22]

The meaning of this statement is not entirely clear. Do "elements of concerted practice and coordination" amount to something less than a concerted practice *tout court*? It is hard to imagine how they could, given the exiguous nature of the "practical co-operation" which suffices to establish the existence of such practices.[23] On the other hand, if a continuing concerted practice is necessary for the application of Article 85, what purpose is served by harking back to the original agreement? A possible explanation has been suggested.[24] Normally, it is unsafe to infer the existence of concertation purely from the fact that the parties concerned are conducting their business in a similar or mutually beneficial way, because this might represent nothing more than a prudent reaction to the conditions of the market to which both are subject. However, the objection falls away if the parties are merely continuing a course of conduct which they embarked upon as a result of a restrictive agreement now formally terminated. The pre-existing agreement would raise a presumption of collusion which it would be for the parties to rebut by showing that, in fact, they had been acting independently.

Licensing intellectual property

In the field of intellectual property the greatest practical impact of the EEC competition rules has been upon the terms of licensing agreements. In its enforcement activity the Commission has been concerned mainly with patent licensing[25]; but many of the principles it has developed are capable of being applied to other property forms, while there have been important decisions of the Court of Justice on the licensing of trade marks,[26] copyright[27] and plant breeders' rights.[28]

---

[22] [1976] E.C.R. at pp. 848–849.

[23] See Chap. 14, *supra.*

[24] By Laddie, (1975–76) 1 E.L.Rev. 499 at p. 502.

[25] The Commission's preoccupation with patent licensing goes back to the earliest days of the competition policy. A notice on Patent Licensing Agreements, setting forth its views on the application of the competition rules to such agreements, was issued on December 24, 1962. Over the years those views came to be modified in important respects and the Notice ceased to be a reliable guide. It was withdrawn, following the adoption of the Block Exemption Regulation on Patent Licensing Agreements: O.J. 1984, C220/14.

[26] Joined Cases 56 and 58/64, *Consten and Grundig* v. *Commission loc. cit.* note 8, p. 595, *supra*; Case 28/77, *Tepea* v. *Commission* [1978] E.C.R. 1391; [1978] 3 C.M.L.R. 392; Case 10/89, *CNL-SUCAL* v. *Hag* [1990] 3 C.M.L.R. 571.

[27] Case 262/81, *Coditel* v. *Ciné Vog Films (No. 2) loc. cit.* note 70, *supra*; Case 53/67, *CICRA and Maxicar* v. *Renault* [1988] E.C.R. 6067; Case 238/87, *Volvo* v. *Erik Veng (U.K.) Ltd.* [1988] E.C.R. 6067; Case T–69/89, *Radio Telefis Eireann* v. *Commission* [1991] 4 C.M.L.R. 586; Case T–70/89, *BBC* v. *Commission* [1991] 4 C.M.L.R. 669; Case T–76/89, *Independent Television Publications Ltd.* v. *Commission* [1991] 4 C.M.L.R. 745.

[28] Case 258/78 *Nungesser* v. *Commission (Maize Seeds) loc. cit.* note 77, *supra*; Case 27/87, *Erauw-Jacquery* v. *Hesbignonne* [1988] E.C.R. 1919.

A licensing transaction consists essentially of the granting by the owner of an intellectual property right of permission for a third party to exploit the right, in consideration of the payment of a royalty. The possibility of exploitation through licences was explicitly recognised by the Court in *Centrafarm* v. *Sterling Drug* as an element in the specific subject-matter of a patent[29]; and the same is true, it is submitted, of all intellectual property. It would follow that any terms in a licensing agreement that may be recognised as indispensable to this indirect method of exploitation would enjoy immunity from the competition rules. These, however, as we shall see, represent a minority of the terms that may be included in such agreements. The rest, if they fulfil the criteria of Article 85(1), can only escape prohibition through the gateway of Article 85(3); and on occasion a possible infringement of Article 86 may also have to be considered.

In the present section we examine the application of the competition rules, and more particularly of Article 85, to certain terms commonly found in patent licensing agreements.[30] Following sections explain the provisions of the Block Exemption Regulation on Patent Licensing Agreements and the ways in which the later Block Exemption Regulation on Know-how Licensing Agreements differs from it.

(i) *Exclusivity.* A licensing agreement may seek to provide for the parties various degrees of protection against competition. A licensor may undertake to appoint no other licensees within the contract territory (a "sole" licence); or he may go further and agree that he will not himself exploit the property within that territory (an "exclusive" licence). The licensee's exclusive right may relate to the manufacture of the protected product or it may extend to marketing the product as well. On his side, the licensee may agree not to exploit the product in any territory the licensor has reserved for himself. Finally, an attempt may be made to give each of the parties absolute territorial protection against parallel importers.

A grant of sole or exclusive rights to a licensee is not regarded by the Commission or, it seems, the Court as coming within the specific subject-matter of patents or other forms of intellectual property. This has been explained by the Commission on the ground that contractual terms which fetter the exercise of an intellectual property right by its owner cannot be regarded as necessary incidents of that right.[31] The explanation would not apply to a licensee's obligation to refrain from exploiting the property in territory reserved for his licensor; and it is submitted that such obligations fall under the heading of specific subject-matter, provided that the property in question is protected in the reserved territory.[32]

The rules on competition thus apply in principle to exclusive

---

[29] Case 15/74 [1974] E.C.R. at p. 1162.
[30] See the discussion in Whish, *op. cit.* note 1, p. 570, *supra*, pp. 653–656.
[31] See, in particular, *Re AOIP/Beyrard* O.J. 1976 L6/8; [1976] 1 C.M.L.R. D14. The Court's view is implicit in the approach it adopted in Case 258/78, *Maize Seeds loc. cit.* note 77, *supra*.
[32] Case 198/83, *Windsurfing International* v. *Commission loc. cit.* note 14, p. 596, *supra*.

manufacturing or marketing licences. Whether a given licence fulfils the criteria in Article 85(1) will depend on the particular circumstances in which the agreement is made. On the one hand, the inability of the licensor to grant further licences in the contract territory means that potential competitors of the licensee will have no opportunity of exploiting the property there.[33] On the other hand, the financial risks of exploitation may be such that, without protection at least against direct competition, no one may be willing to accept a licence: in such a case, the grant of an exclusive right, far from restricting competition, actually enhances it by bringing a new participant into the market. The Commission has often been criticised for giving too little weight to this latter consideration. Its approach has been, broadly, that exclusive licences can normally be expected to have the object or effect or restricting competition within the meaning of Article 85(1), though they may well qualify for exemption under Article 85(3).[34] A more nuanced approach is, however, apparent in the Preamble to the Block Exemption Regulation on Patent Licensing Agreements[35] reflecting the judgment in *Maize Seeds*,[36] where a sharp distinction was drawn by the European Court between two kinds of licensing arrangement—"open exclusive licences" and "absolute territorial protection."

Under an "open exclusive licence," the licensor agrees not to allow any other undertaking to exploit his property within the contract territory; and he agrees not to manufacture or market the protected product himself within that territory. Here the exclusivity is a matter between the contracting parties: the market in the contract territory remains open to parallel imports by third parties, including licensees for other territories. Such an arrangement, the Court held, would not infringe Article 85(1) in the circumstances of the *Maize Seeds* case. Those circumstances involved "the cultivation and marketing of hybrid maize seeds which were developed by INRA after years of research and experimentation and were unknown to German farmers at the time when the co-operation between INRA and the applicants was taking shape."[37] The Court concluded that, unless it were able to obtain an open exclusive licence, an undertaking might be deterred from running the risk of introducing the product onto the German market, a result which, it said, "would be damaging to the dissemination of a new technology and would prejudice competition in the Community between the new product and similar existing products."[38] It remains to be seen whether

---

[33] This argument has been repeatedly used by the Commission to justify the application of Art. 85(1) to exclusive licences. See, *e.g.* Re *Davidson Rubber Co.* [1972] J.O. L143/31; [1972] C.M.L.R. D52; *Re Kabelmetal/Luchaire* O.J. 1975, L222/34; [1975] 2 C.M.L.R. D40; *Re Eisele-INRA Agreement (Maize Seeds)* O.J. 1978 L286/23; [1978] 3 C.M.L.R. 434; *Rich Products/Jus-rol* O.J. 1988 L69/21; *Delta Chemie/DDD* O.J. 1988 L309/34.

[34] The Notice of December 24, 1962 on Patent Licence Agreements stated that, on the basis of the facts then known to it, the Commission did not consider undertakings by a licensor not to authorise anyone else to exploit the invention and not to exploit the invention himself to be covered by Art. 85(1). However, the experience of dealing with the first batch of notified licensing agreements, in the aftermath of the decision in Joined Cases 56 & 58/64, *Consten and Grundig* v. *Commission loc. cit.* note 26, p. 598, *supra*, seems to have brought about a change of mind.

[35] See the 11th recital; See also 6th recital to Reg. 556/89 on Know-how Licensing Agreements.

[36] Case 258/78, *Nungesser* v. *Commission loc. cit.* note 77, *supra*.

[37] [1982] E.C.R. at p. 2069.

[38] *Ibid.*

the Court will acknowledge the pro-competitive effects of such licences in the exploitation of less sensitive products.

The notion of "absolute territorial protection" has been encountered in Chapter 14, *supra*, in connection with distribution agreements. In the present context it refers to arrangements under which, by means of export bans or more informal pressure on his other licensees and his customers, a licensor does his best to seal off the contract territory from parallel imports. The Court found in *Maize Seeds* that an undertaking to this effect had been given by the French licensor, INRA[39]; and concrete steps had been taken to prevent third parties who purchased INRA seeds in France from exporting them to Germany. No licensee is entitled to demand such complete protection. The Court affirmed its consistently held view "that absolute territorial protection granted to a licensee in order to enable parallel imports to be controlled and prevented results in the artificial maintenance of separate national markets, contrary to the Treaty."[40] Subject to the *de minimis* rule, any such agreement is bound in practice to be caught by Article 85(1).

Between these two extremes are intermediate forms of exclusivity, for example a ban on direct sales by other licensees, which the Court did not consider in *Maize Seeds*.

In *Erauw-Jacquery*[41] a restriction on a licensee of plant breeders' rights from selling or exporting basic seeds was held not to come within Article 85(1). However, it seems that the decision is restricted to those rights. Given their special nature, the Court held[42] that the breeder must be able to restrict propagation to the growers selected as licensees. Thus the restriction went to the existence rather than the exercise of the right.[43]

It seems unlikely from the tenor of both the *Maize Seeds* and *Erauw-Jacquery* decisions that bans on direct sales by licensees of other types of intellectual property rights would be found compatible with Article 85(1).[44]

Exclusive licences which are caught by Article 85(1) may qualify for exemption under Article 85(3). In the past, while its treatment of exclusive manufacturing rights has been relatively generous, the Commission has been reluctant to grant exemption in respect of exclusive selling rights.[45] As to the latter, however, the Block Exemption Regulations on Patent

---

[39] The initials stand for "Institut National de la Recherche Agronomique."
[40] [1982] E.C.R. at p. 2070. The point has been clear since Joined Cases 56 and 58/64, *Consten and Grundig* v. *Commission loc. cit.* note 8, p. 595, *supra*. See also Case 28/77, *Tepea* v. *Commission loc. cit.* note 26, p. 598, *supra*.
[41] Case 27/87, *Erauw-Jacquery* v. *La Hesbignonne* [1988] E.C.R. 1919.
[42] [1988] E.C.R. 1919 at p. 1939.
[43] This restriction is sanctioned by the Commission's Standard Seed Production and Sales Agreement O.J. 1990 C6/3.
[44] *Cf.* Case 262/81, *Coditel* v. *Ciné Vog Films (No. 2) loc. cit.* note 70, *supra*, where it was held that a contract under which the owner of the copyright in a film grants an exclusive right to exhibit the film for a specific period in a Member State is not, as such, subject to the prohibition in Art. 85. The Court said that the exercise of the exclusive right may fall within the prohibition "where there are economic or legal circumstances the effect of which is to restrict film distribution to an appreciable degree or to distort competition on the cinematographic market, regard being had to the specific characteristics of that market": [1982] E.C.R. at p. 3402.
[45] See, *e.g. Re Davidson Rubber Company loc. cit.* note 33, p. 600, *supra*; *Re Kabelmetal/Luchaire ibid.*; *Re AOIP/Beyrard loc. cit.* note 31, p. 599, *supra*.

Licensing Agreements and Know-how Licensing Agreements show a significant change of attitude[46]; and this seems likely to be reflected in the Commission's treatment of agreements relating to other forms of intellectual property.[47] Any attempt to provide protection against parallel imports remains beyond reasonable hope of exemption.

(ii) *Royalties.* A patentee makes the profit to which he is entitled by "selling" permission to work his patent. An obligation on the licensee to pay a royalty thus clearly belongs to the domain of specific subject-matter.[48] However, Article 85 may be infringed if products not covered by the patent in question are taken into account in calculating the sums payable.[49] In *Windsurfing International* v. *Commission*[50] the Court took the view that the licensor had not been justified in charging royalties on the basis of the net selling-price of complete sailboards when the patent related only to "rigs."[51] A provision for the continuance of royalty payments after the expiry of a patent is similarly liable to fall foul of Article 85,[52] unless the payments relate to secret know-how still being used by the licensee,[53] or if the licensee is able to terminate on reasonable notice.[54]

(iii) *Duration.* The Commission has written that "Article 85(1) does not in principle touch upon the contractually fixed duration of a patent licence agreement, if this is for the life of a single licensed patent or a shorter term"[55]; though it notes that, exceptionally, Article 86 might apply to abusively short contract periods.[56] On the other hand, a clause extending the duration of an agreement beyond the life of the patent to which it relates obviously cannot be regarded as indispensable to the patent's exploitation. Thus in *Re AOPI/Beyrard*[57] the Commission condemned a clause which enabled a licensee to extend indefinitely an agreement with a number of restrictive features by granting successive licences in respect of patented improvements.[58]

(iv) *Quality controls.* An obligation on a licensee to meet prescribed

---

[46] See Reg. 2349/84, Art. 1(1)(5) and (6), discussed, *infra.*
[47] The solution in Art. 1(1)(5) of Reg. 2349/84 was anticipated in *Re Campari* O.J. 1978 L70/69; [1978] 2 C.M.L.R. 397.
[48] See Comp.Rep. 1975, p. 20.
[49] See Block Exemption Reg. 2349/84, Art. 3(4).
[50] Case 198/83, *loc. cit.* note 14, p. 596, *supra.*
[51] The "rig" is defined in the judgment as "an assemblage consisting essentially of a mast, a joint for the mast, a sail and spars." This is distinguished from the "board," defined as "a hull made of synthetic materials equipped with a centreboard." See [1986] 3 C.M.L.R. at p. 524. In the event, the method of calculating the royalties did not result in the infringement of Art. 85, since the sum charged was no higher than it would have been if it had been based solely on the price of the rigs. See [1986] 3 C.M.L.R. at pp. 535–536.
[52] *Re AOIP/Beyrard loc. cit.* note 31, p. 599, *supra.*
[53] *Re Kabelmetal/Luchaire loc. cit.* note 33, p. 600, *supra.* See Block Exemption Reg. 2349/84, Art. 3(2).
[54] Case 320/87, *Kai Ottung* v. *Klee,* [1989] E.C.R. 1177; [1990] 4 C.M.L.R. 915.
[55] Comp.Rep. 1975, p. 23. See Block Exemption Reg. 2349/84, Art. 2(4).
[56] Comp.Rep. 1975, p. 23, note 1.
[57] *Loc. cit.* note 31, p. 599, *supra.*
[58] See the reasoning of the Commission at [1976] 1 C.M.L.R. D23. See also Block Exemption Reg. 2349/84, Art. 3(2).

standards of production will come within the specific subject-matter of a patent if it is genuinely necessary to ensure that the technical instructions in the patent are carried out.[59] On the other hand, quality controls are liable to infringe Article 85 if they relate to products not covered by the patent. The criteria to be applied must be agreed in advance and must be objectively verifiable. In *Windsurfing International* v. *Commission*[60] an obligation on licensees to obtain Windsurfing's approval of the boards incorporated into their sailboards was held by the Court to infringe Article 85 because the patent was considered to cover only the rig. Even if the whole sailboard had been covered, the controls in question would still have been outside the specific subject-matter of the patent, owing to their discretionary character, which made it possible for *Windsurfing* to impose its own selection of models on the licensees.[61]

Quality controls are of particular importance in relation to trade marks because of the licensor's interest in preserving the reputation associated with the mark. Thus in its *Campari* Decision[62] the Commission raised no objection to an obligation on trade mark licensees to observe instructions from the licensor regarding the manufacturing process and ingredients of the famous drink.

(v) *Tying*. A licensee may be put under an obligation to work a patent or sell patented products only in conjunction with other products or services specified in the agreement. Tie-in clauses which are necessary for a technically satisfactory exploitation of the licensed invention are closely allied to quality controls and belong to the specific subject-matter of the licensor's patent.[63] An example from the sphere of trade marks is, again, provided by the *Campari* Decision[64] where the Commission did not object to a requirement that certain secret ingredients be purchased from the licensor.[65] Where, however, tying cannot be justified in any way, it falls within the express terms of Article 85(1)(e) and is likely to prove irredeemable.[66] Such was the fate of the obligation imposed on the licensees of Windsurfing International in Germany to supply the rig covered by the patent only in conjunction with approved varieties of board.

(vi) *Field of use restrictions*. Where a patent is capable of being worked in two or more distinct applications, a right to grant licences limited to a particular field of use will form part of its specific subject-matter.[67] On the other hand, restrictions on the use of a patent which are not technically

---

[59] See Block Exemption Reg. 2349/84, Art. 2(9). Genuine quality controls have been favourably treated by the Commission since its earliest decisions on patent licensing: see *Re Burroughs/Delplanque* J.O. 1972 L13/50; [1972] C.M.L.R. D67.
[60] Case 198/83, *loc. cit.* note 14, p. 596, *supra*.
[61] See [1986] 3 C.M.L.R. at pp. 532–533.
[62] *Re Campari loc. cit.* note 47, p. 602, *supra*.
[63] See Block Exemption Reg. 2349/84, Art. 2(1).
[64] *Loc. cit., supra*.
[65] [1978] 2 C.M.L.R. at p. 409.
[66] See Block Exemption Reg. 2349/84, Art. 3(9).
[67] Comp.Rep. 1975, p. 22. See Block Exemption Reg. 2349/84, Art. 2(3).

justified are liable to have the object or effect of dividing up the market between licensees. This was the main burden of the Commission's objection to the requirement that rigs covered by the *Windsurfing* patent be used only in conjunction with certain boards.[68] The Court agreed with the Commission that "Windsurfing International's real interest lay in ensuring that there was sufficient product differentiation between its licensee's sailboards to cover the widest possible spectrum of market demand."[69]

(vii) *Grant-back clauses.* A clause requiring the licensee to grant back to the licensor a licence in respect of any improvements for which he may obtain patents can hardly be regarded as essential to safeguard the specific subject-matter of the original patent. The Commission takes the view, however, that such clauses are not normally restrictive of competition, provided that the licensor is put under a corresponding obligation, and the licences to be granted by either party are non-exclusive.[70] On the other hand, the Commission will insist on the removal from an agreement of a clause requiring the licensee to cede the property in improvements, or to license them exclusively, to the licensor.[71]

(viii) *Licensed-by notices.* Some of the licensees in *Windsurfing International* were under an obligation to place on boards manufactured by them a notice which referred to the licence.[72] This, in the Commission's view, gave the erroneous impression that the boards as well as the rigs were covered by the patent. The licensees were thus made to appear less technically independent than they were, and their position on the market was affected. Addressing this point, the Court of Justice said:

> ". . . such a clause may be covered by the specific subject-matter of the patent provided that the notice is placed only on components protected by the patent. Should this not be the case, the question arises whether the clause has as its object or effect the prevention, restriction or distortion of competition."[73]

In the instant case, it was held, the notice encouraged uncertainty as to the scope of the patent and was therefore likely to diminish consumer confidence in the licensees, allowing *Windsurfing* to gain a competitive advantage for itself.[74]

(ix) *No-challenge clauses.* Because of his privileged access to

---

[68] Windsurfing International sought to justify the requirement as a quality control measure, as well as a form of protection for individual licensees against slavish imitation of their products.
[69] [1986] 3 C.M.L.R. at pp. 533–534.
[70] See Block Exemption Reg. 2349/84, Art. 2(1)(10). See also *Re Davidson Rubber Company loc. cit.*, note 33, p. 600, *supra.*
[71] *Re Raymond/Nagoya* J.O. 1972 L143/39; [1972] C.M.L.R. D45; *Re Kabelmetal/Luchaire loc. cit.*, note 33, p. 600, *supra.*
[72] [1986] 3 C.M.L.R. at pp. 536–537.
[73] [1986] 3 C.M.L.R. at p. 537.
[74] See Block Exemption Reg. 2349/84, Art. 2(6). See also *Re Burroughs/Deplanque* J.O. 1972 L13/50; [1972] C.M.L.R. D67; *Re Burroughs/Geha* J.O. 1972 L13/53; [1972] C.M.L.R. D72.

information and his experience of working the patent, a licensee is particularly well placed to detect any possible flaws in the patentee's title. Licensors may, accordingly, seek to protect themselves by exacting an undertaking from their licensees not to challenge the validity of the patent. Such "no-challenge" clauses, the Court has held, do not come within the specific subject-matter of a patent "in view of the fact that it is in the public interest to eliminate any obstacle to economic activity which may arise where a patent was granted in error."[75] That being so, a no-challenge clause is likely to be caught by Article 85(1), with no realistic prospect of exemption under Article 85(3).[76] However, in *Bayer* v. *Süllhöfer*[77] the Court held that no-challenge clauses which cannot affect the licensee's economic activity may escape Article 85(1); for example, if no royalties are payable by the licensee or the licensee does not use the patented process because it is technically outdated. This seems to take a narrower view of the public interest, which previously was equated with the desirability of not maintaining the registration of invalid patents as a deterrent to the use by anyone of such technology.

The Block Exemption Regulation on Patent Licensing Agreements[78]

The Regulation covers patent licensing agreements and agreements combining the licensing of patents and the communication of know-how, to which only two undertakings are party.[79] It entered into force on January 1, 1985 and applies until December 31, 1994.[80]

Article 1(1) of the Regulation lists seven types of clause that benefit from the block exemption. Six of these are concerned with aspects of exclusivity. Although, as we have seen, open exclusive licences do not always require exemption, the terms characteristic of such licences are included in the list. These are: an obligation on the licensor not to appoint other licensees for the contract territory; an obligation on the licensor not to exploit the licensed invention himself within the contract territory; and an obligation on the licensee not to exploit the licensed invention in territories reserved for the licensor. Also exempted is an obligation on the licensee not to manufacture or use the patented product in the territories of other licensees. This reflects

---

[75] Case 198/83, *Windsurfing International* v. *Commission* [1986] 3 C.M.L.R. at p. 540. The Court struck down no-challenge clauses relating to certain word and design marks and to the patent itself; see [1986] 3 C.M.L.R. at, respectively, pp. 537–538 and 539–540.

[76] See *Re Davidson Rubber Co. loc. cit.* note 33, p. 600, *supra*, where the parties removed a no-challenge clause from their agreements under pressure from the Commission. See also the reasoning of the Commission in *Re AIOP/Beyrard* [1976] 1 C.M.L.R. at D23. On the other hand, such a clause may be acceptable in a "delimitation agreement" between the owners of trade marks that are liable to be confused. See Case 35/83, *BAT* v. *Commission* where the Court took the view that a purported conflict over trade marks was purely "contrived," the real purpose being to exclude the products of one of the parties from the other's market; [1985] E.C.R.; [1985] 2 C.M.L.R. 470.

[77] Case 65/86, *Bayer* v. *Süllhöfer* [1988] E.C.R. 5249.

[78] O.J. 1984 L219/15. A proposal to amend Regulation 2349/84 to enable it to be applied to more joint venture agreements has been published at O.J. 1992 C207/11.

[79] Power to apply Art. 85(3) to, *inter alia*, categories of bilateral patent licensing agreements was conferred on the Commission by Reg. 19/65, O.J. 1965–66 35 J.O. 1965, 533.

[80] Art. 14.

the established approach of the Commission to exclusive manufacturing rights. More surprising, perhaps, is the acceptance in the Regulation of the need for a large measure of protection for licensees against sales into their territories by a licensee for another territory. Exemption is given to an obligation on the licensee not to pursue an active sales policy in other licensees' territory so long as the product is protected there by a parallel patent: he may thus be prevented from advertising or establishing a branch or depot or from canvassing for custom, but not from responding to unsolicited orders.[81] But the Commission has gone further. The block exemption also covers a ban, during the first five years after the launching of the protected product on the common market, against all sales in the territories of other licensees. Where a product is new, full protection may, therefore, be given against competition from fellow licensees, passive as well as active.

The seventh item on the list of exempted clauses in Article 1(1) is a requirement that the licensee use only the licensor's trade mark and get-up to distinguish the protected product. Exemption is conditional on the licensee's being permitted to identify himself as the manufacturer of the product. This is to enable him to retain the goodwill attaching to the product after the expiry of the patent, without being forced to enter into a new trade mark agreement with the licensor.[82]

Obligations whose inclusion in a licensing agreement does not affect the availability of the block exemption are listed in Article 2(1). The Commission considers that the obligations in question are not generally restrictive of competition. Should they happen, because of particular circumstances, to fall within Article 85(1), the block exemption will apply to them, irrespective of whether they are accompanied by obligations exempted pursuant to Article 1 of the Regulation.[83] The obligations on the list comprise: tying, where this is necessary for a technically satisfactory exploitation of the licensed invention; an obligation on the licensee to pay a minimum royalty or to produce a minimum quantity of the protected product; restriction of the field of use of the licensed invention; an obligation on the licensee not to exploit the patent after the expiry of the agreement; an obligation on the licensee not to grant sub-licences or to assign the licence; an obligation to mark the protected product with an indication of the patent or the patentee; an obligation on the licensee not to divulge know-how communicated by the licensor (this may be made to continue after the agreement has expired); obligations on the licensee connected with the defence of the patentee's interest against third party infringers; quality controls necessary for a technically satisfactory exploitation of the licensed invention; an obligation on the licensor and the licensee to communicate experience gained in exploiting the licensed invention and to grant one another licences in respect of improvements or new applications; in both cases on a non-exclusive basis; finally, an obligation on the licensor to extend

---

[81] *Cf.* Reg. 1983/83, Art. 2(2)(*c*).
[82] See Preamble, 10th recital.
[83] Art. 2(2).

to the licensee any more favourable terms it may subsequently grant to other licensees (a "most-favoured licensee clause").

A "black list" of terms that prevent the application of the block exemption is found in Article 3. These consist of: no-challenge clauses (though the licensor may be entitled, in the event of a challenge, to terminate the licence); clauses that allow the agreement to be extended beyond the life of the patents existing at the time it was entered into through the inclusion of new patents obtained by the licensor, except where both parties are given a right at least annually to terminate the agreement once the original patents have expired[84]; no-competition clauses (other than those covered by the provisions on exclusivity in Article 1); the charging of royalties on unpatented products or on know-how that has entered into the public domain; the imposition of an upper limit on the quantity of the protected products the licensee may manufacture; the fixing of prices for the protected products; restrictions on the classes of customers to whom the products may be supplied; an obligation on the licensee to assign to the licensor patents for improvements or for new applications of the licensed patents; tying which is not necessary for a technically satisfactory exploitation of the licensed invention; a ban on marketing the protected product in the territories of other licensees for a period exceeding that permitted under Article 1(1)(5); and, lastly, an obligation on either party to refuse supplies within their respective territories to parallel exporters or to make it difficult for parallel importers to obtain supplies elsewhere in the common market.

Other provisions in the regulation may be described more shortly. An "opposition procedure" is provided by Article 4. Agreements containing obligations restrictive of competition which are not covered by Articles 1 or 2 and which do not figure on the black list in Article 3 may be notified to the Commission and will automatically be exempted if within six months the Commission does not oppose this. Article 5 excludes from the scope of the Regulation licensing agreements relating to patent pools[85] or joint ventures, reciprocal licensing between competing undertakings and licences in respect of plant breeders' rights. Transitional provisions giving exemption retrospectively to existing agreements that fulfil the conditions of the Regulation, or are amended in order to do so, are contained in Articles 6 to 8. Under Article 9 the Commission may withdraw the exemption from agreements which, although they fulfil the conditions of the Regulation, are nevertheless found to have effects incompatible with Article 85(3). Among the factors mentioned in the Article as likely to justify such withdrawal are: the absence of effective competition in the licensee's territory from products identical, or considered by users as equivalent, to the protected product; the refusal by the licensee, for no objectively valid reason, to meet unsolicited

---

[84] The licensor has the right to charge royalties for the continuing use by the licensee of know-how which has not entered into the public domain.
[85] Broadly, arrangements under which the leading firms in an industry have access to one another's patents, while denying their use to other firms. See Cornish, *op. cit.* note 1, *supra* at p. 570.

orders from the territories of other licensees; or behaviour by either party intended to frustrate the efforts of parallel exporters or importers.[86]

A patent licensing agreement which falls outside the block exemption may still qualify for individual exemption under Regulation 17. In order to do so, the agreement must have been notified to the Commission, unless it falls within the narrow category of non-notifiable agreements defined by Article 4(2)(2)(*b*) of that Regulation.[87]

The Block Exemption regulation on Know-how Licensing Agreements[88]

A similar block exemption was subsequently introduced to cover know-how licensing agreements. The Patent Licensing Agreements Block Exemption only covered provisions relating to the use of know-how (*i.e.* unpatented technical information, protectable under the law relating to confidential information and trade secrets)[89] to the extent that it permitted a better exploitation of the licensed patents.[90] Accordingly agreements for the licensing only of know-how or where the know-how formed the greater part of the technology transferred under the agreement were not exempted under the Patent Licensing Agreements Block Exemption. The Know-how Licensing Agreements Block Exemption[91] filled that gap. It applies to pure know-how licensing agreements and mixed patent and know-how licensing agreements, unless such a mixed agreement is covered by the Patent Licensing Block Exemption.[92]

The Know-how Licensing Block Exemption broadly follows the Patent Licensing Block Exemption. Where there are differences, these stem from the fact that while a patent is necessarily limited in duration, know-how potentially is perpetual in that it remains protected unless it comes into the public domain. Hence Article 1(1), which lists eight types of clauses benefiting from the block exemption, qualifies these by allowing them only if the restrictions in the agreement are for no more than a certain duration. The duration permitted varies according to the restriction. Restrictions on the licensor not to exploit the licensed technology in the licensee's territory either itself[93] or through grant of licences[94] and on the licensee not to exploit

---

[86] In *Tetra Pak* O.J. 1988 L272/27 the Commission noted that had Tetra Pak not complied with the Commission's request that it renounce exclusive rights under a patent licence to avoid a breach of Art. 86, the Commission would have used its powers under Art. 9 to withdraw the benefit of the block exemption. See further p. 613, below.

[87] In Case 198/83 *Windsurfing International* v. *Commission* it was held the clauses in question did not fall within the non-notifiable category because they went beyond the subject-matter of the patent: [1986] 3 C.M.L.R. at p. 541. See also *Re Advocaat Zwarte Kip* O.J. 1974 L237/12; [1974] 2 C.M.L.R. D79; *Re Vaessen/Moris* O.J. 1979 L19/32; [1979] 1 C.M.L.R. 511.

[88] O.J. 1989 L61/1. See also proposed amendments at O.J. 1992 C207/11, note 78, p. 605 *supra*.

[89] Art. 1(7)(1), Reg. 556/89 defines know-how for the purposes of the Regulation as "a body of technical information that is secret, substantial and identified in any appropriate form."

[90] Recital 9, Reg. 2349/84. In *Boussois/Interpane* O.J. 1987 L50/30, the Commission held that a licensing agreement where the know-how formed the dominant element of the technology involved was not exempt under Reg. 2349/84 citing this recital.

[91] Also adopted under Reg. 19/65.

[92] Recital 3, Reg. 556/89.

[93] Art. 1(1)(2).

[94] Art. 1(1)(1).

the licensed technology in the licensor's territory[95] are exempted only if they are for no longer than 10 years from the date when the licensor first licensed the technology in that territory.[96]

A lesser period of exemption is provided for in respect of restrictions on the licensee from manufacturing in other licensees' territories[97] and from actively marketing licensed products into other licensees' territories.[98] Such restrictions can only be imposed for up to 10 years from the date the technology was first licensed by the licensor anywhere in the Community.[99] A complete ban on passive marketing by a licensee into other licensees' territories is permitted for five years from the date the technology was first licensed by the licensor anywhere in the Community.[1] The different starting dates for these lesser periods of exemption appears to be because of the need to have uniformity in the date on which these restrictions on manufacturing and marketing end for a particular licensed technology throughout the Community. The periods chosen in themselves seem to have no inherent justification and if a longer period of protection is desired, it may be granted by an individual exemption.[2]

As in the Patent Licensing Agreements Block Exemption, the licensor is allowed to require that the licensee is to use only the licensor's trade mark and get-up to distinguish the licensed product, provided that the licensee can distinguish itself as the manufacturer.[3]

Finally, an additional restriction is included which does not appear in the Patent Licensing Agreements Block Exemption. This entitles the licensor to restrict the licensee to using the know-how only to manufacture components of the licensee's own products and sell them either as integral or as replacement parts for those products,[4] this being conditional on no limitation of the licensee's output.

The Block Exemption then proceeds to set out a white-list of exempted restrictions in Article 2 and a black-list of restrictions under Article 3 whose inclusion will preclude the application of the Exemption. These are broadly the same as those in the Patent Licensing Agreements Block Exemption, to which reference is made,[5] but there are some noteworthy differences.

In the white-list, the inclusion of an obligation on both parties to communicate improvements to each other and to license use of those improvements on a non-exclusive basis is narrower in ambit than under the Patent Licensing Agreements Block Exemption. The Know-how Licensing Agreements Block Exemption only allows such a clause to be included if it is made subject to the condition that if the licensee's right to use the licensor's know-how is brought to an end, then the licensor's right to use the licensee's

---

[95] Art. 1(1)(3).
[96] Art. 1(2).
[97] Art. 1(1)(4).
[98] Art. 1(1)(5).
[99] Art. 1(2).
[1] Art. 1(1)(6) and 1(2).
[2] In *Delta Chemie/DDD* O.J. 1988 L309/34 a twenty-year exemption was granted.
[3] Art. 1(1)(7).
[4] Art. 1(1)(8).
[5] See pp. 605–607, *supra*.

improvements to that know-how must also terminate, although it is permissible for the licensor to exercise an option to continue using those improvements provided appropriate royalties are paid.[6] The black-lists in both Block Exemptions contain provisions preventing automatic prolonging of an agreement by the inclusion of new patents or know-how by the licensor, stating that the licensee must have the right to terminate at the expiry of the initial term of the agreement; but, if the licensee does not terminate then, whereas under the Patent Licensing Agreements Block Exemption either party may terminate annually thereafter,[7] under the Know-how Licensing Agreements Block Exemption the right to terminate need only be granted once every three years.[8]

Under the Know-how Licensing Agreements Block Exemption, there are broader grounds for imposing quality requirements on a licensee. Whereas under the Patent Licensing Agreements Block Exemption, quality control was permitted to the extent it was necessary for a technically satisfactory exploitation of the licensed technology,[9] under the Know-how Licensing Agreements Block Exemption this may also be done to ensure compliance with "quality standards that are respected by the licensor and other licensees."[10] This is reflected in the black-list where under the Patent Licensing Agreements Block Exemption, the licensor may only "tie-in" further patents, goods or services if necessary for a technically satisfactory exploitation of the licensed invention,[11] whereas under the Know-how Licensing Agreements Block Exemption tying-in may also be allowed if it is necessary to ensure that the licensee's production meets the aforementioned quality standards.[12]

Moreover, whereas under the Patent Licensing Agreements Block Exemption, a licensor could only restrict a licensee to using the licensed technology to a particular technical field or fields of application,[13] the Know-how Licensing Agreements Block Exemption allows the licensor to go further and restrict a licensee to a particular product market or markets.[14]

There are provisions which are substantially common to both Block Exemptions. In the Know-how Licensing Agreements Block Exemption these are: an opposition procedure in Article 4, a list of agreements in Article 5 which are not covered by the block exemption, confirmation in Article 6 that the exemption extends to certain other agreements such as sub-licensing agreements and, finally, Article 7 which reserves the Commission's right to withdraw the benefit of the exemption in certain cases. There are also transitional provisions in Articles 8–10 and provisions regarding confidentiality in Article 11.

It seems therefore that the Patent and Know-how Licensing Agreements

---

[6] Art. 2(1)(10), Reg. 2349/84; Art. 2(1)(4), Reg. 556/89.
[7] Art. 3(2), Reg. 2349/84.
[8] Art. 3(10), Reg. 556/89.
[9] Art. 2(1)(9), Reg. 2349/84.
[10] Art. 2(1)(5), Reg. 556/89.
[11] Art. 3(9), Reg. 2349/84.
[12] Art. 3(3), Reg. 556/89.
[13] Art. 2(1)(3), Reg. 2349/84.
[14] Art. 2(1)(8), Reg. 556/89.

Block Exemptions do contain some significant differences which may affect which form parties to an agreement wish to adopt, in order to be able to include those restrictions which are considered most important in a particular transaction. This lays the block exemption open to criticisms of formalism in approach, criticisms which are more usually levelled at the equivalent provisions of the United Kingdom's domestic legislation.[15] It is to be hoped that when the Patent Licensing Agreements Block Exemption is reviewed prior to its expiry on December 31, 1994[16] consideration is given to the possibility of incorporating the two block exemptions into one. In practice, it is often a matter of chance whether technology is protected by a patent or left subject to the protection given to know-how. When it comes to transferring that technology, whether by licensing or otherwise, it would seem desirable that the same legal regime should apply to both, irrespective of form.

Limits on exercise of intellectual property rights under Article 86

It has been seen that assignments and licences of intellectual property rights can be subject to Article 85. Article 86 may impose limits on the unilateral exercise of intellectual property rights.

The issue of the extent to which an intellectual property right itself is evidence of the existence of a dominant position has already been referred to above.[17]

Two principal questions arise once the existence of a dominant position is established: is the existence of rights granted under national intellectual property laws capable of constituting an abuse, and can exercise of those rights constitute an abuse?

The answer to the first question was then considered in two references to the Court of Justice, from Italy in *CICRA* v. *Renault*[18] and from the United Kingdom High Court in *Volvo* v. *Veng*,[19] in answer to which the Court handed down its judgments on the same day. The facts of both were essentially the same. Renault and Volvo had the benefit of design copyright in the respective Member States for motor vehicle spare parts, as well as for the complete motor vehicles. Both manufacturers sought to rely on their rights to prevent other automotive component manufacturers from copying their spare parts. The effect of this, given the nature of car spare parts which demands that, except for the most standard components, a spare part must be an exact copy of the manufacturer's original design, was to exclude any competition for the manufacturer's own spare parts. The spare part manufacturers argued in both cases that this constituted an abuse of a dominant position.

---

[15] See Whish's criticism of the Restrictive Trade Practices Act 1976: *Competition Law* (2nd ed., 1989) at pp. 134–135 and the Appendix.
[16] Art. 14, Reg. 2349/84.
[17] p. 595, *supra*.
[18] Case 53/87, *CICRA and Maxicar* v. *Renault* [1988] E.C.R. 6039.
[19] Case 238/87, *Volvo* v. *Erik Veng (UK) Ltd.* [1988] E.C.R. 6211.

The Court ruled, citing *Keurkoop* v. *Nancy Kean Gifts*,[20] that in the absence of Community standardisation or harmonisation of laws, it was solely a matter for national law to determine what protection to grant to designs, even for such functional items as car spare parts. Moreover, it was part of the subject-matter of such rights that the owner be allowed to prevent others from manufacturing, selling or importing spare parts which copied such designs. Accordingly, taking action to protect the existence of the intellectual property right could not constitute an abuse of a dominant position.[21]

The Court then turned to deal with the second question, namely the effect of Article 86 on the exercise of intellectual property rights. It held that exercise of a right could be an abuse, for example arbitrary refusal to supply spare parts to an independent repairer, unfair pricing of spare parts or refusal to continue supplying spare parts for a model of motor vehicle of which many were still in circulation.[22] As there was no evidence of such conduct in either of the cases referred to the Court, no finding of abuse was made.

These rulings were considered by the Court of First Instance in the *Magill TV Guide* cases[23] which considered at greater length the circumstances in which the exercise of intellectual property rights could be considered an abuse.

The *Magill TV Guide* cases involved an attempt by an Irish magazine publisher to introduce a weekly advance TV listings magazine of that name to cover all TV programmes capable of being received in both the Republic of Ireland and Northern Ireland. At this time that involved three broadcasting authorities' programmes, the Irish State broadcaster RTE, the BBC which is the United Kingdom equivalent and the Independent Broadcasting Authority which was responsible for the output from independent television in the United Kingdom. Each of these three authorities owned copyright in the advance listings of their programmes (in the case of the IBA, through its subsidiary Independent Television Publications Ltd.) and produced their own separate weekly advance guide. In response to advance listings being published in the Magill TV Guide, each obtained an interim injunction in the Irish High Court preventing its future publication in breach of their respective copyrights. The Commission launched an investigation on receiving a complaint from Magill and concluded that the exercise of copyright in this way constituted a breach of Article 86, as it exceeded the scope of the specific subject matter of that

---

[20] Case 144/81, *Keurkoop* v. *Nancy Kean Gifts* [1982] E.C.R. 2853.
[21] Case 53/87, *CICRA and Maxicar* v. *Renault* [1988] E.C.R. at pp. 6071–2, paras. 10, 11 and 15 of the judgment; Case 238/87, *Volvo* v. *Erik Veng (UK) Ltd.* [1988] E.C.R. at p. 6235, paras. 7 and 8 of the judgment.
[22] Case 53/87, *CICRA and Maxicar* v. *Renault* [1988] E.C.R. at pp. 6073, para. 18 of the judgment; Case 238/87, *Volvo* v. *Erik Veng (UK) Ltd.* [1988] E.C.R. at p. 6235, para. 9 of the judgment.
[23] Case T–69/89, *Radio Telefis Eireann* v. *Commission* [1991] 4 C.M.L.R. 586; T–70/89, *BBC* v. *Commission* [1991] 4 C.M.L.R. 669 and T–76/89, *Independent Television Publications Ltd.* v. *Commission*, [1991] 4 C.M.L.R. 745; see Robertson, (1992) 108 L.Q.R. 39; Cases T–69/89 and T–76/89 have been appealed to the Court of Justice.

right.[24] On appeal by each of the broadcasting authorities, the Court of First Instance upheld the Commission's finding of an abuse of a dominant position. Noting the Court of Justice's decisions in *CICRA* v. *Renault* and *Volvo* v. *Veng*, the Court of First Instance agreed that ". . . in principle the protection of the specific subject-matter of a copyright entitles the copyright holder to reserve the exclusive right to reproduce the protected work."[25] However, the Court continued, the exclusive right to reproduce could constitute an abuse ". . . when, in the light of the details of each individual case, it is apparent that the right is exercised in such ways and circumstances as in fact to pursue an aim manifestly contrary to the objectives of Article 86. In that event, the copyright is no longer exercised in a manner which corresponds to its essential function, within the meaning of Article 36 of the Treaty, which is to protect the moral rights in the work and ensure a reward for the creative effort . . ."[26]

In this case, because each of the broadcasters allowed publication of their programme listings on other publications, such as newspapers, on a day-by-day basis and allowed their publication in other Member States on a weekly basis, it appeared to the Court that they were using their respective copyrights to exclude the competition in their own Member States for their own weekly programmes listings magazines. It was held that this went beyond what was necessary to fulfil the essential function of the copyright in question.

Subject to what might be said by the Court of Justice on appeal, it thus appears that the exercise of an intellectual property right may now be limited to doing no more than either is implicit in the specific subject-matter of that right or is proportionate in fulfilling the essential function of that right. Exercising a right in any way which extends beyond those boundaries will be abusive and caught by Article 86 subject, of course, to the other requirements for the application of that Article being satisfied.

Intellectual property and the interplay between Article 30 and Articles 85 and 86

There are two issues relevant to intellectual property rights to be dealt with here: first, what is the relationship between Articles 85 and 86, and, second, what is the relationship between those two Articles and Article 30?

The first issue was dealt with by the European Court of First Instance in Tetra Pak.[27] The case arose out of the take-over by Tetra Pak, which occupied a dominant position in the Community liquid food packaging

---

[24] *Re Magill TV Guide* O.J. 1989 L78/43; the Commission's decison only devotes the most cursory attention to the copyright issue however, see p. 50.

[25] Case T–69/89, *RTE* v. *Commission* [1991] 4 C.M.L.R. at p. 617, para. 70 of the judgment; the same statement is made at para. 57 of Case T–70/89 and para. 55 of Case T–76/89.

[26] Case T–69/89, *RTE* v. *Commission* [1991] 4 C.M.L.R. at p. 617, para. 71 of the judgment; the same statement is made at para. 58 of Case T–70/89 and para. 56 of Case T–76/89; See criticism of this characterisation of essential function by Robertson, (1991) 108 L.Q.R. at p. 42.

[27] Case T–51/89, *Tetra Pak Rausing SA* v. *Commission* [1991] 4 C.M.L.R. 334.

market, of one of its competitors, Liquipak. Liquipak was exclusively licensed under an agreement which complied with the provisions of the Patent Licensing Block Exemption to use a new process for sterilising milk cartons prior to filling. The effect of the take-over was that Tetra Pak also acquired exclusive rights to use the new process, to the exclusion of its other competitors. One of these complained to the Commission which, after investigation, held that the acquisition of exclusive patent rights was an abuse of Tetra Pak's dominant position. It also indicated that had Tetra Pak not renounced exclusivity under the patent licence, thus allowing the patent owner to license its competitors under the patent as well, it would have withdrawn the benefit of the Patent Licensing Block Exemption using its power under Article 9 of that Regulation.[28]

This decision was challenged by Tetra Pak which argued that as Articles 85 and 86 pursue the same objective, it was not open to the Commission to apply Article 86 to an agreement exempted under the provisions of the Patent Licensing Agreements Block Exemption Regulation. The Court rejected this argument holding that Articles 85 and 86 "constitute, in the scheme of the Treaty, two independent legal instruments addressing different situations."[29] It ruled that although the acquisition of an exclusive patent licence by a dominant business could not constitute an abuse *per se*,[30] in the specific circumstances of this case it did, given that the effect would have been to deprive other businesses of the means of competing with Tetra Pak.[31] To have held otherwise, the Court observed,[32] would have been in effect to incorporate into Article 86 a means of obtaining an exemption from liability for an abuse of a dominant position.

Turning to the second issue, it will be apparent that reliance on intellectual property rights to exclude imports coming from other Member States may fall foul of the EEC Treaty provisions on both freedom of movement and competition. In the *Maize Seeds* case[33] the Government of the United Kingdom argued, *inter alia*, that the licensing agreement in question could not be regarded as incompatible with Article 85 because it would be possible for third parties to invoke Article 30 in order to prevent the enforcement of the terms designed to achieve absolute territorial protection. In other words, even if the parties had anti-competitive intentions, these would inevitably have been frustrated through the operation of the exhaustion of rights principle. Rejecting that argument, the Court of Justice said it failed to take into account:

"... the fact that one of the powers of the Commission is to ensure, pursuant to Article 85 of the Treaty and the regulations adopted in implementation thereof, that agreements and concerted practices

---

[28] *Elopak/Tetra Pak* O.J. 1988 L272/27; [1990] 4 C.M.L.R. 47; see pp. 607–608, *supra* Re Art. 9, Reg. 2349/84.
[29] [1991] 4 C.M.L.R. at p. 383, para. 22 of the judgment.
[30] [1991] 4 C.M.L.R. at p. 385, para. 23 of the judgment.
[31] [1991] 4 C.M.L.R. at p. 385, para. 23 of the judgment.
[32] [1991] 4 C.M.L.R. at p. 365, para. 25 of the judgment.
[33] Case 258/78, *loc. cit.* note 77, p. 588, *supra*.

between undertakings do not have the object or the effect of restricting or distorting competition, and that that power of the Commission is not affected by the fact that persons or undertakings subject to such restrictions are in a position to rely upon the provisions of the Treaty relating to the free movement of goods in order to escape such restrictions."[34]

The prohibitions in Article 30 and in Articles 85 and 86, therefore, apply cumulatively.

What if the application of the two sets of rules to the exercise of an intellectual property right leads to conflicting results? This is unlikely in the case of attempts to exclude parallel imports, since the exhaustion of rights principle seems to be on all fours with the authorities on absolute territorial protection.

As the Court pointed out in the quoted passage, it is a feature of the competition regime that the Commission enjoys executive powers which can be used against individual undertakings. Anti-competitive exploitation of intellectual property may, for example, be the subject of an order under Article 3(1) of Regulation 17 to terminate an infringement of Article 85 or Article 86; or it may provide grounds for the imposition of a fine under Article 15(2) of the Regulation.[35] No such powers exist in relation to Article 30 (or Article 59). The only action open to the Commission, if national legislation on intellectual property represents an unjustifiable barrier to intra-Community trade, is to bring proceedings under Article 169 against the Member State concerned.

In the definitive phase of the Community both the rules on freedom of movement and the rules on competition are directly effective. However, to make out a case under the competition rules, an individual resisting the exercise of an intellectual property right must be able to show that the right is "the subject, the means or the consequence" of an agreement or concerted practice or that its owner is abusing a dominant position in a substantial part of the common market.[36] Where a choice exists, therefore, Article 30 is likely to be seen by importers as providing a simpler and surer route to success in national proceedings.[37]

---

[34] [1982] E.C.R. at p. 2070.
[35] See Whish, *op. cit.* note 1, p. 570, *supra* at pp. 367–370.
[36] See the discussion at pp. 595–596, *supra.*
[37] The point was first brought home in the *Deutsche Grammophon* judgment: Case 78/70, *loc. cit.* note 57, p. 583, *supra.*

CHAPTER 21

SEX DISCRIMINATION

Article 119—rationale

Article 119 EEC provides that each Member State shall during the first stage ensure and subsequently maintain the application of the principle that men and women should receive equal pay for equal work. According to the Court of Justice, this article pursues a double aim.[1] First, it seeks to avoid a situation in which undertakings established in States which implement the principle of equal pay suffer a competitive disadvantage as compared with undertakings established in States which fail to do so. Secondly, the provision forms part of the social objectives of the Community, which is not merely an economic union, but is intended to ensure social progress and seeks the improvement of the living and working conditions of its peoples. The principle of equal pay thus forms part of the "foundations of the Community," and requires the "levelling up" of women's salaries, rather than the "levelling down" of men's.[2] Fundamental as the principle is, it is limited, as its terms suggest, to pay, and does not extend to securing equality in other terms and conditions of employment. The ingenious argument that the guarantee of equality in pay presumed, and therefore secured implicitly, equality in all conditions of employment has been rejected by the Court.[3]

Direct effect of Article 119

In the landmark judgment of *Defrenne* v. *Sabena*,[4] the Court of Justice upheld the direct effect of Article 119. Miss Gabrielle Defrenne, an air hostess formerly employed in the airline Sabena, had sued her former employer before a Belgian court, claiming compensation for discrimination in terms of the pay she received as compared with male colleagues doing the same work as "cabin stewards." The Belgian court asked the Court of Justice whether Article 119 could be relied upon before national courts, independently of national legal provisions. The Court's answer was a qualified affirmative. The article could be relied upon, as least to the extent that the discrimination alleged was "direct and overt discrimination" which could be identified "solely with the aid of the criteria based on equal work and equal pay referred to by the article in question." In such cases, Article 119 was described as directly applicable and as giving rise to individual rights which national courts must protect. In other cases—described by the Court as cases of "indirect and distinguished discrimination"—judicial

---

[1] Case 43/75, *Defrenne* [1976] E.C.R. 455.
[2] *Ibid* at p. 472, para. 8–15.
[3] Case 148/77, *Defrenne* (No. 2) [1978] E.C.R. 1365.
[4] See note 1.

implementation of Article 119 would have to await the passage of appropriate legislative measures at the Community and national level.

The terminology of "indirect and disguised discrimination" is potentially misleading. It refers in this context only to discrimination which cannot be detected by judicial inquiry in ordinary legal proceedings. It does not refer, for example, to pay structures which can be established to the satisfaction of a judge to be discriminatory in fact, but which apparently provide for equal pay regardless of sex. This latter variety of "indirect" discrimination is certainly caught by directly effective provisions of the Treaty prohibiting discrimination on grounds of nationality,[5] and Article 119 has a similar scope.[6] Thus if an employer pays full-time workers more per hour than part-time workers, and the full-time workers are men, and the part-time workers are women, Article 119 would be directly effective if the employer were unable to establish that the difference in pay was attributable to factors other than sex. This would be the case of indirect discrimination in the more normal sense of the term.[7] If, however, a woman claims that she is being discriminated against by comparison, not with a man actually employed in the undertaking, or even previously employed in the undertaking, but by comparison with what a man would be paid were he in her position, the alleged discrimination is indirect and disguised in the sense that that term is used in *Defrenne*, and while there may indeed be a violation of Article 119, that provision cannot be directly invoked before national courts in such a case.[8]

The Court of Justice gave as examples of direct discrimination which might be identified solely by reference to the criteria laid down in Article 119 "those which have their origin in legislative provisions or in collective agreements and which may be detected on the basis of a purely legal analysis of the situation." This would be the case where men and women received unequal pay for equal work carried out in the same establishment or service, whether public or private.[9] This latter principle will sustain the direct effect of Article 119 in cases where a woman receives less pay than a formerly, but not contemporaneously, employed man doing the same job[10]; where male employees receive an increment to their salary to fund a retirement scheme, which is non-contributory in the case of women[11]; and where part-time workers are paid a lower hourly rate than full-time workers because of their sex.[12] Similarly, where recourse to the criteria of equal work and equal pay, without the operation of Community or national measures, enables a court to establish that the grant of concessionary transport facilities for the families of retired male employees but not for the families of retired female

---

[5] Case 152/73, *Sotgiu* [1974] E.C.R. 153.
[6] The point is made by Adv. Gen. Warner in Case 96/80, *Jenkins Kingsgate (Clothing Productions) Ltd.* [1981] E.C.R. 911 at p. 937.
[7] Case 96/80, note 6.
[8] Case 129/79, *McCarthys* v. *Wendy Smith* [1980] E.C.R. 1288 at p. 1289, para. 15.
[9] Case 53/75, *Defrenne* [1976] E.C.R. 455 at p. 473, paras. 21, 22.
[10] Case 129/79, *McCarthys* v. *Wendy Smith* [1980] E.C.R. 1288.
[11] Case 69/80, *Worringham & Humphreys* v. *Lloyds Bank* [1981] E.C.R. 767.
[12] Case 96/80, *Jenkins* v. *Kingsgate (Clothing Productions) Ltd.* [1981] E.C.R. 911.

employees amounts to discrimination on grounds of sex, the provisions of Article 119 are directly applicable.[13]

Article 119 provides that each Member State shall "during the first stage" ensure sex equality in matters of pay. Thus, for the original six, the equal pay principle was to be "fully secured and irreversible . . . by January 1, 1962."[14] The Resolution of the Member States of December 31, 1961, calling for the phasing out of discrimination in pay by December 31, 1964, was incapable of modifying the time-limit fixed by the Treaty, since, apart from any specific provisions, the Treaty can only be modified by means of the amendment procedure carried out in accordance with Article 236 EEC.[15] Nor could Directive 75/117, designed to eliminate in particular indirect discrimination in pay, modify either the content of Article 119 or the time-limit specified therein.[16]

In the course of the proceedings before the Court in *Defrenne*, both the United Kingdom Government and the Commission argued that Article 119, even if directly effective, could only be invoked as between individuals and the State; it could not be invoked in relations between individuals. The Court rejected this distinction, declaring that:

> "since Article 119 is mandatory in nature, the prohibition on discrimination between men and women applies not only to the action of public authorities but also extends to all agreements which are intended to regulate paid labour collectively, as well as to contracts between individuals."[17]

The way was now clear for individuals to challenge their employers directly on the basis of the EEC Treaty in national courts in cases where they believed themselves victims of sex discrimination in matters of pay.

Despite the applicability of Article 119 from January 1, 1962, objections were raised to its direct effect from that date before the Court in *Defrenne*. The Court held for a number of reasons, discussed elsewhere,[18] that the direct effect of Article 119 could not be relied on in order to support claims concerning pay periods prior to the date of its judgment, except as regards workers who had already brought legal proceedings or made an equivalent claim.[19] Similarly in *Barber* v. *Guardian Royal Exchange Assurance Group*[20] the Court held that the direct effect of Article 119 could be relied upon in order to claim entitlement to a pension with effect from May 17, 1990, the date of the judgment in that case, except in the case of persons or those claiming under them who had already commenced legal proceedings or raised an equivalent claim. Given the duration of the period over which title to an occupational pension is acquired, and the many requirements which

---

[13] Case 12/81, *Garland* v. *BREL* [1981] E.C.R. 359.
[14] Case 43/75, *Defrenne* [1976] E.C.R. 455 at p. 478, para. 56.
[15] *Ibid* at para. 58.
[16] *Ibid* at para. 68.
[17] *Ibid* at para. 39.
[18] See *supra* at p. 63.
[19] Case 43/75, *Defrenne* (1976) E.C.R. 455 at p. 481, para. 75.
[20] Case C–262/88 1990 E.C.R. 1889.

have to be satisfied to acquire a pension, it was unclear when precisely the principle of equality of treatment took effect. Accordingly, the Member States adopted a Protocol to the Treaty of European Union which states that benefits under occupational social security schemes were not to be considered remuneration insofar as they were attributable to periods of employment prior to May 17, 1990 for the purposes of the Treaty establishing the European Community. This limitation does not apply in the case of persons who have, before May 17, 1990, initiated legal proceedings or introduced an equivalent claim under national law.

Equal pay for equal work

Article 119 requires that men and women receive equal pay for equal work. This guarantee extends to both the private and public sectors.[21] The Court of Justice has confirmed in *MacCarthys* v. *Wendy Smith*[22] that a requirement of contemporaneity of employment is not to be read into the Article. Wendy Smith was employed at a salary of £50 per week in a job in which her male predecessor had received £60. The Court of Appeal[23] took the view that the Equal Pay Act 1970 only contemplated comparison between men and women doing the same job at the same time, and asked the Court of Justice for an interpretation of Article 119 EEC in order to establish whether or not it was to be so construed. The Court held that it was not. The only relevant issue was whether or not the work was "equal," and it did not matter whether or not the man and woman whose work and pay were to be compared were employed at the same time in the undertaking or not.

It is unclear whether comparisons may be made with workers in other establishments. In *Commission* v. *Denmark*[24] the Advocate General remarked that Article 119 extended its comparisons to outside the workers' immediate workplace. In *Commission* v. *United Kingdom*,[25] the Court ruled broadly that Directive 75/117 required a worker to be "entitled to claim before an appropriate authority that his work has the same value as other work." *Murphy* v. *An Bord Telecom*[26] established that the principle of equal treatment in Article 119 enabled a comparison to be made between a worker who is engaged in work of higher value than that of the person with whom he or she is being compared.

A problem of "indirect discrimination" in the conventional sense was confronted by the Court in *Jenkins* v. *Kingsgate (Clothing Productions) Ltd.*[27] for the first time. Suppose that all or most part-time workers are women, and part-time workers receive a lower rate of pay then full-time workers. On the face of it, all workers are paid according to criteria which

---

[21] Case 43/75, *Defrenne* (1976) E.C.R. 455; Case 58/81, *Commission* v. *Luxembourg* (1982) E.C.R. 2175.
[22] Case 129/79 [1980] E.C.R. 1288.
[23] [1979] 3 All E.R. 325.
[24] Case 143/83 1985 E.C.R. 437.
[25] Case 165/82 1983 E.C.R. 3426.
[26] Case 157/86 1988 E.C.R. 673.
[27] Case 96/80 [1981] E.C.R. 911.

apply independently of sex. But is the indirect effect of the full-time/part-time differential to discriminate on grounds of sex? In the course of the proceedings before the Court of Justice, the Advocate General observed that in the Community as a whole, about 90 per cent. of part-time workers were women, being mostly married women with family responsibilities. The Court of Justice held that lower rates of pay for part-time workers did not *per se* offend the principle of equal pay insofar as the difference in pay between part-time and full-time work was attributable to factors which were objectively justified and in no way related to discrimination based on sex. In *Rinner-Kuehn*[28] the Court held that if a Member State can show that the means that it has chosen to meet a necessary aim of its social policy are suitable and requisite for that aim, the mere fact that the provision affects a much greater number of female workers than male workers cannot be regarded as constituting an infringement of Article 119.

Whether or not such a provision is objectively justifiable is a matter for national courts to decide. In *Bilka-Kaufhaus*[29] the courts held that it was for national courts to determine whether and to what extent the pay practice of an employer which was applied independently of a worker's sex but in fact affected more men than women could be regarded as objectively justified.[30] Likewise national courts must determine whether, and to what extent, a legislative provision which, although couched in gender-neutral terms, in fact prejudices women more than men, can be objectively justified.[30]

From this case-law it would appear that even if an employer introduced, in good faith, and genuinely believed that his pay policy, comprising pay differentials which adversely affected women, was justified, it could still be struck down as contrary to the principle of equal pay if he could have achieved his objective by other means which would not have resulted in discrimination between men and women in the matter of pay. Where there are several means of attaining a particular objective an employer, or the legislature, must choose that which avoids introducing pay differentials between men and women doing the same job.

The definition of "pay"

Article 119 EEC provides the following definition of "pay":

> "For the purpose of this Article, 'pay' means the ordinary basic or minimum wage or salary and any other consideration, whether in cash or in kind, which the worker receives, directly or indirectly, in respect of his employment from his employer."

The word "consideration" is not used in its English technical contractual sense,[31] and payments in cash or kind in fact made to employees in respect of

---

[28] Case C–171/88 1989 E.C.R. 2743.
[29] Case 170/84 1986 E.C.R. 1607.
[30] *Op. cit.* note 28.
[31] Adv. Gen. Warner in Case 69/80, *Worringham & Humphreys* v. *Lloyds Bank* [1981] E.C.R. 767 at p. 804.

their employment will amount to "pay" whether such payments are legally obligatory or not.[32]

The Court, in the first case which came before it on sex discrimination,[33] held that contributions paid to a State social security scheme by an employer on behalf of his employees were not "pay" in that ". . . the worker will normally receive the benefits legally prescribed not by reason of the employer's contribution but solely because the worker fulfils the legal conditions for the grant of benefits." Likewise social security schemes or benefits were not "pay" because the worker ". . . will normally receive the benefits legally prescribed not by reason of the employer's contribution but solely because the worker fulfils the legal conditions for the grant of benefits."

Any sum which is included in the calculation of gross salary of the employee and directly influences the calculation of other advantages linked to salary forms part of a worker's pay. Such sums do not have to be paid over to the employee. Thus, for example, in *Worringham and Humphreys*,[34] the Court ruled that a contribution to a retirement benefit scheme which was paid directly by an employer in the name of the employee directly to the pension fund but which was included in the calculation of the gross salary of the employee and helped to determine the level of other advantages linked to that salary, such as redundancy payments, unemployment benefits, family allowances and credit facilities, constituted "pay" within the meaning of Article 119. A reduction in the net salary of a male worker because of a contribution paid to a widow's pension fund which in no way affects the amount of gross pay on the basis of which salary-related benefits are calculated, does not offend against Article 119.[35]

In *Rinner-Kuehn*[36] a German law on the continued payment of wages provided that an employer must continue to pay wages for a period of up to six weeks to any employee who, after the commencement of employment and through no fault of his own, is incapable of working. Thereafter the social security system paid, for a statutorily defined period, 80 per cent. of the normal earnings of the worker. The question arose as to whether this continued payment of wages constituted pay for the purposes of Article 119. The Court held that it did. In doing so no distinction was drawn by the Court between the period during which the full salary was being paid by the employer and the subsequent period during which a percentage of it was paid by the social security system. In view of the Court's ruling in *Defrenne*[37] to the effect that benefits payable under a social security system were not pay it seems somewhat surprising that the Court did not choose to make such a distinction. Can one conclude from *Rinner-Kuehn* that a social security

---

[32] Case 69/80, *Worringham & Humphreys* [1981] E.C.R. 767; see Snaith, (1981) E.L. 193. Case 12.81, *Garland* [1982] E.C.R. 359.
[33] Case 80/70, *Defrenne* v. *Belgian State* [1971] E.C.R. 445.
[34] Case 69/80, *Worringham & Humphreys* [1981] E.C.R. 767; Case 23/83, *Liefting* [1984] E.C.R. 5225; Case 170/84, *Bilka-Kaufhaus* [1986].
[35] Case 192/85, *Newstead* 1987 E.C.R. 4753.
[36] Note 28.
[37] Note 33.

benefit, the amount of which is based on a claimant's previous salary and which is designed to replace that salary for a given period of time, is "pay?"

Pay includes benefits paid after the termination of employment. In *Barber*[38] the Court held that it included both redundancy benefits and occupational pensions. The *Barber* case is important in that it establishes finally, after many years of debate in many fora, that occupational pensions are to be considered "pay." Mr. Barber was a member of a pension fund established by the Guardian Royal Exchange Assurance Group ("the Guardian"). Under that scheme the normal pensionable age was 65 years for men and 60 for women. In the event of redundancy members of the pension fund were entitled to an immediate pension subject to having attained the age of 55 for men and 52 for women. Staff who did not fulfil these conditions received certain cash benefits calculated on the basis of their years of service and a deferred pension payable at the normal pensionable age. Mr. Barber was made redundant at the age of 52 years. The Guardian paid him the cash benefits due to him, a statutory redundancy payment and an *ex gratia* payment. He would have been entitled to a retirement pension as from the date of his 62nd birthday. It was undisputed that a woman in the same position would have received an immediate retirement payment and the total value of those benefits would have been greater than the amount paid to Mr. Barber. When the case came before the Court of Justice, by way of a reference for a preliminary ruling from the Court of Appeal, the Court held that the benefit paid by an employer to an employee in connection with the latter's redundancy fell within the scope of Article 119 as did "A pension paid out under a contracted out private occupational scheme . . ."[39]

Conclusion

The Court of Justice has interpreted the concept of pay within the meaning of Article 119 broadly as meaning any consideration received from an employer in respect of employment which affects the level of gross salary and any advantages calculated on the basis of that sum. Benefits which an employee may be entitled to because of his employment but which are not provided by virtue of a contractual relationship with his employer are not pay. An example of such payments would be social security benefits title to which arises under legislation rather than by way of an agreement between employers and their employees.

Although Article 119 requires equal pay for work of equal value, it may be necessary, in order to achieve true equality between the sexes, to discriminate in favour of women in order to enable them to overcome any disadvantages they may suffer in their professional lives which adversely affect their earning power, due to the difficulties of combining responsibilities in the place of work and home.[40] The need for positive discriminatory measures has been recognised under the Protocol on Social

---

[38] Note 20.
[39] *Ibid* at p. 1952, para. 30.
[40] See in general Fredman S., *European Discrimination Law : A Critique* 21 I.L.J. pp. 119–134.

Policy to the Treaty of European Union. It is provided in Article 6(3) of that Protocol that Member States are not to be prevented from

> "maintaining or adopting measures providing for specific advantages in order to make it easier for women to pursue a vocational activity or to prevent or to compensate for disadvantages in their professional careers."

Presumably this provision refers primarily to payments for child care, extra paid holiday to care for children during illness or school holidays, grants to pursue a vocational training course etc. Such extra payments, even if they lead to difference in the gross salary paid to men and women, would not offend against the principle of equality of treatment since their ultimate objective would be to place women in a position where they can compete on an equal footing with men and realise their true earning potential by removing some of the disadvantages to which they are subject by reason of family responsibilities.

Directive 75/117 on equal pay for work of equal value

Article 119 was described by Advocate General Warner in *Worringham & Humphreys* as the "translation" into Community law of the International Labour Organisation's Convention No. 100 dated June 29, 1951 "Concerning equal remuneration for men and women workers for work of equal value."[41] Article 119 provides for equal pay for equal work, irrespective of sex. Article 2 of the ILO Convention provides that "Each Member shall . . . promote and . . . ensure the application to all workers of the principle of equal remuneration for men and women workers for work of equal value." In accordance with this requirement[42] Article 1 of Directive 75/117 provides in part as follows:

> "The principle of equal pay for men and women outlined in Article 119 of the Treaty, hereinafter called "principle of equal pay," means, for the same work or for work to which equal value is attributed, the elimination of all discrimination on grounds of sex with regard to all aspects and conditions of remuneration."

The principal purposes of Directive 75/117 are to make it clear that Article 119 extends to work of equal value as well as the same work, and to facilitate the operation of Article 119 in the field of indirect discrimination, *i.e.* in those situations in which discrimination on grounds of sex cannot be directly determined by national courts without elaboration of further criteria at the legislative level.[43] It would seem to follow that Article 119, properly construed, itself requires equal pay for the same work or work of equal

---

[41] The Convention entered into force on May 23, 1953, and has been ratified by 107 States. See Brownlie, *Basic Documents on Human Rights*, p. 200. UNTS Vol. 1651, p. 304. Bowman & Harris, *Multilateral Treaties*, p. 1951, and Supplements. All Member States have ratified.
[42] Case 43/75, *Defrenne*, [1976] E.C.R. 455 at p. 473, para. 20.
[43] Case 43/74, *Defrenne*, note 33; Case 61/81, *Commission* v. *United Kingdom* [1982] E.C.R. 2601, at p. 2621, *per* Adv. Gen. VerLoren van Themaat.

value.[44] Ensuring equal pay for work of equal value will sometimes involve the direct effect of Article 119, where the discrimination is "direct and overt," that is to say, capable of being identified by reference to Article 119 alone, for example where a collective agreement ascribes equal value to categories of work, but men and women do not receive equal pay for doing work within these categories. On other occasions, securing equal pay for work of equal value will involve eliminating indirect and disguised discrimination, that is to say, discrimination which cannot be detected solely by reference to Article 119, for example by the use of a job classification scheme as provided by national law.[45] In such cases, Article 119 is not of course directly effective, but can only secure equality with the assistance of national implementing rules.

While Article 1 of Directive 75/117 declares that the concept of "same work" contained in the first paragraph of Article 119 EEC includes cases of "work to which equal value is attributed," it does not affect the concept of "pay" contained in the second paragraph of Article 119, but refers by implication to it.[46]

The second paragraph of Article 1 of Directive 75/117 provides:

> "In particular, where a job classification system is used for determining pay, it must be based on the same criteria for both men and women and so drawn up as to exclude any discrimination on grounds of sex."

It was this provision which lay at the heart of a dispute as to the effect of Directive 75/117 between the Commission and the United Kingdom, culminating in legal proceedings before the Court of Justice.[47]

When the terms of the Directive were adopted the United Kingdom secured the inclusion in the minutes of the Council meeting a statement on the interpretation of the words "work to which equal value is attributed" which read:

> "The circumstances in which work is considered in the United Kingdom to have equal value attributed to it are where the work is broadly similar or where pay is based on the results of job evaluation."

Under the British legislation giving effect to Directive 75/117[48] equal pay was required in cases both of a man and woman employed on "like work," and of a man and woman employed on work "rated as equivalent" on the basis of a job evaluation scheme undertaken with the consent of the employer. The Commission took the view that since "like work" did not extend to "work of equal value," and since the latter could only be established if the employer consented to a job evaluation scheme, the United Kingdom had failed to implement Directive 75/117. The matter came before the Court of Justice in proceedings instituted under Article 169 of the Treaty. The United

---

[44] Case 69/80, *Worringham & Humphreys* (1981) E.C.R. 767 at p. 792, para. 23.
[45] See, *e.g.* S.I. 1983 No. 1794, the Equal Pay (Amendment) Regulations.
[46] Case 69/80, *Worringham & Humphreys* [1981] E.C.R. 767 at p. 791, para. 21.
[47] Case 61/81, *Commission* v. *United Kingdom* [1982] E.C.R. 2601. See also on job classification, Case 237/85, *Rummler* 1986 E.C.R. 2101.
[48] The Equal Pay Act, as amended by the Sex Discrimination Act 1975.

Kingdom denied that Article 1 of the Directive gave a right to job evaluation, stressing that the provision referred to work to which "equal value is attributed," which is plainly not the same as work "of equal value." The Court of Justice took the view that the United Kingdom's interpretation amounted to a denial of the very existence of a right to equal pay for work of equal value where no job classification has been undertaken. Where there was disagreement as to the application of the concept of work of equal value to the general scheme, the provisions of Directive 75/117 required that the worker be entitled to claim before an appropriate authority that his work had the same value as the other work in issue. Such a right had not been secured in the United Kingdom, which had accordingly failed to comply with its obligation to implement the Directive. The response to the Court's judgment was the promulgation of the Equal Pay (Amendment) Regulations 1983, which entered into force on January 1, 1984.[49] These Regulations provided, *inter alia*, that an industrial tribunal be empowered to require a member of a panel of independent experts to prepare a report with respect to the question whether or not any work was of equal value to that of a man in the same employment.[50]

Directive 75/117 requires Member States to introduce into their national legal systems such measures as are necessary to enable all employees who consider themselves to have been wronged by failure to apply the principle of equal pay to pursue their claims by judicial process after possible recourse to other competent authorities.[51]

Article 4 of the Directive states:

> "Member States shall take the necessary measures to ensure that provisions appearing in collective agreements, wage scales, wage agreements or individual contracts of employment which are contrary to the principle of equal pay shall be, or may be declared, null or void or may be amended."

This mode of implementation of a non-discrimination guarantee is not unique. Article 7(4) of Regulation 1612/68 provides that classes of collective or individual agreements which discriminate against workers who are nationals of other Member States shall be null and void. Directive 76/207 on equal treatment for men and women in access to employment, etc., has similar provisions.[52] In the case of Article 4 of Directive 75/117 and Article 7(4) of Regulation 1612/68, it is submitted that the provisions in question merely restate guarantees implicit in Article 119 and Article 48 EEC respectively. If discriminatory clauses in agreements are given effect, they are clearly incompatible with the Treaty. If they are not actually enforced, but are nominally in force, or even stand unamended in non-binding

---

[49] S.I. 1983 No. 1794.
[50] Regulations 2 and 3.
[51] Case 43/75, *Defrenne* [1976] E.C.R. 455; Case 58/81, *Commission* v. *Luxembourg* [1982] 2175 at p. 2186, *per* Adv. Gen. VerLoren van Themaat.
[52] Art. 3(2)(b); Art. 4(b); Art. 5(2)(b).

agreements, they are capable of misleading those subject to the law and this is in turn at odds with the non-discriminatory guarantees of the Treaty.[53]

The requirement that Member States take "the necessary measures to protect employees against dismissal by the employer as a reaction to a complaint within the undertaking or to any legal proceedings aimed at enforcing compliance with the principle of equal pay"[54] reiterates a duty inherent in Article 119 itself, as do the terms of Article 6 of the Directive, which enjoins Member States to "take the measures necessary to ensure that the principle of equal pay is applied (and to) see that effective means are available to take care that this principle is observed." Only in its final substantive Article does Directive 75/117 appear to go beyond the requirements of Article 119. Member States are to:

"take care that the provisions adopted pursuant to this Directive, together with the relevant provisions already in force, are brought to the attention of employees by all appropriate means, for example at their place of employment."

It is submitted that the principle of legal certainty combined with Article 119 requires both the amendment of misleading provisions of national laws, regulations, collective agreements, etc.,[55] and the formal publication of national laws clearly implementing Community obligations.[56] Pending such amendments where there are any provisions which indirectly discriminate against one group of workers, the members of that disadvantaged group must be treated in the same way as the group which is not so disadvantaged. In the case of part-time workers which are treated less favourably than full-time workers, they must be treated in the same way and have the same pay system applied to them as that applicable to other workers in proportion to their hours of work.[57]

Directive 76/207 on equal treatment in employment

Article 117 EEC states:

"Member States agree upon the need to promote improved working conditions and an improved standard of living for workers, so as to make possible their harmonisation while the improvement is being maintained.

They believe that such a development will ensue not only from the functioning of the common market, which will favour the harmonisation of social systems, but also from the procedures provided for in this Treaty and from the approximation of provisions laid down by law, regulation or administrative action."

---

[53] Case 167/73, *Commission* v. *French Republic* [1974] E.C.R. 359; Case 165/82, *Commission* v. *United Kingdom* [1983] E.C.R. 3431.
[54] Art. 5.
[55] Case 167/73, *Commission* v. *French Republic* [1974] E.C.R. 359.
[56] Case 143/83, *Commission* v. *Kingdom of Denmark* [1985] E.C.R. 427 at p. 435, paras. 10, 11.
[57] Case 102/88, *Ruzius Wilbrink* 1989 E.C.R. 4311; Case 33/89, *Kowalska* 1990 E.C.R. 985.

The Council of Ministers has concluded that the principle of harmonisation of living and working conditions while maintaining their improvement entails the principle that male and female workers receive equal treatment in access to employment, vocational training, and promotion, and in respect of working conditions.[58] Since the Treaty does not confer the necessary specific powers for this purpose, the Council resorted to Article 235 EEC as the basis of Directive 76/207 on the implementation of the principle of equal treatment for men and women as regards access to employment, vocational training and promotion, and working conditions.[59] The "core" of the Directive constitutes the guarantee of equal treatment in three areas:

— access to all jobs or posts, whatever the sector or branch of activity, and to all levels of the occupational hierarchy (Article 3);
— access to all types and levels of vocational guidance, vocational training, advanced vocational training and retraining (Article 4);
— working conditions, including the conditions governing dismissal (Article 5).

The principle of "equal treatment" is defined as meaning "that there shall be no discrimination whatsoever on grounds of sex either directly or indirectly by reference in particular to marital or family status."

In *Dekker*[60] the Court held that equality of access to jobs meant that an employer could not refuse to engage a pregnant woman who was otherwise suitable for the employment in question. The unfavourable treatment of women on grounds of pregnancy constituted direct discrimination on grounds of sex. With respect to the right of equal treatment in vocational training, the Court in *Danfoss*[61] held that an employer may justify remuneration for special training paid to some employees but not to others by showing that it is of importance for the performance of specific tasks which are entrusted to the employee. Consequently, the fact that vocational training has been made available to a group of employees who are for the most part male, does not necessarily mean that the principle of equality of treatment has been violated provided that the employer has an objective reason for offering that training to that group of workers rather than to any other members of the workforce.

The concept of dismissal in Article 5(1) of the Directive must be given a wide interpretation. The question arose in *Burton* v. *BRB*[62] whether or not the word "dismissal" in Article 5(1) of the Directive could be construed to include termination of the employment relationship between a worker and his employer even as part of a voluntary redundancy scheme. The Court held that it did indeed extend to access to a voluntary redundancy scheme. Similarly an age limit for the compulsory redundancy of workers as part of a

---

[58] Directive 76/207, preamble.
[59] O.J. 1976 L39/40. Art. 2(1), in conjunction with Arts. 3(1), 4(1), and 5(1), may be relied on in national courts, at least as against public authorities: Case 152/84, *Marshall* 1986 E.C.R. 723; Case 222/84, *Johnston* 1986 E.C.R. 1651.
[60] Case 177/88 1990 E.C.R. I 3941.
[61] Case 109/88 1989 E.C.R. 3199.
[62] Case 19/81 1982 E.C.R. 555.

mass redundancy falls within the term "dismissal" even if the redundancy involves the granting of an early retirement pension.[63] Compulsory retirement also constitutes "dismissal."[64]

A woman is protected from dismissal during the period of maternity leave accorded to her under national law. The Directive does not preclude dismissals resulting from absences from work due to illness which originated in pregnancy or confinement.[65]

Application of the principle of equal treatment in the three areas referred to above—access to employment, vocational training, and working conditions—is to be secured in each case by Member States taking the measures necessary to ensure that:

— any laws, regulations and administrative provisions contrary to the principle of equal treatment shall be abolished (Articles 3(2)(a); 4(a); 5(2)(a));
— any provisions contrary to the principle of equal treatment which are included in collective agreements, individual contracts of employment, internal rules of undertakings or in rules governing the independent occupations and professions shall be, or may be declared, null and void or may be amended (Articles 3(2)(b); 4(6); 5(2)(b)).

The Court has held[66] that in order to comply with the above requirements, it is not enough that national law ordains the invalidity of binding agreements containing offending clauses. National rules must go further and secure that where such clauses are to be found in non-binding agreements (as are most collective agreements in the United Kingdom) they can be "rendered operative, eliminated or amended by appropriate means." The reasoning of the Court was to the effect that even non-binding collective agreements have important *de facto* consequences for the employment relationships to which they refer.

With respect to equal treatment in access to employment, and in working conditions, Member States are required to take the measures necessary to ensure that:

"those laws, regulations and administrative provisions contrary to the principle of equal treatment when the concern for protection which originally inspired them is no longer well founded shall be revised; and that where similar provisions are included in collective agreements labour and management shall be requested to undertake the desired revision." (Articles 3(2)(c); 5(2)(c)).

In the case of vocational training, this provision is not appropriate, and it is instead the duty of Member States to take measures to ensure that, without prejudice to the freedom granted in certain Member States to certain private

---

[63] Case 151/84 1986 E.C.R. 703.
[64] Case 152/85 1986 E.C.R. 723.
[65] Case C–177/88, *Vibeke Hertz* 1990 E.C.R. I–394.
[66] Case 165/82, *Commission* v. *United Kingdom* [1983] E.C.R. 3431.

training establishments, vocational guidance, training and retraining shall be accessible without discrimination on grounds of sex (Article 4(c)).

Article 2(2) of Directive 76/207 provides that the Directive shall be "without prejudice to the right of Member States to exclude from its field of application those occupational activities and, where appropriate, the training leading thereto, for which, by reason of their nature or the context in which they are carried out, the sex of the worker constitutes a determining factor." The Court was called upon to define the ambit of the provision in *Commission* v. *United Kingdom*.[67] The Sex Discrimination Act 1975 provided for exceptions to the principle of equal treatment: (i) where employment was in a private household; (ii) where the number of persons employed by an employer did not exceed five[68] and (iii) where the employment, promotion and training of midwives was concerned.[69] In the first two cases, the Court held the British legislation to be incompatible with Directive 76/207. It observed that the "private household" exception was designed to reconcile the principle of equality of treatment with the principle of respect for family life, which was also fundamental, and acknowledged that, for certain kinds of employment in private households, that consideration might be decisive. However, that could not be the case for all the kinds of employment in question. As far as the "small business" exception was concerned, the Court noted that the United Kingdom had not put forward any argument to show that in such undertakings the sex of the worker could be a determining factor by reason of the nature of his activities or the context in which they were carried out. It followed that the "private household" and "small business" exceptions contained in section 6(3) of the 1975 Act, by their very generality, went further than was necessary to secure the objectives of Article 2(2) of the Directive. The Court took a different view of the restrictions imposed in the United Kingdom upon the entry of men into the midwifery profession. Under the 1975 Act[70] until a day to be specified by order of the Secretary of State, men were granted access to the occupation in question and could be trained for that purpose only in certain specific places. It was argued that this situation was due to the fact that in the United Kingdom the occupation in question was not traditionally engaged in by men. Fears were expressed in particular that women from ethnic minorities might refuse medical services provided by male midwives. Since patients' sensitivities were of particular importance, the United Kingdom argued that the restrictions in issue were consistent with Article 2(2) of the Directive. Advocate General Rozés did not think that a restriction on entry for men was justified, and expressed the view that the guarantee of a free choice for patients, while admittedly necessary, would also be sufficient to allay the fears expressed by the United Kingdom Government. The Court upheld the position of the latter. It recognised that at the present time personal sensibilities played an important rôle in relations between midwife

---

[67] Note 66.
[68] s.6(3).
[69] s.20.
[70] Sched. 4, para. 3.

and patient, and that accordingly the United Kingdom had not exceeded the limits of the power granted to Member States under Article 2(2) of the Directive. It is interesting to note that the United Kingdom had, before judgment was given, issued orders under the 1975 Act bringing to an end the restrictions on access by men to the profession of midwifery.

The Court has held that a policy of not recruiting women for armed police duties on the grounds that women would make easy targets for terrorists, who might then acquire their firearms, was capable of justification under Article 2(2) of the Directive.[71]

It is clear that the Court will construe broadly the guarantees of equality contained in the Directive, and narrowly the exceptions referred to therein.

The Directive is stated to be "without prejudice" to: (i) provisions concerning the protection of women, particularly as regards pregnancy and maternity[72]; (ii) measures to promote equal opportunities, in particular by removing existing inequalities which affect women's opportunities.[73] Without referring expressly to the Directive's proviso for measures concerning the protection of women, the Court has upheld "maternity" leave for women, but not for men, immediately after a child under six years of age is adopted into the family. This differentiation between men and women was said to be justified "by the legitimate concern to assimilate as far as possible the conditions of entry of the child into the adoptive family to those of the arrival of a newborn child in the family during the very delicate initial period."[74] The case may turn on the protection of women proviso, or on the Court's concern for the integrity of family life,[75] or on the broader principle that differentiation on objective grounds compatible with the Treaty is not unlawful discrimination.[76] The Court has upheld maternity leave after childbirth for women, on the basis of the Directive's proviso for measures concerning the protection of women, and confirmed that such leave may be denied to men, even if such leave is claimed as an alternative to leave by the mother.[77]

The Directive's proviso for the protection of women is to be construed strictly. It is intended to protect a women's biological condition and the special relationship which exists between a woman and her child. It does not allow women to be excluded from a certain type of employment on the ground that public opinion demands that women be given greater protection than men against risks which affect men and women in the same way and which are distinct from women's specific needs of protection.[78]

Although Directive 76/207 conditions the interpretation and application of legislation adopted to give effect to its terms, it does not contain any sufficiently precise obligation to enable an individual to obtain a specific

---

[71] Case 222/84, *Johnston* 1986 E.C.R. 1651.
[72] Art. 2(3).
[73] Art. 2(4).
[74] Case 163/82, *Commission* v. *Italian Republic* [1983] E.C.R. 3273.
[75] *Commission* v. *United Kingdom*, note 66.
[76] Case 172/73, *Sotgui* [1974] E.C.R. 153.
[77] Case 184/83, *Hofmann* [1984] E.C.R. 3042.
[78] Note 71.

remedy under the Directive when that is not provided for or permitted by national law.[79]

Directive 79/7 on equal treatment in social security matters

The Commission's first draft of what was to become Directive 76/207 applied also to equality in social security matters.[80] But the Member States objected, and it was excluded from the draft Directive in 1976.[81] Article 1(2), Directive 76/207 provided only that "with a view to ensuring the progressive implementation of the principle of equal treatment in matters of social security, the Council, acting on a proposal from the Commission, will adopt provisions defining its substance, its scope and the arrangements for its application." In accordance with this mandate, the Council promulgated Directive 79/7 on the progressive implementation of the principle of equal treatment for men and women in matters of social security.[82] The Member States were obliged to bring their laws into line with the Directive by December 23, 1984. In fact by that date many Member States had done little to implement it. Inequalities still abound leading to not inconsiderable litigation before national courts which in turn resulted in references for preliminary rulings to the Court of Justice. The essential question raised in the earlier cases concerned the direct effect of the principle of equality of treatment set out in Article 4(1) of the Directive. Could that provision be relied upon by claimants to enforce their rights under the Directive after December 23, 1984 in the absence of national implementing measures? The Court held that it could. In the *FNV* case[83] the Court held that Article 4(1) precludes generally and equivocally all discrimination on the grounds of sex as from the date of its required implementation into national law:

> "Article 4(1) of the Directive does not confer on Member States the power to make conditions or to limit the application of the principle of equal treatment within this field of application and so is sufficiently precise and unconditional to allow individuals, in the absence of implementing measures adopted within the prescribed time, to rely upon it before national courts as from December 23, 1984 in order to preclude the application of any national provision inconsistent with that Article."

The Court confirmed this ruling in the subsequent cases of *Borrie Clark*[84] and *McDermott and Cotter*,[85] stressing in the latter that in the absence of

---

[79] Case 14/83, *Von Colson* [1984] E.C.R. 1891; Case 79/83, *Harz* [1984] E.C.R. 1921.
[80] COM (75) 36 Final, February 2, 1975.
[81] O'Donovan, "The Impact of Entry into the European Community on Sex Discrimination in British Social Security Law" in J. Adams (ed.), *Essays for Clive Schmitthoff*, p. 87. The "social security" exception to Dir. 76/707 is to be strictly construed: Case 152/84, *Marshall* 1986 E.C.R. 723; Case 151/84, *Roberts* 1986 E.C.R.703 4; Case 262/84, *Beets-Proper* 1986 E.C.R. 773.
[82] O.J. 1979, L6/24.
[83] Case 71/85 1986 E.C.R. 3855.
[84] Case 384/85 1987 E.C.R. 2863.
[85] Case 286/85 1987 E.C.R. 1453.

national measures implementing the principle of equal treatment women are entitled to have the same rules applied to them as men who are in the same situation since, where the Directive has not been implemented, these rules remain the only valid point of reference.

Thus in *Cotter and McDermott*[86] the Court ruled that, after December 23, if married men were entitled under national law to receive automatically increases in social security benefits in respect of their spouses and children without having to prove actual dependency, married women in the same circumstances without actual dependants are entitled to such increases even if this results in the double payment of such increases to some families.

The direct applicability of the principle of equal treatment in Article 4(1) of the Directive means that national procedural rules cannot bar any claims made on the basis of the Directive where it has not been implemented. In *Emmott*[87] the Irish Government had argued before the High Court in Ireland that a claim by Mrs. Emmott to the same amount of invalidity benefits as a married man was time-barred. Fortunately when the case was referred to the Court of Justice, it rejected the argument. Any other result could potentially have reduced the rights of individuals to enforce their directly effective Community Law rights before national courts.

The purpose of Directive 79/7 is the progressive implementation of the principle of equal treatment for men and women in matters of social security.[88] It applies to the working population, employed and self-employed alike, and includes those whose work has been interrupted by illness, accident or involuntary unemployment. It also applies to persons seeking employment, and to retired and invalided workers.[89]

In *Drake*,[90] Mrs. Drake gave up paid employment to look after her severely disabled mother. The question arose as to whether Mrs. Drake could be considered to be a person covered by Article 2 of the Directive; she had been in paid employment but was not actually working at the time that she sought to enforce the principle of equal treatment under the Directive nor was she actively seeking employment. In spite of this the Court held:

> "Under Article 2 the term 'working population' which determines the scope of the Directive, is defined broadly ... That provision is based on the idea that a person whose work has been interrupted by one of the risks referred to in Article 3, namely the invalidity of her mother. She must therefore be regarded as a member of the working population for the purposes of the Directive."

It is plain, however, that only those who have been and are normally economically active will fall within the scope of the Directive. In *Acterberg-te-Riele*,[91] the Court held that Article 2 covered only those persons who were working at the time they became entitled to claim an old-age pension or

---

[86] Case C–377/89 1991 E.C.R. 1155.
[87] Case C–208/90. I–4269.
[88] Art. 1.
[89] Art. 2.
[90] Case 150/85 1986 E.C.R. 1995.
[91] Case 48/88 1989 E.C.R. 1905.

whose occupational activity was previously interrupted by one of the risks set out in Article 3 of the Directive.

Benefits

Article 3(1) provides that the Directive shall apply to:

"(a) Statutory schemes which provide protection against the following risks:
— sickness;
— invalidity;
— old age;
— accidents at work and occupational diseases;
— unemployment.
(b) social assistance, insofar as it is intended to supplement or replace the schemes referred to in (a)."

Article 3(2) adds that:

"This Directive shall not apply to the provisions concerning survivors' benefits nor to those concerning family benefits, except in the case of family benefits granted by way of increases in benefits due in respect of the risks referred to in paragraph 1(a)."

The principle of equal treatment, set out in Article 4(1), means that there shall be no discrimination whatsoever on grounds of sex either directly, or indirectly, by reference in particular to marital or family status.[92] This guarantee of equal treatment applies in particular to the scope of social security schemes, and the conditions of access thereto, to the obligations to contribute and the calculation of contributions, and to the calculation of benefits, including increases due in respect of a spouse and dependants, and the conditions governing the duration and retention of entitlement to benefits.[93] The principle of equal treatment, however, shall be without prejudice to provisions relating to the protection of women on grounds of maternity. Both direct and indirect discrimination are prohibited. In *Teuling Worms*[94] the Court held that a system of benefits in which supplements are provided, which takes into account the marital status or the family situation of the claimant with the result that a considerably smaller proportion of women than of men are entitled to such supplements, is contrary to Article 4(1) unless it can be objectively justified. In *Ruzius-Wilbrink*[95] the Court found that no such objective justification existed for treatment of the entitlement to invalidity benefits of part-time workers differently from that of full-time workers. Under Dutch law a minimum subsistence income

---

[92] Art. 4(1).
[93] Art. 4(1). Art. (4)(1) may be invoked before national courts against incompatible national legislation: see Case 71/85, *Federatie Nederlandse Vakbeweging*, 1986 E.C.R. 3855.
[94] Art. 4(2).
[95] Case 30/85 1987 E.C.R. 2497.

benefit was paid in respect of invalidity except in the case of part-time workers who received a rate of benefit linked to their previous salary. The Court rejected the argument of the Dutch Government to the effect that the system was designed to prevent part-time workers from receiving benefits which were worth more than their previous salary.

In *Drake*[96] the Court held that the Directive applied to an invalid care allowance payable to a person caring for an invalid, where the allowance was not payable to a married woman living with her husband and maintained by him, but was payable to a married man in similar circumstances.

In *Smithson*[97] the Court ruled that a benefit, in order to come within the scope of Directive 79/7, had "to be directly and effectively linked to the protection provided against one of the risks specified in Article 3(1)." Consequently a housing benefit, the amount of which was calculated on the basis of the relationship between a notional income to which the beneficiary was deemed to be entitled and his or her actual income, was not within the scope of the Directive even if the benefits paid in respect of some of the risks covered by the Directive, such as sickness and invalidity, were taken into account in order to determine the amount of the notional income. There must therefore be a direct link between the benefit and one of the risks covered by the Directive. Similarly in *Jackson and Cresswell*[98] the Court held that a general benefit such as a supplementary allowance or income support granted to persons whose means are insufficient to meet their needs as defined by statute did not come within the scope of Article 3(1) of Directive 79/7. From *Smithson*[99] and *Jackson and Cresswell* it can be concluded that a general benefit, designed to provide for those who have insufficient resources to provide for their own needs, falls outside the scope of the Directive: to come within the Directive the benefit must be designated to cover one of the risks enumerated in the Directive.

Exceptions

The Directive has a number of exceptions to the principle of equal treatment; for example it is "without prejudice to the right of Member States to exclude from its scope . . . the determination of pensionable age for the purposes of granting old-age and retirement pensions and the possible consequences thereof for other benefits."[1] The effect of this proviso was illustrated in *Burton* v. *BRB*.[2] British Rail had offered voluntary early retirement for workers whose jobs had been the subject of reorganisation. The qualifying age was 55 for women, but 60 years for men. Mr. Burton, aged 58 years, applied for voluntary early retirement, but was rejected as being ineligible. He claimed that he had been discriminated against on grounds of sex. The Court of Justice held that access to the voluntary early

---

[96] Note 90.
[97] Case C–243/90. Judgment of February 4, 1992.
[98] Joined Cases C–63/91 and C–64/91. Judgments of July 16, 1992.
[99] *Ibid.*
[1] Art. 7(1)(a).
[2] Case 19/81 [1982] E.C.R. 555.

retirement scheme fell within the scope of Directive 76/207, but that the differential qualifying ages were justified in Community law because they were linked to the differential minimum qualifying ages for a State retirement pension—60 for women and 65 for men. The link was established by the availability of a number of social security benefits for those taking advantage of the early retirement scheme, provided they retired within five years of the normal retirement age. Since Directive 79/7 excluded retirement age from the principle of equal treatment, an early retirement scheme linked to pensionable age fell outside the ambit of Directive 76/207. However, the Court has held that the proviso cannot justify compulsory retirement at a discriminatory pensionable age.[3] In *The Queen* v. *Secretary of State for Social Security*,[4] the Court held that Article 7(1) could justify inequality with respect to the number of contributions required to be paid in order to gain title to a full retirement pension: men could be lawfully obliged to pay contributions for 44 years but women only for 39 years for the same amount of benefit.

Directive 86/378 on equal treatment in occupational social security schemes

In the first *Defrenne* case the Court held that Article 119 did not apply to statutory social security schemes.[5] For certain such schemes the principle of equal treatment is, however, applicable by virtue of Directive 79/7.[6] But this Directive does not apply to occupational schemes based on private law. These latter schemes will fall within the scope of Article 119 to the extent that the benefits can be regarded as deferred earnings, and hence "pay." To the extent that the discrimination in question is "direct and overt,"[7] Article 119 can be relied upon before national courts, but in the case of "indirect and disguised" discrimination[8] the adoption of additional measures is required to secure implementation of the principle of equal pay. Directive 86/378[9] is calculated to provide such an additional measure, and thus to apply the principle of equal treatment to occupational social security schemes which fall outside the scope of Directive 79/7.

The scope of application of Directive 86/378 has been reduced as a result of the decision of the Court of Justice in *Barber*[10] to the effect that "occupational pensions" are to be considered "pay." Henceforth the Directive, in the sphere of pensions, will be confined to those situations which involve indirect discrimination and so cannot be dealt with purely on the basis of Article 119.

"Occupational social security schemes" are schemes which are not

---

[3] Case 152/84, *Marshall*; Case 262/84, *Beets-Proper*, Note 81.
[4] Case C–9/91. Judgment of July 9, 1992.
[5] *Supra* at p. 621.
[6] *Supra*.
[7] *Supra* at pp. 623–624.
[8] *Supra* at p. 269.
[9] O.J. 1986 L225/40.
[10] Note 20.

governed by Directive 79/7, and whose purpose is to provide employed or self-employed persons with benefits intended to supplement the benefits provided by statutory social security schemes or to replace them, whether membership of such schemes is compulsory or optional.[11] The Directive does not, however, apply to: (a) individual contracts; (b) schemes having only one member; and (c) in the case of salaried workers, insurance schemes offered to participants individually to guarantee them either additional benefits, or a choice of date on which the normal benefits will start, or a choice between several benefits.[12] The Directive applies to members of the working population, including self-employed persons, persons whose activity is interrupted by illness, maternity, accident or involuntary unemployment, and persons seeking employment, and to retired and disabled workers.[13]

The following schemes are covered by the Directive:

> (*a*) occupational schemes which provide protection against the following risks:
> — sickness,
> — invalidity,
> — old age, including early retirement,
> — industrial accidents and occupational diseases,
> — unemployment;
> (*b*) occupational schemes which provide for other social benefits, in cash or in kind, and in particular survivors' benefits and family allowance, if such benefits are accorded to employed persons and thus constitute a consideration paid by the employer to the worker by reason of the latter's employment.[14]

Under the conditions laid down in the Directive, the principle of equal treatment requires that there shall be no discrimination on the basis of sex, either directly or indirectly, by reference in particular to marital or family status, especially as regards:

> — the scope of the schemes and the conditions of access to them;
> — the obligation to contribute and the calculation of contributions;
> — the calculation of benefits, including supplementary benefits due in respect of a spouse or dependants, and the conditions governing the duration and retention of entitlement to benefits.[15]

Examples of provisions of schemes covered by the principle of equal treatment are listed,[16] and include:

---

[11] Art. 2(1).
[12] Art. 2(2).
[13] Art. 3.
[14] Art. 4.
[15] Art. 5(1). The principle of equal treatment shall not however prejudice the provisions relating to the protection of women by reason of maternity.
[16] Art. 6.

— setting different conditions for the granting of benefits or restricting such benefits to workers of one or other of the sexes[17];
— fixing different retirement ages[18];
— suspending the retention or acquisition of rights during periods of maternity leave or leave for family reasons which are granted by law or agreement and are paid by the employer[19];
— setting different levels of benefit, except insofar as may be necessary to take account of actuarial calculation factors which differ according to sex in the case of benefits designated as contribution-defined.[20]

Where the granting of benefits within the scope of this Directive is left to the discretion of the scheme's management bodies, the latter must take account of the principle of equal treatment.[21] Member States are obliged to take all necessary steps to ensure that:

(a) provisions contrary to the principle of equal treatment in legally compulsory collective agreements, staff rules or undertakings or any other arrangements relating to occupational schemes are null and void, or may be declared null and void or amended;
(b) schemes containing such provisions may not be approved or extended by administrative measures.[22]

All necessary steps are to be taken by Member States to ensure that the provisions of occupational schemes contrary to the principle of equal treatment are revised by January 1, 1993.[23] However, the Directive does not preclude rights and obligations relating to a period of membership of an occupational scheme prior to revision of that scheme from remaining subject to the provisions of the scheme in force during that period.[24] Application of the principle of equal treatment may be deferred in several cases, in particular with respect to the determination of pensionable age for the purposes of granting old-age or retirement pensions.[25] Member States are obliged to introduce measures to comply with the Directive by July 30, 1989.[26]

Directive 86/613 on equal treatment in self-employment

The purposes of Directive 86/613[27] are to extend the application of Directive 76/207 to self-employed persons, and to secure application of the

---

[17] Art. 6(1)(e).
[18] Art. 6(1)(f).
[19] Art. 6(1)(g).
[20] Art. 6(1)(h).
[21] Art. 6(2).
[22] Art. 7.
[23] Art. 8(1).
[24] Art. 8(2).
[25] Art. 9.
[26] Art. 12(1).
[27] O.J. 1986 L359/56.

principle of equal treatment in cases where the self-employed person and his or her spouse are engaged together in the same work.

The Directive applies to self-employed workers, *i.e.* to all persons pursuing a gainful activity on their own account, including farmers and members of the liberal professions, and to their spouses, not being employees or partners, where they habitually participate in the activities of the self-employed worker and perform the same tasks or ancillary tasks.[28]

For the purposes of the Directive the principle of equal treatment requires the absence of all discrimination on grounds of sex, either directly or indirectly, by references in particular to marital or family status.[29]

As regards self-employed persons, Member States are obliged to take all necessary measures to ensure the elimination of all provisions which are contrary to the principle of equal treatment as defined in Directive 76/207, especially in respect of the establishment, equipment or extension of the business or the launching or extension of any other form of self-employed activity including financial facilities.[30]

Without prejudice to the specific conditions for access to certain activities which apply equally to both sexes, Member States shall take the measures necessary to ensure that the conditions for the formation of a company between spouses are not more restrictive than the conditions for the formation of a company between unmarried persons.[31]

Where a contributory social security system for self-employed workers exists in a Member State, that Member State shall take the necessary measures to enable those spouses who participate in the work of the self-employed worker and who are not protected under the self-employed worker's social security scheme to join a contributory social security scheme voluntarily.[32]

Member States are obliged to bring into force the measures necessary to comply with the Directive by June 30, 1989.[33]

Conclusions

In spite of the Community's extensive legislative programme differences in the pay and employment conditions of men and women persist. Accordingly the Commission, since 1982, has adopted a series of Action programmes designed to make equality in the workplace a reality. The latest of these programmes, entitled "Equal Opportunities for Men and Women: Third Action Programme" (1991–1995) lays down three priority courses of

---

[28] Art. 2.
[29] Art. 3.
[30] Art. 4.
[31] Art. 5.
[32] Art. 6.
[33] Art. 12(1); if a Member State has to amend its legislation on matrimonial rights and obligations in order to secure the principle of equal treatment in the formation of companies the final date for compliance was June 30, 1991.

action: (1) application and development of existing legislation; (ii) the promotion of the occupational integration of women; (iii) improving the status of women in society. In addition the Commission has proposed to the Council the adoption of a Recommendation on Child Care to enable women with small children to maintain or to re-enter the labour market.[34]

---

[34] COM (91) 233 Final.

CHAPTER 22

VOCATIONAL TRAINING

Article 128 EEC empowers the Council, acting on a proposal from the Commission and after consulting the Economic and Social Committee to "lay down general principles for implementing a vocational training policy capable of contributing to the harmonious development of both the national economies and of the common market." For many years little activity, on a Community level, occurred in the field of vocational training; the wording of Article 128 was broad and general, consequently the extent of the powers of the Commission to propose, and the Council to adopt, measures dealing with vocational training were uncertain. Apart from Decision 63/266[1] which stated that ". . . every person should, during different stages of his working life be able to receive adequate basic and advanced training and any necessary retraining," there was no serious effort to formulate a Community vocational training policy until the Court had indicated firmly in a series of preliminary rulings during the 1980s that vocational training fell within the scope of the EEC Treaty and that budgetary provision could be made for the realisation of Community vocational training programmes.[2]

This chapter will discuss the role of the Community in the field of vocational training under two headings: the right of students to move freely throughout the Community, to take up residence and to pursue a course of vocational training studies in any Member State and the creation, by means of legislation, of a Community vocational training policy which sets minimum standards for such training. To these two aspects of vocational training a third dimension must be added: the prohibition, under Community law, of any discrimination between men and women on the one hand, and nationals and non-nationals on the other, with regard to access to vocational training courses. It will be recalled[3] that Article 7(3) of Directive 1612/68[4] gives migrant workers the right to vocational training on the same conditions as nationals of the host Member State. Similarly by virtue of Article 12 of the same Regulation the child of a migrant worker has the right to be admitted to the host State's ". . . general, educational, apprenticeship and vocational training courses under the same conditions as nationals of that State." Directive 76/207 on equality of treatment between men and women,[5] provides, in its Article 4, that male and female workers should be given equality of treatment with respect to access to all types and levels of vocational training.

---

[1] O.J. English Sp.Ed. 1963/64 at p. 25.
[2] Case 242/87, *Commission* v. *Council* 1989 E.C.R. 1425.
[3] See Chap. 9.
[4] Reg. 1612/68 on the free movement of workers within the Community, J.O. 1968 L257/2.
[5] O.J. 1976 L39/40.

COMMUNITY—WIDE VOCATIONAL TRAINING: FREE MOVEMENT FOR STUDENTS

The right of students to move freely throughout the Community in order to take up and pursue vocational training studies in any Member State of their choice has been affirmed by the Court of Justice in a fairly sizeable, but complex, body of case-law beginning in 1983 with the case of an Italian national, resident in Belgium who wished to pursue, in that country, a three-year course which would qualify her to practice as a social worker. Mrs. Forcheri was married to a Commission official, also of Italian nationality.[6] When she applied to the Institut Superieur de Sciences Humaines Appliquees she was required to pay an enrolment fee described as a "fee for foreign students," commonly known in Belgium as the "Minerval." The fee was not charged to Belgian students. Mrs. Forcheri contested the right of the Belgian authorities to charge this fee in the light of Articles 7, 48 and 49 of the EEC Treaty. The Court ruled that ". . . although educational and vocational training policy is not as such part of the areas which the Treaty has allotted to the competence of the Community institutions . . ." the Treaty did, in Article 128, empower the Council to "lay down general principles for implementing a common vocational training policy."

> "Consequently if a Member State organizes educational courses relating in particular to vocational training, to require a national of another Member State lawfully established in the first Member State an enrolment fee which is not required of its own nationals in order to take part in such courses constitutes discrimination by reason of nationality, which is prohibited by Article 7 of the Treaty."

Subsequently case-law has clarified the precise scope of the concept of vocational training. In *Gravier* v. *City of Liege*[7] a case involving a French national who wished to study the art of strip cartoon design in Liege, the Court defined vocational training as ". . . any form of education which prepares for a qualification for a particular profession, trade or employment or which provides the necessary skills for such a profession, trade or employment is vocational training whatever the age and level of the pupil or student."

In *Blaizot*[8] the Court was confronted with the interesting question of whether a course of studies, the first part of which was general in nature and therefore not in itself leading to any qualification for a particular trade profession or employment, and the second part of which did lead to such a

---

[6] Case 152/82 1983 E.C.R. 2323. It is of interest to note that the Court held that Community officials, although not strictly speaking workers within the meaning of the Treaty, did fall within the scope of the latter and must therefore enjoy all the benefits flowing from Community law for the nationals of Member States relating to the free movement of workers.

[7] Case 293/83 1985 E.C.R. 606. See *ERASMUS* judgment, Case 242/87, note 2, paras. 24–26. It is of interest to note that the concept of vocational training in Art. 7(3) of Reg. 1612/68 is narrower than that contained in Article 128 of the EEC Treaty. See Case 39/86, *Lair* 1988 E.C.R. 3161. Judgment, para. 26.

[8] Case 24/86 1988 E.C.R. 355.

qualification, was to be classified as being vocational as a whole or whether only the second part could be so classified. The course in question was that of veterinary medicine. Blaizot and 16 other students, all of French nationality, were studying veterinary medicine in four Belgian universities. In the wake of the *Gravier* judgment they brought an action against the refusal of their respective universities to repay them the supplementary enrolment fee, the "minerval," which they had paid prior to February 13, 1985, the date of the judgment in *Gravier*. The question arose as to whether university studies in veterinary medicine fell within the meaning of the term "vocational training." It appears that a course of studies in leading to a qualification in veterinary medicine in Belgium consists initially of three years of study leading to the award of a preliminary diploma entitled a "candidature" and a further three years leading to the award of a doctorate. The Belgian universities in question and the Belgian government argued that the candidature and the doctorate represented two separate types of studies, one academic, the other vocational. Studies leading to the "candidature" could not be regarded as vocational training since in order to take up and pursue the profession of veterinary medicine a student must complete the further period of study leading to the doctorate, his final degree. The Court did not accept this argument. It held that vocational training included studies ". . . not only where the final examination directly provided the required qualification for a particular profession, trade or employment but also in so far as the studies in question provide specific training and skills, that is where a student needs the knowledge so acquired for the pursuit of a profession, trade or employment . . ." University studies, in general, the Court held fulfilled these criteria. The only exception would be certain courses of study which, because of their general nature, were intended for persons wishing to improve their general knowledge rather than prepare themselves for an occupation. The fact that university studies were divided into two stages could not be taken into account in deciding whether they were of a vocational training nature or not. Access to a second state leading to the final diploma or degree, is conditional on completion of the first stage so that the two stages together must be regarded as a single unit. It was not possible to make a distinction between one stage which did not constitute vocational training and a second which did.

The Court's ruling in *Blaizot* thus brought most university studies within the scope of the concept of vocational training and so required access to university education to be made available on the same terms to nationals and non-nationals alike. It is of interest to note that in *Lair* v. *University of Hanover*[9] it was not disputed in proceedings before the Administrative Court of Hanover that a course in Romance and Germanic languages and literature constituted vocational training. One would imagine that this was precisely the type of course that the Court had in mind in *Blaizot* as being outside the ambit of the concept of vocational training, since it appears to

---

[9] Case 39/86 1988 E.C.R. 3161.

have as its objective the improvement of the general knowledge of the student rather than to equip him for a particular profession.

In *Belgian State* v. *Humbel*[10] the Court reiterated its ruling in *Blaizot* to the effect that the various years of any study programme which forms "a single coherent unit" cannot be split up into "academic years" and "vocational training years." It is for national courts to determine whether a particular course of study is or is not a single coherent unit. In that particular case the Court had to consider the nature of secondary education, which consisted of a programme of study lasting a total of six years made up of three consecutive stages—an "observation" stage, a "guidance" stage and a "determination" stage. The latter stage, it would appear, consisted of technical training and was regarded under national law as being vocational training. Could therefore the whole course of studies be so classified? The Court held that the various years of a study programme could not be assessed individually but must be considered within the framework of the programme as a whole "particularly in the light of the programme's purpose, provided that the programme formed a coherent single entity." Whether this was the case or not was for the national court to decide.

Grants and scholarships

The right of a Community citizen to equality of treatment with respect to grants and scholarships awarded by the host Member State to its nationals and residents is dependent upon two factors: firstly, the purpose of the grant or scholarship and secondly, upon the status of the student in question.

Financial assistance for the purpose of meeting the cost of registration and other fees charged for access to vocational training courses must be granted to non-nationals on the same terms as nationals: such grants form part of the conditions of access to vocational training and therefore discrimination on the grounds of nationality is prohibited by virtue of Article 7 of the EEC Treaty.[11]

The determination of rights to maintenance and training grants is a more complex issue. A migrant worker may claim such a grant from the host Member State on the basis of Article 7(2) of Regulation 1612/68, which, it will be recalled, gives him the right to the same social and tax advantages as nationals of the host Member State. However, this right is subject to two conditions: firstly there must, in general, be "some continuity between the previous occupation and the course of study"[12] and secondly the migrant worker must have pursued his employment as an end in itself. Where a person becomes employed in a Member State with a view to undertaking studies there, that employment being ". . . merely ancillary to the studies to be financed by the grant" does not entitle him to receive, by virtue of Article 7(2) of Regulation 1612/68, the same maintenance allowance as students who are nationals of the host Member State.[12] However, provided the

---

[10] Case 263/86 1988 E.C.R. 5365.
[11] Note 9.
[12] *Ibid.*

employment is genuine the right to social advantages, including educational grants, may not be made conditional upon the completion of a minimum period of employment in the host Member State. In *Bernini*[13] the Court ruled that an Italian national who had worked for 10 weeks in a factory in The Netherlands as a trainee could be considered to be a worker and retained that status even when she left that employment, in order to take up, after a certain lapse of time, a course of full time study provided there is a link between that employment and the studies in question. Whether that is in fact so, is presumably for the grant awarding authority to decide on a case by case basis.

The right to grants for vocational training under Article 7(2) includes the right to grants for study abroad. In *Matteucci*,[14] an Italian national, herself the child of an Italian migrant worker who had been born and brought up in Belgium where she subsequently worked as a teacher of rhythmics, was refused a scholarship to study singing and voice production in Berlin. The scholarship in question was provided under a bilateral cultural agreement between Belgium and Germany and was expressed to be confined to nationals of those countries. The Court held that Article 7(2) of Regulation 1612/68 laid down a general rule of equality of treatment under the law of the host Member State with regard to social benefits with respect to every worker who is a national of another Member State and who is working in that State. Consequently, where a Member State gives its national workers the opportunity of pursuing training provided in another Member State, that opportunity must be extended to Community workers established in its territory.

> ". . . a bilateral agreement which reserves the scholarships in question for nationals of the two Member States which are parties to the agreement cannot prevent the application of the principle of equality of treatment between national and Community workers established in the territory of one of those two Member States."

Children of migrant workers have the same rights to all types of educational grants as nationals of the host Member State. In *Casagrande*[15] and *Alaimo*[16] the Court held that Article 12 of Regulation 1612/68 giving the child of a migrant worker the right to be admitted to that State's general educational, apprenticeship and vocational training courses under the same conditions as nationals of that State providing that he is residing there, refers not only to rules governing the admission to courses but also to other educational facilities such as educational grants. To this could be added other advantages given to students, such as cheap travel between home and school or college. The concept of education in Article 12 is broad, comprising "any form of education, including university courses in economics and advanced vocational training at a technical college."[17]

---

[13] Case C–3/90 1992 E.C.R. I–1071.
[14] Case 235/87 1988 E.C.R. 5589.
[15] Case 9/74 1974 E.C.R. 773.
[16] Case 68/74 1975 E.C.R. 109.
[17] Case 389/87, *Echternach and Moritz* 1989 E.C.R. 723.

Rights under Article 12 of Regulation 1612/68 can be enforced only against the Member State in which the migrant worker resides. Thus in the *Humbel* case,[18] Frederic Humbel, the child of a French father working and residing in Luxembourg could be required to pay an enrolment fee as a condition for admission to a Belgian school even where a Belgian child could not be obliged to pay such a fee.

Grant and scholarships for studies in a Member State other than that in which the child of the migrant worker is currently residing can be claimed by virtue of either Articles 7(2) or 12(2) of Regulation 1612/68.[19]

Entry and residence

In spite of the fact that the Court established 10 years ago that Community nationals had the right of access to vocational training courses on equal terms with nationals of the Member State in which the educational establishment which they wished to attend was, it is only recently that it has ruled that students have the right to enter and take up residence in that Member State in order to pursue those studies. One would have imagined that the right of entry and residence was implicit in the right of equality of access but this does not appear to have been so leading the Council to adopt a Directive in June 1990[20] giving students the right to enter and reside in the Member State in which they wish to pursue their studies and the Court to pronounce upon the matter in reply to a request for a preliminary ruling from a Dutch Court in February 1992.[21]

As we have seen in our discussion of the right of access to vocational training and the right to financial assistance for the duration of such training from the host Member State, students rights, in respect of these matters, are dependent on their status within the Community legal order. Likewise the conditions under which a student may enter and reside in a Member State are governed by his status, the migrant worker enjoying the most liberal conditions followed by the members of his family.

The migrant worker has the right to enter and take up residence in a Member State in order to take up employment there. Once in employment he has the right, under the same conditions as a national of the Member State, to vocational training. In addition, as we have seen his right to social and tax advantages accords him the right to financial assistance from the host Member State on the same terms as nationals of that Member State. Retired workers who have been employed in the host Member State for a certain period of time have the right to continue to reside on the territory of that State and to continue to enjoy the right to equality of treatment prescribed in Regulation 1612/68.

Let us suppose however that a migrant worker decides to give up his

---

[18] *Op. cit.* note 10.
[19] Case C–308/89, *di Leo* v. *Land Berlin* 1990 E.C.R. 4185, *Bernini*, Note 13.
[20] Directive 90/366 on the right of residence for students O.J. 1990 L180/30. This Directive has been declared void by the Court in Case C–295/90, *Parliament* v. *Council* Judgment of July 7, 1992 but its effects are to be maintained until it has been replaced by another measure.
[21] Case C–357/89, *Raulin* 1992 E.C.R.

employment in order to pursue studies on a full-time basis either in the host Member State or any other Member State (for example his Member State of origin) does this mean that he loses his status as such? It appears not. As long as a worker has been in genuine employment, that is if he has pursued "... an activity which is effective and genuine, to the exclusion of other activities on such a small scale as to be regarded as purely marginal and ancillary" in respect of which he has received remuneration, he retains his status as a migrant worker. Thus in *Lawrie—Blum*,[22] a trainee teacher who gave lessons whilst training to be a teacher for which she was paid a salary below the starting level of a qualified teacher was a worker and remained so when she began the second part of her studies leading to appointment as a secondary school teacher. Similarly employment as a bank clerk for two and a half years followed by intermittent periods of other employment qualified a person to be considered to be a "worker" and to retain that status during a subsequent university course in languages and literature.

> "Persons who have previously pursued in the host Member State an effective and genuine activity as an employed person . . . but who are no longer employed are nevertheless to be considered to be workers . . . it is therefore clear that migrant workers are guaranteed certain rights linked to the status of worker even when they are no longer in an employment relationship."[23]

In *Brown* v. *Secretary of State for Scotland*,[24] the Court held that a student who enters a Member State and works therefore a short period with a view to subsequently undertaking studies in the host State in the same field of activity and who would not have been employed by his employer if he had not already been accepted for admission to university is to be regarded as a worker. Steven Brown had dual French and British nationality. For eight months prior to commencing studies leading to a degree in electrical engineering in the University of Cambridge he was employed as a trainee engineer with Ferranti Plc in Edinburgh. His employment was described as "pre-industrial training." It was a pre-condition for such training that he should have been awarded a university place. The Court held that Mr. Brown was a worker.

The members of the family of a migrant worker all have the right to enter and reside in the host Member State with him. Under Regulation 1612/68, they are granted, in Article 12, the right to be admitted to ". . . general, educational, apprenticeship and vocational training courses under the same conditions as nationals of that State." But what of the child whose parent leaves the host Member State whilst he is still pursuing his studies there? Since he derives the right to be in that Member State from his parent must he leave with him? This question arose in *Echternach and Moritz*[24] where the Court held that education in the host Member State was to be regarded as a continuous process, so granting the child of a migrant worker the right to

---

[22] Case 66/85 1986 E.C.R. 2121.
[23] *Lair*, Note 9; *Bernini*, Note 13.
[24] Case 125/87 1988 E.C.R. 1619; 1992 E.C.R.

continue to reside and to pursue studies in the host Member State even after the return of his parents to their Member State of origin. In coming to this conclusion the Court was influenced by the fundamental aim of Article 12 of Regulation 1612/68 which is to ensure "as complete an integration as possible of workers and members of their families" in the host Member State. Such integration requires that the children of migrant workers be able to complete their education in the host Member State.

Although it was clear, from Community legislation and the case-law of the Court of Justice, that Community workers and their families had the right to reside in the Member State in which they intended to pursue studies, the same was not true of the Community citizen who was neither a worker nor a member of the family as such. Accordingly the Council adopted Directive 90/366[25] on the right to residence for students, which granted students, their spouses and their dependent children, who do not enjoy a right of residence under any other provision of Community law, such a right in the Member State in which vocational training studies are to be pursued for the duration of those studies, provided two conditions are satisfied, firstly that the student has sufficient resources to avoid becoming a burden on the social assistance scheme of the host Member State and secondly that the family as a whole are covered by sickness insurance for all the risks on the host Member State.

Subsequently, the Court of Justice in *Raulin*[26] held that a Community citizen who is neither a worker nor a member of the family of such has the right to enter and reside in a Member State for the purpose of pursuing a vocational training course. This right may be subject to certain conditions which the Court did not specify except to say that they must not infringe the principle of equality of access to vocational training.

COMMUNITY VOCATIONAL TRAINING POLICY

As we have mentioned above the first concrete application of Article 128 was Council Decision 63/266[27] setting out general principles for a Community policy on vocational training. At the same time a tripartite Advisory Committee on Vocational Training was created with the rôle of assisting the Commission to implement that policy. In 1977, following a sharp increase in levels of unemployment throughout the Community, the Commission addressed a Recommendation to the Member States on vocational preparation for young people who were unemployed or threatened with unemployment.[28] This instrument was concerned more with improving the literacy and numeracy skills of the Community's youth and preparing them for the discipline of employment rather than with the teaching of any skills than might be required by the labour market. Council Resolution of June 2, 1983 concerning vocational training measures relating

---

[25] Note 1.
[26] Case C–357/89 1992 E.C.R.
[27] Note 1.
[28] Commission Decision 77/467 1977 L180/18.

to new technology[29] called upon Member States in implementing their policies on vocational training in new technologies to have regard to the requirements of industry with respect to training in new technologies and to help (i) the young unemployed; (ii) skilled workers whose employment was likely to be affected by industrial restructuring and; (iii) retraining for re-entry of women into the employment market to acquire new technology skills and so increase their employability.

Following the decisions of the Court of Justice, which have been discussed above, which clarified the powers of the Community institutions with respect to vocational training, the Community's legislative programme became more ambitious. This programme does not aim to harmonise vocational training within the Community but rather recognises the value of the diversity of education and training schemes of the different Member States. Community training policy has therefore been built on the following three principles: co-ordination of national vocational training policies, the convergence of national initiatives and transnational co-operation.[30]

Main Legislative Instruments adopted

1987 saw the adoption of a Commission Recommendation on vocational training for women,[31] an instrument which had been envisaged in the "Equal Opportunities for Women Medium-Term Community Programme 1986–1990." The Recommendation, in its Article 1 states that the Member States should adopt a policy designed to encourage the participation of young and adult women in training schemes. The latter should, in particular, be "relevant to occupations of the future" and "occupation in which women are under-represented." Specific courses should be provided for under-privileged women and women returning to work.

Again in 1987 the Council adopted a Decision setting up a five-year action programme for the vocational training of young people and their preparation for adult and working life.[32] The purpose of this programme was ". . . to support and supplement, through measures at a Community level, the policies and activities of the Member States in doing their utmost to ensure, that all young people in the Community who so wish receive . . . vocational training in addition to their full-time compulsory education."

More recent initiatives in the sphere of vocational training have marked a move away from the Community's previous policy, which had been to set up training programmes on a Community level for specific groups of people, to a more broad approach consisting of general programmes designed to equip the citizens of the Community with the skills required in the single integrated market. Beginning with the *ERASMUS* programme in 1987, the

---

[29] O.J. 1983 C166.
[30] Commission Memorandum on Vocational Training in the European Community in the 1990s. Commission of EC 1992.
[31] O.J. 1987 L166/22.
[32] Decision 87/567 Petra Programme O.J. 1987 L346/31.

Community has gone on to establish, amongst others *TEMPUS, COMMETT, EUROTECHNET, LINGUA, PETRA* and *FORCE*.

ERASMUS, set up by Council Decision 87/327,[33] has as its objective a significant increase "in third level student mobility between Member States; the promotion of broad and intensive co-operation between universities in all Member States and the improvement in the quality of education and training provided by the universities by encouraging the mobility of their staff with a view to increasing the competitivity of the Community in the world market." The task of executing the programme was entrusted to the EEC Commission which was required to set up a European University network consisting of agreements for exchanges of students and teachers between universities in different Member States. The programme is financed out of Community funds. The budget for the period 1990–94 being in the order of ECU 192 millions.

The *TEMPUS*[34] (Trans-European Mobility Scheme for University Studies) extended the *ERASMUS* programme to the countries of Central and Eastern Europe.

Council Decision 89/489[35] set up the *LINGUA*[36] programme with the aim of improving the language skills of Community citizens by increasing the mobility of teachers and students of language with a view to improving the initial training of foreign language teachers.

Other Community programmes included *COMMETT*[35] which sponsors links between business and universities and colleges with advanced technology courses. *COMMETT* extends to *EFTA* countries. *EUROCTECHNET*[37] (European Technology Network) aims at stimulating exchanges and research on new technology in the field of vocational training whilst *PETRA*[38] provides funds for vocational training projects with a Community dimension for young people.

The Social Charter and its Action Programme advocated another approach to vocational training—that of granting to workers the right of equal access to such training on a continuous basis all their working lives. Accordingly in May 1990 the Council adopted a Decision establishing a three-year action programme for the development of continuing vocational training in the European Community (*FORCE*).[39] The main objectives of the *FORCE* programme is to encourage greater and more effective investment in continuing vocational training, to demonstrate and disseminate examples of good vocational training practice in continuing vocational training to those economic sectors or regions of the Community where access to or investment in such training is currently inadequate, and to take better account of the needs of the internal market, in particular by

---

[33] O.J. 1987 L166/20; Case 242/87, *Commission* v. *Council* 1989 E.C.R. 1425.
[34] Decision 90/233 O.J. 1991 L131/21.
[35] Council Decision 89/489 1989 L239/24.
[36] Council Decision 86/365 1986 L222/17 (*COMMETT* 1), Council Decision 89/27 1989 L13/28 (*COMMETT II*). Joined Cases C51/89, C90–89 and C–94/89, *United Kingdom* v. *Council* 1991 E.C.R.
[37] Council Decision 89/657 1989 L393/29.
[38] Council Decision 87/569 O.J. 1987 L346/31.
[39] O.J. 1990 L156.

supporting transnational and transfrontier continuing vocational training projects.

The Treaty on European Union empowers the Community to set up a vocational training policy to:

— facilitate adaptation to industrial changes, in particular through vocational training and retraining;
— improve initial and continued vocational training in order to facilitate vocational integration and re-integration into the labour market;
— facilitate access to vocational training and encourage mobility of instructors and trainees and particularly young people;
— stimulate co-operation on training between educational or training establishments and firms;
— develop exchanges of information and experience on issues common to the training systems of the Member States.

The Council may adopt measures which contribute to the achievment of any of these objectives ". . . excluding any harmonization of the laws and regulations of the Member States."

PART V: EUROPEAN UNION

CHAPTER 23

THE TREATY ON EUROPEAN UNION

Background

The negotiations which led to the signing of the Treaty on European Union (hereinafter, "the T.E.U.") were formally opened in Rome on December 15, 1990. They were pursued through 1991 and were brought to a conclusion in December of that year by the Heads of State or Government of the Member States meeting in the Dutch city of Maastricht. Revised versions of the texts in the nine official languages of the Communities were then prepared and the Treaty was signed, again in Maastricht, on February 7, 1992.[1]

The earliest date for the entry into force of the T.E.U. was January 1, 1993, assuming that the process of ratification by the Member States, in accordance with their respective constitutional requirements, would be completed by then.[2] This was put in doubt by the negative outcome of the referendum on the ratification of the Treaty that was held in Denmark in June 1992. Subsequent referenda in Ireland in June and in France in September 1992 brought votes in favour of ratification, although in the latter case by a narrow margin. Political and economic uncertainty increased as a result of turbulence in the international money markets during the period immediately preceding and following the French referendum, and this led to the suspension by Italy and the United Kingdom of their membership of the exchange rate mechanism of the European Monetary System and to the reintroduction of exchange rate controls by Spain and Ireland. However, at an extraordinary meeting of the European Council at Birmingham on October 16, 1992, the Heads of State or Government reaffirmed their commitment to the T.E.U. It was agreed that the Community must develop together as Twelve, on the basis of the T.E.U., while respecting, as the Treaty does, the identity and diversity of Member States.[3]

That positive development was confirmed by the European Council held in Edinburgh on December 11 and 12, 1992. Agreement was reached in Edinburgh on texts establishing interpretations of various provisions of the T.E.U. which the Danish authorities announced would make it possible to hold a second referendum, with a good prospect that Denmark would be in a position to ratify the Treaty. The European Council also approved texts on the application by the Council of the principle of subsidiarity (see below)

---

[1] The text of the T.E.U. that was signed in Maastricht, with the Final Act and the Declarations annexed to it, has been published in the Information section of the Official Journal of the European Communities: see O.J. 1992 C 191/1. It has also been published "for documentary purposes," as a booklet, by the Office for Official Publications of the European Communities. In addition, a version of the T.E.U., together with a consolidated text of the EC Treaty, as amended, has been published in O.J. 1992 C 224/1.

[2] T.E.U., Art. R(2).

[3] The text of the "Birmingham Declaration", and of the Presidency Conclusions to which it was annexed, can be found in *Agence Europe* (Special Edition), October 18, 1992.

and on greater "openness" in the legislative process. Finally, there was agreement on the financial arrangements that will apply for the 7-year period to 1999 ("the Delors II package"), and this, in turn, opened the way for the launching, early in 1993, of negotiations with the EFTA applicants for Community membership.[3a]

In the light of that outcome, it seemed, at the time of writing, there was a good chance that the T.E.U. would be in force before the end of 1993.

The Treaty

The Treaty in its final form brings together two texts that were negotiated separately by parallel conferences. One text, relating to what was known as "political union" was negotiated by personal representatives of the Foreign Ministers of the Member States under the auspices of the General Affairs Council, while the other text, relating to economic and monetary union, was negotiated by personal representatives of Finance Ministers under the auspices of the Economic and Financial Affairs Council.

The T.E.U. is a lengthy and complex instrument, comprising seven titles, with articles identified by capital letters to avoid confusion with the numbering of the founding Treaties. Title I (Articles A to F) contains Common Provisions. Title II lists, under a single Article G, amendments and additions to the EEC Treaty representing by far the most radical revision of that Treaty in its history. Consequential amendments to the ECSC and Euratom Treaties are found, respectively, in Title III (under Article H) and Title IV (under Article I). Title V contains, in Articles J.1 to J.11, provisions relating to a common foreign and security policy and Title VI, in Articles K.1 to K.9, provisions relating to co-operation in the fields of justice and home affairs. Title VII (Articles L to S) contains the Treaty's Final Provisions. Besides the main body of the Treaty, there are 17 Protocols, some of considerable legal and political importance, while 33 Declarations were annexed to the Final Act.[4]

The three pillars

One of the key issues in the negotiations was whether the new policy areas to be covered by the Treaty, or any of them, should be brought within the compass of the EEC Treaty; and, to the extent that they were not, what the relationship should be between those policy areas and the legal order of the Communities. The four areas principally in question were citizenship, economic and monetary union, foreign and security policy and justice and home affairs.

It was eventually decided that the provisions relating to citizenship and to economic and monetary union should be integrated into the EEC Treaty as amended by the T.E.U. On the other hand, as regards foreign and security policy and justice and home affairs, while wishing to create a framework for

---

[3a] The Presidency Conclusions of the Edinburgh European Council have been published in *Agence Europe* (Special Edition), December 13 and 14, 1992.
[4] The Protocols and Declarations will be referred to by the numbers they were given when listed in the Final Act.

more intensive co-operation and, where appropriate, for joint action, Member States were not ready to cede competence to the Community. Accordingly, the provisions on a common foreign and security policy (C.F.S.P.) and on co-operation in the fields of justice and home affairs remain, for the time being at least, outside the amended EEC Treaty, in separate Titles of the T.E.U.

The T.E.U. thus embraces three distinct spheres of competence—the European Communities, the C.F.S.P. and co-operation in the fields of justice and home affairs. The inclusion, within the same text, of amendments to the European Community Treaties and provisions relating to matters not covered by those Treaties is not unprecedented: as we have seen, in the S.E.A. matters of Community competence are juxtaposed with European Political Co-operation (E.P.C.), the forerunner of C.F.S.P. However, whereas the S.E.A. placed the European Communities and E.P.C. in compartments that were, legally and functionally, nearly watertight, the three "pillars" of the T.E.U. are incorporated into a new structure, the European Union. The reference to "pillars" is explained by the image of a Greek temple façade which has been used to illustrate the structure of the Union.[5] It conveys neatly, if over-simply, the idea that the European Communities and the new areas of co-operation and common action are linked by the T.E.U. in a constitutional order.

European Union[6]

According to Article A, third paragraph of the T.E.U., "The Union shall be *founded* on the European Communities, *supplemented* by the policies and forms of co-operation established by this Treaty." That wording brings out the complex character of the Union and the preponderant influence of the European Communities within it. The paragraph goes on to describe the Union's task as being, "to organise, in a manner demonstrating consistency and solidarity, relations between the Member States and between their peoples." Unifying factors (represented by the pediment of the temple image) consist of common objectives, common principles, a single institutional framework and certain common procedures.

The objectives of the Union are listed in Article B, first paragraph of the T.E.U. The first four indents of the paragraph refer to the main categories of activity to be pursued under the different pillars. More interesting is the fifth indent which makes it an objective of the *Union* to maintain in full, and build on, the *acquis communautaire*. The latter expression (of which there exists

---

[5] A rival conception of the Union, involving a higher degree of integration, was illustrated by the image of a tree, with three branches growing out of the same trunk.

[6] On the political union negotiations and their outcome, see P. de Schoutheete de Tervarent in J. V. Louis (ed.), *L'Union européenne après Maastricht* (journée d'études Bruxelles, February 21, 1922), p. 17; C. Timmermans, *ibid.* p. 49. For a commentary on the "political union" aspect of the Treaty in the draft put forward by the Luxembourg Presidency to the European Council in June 1991, see D. Vignes, (1991) R.M.C., p. 504. The Addendum on the T.E.U. in de Cockborne *et al.*, *Commentaire Mégret* (2nd ed.), Vol. 1 (1992, Editions de l'Université de Bruxelles) contains at pp. 369 *et seq.*, a commentary on the Preamble and Common Provisions of the T.E.U.

no adequate rendering into English) describes the sum of what has been achieved in giving effect to the founding Treaties. A fresh inter-governmental conference is to be convened as early as 1996 to consider, *inter alia*, to what extent it may be necessary to revise the second and third pillars "with the aim of ensuring the effectiveness of the mechanisms and the institutions of the Community."[7] In addition, the Council will be empowered to transfer into the European Community sphere certain matters which are to fall, initially, under the provisions of co-operation in the fields of justice and home affairs.[8] The Union, therefore, has an internal dynamic operating in one directive only—towards alignment on, and further development of, the Community model of European integration.

Among the principles that constitute a common ideology for the Union, three in particular need to be mentioned. First, the Union is required to "respect the national identities of its Member States, whose systems of government are founded on the principles of democracy."[9] That principle directly safeguards the multifarious political and cultural traditions of the Member States; indirectly, it makes clear that possession of a democratic system of government is a *sine qua non* of Community membership. Secondly, the Union must respect, as general principles of Community law, the fundamental rights guaranteed by the European Convention for the Protection of Human Rights and Fundamental Freedoms, as well as those resulting from the constitutional traditions common to the Member States.[10] It has long been established that fundamental rights must be respected by the European Community institutions, and by national authorities when exercising powers derived from Community law, and that principle is to apply also under the two new pillars erected by the T.E.U. Thirdly, the objectives of the Union are to be achieved "while respecting the principle of subsidiarity."[11] That principle is referred to, directly or indirectly, in various provisions of the T.E.U. and a definition is to be inserted into the amended EEC Treaty, as the second paragraph of Article 3b.[12] The definition, and the general significance of the principle, will be examined below, in the context of the discussion of amendments to that Treaty.

The Union will have a single set of institutions—those of the European Communities, which will act for the purposes of the other two pillars in so far as they are given power to do so by the T.E.U.[13] The single institutional framework is designed to provide consistency and continuity as between the Union's different spheres of activity. There is a particular need for such consistency in the external relations field.[14] For instance, a joint action adopted in the future under the provisions of the T.E.U. relating to the C.F.S.P., in response to a crisis such as the Iraqi invasion of Kuwait, may

---

[7] T.E.U., Art. B, first para., fifth indent, which refers to Art. N(2).
[8] T.E.U., Art. K.9. See *infra*.
[9] T.E.U., Art. F(1).
[10] T.E.U., Art. F(2).
[11] T.E.U., Art. B, second para.
[12] See, in particular, Art. K.3(2)(b).
[13] T.E.U., Arts. C and E.
[14] The point is emphasised in Art. C, second para.

require the interruption of economic relations with one or more third countries, which is a matter falling within European Community competence. It obviously makes sense that all aspects of an international situation should be dealt with by the same institutions—the Council and the Commission—although their respective powers may vary in relation to the different matters to be decided. The fact that co-operation and common action under the two new pillars will be the responsibility of *Community* institutions will also help to further the objective of maintaining and building upon the *acquis communautaire*.

The role of providing the Union with the necessary impetus and political guidance for its development is given to the European Council, which brings together, normally once in six months, the Heads of State or Government of the Member States and the President of the Commission.[15] It has been pointed out that the European Council is the only "institution" that can be said really to belong to the Union (rather than being lent to it by the European Communities).[16]

The Final Provisions of the T.E.U. include provisions relating to the amendment of the European Community Treaties[17] and to the accession of new Member States[18] which replace the equivalent provisions in the founding Treaties. In future, therefore, there will be a uniform procedure for amending the various Treaties, and accessions will be to the Union and not, as hitherto, to the individual Communities.

On the other hand, the T.E.U. does not give the Union legal personality. International agreements will, accordingly, still be concluded, in matters of European Community competence, by the relevant Community and, in matters to which the C.F.S.P. applies, by the Member States (or, where areas of competence overlap, in the form of "mixed" Community/Member State agreements).

Nor is the Union to have its own financial resources. Administrative expenditure in the two new areas of co-operation and common action will be charged to the budget of the European Communities, while the Council is given power to determine whether operational expenditure in those areas should be charged to the Community budget or to the Member States.[19]

The various factors considered in the previous paragraphs show that the European Union to be established pursuant to the T.E.U. will be a relatively light structure but one into which the two new pillars can be fitted without destabilising the Community pillar or altering its central place in the overall design. As such, it seems well adapted to this "new stage in the process of creating an ever closer union among the people of Europe."[20]

---

[15] T.E.U., Art. D. See the discussion of the European Council in Chap. 2, *supra*.
[16] By Timmermans, *op. cit.* note 5, *supra*, p. 51.
[17] T.E.U., Art. N(1).
[18] T.E.U., Art. O.
[19] See T.E.U., Arts. J.11(2) and K.8(2).
[20] T.E.U., Art. A, second para., reiterating wording in the preamble to the EEC Treaty.

Amendments to the EEC Treaty

Considerations of space make it impossible to provide a full picture of the numerous and far-reaching amendments to the EEC Treaty contained in Title II of the T.E.U. The present section is intended only to draw attention to certain matters that seem of particular interest. It should be added that the important changes the T.E.U. will bring to the institutional structure and the law-making process of the Communities are not dealt with here but as part of the wider discussion in Chapters 2 and 3, above.

The Community's change of name

First and foremost, the Community is to change its name. The adjective "economic" will be dropped and it will be known simply as "the European Community" (or EC).[21]

The change of name acknowledges a reality which has been clear for some time. As long ago as 1976 the Court of Justice said, in a case relating to the right of equal pay under Article 119 EEC, ". . . this provision forms part of the social objectives of the Community, which is not merely an economic union, but is at the same time intended, by common action, to ensure social progress. . . ."[22] At the same time, the change does mark a shift in the focus of Community activities: this can be seen from the extended list of those activities in Article 3 of the Treaty, as amended by the T.E.U., and from the creation of specific new legal bases for measures to be adopted by the Community in fields such as education,[23] culture,[24] public health,[25] consumer protection[26] and development co-operation.[27]

In future, moreover, if the competence of the Community to legislate on certain matters should be disputed, it will no longer be an argument against such competence that the matters in question do not belong to the economic domain.

The principle of subsidiarity

The second paragraph of the new Article 3b establishes the principle of subsidiarity as a general principle of European Community law. Under the principle, the Community may only take action "if and in so far as the objectives of the proposed action cannot be sufficiently achieved by the Member States and can therefore, by reason of the scale or effects of the proposed action, be better achieved by the Community." The principle does not apply in areas falling within the Community's exclusive competence: its extension to those areas would have deprived the Community of

---

[21] T.E.U., Art. G(1).
[22] Case 43/75, *Defrenne* v. *Sabena* [1976] E.C.R. 455 at p. 472.
[23] EC Treaty, as amended, Arts. 126 and 127.
[24] EC Treaty, as amended, Art. 128.
[25] EC Treaty, as amended, Art. 129.
[26] EC Treaty, as amended, Art. 129a.
[27] EC Treaty, as amended, Arts. 130u to 130y. The extensive activities of the EEC in the field of development co-operation, insofar as they have not taken place within the framework of association agreements pursuant to Art. 238 (the best known being the series of Lomé Conventions), have been based on Art. 235.

existing powers, which would have been inconsistent with the general principle of the Union requiring that the *acquis communautaire* be respected.

The principle of subsidiarity clearly has a part to play in the legislative process. There will be a general duty, on the Commission before putting forward a proposal, and on the Council before finally enacting the measure in question, to consider whether its objectives could be as well achieved by action at national level. As we have seen, the European Council in Edinburgh adopted a text setting out procedures and criteria for the application of the principle in the future practice of the Council.[28]

A more difficult question is whether the principle of subsidiarity is justiciable. The better view is, perhaps, that the content of the principle is too imprecise for it to constitute, on its own, grounds for reviewing the validity of an act of the Council or the Commission. It will, however, serve as a new and useful tool for the interpretation by the Court of Justice and by national courts of the Treaties and of Community legislation.

Citizenship of the Union

The T.E.U. establishes a citizenship of the Union and confers that citizenship on all persons holding the nationality of a Member State.[29] The new status brings with it a bundle of rights which, initially, are fairly modest in their scope. However, the recognition of a Union citizenship has considerable symbolic importance, as reactions in certain national Parliaments during proceedings for the ratification of the T.E.U. bore witness; and it seems likely that the content of Union citizen's rights will develop in the years ahead.

According to Article 8a of the EC Treaty, as amended by the T.E.U., every Union citizen is to have the right to move and reside freely within the territories of the Member States, subject to the limitations and conditions laid down by the Treaty and by legislation adopted under it. The new right thus created will not significantly extend the rights of free movement and residence already accorded to nationals of Member States under the EEC Treaty[30] or pursuant to Council Directives.[31] In particular, Article 8a has been so worded as to allow the continued application of conditions imposed by existing legislation to prevent persons who are not economically active from becoming a burden on the social services of the host State.[32] However,

---

[28] See note 3a, *supra*.
[29] EC Treaty, as amended, Art. 8.
[30] Such rights are enjoyed by nationals of Member States for the purposes of employment or of setting up in business or a profession, as providers or recipients of services or as students pursuing a course of vocational training. See, as to the limited nature of the right of residence of students, Case C–357/89, *Raulin*, judgment of February 26, 1992 (not yet reported). Rights of free movement and residence are more fully analysed in Chaps. 9, 10 and 22, *supra*.
[31] See Dir. 90/364 (right of residence in general) O.J. 1990 L180/26; Dir. 90/365 (right of residence for retired people) O.J. 1990 L180/28; Dir. 90/366 (right of residence for students) O.J. 1990 L180/30.
[32] Art. 8a(2) empowers the Council to adopt provisions with a view to *facilitating* the right of free movement and residence. Except as otherwise provided by the Treaty, the Council is to act unanimously on a proposal from the Commission and after obtaining the assent of the European Parliament. On the assent procedure, see Chap. 3, *supra*.

it will not be open to the legislator to make those conditions more restrictive, to a point where they would substantially interfere with the general right conferred by the T.E.U.

Entirely new rights the T.E.U. will bring to a Union citizen residing in a Member State of which he is not a national are the right to vote and the right to stand as a candidate in both municipal elections and elections to the European Parliament in that State.[33] Detailed arrangements for the exercise of those rights are to be laid down by the Council: this is to be done, as regards municipal elections, before December 31, 1994 and, as regards European Parliamentary elections, before December 31, 1993. Slightly ominously, it is stated that those arrangements "may provide for derogations where warranted by problems specific to a Member State."

A Union citizen will also be entitled, in a third country where the Member State of which he is a national is not represented, to protection by the diplomatic or consular authorities of any Member State, on the same conditions as that State's own nationals.[34] For the right of protection to have substance, it is necessary that it should be recognised by third countries, and Member States are required to set in train international negotiations with that in view, before December 31, 1993.[35]

Finally, Union citizens will have the right to petition the European Parliament and to apply to the Ombudsman who is to be appointed pursuant to the T.E.U.[36] However, they will share that right with any legal or national person residing or having his registered office in a Member State.

Economic and social cohesion

A new Title on economic and social cohesion was introduced into the EEC Treaty by the S.E.A.[37] The reduction of disparities between the levels of development of the various regions and the backwardness of the least favoured regions, which was necessary in order to ensure that the benefits of the internal market would be fairly spread throughout the Community, has become still more urgent with the acceptance, in the T.E.U., of the principle that the third stage of economic and monetary union will begin automatically for all the Member States (with the possible exception of Denmark and the United Kingdom) on January 1, 1999 at the latest.[38]

The Treaty provisions on economic and social cohesion are accordingly to be strengthened,[39] and action through the existing structural Funds is to be

---

[33] EC Treaty, as amended, Art. 8b. The term "municipal" was chosen with a view to excluding regional as well as national elections.

[34] EC Treaty, as amended, Art. 8c.

[35] Member States are to establish the necessary rules among themselves before the same date.

[36] EC Treaty, as amended, Art. 8d. As to the right of petition, see EC Treaty, as amended, Art. 138d. As to the Ombudsman, see EC Treaty, as amended, Art. 138e.

[37] Title V of Part Three of the EEC Treaty, comprising Arts. 130a to 130e.

[38] See the discussion of economic and monetary union, *infra*, Member States that do not fulfil the convergence criteria laid down by the T.E.U. will be exempted, in principle, on a temporary basis, from the rigours of participation in the single currency.

[39] The strengthening of economic and social cohesion is mentioned in Art. B of the T.E.U. as one of the means of pursuing the objective of promoting economic and social progress. There are also references to economic and social cohesion among the Community's tasks as defined by Art. 2, and among its activities listed in Art. 3, of the EC Treaty, as amended. The

supplemented by the creation of a new Cohesion Fund to provide a financial contribution to projects in the fields of the environment and trans-European transport infrastructures.[40] A feature of the Cohesion Fund, as provided for in a Protocol to the T.E.U.,[41] is that its resources are to be concentrated in those Member States with a *per capita* G.N.P. of less than 90 per cent. of the Community average, *i.e.* Greece, Spain, Ireland and Portugal. The Treaty itself, therefore, imposes on the more prosperous Member States an express obligation for the transfer of resources, which are likely to be substantial, to less prosperous Member States.

Economic and monetary union

Previous developments. The idea of going on from the completion of the internal market to the establishment of an economic and monetary union (or E.M.U.) is not a new one. The wish to see such a development was expressed in the final communiqué of the Conference of Heads of State of Government held in December 1969 in The Hague, and the following year a working group was set up under the chairmanship of Luxembourg's Prime Minister and Minister of Finance, Mr. Pierre Werner, to study ways and means of achieving E.M.U. The Werner Committee presented an interim report in May 1970 and its final report in October of that year,[42] and in March 1971 a first Resolution on the attainment by stages of E.M.U. in the Community was adopted by the Council and the representatives of the governments of the Member States.[43] The Resolution looked forward to the establishment of E.M.U. before the end of the decade and set out a number of measures to be taken with that in view, including the strengthening of the co-ordination of short term economic policies, the reduction of the margin of fluctuation between Member States' currencies and the organisation of a European Monetary Co-operation Fund. Those provisions were supplemented by a second Resolution, adopted in March 1972.[44]

Although steps that were taken to implement the Resolutions of 1971 and 1972 helped to prepare the way for later developments, little headway could be made in the economic and political circumstances of the early and mid-1970s. Fresh impetus was given to E.M.U., however, by the introduction in March 1979 of the European Monetary System (or E.M.S.).[45] This was based on guidelines laid down at the meeting of the European Council in Bremen in July 1978 and further elaborated in a

---

substantive Articles on economic and social cohesion, still numbered 130a to 130e, are found in Title XIV of the EC Treaty, as amended.

[40] Art. 130d, second para. requires the Council, acting unanimously on a proposal from the Commission and after obtaining the assent of the European Parliament and consulting the Economic and Social Committee and the Committee of the Regions, to set up the Cohesion Fund before December 31, 1993.

[41] See Protocol No. 15.

[42] Bull. EC Suppl. 11/70.

[43] O.J. English Sp.Ed. (Second Ser.) IX, p. 40.

[44] O.J. English Sp.Ed. (Second Ser.) IX, p. 65.

[45] The E.M.S. replaced an earlier, less successful, system of monetary co-operation which had been set up in 1972, the so-called "snake in a tunnel."

Resolution at the Brussels meeting in December of the same year.[46] The main objective of the E.M.S. is "the creation of closer monetary co-operation leading to a zone of monetary stability in Europe." This is to be achieved, notably, by an exchange rate mechanism under which fluctuations in exchange rates are limited to 2.5 per cent. above or below a "central rate" fixed for each pair of participating currencies. It is possible to opt for a wider margin of fluctuation of up to 10 per cent.; and if margins become too difficult to defend, the central rates of the national currencies concerned can be adjusted, although this requires the agreement of all participants in the mechanism. To help finance interventions by monetary authorities in currency markets in order to prevent margins from being exceeded, various credit mechanisms are available. Last but not least, a European Currency Unit (the ECU), defined as a weighted basket of European Community currencies, serves as the denominator for different operations under the E.M.S., although its uses now extend much more widely: for instance, the statements of revenue and expenditure in the Community budget are expressed in ECU, as also are Community loans and aid to third countries, while the ECU is also playing an increasingly important part in private transactions.[47]

Participation in the exchange rate mechanism is optional for the Member States of the Communities. In 1979 all the then Member States except for the United Kingdom decided to take part, and they were joined by Spain in 1989, by the United Kingdom in 1990 and by Portugal in 1992. For the time being, Greece remains outside the mechanism and in September 1992 Italy and the United Kingdom were forced to suspend their participation. Non-participants in the exchange rate mechanism are not, however, excluded from other aspects of co-operation within the E.M.S. and their currencies are included in the ECU basket.[48]

The Brussels Resolution on the E.M.S. refrained (no doubt wisely) from defining the steps whereby the system might evolve towards a fully fledged monetary union in which exchange rates would be fixed irrevocably and the national currencies would ultimately be replaced by a single currency. Nor, on this point, were matters taken much further by the S.E.A. A new chapter, containing only one article (Article 102a) was added to the EEC Treaty, but this amounts to hardly more than a reminder of the desirability of the convergence of Member States' economic and monetary policies and the usefulness, to that end, of experience gained from co-operation within the framework of the E.M.S. and in developing the ECU. Paragraph

---

[46] The text of the Resolution and other relevant documents were published by the Committee of Governors of the Central Banks. See *Texts concerning the European Monetary System*, 1979.

[47] For a fuller exposition of the E.M.S., see J-.J. Rey, (1980) C.M.L.Rev. 78. See, in particular, the explanation of a "basket-type" unit of account at pp. 14 *et seq.*

[48] In the light of the financial turbulence experienced in September 1992, the Birmingham European Council called for "reflection and analysis" to be undertaken. This was to cover recent economic and financial developments within Europe and in the major industrialised countries as well as the implications of changes in the general economic and financial environment, notably the impact of the increasing size and sophistication of financial markets and greater capital liberalisation.

(2) of the Article recalled that, insofar as further development in the field of economic and monetary policy necessitated institutional changes, these would have to be achieved by fresh amendment of the Treaty.

It was at the European Council in Hanover in June 1988, in the light of progress made towards the completion of the internal market, and of the successful adoption of the financial package necessary to implement the policies introduced or developed by the S.E.A.,[49] that the decisive step was taken of inviting a committee chaired by the President of the Commission, Mr. Jacques Delors, to study and put forward proposals for concrete stages leading to economic and monetary union.[50] The plan formulated by the Delors Committee for the attainment of E.M.U. in three stages was put to the European Council in Madrid in June 1989, where it was decided that the first stage, which did not require any Treaty amendments, would begin on July 1, 1990. Preparations were to be made for an inter-governmental conference that would meet, once the first stage had begun, to lay down the subsequent stages. As we have seen, that conference came to be held in parallel with another relating to "political union," and the final outcome of the two conferences was the T.E.U., to whose provisions on E.M.U. it is necessary now to turn.[51]

Article 3a of the EC Treaty. The two aspects of E.M.U. are defined by a new Article 3a, added to the EC Treaty as amended by the T.E.U. According to that Article, the activities of the Member States and the Community shall include, in accordance with the timetable laid down by the Treaty:

— the adoption of an economic policy which is based on the close co-ordination of Member States' economic policies, on the internal market and on the definition of common objectives, and conducted in accordance with the principle of an open market economy with free competition;
— concurrently with such a policy, the irrevocable fixing of exchange rates leading to the introduction of a single currency, the ECU, and the definition and conduct of a single monetary policy and exchange-rate policy the primary objective of both of which shall be to maintain price stability and, without prejudice to this objective, to support the general economic policies in the Community, in accordance with the principle of an open market economy with free competition.

It is added that the activities of the Member States and the Community in economic and monetary matters shall comply with the guiding principles of stable prices, sound public finances and monetary conditions and a sustainable balance of payments.

---

[49] Known as "Delors I," to differentiate it from the "Delors II" package of financial measures to allow implementation of the T.E.U.
[50] See Committee for the Study of Economic and Monetary Union, *Report on economic and monetary union in the European Community* (the "Delors Committee Report").
[51] There is a full and clear survey of the provisions of the T.E.U. relating to E.M.U. by G. Brouhns in J.V. Louis (ed.), *op. cit.* note 5, *supra*.

There is a striking contrast between the rather general terms in which the economic aspect of E.M.U. is defined and the more specific and coercive terms used in defining its monetary aspect. This difference of approach comes out even more clearly in the detailed provisions on E.M.U. contained in Title VI of Part Three of the amended Treaty.[52] As we shall see, while economic policy remains decentralised, with the emphasis on effective co-ordination and "peer group" pressure on Member States to manage their economies responsibly, decisions on monetary and exchange-rate matters will be highly centralised, with a virtually complete transfer of powers, in the third stage of E.M.U., from the Member States to the European System of Central Banks (ESCB) or, as the case may be, to the Community institutions.

The timetable. The T.E.U. establishes a strict timetable for the attainment of E.M.U. in three stages.

No date is mentioned for the beginning of the first stage, since this is assumed to be under way, in accordance with the decision of the European Council in Madrid in June 1989. The second stage will begin on January 1, 1994.[53] A controversial issue in the negotiations was the transition to the third stage which, it was eventually agreed, will take place in one of two ways. Up to the end of 1997, the decision whether to move to the third stage will be for the Council, meeting in the formation of Heads of State or Government, which must consider the matter not later than December 31, 1996.[54] A positive decision can only be taken if the Council is satisfied that a majority of the Member States fulfil the conditions for the adoption of a single currency, which is to be judged on the basis, *inter alia*, of certain economic criteria indicating the attainment of a high level of economic convergence.[55] If by the end of 1977 the Council has not yet fixed a date for the transition to the third stage, this will take place automatically on January 1, 1999.[56]

The timetable is thus ineluctable. Entry into the third stage of E.M.U. cannot be delayed beyond January 1, 1999, even if only a few of the Member States fulfil the conditions for the adoption of a single currency on that date. Even before 1999, no Member State will be able to veto the fixing by the

---

[52] EC Treaty, as amended, Arts. 102a to 109m.
[53] EC Treaty, as amended, Art. 109e(1).
[54] EC Treaty, as amended, Art. 109j(3).
[55] The four "convergence criteria" are:
  — the achievement of a high degree of price stability, evidenced by a rate of inflation of not more than 1½ per cent. above that of, at most, the three best performing Member States;
  — the sustainability of the government financial position, evidenced by the fact that the Member State in question is not the subject of a Council decision that it is running an excessive deficit (as to the excessive deficit procedure, see *infra*);
  — the observance of the normal fluctuation margins under the exchange-rate mechanism of the E.M.S., for at least two years, without devaluing against the currency of any other Member State;
  — convergence of interest rates, evidenced by an average nominal long term rate not more than 2 per cent. above that of, at most, the three best performing Member States.
  (See EC Treaty, as amended, Art. 109j(1) and Protocol No. 6.)
[56] EC Treaty, as amended, Art. 109j(4).

Council of a date for the transition to the third stage, since the decision can be taken by a qualified majority.[57] In addition, there is a Protocol to the T.E.U. expressly binding all Member States, whether they fulfil the conditions for the adoption of a single currency or not, to respect the will for the Community to enter swiftly into the third stage, and therefore not to prevent that from happening.[58] Pursuant to that Protocol, it is thought, a Member State would be under a duty not to oppose, for political reasons, the setting of a date for the beginning of the third stage, if it was clear that a majority of Member States fulfilled the necessary conditions.

The corollary of establishing such a timetable was that special arrangements had to be made to allow certain Member States to escape, or at least to defer, acceptance of the full rigours of participation in the third stage. There are two cases to consider.

The first is that of Member States which, at the relevant time, do not fulfil the conditions for the adoption of a single currency, for example because their rate of inflation or the level of their government deficit exceed the limits prescribed by the T.E.U. For those Member States to participate in the single currency would not only be damaging to their own economies: it would threaten the stability of the monetary union. Provision is, therefore, made under Article 109k of the EC Treaty, as amended, for the Member States concerned to have, for as long as they need it, a derogation from the relevant provisions of the T.E.U. and of the Protocol on the Statute of the European System of Central Banks. Member States with a derogation, and their Central Banks, will be excluded from rights and duties within the European System of Central Banks and will be authorised to continue managing their monetary policy in accordance with national law.[59] On the other hand, provisions belonging to the third stage but which are not closely linked to the adoption of a single currency, will apply to such Member States.[60]

The other case is that of two Member States, Denmark and the United Kingdom, which were unable or unwilling to accept, from the entry into force of the T.E.U., a firm commitment in principle to full participation in the third stage of E.M.U. Solutions to the problems of these two Member States are found in separate Protocols.

According to Protocol No. 12, "the Danish Constitution contains provisions which may imply a referendum in Denmark prior to Danish participation in the third stage. ..." To allow for the holding of a referendum and a possibly negative outcome, Denmark will have a right, if it notifies the Council that it will not be taking part in the third stage, to treatment corresponding, for most purposes, to that of Member States with a derogation pursuant to Article 109k.[60a]

Protocol No. 11 goes somewhat further, by "Recognising that the United

---

[57] EC Treaty, as amended, Art. 109j(3).
[58] Protocol No. 10.
[59] See EC Treaty, as amended, Art. 109k(3) and Statute of the ESCB, Chap. IX.
[60] E.g. the obligation under Art. 104c(1) to avoid excessive government deficits.
[60a] By the Decision adopted at the Edinburgh European Council, Denmark effectively exercised its option not to take part in the third stage.

Kingdom shall not be obliged or committed to move to the third stage of economic and monetary union without a separate decision to do so by its government and Parliament." The effect of the Protocol is to entitle the United Kingdom, if it does not opt into the third stage, to the treatment *mutatis mutandis*, of a Member State in the second stage. This would mean that, unlike Member States with a derogation the United Kingdom would not be subject to obligations that become applicable in the third stage but that are not closely linked to the adoption of a single currency.

Economic policy. Without going into too much detail, something must be said about the actions the T.E.U. requires to be taken in the field of economic policy during the different stages of E.M.U.

In what remains of the first stage, there is to be a strengthening of existing procedures designed to bring about the convergence of Member States' economic policies and performances. Following a procedure laid down by Article 103(2) of the EC Treaty, as amended, the Council is to adopt a recommendation setting out broad guidelines of the economic policies of the Member States and of the Community. Those guidelines are to serve as a frame of reference in the process of "multilateral surveillance" under which the Council monitors economic developments.[61] If it is found that a Member State's economic policies are not consistent with the broad guidelines or that they risk jeopardising the proper functioning of economic and monetary union, the Council will have power to make recommendations to the Member State concerned; and, to increase the political pressure on that Member State, it may decide to make its recommendations public.[62]

In the second stage, various rules intended to enforce budgetary discipline by public bodies at all levels in the Community will come into play. Thus it will be forbidden for Community institutions and for central or local government or public undertakings in the Member States to be granted credit facilities by central banks[63] or, generally, to enjoy privileged access to financial institutions.[64] It will also be forbidden for the Community or a Member State to be liable for, or to assume, the commitments of central or local government or public undertakings (the so-called "no bailing out" rule).[65]

Another mechanism to impose budgetary discipline on the Member States is the excessive deficit procedure laid down by Article 104c. From the beginning of the second stage, Member States will be under a duty to endeavour to avoid excessive deficits. Quantitative criteria for judging whether a Member State is observing budgetary discipline are provided for by Article 104c(2), supplemented by Protocol No. 5, namely:

---

[61] See Council Dec. 90/141 of March 12, 1990 on the attainment of progressive convergence of economic policies and performance during stage one of economic and monetary union: O.J. 1990 L78/23. If necessary, Member States are required to adopt, before the beginning of the second stage, multi-annual programmes intended to ensure lasting convergence: EC Treaty, as amended, Art. 109e(2)(a), second indent.
[62] EC Treaty, as amended, Art. 102a(4).
[63] EC Treaty, as amended, Art. 104.
[64] EC Treaty, as amended, Art. 104a.
[65] EC Treaty, as amended, Art. 104b.

— a ratio of the planned or actual government deficit to gross domestic product not exceeding 3 per cent.;
— a ratio of total government debt to gross domestic product not exceeding 60 per cent.

"Government" is defined as including central and local government and social security funds.[66] The criteria are to be applied "dynamically": thus the appreciation may be positive if the ratio has been moving steadily downwards and is approaching the reference value. The Commission will have responsibility for monitoring the development of the budgetary situation and of the stock of government debt in the Member States and, where necessary, for setting the excessive deficit procedure in motion.[67] The procedure may lead to a decision by the Council, "after an overall assessment" (implying a political judgment, not the mechanical application of the quantitative criteria), that an excessive deficit exists in the Member State concerned.[68] In that event, recommendations must be made to the Member State, with a view to bringing the excessive deficit situation to an end within a specified period.[69] When it is established that no effective action has been taken in response to its recommendations, the Council may proceed to make them public.[70]

Reinforcement of the excessive deficit procedure is the most significant development, as regards economic policy, the third stage of E.M.U. will bring. Member States will then be under a positive duty to avoid excessive government deficits,[71] and the Council will have additional powers to force deficit reductions. If recommendations made with a view to bringing an excessive deficit situation to an end are not complied with, the Council will be empowered to give notice to the Member State concerned to take, within a specified time, measures to achieve the reduction which it judges necessary[72]; and, in case of non-compliance with such a notice, there is provision for the imposition by the Council of sanctions of various kinds, including fines of an appropriate size.[73]

Monetary policy. The monetary aspect of E.M.U. entails setting up new institutions and procedures.

There is to be established, in time for the third stage, a European System of Central Banks (ESCB) and a European Central Bank (ECB).[74] The ESCB will be composed of the ECB and of the Central Banks of the Member States[75] and will be governed by the decision-making bodies of the ECB—its

---

[66] Protocol No. 5, Art. 2.
[67] EC Treaty, as amended, Art. 104c(2) and (3).
[68] EC Treaty, as amended, Art. 104c(6).
[69] EC Treaty, as amended, Art. 104c(7).
[70] EC Treaty, as amended, Art. 104c(8).
[71] EC Treaty, as amended, Art. 104c(1), read with Art. 109e(3), second sub-para.
[72] EC Treaty, as amended, Art. 104c(9).
[73] EC Treaty, as amended, Art. 104c(11).
[74] The Statute of the ESCB and the ECB (hereinafter "ESCB Statute") is contained in Protocol No. 3.
[75] EC Treaty, as amended, Art. 106(1); ESCB Statute, Art. 1(2).

Governing Council and Executive Board.[76] The Governing Council of the ECB will comprise the members of the Executive Board and the Governors of the national central banks,[77] while the Executive Board will comprise a President, Vice-President and four other members, appointed by common accord of the governments of the Member States at the level of Heads of State or Government.[78] The ECB will have certain law-making powers on aspects of monetary policy.[79]

Important tasks for the preparation of the third stage are to be entrusted to a European Monetary Institute (EMI) which is to be established at the start of the second stage and wound up at its end.[80] The EMI will be directed and managed by a Council, consisting of a President, appointed by common accord of the governments of the Member States at the level of Heads of State or Government, together with the Governors of the national central banks. It will be required to specify, at the latest by December 31, 1996, the regulatory, organisational and logistical framework necessary for the ESCB to perform its task in the third stage.[81]

A fundamental principle of the ESCB will be the independence of the ECB and of national central banks, in performing the tasks and duties conferred on them by the T.E.U. and the ESCB Statute, both from the Community institutions and from national governments.[82] There is an explicit Treaty undertaking by the Community institutions and by governments to respect that principle and not to seek to influence the members of the decision-making bodies of the ECB or of national central banks. A duty is placed on the Member States to take the legislative steps necessary to ensure the complete independence of their national central banks, not later than the date of the establishment of the ESCB.[83]

Member States will retain control over their monetary policies during the second stage, although the EMI will be required to strengthen the co-ordination of national policies.[84] In the third stage, it will be for the ESCB "to define and implement the monetary policy of the Community."[85] Other "basic tasks" of the ESCB will be the conduct of foreign exchange operations, holding and managing the official foreign reserves of the Member States and promoting the smooth operation of payment systems.[86]

The passage to the third stage will be marked by a Council decision adopting the conversion rates at which national currencies will be irrevocably fixed and at which the ECU will be substituted for them.[87] The

---

[76] EC Treaty, as amended, Art. 106(3); ESCB Statute, Art. 8.
[77] EC Treaty, as amended, Art. 109a(1); ESCB Statute, Art. 10.
[78] EC Treaty, as amended, Art. 109a(2); ESCB Statute, Art. 11.
[79] EC Treaty, as amended, Art. 108a.
[80] EC Treaty, as amended, Art. 109f. The Statute of the EMI (hereinafter "EMI Statute") is contained in Protocol No. 4. As to the liquidation of the EMI, once the ECB is established, see EC Treaty, Art. 109 1(2); EMI Statute, Art. 23.
[81] For the primary tasks of the EMI, see EC Treaty, as amended, Art. 109f(2) and (3); EMI Statute, Art. 4.
[82] EC Treaty, as amended, Art. 107; ESCB Statute, Art. 7.
[83] EC Treaty, as amended, Art. 108.
[84] EC Treaty, as amended, Art. 109f(2), second indent; EMI Statute, Art. 4(1), second indent.
[85] EC Treaty, as amended, Art. 105(2); ESCB Statute, Art. 3(1).
[86] *Ibid.*
[87] EC Treaty, as amended, Art. 109 (1)(4).

decision will require the unanimity of the Member States which do not have a derogation and will only affect those Member States' currencies.[88] The ECU will immediately become a currency in its own right, but not necessarily the *single* currency of the Member States concerned. The necessary measures must be taken by the Council in order rapidly to achieve that final objective, and thus to complete the monetary union.[89]

The Social Protocol[90]

This was an expedient devised in the final hours of the negotiations in Maastricht, to break a political deadlock. While 11 of the Member States wanted to strengthen the provisions of the Social Policy chapter of the EEC Treaty along lines laid down in 1989 by the European Social Charter[91] (itself agreed between the same Member States), the changes it was proposed to make were unacceptable to the United Kingdom. The solution eventually found was for the Social Policy chapter of the Treaty to be left substantially intact,[92] while the 11 entered into an Agreement incorporating the disputed amendments. The Agreement is annexed to a Protocol agreed by all 12 Member States which, in turn, is to be annexed to the EC Treaty, as amended. The Protocol authorises the 11 to have recourse to the institutions, procedures and mechanisms of the EC Treaty for the purpose of taking among themselves and applying as far as they are concerned the acts and decisions required for giving effect to their Agreement. The United Kingdom is to be excluded from the Council's decision-making process in respect of measures proposed by the Commission under the Protocol and Agreement, and it will not be required to contribute towards the financing of such measures.

It is a new departure for the Community institutions to make and apply rules that will have the force of law in only 11 out of the 12 Member States.[93] Whether this will give rise to problems remains to be seen: for instance, the adoption of onerous measures affecting employers in all Member States other than the United Kingdom might tend to distort competition within the internal market. However, it is likely that maximum advantage will be taken of the potentialities of Article 118a of the Treaty as a basis for the adoption of legislation establishing minimum health and safety standards for workers, which will be applicable in all 12 Member States. If Article 118a is broadly interpreted, the need for the 11 to have recourse to the Protocol and Agreement (and hence the practical importance of the latter, though not their legal interest) will be considerably reduced.[94]

---

[88] Similar decisions will have to be taken for Member States with a derogation, if and when that derogation is abrogated. It will be the same for Denmark and the United Kingdom, if they "opt in" after the third stage has begun.

[89] EC Treaty, as amended, Art. 109(1)(4), final sentence.

[90] Protocol No. 14.

[91] Printed as a booklet by the Office for Official Publications of the European Communities.

[92] There is a purely formal amendment to Art. 118a(2), first sub-para.

[93] The technique is known, in Community jargon, as "variable geometry." If, owing to difficulties in meeting the conversion criteria, certain Member States remain indefinitely outside full E.M.U. that will be another, and far more significant, example of "variable geometry."

[94] For example, at the time of writing, the adoption on the basis of Art. 118a, of a directive limiting the working week in the Community to 48 hours seemed imminent. If this could be

The two new pillars

The second pillar: a common foreign and security policy

The Common Foreign and Security Policy (C.F.S.P.) to be established pursuant to the T.E.U. will represent, in several respects, an advance on European Political Co-operation as it was organised under the S.E.A. It will allow more systematic and structured co-operation over a wider field of policy, while also providing a legal basis for taking joint action; and that co-operation will take place, and joint action will be determined, within Community institutions.

The potential scope of the C.F.S.P. extends to all areas of foreign and security policy.[95] All questions related to the security of the Union will be covered, including the eventual framing of a common defence policy, which might in time lead to a common defence.[96] In a lengthy Declaration, the Member States which are Members of the Western European Union (WEU) state their objective of building up that organisation in stages "as the defence component of the European Union."[97] To that end, an invitation is issued to the WEU to elaborate and implement decisions and actions having defence implications.[98]

The European Union is to pursue its foreign and security objectives in two ways: by establishing systematic co-operation between Member States; and by gradually implementing joint action in areas where the Member States have important interests in common.[99] Various obligations will be imposed on Member States to ensure that co-operation is effective. They will be required to inform and consult one another within the Council on any foreign or security matter of general interest and, where a common position has been defined by the Council, they will be under a duty to defend that position and to ensure that their national policies are in conformity with it; and in international organisations and at international conferences, they will be required to co-ordinate their action and to uphold common positions.[1] It will be the Council's task to decide, on the basis of general guidelines from the European Council, that a certain matter should be the subject of joint action and, having done so, to define the scope of such action, the general and specific objectives of the Union in carrying it out, if necessary its duration, and the means, procedures and conditions for its implementation.[2]

Representation of the Union in matters coming within the C.F.S.P. is to be undertaken by the Presidency.[3] This means that in international

---

regarded as a health and safety measure, there is obviously considerable scope for legislating, under Art. 118a, on general working conditions.

[95] T.E.U., Art. J.1, para. (1).

[96] T.E.U., Art. J.4, para. (1).

[97] Declaration No. 30. The Member States not belonging to WEU are Denmark, Greece and Ireland. It is proposed, in a separate Declaration, that those Member States either join WEU or become observers.

[98] T.E.U., Art. J.4, para. (2). Under the Decision adopted at the Edinburgh European Council, Denmark will not participate in the elaboration or implementation of Union action in the sphere of defence.

[99] T.E.U., Art. J.1(3).

[1] T.E.U., Art. J.2.

[2] T.E.U., Art. J.3.

[3] T.E.U., Art. J.5(1).

organisations and at international conferences, the Union may have two spokesmen—a member of the Commission, dealing with matters falling within Community competence, and the President of the Council, dealing with matters covered by the C.F.S.P. In performing its representative tasks, the Presidency may be assisted by the previous and next Member States to hold the presidency[4]—the practice known as the "troïka," which may give added political weight to the Union's position. It must be remembered, however, that, since the Union will lack legal personality, the parties to any international agreements entered into pursuant to the C.F.S.P. will be the Member States.

The third pillar: justice and home affairs

Under the heading "Co-operation in the fields of justice and home affairs," the T.E.U. groups together a variety of matters concerning the treatment of third country nationals and aspects of law enforcement and the maintenance of public order which, although regarded as falling outside Community competence, nevertheless have an important bearing on the establishment of a single market with no internal frontiers. Co-operation in respect of these matters, which has been taking place in ad hoc intergovernmental working parties, is to be put on a more systematic footing within the institutional framework of the Union.

Nine areas of activity are identified as ones which the Member States are to regard as being of "common interest."[5] These include: aspects of the free movement of persons, such as asylum policy, the control of the Community's external frontiers and immigration policy; combating drug addiction and international fraud; judicial co-operation, which could for example, bring some easing of extradition procedures; and customs co-operation. Of particular interest is the provision made for police co-operation in the fight against terrorism, drug trafficking and other serious international crime, through the organisation of a Union-wide system of information exchange within a European Police Office (or "Europol").

There is a subtle difference in the drafting of Article K.3 of the T.E.U., as compared with the corresponding provisions under the second pillar, indicating some additional reticence on the part of Member States to restrict their freedom of action. In the areas of common interest Member States will be under a duty to inform and consult one another within the Council with a view to co-ordinating their action; and to that end, they are to establish collaboration between the relevant departments of their administrations.[6] The Council may adopt joint positions relating to those areas and it may promote co-operation "using the appropriate form and procedures."[7] It may also adopt joint action, the principle of subsidiarity—that Union objectives can better be attained in this way than by Member State action—being

---

[4] T.E.U., Art. J.5(3).
[5] T.E.U., Art. K.1.
[6] T.E.U., Art. K.3(1).
[7] T.E.U., Art. K.3(2)(a).

expressly recalled.[8] Another technique, mentioned by Article K.3(2)(c), is the drawing up of conventions, to be recommended to the Member States for adoption in accordance with their respective constitutional requirements.[9]

The Council is expressly given power[10] to decide that action in certain of the areas of common interest listed in Article K.1 may in future be taken under Article 100c of the EC Treaty, as amended, a new provision the scope of which will initially be limited to visa policy. It will thus be possible for matters to be transferred from the justice and home affairs pillar to the Community pillar, without the need for amending the Treaty.

Institutional arrangements

As we have seen, it is one of the organising principles of the European Union that there be a single set of institutions acting for the purposes of all three pillars.[11] However, the institutions will function under the two new pillars in ways that differ significantly as compared with their functioning under the Community pillar. Certain key differences are briefly noted here, and should be borne in mind in relation to the wider discussion of the institutions and their respective powers in earlier chapters.

Contrary to the trend under the EC Treaty, where the range of matters that can be decided by a qualified majority has been progressively enlarged, the rule of unanimity applies to Council decisions under the new pillars. The only exceptions to the rule will be in specific cases where the possibility of reaching majority decisions has been unanimously agreed by the Council in advance. For instance, when adopting a joint action, or at any stage during the development of such an action, the Council may define matters on which decisions are to be taken by a qualified majority.[12] Similarly, where the Council chooses to act in the field of justice and home affairs by drawing up a convention under Article K.3(2)(c), a majority of two thirds of the High Contracting Parties will be sufficient, in the absence of contrary provision, for the adoption of implementing measures.

The Council will have a more than usually dominant role under the new pillars, while the other institutions will have correspondingly reduced opportunities for influencing the development of policy and leaving their mark on the measures finally adopted. Thus the Commission is to be fully associated with the work carried out, and will have a right of initiative but not the exclusive right it enjoys for most purposes under the European Community Treaties.[13] Member States will also have a right of initiative and, in the field of justice and home affairs, this will be more extensive than the Commission's.[14] The European Parliament will have the right to be

---

[8] T.E.U., Art. K.3(2)(b).
[9] T.E.U., Art. K.3(2)(c).
[10] By T.E.U., Art. K.9.
[11] See the discussion of the Union structure, *supra*.
[12] T.E.U., Art. J.3(2). There is a corresponding provision concerning measures for the implementation of joint action decided under the third pillar: see T.E.U., Art. K.3(2)(b).
[13] See T.E.U., Arts. J.8 and J.9; Arts. K.3(2) and K.4(2).
[14] According to Art. K.3(2), second indent, the Commission will have no right of initiative in the following areas: judicial co-operation in criminal matters (Art. K.1(7)); customs co-operation, (Art. K.1(8)); Europol (Art. K.1(9)).

consulted by the Presidency on the principal aspects of Council activities, and to have its views duly taken into consideration, and it must be kept regularly informed by the Presidency and the Commission of relevant developments and discussions[15]; but it will not be directly involved in decision-making on specific matters.

The provisions of the T.E.U. relating to the new pillars are not brought within the jurisdiction of the Court of Justice.[16] The only exception will be where the Council acts under Article K.3(2)(c) by means of a convention in which it is expressly provided that the Court be given jurisdiction. It will, however, be for the Court itself, in defining the scope of its European Community jurisdiction, to establish the dividing line between the Community pillar and the two new pillars. That may give rise to some interesting case-law, especially in relation to the free movement of third country nationals within the internal market.

Specialised committees composed of senior national officials— respectively, the Political Committee and the Co-ordinating Committee— will contribute to the preparation of the work of the Council under the second and third pillars.[17] However, this will be without prejudice to the preparatory role of the Committee of Permanent Representatives (or COREPER) which, in principle, covers the whole of Council business.[18]

From this survey of the special institutional arrangements laid down by the T.E.U. for the two new pillars, it is plain that the supranationalism of the European Community order, which gives the Commission a privileged role in the formulation of policies, which enables the Council to act regularly by a qualified majority and which entrusts to the Court of Justice the task of ensuring that the law is observed, will be missing: in short, the Member States have not agreed to limit their sovereign rights in the way the Court has said they have done under the EEC Treaty.[19] On the other hand, the single institutional framework will facilitate the co-ordination of activities pursued under the different pillars. It also means that decisions on matters falling under the second or third pillar will be prepared within Council bodies under the same conditions as apply under the Community pillar. Proposals will be examined at technical level by Council working groups and will pass through COREPER to the Council, all of this in the presence of representatives of the Commission who will be able to contribute to the discussion at any stage; and the different preparatory bodies and the Council itself will be assisted by permanent officials belonging to the Council's General Secretariat. The influence of working habits developed, and of mutual confidence gained, under the more integrated system of the European Communities will thus be felt in the new areas of co-operation and common action.

---

[15] T.E.U., Art. J.7; Art. K.6.
[16] T.E.U., Art. L.
[17] See, respectively, T.E.U., Art. J.8(5) and Art. K.4(1).
[18] As to the role of COREPER, see Chap. 3, *supra.*
[19] This was first asserted by the Court in Case 26/62, *Van Gend en Loos* v. *Nederlandse Administratie der Belastingen* [1963] E.C.R. 1, at p. 12. It was recently reiterated in Op. No. 1/91 on the draft E.E.A. Agreement: see O.J. 1992 C110/1.

INDEX